"Oh, For a Touch of the Vanished Hand"

Best wishes,
Dana M. Morgan

"Oh, For a Touch of the Vanished Hand"

Discovering a Southern Family
and
the Civil War

by
Dana M. Mangham

Southern Heritage Press, Inc.
4035 Emerald Dr.
Murfreesboro, TN 37130

Library of Congress Cataloging-in-Publication Data

**"Oh, For a Touch of the Vanished Hand": Discovering a Southern
Family and The Civil War** by Dana Mangham.
Vol. 23 of The Journal of Confederate History Book Series
John McGlone, Series Editor

p.cm includes index, genealogical guide, footnotes, and bibliographical
references.
    ISBN 1-889332-40-2 (paper)
    1. United States - History - Civil War, 1861-1865, Family History.

Oh, for a touch of the vanished hand and the sound of the voice that is stilled.

-Epitaph of Betty Carlisle Webster

To the men and boys in blue and gray who fought for the right,
as God gave them the light to see it,
and
to my family, then and now.

John Willis Mangham
Sergeant, "Upson Guards,"
Company B, 2nd Georgia Battalion Sharpshooters
1862-1865

Contents

Part I

From Carolina to the Oconee River: Solomon Mangham Comes to Georgia

Part II

On the Trail of Uncle Solomon: Joseph Mangum's Descendants Move South

Illustrations

Pictures

Maps

Genealogical Charts

(Individual reference numbers on charts are keyed to Genealogical Appendix)

Preface

The conscious decision to undertake this book arrived with enough leisurely detours to put one in mind of a journey across the ramshackle Confederate transportation network in 1861. It was just over a century later that I first felt the magnetic attraction of the war that, for a time, rent the United States asunder, and centennial books and movies may have played a major role in awakening a young boy's interests. More mesmerizing in effect, however, were the sensations produced by our summer vacations throughout the 1960s, when each visit to grandparents, great-aunts and -uncles, and distant cousins seemed to lead me back to the 19th century. The annual migration took me from our home in Baton Rouge down the older roads of the Deep South, dotted with glimpses of decaying cemeteries and tumbledown farmhouses that seemingly bore no similarity to the suburbs where I lived. These roads always led us to Georgia and its Cyclorama, Stone Mountain, and to places whose names evoked desperate struggles of a hundred years ago: Atlanta, Peachtree Creek, Kennesaw.

Much of our time was spent in the hot summer sunshine of rural Georgia, however, and the very air of Talbot County always seemed to say that the Civil War was not so long ago after all. This feeling had nothing whatsoever to do with the civil rights struggles that highlighted the difference a century could make, as well as the existence of perspectives on the war that had nothing to do with a young boy's romantic musings. All that was beyond my ken, thankfully, and how was I to know that my mother's old hometown, Junction City, had never even seen the light of day until the 20th century? It certainly felt, looked, and smelled like "long ago and far away" to me.

After my grandfather, Matthew Martin Webster, died in 1965, I had occasion to note the headstones near his when we made our annual pilgrimage to place a wreath in the little country cemetery. Some of the weathered gravestones bore dates that made me wonder if an "Old Confed" rested beneath their shade, and many markers throughout Talbot County proudly bore an inscription that left no doubt: Co. K, 27th Ga. Inf., CSA. Poignant reminders of what had been, such monuments always made me wonder whether any of my own relatives had fought in the war, and what they experienced during those times. When we recently rediscovered the quiet graveyard where my great-grandmother, Betty Carlisle Webster, was laid to rest over a century ago, we realized that her dimly-etched epitaph was another gentle admonition that those who went before remain, invisibly but powerfully, still a part of us: *Oh, for a touch of the vanished hand and the sound of the voice that is stilled.*

My mother, Ethel Shealy Webster Mangham, had everything to do with my reverence for the past, and her cultivation of family values intertwined with family memories was the same that she had learned at her mother's knee. I believe that such oral traditions formed the centerpiece of the fabled sense of regional identity that characterized the South in my youth. Combat veteran, Secretary of the Navy, and author James Webb drew directly upon such traditions, linking military service and masculine honor, for the character of Marine Lieutenant Robert E. Lee Hodges, a protagonist in his modern classic about the Vietnam War, *Fields of Fire.*

My mother's own childhood memories of a colt named "Joe Wheeler" never ceased tickling my reveries throughout the years, and my inspiration to act finally came in 1994. I was teaching European and world history at the United States Military Academy at West Point, but still read occasional books about the Civil War. One night I lay reading an account of a Georgia regiment undergoing a deadly ordeal by fire at Antietam, and the old memories and questions came flooding back. I decided it was time to learn if I had ancestors there during America's hour of trial.

I began researching my Mangham ancestors that spring, suspecting that they may have been in Georgia during the war, but knowing only that my grandfather had been born there in the 1880s. Little did I realize that his very name, Henry Gordon Mangham, was probably a tip-off. Grandpa apparently was named for Georgia's famous governor of that time, General John B. Gordon, who had risen from captain of volunteers to Robert E. Lee's only non-West Point corps commander. Grandpa's own grandfather, John Willis Mangham, had served in a Georgia Sharpshooter battalion in the Army of Tennessee, but John's brothers Will and Charles ("Nat") had fought in the 13th Georgia Volunteer Infantry, which helped make General Gordon's reputation in Lee's Army of Northern Virginia. I was amazed to learn that both had suffered serious wounds at Sharpsburg (Antietam), where their regiment suffered the second-highest casualty rate of the 180-odd Confederate regiments engaged in a battle that still ranks as the single bloodiest day in America's history. After writing three historical and genealogical articles concerning Mangham Confederate soldiers by 1996, I realized that I wanted to develop a broader perspective on the men and women whose countenances glimmered in the shadows of my initial research.

I am indebted to many for their assistance in my quest. For their friendship, encouragement, and historical acumen, my appreciation is due to many former colleagues at West Point, including Colonels Bob Doughty and Scott Wheeler, as well as Lieutenant Colonels Rich Coon, Dave Cotter, Rick Lechowich, Frank Siltman, and Tom Ziek. Lieutenant Colonel Bill Bassett, another old friend from the West Point faculty, helped me greatly in my work on Willoughby Hill Mangham of the 11th Georgia while I was a student-officer and he was a faculty member at the U. S. Army Command and General Staff College, Fort Leavenworth, Kansas.

Others whose contributions have made this work possible are the ever-helpful staffs of the Florida, Georgia, Alabama, Mississippi, Louisiana, and Texas state archives, as well as the staff at the National Archives. Jeanell Strickland of the East Baton Rouge Parish Library's Bluebonnet Branch, Genealogy Section, and a friend of my sister Gloria since high school days, has responded to my requests with unfailing alacrity and indispensable advice. Another friend of Gloria's, Miriam Davey, provided critical information on Wiley Person Mangham. Mr. Bennie Hixon of Monroe and Shirley Lobrano of the Richland Parish branch library in Mangham, Louisiana helped me research Wiley and his brothers, Tom and Henry. Additionally, thanks are due to Dr. John McGlone of Southern Heritage Press for his patient assistance with the publishing process.

This project never would have entered the realm of possibility if I had not encountered the genealogical foundations laid by Vaughn Ballard, of Arlington, Texas, Lynn Parham of Huntsville, Alabama, and John Palmer, of Santa Rosa, California. Ballard's book on Solomon Mangham opened my eyes to broad genealogical vistas I had never suspected. As he acknowledged in his book, his own research depended heavily upon Parham's quarter century of labor on his *Mangum Family Bulletin*, and Palmer's work expanded the body of corporate knowledge still further. Without attempting to compare our achievements to those of the great scientists, it seems nonetheless appropriate to borrow Isaac Newton's praise of Copernicus, Kepler, and others: "If I have seen further, it is by standing on the shoulders of Giants."

By combining the genealogical and historical disciplines in this work, I have attempted to use the strengths of each to complement the other. In the process, I have unashamedly accepted limitations in source material that would deter many historians. The resulting ambiguities challenge the boundaries normally imposed by the historical discipline, in favor of telling my family's story as fully as it can be told. It is my hope and belief that the resulting narrative offers a useful model to family historians, while providing grist for the mills of analytical historians, unit historians, and Civil War enthusiasts who seek to deepen their understanding of Southerners at war.

Although I owe thanks to many whose mention must fall victim to brevity, I cannot close without expressing my undying gratitude to and admiration for my parents, Dr. and Mrs. J. Roger Mangham of Baton Rouge. Special thanks are due also to my brothers and sisters, Gordon, Barry, Beverly and Gloria, and their families, who all taught me the value of love and tradition.

My love and gratitude are due my wife, Nan, and our daughters Carolyn and Amanda, for their unstinting support at every bend in the road. All three have withstood the years I devoted to this book, accepting the heavy long distance costs run up by a husband and father with a non-stop connection to the 19th century. Both of our daughters are modern proof, if I may paraphrase Jeanell Strickland's conclusion, that we "Georgians sure do recycle names!" After reading this book, you, too, will understand why.

Confederate Units Featured in the Text

Alabama troops:
* Artillery
  - Ashville Artillery (Co. D, 1st Ala. Bn.)
  - 4th Bn. (Hilliard's Legion)
* Cavalry companies
  - Young's Co. (Mounted Infantry)
  - Young's Co. (State Reserves)
* Infantry Companies
  - Ashville Blues (Co. D, 1st Ala. Bn.; later Co. D, 25th Ala.)
  - Ashville Guards (Co. A, 10th Ala.)
  - Cusseta Greys (Co. A, 14th Ala.)
  - George Player Cavaliers (Co. A, 30th Ala.)
  - Tom Watts Rifles (Co. F, 18th Ala.)
* Infantry Battalions
  - 1st Bn. (Loomis's)
* Infantry Regiments
  - 1st Regt.
  - 10th Regt.
  - 14th Regt.
  - 18th Regt.
  - 25th Regt.
  - 30th Regt.
  - 59th Regt.
  - 61st Regt.
* Infantry Brigades
  - Battle's
  - Forney's
  - Gracie's
  - Holtzclaw's
  - Pryor's
  - Hilliard's Alabama Legion

Florida troops:
Leon Rifles (Co. D, 2nd Fla. Inf.)

Georgia troops:
* Artillery
- Bartow Arty. (Co. A, 22nd Hvy. Arty.)
- Jackson's Artillery
- Wise Guards (Co. B, 22nd Hvy. Arty.)
- 22nd Bn.
* Infantry Companies
  - Alexander Rifles (Co. G, 27th Ga.)
  - Bailey Volunteers (Old Co. B, new Co. A, 30th Ga.)
  - Brunswick Rifles (Old Co. L, new Co. K, 13th Ga. [Styles's]; later Co. A, 26th Ga.)
  - Coast Rifles (Co. F, 1st Ga. [Olmstead's])
  - Confederate Guards (Co. A, 13th Ga.
  - County Line Guards (Co. G, 27th Ga.
  - Doyal Volunteers (Co. A, 53rd Ga.)
  - Griffin Light Guard (Co. B, 5th Ga.)
  - Jackson Guards (Co. I, 53rd Ga.)
  - Jeff Davis Rifles (Co. I, 53rd Ga.)
  - Macon Volunteers (Co. B, 2nd Ga.
  - Mangham's Co. (Spalding Inf., 6th St. Gd.)
  - Quitman Greys (Co. I, 11th Ga.)
  - Rucker's Company (5th St. Gd.)
  - Spalding Infantry (6th St. Gd.)
  - Taylor Infantry (5th St. Gd.)
  - Upson Guards (Co. B, 2nd Ga. S.S.)
* Infantry Battalions
  - Mangham's
  - 2nd Bn.
  - 2nd Bn. Sharpshooters
* Infantry Regiments
  - 1st Regt. (Olmstead's)
  - 1st Regt. Reserves (Fannin's)
  - 5th Regt.
  - 5th Regt. (State Gd.)
  - 6th Regt. (State Gd.)
  - 11th Regt.
  - 13th Regt. (Ector's)
  - 13th Regt. (Styles's, later 26th)
  - 27th Regt.
  - 29th Regt.
  - 30th (aka 39th) Regt.

xv

- 53rd Regt.
* Infantry Brigades
  - Evans's
  - Floyd's
  - Jackson's (John K.)
  - Jones's (D. R.)
  - Gordon's (John B.)
  - Lawton's
  - Wilson's
* Militia
  - Georgia
  - Pike County
  - 109th Regt.

Louisiana troops:
* Artillery Battery
  - Benton's (aka Bell Bty., aka 3rd Field Arty.)
* Infantry Companies
  - Claiborne Invincibles (Co. D, 28th La.)
  - Claiborne Volunteers (Co. C, 19th La.)
  - Walmsley Guards (Co. B, 11th La. Bn.; Co. K, Consol. Crescent Regt.)
* Infantry Battalions
  - 11th Bn.
* Infantry Regiments
  - 19th Regt.
  - 28th Regt.
  - Consolidated Crescent Regt.
* Infantry Brigades
  - Mouton's
  - Gray's

Mississippi troops:
* 1st Light Artillery (Withers's) Regt.
  - Co. A (Jackson Light Artillery)
  - Co. I (Ridley's)
* Infantry
  - Rankin Rifles (Old Co. G, 10th Miss. Inf.)

Texas troops:
* Cavalry companies
  - Trinity County Cavalry (Co. E, 7th Cav.)
* Cavalry Regiments
  - 7th Regt.
  - 8th Regt. (Terry's Rangers)
  - 21st Regt.
* Parsons's Cavalry Brigade

Virginia troops:
  - Anderson's Battery (aka Botetourt Artillery)

Chronology

1862

Feb. 6, Feb. 16	Forts Henry and Donelson fall, opening Tennessee and Cumberland Rivers to Union fleets
Apr. 6-7	Battle of Shiloh (Tennessee)
Apr. 25	Fall of New Orleans (*U.S.S. George Mangham* is part of Union fleet)
May 31- June 1	Battle of Seven Pines stops McClellan's advance at Richmond
June 25-July 1	Seven Days' Battles drive McClellan back from Richmond
Aug. 28-30	Battles of Groveton and Second Manassas end in rout Army of Potomac
Sept. 17	Battle of Sharpsburg (Antietam) ends Lee's invasion of Md.
Sept. 22	Lincoln issues preliminary Emancipation Proclamation
Oct. 8	Battle of Perryville ends Bragg's invasion of Kentucky
Dec. 13	Battle of Fredericksburg repulses Burnside's advance on Richmond
Dec. 31-Jan. 2	Battle of Murfreesboro, Tenn. Bragg retreats to Chattanooga.

1863

April 13-14	Battle of Bisland. (Pvts. Arthur G. and William J. Mangham, 11th La. Bn., and Josiah Thomas Mangham, 28th La., captured)
April 26	Battle of Cape Girardeau—Marmaduke's cavalry retreats from Missouri
Apr. 30- May 4	Battle of Chancellorsville repels Hooker's advance on Richmond (Pvt. John S. Mangham, 53rd Georgia, mortally wounded)
July 1-3	Battle of Gettysburg ends Lee's invasion of Pennsylvania. (Pvt. Willoughby H. Mangham, 11th Georgia, wounded and captured)
Sept. 18-20	Battle of Chickamauga ends in Federal flight to Chattanooga (Col. Thomas W. Mangham, 30th Georgia, wounded)
Nov. 24-25	Battles at Lookout Mountain and Missionary Ridge drive Bragg's Army of Tennessee in rout from Chattanooga to Dalton (Cpl. Charles A. Mangham, 18th Alabama, captured)

1864

April 8-9	Battles of Mansfield and Pleasant Hill result in rout of Banks and are the turning point of Red River Campaign
May 5	Battle of the Wilderness opens Grant's Overland Campaign against Richmond (Pvt. William A. Mangham, 14th Alabama, wounded)
May 7	Sherman commences Atlanta Campaign
May 8-21	Battles at Spotsylvania continue Grant's campaign (Pvt. William T. T. Mangham, 61st Alabama, wounded)
May 18	Battle of Yellow Bayou concludes Red River Campaign

May 25-June 3	Battles of Dallas and New Hope Church—Johnston halts Sherman
June 15-18	Grant's advance stopped at Petersburg—beginning of siege
July 13	Rousseau's raiders seize the office of Tom and Wiley Mangham's *Ashville Vidette* en route to rendezvous with Sherman near Atlanta
July 20	Battle of Peachtree Creek: Hood's first counterattack
July 22	Battle of Atlanta ("Bald Hill"): Hood's second counterattack
July 28	Battle of Ezra Church: Hood's third counterattack
Aug. 31-Sept. 1	Defeat at Jonesboro results in Hood's evacuation of Atlanta (Sgt. Willis A. Mangham, wounded)
Sept. 29	Army of Tennessee begins march towards Tennessee
Nov. 30	Battle of Franklin guts the Army of Tennessee
Dec. 15-16	Battle of Nashville results in rout of Hood's army, which retreats to Mississippi

1865

March 25	Attack on Fort Stedman, near Petersburg: last offensive of Lee's Army (Pvt. Wm. T. T. Mangham, 61st Ala., captured)
Apr. 2	Federals break through at Petersburg; Lee retreats towards Appomattox
Apr. 9	Lee's Army of Northern Virginia surrenders at Appomattox (Pvts. Chas. A. Mangham, 13th Ga., and William A. Mangham, 14th Ala., released on parole)
Apr. 14	John Wilkes Booth assassinates President Lincoln
Apr. 26	Johnston surrenders Army of Tennessee at Greensboro, North Carolina (Sgt. John W. Mangham, 2nd Georgia Sharpshooters, released on parole)
May 26	Gen. Edmund Kirby Smith surrenders the Trans-Mississippi Department. Organized Confederate resistance ends.
1865-1877	Reconstruction (Federal forces occupy ex-Confederate states)
1898	Spanish-American War
1914-1918	First World War
1929	Wall Street Crash precipitates America's Great Depression
1931	Charles A. Mangham, formerly 18th Ala., dies in Texas (last surviving fully-documented Mangham Confederate soldier)

Abbreviations

ADAH	Alabama Department of Archives and History
AHQ	*Alabama Historical Quarterly*
A&IGO	Adjutant and Inspector General's Office
B&L	*Battles and Leaders of the Civil War*
CMH	*Confederate Military History*
CRC	Confederate Research Center
CV	*Confederate Veteran*
CWR	*Civil War Regiments: A Journal of the American Civil War*
CWTI	*Civil War Times Illustrated*
FHQ	*Florida Historical Quarterly*
FSL	Florida State Library
GDAH	Georgia Department of Archives and History
GHQ	*Georgia Historical Quarterly*
LSA	Louisiana State Archives
MFB	*Mangum Family Bulletin*
MDAH	Mississippi Department of Archives and History
MDT	*Macon Daily Telegraph*
NARA	National Archives and Records Administration
OR	*Official Records: War of the Rebellion*
OR Navies	*Official Records (Navies)*
ORS	*Official Records–Supplement*
SHS	Southern Historical Society
TSA	Texas State Archives
TSL	Texas State Library
UCV	United Confederate Veterans
UDC	United Daughters of the Confederacy
VNMP	Vicksburg National Military Park

Discovering the "Vanished Hand and the Voice That is Stilled"
Researching Your Civil War Ancestors

Did you ever wonder about your own Civil War ancestors and their experiences? Don't assume it's too tough or complicated for you to find out lots of intriguing information about them! One good day's research on the Internet, in a genealogical library, or at the state archives will turn up more intriguing information than you may imagine.

This appendix is a good starting point to help you begin your search, containing tips about genealogical, historical, and military sources, as well as some observations about organization and technique. You may wish to skip directly to the endnotes and bibliography, and use them to direct you straight to the sources you need. After all, this book comprises thirty-seven related, but separate, case studies in the genealogical and historical research techniques outlined here.

Each researcher has personal reasons for pursuing such a project. Shape your project the way *you* want to shape it, based on your own research goals. Select what *you* need, rather than feeling constrained to follow a "connect-the-dots" approach that locks you into a method that worked for someone else. If you simply want to find out the identity of your Civil War ancestor and his unit, this appendix will show you how to do it. Likewise, if you intend to replicate the scope of this book, you can find what you need to undertake the task.

Although it is important to try your best to identify your goals right at the beginning of your work, don't be surprised to find your interests growing as the project takes on a life of its own. This is why most genealogical primers stress an organizationally intensive approach that ensures maximum efficiency in record keeping. The prospective beginner is often intimidated by complex procedural outlines that imply weeks or months of exhausting study before even beginning research! If you are unsure what you want to learn about your Civil War ancestor, just jump right into the middle of it without worrying too much about efficient search procedure. Wade into the existing sources and grab up everything that seems relevant from Internet websites, library books, or archival records. If you enjoy the discoveries of your first few hours of research, you can always stop and reorganize your initial material to facilitate further work.

*   *   *   *   *

To help you in your quest, consider four levels of research that will match your goals to the appropriate methods and resources.

BASIC RESEARCH:

Level One assumes you wish to identify your Civil War ancestor; obtain his military service and pension records; identify and obtain any existing regimental history; and find secondary sources, such as battle or campaign histories, that will help you understand what he experienced.

Level Two is the same as Level One, but with the intention of *broadening* your research to learn about your ancestor's relatives in a similar degree of detail.

ADVANCED RESEARCH:

Level Three is similar to Level One, but with a view to *deepening* your research on *one specific ancestor* by delving more thoroughly into primary historical and genealogical sources.

Level Four compares to Level Two, but with the intention of digging into primary historical and genealogical sources to *deepen your research on your ancestor and his relatives*.

Although I distinguish between genealogical and historical sources for organizational clarity, they often overlap in content. The published county history that identifies your ancestor's brother may also include his life story. Likewise, the history of his regiment may include a detailed character sketch of your ancestor.

A NOTE ON INTERNET RESOURCES:

When I began my research in 1994, the Internet was in its infancy, so I commenced my search in the "traditional" way, combing through county histories, census records, state archives, and genealogical libraries. These methods are still useful, and you certainly need to do a lot of this type of work if you wish to progress far beyond Level One research. Anyone *beginning* their search now, however, should use some simple search techniques on the Internet to save time. You may find critically important information within a few hours (or even minutes) of deciding to commence work, which was unimaginable just a few years ago. Any librarian can teach you basic search techniques in just minutes.

Read about the basic research methods of Levels One and Two at the conclusion of Part I, or consult advanced research techniques (Levels Three and Four) after the Epilogue.

Introduction

On July 23, 1931, the citizens of San Antonio, Texas, went about the business of making ends meet in the midst of an era of economic hardship later known simply as the Great Depression. At 8:45 on this Thursday morning at his home at 120 Fairplay Avenue, Eugene Mangham bade a sad farewell to his elderly father, 86-year-old Reverend Charles Arthur Mangham, who breathed his last after a month-long struggle with the hemiplegia that paralyzed one side of his body. Reverend D. B. South conducted the funeral services at Eugene's home on the following day, and the bereaved family lay their beloved father to rest in the city's San Jose Cemetery.[1]

The old gentleman left behind a grand family of four children, thirteen grandchildren, and eight great-grandchildren, some of whom perhaps recalled tales about a long-ago day summer day 70 years previously when he had left home and family during times of even greater uncertainty. In August 1861, Charles Mangham was a mere boy of sixteen when he marched off to war with his friends and neighbors of Butler County's "Tom Watts Rifles," a company accepted by the Provisional Army of the Confederate States as Company F, 18th Regiment Alabama Volunteer Infantry.[2] Mustering into service at the start of America's greatest national drama, the young lad was among the first of thirty-seven Mangham men and boys to join the Confederate service from the states of the Deep South.

Little could the boy have imagined the stern tests he would face in the months and years ahead: near a one-room country church in Tennessee known as Shiloh Meeting House, where his regiment suffered 120 killed, wounded or missing in April 1862. Or along the banks of a north Georgia creek known as Chickamauga, the "River of Death," where they lost another 297 killed and wounded out of 527 men present for duty. Or at Missionary Ridge, where the young veteran, now a corporal, was captured along with his regimental colors in a desperate action that left but seven privates from the once-proud Tom Watts Rifles to answer roll call.[3] Still less could he have known that he would be one of the very last of his clan to return home in the bitter days of June 1865, after four years of privation and sacrifice had reduced his beloved Southland to ruin and despair.

At least five Manghams never returned home from the service, and wounds or disease broke the health of several others. Many more bore the scars of old wounds and injuries along with their memories of camp and field, victory and defeat. The Confederacy's death agony in the spring of 1865 engulfed at least one veteran in the eerie darkness of mental despair, resulting in his commitment to Georgia's state asylum for the insane until 1867. Most returned successfully to the pursuits of peace, however, and many left marks on the local, state, or regional levels which are clearly visible 135 years later. Many of these men—such as Charles Mangham—were avowedly proud of their service under the Stars and Bars, as evidenced by their membership in the United Confederate Veterans organization that flourished beginning in the 1880s. The ranks of the Mangham veterans slowly thinned out, however, as a new century dawned and the deeds of the 1860s passed slowly into the realm of the history books. Sixty-six years after the war's end, this inexorable process reached its appointed end. Charles A.

Mangham became, as far as is known, the last of the family's Confederate veterans to "cross over the river and rest under the shade of the trees."[4]

*　　*　　*　　*　　*

The purpose of this narrative is to explore the experiences of Manghams who wore the gray those many years ago, to the extent that surviving source material makes this possible, and to show what modern researchers can learn about a family's past. In the process, I have tried to learn whatever I could about these men as human beings, as family men and as soldiers, in order to recreate something of their essential natures, as well as to reach some conclusions about their war, their cause, and their society. I suspected my findings would reflect the classic interpretations of the Confederate experience portrayed by Bell Irvin Wiley's study *The Life of Johnny Reb: The Common Soldier of the Confederacy*, and indeed they have in large degree. Since the various branches of the Mangham family comprised a passable cross-section of the Deep South's lowland farmers, plantation owners, and tradesmen, it is unsurprising that their individual military careers reflected most of the strengths and weaknesses of the Southern fighting man and his variegated military organizations. As students of the Civil War realize, the distinction between the two is not merely academic.

The resulting narrative thus seeks to develop the separate (but overlapping) stories of thirty-seven different men. They were primarily yeoman farmers, of course, but Frank Mangham was a Mississippi wheelwright and James A. Mangham was a sawyer in Mobile. James O. Mangham was a young plantation owner and schoolteacher in Taylor County, Georgia, while John H. Mangham was a judge in nearby Pike County. Two brothers, Thomas J. and Wiley P. Mangham, owned and edited the *Saint Clair Diamond* in Ashville, Alabama, prior to enlisting with their employees in May 1861.

Their military ranks spanned the spectrum from private to colonel, including Sam Mangham, who left his prosperous business and plantation in Georgia's Spalding County to serve as both. Most served as "webfoot" infantrymen, although some of them were detailed to man artillery pieces or act as marines aboard gunboats. Henry and William R. Mangham served the guns, while Wiley, Tom, and Bush Mangham joined artillery units, but soon found themselves shouldering muskets in the infantry. Willis Mangham "jined the buttermilk cavalry" in Texas, although his life in the saddle certainly was not the pampered one implied by the Rebel foot soldiers' wisecracking jibe, "Who ever saw a dead cavalryman?" Their service ranged across the crazyquilt of parallel, overlapping, competing, and even conflicting organizations that undertook to defend the Confederacy (or specified portions thereof), and which threaten to bewilder modern readers who mistakenly suppose that the Confederate Army was a monolithic, rational organization. Thus, we see Manghams serving not only in the state volunteer regiments that comprised the bulk of the Provisional Army of the Confederate States, but also in militia units, State Guards, or State Reserves. Sam Mangham was again exceptional in this respect: he served in every one of these categories! Manghams aged 16 to 56 enlisted from Georgia, Florida, Alabama, Mississippi, Louisiana and Texas, and they marched and fought in every single state of the Confederacy, plus New Mexico, Missouri, Kentucky, Maryland, Pennsylvania, and the District of Columbia.

4

Given their various backgrounds and experiences, their most obvious shared characteristic was their surname. Even that, however, can be deceptive, for they lived in an era of developing literacy and evolving surnames. The name Mangham, as they

WESLEY MANGRUM, 20TH
TENNESSEE, WOUNDED AT
MURFREESBORO. HIS SON JOHN
ADOPTED THE SPELLING
MANGHAM AFTER THE WAR.
-Courtesy of Timothy Mangham

rendered it, seems to have crossed the Atlantic by the 1660s from England, although family lore then (and since) often identified it as Irish, Welsh, or even French. Probably due to phonetic spelling, *Mangham* often became *Mangum*, a version that predominated in Virginia and the Carolinas long before the Civil War.[5] Many obviously pronounced their name with a trill, thus producing the variants Mangrum or Mangram, which dominated in Tennessee by the same time.[6]

The Solomon Mangham family group, which migrated from the Carolinas into central Georgia in the late 18th century, intentionally revived and formalized the spelling *Mangham*, however, based on their study of existing records. One of Solomon's nephews, James C. Mangham, was a Georgia state senator when he wrote to his close kinsman Willie Person Mangum in 1823, upon the latter's election to the United States Senate. James observed that "on Examining the Register of names from England Ireland and wales—I find that the original name In Ireland—Is Spelt—Mangham—which Has been the cause of the alteration in the Spelling the same—the family is Numerous here." Most of the Southerners who spelled their name Mangham by the time of the Civil War were thus descended from Solomon or James C. Mangham. These wartime Manghams traced their ancestors to Georgia at the turn of the century, and through them to Granville, Orange, and Wake counties in North Carolina, thence to Surry and Isle of Wight counties in Virginia.[7]

Two sons of Solomon's brother Joseph Mangum were the primary exceptions to this rule. One, William Mangham, moved to Georgia about the same time as his Uncle Solomon, and the two maintained close contacts in Hancock and Putnam counties. William and his sons established a solid record of prosperity and public service in Putnam and Henry counties before moving across the Chattahoochee to newly opened territories in Russell County, Alabama. The family of William's brother, Josiah Thomas Mangum, emigrated from Granville County to western Georgia and eastern Alabama in the late 1820s. There, several of his sons adopted the spelling Mangham while living amidst their numerous well-established cousins; several other sons

5

nevertheless retained the spelling Mangum after moving to Texas. The ongoing westward migrations of this period resulted in the influx of numerous other Mangum and Mangrum families into the states of the Deep South, where most retained their now-accustomed spellings alongside their Mangham cousins and neighbors.[8]

My subsequent research on the Civil War connections of the Mangham family has therefore involved a significant amount of genealogical detective work aimed at distinguishing my intended subjects from their much more numerous Mangum and Mangrum relatives. I have placed much of this evidence in endnotes or the Genealogical Appendix, except where it contributes to placing individuals and family groups in the appropriate context. The census data so essential to this aspect of my research played a major role in identifying many aspects of a Civil War soldier's personal life, however, both before and after the war. Especially when combined with information derived from agricultural production schedules, slave censuses, tax rolls and the like, this census material, even with its limitations, provides a gold mine of data about families, occupations, economic status, literacy, and settlement patterns. Published county histories and genealogical publications on Mangham and Mangum families have proved extremely useful in expanding upon these primary sources, as have articles and obituaries from 19th and 20th century newspapers.

The National Archives' official Compiled Military Service Records (CMSR) served as the fundamental source of specific information about each soldier's military service, although I have made use of many other types of unit records from state, local, and national archives. I must stress that the original Confederate muster rolls, which comprise the backbone of the CMSRs, offer us a series of snapshots of unit strength, typically at two- to four-month intervals in the very *best* cases. As such, they fall far short of providing a seamless narrative of each man's service career. A soldier marked "present" on the day of a given muster formation could have been absent for any number of reasons since the preceding muster, and we probably would not know unless his Orderly Sergeant made a notation on the muster roll. Indeed, many units actually mustered weeks or months after the dates *for which they mustered*, and one finds that they did not always record this deviation explicitly, despite regulatory requirements to do so. Therefore, a soldier's presence or absence at any given battle is difficult to determine with absolute accuracy, unless additional evidence (such as records of wounds, capture, or death) provides the necessary confirmation. I have treated this ambiguity with due regard, without unduly cluttering the narrative with caveats.

I have used the justly famous *War of the Rebellion: Official Records of the Union and Confederate Armies* as my primary source of material for each unit's military activities. In many cases, archival sources, published memoirs and unit histories have allowed me to supplement this information to a greater or lesser degree, as have published county histories and other secondary sources. Taken as a whole, these sources have allowed me to depict, at least to a significant extent, the war as each Mangham soldier experienced it, although the quality and quantity of available source materials varied widely from case to case. To my regret, in only two instances have I succeeded in finding a description of the war in the soldier's own words. Since the Georgia Department of

Archives and History has preserved the wartime letters of Pvt. Willoughby Hill Mangham on microfilm, I was able to use his own words to help portray his experiences in the 11th Georgia Volunteers. Thomas Jefferson Mangham wrote a series of letters to his uncle's newspaper in 1861 and 1862, and these missives to the *Jacksonville Republican* provide thoughtful insights about life in the 25th Alabama Infantry. Official correspondence survives from many of their cousins, as do postwar letters and articles, wartime letters by close comrades, and other primary sources.

Willoughby, Tom and their Mangham kinsmen in Confederate uniform served in many different units and at varying times and places, thus posing a major challenge to organizing a coherent narrative of their experiences. The problem is multiplied by the fact that brothers often fought in completely different theaters of war, while cousins sometimes served in the same regiment and shared the same experiences. Consequently, organization by family group risked some repetition in narrating military events. Using a theater of operations as an organizing principle, however, would have isolated close relatives from each other in the narrative, negating much of the human drama inherent in their stories. I have therefore sought to blend both approaches, while retaining my reliance on family groups as the structural framework of each soldier's story. In the process, their widely varying experiences serve to illustrate numerous perspectives of the South at war, as well as providing a significant level of detail on the activities and personalities of many Confederate units.

Of course, the story of Mangham Confederate soldiers and their lives is not one that is explicitly about slavery *per se*, but the South's "peculiar institution" was at the root of the Confederacy's existence. I had hoped to find plentiful evidence of the Manghams' views on the entire issue, but the dearth of anecdotal information has forced me to content myself, in large part, with statistical information about slave ownership. The assiduous search for statistical data, however, facilitated a number of inferential conclusions which are probably more important historically, although much less satisfactory for the task of weaving a historical narrative about individual Mangham Confederates and their families. In the first place, the complex pattern of slave ownership apparent among the various Mangham families in the Deep South highlights potentially serious flaws in commonly cited statistics about the relatively low percentage of Confederate soldiers who "had a stake in slavery." Such statistics commonly rely upon assessments of the number of soldiers who owned slaves. Assertions of this genre are sometimes used defensively, even reflexively, to buttress the argument that the "war wasn't really about slavery after all," since many soldiers never owned slaves. Many serious modern analysts interpret the evidence in this way, based on their evaluation of the available information. Their readers often encounter such assessments of "slavery-connectedness" as a jumping-off point for insightful, even spellbinding, examinations of Confederate motivation for secession, enlistment, or combat. It seems clear, however, that these assessments are ripe for renewed analysis.[9]

Whether the proponents of these statistically based assessments are defensive, scurrilous, or serious in intent, my examination of Mangham Confederates suggests limitations inherent in the "first premises" of such studies. In the first place, any extensive analytical work with ante- or post-bellum census data quickly forces the researcher to wrestle with numerous inaccuracies. Any well-grounded genealogist could tell us this, but I have encountered precious few historians who acknowledge the possible implications for an analysis grounded upon fine distinctions, e.g. exact numbers of slave owners, or minor distinctions between the numbers of slaves they owned. Historians must beware of simple errors in census counts for one thing; the overwhelming number and type of errors relating to their owners' names, genders, ages, birthplaces, literacy, school attendance, and property ownership makes one leery about much of the slave-related data, to be sure! The fault was not all with the census-takers, of course, although some of them were clearly taxed to the limit by the job of organizing, conducting, and recording their enumeration. One senses that they often fell victim to informants who began their answers with, "Well, I reckon. . .", at which point the proceedings took on the nature of educated guesswork.

My research on these Mangham Confederate soldiers involved a great deal of work in tax records, and it soon became utterly unremarkable to note discrepancies between census and tax records regarding every type of property, whether slave or real estate. Part of this results from simple error, and part perhaps from monetary concerns of valuation and taxation. Clearly, however, some of the variation was due to the fact that slave owning was a dynamic business, like any other economic activity. The man who owned five slaves in 1858 tax records might own none in 1860, or he might own ten. Sometimes the cause for the change doubtless was natural increase through birth or decrease through death, and sometimes it was due to the owner's financial status at a given point in time. Additionally, the man who owned a certain acreage and number of slaves in a given county under study often owned significant acreage in other counties or states. Sometimes his slaves lived and worked there, possibly under his name or sometimes under his agent's name, where they remain difficult to trace to the true owner. In any case, it is very easy to miscalculate a man's economic status based on the snapshot view provided by a discrete census entry. John N. Mangham of Pike County, Georgia, owned thousands of acres of land in other counties, but one would never know to look there without examining tax records.

These errors are minor in magnitude, however, compared to a much more fundamental problem with the typical statistics-driven analysis. In no case does a survey of census data allow historians to draw conclusions about slave ownership based on a *family's* propensity for slave ownership, much less the *extended family's* propensity for it. These are crucial distinctions, even in light of the reality that some men and women made purely individual decisions about slave ownership, just as they did on a wide range of other issues, whether it be marriage partner, choice of profession, or the sale price of a bale of cotton. Given the popular history of "rugged individualism" and our modern-day geographic mobility, however, it may be too easy to conclude mistakenly that each man "was an island" in 1860. Despite these powerful modern images, *only one* of the thirty-seven Manghams who enlisted in the Confederate Army lived demonstrably alone and apart from his immediate family, and this man, Willis

8

Mangham, originally moved to Washington County, Texas, on the trail of his deceased brother Nathaniel. On the contrary, most Manghams were absolutely surrounded by an intricate kinship network, and those who emigrated commonly followed (or led the way for) brothers, fathers, uncles, in-laws, and cousins.

Documentary evidence indicates that only nine of the thirty-seven Manghams in the Confederate Army personally owned one or more slaves during or before the Civil War, which seems to support existing studies that emphasize how few soldiers were directly involved in the "peculiar institution." Of the twenty-eight not confirmed as personally owning slaves, however, at least *twenty* were sons of families who did own slaves in 1860. At least six of the remaining eight lived in very close association to aunts or uncles who owned slaves. Only two youngsters have no clear-cut connection to relatives who owned slaves. Bush W. Mangham enlisted in Butler County, amid the cotton lands of Alabama's "Black Belt," and probably near the plantation of his aunt, Rhoda Callaway Mangham Moore. Her deceased husband, Thomas H. Mangham, and her second husband, Seborn Moore, both owned slaves. John S. Mangham, an orphaned youngster in Mary Croley's household in McDonough, Georgia, was apparently a grandson of James M. Mangham, a small farmer and slaveowner in neighboring Butts County. If my genealogical conclusions are correct, then, *every single* Mangham Confederate soldier had close paternal family associations with the institution of slavery. The already one-sided nature of these figures does not even attempt to account for the slave-owning propensities of the Manghams' in-laws. Although such research lay outside the scope of the present inquiry, fragmentary evidence indicates that their story would be essentially the same.

Although limitations of scope obviate any assertion that the Mangham Confederates were statistically "typical" of Southerners in general, it seems clear that they typified Dixie's lowland farmers in many respects. While many lived in or migrated to hilly areas, none lived in the mountainous areas well known for bare subsistence agriculture and Unionist views, such as north Georgia and Alabama, East Tennessee, or the Ozarks. On the contrary, the extended Mangham family largely reflected historian Frank Owsley's thesis in *Plain Folks of the Old South*, in which he asserts that Southern emigrants in the early 19th century sought cheap frontier lands that *looked and felt like the homes they left back east*. Likewise, they strove to gain the prosperity to buy more lands and the slaves necessary to help work them, and thereby rise to the economic level of the comfortable farmer or small planter. The Manghams' specific social aspirations remain unclear, but their families and individual members repeated this economic pattern over and over again.[10] Some may have eschewed slave ownership on principle, and perhaps others manumitted their slaves after a change of heart, but no such evidence ever came to light during my research. Indeed, it seems that just about every Mangham of that era owned slaves if he could afford them.

Unfortunately, the lack of documentary evidence has made it impossible to offer any conclusions about the Manghams' treatment of their slaves, their individual views on the morality of the "peculiar institution," or other related, albeit socially *brissant,* topics. In the absence of documentation that would facilitate worthwhile social analysis, one presumes that most of them exemplified the sternly paternalistic approach that appears to have been common among slave owners who themselves were hard working, God-fearing people. Some may have been lazy, vicious hellraisers or "no accounts," but county histories rarely record such people and most obituaries benignly omit such characterizations. In no case did a Mangham's military or civilian record indicate any such misanthropic tendencies. The Simon Legree image of the vicious slave driver had a basis in reality, of course, and its emotionally loaded, uncompromising quality was one that helped bring the great national debate on slavery to bitter fruition in civil war. Many of slavery's supporters tried to explain to abolitionists, foreigners, and Northerners in general that the Legree-types were social outcasts and faced legal sanction for their misdeeds, and their motivations for such explanations doubtless spanned the entire spectrum. For some, it must have been an essentially accurate reflection of slavery as they practiced it and saw it practiced; for others it was merely a cynical attempt to manipulate opinion, and nothing else.[11]

Nevertheless, every slave owner was a practitioner of a socioeconomic system that was hard-pressed to remain on a firm ideological foundation amidst a Western civilization in the throes of the great liberal revolutions of the 18th and 19th century. The post-Enlightenment Liberal idea, which asserted the grand natural imperatives of liberty and equality, was evolving and expanding continually, as it does still, and some Southerners already had concluded that chattel slavery was morally unsupportable. Although the breadth of such dissent is a disputed issue among modern historians, it seems clear that this was still an *avant garde* opinion at best. Perhaps many worried about it, but relatively few concluded to act upon such doubts by freeing their slaves.

After decades of increasing debate about slavery, which was the primary ingredient of a witches' brew of states-rights issues including tariffs and territorial settlement, the distracted country faced a presidential election in November 1860. In the Deep South, where the Manghams lived, adult white males could vote the Democratic ticket, either for Stephen A. Douglas or John C. Breckenridge, or they could support John Bell, who headed the Constitutional-Union ticket. Bell's platform was vague on the crucial issue of slavery, emphasizing the need to uphold constitutionally protected rights, while remaining politically unified. Since pro- and anti-slavery advocates argued endlessly over the constitutional basis for their views, Bell's stance did little more than hold out the prospect of continued wrangling over the issue that was rending the very fabric of the American polity. Stephen Douglas represented the northern wing of a fractured Democratic Party, and his "popular sovereignty" platform asserted that the settlers of each territory should decide the fate of slavery within its boundaries. Kentuckian John Breckenridge received the nomination of the Southern wing of the Democratic Party, on the constitutional principle that one's rights to property were inviolate in all of the territories, regardless of any locally imposed attempts to restrict the practice. Specifically, Breckenridge supporters insisted that Congress take positive action to reinforce the judicial precedent rendered in the rancorously disputed Dred Scott case of 1857, which confirmed the inviolability of slave property throughout the territories.

Introduction

Abraham Lincoln's name was not even on the ballot in the Manghams' polling places, as his infant Republican Party had no organization in the Southern states. The Republicans comprised abolitionists and Free-Soilers as core-level interest groups, and their platform called for positively prohibiting slavery's expansion into the territories. In a country whose society, economy, and political structures were largely predicated upon geographical expansion and mobility, such a platform promised the ultimate extinction of the "peculiar institution." It was only a matter of time before numerous territories (and future territories) became states, and Republican logic seemed to guarantee that every single senator and representative from the future states would espouse anti-slavery views. The concept of prohibiting slavery in the territories also equated to codifying the moral condemnation of slave owners, since their social and economic organization would thus be adjudged as meriting explicit legal prohibition in most of the country. Although Lincoln expressed his determination to leave the "peculiar institution" unmolested within its existing boundaries, any Republican vote amounted to a vote for the rejection of slavery and condemnation of slave owners.

For anyone who may have owned slaves as a mere matter of convenience, as opposed to conviction, the Republican view promised an economic upheaval at the very least. The loss of slave property, whether sooner or later, thus required a complete reordering of such persons' economic lives. For Southern whites who *embraced* their society as it currently existed, however, any concept of immediate abolition or gradual emancipation opened a veritable Pandora's Box of trials and tribulations. Where would the freedmen live? How would they make a living? What political rights would they have? Where would they attend school to learn the basic skills necessary to exercise their new responsibilities? How would they fit into a society that prided itself that every man was equal to the next, but really meant only *white* men? As chattels, their station was clear, but every single political, social, legal, and economic mechanism in society would require fundamental change after emancipation.

Although these may seem like lame and ineffectual rationalizations to late-20th century Americans, we should tread respectfully and somewhat self-consciously upon the graves of the past. Anyone can see that we continue to struggle today with the tremendously complex socioeconomic problems arising from slavery itself, as well as the nature of its eventual overthrow, and no modern observer dares minimize the impact of economic factors on the democratic process. On the purely practical side, most Northerners in 1860 had little need to seek a solution. Few blacks lived there, so it was not their problem. Many cared little for either abolitionists or slave owners, but abhorred the threat to national unity posed by the festering question of slavery. Southerners did not have the luxury of choosing any such "ostrich" solution even had they wanted one. In 1860, even those who may have favored some mechanism of gradual emancipation found themselves confronted squarely by a Republican Party whose views clashed fundamentally with theirs. Southerners considered that a Lincoln victory would amount to an overthrow of their rights as free and equal citizens in the country, as their society would, in essence, be branded outlaw. The individual signposts

11

along the route to social extinction might remain hazy, but the end of the line seemed clear enough; it would be only a matter of time. Such a conclusion spelled danger indeed for America's body politic, for Dixie still relished the *code duello*, albeit informally rather than as a matter of law, and abolitionist condemnation of their society was both intended and accepted as an insult. In their society, an insulted individual was likely to "demand satisfaction."

In his classic 1941 study *The Mind of the South*, author W. J. Cash sought to dissect the apparently distinctive nature of the 19th century Southerner. He concluded that the prideful individualism of the backcountry frontier and plantation alike had, as its essential quality, "the boast, voiced or not, on the part of every Southerner, that he would knock hell out of whoever dared to cross him." Against the background of a "simple, direct, and immensely personal" society, this character assured the "perpetuation and acceleration of the tendency to violence." Although Cash believed this tendency to be somewhat juvenile in a psychological sense, he emphasized: "I am very far from suggesting that it ought to be held in contempt. For it reached its ultimate incarnation in the Confederate soldier."[12]

Although it is impossible to determine accurately how these and other factors influenced the Manghams as they cast their votes in November 1860, one presumes that some voted for Bell, as did many Southerners, in the hope that something could be worked out eventually. Many doubtless cast their ballots for Breckenridge, insisting that the slavery question be solved once and for all, and in a manner that explicitly supported their society, past, present, and future. When one assesses both their propensity for owning slaves and their subsequent military records, it becomes clear that most Manghams felt a strong motivation to fight and to keep fighting, once Lincoln secured election, secession ensued, and the Federal government sought to "coerce" seceding states back into the Union. At least four Mangham Confederate soldiers had belonged to prewar militia companies; one of them, along with a second who had no known militia connection, enlisted in a volunteer company even before gunfire erupted at Fort Sumter on April 12, 1861. A further sixteen enlisted over the course of 1861, while thirteen more mustered in during the great wave of voluntarism in early 1862, spurred on by a string of Confederate defeats and the passage of the Conscription Act. Of the six who enlisted afterwards, only James M. D. Mangham and James O. Mangham had been of military age earlier in the war; the other four were either young boys or older men.

Of all the Mangham men and boys known to be between the ages of 17 and 45 by 1864, only James Green and Robert J. Mangham did not serve in the army. Lamed by a clubfoot from birth, Bob went to Virginia with his brothers and tried to enlist, but apparently had to content himself with performing camp and courier duties. James may have been exempted from conscription due to his profession, or perhaps his service was undocumented amidst the chaos that engulfed northern Louisiana. The only others of military age who did not serve were Robert H. Mangham, a young Methodist minister in Texas who died in 1863, and John N. Mangham, who turned 50 in 1864. John was duly enrolled as a militiaman in Pike County, Georgia, but he was at the maximum age limit for conscription and his position as county clerk was among those formally exempted from military service.

*   *   *   *   *

To a great degree, these men and boys exemplified the hopes, aspirations, strengths, and weaknesses of lowland Southerners of the ante-bellum era. Although the countenances of many are almost obscured by the shadows of time, they generally seem to have been fair specimens of the pioneer stock whence they came. Most were pleasant enough companions for their peers and humble before God, but they certainly shared with their Northern fellow citizens the contemporary Anglo-American sense of superiority and destiny that bode ill for the non-Western, non-Christian peoples they encountered. Strong currents of confidence and pride combined with a dose of suspicion for "Yankees" in the prewar decades to make a dangerous opponent when the shooting started in 1861. Once it did, their pride in past accomplishments matched their confidence in a bright future as an independent nation. Perhaps Cash captured the essence of their outlook:

> And down to the final day at Appomattox his officers knew that the way to get him to execute an order without malingering was to flatter and jest, never to command too brusquely and forthrightly. And yet—and yet—and by virtue of precisely these unsoldierly qualities, he was, as no one will care to deny, one of the world's very finest fighting men.
>
> Allow what you will for *esprit de corps*, for this or for that, the thing that sent him swinging up the slope at Gettysburg on that celebrated, gallant afternoon was before all else nothing more than the thing which elsewhere accounted for his violence—was nothing more or less than his conviction, the conviction of every farmer among what was essentially only a band of farmers, that nothing living could cross him and get away with it.[13]

This, then, is their story.

---

[1] Death certificate #31904, Charles A. Mangham, Texas Dept. of Health, Bureau of Vital Statistics; *San Antonio Express*, July 24, 1931.

[2] *San Antonio Express*, July 24, 1931; CMSR, Charles A. Mangham, 18th Alabama.

[3] William F. Fox, *Regimental Losses in the American Civil War, 1861-1865* (Albany: Brendow Printing, 1898; reprint, Dayton: Morningside, 1985), pp. 557, 561; Confederate Military Service Memoranda, Robert M. Goodgame, September 24, 1904, 18th Alabama, RG 9, vol. 18, MDAH.

[4] Wiley Paul Mangham died several months after Charles. Although duly counted among the Mangham Confederates, his unit affiliation is unknown. His service is documented by family lore and his United Confederate Veterans' medal.

[5] Vaughn Ballard, comp., *Solomon Mangham: His Ancestors and Descendants* (Arlington: Family Histories, 1989), pp. 31-33; John T. Palmer, *The Mangums of Virginia, North Carolina, South Carolina . . . and Adjoining States* (Santa Rosa: 1992), pp. 1-2.

[6] Several men served in Company H, 20th Tennessee Infantry, whose records reflect them indiscriminately as Mangrum, Mangram, Mangum, or Mangham; typically, the former two spellings predominated. One, Private Wesley Mangrum (shown in a heavily retouched photograph in the text), was severely wounded at Murfreesboro. Although unable to write his name, he clearly pronounced it with the trill. His son John pronounced it that way until his death, although he and succeeding descendants re-adopted the Mangham spelling. (See letters, Timothy Mangham to author, December 2 and December 13, 1995. Tim is a direct descendant of Wes Mangrum.) These Tennesseeans, and others who adopted the Mangham spelling after the war, such as artilleryman Theophilus S. Mangrum and William H. Mangum of the 8th Mississippi, are omitted from this study.

[7] Ibid.; Henry Thomas Shanks, ed., *The Papers of Willie Person Mangum*, vol. 1 (Raleigh: State Dept. of Archives and History, 1950), pp. 84-85. Senator Willie (pronounced "Wiley") Mangum remained a prominent figure in national politics until the Civil War. Upon the death of President Harrison, Sen. Mangum served as acting Vice President of the United States.

[8] Joseph Mangum had a son named William, but my identification of William Mangham as this person remains circumstantial. His age, movements, and legal transactions all establish a close connection to Solomon Mangham and to Joseph's son, Josiah. By 1860, his surviving sons had re-adopted the spelling *Mangum*.

[9] William C. Davis, *The Cause Lost: Myths and Realities of the Confederacy* (Lawrence: Univ. Press of Kansas, 1996), pp. 182-183. Davis, a renowned Civil War historian and prolific author, emphasizes the role of slavery in instigating secession, but asserts, "Probably 90 percent of the men who wore the gray had never owned a slave and had no personal interest at all either in slavery or in the shadow issue of state rights." Although Davis is certainly no apologist for slavery or the South in general, it seems to me that his assessment seriously overstates the case in this instance.

[10] For another prominent historian whose work reflects these views, see Emory M. Thomas, *The Confederate Nation: 1861-1863* (New York: Harper & Row, 1979), pp. 9-11.

[11] Good perspectives on slavery's fundamentally personal and paternalistic qualities are in Ibid., pp. 9-15; Davis, *The Cause Lost*, pp. 183-186; and Kenneth M. Stampp, *The Peculiar Institution: Slavery in the Ante-Bellum South* (New York: Vintage Books, 1956), pp. 162-163, 228-232, 322-330.

[12] W. J. Cash, *The Mind of the South* (Alfred A. Knopf, Inc., 1941; reprint, New York: Vintage Books, 1991), pp. 42-44.

[13] Ibid.

PART I

FROM CAROLINA TO THE BANKS OF THE OCONEE: SOLOMON MANGHAM COMES TO GEORGIA

PROLOGUE: EARLY DAYS IN VIRGINIA, THE CAROLINAS, AND ON THE GEORGIA FRONTIER

Solomon Mangham's exact antecedents remain cloaked in mystery, but existing genealogy accepts him as a son of William Mangum, Sr., whose father was John Mangum of Surry and Isle of Wight counties, in Virginia. John may have been born in England or Ireland about 1670, and possibly was the immigrant ancestor of the Mangum/Mangham families that subsequently spread throughout the coastal and Deep South. John's marriage to Frances Bennett in Isle of Wight County about 1694 was apparently blessed with ten children between 1703 and 1722: John, William, Frances, Joseph, Nicholas, Sarah, James, Mary, Henry and Samuel.[1]

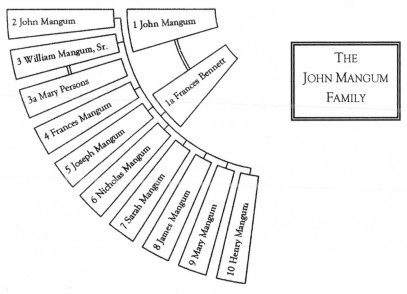

William, the second eldest of the seven boys, was born about 1706. His marriage to Mary Persons about 1731 seems to have resulted in the birth of at least eight male children, with the first six born in Albemarle Parish, Virginia, between 1732 and 1741. Their given names were thoroughly English in origin, and largely repeated those given to William and his siblings: Samuel, John, James, William, Arthur, Henry, Joseph and Solomon. The tentative nature of Mangham/Mangum genealogy in the 17th century is, to a significant degree, a result of this recycling of Christian names, which makes it extremely difficult to distinguish a single individual from a veritable host of close relatives with the same name. This trend established a pattern that typified subsequent generations, in which the given names of parents, aunts, uncles, and grandparents prescribed the great majority of names given to children.[2]

WILLIAM MANGUM, SR.,

AND HIS

FAMILY

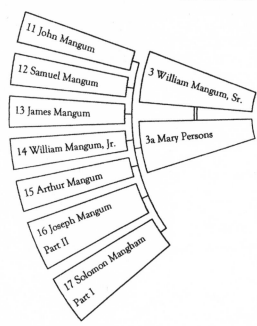

11 John Mangum

12 Samuel Mangum

13 James Mangum

14 William Mangum, Jr.

15 Arthur Mangum

16 Joseph Mangum
Part II

17 Solomon Mangham
Part I

3 William Mangum, Sr.

3a Mary Persons

William and Mary Mangum moved into North Carolina by 1748, settling near the point where the Roanoke River crossed from Virginia into its neighbor to the south. Granville County records from 1754-1755 show him and some of his sons and nephews in the county militia company. His son, William Jr., became a prominent (or notorious) Loyalist soldier in South Carolina, Georgia, and Florida after many British colonists in America rose in revolution two decades later. Indeed, he fought for years against rebels that included some of his own nephews. At least two daughters of "William the Loyalist," Mary and Sarah, married and remained in the newly minted United States after their father was exiled to Spanish Florida and thence to British Nova Scotia about 1785. He remarried and started another family there; a son born in 1798 was named Solomon, in honor of William's youngest brother. Documents surviving from British Nova Scotia routinely refer to William and his family as Mangham, thus using the common English suffix of "-ham" instead of the (apparently) phonetic derivation Mangum that characterized most surviving records from the Southern colonies.[3]

"William the Loyalist's" youngest brothers, Joseph and Solomon, were born in North Carolina about 1750 and 1755 respectively. Both apparently avoided military service during the Revolution, which scourged their family with the hard hand of civil war. George Carrington evidently served as a substitute for Solomon; his father John Carrington later served as guardian for orphaned James C. Mangham, one of Solomon's nephews who followed him when he resettled farther south. One of Joseph's sons bore the name William, like so many of his kinfolk, and he may have been the William Mangham who accompanied Solomon in his eventual move to Georgia (see Chapter VII).[4]

16

Solomon remained in the fertile tobacco-growing areas of North Carolina until about 1782-1783, before settling near Gilkey's Creek in South Carolina by 1784. Making his living as a planter, he remained in the Union County area until about 1790, when he moved south once more. By 1793 he lived in Wilkes County, Georgia, and he moved on to Warren County by the next year. Shortly thereafter, he settled his family for good in the Hancock-Putnam county area, along the banks of the Oconee River.[5]

41 Willis Austin Mangham
Chapter II

42 Thomas Mangham
Ch. VI

43 James M. Mangham
Ch. V

44 Unknown Mangham

45 John C. Mangham
Ch. IV

46 Wiley P. Mangham
Ch. II

47 Henry H. Mangham
Ch. VI

17 Solomon Mangham
Part I

17b Sarah Ann Bennett

THE
SOLOMON
MANGHAM
FAMILY

When Solomon and Sarah Ann arrived in Georgia with their sons Willis, Thomas, and James M. Mangham, along with nephews William and James C. Mangham, they carried with them the agrarian traditions of North Carolina. Moderately prosperous landholders, they used black slaves to help tame the wilderness they found on the Cherokee frontier. They kept weapons handy, of course, as both common sense and the militia tradition dictated that adult males bear the burden of local defense. As the Creek War of 1836 would re-emphasize, conflicts between Indians and white settlers were an ever-present possibility, and a half-dozen or more Mangham men enlisted in the state militia and volunteer units that responded to the emergency.

Frontier life offered other dangers, as well, to include outlawry, disease, and wild animals. These dangers did not abate for some decades, as lawyer and farmer Nathaniel Mangum could attest. Nat, a son of Solomon Mangham's grand-nephew James

17

Mangum, spent a harrowing night in the woods of north Georgia's Gilmer County, after devoting an idyllic afternoon to gathering chestnuts from mouse den trees atop Cowpen Mountain. As the shadows gathered in early evening, Nat built a small shelter of saplings to protect himself against prowling animals and lay down to sleep as best he could. Just as he was dozing off, he felt a stinging pain in his leg; a prowling panther had slipped its paw through an opening in Nat's improvised pen and slashed his pants open from knee to shoetop, slicing open his leg in the process! Far from any help, Nat drew his heavy machete-like knife, fashioned from a sickle blade, and held it ready as he waited breathlessly in the moonlit pen. Before long, the big cat eased a paw through another crack and Nat swung his knife with the strength of desperation. The heavy blade cut cleanly through the big cat's leg, sending the wounded animal screeching into the forest. Nat survived that long night and doubtless greeted the dawn with heartfelt relief, before limping home with his hard-won chestnuts and a renewed respect for the dangers inherent in even the most innocuous aspects of frontier life.[6]

Besides the scar on his leg, however, Nat Mangum bore incontrovertible evidence of the Southern frontiersman's ability to vanquish those dangers if he used his weapons with a steady nerve . Neatly tucked into his chestnut bag was the panther's paw.[7]

---

[1] Vaughn Ballard, comp., *Solomon Mangham: His Ancestors and Descendants* (Arlington: Family Histories, 1989), pp. 31-33; John T. Palmer, *The Mangums of Virginia, North Carolina, South Carolina . . . and Adjoining States* (Santa Rosa: author, 1992), pp. 4ff., 75; James L. Parham, *Pleasant Mangum and All His Kin: The Story of the Bennetts, the Mangums and the Parhams* (Baltimore: Gateway Press, 1997), p. 213.

[2] Ballard, *Solomon Mangham*, pp. 41-46; Palmer, *The Mangums*, pp. 5ff.; Parham, *Pleasant Mangum*, p. 213.

[3] Ballard, *Solomon Mangham*, pp. 42-47; Palmer, *The Mangums*, pp. 5, 34-36; *MFB* 35: 9-11; *MFB* 36: 3-6; *MFB* 37: 3-5. Thomas L. Hughes researched and wrote the various excellent *MFB* articles on "William Mangum the Loyalist." For additional analysis of William and his outlawed comrades in revolutionary Georgia and Spanish Florida, see Carole Watterson Troxler, "Loyalist Refugees and the British Evacuation of East Florida, 1783-1785," *FHQ* 60, no. 1 (July 1981): 1ff.; Joseph B. Lockey, "The Florida Banditti, 1783," *FHQ* 24, no. 2 (October 1945): 87ff. Most of Granville County where the early Mangums settled now belongs to Warren and Orange counties.

[4] Ballard, *Solomon Mangham*, p. 42; Palmer, *The Mangums*, pp. 37, 48, 57, 75, 85; Parham, *Pleasant Mangum*, p. 216.

[5] Ballard, *Solomon Mangham*, pp. 47-48; Palmer, *The Mangums*, p. 75.

[6] Palmer, *The Mangums*, p. 102; Parham, *Pleasant Mangum*, pp. 215, 218; Lawrence L. Stanley, *A Little History of Gilmer County* (N.p.: 1975), pp. 15-16.

[7] Palmer, *The Mangums*, p. 102; Stanley, *Gilmer County*, pp. 15-16. Nat's luck ran out on March 20, 1864, when army deserters murdered him at his home in Fannin County. He was 55 years old, and had served as a captain in the 16th Battalion, Georgia State Guard cavalry (see CMSR).

Chapter I: "The First Stations in Publick Searvice": The James C. Mangham Family of Glynn County

1. AN ORPHAN FINDS HIS ROOTS: JAMES C. MANGHAM AND THE FAMILY NAME

When Solomon Mangham died in Putnam County in 1810, he bequeathed five slaves and a moderate estate to his wife Sarah Ann and their large family. As the patriarch of the Georgia Manghams passed away, his nephew James C. Mangham was just beginning his rise to local prominence. Born about 1771, James was orphaned early in life; Nathaniel Carrington, who apparently was James's uncle, took charge of the young boy at his dying father's request. A surviving letter from James indicates that his life in the Carrington household was a rough one, and Orange County records show that Nathaniel passed the mantle of guardianship to his brother John C. Carrington in 1782. Later, James apparently moved into South Carolina and Georgia with his Uncle Solomon, and surviving evidence shows a close relationship between the two. Whereas Solomon settled permanently in central Georgia, however, James moved farther eastward to the sugar-producing lands along the coast. Establishing a fine plantation near Brunswick, he was elected to the legislature from Glynn County in 1813, beginning many years of public service as a state assemblyman and senator. Although he was promoted in 1824 to lieutenant colonel of Glynn County's 3rd Regiment, Georgia Militia, newspaper articles consistently referred to him as "Major Mangham" until his death.[1]

Upon hearing of the 1823 election of his cousin's son, Willie P. Mangum, to the United States Senate from Orange County, North Carolina, James penned an intriguing letter to his younger relative. In it, he made clear that a conscious decision underlay the spelling of the family name in Georgia:

> Milledgeville, December the 11th 1823
>
> Dr Sir on Examining the Congressional election of My Mother State I find you have been elected from the Eighth District. I on this occasion open a correspondence with you—and have to State that on Examining the Register of names from England Ireland and wales—I find that the original name In Ireland—Is Spelt—Mangham—which Has been the cause of the alteration in the Spelling the same—the family is Numerous here—and some of them fills the first Stations in publick Searvice—if my memory serves me—I saw you when a small boy—and am Proud to hear of your prosperity—and would that I could personaly

commune with your Grand Ma Ma—and others—I have been in the Legislature of Georgia alternetly since the year 1813—and have been in the Senate for the Last 2 years. . . .I will thank you to attend in any shape or way—to the Interest of the Citizens of Georgia who lost negroes by the British In the late war—as the Majority was Taken from the Small County of Glynn—in which I live—my connections there lost considerable & yours also—by the name of Piles—is—the Daughter and Grand Children of old Wm. Mangum—your Grand fathers brother. . . .[2]

/s/ Jas. C. Mangham

P.S.   The number of negroes taken from our small county is about five hundred which Mr. Cuthburt of Tatnal[l] can certify.

James's 17-year-old daughter Caroline died the year he penned this letter, apparently preceded by her mother some years earlier. A September 1827 schedule of property shows that his second wife, Anne McKenzie, a widow three years his junior, owned nine slaves when she married James. Since one of these slave women had borne eight children by 1827, it is probable that James and Anne married by 1815.[3]

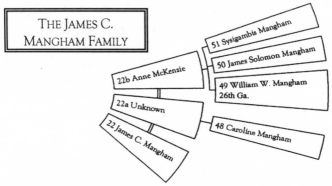

THE JAMES C. MANGHAM FAMILY

51 Sysigambis Mangham
50 James Solomon Mangham
49 William W. Mangham 26th Ga.
48 Caroline Mangham
22b Anne McKenzie
22a Unknown
22 James C. Mangham

Another of James's surviving letters from two decades later displays the strident expansionist, sectionalist, pro-slavery tone typical of the prewar Southern fire-eater after two decades of simmering unrest over the slavery issue. In it, the now elderly planter castigated North Carolina Senator Willie Mangum for his support of Henry Clay, a founder of the Whig Party and noted architect of its pro-business "American System,"[4] which many Democrats found so odious. Writing from his plantation at Bethel on October 13, 1844, James addressed his cousin's son as the "Honorable W. P. Mangum":

Dr Sir I am well & a bold plebian & truly hope this may find you & your sweat family in the same good health—please excuse my Boldness in atempting to trouble you with reading my imperfect Letter the time has been when I felt proud to heare of your High Station in Life, but now feel mortifyed to find you side with Mr. Clay—you as a southern Man 2d in command. In administering the general government, & could turn the tables in my oald beloved state are you to yield to the will of the self styled whigs of the grate Union—may God for Bid it, you have been chided By Mr Clay on the Senate floor, you in the Last Whig convention have been over Lookt by that party an ordinary man taken in your stead, for your Honours sake your countrys sake come and go with us we will Doo the Good-, can you Indorse the public conduct of Mr Clay & vote for him for president Oh that your God may Guide you Right. . . .for the sake of your free Blood that follows after you, I would not try to have you change policy as knowing you have Sterling worth, but the wisest man may be Deceived—the south would a have been pleased to a have made you president some years ago— and would yet if you would take the right side. . . .I have Laboured 40 years for the public in Glynn County, Ga—have never changed my policy for the sake of office Neither do I wish you to Doo it but I can tell you that the flatterey of J. M. Berrien, will never benefit you, Neither will the Clay party—his ambition is known—the former—Deceipt is known Clays changes & British Guilt is known— Mr. Berriens federalism is known—his changes is known—he was opposed to the last war—would brook the British insults—and oppression—the Decendence of Britons & France, here—is whigs—the first from hatred to Jackson the 2d from Hatred to Jackson & Vanburen, from giving payment by the french of the 25 millions of francks—the 3d party is under T. B. Ks Controll, same stripe yankeys.—Soft sawder & Ham oriaturecrates (these 3 partys rules the County— and trys to rule the whole seabord of Georgia—but cant Cum it—I wish you to answer this Letter—or the Next will be but short—as I will [illegible] then write and to the purpose—I Love you and all that has my Blood in there vains—Both the Carringtons & Mangums—our worthy old Gramp is for us

I am your obt Sevt   /s/ Jas. C. Mangham

. . .all the South, that has rightly judged—is for us   the northern Whigs [illegible] against us   then Let us be unitted at the South for the sake of our Dearest rights and not promote the whigs for the sake of office Nor suffer Adams & Clay to Dictate   save the Republic for Gods sake & your Country sake. . .Oh our Best Blood is in Texas holding out thare Hands to us as Drownding men for help—Doo grant it.-

[P. S.] I nurst you on my knees many be the times I have workt for your father under the whip as a poor orphan. I have been abused by your uncle Nathaniel Carrington many years. . . .I must quit—though have not said half anough if I am Drunk you must Excuse it, for it is with Ignorance and not with spirits for I have not taken a Drink for the sake of Drink in 73 years. During which time I have watcht every public man in the union Even the old Roman Jackson—watcht Clays Disobedience to his State and you to yours—both was wrong.[5]

James Mangham clearly had no use for compromise with the Free Soil movement, which he and many other Southerners viewed as a threat to their way of life. When he died four years later at age 76, his personal holdings amply reflected that way of life: sixteen slaves, 5046 acres of land, 1000 pounds of sugar, 6000 pounds of seed cotton, twelve guns, and 120 head of cattle were the most noteworthy items of an estate worth almost eleven thousand dollars. He left this legacy to his children William W., James Solomon, and Sysigambis, along with a small allotment for his widow. Anne was living in Ocala, Florida at the time of his death, residing with the son and daughter-in-law of James's sister (or cousin), Mary Mangum Piles. Since Anne maintained a separate estate in Glynn County as early as 1830 and moved to Florida at least two years before James died, it is likely that their marriage had effectively broken up before his death.[6]

Fifteen-year-old Sysigambis also lived near a number of her Piles relatives in 1850, while attending school in neighboring Wayne County. She was attending the Chalmers Institute in Scottsboro when she died on July 25, 1852 at the home of Mrs. Catherine Fitzgerald, and was laid to rest in Old Midway Cemetery near the state capital of Milledgeville. Her death left William alone, as 17-year-old James Solomon had succumbed to brain inflammation in Savannah in May 1848, and Anne Mangham passed away in Ocala on November 5, 1850. An examination of Marion County tax records makes it clear that Anne's 34 slaves and 160 acres of land went to Frances Piles, although no surviving probate documents record the administration of her estate.[7]

2. STANDING WATCH ON THE ATLANTIC COAST: PVT. WILLIAM W. MANGHAM, "BRUNSWICK RIFLES," STYLES'S 13TH (LATER 26TH) GEORGIA

William was still living in the coastal town of Brunswick in April 1854 when he filed a claim to settle his minor siblings' estates. Although he was almost 30 years old when his father died in 1847, James willed slaves to William in trust to Robert Hazlehurst, rather than directly to his mature eldest son. Apparently William never married or established a household of his own, and perhaps this was the reason for his father's action. He was working as a farmer while living with his Poncell (or Ponsell) relatives in 1850, and ten years later the census found him living in the household of Moses Wright, a farmer five years his junior. By this time, William was making his living as a carpenter, and he apparently no longer owned any land. His personal estate was valued at $1200, however, which was a handsome sum for a carpenter in that era! Most likely, this represented the remainder of his portion of James Mangham's estate.[8]

Whatever else William may have retained of his father's inheritance, he apparently kept his dislike of "Yankeys" and abolitionists, for he was one of the very first Manghams to enlist when war broke out in 1861. Only six weeks after the fateful bombardment of Fort Sumter on the South Carolina coast, William was mustered into service as a private in Capt. B. F. Harris's "Brunswick Rifles," many of whose men came from a militia company organized on October 28, 1860. Reflecting the popular misconception that the war would end quickly, William and the Brunswick Rifles enlisted for a period of only sixty days. As one Texan recalled long after the war, it was common to hear campfire talk in '61 that asserted, "we would only have a breakfast spell and all those who enlisted first would see the fun."[9]

After two months of picket duty at Carteret Point on the Altamaha River north of Brunswick, the Riflemen had fought nothing more than the pestiferous swarms of sand flies, which their inland brethren could scarcely tolerate. A member of Pike County's Jackson Artillery wrote from Brunswick in October, conceding that "These little creatures have almost annoyed the life out of us for the past few days. If you never saw one it would puzzle you to conceive how so small an insect can perpetrate so large a bite." Sand flies notwithstanding, William and the majority of the company re-enlisted for twelve months at the beginning of August. In keeping with a common practice of the time, the "Riflemen" were assigned to man a battery of heavy coastal defense artillery at the southern end of Cumberland Island, southeast of Brunswick. To protect a Southern economy perennially dependent on foreign commerce, it was essential to man coastal defenses protecting the Atlantic and Gulf ports.[10]

During their stay ashore at Brunswick, William's company had belonged to Colonel Semmes's 2nd Georgia Volunteers, but this organization dissolved soon afterwards. Shortly after their arrival on Cumberland Island, the Riflemen joined with seven other companies to organize Styles's 13th Georgia Regiment, which assumed responsibility for defending that portion of the Georgia coastline. There was little to do but drill, however, as no Federal vessels appeared off the coast until October. Even then, the *U.S.S. St. Lawrence* cruised for months tantalizingly out of range of the Brunswick Rifles' cannon, while the frustrated Georgians watched her run aground a Southern schooner laden with a delectable Christmastime cargo of coffee, cigars, and leather.[11]

Coastal defense duty remained dull until February of 1862, when increasing Federal raids on Southern seaports caused Confederate and state authorities to agree to evacuate Brunswick. Most townsmen had abandoned their homes and businesses anyway, and the troops thus made available could concentrate on protecting Savannah, Georgia's most vital port. Through a mistake in orders, the 13th Georgia was dispatched towards Savannah in late February, but was ordered back to Brunswick after marching to within 35 miles of Savannah. Apparently during these movements, Pvt. William Mangham fell gravely ill and was hospitalized. Two days after the regiment evacuated his hometown of Brunswick for the second and final time, he became the second Mangham to die in the service of the Confederacy, although he probably never fired a shot in anger. It was March 11, 1862.[12]

William Mangham's misfortune was all too typical of a soldier's fate in the Civil War, for by the end of the war many more Confederates had died of disease than of combat injuries. Indeed, some authorities have suggested that the average Southern soldier was ill or wounded six times during the war, with cases of sickness outnumbering battle injuries by a ratio of five to one. Confederate forces suffered perhaps three deaths from sickness for each combat-related fatality.[13]

---

[1] Ballard, *Solomon Mangham*, pp. 169-173, 191-95; Palmer, *The Mangums*, p. 57; State of Georgia, Military Records, Commissions 1824-1825, drawer 40, reel 5, GDAH.

[2] Henry Thomas Shanks, ed., *The Papers of Willie Person Mangum*, vol. 1, *1807-1832* (Raleigh: State Dept. of Archives and History, 1950), pp. 84-85. Willie P. Mangum's grandfather was Arthur Mangum, a brother of Solomon Mangham. Arthur Jr. married Dicey Carrington; Solomon's first marriage was apparently to Ann Carrington. One of

Solomon and Arthur's brothers was William Mangum, Jr. ("the Loyalist"), whose daughter, Mary Mangum Piles, lived in Glynn County after he was exiled. She was probably James's sister, or possibly his cousin. See Palmer, *The Mangums*, pp. 34-37.

[3] *The Savannah Georgian*, August 31, 1824; Glynn County, Court of Ordinary, Estate Records (Unbound), 1800-1928, drawer 302, reel 28, GDAH.

[4] James M. McPherson, *Battle Cry of Freedom: The Civil War Era* (New York: Ballantine Books, 1988), pp. 54-60. Clay's opposition to the war with Mexico and annexation of Texas was a mortal sin in the eyes of expansionist Southern Democrats. One of the most prominent, rabid secessionist Robert Toombs of Georgia, growled that Clay "has sold himself body and soul to the Northern Anti-Slavery Whigs."

[5] Shanks, ed., *The Papers of Willie Person Mangum*, vol. 4, *1844-1846* (Raleigh: State Dept. of Archives and History, 1955), pp. 210-212.

[6] Glynn County, Court of Ordinary, Estate Records (Unbound), 1800-1928, drawer 302, reel 28, GDAH. See note 2 for the relationship between James and Mary Mangum Piles.

[7] 1850 Census, Wayne County; Willard R. Rocker, *Marriages and Obituaries from the Macon Messenger, 1818-1865* (Easley: Southern Historical Press, 1988), p. 142; Genealogical Committee, Georgia Historical Society, comps., *Register of Deaths in Savannah, Georgia*, vol. 6, *1848-June 1853* (N.p.: Georgia Historical Society, 1989), p. 7; Annie B. Norman and Mr. and Mrs. David N. Brown, *Cemeteries of Marion County, Florida*, vol. 2 (N.p.: Ocala Chapter, NSDAR, 1979), p. 47; Tax Rolls, Marion County, 1845-1852, FSL. On-line burial records indicate that Sysigambis is buried on the cemetery's second row, along with other pupils who died while attending school. See http://searches.rootsweb.com/cgi-bin/ifetch2?/u1/data/ga+index+ 4334350129+F.

[8] Ballard, *Solomon Mangham*, pp. 191-195; 1850 and 1860 Censuses, Glynn County.

[9] CMSR, William W. Mangham, 26th Georgia; Alton J. Murray, *South Georgia Rebels: The True Wartime Experiences of the 26th Regiment Georgia Volunteer Infantry, Lawton-Gordon-Evans Brigade, Confederate States Army, 1861-1865* (St. Mary's: Author, 1976), p. 13; William A. Fletcher, *Rebel Private Front and Rear: Memoirs of a Confederate Soldier* (Beaumont: Press of the Greer Print, 1908; reprint, New York: Meridian, 1995), p. 3.

[10] CMSR, William W. Mangham, 13th Georgia (Styles's); Murray, *South Georgia Rebels*, pp. 13, 25-28; MDT, October 26, 1861.

[11] Murray, *South Georgia Rebels*, pp. 13, 25-28; *Georgia Regimental Journal*, July 21, 1861, in the Burwell Atkinson Collection, drawer 76, reel 8, GDAH.

[12] Murray, *South Georgia Rebels*, pp. 28-30; CMSR, William W. Mangham. When the Brunswick Riflemen mustered at the end of April, another thirteen men were absent, sick. They represented almost twenty percent of the company's aggregate strength of 82 officers and men. See 13th Georgia (Styles's) Muster Rolls, NARA.

[13] Bell Irvin Wiley, *The Life of Johnny Reb: The Common Soldier of the Confederacy* (Baton Rouge: LSU Press, 1978), p. 244.

Chapter II: Making a Mark in Dixie: Willis A. Mangham, Wiley P. Mangham and Their Families

1. NEW LAND IN WEST GEORGIA!

Willis Austin Mangham was born to Solomon and Sarah between 1775 and 1785, and accompanied his parents from the Carolinas into Georgia in the late 18th century. Solomon settled in Hancock County on a 287-acre farm on the south bank of the Oconee River, known in that locality as Sandy Run. In November 1802, Willis bought 74 acres of land along Sandy Run from Solomon's neighbor George Brewer; just over six years later, on February 26, 1809, Willis married Brewer's daughter Temperance ("Tempy"). Their union soon was blessed with the arrival of a baby boy, James Pendleton Mangham, on June 29, 1810, but old Solomon did not live to see his grandson. The patriarch of the Georgia Manghams died in the spring of 1810, and Willis and his brother-in-law Philip Graybill served as executors of his will in Hancock and Putnam Counties. Four years later, John N. Mangham was born to Willis and Tempy, and another son, William D. Mangham, arrived about 1816; daughters Jane Amanda (b. December 14, 1813) and Frances Ann rounded out the family. Tempy may have been married previously, perhaps even to an unknown brother of Willis, for her father's 1810 will identified "Tempy Mangham's oldest son" as Wiley, yet Wiley E. Mangham was born January 5, 1805, four years before Tempy's marriage to Willis. Other evidence implies strongly that Henry C. Mangham, born about 1804, and Thomas R. Mangham, born some two years later, likewise were Willis's or Tempy's sons by an earlier marriage.[1]

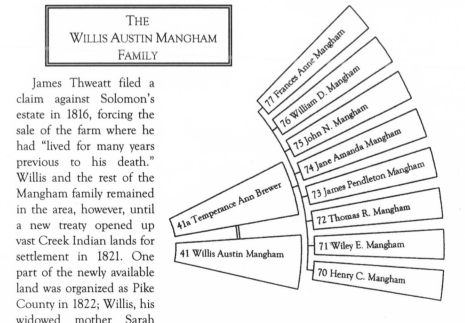

THE
WILLIS AUSTIN MANGHAM
FAMILY

James Thweatt filed a claim against Solomon's estate in 1816, forcing the sale of the farm where he had "lived for many years previous to his death." Willis and the rest of the Mangham family remained in the area, however, until a new treaty opened up vast Creek Indian lands for settlement in 1821. One part of the newly available land was organized as Pike County in 1822; Willis, his widowed mother Sarah

Ann, and his brother Wiley P. Mangham with his new bride, Cynthia Gray Mangham, were some of Pike's first settlers and organizers. They were among the earliest settlers of the Springs District (later known as Lifsey Springs) in the southern part of the county, where they and their descendants have remained prominent for the ensuing century and a half.[2]

The 1820s saw Willis's family continue to prosper and grow. Son Thomas was 19 when he married 18-year-old Matilda Dandridge Grant in March 1825, and the young couple moved on to newly organized Randolph County by 1829 (see Chapter III). Willis's son Wiley E. Mangham married Malinda Holmes five days before Christmas 1827, and he and his family soon became fixtures in the daily life of Zebulon, Pike's county seat. Son James Pendleton Mangham was not yet nineteen when he married Winfred Ennis just four days after she turned seventeen, on April 16, 1829. Seven years later, James's brother John N. Mangham married Rebecca Adams in July 1836, shortly after he returned from militia service in the Creek Indian War.[3]

The Creek War had erupted in the late spring of 1836 in the easternmost counties of Alabama, and the ensuing Indian raids across the Chattahoochee into Georgia caused both states to call out troops to quell the increasingly bloody disturbance. Pike County's militia provided two companies of infantry and one of cavalry. Willis's relative Arthur C. Mangham served in one of the infantry companies, while sons Wiley and John joined the cavalry. Commanded by Capt. Berry E. Lynch, the Pike County troopers formed part of Colonel Beall's 1st Georgia Mounted Volunteers; Thomas served in Company I of the same regiment. It is probable that all of them belonged to the force sent by Gen. Winfield Scott to combat Creeks filtering through Stewart County (below Columbus) towards Florida.[4]

Like so many other Georgians, Willis had numerous close relatives in harm's way on the Georgia-Alabama frontier. His brother John C. Mangham resided in Columbus, where he raised a cavalry company to fight the Creeks. Their first cousin (once removed) Bryant S. Mangham lived in Russell County, Alabama, as did Willis's son Thomas, before the outbreak of war drove him and hundreds of others back across the Chattahoochee to refuge in Georgia. Willis's brother Wiley also had moved west from Pike County to Chambers County, Alabama, in the early 1830s, and thus was one of the thousands of settlers whose presence sparked the outbreak of war.[5]

At home on horseback and carrying a rifle, Wiley had left a lasting impression as one of Pike County's earliest settlers. He and his brothers-in-law James R. and Seaborn Gray had participated in the county's first election in January 1823, when the voters had "nothing to guide them over the pathless wilderness except the blazes and notches recently made by the surveyors." These same frontier instincts led him across the Chattahoochee, where he cleared about sixty acres of land and settled down with Cynthia, their six children, and half a dozen slaves. The eldest child was *John Henry Mangham*, who was born in Pike County about 1827, followed the next year by Emily Jane Mangham. Wiley Adams was born in 1830, and James G. Mangham soon thereafter. The ages of Elizabeth and Martha remain unknown, but Cynthia Ann was born about 1835.[6]

Not long after their arrival in Alabama, however, their father Wiley died, and his widow Cynthia passed away by mid-1835. Her brother, Seaborn B. Gray, had lived next door to Wiley and Cynthia back in Pike County, and he administered her $4188 estate in Chambers County beginning in July 1835. As was customary in those times, relatives assumed guardianship of the seven orphans, with Seaborn taking charge of Elizabeth. Her brother James G. Mangham was placed in the home of another of Cynthia Mangham's brothers, Archibald Gray of Talbot County, Georgia, while Emily Jane and Cynthia Ann went to Crawford County to live with their aunt and uncle, Susannah Gray Howe and Robert Howe. Willis Mangham's eldest son, Wiley E. Mangham, brought his little cousins Wiley Adams and Martha to live at his home in Zebulon; his younger brother John N. Mangham posted the additional security bond required for the legal administration of the orphans' estate. Sometime after Archibald Gray's death in about 1845, James G. Mangham was placed under the legal supervision of his eldest brother, John, and Emily came to Zebulon as well. Only three years later, however, John had the sad duty of administering his younger brother's estate, as James passed away in late 1848 before reaching age 21. About a year later, the same sad fate befell Wiley Adams Mangham, who died in Zebulon at age 19 in May 1849. Almost precisely twelve months later, their sister Emily died at age 21.[7]

105 John Henry Mangham 13th Ga.

46 Wiley P. Mangham

106 Emily Jane Mangham

46a Cynthia Gray

107 Wiley Adams Mangham

108 James G. Mangham

109 Cynthia Ann Mangham

110 Elizabeth Mangham

111 Martha Mangham

THE
WILEY P. MANGHAM
FAMILY

With the deaths of both parents and at least three of his six known siblings in the span of 12 years, John H. Mangham was the sole male survivor of the Wiley P. and Cynthia Mangham family. He lived in Zebulon with his elder cousins Wiley E. and John N. Mangham, and their lives reflect many similarities. John N. and John H. Mangham were both prominent figures in the Pike County militia. The elder cousin served as a lieutenant and later captain of the cavalry company in the 1850s, while the younger man, a merchant in civil life, rose rapidly from second lieutenant of the "Georgia Defenders" in 1847 to colonel of Pike County's 56th Regiment of Georgia Militia in 1850. John N. Mangham was extremely active in business and politics as well, winning election as a Democrat to the state legislature in October 1842, and serving as judge of the county Inferior Court and later as clerk of the Superior Court. Wiley was likewise active in public service, serving as clerk of the county Inferior Court from 1840 until 1850. At this point, the Court of Ordinary was established, and Wiley secured election as the first Judge, or Ordinary. When he resigned in 1854, his younger cousin, Col. John H. Mangham, soon followed in his footsteps; he was the postmaster by 1858, County Ordinary by 1860, and secretary-treasurer of the county's first Board of Education.[8]

THE WILEY E. MANGHAM HOME. ZEBULON, GEORGIA.
(SEE APPENDIX, REF. #71)

- Courtesy of Vaughn Ballard

By the standards of their time and place, all three men certainly were well educated, prominent, and financially affluent. John N. Mangham had a reputation for knowing more about land and deeds in the county than anyone else, and his extensive holdings of land and slaves lend convincing support to this conclusion. In 1859, he owned 2587 acres of land in Pike County alone, plus another 2292 acres in ten other counties. Thirty-nine slaves, whose valuation at $18,700 surpassed the $10,000 taxable value of John's real property in Pike County, farmed his extensive plantation. That year they made a crop that included 35 bales of cotton, as well as more than 2400 bushels of provisions such as wheat, corn, oats, and sweet potatoes. By 1860, John's real property and personal property were valued at $12,000 and $35,000, respectively. His brother Wiley was likewise a prosperous planter, with 1159 acres of land farmed by 25 slaves in 1859. In the following year, his lands were valued at $6000, whereas his personal property was worth $17,000.[9] Wiley E. Mangham was now 55 years old, and he lived with his wife Malinda at their home on Concord Street after the marriage of their only daughter Mary Jane to Capt. Charles F. Redding in 1848.[10]

Their younger cousin John H. Mangham had no farm, but kept two slaves as servants in his nice Zebulon home, which was valued at $1800. Aged 33 in 1860, he lived there with his 29-year-old wife, Rebecca Caldwell Mangham, and their young children Mattie, Wiley, and Emmie, whose names poignantly evoked those of his deceased father, brother, and sister.[11] (See map on page 566.)

2. ON THE FRONTIER AGAIN: THE JAMES PENDLETON MANGHAM FAMILY IN PIKE COUNTY

John N. Mangham's wife Rebecca Adams Mangham died in 1858, leaving her 44-year-old husband to care for two young daughters and a teenage nephew. The nephew was *Absalem Charles N. Mangham*, a son of James Pendleton and Winfred Ennis Mangham. The young man rendered his name as "Charles A. Mangham" and was known to the family as "Nat," apparently due to his diminutive size: family lore has it that he weighed a mere pound and a half at his birth on December 30, 1841. His nickname supposedly stemmed from the exclamation of an astonished visitor, who exclaimed, "He's no bigger than a gnat!" Nat evidently was placed with his Uncle John in Zebulon soon thereafter, so that John's brother-in-law, Dr. Jefferson Adams, could look after the tiny boy, who lay swaddled in a basket filled with sheep's wool.[12]

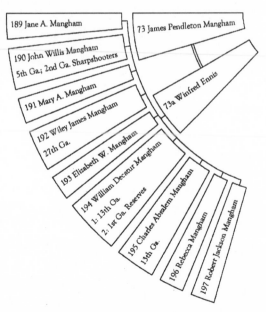

THE JAMES P. MANGHAM FAMILY

Nat was James P. Mangham's fourth son, and the sixth of nine children. His older brother *William Decatur Mangham* was born on March 2, 1840, and clearly was named for his uncle William D. Mangham, who had died in Macon on March 8, 1838, at age 21. In 1860, Will was the eldest son remaining on his father's prosperous 880-acre farm in the Springs District of southwestern Pike County. On the 175 acres under active cultivation that year, Will and his 14-year-old brother *Robert Jackson "Bob" Mangham* helped their father and his seven slaves raise fine crops of wheat, Indian corn, cotton, sweet potatoes, and other staples. Elder brother *Wiley James Mangham* helped farm this land too, but he lived in a small

29

cabin with his young wife Susan and their infant son, James Pendleton Mangham II. The extended Mangham family also may have obtained additional help from Anderson, Sarah Ann, and Elizabeth King, free persons of color for whom James served as legal guardian.[13]

Wiley and Susan had married in October 1858, and were just getting their family started when war fever boiled over in the spring of 1861. The newly minted Confederate Congress called for an army of 12-months' volunteers on March 6, and

HOME OF JAMES P. MANGHAM. SPRINGS DISTRICT, PIKE COUNTY, GEORGIA
(SEE APPENDIX, REF. #73)

- Courtesy of Vaughn Ballard

the first shots were fired at Fort Sumter on April 12. On May 6, President Jefferson Davis approved an act of Congress recognizing that a state of war existed between the United States and the Confederate States of America.[14]

3. SLAUGHTER AT SHARPSBURG; SURRENDER AT APPOMATTOX: CAPT. JOHN H. MANGHAM AND CPLS. CHARLES A. AND WILLIAM D. MANGHAM, "CONFEDERATE GUARDS," CO. A, 13TH GEORGIA

Amidst all the excitement, a volunteer company dubbed the "Confederate Guards" organized in Pike County, where secession fever had been strong. Wiley remained home to help lay by the crop, but his brothers Will and Nat joined their father's first cousin, Col. John H. Mangham, as members of the new company. Apparently the men enlisted for the prescribed twelve-month term and tendered their services to the governor of Georgia, but then ran afoul of new legislation approved on May 9, requiring units to volunteer for three years or the war. Arms and equipment were scarcer than recruits in any case, and the Confederate Guards were only one of many companies competing to obtain them in order to expedite their acceptance into service. Since every passing day seemed to reduce their chances to "see the elephant" before a decisive battle might end the war, the neophyte soldiers were eager to resolve these issues as fast as possible. As a colonel in the state militia and Ordinary of Pike County, John Mangham was a natural choice to clarify these problems for the anxious Confederate Guards. Four days after passage of the new three-years' service law, the company chose him to draft a letter to Col. Henry C. Wayne, Georgia's Adjutant and Inspector General:

> Zebulon Ga.
> May 13th 1861

Dear Sir

We the undersigned were appointed a committee to ask of you your opinion in relation to the late act of Congress concerning the term of service of volunteer companies hereafter received. We desire also to know whether or not our company will be received without a new tender of service. We have now 80 men rank and file, all uniformed, but have received only 60 Guns. 20 more have been ordered but we have not heard from them. An early answer will greatly oblige

Your Frd.[s] & obt. Serv[rts].

> /s/ *John H. Mangham*
> *R. V. Reid*
> *L. J. Green*
> Committee of the Confederate Guards
> Pike Co. Ga[15]

In the general frenzy to have their company accepted for service by someone, somehow, somewhere in the infant Confederacy's nascent bureaucracy, the eager Georgians authorized another committee to fire off a letter just one week later to the Secretary of War:

> Zebulon Pike Co. Ga.

May 20th 1861
Hon. L. P. Walker
    Secretary of War
    Confederate States
        Montgomery Ala.
    Dear Sir,

We the undersigned have been appointed a committee on behalf of the Confederate Guards an Infantry company organized in the County of Pike for the defense of the Confederate States, to tender to the President, through you, the Services of the company for twelve months. The company numbers eighty one (81) rank and file—all stout, healthy men, and pretty well drilled—The services of the company have been tendered to the Governor of this State for twelve months, and arms received for sixty men, but orders have since been issued declaring all such tenders cancelled, and forbidding any arms to be carried beyond the limits of the State by any company which has tendered its services to any other State or Government. We are authorized to say that the Confederate Guards hold themselves subject to your order for twelve months provided they are furnished with suitable arms and accoutrements. And on behalf of the company we earnestly solicit an early reply.

With the Highest regards,

We are Your Obt. Servt[s].

/s/ J. H. Mitchell

L. Sims

J. H. Mangham

Committee

P.S.   We enclose herewith a Muster Roll of the company headed with the form of the tender.[16]

CPL. WILL MANGHAM.
REVERSE IMAGE: NOTE "CG" ON CAP.
(SEE APPENDIX, REF. #194)
–Courtesy of Frances Greene

Just three days after they posted their appeal to Walker, his office admitted its inability to accept the company. New governments at all levels were passing laws, raising men, requisitioning guns, and issuing equipment in accordance with a bewildering variety of rapidly changing procedures and competing requirements, desperately trying to field an army to fight the Yankees before it was too late.

Apparently, Colonel Wayne responded soon after Walker's office, observing that the requirement for three-year enlistments indeed applied in this case. His response probably necessitated the dissolution of the company and its reorganization for the longer term of service. Ironing out all these difficulties cost almost two months' time, and it was July 8 before the Confederate Guards formally mustered into Confederate service at the prescribed regimental rendezvous in Griffin. Upon completion of the new regiment's organization, the Guards became Company A, 13th Georgia Volunteer Infantry, and elected Nat as second corporal and Will as third corporal. John resigned his position as Pike County Ordinary to enlist as a private, but his military, business, and government background resulted in his immediate appointment as captain and Assistant Commissary of Subsistence (A.C.S.) for the regiment. As such, it fell to him to obtain food through army channels and manage its distribution to all ten companies. Given the stresses placed on the Confederate commissary system, this proved to be a daunting task indeed.[17]

Several weeks after the regiment's organization, it was on the way to the "seat of war" in Virginia. After spending a short time in camp near Richmond, the regiment was assigned to Gen. John B. Floyd's brigade in the western part of the state, where the Georgians served until late December of that year. They suffered badly from exposure and disease during the hard months in western Virginia's mountains, losing large

numbers of men to the "camp diseases" that riddled the infant Confederacy's raw legions. After all, the men hailed from rural areas and most never had developed immunity to the diseases rife in crowded encampments. Although their 20th century descendants view the measles as a mere childhood inconvenience, the Confederate Guards feared such infections as potentially lethal killers. In this environment, the sick lists quickly reduced every regiment's nominal strength from 800-1000 men to roughly half (or a quarter) of that number at any given time, even before the men faced combat.[18]

As an Army inspector noted in his mid-December report on conditions in Floyd's Brigade, "I would recommend that the Thirteenth Georgia Regiment [and two other Deep South regiments] be ordered

CPL. CHARLES A. "NAT" MANGHAM
(SEE APPENDIX, REF. #194)
—Courtesy of Joseph Reichert

into a milder climate. The severe winters of Western Virginia will be fatal to those Southern men."[19] Captain John Mangham would have agreed wholeheartedly, as he had suffered badly during his first campaign, in more ways than one. Explaining his irregular subsistence reports to the crusty, bureaucratic, Col. Lucius Northrop, Commissary General of the Confederate Army, John pleaded his case in terms that clearly imply that the paperwork war was unrelenting in its own right. His letter from camp at Causton's Bluff, near Savannah, was dated April 5, 1862:

Dear Sir,

Your communication of the 26th Oct. was recd. two days ago. I would have replied immediately, but was waiting to get some information from the young man who has been acting as my Sergeant. He is at home, but will return in a few days, and with his assistance I will endeavor to make up the Returns required. After hearing a statement of the matter I hope you will bear with me for a while until I can arrange the Returns and forward them. In the latter part of August as our Regiment was going from Richmond to North-Western Va. I was taken very sick and was compelled to stop at Staunton where I was confined to my bed two weeks with a severe fever. As soon as my Physician would permit me to leave my room I started forward to rejoin the Regiment. At Lewisburg I was taken with measles which kept me confined to the house about three weeks, and after going to the mountains I contracted a cold which settled on my lungs and I feared would prove fatal. I therefore on the 31st day of October tendered my resignation and got leave of absence. I went home and was sick for a long while and did not receive any notice of the rejection of my resignation until I wrote to the Secretary of War on the 27th of January and received a reply in February. The young man who acted for me during my sickness was inexperienced in the business, as most of us were, and having many difficulties to encounter, did not get all the invoices he ought to have had. Consequently I could not make up my Returns precisely as I should have done it. Capt. Jones who was appointed in my place when I tendered my Resignation acted until about the middle of Febry., and I have been trying to get him to make out Returns for the time, but for some reason he has not done so. He transacted all the business in his own name and of course it would be difficult for me to make up the Returns for the time he served. Will you receive a Return from him? I have delayed my Returns for Febry. and March in order to have his forwarded first. I hope under all the circumstances you will be as lenient with me as you can consistently with your duty as an officer. Capt. Jones is absent at present. as soon as he returns I will use my utmost exertions to straighten up the whole matter. I will do what is right about it as far as I possibly can I assure you.

Your obedient Servant,   /s/ *J. H. Mangham*
Capt. & A.C.S. 13th
Regt. Ga. Vols.[20]

Nat also was worn out by his initial experience with war, and went home on sick furlough for four weeks beginning on New Year's Eve, 1861.[21] His was not a terribly long trip, however, for the regiment already had gotten orders to head for Savannah in mid-December. The move was dictated by strategic concerns for the great seaport's safety, and perhaps the inspecting officer's climate-related recommendations played a role, too. In any case, the Confederate Guards were glad to be going home to Georgia. As Cpl. Dick Milner observed in a letter to his wife Sallie, "Some of the Boys could not help but shout when we crossed the Savannah River on our way from Virginia."[22]

The ranks of those returning home were slimmed drastically by the numbers lost to camp diseases, but the West Virginia campaign had given the Confederate Guards their first taste of combat, too; they had lost several men in skirmishes at Sewell Mountain and Colton Hill. It also had given them their first experience under the overall direction of Gen. Robert E. Lee, as well as their first exposure to Union troops commanded by Maj. Gen. George B. McClellan. Although the Federals wound up securing West Virginia, and thereby McClellan's early reputation as a successful commander, the Georgians nonetheless thought themselves clearly superior to their opponents in warlike qualities. As Dick Milner observed after one of their early engagements, ". . .the Yankees took there heels—as they usually do—, but the way the rascals fought the other day when they attacked Gen. Floyd was not a little and quit— but they were sure of success." This cocky attitude, so typical of Southern troops, was one of the main ingredients of their many successes on later battlefields (and some of their setbacks, as well).[23]

Their next exposure to combat was at the end of March at Whitemarsh Island, off the coast of Savannah, and the results helped confirm the Confederate Guards' confidence in themselves and their leaders. They landed on the island with several other companies of the regiment to repel a Federal reconnaissance force. In a running fight with seven companies of the 8th Michigan, the Georgians suffered four killed and fifteen wounded, but killed ten and wounded 35 of their numerically superior opponents. The Michiganders withdrew to lick their wounds, leaving the outnumbered but thoroughly aroused Georgians in possession of the island. As April progressed, other such skirmishes kept the 13th Georgia on its toes. Amidst the uncertainties of combat, a harried Captain Mangham still was struggling to straighten out tangled commissary returns, dashing off another hasty alibi to Northrop to excuse the missing reports: "Our Regt. is in a state of confusion at this time. been engaged in a fight a day or two. Some men killed yesterday." In one of these actions the Georgians captured a group of marines and their small launch, which Savannah's Confederate garrison dubbed the "Thirteenth Georgia" and used as a picket boat for the rest of the war.[24]

Such minor encounters seemed dramatic at the time, and commanders on both sides submitted detailed reports of these events. Several weeks later, however, John was still ensnarled in red tape from the West Virginia campaign!

Camp Causton's Bluff Near Savannah Ga. May 8th 1862

Hon. L. B. Northrop
  Commissary General
    Richmond Va.
      Sir:

Having delayed thus long the forwarding of my Returns I feel it to be due that I should make a further explanation. Since the return of Capt. Jones (the former A.A.C.S.) I have been ordered to take possession of his papers and see that his returns are made and properly forwarded. This is requiring a considerable time and is also requiring the entire attention of the Comsry. Sergeant. As soon as the matter is arranged I will make up my returns and forward them. In the mean time I hope you will extend to me the same leniety [leniency] which you have so kindly extended heretofore. Every thing shall be satisfactorily arranged soon I assure you.

Very Respectfully, Your Frd. & Ob't. Serv't.,

/s/ J. H. *Mangham* Capt. & A.C.S. 13th Regt. Ga. Vols.[25]

Within weeks of John's latest plea for understanding from the labyrinthine bureaucracy of the Confederate Commissary Department, the situation heated up again for the 13th Georgia. In June the regiment transferred to Gen. A. R. Lawton's brigade and returned to Virginia, where their war quickly assumed a scope out of all proportion to their earlier experiences. They were summoned to Virginia because McClellan's Peninsula Campaign was threatening the capital at Richmond, while other Union forces were on the loose in the lush Shenandoah Valley. The fledgling Confederacy was facing the greatest crisis of its youthful existence.

4. RIDING FOR LEE AND JACKSON? ROBERT J. MANGHAM'S TRIP TO VIRGINIA

It was probably when Will and Nat returned to Virginia that their 16-year-old brother Bob came with them, seeking to join the army. His brothers had experienced enough hard marching to know that Bob stood little chance of serving in ranks with the Confederate Guards, however, for the boy suffered from a club foot. Apparently, Bob remained some time with the army, taking care of horses and perhaps serving as a courier. Many years after the war, ex-Private W. C. Minter of the Confederate Guards testified that Bob had indeed come to Virginia in the spring of 1862 to enlist in the company. According to this testimony, Bob was detailed the next day to Jackson's (Georgia) Artillery, where he was soon assigned as a courier for Generals Lee and Jackson. Minter stated under oath, "I saw him every few days for more than 12 months. I was there." Although Bob claimed to have served until the spring of 1864, no official records exist to confirm the claims he made in his two surviving pension applications. One of these was denied because the Ordinary of Upson County had incorrectly entered "47th Alabama" instead of "13th Georgia" on the witness statement.[26]

Although Bob may never have enlisted formally in the Confederate Guards or the Jackson Artillery, he may have remained with the army for quite some time in an unofficial capacity. Such irregularities were not uncommon in the Confederate Army, and numerous crippled and maimed men performed light duty of various sorts. Although Bob Mangham could not march, he was otherwise a healthy farm boy capable of helping out around camp.[27]

*   *   *   *   *

In any event, the Manghams probably arrived with their regiment to reinforce Gen. Thomas J. "Stonewall" Jackson's small force in the Shenandoah on June 10, 1862, just as he concluded his astoundingly successful Valley Campaign. They turned eastward for Richmond almost immediately upon joining Jackson's command, and soon learned the meaning of the term "Jackson's Foot Cavalry," as they hotfooted it to reinforce the main army east of the capital. Undertaking a series of exhausting forced marches across the state, they arrived in time to participate in the series of ferocious counterstrokes known to history as the Seven Days Battles, which showcased the relentlessly aggressive style of General Lee. To the regret of its opponents, this style of fighting soon became the trademark of the Army of Northern Virginia.[28] (See map on page 285.)

After a four-hour approach march on June 27, the 13th Georgia hustled three miles at the double-quick to the sound of the guns at Gaines's Mill. The developing battle raged just seven miles northeast of Richmond, where Lee was making a mighty effort to destroy McClellan's army, in retreat after the previous day's battle at Mechanicsville. Immediately upon arrival, the Georgians and their comrades of Lawton's Brigade were flung into an attack towards the center of the Federal line, located in entrenchments that lay beyond a field in deep woods. Under fierce artillery fire, the Georgians surged forward shrieking a battle cry that Cpl. Richard Robins of the 11th U.S. Infantry remembered as "that fiendish yell," better known to history as the "Rebel Yell." Colonel Douglass and his 13th Georgia arrived at the base of a hill and prepared to launch a bayonet assault, when unseen Union troops poured in a volley at 30 or 40 yards range. In the smoky bedlam of the ensuing fight, the cry arose that the Georgians were firing on friendly troops, and the regiment ceased fire and soon pulled back. In this brief but fierce action, the regiment suffered six men killed and 54 wounded, including at least two killed and four wounded from the Confederate Guards.[29]

Soon thereafter, the Union line crumbled under these unremitting assaults, and McClellan pulled his battered army back under cover of darkness. Desperate fighting continued over the next several days as Lee tried to bring McClellan's force to bay, but the 13th Georgia was not committed to battle again until July 1 at Malvern Hill. Even then, the regiment was the only one of Lawton's Brigade to see action, as the Army of Northern Virginia continued to experience difficulties marshaling its whole force simultaneously to strike a concentrated blow. Their Federal opponents were concentrated in compact defensive lines, however, with thirty-seven pieces of field artillery arrayed to cover 1200 yards of breastworks on their northern flank. This lethal concentration gave the Battle of Malvern Hill a unique character, as massed artillery bore the primary burden of defense against massed infantry attacks.[30]

For the 13th Georgia, this meant charging through the remnants of Virginia, North Carolina, and Louisiana regiments towards Union batteries nearly hidden in the deepening twilight. The regiment's alignment disintegrated in the darkness and the attack dissolved into groups of men scrambling through the woods, guiding towards the sound of the Federal batteries. Under these conditions, only some 75 or 100 men ever reached the field in which the batteries stood, and where they were blasted at close range by canister and rifle fire. Some of the men, led by the Confederate Guards' Lt. E. L. Connally, surged nonetheless into the Union position and briefly fell captive, but they broke away in the darkness. The Georgians fell back and consolidated on the nearby high ground, with Colonel Douglass assuming command of the remnants of other units in the vicinity. As the scattered regiment rallied that night, the survivors

37

counted nine killed and forty-six wounded as the cost of their unsupported effort. Three of the dead and seven of the injured were Pike County boys of Company A. General Lawton witnessed the regiment's headlong attack, and proudly reported afterwards that ". . .nothing could exceed the energy, valor, and zeal exhibited by officers and men during their impetuous charge," which apparently penetrated farther than any other unit under Jackson's command.[31]

Confederate casualties at Malvern Hill were appalling, but they still had not managed to break the Federal lines. They had sufficed, however, to break the morale of General McClellan, and he ordered his troops to retreat once more. The 13th Georgia was not involved in any more combat in the ensuing actions that brought the Seven Days' battles, and McClellan's Peninsula Campaign, to a climax. The ferocious fighting had cost Lee more than twenty thousand casualties, or some twenty-two percent of his force, but Richmond was saved. As the Army of the Potomac withdrew down the James River to safety, Southern confidence soared to new heights. They had faced the largest army ever assembled in the New World and had whipped it resoundingly. As historian Stephen Sears has written, "While they mourned their many dead, the men accepted it as the price of victory, and morale was high."[32]

Their morale rose even more as General Lee led them into northern Virginia to face General Pope's Federal army. Will, Nat, and John Mangham almost certainly participated in the ensuing series of engagements during August 1862, as Lee and Pope maneuvered for advantage. These movements culminated in serious fighting for the 13th Georgia at Groveton on August 28 and again at Second Manassas on the two succeeding days, costing the regiment seven killed, thirty-five wounded, and four missing in unrelenting combat.[33] Fighting in Ewell's Division of Jackson's Corps, their sacrifices helped achieve a smashing victory over Pope's force that sent the Union army hustling back to the safety of the Washington defenses. With the Federals narrowly escaping total destruction once more, Lee continued northward to take the war into Maryland in September. This time he sought to deliver a major blow on northern soil, hoping that this could prove decisive in the struggle for Southern independence.

Since a primary motivation for most Confederate soldiers was the determination to defend their homes against Yankee invaders, many of them considered Lee's move north a questionable undertaking. These men had proved steadfast in the preceding engagements on Virginia soil, but now they straggled in great numbers as the army wended its way into Maryland. The steady leakage was swelled further by the sick, halt, and lame, worn out by long months of campaigning, poor food, and exposure. After entering Maryland, most of the men tried to keep body and soul together with roasting ears and green apples, and the resulting diarrhea weakened them still further. Under these conditions, Lee's hard-marching army was reduced to approximately 40,000 men. As Stonewall Jackson force-marched his men to Sharpsburg to rendezvous with the rest of the army, the regiments of Lawton's Georgia Brigade averaged less than 200 men present for duty.[34] (See map on page 258.)

Corporals Nat and Will Mangham were in the hot and dusty columns that came swinging up the road from Harper's Ferry on the evening of September 15. Supremely confident, the men in butternut and gray had resurrected their country's waning fortunes and brought Southern arms to the verge of victory with their hard-fought victories of the previous three months. But for now they were famished and footsore, and they slumped wearily into their blankets near the Mumma Farm, amid trees now known as the West Woods. Over the next 24 hours, the Union army, once more led by McClellan after Pope was relieved of command, closed into the area and prepared to give battle. The 13th Georgia wound up in a field of clover just south of D. R. Miller's cornfield ("the Cornfield") and east of the Hagerstown Turnpike by the evening of September 16, and those who could "slept on their arms" in line of battle. All night long, the popping musketry on the skirmish line warned of danger on the morrow.[35]

The rattle of muskets increased ominously as the new day dawned, and the skirmishers hustled back to the line with the news everyone had expected: the Yankees were coming in force! A major attack was rolling in through the Cornfield, with Duryea's brigade leading the blue tide. If Nat and Will were in their prescribed places, rather than filling in for absent sergeants or serving in the color guard, they were in the front rank, with nothing between them and Yankee bullets but their gray jackets. At the critical moment, Lawton's Georgians rose from the clover and delivered a devastating volley at point-blank range. Stunned New Yorkers recoiled and took cover behind the rail fence separating the Cornfield from the clover field to its south, and began trading volleys with the exposed Georgians at 250 yards range. As the fight continued and artillery batteries poured in shot and shell, Duryea's shocked men began drifting back through the corn, leaving a hole in the Union line; in half an hour, almost a third of his 1100-man brigade had been shot down. Wisconsin troops of Gibbons's brigade wheeled into the developing gap, but the Georgians' intense musketry drove the disorganized remnants of Phelps's brigade into the rear columns of the Wisconsin men, who began another close-range, stand-up fight with the Georgians.[36] As the 6th Wisconsin's Maj. Rufus Dawes recalled,

> Men, I can not say fell; they were knocked out of the ranks by dozens. . . .
> . . .Men and officers of New York and Wisconsin are fused into a common mass, in the frantic struggle to shoot fast. . .Every body tears cartridges, loads, passes guns, or shoots. Men are falling in their places or running back into the corn.[37]

As Lawton's Georgians ran low on ammunition, they scrounged more from the fallen and began pulling back slowly towards the Hagerstown Pike and the Smoketown Road to the south. Hays's Louisiana Brigade provided some timely help at this point, though, and their fire helped Lawton's men break the renewed momentum of the Federal attack. As the Wisconsin troops reeled back through the shattered cornstalks, the Georgia and Louisiana troops pushed forward to their original line in the clover field. Almost immediately, they faced yet another attack, as Hartsuff's brigade of Pennsylvania, Massachusetts and New York troops surged back through the Cornfield. It was not yet 7:00 a.m., but Lawton's brigade already was facing its fourth point-blank fight with a fresh Federal brigade. In the half-hour melee, the Federals shot down the colors of the 13th Georgia, and the bullet-riddled standard fell into a small fold in the ground just several yards south of the Cornfield. Colonel Marcellus Douglass, who had led the 13th Georgia before assuming command of Lawton's Brigade, asked a young soldier to break ranks and recover the flag. The boy dashed to within a few feet of Hartsuff's line, snatched up the colors amidst a hail of fire, and raced back to the regiment's painfully reduced line of battle. In the process he was hit by two bullets, while Colonel Douglass was hit for the eighth time that morning.[38]

As the mortally stricken Douglass breathed his last, his men continued to shoot down their opponents in windrows, but the crisis was now at hand. Just at this moment, other Confederate brigades surged into a counterattack, crashing into the Federal flank from the West Woods. When General Hood's division followed up the initial surge with a bayonet attack, the hard-pressed Yankees dissolved in rout and fled the Cornfield as best they could.[39] Although the two armies continued to hammer each other throughout the day, neither side could gain a decisive advantage in combat of unprecedented intensity. Lee took one of the most desperate gambles of the war by remaining in position to offer battle the next day, but he had judged his opponent well; McClellan hesitated to attack, fearful that his numerically superior force was actually outnumbered. Lee's army moved unmolested back into Virginia beginning that night, effectively terminating their short-lived invasion of the North.

The Battle of Sharpsburg (Antietam) has remained the single bloodiest day in America's history, with the two sides suffering some 24,000 casualties. The 13th Georgia and its sister regiments in Lawton's Brigade played no further active part after their actions at the Cornfield, but the brief span of time between dawn and 7:00 a.m. saw their ranks evaporate under the intense musketry and cannon fire. The brigade was shattered, and the 13th Georgia was shot literally to pieces as its ranks fought back wave upon wave of the blueclad tide. It is not known exactly how many men the regiment took into action that morning, although it was probably about 250 to 300. Of this number, 48 were killed in action, 166 were wounded, and two were missing, totaling 216 casualties. Of some 176 Confederate infantry regiments engaged that day, only the 3rd North Carolina suffered more than the 13th Georgia. Lawton's entire Georgia Brigade was cut up badly, losing 49 percent of the 1150 men who saw action.[40]

Corporal Dick Milner of the Confederate Guards missed the battle due to illness, but met up with several of his friends shortly after they returned to Virginia. As a shocked Milner reported in a letter home, "They say that our company went into the fight with 38 men & came out with three, 8 killed & twenty-five wounded." The Confederate Army lacked official procedures for notifying next of kin in such situations, relying instead on men like Milner to write home with information about the injured, and asking their family members to pass the news within the community. Further sources of information for the home folks were soldiers going home on wounded furlough to recuperate with their loved ones, who could provide better care than the overtaxed army hospitals. As Dick told Sallie, ". . .you will see some of the wounded & they can tell you all about it."[41]

Another source of information was the casualty lists provided by brigade or regimental officers to hometown or regional newspapers for publication. One published in Savannah on October 4, 1862 sent word back to Pike County that the thousands of casualties at Sharpsburg included Cpl. Will Mangham, whose arm had been broken. Known to military doctors of that era as a gunshot fracture, such wounds commonly necessitated amputation in order to prevent the onset of gangrene. Will was extremely lucky not to lose his arm; indeed, he was lucky to be alive at all, for doctors who examined him later noted that he had suffered "a Gun Shot wound through the left arm near the shoulder & entering the side into the lungs." He must have possessed a strong constitution and an equally strong will to live, in order to survive such a ghastly wound in the era before antibiotics and sterilization. He doubtless was evacuated in a jolting ambulance wagon to northern Virginia, where he probably was stabilized at a temporary army hospital before being put on a train to Richmond. He was admitted to the Receiving and Wayside Hospital (General Hospital No. 9) on October 13 and was transferred to General Hospital No. 1 on the same day for further treatment. A month and a half after Will was wounded at Sharpsburg, he finally had recovered enough for the attending surgeon to authorize him a 60-day furlough, which would allow him to recuperate at home.[42]

Other records show that Nat was wounded at Sharpsburg as well, although the nature and extent of his injury are unknown. But as Will underwent treatment and headed south to recuperate, Nat was on his way east to Washington as a prisoner of war. Probably disabled and left behind as the Federals entered the Warrenton area, he was paroled and released to Confederate exchange agents at City Point, Virginia, on November 18, 1862. Luckily for him, he was captured at a stage of the war when the exchange cartel was functioning well, so he did not languish in Union captivity for any great length of time. Some of his cousins were less fortunate later in the war. Soon thereafter he may have gone home to recuperate, as did the two soldiers assigned to help John in his endless struggle to square accounts with the Commissary General:[43]

> Camp Near Port Royal Va.   January 20th 1863
> Sir:
>   My monthly Returns for October, November & Dec[r]. and last Quarterly Returns for 1863 [1862] have been due for some time. Until lately we have not remained long enough at any one point to make up the returns, and since we have been at this camp I have had all the duties of my office to look after as both the young men who have been assisting me are absent, sick. Besides that, I have been for some time performing the duties of Brigade Commissary also. Major Reid (Brig. Comsry.) will return to duty next week and I will then make up my returns and forward them.
>   Hoping you will excuse the delay,
>   I remain, Very Respectfully,
>   Your Obt. Servt.   */s/ J. H. Mangham*
>   Capt. & A.C.S. 13th Ga. Regt.[44]

41

Just a month before John had penned this latest missive to Colonel Northrop, the 13th Georgia had been engaged in the Battle of Fredericksburg, where it had helped dispatch Burnside's shattered legions back across the Rappahannock River. Nat probably missed this engagement, in which the regiment took only a small part; he may have been back at home with Will, who was still struggling to recuperate from his dreadful wounds. Indeed, by the spring of 1863 it was clear that Will's injuries had disabled him for active field service, and he was detailed to non-combat duties in Georgia. Regimental muster rolls carried him as "assigned to the collection of stragglers in Georgia," and records maintained by the Camp of Instruction at Macon showed that he was on detached duty from April through December 1863. He was under the supervision of the state Commandant of Conscripts, and probably lived at home and assisted the enrolling officer responsible for military conscription in Pike County.[45]

Although no regimental muster rolls survive from 1863, other evidence indicates that Nat was back in ranks no later than June. Perhaps both he and his cousin Capt. John Mangham were with the regiment for the second Battle of Fredericksburg in May 1863. Jubal Early's Division held the Confederate lines near the town, while Gen. Stonewall Jackson maneuvered the majority of the army to strike the Federals a surprise blow several miles to the west at a desolate crossroads called Chancellorsville. As the picket force for Brig. Gen. John B. Gordon's Brigade (Lawton's old command), the 13th Georgia fought doggedly to delay the famed Federal "Iron Brigade" that stormed across the Rappahannock River at Fredericksburg. In this hard-fought action, as well as a spectacular counterattack by Gordon's men several days later, the Georgians played a central role in thwarting Union intentions to block Lee's rear at Fredericksburg, while Jackson's men routed Federal forces in the main attack at Chancellorsville.[46]

As Union forces reeled in confusion, General Lee again seized the initiative and struck northward. With the rich Shenandoah Valley serving once more as an axis of advance, June 1863 saw the Army of Northern Virginia streaming northward towards Maryland, Pennsylvania . . . and Gettysburg. Corporal Nat Mangham and his Pike County friends marched in Gordon's Brigade of Early's Division. Since Stonewall Jackson's death from wounds received at Chancellorsville, Lt. Gen. Dick Ewell was their new corps commander. Unbeknownst to the long columns of gray and butternut snaking through the lush farmlands of the North, they were moving towards a rendezvous with the oft-defeated Army of the Potomac at the modest crossroads town of Gettysburg.[47]

As the men of Gordon's 61st Georgia led the way through Chambersburg in late June, Pvt. George W. Nichols overheard a small girl ask her mother, "Mamma, are those men rebels?" When told that they were, the surprised child replied, "Why, mamma, they haven't got horns; they are just like our people." Other civilians, in the form of some 1200 Pennsylvania militiamen, might well have imagined that Gordon's men had horns on their heads like so many devils. They tried to stop the Georgians on their way into Wrightsville, but the raw levies met a predictable fate at the hands of the hard-marching veterans, who brushed them aside and sent them fleeing for their lives.[48]

Matters got much more serious, however, as Lee's army began concentrating for battle near Gettysburg itself on the first day of July. For Nat and the 13th Georgia, this day was marked by hard fighting north of town against men of General Barlow's Federal division. As Private Nichols recalled, "We attacked them immediately, but we had a hard time in moving them. We advanced with our accustomed yell, but they stood firm until we got near them. . . .They were harder to drive than we had ever known them before." General Gordon noted the Yankees' "obstinate resistance" as well, but the veteran officer reported that his brigade "rushed upon the enemy with a resolution and spirit, in my opinion, rarely excelled." The future governor of Georgia observed that the "colors on portions of the two lines were separated by a space of less than fifty paces" when the Federal line finally crumpled and disintegrated in "the greatest confusion, and with immense loss. . . ." He reported that nearly 300 enemy soldiers were buried on the ground where the Georgians attacked, adding proudly that the division inspector credited his 1200-man brigade with capturing 1800 prisoners. Gordon's men helped drive the remaining Federals out of Gettysburg onto Cemetery Ridge, just south of town, where the pursuit halted. The day's fighting cost Gordon's six Georgia regiments seventy killed and 269 wounded; combined with the 39 missing, these losses represented some thirty percent of his force. The 13th Georgia suffered the heaviest casualties in the brigade, counting twenty dead and 83 wounded out of approximately 400 men engaged. Despite these terrible losses, their attack is counted as one of the exemplary actions of the Civil War. No less an authority than General Ewell himself considered that "Gordon's Brigade that evening put *hors de combat* a greater number of the enemy in proportion to its own numbers than any other command on either side ever did from the beginning to the end of the war."[49] (See map on p. 379.)

Although the next two days of combat saw Gordon's men engaged in heavy skirmishing and dodging heavy enemy artillery fire, they were spared any further general engagement. The Confederate Guards nonetheless lost seven men wounded during these two days, in contrast to one killed and two wounded in the assault of July 1. Several additional men fell captive as the army withdrew from the Gettysburg area over the next several days. Since the Army of the Potomac was content to follow up cautiously, the 13th Georgia marched back into Virginia at a relatively leisurely pace.[50]

Lee's invasion of the North was over, and for all practical purposes so was the campaign of 1863 in Virginia. Although the Confederate Guards saw some action when General Meade attempted to flank Lee's army in late November, the Union attempt to maneuver was quickly stymied by troops repositioned near Mine Run. The Georgians spent the remainder of the winter in the bleak forests of Virginia's Wilderness, occasionally standing picket guard at fords on the Rapidan River near Clarke Mountain, six to eight miles above their camps.[51]

Sometime in 1863 or early 1864, Capt. John H. Mangham's talents had been recognized by giving him increased responsibility. Originally the Assistant Commissary for Subsistence (A.C.S.) at the regimental level, he had become Acting A.C.S. for the brigade as early as 1862; by 1864, he was the man responsible for feeding Maj. Gen. Jubal Early's entire division. On March 5, however, he submitted the following letter

43

through channels to Gen. Samuel Cooper, the Confederacy's Adjutant & Inspector General:

> I hereby tender my resignation as Capt. & A.C.S. in the Provisional Army of the Confederate States on the grounds that I have been elected Ordinary (i. e. Judge of the <u>Court</u> of Ordinary) of Pike County Georgia.
>
> In proof of which I append the accompanying order.
>
> Very Respectfully, Your Obt. Servt.
>
> /s/ *Jno. H. Mangham*
>
> Capt. & A.C.S.
>
> Early's Division

The attached certificate evidenced his re-election to the position he had held before the war. Since those holding such positions were exempt under Confederate conscription laws, election was a valid basis for discharge of a soldier already in service. The back of John's resignation letter was endorsed by Brig. Gen. Harry Hays, a noted Louisiana officer temporarily exercising division command, as well as by Lt. Gen. Dick Ewell, the corps commander. The final chain of command endorsement read:

> Head Qrs. Army No. Va.
> 8 March 1864
> Res. fwd. for action under the law.
> /s/ *R. E. Lee*
> Genl.

After the Confederacy's Commissary General verified that John had duly submitted returns "to the close of 1st Quarter 1864," he was released from service to assume his duties as Ordinary. After almost three years in the army, he was returning home to Rebecca and their children.[52]

Many other soldiers remained with Confederate regiments in the field, but transferred into non-combat roles due to their special talents, physical impairments, or both. One of these was Nat Mangham, John's first cousin (once removed) and long-time friend from their days together in Zebulon. Nat was the last of the three Manghams remaining on duty with the 13th Georgia as the spring campaigning season approached, and he was a man capable of writing with both hands and carrying on a conversation all at the same time! Naturally, such skills made him the perfect soldier to detail as clerk for the Assistant Commissary of Subsistence, especially since he also had developed a debilitating case of erysipelas. This disease was potentially fatal, but in Nat's case it apparently weakened his left hand and generally rendered him unfit for strenuous field duties. Probably this condition developed during the winter of 1863, and it was natural for Nat to go to work at brigade headquarters for John. In any event, he was detailed for extra duty in the brigade commissary department from April through November of 1864.[53]

Nat probably rode with the brigade wagon trains as his friends fought in the savage engagements that ensued at the Wilderness and Spotsylvania during May and June

1864, although he may well have shouldered a musket during the emergencies that threatened the survival of Lee's army. As a member of Gen. Jubal Early's 2nd Corps (renamed the Army of the Valley), he apparently was present for the daring July raid to the outskirts of Washington D. C., as well as for the hard fighting at Winchester which resulted from "Old Jube's" Valley campaign. The autumn of that year saw him and his old friends of the 13th Georgia participating in engagements at Fisher's Hill and Cedar Creek, where routed Federals rallied miraculously behind Gen. Phil Sheridan and routed Early's initially victorious force.[54]

After the October 19 debacle at Cedar Creek, Virginia, Jubal Early's once proud corps was reduced to an ineffectual remnant. General Lee was desperate to remedy his shortage of troops, and issued orders requiring all detailed men between 18 and 35 back into ranks with their muskets. Nat accordingly was returned to the ranks, but the 13th Georgia's surgeon emphasized that he was truly unfit to return to combat duty. Writing at camp near New Market on November 2, he verified that Nat was still "suffering from the effects of erysipelas causing weakness of the left hand with gen'l. debility. In consequences of which he was [detailed to] the commissary department of Evans' Brigade. I respectfully recommend that he be retained in his present position." Subsequent records show that Nat returned to the brigade commissary department, so he must have been suffering a significant infirmity indeed.[55]

As Nat saw Early's hard-fighting corps decay under the incredible stresses of the 1864 campaign, his brother Will witnessed the erosion of Confederate fortunes in Georgia, where the Army of Tennessee faced Sherman's forces. Will officially remained on the rolls of the 13th Georgia as a convalescent, collecting conscripts and working under supervision of the commandant of the Camp of Instruction at Macon. Although disabled by the arm and lung wounds he suffered at Sharpsburg in September 1862, he nevertheless undertook a mission of mercy in early January on behalf of the Howell family. Close neighbors of the Manghams in the Springs District, the Howell family's son James was also a corporal in the 13th Georgia, and son Samuel was in the army as well. Their father William was wounded while serving in the 66th Georgia Infantry in the Army of Tennessee, and he died in early January of complications culminating in a fatal case of pneumonia. With both of her grown sons away in service, Mrs. Mary Howell asked the Manghams for help in bringing the body back home from the hospital outside Atlanta. Will drove his mule and wagon the 75 miles to Marietta, picked up the charcoal-packed remains, and brought them back home for burial in the Mangham family cemetery, where they still rest today.[56]

As the campaigning season approached in the Deep South, it was clear that Sherman would seek decisive engagement with Gen. Joe Johnston's army on Georgia soil. As Governor Joe Brown and Confederate authorities strained to identify every remaining scrap of manpower for the coming campaign, they reorganized the Georgia militia by enrolling all boys aged 16-17 and men aged 45-55 into local militia companies. Pike County's militia rolls for January 1864 do not reflect the name of John H. Mangham, who was still on active service when they were compiled, but his resignation from the army caused his status to revert to colonel of Georgia militia. As such, he was liable to militia duty but exempt from conscription, a fact that John verified with the State Adjutant and Inspector General. As a judge, he also was exempt from the governor's later mobilization of the militia. County militia rolls do reflect the enrollment of 53-year-old James P. Mangham and his 50-year-old brother, John N. Mangham, who also was appointed a Pike County representative to the Soldier's Relief and Aid Association of Griffin that spring. John already was serving as Deputy Clerk of the Pike County Superior Court, and this status probably exempted him from the governor's mobilization orders that summer and fall. James's youngest son Bob also enrolled in the 581ˢᵗ Georgia Militia District company, but was exempted from service due to his physical disability.[57]

At about the same time, Will joined a reserve company organizing for local defense in Pike County. This unit mustered into Confederate service on April 28, 1864, as Company G, 1ˢᵗ Georgia Reserves. Comprising young boys under conscription age, men aged 45-50, and a leavening of disabled veterans like Will, they elected the regular complement of company officers, including a junior second lieutenant (also known as third lieutenant). As a veteran of the West Virginia campaign, Whitemarsh Island, Gaines's Mill, Malvern Hill, Second Manassas and Sharpsburg, Will Mangham was elected to this position, while his old Confederate Guards comrades J. T. G. Caldwell and W. F. Connally assumed duties as first and second lieutenant, respectively. Combined with a medical certificate of his disability for active field service, this commission was the basis for Will's request for official transfer from Company A, 13ᵗʰ Georgia, to the reserves on October 22, 1864. His discharge from active duty and transfer to the reserves finally was approved on January 17, 1865.[58]

Apparently, however, Will was still too badly debilitated to spend much time with his new regiment. Muster rolls and inspection reports for the period from April 28 to September 1 show him as absent on sick furlough in Pike County, based on a surgeon's certificate of disability. This was unfortunate for his unit, which badly needed mature veterans to impose the necessary level of discipline and training. For Will personally, however, his absence was a veritable godsend. His regiment's post of duty was at the little village of Anderson, a rail station eleven miles northwest of Americus in Sumter County. This remote post soon became infamous as Andersonville, the hellhole prison stockade where Union captives perished by the thousands in 1864 and early 1865.[59]

The Georgia Reserves suffered terribly from disease as well, with a mortality rate approaching that of their prisoners. The notorious unreliability of the Reserves made them the bane of Brig. Gen. J. H. Winder, post commander at Andersonville, who was beside himself over the terrible conditions that mocked his every effort. As he reported in June, "The state of affairs at this post is in a critical condition. We have here largely over 24,000 prisoners of war, and 1,205 very raw troops (Georgia Reserves), with the measles prevailing, badly armed and worse disciplined, to guard them. . . ." In August, an inspecting officer agreed, reporting that the Reserves "are entirely without discipline, and their officers are incapable of instructing them, being ignorant of their own duties. I recommend that one competent officer from the Invalid Corps be assigned to each regiment as drill officer and instructor." Winder was absolutely desperate by October, when he reported his plight to Gen. Samuel Cooper, the Adjutant and Inspector General of the Confederacy. Commenting acidly on the 1st and 2nd Georgia Reserves, he stated bluntly: "They are the most unreliable and disorganized set I have ever seen. They plunder in every direction and are creating a very bitter feeling against the Government. . . .the officers will not exercise any authority, and some of them even encourage it."[60]

Demoralization was spreading through much of the South's civilian population by this stage of the war. Reserve troops certainly reflected this trend, since they lacked the spirit and cohesion of early volunteer units and their traditions of battlefield success and shared sacrifice. As the military situation deteriorated in mid-September, Will's uncle John N. Mangham wrote to his first cousin John Grier Mangham (see Chapter VI) in Randolph County asking about the availability of farms in western Georgia:

Zebulon, Sept. 18, 1864

Cous. Jno. G. Mangham
Sir
Do you know of a good Farm well improved of about 600, 800, or 1000 acres of Land for Sale or that could be bought in your Section of the State, at a fair good price. I Shall have to refugee from here unless the Yankee Army is Stoped or held at or in Atlanta by Our Army. Please look out for me and if you can hear of a Farm for Sale that a man Can Make a good living on, Let Me know. I Shall want to buy Corn on the Place. I would buy Farm Crop & all[.] If I cant get a place as Large as I would like, a Small place well improved so as to give me House Room would answer. I have no Family but Myself and two Little Daughters 13 & 7 years old, (My wife's been dead Six years) and about Forty Negroes. Let me hear from you Soon. Some Little Sickness in My Family, not dangerous.

Very Respt &c.
/s/ John N. Mangham

Atlanta actually had fallen already, and Sherman's hard-bitten Westerners were about to make good on his threat to "make Georgia howl." Since the Confederates feared Sherman might seize Andersonville and liberate the prisoners there, they desperately evacuated the prison from September through November. Both captives and guards relocated to a new enclosure at Millen, Georgia, not far from the South Carolina state line.[61]

As the Federals subsequently cut a swath of destruction from Atlanta to Savannah and then north into the Carolinas, elements of the Millen garrison escorted the prisoners southwards again, while the remainder stayed to help defend Savannah. Will Mangham's Company G was part of the latter contingent, and eventually they engaged in combat with Federal landing parties northwest of Beaufort, South Carolina, in early December. In these two successful engagements at Coosawhatchie, Will's company lost at least two men wounded and one killed in action, but it is unclear whether Will was present. He was certainly on duty with his unit during the last weeks of the war, however, as the ragged Reserves returned their prisoners to Andersonville, then marched and countermarched their captives between Andersonville, Albany, and Thomasville in desperate efforts to avoid Union raiding forces. Many of the luckier prisoners were paroled and exchanged during this time, while their guards increasingly slipped away to their homes as the Confederacy collapsed.[62]

5. A Crushing Burden of Despair: Coming Home from Appomattox and Andersonville

On May 4, garrison commander Col. George Gibbs left his post, and the last vestiges of the guard force dissolved. When the remnants of his company and regiment surrendered near Albany, the war was finally over for Will Mangham. As his comrade Samuel Howell remembered, Will "came home after the surrender with his company they all walked through the country from Albany to Pike County. he made a good Officer and soldier always ready to do any duty to which he was detailed."[63]

Will's brother Nat probably arrived home about the same time, having surrendered with General Lee's Army of Northern Virginia at Appomattox Court House, Virginia, on April 9, 1865. His brigade had fought doggedly through the long winter's siege at Petersburg, and had suffered badly in the retreat that ensued when the army's position collapsed in early April. Nat's last brigade commander, General Evans, wrote after the war to one of the brigade's officers about the final moments of combat at Appomattox:

> There is no question in my mind of the fact that the last shot fired and the last capture made by the army under Gen. Lee were through you and your picked corps of sharpshooters. . . .It is one of the proudest of my thoughts that we were shooting with all our might when the army was surrendered; and I have not the slightest doubt, captain, that you burned the last grain of powder and directed the last Confederate bullet from the great old army of Gen. Lee.[64]

When Nat Mangham surrendered with the 21 remaining Confederate Guards of Company A, only 12 officers and 161 men remained in the entire 13th Georgia.[65] Their four years of war were over, and the world as they had known it had come to an end. It was time for the long journey back to their devastated homeland. After four years of sacrifice, the anguish and uncertainty proved a heavier burden than some could bear.

*   *   *   *   *

As Nat stacked arms for the last time at Appomattox and began the long trek home, Rebecca Mangham undertook what was probably the saddest journey of her life, arriving in the forlorn state capital of Milledgeville two days after the surrender. She had come to the state asylum for the insane, bringing her husband, John Henry Mangham. As the official record of admission stated:

> Capt. Jno. H. Mangham Lunatic of and from Pike County Geo. Age about 37 years. Married has four Children. He is the Ordinary of Pike County and has been for more than a year. He previously occupied that position, for some years, but resigned it in 1861. to take a position in the Army. which he left in January 1864. No manifestations of derangement were observed until Oct'r last. There is

beleived to exist some hereditary predisposition to insanity in his family. The cause of his derangement is not known. Unless it was the anxiety and excitement growing out of the State of the Country. He is always quiet and orderly, he has no tendency to violence. Nor destructiveness. His health is very feeble has eaten a few mouthfulls. oncce only in ten days past. Does not sleep but very little. has stood on his feet for a month past at least 18 hours out of every 24.

Almost two years later, a brief notation was appended: "Removed Jany 11th 1867."[66]

*　　　*　　　*　　　*　　　*

Some 30 years later, the Confederate Guards' roster committee noted discreetly that John H. Mangham had "Died at home since war." One Pike County history stated only that John's family "returned to Alabama" after the war, offering no further explanation. In 1900, John's son Wiley C. Mangham and his wife Delilah lived with their adopted daughter Daisy Bolton and nephew Travis A. Hudson in DeArmanville, Calhoun County, Alabama, where Wiley was a general merchant. I have found no

other record of the once-prominent John H. Mangham family of Georgia and Alabama.[67]

His cousin and mentor, John N. Mangham, died in Pike County within a year of the war's end. Only 51 years old when he passed away, he left behind his young daughters Luella Ann and Rebecca Elizabeth. He had prepared a last will and testament in 1859, bequeathing each of them a number of slaves. John had lived to see these provisions made irrelevant by military defeat, emancipation, and Federal occupation.[68]

Ex-corporal Will Mangham married Martha Jane Hagan (or Hagins) on February 4, 1868, with his old lieutenant T. J. Barrett presiding over the nuptials as Justice of the Peace. The young couple settled down to farm and raise a family of

LULA STEGER MANGHAM
-Courtesy of Joseph Reichert

three children on 66 acres that Will obtained from his father, James P. Mangham. James died on April 7, 1874, preceding Will by only seven months. The young veteran was but 34 years old, and possibly never recovered fully from the grievous wounds he suffered at Sharpsburg twelve years earlier. Only 31 years old and seven months pregnant when her husband died suddenly, Martha never remarried. When her mother-in-law, Winfred Mangham, died in 1884, she left a small inheritance to her grandchildren Lou Emma, Leola, Mary Anna, and James William "Bud" Mangham.[69]

Martha applied for a Confederate Widow's pension ten years after the dawn of the new century. The man who processed her application was Pike County Ordinary J. W. Means, Will's old first sergeant in the Confederate Guards. Martha, known affectionately as "Aunt Sis" by her many nieces and nephews, died on July 28, 1926. She lies buried alongside her husband in the old Mangham family cemetery in Lifsey Springs.[70]

*   *   *   *   *

After returning home to Pike County, Nat Mangham married a neighbor girl, 15-year-old Lula Steger, in 1866. They lived in the Springs District until the early 1870s, when they joined the exodus to Texas. There, cheap land beckoned Southerners desperate to escape crop failures and start new lives away from the desolation of war and Reconstruction. For Nat and his family, the chosen destination was Panola County, Texas. Settling near Irons' Bayou on the Carthage-Henderson Road, Nat was active as a teacher, Methodist minister, bookkeeper, and land developer. Earning a reputation as a serious man of strictly conservative views and Christian devotion, the young Georgia veteran brought the same hard-working approach to postwar life as he had to his service in the "Lost Cause." Despite his pride in his military service, however, Nat later became known for his patriotic support of the reunited country, in the manner exemplified by his old commander, Gen. John B. Gordon. Nat even took a position with the United States government, serving as postmaster at Stones Mill, Texas, from 1886 until the post office closed in 1900.[71]

His beloved Lulabee died in March 1895, two weeks after the birth of their fourteenth child. Nat remarried the next year, and later lived with his eldest son Jim and his family in Kaufman County. His later years apparently were wracked with the pain of his war wound, possibly aggravated by other injuries, and he trained a horse to support his limping gait by leaning to one side. Forty-one years after the surrender at Appomattox, Nat went to visit Jim, riding horseback through bone-chilling winter rains that must have recalled earlier days in uniform. Although he reached Kaufman, he fell sick and never recovered. Nat "crossed over the river" on November 27, 1906, one month shy of his 65th birthday. When he passed away, twelve children survived him, all but three of whom were grown.[72]

Although most of Nat's many children were named in honor of other family members, one's name evoked those long-ago years in Virginia: Robert Lee Mangham.

*   *   *   *   *

Nat clearly meant for his son's name to honor the memory of his old general, but it probably was intended as a compliment to his youngest brother Bob as well, since Nat often spoke of him after moving to Texas. Bob was 24 when he married 15-year-old Eliza Elliott five years after the war ended, and they settled down to farm 36 acres of

50

his father's property and raise a family. Indeed, he proceeded to ensure personally that the Manghams would remain a force in Pike County for many years to come: Bob and Eliza had twelve children by the time of her death in 1890. After Bob married Lucy Abigail "Abby" Littlejohn the following year, they proceeded to have eleven more children, with the last arriving in 1910 when Bob was 64 years old. Ten years later he applied for a Confederate veteran's pension from the state of Georgia, but was denied due to the lack of documentary evidence to prove his service. He renewed his application in 1927, but was denied again for the same reason. Eight months after his second application was denied, Bob passed away on July 19, 1929.[73]

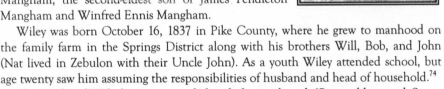

BOB MANGHAM AFTER A HARD DAY'S WORK IN THE FIELDS. THIS PHOTO DATES FROM THE EARLY 1920S. (SEE APPENDIX, REF. #197)
-Courtesy Ray Mangham

6. DEATH AT MANASSAS: SGT. WILEY JAMES MANGHAM, CO. G, "ALEXANDER RIFLES," ALSO KNOWN AS "COUNTY LINE GUARDS," 27TH GEORGIA

Four years after Bob passed away, his sister-in-law Susan Marshall Mangham died in Appleby, Texas, where she had lived for many years with her children and grandchildren. She was the widow of Wiley James Mangham, the second-eldest son of James Pendleton Mangham and Winfred Ennis Mangham.

Wiley was born October 16, 1837 in Pike County, where he grew to manhood on the family farm in the Springs District along with his brothers Will, Bob, and John (Nat lived in Zebulon with their Uncle John). As a youth Wiley attended school, but age twenty saw him assuming the responsibilities of husband and head of household.[74]

The apple of Wiley's eye was a slight, dark-complected 17-year-old named Susan Glen Marshall, daughter of the Manghams' neighbors, Pendleton J. and Nancy Barrett Marshall. Susan and Wiley were married in Zebulon on October 6, 1858, just a week before Wiley turned 21. The young couple built a cabin on James Mangham's property and settled down to farm and raise a family of their own. Their first-born child was a boy, and Wiley's father was doubtless proud to learn that his first grandson was christened James Pendleton Mangham II. The baby was entering his second spring in 1861 when the storm clouds of sectional conflict darkened the skies over his parents' little twenty-two acre, two-horse farm. Susan was four months pregnant in June when Wiley's younger brothers Will and Nat joined their cousin John H. Mangham in the

51

ranks of Pike County's "Confederate Guards." With his modest crop of corn, peas, sweet potatoes and cotton ripening in the midsummer sunshine, Wiley apparently stayed behind long enough to ensure the success of his harvest, then followed his bachelor brothers into Confederate service.[75]

CPL. WILEY JAMES MANGHAM, PHOTOGRAPHED IN UNIFORM
AND FRATERNAL ORDER [?] GARB. (SEE APPENDIX, REF. #192)

–Courtesy of Waymon Campbell

Wiley enlisted in Pike County's "Alexander Rifles" in August 1861. Captain William D. Redding, whose family had very close connections to the Manghams, commanded the new company. His brother Charles, a lieutenant in the company, had married Mary Jane Mangham, the daughter of Wiley's prominent uncle, Wiley E. Mangham. Another brother, John C. Redding, married Cynthia Ann Mangham, a sister of Capt. John H. Mangham.[76]

The company proceeded to Griffin, the county seat of neighboring Spalding County, where a number of men apparently enlisted under Captain Redding before the unit was mustered formally into service. These additions evidently led to the company's redesignation as the "County Line Guards," as well as to Wiley's reduction to the rank of private. He apparently had been elected fourth corporal of the original "Alexander Rifles," but integration of the Spalding men seems to have bumped him from the non-commissioned ranks, reflecting the spirit of office-sharing that typified Southern units organized from different localities. The men officially mustered into Confederate service near Griffin at Camp Stephens on September 9 and 10, 1861, and thereby became Company G of the newly minted 27th Georgia Volunteers.[77]

As sickness started to claim its first victims among the raw recruits, rumors reached Camp Stephens that the regiment would entrain soon for the threatened coastal town of Brunswick, where Wiley's second cousin (once removed) *William W. Mangham* was stationed with Styles's 13th Georgia Volunteers (see Chapter I). September, however, wore into October before the call finally came to move out, and when they left Griffin on the last day of October their destination was Richmond, Virginia. The 27th Georgia quickly passed through the Confederacy's capital, heading for camps located on the old battlefield of Manassas. The still-unarmed troops reached camp on November 15, where they soon went to work building a bridge across the Occoquan River. They completed the span after a month's labor, then went into winter quarters at nearby Camp Pickens. November saw a truly catastrophic epidemic ravage the 27th Georgia's encampments: of an aggregate strength of 799 officers and men, 637 required hospital care! Thirty-five unfortunates succumbed that month alone, followed by four more in December and another eight in January 1862.[78]

After a month of garrison and picket duties at Camp Pickens with the stricken regiment, Wiley was promoted to second sergeant of Company G on January 18. His friend William H. Means wrote home several weeks later, observing to his family that Camp Pickens was "the muddiest place I ever saw and it gets muddier every day," which made it tough for the healthy men to withstand the ever-increasing guard details. Given the constant exposure to cold, rain, mud, and a stunning variety of communicable diseases, it is not surprising that Means also noted: "Sergeant W. J. Mangham and H. Y. Lifsey are both sick with pneumonia but not dangerous I hope. They have been sick three days." Exactly two hundred other men reported sick that month, along with another two hundred sick and convalescent from January. Sergeant David Green of Company K wrote home on February 9 that about 200 men remained fit for regimental drill that day, which represented the first such drill the 27th Georgia had even attempted while at Manassas.[79]

Given the paucity of medical resources and care available at Camp Pickens, Wiley and other sick soldiers were heavily dependent on the ministrations of friends and relatives in the same unit. Private David Steger, whose niece Lula later married Wiley's brother Nat, scared up a pint of poor brandy for Wiley, and the three dollars he paid for it represented more than one-fourth of a private's meager monthly pay of eleven dollars. Steger's kindness was in vain, however, for Wiley's condition worsened into a severe case of typhoid pneumonia.[80]

The end came for 24-year-old Wiley James Mangham on February 14, 1862, before he had completed six months in service and two months before his regiment entered combat for the first time. His widow Susan was only 20, and was left on their little farm to raise two-year-old Jim and his three-month old brother William Wiley Mangham. Young Will was born on November 3, 1861, when his father's regiment was en route for Virginia. It is not known whether Wiley ever got a furlough home to see his son and namesake.[81]

About a week after Wiley's death, his elder brother John Willis Mangham arrived from Georgia to bring the remains home for burial. After several days fruitlessly contending with the irregular train schedules out of Manassas, John was able to get his brother's charcoal-preserved remains aboard a train in late February. Wiley was laid to rest in the Mangham family cemetery in early March 1862.[82]

*   *   *   *   *

Susan Mangham applied to the War Department in early August 1862 for a settlement of Wiley's pay and allowances, but it was November 1863 before the Confederate bureaucracy was able to determine that it owed the young widow $71.53 in back pay and bounties. Susan made shift through the remainder of the war, and family lore records her complaints about the depredations of Union soldiers who later took her livestock and crops, and her fears that they would harm her little sons. As one descendant has noted, "She had a low regard for Yankees. She did, however, compliment a Yankee officer for once preventing a group of soldiers from taking a sack of cornmeal from her."[83]

Shortly after the war's end, she had two more sons who bore the Mangham name, but she never revealed the identity of their father. She never remarried, and thus was eligible for a Confederate widow's pension when the state of Georgia instituted this procedure in the 1880s. She drew $100 annually in Pike County from 1891-98, and then enrolled on the Spalding County pension list from 1899-1907. She moved to Texas in 1899 with son Will, and lived in Nacogdoches and later Appleby for many years with her children and grandchildren. From 1925 until her eventual death of "old age and heart failure" on July 12, 1933, she drew a widow's pension from the state of Texas. The descendants of Wiley and Susan are still numerous in the Nacogdoches area.[84]

7. ONE OF "COX'S WILD CATS": SGT. JOHN W. MANGHAM, "UPSON GUARDS," CO. L, 5TH GEORGIA; AND CO. B, 2ND BATTALION GEORGIA SHARPSHOOTERS

After John Willis Mangham brought Wiley's body back home for burial in Pike County, he doubtless returned to his own home in neighboring Upson County. He had moved there about 1856 and acquired a farm near Thomaston, in a community known as Hendricks. About this time he lost his first wife, Amanda G. Barrett Mangham, who left him with their infant daughter Rebecca. Within two years the young widower remarried, this time to 19-year-old Amanda Elizabeth Zorn. By the spring of 1862, John and Amanda had two more children, Charles and Eliza, to raise on their small farm.[85]

It is uncertain whether John declined to enlist during the war's first year due to personal or political convictions, or whether he simply believed it impossible to care for his family on a private's meager eleven dollars a month. In any event, the government was about to add a new variable to the equation: conscription. In an act approved on April 16, 1862 and published twelve days later, the Confederate Congress made liable for military service every fit, white male citizen of its constituent states, excepting those specifically exempted under provisions of the act. This first military conscription act in American history left John and many other Southerners the choice of enlisting voluntarily in a regiment of their choice, or awaiting enrollment at the convenience of the government and assignment to any unit the authorities deemed fit. Given Americans' abhorrence for the Old World's conscript armies and their antidemocratic traditions, motivation was strong to volunteer and avoid the stigma of conscription.[86]

The conscription act was timed to prevent the dissolution of Confederate forces in the field, as many of the initial volunteers had signed up in the spring of 1861 for twelve months service. These men faced the option of re-enlisting for three years, or accepting discharge and probable conscription in the near future. The Upson County men of the 5th Georgia's Company K were re-enlisting in large numbers, and many of their fellow Upsonians journeyed to Mississippi to enlist with their friends, neighbors and kinsmen. The number was large enough to fill out Company K and still require the establishment of an eleventh company (Co. L) in the regiment; each company comprised a mixture of Company K veterans along with many of the new men. One of the soldiers in newly organized Company L was John Willis Mangham, who was sworn into Confederate service for a term of three years on May 15, 1862 at Corinth, Mississippi. John was unique among the new men in at least one sense, however; he was the only recruit with the same last name as the man who swore them in. This officer was the commander of the 5th Georgia Infantry, *Col. Samuel Watson Mangham*, a first cousin of John's father, James Pendleton Mangham. Swearing in the new recruits was one of Sam's last official acts as regimental commander, as health problems (perhaps combined with his child's recent death) led to his resignation from service just several days later.[87] (See maps, pp. 483 and 566.)

Private John Mangham underwent his initiation to military service in the trenches (commonly known as "ditches" in Civil War parlance) near Tupelo, since Brigadier

General Jackson ordered "Colonel S. W. Mangham with his entire available force" to occupy the trenches at 6:30 p.m. the very day John enlisted. Here in northern Mississippi, the 5th Georgia and other units of the Confederate Army of the Mississippi sought to block any advance by their opponents, the recent victors of Shiloh. John served with the 5th Georgia until July 18, when the regiment's three excess companies (L, M and N) were transferred to form the bulk of a new battalion of sharpshooters. John and his Upson County friends thereby became the battalion's Company B.[88]

The Confederate Congress had authorized the establishment of one such sharpshooter battalion per brigade. The three to six companies of sharpshooters were to carry long-range rifles, with which they could cover the movements of their brigade's several line infantry regiments. Given the close-order battle tactics of that era, infantry regiments were especially vulnerable to attack while changing from fast moving column formations into the lines of battle that allowed them to deliver effective fire. Sharpshooter battalions could protect their line regiments admirably, flinging out companies of trained skirmishers to "feel out" the location and strength of the enemy, delay and give warning of his advance, or harass his retreat. If the brigade commander thought it desirable, he also could deploy his sharpshooters in normal line of battle.[89]

The three excess companies of the reorganized 5th Georgia joined another composite company of other men from their regiment, reinforced by troops from each of the brigade's four Alabama regiments. The brigade's morning report for July 18, 1862 showed the newly-minted battalion at a strength of 15 officers and 275 men, as 191 Georgians had joined the 99 men of Capt. Octavus C. Myers's original company. Although this would not be the final reorganization in the unit's history, the men of these four companies would be the ones that won the battalion's battle honors from the bloody battlefield of Murfreesboro through the hardships of Hood's Tennessee campaign. Most of the Alabamians in Myers's command, now redesignated as Company D, had enlisted in September or October 1861 in Montgomery or Mobile, although they hailed from many other parts of the state as well. They had "seen the elephant" under Jackson at the Battle of Shiloh, to include the bitter combat at the "Hornet's Nest." The resulting four-company battalion was known as Cox's Battalion of Sharpshooters, after their commanding officer, Maj. Jesse J. Cox. Their brigade commander, Brig. Gen. John K. Jackson, Sam Mangham's predecessor as commander of the 5th Georgia, directed that his Sharpshooters waste no time getting ready: they were to "commence drilling as skirmishers without delay."[90]

July and August saw the redeployment of these Confederate forces into the vicinity of Chattanooga, where Gen. Braxton Bragg was marshaling his forces for a strike into Kentucky. Young Charles H. George, the second lieutenant in Captain Whiteley's Company A, wrote on July 17 to his sister Mary, reporting the battalion's just-completed rail movement from Mississippi to a camp near Tyner's Station, Tennessee. Charlie, a Marietta native, was grateful to leave the dusty conditions and poor water of Mississippi and looked forward cautiously to the coming campaign. As he reported, "The word is forward so they say on to Cincinnati I <u>dont know</u> wheather I will ever see the place or not but would like as there is no chance of getting home to go there[.] I have my doubts though as to our geting there." Divisional inspection reports from late August indicate that Cox's Sharpshooters were shaping up into an efficient unit, but noted alarmingly that "The Batt[alion] of Sharpshooters is miserably armed. Many efforts have been made to get rifles for it but without success." This was unfortunately typical of the Army of the Mississippi at that time, and many of its troops still lugged smoothbores into action two years later. Ready or not, however, the Sharpshooters prepared to move north.[91] (See map on page 483.)

Captain Joseph B. Cumming, Jackson's assistant adjutant general, recalled after the war that the brigade's infantrymen staged into Tennessee by rail, leaving the supply and artillery trains to move up by road. Sixty men, including ten from the Sharpshooters, were detailed as teamsters and pioneers to assist this movement at the end of July. The remainder worked to get ready for the commencement of active operations, conducting a daily regimen of two company drills and one battalion drill. Surgeon John G. Griggs of the 5th Georgia was dispatched to Atlanta to procure medical supplies for his regiment and for the Sharpshooters, in order to prepare for the campaign's inevitable medical emergencies.[92]

For John Mangham and his Sharpshooter friends, the Kentucky Campaign of September and October 1862 tested their shoe leather more than their marksmanship, combining a little skirmishing with huge doses of physical hardship. Recalling the lack of combat action, Captain Cumming of Jackson's staff afterwards considered that the "campaign was largely in the nature of a pic-nic." Jackson's troops had some excitement at Munfordville, where they helped to invest the Federal garrison and force its surrender. Cumming's view of the proceedings was probably representative, as he recalled:

> At Mumfordsville [sic], Kentucky, we captured every officer and man of 7,000 troops, under circumstances reflecting little credit, at least in the matter of vigilance, on the part of the captives. They were posted there to protect a railroad bridge over the river. Their camp was surrounded by hills which commanded it. The camp awoke one September morning to find these hills occupied by the mass of the Confederate Army and crowned by its artillery. There was nothing left for the camp but to surrender. . . .Here I witnessed a sight which, perhaps, was not seen elsewhere during the war, viz., the ceremony of "grounding arms." At the word of command from their own officers, these long lines deposited their muskets, pointed to the front, on the ground in front of them. The cartel for the exchange of prisoners was then in force; the men were paroled, formed from line into column, and marched away.[93]

After this taste of war according to "Marquis of Queensbury" rules, the Sharpshooters also got a close-range view of the nastier side of internecine conflict during their ensuing retreat through eastern Tennessee in October. These parts were contested territory in the fullest sense of the word, as partisans of both sides engaged in irregular guerrilla warfare with a brutal ferocity rarely noted in the picture book histories of the Civil War. The wanton looting, arson and robbery that characterized

57

partisan warfare in such areas usually had little, if anything, to do with the war's greater issues. Such activities accordingly were viewed dimly by regular forces of both sides, who considered such "bushwhackers" as murderers and thieves, rather than proper combatants. As such, it is unsurprising that Sharpshooter Bill Hay, of Company D, recalled that such "bushwhackers" were "shot in short order, without a trial." Brigade staff officer Captain Cumming declined an invitation from his servant Lucius, who wanted him to see a "heap of thirteen 'Bushwhackers' who had been hanged by our men with one rope, over one limb, one at a time."[94]

On their way out of the mountainous wilds of east Tennessee that October, Cox's Sharpshooters were reduced to "subsisting on acorns and things." As Private Hay observed, "Marching three days without eating anything is something else." The great majority of the starving men remained in ranks, however, and even the sizable minority who straggled on the line of march eventually caught up with the battalion again. Major Cox's November 18 report showed that companies A, B, and C, nominally mustering about sixty men each, reported 21, 14, and 18 absentees, respectively. The great majority of absentees were reported as "left, sick" at various hospitals, from which sixteen never returned. Seven men in these companies were reported as absent without leave, but these were ailing men who had straggled on the line of march; all but one eventually returned to the ranks. Myers's Company D, with its larger 100-man roster, had 21 "left, sick" plus eleven more absent without leave. Almost all of the unauthorized absentees simply had fallen out along the badly rutted tracks, and all but one returned to the battalion. Cox submitted a separate report naming the sixteen men who actually had deserted from the Sharpshooters since the unit's formation. Seven of these men never returned to the battalion and eventually were dropped from the rolls. As the Sharpshooters eventually settled in to help garrison Bridgeport, an important crossing point on the Tennessee River in northeastern Alabama, they had gathered valuable campaign experience at a low cost in lives. Unfortunately, however, they also had witnessed their first taste of warfare, Braxton Bragg style: hard marching, hard (but indecisive) combat at Perryville, followed by a frustrating withdrawal from a still-contested field.[95]

Equally ominous, perhaps, were the apparent effects on the Army of Tennessee's morale. The Sharpshooters watched bemusedly as President Jefferson Davis alighted in their midst at Bridgeport, and Lt. Charlie George wrote with disappointment that Davis ". . .made no speach nor took any notice of the crowd of soldiers who came from their camps to see him[.]" The concerned lieutenant also added that "No one cheered him some one tried to get up a cheer for him but failed I thought that his reception was rather a cool one though I do not know that it was so meant at least I hope that it was not[.]" In a society that expected its leaders to give rousing ovations to crowds that responded by cheering them to the echo, Davis's lukewarm reception clearly was a disquieting indicator of underlying problems. Further problems arose later that month with the 81 men of the Sharpshooters' newly acquired Company E. The new company was under the command of Capt. Stephen D. Oliver, erstwhile first lieutenant of Cox's old outfit, the "Prattville Dragoons" of the 3rd Alabama Cavalry. This addition brought the Sharpshooters up to an aggregate strength of 352 men, of whom 262 were present for duty with the battalion. Over and above the welcome increase in strength, the addition of Company E changed the Sharpshooters' complexion in two additional ways: Alabamians now comprised some 45 percent of the unit's strength, and many of them were reluctant conscripts from the hills of northern Alabama. Unionist sentiments ran strong in their home region, and nasty implications soon developed.[96]

Many of the new men of Oliver's Company E were willing to take to "shank's mare" to avoid service in the Confederate Army, as evidenced by a mass desertion that occurred on December 10. As Lieutenant George put it: "There is a new company in our battalion of <u>cons scripts</u> and just (19) nineteen of them deserted two nights ago at one time we sent a party after them who I hope will catch them and bring them back." Of course, the flight of one-fourth of the newly arrived company, under conditions reeking of conspiracy, was sure to provoke commanders to stern action. The day after the conscripts took flight, Jackson dispatched Captain Oliver with an armed detail to track down and arrest the runaways. Several days later, Company B's Second Lt. Willie Sandwich was ordered to "proceed to places in Alabama and Georgia where he may ascertain that there are absentees from the Battalion without authority and bring or send them to their command under arrest." At least nine of the runaways were corralled eventually, as courts-martial documents show. Captain Richard H. Whiteley, commander of Company A and a prominent Bainbridge, Georgia, lawyer before the war, acted as judge advocate in the March 16, 1863 court-martial which found privates Miner, Rolin and Henry Kite, Ruben and Thomas Aldridge, Motes, Robertson, Mims, and Wyatt guilty of desertion. Most of the defendants had evaded capture until February or early March; their sentences of sixty or ninety days' hard labor in the Chattanooga guard house, however, were pleasant compared to the ordeal their comrades had faced in the interim at Murfreesboro, Tennessee.[97] (See map on p. 483.)

Garrison routine in middle Tennessee had halted abruptly on Sunday, December 28, when Jackson received orders to move his brigade by rail to Murfreesboro at once, leaving only a small garrison at Bridgeport. As a large number of the Company E deserters remained at large, apparently with Captain Oliver and his posse still in pursuit, this company was clearly less than combat ready. The Sharpshooters' newest company therefore remained behind with 165 other officers and men detailed from the 5th Georgia, 5th Mississippi, and 8th Mississippi regiments. John Mangham and the remainder of the brigade moved to join the army, detraining at Murfreesboro on Sunday night and bivouacking in a drizzling rain. Over the next two days of bitter combat, Jackson's command moved to "various parts of the field, and at different times occupied positions in the front line, on the extreme right, on the left of the right wing, on the right of the left wing, and on the extreme left."[98]

Their moment of truth came late on the morning of December 31. Orders came to ford Stone's River and support Donelson's Brigade by attacking the Federal troops standing firm in the Round Forest, north of the Cowan House on the left wing of the embattled Union line. Cox's Sharpshooters took thirteen officers and 139 men into the unsupported assault by Jackson's little brigade, which numbered only 874 men of all ranks. Little did they know that this would prove to be one of their grimmest days of the war, as they were merely the latest in a series of unsupported brigades flung against the compact Federal position. In the initial advance, they encountered the detritus of Donelson's, Chalmers's and Coltart's shattered brigades as they crossed a quarter mile of open ground under intense cannon and small-arms fire. Captain Cumming, the brigade's assistant adjutant general, recalled proudly: "I have never seen on Broad Street troops on parade move more steadily and evenly than did our little brigade," despite the deadly fire that seemed to "swamp every foot of space." Gilbert Stormont, a soldier in the ranks of the 58th Indiana, recalled seeing his grayclad opponents "falling like leaves" until they finally "retired in good order, leaving their dead on the field."[99]

The Sharpshooters fell back a short distance with their brigade, before standing firm on the edge of a cedar forest and exchanging heavy fire with the nearby Federals. Private Hay of Company D blazed away from the cover of a small cedar tree, loading and firing as fast as he could. "I had shot fourteen times at a solid mass of the enemy," he recounted years later. "As I was ramming the fifteenth cartridge into my rifle, I was struck on the head by a ball and fell to the ground as flat as a flounder." He was carried to the rear by litter bearers, through what Cumming described as a "din augmented by crashing and falling limbs. . .such as I heard no where else during the war." A proud Major Cox reported that his Sharpshooters stood "under a heavy fire from the enemy" from noon until three o'clock, until ordered to fall back on the brigade after silencing the enemy's infantry fire. After another unsupported assault whose failure mirrored the first, the Sharpshooters resumed their positions on the edge of the cedars.[100]

As they fell back, no one noticed the absence of Color Sgt. Ed Hall of Company C, who had fallen mortally wounded in the forefront of the action. Battalion Sgt. Maj. Charlie Roberts and two men from Company C dashed back under heavy fire and retrieved the colors, thus saving the Sharpshooters the mortification of losing their banner in their first major engagement. Additionally, Roberts's action built upon the reputation that he had begun to develop among the Sharpshooters during the Kentucky campaign, which had occasioned his promotion for gallantry in action.[101]

Cox, a veteran of Shiloh, observed that his "men were very calm, and obeyed every order promptly." In the four hours of combat, the brigade suffered 32 percent casualties; the Sharpshooters' horrific twenty percent losses paled by comparison to the slaughter in the line regiments. Their parent regiment, the 5th Georgia, lost 64 of the 173 men taken into action, and suffered *less* than the two Mississippi outfits! Among those mortally wounded was Col. William T. Black, who had replaced Sam Mangham as regimental commander, along with three color-bearers in the 5th Georgia and another in the Sharpshooters. The Sharpshooters remained under fire throughout January 1, 1863, but without loss. They were not committed to action again until the next day, when John Mangham's Company B lost Pvt. Harvey Teat to a severe thigh wound. Teat, the last casualty in the entire brigade, was felled while the Sharpshooters were skirmishing across the brigade front on the extreme left flank of Bragg's army.[102]

The armies had fought each other to a bloody standstill, but Bragg blinked first. When he ordered his troops to withdraw to Chattanooga, many felt that their battlefield achievements were again being wasted. As Lieutenant George wrote home later that month, "Why we left Murfreesboro I dont know. . . .he [Bragg] was the only one the Yanks whiped his men were all right and expected to be let at the Yanks any moment but instead we had to skedaddle." The nettled Sharpshooter lieutenant added, "I hope that my skedaddlin days are over as I have had enough of it and had much rather fight them." His aggressive sentiments were not the mere posturing of a "fire-eater," however, as he confessed to his very human reaction to his first taste of real combat: "I dont mind fighting as much as I thought I should but I assure you that I am very well satisfied to put a stop to my part of it. I can stay in C[hattanooga] or anywhere else that they see proper to put me with a very good grace." There can be little doubt that the dilemma that he described was representative of the great majority of soldiers in his battalion and, indeed, in both armies. Those who lived through a pitched battle learned to respect the enormity of the consequences; however, in good units, a sense of pride, stubborn determination, and a sense of duty kept most men at their posts.[103]

This spirit was apparently widespread in the battalion, which by now bore the proud nickname "Cox's Wild Cats." They had little opportunity to get at their antagonists through the ensuing months spent on provost guard duty in Chattanooga, however, which a disgusted Charlie George characterized as "the lowest, dirtiest, filthiest hole now in the Southern Confederacy[.] if it has any other hole like it in it I hope that it will not be my misfortune to have to stay there." He snorted, "The town is full of cakes & Beer ginger cakes and I dont know what kind of beer it is, but suffice to say that any of it would kill any man who wasnt a soldier. . . ." The Sharpshooters remained in and around the town through July 1863, detached from the main body of the brigade, which again garrisoned Bridgeport. A soggy Lieutenant George grumped, ". . .our camp is a dry one when it is not raining and allow me to inform you by way of the possibilities that it is raining here nearly all the time. . . ." A few weeks later he joked sardonically: "Variety though you know is the spice of life but to tell the truth I am getting rather tired of so much of the spice and would rather have a little more of the substantials."[104]

Their outlook could not have been improved much by a foray launched against bushwhackers, deserters, and draft evaders holed up downriver in "Buck's Pocket," a natural cave of vast dimensions. A civilian informed Cox of their presence; smelling a chance for action, the hard driving major wasted no time selecting fifty men and starting in pursuit. The Sharpshooters marched downriver about fifteen miles, arriving at the banks of the Tennessee at about 9:00 a.m. They crossed the river via flatboat, then marched through driving sleet and snow to the foot of the mountain, arriving near sundown. They surprised and captured two of the skulkers at a small settlement there, but others fled before Cox's men could surround the few buildings. Sergeant Caleb Peacock remembered the atrocious conditions as the Sharpshooters began to struggle up the mountainside:

> . . .the rain poured in torrents for half an hour, and in less than ten minutes after the rain ceased the wind was blowing a gale from the north, and the water

from the mountain side, which only a few moments before was running like a creek, was frozen hard. The moon shone almost as bright as day, and the mountain seemed to be a solid ball of ice.

One of the prisoners made good his escape in the rough terrain, and the weary Sharpshooters found Buck's Pocket deserted when they finally reached it at four o'clock the next morning.[105]

What they saw when they reached the cavern was nonetheless astounding: abandoned bedding and cooking utensils indicated that at least 150 men had been hiding in the cave, which was spacious enough to hold two or three hundred men! The wary soldiers left the mountaintop that morning, but nightfall found them still working their way down the precipitous mountainside, far above the valley below. Major Cox decided to bivouac another night on the mountain, but soon thereafter learned that the bushwhackers had gathered some 250 men and planned "the massacre of the command." This news gave their feet wings, for the Sharpshooters hustled down the treacherous slopes that night, eventually collapsing exhausted into their bedrolls without anything to eat. They left the next morning with no breakfast and a meager haul of prisoners, well aware that the war confronted Confederate soldier s with many hazards besides those that stirred them to enlist in the heady days of 1861 and 1862. While waiting for the flatboat to carry them back across the river, a freak accident reinforced this glum conclusion. Sergeant Peacock's messmate, Sim Roper, struck the hammer of his rifle on a fence rail as he hopped down from his perch. The gun discharged, striking Roper in the head and killing him. The remainder of the little band of soldiers must have felt lucky to escape to Chattanooga with hides intact.[106]

Major Cox resigned soon afterwards due to ill health, and trouble-prone Company E transferred out in late July to form the cadre of the 58th Alabama Infantry. Although the Alabamians of Company D remained with the battalion, it was officially renamed the 2nd Georgia Battalion Sharpshooters at this time. Under newly promoted Maj. Richard H. Whiteley, a 32-year-old fighting Irishman from Bainbridge, Georgia, the battalion's remaining four companies continued the thankless work as the provost guard at Chattanooga. One of these men was Third Cpl. John Mangham, who was promoted on August 1 after spending the months of March through June detailed to special duties. The extended quietude of spring and summer came to an end after Rosecrans flanked Bragg out of his Duck River line in Middle Tennessee, and the armies began maneuvering down towards Chattanooga. Assisted by a masterful feint and aggressive leadership, blueclad soldiers soon poured across the Tennessee River west of town, forcing Bragg to abandon it and withdraw into north Georgia. John and his comrades now steeled themselves to fight for their homes and firesides. Literally.[107]

Although the months spent patrolling the lawless streets and mountainous environs of wartime Chattanooga must have done little to boost their fighting spirits, the ensuing melee along Chickamauga Creek found the "Wild Cats" ready to meet the test. Company D was detached to army headquarters just before the collision in the north Georgia forests, so Whiteley led only 108 of his 208 men into action on

September 18, 1863. As the opposing armies groped towards each other in the dense woods, the Sharpshooters encountered Union outposts just 500 yards from Gordon's Mills on the Chattanooga road. Whiteley struck fast to drive in the blueclad picket lines, but recoiled when six cannon opened fire on his small battalion, wounding two men of Upson County's Company B.[108]

The sharp skirmish was nothing compared to the next day's action, which saw the main armies collide in action of murderous intensity. When General Bragg dispatched Maj. Gen. Frank Cheatham's division to the far right of the developing line of battle, Jackson's Brigade led the column. The Sharpshooters marched as the brigade's advance guard, thus forming the extreme right flank unit of the Confederate battlefront when Jackson wheeled his brigade by the right into line near the Winfrey Farm. Jackson's 1405 officers and men moved forward about 150 yards before Croxton's Federals struck the left of the brigade line, staggering the 5th Georgia Volunteers and their neighbors, the 2nd Battalion, 1st (Georgia) Confederate Regiment. The Sharpshooters' parent regiment was comprised of their neighbors, friends, and relatives, and the sorrow in their homes would be great when news of the fighting arrived there: the Upson Guards of Company K lost six killed, four severely wounded, and another ten slightly wounded. The 5th Georgia as a whole lost 194 of the 317 men who went into battle, or some 61 percent.[109]

Jackson's men continued forward despite the initial shock, and the ensuing advance of more than half a mile saw John and his Sharpshooter comrades help the 8th Mississippi overrun three Parrott guns and six artillery horses, which they sent to the rear. To capture an enemy battery was the ultimate honor for Civil War infantrymen, and Jackson's hard-fighting troops pressed forward in renewed pursuit of their dissolving foe. As they topped a ridge in pursuit of Croxton's men, however, they halted in the face of Brig. Gen. August Willich's fresh troops, standing firm 200 yards to the front and left. As Willich pushed back Smith's Brigade on Jackson's left flank, the Georgian worked hard to stabilize his line. Fresh Union brigades led by colonels Dodge and Baldwin began turning Jackson's left and right flanks, respectively, causing him to call for reinforcements. Upon the arrival of Maney's Tennessee brigade, Jackson's troops were able to conduct a retirement "slowly and in good order." The brigade reformed its line of battle at the original line of departure, helping repulse the Federal advance at this point "with heavy slaughter."[110]

The advancing twilight saw the Sharpshooters advancing yet again under Lt. Gen. Leonidas Polk's orders, this time as part of a two-division attack which saw the hard-fighting Confederates strive vainly to break the Union lines to their front. Jackson's troops advanced 600 yards against a heavy fire as part of a line formed by Cleburne's Division, but the Sharpshooters were spared any further losses in this attack. At about 9:00 that night, Jackson pulled his men out of line to allow Cleburne's Division to reform in its proper configuration. The Georgians and Mississippians returned to their original positions where they "slept on their arms," ready for battle. Whiteley reported proudly that his Sharpshooters "illustrated in an eminent degree those soldierly qualities for which Georgians have become so justly celebrated" during this long day of fierce combat. The mid-day phase of the engagement cost the battalion one killed and ten wounded, with the latter including Lt. James Ogletree of George's Company A.[111]

Darkness provided but a brief respite before the combatants closed with each other yet again. After a morning spent moving to various parts of the battlefield, Jackson's Brigade settled into line in the early afternoon between Cleburne's and Liddell's divisions, in the woods just northeast of the Kelly Field. The "Wild Cats" deployed as skirmishers across the entire brigade front, trading shots with their Union counterparts posted in the woods across one hundred yards of intervening open ground. Their fighting blood was up already when Jackson attached two companies of the 1st Battalion, First Georgia (Confederate) to Whiteley's command, ordering him to clear out the enemy skirmishers in preparation for a brigade attack. The result was devastating: as soon as the young Irish major gave the word, his Sharpshooters responded with the élan that has secured the reputation of the Confederate soldier ever since. Sprinting forward in a headlong charge, they gave tongue to their weirdly pitched battle cry, a shrill yipping that contrasted with the deeper "hurrah" used by their foes. The Rebel Yell sent chills down the spine of Federals who had to face it up close, and it combined with the Georgians' do-or-die determination to drive the Union pickets in precipitate flight after they loosed a single ragged volley. It was moments like these that caused Company C's Sgt. Martin V. Calvin to reflect in later years, "My observations afield, when the battle raged fiercest, gave me this thought: that, at a time so trying, yet not confusing or demoralizing, combatants are transformed into the spiritual almost. Otherwise, plain human nature could not stand shocks so terrific."[112]

The "Wild Cats" stormed through the clutter of blankets and knapsacks left by their fleeing foes, but then slammed head-on into entrenchments held by Yankee infantrymen determined to hold their ground. Supported by a battery firing from the left flank, they held on doggedly as the Georgians' fire swept across their breastworks. Whiteley's men comprised only a thin skirmish line, with no real chance of prevailing in an uphill charge against an entrenched line of battle. Instead of falling back, however, they strove desperately to protect their brigade's advance by pinning the bluecoats in their trenches. A "galling fire" poured downslope and flanking units "enfilad[ed] the entire line with canister and small-arms," but Jackson reported that his men "stood nobly to the work before them, and steadily advancing surmounted the hill on which the enemy's breastworks were." As shaken Federals began slipping rearwards out of their entrenchments, Maney's Brigade charged through Jackson's line and administered the finishing blow to this section of the Union line.[113]

The hard-bitten bluecoats disintegrated under a multitude of such hammer blows, and the long-suffering troops of the Army of Tennessee sensed complete victory within their grasp. As a young officer of Ector's Brigade wrote home:

> Suddenly, miles away on our extreme right, Hood's boys sent a shout—a shout of triumph, solid, invigorating unmistakeable. 'Twas peculiar to Southern troops, and all instantly knew what it meant. Quickly it was caught by the next command, and the next, and thus with increased volume, it passed on to the

left. . . .None can describe the electric, thrilling effect of this Southern anthem as it echoed among those grand old mountains.[114]

John Mangham and the rest of the "Wild Cats" doubtless added their voices to this chorus of victory, but the 95 Sharpshooters who entered the third day of battle had been reduced by a further seventeen killed and wounded. Their total of 33 casualties included ten wounded from John's Company B, and comprised some thirty percent of the men who had gone into battle. Whiteley was justifiably proud of his battalion's performance, singling out nineteen non-commissioned officers and men as "conspicuous for good conduct in the two days' engagement." He was pleased with his "Wild Cats," adding: "The conduct of the entire command. . .was highly commendable to both officers and men, and I am proud to say that I witnessed no instance of bad conduct or want of appreciation of duty during the battle."[115]

The Sharpshooters' shattering losses accurately reflected the sustained ferocity that characterized the Battle of Chickamauga, and they were typical for the Confederate units engaged there. Unfortunately for the Southern cause, the resulting chaos helped convince their commanding general to pause for reorganization, instead of pursuing the shattered remnants of Rosecrans's Army of the Cumberland in their headlong flight to Chattanooga. Bragg's dilatory pursuit was one of the most fateful blunders of the war, for it ensured the survival of the routed Unionists, while triggering a near-mutiny among Confederate commanders subordinate to Bragg. For the hard-fighting troops of the Army of Tennessee, it meant that Chickamauga followed Shiloh, Perryville, and Murfreesboro as evidence that their battlefield prowess would go for naught, denied the fruits of victory by circumstances beyond their control.[116]

For Cpl. John Mangham and the 2nd Georgia Sharpshooters, these evil omens may not have been immediately apparent as they moved northward to besiege their defeated opponents at Chattanooga. The battalion remained in Jackson's Brigade, but a widespread reshuffling eventually brought in the 47th Georgia and 65th Georgia to join them, the 1st Georgia (Confederate), and the 5th and 8th Mississippi regiments under the command of the Georgia lawyer-turned-soldier. Although their opponents in the Army of the Cumberland were threatened with outright starvation, the Confederates on the wind-swept high ground around the city soon faced similar scarcity. The shortages were shocking: letters and memoirs written by the Southern troops positioned on Missionary Ridge speak of starvation as an imminent possibility, not merely as a literary turn of phrase. Some men considered themselves fortunate to catch barn rats for a stew, while others scavenged bits of parched corn from the dirt beneath equally hungry horses. Sam Watkins of the 1st Tennessee saw the whole war from start to finish, and recalled: "I cannot remember of more privations and hardships than we went through at Mission Ridge."[117]

As both armies settled in for the uncertainties of a long, hungry winter, reminders of a more normal existence arose even amidst the universal misery. On October 7, 1863, the Sharpshooters lined up at Camp Missionary Ridge to cast their ballots in state elections, and Lt. Frank Vining and Capt. Mitchell Hester certified that "J. W.

Mangum" was one of those exercising this fundamental right of citizenship, which Confederate soldiers guarded so jealously.[118]

By late November, the reinforced and resupplied Federals were prepared to take the offensive once more, now under the command of Maj. Gen. Ulysses S. Grant. John and the rest of the Sharpshooters stood with Jackson's Brigade at the bottom of Lookout Mountain's eastern slope during the debacle of November 24, when superior Union forces made skillful use of the terrain and foggy weather to sweep the mountain clear of resistance in a spectacular maneuver. Jackson's men crossed Chattanooga Creek about 2:30 a.m. the next morning and stumbled into positions in the main Confederate lines atop Missionary Ridge. Forming the extreme left-flank element of Cheatham's Division and Hardee's Corps, John and the "Wild Cats" were fated to watch in agony once more as the Confederate defenses to their immediate left unraveled, when Union forces pierced Maj. Gen. Patton Anderson's undermanned and ill-positioned line. Corporal Mangham and his comrades hurried to refuse their line to face southward down the long axis of Missionary Ridge, as Jackson's Brigade was the only barrier preventing the Federals from rolling up Hardee's entire corps from south to north. They got help in the nick of time from Moore's Brigade, which arrived to steady their wavering front and extend a line shaken by confusion, as well as by heavy casualties inflicted in stand-up fighting which the victorious Ohioans considered the "hardest of the day." The Sharpshooters' distinguished contribution to the survival of the Army of Tennessee was a small but significant one, yet this could not erase the bitter truth that the damage to their army's fortunes was stunning. The rout was nearly complete, as the Confederate forces pulled back under extreme pressure, many units practically dissolving along the way. It was a terrible and demoralizing turnabout after the great victory just two months earlier at Chickamauga.[119]

It is impossible to determine the Sharpshooters' exact losses in their desperate holding action atop Missionary Ridge, although at least five were wounded and eight captured out of some 122 men present for duty with Companies A, B and C. One of those wounded was Major Whiteley himself, who was shot through the shoulder. Comparing the brigade morning report from November 16 with the next existing report from mid-December, the battalion's rolls reflected a further eighteen men absent without leave and twenty more listed as "absent, sick." In all likelihood, the reported absentees included some men taken prisoner in the confusion of close combat and the ensuing retreat. Likewise, the sick doubtless included a number of others wounded in action. Overall, it is probable that the battalion's actual casualties greatly exceeded the ten percent known to have suffered wounds or capture.[120]

Most of the absentees returned to the Sharpshooters' rolls during the winter, and ranks thinned to a mere 84 men in December had swollen to 111 by January 9, 1864. The welcome return of Company D from detached service soon boosted the numbers present for duty back to 176. Corporal Mangham was one of those present, as he was the first man listed on the voting rolls of Company B's Upson Guards when they cast ballots in elections for local office just six days into the new year.[121]

It was bitterly cold in the army's encampment at Dalton, Georgia, and Charlie George, captain of Company A since Whiteley's assumption of battalion command, wrote painfully to his sister, ". . .the wind blows so keen through the cracks in my cabbin that I cannot hold my pen well because my fingers are too cold"[.] The men had trouble with both the quality and quantity of their rations, with Charlie observing sardonically that "I am geting on as usual have plenty to do and not much to eat but I am somewhat used to this if one could be used to it but it is something like getting used to burning and hurts right bad. . . ." Such scarcity, combined with the Confederacy's shaky financial system, forced one group of Sharpshooters at "Camp Wild Cat" to ante up three hundred dollars for a five-gallon keg of cane syrup to vary the deadly monotony of beans and cornbread.[122]

The army that went into winter quarters near Dalton, Georgia, was haunted by the specter of the Missionary Ridge debacle, and its men had little to sustain themselves except their wounded pride. As Maj. Gen. Thomas C. Hindman noted in a general order to his corps, "Rations may be scanty, the supply of clothing inadequate; but the Confederate soldier wraps himself in his Spartan fortitude, and defies all hardships." The resignation of General Bragg and Gen. Joseph E. Johnston's ensuing assumption of command signaled a renewed determination to restore the army's battle worthiness, however. Johnston's General Order No. 5 of January 8, 1864 made his program clear: he would restore the morale of the Army of Tennessee by restoring its discipline. This directive was eight pages long and spelled out camp routine and drill schedules in astonishing detail. At the core of Johnston's approach was his view of officership: "The test of [officers'] fidelity is in the condition of the troops which they command. Men well disciplined, well instructed, and well cared for, point out the honest officer and true patriot. The reverse shows an officer unworthy of his position, and faithless to the cause." This view signaled Johnston's commitment to his army's most precious resource, the men in the ranks, and they loved him for it.[123]

Reflecting a general spirit of rejuvenation that did wonders for morale and *esprit de corps*, youthful Sharpshooter Frank Roberts joined with his older brother Charlie (the battalion adjutant), First Sgt. "Griff" Griffin and "Buck" Buchanan to form a singing quartet that entertained audiences numbering in the hundreds. Old salt Bill Hay found his fun in earthier sport, playing pranks at the expense of young soldiers arriving in the veteran battalion:

> Some of us would tell the new young recruits that some of these old soldiers had fits, and they would take after a new man if he was near by.
> One day a fit came on one of the old soldiers and he made for the new man. The latter was in a position where he could not get to the door, but he made for the chimney, which was about ten or twelve feet high, went out at the top and down to the ground. We found him later on in another company.[124]

Hay, Roberts, George, Mangham and the rest of the men of Jackson's Brigade were now in Maj. Gen. William H. T. Walker's division, which was "attacked" by the serried ranks of Cheatham's Division in the famous snowball battle of March 1864. Charlie

George took a few minutes to write home about the event, which illustrated that the army was recovering its morale:

> While the snow lasted we had plenty of fun fighting battles with snow balls. Our division and Genl Cheatham had a good fight the first day of it but as they took us rather by surprise they whipped us before we could collect all of our snow together If we had been looking for it we could have had the different brigades formed and would have then given them as good as they could send if not a little better As it was they went to first one camp and then the other and whipped us one brigade at a time[.]

In the same letter, he noted that ". . .the Yankees. . .are all over at Chattanooga behaving themselves very well so far as their troubling us is concerned. . . ." In this atmosphere of safety and snowball wars, the men were called to the colors for a sham battle, apparently to test their readiness. As Captain George observed, some of the men appeared less than eager to cross swords with their antagonists:

> We had a show fight not long ago and a good many did not know that it was to come off and thought the Yankees had go[t] in between us and Atlanta and some of them were pretty badly frightened I can tell you, and especially those that generally go to the hospital when ever they hear Yankee guns begin to open these fellows thought their time had come and looked as wild as bucks but did not have much to say[.][125]

The young commander of the Sharpshooters' Company A believed the army had come a long way towards recovering from the post-Missionary Ridge doldrums. It was a timely improvement, too, because he believed the improving weather would ". . . bring on the Yanks who like Snakes begin to crawl as soon as warm weather approaches. I hope that by the next winter God helping us that we will have them in their dens north of 36° 30' never again to pollute our soil by their presence." Captain George retained a healthy respect for his foe despite his fiery rhetoric, however, telling his sister that the Confederate Army's "greatest bragarts" generally belonged to the commissary or quartermaster departments, adding that even "Genl J[ohnston] dont allways whip the Yankees either." Nonetheless, by May, Charlie believed that the army had recovered from the low point of November 1863 and was once more in "excellent health and spirits." Private Frank Roberts felt confident, too, as he opined that ". . .a practically new machine had been evolved out of the broken one that came limping from Missionary Ridge a few months previously." April's grand review, in which General Johnston trooped the lines of the assembled Army of Tennessee, provided a confidence-inspiring spectacle that the young Sharpshooter never forgot; more than fifty years later, Roberts still remembered it as "the most magnificent sight I ever witnessed."[126]

It was not long before the bold and craven alike had to face the music in earnest, as the onset of warm weather proved Charlie George correct in his estimate of Union intentions. The mettle of Johnston's revitalized army would be tested in sustained combat from May through early September of 1864. For the Sharpshooters, whose specialty was the skirmish line, this meant a steady drain of casualties that slowly eroded their butternut-clad ranks. Johnston's "drills and inspections without end," which had kept Sharpshooter veterans in shape while acclimating new recruits like Frank Roberts, ceased when the drums beat the long roll on May 8. Although their ensuing rapid march to Dug Gap turned out to be a false alarm, it signaled the onset of a campaign that would demand every ounce of leg power, will power, and valor that the "Wild Cats" could muster. (See map on page 566.)

For the 171 Sharpshooters present for duty, the forced march to Dug Gap preceded subsequent moves to Resaca and the Oostanaula River, where they guarded a battery of Hallonquist's artillery overlooking a ford, while battle raged at nearby Resaca. One of their brigade mates, who signed his letter as "5th Mississippi," noted that the infantry regiments missed their Sharpshooters at Tanner's Ferry in a ferocious engagement on May 15, when the 5th Georgia's smoothbore muskets had proven woefully inadequate for skirmishing duties. "Had our gallant battalion of sharpshooters (Cox's Wild Cats) been but with us, the Yankee skirmishers would have had some work to do." He went on to note proudly, "there is a feeling of security which creeps over all the brigade, when we know that the 'Cats' are in front of us as skirmishers."[127]

"Mignonne," an anonymous member of the Sharpshooters, reported in a letter on May 21 that the battalion remained "constantly in the extreme front or on the march." Although he made no mention of casualties, the skirmishing of the preceding days had taken a toll of Whiteley's battalion. After losing a pair of men captured near Calhoun on May 16 and 17 in the rearguard actions of Lieutenant General Hardee's corps, disaster struck the Sharpshooters on May 19 at Cass Station. Possibly in the "heavy skirmishing" that attended Johnston's attempt to bring Sherman to battle along a line just east of Cassville, Myers's Company D lost thirteen men as prisoners in one day. Prisoner of war records indicate that five of the men were deserters and two more soon became "galvanized Yankees," enlisting in the U. S. Army for frontier service in May and June 1864. Since Myers's company suffered no known killed or wounded at Cass Station, it is apparent that most or all of those captured had decided that they had seen enough war. Clearly, Johnston's restorative measures at Dalton had not convinced every Sharpshooter to stand firm.[128]

As the 1864 campaign got into full swing, Third Cpl. John Mangham was serving on special duty with the battalion's Infirmary Corps, and he apparently remained in this position throughout the long succession of battles that summer. General Johnston had ordered the establishment of regimental-level Infirmary Corps on March 21, 1864, directing the selection of "three good men" for each 100 effective men. A non-commissioned officer was to be in charge of each regiment's detail, and was its sole member who bore arms; as a corporal, John filled this position for the "Wild Cats." An officer was in charge of each brigade's consolidated Infirmary Corps, which operated under the control of the Brigade Surgeon. These detailed men were tasked to collect the wounded from the battlefield and get them to the battalion surgeon for treatment. The duty certainly was no picnic, as attested by the fact that at least one of the Sharpshooters' four Infirmary Corps men was killed in action in 1864, while the battalion's assistant surgeon was wounded in action. Colonel James Cooper Nisbet, who served in the 21st Georgia before organizing and commanding the 66th Georgia Infantry, observed that company commanders in the 21st "selected the strongest and bravest men for this duty," as they had to go into harm's way without the psychological comfort of fighting back. Hard-bitten Texan William Fletcher echoed these sentiments when he declined the honor of serving as his regiment's color-bearer, allowing, "I find the oftener I can load and shoot the better able am I to maintain my honor."[129]

John had plenty of opportunities to mull over all of this while carrying wounded Sharpshooters out of harm's way, as the scorching Georgia summer witnessed a seemingly endless series of maneuvers, skirmishes, and pitched battles. Less than ten days after the debacle at Calhoun, the Sharpshooters were on the move near Dallas and New Hope Church. Johnston's army had fallen back from Cassville, crossed the Etowah River, and concentrated to offer battle again. The new line stretched from a southern terminus just east of the town of Dallas, running generally northeastwards to the vicinity of New Hope Church some four miles away. Hardee's Corps took position on the army's left, or southern, flank. The Sharpshooters spent May 25 and 26 on skirmish and picket duty on the relatively quiescent southern flank, while the bloody engagements to their north began to earn this sector the grim title of the "hell hole" among Sherman's troops. On the morning of May 27, Sherman ordered parts of his IV and XIV Corps, facing Hardee, to pull out of line and move towards the hornet's nest around New Hope Church. In the mistaken belief that these movements signified a Federal retreat, Johnston decided to strike. His decision heralded what Company D's Sgt. Bill Hay later remembered as "one of the most miserable days of my life."[130]

Jackson's Brigade had occupied positions in the front-line breastworks just after sunrise on May 27, deploying the Sharpshooters forward of the main position. The "Cats" filed downhill, crossed a stream (probably Pumpkin Vine Creek), and climbed the opposite slope. There they established a skirmish line, relieving the scattered pickets who had stood guard the previous night. Asking the departing men about the nature of the sector, Hay and his comrades were pleasantly surprised to learn that "all had been quiet along that little Potomac," as the Sharpshooters "were seldom ever fortunate enough to find such a place." After posting sentries, the men settled down to a breakfast of hardtack and beef. Within minutes, however, the picket near Hay's group gave the alarm: Federals were moving in the brush just 75 yards to the front! As the sentinel aimed and fired, the Sharpshooters dodged for cover from the inevitable return fire. Within minutes, the deploying northerners rushed the Sharpshooters and drove them down the hill to the creek bottom.[131]

Ordered to retake their positions, the Sharpshooters pushed back uphill through the heavy undergrowth, closing to nearly point-blank range as they neared the top. The two men on Hay's left were badly wounded; another comrade three steps to his right was desperately loading his rifle when he was shot in the hands and top of the head by two opponents just fifteen yards away. As the two Federals turned to run, Hay fired at one and dived behind a pile of rocks, which stopped a bullet sent his way by yet

70

another "Blue coat" just fifteen yards away. Hay frantically rammed a fresh load home and popped back up, only to find that his antagonists had disappeared. The only other men Hays could see were Orderly Sgt. James O. Cauthren, about thirty yards to his right, and another badly wounded Sharpshooter a few yards beyond Cauthren. Within a few minutes, the Federals rallied and began to push through the woods to Cauthren's right, so the two Sharpshooter sergeants pulled back down to the creek bottom.[132]

The bitter small-unit fighting continued through the rest of the day, with the Sharpshooters eventually regrouping to drive their foes off the contested hill. Reinforced by Colonel Wilkinson's 8th Mississippi, they were then sent against the main enemy breastworks,[133] apparently as a result of Johnston's aforementioned belief that the Union force was falling back. As Captain George reported to his sister:

> Our battalion and the 8th Miss Regt. charged the Yankees near New Hope Church in their breast works but were repulsed as we had only a line of skirmishes. They—two lines of battle and in their entrenchments We carried a part of it then we soon had to abandon it We lost seventeen men out of our battalion three of them from my company one wounded two missing[.][134]

Although the Sharpshooters and their Mississippi comrades suffered badly in this fierce engagement, they brought out their dead and wounded, along with some Federal prisoners. Frank Roberts of Company C remembered that the day's action wiped out the squad on the right of Company B's line. As he wrote the *Thomaston Times* in 1912, the right four of the company at Dallas comprised "two brothers Smith, Ben Kilcrease who was of giant proportions. . .with one other whose name I do not recall. . . . One of the Smiths was killed and the other three were captured." Indeed, the records show that Captain Brown's company lost four men that day: William G. Smith, killed, and William O. Smith, Samuel Johnson, and Ben Kilcrease, captured.[135]

As the interminable afternoon wore on, the pressure finally began to ease. Wilkinson's men were withdrawn to the brigade's main position, leaving the "Wild Cats" out on the skirmish line, where they traded shots with their opposite numbers until the sun went down. As they stood together behind a large oak tree, Cauthren commented to Hay that they should be thankful to be spared after the long and bloody day. Hay agreed, but hastened to add that they still were "in what Joe Brown's Militia would have considered 'a very dangerous position,'" as the bullets were flying thick and fast. A few moments later, just after Cauthren had moved behind a small tree a few steps to the rear, Hay heard a bullet whiz past and strike home with the sickening thud that veteran soldiers dreaded. He turned in time to see Cauthren sink moaning to the ground with a shattered thighbone.[136]

As the weary Sharpshooters washed up that night after being relieved on the picket line, Hay and his friends remembered that Cauthren had been shaken badly by a dream one night in late April before the army left Dalton. Apparently, he awoke convinced that something would happen in exactly one month's time to end his service in the army. Of course, it is impossible to verify the accuracy of Hay's recollection, but it is clear that First Sgt. James O. Cauthren died in Fair Ground Hospital No. 2 from wounds received at Dallas on May 27. When Bill Hay passed through the hospital with a thigh wound received several days later in the continued skirmishing near New Hope Church, he learned that a hospital orderly had been surprised to meet Sergeant Cauthren; a Private Cauthren had died in the same bed only a short time previously. An examination of surviving records indeed shows that James Cauthren's younger brother, Pleasant, succumbed to typhoid fever in this hospital in early May, after only two months' service with the Sharpshooters.[137]

The continuing heavy combat saw the Sharpshooters shift to the skirmish lines near New Hope Church, until Sherman managed to disengage his army and begin another flank movement. In response, Johnston redeployed his army on the night of June 1 to a new line near Lost Mountain. The movement began at 11:00 p.m., but Johnston's order specified: "The skirmishers will be left on the line until two o'clock [a.m.], and until the Infantry of the line has been put in march." The skillfully masked withdrawal was successful, and Hardee's Corps eventually occupied the portion of the new line that stretched from Lost Mountain on the left to Pine Mountain in the center.[138]

Charlie George wrote his sister on June 9 from camp in their new sector, noting his recent participation in one skirmish that lasted "from daylight till dark," and another that lasted "two days and nights." He excused his tardy letter writing by summarizing:

> . . . we have now and have had as much as we could attend to to keep up with the movements of Genl Sherman. I can assure you that we have had a right hard time of it but we have rested for the last three or four days and now feel a little more like going into it again.[139]

Indeed, he would soon be called upon to "go into it again," as another series of sharp skirmishes ensued at mid-month when Sherman closed on the new Confederate position. In these engagements near Pine Mountain, the Sharpshooters lost three killed and one wounded on June 15, and another killed and four wounded in the following day's skirmishing and artillery bombardment. Company A was especially hard-hit in this latter engagement, losing Lt. Charles Cobb killed in action, and Captain George and First Sergeant Griffin seriously wounded. Company A's commander, the son of a minister, had recently written his young bride, "If it is God's will I want to live to show the world that I love the Saviour." His hopes and dreams were to remain tragically unfulfilled, however; Capt. Charles H. George died of his wounds at his father's home in Griffin, Georgia, on June 29, 1864.[140]

The steady losses on the skirmish lines from Dallas to Lost Mountain and Pine Mountain had bled the Sharpshooters almost dry by mid-June. By the nineteenth of that month, the "Wild Cats" were in position on a chain of hills overlooking Nose's Creek, just southwest of Little Kennesaw Mountain, where Walker's Georgia Division again formed the right of Hardee's Corps. Fierce skirmishing and artillery bombardments began on June 19, as Federal troops sought to "develop" the new Confederate line. The Sharpshooters were in the midst of the continuous skirmishing, losing at least two killed and eight or nine wounded, including assistant surgeon W. R. Lide. Company C's men had a particularly grim day: they had lost Pvt. Charles Dortic to a leg wound the day before, and now suffered four more wounded, including their commander, Capt. Mitchell Hester, whose right arm was broken by a bullet. Private Frank Roberts watched as his comrade W. H. Hendrix was led from the field in front of Kennesaw with blood streaming down his neck from a head wound; the next time the two met was in Washington, D. C., in 1917. Roberts never again saw his wounded messmate, Sgt. Henry Miller, whose tasty cooking made such an impression on the young soldier while at Dalton. Frank's brother, Charlie Roberts, compiled a list of casualties for his hometown newspaper for the period May 8 to June 21, observing that the battalion had lost nine killed, six wounded "mortally and dangerously," and another 36 wounded slightly or severely. The hard-fighting adjutant summed up the relentless logic of the campaign for Atlanta: "One hundred and seventy-one was the total effective number when we left Dalton, one hundred and sixty-two is the greatest number carried into action, fifty-one of which have been killed and wounded, about one-third of the command." Since another nineteen had been captured in the six weeks of fighting, the "Wild Cats" actually had suffered 41 percent casualties.[141]

The Sharpshooters lost several more men in the succeeding days, but apparently none in Sherman's general assault of June 27, which did not target Walker's Division directly. Several days later, however, Whiteley's command ended its long association with Brigadier General Jackson, as his badly attrited brigade of Georgians and Mississippians was dissolved. The ensuing reorganization saw the Sharpshooters assigned to Brig. Gen. States Rights Gist's brigade within Walker's Division. Gist, a hard-fighting South Carolinian whose very name breathed anti-Northern sentiment, had an excellent brigade consisting of the 16th and 24th South Carolina regiments, the 46th Georgia regiment, 8th Georgia Battalion, and the 2nd Georgia Sharpshooters. Under the fiery South Carolinian's command, the Wild Cats fought a grinding war of attrition throughout the long months of July and August. The battalion's picket and skirmish duties exacted a toll in ones and twos, eventually mounting up to at least four killed, seven wounded, and six captured. Most of these were minor actions now lost to history, aside from the desperate but mistimed attack at Peachtree Creek on July 20 (see map on page 224), along with the Battle of Atlanta just two days later. These two ferocious battles punctuated the steady flow of casualties resulting from nearly continuous service on the skirmish lines facing Sherman's army.[142]

In the bitter struggle of July 22, Walker's Division launched another well-conceived but ill-fated and ill-coordinated assault against Sherman's left wing, near Decatur. Difficult terrain deprived Gist's Brigade of support on either flank when it went into the attack, but his Georgians and South Carolinians surged to a point just forty yards from the Union line before the blast of thousands of muskets repulsed the desperate onslaught. Some accounts indicate that General Walker was killed while rallying the 24th South Carolina, and another bullet dropped Gist from the saddle with a painful wound; John Mangham may have witnessed these events firsthand. Both the savagely contested Battle of Atlanta and the preceding fight at Peachtree Creek found the Army of Tennessee marching under the orders of Gen. John Bell Hood, a headlong fighter who had replaced the much-loved Joe Johnston on July 17. President Davis wanted a general who would spare nothing to defend Atlanta, and Hood soon proved that no casualty list could be long or bloody enough to deter him from a fight. Tragically for his men, however, his willingness to fling them into attacks was not matched by his ability to judge the right place and time. His record would lead to a proud but bitter characterization by his soldiers: the Army of Tennessee would "charge Hell with a cornstalk."[143]

Soon after Walker's death in the Battle of Atlanta, his division was dissolved, and Gist's Brigade was reassigned to Cheatham's Division. They continued the daily grind in trenches spaded from the red Georgia dirt, where the broiling heat and constant glare pounded down upon the beleaguered city's defenders. After six more weeks of successful defense, the overnight disappearance of Federal troops in their front gave rise to the rumor that Sherman was retreating. These hopes were dashed soon thereafter, when new reports indicated that his massive flanking columns had appeared at Jonesboro, where they threatened the last railroad artery leading into Atlanta. The Georgians and South Carolinians were pulled rapidly out of the lines, along with the rest of Hardee's and Stephen D. Lee's corps, and marched south to Jonesboro. Cheatham's Division was held in reserve on the first day of fighting, but the next day saw it engaged in a desperate defensive struggle against impossible odds, as Lee's Corps had been ordered back to Atlanta. With the remainder of Hood's army a day's march away from Hardee's men, the unexpected convergence of most of Sherman's army on Hardee's front and flanks threatened "Old Reliable's" army corps with extinction.[144]

The corps line of battle was posted west of Jonesboro, running roughly north to south. As Hardee became aware that Federal troops were flowing north of town around his right flank, he dispatched Gist's Brigade to protect the threatened point. The brigade anchored its left flank on the Macon and Western railroad line, then refused its right flank until it was facing nearly due east. Corporal John Mangham was present, and may have helped set up the battalion field infirmary before standing by on the skirmish line to help carry the stricken to safety. Those men not on skirmish duty began feverish preparations to receive an assault, throwing up breastworks with a haste learned through hard experience; as some heaved rails and logs into position, others used pocketknives to girdle saplings and then bent them over to form an abatis. The Sharpshooters dug in adjacent to the railroad cut, which comprised a dangerous avenue of approach past their left flank and into the rear of Hardee's main position, which faced westward.[145]

The "Wild Cats" had less than two hours to prepare before rapid fire on the skirmish line warned of the coming onslaught. Elements of two Federal army corps felt their way into contact with Gist's Brigade and the neighboring brigades, commanded by Lewis and Govan. The latter two brigades were posted west of the tracks facing north and northwest, and combined with Gist's men to create a fishhook-shaped right flank for Hardee's position. Only fifteen or twenty Sharpshooters of Company D, adjacent to the railroad cut, could fire down into the cut itself, but Pvt. James Davison later recalled that he and his comrades quickly forced the onrushing Yankees to conclude that it "was not a healthy place."[146]

The 69th Ohio was coming up the railroad towards the Sharpshooters, and its commander rapidly realized that the easy pickings of that morning were but a pleasant memory. After sweeping through the skirmishers and into the woods lining the railroad, they ran smack into the Sharpshooters and the leftmost companies of the 24th South Carolina. Closing to within fifty yards of the Rebel line, the Ohioans withstood "a murderous fire, which speedily decimated our ranks" during a fifteen-minute fight. Elements of two Federal brigades swirled against the Georgians and South Carolinians, threatening to overwhelm their front and both flanks; the color-bearer of the 69th Ohio stood defiantly waving his flag in their faces, only fifty or sixty yards away. Private Davison remembered a dozen Sharpshooters shouting "Shoot him down!", but everyone within range was frantically reloading at the time. The respite was brief, however, and half a dozen rifles cracked at the same time Davison pulled his trigger. The flag and its bearer, Color Sgt. Allen L. Jobes, crumpled to the ground, but another man quickly picked up the ensign before suffering the same fate in his turn. It seemed to privates Davison and Frank Roberts that five or six color-bearers were shot down in rapid succession. Another may have been Sgt. George Field, who died as he planted the colors of the 38th Indiana atop the opposite embankment. As Davison recalled grimly, "our rifles were true, with men behind them that knew how to use them," adding, "We did not want them to go back home and say we slighted them." The onrushing assault waves crested ever closer to the Sharpshooters' line, until finally the 69th Ohio's flag dropped, abandoned, some thirty-five yards from Davison's position.[147]

Twenty-five-year-old Adjutant Charlie Roberts was just coming down the Sharpshooters' line from the right flank as the blueclad infantrymen recoiled into the woods, and he wasted no time in sizing up the situation. Shouting "Hold up boys, I'm bound to have that banner!", he vaulted the breastworks and scrambled down into the railroad cut to seize the abandoned trophy. Davison screamed vainly, "Stop, Charley; there are five hundred yanks right round the curve"! The continuing din of battle drowned out his words of caution, however, and Roberts made his dash for the flag. His teenaged brother Frank and many others watched in horror as Charlie snatched up the colors, then went down hard amid a storm of musketry unleashed as the opposing lines opened fire on each other. First Sergeant Fayette Taylor and Pvt. Sam Ellerbee, of Company B's Upson Guards, jumped over the breastworks in an attempt to bring Roberts back, dead or alive, but they were unable to reach him before another wave of Federals surged forward over the prostrate form of the young adjutant. The veterans of the 69th Ohio had fallen back into the protection of the woods before rallying at a point from which they could cover their abandoned flag and prevent its capture. As other blue-coated infantrymen poured into the Confederate positions west of the railroad, the entire position became a maelstrom of close-range combat. This attacking wave, or perhaps a succeeding one, drove the single rank of Sharpshooters back a hundred yards, threatening to collapse the entire right flank of Hardee's position. The 24th South Carolina managed to hold firm behind their adjacent traverses in hand-to-hand fighting, and the regrouped "Wild Cats" soon surged back to help the desperate Carolinians drive the Yankees out of their critical position alongside the railroad cut.[148]

It was a near-run thing, given that the main blow of two brigades had struck the four companies of "Wild Cats" and three companies of South Carolinians in the front and flank, while the remainder of Gist's Brigade initially faced no direct assault. It speaks very highly of both commands that they withstood such pressure, and then rallied to repulse the superior numbers that threatened to swamp them. Since Govan's Arkansans were overwhelmed west of the railroad cut, the stand of a few companies of South Carolina and Georgia troops made a crucial contribution to the salvation of Hardee's right flank. Indeed, units such as the 38th Indiana found themselves unable to hold their positions west of the railroad cut, deeming it "but slaughter of the men who had done so gallantly to remain longer exposed to the terrible enfilading fire from the left." The Confederates had staved off total disaster by a razor-thin margin, with the 24th South Carolina earning the personal thanks of General Hardee for its stand. There was no question, however, of his isolated corps attempting to hold the same ground the next day.[149]

When John Mangham and the rest of the "Wild Cats" mustered down the line in new positions at Lovejoy Station four days later, the 142 men present in ranks had fought their last battle on Georgia soil. After some skirmishing and artillery fire at Lovejoy, they stood fast in camps at Palmetto, Georgia, for most of September, before heading back north as Sherman's legions turned east to Savannah and the coast. Army of Tennessee inspectors noted that the Sharpshooters were ill clad, poorly shod, dirty, and badly fed as they prepared for their next campaign. They also noted, however, that men who had no soap for washing still found a way to keep their rifles clean, and they were well-trained and disciplined in their use. Given 135 years of hindsight, today's reader might consider them merely a doomed and hopeless, even helpless, remnant of an army. But long odds or not, they still had plenty of fight left. At the little crossroads town of Franklin, Tennessee, they would show just how much.[150]

After breaking camp at Palmetto on September 29, they marched 361 miles to Tuscumbia, Alabama by the end of October, where they rested a while and waited for orders in the cold, rain, and mud. Jim White, a soldier in Gist's 46th Georgia, remembered the makeshift food situation: "the black peas from the river bottoms that was so black & strong we boill them twice & they was splended without salt and very little bread. A pocket full of parch corn gave another very good days rashions to him who could get it." After a pontoon bridge was built to allow the army to cross the Tennessee River, the "Wild Cats" slogged northwards another hundred-odd miles to Spring Hill, Tennessee by late November. Although Hood's attempt to destroy Sherman's supply lines had failed to deter his infamous march to Georgia's coast, the Southern general decided to take the war back into Tennessee.[151] (See map on p. 566.)

The last few miles of their march had placed the Sharpshooters in a cornfield near the road to Franklin, where the Army of Tennessee was poised to cut off and destroy Schofield's Federal army. In one of the most fateful blunders of the war, however, the Southern commanders bungled the opportunity and left the trap unsprung. With two army corps positioned directly on Schofield's flank, his men pulled out unmolested during the night of November 29. Men of Gist's Brigade lay in growing disbelief just seventy yards from the road, obedient to orders to withhold their fire. Colonel Ellison Capers, commanding the 24th South Carolina, raged helplessly in his journal, "Somebody in authority ought to be shot! Marched 18 miles to strike the enemy's rear, reached it, but did not attack a retreating enemy in flank, and in full sight!" Presumably, John Mangham was one of the frustrated "Wild Cats" who moved north up the road the following day, passing through the debris of an army in flight. They helped push the Union rear guard off of Winstead Hill that afternoon, and covered the front of Gist's Brigade as it formed into line of battle just two miles south of the town of Franklin.[152]

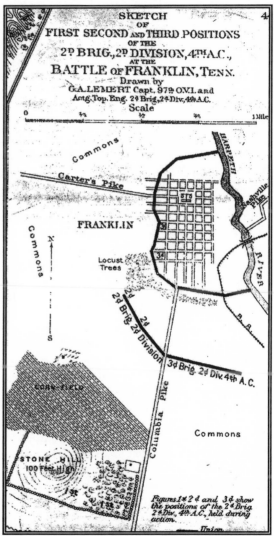

The brigade formed a small part of an awesome sight: some 20,000 troops of two corps, lined up in serried ranks as if on parade. Gist's veterans were to march northward, guiding along the left of the Columbia-Franklin Pike, separated from the road by one other brigade. The "Wild Cats" were ordered to clear Yankee skirmishers from Gist's path, then stand clear as the main line of battle stormed the Federal works. For Whiteley's Georgia and Alabama soldiers, this meant clearing out a "strong line of skirmishers" sheltered behind a stone wall on Privet Knob, which stood halfway between Winstead Hill and Franklin. After trading shots at long range, the "Wild Cats" closed with a rush across the open fields south of the 100-foot high outcropping. Frank Roberts saw several comrades felled by a

CPL. JOHN MANGHAM AND COX'S WILD CATS SEIZED THE "STONE HILL" SHOWN AT LOWER LEFT. (SEE APPENDIX, REF. #190)

77

"very hot fire" during the charge, but the "Cats" drove their opponents back from the wall. After a short pause, they pushed uphill and secured the crest, scattering the remainder of the bluecoated skirmishers. Roberts and his comrades found at least one 16-shot Henry repeating rifle among the equipment abandoned by the Federals.[153]

It is unclear whether the Sharpshooters then remained atop Privet Knob, or whether they continued 500 yards further north to help drive Union troops from their ill-advised forward position. Their mission complete, they watched in awe as the main assault swept past to storm the main Union breastworks. In sustained fighting of almost unparalleled ferocity, the Army of Tennessee proved itself the equal of any in the Civil War for raw valor. Unfortunately, however, Hood had committed them foolishly once more; possibly in a cold fury of frustration after the failure at Spring Hill, he determined to "teach" his army how to charge breastworks. Choosing to launch a headlong assault across two miles of open ground instead of flanking his foe out of impressive positions, he got a valiant performance from his men: a performance that he had no right to expect. In what historians James L. McDonough and Thomas Connelly so aptly called the "five tragic hours" of combat at Franklin, the officers and men of the Confederacy's western army resolutely refused to flinch. Although they proved unable to rout their hard-fighting opponents from their breastworks after Opdycke's Federal brigade plugged the initial gap, the desperate attackers remained there in a fight to the death that persisted long after night fell. It was a frenzied melee at point-blank range, with men thrusting muskets through gaps in the logs and firing into the very faces of their foes, while others savagely stabbed and slashed with bayonets and swung rifle butts.[154]

When Sharpshooter Sgt. Bill Hay walked the battlefield the next day after the Federals had pulled out during the night, he saw corpses stacked in windrows, twin rivers of blood streaming down the turnpike, and a dead officer wedged upright among the fallen who jammed the breastworks. The five hours of combat had destroyed the command structure of the Army of Tennessee: sixty-five regimental, brigade, and division commanders were lost in the butchery, including Gist. Their formations were likewise gutted. Of the 20,000 men committed to the assault at 4:00 p.m. that afternoon, some 7000 were casualties by nine o'clock that night. Years afterward, General Schofield told the German Kaiser bluntly what he thought of the men he faced that day: "The highest exhibition of human courage in the history of the world was the Confederate attack on my breastworks at Franklin."[155]

Private Sam Watkins, later renowned for his memoir *Company Aytch*, was a skirmisher that day in front of Carter's Brigade of Brown's Division, and thus went into action on the Sharpshooters' immediate left. Although these skirmishers had to go all the way to the main Federal works, they did not have to advance within the dressed and covered ranks of the 1st Tennessee. Undoubtedly, many a man of the 2nd Georgia Sharpshooters later echoed Watkins's sentiments as he mused, "If I had not been a skirmisher on that day, I would not have been writing this today, in the year of our Lord 1882."[156]

Despite its horrific casualties, the famished and ragged army moved northward once more, gamely following Schofield's Federals to Nashville itself. As the "Wild Cats" marched wearily towards Tennessee's capital city, many must have recalled an incident that had occurred only the week before. Gist's men and the other troops of Brown's Division heard cheering from the head of the column as they marched north out of Alabama, and had wondered at the cause until they hove within sight of the state line. There they passed under a crudely painted canvas sign stretched above the road, bearing an inscription that captured the nature of Hood's desperate enterprise: "Tennessee, a Grave or a Free Home." In many respects, these stirring words had posed the essential question facing the proud but ragged butternut columns as they approached Spring Hill. For the desperate remnant of an army that dug in south of Nashville in early December, however, the answer appeared increasingly clear after the slaughter of Franklin. The army was, almost unbelievably, still game, but its staying power was finally nearing an end.[157] (See map on p. 576.)

In the freezing hills south of the city, the Sharpshooters took their accustomed place on the picket lines, as their opponents marshaled their strength and prepared to smite the pesky army of starvelings who had the temerity to "besiege" a much superior force. Posted several hundred yards in front of the breastworks of Cheatham's Corps, the Georgians were near the right of Hood's line, and Frank Roberts recalled that it "was no picnic doing picket and vedette duty out there in our threadbare and ragged clothes." Several of the men managed to "organize" some fresh food from farms between the opposing lines, but the days were otherwise dreary. The Federals' heavy guns in Fort Negley made the days even longer, shelling the Sharpshooters' lines and leaving fearsome holes "deep enough to bury a mule."[158]

When mid-December finally saw Gen. George Thomas move his blueclad legions out to assault their besiegers, the outcome was hardly in doubt. The long-awaited Federal attack finally came against Hood's army on December 15, but the Sharpshooters remained unengaged on the right flank. Since the main effort was clearly directed against the left, Cheatham's Corps shifted over to help face this threat. Gist's Brigade, whose senior officer was now Lt. Col. Zachariah Watters of the 8th Georgia Battalion, arrived in its new position just before dark that evening. The men began to throw up a line of breastworks just south of Shy's Hill, facing to the west, while the Wild Cats resumed skirmish line duties on the brigade front. Just as he had at Spring Hill only two weeks before, Pvt. Frank Roberts listened to the sound of Federal troops moving in force during the night. Again, the sounds bore tidings of impending disaster for the Confederates. As day broke on December 16, long blue columns were visible moving around Hood's left. During the day's fighting, Gist's and Maney's brigades shifted south to try to refuse and cover the exposed flank, but the Sharpshooters did little if any fighting before Bate's overstretched division broke in their rear, on the northwest slopes of Shy's Hill. As Roberts recalled: "From our position on the left we could see General Bate's line very distinctly, and when it broke the men seemed to rise like a flock of big birds and fairly fly down the hill."[159]

"Oh, For a Touch of the Vanished Hand"

The collapse was sudden, for most of the butternut-clad troops on Shy's Hill could see quite plainly that heavy Union flanking columns were moving almost unmolested upon the sole possible path of retreat. The penetration of the thinly-manned Confederate center thus gave the signal for general flight, as two army corps dissolved in rout and ran southward down the Granny White Pike, striving to escape before the road was blocked. Joseph Cumming, now a major on Cheatham's staff, was one of those who tried unsuccessfully to rally the fugitives as they ran for their lives. Sharpshooter Sgt. Evan Morgan encountered Cumming after the war, and told him:

> Major, I saw you on one occasion when I thought you were a perfect damn fool! It was at the battle of Nashville. You were dashing about on a white horse trying to stop the men. I said to myself "what a damn fool! If I had that horse I would make a better use of it!"[160]

John Mangham must have been among the thousands of refugees, as was Private Roberts, who legged it through scenes of "wild confusion" on the Granny White Pike. Frank made it to Brentwood that night, then continued on to Franklin the next day. Many other Sharpshooters were either less fortunate or less determined to escape. Captain Octavus C. Myers, commander of Company D and the original "Company of Sharpshooters" of June 1862, had his right arm fractured by a Minie ball in the fracas and fell captive in Franklin the next day. It is unclear whether other Sharpshooters were killed or wounded at Nashville, although it is hard to imagine otherwise. Prisoner of war records do indicate that at least eighteen Sharpshooters fell captive on December 16, marking Nashville as the darkest, though not the bloodiest, day in the unit's history. One of those captured was Sgt. Bill Hay, who now had to turn his skirmish line savvy to the struggle for survival in notorious Camp Douglas prison.[161]

Reminiscent of the debacle at Missionary Ridge in November 1863, however, elements of the Army of Tennessee miraculously managed to hold fast, slow the Federal pursuit, and save the army from destruction in detail. John Mangham's third cousin *Thomas H. Mangham*, a private in the 19th Louisiana, was one of those who helped stave off the army's extinction that day. But like a rubber band stretched too far, most of Hood's force no longer had the ability to bounce back to fighting trim. The losses were too great and the South's dearth of men and resources too severe; the odds were now simply too long, and those who fought on did so despite an increasing sense that the Confederacy was "gone up the spout." Although some units retained cohesion sufficient to stymie the Federal pursuit, further offensive action was utterly out of the question. The remaining "Wild Cats" helped secure a battery posted to protect the retreating army from marauding Union gunboats as the gray columns shuffled across pontoons over the Tennessee River at Bainbridge, but they doubtless knew that their future was bleak. General Cheatham complimented their steadfastness amidst the ruins of the army, recalling that "Gist's Brigade was the only body of troops" in his entire corps "which crossed the Tennessee. . .marching in order. . .and under its officers. . .armed, obedient and organized."[162]

The two ensuing months were spent in northern Mississippi, not far from the place where John Mangham had enlisted three years previously. Most of the troops from the Trans-Mississippi states were furloughed, in order to provide a facade of legitimacy to their spontaneous exodus to their homes. Many of the Sharpshooters had fallen prisoner at Nashville or in hospitals at Franklin, while others were sick and unable to continue in service. Some remained with the colors, but rampant rumors of Sherman's atrocities in Georgia drove them almost literally to distraction. Most of the men were glad to set their faces eastwards once more as they moved to join Gen. Joe Johnston's scratch force opposing Sherman's march through the Carolinas.[163]

John was one of those remaining, and he may well have been among the remnants of Cheatham's Division which arrived on the field at Bentonville, North Carolina, on March 21, 1865. A lieutenant of the 10th Illinois, participating in a Federal counterattack which threatened Johnston's force with disaster, remembered Cheatham's men "came down in a heavy mass hooping and yelling. . . .We ingaged them with all the determination in our power. . .but to no use. . . .[We] soon found the enemy comeing down on our left flank, and swinging around in our rear." After the rebels pressed to within twenty yards of the Illinoisans' line and began calling for their surrender, the lieutenant reported that he and his men "about faced and made for the rear as fast as we could."[164]

The battle petered out with both armies intact, and it proved to be the last major fight before Johnston's force surrendered at Greensboro, North Carolina, on April 26, 1865. It was seventeen days after Lee's army had surrendered at Appomattox, and only four dozen weary "Wild Cats" remained to form up behind their battle-worn Southern Cross when the end finally came for the Army of Tennessee. Of the approximately 26,000 men remaining on the army's rolls at the surrender, a mere 51 soldiers in companies C and D of the awkwardly named "65th Regiment, 2nd and 8th Battalions Consolidated Georgia Volunteers," comprised the sad remnant of the 2nd Georgia Battalion Sharpshooters. The forty-eight soldiers present for duty in the two companies had successfully defied the long odds faced by infantrymen of the Civil War; they were the remnant of the 526 who had served in the battalion during its three-year existence. Many of those absent were on the list of 210 killed, wounded, or captured. Many of the others had been transferred, some deserted, and the rest had run afoul of the innumerable pitfalls posed by the line of march, army discipline, bushwhackers, accidents, and an array of health hazards that boggles the minds of their 21st century descendants. Only a few had been with the battalion from start to finish, and fewer still were those whose names were marked "present" on every surviving muster roll from 1862 to 1865. One was Fourth Sgt. John Willis Mangham.[165]

Another of those present as the Army of Tennessee faded into history was color bearer Andrew J. Boland, who had soldiered with the 5th Georgia and the 2nd Georgia Sharpshooters since May 1861. Perhaps it was Boland who carefully folded the battalion's battle flag, placed it in a black carpetbag, and hid it in a pile of brush as the end approached in North Carolina. Thomas D. Bivins, a soldier in the 12th Michigan, found it there and carried it home as a war trophy. In 1902, his family wrote the

Atlanta Constitution, seeking help in contacting any surviving Sharpshooters. The "relic of red battle" recently resurfaced after a century in obscurity.[166]

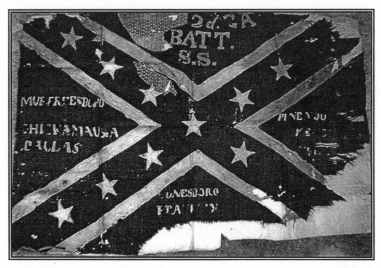

DAMAGED BATTLE HONORS INCLUDE JONESBORO AND FRANKLIN
(BOTTOM); PINE MOUNTAIN, KENESAW, AND ATLANTA (RIGHT).
MORE CLEARLY LEGIBLE ARE MURFREESBORO, CHICKAMAUGA,
AND DALLAS.

–Photo courtesy of Bill Russell

John Mangham was 32 years old when he finally made his way back to home and family in Upson County, where Wilson's great cavalry raid had overrun the county seat of Thomaston on April 18-19. Fortunately the blueclad horsemen had limited their destructive efforts there to three textile mills and a train filled with supplies, sparing Upson County the ravages that laid waste much of Georgia and the South. John came home to a family that now included little Lella, born in the spring of 1864, and Dora and Amos came soon thereafter. By five years after the war's end, John had forty acres of land under cultivation to support his wife and six children, while 100 acres of woodlands and another 110 unimproved acres rounded out his $1000 farm. The pasturage supported the horses and oxen with which he worked the farm, as well as the sheep and pigs that helped feed his growing family.[167]

Son William Augustus was born the next year, and in 1874 John and Amanda had another son, Wiley Thomas Mangham, apparently named after John's deceased brother and their beloved Uncle Wiley of Zebulon, Georgia. The same year saw tragedy befall the Mangham family, however, as John's father James died in April and his younger brother Will passed away in November. Three years later, the still-growing family welcomed little John Jackson Mangham, some 15 years after his father had enlisted in the brigade commanded by Brig. Gen. John Jackson. Although the general's role in the Missionary Ridge disaster was severely criticized by some in the army, the former Sharpshooter apparently felt differently about the brigade commander he had followed for two years. John Jackson Mangham would make the family name well known throughout Georgia in 1932, when he made a strong, but eventually unsuccessful, bid for the governorship.[168]

JOHN MANGHAM (TOP ROW, THIRD FROM LEFT) WITH HIS SON CHARLES B.
"PONY" MANGHAM (TOP, CENTER) AND FAMILY. UPSON COUNTY, GEORGIA.
(SEE APPENDIX, REF. # 190)

- Courtesy of Betty Wiltshire

In so doing, he was emulating his father's example of political involvement, as John Willis Mangham had become a prominent figure in Upson County during the 1880s. By 1887, he was a member of the Board of Trustees that visited the school in Hendricks, where John had lived for thirty years. As the *Thomaston Times* noted, the "instructive talks" delivered by John and Dr. Means made a favorable impression, observing, "It is not necessary to say that such visits are inspiring alike to preceptor and pupils. . . ." John also served as President of the Hendricks Alliance from September 1889 to late 1890, when he became vice president. This organization was a local chapter of the Georgia Alliance, itself a part of the larger agrarian-populist antitrust movements of the late 19th century. The specific issue that put John's name in the paper on September 12, 1889, was the Alliance's boycott of merchants who sold imported jute as an alternative material for bagging cotton. A year later, the *Thomaston*

Times reported that a "mass meeting" of the citizens of Hendricks had selected *Judge* John W. Mangham as chairman of a committee established to persuade the Macon & Birmingham Railroad to build a station in the little town. By that time, John was prominent enough in the county to stand for election as County Commissioner on the Democratic ticket, and he garnered 217 of 221 votes cast. He served in this capacity for much of 1891, and did so again in 1896.[169]

John was a devout Christian who was very active in church affairs as well as local politics. He and his son Charles Banks "Pony" Mangham attended a camp meeting in Bluff Springs in late August 1887, and John sent word to the local newspaper that it was a "good meeting." He was a long-time member of the Methodist church, and his family's names are prominent among those listed as early members of Bethel Methodist Church in Hendricks. Late in the 1880s, however, the church membership divided acrimoniously over the issue of conference membership. As a lifetime Hendricks resident recalls her mother saying feelingly, "That was some *passing words*." John Mangham may well have been foremost among those upset over the issue, for on August 21, 1889, he called to order a meeting for the purpose of organizing a new Congregational church. An old Sharpshooter comrade, Drury Womble, was among the deacons, and John Mangham was a trustee, first Sunday school superintendent, and deeded an acre of land for the erection of the church building itself. Just six weeks later, John hosted a Reading Club entertainment for the young people's Society of Christian Endeavor, which met at his home to receive Reverend William Show, a Congregationalist Sunday school lecturer for Georgia and Florida. John's son Amos played the organ for the assemblage.[170]

Amos was 21 years old at this time, but had only thirteen more years to live. When he died unexpectedly in 1902, he left behind six children and saddened parents. John wrote his son's obituary notice, which noted sadly:

> He was a good boy to his father and mother. . . .but we feel our lost is his eternal gain. . . .The life that he lived for the last 2 or 3 years tells the truth of his nearness to the Christian religion as taught in the Bible bears out to us that he has gone to live with God and angels in the house prepaired for all the good that went before or that will come after.

> May all his relatives live the life that is taught in the Bible that will give a home in that house not made with hands where we may meet with Amos and the good that have gone before. May God's blessings rest upon his aged parents that their last day on earth may be their best days. . . .171

Not quite three years later, John lost Amanda, his companion of forty-seven years. Her obituary noted that "Mrs. Mangham has been a great sufferer for years, but bore her suffering with true christain [sic] fortitude." The writer also noted that "The large concourse of friends and neighbors, who gathered to sympathize with family, and pay the last tribute of love, showed more forcibly than words, the high esteem, in which Mrs. Mangham was held, by all who knew her."[172]

Just months after Amanda's death, John remarried on December 3, 1905, this time to her widowed sister Sophronia Victoria Zorn Smith, who lived in Saint Petersburg, Florida. Leaving his eldest son Charles B. "Pony" Mangham as the sole remaining family member in Hendricks, John and Sophronia apparently lived in Florida, although he also may have stayed with his son Wiley in the town of Omega in southern Georgia's Tift County. His move south probably caused him to miss a big event on May 2, 1908, when Upson County unveiled a memorial in honor of the more than 1200 men who filled the ranks of her eleven wartime companies.[173]

John probably saw the statue commemorating his service when he came back to Upson in 1910 to visit the "Pony" Mangham family. While visiting in the winter of that year, however, he suddenly took to the sickbed. Despite the best efforts of Dr. J. M.

McKenzie, the old Sharpshooter had fought his last fight. At 3:00 p.m. on Monday, November 14, 1910, John Willis Mangham closed his eyes for his final rest.[174]

John lies buried alongside his beloved Amanda in the cemetery at Hendricks Baptist Church, near their sons James Amos and William Augustus Mangham. John's Sharpshooter comrades Charles V. Collier, Samuel Ellerbee, and Arch Daniel lie nearby. Memorial crosses emplaced by the Sons and Daughters of Confederate Veterans mark their graves.

The Hebron Congregational Church stands near the graveyard, a visible reminder of John Willis Mangham's religious convictions. He donated the land for this house of worship just fifteen years after his father, James Pendleton Mangham, donated acreage for Beulah Baptist Church, near the old home place at Lifsey Springs.

GRAVE MARKERS OF JOHN WILLIS AND AMANDA ZORN MANGHAM , UPSON COUNTY, GEORGIA.

- Author's collection

[1] Vaughn Ballard, comp., *Solomon Mangham: His Ancestors and Descendants* (Arlington: Family Histories, 1989), pp. 69-77; Hancock County, Deeds and Mortgages, Book A (1794-1838), pp. 215-216, drawer 106, reel 52, GDAH. For the story of the Thomas R. Mangham family, see Chapter III.

[2] Hancock County, Deeds and Mortgages, Book A (1794-1838), pp. 215-216, drawer 106, reel 52, GDAH; *A History of Pike County, 1822-1989* (N.p.: Retired Teachers of Pike County, and "The Pike County Journal & Reporter," 1989), pp. 184, 572; Lizzie R. Mitchell, *History of Pike County Georgia, 1822-1932* (Spartanburg: The Reprint Co.,

1980), pp. 3-4, 7-8; Rubye S. Snead, ed., *Pike County, Georgia, Sesquicentennial, 1822-1972* (Zebulon: Pike County Sesquicentennial Assoc., 1972); Marriage records, Putnam County. The Lifsey Springs area is just east of Molena, Georgia, on Hwy. 109. Mail addressed to Wiley P. Mangham was in the dead letter files at Madison, GA in 1818 and 1819. Since the location and dates are consistent with the Wiley Mangham discussed here, I have tentatively identified his middle initial accordingly. See Fred R. Hartz, *Genealogical Abstracts from the Georgia Journal (Milledgeville) Newspaper, 1809-1840* (Vidalia: N.p., 1992), vol. 1, pp. 890-891; vol. 2, pp. 17, 285.

[3] Marriage records, Pike County; Iva P. Goolsby, comp., *Randolph County, Georgia* (N.p., 1976-77); Mitchell, *History of Pike County*, pp. 37, 54.

[4] Mitchell, *History of Pike County*, p. 24; CMSR Index, Indian Wars 1815-1838, series M629, reel 23, NARA; Mrs. J. E. Hays, comp., *Georgia Military Record Book, 1779-1839* (typescript), vol. 7, pp. 75, 296-298, 343; Anne Kendrick Walker, *Russell County in Retrospect: An Epic of the Far Southeast* (Richmond: Dietz Press, 1950), pp. 121-124. References to John N. Mangham's service in the Creek Wars show him as a private and first sergeant in Lynch's cavalry company, but he voted in elections held by Varner's company of Pike County volunteer militia infantry as well. His relative Arthur C. Mangham voted in the latter elections also, although other evidence indicates he served in Capt. Young Allen's company of drafted militia.

[5] Willis's wife, Temperance Mangham, died on June 13, 1835, just as the Creek troubles were beginning. See Ballard, *Solomon Mangham*, pp. 83, 285. See more on John C. Mangham and Bryant S. Mangham in Chapters IV and VII.

[6] Mitchell, *History of Pike County*, p. 8; Ballard, *Solomon Mangham*, p. 71; Chambers County, Miscellaneous Probate Records, Inventory Records (1834-1840), vol. 1, pp. 56-58, 116-119, LGM 113, reel 4, ADAH. Elizabeth may have been an orphan child of Wiley, adopted by his sister and brother-in-law James R. Gray. See Joyce Hill Gossett, *Abstracts of Pike County Will Books A and B, Part of C* (N.p.), p. 14. The author is indebted to Gerry Hill for information on Wiley's pursuits in Chambers County.

[7] Chambers County, Miscellaneous Probate Records, Inventory Records (1834-1840), vol. 1, pp. 56-58, 116-119, LGM 113, reel 4, ADAH; Chambers County, Orphans Court Records (1833-1839), vol. 1, pp. 186, 224, LGM 113, reel 7, ADAH; Pike County, Court of Ordinary, Guardians' Bonds, 1829-1955, drawer 168, reel 1, p. 70; reel 2, pp. 137-138, 280-281, 402-403, GDAH; Pike County, Court of Ordinary, Bonds and Letters of Guardianship, pp. 5-6, drawer 125, reel 60, GDAH; Talbot County, Probate Court, Annual Reports (1838), p. 26, drawer 124, reel 30, GDAH; William H. Davidson, *A Rockaway in Talbot: Travels in an Old Georgia County*, 4 vols. (West Point: Hester Printing Co., 1983-1990), vol. 4, p. 196. Seaborn Gray also purchased five slaves, Billy, Lavisa, and her three children, from Cynthia's estate. William Brown bought the last slave, a man named Oliver. Wiley's brother, John C. Mangham, bought a small lot of books at the estate sale in October 1835. The author

is indebted to Mrs. Gerry Hill for information on Robert Howe's guardianship of the Mangham orphans. Wiley A. and Emily are buried in Zebulon.

[8] State of Georgia, Military Records, Commissions 1846-1849, drawer 40, reel 14, GDAH; Commissions, 1849-1860, drawer 40, reel 15, GDAH; Mitchell, *History of Pike County*, pp. 37, 40, 50, 110, 112; Snead, ed., *Pike County, Georgia, Sesquicentennial*; Rev. R. W. Rogers, comp., *History of Pike County from 1822-1922* (Zebulon: N.p., [1922]), p. 67.

[9] Mitchell, *History of Pike County*, p. 42; Pike County, Tax Digests, 1859, drawer 148, reel 39, GDAH; 1860 Census, Slave Census, and Agricultural Schedule, Pike County.

[10] Pike County, Tax Digests, 1859; 1860 Census and Slave Census, Pike County; Ballard, *Solomon Mangham*, p. 73; Marriage records, Pike County.

[11] The first three children born to John and Rebecca each died between the ages of nine and thirteen months: Willie, a little girl, died just after her first birthday in 1852. M. Eliza and Mary Willie died in 1854 and 1855, respectively (data transcribed from gravestones in Zebulon).

[12] Letter, John N. Mangham to cousin John G. Mangham, September 18, 1864, in Willoughby Hill Mangham Letters, drawer 154, reel 27, GDAH; 1860 Census, Pike County; Ballard, *Solomon Mangham*, pp. 96-98. Birth records in the James P. Mangham family Bible (photocopied in Ballard) provide the only known reference to Nat's given name.

[13] 1860 Census, Slave Census, and Agricultural Schedule, Pike County; Ballard, *Solomon Mangham*, pp. 81-83; *The Georgia Messenger* (Macon), March 15, 1838, drawer 51, reel 72, GDAH; Pike County, 1859 Tax Digest.

[14] OR IV, pt. 1, pp. 126-127; E. B. Long, *The Civil War Day by Day: An Almanac, 1861-1865* (Garden City: Doubleday & Co., 1971), pp. 56-59.

[15] CMSRs, Charles A. Mangham, John H. Mangham, William D. Mangham, 13th Georgia; Long, *Civil War Day by Day*, p. 71; Letter, John H. Mangham to Henry C. Wayne, May 13, 1861, in State of Georgia, Adjutant General, Incoming Correspondence, series 22-1-17, box 17, GDAH. Elections for the state secession convention had seen the "immediate secession" ticket poll a 250-vote majority in Pike County (see *MDT*, January 4, 1861).

[16] Letter, John H. Mitchell, et. al., to Secretary of War Leroy P. Walker, May 20, 1861, Letters to the Confederate Secretary of War, file no. 814 –1861, NARA.

[17] CMSRs, Charles A. Mangham, John H. Mangham, William D. Mangham.

[18] OR 5, pp. 995-996.

[19] Ibid.

[20] CMSR, John H. Mangham; Letter, J. P. Garner, November 30, 1861, cited in *Confederate Reminiscences and Letters*, vol. 1 (Atlanta: Georgia Division, UDC, 1995), pp. 138-139. Garner was in a different company, but knew many of the Confederate Guards. Referring to John by his militia rank, he noted that "Col. Mangham" was one of at least five men of that company home sick at the time of writing. Only one of

them was expected back soon. An examination of Pike County records reveals that John was conducting business as County Ordinary from December 1861 until early April 1862. See Pike County, Court of Ordinary, Probate Records, 1829-1955, drawer 167, reel 51, GDAH.

[21] CMSR, Charles A. Mangham.

[22] OR 5, pp. 1000-1001; letter, Richard Milner to wife Sallie, December 24, 1861, in Richard W. Milner Papers, drawer 171, reel 40, GDAH.

[23] Letter, Richard Milner to wife, undated (October or November 1861).

[24] OR 14, pp. 4-13; CMSR, John H. Mangham; G. W. Nichols, *A Soldier's Story of His Regiment (61ˢᵗ Georgia), and Incidentally of the Lawton-Gordon-Evans Brigade, Army Northern Virginia* (Jesup: c. 1898), p. 14.

[25] CMSR, John H. Mangham.

[26] Confederate Pension Records, Pike County, R. J. Mangham, drawer 275, reel 59, GDAH.

[27] William C. Oates, *The War Between the Union and the Confederacy and its Lost Opportunities* (1905; reprint, Dayton: Morningside, 1985), p. 285; Letter, Raymond L. Mangham to author, November 14, 1995. Ray is Bob Mangham's grandson. His Uncle Harvey Mangham, Bob's son, told him that Bob accompanied an older brother back to the army. Harvey said Bob was refused enlistment due to his clubfoot, so he took care of horses for Stonewall Jackson until he was sent back to Georgia.

[28] Nichols, *Soldier's Story*, pp. 36-37; Stewart Sifakis, *Compendium of the Confederate Armies: South Carolina and Georgia* (New York: Facts on File, 1995), pp. 210-211. For first-person accounts of the regiment's peregrinations in northern Virginia, see letters dated June 16 and June 22, 1862 in Kenneth C. Collier, *The 13ᵗʰ Georgia Regiment: A Regimental History of the 13ᵗʰ Georgia Infantry Regiment, a Part of the Lawton-Gordon-Evans Brigade* (N.p.: Author, 1997).

[29] OR 11, pt. 2, pp. 599-600, 974; Nichols, *Soldier's Story*, pp. 41-44; Stephen W. Sears, *To the Gates of Richmond: The Peninsula Campaign* (New York: Ticknor & Fields, 1992), pp. 238-239, 249; Lillian Henderson, comp., *Roster of the Confederate Soldiers of Georgia 1861-1865* (N.p.: State of Georgia, 1959-64), vol. 2, pp. 247-257. Confederate and Union casualties in less than nine hours of combat at Gaines's Mill totaled 15,223 men of the 96,100 committed to action. The Henderson rosters were compiled primarily from surviving muster rolls and pension records, and serve as an invaluable source of information. They are not definitive, however, as missing (or flawed) source documents made it impossible to reconstruct casualty records comprehensively. In short, casualties were usually *higher* than indicated in Henderson. For a participant's description of the charge of Lawton's Brigade at Gaines's Mill and Malvern Hill, see letter dated August 8, 1862 in Collier, *13ᵗʰ Georgia Regiment*.

[30] Sears, *Gates of Richmond*, pp. 249-250; OR 11, pt. 2, pp. 597-598.

[31] OR 11, pt. 2, pp. 597-598, 600-601.

[32] Sears, *Gates of Richmond*, pp. 337-338, 343, 349.

[33] OR 12, pt. 2, pp. 642-648, 703-717, 811-813; John J. Hennessy, *Return to Bull Run: The Campaign and Battle of Second Manassas* (New York: Simon & Schuster, 1993), pp. 72, 84, 131-134, 261, 283-285; *MDT*, September 16, 1862. See also Collier, *13ᵗʰ Georgia Regiment*.

[34] Many of the men who fell out of Lee's columns were truly sick, and the corn and green apples which comprised much of the army's rations in Maryland did precious little to sustain those who made it that far. Others, however, purposefully "lost" their shoes to avoid having to cross into the North, as they objected to waging an "offensive" war. For an excellent discussion of the problem, see Stephen W. Sears, *Landscape Turned Red: The Battle of Antietam* (New Haven: Ticknor & Fields, 1983), pp. 70-71, 175-76; John Michael Priest, *Antietam: The Soldiers' Battle* (New York: Oxford Univ. Press, 1989), pp. 2, 4-5.

[35] Priest, *Antietam*, pp. 1-2, 38-50; OR 19, pt. 1, pp. 975-976; Sears, *Landscape*, pp. 186-190, 193-194.

[36] Ibid.; Major William Gilham, *Manual of Instruction for the Volunteers and Militia of the United States* (Philadelphia: Charles Desilver, 1861; reprint, n.d.), pp. 32-33.

[37] Cited in Sears, *Landscape*, p. 193.

[38] Ibid., pp. 188-194; Priest, *Antietam*, pp. 44-50.

[39] Priest, *Antietam*, pp. 49-55; Sears, *Landscape*, pp. 194-201.

[40] OR 19, pt. 1, pp. 975-976; Priest, *Antietam*, pp. 343, 318-331; Sears, *Landscape*, pp. 294-296; William F. Fox, *Regimental Losses in the American Civil War, 1861-1865* (Albany: Brandow Printing, 1898; reprint, Dayton: Morningside, 1985), p. 565. See also a regimental casualty list transcribed from a contemporary Savannah newspaper, in *Savannah Newspaper Digest*, January 1 to December 31, 1862, drawer 293, reel 35, pp. 66-67, GDAH. Minor variations exist between all of these sources.

[41] Letter, Richard Milner to wife, September 27, 1862. It is unclear whether Milner simply miscounted the casualty totals, or whether the illegibly faint sentences that followed may have contained further explanation. The regimental casualty report submitted for newspaper publication listed the company's casualties by name, reflecting seven killed, 22 wounded (one mortally) and two missing. The Henderson rosters, by contrast, record nine killed and 14 wounded, and show that one of the missing was in fact killed in action. The Henderson rosters are invaluable for researchers, but their necessary reliance on surviving official records makes them only as good as those (very incomplete) records. See *Savannah Newspaper Digest*, pp. 66-67; Henderson, *Georgia Rosters*, vol. 2, p. 254.

[42] CMSR, William D. Mangham.

[43] CMSR, Charles A. Mangham. Nat's name does not appear in the transcribed newspaper casualty report, but an 1898 Pike County Veterans' Roster Committee produced an annotated roster stating that Nat was wounded at Sharpsburg. Since the committee consisted of two former officers and a sergeant of the Confederate Guards, and its work was approved by the County Ordinary (a former sergeant of the company),

and three of these four men were themselves wounded at Sharpsburg, I consider their information reliable. See Pike County, Court of Ordinary, Roster of Confederate Guards, December 5, 1898, pp. 1-6, drawer 168, reel 8, GDAH. Also, Mrs. Louise Carson (a granddaughter of Nat's) provided me a letter from his daughter-in-law Mrs. Roy Mangham, who stated that he was wounded during the war (letter, Mrs. Roy Mangham to Ellen Mangham, Beckville, Texas, July 24, year not stated). Regarding his later capture by Federal troops, the documents in his CMSR simply indicate that he was exchanged with a group of Confederates "captured at Warrenton since Oct. 1st, '62."

[44] CMSR, John H. Mangham.

[45] OR 21, pt. 1, pp. 664-665, 670; CMSR, William D. Mangham. Lawton's Georgia Brigade delivered a spectacular counterattack that saved the victory at Fredericksburg, but the 13th Georgia never received the order to advance. George F. Cooper, the brigade surgeon, described the 13th as the brigade's largest and best regiment in his account of the battle (see *MDT*, May 4, 1863).

[46] Ernest B. Furgurson, *Chancellorsville 1863: The Souls of the Brave* (New York: Vintage Books, 1993), pp. 99, 102, 289-290, 297-298; Nichols, *Soldier's Story*, pp. 80-86. The 13th Georgia lost three killed and 27 wounded in the battle they knew as Second Fredericksburg (see OR 25, pt. 1, p. 808).

[47] Furgurson, *Chancellorsville*, pp. 345-346; Leila S. LaGrone, *This Very Unreasonable War: A History of Panola County During the Civil War* (Carthage: N.p., 1972). The latter book contains a roster of Confederate veterans who lived in Panola County, Texas, where Nat lived after the war. The roster was compiled from data provided by veterans' descendants, and Nat's entry states that he "fought in the 'Battle of Gettysburg."

[48] Nichols, *Soldier's Story*, pp. 115-116; OR 27, pt. 2, pp. 491-492. For an itinerary of Gordon's Brigade during its two weeks in Pennsylvania, see Wilbur S. Nye, *Here Come the Rebels!* (Baton Rouge: LSU Press, 1965; reprint, Dayton: Morningside, 1988), pp. 266-297.

[49] Nichols, *Soldier's Story*, pp. 116-118; OR 27, pt. 2, pp. 341, 474-475, 492-493. For calculations estimating the regiment's strength, see John W. Busey and David G. Martin, *Regimental Strengths at Gettysburg* (Baltimore: Gateway Press, 1982), p. 128; David G. Martin, *Gettysburg July 1* (Conshohocken: Combined Books, 1995), p. 306.

[50] Nichols, *Soldier's Story*, pp. 117, 120-125; OR 27, pt. 2, p. 493; Henderson, *Georgia Rosters*, vol. 2, pp. 247-257; Pike County, Roster of Confederate Guards.

[51] Nichols, *Soldier's Story*, pp. 130-131, 137-138; Long, *Civil War Day by Day*, pp. 438-441; Henderson, *Georgia Rosters*, vol. 2, p. 257.

[52] CMSR, John H. Mangham. In many cases, soldiers holding humbler stations in life secured discharges based on the needs of their home communities. In the commodity-starved Confederacy, it was not uncommon for the local citizenry to petition for the release of skilled tradesmen from the army, since their low density in Southern society combined with the sweeping conscription laws to deprive

communities of life's necessities. John N. Mangham, in his capacity as Deputy Clerk of the Pike County Superior Court, forwarded such a petition in November 1863 on behalf of Pvt. Thomas M. Carter of the 32nd Georgia, requesting his discharge or detail to make shoes in his home community. The locals signing the petition included Winfred Mangham (mother of Will and Nat), Rebecca (wife of John H. Mangham), Susan (widow of Wiley J. Mangham), Jane A. T. Chapman (eldest sister of Will and Nat), and Martha Hagan (Will's future wife). See letter from John N. Mangham, November 20, 1863, in Letters to the Confederate Secretary of War, file no. 943-C-1863, NARA.

[53] CMSR, Charles A. Mangham; Ballard, *Solomon Mangham*, p. 94.

[54] CMSR, Charles A. Mangham; Henderson, *Georgia Rosters*, vol. 2, pp. 257-258; Pike County, Roster of Confederate Guards. For analyses of the spectacular performance of Gordon's Brigade at the Wilderness and Spotsylvania, see Gordon C. Rhea, *The Battle of the Wilderness, May 5-6, 1864* (Baton Rouge: LSU Press, 1994), and William D. Matter, *If It Takes All Summer: The Battle of Spotsylvania* (Chapel Hill: UNC Press, 1988). For Early's Valley Campaign and the Cedar Creek disaster of October 1864, see Benjamin F. Cooling, *Jubal Early's Raid on Washington, 1864* (Baltimore: Nautical & Aviation Publishing Co. of America, 1989), and Thomas A. Lewis, *The Guns of Cedar Creek* (New York: Harper & Row, 1988; reprint, Dell Publishing Co., 1991). For anecdotal information on these engagements, see Nichols, *Soldier's Story*.

[55] J. Tracy Power, *Lee's Miserables: Life in the Army of Northern Virginia from the Wilderness to Appomattox* (Chapel Hill: UNC Press, 1998), pp. 212-213, 226; transcript of medical evaluation provided by Mrs. Louise Carson, Nat's granddaughter, from original document in her possession; CMSR, Charles A. Mangham.

[56] CMSR, William D. Mangham; *A History of Pike County, 1822-1989*, p. 526.

[57] Adjutant General's Letter Book, number 22, February 2, 1864-April 4, 1864, typescript, comp. Mrs. J. E. Hays, 1942, p. 336, GDAH; 22nd Senatorial District, Pike County, Enrollment of Present Militia Company, District No. 581, drawer 245, reel 8, GDAH; *MDT*, January 5, February 13, 1864; Letter, John N. Mangham, November 28, 1863, in Letters to the Confederate Secretary of War, file no. 943-C-1863, NARA; Allen D. Candler, comp., *The Confederate Records of the State of Georgia* (Atlanta: Charles P. Byrd, State Printer, 1909), vol. 2, pp. 703-704, 800. Although the Pike County militia companies were called into service to help defend Atlanta in the summer of 1864, no existing records identify the individuals who actually reported for duty. Unless James was unfit for service, he probably spent months in the trenches during the siege, as well as several more months in service as Sherman marched on Savannah.

[58] CMSR, William D. Mangham, 13th Georgia and 1st (Fannin's) Georgia Reserves; Pike County, Court of Ordinary, Roster of Company G, 1st Georgia Reserves, December 5, 1898, pp. 31-33, drawer 168, reel 8, GDAH.

[59] CMSR, William D. Mangham; William Marvel, *Andersonville: The Last Depot* (Chapel Hill: UNC Press, 1994), pp. 14, 62-65.

[60] OR II, vol. 7, pp. 392-393, 410-411, 548-549, 993; vol. 8, pp. 606-625. Of course, the primary tragedy at Andersonville was the horrendous plight of the Federal prisoners, and the Confederate health and inspection reports cited here emphasized this fact. The garrison of Georgia Reserves nonetheless suffered terribly, too. A horrified inspector noted that 66.4 percent of the garrison had been on the sick lists for July and August alone, with a mortality of 2.3 percent. He concluded, "If the same mortality continued throughout the entire year the command would lose by death alone 13.2 percent of the mean strength. Such mortality would ensure the complete obliteration of a command by disease alone in the short period of about seven years and seven months" (vol. 8, p. 616).

[61] Letter, John N. Mangham to cousin John G. Mangham, September 18, 1864, in Willoughby Hill Mangham Letters, GDAH; Marvel, *Andersonville*, pp. 198, 211-220. For more about John G. Mangham, see Chapter VI and Appendix, reference # 78.

[62] Marvel, *Andersonville*, pp. 222, 226-228, 236-239; Pike County, Roster of Co. G, 1st Georgia Reserves; Confederate Pension Records, Pike County, Mrs. M. J. Mangham, drawer 277, reel 11, GDAH.

[63] Pension Records, Pike County, Mrs. M. J. Mangham.

[64] Major William S. Dunlop, *Lee's Sharpshooters; or, the Forefront of Battle* (Little Rock: Tunnan & Pittard, 1899), pp. 480-482.

[65] R. A. Brock, ed., "Paroles of the Army of Northern Virginia," SHSP 15 (1887; reprint, New York: Kraus Reprint Co., 1977), pp. 213-216.

[66] Records of Admission to State Asylum at Milledgeville, Capt. Jno. H. Mangham, April 11, 1865, volume 3, p. 127, RG 26-12-29, GDAH. The current author has found one other reference to insanity in the Mangham family of that era, although one presumes that elderly William Mangham of Russell County, Alabama, actually suffered from what we now know as Alzheimer's disease (see Chapter VII and Appendix, reference # 38).

[67] Pike County, Roster of Confederate Guards; Mitchell, *History of Pike County*, p. 110; 1900 Census, Calhoun County.

[68] Pike County, Record of Wills, John N. Mangham, drawer 167, reel 45, pp. 411, 413, GDAH.

[69] Pension Records, Pike County, Mrs. M. J. Mangham; 1870 Census and Agricultural Schedule, Pike County; Pike County, Probate Records, Record of Wills, Book B (1844-1898), p. 385, drawer 168, reel 1, GDAH.

[70] Pension Records, Pike County, Mrs. M. J. Mangham; Ballard, *Solomon Mangham*, pp. 83, 95. The family cemetery is located about a mile north of Beulah Baptist Church, which stands several miles east of Molena on State Highway 109. James P. Mangham donated the land for this church, and his old home place still stands several hundred yards east of it on the south side of the highway. (See photo on page 30.)

[71] Ballard, *Solomon Mangham*, pp. 95-111; Grady McWhiney, Warner O. Moore, Jr., and Robert F. Pace, eds., *"Fear God and Walk Humbly": The Agricultural Journal of James*

Mallory, 1843-1877 (Tuscaloosa: Univ. of Alabama Press, 1997), p. 437; letter, Joseph W. Reichert to author, July 19, 1996.

[72] Ballard, *Solomon Mangham*, pp. 95-111; letter, Joseph W. Reichert to author, July 19, 1996; letter, Mrs. Roy Mangham to Ellen Mangham, Beckville, Texas, July 24 (year not stated). After the war, Stonewall Jackson's dying words, "Let us cross over the river and rest under the shade of the trees," became a favorite formulation to announce the passing of elderly Confederate veterans.

[73] Letter, Mrs. Roy Mangham to Ellen Mangham; 1870 Agricultural Schedule, Pike County; Ballard, *Solomon Mangham*, pp. 112-120; *A History of Pike County, 1822-1989*, pp. 573-574.

[74] James P. Mangham family bible records (photocopied in Ballard, *Solomon Mangham*), pp. 81, 121; 1850 Census, Pike County.

[75] Ballard, *Solomon Mangham*, pp. 121, 129; 1860 Agricultural Schedule, Pike County.

[76] CMSR, Wiley J. Mangham, 27th Georgia; Pike County, Court of Ordinary, Roster of Alexander Rifles, December 5, 1898, pp. 14-18, drawer 168, reel 8, GDAH; Ballard, *Solomon Mangham*, pp. 65-66.

[77] James M. Folsom, *Heroes and Martyrs of Georgia: Georgia's Record in the Revolution of 1861* (Macon: Burke, Boykin & Co., 1864), pp. 62-63; Henderson, *Georgia Rosters*, vol. 3, p. 330; W. J. Tancig, comp., *Confederate Military Land Units, 1861-1865* (Cranbury: Thomas Yoseloff, 1967), p. 33; CMSR, Wiley J. Mangham; Pike County, Roster of Alexander Rifles.

[78] Folsom, *Heroes and Martyrs of Georgia*, p. 63; Scott Morris, Jr., *John Thomas Pound, Confederate Soldier* (Macon: Southern Press, 1964), pp. 19, 26; Regimental Reports of Sick and Wounded, November 1861-January 1862, in 27th Georgia Muster Rolls, NARA. John T. Pound died of fever in the summer of 1862. See William W. Mangham's story in Chapter I (reference # 49).

[79] CMSR, Wiley J. Mangham; letter, William H. Means, February 5, 1862, cited in *Confederate Reminiscences and Letters*, vol. 2, (Atlanta: Georgia Division, UDC, 1996), pp. 147-148; Regimental Reports of Sick and Wounded, January-February 1862, in 27th Georgia Muster Rolls, NARA; Letter, David Green to sister, February 9, 1862, cited in Robert H. Jordan, *There Was a Land: A Story of Talbot County, Georgia and Its People* (Columbus: Columbus Office Supply Co., 1971), p. 235. H. Y. Lifsey survived his bout with pneumonia and was promoted to lieutenant later in 1862. A scion of the family for whom Pike County's Springs District was renamed Lifsey Springs in the postwar era, Lifsey was killed at Cold Harbor in 1864 (see Pike County, Roster of Alexander Rifles).

[80] Letter, William H. Means, February 19, 1862, cited in *Confederate Reminiscences and Letters*, vol. 2, pp. 148-149; 1860 Census, Pike County. David R. Steger was 29 in 1860; Lula B. was listed as "Lucy B." in the household of 37-year-old James C. Steger, who was probably David's brother. Private Steger fell victim to smallpox later in 1862.

William H. Means, the author of these letters, was killed at Sharpsburg in September of the same year (see Pike County, Roster of Alexander Rifles).

[81] Regimental Report of Sick and Wounded, February 1862, in 27th Georgia Muster Rolls, NARA; CMSR, Wiley J. Mangham; 1860 Census, Pike County; Folsom, *Heroes and Martyrs of Georgia*, p. 63; Ballard, *Solomon Mangham*, p. 129, 153. Military and pension records list Wiley's cause of death variously as typhoid pneumonia or yellow jaundice, just as they refer to him either as Wiley James or James Wiley Mangham. Indeed, even his gravestone reads "James Wiley Mangham," although family Bible records (supported by Susan's memory) confirm that his given name was in fact Wiley James. His gravestone also indicates that he died on February 14, *1861*, which is patently incorrect.

[82] Ballard, *Solomon Mangham*, pp. 225-226; Letter, William H. Means, February 21, 1862, cited in *Confederate Reminiscences and Letters*, vol. 2, p. 149.

[83] Ibid., p. 257; CMSR, Wiley J. Mangham; letter, Craig S. Mangham to author, December 9, 1995.

[84] Ballard, *Solomon Mangham*, pp. 126-127, 256-257; Confederate Pension Records, Pike and Spalding Counties, Mrs. Susan G. Mangham, drawer 276, reel 13, GDAH; Confederate Pension records, file no. 41466, TSA.

[85] The identity of John's first wife is not documented in any primary source. The information here comes from handwritten notes found by the present author and his aunt, Lora Mangham Brantley, in papers left by her sister Linda Mangham Johnston. Marriage records in the James P. Mangham family Bible show that John N. W. Mangham married Amanda on October 19, 1852; her maiden name is not given, but the date and year cited differ from his later marriage to Amanda Zorn. (See also Ballard, *Solomon Mangham*, p. 82.) Since John dropped off the Pike County tax rolls in 1855, he presumably moved to nearby Upson County about 1856. See Pike County, Tax Digests, drawer 148, reel 39, GDAH.

[86] OR IV, vol. 1, pp. 1081, 1095-1100; vol. 2, pp. 160-168.

[87] CMSR, John W. Mangham, 5th Georgia and 2nd Georgia Battalion Sharpshooters. For more about Col. Sam Mangham, see Chapter IV and reference # 100.

[88] Order Book of Brigadier John K. Jackson's Brigade (hereinafter Jackson's Order Book), Withers's Division, March 13, 1862-January 10, 1863, Special Order (S. O.) 49, May 15, 1862, and S. O. 98, July 17, 1862, Jackson-McKinne Papers, 1817-1871, UNC. For a history of the Sharpshooters, see Dana M. Mangham, "The 2nd Georgia Battalion Sharpshooters," *CWR* 7, no. 1 (2000). This article is edited for use here by permission of *CWR*. See also Dana M. Mangham, "Roster of the 2nd Georgia Battalion Sharpshooters, C. S. A.," *Georgia Genealogical Magazine* 35, no. 1-2 (Winter/Spring 1995): 65-82; Henderson, *Georgia Rosters*, vol. 1, pp. 704-749.

[89] OR IV, vol. 1, pp. 1110-1111.

[90] Jackson's Order Book, S. O. 98, July 17, 1862; CMSR, Confederate General and Staff Officers and Non-Regimental Enlisted Men, M331, reel 139, NARA; Henderson,

Georgia Rosters, vol. 1, pp. 704-749; *Middle Georgia Times,* August 28, 1886; Walter A. Clark, *Under the Stars and Bars or, Memories of Four Years Service with the Oglethorpes, of Augusta, Georgia* (Augusta: Chronicle Printing Co., 1900), pp. 214-216, 219-224.

[91] Letter, Charles H. George to sister Mary, July 17, 1862, from Camp Gadsen, Tennessee, in Charles H. George Confederate Letters, 1859-1866 (typescript), Auburn University Archives. (In order to preserve the flavor of these letters, the original grammar and spelling is rendered without correction or use of [sic], except as needed for clarity.) See also Inspection Report, Reserve Division, Army of the Mississippi, August 28, 1862, M935, reel 18, NARA.

[92] *Major Joseph B. Cumming War Recollections, 1861-1865,* in Southern Historical Collection, UNC, p. 19.

[93] Ibid., pp. 19-20. Cumming overstated the bag of prisoners significantly, as the actual number was slightly more than four thousand (OR 16, pt. 1, pp. 967-968).

[94] W. C. Hay, *Reminiscences of the War, In Letters to the Children of Cuthbert, Ga.* (N.p.: Confederate Soldiers' Home of Georgia, 1920), pp. 20-21; Cumming, *Recollections,* p. 22.

[95] Hay, *Reminiscences,* pp. 20-21; Muster Rolls, 2nd Georgia Battalion Sharpshooters, Special Report, November 18, 1862, NARA; CMSR, 2nd Georgia Sharpshooters.

[96] C. H. George Letters, December 13, 1862; Letter from Maj. Jesse J. Cox to Attorney General Watts, January 29, 1863, in Letters to the Confederate Secretary of War, file no. M122-1863, NARA; Departmental Records, Army and Department of Tennessee, Chapter II, vol. 245, Morning Reports of Brigadier General John K. Jackson's Brigade, 1862-1864, December 12, 1862, NARA (hereinafter cited as Morning Reports, Jackson's Brigade).

[97] Charles H. George to sister Mary, December 13, 1862; Jackson's Order Book, S. O. 56, December 11, 1862; S. O. 58, December 15, 1862; Departmental Records, Department and Army of Tennessee (Bragg-Hardee), November 1862-December 1863, General Order (G. O.) 112, May 20, 1863, NARA.

[98] Cumming, *Recollections,* pp. 24-25; Jackson's Order Book, Brigade Circular, December 27, 1862.

[99] Cumming, *Recollections,* pp. 24-25, 27; Jackson' s Order Book, S. O. 56, December 11, 1862, and Brigade Circular dated December 27, 1862; OR 20, pt. 1, pp. 838-841; Thomas Lawrence Connelly, *Autumn of Glory: The Army of Tennessee, 1862-1865* (Baton Rouge: LSU Press, 1971), pp. 56-61. Stormont's account quoted in Peter Cozzens, *No Better Place to Die: The Battle of Stones River* (Urbana: Univ. of Illinois Press, 1990), p. 164.

[100] OR 20, pt. 1, pp. 838-839; Hay, *Reminiscences,* p. 7; Cumming, *Recollections,* p. 27.

[101] Frank S. Roberts, "C. P. Roberts, Adjutant Second Georgia Battalion," CV 22: 112.

[102] OR 20, pt. 1, pp. 838-841; Battalion Report dated January 10, 1863, and Brigade Report dated January 12, 1863, in Confederate States Army Casualties: Lists and

Narrative Reports, 1861-1865, M836, reel 4, NARA; Captain John A. Fulton, "The Roll of Honor," filed under Pvt. Thomas J. Brantley, Civil War Miscellany, Personal Papers, drawer 283, reel 18, GDAH. A newspaper account of the 5th Georgia's action asserted that only 117 men went into action, rather than the 173 officially reported (see *MDT*, January 13, 1863).

[103] C. H. George Letters, January 24, 1863.

[104] Morning Reports, January-July 1863; Roberts, "C. P. Roberts, Adjutant Second Georgia Battalion," CV 22: 112; C. L. Peacock, "Conscription in the Mountains," CV 23: 171; Charles H. George to sister Mary, January 24, 1863, from Camp Ansley, Chattanooga; Charles H. George to sister Mary, March 6, 1863, from Chattanooga.

[105] Peacock, "Conscription in the Mountains," CV 23: 171.

[106] Ibid. For a fuller discussion of the fight against Unionists in East Tennessee, see Noel G. Fisher's chapter in Daniel E. Sutherland, ed., *Guerrillas, Unionists, and Violence on the Confederate Home Front* (Fayetteville: Univ. of Arkansas Press, 1999).

[107] CMSR, Jesse J. Cox; CMSR, 2nd Georgia Sharpshooters; CMSR, 58th Alabama; *Who Was Who in America: Historical Volume 1607-1896* (Chicago: Marquis Who's Who, 1963), p. 576; Frank S. Jones, *History of Decatur County Georgia* (N.p., c. 1971), p. 190; CMSR, John W. Mangham. For an analysis of Bragg's difficulties on the Duck River line, see Connelly, *Autumn of Glory*, pp. 112-134.

[108] OR 30, pt. 2, pp. 89-91; Morning Reports, September 15, 1863.

[109] OR 30, pt. 2, pp. 77-80, 83-85, 89-91; Fox, *Regimental Losses*, p. 556; *MDT*, October 7, 1863.

[110] OR 30, pt. 2, pp. 77-80, 83-85, 89-91; *Atlanta Daily Intelligencer*, October 24, 1863; Peter Cozzens, *This Terrible Sound: The Battle of Chickamauga* (Urbana: Univ. of Illinois Press, 1992), pp. 157, 171.

[111] OR 30, pt. 2, pp. 77-80, 83-85, 89-91; *Atlanta Daily Intelligencer*, October 24, 1863; Cozzens, *Terrible Sound*, pp. 157, 171; CMSR, James Ogletree.

[112] OR 30, pt. 2, pp. 77-80, 83-85, 89-91; Martin V. Calvin, "The Bloody Angle, Thrilling Events of the Twelfth of May, 1864," CV 32: 460.

[113] OR 30, pt. 2, pp. 77-80, 83-85, 89-91; *Atlanta Daily Intelligencer*, October 24, 1863.

[114] *Atlanta Daily Intelligencer*, November 22, 1863. See also Cozzens, *Terrible Sound*, p. 501.

[115] *MDT*, October 7, 1863; OR 30, pt. 2, pp. 89-91; CMSR. Minor inconsistencies exist in these casualty returns. I have relied primarily on Adjutant Charlie Roberts's report published in the *MDT*, but I have added three wounded men based on the CMSR.

[116] Glenn Tucker, *Chickamauga: Bloody Battle in the West* (Bobbs-Merrill, 1961; reprint, Dayton: Morningside, 1992), pp. 376-382; Peter Cozzens, *The Shipwreck of Their Hopes: The Battles for Chattanooga* (Urbana: Univ. of Illinois Press, 1994), pp. 23-28;

Wiley Sword, *Mountains Touched with Fire: Chattanooga Besieged, 1863* (New York: St. Martin's Press, 1995), pp. 27-35.

[117] *OR* 31, pt. 3, p. 822; Cozzens, *Shipwreck of Their Hopes*, pp. 29-31; Sword, *Mountains*, pp. 107-111; Sam Watkins, *"Co. Aytch": A Side Show of the Big Show* (reprint, New York: Collier Books, 1962), p. 113.

[118] Tallies of Votes Cast in State and Regimental Elections, 1862-1864, drawer 283, reel 60, GDAH.

[119] *OR* 31, pt. 2, pp. 684-691, 704-706, 733-738; pt. 3, p. 822; Sword, *Mountains*, pp. 313-314.

[120] Muster Rolls, 2nd Ga. Bn. S.S., NARA; Morning Reports, Jackson's Brigade; CMSR; *OR* 31, pt. 3, p. 822. The 5th Georgia reported 21 killed and wounded, and another 42 missing in action. The wounded included Colonel Daniel and Maj. D. H. Ansley (see *MDT*, December 4, 1863).

[121] Morning Reports, Jackson's Brigade; Tallies of Votes Cast in State and Regimental Elections, 1862-1864, GDAH.

[122] C. H. George Letters, March 13, 1864; Frank S. Roberts, "In Winter Quarters at Dalton, Ga., 1863-64," *CV* 26: 274-275.

[123] Departmental Records, Army of Tennessee (Hardee's Corps), Orders and Circulars, February 1863-March 1865, Chapter II, vol. 272, G. O. 9, January 18, 1864, NARA; Army of Tennessee (Johnston's Headquarters), General Orders and Circulars, December 1863-January 1865, Chapter II, vol. 350, G. O. 5, January 8, 1864, NARA.

[124] Roberts, "In Winter Quarters at Dalton," *CV* 26: 274-275; Hay, *Reminiscences*, p. 9.

[125] C. H. George Letters, March 27, 1864.

[126] C. H. George Letters, March 13, March 27, and May 7, 1864; Frank S. Roberts, "Review of the Army of Tennessee at Dalton, Ga.," *CV* 26: 150.

[127] *Augusta Constitutionalist*, June 24, 1864; *Daily Constitutionalist*, May 26 and June 19, 1864; Russell K. Brown, *To the Manner Born: The Life of General William H. T. Walker* (Athens: UGA Press, 1994), pp. 225-235.

[128] *Daily Constitutionalist*, May 26, 1864; Muster Rolls, Company D, June 1864; Richard M. McMurry, "Cassville," *CWTI* 10, no. 8 (1971), pp. 8-9; Albert Castel, *Decision in the West: The Atlanta Campaign of 1864* (Lawrence: Univ. Press of Kansas, 1992), pp. 199-202. For a discussion of Confederate prisoners who enlisted for frontier service in the U. S. Army, see D. Alexander Brown, "Galvanized Yankees," *CWTI* 4, no. 10 (1958), pp. 12-21.

[129] CMSR, John W. Mangham; Departmental Records, Army of Tennessee, General Orders and Circulars, December 1863-January 1865, Chapter II, vol. 350, Circular dated March 21, 1864, NARA; *Augusta Constitutionalist*, June 24, 1864; James Cooper Nisbet, *Four Years on the Firing Line* (Chattanooga: Imperial Press, n.d.), p. 125; William A. Fletcher, *Rebel Private Front and Rear: Memoirs of a Confederate Soldier* (Beaumont: Press of the Greer Print, 1908; reprint, New York: Meridian, 1995), p. 57.

[130] Richard M. McMurry, "'The Hell Hole': New Hope Church," CWTI 11, no. 10 (1973), pp. 38-39; Castel, Decision, pp. 220-231; Brown, To the Manner Born, pp. 238-240; Hay, Reminiscences, p. 37.

[131] Hay, Reminiscences, pp. 5-6, 36-38.

[132] Ibid.

[133] Ibid.; Daily Constitutionalist, June 19, 1864.

[134] Charles H. George to sister Mary, June 9, 1864, from camp near Marietta.

[135] Hay, Reminiscences, pp. 5-6, 36-38; Frank Roberts to editor, Thomaston Times, April 26, 1912; CMSR.

[136] Hay, Reminiscences, pp. 5-6, 36-38.

[137] Ibid.; CMSRs, James O. and Pleasant E. Cauthren. Hospital records and muster rolls indicate that James died on May 31 or June 3, 1864, and Pleasant died on May 1 or 7 of that year.

[138] Hay, Reminiscences, pp. 5-6, 38; Richard M. McMurry, "Kennesaw Mountain," CWTI vol. 8, no. 9 (1970), pp. 8-9; Departmental Records, Army of Tennessee (Johnston's Headquarters), General Orders and Circulars, December 1863-January 1865, Chapter II, vol. 350, Confidential Circular dated June 1, 1864, NARA.

[139] Charles H. George to sister Mary, June 9, 1864, from camp near Marietta.

[140] McMurry, "Kennesaw Mountain," pp. 22-23; CMSR; Flora George to sister-in-law Mary George, June 22, 1864, Griffin, and undated transcribed newspaper obituary, C. H. George Letters.

[141] Castel, Decision, pp. 285-287; McMurry, "Kennesaw Mountain," p. 23; Brown, To the Manner Born, pp. 242-244; CMSR; Roberts, "In Winter Quarters at Dalton," CV 26: 274; Augusta Constitutionalist, June 24, 1864.

[142] CMSR; Hay, Reminiscences, pp. 5-6, 36-38; Augusta Constitutionalist, June 24, 1864; Castel, Decision, pp. 280-285.

[143] Brown, To the Manner Born, pp. 268-274; Eugene W. Jones, Enlisted for the War: The Struggles of the Gallant 24th Regiment, South Carolina Volunteers, Infantry, 1861-1865 (Hightstown: Longstreet House, 1997), pp. 180-184; OR 38, pt. 3, p. 661; CMSR, 2nd Georgia Bn. S. S.; Castel, Decision, pp. 360-361, 395-397.

[144] OR 38, pt. 3, pp. 661, 701-702, 708-712; Castel, Decision, pp. 512-520.

[145] Ibid.; James A. Davison to editor, Atlanta Constitution, October 17, 1902.

[146] OR 38, pt. 3, pp. 701-702, 708-712; Castel, Decision, pp. 512-514; Davison to editor, Atlanta Constitution, October 17, 1902.

[147] Ibid.; Roberts, "C. P. Roberts, Adjutant Second Georgia Battalion," CV 22: 112; OR 38, pt. 1, pp. 566, 611; Whitelaw Reid, Ohio in the War: Her Statesmen, Generals and Soldiers, vol. 2 (Cincinnati: The Robert Clarke Co., 1895), p. 402; Frank Roberts to editor, Thomaston Times, April 26, 1912.

[148] Roberts, "C. P. Roberts, Adjutant Second Georgia Battalion," CV 22: 112; OR 38, pt. 1, pp. 566, 601, 610; pt. 3, pp. 708-712; Frank Roberts to editor, Thomaston Times, April 26, 1912. Charlie Roberts survived to share a blanket that night with

Davison, as they both fell captive during the melee at the railroad cut. The 21st Ohio, another regiment involved in the attacks against the Sharpshooters, claimed the capture of a "rebel adjutant," who was probably Lieutenant Roberts. See Davison to editor, *Atlanta Constitution*, October 17, 1902; OR 38, pt. 1, p. 614.

[149] OR 38, pt. 3, pp. 610, 701-703, 718-720; Jones, *Gallant 24th Regiment*, pp. 192-195.

[150] Muster Rolls, 2nd Georgia Bn. S. S., NARA; Inspection Reports (Cheatham's Division and Gist's Brigade), Army of Tennessee, September 23, 1864, M935, reel 6, NARA.

[151] OR 45, pt. 1, pp. 733-739; Jim Smith, unpublished reminiscences, 46th Georgia, p. 11. The author is indebted to Bobby C. Smith of Thomaston, Georgia, for providing a copy of this typescript. For a detailed travelogue of the march of Gist's Brigade, see also Jones, *Gallant 24th Regiment*, pp. 196-215.

[152] OR 45, pt. 1, pp. 733-739; Y. P. Young, "Hood's Failure at Spring Hill," CV 16:25-41; Frank S. Roberts, "Spring Hill-Franklin-Nashville, 1864," CV 27: 58; Wiley Sword, *The Confederacy's Last Hurrah: Spring Hill, Franklin, and Nashville* (Lawrence: Univ. Press of Kansas, 1992), pp. 134, 146; Jim Smith, unpublished reminiscences, p. 12; Jones, *Gallant 24th Regiment*, pp. 217-218.

[153] OR 45, pt. 1, pp. 231-232, 255-257; Roberts, "Spring Hill-Franklin-Nashville, 1864," CV 27: 58-59; Hay, *Reminiscences*, p. 8; Sword, *Confederacy's Last Hurrah*, pp. 158-159, 170-173, 178-181.

[154] Roberts, "Spring Hill-Franklin-Nashville, 1864," CV 27: 58-59; James Lee McDonough and Thomas L. Connelly, *Five Tragic Hours: The Battle of Franklin* (Knoxville: Univ. of Tennessee Press, 1983).

[155] OR 45, pt. 1, pp. 255-257, 684-686; Hay, *Reminiscences*, pp. 8, 21-22; Sword, *Confederacy's Last Hurrah*, pp. 173, 176, 269; Roberts, "Spring Hill-Franklin-Nashville, 1864," CV 27: 58-59. Schofield cited in Jones, *Gallant 24th Regiment*, p. 231.

[156] Watkins, *"Co. Aytch"*, p. 233.

[157] H. K. Nelson, "Tennessee, A Grave or a Free Home," CV 15: 508-509.

[158] Roberts, "Spring Hill-Franklin-Nashville, 1864," CV 27: 59-60; Hay, *Reminiscences*, p. 22.

[159] Roberts, "Spring Hill-Franklin-Nashville, 1864," CV 27: 59-60; Sword, *Confederacy's Last Hurrah*, pp. 370-374.

[160] Roberts, "Spring Hill-Franklin-Nashville, 1864," CV 27: 59-60; Hay, *Reminiscences*, pp. 6-7, 23; Sword, *Confederacy's Last Hurrah*, pp. 370-378; Cumming, *Recollections*, p. 76.

[161] Roberts, "Spring Hill-Franklin-Nashville, 1864," CV 27: 59-60; Sword, *Confederacy's Last Hurrah*, pp. 375-378; CMSR, Octavus Myers; Hay, *Reminiscences*, pp. 6-7, 23. Extant hospital records additionally show that at least two Sharpshooters were treated for gunshot wounds in January 1865. Although it is likely that these were combat casualties from the Tennessee campaign, it is not verifiable.

[162] "Frank Stovall Roberts," CV 32:25. Cheatham cited in Jones, *Gallant 24*[th] *Regiment*, p. 240. For Thomas H. Mangham's story, see Chapter IX.

[163] Ibid.; Sword, *Confederacy's Last Hurrah*, pp. 425-430; CMSR; Mark L. Bradley, *Last Stand in the Carolinas: The Battle of Bentonville* (Campbell: Savas Woodbury Publishers, 1996), pp. 29-30, 386; Jones, *Gallant 24*[th] *Regiment*, pp. 240, 244.

[164] Bradley, *Last Stand*, pp. 386-390.

[165] CMSR. The figures given are the best approximations possible, based on painstaking examination of the CMSR, unit muster rolls, and casualty reports from a variety of sources. Given the incomplete nature of the sources, definitive statistics remain elusive. It is certain that casualty figures were, in actuality, significantly higher than those given here.

[166] CMSR, Andrew J. Boland; "Relic of Red Battle May Soon be Sent to Georgia," *Atlanta Constitution*, August 6, 1902.

[167] James Pickett Jones, *Yankee Blitzkrieg: Wilson's Raid Through Alabama and Georgia* (Athens: UGA Press, 1976), pp. 160-163; 1870 Census and Agricultural Schedule, Upson County.

[168] Gravestones, Mangham Family Cemetery, Pike County; J. P. Mangham Bible records, photocopied in Ballard, *Solomon Mangham*, pp. 83, 304; personal papers of J. Roger Mangham, Linda Mangham Johnston, and Lora Mangham Brantley; *Atlanta Journal-Constitution*, February 24, 1985.

[169] *Thomaston Times*, August 13, 1887, September 12, 1889, December 26, 1890, January 9, 1891, October 7, 1896; Carolyn Walker Nottingham and Evelyn Hannah, *History of Upson County, Georgia* (1930; reprinted Vidalia: Georgia Genealogical Reprints, 1969), p. 56.

[170] *Thomaston Times*, August 13, 1887, October 4, 1889; letter, Mrs. Grady Fowler to author, August 11, 1996; Nottingham, *Upson County*, pp. 345-346, 366-367; Upson County, Deed Book W, pp. 278-279 (provided by Mrs. Bobbie McCrary). Mrs. Fowler has fond memories of her first-ever automobile ride, provided by "Mr. Pony" Mangham in the early 1900s.

[171] *Thomaston Times*, October 31, 1902.

[172] Ibid., May 26, 1905.

[173] Confederate Pension Records, Pinellas County, Florida, Mrs. Sophronia V. Mangham, FSL; 1910 Censuses, Tift and Upson Counties; J. E. F. Matthews, "Address Delivered at the Unveiling of Confederate Monument, Thomaston, Georgia, May, 1908: Roster of Companies going to the War from Upson County" (Macon: J. W. Burke Co., 1908), p. 6. Upson County's 1200 soldiers outnumbered her population of male citizens in 1860. The Florida Pension Department approved Sophronia's request for pension in November 1913, allotting her a stipend of ten dollars a month.

[174] *Thomaston Times*, November 25, 1910.

CHAPTER III: "WARM SECESSIONISTS" AND COUNTRY EDITORS: THE THOMAS R. MANGHAM FAMILY

1. BLAZING THE TRAIL IN WEST GEORGIA: FROM PIKE COUNTY TO THE CHATTAHOOCHEE FRONTIER

James Pendleton Mangham's elder brother, Thomas R. Mangham, shared his talent for agricultural success, and Thomas established a record of civil and military service similar to their brothers Wiley E. and John N. Mangham.[1] Born in late 1806 or 1807, Thomas was in his mid-teens when Willis Mangham moved the family from Putnam County to the raw frontier of Pike County, Georgia. The young man thrived in this environment, and sought out new frontiers soon after marrying eighteen-year-old Matilda Dandridge Grant on March 10, 1825. When the following year saw Georgia acquire Creek Indian lands extending to the Chattahoochee River, Thomas and Matilda were among the pioneers of the new territories, along with Thomas's brother, Henry C. Mangham. Thomas cut the first road into the forests of newly minted Lee County, and it carried the name "Mangham's Trace" for many years thereafter.[2]

Regardless of written agreements, of course, the Creeks continued to roam the woodlands, and Federal records are full of affidavits filed by aggrieved settlers claiming compensation for Indian depredations. Thomas was among the claimants in July 1828, after he and Michael Hinch found one of his heifers and several other cows dead, with a large number of Creeks camped nearby. Government agent Mansfield Torrance noted that Thomas told him that the "Indians were all in the woods around where he lived and were killing cattle quite often." Thomas's uncle, Valentine Brewer, was living with the Manghams at the time and testified to the accuracy of the claim.[3]

When Randolph County was created from the western part of Lee County on December 20, 1828, Thomas and Matilda were among those residing in the lands allotted to the new county, along with their newborn son, *Henry Grant Mangham*. When the Randolph County settlers elected their first officers a year later, they chose 22-year-old Thomas as the county's first Clerk of the Superior Court. In all likelihood, the Manghams lived in or near the county town of Lumpkin, and thus fell under the jurisdiction of Stewart County when it was organized from the northern portion of Randolph in 1831. Thomas continued to serve as Clerk of the Superior or Inferior Courts in Stewart County for several more years, before succumbing once more to the allure of life on the frontier.[4]

This time, Thomas moved Matilda, young Henry, and little Ann (born about 1832) across the Chattahoochee River into Russell County, Alabama. He may well have accompanied his brother Henry and their relatives William, Bryant, and Arthur Mangham, although documentary evidence is insufficient to establish the exact timing of their movements. Thomas quickly established himself as a thriving farmer, stock raiser, and successful real estate speculator in the booming young county. As such, he represented in microcosm the pressures and motives that attracted Americans to the frontier in overwhelming numbers. After all, the Mangham family migration was but a small part of the flood of settlers that helped ignite a terrible backlash by the Creeks in

1836. Although the 1832 Treaty of Cusseta laid the foundation for cooperation between Creeks and whites, many settlers ran roughshod over the agreement and pushed the Creeks contemptuously aside. Heated exchanges occurred between the Federal government and the State of Alabama over these treaty violations, but outbreaks of violence against the settlers helped ensure the whites eventually closed ranks. A series of Indian attacks cast a pall of gloom and terror over Russell County that spring, as slaughtered cattle, murdered families, and burning bridges and farmsteads betokened the collapse of the tenuous relationship between Creeks and whites.[5]

THE THOMAS R. MANGHAM FAMILY

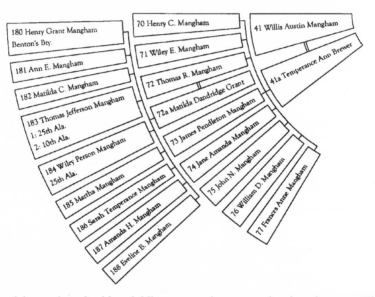

One of those whose livelihood fell victim to the rising tide of mayhem was Thomas Mangham, who lost more than $3300 worth of property when his house was burned and his estate sacked. Apparently, he fled with Matilda and their little brood in 1835 or early 1836 as the violence spiraled out of control. The refugee family now included little Matilda (born c. 1834) and *Thomas Jefferson Mangham*, born in Harris County, Georgia, on February 25, 1835. The infant boy's father and namesake clearly had a score to settle with the Creeks, and he enlisted in Company I of Colonel Beall's 1st Georgia Mounted Volunteers. His brothers Wiley and John were in the same regiment, and may have accompanied Thomas into Florida in pursuit of the Creeks as they fled to join the Seminoles. Thomas took part in the decisive engagement at Chichasahatchee Swamp, receiving a land warrant for his meritorious service in battle.[6]

After the war ended, the Manghams moved back to Alabama to rebuild. New Year's Day of 1838 saw another addition to the family, when *Wiley Person Mangham* was born in Russell County. Although the parents may have intended his name to honor Thomas's brother Wiley E. Mangham (of Pike County) and their recently deceased uncle, Wiley P. Mangham, late of Chambers County, the youth's name also drew a connection back to the family's North Carolina roots. By 1838, Willie (pronounced Wiley) Person Mangum of North Carolina had served most of the preceding fifteen years in the United States Senate, pursuing a career that led him nearly to the pinnacle of American politics. Serving as President pro tempore of the Senate, he assumed duties as acting Vice President of the United States when President William Henry Harrison died in 1843.[7]

When little Wiley was ten years old, he moved with his family to Read's Mills in western Benton County (later renamed Calhoun County), Alabama, where Thomas and Matilda farmed sixty acres of a spread six times that size. Assisted by sons Henry, Tom, and Wiley, as well as daughters Ann, Matilda, Martha, Amanda, and Eveline, Thomas raised fine crops of wheat, corn, rice, and sweet potatoes. Many years later Wiley recalled searching in vain for his father's sheep over hill and dale, before realizing that the ever-receding sound of bells was in fact the hum of locusts echoing among the mountains. In the fall of 1857, his eldest brother Henry showed that he shared the same wanderlust that had kept his father seeking new frontiers: he departed Alabama to go west, where he settled in the rich lands of Franklin Parish, Louisiana.[8]

Wiley attended the Baptist high school in the county seat of Jacksonville, where his uncle, James F. Grant, owned and operated the *Jacksonville Republican*. In the early 1850s, both Wiley and his elder brother Tom began learning the intricacies of the newspaper business from their uncle, and Wiley also spent some time sharpening his skills as a printer's devil in Rome, Georgia. By 1859, the brothers were ready to strike out on their own. With a forty-year-old cast iron Smith printing press obtained from his uncle for the sum of $250, Tom set up shop in nearby Ashville as editor of the *St. Clair Diamond*, the first newspaper published in St. Clair County. With Wiley's assistance, Tom produced a good country newspaper that provided news of local affairs and momentous occurrences on the national scene.[9]

As the country writhed in the throes of the secession crisis, Calhoun and St. Clair counties reflected the political, economic and social fissures that divided many of the South's mountainous regions from their lowland neighbors. Situated in the lower reaches of the Appalachian Mountains, many citizens of the northern Alabama hill country perceived little common interest between their isolated communities and the vocal cotton planters of the state's Black Belt. Many mountaineers simply resented any governmental intrusion in their lives, and cared little for any lowlanders' political conceptions. Others, however, feared the abolitionist specter of "Negro equality" that haunted many Southerners and evoked passionate resistance to Lincoln's new Republican Party, and therefore viewed secession and states' rights as the best security for their social system and values. Still others considered that the greater danger lay in giving more authority to the haughty Black Belt planters so prominent in the secessionist movement, however, and thus rejected calls to break up the Union.[10]

All things considered, Saint Clair and Calhoun counties were a volatile mix in the election year of 1860. Although Thomas Mangham's family was a product of the frontier and its strong admixture of egalitarianism, he and his sons were steeped in the values of a society that passionately embraced personal honor as its touchstone, and an economy that was based largely on the practice of black slavery. Thomas apparently owned no slaves in 1860, but he kept two hands on behalf of his brother Henry C. Mangham, now earning a living as a bookkeeper in Warm Springs, Georgia.[11] Their father, Willis, and brothers James, John, and Wiley all owned slaves back in Pike County, as well. Perhaps most importantly, however, the family's strong tradition of political activity and active militia service cultivated roots that nourished, and drew nourishment from, the mainstream of Southern society. There was nothing in them of the clannish mountaineer that populated much of St. Clair and Calhoun counties.

Unsurprisingly, the Manghams took an unequivocal stance in favor of secession as the long-simmering debate reached crisis proportions, and Thomas "warmly espoused the cause of the Southern Confederacy." His sons used the bully pulpit of the *St. Clair*

WILEY PERSON MANGHAM
(SEE APPENDIX, REF. # 184)

Diamond to declare their separatist views. The edition of December 5, 1860 carried an editorial from the *Southern Democrat* about Vice-President-elect Hannibal Hamlin's widely alleged status as a "free Negro." An appended editorial comment stated baldly, "No matter whether or not he has a single drop of negro blood in his veins, he believes the man is equal with himself, and consequently is too much degraded to be Vice President of these United States." Although the layout of the article leaves it open to question whether the editorial commentaries are attributable to Tom and Wiley or to the editors of the *Southern Democrat*, the lack of opposing commentary makes it clear that the two brothers agreed with the sentiment, at the very least.[12]

Another barometer of the national crisis was the proliferation of volunteer companies forming across the South as the critical election of 1860 approached. The fever already took Ashville in its grip on May 26, 1860, and Tom was one of fifty-eight men who assembled that day to form the "Ashville Guards." The town elite filled the company's ranks, which included a county commissioner, the sheriff, the clerk of the circuit court, four lawyers and three doctors, as well as Tom, its newspaper editor and proprietor.

The Guards were preparing to back their secessionist sentiments with action, even before the election took place.[13]

2. WIELDING THE PEN & SWORD: LIEUTENANTS THOMAS J. AND WILEY P. MANGHAM, "ASHVILLE ARTILLERY," LATER THE "ASHVILLE BLUES," CO. D, 1ST ALABAMA BATTALION, LATER THE 25TH ALABAMA REGIMENT

By June 1861, the secession crisis had boiled over into a shooting war, and the Ashville Guards left town for Montgomery, where they became Company A of the 10th Alabama Infantry. Tom and Wiley Mangham had other plans, however. Along with some other members of the original Guards, they remained in town to organize a second company, the "Ashville Artillery." Tom signed on as a private, while Wiley was unanimously elected second lieutenant when the company organized in July 1861. The men remained at home for some time, apparently waiting for the governor to accept their services, but their long-awaited marching orders finally arrived later that summer.[14] On August 29, Tom prepared an editorial adieu in the last issue of the *Diamond*, under the title "Valedictory":

> Having determined to go into the service of the Confederate States as a soldier, and thinking I could do my country more affectual service with the musket than with that powerful engine, the Press, I have attached myself to a volunteer company—the Ashville Artillery—who have orders to take up the line of march on Monday next, the 2nd of September. Therefore, I exchange the quill for a musket, and my editorial chair for the camp stool—or the ground, as the case may be; and this I do cheerfully as though I were making an exchange of one of the most arduous professions for one of the easiest and most lucrative.
>
> My friends and acquaintance know that I would long since have been upon the battle plains of Virginia if I had not been advised by my physicians and other friends not to go, assigning as their reasons my inability to perform the duties of a soldier, saying that it would result in certain death before I should even have the pleasure of shooting at a Yankee. My health has improved since that time, and the temptation is so great that I cannot resist it. Hence, I go fully determined never to return until I have done all I can in repelling the ruthless invaders from our beloved soil, let the consequences be what they may, conscious that I have performed my duty to the best of my ability, and if I should die either from the bullet of the enemy or from disease, I shall die satisfied that my duty has been performed and that I die in a just and righteous cause.
>
> We have all seen and heard great speeches and editorial articles in relation to the invasion, devastation, etc. of our country—this is all well enough, but the time, in my opinion, has come for some of us to act as well as talk and write, and I for one, feel it to be as much my duty to assist in repelling the invasion as encouraging others to do so.
>
> I know there are some of our citizens who desire that the paper should not be suspended—to such I am very thankful for their appreciation of my ability and

merits and for their proper estimate of the value of a paper in their county—but I hope they will better appreciate my motives in suspending the paper to engage in what I conceive to be a more patriotic enterprise and be satisfied to wait until we (myself and brother) return to our post as editors and publishers. Then I trust they will show their loyalty and appreciation by subscribing liberally for our paper, if we should survive the struggle for independence.

I trust that neither of us have an enemy behind—we have endeavored to conduct ourselves, as much as possible, in such a manner as not to gain an enemy—if he was an honorable and loyal citizen; yet at the same time we held our course onward in the direction which we deemed to be the most honorable, unbiased by few or favor; but if we have gained enemies by this, I, for myself, say I desire not their friendship or favors, feeling conscious that I done my whole duty, and nothing but my duty. And if ever I return I shall pursue the same course regardless of consequences, even if we should be subjugated, which I think is impossible.

I know I have gained many warm hearted friends, for which I am much gratified, and to such I make a polite bow, on leaving my editorial chair, wishing them all the blessings of a divine and gracious Providence, promising to resume it and issue the next number of the Diamond when I can have the pleasure of publishing the recognition of the Confederate Government by all the nations of the earth. So mote it be.

THOS. J. MANGHAM[15]

His editorial resounded with a clarion call that any West Point cadet would have understood clearly: Duty, Honor, Country. A week later, Tom and Wiley were in ranks among the 107 officers and men of the new company as it marched out of town, bound for Fort Gaines, on the Gulf Coast near Mobile Bay. At their head was Dr. Andrew W. Nickson, another member of the original Ashville Guards.[16]

Just a few days after their departure, Thomas R. Mangham placed a notice in his brother-in-law's *Jacksonville Republican*, stating his intention to travel to Fort Gaines in mid-October. He announced that he would "take great pleasure" in delivering packages to members of the Ashville Artillery, and asked that any such items be left at Ashville's hotels for him to collect before departing.[17] In the meantime, Pvt. Tom Mangham was writing from camp to his uncle's newspaper, using it as a medium to transmit news to the company's well wishers at home. Taking up his pen at Fort Gaines on September 11, he addressed his uncle:

Dear Sir:[18]

Having had solicitations, when I left home, to write to so many of our friends in old St. Clair as to render it impossible to comply with the requests of all, I desire to use the Republican as a medium for that purpose, if you will give my letter an insertion—by so doing you will give great satisfaction to a number of your friends and patrons of that county.

On Thursday the 5th inst. Capt. A. W. Nickson's company—Ashville Artillery—of which I am a member, took up the line of march for Ft. Gains. Nothing of importance occurred on the way, except it rained upon us the two first days, giving us a real drenching. It was raining very hard when we reached Talladega, but we were met by the Walker Reynolds Guards and escorted to a shelter, and were shown all the courtesy and hospitality which the citizens could extend to us. We remained there until morning, when we took the train for Selma, when we arrived safe at the usual hour. The rain fell in torrents upon us before we reached Selma, giving some of our men a real baptising, as we rode upon open cars. We took passage upon the Virginia, for Mobile, and left Selma some time after dark on Saturday night, and arrived at Mobile about 4 o'clock on Monday morning. You must indulge me in giving praise to the courteous, gentlemanly and accommodating commander of the Virginia, Capt. Buckley, who gave us bedding and all the accommodations possible, for which I hope our friends will remember him when they are travelling in this direction.

While in Mobile, which was a short time, I went on board the prize vessel Danube, captured at Ft. Morgan some time since, which was towed up from this place a few days since and on Saturday last was sold to a French company, who are now having it fitted out for shipping a cargo of cotton, and, I learn, they say they will go out of port with it, if they have the blockade to run.[19]

We found the *Wm. Bagley*, which is now under the employ of the Confederate States, lying at the wharf in Mobile, hence we only had to reship baggage and start, which we did about 9 o'clock and arrived here at about 11 or 12.

I learned on reaching the beach, that there were something like a thousand troops stationed on this island, though I have not seen much more than half that number. Some of them, I suppose, are quartered some miles west of us, at a point which commands Grant's Pass. We are quartered just outside the fort, as are several other companies, including Capt. Pope's company from Columbiana. The fort is not large enough to contain more than half the men who are upon the island. We have plenty to eat: light-bread, bacon, beef, rice, beans, sugar and coffee. We have two tents to each mess, and they are too small for comfort, having to sleep six to a tent; and in fact, it might be called hard living, but we are willing to endure all for the good of our country.[20] We all knew partly what we would have to endure, and came prepared for it, and, I believe, general satisfaction prevails in our company. Our Captain is a noble fellow, and, if I mistake not, will always have the friendship and esteem of his company; in fact, all our officers are good, clever fellows—Wiley Mangham and (Dick) Jas. E. Banks have gained great favor with the company.[21] "Dick" has exalted himself in my estimation since we left more than I had any idea he ever would—he is a fine fellow. I must say, while we were being mustered into service yesterday, some one remarked our Captain was the finest looking man in the fort, the Col. not excepted.

We were all mustered in yesterday, and only one objected to, which was the little cripple, Jack Inglet, our "devil."[22] Our company is the largest, and composed of the best material on the island; and all are in better health than when they left—those who had chills when we left home have had none since, notwithstanding the oppressive heat, which it seems, would be almost unbearable, if it were not for the breeze which is continually stirring. The sun shines distressingly hot upon this sandy beach, and those who have been here during the summer are tanned until they are as dark as creoles.

This fort is situated upon an island some 10 miles in length, 30 miles south of Mobile, 4 miles from Fort Morgan, which is in full view.[23] The neck of land on the western shore of the bay is just visible from this point, and we have a picturesque view on every side, upon one hand we can just perceive the headland below Mobile, upon another the point at Fort Morgan, and upon another nothing but the broad expanse of the mighty deep. Just south east of our wharf, and in sight, near the light house the haughty blockade steamship lies at anchor in the outlet from our port,[24] but she keeps at her distance as well she may, for if she comes as near with her taunts as she has formerly, she is ours or sunk in the waters of the deep. Our boys are anxious to see her blown up. The fort is being repaired—a great many hands working upon it—and guns are being planted upon the walls which will send terror to the Yankees, if they come near us.

Fish, of the finest quality, and oysters are plentiful, and we have the finest place for bathing almost in the world. And it is amusing to hear the boys singing out, "Come boys, let's go to the branch fishing," or "bathing." They all call it the branch.[25] Joel Galbreath says they dammed up the Alabama river while we were lying over at Mobile.[26]

We are all doing finely, and I hope our friends will give themselves no unnecessary trouble about us.

The ladies of Mobile visit the fort occasionally, two boats were down yesterday, freighted with this precious material. Some of them were fine looking ladies, and I suppose were considered the fairest of the fair of that city; but they will not do to compare with the North Alabama girls.

We have not been armed yet, nor do we know when it will be done. We feel the necessity of such things. We are in a helpless condition until we can get them.[27] Col. Gardner is commander of this post.

THOS. J. MANGHAM

About six weeks later, Third Lt. Dick Banks sent news of the company for publication in the *Jacksonville Republican*. The Ashville Artillery was no more; the company had been renamed the "Ashville Blues" sometime after mustering into Confederate service on September 10. Captain Nickson's men gave up their hopes of manning the heavy artillery along Fort Gaines's glowering ramparts, and now comprised Company D of the 1st Battalion Alabama Infantry.[28] As Banks explained to friends and relatives in a letter published on October 24, the Blues finally had received arms in mid-October:

> Dauphin Island, (Near) Fort Gains, Ala. Oct. 31, '61.[29]
>
> Mr. Grant:
>
> Dear Sir: I take this method of informing my people at home together with a number of other relatives, and friends, that I am well, and have been since I landed on Dauphin Island. We have hitherto been stationed very near the Fort, because of our defenseless condition, but we received our arms the other day, and provisions were immediately made for our Battalion to march out on the west end of the Island, about three or four miles from the Fort. So we, the Ashville Blues, struck our tents yesterday morning about 6 o'clock, and by seven, we took up the line of march, accompanied by Capt. Walker's company of Maj. Gee's Battalion,[30] for our new place or home, where we arrived in due time; the ballance of our Battalion will come out today. We had not long eaten our supper, last night, when we heard three cannon from Fort Morgan. Capt. Walker ran out on the beach to see what was the matter, and while he was there, he saw them throw up some sky rockets, and in a very short time we were ordered to arms; in a few moments we were all under arms, and ready for a fight. Skirmishers were soon placed out around our encampment, though our boys were few in number, they were anxious for the Yankees to come on; I entertain no fears whatever, of their taking Fort Gains as long as we keep it garrisoned with such material as we have here at present, our men acted with as much calmness as though they were loading their pieces to shoot for a prize; but we were relieved about midnight with orders to sleep upon our arms; and we were not disturbed any more. If they will stay away a few days longer, we will erect our Batteries out here on the beach, and then we will be prepared to give them a hearty welcome to watery graves; if we get our guns mounted out here; the Yankees will never be delighted with the sight of Fort Gaines, for before they can land, we will send them to keep company with the hordes of vandals who fell at the battle of Manassas. We have but little work to do, to prepare as good and effective defences as we have in the Fort. Nature has done much for us here; she has thrown up our breast works to a sufficient height along the shore, with a very little work they are ready to mount guns upon. We hope our friends will not give themselves any uneasiness about us, as we are well provided for, and are well satisfied, we have plenty to eat; our provisions consist of corn bread, flour bread, bacon, beef, beans, peas, sweet potatoes, rice, sugar, coffee, fish and oysters in abundant quantities, so you see we are at home. I was pleased to see a letter in the Republican of the 26th Sept., from under the pen of my esteemed friend, Thos. J. Mangham, he gives a glowing description of our trip to this beautiful little Island; he also gives our gallant Capt. great praise, which I assured my friend he is worthy of. ____ when he says he is a noble fellow, a truer heart than his, never beat within the breast of man, and we will follow him even to death.

My noble friend (Mr. Mangham,) also says, "all our officers are good clever fellows." Our company is the largest one on the Island, and I flatter myself that whenever we are called into action, we will all prove ourselves worthy the love and esteem, of all our friends behind, God forbid that it will ever be said the Ashville Blues, fell short of their duty in defending their country. We will never surrender nor retreat as long as we have one load of ammunition, or power to charge bayonet. Just as I have finished my letter, my friend Joseph M. Alexander, who has been taking a nap in my tent, asked me to mention his name in my letter, for the benefit of his friends in St. Clair. Selus, (for that is what we call him) has been out on picket guard last night, come in this morning wet and sleepy.[31] I gave him a dram and my bed to rest upon. He has just awaked from a sweet sleep, and says he feels very much refreshed. He is a good soldier, he is ever attentive and obedient to the commands of his officers, and is beloved by all the company.

JAMES E. BANKS

In the same issue of the *Jacksonville Republican*, Second Lt. Wiley Mangham passed along a report that graphically illustrated the danger attendant to life in camps:

Camp Loomis (near) Ft. Gains, Ala., Oct. 12th, 1861.
Mr. Grant:
It pains me to record the sad accident, that happened in our camp yesterday morning about daylight.
The facts as stated to me are these:
Sergeant Green, a member of our company—was coming out of his tent with his gun in hand, when the hammer caught against the upright piece of the tent and was raised from the cap. The hammer then falling on the cap again, caused the gun to go off. A ball stuck the ground some 15 feet from the tent, and glancing from thence, inflicted a severe wound in the leg of Robt. Dunn, a member of our company. The whole cartridge went through his leg just above the knee, breaking the bone entirely into [sic]. The Physicians give it as their opinion, that his leg will have to be amputated. A ball also took effect in Malone Smith's thigh, but the wound is not considered serious.[32]

Yours in haste, WILEY

A short time later, Tom sent further news via the *Republican*. Displaying a keen sense of humor and a patriotic tolerance for the problems of camp life, he obviously reveled in an opportunity to poke fun at the Union blockade. With a true editorialist's sense of irony, however, his broadsides against Lincoln's blockade aimed to convince his readers that the blockade was ineffective, and thus unworthy of recognition by European powers. As many Southerners pointed out, a formally declared naval blockade amounted to *de facto* recognition of the Confederate States as a belligerent power, rather than merely a rebellious section of a sovereign country. Furthermore, under international law, a naval blockade had to be effective to require neutral powers

110

to respect it. If the Confederacy could convince France and England that the coastal quarantine was a sham, there was hope that European traders would disregard the embargo and keep crucial trade routes open, simultaneously promoting intervention on the South's behalf. Thus, while providing the home folks with news of the Ashville Blues, Tom also gave vent to the aggressive partisanship that made Southern newspapermen such a notable source of secessionist sentiment and morale. Many soldiers also sought to boost confidence on the home front, and Tom's November 2 letter from Fort Gaines showcased this tendency as well:

Dear Republican:

It was my intention, when I first arrived at this place, to have written an article for your columns every week; but nothing having transpired worthy of placing upon record—especially of occupying the space of so valuable a paper—I have remained silent for some time. But, lest my friends all arrive at the conclusion that I have been stowed away in the sand of Dauphin Island, been devoured by a shark, or like Jonah, taken up my abode in the enormous stomach of some mamoth whale, I will again "drop you a short epistle," just merely to communicate to you the very important intelligence that I am still living and that the Yankees have not yet taken this post.

I will, according to the usual custom of letter writing, begin by informing the friends of the Ashville Blues that the members of that company are none of them dangerously ill, only four of them reported sick this morning—in fact, there are but three—the fourth being the man who was accidently shot—and those who are sick have nothing seriously the matter. Yet I entertain some fear that they will have the measles as it has made its appearance in our Battalion, and if they do take it, they will doubtless suffer severely; for we are still in tents and the weather is getting pretty chilly. None of the A.B's. have had it yet, and those of our Battalion who have taken it, were conveyed immediately to the Hospital inside the Fort, where they received all the attention requisite—good physicians and nurses. Dr. Benson is there, and I am confident this information will greatly relieve the anxious minds of our friends at home; for they know the value of his professional services.[33] It is the desire of the majority of this Battalion that he remain with us, and I hope he will do so.

I presume our friends generally, have been informed of the fact that some weeks since we had a general ["]stir round," in consequence of an alarm being given at night &c.—yes, I remember now, seeing in my friend Lieut. Bank's letter to you,—But to the "point." None of us "small fry" knew the intention of the alarm until a few days since; when a little Southern schooner arrived in port, laden with coffee and cigars, from Cuba, we learned that the alarm was given and rockets sent up to attract the attention of the blockade's crew in order to give the schooner a chance to pass out to sea; the plan succeeded admirably, and within about a fortnight after she stood out to sea the gallant little schooner hove into port, safe and sound, laden with some twelve hundred sacks of coffee,

I learn, and some important messages for our President, though I can't say this is true; but I can say that the schooner came in, and that in open daylight, with the old blockade steamer lying in plain view. So, you see the Yankee blockade is no obstacle in the way of men of daring and skill—Where is their boasted fleet, which was sent to cruise upon Southern waters, that they did not overhaul this little vessel?

Will Europe recognize Lincoln's blockade as effective now, or will she want more proof to satisfy her upon this subject? If she wants more proof she will doubtless get it, if we can find enough little schooners large enough to live at sea. All we are in need of are the vessels; there are those here who are willing to man them. The Confederate States will never lack for bravery. I hear several of Capt. Nickson's company—the Ashville Blues—say they would be willing to lose a nights sleep any time to see the blockade run.

I thought, when we came here, that we would have no cold weather upon this island; but, if this is not a cold day, I have forgotten what we used to call cold days. On the night of the 31st ult. there came upon us, about two o'clock, a real storm—such a one as is only known to those who have been placed in a similar condition to that in which we were placed, and to the storm-tossed mariner—out upon an open plain, upon a little island in the sea, with nothing to shield us from the fury of the tempest, save our little cloth tents, some of which were leveled by the first gust of wind with the ground; and when day dawned so that we could see the effects of the storm, I turned my eye upon the camp, and behold, not more than half the tents were standing, and seemed as if they were just ready to be carried off by the howling tempest, leaving their occupants to the mercy of the storm—and they would certainly have been drenched with the chilling rain if nothing more. Some of the boys who wure [sic] so unfortunate as to have their tents blown down were stalking around as "wet as rats," and presented a laughable, though sad, appearance. The rain did not continue to fall long, and the men were soon busied in erecting their tents again and drying their clothing; and I think they were more careful in replacing and fastening down their tents; they will not be blown down again soon.

We would not have fared so bad in the storm, if we had remained out upon the island, where we were ordered some few weeks since; but we were here, just outside the fort, where there was no timber to protect us. We were ordered back to this place by Gen. Bragg, and had been here but a few days. The authorities keep us moving about on the island continually, and if we were on the main-land they would certainly have us to traverse the whole Continent; but, of course, they know best, and none of us are disposed to grumble at it.[34]

There are upon the island at this time two Battalions—one of Regulars, commanded by Lieut. Col. Garner—I do not know the number of men composing this Battalion—and one of volunteers—known as the 1st Battalion of Infantry Ala. Vols., numbering about 416, commanded by Lieut. Col. J. Q. Loomis—who is by the way, one of the noblest fellows, and best commanders, in the Confederate service. He has, by his kindness and noble bearing, won the confidence, esteem and respect of his whole Battalion. His men would follow him where no other man could lead or drive them. His deportment is such as is only characteristic of a true gentleman and officer. His men all love him for his true worth, and all who know him admire him as an officer. He is in his true element and knows how to govern his men. We, indeed, have good officers in our Battalion. Our Adjutant is one of nature's noblemen—a stern and unflinching patriot, with a heart overflowing with kindness; and he takes great pride in seeing his men deport themselves as become soldiers, and is always ready to defend them when any one presumes to impeach their characters as gentlemen and soldiers.

Whenever an opportunity presents itself, if I am not sadly mistaken, you will hear of our Battalion acquitting themselves with honor, and of their making a display of valor and bravery.

TOM

Tom's next letter arrived just prior to publication of the November 28 issue of the *Jacksonville Republican*, so Grant summarized it briefly for his readers. He published it in full on December 5, 1861:

Camp upon Dog River, (near) Hall's Mills, Mobile Co., Ala., Nov. 23, 1861.

Dear Republican:

We have been moving and removing so much of late, and having arrived here during the night, I hardly know how to designate the present locality of our camp; though it is at the head of navigation of a small stream, called Dog River, which empties into Mobile Bay something like 30 miles south west of the city—I only suppose the distance to be that. How, or why we came here, I will state as near as I can for the information of our friends at home.

Some days since—I am not a good hand to remember dates—we were ordered to strike tents and get ready to take shipping. The removal was delayed after we received orders until Col. Crawford's Regiment had landed at Ft. Gaines,[35] to take the place of our Battalion, (Lieut. Col. Loomis'); but when this Regiment had all arrived there, which was on Saturday evening the 17th inst., the drum was beaten for the striking of our tents, and they were soon down and on board the steamer *Bagley*; and awhile after dark we steamed up the Bay for the Mouth of Dog River, where the *Dixie* was lying in wait for us to convey us to this place. Our baggage &c., was soon transported from the *Bagley* to the *Dixie*, and we started up this little winding stream, which is scarcely broad enough to be called a creek, and so crooked it is difficult for the boats to make the turns; but we landed here safe between two and three o'clock on Sunday morning, pitched a few tents on the banks of the stream, and a few threw themselves into them, others upon the ground in the open air, and as is usual in camp life, some of us slept till day, while others sat around the camp fires, telling yarns & singing camp songs.

When the darkness began to break, I noticed that Col. Beck's [sic] Regiment were encamped near at hand.[36] This is a very fine looking Regiment, but the men do not seem to be used to camp life, and they need drilling—By 2 o'clock P.M. we had succeeded in bringing order out of confusion, and had pitched our tents in something like order, though we have very bad ground for an encampment, nor were we very careful in laying off the ground, as we did not expect to remain long here; though we are still here, but I suppose we will be removed a few miles within a few days.

The day we arrived here (about 12 o'clock, I suppose) the *Clipper* hove up to our landing with a regiment on board, and I soon learned it was Col. Wheeler's.[37] Judge of my surprise, on going down to the water's edge, to hear my name so familiarly called out by voices in the crowd, and upon close examination I saw the faces of many old familiar friends. None only the soldier can judge of the feelings produced when beholding the forms and faces of those with whom we have associated in bygone days of peace and happiness—those around whose firesides we have sat and conversed familiarly upon cold winter days, surrounded by friends and relatives. I say, none can judge of our emotion upon meeting with such friends, far away from home and friends upon the tented field, save those who are or have been similarly situated; and you can scarcely imagine the joy with which we clasped each others hands upon meeting. It seemed as though I was at home again with my friends.

Those boys of whom I speak are members of Capt. Hollingsworth's Company of Gadsden, and all those at home, who read this, will know of whom I speak without me naming them. They are all pretty well, I believe; have had the measles and recovered. The boys indeed looked very healthy and fine.[38]

Oliver's company is also here in Bullock's Regiment.[39] I have not seen the boys of that company, but some of our boys have been over to see them and bring back good reports, I believe, as to health etc.

As to the reason why we were ordered to this place, I have not been informed, and am unable to arrive at a satisfactory conclusion of my own in regard to the movement; though some say it is for the purpose of having us [at] a point from which we can be transported with more dispatch, if we should have an attack upon the coast; but this does not seem to me to be a reasonable conclusion, for we could have been more speedily transported from the Fort than here, unless they have means of transportation, unknown to me, more speedy than that by which we were brought here. It seems to be a very good hiding place from the Yankees; for I am sure they will never find us here, unless it is by accident, or we are carried away. But laying jesting aside, I suppose the above conclusion, together with the following, are the most obvious; we are, I suppose, quartered here for the purpose of cutting off any possible chance of land forces attacking Mobile; and this I think we can do effectually. I think the city of Mobile is perfectly secure from the ravages of any forces of the vandals which may be brought against her; for she is guarded by enough boys who have the right kind of "sand in their craws," who are anxious for a fight, which renders some of them uneasy; they wish to be in active service. But we may get a fight here as soon as anywhere else.

The measles is very prevalent in our Battalion now, and in fact throughout the encampment, I believe, but none of our boys are dangerously ill, I think. Those who were very sick when we came here, were sent on up to Mobile to remain in the Hospital till they recovered, and are very tenderly cared for there.

I am really gratified to know, that wherever we may go, the Republican finds its way to our camp, where it is always a welcome visitor, and gives great satisfaction to many of our company. It is true it does not come regularly, but then a copy, now and then, finds its way to us, for which we are exceedingly thankful to its proprietors.

You can just say to our friends, our present address is Mobile. This mail is brought from the city out to us. He should be careful to direct to the Capt. of the company always.

For the satisfaction of our friends, I would say to them that we are well cared for in the way of provisions; indeed we have many little things which I never would have thought of myself if I had been required to prepare necessaries for a camp, such as Sugar, Molases, Rice, Soap, Potatoes &c. &c. No one has any room for grumbling on this score, nor do I believe there is any dissatisfaction among our troops.

You will probably hear from me again soon, if I continue to live and breathe.

TOM

Tom was witnessing a concentration of troops near Mobile that bespoke Confederate fears of a Federal attack on Alabama's coast. Although he affected scorn for the Union navy's blockade, its supremacy on the seas gave Federal forces the option to swoop down unopposed on the South's seaports. Hindsight tells us that Mobile was to be spared until 1865, but Confederate sentinels in the winter of 1861 had to agree with Tom's view, that "we may get a fight here as soon as anywhere else."

While a Federal invasion fleet remained but a looming menace beyond the murky horizon, the grim-visaged specter of disease was an immediate threat. It was spreading disaster through Loomis's battalion and into the Mangham home. Writing from camp at Barlow's Mills on December 2, Tom passed on the sad tidings to the *Republican*:

Since I last wrote to you my heart has been made sad because of the death of two of our best soldiers, and the receipt, shortly after the death of the last one, of the sad intelligence of the death of my beloved father, at home, who parted with me sick something like a month since, at Ft. Gains, Dauphin Island. He left his two sons then upon the tented field, never to see them again until we meet in that better world, never to be parted again. May God be a husband indeed to my widowed mother, and a father to to [sic] my orphan sisters, who are alone without even a brother to protect them.

Our camp now presents a sad scene—my fears, as expressed in my last letter written at Ft. Gaines, are realized.—More than half our Battalion are sick with measles, pneumonia, and other camp diseases; and I think we average at least one death per day.[40] But, thank heaven, some of them are getting well. Those who were sick when we arrived at this place fared very bad, as the Hospital had not been furnished with even a substitute for—the sick having to lie upon straw thrown down upon the floor; but our noble Col. and Surgeon used every exertion to have them provided for, and now they have very neat, comfortable cots and mattresses to lie upon; but the hospital will not hold half our sick—being a small dwelling with some four rooms, and kitchen—in consequence of which those who are not considered dangerously ill, together with all who wish to do so, remain in quarters, where their fellow soldiers attend them as best they can; but the chances are bad there to render any material aid, and their tents being made of material too thin to protect them well in time of a storm or hard rain. We have very wet weather now, but one thing which I consider favorable to those who have the measles, is the weather is very warm yet. We have had but one frost, and that was light.

There are at this time several Regiments encamped near us, and they are all, more or less sick. I learn that one of these Regiments buried seven men one day last week. Surely more soldiers are slain by disease than by the sword or musket.[41]

Notwithstanding the sickness and deaths in our camps most of our men appear cheerful and very well satisfied. Of course, some of those who are rather given to despondency and would like to be at home, but this is only natural.

We have been here very near three months—some of us more than than [that]—and have never been paid off yet, but we are expecting the money in a few days. It is a pity our men have not been paid before now, for money is very scarce with us, and now is a time when it is needed very much. But I suppose there are so many soldiers to pay off we will be treated like the miller treats his patrons, and will be served when our time comes.[42]

Enclosed I send the obituarys [sic] of two members of the Ashville Blues, which I hope will find a place in your columns.[43] As I have no news except that which is sad I will close my epistle hoping I will have more cheering news when you hear from me again.

TOM

While the Ashville Blues mourned the deaths of Pvts. Thomas Simpson and J. M. Galbreath, Tom and Wiley were afflicted particularly by the loss of their father. He came down with typhoid fever visiting his sons at Fort Gaines in October, but set out for home despite his weakness, reaching the home of Judge Thornton in Talladega before he had to take to his sickbed. Recovering enough to resume his journey, Thomas reached his Calhoun County home, where he collapsed again. He died ten days later, on November 22, 1861, leaving behind his wife Matilda, five daughters, and three sons. His obituary appeared in his brother-in-law's newspaper shortly afterward, praising him as "a man of decided character, a warm and devoted friend and generous and forgiving to his enemies—a good and generous neighbor—a kind and affectionate husband and father." This testimonial also noted that Thomas "warmly espoused the cause of the Southern Confederacy," and that he had "experienced and manifested much anxiety for the success of the Southern cause" in the last days of his life.[44]

It was not long after his father's death that Wiley fell sick in camp. Considered one of the "best drilling officers in the battalion," he had been present for duty until December, when he fell ill and left for home on a sick furlough. Just twenty-four on New Year's Day, 1862, he permanently lost the use of one lung as a result of his illness. Persuaded by Surgeon Josiah C. Nott to resign his commission due to his disability, Second Lt. Wiley Person Mangham was honorably discharged on January 15, 1862. Loomis's 1st Alabama Battalion combined with McClellan's 6th Alabama Battalion on January 8 to form the 25th Alabama Volunteers, so Wiley's discharge officially was from Company D of that regiment.[45]

Just four days later, Tom Mangham sat down to update the readers of the *Jacksonville Republican*. Appointed sergeant major of the 1st Alabama Battalion in December, Tom became sergeant major of the newly-organized 25th Regiment when Loomis's battalion combined with McClellan's.[46] While he wished to inform his readers of this reorganization, Tom also seized the chance to comment on the price gouging and speculation that was scandalizing the Confederacy. His scathing critique, written at Camp Memminger (near Mobile) on January 19, appeared in the *Republican* on February 6, 1862:

> Dear Republican:
> Doubtless your readers have forgotten that I was ever in existence, or that there is such a regiment in the service as the 25th Ala. Kin always excepted, of course; —and this would be a sad[?] pity, as it is composed of such good material and one company from your own county, while there are several companies from your neighboring counties. For the information of your readers, I will give you the names or at least the rank of our companies, and the names of their Captains and counties. They are as follows: Co. A. Capt. Harper, Covington; B. Lieut. House, Pike; C. Capt. Pope, Shelby; D. Nickson, St. Clair; E. Richards, Pickens; F. Hundley, Randolph; G. McCann, Talladega; H. Turner, Talladega and St. Clair; I. Alexander, Calhoun; K. Castello [sic], Coffee. So, you see we have a full regiment, and that of good material and good officers. Col. Loomis is well known in South Alabama as being one of the first men in the state. As a distinguished lawyer, a gentleman of brilliant intellect, and an efficient military officer, who for merit and ability, has risen from an Orderly Sergeant to the position of a Col. during his military career. Our Lieut. Col. is well known to many of your readers as a quiet, and unique, retired citizen of Talladega county.[47] He is several years the senior of our Col., and is a veteran of the "old school," is, I believe, a graduate of West Point, and has served as an officer in the United States service. Our other officers are good tacticians and men with whom we are well pleased.

Dr. J. T. Reese [?] of Selma, and 1ˢᵗ Surgeon at Ft. Gaines, is our Surgeon, (Capt. Nickson, Co. D, having resigned that position, preferring to remain Capt. of his company) and now has ___ of our ___, who has wonderful ___ __, notwithstanding he has a great many ____ ____ of ___ ___ ___. He has the reputation of being one of the first Surgeons in the Confederate service.

We belong to Gen. Walker's (1ˢᵗ Alabama) Brigade, who are all encamped upon a line, some 2 miles in length, upon the camping ground of Gen. Jackson in ___;[48] 38 [?] years ago, in a fine forest, convenient to to good spring water, and our Regt. in my opinion, have a ____ advantage in ground, being upon an eminence, about the centre of the encampment, just above the springs, which gush out in a deep ravine just to rear of our quarters. The water is the best of __ water, and this is a luxury to our boys, who have not had good water since they have been in the service until they came here. Some of the regiments in this Brigade have erected good winter quarters for the men and are building officers' quarters; but, in my opinion, by the time they have finished they will not need them for the present winter.

The citizens of Mobile—some of them—presented one of our Regiments (Col. Deas') with a very nice flag yesterday;[49] and many of the "Mobile fair" were in attendance upon this occasion, and, I learn, one of these very interesting and beautiful ladies for which the city is famous, Miss Sue Tarleton, delivered quite an entertaining and patriotic presentation address. It was quite refreshing to see so many interesting and beaming countenances passing through our encampment; and our sentinels all had orders to permit "silk" and "callico" [to pass?] at will, unmolested. God bless the ladies! I believe they are all patriotic—all greater lovers of their country than the male population. The fair daughters of Rome sacrificed their jewels in defence of their city, and this was a sacrifice of great magnitude, for a great number of them cling to these articles of aparel as tenaciously as a man does to the same material moulded into coin, which in a great many instances is dearer than life. I wish I could say as much for all of the sterner sex; but it is a sad fact that a large number of them, instead of making sacrifices in defense of their country, are growing rich off of the distress of that country, filling their coffers from the pockets of the soldiery of their country, taking advantage of the misfortunes of their country and people and turning them into profit to themselves—extortioning upon the noble soldiers who have left their houses and families, in defense of their country and the families and property of these same "jayhawkers," by placing such prices upon articles of necessity as to draw the last cent from the pockets of poor soldiers, whose families doubtless are suffering from want at home. Mobile is probably no worse than most other cities, but [still?] it is infested with those "vampires," who regardless of the "__ small voice," seize, with the tenacity of a horse[leach?] upon every soldier which visits their city, until they have denuded[?] his purse of its entire contents. It is true there are a great many good and loyal citizens in Mobile; but they are so few, when compared with those innumerable "leaches," that it reminds one of the day of a certain man by the name of Lott, and, if it was not for those honest individuals and the ladies, the majority of the soldiers here would not be grieved very much if it was to meet with the same calamity that befell a certain city we read of in the Bible.

Those characters are very numerous throughout the Confederacy, and even surpass the Yankees in cunning and extortion, if I may judge from articles upon this subject, which I see in every paper I pick up—the papers are all crying out against extortioners and still the practice is continued. Have you ever thought of the reason, or do you know why it has not been put down? If not, let me whisper in your ear what I perceive to be a very obvious reason. If, when an article upon this subject is published, a few of those "bloodsuckers" were personally named, I think it would eventually result in putting a final period to this dishonest business; for there is scarcely a business man, no matter how avaricious, that would like to be regarded as an extortioner; if for no other, for pecuniary interest. But what do they care for the tauntings of a paper, if they are not personally assailed? It is the worst of folly to suppose such a man will quit a business that pays so well, unless he has some fear of his dishonesty being discovered; or even being singled out as one of a numerous class.

Conductors of newspapers ought to devote a column each day to the benefit of such individuals, giving their name, line of business, streets and numbers, to warn the unsuspecting against falling in their hands.

TOM

The 25th Alabama remained in the pine forests and enjoyed the Gulf breezes of Camp Memminger for the remainder of January and February, and it was March before Tom wrote again.[50] After the long months of dreary garrison duty near Mobile, change was in the air. General Ulysses S. Grant had conquered Forts Henry and Donelson, and his ensuing push down the Tennessee and Cumberland Rivers had unhinged the Confederate defense of southern Kentucky and most of Tennessee. With springtime approaching, the resumption of active campaigning was at hand, and Confederate forces were concentrating for a desperate battle in northern Mississippi or southern Tennessee. Tom's next letter to the *Republican*, datelined "Camp of the 25th Ala. Vols., Corinth, Miss., Mar. 11th 1862," clearly showed that he and his comrades were nerving themselves for the impending test:

As it has been sometime since I wrote to you, and our regiment having changed locality, I beg enough space in your columns to inform your readers of our whereabouts, what we are doing and what has transpired under my observation, of late.

I will say but little about what happened to us at Camp Memminger, since I wrote to you, as you have doubtless heard all about the terrible and disastrous hurricane which visited us there on the morning of the 26th ultimo, killing some of our men and frightfully mangling and bruising others; blowing down houses,

119

etc.; but will commence with the 1st day of March and give you a brief detail of what has transpired since that time.[51]

On the first day of March (Saturday,) we received orders, about noon to pack up and travel, and by three o'clock, P.M., we were, like terrapins with all we possessed upon our backs,, [sic] formed upon the parade ground, awaiting orders to start. Our Maj: (Geo. S. Johnson) soon gave the command: "Forward—march," and we moved off to the tune of "Dixie", for Hall's Landing, on Dog River, some 2 1-2 miles distant. The steamer Dixie arrived at the landing about the time we did, and our men and baggage were soon on board; and we steamed down the river for Mobile Bay. If I was competent, and felt inclined to do so, I might give you a romantic description of our trip down the river and up the bay, and the desolate appearance of Camp Memminger, occasioned by the effects of the late storm and our departure; but as that does not concern your readers, I will proceed with the details of our removal, &c.

We arrived at Mobile about 8 1-2 o'clock, P. M., wearied and hungry, and were comfortably quartered in a large building upon Water Street, which afforded ample room for the quartering of the whole Regiment; and here we found a quantity of salt beef and hard bread which had been prepared for us; we soon devoured it, and sought repose, for we were somewhat fatigued by the labors and march of the day. We found several nice mattresses packed away up stairs; and those of us who were so luck-[y] as to be in first, appropriated them to our use for the night, upon which we reclined our weary limbs and were soon in the arms of Morpheus, some doubtless dreaming of home and friends, while others were dreaming of a bloody battle upon the banks of the Mississippi or Tennessee—of victories achieved and laurels won—of triumph and glory.

We were upon our feet before day, and by 7 1-2 o'clock A. M., had our men and baggage transferred onto an extra train upon the Mobile and Ohio railroad and were off to Corinth, Miss. All went on "as merry as a marriage bell," until about 12 1-2 o'clock P. M., when I being in the rear box, was startled by the cry ahead, of, "Man off the train." We had passed the place where he fell of a mile or more; the cars ran back, and as we neared the spot, I beheld a sight which I hope I may never see again. What was a few moments before a young man in youthful vigor and health, was now a gory mass of human flesh, with but little sign of vitality. I have seen a great many corpses, some dying of diseases and others killed, torn and mangled; but I have never seen one so frightfully mangled as this poor fellow.—He was placed on board the train, and we started; but his case was beyond the reach of the skill of our surgeon, and ere we proceeded 10 miles, his spirit had taken its flight, and his remains were taken off and burried among strangers, where no relative will ever drop a tear of grief, for his mother is far away in the North, and his brothers are in the Federal army. He was a member of Capts. [sic] Popes company—name Kuyler and was admired and respected by all the regiment, who knew him, for his noble bearing as a soldier and upright walk as a Christian.[52]

After passing Enterprise, Miss., we passed over some of the most beautiful county [country] in the Confederacy; and spent the night (Sunday) in rumbling and dashing along through prairies, and farms and woodlands, amid storms of wind and rain, which rendered the ride quite disagreeable.[53] We were three days and nights upon the train; and when we arrived here the weather was extremely cold—almost, or quite, freezing—the coldest weather by far, that I had experienced since I entered the service; the ground was cold and muddy, being very wet from the late rains. We came up 1 mile north of the city, took off our baggage, and packed it over to where we are—about a quarter of a mile from the Railroad,—and pitched our tents. The first night was very severe upon us, having exchanged a very warm climate for a cold one, and comfortable quarters for disagreeable quarters—and floored tents for the cold damp ground—and some of us good warm mattresses and beds for a single blanket spread upon oak leaves. And when I awoke next morning I saw the ground was covered with snow—the first I had seen during the winter—and it still falling. The efficient men only for service were brought; but the next morning after our arrival, Capt. Nixon's company had one man less in it, poor Jefferson Crow having died of congestion. -He was a good soldier—several are now sick.

The whole Confederate Army seemed to be concentrating here when we arrived. Gen. Gladden's forces were all here,[54] and besides these, a great many more;—from two to three Reg'ts arriving each day.—But there are but few coming in now. The third day after our arrival here, I heard that the 10th Ala had arrived in town; I immediately obtained leave, and proceeded to the depot hoping there to see the familiar faces and shake the hands of those dear friends and relations of that Regiment; but what a sad disappointment, when upon reaching the place, I learned, that it was the 10th Mississippi, and 2d Tennessee had come in, that night! I felt almost like shedding tears over my disappointment. But in the army we are subject to such disappointments—and should always be prepared to meet them with fortitude;—for if we had met then, we would probably have been separated the next day. For in the army no one knows to-day what the orders of to-morrow may be—or, as the old adage goes, "no one knows to day what to-morrow may bring forth."

For the satisfaction of those who may have relatives and friends in the 18th and 19th Alabama Regiments, I would state that they are here—but as to the number of troops here, if I knew precisely, it might not be expedient for me to state. Those of the 18th, with whom I am acquainted, I believe are well, but I have not seen the 19th since they came here.[55]

There may be those of your readers who do not know where Corinth is situated. To such I would say, it is in the upper part of Tishamingo county—5 or 6 miles from the Tennessee line—where the Mobile and Ohio Railroad crosses the Memphis and Charleston road, in a very fertile section; but a very low, flat, muddy country—or appears so to those who have been so long in the sandy regions of the coast.—The regiment to which Capt. Geo. Forney's company is attached passed out the road towards Memphis on the 7th inst., and the one to which the Old Calhoun Guards belong went the same direction the next day. I did not see them, but several of our boys did, and they were looking finely, anxious for a fight; which anxiety will doubtless be gratified in a short time. For everything betokens a fight; and if the Yankees don't change their position, and "right about march," in a few days "some-body's going to be injured." I could give very obvious reasons for such a conclusion, but as it may not be prudent to do so, I will withhold them for the time. But suffice it to say, that those of our friends who may feel solicitous for our well being, need not be shocked or surprised to hear of our being "in at the ball."

Although I, unlike some of the boys I have seen and heard of, do not feel any great desire to get into a "muss," with the Yankees, I do not, like some other illustrious friends, "feel my courage gradually oozing out through my fingers' ends," but feel calmer and more determined "to do or die" the nearer I approach the conflict, and I believe this is the prevailing sentiment throughout the camps.[56]

We are very vigilant—pickets, scouts &c, are continually on the alert—our sentinels are more careful and explicitly instructed, and parties of men are continually travelling on the cars, while others are posted all along the the [sic] roads to examine passengers, and see that nothing goes wrong.

Some of our advanced pickets had a little skirmish with the enemy's gun boats on the Tennessee river on the 3[d] inst., in which we suffered but little; but nothing has occurred since. Some of their spies are picked up occasionally and brought into town—just enough to keep our boys employed, and give them encouragement.[57] This is the busiest little place now I ever saw, in the way of a stir, —cars are arriving and departing at almost every hour in the day and night— dashing by and whistling continually.

I would close this lengthy, and I fear disinteresting epistle; but cannot get my consent to do so, without paying a passing but merited compliment to the ladies of Mississippi. This State proves to be as productive of heroines as heroes. True patriotism and loyalty are exhibited by them on all occasions. The daughters of Mississippi are as noble, brave and patriotic as her true and gallant sons, of whom the world speaks in such high praise. And they are no less beautiful and patriotic than they are heroic, and the fair daughters of Alabama need not be surprised if they are somewhat neglected by their lovers, if they have any in the 25th, 19th or 18th, while in this State; for such rare beauty and loveliness are calculated to fascinate the truest hearts, and while moving within the orbs of a such brilliant constellation, it will be no wonder if they forget for a time, that there are other lights which seemed once to obscure all others with their brilliant lustre, or that there are other hearts to which they have sworn eternal love.

For example of their patriotism and loyalty, I will give one or two of a thousand instances. As we came up the road, the train stopped at a little station for a few minutes—it was raining hard—and while there one of these noble, self-sacrificing creatures came to the cars with a bundle of warm woolen socks, which she had knit. Some of the boys, supposing she had them for sale, began to offer to buy them. She seemed mortified, and said, "Those who are able to buy socks can get them elsewhere; mine are not for sale, but to give to those who need them, and have not the money to buy them with;" and she gave them to such. While she was engaged in this charitable work, her little children were filling our canteens with water. Her husband was then in the house a cripple for life, from a wound received upon the battle-field, fighting for his home, his wife and those little children. God bless this noble woman—I wish I knew her name—and those children! Who would not be a soldier and fight for her and her little ones? How are they? How peaceful their repose when they retire at night knowing they have been engaged in such a noble work during the day, even in giving the weary, poor, thirsty soldier water to drink! God—their Heavenly Father—whose name they doubtless lisp each night—will send ministering angels to watch over their couch as they sleep, and will care for them through life; for He will never forsake such good and noble beings.

A few miles below this place, seated, in a reflective and melancholly [sic] mood, was one of those beautiful and lovely beings who excite admiration in all who behold them, whose father and lover had both been take prisoners at the battle of Fort Donelson. They were among those noble Mississippians who stood at the point of the bayonet, and pulled down the flag of truce three times when it was hoisted by their comrades.[58] As the train passed she threw our boys the following note:

To some dear soldier,

"You are going to fight for liberty. May Angels guard you. Yes, go, and redeem our loss at Fort Donelson. My lover is a prisoner, but it is not because he is not brave. I want you to go and release him. Cheer up brave boys, and may Heaven protect you. God bless the noble soldiers, and bring them back to their homes and loved ones again."

Her name was signed in full; but I do not feel at liberty to publish it. It seems to me it would be a pleasure, even in a dark Northern prison, to have the assurance of the devotion of one so lovely—so constant. Who would not fight for such a sweetheart.

Our boys will rescue her lover at the point of the bayonet if an opportunity presents itself.

TOM

Tom's letter superbly illustrates the feelings that animated him and so many others gathered around Confederate campfires in the spring of 1862. Above and beyond considerations of states' rights, tariffs and slavery were more concrete realities: their land literally was being overrun and their loved ones exposed to occupation, humiliation, and ruin. Tom's choice of anecdotes likewise provides the modern-day reader a telling insight into the way that the men in gray perceived such threats. They were products of a society that idolized womanly virtue, even as they maintained a degree of female subordination that seems oppressive by today's standards. A corollary of Southerners' idolization of women and womanly virtues was their emphasis on a man's personal honor, which was tied to a fierce sense of personal independence and placed a high premium on physical bravery. The idea that their women would be subjected to "insult," as Southerners typically phrased it, personalized the sense of danger and magnified the sense of mission that characterized so many of these soldiers. Tom couched these concepts in a manner that identifies him clearly as a member of the South's social elite, but his flowery turn of phrase was of a kind that resonated with a great many men from humbler social and economic circumstances. Although desertion and draft evasion would later make it clear that many Southerners, especially poor ones, rejected part or all of the secessionist program, the duration and tenacity of the Confederate war effort evidence that many more felt keenly the threats which Tom Mangham portrayed in his letter home.[59] As he composed his missive, the soldiers in ranks at Corinth, Richmond, Savannah, Mobile and elsewhere were volunteers to a man. With their firesides threatened, the men of the 25th Alabama nerved themselves for the contest that seemed inevitable if the "Yankees don't change their position, and 'right about march'."[60]

Tom Mangham had read the handwriting on the wall when he predicted that, within a few days, "some-body's going to be injured." When his letter was published in his uncle's newspaper on March 27, 1862, it was only ten days until Confederate and Union forces collided near the hamlet of Pittsburg Landing on the Tennessee River. In two days that shook the warring populations to their very roots, more than 23,000 men and boys fell killed, wounded, or prisoner. This holocaust exacted a higher price in blood than the combined totals attributed to every war, battle, and skirmish fought on the American continent to that time, in ironic contrast to the fact that it took its name from a humble whitewashed meeting-house dedicated to the brotherhood of man. Its name was Shiloh.[61]

*　　*　　*　　*　　*

The men of the 25th Alabama had come to Corinth to help protect the critical railroad junction that Tom identified in his letter. As a glance at any map of Southern railroads in 1860 will show, the Mobile and Ohio Railroad and the Memphis and Charleston line comprised critical arteries pumping the life's blood of the Confederacy. Connecting Kentucky with the Gulf and the Trans-Mississippi with the Atlantic seaboard, these railroads were critical to commerce and military movement within the South. Grant's victories at Forts Henry and Donelson had brought Federal armies into southern Tennessee just above Corinth, and threatened not only the crucial railways, but also a penetration along the Tennessee River across northern Alabama to the great rail hub at Chattanooga. Indeed, early February saw Union gunboats push all the way up the Tennessee past Florence, Alabama, where they captured several steamers and forced the destruction of numerous others.[62]

Since the Union penetrations along the Tennessee and Cumberland Rivers threatened to divide his forces and disembark a Federal army in his rear, Lieut. Gen. Albert Sidney Johnston was forced to pull his army back from Kentucky and middle Tennessee. As Johnston pulled back, he sent Lieut. Gen. Pierre Gustave Toutant Beauregard, the hero of Bull Run, to organize the defense of the Mississippi River

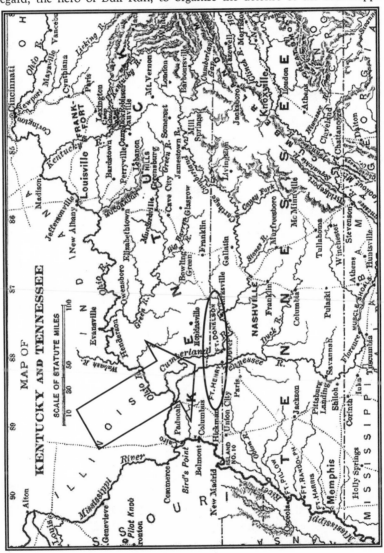

CONQUEST OF FORTS HENRY AND DONELSON OPENS UP THE
CONFEDERATE HEARTLAND TO INVASION.

125

valley. The Creole general quickly began lobbying for troops from Deep South governors, who responded by sending forces to concentrate around Corinth, Mississippi. Leading the way to the critical rail junction was Braxton Bragg, who had volunteered ten regiments from his Mobile and Pensacola garrisons.[63]

Although Bragg's troops had a reputation for drill and discipline that made them the envy of other commanders, Sgt. Maj. Tom Mangham and his comrades in the 25th Alabama must have presented a ragged appearance by early April 1862. Upon their arrival in March, Bragg had pushed them north into Tennessee to secure Bethel Station against a Federal force of unknown intentions on the Tennessee River, while Confederate forces at Corinth started digging in. The spring rains had turned the roads into swampy morasses, and the soaking wet Alabamians got little benefit from the rigorous exercise of plowing through the muddy Tennessee backwoods. To the contrary, they suffered terribly from exposure, and the attendant pulmonary illnesses

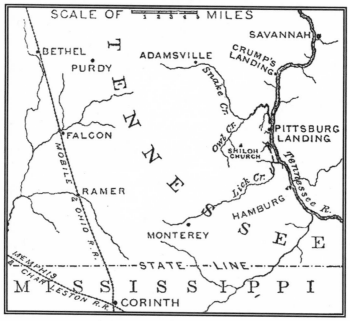

THE BATTLE OF SHILOH, APRIL 6-7, 1862.

doubtless laid low many men who had made the trip from Mobile. Measles also continued to plague the Alabamians, and Captain Costello's Company K alone had forty-five men prostrated with the virulent disease on March 12.[64]

The massive concentration of reinforcements flooding into Corinth impressed Grant as merely defensive in nature, and this ignorance of his true peril permeated down to his junior commanders. Ensconced in ill-deployed camps outside of Pittsburg Landing, the Federal troops had little apprehension of a possible enemy attack. The clumsy and noisy Confederate concentrations in late March and early April seemed certain to give away the element of surprise,[65] and General Beauregard actually determined to cancel the attack while in conversation with Generals Polk, Bragg and Breckenridge. Johnston overruled him, however, ending the debate with the words: "Gentlemen, we attack at daylight tomorrow." Walking away from the group, he emphasized "I would fight them if they were a million." The next dawn, April 6, 1862, brought sharp skirmishing as his marshaling troops encountered enemy scouts. Unbeknownst to the Union commanders, it portended a truly nightmarish day.[66]

As Confederate forces moved against the roughly semicircular Federal position before seven o'clock that morning, Prentiss's Union division took position across the Eastern Corinth Road in front of Spain Field, on the left flank. After an hour's combat to their right, Prentiss decided to pull back to the north edge of the field and change front to the right to support the buckling line there, while Miller's brigade and two artillery batteries protected his left at the Spain Field. As his units were reorienting themselves to their right, those near the field saw a wave of light blaze from the woods to their front. It was the sunlight reflecting from hundreds of musket barrels, carried at right shoulder shift by a long line of men dressed in earthen tones of brown and gray.[67] These men were troops of Gladden's Brigade, which had pushed forward on the extreme right flank of the Confederate army. The men from Wisconsin and Illinois were "seeing the elephant" for the first time, and many began blazing away without orders at Gladden's Alabama and Louisiana troops. After firing only a few rounds, however, Prentiss's earlier order to pull back to the northern edge of the field reached Miller's men. Pulling back in the face of the first Confederate attack they ever faced, Miller's greenhorns began falling into confusion. One Michigan regiment had marched to the front without ammunition for their Austrian rifles, so they stood at order arms and absorbed bullets helplessly, unable to answer the fire. The 18th Wisconsin and most of the 18th Missouri fell apart in headlong rout as they withdrew across Spain Field, but their musketry and the supporting fire of the two batteries exacted a heavy toll before they broke.[68]

One of these supporting batteries was Hickenlooper's 5th Ohio Independent Battery, a Cincinnati outfit equipped with four six-pounder rifles and two six-pounder smoothbores. Along with Munch's 1st Minnesota Battery, they blasted explosive shells into Gladden's men during the initial assault. One shell nearly ripped off Gladden's left arm as he rode behind the line of battle formed by the 305 men of Colonel Loomis's 25th Alabama Regiment. Since the sergeant major's prescribed position was behind the left flank of the regimental line of battle, Gladden probably fell just yards from where Tom marched behind the junior officers and sergeants who served as file closers. The mortally wounded Mexican War veteran was replaced by Col. Dan Adams of the 1st Louisiana. Waving the Pelican flag of his regiment, Adams led the brigade back into the field against a rising tide of Federal musketry. Every thirty seconds, one of Hickenlooper's guns cut loose with a blast of canister. By the time the charging Confederates reached the middle of the Spain Field, the Ohioans were frantically ramming two cans of the lethal slugs down the gaping muzzles of their guns. Priming the vents and jumping clear of the recoil, they blasted double canister into the howling faces, each shotgun-like discharge spraying fifty-four one-inch slugs in a lethal sheet of iron.[69]

Captain Pierre Costello of the 25th Alabama had written his wife a month previously that the soldiers' "registered vow is that this shall be the crowning victory of the war," and the men now acted as though they meant to back up Costello's claim. Hickenlooper's gunners desperately changed front at Prentiss's order when the Alabamians surged right up to their guns, screaming the Rebel yell as they came. Hickenlooper recalled that the sound "caused an involuntary thrill of terror to pass like an electric shock through even the bravest hearts." The shrieking Southerners were black-faced from gunpowder and grime as they reached the guns, and the first man there was Pvt. John Vann of the Ashville Blues. Vann captured the battery color bearer's horse, and his comrades unleashed a withering volley of musketry that downed all twenty-four horses of Lieutenant Blackburn's left gun section in a writhing mass. The 25th Alabama overran Blackburn's two immobilized guns, as Hickenlooper's men struggled desperately to get the other four out of harm's way. Somehow they succeeded, despite a hail of fire that dropped another thirty-five horses, leaving the battery only twenty-one able to pull the guns.[70]

Although the 25th Alabama suffered severe casualties in the melee at Spain Field, they helped smash a gaping hole in the Federal left, and only paused after fighting their way through the camps of the fleeing enemy. A soldier in the 26th Alabama noted that the camps of Miller's brigade were strewn thickly with dead and wounded Federals, who "were mangled in every conceivable form." Only the 18th Missouri and a portion of the 18th Wisconsin retained their organization in the flight; the rest of Miller's brigade withered under the impact of the attack by Gladden's Brigade, which was assisted near the end by Chalmers's Mississippians. Prentiss's whole division was virtually wrecked, and the remnants were fleeing for Pittsburg Landing. Many would fight again that day, but not as a coherent unit.[71]

After a short halt in Miller's encampment, Colonel Adams moved the brigade forward again several hundred yards to the verge of Daniel Davis's wheat field and Sarah Bell's cotton field, where two fresh Union brigades under Brig. Gen. Stephen Hurlbut were arriving just in the nick of time. Here, a half-mile beyond Miller's camps, Hurlbut's men and some artillery were the only thing between three Confederate brigades and the Tennessee River, and a hard-fought artillery duel and long-range musketry contest held them up for about an hour. Later that morning, Jackson's and Chalmers's Confederate brigades were shifted elsewhere, leaving the 25th Alabama and the remnants of their brigade facing Hurlbut. The tired Alabama and Louisiana troops were unable to push through this fresh resistance, and additional Union troops continued to arrive.[72]

Along with the remnants of Prentiss's returning men, these bluecoats rapidly built up a line that would become known as the "Hornets' Nest." Vicious fighting ensued there through the remainder of the morning and much of the afternoon, which saw a series of Confederate brigades fling themselves in desperate, uncoordinated attacks against the Federal line. In all likelihood, the 25th Alabama participated in some of these charges, but the accidents of battle (including the wounding of Colonel Adams) caused the brigade to splinter into several pieces, each of which continued the fight independently. The first three assaults against the Hornets' Nest line featured Cheatham's Tennesseeans and Gibson's Louisiana brigade. The latter swept up into the Union line and engaged in ferocious hand-to-hand combat, and there shot down almost every horse and gunner remaining in Hickenlooper's 5th Ohio Battery, before ebbing back in the face of a deadly fire which heaped them up in piles. These Louisianians bestowed the famous "Hornets' Nest" nickname on the enemy stronghold, and the blood they spilled there backed up their claim.[73]

The desperate contest continued to grow as both sides marched more and more units to the sound of the guns, and the unrelenting pressure bent the Federal line into a U-shaped line. Braxton Bragg found the 25th Alabama and other remnants of Gladden's Brigade resting near the Manse George cabin, and hurled them into an assault that almost overran the 3rd Iowa Regiment, which stood in an exposed position in the woods. The close quarters fighting saw the Iowa officers using their pistols against the Alabamians, but the bitter Midwesterners soon "beheld the enemy's hated flag floating above the house," and the Southerners had overrun Myer's Ohio Battery in the process. Another piece of the shrinking Federal perimeter was gone. After more hard fighting, the outgunned defenders were brought to bay at about 5:30 that evening. Over two thousand exhausted men shuffled into captivity, as fighting came to a halt on this portion of the Union line.[74]

With about an hour of daylight remaining, all that was left between the victorious Confederates and the Tennessee River was a line of guns and men known as "Grant's Last Line." His right had crumpled under a series of blows like those that had smashed his left, so this makeshift line was Grant's sole remaining hope. Initial Confederate probes brought on a storm of cannon fire from field and siege artillery emplacements, as well as a terrifying barrage of heavy mortar fire from Union gunboats on the river. General Beauregard, commanding Confederate forces after Johnston was mortally wounded, believed that the disorganization and exhaustion of his forces dictated a cessation of the attack for the day. After all, Grant's battered remnants would still be ripe for the plucking in the morning.[75]

Had Beauregard been able to see the seven to ten thousand Federal skulkers jamming the riverbanks at Pittsburg Landing, he would have been reinforced in his conviction that little more than mopping up remained for his victory to be complete. Many, perhaps most, of Grant's men felt the same way. One man who considered Grant's men little more than whipped curs was Union Brig. Gen. William "Bull" Nelson, who landed at Pittsburg Landing about four o'clock that afternoon. With his craft almost immersed by a panicked mob shouting "We're whipped!" and "The fight is lost!", the disgusted Nelson barked an order to his staff: "Gentlemen, draw your sabers and trample these bastards into the mud!—Charge!"[76]

Behind Nelson's staff came the 36th Indiana, the vanguard of a reinforcing army under Maj. Gen. Don Carlos Buell.[77] Nobody on the fighting line knew it, but Grant's salvation was at hand. As thousands of Buell's troops crossed the river that night, the tide turned irrevocably. Although it took hard fighting the next day to reverse the course of the battle, the outnumbered, disorganized, and exhausted Confederates were unable to stand up against a fresh army determined to win. The 25th Alabama took part in some sharp fighting on the right flank near the Davis wheat field, spending much of the day alongside a Missouri Confederate regiment, since Gladden's Brigade was badly fragmented in the previous day's melee.[78] Overall, however, the powerful Union reinforcements proved more than equal to the task. By mid-afternoon, the overwhelming force in his front had convinced Beauregard to break contact and withdraw his army to Corinth while it remained intact.

It was a stunning reversal of roles unlike any other that occurred during the war, and the failure of the Confederate counteroffensive at Shiloh set the stage for the fall of New Orleans and the eventual Federal reconquest of the Mississippi River. One wonders to what extent this debacle also set the stage for so many battles fought by the Confederacy's western army, where hard-fought battlefield victories remained barren of results, and close-run battles caused Southern commanders to concede the initiative to their enemies and pull back.

All of these post-mortems remained in the future, however, as men of Beauregard's Army of the Mississippi wrote home proudly of their hard-fought victory on the first day at Shiloh. One of those was Lt. William J. Borden of the 25th Alabama, whose April 10 letter to the Jacksonville *Republican* evinced nothing so much as pride in his regiment's success:

> Thinking that you might have an interest in all the Calhoun boys, I write to give you the particulars of the fight at Monterey on the 6th and 7th inst. As you already know we have had a most terrible engagement here. The contending armies were composed of western men and southern farmers, both of whom had learned the use of fire arms in boyhood. They too, had been taught to believe they had no superiors in marksmanship. After manoeuvering for several days the opposing armies were drawn up face to face, presenting the appearance of two winding columns nearly six miles in length. The hour of suspense was upon us all. Scarce four hundred yards separated the combatants. Our brigade (Gen. Gladden's) occupied the centre, and our regiment had the honor of carrying the Brigade battle flag, which was gallantly borne aloft between the companies from Calhoun and St. Clair. Ten thousand glistening bayonets shown [sic] in the morning sun—ten thousand hearts beat high with the fate of an infant nation—ten thousand strong arms were nerved for the contest; and scarce had time elapsed for our brave boys to think of home, father, mother, wife and babes and utter an earnest prayer to the God of battles, when ran along the lines the ominous word "forward!" and soon the foe poured a deadly fire upon us, we also halted and returned the fire with destructive precision. Scarce half a dozen rounds had been fired when again the word "forward!" rang out with clarion notes from the lips of our gallant Colonel. Advancing near one hundred and

fifty yards, again, above the crack of the rifle and roar of musketry, that well known voice was heard, "Charge, my men, Charge!" With a shout of triumph our boys charged the flying foe until they had fled near half a mile. All our troops fought well, but the little 25th was first in the charge; and first to take possession of the enemy's camp, and last to leave the chase. We took a few moments rest, but soon the enemy was discovered reforming his broken lines, and planting a battery in our front. Gen. Gladden gave orders to attack them in their new position. We were at them again and ere long, in the face of ten thousand deadly rifles; and the missiles of death from their long parrot guns, we were in full charge at them, and soon drove them from their position, in hot haste, and captured one of their finest batteries. In this charge Gen. Gladden had his left arm shot nearly off and even while the old heroe's [sic] was dangling by his side he waved his cap in triumph to the little 25th. The battle raged along our whole lines throughout the day; the enemy always retreating before us. The 25th during the fight made seven successful charges, always against double and sometimes tripple [sic] their number. I must mention that in one of the charges, Private Vann of the "Ashville Blues" ran forward, captured the banner horse of the 5th Ohio battery. Private Sullivan of the "Mountain Guards," was sent forward to reconnoitre, and soon returned with an artillery horse and equipments, having taken him from a battery near their lines, directly under the fire the [sic] of their guns.[79]

Late in the afternoon, when our men nearly exhausted, from hunger fatigue and thirst, and all but 82 of the 25th were either wounded or worn out, Gen. Bragg ordered it alone to charge about two thousand Federals in an underwood, Col. Loomis having retired from the field on account of a severe wound, our Major the gallant Geo. D. Johnston of the 4th Ala said to Gen. Bragg, "Sir I have but 82 men, nearly worn down by fatigue." "No difference" replied Gen. Bragg, "make the charge." They did make that charge and put the vaunting two thousand, to instant flight.[80] In short, veterans never fought better than the 25th Ala. Most of our troops fought well, but this little reg't. was first in the fight, and last out—was in every charge, and assisted in taking every battery taken by the brigade; and when by accident any one of the Reg't was cut off from his command, he would fall into another regiment or brigade and fight on. Each seem to have adopted Ned Ruffins' policy at Charleston, when asked what command he belonged to, replied, "wherever there is room."[81] The company from St. Clair lost but one man killed instantly, and the Calhoun company had none killed, but both had several wounded. Our loss in killed and wounded I suppose is near five thousand, that of the enemy in killed wounded and prisoners must be near twenty-thousand, and their loss of Government property about five millions of dollars. The Federals will never attack Corinth, while we have an army. We in my opinion, will have but few more fights in this war. I know they are very tired of us, and now since their best army, (the finest in the world) has been so cut up, I do think they will get some sense. I write this, not for publication but for your own use. If you find any part or fact of importance, I have no objection to your publishing it.

Very truly, &c

W. J. Borden

In the same issue was a letter from Wiley Mangham, who had hastened to Corinth to check on his brother and their friends in the Ashville Blues. Just as in Borden's letter, Wiley's of April 20 offers the *Republican*'s readers no intimation that Shiloh was viewed as a defeat for the South:

> I arrived here on Friday the 18th inst., and found the boys very much fatigued having just re-returned [sic] from Monterey—a distance of ten miles from this place, in the direction of Shiloh. They describe the battle as being furious.
>
> Capt. Morris, who is now in command of Co. D. of 25th Ala. Vols., commanded said company in the engagement both days—(Sunday and Monday) losing one man and having eight others wounded, all on Sunday, and no one hurt on Monday.
>
> Capt. Morris was with his men both days, and acted so as to gain the esteem of all. It is useless for me to speak of Captain Morris' meritorious conduct, for all who know him, know him to be a noble fellow.[82]
>
> Lieut. R. A. Green, of the Ashville Blues was wounded in the foot, but I hope it is not very serious. Lieut. Hayden was in the engagement on Sunday, and came out unhurt.[83]
>
> I now take this opportunity of informing your readers that the 25th Ala. Regiment crowned herself with glory as well as the 21st. The 25th took the celebrated 5th Ohio battery, and assisted in taking several others.
>
> John W. Vann of the Ashville Blues captured the color-bearer's horse of the 5th Ohio Battery.
>
> The man killed of the Ashville Blues was Preston C. Pinson, he was shot through the bowels—he lived till some time Sunday night—he said he had rather die that way than any other. He was a good soldier, ready always to do his part. The members of the Ashville Blues buried him decently. His kindred and friends have the sympathy of the company.
>
> I have just received the intelligence of the death of Joseph Mauldin, a member of the Ashville Blues.

Yours &c.

WILEY

More than a month passed before Tom Mangham wrote to the *Republican* again, and this time he did so as first lieutenant of the Ashville Blues. Commissioned on May 6, it is probable that Tom earned promotion by his meritorious service as regimental sergeant major at Shiloh; had his conduct been found wanting, he never would have earned promotion over others who had done well. After all, the 25th Alabama had lost thirteen killed and seventy-five wounded of the 305 men engaged at Shiloh, and

132

claimed to have made "eight different and distinct charges." In the process, they claimed three stands of Federal colors and helped capture four enemy batteries. As Tom pointed out in his letter, the regiment also had fought a series of skirmishes at Farmington in the meantime, in which they helped stop the Union advance against Corinth. In the process, he took the opportunity of schooling his readers on a point of military procedure that showed a typical Confederate officer's concern for points of honor; namely, let nobody doubt that the Ashville Blues alone were the color company of the 25th Alabama Regiment. Although Tom was a hot-blooded secessionist who demanded his just due as a gentleman of honor, it is instructive to see that he made his point in a way that granted the Calhoun company its full measure of respect for the danger it shared in line of battle.[84]

All in all, Tom's treatment of this situation was absolutely congruent with Southerners' views of an officer's duty to his men, for they certainly expected officers to insist upon all rights and privileges due the unit, and woe betide the officer who failed in this responsibility. Likewise, Tom's response to Federal outrages in occupied New Orleans provides a window into the minds and mores of Southerners of that era, and his reaction was certainly typical. General Butler's directive regarding the ladies of the Crescent City created an uproar throughout the country, and it struck at the very heart of many Confederate soldiers' core motivation: the defense of their loved ones:

Camp of the 25th Ala. Reg't
Corinth, Miss., May 21st, '62,
Dear Republican:

I hardly know what to write, as each day brings forth something "startling" and "full-grown" which was never dreamed of the day previous. But as the address of the Rev. Dr. Palmer, of New Orleans, and the publishing of Picayune Butler's infamous order, relative to the treatment of the ladies of the Crescent City, have created quite a sensation in our army, food for comment has been furnished those who desire to scribble for newspapers.

The Rev. Dr. Palmer, whose name is already familiar to most of your readers as one of the ablest divines of this continent, it was announced would address the army of the Mississippi at 11 o'clock yesterday morning, at, or near the encampment of the 25th Alabama. It was not announced what the subject of the discourse would be, nor was such an announcement necessary to inspire all with a desire to hear him. It was 10 when we received notice;—in 15 minutes nearly all of the men of the 25th Ala. were in lines to proceed to the place designated, where we soon arrived and found a rude log rostrum, formed of oak logs, for the accommodation of the speaker. It was soon mounted by the distinguished orator who entertained an immense audience of soldiery, in that strain of eloquence which can fall only from the lips of such a man as Palmer, upon such an occasion, and inspired by such a religious and patriotic devotion. He deplored the condition of the ladies of his own native city, and appealed to us to save our own people from the insult and injury to which his were exposed, (here he read the disgraceful order of the infamous and villainous Butler, subjecting those so near and dear to him to the treatment of "women of the town, plying their avocation;")[85] and many a manly bosom was seen to heave with emotions of sympathy, and many eyes were moistened with the 'briny tear.' I could see the fire of indignation burning in every eye, and the spirit of revenge mirrored in every countenance. Can such insults to innocent virtue be borne by such lovers of virtue and innocence as compose the soldiery and citizens of the Confederate States? I think not. Such acts of barbarity will convert us into fiends and nev-[er] will we submit to such injury until the earth shall have drunk the last drop of Southern blood. I know this is the case with the army at Corinth, and hope it is with the citizens at home. Citizens, it may be that you will have an awful responsibility resting upon your shoulders ere this conflict shall end[.] If our army should be overridden here, and the invader pour his hordes of brutal soldiery down upon our homes it will be your sacred and imperative duty to defend from insult and rapine your sacred domicile and those of your soldiers.

I am highly gratified to see the effect of the following just and commendable order published by Gen. Beauregard. It inspires a feeling of honor and aspiration never before exhibited in our ranks:

Headqr's Western Departments.

Corinth, Miss., May 18 '62

General Orders No. 43

I. To do full justice to the private soldier, who is seldom accorded his meed of praise, and who rarely receives full credit for his gallant deeds; and to place him in this respect, more nearly on an equality with the commissioned officer, the commander of the forces has determined to distribute a badge of merit, in person, in the presence of the troops, to every officer and every private soldier who shall greatly distinguish himself in any engagement with the enemy.

II. This badge will have inscribed upon it, the name of the battle in which it was won. During the war it will be a proud testimonial of the wearer's heroism, and will place his name upon the list of those entitled to promotion in the army; when the invader is driven back, and our independence secured, it will gloriously prove his title to the gratitude of his countrymen, and to the highest civic honors.

III. Commanders of corps, divisions, brigades, regiments and companies, will immediately after each engagement, carefully report their bravest men to a military commission, to be appointed for that purpose, upon whose report that their conduct has been *preeminently* brave, they will receive the reward of their patriotism at the hands of their General.

G. T. BEAUREGARD

General Commanding

(Official)

F. H. Jordan, A. A. G.

The boys of of [sic] the 25th are all aspirants for the badge, and I hope to be able to chronicle the fact to you soon, not only of there being many badges awarded to our reg't., but that our flag also has inscribed upon it, in golden letters, the name of the impending battle. And while upon the subject of the flag, I would correct a probable unintentional, error of Lt. Bordon [sic] in regard to it. The error has been repeated by him, or I would never have noticed it. He states that the honor of being color company is divided between the two companies from St. Clair and Calhoun Counties, or makes that impression whether he makes the positive assertion or not, which is a mistake; the St. Clair company alone is the color company—it being the "right centre company"—and the Calhoun boys have no right to the color, unless its being the "left centre company", and consequently touching the St. Clair company on the left where the colors are carried, entitles them to that honor. All military men know that the colors belong exclusively to the "right centre company" and maneuvers accordingly—the colors are to remain with this company and be borne with it wherever it goes, no matter who carries them. The ensign or color bearer, is selected from the sergeants of a regiment, and if taken from another company, is attached to the "right centre company" in action, upon drill or dress parades. This of course does not remove honor from the "left centre company" of being exposed to as much danger as the color company; for when the regiment is not divided into two independent battalions in action, its close proximity to the colors exposes it to all the dangers of the company who carries them. The colors are now carried by a private of the St. Clair company, (Benj. F. Smith,) who volunteered to carry them at Farmington. They were borne upon the battlefield of Shiloh by Rob't. Stringfellow, (a native of St. Clair, but a member of Capt. Turners [sic] company of Talladega,) until he was wounded, and they were then taken up by one of the Calhoun boys.

To judge from orders received, from "These Head Quarters" yesterday evening, one would suppose we were upon the eve of an important battle—which is that we be ready, with five days cooked ration, to go into "bivouac" at 6 o'clock this evening—but we have been ordered so often lately, and only got into skirmishes occasionally that we are never certain of anything important. I hear tremendous cannonading in the direction of Monterey, about 3 miles distant probably. After this is over, if I survive, you will hear from me again.

Health is some better than when I last wrote; but we are actually suffering for vegetables, and if our friends along the road between this place and Mobile, could furnish us with them, they would be well paid for their trouble and receive the thanks of many grateful hearts.

The Republican of the 15th inst., is the only copy of that paper I have received for at least two months.

TOM.

The cannonading that Tom heard as he wrote this letter came from the latest skirmish outside the Corinth defenses, but no climactic battle ever came to pass. After the regiment participated in further sharp skirmishing near Bridge Creek on the Monterey Road on May 28 and 29, it pulled back fifty-two miles to Tupelo with the rest of Beauregard's army. The steadily encroaching Union forces under General Halleck had convinced the Creole general that he could not break the siege of Corinth, so he skillfully withdrew his forces to prevent their envelopment. Clearly, there was no point in sacrificing his army to defend the once-vital railroad center, since Union forces already had occupied Memphis to the north and New Orleans to the south, as well as Huntsville, Alabama, to the east. The Confederacy's best hope lay not in defending Corinth, but in preserving the field army that could redeem its conquered lands.[86]

As both armies caught their collective breath that summer, Tom remained with the regiment in Tupelo, acting much of the time as commanding officer of the Ashville Blues. Major changes were in the offing, however, as President Davis relieved Beauregard in mid-June due to his displeasure over the retreat from Corinth, as well as a misunderstanding over the general's subsequent convalescent leave near Mobile. Davis appointed Braxton Bragg to command the army, and he immediately initiated harsh measures designed to whip the conglomeration of units into shape. Bragg was indeed talented as an organizer and trainer, but his hard-bitten Regular Army brand of discipline smacked of tyranny to many of the independent spirits under his command. When he lined up his units to watch firing squads dispense leaden justice to deserters, many rebelled at his apparent heartlessness. Despite widespread resentment, however, Bragg's methods increased the army's efficiency in rapid order. Every improvement was critical, too, for Bragg was about to take his army on a daring offensive to regain middle Tennessee, liberate Kentucky, and perhaps invade Ohio![87]

The great movement got underway in August, as the army moved to Chattanooga in preparation for the offensive. The 25th Alabama was encamped at Camp Loomis, and a muster roll for the Ashville Blues shows that twenty-eight of its 72 officers and men were absent due to sickness or wounds, while one other man was absent without leave. One of the sick was First Lt. Tom Mangham, who apparently remained at his home throughout the month of August. Bragg, however, was set to launch the army across the Tennessee River on August 28, and Tom felt the lash of Bragg's uncompromising discipline on the previous day: he was dismissed from the service for absence without leave.[88]

Had he requested a furlough extension and been denied? Was his application misrouted, or his doctor's recommendation rejected by military authorities? Had he submitted his resignation and believed it was approved, as he later testified? Or had he simply overstayed his leave? Unfortunately, it is impossible to determine whether his dismissal was warranted or not. In all probability, however, the hot-blooded secessionist believed himself a victim of injustice, for his subsequent actions evidenced his continued support for the Confederate cause and his antipathy towards those who sought to avoid military service.[89]

Wiley obviously felt the same way, for just a month after Tom's dismissal, he dashed off a quick letter from Jacksonville, Alabama. Dated September 28, 1862, he addressed it to "Gen. George W. Randolph, Secretary of War, Richmond, Va.":

> Sir:—I have the honor to ask of you the authority to raise a company of Partisan Rangers (Cavalry), as there are a great many men in this section of the country between the ages of 35 & 45.
>
> I think it proper, however, to state that I have served five months in the Confederate Army as a Lieut., and have some experience in the matter.
>
> Address Wiley P. Mangham, Jacksonville, Ala.

Wiley was one of many throughout the South who sought to serve in such units, which were authorized by the Confederate Congress on April 21, 1862. The "Act to Organize Bands of Partisan Rangers" empowered the president to commission "such officers as he may deem proper with authority to form bands of partisan rangers, in companies, battalions or regiments, either as infantry or cavalry." Although these units were to be "regularly received into service" and paid and disciplined accordingly, they were authorized to be paid full cash value for arms captured from the enemy, much as sailors were entitled to prize money when their ship captured enemy property. Even more enticingly, partisan rangers served in detached units under independent command, free of the rigors of camp life, army bureaucracy, and the steady campaigning faced by the Confederacy's field armies. Wiley wrote his letter just one day after Congress amended the conscription act, extending its provisions to include those from 35 to 45 years of age. He was evidently aware of this amendment, and hoped to obtain authority to enlist men of this age group before they were formally called into regular service. In fact, the War Department received his letter on October 6, almost a full month before the Adjutant and Inspector General's Office issued its General Orders No. 82, implementing the new conscription law.[90]

As historian Albert Burton Moore has noted, however, the Confederacy had more partisan ranger units than it needed by the summer of 1862, so it is not surprising that the War Department simply filed Wiley's request without taking further action. Additional partisan ranger units formed without authority in many localities, making the job of conscription officers even more difficult, as men they sought to enroll claimed to be in service already. Many of these partisan bands, such as Mosby's Rangers, made a significant contribution to the war effort in areas occupied or threatened by Federal forces. Others, however, were little more than brigands operating outside of the law and answerable to neither government, and their major opponents in the Southern states were local militia, state troops, legitimate partisan ranger companies, and leading citizens, banded together for self protection against their rampant depredations.[91]

Wiley and Tom Mangham may have served in such capacities in St. Clair and Calhoun counties in late 1862, given the nature and scope of lawlessness and draft resistance that was developing in the north Alabama hill country. Union forces had occupied much of the northern part of the state in the summertime, burning Gadsden itself on May 2, before Bragg's move into middle Tennessee and Kentucky pushed them back.

Exactly a year later, 1700 Union cavalry raiders under Colonel Abel D. Streight were fighting near Gadsden once more. Departing Nashville in mid-March, they were bound for Rome, Georgia, to disrupt Confederate railroad operations. By the time Streight's men swung past Gadsden on May 2, however, they were nearly worn out. Continually harassed by a small command under Nathan Bedford Forrest, the Federals nonetheless composed a fearsome threat to the various home defense and militia units that found themselves in the way of the onslaught. One of these ad hoc groups was composed of sick soldiers from Rome's military hospitals, as well as a few militiamen and citizens, one of whom was Wiley Mangham. As he recalled it some years later, he had "less fear than discretion" as he crossed the Oostanaula River and "went along with the crowd who were to be slaughtered in the defence of the city of Rome." Observing wryly that many others headed south across the Etowah River as they suddenly determined they "had business in that direction," Wiley had enough military training to know that the city's would-be defenders were in a bad fix. To the rear "was a torn up bridge and the river," with a host of first-class Yankee cavalrymen bearing down on them from the front. He thought it the better part of valor to "cast about for something to assist in riding on the water," since it was obvious that he and his comrades would be scattered by the impending collision. "Imagine our feelings," he related over a quarter-century later, "when a courier rode up and informed us that Gen. Forrest had captured Straight's [sic] entire command." In a stratagem that became part of the legend surrounding the Confederacy's "Wizard of the Saddle," Forrest had bluffed Streight into surrendering to a force one-third the size of his! As Wiley gratefully observed in 1889, "thanks to the strategy of Gen. Forrest we were not sacrificed, and some of us are still living to-day."[92] (See map on page 566.)

When late summer of 1863 found Union Major General Rosecrans maneuvering Bragg out of Tennessee again, Wiley Mangham tendered his services once more:

> Rome, Ga. July 24, 1863
> Hon. James A. Seddon, Secretary of War
> Sir,
> I have the honor to respectfully ask of you the authority to raise a cavalry company to enter the Confederate service for three years or during the war, in the State of Alabama, from all classes conscripts, non conscripts and exempts.
> I have been an officer in the Confederate service, but resigned, and now have a certificate of exemption under the act of Congress.
> Please write me soon at Rome, Ga.
>
> Respectfully Your Obt. Servt.
> /s/ *Wiley P. Mangham*
> I expect to form my company mostly of non conscripts.
> /s/ W.P.M. [93]

Although the War Department's reply does not survive, the endorsement scribbled on Wiley's letter makes it clear that the response was negative: "The department cannot free a commission to raise a new company from conscripts. The acts of conscription appropriate conscripts to the ranks of the old companies—When a company of non conscripts is organized and ready for service it will be accepted, but the department will not free a commission as authority." Since postwar records indicate that Wiley never served in the army after his discharge from the 25th Alabama in January 1862, it is apparent that his attempts to organize partisan ranger or volunteer cavalry companies never reached fruition. Likewise, his medical condition and his draft-exempt status as a newspaperman prevented his involuntary conscription into the army in some other capacity.[94]

The combination of toryism in the hills of north Alabama and the renewed Federal presence in that region probably stimulated Wiley's desire to raise a company, and he probably assisted Tom in his attempts to help enforce conscription laws in St. Clair County. Although it is little remarked in many histories of the war, the struggle between secessionists, Unionists, and draft evaders within Confederate territory was grim evidence of a war within a war. An intriguing letter from a St. Clair man named James Ash demonstrates that Tom was engaged in the nasty infighting that raged outside the limelight of the major battlefields. Ash's account provides rare insight into the harsh realities of conscription in Alabama's hill counties, where the "good men set," including Tom Mangham, mobilized the militia, partisan cavalry bands, and tracking dogs to hunt down deserters and draft evaders and dispense justice:

Branchville, Ala.
Nov. 15th 1863 [95]
Mr. George W. Ash

. . .I reach home on Sunday night after I left you, and commence sowing wheat on Monday and that evening got orders to report up at headquarters next morning at 9 o'clock. . . .So I left next morning. . .went up to headquarters which was old Mrs. Lankford place[96] And there I found the old house a guard house They had the men and women all in a room to gether, and a guard at the door. Some was hawling wood some cutting up beef some cooking and some lofering around doing nothing. I enroll my name And then got leave and went down to Paps and had to be back next morning by Sun up. . . .So that was to be the big day or the day the big raid was to be made on the Blunt mountain.[97] Capt. Frank Morris was to command the sitzens and Liut. Brooks the Cavaldry or his own squad.[98] So Morris call out his men in to a line and I did not goe in so he got all ready and a way he went. And then Lieut. Brooks fill a two horse waggon full of dogs and Arden Sanders to drive it and then whistle for his men and then they started. And now the Corporal call us all in to a line and then pict out twelve men for guards and told the balance to goe home so I was one of them told to goe home so you better believe we got a way quick. . . .We meet all the Springville trash going up. And then we came on a little farther and meet a

Branchville squad and men. we just keep meeting of them untill we got down to John Hardens. . . .The whole county was summons but I don't know whether they all got there or not.

George, they was a commity to be there that day to try all the deserters or to doe something I don't know what hardly. George Vandegrift was there a little while he said they was in the meeting house doing of something of that sort. And it was just as Dr. Lloyd said it would be. They pict their crowed [crowd]. I will give you some of their names. I will commence at God Byers[,] John I Thomason, Judge Turner[,] Thos. Mangham[,] Jackson Philips[,] L.W. Herring[,] Dr. Freeman[,] Willis W. Landford[,] and Wily Truss And the ballance was all just such men. . . .Next Saturday is to be another big day I don't know what they will do, But let me tell you the other day them good men set, or that's what old Byers called them. . . .It is thought by some that they Hang Joe Taylor, but I hope not. Ed byers told me that they was trying to but he [al]lowed to interfear and not let them do it if he could help it. George it is no use to make lawes and have them over run the way they are doing in this country. I don't believe we will have any malitia. For they are a few men in this county that has more power than the governors It is no use to have a governor &c.

George thay have taken up nearly all the women where they have any one out or deserted. . . .So they have a fine house full up at head quarters.[99]

George They aught to be something done with our enrolling officers and Cavaldry if a body only knowed [what] to doe &c. I will hush about our times up here. . . .But I look every day to see if the Sheriff a coming or the Cavaldry one, to hinder us but I do hope they let us a lone this week. . . .[100]

The Mangham brothers continued to voice their support for the Southern cause through the newspaper they owned and edited, the *Ashville Vidette*. Tom had closed down the *St. Clair Diamond* when he, Wiley, and the rest of their staff joined the army in 1861, but the brothers went back into the newspaper business sometime after Tom left the service in 1862. With its very name evoking the image of militant watchfulness, the *Vidette*'s secessionist tone and content made it a natural target for Yankee cavalrymen when Gen. Lovell Rousseau's raiders came to Ashville in July 1864.[101]

Tom and Wiley left town or hid out with most of the rest of the populace, when a cavalry patrol warned them that Rousseau's 2700 horsemen were riding toward Ashville during the night of July 12. These men had departed the Federal garrison at Decatur on July 10, seeking to disrupt Confederate operations in eastern Alabama and western Georgia en route to a junction with General Sherman's army near Atlanta. There was no appreciable opposition to their advance through northern Alabama, and the troopers of the 4th Tennessee (U.S.) Cavalry met no resistance when they charged down Ashville's deserted streets at midnight.[102]

The main body of Rousseau's force entered town at 10:00 a.m. on July 13, and the hungry raiders made quick work of distributing the food supplies they found there. Other men ransacked the jail and post office, while Pvt. John Matz of the 8th Indiana

Cavalry strolled about wearing the cap of a Confederate lieutenant, which very possibly belonged to Tom or Wiley Mangham. One group broke into the offices of the *Ashville Vidette*, where they found that the Mangham brothers had departed in such haste that they had left the coming weekly edition partially typeset, with forms locked into place. The paper featured the text of a recent speech by former Congressman Clement Vallandigham, an Ohio "Copperhead" whose outspoken denunciations of the Lincoln administration and the war led to his expulsion from the United States in 1863. He had returned to Ohio from Canada in June 1864, when his gubernatorial bid evidenced the relative power of the peace movement in much of the war-weary Midwest.[103]

Next to Vallandigham's speech in the *Vidette* was an editorial by the Manghams, who praised him as a "gifted statesman, orator, and patriotic exile." They went on to editorialize:

> It is our desire to see the names of Fernando Wood and C. L. Vallandigham, or some of their co-laborers, placed upon the ticket of that party at the Chicago convention, for President and Vice-President of the United States, supported by such men as Long and Harris; and just in the proportion to the support they receive will the North exhibit signs of returning reason and humanity. If they are elected we expect to have peace, independence, and constitutional liberty.[104]

Rousseau detailed some printers from his unit to commandeer the services of the Manghams' old Smith printing press, which they promptly used to print some blank forms and special orders. Amused at the opportunity to use their typesetting skills against the enemy, some of the Federal troopers proceeded to rewrite the *Vidette*'s front page. Adding a satirical piece lampooning Jefferson Davis and his cabinet as the "offscouring of Goths and Vandals," they also inserted an article entitled "Distinguished Arrival":

> Maj. Gen. L. H. Rousseau, of U.S. Army, paid our town the honor of a visit this morning, accompanied by many of his friends and admirers. The General looks well and hearty. It is not known at present how long he will sojourn in our midst. He expressed himself much pleased with the hospitality and kindness of the citizens of Ashville and the vicinity, and was apparently well satisfied with the manner in which he was entertained.
>
> The Staff of Maj. Gen. L. H. Rousseau, U.S.A., paid our office a visit this morning and kindly assisted us to issue our paper for to-day. . . .[105]

After having their fun at the Manghams' expense, the Federals torched all of the Confederate commissary supplies they could not eat or carry before riding out of town at two o'clock that afternoon. Rousseau's raiders would pass through or near the hometowns of *John Henry Mangham, Solomon R. Mangham,* and *James M. D. Mangham* in the coming days, en route to a rendezvous with Sherman at the gates of Atlanta on July 22. With Grant's Army of the Potomac ensconced in siege lines outside of Petersburg, Virginia, it was clear that the Confederacy had its back to the wall.[106] (See map, p. 566.)

Perhaps Tom Mangham's draft exempt status as a newspaperman expired along with the *Ashville Vidette*, as Wiley loaded their Smith press into a twelve-ox wagon and drove it to safety in Oxford, where he resumed publication until the end of the war. More likely, the fall of Atlanta in early September led Tom to conclude that it was time to go back to the war, as men were needed to fight "to the last ditch." In any event, he traveled to Jacksonville, Alabama, where he found his friend, Col. William H. Forney, now commanding the 10th Alabama Volunteers. On September 19, 1864, Tom Mangham enlisted for the war as a private in his old prewar unit: Company A, the "Ashville Guards."[107]

Within a week, Tom was in Virginia, where he spent a day in a Richmond hospital before returning to duty. Once more in the ranks of the company he had joined in the long ago days of May 1860, he found that many of his old friends were long since gone: killed, wounded, or rendered unfit for duty during three years' hard service in the Army of Northern Virginia. A number of the original commissioned and non-commissioned officers were still in ranks, however, such as Capt. Wilson Brewster, Lt. Samuel Wyatt, and Assistant Quartermaster Thomas Hayden. Tom doubtless enjoyed the long-delayed reunion with his old friends, and must have remembered the disappointment he had felt at Corinth in 1862, when camp rumors about the arrival of the 10th Alabama turned out to be incorrect.[108]

He also may have been struck with the similarity of the tactical situation, as the trenches and sharpshooters at Petersburg certainly evoked memories of the same pests at Corinth in 1862. Tom got his first chance to compare the fighting qualities of the 10th Alabama with his old comrades of the 25th Alabama just a month after his arrival, when generals Grant and Meade launched three army corps into action on October 27. Their intention was to push past Lee's overextended right (western) flank where Hatcher's Run flowed past Dabney's and Burgess's mills, in hopes of cutting the Boydton Plank Road and seizing the South Side Railroad. If successful, this attack would effectively close the ring around Lee's army and bring Federal troops squarely up against Petersburg's inner belt of fortifications (see map on page 512).[109]

The crackle of gunfire along the southwestern portion of the Confederate line that morning announced their readiness to receive the attack of Maj. Gen. John Parke's IX Corps. Even though the defenders' lines were believed to be incomplete and unmanned, it soon became clear that these estimates were sadly mistaken; Warren's V Corps and Hancock's II Corps would have to bear the burden of success. With Parke's men bogged down in what had unexpectedly turned into a frontal attack, Warren and Hancock aimed to sweep west below the southern end of Lee's line, then pivot north to envelop the defenders and seize the railroad. As their units deployed into action against units of A. P. Hill's Corps under the control of Maj. Gen. Henry Heth, the entire line along the Boydton Plank Road began to blaze with gunfire.[110]

Although Hill was sick and unable to exercise field command that day, he directed Maj. Gen. William "Fighting Billy" Mahone to take three brigades from the line north of the Appomattox River and move to the intersection of Cox Road and the Boydton Plank Road. Once there, just below the South Side Railroad tracks, he was to "await further orders." By the time Mahone reached the intersection, however, he could hear that the boom of cannon now punctuated the rattle of musketry near Burgess's Mill. Accordingly, he pushed his brigades south towards the sound of the guns. One of the outfits toiling down the muddy road under Mahone's orders was Sanders's Alabama brigade, comprising the 8th, 9th, 10th, 11th, and 14th Alabama regiments. Unit records document that Pvt. Tom Mangham was in the grayclad ranks of Forney's regiment, and his father's first cousin, *Pvt. William A. Mangham*, probably slogged along in the trail regiment, the 14th Alabama. The veterans of the Ashville Guards were heading into their twenty-ninth engagement of the war; for Tom Mangham, however, it was the first time he had marched toward the guns since the long-ago days of Shiloh, Farmington, and Corinth.[111]

General Heth directed Mahone to move his men down an abandoned road toward the right (northern) flank of Hancock's penetration, which was blocked in front by Wade Hampton's cavalry and to the south by Fitz Lee's troopers. Flailing their way through the swampy undergrowth, Weisiger's Virginia brigade and Sanders's Alabamians emerged about 4:30 p.m. on Hancock's flank. Scattering two regiments that had probed into the woods to scout for lurking rebels, Mahone's men overran Metcalf's battery, pushed back Pierce's brigade, and hauled off the colors of the 5th Michigan, 63rd Pennsylvania, and the 105th Pennsylvania, along with dozens of prisoners. Hancock ordered his men to dig breastworks, but one veteran asked pointedly, "General, which way will you have them face?" The hard-pressed Federals were assailed on all sides, and the survivors bitterly referred to the spot as the Bull Ring or Bull Pen.[112]

Unluckily for Tom and his comrades, however, no supports were readily available to protect Mahone's spearhead brigades. Their penetration into Hancock's flank left them vulnerable in turn to Federal counterattacks, and that is precisely what occurred. Spirited thrusts against Mahone's right and front drove much of his line back in disorder, and nightfall finally caused both sides to stop to catch their breath. Faced with Confederate threats to his flanks and rear, Hancock decided to withdraw that night, despite his inability to evacuate many of his wounded. When the last Federal pickets pulled out just after midnight on October 28, the Battle of Burgess's Mill was over. Hancock's II Corps suffered more than a thousand casualties that day, and Federal losses totaled 1758. Confederate losses in the sharp combat exceeded 1300, although the Ashville Guards suffered only one man wounded of the twenty-five in ranks. What Tom Mangham saw that day began to convince him that "General Billy" was a "brave soldier and a good general," which might have helped prepare him for Lee's subsequent employment of Mahone's men in one tactical emergency after another.[113]

Although Grant reported that Hancock's action had been a successful reconnaissance in force, few participants in the heavy combat accepted that explanation. Charles Wainwright, chief of V Corps artillery, noted that Grant's lame assertion "affords a vast deal of amusement in the army, considering there were greater exertions and preparations made for this expedition than any previous one." A

Confederate who walked the battlefield assessed the Federal withdrawal as "a perfect stampede." After all, "Their dead were left unburied, hundreds of wounded were abandoned, guns, cartridge boxes, ammunition. . .strewed the ground; three of their ambulances were burned and their videttes were abandoned to be captured." Tom Mangham's second crack at Ulysses S. Grant had turned out much more successfully than the first.[114]

After helping repulse the thrust at Burgess's Mill, Tom and the Ashville Guards settled down to a long cold winter in the Howlett Line trenches northeast of Petersburg. They whiled away the fourth winter of the war, with the terrible ration shortage adding to the miseries inflicted by sharpshooters, lice, rain, and snow. In accordance with a state initiative to record the deeds of Alabama units during the war, the 10th Alabama took the time to compile comprehensive rosters of personnel, engagements, and casualties through January 1, 1865. By that time, 142 men had served in the Ashville Guards, of whom eighteen had been killed in action, while another 24 had died of disease. Eight of the 46 wounded men had died of their injuries, and four of the sixteen men captured by the enemy had died in captivity.[115]

The casualty toll mounted once more in early February 1865, when a renewed Union thrust towards Hatcher's Run sought to support a cavalry raid aimed at Confederate wagon trains. The cavalrymen reached Dinwiddie Court House as planned on February 5, only to learn that the hoped-for wagon trains were nowhere to be found. Several divisions of Warren's V Corps engaged Confederate forces near Dabney's Mill, just east of the old battleground at Burgess's Mill (see map, p. 512). Again, Mahone's Division hit the road heading south, crossing the Appomattox River and approaching the threatened area. When the morning of February 6 gave no sign of a serious Federal onset, Mahone's men started back for the north side of the river.[116]

Late morning saw Crawford's Federal division renew its reconnaissance efforts, however, and the probe turned into a full-scale battle as both sides reinforced the engaged units. By the time Mahone's Division was back at the scene of the action, Crawford's Federals were barely holding together. Floridian Joseph Finegan was in command of Mahone's Division this day, and the men long remembered him sitting astride his horse, dressed in a civilian coat and beaver hat and carrying a walking stick. Repeating "On ye go you brave lads," he cheered them into a stunning attack against Crawford's wavering lines. Sanders's Alabama brigade, commanded by Col. William H. Forney of the 10th Alabama, led the way again with Weisiger's Virginians on their flank. Backed up by Sorrel's Georgians and Harris's Mississippi brigade, they shattered Crawford's division and threw its remnants back onto Ayres's division, which collapsed in turn. Defeat quickly became rout, and the fleeing Federals disorganized Wheaton's VI Corps division as it tried to make a stand in their rear. Eventually, Griffin's division arrived to stay the panicked mobs of fugitives and halt the pursuing Confederates, stabilizing the line just east of Dabney's Mill. One of Forney's Alabamians reported simply, "We drove them back easily and did it handsomely, nothing easier."[117]

One of the men doing the driving apparently was Tom Mangham, who later wrote proudly of standing "side by side with Harris's Brigade upon many a hard fought battle field." He added, "We have often thought a braver and more gallant set of men never made or withstood the shock of a desperate charge or hail of lead than these same Mississippians, and shall never cease to admire their courage." Perhaps the dispirited Federals felt the same way, after a fashion. After delivering a minor riposte the following day, Warren pulled his men back across Hatcher's Run. The Army of the Potomac had lost more than 1500 men in the three days' fighting, but had inflicted about a thousand casualties on the three Confederate divisions facing them. Some fifteen or twenty of the disabled belonged to the 10th Alabama.[118]

Tom Mangham and his friends returned to the Howlett Line northeast of Petersburg after this engagement, and probably participated in no more major engagements until the southwestern portion of Lee's defensive line finally collapsed on April 2, 1865. Mahone's Division evacuated its positions at Bermuda Hundred and marched west, crossing the Appomattox River on Goode's Bridge. After several days on the road with little or no food, Tom found himself as part of a rear guard posted to defend a colossal structure known as High Bridge, just east of Farmville. Twenty-five hundred feet long and 126 feet high, the gigantic railroad bridge rested on twenty-one brick piers spanning the Appomattox River.[119]

The rear guard successfully held the bridge open for Lee's retreat, and managed to burn three of the twenty-one spans on the northern end before the pursuing Federals captured it. The defenders also set fire to the small wagon bridge down below, but men of the 19th Maine managed to get there in time to douse the flames by bailing water with their hats, dippers, and canteens. When the remainder of Barlow's Federal division arrived to stake their claim to the structure, further Confederate counterattacks yielded to superior force. The bridge was now in Union hands, and so was Tom Mangham. Captured in the fracas at High Bridge on April 7, 1865, his Civil War odyssey ended twenty miles east of Appomattox Court House, where Lee surrendered the Army of Northern Virginia two days later. The 10th Alabama furled its colors with ten officers and 208 men present.[120]

*   *   *   *   *

Tom was marched to Burkesville Junction after his capture, and was among a crowd of 1614 prisoners paroled by the IX Corps Provost Marshal in mid-April. After he signed a statement on April 14 vowing not to take up arms against the United States until regularly exchanged, he started home for Alabama. On the very day he began his long trek home, the United States flag was raised over Fort Sumter, four years to the day after it had been hauled down. In 1865, April 14 was Good Friday, and President and Mrs. Lincoln had plans to visit Ford's Theater that evening.[121]

When Tom finally got home to Ashville, he found shocking scenes that testified to the lawlessness of the guerrillas he had fought before leaving home. Just after he and the rest of the Ashville Guards had driven back the Yankees at Dabney's Mill in early February, a band of Tories (Southern Unionists), deserters, and draft evaders had overrun his hometown in a vicious nighttime raid. Amid scenes of panic and terror, they had burned down the county courthouse and looted much of the town. With

145

little room left for fervent secessionists there as the Confederacy collapsed, Tom wasted little time in getting married and heading west to Texas to start a new life.[122]

*   *   *   *   *

Four years after the surrender, Tom struck out on yet another journey. This time he was bound for Louisiana, where Wiley had gone to join their brother Henry shortly after the war ended. They had buried their father in Alabama in 1861, and their mother had passed away in January 1864. With their parents dead and gone, and the fabric of Alabama society torn asunder by defeat and occupation, it was time to start afresh on the fertile lands along Bayou Boeuf in northern Louisiana.

3. Church Bells and Cannoneers: Cpl. Henry G. Mangham, "Bell Battery," aka "Benton's Battery," 3rd Louisiana Light Artillery

Henry Grant Mangham had left Alabama in the fall of 1857, attracted to the fertile bottomlands and fresh promise of northeast Louisiana. Born in Lee County, Georgia on December 9, 1828, Henry's youth was marked by his family's migration to new lands in Georgia and Alabama. Apparently he imbibed his father's love of the frontier and its unique challenges and opportunities, for he was the first of Thomas and Matilda Mangham's sons to strike out westward.

He fetched up in Franklin Parish, Louisiana, in the Red Mouth district along Bayou Boeuf. In an area where today's road signs still proclaim cotton's status as "white gold," Henry secured a job as overseer on the new plantation of James H. Montgomery. The Montgomery family had come from Jefferson County, Mississippi, in 1856, and James owned a prosperous spread valued at $5200 in 1860. Henry helped oversee the labor of 34 slaves, whose appraised worth was five times greater than the land itself. It was a ratio common on Southern plantations, where land was relatively cheap but labor was precious.[123]

On April 21, 1859, Henry married Montgomery's 16-year-old daughter Telitha Ann and the following year saw the arrival of their first child, Thomas H. Mangham. Thus continued the Mangham family tradition of naming children almost exclusively after their close relatives, as the boy's namesakes included his uncle, grandfather, and Henry's great-uncle. The little family lived in a log cabin Henry built on a gentle slope near the Boeuf, clearing the surrounding farmland from its wilderness state with ax and grubbing hoe. His personal estate was valued at $180 in 1860, reflecting his modest means, if not necessarily his future prospects as the son-in-law of a prosperous planter.[124]

The outbreak of war a year later did not move Henry to enlist immediately, although it is safe to say that his family and cultural heritage all but guaranteed his dislike for Yankees. In his book *Civil War Soldiers*, Reid Mitchell has characterized the complex views ante-bellum Southerners held towards their neighbors to the north:

> The Yankee was the symbol of all that the South hated. He was, of course, the abolitionist. Even the nonslaveholder, who may have resented the planter, very

rarely had love for the slave. He too could be stirred by tales of abolitionist incendiarism. For those Southerners who saw the future of the South in terms of prosperity and economic development, the Yankee was a villain who resisted Southern progress. At the same time, ironically, the Yankee also embodied the capitalistic values that those troubled by economic transformation had come to fear. Finally, after the war began, the Yankee became the invader. The usefulness of the Yankee as an ideological symbol lay precisely in the fact that he could represent all that threatened white Southerners, no matter what their politics.[125]

Although Henry left no record of his personal views, it is highly likely that he mirrored the general antipathy towards the North that typified so many Southerners. He was almost thirty years old when he left Alabama, and his father and brothers viewed the world through cultural and political lenses that Henry probably shared. In this light, Mitchell's interpretation of the "Yankee" as a symbol is a useful one, in that he emphasizes the particular roles of the abolition movement, Free Soil politics, and modern industrialism in evoking Southern mistrust, fear, and wrath. Henry probably held little ill feeling towards any northern-born farmer he may have encountered, but his blood almost certainly boiled when abolitionist doctrines were discussed. Not only did abolitionists vilify the society in which he grew to manhood as a savage and unjust one, but also they specifically seethed with contempt for white Southerners in his position. As an overseer on a Louisiana cotton plantation, Henry Mangham qualified as the prototypical "Negro driver" whom abolitionists viewed as the instrument of inhumanity in the South. For those whose emotions rose to fever pitch while reading Harriet Beecher Stowe's *Uncle Tom's Cabin*, Henry was a real-life Simon Legree.

He eventually enlisted in an artillery battery raised by Thomas O. Benton at Monroe in May 1862.[126] Benton, a graduate of Virginia Military Institute and former superintendent of the Arkansas Military Institute, had accepted a colonel's commission from Governor Letcher of Virginia before Secretary of War Judah P. Benjamin convinced him to raise an artillery battery in the Trans-Mississippi Department. Like others who enlisted in the spring of 1862, Benton's recruits probably were motivated by the wave of Union victories that threatened the Confederacy's survival, as well as the conscription law that sought to mobilize men aged 18 to 35 years. Defeats such as Tom Mangham endured at Shiloh in April evoked a huge wave of voluntarism in the South, and Captain Benton capitalized on the outpouring of patriotic feeling to obtain the donation of every bronze church bell in Ouachita, Caldwell, and Morehouse parishes. These bells were melted down in Vicksburg and cast into six cannon for Benton's "Bell Battery" in early 1862, but the raw cannoneers never saw them. The guns were diverted elsewhere, while caissons and other equipment intended for Benton's men were lost with the fall of New Orleans.[127]

In July 1862, however, Lieut. John D. Girtman proceeded to Columbus, Mississippi to sign for a fresh consignment of guns for the battery. He duly receipted for one 3-inch iron rifle, one 3-inch bronze rifle, two 6-pounder bronze guns, and two 12-pounder bronze howitzers. General Bragg also provided other equipment to outfit the Bell

Battery properly, and they trained in Monroe before moving to Richmond in nearby Madison Parish. Here, not far from Vicksburg, the battery comprised the sole artillery available to Confederate authorities in northeastern Louisiana in the fall of 1862. The tiny infantry force of two regiments, two battalions, and one Partisan Ranger company included Henry's third cousins *Arthur G. Mangham, William J. Mangham,* and *Josiah T. Mangham* (see Chapter IX). Tiny as they were, these forces were tasked to interfere with Federal traffic on the Mississippi River from positions on the Louisiana shore. Had they been in position a little sooner, the Mangham boys could have found themselves exchanging shots with the Federal mortar schooner *U.S.S. George Mangham!*[128] At Christmastime, however, the detachments near Richmond pulled back to Monroe by order of Gen. Albert G. Blanchard, when Federal troops landed in force to clear the westward approaches to Vicksburg. Afterwards, as General Grant's engineers worked tirelessly to build canals to bypass the Confederate bastion on the river, Benton received orders to move his battery to Fort Beauregard, at Harrisonburg on Bayou Macon, just north of its confluence with the Tensas, Ouachita, and Black Rivers (see map on page 558).[129]

Major General Richard Taylor, son of ex-General and President Zachary Taylor, described Fort Beauregard and similar installations as "mere water batteries to prevent the passage of gunboats." Taylor had assumed command of the District of Western Louisiana in the Trans-Mississippi Department in August 1862, and would later take charge of operations in the northern part of the state as well. As he noted, his district was "penetrated in all directions by watercourses navigable when the Mississippi was at flood." Accordingly, "every little bayou capable of floating a cock-boat called loudly for forts and heavy guns." Given the paucity of men and arms in a state whose political and economic structures were thrown into chaos by the early Federal capture of New Orleans and Baton Rouge, Taylor was hard-pressed to answer the cries for help.[130]

Engineer Lieutenant Alphonse Buhlow had designed Fort Beauregard, whose heavy cannon frowned from positions designed to sweep the river. Company F, 11th Louisiana Battalion, had drilled as artillerymen and manned the heavy guns. The Bell Battery's light artillery complemented the heavies, and consisted of two 3-inch rifled cannon (one bronze and one iron), along with two light 12-pounder howitzers. Major Harrison's cavalry battalion rounded out the little fort's complement of men.[131]

Benton's men had seen no action during their service to this point, but Grant's latest stratagem in the Vicksburg campaign changed that in May 1863. Grant managed to cross his army from the west bank of the Mississippi to the east bank in late spring, and Maj. Gen. Nathaniel Banks's troops in southwestern Louisiana were pushing northwards to Alexandria to apply pressure from that quadrant. Admiral David D. Porter moved his fleet of gunboats and transports up the Red River in support of Banks's operations, pushing Taylor's little army before him and arriving at Alexandria on May 7. Since shallow rapids made the Red unnavigable beyond that point, Porter broke off his pursuit of Taylor and sent four gunboats north up the Black River in search of Confederate boats and supplies.[132]

Commander Selim E. Woodworth led the ironclad *Pittsburg*, along with the *Arizona*, *General Price*, and the ram *Switzerland* up the Black River and hove into view of Fort Beauregard at 1:00 p.m. on May 10. Already warned of the ships' progress on the preceding day, the garrison's drummers had beaten the long roll and the troops were standing by for action. Clearly visible in line of battle at two miles range, the Federal ships paused a mile and a half from the fort to dispatch a yawl bearing a flag of truce. Post commander George W. Logan, formerly lieutenant colonel of the Chalmette Regiment, Louisiana Militia, deputized his adjutant, Lieut. James Blanchard, and Captain Benton to meet the yawl. Benton and Blanchard met Lieutenant Fowler at the riverbank, and there received Commander Woodworth's summons for the fort to surrender unconditionally: if they refused, they had one hour to evacuate women and children from the town. In accordance with Logan's instructions, Benton advised Fowler that the garrison "would be defended at all hazards" and informed him that the women and children were already out of harm's way.[133]

Thirty minutes later, the boats commenced firing on Fort Beauregard and began a slow advance up the river. Their 9- and 10-inch rifled guns outranged anything in the garrison's arsenal, so Logan held fire for thirty minutes until he judged that the Federal ships had approached within range. From his position in the lower casemate, Logan sighted and fired the signal gun, unleashing the fire of every gun that could reach the enemy. Benton was supervising the whole of the fort's artillery, and his men sent round after round thumping into the ships, which soon dropped downriver out of range and continued firing. Approaching once more, they attracted another barrage of fire from Beauregard's gun emplacements and withdrew yet again. Despite having poured 122 well-directed rounds into the little Confederate emplacement that day, the frustrated Federal gunners could not penetrate the well-designed earthworks. One large fragment mortally wounded Second Lt. W. J. Carter of the Bell Battery, but he was the only man in the fort injured by the heavy fire.[134]

Woodworth withdrew his ships four miles downriver that night, while Henry Mangham and his comrades stood to their guns in case the Federals tried to pass upriver under cover of darkness. Just before noon the next day, Woodworth brought his three gunboats back for another try, leaving the ram *Switzerland* out of range. In Logan's estimation, the Federal gunners fired even more "briskly and accurately" this time, and "exploded most of their shells in the fort." Although the gunboats poured about ninety shells into Fort Beauregard in an hour of intense firing, Benton's cannoneers returned fire with a will, "striking the boats repeatedly and exploding rifled shells in their midst." As broken timber from the boats floated in the water after three hours' heavy firing, Confederate sharpshooters crept into position behind an Indian mound and began to sweep the decks with rifle fire.[135]

The sharpshooters' attack was the last straw, and Woodworth pulled his boats back downriver. Apparently, his crews buried six to eight men just north of the town of Trinity, and they told townspeople that they had suffered another thirty or forty wounded. After destroying some provisions in the town, the battered expedition proceeded downriver and soon passed out of the Black River. The citizens of Trinity saw that one of the boats was limping along with one wheel disabled, while the "general hammering on all the boats" indicated that many of Benton's shot and shell had struck home. Most of the Federal shells had failed to penetrate Beauregard's parapets and casemates, and only three other Confederates were wounded besides Lieutenant Carter. The heavy gunfire, however, took a grim toll on the town of Harrisonburg.[136]

The sharp engagement along the banks of Bayou Macon typified much of the combat in Louisiana, where the ubiquitous waterways offered Federal vessels plentiful avenues into the depths of the state. The Confederates, severely constrained by the paucity of their naval resources, struck back by designing defenses to contest the waterways. Positioning batteries to blast passing boats with cannon fire, they augmented them with infantrymen for local defense and sharpshooter duties. Cavalry played an important role in this scheme of defense, too, as small parties of partisan rangers were well suited to scout Federal approaches and snipe at passing ships.

Benton's artillerymen remained at Fort Beauregard until its abandonment on September 4, after which they moved back to the banks of the Mississippi River, helping man emplacements along the levee near Pointe Coupee.[137] Here, some thirty miles above Baton Rouge, the men of Bell Battery joined with several other batteries to make things hot for Union transports along the river in late 1863. After Vicksburg and Port Hudson had fallen in July, General Banks had pulled his forces out of range of the Red River area and Taylor could move into the resulting vacuum. His batteries poured shot and shell into the transport *Black Hawk* as she moved downriver on November 21, with gunners under Capt. Thomas A. Faries in Battery No. 1 claiming nine hits as she passed their emplacements. Lieutenant John D. Girtman of Benton's Battery asserted that his iron 3-inch rifle hit the *Black Hawk* with five solid shot of the six it fired, while his bronze rifle fired two solid and three capped shots. Girtman saw two of the latter explode and believed they may have set the boat on fire, as she was seen in flames as she passed Battery No. 3. Captain William Edgar commanded the latter battery, and claimed to have set the fire with his 12-pounder howitzer shells. He also hammered the ship with his 6-pounder guns, and poured on spherical case and even canister from his howitzers in an attempt to sweep her decks. Edgar saw the *Black Hawk* run aground on the east bank opposite Hog Point, as the surviving crew and passengers bailed out into the woods, dragging out many wounded and dead comrades. Although Edgar limbered up his battery to move within range of the grounded vessel, the gunboat *Choctaw* roared into action and drove back his guns and sharpshooters.[138]

Three weeks later the cannoneers meted out similar treatment to the transport *Henry Von Phul*, with Captain Daniel's Consolidated Texas Light Battery claiming 34 hits on the steamer. Lieutenant Girtman's men of Benton's Battery used their 3-inch iron rifle to inflict three hits on the boat, before the gun burst spectacularly upon firing its fourth shot. The explosion completely blew out the top of the piece from cascable to trunnions, and split the tube a further eight inches beyond the trunnions. Luckily for Benton's men, the catastrophic failure inflicted only slight scratches on the crew and its horses, since the force of the explosion went straight up into the air.

Girtman's bronze rifle fired an additional seventeen solid shot at the *Von Phul*, hitting it numerous times and cutting its steam pipes. Lieutenant Hall's howitzer section of Edgar's Battery was located with Girtman's rifle section, and raked the ship with shells that wrecked the pilothouse and killed the ship's captain.[139]

Admiral Porter wrote General Grant from Cairo, Illinois on December 15, noting that the *Von Phul* had just arrived in port "with 40 shot-holes in her, captain and clerk killed." Porter was angry that "Banks has left the country about Red River without any troops, and the rebels have it all their own way." He added, "Dick Taylor has come in with 4,000 men and twenty-two pieces of artillery, and has planted them behind the levee to great advantage. He don't trouble the gun-boats. . .but the transports get badly cut up, even when they are convoyed."[140]

*   *   *   *   *

Porter would get even angrier with Banks the following spring, when the combined army-navy Red River Campaign ground to a halt after pushing Taylor's little army all the way to Mansfield, just thirty miles below Shreveport. Porter sailed some of his heaviest boats beyond Alexandria, where the shallows put them at extreme risk. Banks, for his part, was lulled by his overwhelming numerical superiority into the belief that Taylor could not strike a serious blow even if he tried, and seemingly felt little compunction about veering away from the Red River where he could cooperate with the gunboats. General Grant, now exercising overall command of the Union war effort, foresaw Banks's campaign as the southernmost of three simultaneous offensives aimed at destroying the Confederate armies in Virginia, Georgia, and Louisiana. While Grant and Sherman closed with Lee and Johnston in sustained combat that began in May and lasted all summer, Banks got an earlier start and met with disaster at Mansfield and Pleasant Hill on April 8-9, 1864.[141] (See map on p. 594.)

Corporal Mangham and the men of Benton's Battery were in reserve and thus remained unengaged during these two decisive battles, which all but routed Banks from the field. As the overmatched political general began a desperate retreat back to Grand Ecore, Taylor sought to cut off his 25,000-man army and destroy it with his puny 5,000-man force. Wherever possible, Confederate infantry and cavalry forces struck at Banks's retreating soldiers and sailors, turning the withdrawal into a continuous series of nerve-wracking skirmishes.[142]

On the night of April 25, Confederate scouts along the Red River near DeLoach's Bluff spotted Federal gunboats and sent for help. Major General Polignac, a hard-fighting Frenchman commanding the 2nd (Louisiana) Infantry Division, sent word for Captain Benton to report with his battery to Col. Joseph Brent, Chief of Artillery, at Mrs. Griffith's house on the Natchitoches Road. Urging their teams to their best speed, Benton's cannoneers left their camp beyond Cane River just after midnight and marched through the darkness to reach the Griffith place. After receiving his orders from Brent, Captain Benton moved his men to a point near DeLoach's Bluff, where the sweating gunners wheeled their two rifled 3-inch guns into position shortly after eight o'clock that morning.[143]

The gun crews could see an eight-gun Federal tinclad gunboat just 450 yards away in mid-river, while another gunboat stood beneath their very muzzles, just under the bluff. The latter boat was apparently the ironclad monitor *Osage*, and her position made it impossible for Benton to depress his guns sufficiently to hit her. Apparently, he tried to wait for the monitor to move into his field of fire, but at 10:30 a.m. he finally gave the order to open fire at the more exposed and less-heavily armored tinclad. Two 6-pounder guns of Captain Nettles's Valverde Battery added their fire to Benton's, as did a detachment of sharpshooters. The tinclad immediately returned fire, and the *Osage* cut loose with canister and grapeshot at her tormentors in the ensuing half-hour of intense close-range action. One can almost hear Benton's gunners swearing in frustration at their faulty friction primers, since the notoriously unreliable products provided by Confederate arsenals repeatedly failed to function. This problem dogged Southern artillerymen throughout the war, and this morning it slowed Benton's rate of fire considerably. His iron rifle went silent after firing just eighteen rounds, when a particle of faulty primer jammed in the gun's air vent and prevented further firing.[144]

Their gunnery was nonetheless accurate, and the crew of the bronze 3-inch rifle managed to fire thirty rounds in a half-hour, despite the unreliable primers. Many of the battery's 48 shots struck and penetrated the tinclad, and one such hit forced it to cease fire and retreat downriver to a new position a mile away. The Federal gunfire had killed one of the battery's horses and slightly wounded two others, while killing two men and wounding several in the small force supporting Benton. After the tinclad retreated, Benton pulled his exposed gun section back into defilade, but he repositioned his bronze rifle and two 12-pounder bronze howitzers at 2:00 p.m. that afternoon. This time he emplaced them to range upriver against any boats trying to pass DeLoach's Bluff, but his gunners spent the evening undisturbed by enemy action, except for three rounds fired by the persistent *Osage*. Three boats came upriver to the battered tinclad's assistance that evening, and all withdrew to Alexandria that night. Benton's Battery had faced disbandment just several months previously due to deficiencies in equipage and drill, but renewed efforts had made for a "remarkable" improvement in efficiency; in their first action since that time, the soldiers' dedication had paid off handsomely.[145] (See maps, pp. 397 and 400).

Banks's forces were hemmed up in a defensive position at Alexandria for several weeks. While they tried to regroup and protect the numerous naval vessels stranded by low water, Taylor sought to gather the forces necessary for the decisive victory that was almost within his grasp. The five to six thousand Confederates under Taylor's command now penned up some 31,000 Federals, as Banks had received reinforcements before the ever-tightening web along the waterways stopped all Federal traffic along the Red River. Benton's gunners helped hold the "siege" lines tight on May 5 at Chambers's (or Polk's) Plantation on the Bayou Robert Road, eleven miles below Alexandria. Henry and his fellow cannoneers pulled into battery after a night march of twenty-two miles, and then participated in a "brisk and well sustained" fight of several hours against Federals probing southwards out of town. Firing in support of three cavalry brigades of Bee's Division, Benton's men again cooperated with Nettles's

Battery. The Louisiana cannoneers "severely punished" the Federal advance, eventually reaching into their ammunition chests to pull out the munitions they reserved for the most desperate of close-range actions: canister. Blasting the tin cans filled with heavy iron slugs into the advancing blue skirmish lines, the battery helped drive the Federal force back to its lines at Alexandria.[146]

The following day found Benton's Battery in another hot action at Bayou Lamourie, where a renewed Federal thrust threatened to overpower Bee's horsemen. Although the "battery was exposed to a heavy and flank fire of the enemy's much more numerous artillery," the men "stubbornly sustained the engagement until both rifle guns were disabled by rapid firing." As their supporting cavalry pulled back across Polk's Bridge, Benton's two howitzer crews continued to fire on the advancing enemy until one of the howitzers failed as well. With only one serviceable piece remaining in action and all supports withdrawn, the battery held its position with deadly canister fire until finally limbering to the rear, eliciting praise for the daring manner in which they brought off their guns in the face of the advancing enemy.[147]

Although more severe fighting continued around Alexandria, the shortage of serviceable cannon kept Benton's Battery out of further action.[148] Most of Porter's fleet finally escaped down the Red River after enterprising engineers built a series of wing dams and locks that succeeded in raising the water level to a sufficient depth. Banks's army also managed to push aside Taylor's little force after severe fighting at Mansura and Yellow Bayou. Finally retreating across the Atchafalaya River at Simmesport from May 19 to 21, Banks's Red River Campaign was over. An utter disaster for the Federals, the outcome was much better for them than it could have been. They were very fortunate to escape complete destruction at Taylor's hands. Had Kirby Smith not deprived Taylor of Churchill's and Walker's divisions as Banks fell back after Pleasant Hill, it is likely that the Federal fleet and army would have been destroyed.[149]

Two days after the Federals escaped destruction at the hands of his forces, Gen. Dick Taylor published general orders praising his men for their accomplishments:

Headquarters District Western Louisiana,
In the Field, May 23, 1864

Soldiers of the Army of Western Louisiana!
On March 12 the enemy, with an army of 30,000 men, accompanied by a fleet of ironclads, mounting 150 guns, moved forward for the conquest of Texas and Louisiana. After seventy days continued fighting, you stand a band of conquering heroes, on the banks of the Mississippi. Fifty pieces of cannon, 7,000 stand of small arms, three gunboats and eight transports captured or destroyed, sixty stands of colors, over 10,000 of the enemy killed, wounded or captured—these are the trophies which adorn your victorious banners. Along 300 miles of river you have fought his fleet, and over 200 miles of road you have driven his army. You have matched your bare breasts against his ironclads and proved victorious in the contest. . . .

The devotion and constancy you have displayed in this pursuit have never been surpassed in the annals of war, and you have removed from the Confederate soldier the reproach that he could win battles but not improve victories.

Along 100 miles of his path the flying foe, with more than savage barbarity, burned every house and village within his reach. You extinguished the burning ruins in his base blood, and were nerved afresh to vengeance by the cries of women and children, left without shelter or food.

Long will the accursed race remember the great river of Texas and Louisiana. The characteristic hue of his turbid waters has a darker tinge from the liberal admixture of Yankee blood.

The cruel alligator and ravenous garfish wax fat on rich food, and our native vulture holds high revelry over many a festering corpse.

. . . .Our artillery has been the admiration of the army. Boldly advancing, without cover, against the heavy metal of the hostile fleet, unlimbering often without support within the range of musketry, or remaining last on the field to pour grape and canister into the advancing columns, our batteries have been distinguished in exact proportion as opportunity was afforded.

Soldiers! These are great and noble deeds, and they will live in chronicle and in song as long as the Southern race exists to honor the earth. . . .

Soldiers! This army marches towards New Orleans, and though it does not reach the goal, the hearts of her patriotic women shall bound high with joy, responsive to the echoes of your guns.

TAYLOR, Major-General[150]

Henry Mangham and his friends in Benton's Battery indeed must have felt proud of their role in saving western and northern Louisiana from occupation, but they also were exhausted after seventy days of sustained marching and fighting. Little could they have known just how much rest they would get after drubbing Banks, however. Although they marched into Arkansas that winter as part of Polignac's Division, they returned to camps at Collinsburg, near Shreveport, by January 1865. There they turned in their field guns and moved to Grand Ecore to assume duties with the heavy artillery batteries covering the Red River near Natchitoches. Having triumphed in western Louisiana, they whiled away the time as the exhausted Confederacy staggered to its final defeat.[151]

Benton's Battery had fired its last shot of the war on May 7, 1864 at Bayou Lamourie. A year later, the Trans-Mississippi Army dissolved after hearing that Lee had surrendered in Virginia and Johnston's army had stacked arms in North Carolina. Although many of the men reported later to towns such as Monroe, Natchitoches, and Alexandria to receive formal paroles, there was never a formal surrender ceremony. With the "blackened country between the Mississippi and the Ouachita" literally ruled by large bands of jayhawkers and nightriders, the Yankees were no longer Henry's worst enemy. Telitha and the children were helpless and alone, in much greater danger of attack than was the army rotting in garrisons at Grand Ecore, Natchitoches, and Alexandria. Along with many of his comrades, Henry simply went home.[152]

4. "JUST BEYOND THE RIVER": REUNION IN LOUISIANA

Soon after Henry returned to Franklin Parish, his brother Wiley struck out for Louisiana on horseback. Appalled at the wreckage of the Southland he knew and loved, Wiley was dismayed at the spectacle of armed freedmen jeering at their former masters as they returned home from the army. He was a devout Baptist, and often sought comfort during his journey by singing one of his favorite hymns, "Near the cross I'll watch and wait, Hoping, trusting ever Till I reach the golden strand, Just beyond the river."[153]

Joyously reunited with Henry upon his arrival, Wiley spent many pleasant hours with him and his family at their home near the village of Girard. He soon obtained employment as a printer in the *Telegraph and Intelligencer* offices at Monroe, but maintained his close contacts with Henry. Dressed up in his Sunday best one evening for a neighborhood dance near Henry's home, he met and fell in love with Miss Carolyn Frances Emmeline Lynn. "Miss Fannie" was sixteen or seventeen when she and Wiley were married at her mother's house on October 18, 1866. Their first daughter, Jennie L. Mangham, was born on their first wedding anniversary, but she died on June 27 of the following year. Wiley and Fannie buried her on Henry's farm near Girard.[154]

A little more than a year later Richland Parish was created, its area encompassing the Boeuf River bottomlands where Henry lived. The settlement of Little Creek was renamed Rayville and established as the parish seat, and Wiley moved there and bought land across from the courthouse. He built a two-room house there for his family and a little newspaper office next door. When a Washington Hand Press arrived for typesetting, Wiley was ready to go back into business: he published the first issue of the *Richland Beacon* on January 14, 1869. Using the motto *Libertas et Natale Salum* (Liberty and Native Soil) as a proclamation of his Democratic politics in an era of Republican Reconstruction, Wiley's newspaper would remain in family hands for more than a century.[155]

Wiley helped organized the Baptist Church of Rayville, which originally met in his home, and soon he was elected recorder of the new parish. He busied himself recording the numerous deeds and grants attendant to the establishment of the new parish. He contacted his brother Tom, who had moved to Texas after the war, and arranged for him to come take over the newspaper. Tom and his wife Jennie arrived in Rayville on September 27, 1869 and he immediately assumed duties as editor and publisher, although Wiley remained the nominal editor for another year. Tom leased the entire establishment from Wiley until 1872, before releasing it back to him and moving to Delhi that fall. There, on the railroad just a few miles west of Rayville, Tom founded the *Delhi Chronicle*, but folded it in 1874 as "an unprofitable enterprise." He returned to Rayville and resumed editing the *Beacon*, which he finally purchased outright in the fall of 1876.[156]

That autumn, Wiley and Fannie lost two more children: nine-month old Callie (Fannie C.) and three-year-old Sammie (Wiley Samuel). They, too, were buried in the little plot on Henry's farm. Four-year-old Alice (Mary A.) had died in September 1873, and Jessie H. died sometime in the 1870s, too; Wiley's first five children had fallen victim to the ever-present threats of cholera and "swamp fever." Tom and Jennie had an adopted son named Robert in their household in 1880, but he also seems to have died

young. Their only other child, John Wiley Mangham, died in September 1882, aged three months. Henry and Telitha also lost two of their five children before they reached adulthood. Such tribulations were terrible to bear, despite the ever-present reality of death, and the heart-rending obituaries of the Manghams' little children bear eloquent testimony to their bereaved parents' reliance on an eventual reunion in Heaven.[157]

In the decade from 1878 to 1888, however, Wiley and Fannie had four more children, and Eunice, Irma, Horace, and Hervey all survived the horrible threat of disease that had carried off their elder siblings. Meantime, both Wiley and Tom remained active in practically every aspect of Richland Parish life. Wiley was a partner in Mangham & Davis's general store, treasurer of the local Masonic lodge, and member of the Knights of Pythias and American Legion of Honor, all

WILEY PERSON MANGHAM
(SEE APPENDIX, REF. # 184)

while playing a very prominent role in local Democratic Party politics as Justice of the Peace, school board member, and town councilman. He retained his position as parish recorder for three terms, until the office was abolished in 1879 through consolidation with the parish clerkship. Tom was a tireless political organizer as well, often serving as Secretary or President of Richland Parish Democratic conventions, plus a term as Parish Treasurer. He held office in the local Baptist convention and served as Sunday school superintendent, while finding time to fire off editorial volleys embracing economic and social progress of all kinds. He advocated university education for women, religious tolerance towards members of the Jewish faith, establishment of a humane state mental institution, the prohibition of dueling and suppression of lynch law, and even the prohibition of pistols.[158]

Although Wiley's editorials also demanded due process and fair treatment for all men of good will, he often bluntly asserted white supremacy in terms typical of that age and place. Tom, on the other hand, rejected membership in the Democratic White League and took a different stance on the racial issues facing the state. After the end of Reconstruction in 1877 and the restoration of self-government to Louisiana, he began voicing concerns that the Democratic "Solid South" would be better off "if it were not quite so solid." In 1881, he even sparked a local controversy by criticizing Jefferson Davis's memoirs on the grounds that the book attempted "to defend slavery as an abstract principle." Called to task by a local pastor who elucidated the Biblical defense of slavery that had been an important part of the ante-bellum South's view of its "peculiar institution," Tom engaged in a prolonged editorial defense of his assertion that slavery had been a "relic of barbarism." While granting the fact that slavery had existed in Biblical times and had prospered into the current century for reasons known to a wise and just God, he maintained that the institution was "wholly incompatible with the advanced state of civilization of the present age." He added, "We do not blame people for having once owned slaves, nor do we accuse them of barbarity—many of them were cruel, but perhaps a majority were not. What we object to is the defence of slavery as an abstract principle—only that, and nothing more." At the end of the year, he decried the fact that "the sword of justice scarcely ever falls upon a violator of the law unless his skin is black, or he is some poor wretch who has descended almost to the level of the brute in the social scale." In a different context, Tom lamented that "the negro has ever been a subject of contention, the innocent cause of a terrible sectional war, and seems likely to be a source of trouble as long as our government exists. Now that he is a free man, why not let him alone and let him work his way in the world as other men do?"[159]

At the end of December 1884, Wiley bought back the *Beacon* from Tom, and resumed his active work as a newspaperman. Tom moved on to Gibsland, in nearby Bienville Parish, where he founded the *Bienville New Era* in 1885. As early as 1875, Wiley had used his editorial pen to advance the cause of sectional reconciliation, writing an appeal for the locals to observe the Fourth of July, and he reaffirmed ten years later that he felt "more disposed to poor oil on the wounds than to open them." Both of the Manghams had supported the presidential candidacy of General Winfield S. Hancock, Tom's opponent on Virginia's battlefields in 1864. "We all know that Gen. Hancock led brave men against us during the war and that they killed many of our brave boys, but we killed them too; still we admired and yet admire them and him for their courage. . . ."[160]

While his younger brothers pursued their agendas through the columns of the *Richland Beacon*, Henry limited his political activity to service as a school trustee, member of the Parish police jury, and Democratic delegate from the 4th Ward.

Although he loved to fish and hunt, he was a hard-working man who built his farm into a large and profitable enterprise. In 1870, he tilled 76 of his 266 acres, producing 500 bushels of corn along with thirty-five bales of cotton, among other products. Ten years later, he was cultivating 125 acres of a 402-acre plantation, harvesting 1200 bushels of corn and forty-three bales of cotton from property valued at five thousand dollars. He also owned $1500 worth of livestock, including eleven horses, five mules, and 67 head of cattle. In each of these census years he paid about $1300 for farm labor to help make his crop, an indication that his successful cotton crops helped generate the ready money so often lacking on Southern farms. His fruit harvests were a boon to his brothers and their families, and their local interest columns often noted their good fortune when Henry brought them a load of melons and peaches. Likewise, Wiley loved to hunt deer and go fishing with Henry, and Tom often used his wry sense of humor to compose a column dedicated to the Mangham brothers' hunting and fishing (mis)adventures. Louisiana's plentiful water moccasins nearly got the better of them on one occasion, when Tom pronounced himself "somewhat demoralized" by their numbers and "indifference to our presence." One huge snake even seized Henry's string of fish and glided away into midstream with them, before returning with them to the bank and eventual recapture.[161]

As new vistas continued to open up for Tom and Wiley during the mid-1880s, a premature end came for Henry. In the *Beacon* dated December 12, 1885, Wiley wrote:

> DEATH—This monster has again invaded the family of this writer. Sad is it that we are called upon to consign to the tomb our elder brother H. G. Mangham who departed this life Dec 10th, 1885, at 2 a.m. He left Ala. in the fall of 1857, came to Richland parish, where he engaged in planting and has remained here since that time. He was one of the best men in our parish and the universal expression from the people is "He was one of the best men in the parish." A suitable obituary will be published in the Beacon.
>
> The subject of this notice was only 2 hours over 57 years. How strange that he should die on the very night of which he arrived at the 57th year. Men's days are surely numbered.[162]

Henry Grant Mangham died of pneumonia, and rests in a grove of trees on his old homestead alongside Wiley's children. Another small marker inscribed "H.G.M." denotes the spot where Henry's infant son and namesake lies buried. His son Thomas attended college and grew to manhood, but died an untimely death in a streetcar accident in Oklahoma City in 1918. Telitha Ann received a modest Confederate widow's pension from 1914 until she passed away on January 25, 1928. Surviving Henry by 43 years, she was 85 years old at her death. She was survived by her daughters, Mrs. Hattie Louvent and Mrs. Carrie Binion, and was laid to rest next to Henry on their old home place.[163]

*   *   *   *   *

Tom Mangham's newspaper office in Gibsland burned down the year after Henry died, so he moved his fledgling newspaper to Sparta. He settled in Ruston in May 1890 and started yet another newspaper, the *Progressive Age*, whose initial issue appeared on August 16. With its circulation of six hundred copies, his solidly Democratic paper was the official organ of the Farmer's Union and Lincoln Parish. A devout Baptist like his brothers, Tom was a Past Master of Ruston Lodge No. 106 of the Masonic Order.[164]

As Tom was founding the *Progressive Age*, whose title reflected the "New South" outlook that characterized his editorial approach with the *Beacon*, Wiley was acting to build north Louisiana's prospects in a material way. He had purchased hundreds of acres of land about twelve miles south of Rayville and surveyed the property into twenty-four blocks, each 300 feet square. After further subdividing each block into twelve lots and laying out streets, he began donating lots to people on the condition that they erect buildings within a specified time. He also deeded land to the New Orleans, Natchez and Fort Scott Railroad to establish a station at the place, which he foresaw as a prime location for shipment of the area's abundant cotton crop. Wiley began giving away these lots in the fall of 1890, and soon a post office and flag station gave further shape to the little village. Established as the village of Mangham in that same year, it soon boasted a sawmill, gristmill, shingle mill and cotton gin.[165]

Six years after the establishment of the village that bore his name, however, Wiley fell sick while on a trip out west. He had long wanted to view Pike's Peak, and took the opportunity to travel to Colorado Springs in September 1896 to attend a meeting of the National Press Association. He contracted a bad cold on the trip, and it worsened into pneumonia by the time he returned home late in the month. Given that he had lost the use of one lung while in service at Fort Gaines in 1861, he was particularly vulnerable to pulmonary illness. He died at 11:30 on the morning of September 26, 1896, felled by the same disease that had killed his brother Henry.

Wiley Person Mangham was 58 years old when he was laid to rest at Oak Ridge in Morehouse Parish, Louisiana. At the time of his death, he was serving as adjutant of the Richland Camp of the United Confederate Veterans. As one newspaper obituary commented, "He was a confederate soldier and proud of it."[166]

*   *   *   *   *

It was Tom's sad duty to write a brief history of the *Richland Beacon* in commemoration of Wiley's contributions to journalism in northern Louisiana. Now sixty-one years old, he set the record straight in a fashion characteristic of his sense of pride, duty, and honor. Writing from Ruston on October 14, he began:

> Owing to the fact that some of the Louisiana papers have fallen into the error, unwittingly, of stating that Wiley P. Mangham, my beloved and last brother, had edited the Richland Beacon and Beacon-News continuously from the establishment of the former until the day of his death, suggests the idea to me, by permission of the present editor, of giving a brief history of the paper.

Tom then proceeded to clarify his role and Wiley's in the first fifteen years of the paper's existence. He also explained the parts played by W. R. Baird, a part owner of the *Beacon* in 1884-1885, and Rhyme's and Faulk's *Richland News*, which existed briefly before its consolidation with Wiley's paper as the *Richland Beacon-News*. Tom wrote the article while convalescing from "a similar illness to that which took my brother off," and concluded with heartfelt thanks to "the press for its favorable notice of my brother, and my old friends and patrons for their love and esteem for him."[167]

* * * * *

Ten years after Tom composed Wiley's journalistic epitaph, he sat down to write something that may have nearly as painful in its own way: he was requesting a veteran's pension due to the infirmities of old age. He and Jennie resided in a house she owned in Ruston, and his personal estate consisted of nothing more than a watch. Unable to make a living due to old age and "want of employment," he had supported himself during the previous five years by selling books and doing odd jobs. He also noted, "I work the garden and make the vegetables." In response to the question, "Do you use intoxicants to any extent?", the old veteran fairly bristled: "None whatever."[168]

Tom attached a certificate from his old colonel in the 10th Alabama, William T. Smith, but to no avail. His pension application was marked "R," denoting "Rejected." Apparently, his dismissal from the 25th Alabama in August 1862 had disqualified him from a pension for honorable service, and one can sense the sting of shame even over the intervening years. When he renewed his application in December 1907, he wrote:

Hon. C. K. Lewis
Dear Sir & Friend:
Allow me to trouble you with a request; and this is that you search for a paper for me.

I believe it was more than a year ago I sent to the Secretary of Pensions—or whatever his title may be—an application. Accompanying that application was a certification of my Colonel, W. __ Smith, Col. 10th Ala. Volunteer Infantry, C.S.A. Strange as it may seem I have forgotten his middle name; we called him Billie Smith. Now, will you please go to the office and try to find that certificate for me? I value it more highly than you could appreciate unless you were a veteran to whom such a certificate had been given. I think the colonel is now dead.

They rejected my application for reason; and I would not undergo the humiliation of renewing it unless it [were] to save my wife from suffering; not to save myself, I know.

I have been down sick over three weeks and am just able to sit up.

Excuse prolixity and the consuming your time.

May you be guided by wisdom and patriotism in discharge of your duty.

Respectfully Yours,

/s/ *Thos. J. Mangham*

This renewed application for pension showed that he had worked as a book agent and in a printing office, although his recent illness had prevented him from working for several weeks. He was requesting a pension due to "Old age and more or less physical weakness, on account of which cannot get employment," and again answered the question about use of intoxicants with an emphatic, "None at all of any kind." A veteran of Shiloh, Farmington, the siege of Corinth, Burgess's Mills, Dabney's Mills, the siege of Petersburg, and High Bridge, Tom was lucky to be able to state that he had suffered no wounds while in service.[169]

Ten days after Tom submitted his second application, it was approved by the state pension board. In this same year, the Governor of Louisiana proclaimed the incorporation of the Village of Mangham.[170]

MANGHAM, LOUISIANA.
NAMED FOR WILEY P. MANGHAM, WHOSE EFFORTS TO IMPROVE
RICHLAND PARISH RESULTED IN THE ESTABLISHMENT OF THIS SETTLEMENT.
-Author's collection

The old Confederate lived to witness an even bigger war from 1914 to 1918, but he crossed over the river as Alabama's young men were marching once more to the sound of the guns. On January 12, 1918, Thomas Jefferson Mangham succumbed to renal calculary cystitis, aged 82 years, 10 months, and 17 days. His wife Jennie died the following year, and is buried alongside him at Greenwood Cemetery in Ruston, Louisiana. Fittingly, the cemetery is located on Alabama Street.[171]

*   *   *   *   *

Wiley Mangham's wife Fannie received a Confederate widow's pension from the state of Louisiana from 1922 until her death on May 26, 1931. She is buried in Rayville. One of their daughters, Eunice Mangham Trezevant, lived in the old Mangham home place until her death in April 1967. The Richland State Bank purchased the land and razed the building later that year.[172]

Wiley and Fannie's son Horace owned and edited the *Richland Beacon-News* until his death in 1961. His son Hervey S. Mangham then assumed editorship of the paper until the 1980s. The *Beacon-News* remains a mainstay of journalism in northern Louisiana.[173]

*　　　*　　　*　　　*　　　*

In its centennial year of 1990, the census-takers counted 598 residents in the town of Mangham, Louisiana.

---

[1] As noted in Chapter II, the connection between Thomas R. and Willis Mangham was quite close, but some evidence indicates that Thomas and Henry were sons of an unknown cousin or brother of Willis.

[2] *Jacksonville Republican*, November 28, 1861; Pike County, Marriage records; Iva P. Goolsby, comp., *Randolph County, Georgia: A Compilation of Facts, Recollections, and Family Histories* (N.p.: Randolph County Historical Society, 1976), pp. 6-7. For information on Matilda Grant Mangham's family, see http://www.geocities.com/ Heartland/Meadows/4386/freeman1.htm. Stewart County records indicate that Henry G. Mangham registered a cattle brand in October 1829, only eight months after Thomas did so. Presumably this was his brother Henry C. Mangham, not his infant son Henry G. Mangham. Other records also evidence a close relationship between Thomas and his brother. See Helen E. Terrill, *History of Stewart County, Georgia*, vol. 1 (Columbus: Columbus Office Supply Co., 1958), p. 48.

[3] Donna B. Thaxton, ed., *Georgia Indian Depredation Claims*, (Americus: The Thaxton Company, c.1988), p. 268. Valentine Brewer was probably Temperance Brewer Mangham's brother; he was listed as a head of household in the 1820 Putnam County census, as was their father George Brewer. See Ballard, *Solomon Mangham*, p. 69; 1820 Census, Putnam County.

[4] *Jacksonville Republican*, November 28, 1861; Goolsby, *Randolph County*, pp. 6-7; Terrill, *History of Stewart County*, pp. 9-11.

[5] 1840 and 1850 Censuses, Russell County; Walker, *Russell County in Retrospect*, pp. 121-128; *Jacksonville Republican*, November 28, 1861. For more on the other Mangham families in Russell County, see Chapters VII through IX.

[6] *Jacksonville Republican*, November 28, 1861; Robert Scott Davis, Jr., "Alabama Indian Depredation Claims," *AlaBenton Genealogical Quarterly* 10, no. 1 (1993): 60; CMSR Index, Indian Wars 1815-1838, series M629, reel 23, NARA; 1850 Census, Benton County, Alabama; 1860 Census, Calhoun County, Alabama; Mark E. Fretwell, *This So Remote Frontier: The Chattahoochee Country of Alabama and Georgia* (Tallahassee: Historic Chattahoochee Commission, 1980), pp. 243-244.

[7] *Richland Beacon-News*, October 3, 1896; *Biographical and Historical Memoirs of Louisiana*, (Chicago: The Goodspeed Publishing Co., 1892; reprint, Baton Rouge: Claitor's Publishing, 1975), vol. 2, p. 231; John T. Palmer, *The Mangums of Virginia, North Carolina, South Carolina . . . and Adjoining States* (Santa Rosa: author, 1992), p. 41. Thomas and Matilda Mangham also named their daughters after their forebears. Little Sarah Temperance Mangham was the namesake of her great-grandmother Sarah Ann Mangham and her grandmother Temperance Brewer Mangham. The four-month-old infant died on July 11, 1842, and was the subject of a touching obituary published in

her uncle's newspaper. See *Jacksonville Republican*, August 17, 1842, excerpted in Surname Files, reel 359, ADAH.

[8] 1850 Census and Agricultural Schedule, Benton County; 1850; *Richland Beacon*, May 30 and December 12, 1885.

[9] *Richland Beacon*, October 26, 1878, February 25, 1882; *Richland Beacon-News*, October 3, 1896; *Memoirs of Louisiana*, vol. 2, p. 231; Elizabeth W. Gunby, "Wiley P. Mangham," in Louisiana Pen Women, *Louisiana Leaders* (Baton Rouge: Claitor's Publishing, 1970), p. 103; *Memorial Record of Alabama: A Concise Account of the State's Political, Military, Professional and Industrial Progress, Together with the Personal Memoirs of Many of Its People*, vol. 2 (reprint: Spartanburg: The Reprint Company, 1976), p. 222; *The Saint Clair News-Aegis*, April 22, 1976.

[10] The uneasy relationship between denizens of the Confederacy's mountainous regions and those in the more fertile lowlands was an ongoing problem for every state east of the Mississippi River. For a discussion of the problem in Alabama, see Malcolm C. McMillan, ed., *The Alabama Confederate Reader*, (Tuscaloosa: Univ. of Alabama Press, 1963), pp. 26-32. The problem is a major theme of Bessie Martin, *Desertion of Alabama Troops from the Confederate Army: A Study in Sectionalism* (New York: Columbia Univ. Press, 1932).

[11] 1860 Slave Census, Calhoun County.

[12] *Jacksonville Republican*, November 28, 1861; *St. Clair Diamond*, December 5, 1860, ADAH. Although repellent to modern day readers, such overtly racist sentiments typified the views held by white Americans of that era. White men who accepted the idea of racial equality in 1860 were viewed as members of a dangerous lunatic fringe by almost everyone, even in the North. Anyone espousing such radical egalitarian ideas in the South did so at considerable personal risk.

[13] *Memorial Record of Alabama*, vol. 2, p. 222; Muster Roll of Ashville Guards, May 28, 1860, 10th Alabama Unit Files, ADAH; Joseph L. Whitten, ed., *CHERISH: The Quarterly Journal of the St. Clair Historical Society*, vol. 2, no. 2: 66-67.

[14] Unit Historical Roll, Company A, 10th Alabama Unit Files, ADAH; Muster Roll of Ashville Artillery, 1861, 25th Alabama Unit Files, ADAH.

[15] *St. Clair Diamond*, August 29, 1861, ADAH.

[16] *Jacksonville Republican*, August 1, 1861.

[17] *Jacksonville Republican*, September 12, 1861.

[18] This letter appeared in the *Jacksonville Republican*, September 26, 1861. For clarity's sake, I have italicized ships' names mentioned in Tom's letters. I have added other minor clarifications in brackets when necessary, but otherwise have reproduced Tom's and Wiley's correspondence as faithfully as possible. Lacking the original letters, it is impossible to distinguish their stylistic errors from those generated by their uncle's typesetters.

[19] President Lincoln ordered a blockade of the Southern coastline on April 19, 1861, shortly after the fall of Fort Sumter, although Forts Gaines and Morgan had been

occupied by Alabama troops as early as January 5. The *U.S.S. Powhatan* established the blockade off the coast of Mobile on May 26, 1861. See E. B. Long, *The Civil War Day by Day: An Almanac, 1861-1865* (Garden City: Doubleday & Co., 1971), pp. 61, 79; McMillan, ed., *Alabama Confederate Reader*, p. 22.

[20] A "mess" was a small group of men who shared rations and cooking duties. Usually comprised of about half a dozen men, it formed a basic social unit within Civil War companies.

[21] Dick Banks was the company's third lieutenant (see Roll of Ashville Artillery, 1861, 25th Alabama Unit Files, ADAH).

[22] Inglet does not appear on the unit muster roll since he was rejected for service. He had worked for Tom and Wiley at the *Diamond* as a "printer's devil" (see *St. Clair Diamond*, August 29, 1861).

[23] Fort Gaines stands on the eastern tip of Dauphin Island. Fort Morgan is several miles to the east, located on the western tip of a narrow peninsula that projects across the mouth of Mobile Bay.

[24] Presumably he meant the *U.S.S. Powhatan*.

[25] One can almost hear the laughter as the rustics from northern Alabama jokingly referred to the Gulf of Mexico as a "branch," a Southern colloquialism for a creek or stream.

[26] Galbreath was a private in the company (see Roll of Ashville Artillery, 1861, 25th Alabama Unit Files, ADAH).

[27] Like so many companies of Confederate volunteers, the Ashville Artillery had to wait impatiently for the infant government to provide arms. Fort Gaines was likewise ill equipped with artillery at this point. Major Leadbetter, Acting Chief of the Engineer Bureau in Richmond, advised Captain Lockett, chief engineer at Mobile, that he saw "no probability" of obtaining heavy guns for the remaining bastions at Fort Gaines. He thought it unlikely that Gaines would receive guns for the flank embrasures either, and advised Lockett to close the embrasure shutters and loophole them for muskets! On October 18, Leadbetter reported to Col. Josiah Gorgas, Chief of Ordnance, that the fort still lacked sixteen 24-pounder howitzers and three 8-inch Columbiads. See OR 6, pp. 750, 753.

[28] Wiley Mangham's commission dated from September 10, 1861; the battalion was organized a week later. See CMSR, Wiley P. Mangham, 1st Alabama Battalion; Stewart Sifakis, *Compendium of the Confederate Armies: Alabama* (New York: Facts on File, 1995), p. 51.

[29] Since this letter appeared in the newspaper on October 24, it is likely that it was dated October 13, and a typesetting error mistakenly converted it to October 31.

[30] Gee's outfit was the 1st Artillery Battalion (see OR series IV, vol. 1, p. 788).

[31] Alexander was a private in the Ashville Blues (see Roll of Ashville Artillery, 1861, 25th Alabama Unit Files, ADAH).

[32] Sergeant R. A. Green appears on the rolls of the Ashville Artillery, but Dunn and Smith do not. Wiley's discussion of multiple balls implies that the company was armed with smoothbore muskets charged with "buck and ball." Comprising one large musket ball and three buckshot, this load was lethal at close range but unsuited for use in rifled muskets.

[33] Dr. Benson was an Ashville physician (see Whitten, ed., *CHERISH* 2, no. 2: 66).

[34] General Braxton Bragg commanded the Department of Alabama and West Florida, with responsibility for the defense of the vital Gulf Coast ports of Mobile and Pensacola. Thomas R. Mangham's first cousin, Capt. Sam Mangham, was serving at Pensacola with the 5th Georgia at this time (see Chapter IV).

[35] Colonel James Crawford commanded the 21st Alabama, which mustered into Confederate service at Mobile on October 13, 1861 (see Sifakis, *Confederate Armies: Alabama*, p. 66).

[36] Colonel William A. Buck commanded the 24th Alabama, organized at Mobile on October 15, 1861 (see Ibid., p. 91).

[37] Joe Wheeler, later famous as a cavalry commander, was colonel of the 19th Alabama in 1861 (see Ibid., p. 83).

[38] Gadsden, a major communications center in northeastern Alabama, is situated fifteen miles northeast of Ashville.

[39] Captain James Oliver commanded a company from Jefferson County in Col. Edward C. Bullock's 18th Alabama. Jefferson County lies about 25 miles southeast of Ashville, and was well known to many in Saint Clair and Calhoun counties. Charles A. Mangham, a third cousin of Tom and Wiley, was in the 18th Alabama (see Chapter VIII).

[40] As sergeant major, Tom was in the perfect position to know the battalion's status. He probably helped prepare the official report that day, which showed 15 officers and 202 men present for duty. Another 150 were present but unfit for duty, while a further 39 were absent. Thus, only 217 were present for duty out of an aggregate strength of 406 men. See OR 6, p. 772.

[41] Tom was absolutely correct in this assessment, and the ferocious battles yet to come failed to change the reality that disease was a deadlier foe than Federal soldiers. Some authorities estimate that three Confederate soldiers died from disease for every one killed in action. See Bell Irvin Wiley, *The Life of Johnny Reb: The Common Soldier of the Confederacy* (Baton Rouge: LSU Press, 1978), p. 244. Using the Mangham family as a test case provides results that validate this ratio. Only John S. Mangham is known to have died of wounds, whereas Wiley Pendleton Mangham, Wiley James Mangham, William W. Mangham, and John R. Mangham are known to have died of disease.

[42] The Confederate Army never resolved this problem, and it remained common for soldiers to go without pay for six, twelve, or even eighteen months at a time.

[43] Tom wrote obituaries for Simpson and Galbreath, which appeared as requested in the newspaper.

[44] *Jacksonville Republican,* November 28, 1861. Matilda Mangham died shortly afterwards, and was buried next to her husband in the Oak Grove churchyard at Read's Mill. (See *Richland Beacon,* August 24, 1878.)

[45] CMSR, Wiley P. Mangham, 25th Alabama; *Memoirs of Louisiana,* vol. 2, p. 231; Confederate Widows' Pension Records, Richland Parish, Mrs. Fannie L. Mangham, LSA; Sifakis, *Confederate Armies: Alabama,* p. 51; *OR* 52, pt. 2, p. 253. Dr. Josiah C. Nott, who recommended Wiley's discharge, was the highly regarded surgeon of the Mobile garrison. Known for his observation that mosquitoes seemed responsible for transmitting yellow fever, a thesis far in advance of the times, Nott was greatly alarmed at the strange combination of malaria and typhoid which decimated the garrison in early 1862. He reported, "The whole affair now is horrible. . . There is a great deal of *bad* sickness, and if the whole thing is not changed, the whole command will be rendered worthless." See H. H. Cunningham, *Doctors in Gray: The Confederate Medical Service* (Baton Rouge: LSU Press, 1958), pp. 20, 47.

[46] CMSR, Thomas J. Mangham, 25th Alabama; *Jacksonville Republican,* February 27, 1862.

[47] The lieutenant colonel was William B. McClellan. As commanding officer of the 6th Alabama Battalion, he was junior in rank to Loomis of the 1st Battalion.

[48] Tom makes reference here to Gen. Leroy P. Walker of Alabama, as well as to former general and President Andrew Jackson.

[49] Deas commanded the 22nd Alabama (see Sifakis, *Confederate Armies: Alabama,* p. 87).

[50] Letter, Capt. Pierre D. Costello to wife, January 31, 1862, 25th Alabama Unit Files, Letters of P. D. Costello, 1861-1862, ADAH. Costello thought the location "as healthy as Ala. can produce," but nonetheless considered that ". . . living here is as hard as the road to Jordan." He and his company had been in the army only two weeks when he wrote this letter.

[51] Captain Costello was amazed at the fury of the storm that blasted Camp Memminger, noting that the gale had turned over the regiment's hospital building with some one hundred sick men inside. One of his men, James E. Morris, had a "pine pole the size of my arm passed completely through his leg at the calf & stuck so fast it required the united strengt [sic] of two men to pull it out after I sawed off the part that had passed through. . . ." Poor Morris also was struck with a board which cut a "frightful gash" in his thigh (Ibid., March 6, 1862). See also Wilson P. Howell, "History of the 25th Alabama Regiment," (typescript), p. 5, Unit Files, ADAH. Howell served as a lieutenant in Calhoun County's Company I, and later was promoted to a captaincy and company command. See Willis Brewer, *Alabama: Her History, Resources, War Record, and Public Men, from 1540 to 1872* (Montgomery: Barrett & Brown, 1872), p. 630.

[52] Pope's company hailed from Shelby County.

[53] In a letter to his wife, Captain Costello recounted in detail the gloomy realities at which Tom merely hinted: ". . .we had to put mud in the bottom of the RR Cars &

build fires on it & stand the smoke, until our eyes gave out & then put out the fire & stand the cold until about to freeze, and so on if this be a fair sample of the marches I don't wonder at the number of deaths in the army." Costello also reported that many of his men broke out with the measles en route to Corinth. See Letter, Costello to wife, March 6, 1862, ADAH. Lieutenant Howell also recalled the massive measles epidemic (see Howell, "25th Alabama," p. 5, ADAH).

[54] Brigadier General Adley H. Gladden commanded the 1st Brigade in Brig. Gen. Jones Withers's 2nd Division, which was assigned to Bragg's 2nd Corps. Besides the 25th Alabama, Gladden's Brigade comprised the 21st, 22nd, and 26th Alabama regiments and the 1st Louisiana, plus Robertson's Battery. See OR 10, pt. 1, p. 538.

[55] The 18th and 19th Alabama regiments were assigned to Brig. Gen. John K. Jackson's 3rd Brigade, Withers's Division.

[56] Tom's assertion was a highly interesting departure from the norm for Southerners approaching combat for the first time, since they were more likely to publicly proclaim their eagerness for the fray. Writing his wife just five days before Tom penned his letter to the *Republican*, Captain Costello insisted: "Every impulse of my nature rebels against the forced rule they seek to impose on us & I thirst for a showing to give evidence of the faith that is in me." Costello also opined that his was the prevailing sentiment, since "our men are as eager as ever hawk was to pounce on his quarry and the glistening bayonet will be their weapon." See Letter, Costello to wife, January 31, 1862, ADAH.

[57] Captain Costello confirmed that his men were "kept warm by the contiguity of the Yankees, some of whom are brought in every day by our pickets." See Letter, Costello to wife, March 6, 1862, ADAH.

[58] Confederate forces surrendered at Fort Donelson in February 1862 by order of Gen. Simon B. Buckner, unleashing a whirlwind of acrimonious debate. After the besieged Confederates had smashed the Union lines in an attempt to secure a line of retreat to Nashville, Generals Floyd and Pillow decided to return the troops to their old lines, rather than marching to Nashville or attempting to destroy Grant's disorganized forces. This stupendous blunder allowed Grant to reorganize his siege lines, while convincing Buckner that all hope of successful resistance was lost. Floyd passed command to Pillow, who passed it to Buckner, who was left to reap the whirlwind of capitulation. These events inspired Tom's story about the gallant Mississippians. See Stanley F. Horn, *The Army of Tennessee* (Bobbs-Merrill, 1941; reprint, Norman: Univ. of Oklahoma Press, 1993), pp. 87-98.

[59] For a fine synopsis of these influences on the Southern fighting man, see James M. McPherson, *For Cause and Comrades: Why Men Fought in the Civil War* (New York: Oxford Univ. Press, 1997), pp. 95-97, 134-138, 148-151. A basic work on the Southern outlook is W. J. Cash, *The Mind of the South* (Alfred A. Knopf, Inc., 1941; reprint, New York: Vintage Books, 1991).

[60] The phrase "right about, march" alluded to the drill command that caused marching men to immediately turn around and march in the opposite direction. See

also Letter, Costello to wife, March 6, 1862, ADAH. Costello hoped that a month's time would see him in Cincinnati, where he would mail her a letter after "having helped to drive Lincoln's minions" from the city.

[61] Larry J. Daniel, *Shiloh: The Battle That Changed the Civil War* (New York: Simon & Schuster, 1997), p. 305.

[62] Ibid., pp. 24, 29-30, 68; Wiley Sword, *Shiloh: Bloody April* (New York: William Morrow & Co., 1974), pp. 59, 63, 73. No less an authority than Secretary of War Walker called the Memphis & Charleston railroad the "vertebrae of the Confederacy" (see McMillan, ed., *Alabama Confederate Reader*, p. 144).

[63] Daniel, *Shiloh*, pp. 40-47, 60-63; Sword, *Bloody April*, pp. 61-67.

[64] Daniel, *Shiloh*, pp. 63, 94; Sword, *Bloody April*, pp. 76-77; Letter, Costello to wife, March 12, 1862, ADAH; Howell, "25th Alabama," p. 7, ADAH; *Jacksonville Republican*, April 10, 1862. The last-named reference was a March 22 letter from Lt. W. J. Borden; unfortunately, the great majority of this letter is illegible on microfilm.

[65] The 25th Alabama, 22nd Alabama, and 1st Louisiana raided the Union lines in late March, driving in the enemy pickets and hauling off 3500 bushels of corn. Captain Costello related with amazement that the little force had stood unmolested within earshot of the Federal encampments, and could hear "every tap of their drums as they beat Reveillee & Tattoo." See Letter, Costello to wife, April 1, 1862, ADAH.

[66] Daniel, *Shiloh*, pp. 126-129, 143-144; Sword, *Bloody April*, pp. 104-108, 139-144.

[67] Daniel, *Shiloh*, pp. 152-154; Sword, *Bloody April*, pp. 156-158.

[68] Daniel, *Shiloh*, pp. 154-155; Sword, *Bloody April*, pp. 160-62; Howell, "25th Alabama," p. 8, ADAH.

[69] Ibid.; *Jacksonville Republican*, April 24, 1862; Major William Gilham, *Manual of Instruction for the Volunteers and Militia of the United States* (Philadelphia: Charles Desilver, 1861; reprint, n.d.), pp. 34-35; C. S. Ordnance Bureau, *The Field Manual for the Use of the Officers on Ordnance Duty* (Richmond: Ritchie & Dunnavant, 1862; reprint, Gettysburg: Dean S. Thomas, 1984), p. 23.

[70] Letter, Costello to wife, March 6, 1862, ADAH; Daniel, *Shiloh*, p. 155; Sword, *Bloody April*, pp. 162-163, 166-167. Costello was wounded at Shiloh and mentioned for particular gallantry in Colonel Loomis's report of the battle. See OR 10, pt. 1, p. 544; Brewer, *Alabama*, p. 630.

[71] Daniel, *Shiloh*, pp. 155-156; Sword, *Bloody April*, pp. 167-170.

[72] Daniel, *Shiloh*, pp. 192-197; Sword, *Bloody April*, pp. 234-241.

[73] Daniel, *Shiloh*, pp. 235-236; Sword, *Bloody April*, pp. 243-256.

[74] Daniel, *Shiloh*, pp. 221, 235-237; Sword, *Bloody April*, pp. 287-288, 300-307.

[75] Daniel, *Shiloh*, pp. 250-256; Sword, *Bloody April*, pp. 339-345, 361-368; Howell, "25th Alabama," p. 9, ADAH.

[76] Sword, *Bloody April*, pp. 358-359. Later that evening, the mob under the bluffs numbered an estimated ten to fifteen thousand fugitives. See Daniel, *Shiloh*, p. 246.

[77] Sword, *Bloody April*, pp. 358-359.

[78] Daniel, *Shiloh*, p. 269; OR 10, pt. 1, p. 544.

[79] This narrative relates the action in and around Spain Field.

[80] Elements of the 22nd Alabama also participated in this charge near the Manse George House on the afternoon of April 6, when the Alabamians ejected the 3rd Iowa from an exposed position near the Hornets' Nest line. Borden greatly overestimated the number of Federals engaged on this small portion of the line.

[81] Borden apparently referred to Edmund Ruffin, a secessionist firebrand who fought at Fort Sumter in 1861, although he was an elderly civilian. A minor war of words ensued regarding regimental claims at Shiloh. A soldier of the 22nd Alabama, who arrived at the end of the battle, claimed that his regiment and the 1st Louisiana captured every battery taken that day, except one taken by the 25th Alabama. He was angry that the 21st Alabama had claimed all the glory in the Mobile newspapers. See the Corinth Information Database, http://www2.tsixroads.com/corinth/josie.html, copyright Milton Sandy, Jr., (CrossRoads Access, Inc., 1995).

[82] Captain H. Lewis Morris succeeded Captain Nickson, although it appears that the latter retained his rank until resigning in 1864. It is likely that Nickson reverted to his civilian profession and was serving as a physician, since mumps and measles were decimating the regiment. See ORS II, vol. 1, p. 566.

[83] Lieutenant Robert A. Green died of his wounds in Talladega, Alabama, on May 16, 1862. Lieutenant William A. Hayden resigned August 1, 1862, to date from June 10, 1862. See Ibid., p. 567; *Jacksonville Republican*, June 6, 1862.

[84] Special Order No. 57-2, Army of Mississippi, 2nd Army Corps (Bragg), May 6, 1862, NARA; *Jacksonville Republican*, April 24, 1862; OR 10, pt. 1, pp. 544, 839. Colonel Joe Wheeler of the 19th Alabama commanded advance units of Withers's Division, and mentioned elements of the 19th and 22nd Alabama regiments in his May 10 report of the skirmishing in progress at Farmington. Since these regiments were brigaded with the 25th Alabama, it is possible that Tom and his comrades took part in several of these skirmishes.

[85] Butler's Order No. 28 read: "As the officers and soldiers of the United States have been subject to repeated insults from the women (calling themselves ladies) of New Orleans in return for the most scrupulous non-interference and courtesy on our part, it is ordered that hereafter when any female shall by word, gesture, or movement insult or show contempt for any officer or soldier of the United States she shall be regarded and held liable to be treated as a woman of the town plying her avocation." See Long, *Civil War Day by Day*, p. 212.

[86] OR 10, pt. 1, pp. 852-855; Horn, *Army of Tennessee*, pp. 150-152.

[87] Horn, *Army of Tennessee*, pp. 150-158.

[88] Ibid., p. 166; undated Muster Roll, Company D, 25th Alabama, datelined Camp Loomis, Hamilton County, Tennessee, 25th Alabama Unit Files, ADAH; CMSR, Thomas J. Mangham. Although official documents refer to Tom as a lieutenant upon his dismissal, at least one postwar newspaper editor referred to him as a captain. Unit

listings in the Alabama Department of Archives and History also show *Captain* Thomas Mangham as one of the commanding officers of Company D, 25th Alabama. (See *Richland Beacon* quotation on February 23, 1878 from *Vicksburg Herald* of February 20.)

[89] Many years after the war, Tom asserted on a pension application that he had resigned his commission. Existing evidence is inadequate to substantiate or refute his claim. See Confederate Pension Records, Lincoln Parish, Thomas J. Mangham, LSA.

[90] OR IV, pt. 1, pp. 1094-1095, 1098; pt. 2, pp. 160, 585; Albert Burton Moore, *Conscription and Conflict in the Confederacy* (Macmillan, 1924; reprint, Columbia: USC Press, 1996), pp. 121-122.

[91] Moore, *Conscription and Conflict*, pp. 121-122. The literature of the South in the Civil War is filled with references to the depredations of cavalry units, both regular and irregular. Martin identifies Calhoun, St. Clair, and DeKalb counties as particularly vulnerable in northern Alabama, noting that "several cavalry companies composed largely or wholly of deserters" were formed there in 1864 "with the ostensible object of protection against invasion of the enemy and against depredations of deserters." See Martin, *Desertion of Alabama Troops*, p. 68.

[92] *Richland Beacon*, April 27, 1889; Long, *Civil War Day by Day*, pp. 344-348. One of those who headed south across the Etowah River to safety was Charlie Smith, better known as humorist "Bill Arp."

[93] Letter, Wiley P. Mangham to Hon. James A. Seddon, July 24, 1863, in Letters to the Confederate Secretary of War, file no. 593-M-1863, NARA; *MDT*, May 5, 1863.

[94] Ibid.; Confederate Widows' Pension Records, Richland Parish, Mrs. Fannie L. Mangham, LSA.

[95] Branchville is located seventeen miles southwest of Ashville.

[96] Ash apparently was referring to a temporary militia headquarters established for this operation.

[97] Blount Mountain, a continuation of the Appalachian Mountains, extends into northwestern St. Clair County.

[98] The "sitzens," or citizens, comprised the St. Clair County militia, called up for this sweep to capture deserters and draft evaders. The "Cavaldry" probably comprised a partisan cavalry unit that helped with the hunt.

[99] To "have someone out" meant that these women had male relatives hiding out to evade conscription.

[100] "Civil War Letter, James Alexander Jackson Ash to George W. Ash," in *Cherish* 2, no. 2: 50-51.

[101] *Memorial Record of Alabama*, vol. 2, p. 222.

[102] David Evans, *Sherman's Horsemen: Union Cavalry Operations in the Atlanta Campaign* (Bloomington: Indiana Univ. Press, 1996), pp. 98, 105.

[103] Ibid., pp. 105-107; Frank Moore, ed., *The Rebellion Record: A Diary of American Events, with Documents, Narratives, Illustrative Incidents, Poetry, etc.*, vol. 11 (New York: D. Van Nostrand, 1868), p. 191; Long, *Civil War Day by Day*, pp. 355, 523.

[104] Evans, *Sherman's Horsemen*, pp. 106-107; Moore, ed., *Rebellion Record*, p. 191.

[105] Ibid.

[106] Evans, *Sherman's Horsemen*, pp. 106-169. The raiders' path led them directly through Sylacauga and Dadeville, the homes of Henry and Solomon Mangham, respectively. They were first cousins, and first cousins of Thomas R. Mangham. James M. D. Mangham, a brother of Henry Mangham, lived near LaFayette. For the stories of James and Henry, see Chapter V; for Solomon R. Mangham, see Chapter VI. These chapters also feature genealogical diagrams depicting each man's position in the family tree.

[107] *Richland Beacon*, September 16, 1876, June 17, 1882; *The St. Clair News-Aegis*, April 22, 1976; CMSR, Thomas J. Mangham, 10th Alabama. The *Vidette's* career ended conclusively when another Federal cavalry raid burned the telegraph office in Oxford and destroyed one of Wiley's type cases. The brothers sold their printing office in July 1865 before leaving Alabama. Colonel Forney originally served as captain of a Calhoun County company in the 10th Alabama; he and Tom were friends from pre-war days.

[108] Ibid.; Historical Records, Company A, and Muster Roll of Ashville Guards, May 28, 1860, 10th Alabama Unit Files, ADAH.

[109] Noah Andre Trudeau, *The Last Citadel: Petersburg, Virginia, June 1864-April 1865* (Baton Rouge: LSU Press, 1991), pp. 222-223.

[110] Ibid., pp. 230-236.

[111] Ibid., pp. 236-237; Historical Records, Company A, 10th Alabama Unit Files, ADAH; OR 42, pt. 3, p. 1190. See the William A. Mangham story in Chapter V.

[112] Trudeau, *Last Citadel*, p. 245.

[113] Ibid., pp. 245-247, 250; Historical Records, Company A, 10th Alabama Unit Files, ADAH. The company's historical records list each man's name, annotating whether he was present or absent during the company's engagements. Thomas J. Mangham was one of the 25 men listed as present for the battle of October 27, 1864. The Battle of Burgess's Mill was also known as the Battle of Hatcher's Run or the Battle of Boydton Plank Road. For Tom's opinion of Mahone, see *Richland Beacon*, March 19, 1881.

[114] Trudeau, *Last Citadel*, pp. 251-252.

[115] Historical Records, Company A, 10th Alabama Unit Files, ADAH.

[116] Trudeau, *Last Citadel*, pp. 312-317.

[117] Ibid., pp. 319-322; *Richland Beacon*, May 6, 1876.

[118] Trudeau, *Last Citadel*, pp. 319-322; Brewer, *Alabama*, p. 605.

[119] Trudeau, *Last Citadel*, p. 380; Noah Andre Trudeau, *Out of the Storm: The End of the Civil War, April-June 1865* (Baton Rouge: LSU Press, 1994), pp. 89-92, 102, 118-122;

Chris M. Calkins, *The Appomattox Campaign, March 29-April 9, 1865* (Conshohocken: Combined Books, 1997), p. 58.

[120] Trudeau, *Out of the Storm*, pp. 120-122; Calkins, *Appomattox Campaign*, pp. 126-128; CMSR, Thomas J. Mangham; Confederate Pension Records, Lincoln Parish, Thomas J. Mangham, LSA; Brewer, *Alabama*, p. 605.

[121] CMSR, Thomas J. Mangham; Confederate Pension Records, Lincoln Parish, Thomas J. Mangham, LSA; Trudeau, *Out of the Storm*, pp. 220-226.

[122] *MDT*, February 22, February 24, 1865. The attack on Ashville occurred on February 11.

[123] 1860 Census and Slave Census, Franklin Parish.

[124] 1860 Census, Franklin Parish; *Richland Beacon*, undated clipping, 1927, provided courtesy of Miriam Davey of Baton Rouge, Louisiana; Confederate Widows' Pension Records, Richland Parish, Mrs. Telitha A. Mangham, LSA; Gunby, "Wiley P. Mangham," *Louisiana Leaders*, p. 103.

[125] Reid Mitchell, *Civil War Soldiers: Their Expectations and Experiences* (New York: Simon & Schuster, 1988), pp. 8-9.

[126] Confederate Widows' Pension Records, Richland Parish, Mrs. Telitha A. Mangham, LSA. This record indicates Henry enlisted in May 1863 and served as a corporal. If he was appointed corporal upon enlistment, then it is almost certain that he joined the battery upon its organization in May 1862. Additionally, it is likely that he would have been drafted in May 1862 had he not enlisted voluntarily. The pension document also erroneously fixes Henry's death as occurring in 1875, a full ten years before he actually died. These errors are particularly understandable in light of the fact that Telitha Mangham applied for the pension some fifty years after the events in question, and almost thirty years after her husband's death. Although the 1863 enlistment date is possibly correct, I consider it highly probable that Henry enlisted in May 1862.

[127] *CMH* 13 *(Extended Edition)*, *Louisiana*, pp. 345-346; Arthur W. Bergeron, Jr., *Guide to Louisiana Confederate Military Units 1861-1865* (Baton Rouge: LSU Press, 1989), pp. 21-22.

[128] The *George Mangham* helped Admiral Farragut shoot his way past the fortifications at New Orleans in April 1862, and was employed against Confederate artillery positions along the river during the first weeks of July. Built in 1854 and commissioned into naval service at Philadelphia in 1861, the ship probably bore the name of one of the few Manghams who lived in the northeast. Apparently, they descended from different immigrant ancestors than the much more numerous Southern Manghams. (See http://www.uss-salem.org/danfs/sail/mangham.txt.)

[129] CMSR, Bell Battery (Benton's), M320, reel 48, LSA; Bergeron, *Guide*, pp. 21-22; OR 15, p. 805; OR 24, pt. 3, pp. 1056-1057; John D. Winters, *The Civil War in Louisiana* (Baton Rouge: LSU Press, 1963), pp. 171-173. Although documentation shows that Girtman signed for the six guns listed, all later reports indicate that the

battery operated only the two 3-inch rifles and the two howitzers, a mix that typified Confederate battery organizations. Probably the two 6-pounders were transferred to a different unit at some point.

[130] Winters, *Civil War in Louisiana*, p. 152; Richard Taylor, *Destruction and Reconstruction: Personal Experiences of the Late War* (reprint, New York: Longmans, Green and Co., 1955), pp. 140-142.

[131] ORS I, vol. 3, pp. 195-197; vol. 4, pp. 378-382.

[132] Winters, *Civil War in Louisiana*, pp. 196-197; Stewart Sifakis, *Compendium of the Confederate Armies: Louisiana* (New York: Facts on File, 1995), p. 9; ORS I, vol. 3, p. 197.

[133] ORS I, vol. 3, pp. 195-197, vol. 4, pp. 378-382; OR 24, pt. 1, pp. 700-701; Winters, *Civil War in Louisiana*, p. 197.

[134] ORS I, vol. 3, pp. 195-197, vol. 4, pp. 378-382; OR 24, pt. 1, pp. 700-701. In a dispatch composed during the engagement, Logan estimated that the gunboats had fired 150 rounds. A newspaper report written afterwards specified 122, which appears to be based on an accurate count made within the fort.

[135] Ibid.

[136] ORS I, vol. 3, pp. 195-197, vol. 4, pp. 378-382; Winters, *Civil War in Louisiana*, p. 197.

[137] Captain Benton's report, September 9, 1863, Group 55-L, Joseph L. Brent Papers, 1862-1865, Louisiana Historical Association Collection, Special Collections, Tulane University Library (provided by Dr. Arthur Bergeron). Benton's gunners succeeded in evacuating only four pieces from the fort, abandoning four others.

[138] OR (Navies) 25, p. 63; OR 26, pt. 1, p. 455; ORS I, vol. 4, pp. 840-843. Apparently the upper decks of the *Black Hawk* burned, but the vessel (or its namesake) was back in service in April 1864. See Winters, *Civil War in Louisiana*, pp. 297, 331. The 3-inch rifles fired a variety of shot and shell patterns weighing between six and ten pounds (see Dean S. Thomas, *Cannons: An Introduction to Civil War Artillery* (Gettysburg: Thomas Publications, 1985), pp. 38-39.

[139] ORS I, vol. 6, pp. 42-48. The cascable was the rear of the gun tube, which was elevated or depressed on the axis of the trunnions; these supported the tube on the gun carriage (see C. S. Ordnance Bureau, *The Field Manual for the Use of the Officers on Ordnance Duty* (Richmond: Ritchie & Dunnavant, 1862; reprint, Gettysburg: Dean S. Thomas, 1984), pp. 4-5;

[140] OR 31, pt. 3, pp. 421-422.

[141] Ludwell H. Johnson, *Red River Campaign: Politics and Cotton in the Civil War* (Johns Hopkins Press, 1958; reprint, Kent: Kent State Univ. Press, 1993), pp. 42-45, 106-108, 113-118, 139-143, 165-166. Grant actually wanted to direct an offensive against Mobile, but had to submit to political considerations that called for Banks to advance up the Red River.

[142] Johnson, *Red River*, pp. 213-221; Sifakis, *Confederate Armies: Louisiana*, p. 9; Bergeron, *Guide*, p. 22. Taylor's force was reduced from more than 12,000 at Pleasant

Hill to 5000 by the transfer of Walker's and Churchill's divisions to Arkansas, a disastrous miscalculation by the department commander, Gen. Edmund Kirby Smith.

[143] OR 34, pt. 1, pp. 583-584, 632.

[144] Ibid.; *OR (Navies)* 26, p. 177; ORS I, vol. 6, pp. 344, 356; Larry J. Daniel, *Cannoneers in Gray: The Field Artillery in the Army of Tennessee, 1861-1865* (Tuscaloosa: Univ. of Alabama Press, 1984), pp. 72-73, 103. The *Official Records* are replete with complaints from Confederate commanders in all armies about the poor quality friction primers available for their guns.

[145] OR 34, pt. 1, pp. 583-584, 632; *OR (Navies)* 26, p. 177; ORS I, vol. 6, pp. 344, 356; "Louisiana Batteries in Army of Western Louisiana," in Napier Bartlett, "The Trans-Mississippi," in *Military Record of Louisiana, Including Biographical and Historical Papers Relating to the Military Organizations of the State* (reprint; Baton Rouge: LSU Press, 1992), pp. 59-60.

[146] Johnson, *Red River*, pp. 254-266; ORS I, vol. 6, pp. 345-346, 356-357; OR 34, pt. 1, p. 587.

[147] ORS I, vol. 6, p. 357; "Louisiana Batteries," in Bartlett, *Military Record*, pp. 59-60.

[148] One of Benton's disabled guns was replaced by a 12-pounder Dahlgren boat howitzer salvaged from the wreck of a Federal gunboat. See Lieutenant Bryce's report to Colonel Brent, May 8, 1864, Group 55-L, Joseph L. Brent Papers, 1862-1865, LHA Collection, Special Collections, Tulane University Library (provided by Dr. Arthur Bergeron).

[149] Ibid.; Johnson, *Red River*, pp. 260-266, 273-276, 279-281.

[150] "Unpublished After-Action Reports from the Red River," CWR 4, no. 2 (1994): 129-130.

[151] Bergeron, *Guide*, p. 22; OR 41, pt. 3, p. 967; OR 48, pt. 2, p. 963. On November 19, the Trans-Mississippi Department reorganized its artillery and Benton's Battery became the 3rd Louisiana Field Battery, 3rd Artillery Battalion. See OR 41, pt. 4, p. 1064.

[152] Robert L. Kerby, *Kirby Smith's Confederacy: The Trans-Mississippi South, 1863-1865*, (Tuscaloosa: Univ. of Alabama Press, 1972), pp. 400-402. Some of the outlaw bands in north Louisiana numbered as many as 500 men.

[153] *Richland Beacon-News*, January 11, 1969. This centennial issue of Wiley's old newspaper featured a two-page article, "I See By the Beacon," focusing on its founder and the early days of the paper.

[154] Ibid.; *Richland Beacon-News*, October 10, 1896; *Memoirs of Louisiana*, vol. 2, p. 231. The grave is located on the old Henry Mangham farm. Dr. Ron Morgan, the current owner of the property, kindly allowed me to visit the site and photograph the family graves.

[155] *Memoirs of Louisiana*, vol. 2, p. 196; *Richland Beacon-News*, January 11, 1969; *Monroe Morning World*, January 15, 1961; Gunby, "Wiley P. Mangham," Louisiana Leaders, pp. 103-104.

[156] *Richland Beacon-News*, January 11, 1969; Richland Parish Deed Book M, pp. 417-418 (provided by Miriam Davey); *Richland Beacon-News*, undated article (about October 17, 1896), "History of the Beacon-News," written by Thomas J. Mangham, October 14, 1896. Tom and Jennie married before he left Alabama in 1865, and lived on a 240-acre farm in Richland Parish in 1870 (see 1870 Census, Richland Parish; 1900 Census, Lincoln Parish; *Richland Beacon*, July 22 and September 9, 1876).

[157] *Memoirs of Louisiana*, vol. 2, pp. 231-232; *Richland Beacon*, September 6, 1873, December 9, 1876, September 9, 1882; Joseph L. Whitten, *By Murder, Accident, and Natural Causes: Death Notices from St. Clair County, Alabama, Newspapers 1873-1910*, p. 4; 1880 Census, Richland Parish; *Donaldsonville Chief*, October 14, 1882; Undated news clipping entitled "Mrs. T. A. Mangham Dies at Advanced Age," *Richland Beacon-News*, provided courtesy of Miriam Davey. The 1900 census of Lincoln Parish recorded that Tom and Jennie had had two children, neither of which was still living.

[158] *Memoirs of Louisiana*, vol. 2, pp. 168, 231-232; *Richland Beacon*, December 5, 1874; July 10 and 17, 1875; February 19 and June 10, 1876; July 21 and August 11, 1877; March 2, July 6, and October 19, 1878; March 6, March 27, May 22, July 10 and July 24, 1880; January 29, February 5, May 14, May 28, August 6, November 19, and December 10, 1881; January 3, May 16, 1885; *Richland Beacon-News*, October 10, 1896.

[159] *Richland Beacon*, July 4, 1874; February 6, 1875; November 6, 1880; January 8, July 23, July 30, August 6, and December 10, 1881. See some of Wiley's views in May 26, 1888; May 4, May 11, and August 10, 1889. He likewise protested heatedly against post-Reconstruction lynching and "whitecapism," which he considered tantamount to an admission of unfitness for self-rule.

[160] *Memoirs of Louisiana*, vol. 2, pp. 168, 231-232; *Richland Beacon*, June 26, 1875; September 11, 1880; January 3 and January 25, 1885; *Richland Beacon-News*, October 10, 1896.

[161] 1870 and 1880 Agricultural Schedules, Richland Parish, Louisiana; *Richland Beacon*, November 7, 1874; April 22, 1876; August 4, 1877; July 6 and August 31, 1878; June 19 and July 24, 1880. Tom, Wiley, and Henry's son Thomas were central figures in the establishment of a baseball club in Rayville, and their newspaper often carried the results of local games.

[162] *Richland Beacon*, December 12, 1885. Unfortunately, it has proved impossible to find the "suitable obituary" Wiley promised to provide. Only remnants survive from the following week's issue of the *Beacon*, and nothing survives of the issue dated December 26, 1885. I have been unable to find microfilm copies of the *Beacon* from 1886. This unhappy coincidence leaves a major gap in what we know about Henry G. Mangham.

[163] *Richland Beacon*, January 15, 1876, April 20, 1878; Confederate Widows' Pension Records, Richland Parish, Mrs. Telitha A. Mangham, LSA; Undated clipping, "Mrs. T. A. Mangham Dies at Advanced Age," *Richland Beacon-News*; Telephone interview, Billy Grant Mangham with author, November 13, 1995. Billy Mangham is a great-grandson

of Henry Grant Mangham, and kindly provided the information about his grandfather Thomas Mangham's death in Oklahoma City. Billy's father also bore the name Henry Grant Mangham.

[164] *Richland Beacon*, October 24, 1885; *Memoirs of Louisiana*, vol. 2, p. 168; Confederate Pension Records, Lincoln Parish, Thomas J. Mangham, LSA; "Louisiana Masons," *Claiborne Parish Trails* 4, no. 4 (November 1989): 178.

[165] In the *Beacon* of March 21, 1874, Wiley advertised over 1900 acres of land "on easy terms." See also *Richland Beacon-News*, July 17, 1984; March 26, 1985. The author of these articles, Mr. Bennie Hixon, kindly made them available to me. Himself a descendant of the Hixons who settled in Mangham, Louisiana, he is a veritable fount of knowledge about the early days of Richland Parish.

[166] *Richland Beacon-News*, October 3, 1896; October 10, 1896; and undated article (about October 17, 1896), "History of the Beacon-News," written by Thomas J. Mangham, October 14, 1896.

[167] *Richland Beacon-News*, undated article by Thomas J. Mangham, October 14, 1896.

[168] Confederate Pension Records, Lincoln Parish, Thomas J. Mangham, LSA. The 1900 census of Lincoln Parish listed Tom as a farmer.

[169] Ibid. Tom's pension file is annotated "Private papers returned Dec. 5th 1907." Clearly, this referred to Colonel Smith's testimonial regarding Tom's character and military service. Tom's gain was our loss, however, as no record survives today of the document's contents. Obviously laudatory in nature, Smith's recommendation either attested that Tom was wronged by his dismissal from service in 1862 or simply emphasized the quality of his service as a private in the 10th Alabama. In either case, it apparently convinced the state pensions board to grant Tom's request for a pension based on honorable service.

[170] Ibid.; Clare D. Leeper, "Mangham," in *Louisiana Places: A Collection of the Columns from the Baton Rouge "Sunday Advocate" 1960-1974* (Baton Rouge: Legacy Publishing Co., 1976), p. 150; "Governor's Proclamation of Incorporation of the Village of Mangham," March 4, 1907, in unpublished manuscript, Horace B. Chambers, "History of Mangham Louisiana, Richland Parish," June 30, 1951. I obtained this manuscript from Mildred Johns, Clerk of the Town of Mangham, while visiting in 1997.

[171] Death Certificate, Thomas J. Mangham, State Deaths, reel 1, 1918, LSA. Tom's death certificate correctly reflected his birth month and day, but misstated the year as 1836. Since he personally filled out two pension applications giving 1835 as his year of birth, I have accepted that date as definitive. It also is the date inscribed on his gravestone, and is consistent with census and enlistment records. The grave marker indicates Jennie was born in 1844 and died in 1919.

[172] Confederate Widows' Pension Records, Richland Parish, Mrs. Fannie L. Mangham, LSA; *Richland Beacon-News*, January 11, 1969.

[173] *Richland Beacon-News*, January 11, 1969.

CHAPTER IV: MERCHANTS & THE SOUTHERN MILITIA TRADITION: THE JOHN C. MANGHAM FAMILY OF SPALDING COUNTY

1. FROM MILLEDGEVILLE TO GRIFFIN: JOHN C. MANGHAM AND THE SETTLEMENT OF WEST GEORGIA

Whereas Thomas R. Mangham's sons left their mark in Alabama and northern Louisiana, his uncle John C. Mangham remained in Georgia from start to finish. A younger brother of Willis Austin Mangham and son of Solomon Mangham, John was born in Hancock County about 1797 and grew to maturity in the Hancock, Putnam, and Baldwin county areas. By 1820, he was operating a stage line in Milledgeville, displaying at an early age the wide-ranging business acumen that came to characterize his entire adult life. Like so many of his relatives, John also spent much of his life in positions of public service, beginning in 1821 with his election as deputy sheriff of Baldwin County; by the following year, he had risen to the position of sheriff. In February of 1822, John departed the ranks of Milledgeville's eligible bachelors, marrying Isaac Barrett's daughter Nancy (Ann).[1]

John and Ann were blessed shortly thereafter with a son, John C. Mangham, Jr., who was born about the same time that his proud father was commissioned second lieutenant of the cavalry troop attached to the 33rd Regiment of Georgia militia. These part-time military duties were more than simply ceremonial in a state whose western and southern reaches were still very much on America's frontiers. On December 24, 1826, Second Lt. John C. Mangham reported for duty when the governor ordered Capt. William F. Scott's cavalry troop into active service "for the protection of the southern frontier" against Indians raiding from Florida; the militiamen remained afield until January 27 of the following year. For one month and five days on active duty, Lieutenant Mangham received the sum of precisely 38 dollars and 88 2/3 cents! By the mid-1820s, however, John was making his living as a hotelkeeper, and doubtless earned a great deal more in his civilian avocation. He assumed ownership of the Zebulon Hotel in fledgling Pike County, which his brothers Willis and Wiley had helped organize just several years earlier. While living there, John and Ann had another son, *Samuel Watson Mangham*, born on September 21, 1830. Just one year later, John secured a commission as captain commanding the company of Pike County cavalry attached to the 66th Militia Regiment.[2]

By the mid-1830s, John was attracted to the thriving crossroads town of Columbus, Georgia, one of the main gateways to the trans-Chattahoochee frontier. He obtained a retail license there in 1836-1837, apparently to operate another hotel. The townsmen were increasingly concerned, however, about the "great mobs" of Creek Indians who crossed the Chattahoochee each day from Russell County, Alabama, to wander around town. Their presence in Columbus reflected the tensions building up in Russell County, established in 1832, where white settlement was pushing aside the Creeks. By late 1835, numerous minor incidents had eroded the five-year period of peace, and the Georgia-Alabama frontier was ripe for a major clash. When Creeks killed Maj. William Flournoy in an ambush on May 9, 1836, tensions reached a fever pitch; the ensuing grisly massacre of white women and children at the Big Uchee bridge proved to be the proverbial last straw.[3]

When widespread hostilities erupted along the frontier between whites and Indians, John was as quick to respond to the danger as he had been ten years earlier. A "troop of horse" organized and elected officers in Columbus on May 18, and John was elected unanimously as its captain. His "Muscogee County Cavalry" militia company was the sixth in line to draw arms from the state arsenal at Columbus, of the fifty-five companies outfitted between February 9 and October 1, 1836. The company was assigned to Col. Asa Bates's 66th Regiment of Georgia Militia, in which John had served while captain of the Pike County cavalry. John and his men saw active service for several months during the war, which resulted in the suppression of Indian depredations in western Georgia and eastern Alabama.[4]

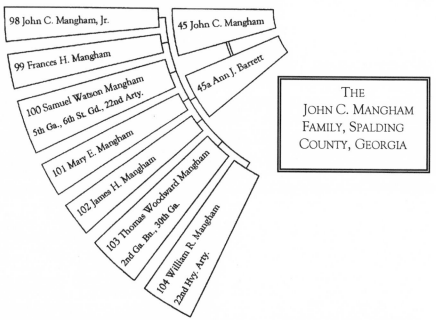

98 John C. Mangham, Jr.

45 John C. Mangham

99 Frances H. Mangham

45a Ann J. Barrett

100 Samuel Watson Mangham
5th Ga., 6th St. Gd., 22nd Arty.

101 Mary E. Mangham

102 James H. Mangham

103 Thomas Woodward Mangham
2nd Ga. Bn., 30th Ga.

104 William R. Mangham
22nd Hvy. Arty.

THE JOHN C. MANGHAM FAMILY, SPALDING COUNTY, GEORGIA

It was probably shortly after his return from the campaign against the Creeks that he and Ann welcomed a fourth son into the family in November 1836, when *Thomas Woodward Mangham* joined John Jr., Sam, and James H. (born c. 1834), along with their sisters Frances and Mary. John served as census-taker for nearby Meriwether County in 1840, and secured election two years later as sheriff of Muscogee County. In that year or the following one, son *William R. Mangham* was born, just a short time before John Jr. went off to serve in the Mexican War as quartermaster of a regular infantry regiment. Their father maintained his establishments in Zebulon and Columbus, as well as one at Warm Springs in neighboring Meriwether County. He advertised the latter hotel in 1847 in the Macon *Messenger*, emphasizing its location in western

Georgia's "fashionable and celebrated watering Place," and offering board, lodging, and bath for twenty dollars per month. In the late 1840s, he established yet another hotel in the town of Griffin, which became the county seat of newly organized Spalding County in 1851 when the legislature created it from Pike and neighboring counties. Sometime before the new county's organization, John reached the pinnacle of his public service by serving as judge of the Pike County Inferior Court.[5]

The 1850s, however, saw two tragedies strike the family. John's fifty-year-old wife Ann passed away in Columbus on Christmas Eve, 1853, leaving the family without a mother. Five years later, their son James died in Griffin, where he was buried with Masonic honors in the family plot. Only twenty-four years old when he died, James already was serving as judge of Spalding County's Court of Ordinary; his collection of law books was the most valuable possession in his modest estate. When James died, his father was about 61 years old, and long since had established himself as a successful businessman, community leader, and public servant. John was also a prosperous farmer and slaveowner, owning twenty-six slaves, 250 acres of cultivated land and two hundred additional acres of unimproved land in Pike County by 1860. With six thousand dollars worth of real estate and $21,700 of personal property in 1860, he was one of the most prominent and well-known men in the county, where he was known commonly by his militia title, "Captain Mangham." Although John was "without those advantages of an early education" and was "considered somewhat eccentric by many people," he "possessed a strong and vigorous intellect, quick perception and ready wit," which made the prominent men of his place and time "his fast friends."[6]

2. Brothers in Arms: Col. Samuel W. Mangham and Pvt. William R. Mangham, 5ᵗʰ Georgia Infantry; 6ᵗʰ Georgia State Guard; 22ᴺᴰ Battalion Georgia Heavy Artillery

As Capt. John C. Mangham established himself as a prominent economic and social fixture in Griffin during the last decade before the war, so did his son Samuel Watson Mangham. Raised with a commercial sense honed by working in his father's hotels, Sam went into business with C. H. Johnson soon after the Mangham family moved to town. Before long, he became a partner of J. H. White and thus co-owner of White & Mangham, a prominent clothing store in town. Like most other Southerners of the ante-bellum era, however, Sam remained firmly rooted in the region's overwhelmingly agricultural economy, and he owned sixteen slaves to work the farm that comprised the other half of his business interests. By 1856, Sam was one of the town's most eligible bachelors; when he tied the knot that year with 19-year-old Pope Reeves, it must have been a significant event for Griffin society.[7]

Sam's younger brother James was a practicing attorney in town, and eventually won election as Spalding County Ordinary. Before his death at age 24 in 1858, James also served as manager of the Concert Hall at the Georgia Hotel on East Broadway Street. The Mangham family thus held a position at the center of local society, as surviving party and cotillion invitations attest. A successful young businessman and gentleman farmer, widely viewed as "the handsome and dashing young man of his time," Sam was

179

a natural candidate for a position of responsibility when Griffin's young bloods decided to organize a new militia company in late 1856. Such companies had begun sprouting up throughout the Deep South in the 1850s, as the increasingly heated rhetoric of sectional debate led many to consider dissolving the Union. These organizations grew from Southern militia traditions not long dormant. After all, when the "Griffin Light Guards" unanimously elected 26-year-old Sam Mangham as their captain in 1856, it was only twenty years since his father had led his Muscogee County cavalry company into action against the Creek Indians.[8]

COL. SAMUEL W. MANGHAM

- Courtesy of Jean Mangham Holzapfel

The Southern militia corps of the 1850s thus sent a strong message evocative of the coiled rattlesnakes and "Don't Tread On Me" mottoes of earlier times, but few of the hotbloods in the ranks foresaw the grim realities of the next decade. Most of these militia units seemed to resemble social clubs more than the eventual combat organizations of the Civil War, and Captain Mangham and his Griffin Light Guards probably were no exception to this pattern. Sam's brother, *Thomas W. Mangham,* himself orderly sergeant of the company, was on the social committee in January 1858 when the dashing young gallants sponsored a gala "Military Party" at Griffin's Marshall College Chapel. Befitting Sam's occupation as a clothing merchant, it is likewise unsurprising that his company proudly claimed a reputation as "one of the most conspicuously ornamental" in the state of Georgia. Sam Mangham was conspicuous for his organizational talents, too, and his well dressed "showy, holiday, corps" claimed to be one of the best drilled in the state. At a drill session in July 1860, the Light Guards "presented quite an imposing appearance" to Griffin's 2855 souls as they paraded through the city streets for several hours "under command of their gallant Captain Mangham. . .performing various evolutions, with good effect."[9]

The Light Guard's drills soon assumed a more earnest aspect, for the end of the year brought the long-threatened crisis of the young republic, when South Carolina seceded from the Union. Georgia followed in January 1861, with Spalding County voters giving a 330-vote majority to the "immediate secession" ticket; the first shots were fired in anger at Fort Sumter just three months later. When President Lincoln called for troops to quell the secessionists and protect Federal property in the seceding states, the call to arms sounded throughout the Southland. As aroused volunteers streamed into cities and towns across Georgia for the purpose of organizing military units, Governor Joe Brown coordinated with Secretary of War Leroy P. Walker to muster a regiment at Macon for service at Pensacola, Florida, one of the fledgling Confederacy's crucial port cities. Sam and his Light Guards were one of the ten companies ordered to rendezvous at Macon, so he clearly tendered their services almost immediately upon the outbreak of war. When the company formally enlisted at Macon for twelve months' service on May 10, 1861, the men elected to retain Sam Mangham as their captain. They were now organized as Company B of the 5th Regiment Georgia Volunteer Infantry. If Griffin's finest shared the dominant sentiments of that time, they must have been supremely confident that a year's time would suffice to thrash their foes.[10]

For 30-year-old Sam, however, May 1861 was only the beginning of a military odyssey that saw him occupy positions both great and small in a bewildering variety of organizations. As such, his military career provides a fascinating glimpse of the nature and complexity of the Confederacy's armed forces. All of that lay in an uncertain future, however, when Sam bade goodbye to his wife of eighteen months, Harriet (Hattie) Reeves Mangham, his three-year-old son Pope Reeves Mangham, and baby John H. Mangham, born only nine months before Sam's departure. The young officer needed to look no further than his little family to see proof of life's uncertainties: Hattie was the sister of Sam's first wife, Pope Reeves Mangham, who died in 1857, just four months after giving birth to the son who bore her name.[11]

The Griffin Light Guard certainly made a favorable impression in Macon, as did the rest of the regiment. The *Macon Daily Telegraph* thought the men were "all *evidently* respectable," and considered it "a shame to pit such material, man for man, against such vagabonds as the North are sending against us, but we will console ourselves with the belief, that one such man as Georgia is turning out for the holy work of self protection, is worth a half score of Northern pick-pockets." Such sentiments were widespread among aggrieved Southerners, who commonly viewed the numerous blue-uniformed Irish and German immigrants as little better than pillage-hungry mercenaries.[12] An article in the same issue of the *Telegraph* reprinted an already widely popular, scathing assessment of Col. Billy Wilson's New York Zouave regiment, which Sam's 5th Georgia soon confronted at Pensacola:

> . . .Well, let [Wilson] bring on his rascals. The scheme of sending off an army of cut purses, foot pads, river thieves, gutter scrapers, to pillage the South, is economical and judicious in several respects. Every man killed is so much clear gain to humanity at large, and particularly in New York, and as the time is coming when what are left will exercise their vocation at home, it is especially

desirable to New York that as few should be left as possible. The list of killed among the New York volunteers will be wound up with a mental ejaculation of "Laus Deo" by every decent New Yorker.[13]

The very day he mustered into Confederate service, Sam bade farewell to Macon and proceeded with the 832 men of the 5th Georgia to reinforce the garrison holding Pensacola. Along the sandy beaches facing the northern shores of Santa Rosa Island, troops of the 1st Alabama Infantry had been watching the glowering ramparts of Federal-occupied Fort Pickens since February. Other troops from the South's Gulf Coast flowed into the area during the spring and summer, which they spent building shore batteries, drilling as coast artillerymen, and generally acclimating themselves to the rigors of active military service. Sam and his men did the same; although his Light

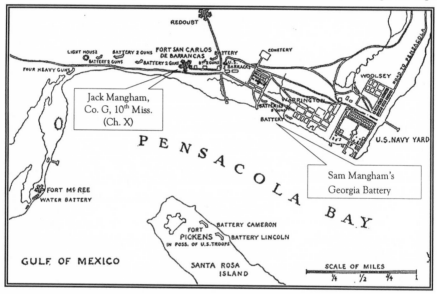

PENSACOLA BAY, MAY 27, 1861. SAM MANGHAM COMMANDED THE "GEORGIA BATTERY" AT WARRINGTON. HIS RELATIVE JOHN C. MANGHAM, 10TH MISSISSIPPI, WAS AT BARRANCAS. PART OF HIS REGIMENT DEFENDED FORT MCREE (SEE CH. X).

Guards were armed with Maynard-primed muskets and organized as an infantry company, the lack of trained artillerymen available to Maj. Gen. Braxton Bragg led him to employ many of his foot soldiers as gunners. Sam accordingly assumed command of the "Georgia Battery," and began drilling his soldiers in the intricacies of their three 8-inch Columbiads. The tubes of these behemoths weighed 9210 pounds exclusive of the carriage, and could hurl a fifty-pound shell almost 3900 yards, or a 65-pound solid shot 3200 yards. These ship-killing coast defense guns were located in Warrington, at the northern end of the harbor next to the Navy Yard. Sam's men may have rotated between their gun emplacements and an encampment at Camp Stephens, situated on a hill one mile north of Pensacola on the Florida & Alabama Railroad.[14]

July saw Bragg form his army of neophytes, ten thousand strong, for a formal review in the blazing Florida sun. Buttoned up to the chin in their early war uniforms, many overheated Southrons collapsed or staggered out of ranks before the ordeal was finally over. These men were fortunate, however, compared to the miserable unfortunates laid low by the epidemics of measles, jaundice, typhoid fever, and malaria that scourged the crowded encampments. These dangers contrasted to the live and let-live attitude which reigned between the Federals on Santa Rosa and the secessionist forces arrayed along Pensacola's beaches.[15]

Union raiders rudely interrupted this quietude on the night of September 14, 1861, when launches from the *U.S.S. Colorado* surprised and burned the Confederate privateer *Judah*. More raiders burned the dry dock at the Navy Yard, adding insult to injury by spiking the guns of the battery there. These daring actions stung the Confederates into responding, and they launched a raid of their own on the night of October 8-9. For Captain Mangham, it began when the regimental commander, Col. John K. Jackson, issued a call to the 5th Georgia's various companies for 150 volunteers to undertake "hazardous work." The volunteers were grouped into a provisional battalion of three composite companies, with Sam commanding the 1st Company. The men filed onto flatboats beginning at 11:00 p.m. that night, and left the wharf at midnight as part of a thousand-man landing force bound for Santa Rosa Island.[16]

Towed by the steamers *McAffie* and *Ewing*, the flatboats glided across the darkened bay, scraping ashore after two hours of tense silence. Forming his men into line on the right of the 5th Georgia contingent, which was positioned on the right and rear of Brig. Gen. Richard H. Anderson's entire landing force, Sam had his men load their muskets and fix bayonets before striking out into the blackness at a rapid pace. They slogged along the beach for several miles through the sand and surf, with the rightmost files struggling against waves which lapped up to their knees at times, until Colonel Jackson shouted "Down men and wait well for the word." Pulses pounding from exertion and excitement, Sam's men knelt, cocked their pieces, and prepared to fire their first shots in defense of their country and their lives.[17]

Whether it was discipline or fear that stayed the Georgians' anxious trigger fingers, it was well that they held their fire, for the foe looming in the darkness proved to be the Mississippians of Col. J. R. Chalmers's column, which was advancing in their front. Regrouping after this scare, Sam and his men moved out again for about a mile, until a shot to their front signaled that a sentry had discovered the Mississippians. General Anderson now ordered Jackson's men to push rapidly through the thickets to the center of the island, where they became the first of three Confederate columns to make significant contact with the enemy. Confronting Sam Mangham's advance were some twelve to fifteen pickets of Col. Billy Wilson's 6th New York Zouaves. Their scattering fire killed two of Sam's men, but triggered a crashing return volley that felled a number of Zouaves. The Georgians continued forward to a wagon road that led to the New Yorkers' camp; at twenty yards range, they poured a volley into the deploying

Federals and charged with lowered bayonets, shrilling the high-pitched battle cries later renowned as the "Rebel Yell." Listening expectantly across the bay at Pensacola, their comrades from the Navy Yard to Fort McRee gave tongue in response. As Sam's company poured into the camp along with the remainder of Jackson's Georgians, they mowed down Zouaves fleeing in panic rout before the surprise attack. The rebel infantrymen then torched the encampment and prepared to resume their advance. Some of the bewildered New Yorkers attempted to rally, but the blazing tents illuminated sand dunes swarming with Confederate soldiers; a chastened Colonel Wilson admitted, "My men, on seeing this, broke for the beach." Luckily for the dazed New Yorkers, the glimmer of approaching sunrise caused General Bragg to fire a cannon at the Navy Yard, signaling the raiding force to fall back to the beach for evacuation; further delay would expose their little steamers to destruction by the Federal naval vessels blockading Pensacola.[18]

Sam's company took part in the ensuing withdrawal, as Union reinforcements attempted to cut off the Georgians from the coast. Private Richard Clayton was marching under Sam's command, and wrote proudly to his father that they ". . .rushed up fired and charged. We killed many of them, the balance ran like dogs. I wish you could have seen them. They would stand very well until the command 'Charge Bayonets' was given—then they would run—run as Yankees alone can run. . . ." The pursuit persisted nonetheless, however, and Union regulars continued to fire on Sam's men as they boarded their flatboats. One shot dropped Lieutenant Nelms of the 5th Georgia's "McDuffie Rifles," and Private Clayton saw an enraged comrade rush the man who had fired the fatal shot. As he recalled the scene a short time later:

> The fellow cried for mercy—The McDuffie threw him to the ground jumped on him—and says, "Yes, I'll show you mercy"—He raised his "large knife" and came down with a lick which cut the Yanks "heart out." He then cut the fellows throat telling him at the same time, "If I had 3 thousand of you I'd do with them all just as I have done with you." (His words as near as I can remember.)

After some other proud comments about the expedition's success, Clayton added, "War is an awful thing but can't be helped with us. We are fighting in self-defense, and it is a crowd of scamps we are fighting. . . ." In words that testified to the depth of feeling that sustained Southerners through four years of war, he defiantly added, "Talk about whipping us that can't be done. 'Three million of (our) people fighting for their country—their firesides are invincible.'" General Bragg would have agreed. Normally sparing in his praise for volunteer troops, the crusty old Mexican War hero reported that their "alacrity, courage, and discipline" at Santa Rosa Island merited "the highest commendation."[19]

In contrast to Bragg's high praise of his volunteer troops, his opposite number at Fort Pickens spoke scathingly of the performance of his hapless Zouaves, Colonel Wilson's 6th New York Volunteers. Colonel Harvey Brown, a Regular U.S. Army officer, barely mentioned the ill-starred regiment in his initial report, later excusing the omission by commenting: "I desired to spare them the stigma of cowardice, which I should have been compelled to inflict." In his view, the men of the regiment were good material, but their leaders were "in every respect unfit for officers." He proposed to break up the regiment and assign its men to Regular Army companies, where they could be made into soldiers in one month, allowing that "I could with confidence lead them into battle, which I should now be very sorry to do."[20]

As for Sam and his men, they had indeed "heard the balls whistle," as Private Clayton commented. The raiding force lost eighteen men killed and thirty-nine wounded from its total strength of 1000-1100, as well as thirty who fell captive; most of the latter were taken prisoner at the hospital complex, where they failed to hear Bragg's signal to evacuate. At least one of the mortally wounded and two of the killed were among the approximately fifty men under Sam's command in his baptism of fire.[21]

Less lethal for his command, but more awe-inspiring in many respects, was the terrific cannonade that ensued in late November. The Griffin Light Guard had recently handed over the "Georgia Battery" to the "Brown Infantry," thus reverting to an infantry role. Only one day after Sam receipted for a consignment of two thousand rounds of "buck and ball" ammunition for his company's muskets at Warrington on November 21, he probably wished he had received two thousand rounds for the Columbiads instead. Early on November 22, every Federal battery on Santa Rosa Island opened fire on the Confederate positions at Pensacola, as did several Union naval vessels.[22] As one gunner of the 1st Alabama, Edward McMorries, remembered many years later:

> The artillery on both sides aggregated about 300 pieces, varying in calibre from 32 to 128 pounders; and as each was fired every few minutes, the deafening roar was beyond description—beyond even conception save to those engaged. Every window light in Warrenton was shivered to atoms by the first few volleys, while those in Pensacola, eight miles distant, were badly shaken up and many broken. In some instances blood poured from the noses of the men working the guns, while the thunder of the conflict was afterwards declared to have been heard at Greenville, Camden, Montgomery, Hayneville, Union Springs, and Troy, distances ranging from one hundred to one hundred and twenty-five miles from the scene of action.

A nightlong hiatus ensued in the bombardment, but McMorries and his fellow Confederates got precious little sleep. Scattering picket fire alarmed the weary troops shortly before midnight, and officers and men listened with growing anxiety. The shooting "rapidly increased until it seemed like the whole picket force was hotly engaged," and regimental drummers furiously began beating the "long roll" for assembly. Just west of Sam's position at Warrington, the 1st Alabama's officers began "shouting to their men to 'fall in,' as if the whole Yankee army was landing about two hundred yards in our front." Private McMorries recalled the sense of danger:

> Men ran hither-thither in hurly-burley style, sometimes knocking each other down in their blind and mad rush for clothing, guns and equipment. As soon as

formed, the companies were "double-quicked" to their respective batteries. On reaching his battery, a certain captain of the regiment made a speech that night to his company that was repeated many a time afterward around the camp-fires of the regiment. As he drew up his company in line, he thus harangued the men at the top of his voice, and in a high key: "Stand firm, men! Stand firm! Think of your homes and firesides! You have done well today, and we expect you to do well tonight."

As the tension waned during the ensuing hour at their gun positions, the realization grew that the wary pickets had been shooting at shadows; the whole thing was a false alarm. McMorries noted that such mishaps were "a very common occurrence in any army in time of war," concluding "that these night alarms, far in the dead hour of night, are more trying to the nerves than a real battle in daytime." In all probability, the confusion in the 1st Alabama mirrored the scenes in Sam Mangham's camp and elsewhere at Pensacola.[23]

The following day saw a repeat of the colossal bombardment, which the awed Alabamian reflected may have been the most intense of the entire Civil War, considering both the number and caliber of the guns engaged. General Bragg, himself a famed Mexican War artillerist, reported: "For the number and caliber of guns and weight of metal brought into action it will rank with the heaviest bombardment in the world." Although both sides suffered material damage to their respective fortifications and losses of personnel, neither was prepared to give way. The stalemate at Pensacola would continue.[24]

In the opening days of 1862, when the Confederate government queried Bragg about transferring to the threatened region of eastern Tennessee, he asked leave to take his best three regiments along; one of these was Colonel Jackson's 5th Georgia Volunteers. Writing to Secretary of War Judah P. Benjamin on January 6, Bragg asserted that these units "would give me a nucleus upon which to form, would set an example of discipline, and would give me the support of excellent officers, who know and trust me, and in whom I place unlimited confidence." Bragg also asked that Jackson, who had commanded the 4th Brigade of the Army of Pensacola for over seven months, be formally advanced to brigade command.[25]

Jackson's ensuing promotion to brigadier general on January 14 meant that the soldiers of the 5th Georgia needed to elect a new colonel. As members of Sam Mangham's Griffin Light Guards preened years later, their captain's "superb management" of their company "gave to it a reputation for all that was soldierly second to that of no command in this Southern land." Accordingly, "After this demonstration of his capacity as an organizer and commander of men, it was no surprise to us that he was selected to take command of the whole regiment, where in a broader field he added increased lustre to his military reputation." Sam's commission as colonel in the Provisional Army of the Confederate States was effective February 1, 1862. As a token of their esteem, the men of his old company presented him a sword engraved with the words: "Presented to Col. S. W. Mangham, 5th Ga. Vols. by Griffin Light Guard Co. B.

Feby. 3rd 1862" The *Macon Daily Telegraph* pronounced itself satisfied with news of Sam's election, averring that "He will make a good officer."[26]

COLONEL MANGHAM'S SWORD, PRESENTED BY THE MEN OF THE
GRIFFIN LIGHT GUARD
- Courtesy of Jean Mangham Holzapfel

His first weeks in command of the 5th Georgia were hectic ones, as orders soon came down for the regiment to move to eastern Tennessee. By February 18, Sam was on his way to Knoxville, an island of secessionist sentiment in a largely Unionist region, as well as a critical node in the Confederacy's tenuous east-west rail network. Shortly thereafter, Sam's regiment marched north to help garrison Cumberland Gap, a strategic location at the point where Tennessee, Virginia and Kentucky intersect, as part of a desperate attempt to protect against an impending Federal offensive. His old company, the Griffin Light Guards, engaged in at least one skirmish while the regiment garrisoned the gap, losing two men wounded in a daylong action on March 22. Most of the picket duty was simply dull routine, however, with moments of tense watchfulness interspersed among hours of drudgery. (See maps, pp. 125 and 519.)[27]

The fast moving Georgians were on the road again within a few weeks, however, as orders came in late March to move to Chattanooga. A despairing Gen. Edmund Kirby Smith, commanding the Confederate Department of East Tennessee, bemoaned the 5th Georgia's removal, but to no avail. Probably Sam and his men did not mind nearly as much, since their health had suffered badly in cold weather that was a bitter contrast to balmy Pensacola.[28]

Sam's regiment was not destined to linger in Chattanooga, although it remained for a short time in garrison there and at the nearby rail junction of Bridgeport, Alabama. In this role, the 5th Georgia helped secure the critically important line of communications to Corinth, Mississippi, where Gen. Albert Sidney Johnston was marshaling forces to contest the Federal advance along the Tennessee River. After Maj. Gen. Ulysses S. Grant captured the Confederate river fortress at Fort Donelson, it was clear that he intended to strike deep into the Southern heartland in an attempt to sever the east-west rail connections holding it together. The Memphis & Charleston Railroad, described as the "vertebrae of the Confederacy," traversed northern Alabama and Mississippi en route to Memphis, the Mississippi River, and the western Confederacy. Corinth lay on this line, offering an advantageous point for Johnston to concentrate his far-flung forces at a point near the Tennessee River where he could turn and give battle.[29]

Johnston struck with a vengeance at Shiloh, a short distance northeast of Corinth, but Sam's 5th Georgia remained at its post far to the east in the Bridgeport area. On April 9, just two days after the ferocious battle resulted in a Confederate withdrawal to Corinth, Sam received orders to depart Alabama immediately and join the main army, which was greatly outnumbered by the Union forces near Shiloh. The latter were now under the command of Gen. Henry Halleck, however, and their timorous advance on Corinth became little more than a siege.[30]

By mid-April, Sam and his men were back under the brigade command of Brig. Gen. John Jackson at Bethel Station, near Corinth. There, they helped bar the way to any further Union advance as April wore into May. By this time, however, the 5th Georgia's time in service was rapidly approaching expiration. Suffering from "greatly impaired health" due to "very extensive varicocele of left side and habitual prolapsus annus," Sam declined to stand for reelection to the colonelcy of the reorganizing regiment. On May 15, 1862, Jackson directed Sam to take his regiment into the trenches near Corinth, where he was to post three reliefs, of thirty men each, across the entire brigade sector, while maintaining the remainder in reserve at a central point. On the same day, Sam welcomed a fresh group of recruits into the regiment's companies K and L, the latter built around a nucleus of veterans reenlisting from Company K. The new recruits were from Upson County's gently rolling hills, and doubtless included a number of names and faces known to Sam. One of them was his cousin's son, *John Willis Mangham* (see Chapter II).[31]

Swearing John into the service of the Confederate States of America was one of Sam's last acts as commanding officer of the 5th Georgia. John may have brought news of the illness of Sam's second son, little John H. Mangham. It is not likely that the two cousins knew just how bad the news was, however, for Sam's twenty-month-old boy had died just five days earlier. On May 20, the 31-year-old colonel was honorably discharged from service at camp near Corinth, Mississippi.[32]

*   *   *   *   *

Sam returned to his bereaved family at Griffin, where he soon resumed work at his farm and business. In Georgia, however, the war was never very far away. Accordingly, Sam secured appointment as colonel of the 109th Regiment of Georgia Militia on July 15, just two months after his separation from active service. In all probability, he viewed his militia post as a patriotic duty, as well as security against subsequent conscription; a discharge for disability did not necessarily exempt him from recall into service, according to Confederate statute. State militia officers, however, comprised a category of men whom Governor Joe Brown strove mightily to protect from Confederate enrolling officers, since he viewed the maintenance of a state-level armed force as critical to state sovereignty. Sam probably shared these sentiments, as they were certainly common among the Southern patriciate. Indicative of his outlook on such matters, the men of the 5th Georgia remembered him fondly as a commander who endeared himself to them "by his tenacious demands for the right of his command and his stubborn resistance to the slightest wrong being done to his command or to the humblest member of his company or regiment."[33]

Such prideful insistence on rights and prerogatives was a common characteristic of many, perhaps most, Southern officers, and it proved a source of great strength and *esprit de corps*, but also of bitter divisiveness at times. When the war surged towards Georgia's borders in mid-1863, Governor Brown's continued, even heightened, insistence on his state's right of self-defense was another perfect example of the two-edged nature of the states' rights position. General Bragg, by now commanding the Army of Tennessee, was falling back towards Georgia, and both he and President Jefferson Davis were looking for that state to strain every resource to reinforce his army in the field. Brown, on the other hand, was acutely aware that Georgians sworn into Confederate service were serving in Virginia, the Carolinas, Mississippi, and Bragg's army, while Georgia's own coastline was but weakly defended. The governor knew it was in Georgia's interest to sustain the Confederacy's field armies, of course, but if the state did so unreservedly, it placed itself at the mercy of strategic decision-makers in Richmond. Given the logic of states' rights that had developed in the ante-bellum South, it should not be surprising that subservience to Richmond in such matters was hardly a reflexive response for Brown and many other Southerners.[34]

Desperately seeking ways to relieve the pressure on the Confederacy's embattled field armies in the early summer of 1863, President Davis called for states threatened with invasion to organize home defense units to combat enemy penetrations on their own soil. These troops were to be comprised of men exempt from normal conscription, but if volunteers from these classes were not sufficiently forthcoming, Davis required them to be raised by a draft. In Georgia's case, he required the state to provide 8000 such troops by the beginning of August.[35]

Governor Brown duly issued a call on June 22 for the organization of the force that became known as the Georgia State Guard. Its recruits enlisted for six months' service on a standby basis, with the specific provision that they should be activated only as long as an enemy threat required their service under arms. After all, the State Guard drew its manpower from those normally exempted from conscription altogether: youths under 18 and men over 45; those certified unfit for field service by medical examining boards; and those exempted by virtue of their trade, profession, or official position. Captains raising companies swore in recruits to defend specifically defined areas within their respective districts, and the companies likewise were grouped into regiments or battalions on a regional basis. These units could be sent outside their specified territorial limits only if the men consented. Predictably, wrangling ensued between Governor Brown and President Davis over the enrollment and employment of the State Guard, with Confederate enrolling officers keeping a sharp eye out for potential conscripts who would much rather volunteer for six months' state service than for the army.[36]

Governor Brown's executive proclamation established specific guidelines for the new force. Pointing out that he did not expect "the troops now called for will be on active duty any considerable proportion of their time," the governor opined that militia officers and civil officials at all levels could join the new organizations without compromising the State's ability to function. Indeed, he authorized any militia officer in the rank of captain or above to raise a company, and furloughed any militia officer wishing to serve in the new force in any capacity, without endangering his status as a state official. Brown directed all militia officers and civil officials to travel through their counties to raise recruits, and pointedly observed the value of a strong example. He admonished his would-be recruiters: "Let no officer forget that he will be more successful in inducing others to volunteer when he can show *his own name* upon the list *as a volunteer*." After a final appeal to patriotism and the volunteer spirit, Brown concluded: "*Georgia expects every man to do his duty*. Fly to arms and trust in God to defend the right."[37]

Colonel Sam Mangham was one who sought to answer Governor Brown's call, but his request for clarification from the State Adjutant & Inspector General, Col. Henry C. Wayne, serves as a barometer of the confusion characterizing the establishment of a completely new category of military force. How was he to raise troops from men who were exempted from conscription under all existing draft laws, if they didn't wish to volunteer?

Griffin, Ga. July 13th 1863

Col. H. C. Wayne
Adjt. & Insp. Genl.
Colonel,

The indisposition manifested in this County to Volunteer under the late call of the Governor, induces me to write you for instructions.

How is the draft to be conducted? Who are liable? Of which Class shall the draft be composed?

We have in the County a number of exempts by reason of holding Militia Commissions, Substitutes, County Offices, etc. Some of these parties claim and m[ake?] reason, that they cannot be drafted. Please give me explicit instructions as to how to proceed. My opinion is that twice the number called for can be had of serviceable good men provided the above objections can be removed. Efforts are being made to organize Volunteers, but little progress is being made.

Very Respectfully,
/s/ S. W. Mangham
Col. 109th Regt. G. M.

Wayne's reply is unrecorded, but it clearly left unresolved many issues of policy. With the August 1 recruitment deadline fast approaching, Sam wrote again on July 24:

Colonel

Efforts are being made to raise two volunteer companies in this county with indifferent success. One has already organized with say twenty (20) men the other not yet having elected officers. Will such companies be recognized at the draft, & will drafted men be apportioned to fill them up? Are Regimental organizations to be effected before or after the draft? An early answer will greatly oblige.

/s/ S. W. Mangham
Col. 109th Regt. G. M.[38]

Despite the difficulties in securing volunteers and defining applicable conscription criteria, Sam found a way to get the job done. He succeeded less than two weeks later in completing the recruitment of a full company of men at Griffin, with himself at their head. Organized on August 4, 1863 for six months' service anywhere within the state of Georgia, "Captain Mangham's Company" became the "Spalding Infantry." The second company completed its organization too, as the "Spalding Volunteers," and the two units emerged as the nucleus of a new command known as "Mangham's Battalion." Accordingly promoted to the rank of major, it was not long before Sam was called into active service, as Bragg's Army of Tennessee fell back into north Georgia before General Rosecrans's advancing Federals. Unfortunately, however, the governor's mobilization order apparently was limited to troops enlisted to defend the area between Atlanta and Tennessee. This confronted Sam (and many others) with yet another administrative hurdle, and one can sense the exasperation in the note he penned to Colonel Wayne:

Griffin Ga. Sept 7th 1863

Col. Wayne
Sir,
The order calling six months troops into service embraces part of my battallion, leaving part at home, thus leaving me without a command. Will you please arrange the matter so as not to cut up my battallion? Your early attention will greatly oblige.

Very Respectfully
/s/ S. W. Mangham
Mjr. Comdg. Bat. Infantry

The matter apparently was resolved, for Mangham's Battalion merged with Lofton's Battalion in September to become the 6th Regiment Georgia Infantry (State Guard). At mid-month, the regiment drew a mixture of smoothbore muskets and Belgian rifles in preparation for active service, and the men elected William A. Lofton colonel and Sam Mangham lieutenant colonel on September 19.[39]

Sam's resumption of active duty came as Federal actions posed a "clear and present danger" to his state's safety, since the Union Army of the Cumberland was pushing into the hills of north Georgia. The date he was elected lieutenant colonel of his regiment, however, marked the very day that the Army of Tennessee turned on its opponents and struck them a staggering blow along Chickamauga Creek. Sam could not have known that his younger brother, *Col. Thomas W. Mangham* of the 30th Georgia, had been seriously wounded at Chickamauga on the very same day. Sam was one of 424 men of the 6th State Guard assembled at Rome, Georgia, with some 2500 other

191

state troops by early October, but the Federal threat had receded by then. When Gen. Howell Cobb, commander of Georgia State Troops, reported the readiness of his State Guard to Bragg's Chief of Staff on October 3, it was two weeks since Rosecrans' invading host had been hurled back to Chattanooga in utter rout.[40]

Sometime after the great victory at Chickamauga, Sam's regiment was transferred to help garrison Savannah, Georgia's tenuous lifeline to the outside world. Although he was absent on sick furlough at year's end, Sam was back in camp in January and serving as regimental commander when the State Guard prepared to end its six month term. Nearly five months of this time had been spent on active service, a situation doubtless caused by Bragg's stunning reverse at Chattanooga in late November 1863, which left open the possibility of renewed Federal invasion. Although some of the State Guard fumed at their extended stay on active duty and Governor Brown protested to President Davis on their behalf, the men were kept in camp for the duration of their terms.[41]

As the time for dissolution of the State Guard drew near, Sam Mangham considered his future options. On January 22, 1864, he submitted a request to raise an artillery company for the Savannah River batteries from among the numerous state troops about to disband. Colonel E. C. Anderson, commanding the river batteries at Fort Jackson, heartily endorsed Sam's petition, describing him as an "officer of experience & intelligence" and asserting that "I should much like to have him associated with me." Brigadier General Hugh Mercer, commander of the District of Georgia, likewise gave a spirited endorsement to Sam's request, noting that the practice of detailing various infantry companies to artillery duty was far less efficient than using permanently assigned gun crews.[42]

Although the endorsements show that Sam's request wended its way through channels all the way to Secretary of War Seddon's office, no record survives of Seddon's response. Clearly, however, it was unfavorable, for Sam's next appearance in Savannah was not as an artillery captain, but as an artillery *private!* This development, as well as its sequels, provides some instructive (and amusing) insights into the labyrinths of competing Confederate military bureaucracies. The men operating within these institutions faced a formidable challenge, struggling to integrate vestiges of prewar United States Army procedures with the idiosyncrasies of politics and personality during a revolutionary emergency.

Sam enlisted on May 10, 1864 in Company B, 22nd Battalion Georgia Heavy Artillery, and was sworn in at Griffin by the company commander, Capt. Daniel A. Smith. Since Captain Smith's command, known as the "Wise Guards," was raised in Macon County and was stationed in Savannah, he probably came to Griffin at the behest of Maj. Thomas D. Bertody, the battalion's second-ranking officer and a resident of the Spalding County seat. Major Bertody, by no coincidence, was also Sam's brother-in-law, having married Mary E. Mangham in 1853, and this family connection doubtless was a significant reason Sam volunteered for service in his battalion. Service with the 22nd Heavy Artillery also promised Sam the opportunity to return to duty in Savannah, where he had first-rate connections with the upper echelons of military command, and thus a good chance of obtaining commissioned rank again. Coastal artillery duties were a known quantity for him as well, and certainly less strenuous than infantry service; given his physical impairment, this had to be an important consideration.[43]

Finally, enlistment in this battalion allowed Sam to look out for his youngest brother, *William R. Mangham* who enlisted as a private in Company A ("Bartow Artillery") on April 13, 1864. At the beginning of the year, young William had been enrolled in Spalding County's militia at age sixteen years and seven months. At or near age seventeen by April, he had the choice of volunteering for a unit of his choice or awaiting conscription and assignment at the convenience of Georgia's Commandant of Conscripts. Since Sam was not currently in service and Tom was being invalided out of the army (see below), William probably selected service in his brother-in-law Thomas Bertody's battalion as the best available option.[44]

Reporting for duty with the Savannah River batteries at Fort Jackson, William went to work mastering the unwieldy .69 caliber smoothbore muskets carried by his company. He also had to learn the other duties of a heavy artilleryman in a fortress mounting two 8-inch Columbiads, two 32-pounder rifled guns, and three 32-pounder naval guns. One can only wonder what the boy soldier thought when a riotous crowd of Savannah's women defied Confederate troops to demand bread, just four days after he mustered into service there. Far from home, with Yankee blockade squadrons to his front and an increasingly restive populace in his rear, William may have wondered just what he was in for. It must have been particularly hard for him to leave home, knowing that Federal forces under Gen. William T. Sherman were encamped in north Georgia, poised for a spring campaign that everyone presumed would aim to conquer the critical rail center of Atlanta. Less than one hundred miles separated Sherman's army from his goal, which in turn lay only thirty miles north of the Mangham home in Griffin.[45]

William had been in Savannah for nearly a month when Sam enlisted in the "Wise Guards" on May 10, but his elder brother apparently remained at home in Griffin for some weeks. By June 8, Gen. Joe Johnston's embattled Army of Tennessee had been pushed back more than halfway to Atlanta, and his hard-pressed command was taking casualties at an alarming rate. Aggravated by the steady leakage of deserters, the army's need to track down and induct reluctant conscripts assumed critical importance. Confederate conscription authorities accordingly authorized the establishment of companies for the purpose of pursuing draft evaders and deserters, as well as conducting other local defense operations; Sam requested permission to raise such a company for the 7th Congressional District. Observing that he had served "in the Army of the Confederacy as Captain & Colonel and as I believe to the satisfaction of my Commanding Officer," Sam stated his intention of serving with the company if allowed to raise it, despite his earlier request for exemption as an "agriculturalist." Lieutenant Newton, the local enrolling officer, noted that such a company was needed, and added a vote of personal confidence: ". . .I know of no man better qualified to raise one, and to command it afterwards, than Mr. Mangham."[46]

The state conscription authorities in Macon approved Sam's request by late June, and he commenced organizing his company. By July 25, he had enrolled 102 men in his company and that day was elected captain by acclamation. Lieutenant Newton then requested the medical authorities to certify him fit for light duty so that he could be commissioned. The examining board examined him and pronounced him "unfit for duty in the field because of very extensive variocele of left side and habitual prolapsus annus." This certificate of disability for active field service was intended to demonstrate clearly that Sam was eligible for this type of auxiliary duty, since those certified as completely fit were required to serve in regularly organized active duty units. With everything apparently in order, Sam reported for duty in Savannah. On August 13, he submitted a formal request to the Secretary of War asking for discharge from Company B, 22nd Heavy Artillery, based on his unfitness for active field service and his election as captain of a supporting force for conscription.[47]

With Thomas Bertody now commanding the 22nd Heavy Artillery, his endorsement was a foregone conclusion at the company and battalion levels, and it sailed through subdistrict and district headquarters as well. Once it reached the Department of Georgia, South Carolina, and Florida, however, Maj. Gen. Lafayette McLaws referred it to his chief surgeon to determine whether a man in Sam's condition could withstand the "exceedingly arduous" duties of such a position.[48]

When Sam's application reached the desk of Chief Surgeon William Henry Cumming, heavy sledding ensued. Cumming complained of a "serious informality about these papers," noting that Private Mangham seemed to have circumvented his battalion commander in the proceedings! (It probably would not have helped matters to explain that the battalion commander in question was Sam's brother-in-law!) Asserting that Lieutenant Newton's directive for a medical board examination was "in direct violation of Law," Cumming then waxed eloquent about Sam's medical condition. Responding to General McLaws's query, he opined: "An extensive variocele would interfere with long marches on foot or on horseback; a 'habitual prolapsus annus' is a still more serious disqualification for such exercises." He went on to editorialize, "If these companies are to pursue and arrest deserters and force the unwilling into the military service, there will be required great energy and activity in their leaders. With so infirm a Captain, little should be expected from the command." By September 20, the application had worked its way through intervening channels, along with an ever-increasing burden of disapproving endorsements, until the War Department formally disapproved and routed it back down the chain.[49]

For whatever reason, a copy of Sam's original request apparently had been routed through Bureau of Conscription channels beginning in August. With the enthusiastic recommendations of Lieutenant Newton, Major Bertody, and Colonel Browne, Georgia's Commandant of Conscripts, the request arrived at Richmond's Bureau of Conscription and was approved by the Acting Superintendent on August 29! It was then referred for opinion to the Confederate Adjutant General, and thus veered back into command channels at the company and battalion levels on September 29, 1864. Captain Smith and Major Bertody again endorsed the application and forwarded it once more into the maze of bureaucracy. Little knowing that Sam's request already had been disapproved in different channels, Bertody stated the case that is obvious to us in retrospect: "This soldier was formerly Col of the 5th Ga Regt. and declined reelection. He was an excellent officer & I am satisfied he can be more useful in the position to which he has been elected—than in the ranks."[50]

By this time, Atlanta had fallen to Sherman's army and the defeated Army of Tennessee was licking its wounds at Palmetto, Georgia. When Sam finally received notification of his rejection on October 10, he was quick to present his case to General Cobb, the commander of Georgia state forces. Cobb referred him back to Colonel Browne, asking him to emphasize that Sam's physical impairment was actually a prerequisite for his command rather than a disqualification. Sam wrote immediately to Browne's office in Augusta, noting:

> General Cobb authorized me to say to Col. Browne that he thought injustice had been done me by the endorsement of Dr. Cumming and that upon return of the paper to him through Colonel Browne he would place such endorsement theron, as would in all probability place me in Command of my Company, and insure a transfer from Savannah.

Sam added that General Cobb had urged him to see Colonel Browne in person, but the requirement for him to report to his command made it impossible for him to travel to Augusta.[51]

Sam therefore returned to duty in Savannah, where he was detailed through November and December as clerk to the battalion commander, Lt. Col. William R. Pritchard, while his brother William continued to serve in the batteries protecting the Savannah River approaches northeast of the city. The two brothers underwent agonies of suspense as Sherman's army ceased sparring with Hood near Atlanta in late October and prepared to move deeper into the state's interior. After all, their homes in Griffin lay on the direct rail line between Atlanta and Macon, one of the Confederacy's primary centers of military industry. And after Hood moved northwest of Atlanta and on towards Alabama and Tennessee in a vain effort to lure his opponent away from Georgia's interior, only "Fighting Joe" Wheeler's cavalry and scratch forces of militia and reserves stood between Sherman's 62,000 men and any destination he might choose.[52]

Sherman had boasted that he could "make Georgia howl," and after destroying Atlanta and cutting his communications with the outside world, he struck out on November 16, 1864 to make good on his claim. Some of his units feinted towards Griffin, where General Wheeler made his headquarters, before moving on to the east. As Sherman's troops marched through Georgia, they systematically gutted the countryside in an effort to punish the secessionist populace itself, while breaking both its willingness and ability to continue the fight. In their occasional encounters with Georgia militia units, they most probably faced Mangham men and boys whose names are unknown to history, due to the nonexistent record keeping of these hastily improvised units. It is certain that Sherman's legions wreaked havoc in the core areas of Mangham settlement during the 1820s, including Hancock, Putnam, Baldwin, and Jasper Counties, where Sam's and William's father John C. Mangham had been born and grown to manhood. Perhaps one awestruck slave summed it up best when he told an amused major on Sherman's staff, "The Yankees is the most destructionest people ever I saw."[53]

By December, it finally became clear that Sherman's goal was the great port city of Savannah, where Lt. Gen. William J. Hardee was scrambling to prepare a landward defense worthy of the name. By December 10, Federal forces had bumped into the city's primary defenses along the thirteen-mile-long front, which ranged in a semicircle just two miles outside the city itself. Ten thousand men and boys held the city against six times their number, but heavy coastal artillery pieces emplaced in Savannah's skillfully engineered landward defenses helped even the odds somewhat. Presumably, William continued to help defend Fort Jackson on the right of the Confederate interior line with his comrades of the Bartow Artillery. Since Federal ground forces never penetrated in this direction, William's company may have remained unengaged. In any case, he and Sam were present for duty on December 13, when Union forces stormed Fort McAllister, which lay just south of town on the Ogeechee River. This victory reestablished Sherman's communications with the Federal navy, ensuring the resupply of his hungry army. The fall of McAllister therefore presaged the doom of Savannah's garrison, and Hardee soon began preparing his troops to evacuate the ill-fated city.[54]

The garrison maintained effective resistance for another week, while secret preparations were made to build an extraordinary pontoon bridge across the mile-wide Savannah River to South Carolina. Confederate engineers collected every barge, skiff, and rice flat in the area and lashed them together. After tearing down the city's wharves and several nearby buildings to provide planking across the tops of the improvised pontoons, they laid a thick layer of rice straw atop the boards to deaden the sound of marching men and rumbling wagons. The exodus began after dark on December 20, 1864, after Savannah's civilians were allowed to cross in daylight. Sam and William probably boarded steamers at nine o'clock that night and crossed over to Screven's Ferry on the South Carolina side, along with the rest of the garrisons of the coastal forts. On the next morning, two Federal brigades arrived at Fort Jackson and hung out the Stars and Stripes on the walls where William had stood guard for the last eight months. The stealthy evacuation saved him, Sam, and 10,000 other Confederate soldiers, but Savannah was lost irretrievably. Ironically, it fell on the fourth anniversary of South Carolina's secession.[55]

By General Sherman's own estimate, his legions had wrought one billion dollars worth of destruction on Georgia, of which some $20,000,000 was of benefit to his forces. The remainder, $880,000,000 in damages, was pure waste. One Union soldier believed, "The destruction could hardly have been worse if Atlanta had been a volcano in eruption and the molten lava had flowed in a stream 60 miles wide and five times as long."[56]

* * * * *

During January 1865, Sam Mangham was appointed battalion ordnance sergeant, a relatively independent position that allowed him to use his considerable expertise to help maintain a high standard of weapons maintenance, inspection, and supply. On January 30, however, the Department of South Carolina, Georgia and Florida issued Special Order 25, finally resolving his status. Paragraph VII of the order read:

> Ord. Sergt. S. W. Mangham 22nd Ga Battl Heavy Arty having been elected Captain in the Georgia Reserves, & his application with certif of disability having been forwarded to the War Dept, is hereby detailed to report for duty to Maj Genl Cobb, as Captain of his Company of reserves until his application is heard from.

Sam probably spent the remainder of the war in command of his reserve company, struggling to maintain some sort of order in Spalding County as the Confederacy tottered on its last legs.[57] The war ended definitively for the citizens of Griffin on April 19, when Wilson's bluecoated cavalrymen rode into town at the end of their great raid through Alabama and western Georgia. After they distributed the contents of a warehouse to blacks and poor whites hovering about, the troopers burned the structure and torched the railroad depot. The occupation of Griffin took place just days before the fourth anniversary of Sam's departure with the Griffin Light Guard in 1861.[58]

* * * * *

William Mangham was present (although sick) with Company A on the final day of 1864, when the unit mustered for the last time on record. Having fired off the last of their artillery ammunition before spiking their guns on the night they evacuated Savannah, the erstwhile cannoneers were now novice infantrymen, organized with remnants of other commands into Elliott's Brigade of Taliaferro's Division. These men served in Charleston until mid-February, when Hardee's Corps pulled back into North Carolina. By mid-March, the seemingly endless retreat had convinced half of Hardee's 13,000 men that further resistance was hopeless, and they had left the army to return home. Perhaps William took part in the sharp delaying action at Averasboro on March 16, when Elliott's Brigade tasted its first combat in the open field. It was brushed back from the second line to the third line after light contact with a strong Federal force, but rallied there until orders came to fall back that night under cover of darkness.[59]

The great test for Elliott's men came several days later, when Gen. Joe Johnston, restored to command of the remnants of the Army of Tennessee and all Confederate forces afield in the Carolinas, struck hard at Sherman in the Battle of Bentonville. The men of Taliaferro's Division were rousted out to march on Bentonville in the predawn darkness of March 19, and one of their officers, Capt. Charles Inglesby, recalled them as a "sleepy, worn-out, hungry and altogether unhappy body of men." Grouchy about missing their breakfast, they cocked their ears as they began to hear the occasional report of cannon in the distance. With the exception of the scrap at Averasboro several days earlier, they had been running from Billy Sherman for three months without offering resistance, and their thinning ranks bespoke the demoralization of mass desertion rather than the wastage of numerous battles.[60]

As they slogged towards Bentonville, the cannon fire grew louder and more frequent. As the realization spread that they were hurrying toward a battle rather than fleeing before the enemy's approach, their step quickened appreciably; the complaining faded away as the stutter of musketry swelled into the steady roar of a large-scale engagement. Filing off to the right of Johnston's heavily engaged battle line, they rested apprehensively near a field hospital as enemy cannonballs screeched overhead. After several hours in this position, their moment came to join in the last great assault of the Army of Tennessee. Grounding their knapsacks and blankets to allow easier movement, they cut loose with the Rebel yell and moved out through thick woods when General Elliott gave the order to advance. Moving at the "double-quick, steadily and in good order," they smashed and scattered the picket line of the Federal brigade to their front, and in conjunction with the troops on their left they drove the left of the enemy line into a regular stampede. In smashing the flank, however, Confederate forces lost alignment and eventually were forced to pause for reorganization.[61]

In the ensuing lull, more Union forces approached the battlefield, closing into supporting distance of their beleaguered left flank. When Elliott's Brigade resumed its assault once more, the men were completely unaware that three enemy brigades had materialized in the woods to their right. As the neophyte infantrymen of the 22nd Georgia Heavy Artillery and the rest of Elliott's men burst from the woods and surged upslope across the Morris Field, they again shrieked the Rebel yell. A shuddering Chaplain Earle of the 21st Michigan recalled: ". . . such fiendish yells never saluted my ears before. Why it seemed to me as though the doors of perdition had been thrown wide open, and that all the devils were out!"[62]

Five hundred yards to the front of Elliott's men, however, was Stephens' Ohio battery. Steady veterans that they were, the Ohio gunners stood to their pieces and fired short-fused case shot into the faces of Elliott's Georgians and South Carolinians, while the Federal infantry line poured a hail of musketry into them as well. Thousands of lead slugs and iron fragments blasted into the charging Rebels, dropping some and blinding others by blasting sand into their eyes. Hunching forward like men breasting a storm, Elliott's men drove onward still, with some men approaching within fifty yards of the Federal lines. The crisis came swiftly and unexpectedly, as the recently arrived Union regiments now arose at point-blank range on the right rear and poured a hail of fire into the stunned Confederates. After several volleys, it proved to be more than they could bear. Elliott's Brigade broke for the rear and was rallied only with difficulty at the edge of the woods. There the troops remained for hours as canister slugs rained around them and showered them with twigs and branches, but they were not fit for a renewed attack. As they lay there in line of battle, many of the shocked and exhausted men fell asleep as shells crashed over their heads. It was late that night before they pulled back, blundering astray through the darkness until finding their proper place at 2:30 in the morning.[63]

Although the exhausted remnants of the 22nd Georgia Heavy Artillery could not have known it then, the stinging blows they had delivered and received at Bentonville were their last of the war. Few remained in ranks at the final surrender a month later. Although he is known to have survived the war, Pvt. William Mangham was not among those paroled at Greensboro in April.[64]

When Georgia's citizens swore loyalty oaths in 1867 and 1868 and registered to vote under the Reconstruction government, William R. Mangham registered in Spalding County. It is believed that he married Fannie Gile of Meriwether County; their only known child was William Gile Mangham. William R. Mangham worked as a building contractor on the railroad between Atlanta and Macon until his death of smallpox soon after the turn of the century.[65]

*   *   *   *   *

His elder brother Sam left a much more noticeable mark on postwar Griffin and Spalding County, serving in a number of positions of civil leadership, just as he had in the army. His prewar prominence and wartime Confederate service had fitted him for his late-war role as reserve officer and protector of public safety, and this role in turn made him an obvious candidate to help the Federal occupation forces determine the extent of the disaster they inherited in prostrated Spalding County. Colonel Ira W. Foster commanded Union forces in the district, and he appointed Sam to conduct a census of inhabitants and supplies. Sam found that 2735 of the county's 4430 whites and 3242 blacks were totally destitute, and another 478 whites had no more than ten days' supplies on hand. In other words, some thirty-seven percent of the populace lacked any sustenance whatsoever, and an additional eleven percent of the white inhabitants, not to speak of the newly emancipated and landless blacks, faced imminent disaster. With Georgia's commercial infrastructure in ruins, money valueless, and the land stripped bare by the competing armies, deserters, and lawless bands, famine was at hand.[66]

Georgia's returning veterans worked to rebuild the state's agriculture, however, and Sam was back in the grocery business in Griffin by 1866. That same year saw the establishment of the Confederate Soldiers Interment Society, one of many groups dedicated to the recovery and proper burial of the numerous soldiers whose deaths in hospital wards and on battlefields were followed by the hastiest of burials. As befitted an officer known for taking care of his men during the war, Sam served as one of the Society's executive committee members dedicated to organizing this noble postwar effort.[67]

Sam also worked to reestablish and expand necessary services in the once-thriving community, serving as Secretary on the Board of Trustees that established the Griffin Male School in 1869. The following year saw the completion of the sixty by ninety foot building, which still stands today, as well as the establishment of the Young America Fire Company No. 2, with Sam Mangham as foreman. Such a position certainly fitted his long-standing record of public service, but perhaps it reflected self-interest as well: Sam was earning his living by this time as a life and fire insurance agent! His firemen turned out in full uniform later that year when he helped organize a memorial service for Gen. Robert E. Lee, who died on October 12, 1870 in the Virginia he fought so hard to protect. The town's Masons and Odd Fellows were present as well; Sam was a prominent member of these two fraternal Christian organizations, serving as Grand Master of the State of Georgia for the Odd Fellows.[68]

Sam and Hattie had been rebuilding their family in the postwar years, too, welcoming the birth of sons Joseph J. Mangham (about 1866) and John Woodward Mangham (about 1868). The boys' father was co-proprietor of one of Griffin's newspapers, *The Middle Georgian*, before selling his interest in the paper in 1872. Sam also served one term as Griffin's mayor pro tem, as well as a number of years as a city alderman. He even resumed his connection with military affairs, securing election in May 1874 as captain of his beloved Griffin Light Guards. Three years later, on July 9, 1877, Sam was elected major of the 5th Georgia Battalion in the reorganized state militia. Perhaps his most remarkable contribution to the well being of his fellow citizens was his service as chairman of the Board of County Commissioners, established in 1873 to oversee county revenues and road maintenance. As one friend remembered years later, ". . .it was here that he showed his devotion to public duty, his love for the people of his county and an executive ability that ranks among the best. The fine condition of our county is due to Col. Mangham more than [any] other man."[69]

His father, Capt. John C. Mangham, passed away on August 14, 1873, just as Sam was beginning his work as a county commissioner. Then as now, obituaries tended to focus on the positive qualities of the deceased, but writers of that era also could be surprisingly blunt at times. In John's case, the person writing his obituary felt compelled to acknowledge that he "may have been considered somewhat eccentric by many people," but went on to assert that "still a truer, and more honorable man or better citizen than he, never lived. His official positions and callings in life threw him in contact with most of the prominent men of the past age, and one, too, composed of honest and pure men, and they were his fast friends." He clearly was a fascinating man, who "had a vast fund of information and incident, and it was a rare piece of good fortune to catch him from business and listen to the recitals of his personal knowledge and recollections of men and measures in days gone by." John was "tenderly attached to his family and friends," and the editor averred that "another evidence of his goodness of heart was the devotion his former slaves always exhibited towards him, and in his last hours they gathered around him with demonstrations of unfeigned grief for one who had been and was still their best adviser and friend."[70]

John's obituary averred that "Few men were better known than Captain Mangham or more universally esteemed," and the old Georgian doubtless was proud to know before he died that his son Sam was numbered as one of these few. The veterans of Sam's old command, the 5th Georgia Volunteers, elected him President of their association in August 1886 at their fourth annual meeting. It was a joint assembly with the 13th Georgia, and it drew three to five thousand spectators to hear a keynote speech by gubernatorial candidate Gen. John B. Gordon. This justly famous Georgian had been the only non-West Pointer to achieve the rank of lieutenant general under Robert E. Lee, and made his military reputation commanding a brigade that included the 13th Georgia, in whose ranks Sam's cousins John, Nat, and Will Mangham had served long and well.[71]

For Sam, it was the latest honor in a life that had seen him earn so many. It proved to be one of his last, however, for late on Thursday morning, January 5, 1888, he passed away peacefully in his beloved Griffin. For the next three days, *The Griffin Daily News* featured articles about Sam on its front page. All the business houses of Griffin closed on Friday afternoon for his funeral at the Methodist Church to which he had belonged. As the newspaper observed, such a tribute was "unknown almost in the history of the city." The survivors of the Griffin Light Guard attended their old commander's funeral services in a body, and prepared resolutions of tribute and respect that movingly expressed their esteem for him as a person and an officer. These resolutions were published on the front page of the newspaper on Sunday morning, and observed that Sam "fully shared all of the trials and vicissitudes of camp life and was always ready to share with his men the contents of 'Canteen or Haversack.'" While conceding to others the "pleasant duty of recording his unswerving devotion and robust ability as a citizen," the Griffin Light Guardsmen demanded that ". . .to us alone be allowed the pleasure of speaking of him who under all circumstances was true, manly, virtuous and brave."[72]

Clearly, Samuel Watson Mangham was an exceptional man and outstanding officer. Numerous written testimonials emphasize these facts, and lest the modern reader tend to discount them as simply speaking well of the dead, one need only think of the many times he was chosen by his men to be their leader. Had he been a merely another fancily uniformed militia officer from a well-to-do family, the men of the 5th Georgia probably would not have elected him as their commander in 1862; most veteran soldiers facing renewed combat knew better than to elect their leaders based on superficial qualities. Likewise, many a charlatan parlayed a flawed war record into personal advantage after the war, but not among those who had seen him on the march, the tented field, and amidst the smoke of combat. However nostalgic old Confederates grew as the myths of the "Lost Cause" blossomed in the 1880s, they did not forget the transgressions of officers who had failed the tests of the 1860s. When the Griffin Light Guards and later the 5th Georgia survivors acclaimed Col. Sam Mangham as their leader many years after the war, they made a statement of trust and respect that echoes across the decades. They would be proud to know that the sword they presented him in February 1862, upon his election as colonel of the 5th Georgia, retains an honored place in his family more than a century later.

Samuel Watson Mangham lies in Oak Hill Cemetery on West Poplar Street in Griffin, near his wives Pope Reeves Mangham (d. 1857) and Hattie L. Reeves Mangham (d. 1893). Also buried in this cemetery are Sam's sons John H. Mangham (1860-1862), and Pope Reeves Mangham (1857-1877), his brother James H. Mangham (1834-1858), and the patriarch of the family, John C. Mangham (1797-1873).[73]

3. COUSINS IN ARMS, OR "COLONEL, WE ARE GOING TO HAVE HOT TIMES JUST OVER YONDER": THOMAS W. MANGHAM, SGT., "MACON VOLUNTEERS," CO. B, 2ND GEORGIA BATTALION, AND COL., 30TH GEORGIA INFANTRY; SGT. WILLIS A. MANGHAM (II) "BAILEY VOLUNTEERS," CO. A, 30TH GEORGIA INFANTRY

One of those present at Samuel Watson Mangham's funeral in January 1888 was Mrs. Ida Louise Winship Mangham, the widow of Sam's younger brother, Col. Thomas Woodward Mangham.[74]

Born in November 1836 while the family resided in Columbus, Georgia, Tom seemed bound from early manhood to continue the military traditions established by his father and two elder brothers, since he was elected orderly sergeant of Sam's militia company, the Griffin Light Guards. Employed in the late 1850s as a conductor on the Macon & Western Railroad, which ran through Griffin on its way between Atlanta and Macon, Tom soon moved to the latter city and accepted a position working in Mr. Isaac Scott's Bank of Middle Georgia. He quickly established himself as a capable young man of good education and solid integrity, thus attracting a lucrative offer from Mr. J. E. Jones of the Bank of Savannah. When Tom informed Scott of this opportunity, Scott went of his own volition to Mr. Jones and offered to serve as bondsman on Tom's behalf.[75]

Clearly, the up-and-coming young Georgian had a bright future in the world of commerce, but he certainly viewed events on the national scene as a threat looming on the horizon. Whereas his brother Sam's actions and characteristics lead one to conclude that he favored the breakup of the Union in 1861, there is not the slightest need for surmise in Tom's case. Described as "a warm secessionist from the outset" by those who knew him best, he took a firm stance on this issue. He also expressed his intent to back it up with action should it come to that, obtaining election in the Macon Volunteers as third lieutenant in July 1859. He was elected fourth corporal a year and a half later, when the company began preparing in earnest to defend Georgia's ordinance of secession. Commanded by Capt. Robert A. Smith in early 1861, the Volunteers were arguably the elite militia company in Macon, which boasted seven militia and volunteer units by that time. Tom's erstwhile employer Mr. Scott, an avowed Unionist, had urged him in the strongest terms to vote against secession when Georgians went to the polls after Lincoln's election. Tom thanked Scott for the advice he had provided on so many occasions; noting that it pained him to differ with his old mentor this time, he affirmed that he had to act in accordance with his conscience and support the secessionists. With their minds made up on the issue, Tom and the Macon Volunteers tendered their services to the Provisional Army of the Confederate States at the beginning of March 1861, drilling incessantly while awaiting acceptance.[76]

Tom was elected first corporal when the company finally mustered into active service on April 20, 1861, just one week after the surrender of Fort Sumter. As Company B, 2nd Independent Battalion Georgia Volunteer Infantry, the sixty-six hot-blooded young volunteers proceeded that very night to the "seat of war" in Virginia, basking in the acclaim of five thousand citizens at the train depot and cheering crowds along the whole route. Upon arrival, they claimed the distinction of being the first Confederate troops to arrive in the newly seceded state. After a brief stay at Norfolk's Naval Hospital, they fetched up at nearby Sewell's Point, where shore batteries barred Union ships from steaming up the Elizabeth River to Norfolk itself. Here the "City Light Guards" participated in the Georgia Battalion's first action on May 18-19, when two Federal vessels bombarded the Confederate shore battery at Hampton Roads; for the other companies, the excitement boiled down to a toilsome slog through rain and mud. Tom remained with the battalion at Norfolk through the frustratingly quiet summer and fall of 1861, during which he attained promotion to third sergeant, but greater opportunities beckoned when Col. David J. Bailey organized the 30th Georgia Volunteer Infantry in October.[77] (See map on page 459.)

Bailey was a prominent Butts County lawyer and senator, and had served as first lieutenant in a company that fought in the 1836 Creek War. In all likelihood, he was a friend or acquaintance of Tom's father John C. Mangham, who had commanded the cavalry company from nearby Pike County. Bailey's hometown of Jackson was but eighteen miles from the Manghams in Griffin, and men of public standing like Bailey and Mangham most probably knew each other before the war. In any case, Bailey moved to Griffin early in the war, and there he certainly came to know John, Sam, and Tom Mangham well.[78]

For Sgt. Tom Mangham, these connections were probably the basis for his discharge from the 2nd Georgia Battalion by order of the Secretary of War, who directed Tom's transfer to Bailey's regiment as first lieutenant and regimental adjutant. Effective November 1, 1861, Tom's transfer brought him into the regiment where he would make his military reputation. It also meant that his Civil War experience would be inextricably intertwined with that of his first cousin, *Willis Austin Mangham (II)*.[79]

*   *   *   *   *

Tom arrived at Camp Bailey in Fairburn, Georgia, to assume duties as adjutant of Bailey's newly organized regiment. There he doubtless met up with Willis Mangham of Captain Dollar's Company B, an outfit recruited from Butts County. Born on February 28, 1840, Willis was the youngest son of James M. and Nancy Mangham of Butts County, who named their boy after James's elder brother, Willis Austin Mangham of Pike County.[80]

By 1860, 70-year-old James Mangham had 225 acres of his 490-acre spread under cultivation, and that year he brought in a harvest of five hundred bushels of Indian corn, four bales of cash-producing cotton, and lesser quantities of produce typical of west Georgia's yeoman farmers. In this last year of peace, James doubtless relied heavily upon Willis and the five slaves of working age to do most of the heavy labor in the fields. By the time Willis helped his father lay by the following year's crop, however, the country had plunged into civil war, and he decided it was time to lay down the implements of peace and shoulder a musket in defense of his home. Willis mustered into the "Bailey Volunteers" on September 25, 1861, leaving his parents at home with his sister-in-law Sarah and her son Charles Thomas Mangham. Since Willis had married twenty-one year old Nancy Thaxton in February 1859, his departure meant a sad farewell to his young wife as well, along with their daughter Mary Malissa, whose first birthday was celebrated just three weeks before his enlistment.[81]

WILLIS A.
AND NANCY
MANGHAM

*-Courtesy of Asa
Mangham*

Willis traveled to the county seat of Jackson to enlist in the company being raised by Henry Hendrick. A locally prominent lawyer and farmer, Hendrick had been elected along with David J. Bailey to represent Butts County in the secession convention of 1860, and it was natural that Hendrick would seek to serve in the regiment Bailey began raising in the summer of 1861. Given James Mangham's lengthy residence in Butts County, as well as his service on the grand jury, it is highly probable that both Hendrick and Bailey knew him. So, when cousins Willis and Tom Mangham reported for duty with Bailey's fledgling regiment, the newly minted colonel doubtless was acquainted with both of their fathers.[82]

*   *   *   *   *

Willis had been at Camp Bailey near Fairburn, Georgia, for about a month when Lt. Tom Mangham assumed duties as regimental adjutant on November 1, 1861. Due to the confusion attending the establishment of dozens of regiments almost overnight, Bailey's regiment initially was accepted as the 25th Georgia. Later it was dubbed the 39th Georgia, and some months passed before it was designated definitively as the 30th Regiment Georgia Volunteer Infantry. The rapid mobilization outstripped the state's ability to arm the troops it raised, and the first months of service saw most of Bailey's men remain unarmed, while others carried a miscellany of rifles, muskets, and shotguns provided by family and friends. This state of affairs prevented the regiment's early deployment to a theater of active operations, but provided time for the officers and men to master the rudiments of drill so essential to effective tactical maneuver, even survival, on the battlefield.[83]

Of course, most of the volunteer officers were as untrained as their men, so accomplished drillmasters were at a premium. In these circumstances, Lieutenant

204

Mangham's star quickly began to shine. His prewar militia service in two well-drilled militia companies, the Griffin Light Guards and the Macon Volunteers, combined with six months' active service to make him the man for the job in Bailey's regiment. Indeed, one would suppose that Colonel Bailey pursued Tom's reassignment from the 2nd Georgia Battalion as a result of learning about Tom's skills from John and Sam Mangham. In any event, Tom was considered the "best drilled officer" in the regiment, and he "was kept busy drilling the officers of the regiment, and frequently the whole command."[84]

Although Governor Brown personally pleaded with the Secretary of War in November to equip Bailey's men with Enfield rifles and post them on the state line to protect Georgia against unruly east Tennessee Unionists, no arms were forthcoming. Furthermore, the threat to Georgia's coast was greater than that posed by "Tories" from the mountains of Tennessee. Therefore, after a brief stint at Camp Griswoldville in Jones County, late January 1862 found Tom and Willis Mangham on a night train bound for Camp Bartow, near Savannah. Over the next several months, the regiment shuffled to other camps around Georgia's key port city, where they helped construct coastal defenses similar to those Sam Mangham was manning at Pensacola. Armed solely with civilian shotguns while performing picket duties along the chilly Atlantic coast that winter, large numbers of men began falling victim to measles, mumps, and the other epidemics that ravaged the armies of the Confederacy in that first winter of the war.[85]

TOM MANGHAM

Sports of all types were nonetheless popular distractions, as was "blockade running." The latter pastime involved visiting the city without proper authorization to do so, and the participants risked punishments of double duty or digging up stumps if apprehended. Although they possessed good tents, uniforms, and adequate rations, some of the high-spirited troops wanted a change of diet and victimized a local gentleman's herd of goats. In the ensuing uproar, many pleaded self-defense, claiming that the goats had tried to run over them! Of course, these Georgia boys were merely indulging in the practice of "foraging," a nuisance that reigned supreme throughout the war. Many an irate farmer or officer caught a soldier red-handed, only to have the miscreant, doubtless struggling to keep a straight face, draw himself up in his scarecrow's dignity to announce self-righteously, "I'll kill any man's hog that bites me!" Again, Tom and the other officers probably did not know whether to laugh or cry when they called an unannounced alert one night, only to watch their men careering through the darkness like scalded cats, unable to find their companies and tumbling headlong over stumps. Perhaps Willis was one of several men in Company B who fell into an old well amidst the chaos. Hollering desperately for help as they imagined Yankees closing in for the kill, the hapless crew doubtless took a ribbing over the incident as long as any two of the regiment's original members ever met in the same room.[86]

Despite the hi-jinks, however, morale suffered that winter due to poor food, lack of pay, miserable arms, nasty weather, and the ennui resulting from inaction. Private Adamson, for one, wanted to tangle with the Yankees who were less than three miles away, but dreaded the prospect of matching his old shotgun against their rifled muskets. Even worse, he was convinced that ". . .old Bailey is willing to risk them even with Lightwood knots. But if he will suffer this regiment to go into battle with the guns they have he is not capable of commanding a regiment." Adamson reported the regiment's problems in a letter home, adding gloomily: "It is reported here that Adjutant T. W. Mangham has resigned but I hope it is not so."[87]

It is not clear whether Tom considered resignation that spring, but the regiment certainly was in ferment over its circumstances. The officers were still trying to get the men suitable weapons, but were apparently told to forget it unless the regiment re-enlisted for "three years or the war." Adamson, for one, was "not quite willing to try it for the war for fear we would get the same staff officers we have got now or some equally as bad for we was blinded before in the Election of officers. . . ." He added, "If we could get a Tidwell, a Mangham, a Hendrick or a Dollar I think there might be some danger of me reenlisting but under other circumstances I could not."[88]

The coming of conscription in April 1862 caused the reorganization of the regiment, which re-enlisted for an additional two years and five months. Although Private Adamson was disappointed that Colonel Bailey was re-elected, he held out high hope for the upcoming election of the regiment's other field officers: "T. W. Mangham [will I think be] our Lieut.-Colonel who is one of the finest men in the world." Tom stood for election against Capt. John Barnett of Company A, a Butts County notable of long standing. Despite Barnett's prior service as adjutant, captain, and colonel in

206

the state militia; sixteen years as judge of the county Inferior Court; a term in the state legislature; and service as a delegate to the 1860 Democratic presidential convention, Tom Mangham secured 252 votes against Barnett's 161. Effective April 24, some two months after his brother Sam was elected colonel of the 5th Georgia Volunteers, Tom was commissioned lieutenant colonel of the 30th Georgia. For Pvt. Willis Mangham, the reorganization was significant in two other respects as well: his Company B soon was redesignated Company A, and he was appointed its fourth sergeant on May 13.[89]

For Willis, drill now required him to learn the evolutions required of a sergeant and file closer, rather than a member of the file. For Tom, now serving as the regiment's second-in-command, it meant an opportunity to enforce higher standards of discipline and training, and he drilled the regiment until its efficiency became a point of pride for them all. Augustus Adamson heard Tom remark that he had never had a "drop of liquor in his life," and concluded several weeks after the election that the new lieutenant colonel was "the finest young man I have ever seen," adding "Everybody loves him." Tom certainly had plenty of opportunities to put his stamp on the regiment, for Colonel Bailey, born in 1812, was often in poor health and absent from his duties. Tom was barely half Bailey's age and possessed a robust constitution; although he was sick in camp in late May, he served as acting regimental commander for most of the time from May through November. Setting his regiment to blockading the river below Thunderbolt, while picketing Dutch Island and Whitemarsh Island, Tom's actions helped raise morale from its wintertime low. Adamson noted that Bailey's absence "leaves Mangham in command who is as good a commander as we could get." He added meaningfully, "I suppose strict military discipline is being enforced in this regiment at last and it is the best for us that it should be." Tom was still in command on July 3, when he receipted for the four hundred Enfield rifles and associated accouterments that finally gave the 30th Georgia the potential to make its mark as a front-line combat unit. Like his cousin, Willis also enjoyed good health; existing muster rolls cover the period from March to December 1862, and he was present for duty at each bimonthly muster.[90]

Willis was probably in ranks on the evening of October 3 when Lieutenant Colonel Mangham read aloud an order he had just received: the 30th Georgia was to leave its camps at Thunderbolt and move to Florida, where Confederate forces had been forced to evacuate Jacksonville. Moving by train as well as covering twenty-two miles by foot march, the 30th Georgia arrived at Baldwin, Florida, by October 6. Just several miles from Jacksonville, they bedded down in the open and Tom posted pickets in expectation of facing an enemy advance. When no further hostile movements developed, however, Tom was directed to move his regiment back to Savannah just four days later.[91]

For Tom and his men, this expedition to Florida must have proved a useful exercise in operational mobility, for the coming months would see the regiment undertake many more such deployments. Late October saw him move his men to Coosawhatchie in response to a Union raid against the railroad between Charleston and Savannah. Colonel Claudius C. Wilson of the 25th Georgia assumed overall command of the three Georgia regiments rushed to Coosawhatchie, but the "small force of the Abolitionists" that had caused the alarm was not interested in pressing the matter. After the Georgians arrived, the raiders pulled back without offering further combat. Tom and his men soon returned to Camp Hardee near Savannah, where their normal tedium of picket duties and unrelenting drill was relieved on occasion by Federal bombardments of Savannah's defenses. Periodically, senior officers inspected the troops, and General Mercer's review in late November was the occasion for the presentation of a battle flag and regimental banner to the 30th Georgia. December 17 saw the regiment rush with the remainder of the brigade to Wilmington, North Carolina, once more in response to a chimerical enemy threat. Back at Camp Young near Savannah on January 3, 1863, the regiment was dispatched to Wilmington again just fifteen days later. With the latest alarm over by early February, Tom moved his regiment back to Savannah once more. Due to derailments on the track in front of them, wheezing locomotives, and other frustrating delays, it took three days to get the regiment's 600-odd men back to Savannah, along with the remainder of Wilson's 1st Georgia Brigade. Not three weeks later, another alarm sent the 30th Georgia on a one-day excursion to the city's outskirts at Causton's Bluff, and April 9 saw the whole brigade, now under the command of Brig. Gen. W. H. T. Walker, deploy to Charleston for ten days. Tom tried to obtain General Beauregard's support to detail the regiment for permanent garrison duty in the city, but the Creole commander had all the troops he needed. April 27 to May 4 saw another deployment, this time to Pocotaligo, South Carolina, where the 30th Georgia dubbed its encampment "Camp Mangham" before departing for the seemingly inevitable return to Savannah.[92]

Indeed, the regiment's peregrinations between October 1862 and May 1863 make the 30th Georgia a minor case study in the Confederacy's operational and strategic use of its critical, albeit rickety and overstressed, railroad system. By the same token, the dizzying sequence of expeditions points out the serious disadvantage under which the South labored due to the lack of any naval force adequate to protect her coasts and ports. Every Federal movement against the Gulf or lower Atlantic coasts, whether it portended a serious landing attempt or merely a feint, required close scrutiny and rapid response by the Confederates. Many regiments such as the 30th Georgia were tied down by an endless series of deployments, and their services were withheld from the Confederacy's field armies throughout 1862 and the first half of 1863. After a year and a half of service, Tom Mangham's regiment had yet to experience its baptism of fire. By the time he and his men finished serving as a fire brigade for the southern Atlantic seaboard, the Army of Northern Virginia had firmly established its famous reputation; indeed, it was commencing the Battle of Chancellorsville and would soon be on its way to Gettysburg. The Army of Tennessee had fought at Shiloh, campaigned in Kentucky, and fought the Battle of Murfreesboro. On the Mississippi River itself, New Orleans had been lost and Vicksburg was facing yet another major Federal attempt to subdue its defenses, developments which were facilitated directly by superior Union naval power.

For Tom and his Georgians, it had been a dizzying six months, even though they had not been engaged in direct combat. And they were officially Tom's men now, for

Colonel Bailey's ill health had forced him to submit his resignation on the day before the December 17 deployment to Wilmington. Tom Mangham assumed the position of commanding officer of the regiment effective December 16, and Brig. Gen. States Rights Gist directed his promotion to the rank of colonel on January 12, 1863. The appointment was made official on April 2, to rank from December 16, 1862, and Tom's official acceptance of the appointment was dated April 28, 1863. It was six days before the regiment returned to Savannah from Camp Mangham for the last time. Three days later, Brig. Gen. W. H. T. Walker received orders to take his whole brigade to Jackson, Mississippi. Since Col. Tom Mangham was absent on leave, Lt. Col. James Boynton was in charge of the regiment for this movement, and Corporal Adamson noted that "The boys are all in fine spirits and appear to be very willing to go." But whether Boynton, Willis Mangham, and their fellow Georgians understood it or not, these marching orders were different from all the ones that had gone before. The only enemy they had seen to date was a group of stranded sailors captured near Wilmington and marched through the 30th Georgia's camp. The next Yankees they would see would not be prisoners of war, and they most certainly would not be sailors. They would be hard-marching, hard-living infantrymen under a hard-fighting general named U. S. Grant. After nineteen months in the army and the long months of picket duty and fruitless alarms, it was time for the men of the 30th Georgia to go "see the elephant." For some of them, the first time would be the last time.[93]

*   *   *   *   *

The regiment's move to Jackson, Mississippi, was part of a much larger effort to defend Vicksburg against Grant's latest stratagem. After months of frustration in his attempts to take the Confederate bastion on the Mississippi River, Grant moved some 35,000 men sixty miles down the west bank of the river and crossed at Bruinsburg on April 30. If he could take Jackson, he would cut off Vicksburg from the east and envelop its powerful river defenses from the landward side.[94] (See map, p. 637.)

Grant's swift-moving forces already had reached Clinton, just ten miles west of Jackson, when the 30th Georgia arrived at nearby Mississippi Springs on May 13. Sergeant Willis Mangham and his friends of the Bailey Volunteers formed up at the station, shouldered their Enfield rifle muskets, and moved out in a hurry to join their brigade near Clinton. After stumbling about in search of the right road, they reached the lines that night only to find that their quartermaster had failed to bring along their mess gear! Seasoned campaigners doubtless would have been little inconvenienced, but the 30th Georgia clearly was accustomed to the more centralized messing arrangements suited to static garrisons. Ignorant of techniques for cooking their raw rations without utensils, they went without supper and breakfast the following morning. About noon that day, the ladies of Clinton came to the rescue of the hungry Georgians as they stood in line of battle, providing a "bountiful dinner for the whole regiment."[95]

Whether they knew it or not, however, Gen. Joe Johnston already had given up the idea of defending Jackson with the 12,000 men available, and Walker's Brigade was one of two ordered to delay the Yankees west of the city. May 14 saw them engaged in light skirmishing as they pulled back to avoid capture. Although it was the 30th Georgia's first time under fire and the situation was clearly a desperate one, the well-trained men "behaved well." Directed to drop their "well-filled knapsacks" and wrap a change of underwear in a blanket slung over the shoulder, they pulled back through Jackson in a driving rain that reduced the roads to a glutinous mass of mud. By the next morning, the neatly uniformed and well-equipped Georgians had been transformed into mud-bespattered shadows, some of whom had lost their shoes in the clinging muck. Although the quartermaster was supposed to bring out their packs in his wagons, it goes without saying that this plan went awry; Willis Mangham and his friends never saw their packs again. Barely ten days after leaving Savannah, their war had assumed a completely different aspect. Even worse, the failure to forge a linkup with General Pemberton's forces meant that the defenders of Vicksburg were now isolated and surrounded. In truth, they were doomed, although rumormongers in the brigade claimed that General Pemberton was reporting plentiful food and ammunition stocks as late as June 24![96]

English Colonel James Fremantle, freshly arrived in the South to observe the combatants in action, saw Walker's men scattered all over the roads as they pulled back from Jackson, and concluded that the "straggling of the Georgians was on the grandest scale conceivable." Excusing their poor march discipline after he learned that their service had been limited to coastal garrisons, Fremantle was impressed by a meeting with their commander. Walker struck him as "a fierce and very warlike fire-eater, who was furious at having been obliged to evacuate Jackson after having only destroyed four hundred Yankees." The fiery Georgian added, "I know I couldn't hold the place, but I did want to kill a few more of the rascals."[97]

As the hot Mississippi summer waxed in strength and the siege of Vicksburg commenced, the 30th Georgia made a grueling 25-mile forced march to Yazoo City over roads topped with fine dust one to two inches thick, tramping through waterless countryside in furnacelike heat. There they remained with Johnston's little army throughout June, suffering in the heat and dust with only scum-covered, mud-choked livestock tanks for a water supply. Predictably, sickness soon began to thin the regiment's ranks. Colonel Mangham returned from furlough to resume command of his regiment, and he and his men performed picket duty in the face of Union forces near Yazoo City, but they did little in the way of active operations. With the Yankees' attention focused on Vicksburg and Johnston refusing to risk his small command until he secured more supplies and field transportation, Tom had his hands full simply helping his men survive the elements. In General Walker's opinion, Mississippi was the "worst country to campaign in I ever knew on account of dust in dry weather, mud in wet, and the almost total absence of good water, and very often on the march from eight to ten miles [with] no water at all."[98]

As the siege of Vicksburg reached a crisis, Johnston ordered his army into motion. Colonel Mangham received orders on July 4 to get his regiment ready to move at midnight that night, and the Georgians understood that they were to cross the Big Black River and attack the rear of Grant's besieging army. Indeed, General Johnston planned to move his army south of the railroad and there create a diversion that might allow Pemberton to cut his way out of Vicksburg. Before they moved out that night, however, they received the dismal news resonating throughout the embattled Confederacy: Vicksburg had fallen! Although its beleaguered defenders had repelled every assault on their lines during the preceding weeks, they had tottered on the brink of outright starvation. Lacking the power to break the siege and rightly despairing of relief from the outside, their commander surrendered the battered city and its garrison on the very day that Johnston prepared to move. Among the 29,000 Confederate

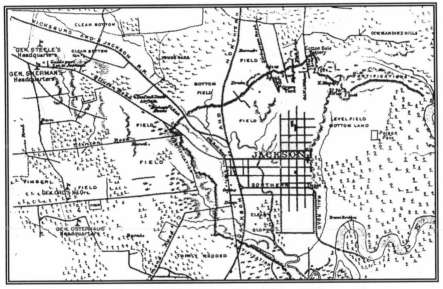

JACKSON, MISSISSIPPI, MAY – JULY, 1863.
TOM AND WILLIS MANGHAM HELD POSITIONS NORTH OF THE CITY. PRIVATE THOMAS H.
MANGHAM OF THE 19TH LOUISIANA WAS WEST OF TOWN, BETWEEN THE CLINTON AND
RAYMOND ROADS (SEE CH. IX AND APPENDIX, REF. # 153).

soldiers who stacked arms in Vicksburg was *Pvt. Francis Joseph Mangham* of the 1st Mississippi Light Artillery (see Chapter X). As Frank marched off to parole camp, his kinsmen Tom and Willis Mangham were retreating once more towards Jackson.[99]

The 30th Georgia marched in the wake of the retreating column as it took the road for Jackson at midnight on July 4, beginning a hellish march that they would long remember. Anyone who has ever marched at the rear of a column has learned to dread the accordion effect that bedevils the unfortunates assigned to that position. The fits and starts of the column are magnified down the line in a slingshot effect, often forcing the hindmost to run just to keep up. On the road to Jackson, this translated into a 24-hour hike in the scorching sun of a Mississippi July. Pausing only ten minutes each hour to rest, Colonel Mangham pushed his men down the road through the stifling dust clouds raised by the army's passage, hiking through waterless country with no relief in sight. The Georgians pushed the army's stragglers to keep up, aiding the sick and disabled as best they could.[100]

The next day brought more of the same, although the regiment gratefully assumed a place farther forward in the column. A Louisianian tramping down these same roads doubtless spoke for them all in his diary entry for July 6: "We have had a terrible march to-day. *No water*—dust, dust, dust. My God it is awful. . . .I didn't get any sleep last night, nor have I had anything to eat for twenty-four hours and I feel pretty well worn out. The heat is intolerable and the dust awful. I never want to be on another retreat." They had to keep moving rapidly, however, for Union forces were reaching towards Jackson in an attempt to cut off Johnston's hard-marching units. When the dusty butternut columns reached Clinton on July 6, they had covered forty to fifty miles in two days, without water. Although many citizens along the route had removed the water buckets from their well ropes to protect their meager water supplies from the passing columns, the townspeople of Clinton allowed the exhausted Georgians to drink freely from their cisterns; some of Tom's swollen-tongued troops literally drank themselves sick. Halting at midnight to rest, the regiment initially must have welcomed the rains which came to relieve the oppressive heat, but their bivouac area soon flooded and the bone-weary men found it impossible to sleep in the standing water.[101]

The morning saw them march into position outside of Jackson, where the exhausted men halted and stacked arms. Within moments of their arrival, however, events made it startlingly clear that a bad time was about to get worse: the boom of a cannon announced the presence of the Yankees. The solid shot mortally wounded two men of the 4th Louisiana Battalion of Wilson's Brigade, before bounding over the heads of Tom Mangham's Georgians. Troops scrambled in confusion as other shots followed the first in rapid succession, but Tom steadied his regiment, formed it into line and marched it rapidly to the left along a dry creek bed. Here they dug into the banks and threw up breastworks to their front, assuming a position in the Confederate line coalescing before Mississippi's capital city.[102]

They remained there for several days under increasing fire from sharpshooters and artillery, while Union forces built up in their front. On July 15, Tom ordered companies A, E, and H out front on picket duty. Sergeant Willis Mangham presumably was among those who thus stationed themselves in the first line of defense that day, and he and his friends of the Bailey Volunteers helped hold the picket lines intact until they were relieved late the next morning by some Tennesseeans and Texans. Picket duty in front of Jackson was only nominally similar to the long tours of guard duty the Georgians had pulled on the Atlantic coast, because they now were in the face of skilled and determined enemy troops who smelled victory in the air. In such a case, picket duty posed a thorny problem for the men posted in small groups between the lines. Their job was to prevent any surprise attack against the main defensive line, by firing on advancing enemy forces in time to give warning to their comrades. If the enemy advanced with skirmishers in front to protect their own main body, the scattered fire between advancing skirmishers and defending pickets formed a sort of prelude to the main assault. On the other hand, a sudden heavy rush by attacking lines could capture, or "gobble," the pickets in their exposed forward positions. Without the firepower to stop an opposing line of battle coming on in a full-blown attack, pickets had to come in fast to allow their own main line to commence firing before the enemy got too close. Any laggards ran a high risk of being caught between the two fires if they fell back too slowly.[103]

As Willis and the other pickets marched back towards the main lines about noon on July 16 with his comrades of companies A, E, and H, oncoming Union troops put the new picket companies on the horns of just such a dilemma. With a sudden dash forward, they caused the Tennesseeans and Texans to make up their minds in a hurry. The alarmed Rebs flew back to the main line, passing Willis and his friends on the run. Corporal Augustus P. Adamson of Company E recalled with amused understatement, that "We, of course, followed them in quick order, and regained our position with the balance of the regiment."[104]

As the rattled Georgians came panting into the trenches, Colonel Mangham doubtless had his drummer beating the long roll for assembly. The eight companies present for duty fell into line to repel the inbound assault columns, but no full-blown attack followed the initial overtures. Apparently, all of the pickets across the brigade front had been driven in as well, leaving General Walker to face the severe tactical problem this posed. If he tried to reestablish his picket line by counterattacking before the Federals could consolidate their hold on it, he might well find himself launching his troops directly into the teeth of an advancing enemy force. On the other hand, failure to restore his picket line would leave him blind to enemy maneuvers and force him to keep his men tensed for imminent assault at any moment. A stealthy approach by night or a quick lunge by day would bring the enemy within arm's length before the defenders could react.[105]

Any soldier with common sense knew that a defending force thus handicapped was easy pickings for a capable opponent. And brigade commander William Henry Talbot Walker was not just any soldier. A West Pointer, long-time Regular Army officer, and combat veteran whose propensity for stopping bullets in the Seminole and Mexican Wars earned him the moniker of "Old Shot-Pouch," the hot-tempered general was perhaps one of the few who really enjoyed war for its own sake. If his native Georgia was waging it against the hated Yankee, then that was so much the better. That evening, he ordered Colonel Mangham to retake the picket line. The old war-horse would be there to watch.[106]

Tom Mangham left no known record of his feelings that July evening, but John W. Hagan of the 29th Georgia wrote that "Col Mangrams of the 30th Georgia was on his way to releave our Skirmishers & tindered his Sirvisses to take back the woods." Tom's secessionist views and oft-remarked sense of personal honor make it extremely likely that he was eager to strike a personal blow against men commonly described as "Vandal invaders," or "defilers of Southern soil." Militarily speaking, he had trained himself for this moment since his days in the Griffin Light Guard. After two full years in service and countless hours spent drilling his regiment and disciplining it thoroughly, he now looked beyond his breastworks in the knowledge that the moment of truth had come. His objective was ground given up by his beloved regiment only hours before, and his mission was critical to the survival of his brigade and this sector of the Confederate lines. Honor was at stake, both personal and regimental. Walker was watching, and the men who had followed Tom's orders since November 1861 were watching, too.[107]

Colonel Thomas Woodward Mangham knew all of these things, and it is almost beyond doubt that he thought of all of them. It is likely that his blood was running nearly as hot as the Mississippi sun that day, but it is certain that he remained cool enough to establish a plan of action and communicate it to his regiment. He planned to use a minimal number of his men as skirmishers, thus reserving most of his regiment's power for the main assault. This was to be delivered in a compact formation from short range, so that his men would not wither in the heat and lose their impetus, or conversely, turn the attack into a wild footrace for the enemy lines. If resistance proved strong, the skirmishers had orders to fire and fall flat, allowing the main line to sweep forward past them without hindrance.[108]

On Tom's order, the 30th Georgia crossed its breastworks and formed line of battle in the field to their front, some 500 yards from thick woods on the opposite side. Private Augustus Adamson and the other men in Company E deployed some seventy-five yards to the front of the regiment, which stepped off at quick time "in splendid order and perfect alignment." Federal pickets posted in the woodline had a clear view of the advancing Georgians, and their popping muskets signaled the opening of the ball. As Company E continued forward to a point about one-third of the way across the field, the scattered musketry was replaced by heavy volleys from the Federal line. John Hagan and the rest of the 29th Georgia were watching closely, and to him it seemed that ". . .the yankees lay in ambush until our troops got within a few yds of them & then pored a volley into our troops but Col Mangrams marchered his men & presed forward. . . ." When some seven of Private Adamson's mates fell wounded, the remainder of the company sighted their Enfields on the woodline and "let drive," their skirmishing mission completed. Upon firing, they dropped to the ground as ordered, and Tom ordered the double-quick. He and his remaining seven companies pushed into the hail of Minie balls, howling the Rebel yell as they crossed the field. Four men were killed outright as they breasted the fire, and another two fell mortally wounded. Twenty-seven more were wounded in the attack, which cost the regiment about seven percent of its total force of some 450 men. Willis Mangham's Company A was one of the hardest-hit, losing Captain Towles, Lieutenant Ham, and five privates wounded.[109]

Despite these sharp losses, the whooping Georgians carried the woodline and drove the Yankees of the 11th Illinois back to their original positions. Consolidating their gains, the regiment reestablished the picket line and stood fast until relieved by troops of the 25th and 29th Georgia regiments. A delighted General Walker issued a general order praising the "fearless manner" they displayed in charging and routing a superior force of the enemy from this important position. Coming from a fiery taskmaster like Walker, this was a heady tonic indeed. As Corporal Adamson observed in a hastily written letter several days afterwards, "We was in no drawn battle but had to charge a

Brigade of Yankees and had the satisfaction to make them skedaddle. . . .Although the bullets whizzed all around us our men went through without a single man flinching." Even so, Adamson acknowledged that the "balls and shells made a very unpleasant music very near me," and admitted ". . .I had as soon been somewhere else."[110]

The elation was short-lived, however, for General Johnston already had decided that his position at Jackson was an untenable one, and the 30th Georgia fell back stealthily with the army to Morton that same night. The ground they regained that afternoon helped provide the space necessary for the army to pull out unnoticed. As Hagan viewed it,

> We fought the Yankees 8 days but was forced to retreat for want of more force. . . .I was confident we could Stand our ground & give the Fedearls a decient whiping but the longer we Stayed & fought them the more reinforcements they got & if we had have Stayed & fought a few days longer I fear we would have Suffered for our lines was so long we did not have men to fill the entrenchments & support our batteries. So we retreated in good order & we had a trying time. . . .the retreat was well conducted & we lost no men nor public property. . . .

After Federal probes ignited a few skirmishes during the next several days, Johnston's 24,000 men settled down to await developments. Tom Mangham and his men had fought hard and well, but Vicksburg and Jackson remained in enemy hands with no apparent hope of redemption. In the ensuing reorganization, Lt. Gen. William J. Hardee assumed command from the ailing Johnston, and Walker was promoted to major general commanding division. His old brigade reverted to the command of its senior colonel, Claudius C. Wilson of the 25th Georgia. Tom remained in command of the 30th Georgia, while the 29th Georgia, 1st Georgia Battalion Sharpshooters, and the 4th Louisiana Battalion rounded out the brigade.[111]

*   *   *   *   *

General Hardee's "Army of the Department of Mississippi and Eastern Louisiana," to cite its cumbersome official title, remained at Morton throughout the remainder of July and most of August. These were daunting months for the Confederacy, as the catastrophe of Vicksburg and the serious repulse at Gettysburg were followed by more ill tidings from middle Tennessee, where Rosecrans's brilliant maneuvers flanked Bragg's Army of Tennessee from its positions astride the Duck River with little fighting. By mid-August, Bragg had fallen back all the way to Chattanooga, abandoning all of fertile Tennessee to the enemy. As this situation worsened, Hardee's command was ordered to join the Army of Tennessee at the strategic rail center just above the Georgia state line.[112]

For Tom and Willis, these developments heralded their departure from Morton on August 24. The journey to Atlanta took four days by rail and steamer, and Tom's valise was stolen from the boat during the process. The case contained numerous regimental records (as well as Tom's commission as colonel of the regiment), and is probably the reason why no muster rolls survive from this period to document Willis Mangham's service. Arrival in Chickamauga Station on August 28 showed that the regiment had lost much more than its papers, though, as almost half of the men had turned up missing! Some 450 men were with the regiment when it left Mississippi, but scores had jumped from the cars at East Point and Fairburn, Georgia, to take a little "French leave." Although the regiment prided itself on its good discipline, the trains were passing within spitting distance of many of the soldiers' homes, and the temptation was simply too strong. Augustus Adamson thought Colonel Mangham was "the maddest man I ever saw," noting that he "considers his regiment disgraced," but Adamson hoped that "his passion will cool down before the boys get back." Nearly all of the absentees returned to the regiment within a few days, but Tom reduced the noncommissioned officers among them to the ranks. Momentous movements were in progress, however, and he could not spare much time to discipline privates who had helped themselves to a few days at home.[113]

After a few days at Tyner's Station, the 30th Georgia returned to Chickamauga Station on the night of September 7 to load commissary supplies onto railcars for shipment south. Bragg was pulling out of Chattanooga that very night, so the regiment marched to Ringgold the next day and then hotfooted it twenty-six miles to Lafayette on September 9. The armies were now engaged in a deadly game of hide-and-seek in the north Georgia mountains, and the regiment alternated rapid marching and countermarching with hours spent drawn up in line of battle, waiting anxiously to launch attacks that never came to pass.[114]

The long-awaited clash began in earnest on September 18 along the banks of Chickamauga Creek, when Confederate forces began to probe for Rosecrans's left flank along the Reed's Bridge Road. Just more than a mile to the south, Wilson's Brigade was one of the units of Walker's Division stacked up along Alexander's Bridge Road south of the bridge itself, where Col. John T. Wilder's Federal brigade fought a crucial delaying action against Johnson's Division. Wilson's men finally crossed the Chickamauga the next morning about one o'clock, wading through the chill waters at Shallow Ford (also referred to as Byram's Ford) before bivouacking just west of the creek. Colonel Wilson received orders to keep his troops near the ford to guard the division's ordnance trains, and he detached the 30th Georgia to secure the crossing point. Tom posted two companies to secure each road leading down to the creek, then set the rest of his command to work recovering stalled and broken-down wagons at the ford itself. By about eight o'clock that morning, the ammunition wagons were across the river and re-integrated into the brigade column as it pushed forward two miles to the intersection of the Alexander's Bridge Road and the Alexander Road leading to Lee and Gordon's Mills.[115]

Here Wilson received orders to move north along the Bridge Road to support two brigades of cavalry under Gen. Nathan Bedford Forrest, who had been fighting for an hour or more against blueclad infantry comprising the extreme left (northern) flank of Rosecrans's army. It was probably at this point that Cpl. Augustus Adamson, a member of the 30th Georgia's color guard, saw Lt. Rufus Lester, the brigade's acting assistant adjutant general, ride up to Colonel Mangham. Lester's advice was terse and to the point: "Colonel, we are going to have hot times just over yonder; get your men ready."[116]

Wilson marched his brigade up the road and formed line of battle off to the left, as directed by Forrest. As the firing up ahead grew louder, orders came to move up still

"COLONEL, WE ARE GOING TO HAVE HOT TIMES JUST OVER YONDER."
COLONEL THOMAS WOODWARD MANGHAM, 30TH GEORGIA VOLUNTEERS
-Georgia Historical Society, Savannah, Ga

farther to support Forrest's troopers, who were outgunned by two brigades of Yankee infantrymen. Wilson again ordered his brigade to file by the right up the Alexander Bridge Road, with his own 25th Georgia in the van. The 29th Georgia came next, followed by the 26 officers and 308 men of Mangham's 30th Georgia, marching behind Colonel Mangham and T. E. Moore of Company B, who bore the regimental colors presented two years earlier by Colonel Bailey's daughters. The 4th Louisiana Battalion was next in the column, with the 1st Georgia Battalion Sharpshooters bringing up the rear.[117]

After moving in column nearly half a mile up the road, Wilson ordered his brigade to form forward across the Brotherton Road. Tom ordered his command into line by the right flank at the double-quick, forming them behind a fence bordering the Winfrey cornfield. Almost immediately, Yankee skirmishers posted in the field started popping away, and Wilson ordered his brigade to advance. He noted proudly that his "line stepped off with the enthusiasm of high hope and patriotic determination, and the precision and accuracy which only disciplined and instructed troops can attain."[118]

Colonel Mangham put Company E out on the skirmish line to clear the way, and Captain Dollar's "Clayton Invincibles" responded with the verve that Tom expected from men who had volunteered to spend the night scouting for Yankees in the streets of Jacksonville, Florida, back in October 1862. The Clayton County boys were driving back skirmishers from Col. Charles Chapman's 74th Indiana Volunteers of Croxton's brigade, and Chapman was the first to realize the danger that had materialized on their flank. Croxton's five regiments had been pushing east through the woods against Forrest's dismounted cavalrymen, believing that they faced a single misdirected Confederate brigade stranded on the west side of Chickamauga Creek. Only when they saw Wilson's Brigade marching through the Winfrey Field and the surrounding pines did the true gravity of their situation become clear: a full brigade of Confederate infantry was heading straight for their right flank![119]

Chapman was directly in the path of Tom and Willis Mangham and the 30th Georgia Infantry, which was pouring a "terrible fire" into his flank, and he shouted desperately for his rightmost companies to refuse the regiment's flank to face this new threat. Amid the confusion, however, his whole regiment began to pull back, whether from a misunderstanding of orders or from a veteran unit's finely tuned sense of self-preservation. From Wilson's point of view, his troops' "well-directed fire" caused the Indiana men to "break and flee from the field in confusion, leaving dead and wounded covering the field over which we marched." Croxton managed to dispatch the 10th Kentucky at the double-quick from the left of his line, and they arrived alongside the desperate Hoosiers in time to pour a volley into the howling Georgians' faces. Colonel John Croxton was an accomplished commander and his men obviously were made of stern stuff as well, for he managed to disengage them from the cavalry to the east and change the whole brigade's front to the south in time to slow the gray tide. Tom Mangham was at the right of his advancing line, posted slightly to the front and "cheering them to the charge." The color guard saw him "displaying a courage which was characteristic of him and an inspiration to his soldiers." The other regiments of

Wilson's Brigade were keeping pace, and the woods resounded with the roar of musketry and the Rebel yell, while Croxton's hard-pressed men fell back rapidly.[120]

The 31st Ohio Volunteers were moving up to Croxton's aid through the woods, however, having dropped packs at the Kelly farm. Sergeant McNeil of Company F remembered marching "through the woods right toward the wicked noise, which had increased to a steady roll." Hearing a "deafening crash, followed by the familiar rebel screams," the regiment began to move forward at the double-quick. When they arrived on the left of Croxton's beleaguered line, it already had retired some four hundred yards and was threatening to give way altogether.[121]

As the crisis approached, elements of Brig. Gen. John King's U. S. Regulars arrived behind Croxton's wavering line and established a fresh line of battle. Croxton's men were used up by now, and more than glad to step aside and let King's men go to it. This they did with a will, as Wilson noted that "the contest was renewed with great energy and the position disputed with stubborn resolve. The firing at this point was terrific, and many brave officers and men fell while gallantly discharging their duties." Nevertheless, Wilson's Brigade drove forward several hundred more yards before slowing up in front of breastworks hastily fashioned from fallen pines.[122]

As the assault's momentum waned, Wilson received orders from Forrest directing him to break off the pursuit, so he stood fast and continued to slug it out. His ranks were sorely thinned by this time, and the situation was degenerating as he learned of a Federal force forming up on his own exposed left flank. This was another fresh brigade of bluecoats under Col. Benjamin F. Scribner, and their fire rapidly turned Wilson's left into a veritable meat-grinder. Scribner's arrival meant that Wilson's 1800 men had now faced more than 4000 Yankees that morning, and the odds had become simply overwhelming. Wilson called for reinforcements, but it was already too late for the left of his line. The 1st Georgia Sharpshooters and 4th Louisiana Battalion melted away under terrific fire from front and flank, and the 30th Georgia was forced back as well.[123]

Tom's embattled regiment was in a bad fix indeed, as its losses had mounted to staggering proportions by this point. Of the 334 officers and men who went into the attack on September 19, 1863, at least thirty were killed, 78 wounded and two missing by the end of the next day, and almost all of these casualties were suffered in the first day's action. One of those felled in the ferocious combat in the north Georgia woods was the regiment's hard-fighting 26-year-old commander, Col. Thomas Woodward Mangham. In Corporal Adamson's words, "The intrepid Mangham was wounded in the hottest of the fight, while in front, gallantly leading his men." Tom apparently was hit either when Scribner's men enfiladed the brigade's left flank or in the preceding bitter engagement with King's Regulars, and he went down hard indeed. Tom was struck in the right groin with a Minie ball, and it drove his pocketknife into his hip joint, injuring both the bone and the joint itself. Adamson and two other members of the five-man color guard also had been shot down, and the nineteen-year-old corporal lay in the field hospital when Tom was carried in. He recalled the scene almost five decades later:

At the field hospital he showed a kind consideration for the wounded of his men, inquiring as to their wounds and giving to each an encouraging word, and when the surgeon told him he was ready to examine his wound he replied: "Doctor, I have men here who are worse wounded than I. Look after them."

The writer was among the wounded and nearby, and heard this remark, and saw the ball extracted from his wound. Had it not been for a pocket knife, which the ball struck and partly checked its force, the wound would likely have been fatal.[124]

Tom Mangham was extremely lucky to survive his terrible wound, which remained unhealed months later. The young colonel was at home with his family in Griffin, and dictated a letter to the military authorities:

A. P. Mason   April 11th 1864
Major & A. A. Genl.
Sir,

I respectfully request permission to appear before a Board of Medical Officers for examination with a view to being retired under the provisions of an act of Congress approved February 17th 1864.

I was disabled by a severe gunshot wound in my right groin received in the battle of Chickamauga, Saturday September 19th 1863. I have been confined to my bed since that time, not being able to walk on crutches even now, though seven months have nearly passed since receiving my wound. In a word I am perfectly helpless and my Surgeon has given it as his opinion that I will not be fit for field service in less time than eight or ten months.

My address is Griffin, Ga.

I am Major
Very Respectfully
Your Obedient Servant
Written by   /s/ *Thos. W. Mangham*
A. Merritt   Colonel 30th Ga. Regiment

Tom's request to appear before a medical board required endorsements by his military chain of command. Brigadier General C. H. Stevens was now the brigade commander, since Colonel Wilson had fallen fatally ill during the subsequent siege of Chattanooga. Stevens recommended approval, noting that "Col. Mangham is an excellent officer and his services will be a serious loss to the Brigade, but all reports of his condition concur in the statement that he will be very long if not permanently disabled." Major General W. H. T. Walker, the fire-eating Southron *par excellence*, also approved Tom's request, adding the remark that "Col. Mangham behaved with distinguished gallantry."[125]

When the medical examining board met at Griffin on April 24, the surgeons rendered their professional opinion:

Colonel Thomas W. Mangham of the 30th Georgia Regiment. . .was wounded at the battle of Chickamauga Sept. 19th 1863 by a ball striking and driving before it a pocket knife into the right groin lodging near the hip joint materially involving the joint and injuring the bone. The wound continues to suppurate and his general health has become involved.

The hip joint is so much involved as to remain partially anchylosed.

He is unfit for duty in any Department of the Government.

Now officially a retired officer of the Invalid Corps, the war was over for Col. Thomas Woodward Mangham.[126]

*   *   *   *   *

British Lt. Col. Arthur Fremantle spent several months touring the Southern armies in 1863, and thought that a comment by a colleague, Colonel St. Leger Grenfell, aptly illustrated the standards Confederate soldiers expected of their officers:

Colonel Grenfell told me that the only way in which an officer could acquire influence over the Confederate soldiers was by his personal conduct under fire. They hold a man in great esteem who in action sets them an example of contempt for danger; but they think nothing of an officer who is not in the habit of *leading* them; in fact such a man could not possibly retain his position. Colonel Grenfell's expression was, "every atom of authority has to be purchased by a drop of your blood."[127]

When reading the regimental history compiled almost fifty years later by ex-Corporal Adamson, it is abundantly clear that Tom Mangham was exactly the type of officer Grenfell had in mind, and his troops responded just as the Briton described. Tom knew his business and led from the front, and his men loved him for it. The same must be said as well for the other field officers of Wilson's Brigade, only two of whom remained unhurt after the savage combat in north Georgia's bitter woods.[128]

*   *   *   *   *

Although Tom would never again march with his regiment, his cousin, Sgt. Willis Mangham, continued to soldier with Company A, the "Bailey Volunteers." If he was at Chickamauga, then he was lucky to get out alive. He was even luckier that a mix-up on the Federal side prevented Scribner from flinging his brigade full-force into the flank of Wilson's Georgians as they retired through the Winfrey field, because such a blow probably would have bagged the great majority of the survivors. Of course, this miscue was neither the first nor the last in the horrific fighting in the dense forests; an even greater Federal blunder helped ensure the collapse of their line under the never-ending Confederate hammer blows on September 20. Wilson's Brigade and the 30th Georgia were under fire in a supporting role on that second day of combat, but their terrible losses the preceding day helped keep them out of the forefront of action. If Willis was in the ranks that day, he doubtless heard and participated in the tremendous cheers of exultation that swelled from the throats of the men of the Army of Tennessee. For the first and only time in their ill-starred history, they had won a smashing victory in a general engagement. Even now, their victory was won despite their commander's mistakes, rather than because of his skillful employment of his hard-fighting army.[129]

What a bitter contrast Chickamauga posed to the debacle at Missionary Ridge just two months later. Most of Wilson's Brigade, commanded temporarily by Col. James Cooper Nisbet of the 66th Georgia, remained unengaged on the northern reaches of the ridge, but lost a few prisoners in the nighttime withdrawal that followed the Federal penetrations far to their left. The Georgians had not even seen the disastrous breakthrough that precipitated the retreat; on their end of the line, the units of Cleburne's Division had administered a resounding repulse to the main Federal attack, which sought vainly to expel them from the heights on the north end of Missionary Ridge. They were shocked that night to hear that the army was defeated, but the brigade pulled back in good order and marched into Chickamauga Station in the sleet and rain. As Nisbet had the brigade draw rations from the large commissary warehouses there, he had to laugh at the antics of the men scooping sorghum in their hats, tripping unsuspecting soldiers into the sticky mess, and then "sopping" the sweet stuff off of their victims! But all shenanigans aside, it would be a long, cold winter for Willis and his friends who pulled back with the defeated army to Dalton, Georgia. The most positive development during the months of discontent was the appointment of Gen. Joe Johnston to command the Army of Tennessee; the ensuing reorganization did much to dissipate the cloying odor of defeat that clung to the troops after the catastrophe at Missionary Ridge.[130]

*　　*　　*　　*　　*

When William T. Sherman launched his campaign against Atlanta in April 1864, it meant hard marching and hard fighting for the 30th Georgia over the next hundred days. They took part in a nasty little engagement near Calhoun on May 16, in which the regiment lost more than a dozen men in an attack launched to drive back Union troops as they crossed the Oostanaula River and outflanked Johnston's army. Although the Georgians and other troops succeeded in stemming the tide, the previous day's action had secured a solid Union lodgment and Johnston had to abandon his now untenable position at Resaca. The Army of Tennessee was forced to fall back through Adairsville, Cassville and beyond in heavy fighting, but eventually settled into strong positions anchored on Kennesaw Mountain by mid-June.[131]

For almost two weeks, Sherman probed the Kennesaw Line for weaknesses, but few seemed apparent; a morose Indiana surgeon wondered at opponents who "contest every foot of ground and fight with an obstinacy almost unprecedented." Willis Mangham participated in the incessant skirmishing that caused both sides to leak casualties rearward at an alarming rate, but these paled by comparison with the horrific losses resulting from Sherman's direct assault on June 27 at three points along the Confederate lines. The men of the 30th Georgia were posted several hundred yards south of Little Kennesaw that morning with the remainder of Walker's Division, and the attack in their sector passed just to their north. Walker's men had the satisfaction of pouring fire into the flank of Logan's XV Corps as it went past, thus helping disrupt the momentum of the doomed assault. Several men of the 30th Georgia fell while helping to repulse this attack, but their known losses of two killed and eight wounded during the weeks at Kennesaw were mercifully small when contrasted with units at the center of the storm.[132]

After losing nearly three thousand men in the futile assault of June 27, Sherman's renewed flanking maneuvers finally levered Johnston out of the trenches near Kennesaw, and the embattled Rebels fell back steadily to the outskirts of Atlanta by early July. Most of the troops revered "Old Joe" Johnston and believed that his defensive strategy was a wise one in view of their numerical inferiority, but they likewise hoped to strike a major blow to the invaders and drive the hated "Vandals" from Georgia soil. Some fainthearts had faded from the ranks upon resumption of active campaigning in May, and men from Kentucky, Tennessee, northern Alabama and north Georgia were deserting in increasing numbers as the incessant retreat left their homes and families at the mercy of the invading host. As one Federal officer observed, "These deserters have no special love for us, but are tired of war, discouraged, and after years of absence anxious to see home, which is generally within our lines." By July, even the hardened veterans who stood firmly by their colors began to despair; if they could not stop Sherman in the hills of north Georgia, how could they stop him at the very gates of Atlanta? While their letters home often expressed confidence in the eventual outcome, it sometimes sounded as though the writers were "whistling past the graveyard." Sergeant John Hagan of the 29th Georgia had marched in the same brigade as Willis Mangham for nearly two years, and his letters to his wife Amanda clearly evidence his devotion to the Confederate cause. They also offer us a telltale glimpse of the desperation that gripped the men who did the fighting. On July 11, he wrote:

> "Gen Hardees corps is as near concentrayted as posable & it denotes & oppen field fight as Gen Bragg fought at Chickamauga we are ready, & willing to fight any time for evry retreat we make only has a tendeincy to demoralize a po[r]tion of the Army & I am anxious for the fight to come off."[133]

Despairing of Johnston's willingness to stand before Atlanta, President Jefferson Davis replaced him with Gen. John Bell Hood, foretelling a dramatic change in tactics. Hood had made his reputation as an aggressive fighter in numerous battles with the Confederacy's eastern and western armies, and he sought to save the critical rail and manufacturing center of Atlanta by using the same formula. His first attempt came just two days after assuming command, when he launched an attack aimed at destroying elements of three Union army corps under Gen. George Thomas in the vulnerable hours after they crossed Peachtree Creek.[134]

Although Hood often has been condemned roundly for this attack and the others that followed in the weeks and months to come, historian Albert Castel argues that Hood's plan at Peachtree Creek actually held out a very real possibility of success. Planning to smash the Federal forces isolated on the near side of the creek before they could prepare breastworks, he rapidly marshaled Hardee's and Stewart's Corps for the attempt. The 30th Georgia marched in Stevens's Brigade of Walker's Division, one of four divisions assigned to Hardee's Corps. Bate's Division, on the right, initiated the attack in echelon by probing through dense thickets searching vainly for the Union flank. Walker's men were next in line, with Stevens's and Gist's Brigades in the van. Unfortunately, Walker failed to coordinate his attack and these two brigades went in piecemeal, unsupported by the division's second line. Since Bate's attack floundered miserably to their east and Maney's Tennesseeans on their west probed tentatively rather than assaulting vigorously, this meant that Stevens's Brigade had almost no chance of success.[135]

He and his Georgians could not foretell this, of course, and their actions that afternoon bespoke the élan and determination of veteran troops who meant business.

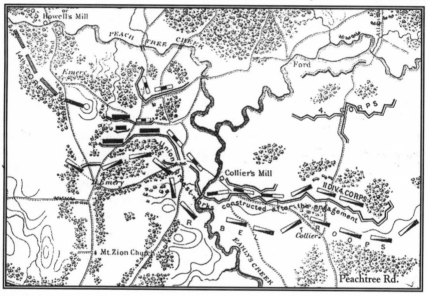

BATTLE OF PEACHTREE CREEK, JULY 20, 1864.
WALKER'S GEORGIA DIVISION ATTACKED UP PEACHTREE ROAD (LOWER RIGHT CORNER).
IN ITS RANKS WERE WILLIS MANGHAM OF THE 30TH GA. AND JOHN WILLIS MANGHAM OF
THE 2ND GA. SHARPSHOOTERS (SEE CHAPTER II AND APPENDIX, REF. # 190).

They came rolling up the right side of Peachtree Road, boiling over a hill so fast and unexpectedly that the two brigades of Yankees on the ridge to their front had to fling down their entrenching tools and pick up their muskets in a hurry. Union General Kimball reported that Walker's Georgia division attacked "with a rapidity and absence of confusion I have never seen equalled." Both sides opened fire simultaneously, and a Union artilleryman thought the terrific detonations sounded "something like the heavens and earth had come suddenly together." Infantrymen standing in the blueclad lines of battle were practically deaf for two days afterwards, and did not recover their

224

normal hearing until almost a week later. Even one hundred miles to the west, where Willis's disabled brother *John Henry Mangham* lived in Talladega County, Alabama, all normal business came to a halt as worried people listened to the terrible rumble of battle from the direction of Atlanta (see Chapter V).[136]

After their first charge was repulsed with heavy casualties, the Georgians came on yet again. Brigadier General George Wagner, commanding the Federal brigade at this point, noted that the "repeated and desperate assaults" mired down in the maelstrom of musketry and cannon fire that his men poured down the slope. The blood-soaked ridge was practically carpeted with the bodies of twenty-nine Confederates who fell within twenty paces of his breastworks. General Stevens himself went down before the lines of the 40th Indiana, dropped from his mount by a bullet in the head. The 1st Georgia Confederate Regiment lost fifty percent of the men who went up the ridge that afternoon, and the 66th Georgia lost one-fourth of its strength in assaults that reached, but could not hold, the enemy breastworks. Records are incomplete for the 30th Georgia, but at least two men were killed and five wounded in their vain attempt to inflict a telling blow on the invaders. Hardee's clumsily managed and unevenly executed attack fetched him perhaps a thousand casualties, most of them from Stevens's Brigade, while gaining nothing. Although Stewart's Corps enjoyed much greater success and badly mauled Fighting Joe Hooker's XX Corps, the overall result was another costly defeat.[137]

Some Confederates believed they had scored something of a victory in the bloody fighting, which seemed to have checked yet another of Sherman's flanking moves. Writing to his wife to inform her that he was "stil among the living," Sergeant Hagan noted proudly that "We attacked the yankees & drove them back some distance," but added significantly that "we finally had to fall back leaving our dead & wounded on the field." For him personally, the battle culminated in a fashion that bore no resemblance to victory: "I come very near falling into the enimys hands & had to lay down my gun & accutiaments & haversacks & Bedcover. I had to leave all & Swim a creek about 3 hundred yards & made my asscape."[138]

While a soaking wet Hagan recovered from his harrowing ordeal, General Hardee received orders to dispatch a division to Atlanta, as cavalry reports indicated that a Federal force approaching from McDonough was practically at the city's gates. Cleburne's Division accordingly moved out to help counter this threat, and the remainder of Hardee's men soon pulled out and followed them off to the east. Within two days, they would be engaged in a still more desperate assault in the Battle of Atlanta. Here, Hood hoped to concentrate his army in time to strike the exposed eastern flank of Gen. McPherson's wing of the Federal Army, rolling it up and allowing him to pinion Thomas against the Chattahoochee. The odds were long, but if the outnumbered Confederates could strike hard and fast, they could make Sherman pay dearly for allowing the two wings of his army to stray outside of supporting distance of each other.[139]

For Willis and the 30th Georgia, this meant marching east on Peachtree Road into Atlanta, then out the McDonough Road towards Decatur in the attempt to get on

McPherson's flank with the remainder of Hardee's Corps. As the weary columns shuffled through Atlanta that night, dreadful scenes of panic and looting broke out, since civilians and army stragglers concluded the army was abandoning the city. The resulting confusion coupled with fatigue, heat, and terrible dust to clog the wheels of movement; after assaulting the Federal lines at Peachtree Creek on July 20, Hardee's men had dug trenches all day on July 21. That night, the lucky ones got three hours' sleep before tramping more than fifteen miles to get into position for the attack. Daybreak on July 22 found Willis and his exhausted comrades of Walker's Division near the Aker's house on the Fayetteville Road, still almost five miles from Decatur.[140]

After additional delays, Hardee determined to send Wheeler's cavalrymen forward to Decatur to complete the envelopment, giving up on accomplishing this with the slower-moving troops of his four infantry divisions. These he planned to swing north towards the flank and rear of the Federals, guiding Walker's Division along the line of Sugar Creek. Walker, dismayed by the morass of briar patches that clogged his route of advance, vainly importuned Hardee for permission to take a different route. Enraged by the brusque dismissal of his request, Walker stormed off, asserting that "Hardee must answer me for this." Notorious at the best of times for his prickly sense of personal honor, Walker exploded in rage after his division slogged through the briars west of Sugar Creek only to encounter an utterly impassable slough filled with fallen trees, named Terry's Mill Pond. Turning on his hapless civilian guide, Walker pulled his pistol and prepared to shoot him on the spot, but his aide, Maj. Joseph Cumming, delayed him long enough to allow the guide to suggest a route around the left side of the morass.[141]

Walker's personal woes were almost at an end, however, for after skirting the quagmire he pulled up to examine the forest some 250 yards ahead. As he peered through his binoculars, a Yankee rifleman dropped him dead from the saddle with a single shot. Almost immediately, the popping of small arms began, signaling the onset of the Battle of Atlanta. Unfortunately for Willis Mangham and his friends, things continued to go awry in the fashion of the uncoordinated attack at Peachtree Creek just two days earlier. It began when Bate's Division on their right lunged out of the blackberry thickets towards McPherson's unprotected flank and rear.[142]

Only it was no longer unprotected.

On the ridgeline several hundred yards away stood two Federal divisions and two batteries of artillery. Sweeny's division had arrived just thirty minutes earlier, sent by an anxious McPherson to reinforce his left flank as it dangled in thin air. Fuller's division was there as well, waiting to move westward into Atlanta's supposedly abandoned defenses; it was not expecting an engagement at all, much less one to the south, but it formed line in a hurry as shooting boiled up from that direction. By the time Walker's Confederates struggled out of the slimy mud of Terry's Mill Pond to get roughly on line with Bate's men, the Yankees were waiting, with Sweeny on the far left wing of a newly refused flank and Fuller just to his right. Supported by artillery, Sweeny's division hammered back Bate's men quickly as they surged unsupported into a frontal assault across several hundred yards of open valley.[143]

First in Walker's column was Stevens's Brigade, led by Col. George A. Smith, and his men went howling for the gap between Sweeny's and Fuller's divisions just as Bate's Division recoiled from the wall of flame. Unsupported, the brigade plunged forward into the fire of six field pieces of the 14th Ohio Battery, as well as elements of two Federal divisions. Their repulse was perhaps only predictable. The Georgians were fighting on their home ground, however; although Colonel Smith was wounded and unhorsed, Colonel Nisbet of the 66th Georgia assumed command and rallied the men to try yet again. With officers waving drawn swords and color bearers flaunting their flags to bring the men to fever pitch, they went forward once more. Still no support came, however, and the blueclad troops they faced were veterans as well. This time, two regiments from Fuller's division and two from Sweeny's pushed forward to attack the Georgians' exposed flanks when they were halfway across the valley. With no artillery or supporting infantry to protect them from this well-timed onslaught, the result was horrible. The once-proud brigade, chewed up badly just two days earlier at Peachtree Creek, was shattered and more than five hundred trapped men were forced to surrender. At least six of those captured were from the 30th Georgia, which suffered at least twelve killed in action and thirteen wounded. Two of the killed and four of the wounded had marched alongside Willis Mangham in the Bailey Volunteers, and two of the injured succumbed to the effects of their injuries. Willis would have been pained to know that his first cousin (once removed), *Cpl. John Willis Mangham* of the 2nd Georgia Battalion Sharpshooters, was in the ranks of Gist's Brigade as it double-quicked past Stevens's remnants just minutes later, destined to meet a similar dismal fate.[144]

The debacle was over in less than forty-five minutes; two veteran divisions were badly mauled for naught. For all the criticism of Hood, this was a patented example of a disaster caused by mismanagement at corps and division levels. The battle grew to much greater proportions over the next few hours and in some places the Confederates came very close to success, but the final result was another costly repulse. The failure meant weeks of continued siege and bitter combat, now at the very gates of Atlanta.[145]

As the noose tightened throughout August, Federal forces managed to cut off all but one railroad to the city. This last tenuous lifeline was the Macon & Western Railroad, on which Tom Mangham had served as a young conductor in the last heady years of peace. And in the waning days of the month, Sherman vacated the trenches on the left of his line and swung a large force west and south of the city to strike at the railroad near Jonesboro. Although it took some time for Hood to determine where the Federal blow would fall, the threat finally materialized with frightening clarity on the evening of August 30. When the Confederate commander received dispatches which made it clear that strong enemy forces were within cannon shot of Jonesboro, he immediately ordered a counterblow aimed at smashing Sherman's force while it was on the move.[146]

That night, Hood ordered Hardee's Corps south to Jonesboro, and Willis soon shouldered arms and headed southward out of Atlanta's defenses for the small railroad depot in Clayton County. For the boys of Company I, the "Clayton Invincibles," any scrap at Jonesboro would take place almost within sight of their homes. Indeed, the town was situated in country that most of the 30th Georgia claimed as home. The "Fayette Volunteers" hailed from the county of that name, just five miles west of Jonesboro, whereas the "Bartow Invincibles" had enlisted in Henry County, a scant five miles east of town. Three other companies came from Campbell (now Douglas) County just west of Atlanta, while another mustered in at Bibb County, whose county seat of Macon was the southern terminus of the railroad that gave Jonesboro its strategic significance. A portion of Company C enlisted from Spalding County, some eight miles south of Jonesboro; the remainder of the company had answered the call from Butts County, along with Companies A and B. For Willis and the Bailey Volunteers, the looming crisis at Jonesboro was only twenty miles from home. Many historians have noted that a common thread of motivation for Confederate soldiers was their sense that they served as a bulwark between the invading "Vandal" hordes and their loved ones at home. The desperate valor of the 30th Georgia's assaults at Chickamauga, Calhoun, and Atlanta produced casualty lists that testify to their grim determination to defend their firesides.[147]

One can only wonder how these Georgians felt that night, tired and hungry as they marched southward through the gathering darkness. Certainly they were exhausted by the time they arrived in Jonesboro at dawn on August 31, having marched twelve miles over rough roads during the dead of night. As they took up positions just west of town that morning, they doubtless understood that their thin ranks were the only thing between the invading host and the homes they had enlisted to defend three long years before. Even though the men could not possibly know whether Hood intended to hold Atlanta or evacuate it immediately, the butternut-clad veterans knew enough about strategy by now to understand what their arrival in Jonesboro meant. Clearly, Sherman was threatening the last means of sustenance for the beleaguered Gate City and its garrison. And if Sherman could choke off the railroad routes into Atlanta, he could prevent escape from the city. Unable to remove their heavy ordnance and commissary trains, the Confederates would be forced to make their way out of town to the south and east under extreme pressure, without adequate means of provisioning tens of thousands of men. In short, Willis Mangham and his comrades were fighting not only for their homes; they were fighting for the very survival of the Army of Tennessee.[148]

The Union forces west of Jonesboro comprised elements of three army corps, which had entrenched the previous evening in a semicircular line whose flanks were anchored on the Flint River at their backs. They lacked the strength to take the town itself once Hardee's and Lee's Corps had arrived, although their copious complement of artillery would guarantee the slaughter of anyone foolish enough to move a train through the depot just 800 yards to their east. Their numbers were roughly equal to the twenty thousand grayclad troops they faced, however, and well-sited entrenchments increased the odds in their favor.[149]

Thousands of footsore or discouraged Southerners had fallen out of ranks on the punishing night march to Jonesboro. Hard-fighting Tennesseean Sam Watkins recalled that Atlanta's haggard defenders were "broken down with their long days' hard marching—were almost dead with hunger and fatigue. Every one was taking his own course, and wishing and praying to be captured. . . .It was too much for human endurance." Many of those who remained in ranks assessed the situation as hopeless once they saw that the enemy forces outside town were entrenched. The sense of misery and hopelessness augured ill for these tired Rebel troops, and when their attack commenced that afternoon, things quickly began to go wrong. Lee's Corps, positioned north of Hardee's men on the Confederate right flank, mistook skirmish fire on Hardee's front as the signal for a general advance. Although Lee's first line stepped off in good order, it soon was shot to pieces by the well-positioned Federals, who then had an easy time repelling the dispirited remnants of the supporting line.[150]

On Hardee's front, one division was lured away from its objective in pursuit of Federal cavalry, leaving Gen. John C. Brown's division to attack without support on either flank. Finley's and Tyler's brigades formed the first line, but a "murderous fire of grape shrapnel and musketry" smashed them in both body and mind. Their assault collapsed almost immediately, with many survivors huddling in a deep gully and refusing to rally on Brown's second assault wave, led by Henry R. Jackson's Georgia brigade. Sergeant Mangham and the 30th Georgia marched in Jackson's Brigade, and the general noted with pride that his men delivered a determined assault, although it was repulsed without penetrating the enemy lines. Both Confederate corps had bogged down in a welter of casualties; some 2200 Confederate troops were killed, wounded or captured in one-sided fighting that cost the Federals a mere 172 casualties. Jackson's Brigade paid a terrible price for pressing its attack home when no support was forthcoming: that day's action cost the little brigade thirty percent of its men. At least five men of the 30th Georgia were killed in action, one man was captured, and another fourteen fell wounded.[151]

Many of these casualties fell victim to the storm of artillery fire that raked the regiment, and one of the bursting shells brought down Willis Mangham hard. A piece of jagged shrapnel struck him in the left temple and another knifed into his back, halfway between his hip and shoulder blade. The company's orderly sergeant, James F. Carmichael, stopped to help Willis. Wincing at the "ugly wound" in his friend's temple, he bathed his face and gave him water to drink, thus reviving him somewhat. After ensuring that the regiment's stretcher bearers would carry Willis to a field hospital, Carmichael returned to his place in line, only to be badly wounded himself later that afternoon. Upon Carmichael's arrival in the field hospital, he noticed that Willis's wounds had been treated in the interim; as veteran soldiers knew only too well, however, there were limits to what medical care could achieve. Perhaps this was particularly the case in battered Jonesboro, whose surviving buildings all were put to use as hospitals in a vain attempt to house the flood of wounded men.[152]

Willis's cousin *John Willis Mangham* and his 2nd Georgia Battalion Sharpshooters were heavily engaged in a bitter defensive struggle that continued throughout the next day at Jonesboro, but for Willis, the war was now reduced to the intensely personal struggle to survive his dangerous wounds. Twenty miles to the south, another cousin, Col. Tom Mangham, still lay crippled at his father's home in Griffin. The hard-fighting young colonel doubtless had become accustomed to hearing the distant rumble of artillery in the prolonged combat around Atlanta, but the thunder from Jonesboro must have told him that the enemy had reached around to the south of the Gate City. He would know what this foretold for the weakened Confederacy.

*   *   *   *   *

Although the regiment he loved would suffer through eight more months of terrible hardship after Jonesboro, Tom Mangham must have focused on regaining his health as the Confederacy writhed in its death throes. About a year after a Yankee Minie ball smashed into his hip at Chickamauga, he was finally able to leave his sick bed with the aid of crutches, but he required their help for a long time to come. By the end of 1864, however, he was well enough to work in some capacity, and went into business with William M. Dunn on Third Street in Macon. As co-proprietor of Dunn & Mangham's, Tom bought and sold wholesale produce, but newspaper advertisements show that his firm traded in a variety of other goods as well, from kegs of nails to barrel staves. In at least one case, their daily advertisement announced the pending sale of a 17-year-old slave girl.[153]

On the second anniversary of Tom's wounding, September 19, 1865, Atlanta was little more than a ruined city in a defeated country, but he was well enough to make a

THOMAS WOODWARD MANGHAM, "RECONSTRUCTED CONFEDERATE."

big step towards a bright future. He married Miss Ida Louise Winship, daughter of a prominent citizen of Atlanta, and the couple made their home in Macon. There, as Georgia slowly revived from the ravages of wartime, Tom returned to the peaceful pursuits of banking, obtaining an appointment as cashier of the newly organized Central Bank of Georgia in December 1869. Once again, he was in the employ of his old friend and mentor, John E. Jones. By now, Tom and Ida were the proud parents of two girls, Fannie Graham and Lizzie Mangham. Thomas Woodward Mangham, Jr., was born a year or two later, and a third daughter, Ida Louise Mangham, joined the family about 1872.[154]

In April of that same year, Tom reestablished the military ties that had done so much to shape his life, joining the newly reorganized "Macon Volunteers" of the Georgia militia as the company's secretary and treasurer. In all probability, his terrible wound prevented him from taking a position as one of the company's line officers. It did not keep him from traveling to Atlanta from time to time, however, and he often met there with Col. James C. Nisbet, the former commanding officer of the 66th Georgia. Since Nisbet's regiment was brigaded with the 30th Georgia from late 1863 until the end of the war, the two young veterans shared many friends, acquaintances, and memories from their military service.[155]

Tom was nevertheless in fragile health for more than ten years due to his wound, and he took to his bed in November 1874, suffering painfully from the onset of consumption. This time, the enemy was one he could not see to fight, and the unequal combat was soon over. Just one week past his 37th birthday, he "passed quietly to his rest." Several days before the end, he asked Ida to have him buried by his comrades of the Macon Volunteers, as near as possible to the soldiers' cemetery in town. Announcing Tom's death, the obituary in the *Macon Telegraph* sadly observed:

> There are few men of his age in Macon who could not have been better spared. He was a man of sound judgment, of sterling integrity and of the most scrupulous exactness in all his transactions. His promise was the criterion of his actions. What he said, he would do. If he once announced a determination it was irrevocable. He knew nothing but the closest adherence to honor, and he had the entire confidence of everyone who knew him.[156]

At three o'clock in the afternoon, his friends and relatives gathered in the Mulberry Street Methodist Church for his funeral service. After the services, the funeral cortege wended its way to the waiting grave. At a crisp word of command, a detail from the Macon Volunteers fired a volley over his grave. As the echoes faded away to silence, Col. Thomas Woodward Mangham was laid to eternal rest in Rose Hill Cemetery.[157]

*   *   *   *   *

Sergeant Willis Austin Mangham remained on the rolls of the 30th Georgia Volunteers until the end, and was even appointed first sergeant of Company D when the tattered remnants of his once-proud brigade were consolidated into a single battalion in April 1865. In actuality, however, his active military service had ended forever with the crippling wounds he suffered at Jonesboro. So badly injured that he remained hospitalized until the war ended, the young veteran returned home deaf in his left ear and with badly impaired vision in his left eye, while suffering partial paralysis in his left side.[158]

His elderly father James M. Mangham deeded Willis one hundred acres of the family farm in December 1866, but the young man's physical disabilities made him rely heavily on others to raise a crop. James Wiley, named for Willis's father and deceased brother, joined Mary Malissa and four-year-old Willis Benjamin Franklin ("Frank") Mangham in March 1866. By 1879, the family had grown to include two more sons and three daughters, and the older children were able to help run the farm.[159]

It is doubtful that Willis ever was able to do much heavy work after he returned from the war, so along with many other disabled veterans he turned to other avocations to support his family. When the County Line Baptist Church opened the first school in the Jenkinsburg area, Willis was one of its earliest teachers. Many years later, in 1902, his educational attainment and public standing led to his selection as Tax Receiver of Butts County. Willis served in this capacity for two years before retiring from public service in October 1904. He was 64 years old by this time, and forty years had passed since the thunderclap of an exploding shell had robbed him prematurely of his youth and health.[160]

WILLIS AUSTIN MANGHAM (SEATED, CENTER) AND HIS EXTENDED FAMILY
-Courtesy of Raymond Mangham

He had qualified for a pension from the State of Georgia in 1899, based on the severe wounds that had rendered him, in the words of his pension application, "practically incompetent to perform the ordinary manual vocations of life." The Butts County Ordinary (i.e., Judge of the Court of Ordinary) who received and forwarded

Willis's original pension application, was none other than James F. Carmichael. He was not only Willis's old orderly sergeant, he was the same man who had stopped to care for Willis when he was wounded at Jonesboro, and he submitted a statement describing the event. The doctors who examined Willis left a sad testimony to the old veteran's shattered physical condition: "Large scar above left temple. Left eye very deficient—Entire deafness of left ear. Left arm & leg parcially paralized from a severe wound in the lumbar region. Entire left side is very weak & perished away. Has a quick & irregular pulse. Accelerated breathing. . . ." Willis Mangham's "Invalid's Pension" from the State of Georgia entitled him to an annual stipend of fifty dollars. In later years, Willis had the check sent under a Power of Attorney to Butts County Ordinary J. H. Ham, the son of Lt. J. G. S. Ham of the old Bailey Volunteers.[161]

Lieutenant Ham had fallen in the company's first major combat at Jackson, Mississippi, "a brave and popular officer" whose early death left him etched in the memories of Company A's veterans as eternally youthful. Willis Mangham left his youth on the field at Jonesboro a year later, but survived nevertheless to raise a large and devoted family in his beloved Butts County. His wife Nancy passed away on May 5, 1905, and the 67-year-old veteran rejoined her on December 8, 1907. They rest beside each other in the cemetery at Towaliga Baptist Church in Butts County, where numerous descendants of theirs still reside at the present day.[162]

---

[1] Vaughn Ballard, comp., *Solomon Mangham: His Ancestors and Descendants* (Arlington: Family Histories, 1989), pp. 61-62; *The Daily News* (Griffin), August 15, 1873; Fred R. Hartz, comp., *Genealogical Abstracts from the Georgia Journal (Milledgeville) Newspaper 1809-1840*, vol. 2, pp. 234, 479, 605; Marriage records, Baldwin County, p. 25. John married Nancy (Ann) on February 26, 1822, in a ceremony conducted by R. Shackleford. His obituary listed his probable birthplace as Jasper County, just west of Putnam, but Jasper was not founded until many years after John's birth.

[2] Ballard, *Solomon Mangham*, pp. 62-63; State of Georgia, Military Records, Commissions 1824-1825, drawer 40, reel 5; and 1830-1834, drawer 40, reel 8, GDAH; *The Daily News* (Griffin), August 15, 1873; CMSR Index, Indian Wars 1815-1838, M629, reel 23, NARA; Mrs. J. E. Hays, comp., *Georgia Military Record Book, 1779-1839* (typescript), vol. 1, pp. 250-251; vol. 5, pp. 207-214, 237-238.

[3] John H. Martin, comp., *Columbus, Geo., From its Selection as a "Trading Town" in 1827, to its Partial Destruction by Wilson's Raid, in 1865* (Columbus: Thos. Gilbert, 1874), pp. 79-80, 129; Anne Kendrick Walker, *Russell County in Retrospect: An Epic of the Far Southeast* (Richmond: Dietz Press, 1950), pp. 121-128.

[4] Hays, comp., *Georgia Military Record Book*, vol. 7, pp. 377-378; vol. 8, p. 256.

[5] A. P. Adamson, *Brief History of the Thirtieth Georgia Regiment* (Griffin: Mills Printing Co., 1912), p. 55; 1850 Census, Pike and Muscogee Counties; *The Georgian* (Savannah), December 31, 1839, drawer 78, reel 55, GDAH; Carolyn Walker Nottingham and Evelyn Hannah, *History of Upson County, Georgia* (1930; reprint, Vidalia: Georgia

Genealogical Reprints, 1969), p. 711; Lizzie R. Mitchell, *History of Pike County Georgia, 1822-1932* (Spartanburg: The Reprint Co., 1980), p. 112.

⁶ Buster W. Wright, comp., *Burials and Deaths Recorded in the Columbus (Georgia) Enquirer, 1832-1872* (N.p., 1984), p. 309; Listing of Burials in Oak Hill Cemetery, Griffin, provided by John P. Jennings, Jr., of the Griffin Historical Preservation Society; Willard R. Rocker, *Marriages and Obituaries from the Macon Messenger, 1818-1865* (Easley: Southern Historical Press, 1988), pp. 158, 232; Spalding County, Court of Ordinary, Inventories and Appraisals, Book A, 1852-1872, pp. 175-176, drawer 164, reel 71, GDAH; 1860 Census, Slave Census, and Agricultural Schedule, Spalding County; *The Daily News* (Griffin), August 15, 1873. According to the slave census, sixteen of John's 26 slaves were mulattos; this was possibly the basis for his "somewhat eccentric" reputation.

⁷ *The Griffin Daily News*, January 6, 1888; 1850 Census, Muscogee County; *The Independent South* (Griffin), March 3, 1859, in papers provided courtesy of John P. Jennings, Jr., of the Griffin Historical Preservation Society (hereinafter cited as "Griffin Historical Society Papers," these documents include photocopies of contemporary newspaper clippings, correspondence and invitations, as well as typescript commentary prepared by the Griffin Historical Preservation Society); Quimby Melton, Jr., *The History of Griffin* (Griffin: The Griffin Daily News, n.d.), p. 92; 1860 Slave Census, Spalding County; Ballard, *Solomon Mangham*, p. 63. Unfortunately the agricultural census taker did not record Sam's holdings and produce in 1860; his ownership of sixteen slaves implies a farm of considerable size, unless his slaves worked on his father's property.

⁸ *The Griffin Daily News*, January 8, 1888; Griffin Historical Society Papers; Richard M. McMurry, *Two Great Rebel Armies: An Essay in Confederate Military History* (Chapel Hill: UNC Press, 1989), pp. 74-76, 95-98.

⁹ McMurry, *Two Great Rebel Armies*, pp. 74-76, 95-98; Griffin Historical Society Papers; *The Griffin Daily News*, January 8, 1888; Melton, *History of Griffin*, p. 103.

¹⁰ E. B. Long, *The Civil War Day by Day: An Almanac, 1861-1865* (Garden City: Doubleday & Co., 1971), pp. 27, 56; OR IV, vol. 1, p. 289; CMSR, Samuel W. Mangham, 5ᵗʰ Georgia; Lillian Henderson, comp., *Roster of the Confederate Soldiers of Georgia 1861-1865* (N.p.: State of Georgia, 1959-64), vol. 1, pp. 653-662.

¹¹ 1860 Census, Spalding County; Ballard, *Solomon Mangham*, pp. 63-64.

¹² MDT, May 9, 1861.

¹³ Ibid.

¹⁴ CMSR, Samuel W. Mangham; MDT, May 11, June 3, 1861; letter, Samuel W. Mangham to Henry S. Wayne, May 9, 1861, State of Georgia, Adjutant General, Incoming Correspondence, series 22-1-17, box 17, GDAH; *Directory of the City of Montgomery and Historical Sketches of Alabama Soldiers* (Montgomery: Perry & Smith, Publishers: 1866), p. 53; Edward Y. McMorries, *History of the First Regiment Alabama Volunteer Infantry C.S.A.* (Montgomery: Brown Printing Co., 1904), pp. 14-21; "The

Pioneer Banner: A Confederate Camp Newspaper," *AHQ* 23 (1961): 211-219; Henry E. Sterkx and Brooks Thompson, eds., "Letters of a Teenage Confederate," *FHQ* 38: 339-341; William S. Smedlund, *Camp Fires of Georgia's Troops* (N.p.: Kennesaw Mountain, 1994), p. 254. For information on Sam's Columbiads, see Dean S. Thomas, *Cannons: An Introduction to Civil War Artillery* (Gettysburg: Thomas Publications, 1985), p. 55; C. S. Ordnance Bureau, *The Field Manual for the Use of the Officers on Ordnance Duty* (Richmond: Ritchie & Dunnavant, 1862; reprint, Gettysburg: Dean S. Thomas, 1984), p. 118.

[15] McMorries, *First Alabama*, pp. 23-27; *Directory*, p. 53.

[16] McMorries, *First Alabama*, pp. 27-28; OR 6, pp. 458-461; letter, Pvt. Richard A. Clayton to father, cited in Smedlund, *Camp Fires*, pp. 254-255; Long, *Civil War Day by Day*, p. 118.

[17] R. A. Clayton to father, cited in Smedlund, *Camp Fires*, pp. 254-255; OR 6, pp. 458-461.

[18] R. A. Clayton to father, cited in Smedlund, *Camp Fires*, pp. 255-256; OR 6, pp. 442-443, 446-449, 458-462; McMorries, *First Alabama*, p. 28.

[19] Ibid.

[20] OR 6, pp. 442-443.

[21] R. A. Clayton to father, cited in Smedlund, *Camp Fires*, p. 255-256; OR 6, pp. 443, 459, 462. Federal casualties in the raid on Santa Rosa Island totaled 13 killed, 27 wounded, and 21 missing in action.

[22] Unfiled Slips (Samuel W. Mangham), CMSR, M347, reel 247, NARA; *MDT*, November 30, 1861; McMorries, *First Alabama*, pp. 28-32.

[23] McMorries, *First Alabama*, p. 31.

[24] Long, *Civil War Day by Day*, pp. 142-143; OR 6, pp. 488-493.

[25] OR 6, pp. 797-798; CMSR, Confederate General and Staff Officers, John K. Jackson.

[26] CMSR, John K. Jackson; CMSR, Samuel W. Mangham; Henderson, *Georgia Rosters*, vol. 1, p. 653; *MDT*, February 10, 1861. The inscription on Sam's sword, as well as its accompanying photo, were provided courtesy of Mrs. Jean Mangham Holzapfel (his great great granddaughter) and Mr. James Mangham (her nephew).

[27] OR 10, vol. 2, pp. 308-309, 405-406; ORS II, vol. 6, p. 207.

[28] OR 10, vol. 2, pp. 376-377, 405-406; Reminiscences of George P. Armstrong (5th Georgia), UDC Typescripts, vol. 13, pp. 130-131, GDAH.

[29] CMSR, Samuel W. Mangham; OR 10, pt. 2, pp. 377, 405-406; Stanley F. Horn, *The Army of Tennessee* (Bobbs-Merrill, 1941; reprint, Norman: Univ. of Oklahoma Press, 1993), pp. 107-110.

[30] OR 10, vol. 2, pp. 406, 409; Horn, *Army of Tennessee*, p. 148.

[31] CMSRs, Samuel W. and John W. Mangham; CMSR, 2nd Georgia Bn. Sharpshooters; Order Book of Brigadier John K. Jackson's Brigade (hereinafter

Jackson's Order Book), Withers's Division, March 13, 1862-January 10, 1863, Special Order (S.O.) 49, May 15, 1862, Jackson-McKinne Papers, 1817-1871, UNC.

[32] CMSR, Samuel W. Mangham; Ballard, *Solomon Mangham*, p. 64.

[33] Henderson, *Georgia Rosters*, vol. 1, p. 653; *The Griffin Daily News*, January 8, 1888; OR IV, vol. 1, pp. 1081-1085.

[34] OR IV, vol. 1, pp. 1082-1085; vol. 2, p. 94.

[35] Allen D. Candler, comp., *The Confederate Records of the State of Georgia*, vol. 2 (Atlanta: Charles P. Byrd, State Printer, 1909), p. 457.

[36] Ibid., pp. 457-458;OR 52, pt. 2, p. 537; OR IV, vol. 2, pp. 160, 584.

[37] Candler, comp., *Confederate Records*, vol. 2, pp. 457-462.

[38] Letters, Samuel W. Mangham to Henry C. Wayne, July 13 and July 24, 1863, State of Georgia, Adjutant General, Incoming Correspondence, series 22-1-17, box 17, GDAH.

[39] OR 52, vol. 2, p. 537; Letter, Samuel W. Mangham to Henry C. Wayne, Sept. 7, 1863, State of Georgia, Adjutant General, Incoming Correspondence, series 22-1-17, box 17, GDAH; CMSR, Samuel W. Mangham, 6th Georgia State Guard; Muster Rolls, 6th Georgia State Guard, NARA; Stewart Sifakis, *Compendium of the Confederate Armies: South Carolina and Georgia* (New York: Facts on File, 1995), pp. 195-196.

[40] OR 52, vol. 2, pp. 536-537; CMSR, Samuel W. Mangham; CMSR, Thomas W. Mangham, 30th Georgia.

[41] CMSR, Samuel W. Mangham; OR IV, vol. 2, pp. 952-954.

[42] CMSR, Samuel W. Mangham.

[43] CMSR, Samuel W. Mangham, 22nd Georgia Battalion Heavy Artillery; Muster Rolls, Company B, 22nd Ga. Hvy. Arty., NARA; Louise Frederick Hays, *History of Macon County Georgia* (1933; reprint: Spartanburg: The Reprint Co., 1979), pp. 716-720; Griffin Historical Society Papers.

[44] CMSR, William R. Mangham, 22nd Ga. Hvy. Arty.; Muster Rolls, Company A, 22nd Ga. Hvy. Arty., NARA; State of Georgia, Adjutant General's Office, Militia Enrollment Lists, drawer 245, reel 9, GDAH.

[45] Muster Rolls, 22nd Ga. Hvy. Arty., drawer 279, reel 62, GDAH; Charles C. Jones, Jr., *The Siege of Savannah in December, 1864* (Albany: Joel Munsell, 1874; reprint, Jonesboro: Freedom Hill Press, 1988), p. 101; Long, *Civil War Day by Day*, p. 486. The 1850 Muscogee County census shows William's name as "Willis R. Mangham." Other census records refer to him as "William," whereas his army and militia records simply reflect "W. R."

[46] CMSRs, William R. and Samuel W. Mangham, 22nd Ga. Hvy. Arty.; letter, Samuel W. Mangham to Lieut. B. H. Newton, June 8, 1864, and letter, Samuel W. Mangham to Secretary of War James A. Seddon, August 13, 1864, in Letters to the Confederate A&IGO, file no. 2358-M-1864, NARA.

[47] Letter, Samuel W. Mangham to Lieut. B. H. Newton, June 8, 1864, and letter, Samuel W. Mangham to Secretary of War James A. Seddon, August 13, 1864, A&IGO file no. 2358-M-1864, NARA.

[48] Ibid.

[49] Ibid.

[50] Letter, Samuel W. Mangham to Capt. J. R. Branham, October 11, 1864, Letters to the Confederate A&IGO, file no. 2499-M-1864, NARA.

[51] Ibid.

[52] CMSR, Samuel W. Mangham; Sifakis, *Confederate Armies: South Carolina and Georgia*, p. 126; Albert Castel, *Decision in the West: The Atlanta Campaign of 1864* (Lawrence: Univ. of Kansas Press, 1992), pp. 552-555; Jim Miles, *To the Sea: A History and Tour Guide of Sherman's March* (Nashville: Rutledge Hill Press), pp. 11-15, 29-30, 139-140.

[53] Miles, *To the Sea*, pp. 59-62, 66-81, 141-142, 169.

[54] Ibid., pp. 199-201, 210-212; Long, *Civil War Day by Day*, pp. 609-610; CMSR, William R. Mangham; *OR* 35, pt. 2, pp. 610-612. William enlisted in Company A at Fort Jackson, but his subsequent service records merely indicate that the company was stationed in Savannah, without specifying which fortification it manned. Official reports from August 1864 show that a company of his battalion was stationed there still, but do not identify specifically which one. There is no reason to suppose, however, that the battalion's companies rotated their positions within these static fortifications.

[55] Miles, *To the Sea*, pp. 225-230.

[56] Ibid., p. 244.

[57] For detailed analyses of the relationship between conscription and the desertion problem in the South, see Albert Burton Moore, *Conscription and Conflict in the Confederacy* (Macmillan, 1924; reprint, Columbia: USC Press, 1996), and Ella Lonn, *Desertion During the Civil War* (New York: Century, 1928; reprint, Lincoln: Univ. of Nebraska Press, 1998).

[58] Departmental Records, Department of South Carolina, Georgia & Florida (Hardee), Special Order (S.O.) 25, January 30, 1865, NARA; James Pickett Jones, *Yankee Blitzkrieg: Wilson's Raid Through Alabama and Georgia* (Athens: UGA Press, 1976), p. 162.

[59] Sifakis, *Confederate Armies: South Carolina and Georgia*, pp. 126-127; Mark L. Bradley, *Last Stand in the Carolinas: The Battle of Bentonville* (Campbell: Savas Woodbury Publishers, 1996), pp. 20-33, 115-116; 127-128, 131-132. Just weeks before Sam was transferred back to militia service, Governor Joe Brown had published desperate orders calling on the militia to restore order to the ravaged countryside. See *MDT*, January 10, 1865.

[60] Bradley, *Last Stand*, p. 192.

[61] Ibid., pp. 192-193, 213-215, 223-224; Nathaniel Cheairs Hughes, Jr., *Bentonville: The Final Battle of Sherman and Johnston* (Chapel Hill: UNC Press, 1996), pp. 140-143.

[62] Bradley, *Last Stand*, pp. 279-280.

[63] Ibid., pp. 280-283, 313-314; Hughes, *Bentonville*, pp. 140-143.

[64] CMSR, William R. Mangham.

[65] William R. Mangham registered to vote on April 7, 1868; he also witnessed a deed in Spalding Co., Georgia, in 1874. See State of Georgia, Executive Department, Returns of Qualified Voters under the Reconstruction Act, 1867, vol. 89, p. 34, drawer 297, reel 22, GDAH. The author is indebted to Frances Mangham Yates, William's granddaughter, for information on his postwar life.

[66] Melton, *History of Griffin*, p. 121.

[67] Ibid., pp. 137-138; *The Southern Herald* (Griffin), July 19, 1866.

[68] Ibid., pp. 144, 149-150; *The Griffin Daily News*, January 6, 1888.

[69] 1900 and 1910 Censuses, Spalding County; *The Griffin Daily News*, January 6-8, 1888; State of Georgia, Adjutant General, Military Records, Roster of Commissioned Officers in Georgia Militia, drawer 40, reel 18, GDAH; Melton, *History of Griffin*, p. 166. See also the AAFA Action newsletter, Fall 1995, p. 24 (courtesy of Jean Mangham Holzapfel).

[70] *The Daily News* (Griffin), August 15, 1873. Sam administered his father's extensive estate, which comprised 402 acres of land and two houses; the whole was appraised at more than $7000. See Spalding County, Court of Ordinary, Inventories and Appraisals, Book B, 1871-1892, pp. 25-26, 240-242, drawer 164, reel 71, GDAH; Spalding County, Court of Ordinary, Letters of Administration (Temporary), Book A, 1859-1881, p. 72, drawer 164, reel 66, GDAH; Spalding County, Court of Ordinary, Administrator's Bonds, pp. 259-260, 288, drawer 164, reel 69, GDAH; Spalding County, Court of Ordinary, Annual Returns and Vouchers, Book C, 1866-1882, pp. 394-396, 419, drawer 164, reel 78, GDAH.

[71] Ibid.; *The Middle Georgia Times* (Thomaston), August 28, 1886; John B. Gordon, *Reminiscences of the Civil War* (Charles Scribner's Sons, 1903; reprint, Baton Rouge: LSU Press, 1993), p. xiii. For more about Sam's relatives in the 13th Georgia, see Chapter II.

[72] *The Griffin Daily News*, January 6, 1888. At the time of his death, Sam's five thousand dollar estate included one-third interest in Mangham & Sons, a millinery business, as well as a house and farm situated on an extension of 6th Street in Griffin. See Spalding County, Court of Ordinary, Inventories and Appraisals, Book B, 1871-1892, pp. 242-243, drawer 164, reel 71, GDAH.

[73] Listing of Burials in Oak Hill Cemetery, Griffin, provided by John P. Jennings, Jr., of the Griffin Historical Preservation Society.

[74] *The Griffin Daily News*, January 10, 1888.

[75] Griffin Historical Society Papers; Adamson, *Thirtieth Georgia*, p. 55. While in Macon, Tom made his home in the Granite Hall Hotel (see 1860 Census, Bibb County).

[76] Adamson, *Thirtieth Georgia*, p. 55; *Georgia Journal & Messenger* (Macon), August 10, 1859; Ida Young, Julius Gholson, and Clara Nell Hargrove, *History of Macon, Georgia* (Macon: Lyon, Marshall & Brooks, 1950), p. 231; *MDT*, January 7, January 21, January 22, February 16, February 23, March 5, 1861. The Macon Volunteers marched in the city's secession celebration in January 1861.

[77] CMSR, Thomas W. Mangham, 2nd Georgia Battalion; *MDT*, April 20, April 22, April 27, May 1, May 2, May 4, May 7, May 24, May 25, June 9, June 15, June 25, August 10, 1861; Long, *Civil War Day by Day*, pp. 75-76.

[78] Adamson, *Thirtieth Georgia*, pp. 49-51.

[79] CMSR, Thomas W. Mangham.

[80] Confederate Pension Records, Butts County, Willis A. Mangham, drawer 271, reel 45, GDAH. The story of the other Butts County Manghams is in Chapter V.

[81] 1860 Census, Butts County; CMSR, Willis A. Mangham, 30th Georgia; Adamson, *Thirtieth Georgia*, p. 23; Georgia Marriage Records, Butts County; Ballard, *Solomon Mangham*, pp. 56-57.

[82] CMSR, Willis A. Mangham; Adamson, *Thirtieth Georgia*, pp. 51, 63; Hartz, comp., *Genealogical Abstracts 1809-1840*, vol. 4, p. 711.

[83] CMSRs, Willis A. and Thomas W. Mangham; Adamson, *Thirtieth Georgia*, pp. 24-25.

[84] Adamson, *Thirtieth Georgia*, pp. 25, 52-53; *MDT*, January 7, 1861.

[85] OR 52, pt. 2, p. 209; Adamson, *Thirtieth Georgia*, pp. 25-26; Letters, Augustus P. Adamson, December 16, 1861; January 19, 1862; January 26, 1862, in *Confederate Reminiscences and Letters*, vol. 1 (Atlanta: Georgia Division, UDC, 1995), pp. 229-231.

[86] Adamson, *Thirtieth Georgia*, pp. 26-27; Bell Irvin Wiley, *The Life of Johnny Reb: The Common Soldier of the Confederacy* (Baton Rouge: LSU Press, 1978), pp. 44-47; H. K. Nelson, "Tennessee, A Grave or a Free Home," CV 15: 508; Frank S. Roberts, "Spring Hill-Franklin-Nashville, 1864," CV 27: 58. One of the funniest "biting hog" stories on record involves Nathan Bedford Forrest's attempts to curb his troops' penchant for unauthorized pork. See William Forbes, *Capt. Croft's Flying Artillery Battery, Columbus, Georgia* (Dayton: Morningside, 1993), pp. 249-250.

[87] Letters, Augustus P. Adamson, February 2; February 17, 1862, in *Confederate Reminiscences and Letters*, vol. 1, pp. 231-232. The regiment drew pay for the first time on February 16, 1862. A mustering officer on April 30 described the Bailey Volunteers' arms as "musketoons & shot guns—inferior" (see Muster Roll, Company B, 30th Georgia, April 30, 1862, NARA).

[88] Letter, Augustus P. Adamson, March 23, 1862, in *Confederate Reminiscences and Letters*, vol. 1, p. 234.

[89] Ibid., pp. 237-238, letters dated April 27; May 5; June 11; July 13, 1862; Adamson, *Thirtieth Georgia*, pp. 24, 53, 124-125; CMSRs, Thomas W. and Willis A. Mangham. The reshuffling of companies occurred in early June, and the regimental

designation changed from 39th to 30th Georgia in the first half of July. Tom was elected lieutenant colonel on April 30 (see *MDT*, May 5, 1863).

[90] Adamson, *Thirtieth Georgia*, pp. 25, 49-51; Letter, Augustus P. Adamson, May 12, 1862, in Richard B. Abell and Fay Adamson Gecik, *Sojourns of a Patriot: The Field and Prison Papers of An Unreconstructed Confederate* (Murfreesboro: Southern Heritage Press, 1998), p. 58; CMSRs Thomas W. and Willis A. Mangham. The Manghams were fortunate to enjoy passable health; citing the mortality statistics for each company in a letter on June 2, Augustus Adamson reported that the regiment had lost some fifty men to sickness. His figures excluded Co. C, since he lacked information on their losses. See Letters, Augustus P. Adamson, June 2; June 22; July 4; September 14; November 21, 1862, in *Confederate Reminiscences and Letters*, vol. 1, pp. 243, 245-247, 250, 257.

[91] Adamson, *Thirtieth Georgia*, p. 24, 27, 53, 124-125; OR 14, pp. 625, 635; Letters, Augustus P. Adamson, October 3; October 7, 1862, in *Confederate Reminiscences and Letters*, vol. 1, pp. 251, 253.

[92] Adamson, *Thirtieth Georgia*, pp. 27-28; Letters, Augustus P. Adamson, November 26; December 1; December 17; December 19, December 22, 1862; March 1; April 27; May 5, 1863, in *Confederate Reminiscences and Letters*, vol. 1, pp. 258-265; Letter, Augustus P. Adamson, April 21, 1863, in *Sojourns of a Patriot*, p. 148; OR 14, pp. 187-188, 774-775, 824, 925; Russell K. Brown, *To the Manner Born: The Life of General William H. T. Walker* (Athens: UGA Press, 1994), pp. 140-141; Report of Detailed Men, May 1, 1863, in Muster Rolls, 30th Georgia, NARA.

[93] Adamson, *Thirtieth Georgia*, pp. 28-29, 53; CMSR, Thomas W. Mangham; OR 14, pp. 929-931. Colonel Bailey had returned to the regiment in mid-November, and accompanied it to Wilmington despite having submitted his resignation the previous day. His last chance to lead his men into battle proved to be one more dashed hope. See Letters, Augustus P. Adamson, November 21; November 25; December 17, 1862; May 7, 1863, in *Confederate Reminiscences and Letters*, vol. 1, pp. 256-258, 260, 265.

[94] Horn, *Army of Tennessee*, p. 214. For the story of the Mangham family's participation in the defense of Vicksburg, see Chapter X.

[95] Long, *Civil War Day by Day*, p. 352; OR 24, pt. 3, p. 870; Adamson, *Thirtieth Georgia*, p. 29.

[96] Long, *Civil War Day by Day*, p. 353; Adamson, *Thirtieth Georgia*, p. 29; *MDT*, July 4, 1863.

[97] Lt. Col. Arthur J. L. Fremantle, *Three Months in the Southern States: April-June, 1863* (New York: John Bradburn, 1864; reprint, Lincoln: Univ. of Nebraska Press, 1991), pp. 113-114, 118.

[98] Adamson, *Thirtieth Georgia*, pp. 29-30; Long, *Civil War Day by Day*, p. 356; Horn, *Army of Tennessee*, pp. 217-218; Brown, *General Walker*, p. 157. The rosters of the 30th Georgia are replete with men who died of disease in Mississippi during the summer of 1863.

[99] Adamson, *Thirtieth Georgia*, p. 30; Long, *Civil War Day by Day*, pp. 378-379; Horn, *Army of Tennessee*, p. 218; CMSR, Francis J. Mangham, 1st Mississippi Light Artillery.

[100] Adamson, *Thirtieth Georgia*, p. 30.

[101] Adamson, *Thirtieth Georgia*, p. 30; Long, *Civil War Day by Day*, pp. 380-382; F. Jay Taylor, ed., *Reluctant Rebel: The Secret Diary of Robert Patrick, 1861-1865* (Baton Rouge: LSU Press, 1987), pp. 119-120. Another Louisianian participating in the retreat to Jackson was Pvt. Thomas H. Mangham of the 19th Louisiana (see Chapter IX).

[102] Adamson, *Thirtieth Georgia*, pp. 30-31.

[103] Ibid., p. 31; Long, *Civil War Day by Day*, pp. 382-383; Bell I. Wiley, ed., "The Confederate Letters of John W. Hagan," *GHQ* 38 (1954): 190-194. In all likelihood, Hagan was a relative of Martha Jane Hagan Mangham, wife of William Decatur Mangham of the 13th Georgia (see Chapter II).

[104] Adamson, *Thirtieth Georgia*, p. 31.

[105] Adamson, *Thirtieth Georgia*, pp. 31-32. Company K had remained in Savannah on detached service, and Company B was detailed to duty in Jackson itself.

[106] Ibid.; Castel, *Decision*, pp. 37, 395; Lee Kennett, *Marching Through Georgia: The Story of Soldiers and Civilians During Sherman's Campaign* (New York: HarperPerennial, 1995), p. 174.

[107] Wiley, ed., "Letters of John W. Hagan," p. 194.

[108] Adamson, *Thirtieth Georgia*, p. 31.

[109] Ibid., pp. 31-32; Wiley, ed., "Letters of John W. Hagan," p. 194. The casualty list cited in Adamson covers the period 8-16 July 1863, and the author notes that the list omits several names. It is clear from the context of his work that the great majority of the regiment's casualties were suffered in this attack, however, so the figures cited here are very good approximations for this single engagement. See also the regimental casualty report in the *MDT*, July 24, 1863.

[110] Ibid.; Brown, *General Walker*, p. 158; Letters, Augustus P. Adamson, July 20; July 24, 1863, in *Confederate Reminiscences and Letters*, vol. 1, pp. 266-267; Letter, Augustus P. Adamson, July 20, 1863, in *Sojourns of a Patriot*, p. 166. The whole purpose of the Federal advance north of Jackson that day was to determine whether Confederate troops still stood fast in their defenses. The response they stirred up answered the question in no uncertain terms. See Edwin C. Bearss, *The Siege of Jackson: July 10-17, 1863* (Baltimore: Gateway Press, 1981), pp. 92-93.

[111] Adamson, *Thirtieth Georgia*, p. 32; OR 24, part 3, pp. 1039, 1041; Wiley, ed., "Letters of John W. Hagan," p. 195; Long, *Civil War Day by Day*, pp. 387-388; Brown, *General Walker*, pp. 158-159.

[112] Adamson, *Thirtieth Georgia*, pp. 32-33; Horn, *Army of Tennessee*, pp. 231, 235-238; Peter Cozzens, *This Terrible Sound: The Battle of Chickamauga* (Urbana: Univ. of Illinois Press, 1992), pp. 17-21.

[113] Adamson, *Thirtieth Georgia*, pp. 32-33; Letter, Augustus P. Adamson, August 30, 1863, in *Sojourns of a Patriot*, p. 183; letter, Thomas W. Mangham to Gen. Samuel

Cooper, April 24, 1864, Letters to the Confederate A&IGO, file no. 1282-M-1864, NARA.

[114] Adamson, *Thirtieth Georgia*, p. 33.

[115] Ibid., p. 34; Cozzens, *Terrible Sound*, pp. 108-110, 128; OR 30, pt. 2, pp. 247-248; Brown, *General Walker*, pp. 168-169.

[116] Adamson, *Thirtieth Georgia*, p. 34-36; Cozzens, *Terrible Sound*, pp. 128-129; OR 30, pt. 2, p. 248.

[117] Ibid. Adamson cites details of the regiment's strength on p. 36, totaling 334 men engaged, but gives the number as 364 on p. 141.

[118] OR 30, pt. 2, p. 248; Cozzens, *Terrible Sound*, p. 133; Adamson, *Thirtieth Georgia*, pp. 34-35.

[119] Adamson, *Thirtieth Georgia*, pp. 27, 35, 91; Cozzens, *Terrible Sound*, pp. 125-127, 131-133.

[120] Adamson, *Thirtieth Georgia*, pp. 35-36, 53; Cozzens, *Terrible Sound*, pp. 125, 133; OR 30, pt. 1, pp. 415-416, 418-419, 422; pt. 2, p. 248.

[121] Cozzens, *Terrible Sound*, pp. 133, 136; OR 30, pt. 2, p. 248.

[122] Cozzens, *Terrible Sound*, pp. 136-137; OR 30, pt. 2, pp. 248-249.

[123] Cozzens, *Terrible Sound*, pp. 137-138; OR 30, pt. 1, pp. 285-289; pt. 2, pp. 248-249. Croxton started the fight with 2400 men; the 31st Ohio added another 517. King's U. S. Regulars committed at least one battalion against Wilson, or perhaps 300 men. Scribner's five regiments added another 1879 men.

[124] Adamson, *Thirtieth Georgia*, pp. 35, 53, 141; OR 30, pt. 2, pp. 248-249; CMSR, Thomas W. Mangham. Colonel Wilson's report mentioned that Lt. Col. James Boynton was in command of the 30th Georgia as it pulled back from the enemy breastworks, but he did not specify where Colonel Mangham was wounded. Adamson reproduces Boynton's official casualty report, which lists each casualty by name. At another place in his narrative, however, he states that the casualty toll reached 126 killed and wounded; Boynton's report in the *Macon Daily Telegraph* of September 29 lists 21 killed, 98 wounded and 6 missing, for a total of 125. A soldier of the 29th Georgia asserted that his regiment lost 130 killed and wounded from the 200 who entered the battle (see Brown, *General Walker*, p. 180).

[125] CMSR, Thomas W. Mangham; Adamson, *Thirtieth Georgia*, p. 38; James Cooper Nisbet, *Four Years on the Firing Line*, ed. Bell Irvin Wiley (reprint: Broadfoot Publishing, 1987), pp. 142-143.

[126] CMSR, Thomas W. Mangham. "Anchylosis" denoted a joint stiffened by "fibrous or bony union."

[127] Fremantle, *Three Months*, pp. 148-149, 159. Grenfell was a well-to-do English officer and adventurer who was serving as General Bragg's Inspector General of Cavalry. For the premier analysis of the centrality of courage in the Civil War soldier's outlook, see Gerald F. Linderman, *Embattled Courage: The Experience of Combat in the American Civil War* (New York: The Free Press, 1987).

[128] Brown, *General Walker*, p. 180.

[129] Cozzens, *Terrible Sound*, pp. 137-138, 501.

[130] Adamson, *Thirtieth Georgia*, p. 38; Nisbet, *Firing Line*, pp. 162-163.

[131] Castel, *Decision*, pp. 178-179, 191; Adamson, *Thirtieth Georgia* (see annotated company rosters).

[132] Castel, *Decision*, pp. 303-304, 309-313; Horn, *Army of Tennessee*, pp. 325, 334-337; Brown, *General Walker*, pp. 227-231; Richard A. Baumgartner and Larry M. Strayer, *Kennesaw Mountain, June 1864: Bitter Standoff at the Gibraltar of Georgia* (Huntington: Blue Acorn Press, 1998), p. 66; *Sons of Confederate Veterans Ancestor Album* (Houston: Heritage Publishers Services, 1986), p. 129; Adamson, *Thirtieth Georgia* (see annotated company rosters). The 30th Georgia's casualties near Kennesaw probably were a great deal higher than those listed in their postwar rosters. Their sister regiment, the 29th Georgia, suffered 83 casualties in the period June 14-21 (see Wiley, ed., "Letters of John W. Hagan," pp. 277-278). Steven Hale, a descendant of Willis Mangham, submitted a biographical statement to the *SCV Ancestor Album*, stating that Willis fought at Kennesaw Mountain. The source of his information is unknown.

[133] Richard M. McMurry, "Confederate Morale in the Atlanta Campaign of 1864," *GHQ* 45 (1970): 230-233; Wiley, ed., "Letters of John W. Hagan," p. 272.

[134] Castel, *Decision*, pp. 360-364, 366-367.

[135] Ibid., pp. 369-376.

[136] Ibid., pp. 360-364, 366-367; OR 38, pt. 1, pp. 337-338; Rice C. Bull, *Soldiering: The Civil War Diary of Rice C. Bull, 123rd New York Volunteer Infantry* (Novato: Presidio Press, 1977), p. 151; Grady McWhiney, Warner O. Moore, Jr., and Robert F. Pace, eds., *"Fear God and Walk Humbly": The Agricultural Journal of James Mallory, 1843-1877* (Tuscaloosa: Univ. of Alabama Press, 1997), p. 338.

[137] Castel, *Decision*, pp. 360-364, 366-367; Nisbet, *Firing Line*, pp. 209-210; Brown, *General Walker*, pp. 259-261.

[138] McMurry, "Confederate Morale," p. 235; Wiley, ed., "Letters of John W. Hagan," p. 287.

[139] Castel, *Decision*, pp. 378-379, 385-387.

[140] Ibid., pp. 378-379, 388-389; Brown, *General Walker*, pp. 262-264.

[141] Castel, *Decision*, pp. 391-394; Brown, *General Walker*, pp. 264-266.

[142] Castel, *Decision*, pp. 395-397; Brown, *General Walker*, pp. 266, 271-275. Brown details the various conflicting accounts of Walker's death, which may have occurred later in the battle while rallying Gist's Brigade.

[143] Castel, *Decision*, pp. 392-393, 396-397.

[144] Castel, *Decision*, p. 397; Nisbet, *Firing Line*, pp. 211-215; Brown, *General Walker*, pp. 267-269; Adamson, *Thirtieth Georgia*, pp. 66-69, 76-79, 81-85, 87-89, 102-107, 110-117, 119-122, 127-131, 132-135. The annotated company rosters cited here are the sources of the regimental casualty figures, but they vary in quality and make no claim to be comprehensive. For more on John W. Mangham, see Chapter II.

[145] Castel, *Decision*, p. 398.

[146] Ibid., pp. 485-486, 495-496; Adamson, *Thirtieth Georgia*, p. 55.

[147] Castel, *Decision*, p. 496.

[148] Ibid., p. 498.

[149] Ibid., pp. 499-502.

[150] Ibid., pp. 499, 502-503; Sam Watkins, *"Co. Aytch": A Side Show of the Big Show* (reprint, New York: Collier Books, 1962), p. 212.

[151] Castel, *Decision*, pp. 503-504; Adamson, *Thirtieth Georgia*, pp. 66-69, 76-79, 81-85, 87-89, 102-107, 110-117, 119-122, 127-131, 132-135.

[152] Adamson, *Thirtieth Georgia* (casualty rosters); Confederate Pension Records, Butts County, Willis A. Mangham, GDAH; A. A. Hoehling, *Last Train from Atlanta* (New York: T. Yoseloff, 1958; reprint, Harrisburg: Stackpole Books, 1992), pp. 394-395.

[153] Adamson, *Thirtieth Georgia*, p. 53; *Macon Daily Telegraph & Confederate*, January 3, January 26, 1865.

[154] Young, *History of Macon*, pp. 44, 311-312; 1880 Census, Bibb County.

[155] Young, *History of Macon*, p. 316; Nisbet, *Firing Line*, p. 144.

[156] Adamson, *Thirtieth Georgia*, pp. 55-56.

[157] Ibid.

[158] CMSR, Willis A. Mangham, 1st Georgia Confederate Battalion (consolidated April 9, 1865 from 1st Ga. Bn. Sharpshooters, 25th Ga., 29th Ga., 30th Ga., and 66th Ga. Infantry Regiments); Confederate Pension Records, Butts County, Willis A. Mangham, GDAH.

[159] Ballard, *Solomon Mangham*, pp. 56-61; Butts County, Superior Court, Deed Book H, p. 370, drawer 6, reel 73, GDAH; Butts County Census Index (SOUNDEX), 1880, 1900, 1910.

[160] Lois McMichael, comp., *History of Butts County Georgia, 1825-1976* (Atlanta: Cherokee Publishing Co., 1978), pp. 114, 197. Willis also joined the John L. Barnett Camp of the United Confederate Veterans, appearing on the roster in 1898 and as Camp Sergeant in 1900 (see United Confederate Veterans Association Records, Louisiana and Lower Mississippi Valley Collections, LSU Libraries, Baton Rouge, LA, Box 57, Camp #1114).

[161] Confederate Pension Records, Butts County, Willis A. Mangham; Adamson, *Thirtieth Georgia*, p. 62.

[162] Confederate Pension Records, Butts County, Willis A. Mangham; Adamson, *Thirtieth Georgia*, p. 62; Ballard, *Solomon Mangham*, p. 56; Jeannette Holland Austin, *30,638 Burials in Georgia* (Baltimore: Genealogical Publishing Co., 1995), p. 402. I owe a debt of gratitude to Willis Mangham's great-grandson, Rev. Asa Mangham of Rome, Georgia, for providing photographs of his great-grandparents and their graves.

CHAPTER V: "SALT OF THE EARTH": THE JAMES M. MANGHAM FAMILY OF BUTTS COUNTY

1. A YEOMAN FARMER OF BUTTS COUNTY

Sergeant Willis Austin Mangham's father, James M. Mangham, was born in North Carolina before 1790 to Solomon and Sarah Ann Mangham. As a boy, James accompanied his parents in their migration to South Carolina and thence to Georgia. He served as a private in Thomas's 2nd Regiment of Georgia Militia during the War of 1812, but he made a much more lasting mark in civil life after that war. When Butts County was laid out from Henry and Monroe Counties in 1825, James Mangham was among the new county's first citizens, and many of his descendants live there to this day.[1]

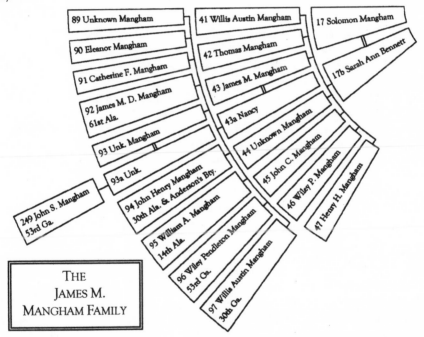

Over the succeeding thirty-five years, he and Eleanor (later Nancy), their daughters Catherine and Eleanor, and sons James, William, Wiley, John Henry, and Willis worked alongside the family's slaves to establish a sizable farm in the western part of the county, in the area known locally as Coody's District. By 1860, James Mangham could look back over his eventful seventy years with a sense of satisfaction. Like his brothers Willis in Pike County and John in Spalding County (Chapters II and IV), he had helped clear Butts County's primeval forests into prosperous agricultural lands. Neither a planter nor a hardscrabble subsistence farmer, James had fully 225 acres of his comfortably prosperous 490-acre spread under cultivation. His hard work in 1860 yielded a bountiful harvest of five hundred bushels of Indian corn and four bales of cotton at 400 pounds apiece, as well as other provisions typical of west Georgia's family farms. In this last year of peace, the patriarch of the Butts County Manghams certainly relied heavily upon his youngest son *Willis Austin Mangham* (see preceding chapter) and the five slaves of working age to do most of the heavy labor in the fields. By this time, his eldest sons *James M.* and *William A. Mangham* had moved west to Chambers County, Alabama, where they operated a modest farm. His fourth son, *John H. Mangham*, had settled just northwest of there in Talladega County, where he worked cutting stone from the area's rich marble quarries. Middle son *Wiley Pendleton Mangham* still lived in Butts County, but he and his young family rented a small farm of their own, and would have been hard-pressed to provide his father any substantial help.[2]

2. GIVING THEIR ALL IN THE OLD DOMINION: SGT. WILEY PENDLETON MANGHAM, "JACKSON GUARDS," CO. I; PVT. JOHN S. MANGHAM, "DOYAL VOLUNTEERS," CO. A, 53RD GEORGIA

In 1860, *Wiley Pendleton Mangham* made his home in the Towaliga District, which bore the name of the river that coursed through the southwestern portion of Butts County. Born about 1832 or 1833, Wiley apparently was named for his uncle Wiley P. Mangham, father of *Capt. John Henry Mangham* (see Chapter II). Young Wiley married a neighbor girl, 21-year-old Mary Ann Heath, in Butts County on October 4, 1855. Over the next four years, the young couple had two children, Eliza R. (born about 1857) and John W. Mangham (born about 1859). Whereas his younger brother Willis remained on their father's farm after marrying Nancy Thaxton, Wiley moved to a tenant farm just a short distance west of there, working a property between the farms of Jonathan B. Carmichael and Dolphin Lindsey. Both the Carmichael and Lindsey families had close contacts with James M. Mangham and his family over many years, so Wiley's rental arrangement doubtless stemmed from these relationships.[3]

Wiley's was the prototypical one-horse farm, and his single milk cow, two "beef critters" and six hogs characterize the modest holdings of Georgia's yeoman farmers of the ante-bellum period. White's 1854 *Historical Collections of Georgia* advertised Butts County's "gray lands" as "admirably suited" for raising cotton, and neighbor John Carmichael harvested 43 bales in 1860, but Wiley raised only four bales of the South's predominant cash crop. Necessarily, he focused his efforts upon the cultivation of staple foodstuffs such as corn, wheat, and rye. He did own one slave, a 50-year-old woman, who doubtless shared in the numerous duties of life on a small farm. The census-taker assessed Wiley's personal estate as a modest three hundred dollars, so his single slave comprised most of his worldly wealth as it was reckoned in those days. Indeed, she probably was a gift from James Mangham, intended to help Wiley and his young family make ends meet.[4]

Working from sunup to sundown in the ancient rhythms that regulated farm life, Wiley must have enjoyed precious little opportunity to ruminate about the Union's impending crisis when the census-taker made his rounds in 1860, and his personal sentiments about secession are lost to history. He and his family were part and parcel of a Southern cotton belt society that was suspicious and resentful about Yankees in general, however, and his status as a slaveowner makes it almost certain that he shared in such views to a considerable extent. Nevertheless, his family depended on him to make the crop and run the farm, so Wiley did not rush to the colors in 1861. Of course, his dilemma typified that facing other small farmers throughout the thinly populated Southern states, and the resulting manpower shortages threatened the young Confederacy's armies with disaster when the war entered its second year.

When the Confederate Congress bowed to necessity by passing the Conscription Act in April 1862, it was careful to allow a thirty-day grace period for newly authorized units to complete their organization. Conscription, after all, was an unprecedented act in American history, and fiercely independent Southerners were known to view the measure with mixed feelings at best; indeed, many viewed conscription as an act of outright despotism. Paradoxically, however, those who waited to be enrolled by conscription officers commonly were viewed as unpatriotic laggards unwilling and unfit to defend their country voluntarily. Virginia Pvt. Carlton McCarthy called conscripts "the most despised class in the army," asserting that "true men" (i.e. volunteers) "could not bear the thought of having these men for comrades." Internal pressures such as these, along with the Union capture of New Orleans, their renewed advance on Richmond, and the Confederate repulse at Shiloh, all combined to produce a second great wave of voluntarism across the South in the war's second spring.[5]

One regiment that grew out of these various stresses was the 53rd Georgia Volunteer Infantry, commanded by Col. Leonard Doyal. A native of McDonough in Henry County, Doyal was a prominent attorney in civilian life, and he moved his thriving practice to Griffin in 1856. The 42-year-old Doyal lived with his family and their five slaves, just two houses down from Wiley's first cousin, Col. Samuel W. Mangham. Doubtless a close acquaintance of Sam's, Doyal entered Confederate service in 1861 as captain of the "Spalding Grays," Company D of the 2nd Georgia Infantry Battalion. In this capacity, Doyal probably renewed his acquaintance with Sam's brother *Thomas W. Mangham*, then a sergeant in the battalion's Company B (see Chapter IV).[6]

Doyal's authority to raise companies for a new regiment predated the April 16 Conscription Act, thus qualifying his unit for acceptance into Confederate service if he could muster the required ten companies by May 17. The second-to-last company to complete recruitment was Captain John M. D. Bond's "Jackson Guards" from Butts County. Named for the town that served as the county seat, this unit's ranks included Pvt. Wiley Mangham. Wiley enlisted on May 10, but his term of service dated from two days later, when his company rendezvoused in Griffin to muster officially into service for three years or the war. Upon the accession of the "Quitman Guards" on the following day, the regiment was completely organized, and the Jackson Guards accordingly became Company I, 53rd Georgia.[7]

*   *   *   *   *

As the Butts County men mingled with the other men of their regiment in Griffin, Wiley Mangham may have met *John S. Mangham*, a private in Company A. John had enlisted on April 28 in the first company to organize for Doyal's regiment, and he and his mates appropriately dubbed themselves the "Doyal Volunteers." The men also may have chosen this title because they could not have agreed on a nickname honoring a single county; census records show that the Doyal Volunteers hailed from at least half a dozen counties. Some of the enlistees resided in Griffin itself, while many others came from Spalding County's Cabin District. Many others came from adjoining districts in western Butts County, such as Wiley Mangham's Towaliga, and Coody's, where James M. Mangham lived. Most of the remaining recruits hailed from Henry County, which adjoined these areas of Spalding and Butts counties.[8]

A large proportion of the Henry County men came from the county seat of McDonough, which lay approximately ten miles from the Spalding and Butts county lines. This was only logical, as many of the men and their families doubtless were well acquainted with Leonard Doyal before he moved his law practice from McDonough to Griffin in 1856. Certainly, he would have sought recruits in a relatively populous area where his name remained well known and highly respected. John S. Mangham was one of these McDonough residents who answered Doyal's call for volunteers. The 1850 census shows five-year-old J. S. Mangham living in Mary Croley's home in Henry County, with the orphaned children of her deceased husband, Spencer Croley. John had lived with the widow Croley since September 1847, when an "orphan child by the name of John S. Mangum" was bound to her as an apprentice until he reached his majority. Living nearby in 1850 was 22-year-old *James M. D. Mangham*, who probably was John's uncle, and the eldest known son of James M. Mangham. Ten years later Mary Croley was 59 years of age, and her McDonough household still included 15-year-old John "Mangam." Although the connection between the Croley and Mangham families remains unclear, the young lad who enlisted in the Doyal Volunteers clearly was John S. Mangham, probably an orphaned grandson of James M. Mangham and thus a nephew of Wiley P. Mangham. When John put down his schoolbooks to shoulder a musket on April 28, 1862, he was either 16 or 17 years old.[9]

Although the 53rd Georgia completed its organization just two weeks later, it remained in the Griffin area until late June, probably waiting for arms, transportation, or both. After all, newly organized regiments across the South were clamoring for these same scarce resources. Orders finally arrived on June 23, directing Doyal to entrain his new regiment for Virginia immediately. Time was short, although Doyal and his men could not possibly have known just how very short it was.[10]

The men and boys of the 53rd Georgia knew that Gen. George B. McClellan's Army of the Potomac had been working its way up the James River to Richmond since landing on the Virginia coast in March. A ferocious engagement at Williamsburg on May 5 had failed to stop McClellan's glacial movement towards the Confederate capital, and Gen. Joseph E. Johnston's fierce counterblow at Seven Pines at the end of the month was likewise indecisive. An artillery burst wounded Johnston in the latter battle, however, and his replacement was Gen. Robert Edward Lee. Once derisively dubbed "Granny Lee" or the "King of Spades" because of his insistence that his troops entrench their positions, the courteous, gentlemanly Lee would prove himself one of

248

the most audacious risk-takers in military history. In fact, he was meeting secretly with Lt. Gen. Thomas J. "Stonewall" Jackson and other key subordinates on the very day the 53rd Georgia was ordered to hasten to Richmond. Unbeknown to anyone but this small inner circle, Lee planned to bring Jackson's men all the way from the Shenandoah Valley to crash like a thunderbolt into McClellan's right flank, just five miles east of Richmond. Jackson's blow was to be the opening move of a general offensive designed to roll up McClellan's army from right to left, with Confederate units attacking in echelon as the Union line unraveled. Allowing time for Jackson's Army of the Valley to march secretly across northern Virginia, the great counteroffensive was scheduled to commence on June 26, 1862.[11]

Rattling up the rails from Griffin, Georgia, Wiley and John Mangham probably were experiencing their first-ever long distance travel, taking in the scenic summer vistas of the Confederacy they had sworn to defend. They were not far from Petersburg, however, when they got a stern lesson in the dangers of movement on the South's overtaxed rolling stock. Private Billie Stillwell told the tale in his first letters home to his wife, Molly: "I feel thankful to Almighty God that I am permitted to write you for the cars have just run off the tracks breaking every box on the train wounding eight or ten men. . . .We would have got to Richmond tonight if the cars had not run off." The amazed Georgian could only wonder how nobody was killed, since pieces of planking and cast iron went flying everywhere while men leapt from the disintegrating train. After changing trains near Petersburg, the regiment arrived in the capital on June 27, finding the city abuzz with the events of the past two days.[12]

Independent of Lee's plans, McClellan had initiated a limited attack at Oak Grove on June 25, intending to seize a good advanced position from which his heavy artillery could batter the main Rebel entrenchments east of Richmond. Less than a mile west of May's Seven Pines battlefield and near the southern flank of the opposing forces, the bloody fighting cost the combatants more than a thousand casualties in the first day of what became known as the Seven Days' battles. The following day saw the commencement of Lee's attack, but since Stonewall Jackson's movements were unaccountably delayed, Maj. Gen. A. P. Hill initiated the attack from the northern end of the Confederate line, near Mechanicsville. His hopes that Jackson would arrive in the enemy's flank and rear proved vain, and Hill's five brigades lost heavily in a desperate series of unsupported assaults.[13]

Incredibly, however, McClellan decided to retreat from forces that he feared outnumbered his own, and he quickly withdrew his right flank several miles from Mechanicsville to the vicinity of New Cold Harbor, known locally as Gaines's Mill. Confederate forces struck hard there on June 27, trying for a knockout blow. Although they finally broke the Federal line in numerous places during some of the most furious fighting of the entire war, they were unable to bring their quarry to bay. When Wiley and John Mangham arrived in Richmond that day with the 53rd Georgia, they probably heard nothing of the battle raging just seven miles away, for acoustic shadows had the strange effect of muffling the sound. McClellan's headquarters stood less than two miles from the storm center, yet he barely heard anything of the fighting that cost the two armies more than 15,000 casualties. The raw Georgia troops were busy equipping themselves with captured Springfield muskets and knapsacks, "which we packed as full as we could ram and cram them."[14]

The following day saw the Army of the Potomac retreating rapidly towards the James River with Lee's troops in pursuit. The 53rd Georgia staggered some twenty miles down the badly cut-up roads under their heavy burdens, learning the hard way that marching infantrymen need to travel light. The scattered fighting that day gave way to full-blown combat on June 29, when Maj. Gen. John Magruder's wing of Lee's army was ordered to overtake and engage the Federals, thus allowing other Confederate forces to outflank McClellan's force and destroy it. The 53rd Georgia was now part of Magruder's command, assigned to Semmes's Brigade of McLaws's Division. McLaws directed his second brigade, under Brig. Gen. Joseph Kershaw, to lead the way, and the South Carolinians ran into a strong Federal rear guard at five o'clock that afternoon. In fact, the 26,000 Yankees positioned to block the Williamsburg Road near Savage's Station outnumbered Magruder's entire force by more than two to one, so Semmes's Brigade was soon ordered into line on Kershaw's right.[15]

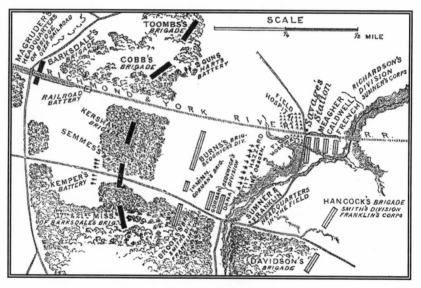

THE BATTLE OF SAVAGE'S STATION, JUNE 29, 1862.
WILEY P. AND JOHN S. MANGHAM SERVED IN SEMMES'S BRIGADE.

Semmes's main striking power comprised veteran regiments such as the 5th Louisiana, 10th Louisiana, 10th Georgia, 15th Virginia, and 32nd Virginia, so he wisely kept Doyal's "fresh fish" in reserve as he committed his brigade on the Williamsburg Road. Since the Federal line stretched well south of the road, Semmes's troops quickly found themselves extending their front southward to face the fire that threatened the flank of Kershaw and his South Carolinians'.[16]

Doyal's men had spent the day alternately marching down roads and floundering through knee-deep swamps and thickets, and the fight at Savage's Station promised more of the same. As he moved into the brambles south of the road in the brigade's second line, Pvt. John Wood of Company B noted that it was "tough working charging through such a place with a knap sack, and it crammed chug full, and also my gun and other equipments." The fight developed rapidly on Semmes's front, and the briars meant not only tough going but short ranges: most of the shooting was at forty yards or less. On the left of the brigade line of battle, hand-to-hand combat erupted; one desperate Yankee lunged for the colors of the 10th Georgia before he was knocked down and killed. On the right, Semmes sent Private Maddox of the 5th Louisiana forward to identify troops spotted forty yards in front. Singing out "Who are you?" to the mysterious command, Maddox received the answer "Friends." Semmes chimed in, demanding "Which regiment?" The answer, "Third Vermont," elicited a blast of fire from the Louisianians, whose volley instigated another close-range shootout.[17]

Wiley and John Mangham, as well as the rest of Doyal's raw troops, must have found the situation almost unbearable. John had been in the army all of eight weeks, and Wiley only six. Just six days earlier they had been in Griffin! Now, after five days crammed aboard trains in the sweltering June heat and one additional day marching to the front, they were in combat on a battlefield which bore no resemblance whatever to the drill field, about which they knew precious little in any case. Although they were technically "in reserve," this translated in the thickets to only fifty yards or so behind the firing line, in a battle where the enemy remained unseen until he stood up and volleyed practically into their very faces. Private Wood noted: "The bombs and bullets, fell in all directions, in front and in the rear, on our right, and on our left, above, and amongst us. There were one half dozen balls fell from one half to two feet from me." One artillery projectile struck within ten feet of Wood; had it exploded, he might never have survived to write his letter home. Private William Head of the Jackson Guards survived a shell exploding almost underfoot, however, suffering nothing but a badly bruised knee and leg.[18]

When General Magruder dispatched the 13th Mississippi to protect the right rear of Semmes's Brigade in the melee south of the Williamsburg Road, a bad day got worse for Doyal's men. Wood recalled, "The Mississippi regt. taking our regt. for the enemy fired several rounds at our regt. and the 10th Ga. regt. Our boys thinking they were fired at by the enemy, never waited for the command, fired a galling volley at the Mississippians." In the confusion, however, Wood believed that "the only damage we done. . .was that of killing our Major's horse." A cannon shot passing under the colonel's horse was apparently the straw that broke the camel's back, for Wood reported: "All our regt. started to run but our Company, and some of them also started." As for his own feelings, he acknowledged being "a little frightened when the bombs came whizzing by me at first, but after the Mississippians fired at us I became so that I did not care for any thing. I fired as cooly as if I had been shooting a squirrel."[19]

By now it was dark, and Semmes ordered his men to cease firing, reform, and rest on their arms. Private James Maddux, in Wiley Mangham's Company I, was one of some 444 Confederates killed, wounded, or captured by the time darkness brought a halt to the firing; the Federals reported 919 casualties in the chaos at Savage's Station. Semmes's men were equipped with smoothbore muskets loaded with one ball and three buckshot, and he attributed the disparity in losses to the "greater efficiency" of this combination in the day's short-range firefights, as well as to the "superior steadiness of our men, and the precision of their fire."[20]

John and Wiley Mangham lay down that night in the open fields behind deserted Union breastworks, soaked by a rain pouring "as hard as it could shower down." Private Wood noted with wonder, "I slept as sound that night as if I had been lying in a feather bed." Stillwell also wondered that he was able to "sleep sound all night on the wet ground [and] get up next morning all right." Worn out by the stress of the last week and their first experience of combat, most of Doyal's men probably slept as soundly as Wood, but they were up again and marching in pursuit of the fleeing "Vandals" as day broke on June 30. "That day was a terrible day to me," wrote Wood, adding, "There was one time, I actually would have given 25 dollars for one half an hours rest. I believe if we had not halted shortly, I undoubtedly, would have fainted." Magruder's men had slogged more than twenty miles through the muggy Virginia heat, first to support an attack at Glendale and then to reinforce General Huger's initial attempt to seize Malvern Hill from the Federals. Although the 53rd Georgia did not fire a shot that day, it was nonetheless a day to try men's souls.[21]

On July 1, an attempt to reposition Magruder's forces at Malvern Hill again ran afoul of bad maps and the local penchant for using the same name for several different roads. It was late afternoon before Semmes's Brigade was in a reserve position on the far right of the Confederate line, where the men stood in a ravine just 1200 yards from an incredible array of Federal guns. Semmes reported that his men were subjected to "a shelling unsurpassed for severity in any conflict during the war." He was not exaggerating, either, as more than forty pieces of field artillery and sixteen heavy guns of the Army of the Potomac's artillery reserve frowned down the northern slopes of Malvern Hill, while 36 additional cannon pointed westward. The gunboats *Aroostook* and *Galena*, which packed a formidable array of 9-inch and 11-inch guns as well as 100-pounder Parrott rifled cannon, backed up the whole. As historian Stephen Sears has observed, "Virtually every Confederate who stormed Malvern Hill and left a record of his experience spoke in awe of the Federal guns." The 53rd Georgia's John Wood was no exception to this pattern, reporting:

> We proceeded to march through a perfect continual shower of grape, canister, shots and shells. One of our company was shot through the head and killed instantly, by a grape-shot. His gun was shot all to atoms. About that time, several pieces of shells struck my head and hat, but they happened to be spent pieces of shells.[22]

This trial by fire also wounded a man in John Mangham's company, probably as the regiment moved with Semmes's Brigade three hundred yards to the right flank, before advancing in line of battle from a point just eight hundred yards from the guns. The brigade became badly mixed up as Semmes attempted to take advantage of folds in the ground and the concealment of the forest, and he lost track of most of his regiments. Private William Head of Wiley Mangham's Jackson Guards found himself stranded in the open with Captain Bond and two others of the company, since "Some had flanked off to the left some to the right, some had lain down in a ditch & some had ran off, while others were shot down by the enemy. . . ." Private Head was experiencing the "empty battlefield" syndrome in spades, where men disappearing behind cover left one apparently alone amid the disorienting roar of combat. To the awestruck Georgian, it seemed that he and his few companions stood "alone on the field for a space of four or five hundred yards, directly in front of a battery of thirty or forty cannon & at least forty thousand muskets & Enfield rifles, at a distance of one hundred yards." When General Semmes finally got his brigade to its assault position just two hundred yards from the Federal gun line, only the 10th Georgia and 10th Louisiana remained under his control, along with Company K of the 53rd Georgia. The charge they launched actually surged into the opposing infantry lines, but eventually was repulsed like every other Confederate assault that day.[23]

Despite the fact that his massed batteries and determined infantrymen had acquitted themselves with distinction at Malvern Hill, George McClellan had long since given up hope of defeating the Rebels who seemingly loomed everywhere in overwhelming numbers. His overriding concern was escape, and the Confederates' inability to synchronize their attacks allowed him to salvage his hard-fighting but ill-managed army by retreating to the James River. In perhaps the most incredible turnabout of the whole war, the gigantic Union army was defeated literally at the gates of Richmond and sent flying in retreat after a week of intense fighting. It was the beginning of the legend of Robert E. Lee and the Army of Northern Virginia.[24]

Wiley and John Mangham, along with the other rookies of Doyal's 53rd Georgia, played only a modest role in the Seven Days' battles, but their baptism of fire was nevertheless a harrowing experience. Just one week after entraining at Griffin, the dangers of the battlefield had passed from the realm of vague supposition to the stark realities of combat in the Chickahominy River swamps. With the regiment encamped on the field of Malvern Hill, Private Wood wrote home: "The sight of the battle field was horrid, to look upon. I could see dead men and wounded in all directions. The groans of the wounded was horrid. Some men I saw with their heads shot off, also hands and feet. Some were shot all to pieces." Later, he admonished his relatives in so many words to count their blessings: "Don't talk of hard times at home, ask a soldier of the peninsular army what hard times are and he will tell you and give you a correct answer. If I have not seen hardships, privations and hard times there are no snakes." As William Head put it, "The boys have seen the Elephant and are satisfied." Noting that he had seen "thousands of acres literally strown with dead and wounded," he nevertheless desired "no peace that does not give us an honorable position among the nations of the earth." He knew that many felt otherwise, however: "It is my opinion that many men in the army, would submit to Lincoln's despotism in any form for the sake of peace, or to ease their own dear selves out of the scraps."[25]

Billie Stillwell was thankful that the regiment had weathered the storm of shot and shell as well as it had, with only "two or three killed and ten or twelve wounded." He added fervently, "I was on the battle field yesterday and God deliver me from ever seeing another battle field. Some think that this fight will end the war and that we will have no more fighting to do. All that I can say is God grant it." Whereas Private Head hinted that there might have been some morale problems in the 53rd Georgia, Stillwell made no bones about it. He opined that the regiment was not really a good fighting outfit, since most of the men "were driven in service by the Conscript [Act]," but stoutly denied home-front rumors that "our Reg ran and that they could not get it in the fight. . . .I don't intend to undertake to defend Doyal or the Reg but simply state facts and then I am done. There is one thing I know and that is that there were lots of Reg that did as bad as ours and old one[s] at that." Nevertheless, he was proud that the army had "routed and whipped the Yankeys." He added, "This is twice they have tried to get to Richmond and they went so far as to have on their flags 'Richmond or Hell by Saturday night.' Some of the boys say that they got to both places. I don't know. I know some of them went to Richmond, the other place I don't know."[26]

Regardless of the fate of the Yankees, the stresses of combat, incessant marching through rugged terrain, steamy weather, exposure, and bad water soon began to take a toll of Doyal's regiment, which suffered every new unit's vulnerability to camp diseases along with the hazards of active campaigning. Private Head tried to describe it to his wife in a letter home on July 12, grumbling that he had been "marching and fighting almost day and night ever since my arrival in Richmond, without tents or blankets exposed to rain & slop, wading knee deep in mud and water, sleeping on the ground in the rain without any covering, etc." Another Georgian sought to summarize the campaign around Richmond to his home folks, commenting wryly, "When standing we were in a bog of mud; when lying down to refresh ourselves in sleep we were in a pool of water." He was one of many whose health was suffering from the "miasma" of the Chickahominy swamps, where surface water often was the only thing available for the troops to drink in the muggy heat. The Army of the Potomac reported a staggering 42,911 cases of disease during July alone as it squatted in the bogs along the James River; its gray-clad besiegers suffered terribly as well.[27]

Among the legions of weakened soldiers tottering into hospitals in Richmond were John and Wiley Mangham, both of whom were taken to the General Hospital at Camp Winder on July 9. John, admitted as "J. S. Mangum," apparently was worn out and sick from the exertions of the preceding two weeks. Not diagnosed with any particular ailment, the boy soldier was treated for "debility" for several days and released on July 12. He probably was fairly well recovered, but he may have decided simply to take his chances with his regiment after witnessing first-hand the horrors of Richmond's shockingly overtaxed hospital facilities. One man in his company, Pvt. F. D. Black, apparently chose to stay in camp while sick; he was the first man in the company to die in service, passing away on the day after John's release from the hospital.[28]

Wiley was promoted to fifth sergeant at about this time, which probably reflected well on his steadiness in action at Savage's Station and Malvern Hill; perhaps he was one of the two who had stood before the Federal guns with Captain Bond and Private Head at the latter place. Wiley had to remain in the hospital after John was released, however, having developed a nasty case of dysentery in the hopelessly unhygienic conditions in the Chickahominy swamps. One historian estimates that North and South combined lost more than five thousand troops to disease during the Peninsular Campaign of summer 1862, mostly to the ravages of dysentery. Although the total number who died in this manner can never be ascertained, they combined with those killed in action to keep Richmond in a state of perpetual mourning throughout July. Church bells which, by all rights, should have rung in celebration of Richmond's deliverance, were instead tolling for the dead. As Constance Harrison remembered, "Day by day, we were called to our windows by the wailing dirge of a military band preceding a soldier's funeral. One could not number those sad pageants. . . ."[29]

Perhaps one of them was for Sgt. Wiley Pendleton Mangham. Wasting away for fifteen days in a hospital whose medical personnel knew nothing of germ theory, not to speak of modern antibiotics, he died of acute dysentery on July 24, 1862. In the army for just 74 days, he was the first member of Butts County's Jackson Guards to die in service; he certainly would not be the last. His widow, Mary Ann Mangham, testified to Butts County officials on August 19 that she was duly entitled to any monies owed Wiley P. Mangham for his military service. Her application wended its way through the Confederate bureaucracy until March 14, 1863, when auditors at the War Department registered her claim. No record of any payment survives, but it could not have exceeded forty dollars.[30]

*   *   *   *   *

In December 1866, Wiley's father deeded 100 acres of land to Mary Ann's father Dawson Heath in late 1866, in trust for her and little Eliza. Apparently, Wiley's young son John W. Mangham already had died, within four years of his father. Mary Ann Mangham married Thomas J. Henderson in Butts County on December 31, 1867.[31]

*   *   *   *   *

When General Lee decided to move the bulk of his forces into northern Virginia to confront Gen. John Pope's Army of Virginia, he left a sizable contingent on the peninsula to keep McClellan's Federals safely penned up. McLaws's Division, including Semmes's Brigade and the 53rd Georgia, thus remained east of Richmond in the steaming Chickahominy swamps during the Second Manassas campaign. But when a resounding Confederate victory there led to Lee's decision to enter Maryland, McLaws was summoned to rejoin the main army for its daring foray into Union territory. As his division hiked northward in the punishing heat, many sick and barefoot men broke down under the renewed strain and fell by the wayside. Others were content to fight in defense of Southern soil, but were perturbed at the idea of invading the North; some of these men, along with skulkers of all stripes, faded away from the army at every opportunity. Others, learning of Lee's order authorizing barefoot men to remain in

255

Virginia, gave new meaning to the phrase "voting with their feet": they sat down, pulled off their shoes, and deliberately threw them away.[32]

If Pvt. John Mangham remained among those willing and able to continue northward, he and his comrades passed through the horrific sights of the recent carnage at Manassas, where hundreds of corpses lay unburied under the blazing sun. A South Carolinian marching in Kershaw's Brigade remembered simply that "the harrowing sights that were met with were in places too sickening to admit of description." Private Billie Stillwell also lamented the destruction, but noted saucily to his wife that the Federals had gotten "all their big dogs whipped, Burnsides and McClelland, Pope and Fremont and they all had to toddle. I guess they will learn after while that we are in earnest about this matter."[33]

By mid-September, Semmes's depleted brigade stood atop South Mountain at Crampton's Gap, helping pen up the Federal garrison at strategic Harper's Ferry. McClellan's Army of the Potomac sought to strike through the mountain passes against Lee's broadly dispersed forces, resulting in a nasty scare for the men of the 53rd Georgia. On September 14, they rushed up to support a couple of McLaws's brigades under attack by the whole of Maj. Gen. William Franklin's VI Army Corps. The badly outnumbered Rebels were lucky to avoid utter disaster in the sharp action that ensued, but the overly cautious Franklin hesitated to pursue a routed foe he believed to be numerically superior. McLaws cobbled together a line several miles away in Pleasant Valley the next day, desperately preparing his five thousand men to attempt a stand against four times their number. The Federal troops, themselves veterans of the Peninsula disasters, had seen the backs of their enemies for the first time on the previous day, and they were eager to follow up their handy victory. But while their generals waffled, nervously wondering why all firing at nearby Harper's Ferry had ceased, they heard the sound of cheering come floating down the valley from the direction of the beleaguered garrison. When McLaws's men began cheering as well, an anxious bluecoat yelled across to them, inquiring, "What the hell are you fellows cheering for?" Came the haughty answer, "Because Harper's Ferry is gone up, God damn you!"[34]

Soon afterwards, McLaws's Division was off for Harper's Ferry, whence it continued on its way to rejoin the main army, and John may have been marching in the long gray columns that streamed past the despondent Federals captured at Harper's Ferry. Captain Edward Ripley of the 9th Vermont remembered watching the hard-marching Confederates stream past him on the Charlestown Pike:

> It was a weird, uncanny sight, and drove sleep from my eyes. It was something demon-like, a scene from an Inferno. They were silent as ghosts, ruthless and rushing in their speed; ragged, earth-colored, dishevelled, and devilish, as though they were keen on the scent of hot blood. . .and thirsting for it; their sliding dog-trot was as though on snow-shoes. The shuffle of their badly shod feet on the hard surface of the Pike was so rapid as to be continuous like the hiss of a great

serpent. . . . The spectral, ghostly picture will never be effaced from my memory.[35]

Lee was striving desperately to concentrate his widely scattered forces, as the Army of the Potomac was closing in to bring him to battle. Outnumbered though he was, Lee spurned the idea of retreat, believing that he and his men were more than a match for the cautious McClellan. The Union commander, on the other hand, had found a copy of Lee's plans wrapped around three cigars, the famous Special Order No. 191. Possession of the Confederate order of march nerved the cautious McClellan to push his army through the mountain passes after the Confederates, boasting, "Here is a paper, with which if I cannot whip Bobbie Lee, I will be willing to go home." Both Lee and McClellan soon would have the opportunity to prove their points along Antietam Creek, just outside the pleasant town of Sharpsburg, Maryland. As the armies concentrated there throughout the day on September 16, 1862, it became increasingly clear that a showdown fight was in the offing.[36]

Private Mangham and his comrades of Semmes's Brigade slumped down for a well-deserved rest that night, several miles short of Boteler's Ford near Shepherdstown, Virginia. With the other brigades of McLaws's Division, they were still miles away from Sharpsburg, as they had been busy helping reduce the Union garrison at Harper's Ferry. Since Richard H. Anderson's and A. P. Hill's divisions were likewise delayed, fully one-third of Lee's nine divisions were absent, and the odds were mounting tremendously against him. Battle losses, sickness, and straggling had reduced the Rebel ranks to some 26,000 at Sharpsburg, plus some 10,000 more in the three divisions still en route. The Army of the Potomac, on the other hand, marshaled some 75,000 men present for duty at Sharpsburg on September 16, with another 25,000 within a day's march. When a courier found McLaws's Division bivouacked for the night, he delivered orders from Lee that unleashed a flurry of activity: they were to immediately commence a forced march to Sharpsburg, some eight miles away. The guns were rumbling already, as Union troops moved into position to launch a full-scale attack against Lee's left flank the next day. Among the men in gray jackets awaiting the onslaught were *Will, Nat, and John Mangham* of the 13th Georgia (Chapter II).[37]

Their second cousin John S. Mangham spent much of that long night tramping down the road leading to the Potomac River. He and the other men of the Doyal Volunteers spent the night south of the river, then moved out again with the rest of Semmes's troops the next morning. Although they had not been heavily engaged in the battles near Harper's Ferry, they were footsore and weary, having been on the road for most of the previous twenty-four hours. They also had dealt with the roughest terrain of any division in the army during their approach march to Harper's Ferry, and their thinned ranks bore testimony to the hardships they had faced. Semmes's Brigade arrived with only 709 officers and men, and the 53rd Georgia's twenty-one officers and 255 men marked it as the only one of Semmes's four regiments with even two hundred men in ranks.[38]

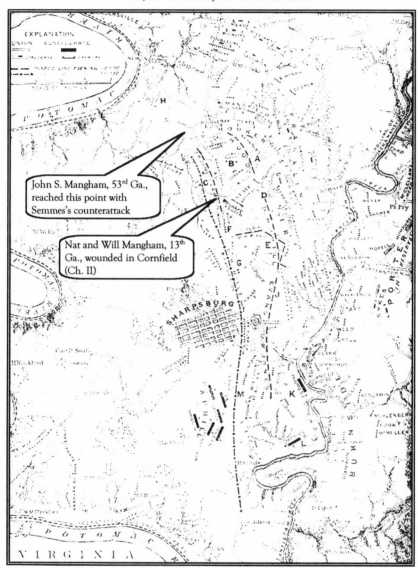

John S. Mangham, 53rd Ga., reached this point with Semmes's counterattack

Nat and Will Mangham, 13th Ga., wounded in Cornfield (Ch. II)

THE BATTLE OF SHARPSBURG (ANTIETAM), SEPTEMBER 17, 1862.

As the opposing forces clashed just north of town along the Hagerstown Turnpike, Semmes's Virginians and Georgians marched to the sound of the guns, splashing across the Potomac River into Maryland at seven o'clock. Pausing only to restore their formations, they got to Sharpsburg about an hour later and were directed towards the far left of the Confederate line, where Stonewall Jackson's men had been engaged in bitter combat in the West Woods and the Cornfield since dawn that morning. Will and Nat Mangham already had been shot down in the Cornfield, along with most of their comrades of the 13th Georgia, and Jackson was flinging newly arrived reinforcements into action in an attempt to smash the jumbled blue columns before they reorganized.[39]

John Mangham and the 53rd Georgia double-quicked at the rear of Semmes's column as it passed through the shattered remnants of Hood's fabled Texas Brigade. Skirting past the westernmost fringes of the West Woods, Semmes's troops filed by the right flank through a gate on Mr. Poffenberger's property, then formed into line on the double. They were approaching the extreme right flank units of the Federal Army, advancing under command of Maj. Gen. "Fighting Joe" Hooker, and the heavy fire from front and flank began dropping men by the dozen, especially on Semmes's right. A stand-up fight commenced, but Semmes kept his men moving forward as the fire intensified. The 53rd Georgia was on the far left of the brigade line of battle, and surged forward when Semmes ordered a charge. Lieutenant Colonel Sloan led the regiment through a hot fire of artillery and musketry, passing through one cornfield, an apple orchard, and yet another cornfield, before receiving a mortal wound while the regiment paused at a fenceline.[40]

Private Stillwell wrote his wife that the men called out vainly to the stricken Sloan, then asked for someone to lead them in a renewed charge. Lieutenant Redd of Semmes's staff stepped forward with drawn sword to lead the way, while the excited men shouted, "Go on!" With the heat of battle upon them, they followed Redd over the fence "with yells like demons" in a pursuit that carried them forward about a mile. There, among the haystacks of the Nicodemus Farm, lack of ammunition brought Semmes's advance to a halt just shy of the North Woods. They had effectively dispersed the enemy infantry in their front, but remained under a heavy fire from two Union batteries whose gunners continued to shower them with canister. After some time in this exposed position forward of Confederate lines, Semmes pulled his men back to the vicinity of the West Woods to regroup.[41]

Semmes's Brigade had hit the extreme right flank of several Union brigades just as other Confederate forces hit their front and left flank, and their combined efforts almost destroyed Sedgwick's Union division. Of some five thousand Northerners who had pushed into the West Woods that morning, 2200 fell dead or wounded in an hour of ferocious fighting which saw them completely routed; most of these men fell in the first twenty minutes of the Confederate assault. Hooker's attack was not just repulsed, it was shattered. Union signalers wigwagged the worrisome news to McClellan's headquarters: "Things look blue. Re-inforcements are badly wanted. Our troops are giving way."[42]

Since Hooker's effort against the Confederate left flank comprised McClellan's main attack, Semmes's slashing counterattack had contributed greatly to stalling the Army of the Potomac and stymieing its commander. The bloodiest day in America's history was far from over, but Pvt. John S. Mangham and his friends in the Doyal

Volunteers had played an important act in a drama which saw the desperately outmanned Army of Northern Virginia stop several times its weight in bluecoats. Although Lee defiantly remained in position to offer battle on September 18, McClellan could not bring himself to tangle with his opponent again. His hesitation may have allowed Lee's army to survive; certainly, it allowed that army to feel that it was more than a match for its larger opponent.[43]

As for the men of the 53rd Georgia, they pointed proudly to a battle flag that bore two shots through its folds, knowing that they had fought creditably in an army grown gamecock-proud of its fighting prowess. Stung by allegations that they had run at Savage's Station, they felt that things were different after Sharpsburg. Private William Stillwell of Company F was a member of Semmes's headquarters guard and thus remained out of the fight, but he wrote home proudly on September 18 that his friends had "fought and fought like men." After observing that some other regiments had "straggled off," he asserted proudly that the Georgians, ". . .that is, what is left of them are ready for them [the Yankees] again." Then he stated the bottom line: "It will be said no more that the 53 Ga Reg won't fight."[44]

Despite his obvious pride, Stillwell was moved by the magnitude of the conflict. From his perspective, Sharpsburg was "one of the most awful battles that was ever fought," and the regiment "was almost cut to pieces." He was not exaggerating. Of the 276 men engaged, eleven were killed and sixty fell wounded, while another six counted as missing. Approximately two hours of heavy combat had cost the 53rd Georgia fully thirty percent of its effective strength. In the holocaust that was Sharpsburg, however, they were almost fortunate, since their position on the brigade left flank shielded them somewhat from enfilading artillery fire that scythed down their sister regiments in windrows. Of Semmes's four regiments, the decimated 53rd Georgia suffered the *lowest* percentage of casualties that day.[45]

*　　　*　　　*　　　*　　　*

Lee's men crossed the Potomac River once more, this time heading southward to rest and refit in the fertile Shenandoah Valley. Spared the continuous marching of August and September and finally eating full rations, the battered army rapidly regained its vitality. By October 10, less than one month after Sharpsburg, more than 64,000 men were present for duty, but Pvt. Mangham apparently was not one of them. Perhaps broken down and sick after marching some 250 miles in August and September, he was in General Hospital No. 17 at Richmond on or about October 31, listed on a muster roll of the sick and wounded present at that place. He was paid shortly afterwards for the first time in his army career, after more than six months of service, and was again present for duty with his company in early November. He may have relapsed later that month, as he was readmitted to the same hospital on November 19. In all probability, he was evacuated to the hospital with the other sick men of Longstreet's 1st Army Corps, since the corps began moving to occupy positions on the heights above Fredericksburg on the very day that John arrived at the hospital. The first day of December found him sufficiently well to return to duty.[46]

Three days after John returned to the regiment, the Jackson Guards took time to remember their dead in a manner typical of the times. The letter that appeared in the December 13 edition of the *Macon Daily Telegraph* tells their story:

Fredericksburg, Va., Dec. 4, 1862.

At a meeting of the Jackson Guards held [t]his day the following preamble and resolutions were unanimously adopted. Capt. J. M. D. Bond was called to the chair, and Lieut. Wm. H. Willis requested to act as Secretary. The Chairman then arose and stated the object of the meeting, when, on motion of Sergeant Wm. A. Pace, a committee of five was appointed to report a suitable preamble and resolution in favor of the gallant dead of the Jackson Guards, that their friends and relatives may know how and where they died, when Capt. Bond reported the following preamble and resolution:

Whereas, as Allwise, merciful and just God has seen fit to take away from us our friends and companions in arms, Sergeant Wyley P. Mangham, privates Thomas G. Cole, Charles Waller, Wm. R. Smith, James R. Henderson, Sanford L. Moore, Rev. William W. Head and James Edwards, all of whom died in and around Richmond during the month of July, August, September and October; also, Charles Nichols, who was killed in the Sharpsburg fight September 17th; also, Josiah Harris, who died in camp near Fredericksburg, Va., and Joseph Cook, who died in Gordonsville. Therefore,

1st *Resolved.* In the death of these our friends we recognize the omnipotent hand of the Great Giver of all things, and bow with humble submission to his Divine Providence.

2[d]. *Resolved.* That not only have their friends and relatives lost true and devoted friends, but the Confederate States have lost true, devoted and valiant soldiers, ever ready to perform a soldier's duty, and always found at their post, with willingness and without a murmur.

3[d]. *Resolved,* That while in the battles around Richmond and in Maryland, they not only evinced a willingness and determination to drive the invaders from our soil, but seemed perfectly willing to undergo any hardship, and if necessary to make any sacrifice to promote Southern independence, and seemed perfectly calm and resigned to their affliction, and died easy, and we hope and have reason to believe, they are resting in a better world.

4th. *Resolved,* That we, the members of Co. I, do join in heartfelt grief with the afflicted relatives and friends, and can assure them that they died like true and chivalrous patriots on the tented field, manfully battling for their homes and firesides.

On the motion of Sgt. Augustus Gray, the men voted to send this preamble to the *Macon Telegraph,* as well as the Atlanta, Augusta, and Griffin newspapers for publication.[47]

As the Jackson Guards remembered their dead, the devil was about to break loose along the Rappahannock River line, for General Lee was building up his forces along the river at Fredericksburg in order to stop a renewed Federal "On to Richmond" campaign. This time his opponent was Maj. Gen. Ambrose Burnside, who replaced McClellan in command following the latter's failure to capitalize on his strategic success at Sharpsburg; this failure was aggravated by McClellan's notorious unwillingness to work amicably with the President. In any case, Lincoln wanted a fighting general who would push the Rebels hard, and Burnside certainly fit the bill. Unfortunately for the Northern troops marshaling along the Rappahannock that December, their new commanding general lacked many other talents needed for high command, and the attack he launched at Fredericksburg was little more than a series of abominably unimaginative, uncoordinated frontal assaults. Although Burnside led some 115,000 men into action against Lee's 78,000 Southerners beginning December 11, 1862, it soon became clear to everyone involved that Burnside's willingness to fight, and fight hard, was no adequate substitute for skill, planning ability, and tactical acumen. His unfortunate soldiers were fated to pay the high price of his incompetence in blood. For Lee's veterans, it would seem absurdly easy, although many of them also were doomed to pay the ultimate price.[48]

As Private Wood of Company B, 53rd Georgia, wrote home on December 18, ". . .as near as I can recollect the ball was opened last Thursday week, the 11th of December, at about 4 o'clock, by the enemy crossing the river, and our pickets firing on them." Burnside had pushed across pontoon bridges in the darkness, and his troops stormed into Fredericksburg's streets to clear out the Confederate picket guard in a nasty little scrap. As drummers beat the long roll for assembly, Private Mangham and the 53rd Georgia formed up about daybreak and moved into line of battle about a mile from their camp in the hills west of town. Building fires to ward off the chill air, they remained in position about three quarters of a mile from the river, while "a few inquisitive bombshells" sought them out with the peculiar whizzing sound that sounded to Georgia ears like a malevolent whisper, calling "Where is you? Where is you?" The following morning they moved a half-mile upriver to support Kemper's Virginia battery, whose fire attracted a counter-bombardment that burst all around the Georgia infantrymen, mercifully without inflicting any casualties. They remained in this position or in line of battle near the edge of town over the next several days of combat, in danger from cannon and small arms fire, but like many of Lee's units, they never directly engaged in the thick of the fray. Even so, Pvt. John Dearing of the Doyal Volunteers was wounded severely in the ankle on December 13, as the climactic Federal assaults surged against the Confederate lines frowning from the heights above. Private Billie Stillwell of Company F was on duty guarding the brigade's baggage train, and he found a convenient elevation from which to view the unfolding drama. The furious musketry blazing from Longstreet's lines on Marye's Heights sounded to him as though someone "had set fire to a canebrake of a thousand acres."[49]

Burnside had set his determined troops an all but impossible task. The slopes leading up to the sunken road soon were carpeted with blue as the relentless assault waves washed up to the very muzzles of the defenders before ebbing away in confusion, with regiment upon regiment shot to pieces. Just fifteen minutes after Union guns stopped shelling Kemper's Battery, Private Wood and other men of the 53rd Georgia filtered down to the killing zone to see the sights. The young soldier wrote his father,

> You can't imagine what a horrible spectacle I witnessed. I saw hundreds of men lying dead, shot in all parts some with their heads, hands, legs arms, etc. shot off, and mangled in all manner and shapes. The ground resembled an immense hog pen and them all killed. It put me in mind of hog killing time more than any thing else. . . .[50]

Wood was among those detailed to scour the battlefield for serviceable muskets, but candidly admitted that the men of Semmes's Brigade "helped themselves to plunder. Some searched the Yanks pockets, and even stripped them to their skin. Nearly every one of our boys helped themselves to Yankee canteens, haver-sacks, overcoats, shoes, and etc." A booming trade sprang up among the victors, as they bought, sold, and traded booty of all descriptions, but the 53rd Georgia soon moved down into Fredericksburg itself to dig rifle pits against the possibility of a renewed Union assault. After several more days of tense duty in close proximity to the enemy's pickets, the Georgians finally could relax a bit, as Burnside's defeated army pulled back across the Rappahannock to lick its wounds during the night of December 15-16. John Wood observed, "I am truly proud that I can write that our company, behaved well in the 6 days fight and skirmish and come out safe and sound." For John Mangham and his friends, the army's resounding triumph meant the end of six days and nights in line of battle along the river. It was high time to kindle roaring campfires and warm up.[51]

The 13,000 names on Federal casualty lists cast a pall over the Army of the Potomac, while brightening the prospects for Confederate success. Sometime after the battle, some wag composed saucy new lyrics to the tune of "Jordan is a Hard Road to Travel." Entitled "Richmond is a Hard Road to Travel," the ditty satirized the numerous Union failures to reach the Confederate capital, and it summarized their difficulties at Fredericksburg tartly, but all too accurately:

> Last of all the brave Burnside, with his pontoon bridges tried,
> A road no one had thought of before him,
> With two hundred thousand men for the Rebel slaughter pen,
> And the blessed Union flag a-waving o'er him.
> But he met a fire like hell, of canister and shell,
> That mowed down his men with great slaughter,
> 'Twas a shocking sight to view, that Second Waterloo,
> And the river ran with more blood than water.
> Now pull off your coat and roll up your sleeves,
> Rappahannock is a hard road to travel,
> Burnside got in a trap, which caused for him to grieve,
> For Richmond is a hard road to travel I believe![52]

The 53rd Georgia completed a tour of picket and provost guard in Fredericksburg in the first week of the new year, and returned to camp to hear the cheering news of victory in the west at Murfreesboro. Although this news later proved to be exaggerated, the Georgians were satisfied that the Yankees along the Rappahannock were cowed sufficiently for the time being. As Private Wood wrote on January 5, "I think they ought to be sufficiently satisfied of Fredericksburg. If they do attack us they will get worse whipped than they did before as we are better fortified."[53]

Most of the ensuing winter months afforded precious little excitement to the men of the regiment, now commanded by Col. James P. Simms. Although they lived in the relative comfort of bell tents and had plentiful (though monotonous) rations, many must have shared Billie Stilwell's feelings:

> We have had more snow, snow. I am so tired of snow and mud and long to see the beautiful spring and summer and dust again and if we can't have peace I want to hear the cannon roar again. One gets so tired lying here in camps and never hearing anything but the same old thing "fall in to roll call", prepare for inspection, "form in third relief" and the old drum that is most always rattling and it makes one want to get off into the dessert of Arabia where they never would hear the roar of camps any more. But the soldier allways looks forward to the time (alas few of them ever see it) when they will get home to where the laurels that they have so nobly won through danger and hardships not afew. Oh Molly, how the soldiers think every sun that rises he knows he is one day nearer his home or his grave. Oh peace, one of the greatest blessings of this world.[54]

*   *   *   *   *

The monotony of winter quarters was broken in due course by renewed Federal maneuvers commencing in late April, this time under the direction of Maj. Gen. "Fighting Joe" Hooker. The result would be the bitterest combat to date for John Mangham and the 53rd Georgia, when the Army of Northern Virginia met the Army of the Potomac at a crossroads west of Fredericksburg, amidst the forlorn tangles of forest and underbrush known forbiddingly as the Wilderness. Its name accurately evoked the dense thickets that lined the area's poor roads and tracks, small farms, and sparse habitations, but belied the fact that the roads themselves were numerous. Since many led to fords across the Rappahannock River, they offered General Hooker an opportunity to get his army across the river west of Lee's formidable concentration of troops at Fredericksburg, with the seemingly impenetrable jungles masking the movements from prying Confederate eyes. If successful, Hooker's gambit could place him between Lee's army and Richmond itself, with consequences perhaps fatal to the Confederate war effort.

In contrast to Burnside's ill-conceived and poorly executed assaults at Fredericksburg in December, Hooker's opening moves placed his forces across the river on both sides of the city by April 29, 1863. John Mangham's second cousin, *Cpl. Charles A. "Nat" Mangham,* may have been in the 13th Georgia's picket line on the river bank south of town, resisting Union troops of the famed "Iron Brigade" as they forced their way across the river in the early morning hours. At eight o'clock, the 53rd moved out with elements of Semmes's Brigade in response to the ruckus along the river line, taking a reserve position next to the Telegraph Road, just half a mile behind the heights overlooking Howison's house, south of town. John and the Doyal Volunteers were pushed forward into the brigade picket line about six o'clock that evening, along with two other companies from their regiment, and they watched as bluecoats streamed across two pontoon bridges flung across the Rappahannock. Private John Wood was among those out front, and scouted to a point within 150 yards of the marching troops, who impressed him as a "savage looking set of blue birds." Private Mangham and the other pickets listened throughout the following night to the sounds of Union regiments crossing the river, while the remainder of Semmes's Brigade moved into line of battle, anchored on an artillery battery directly behind Howison's house.[55]

Things remained quiet in Semmes's sector on April 30, although his men clearly heard cannonading and musketry downriver to their right. Orders came at sunset to move in the opposite direction, however, into the Wilderness west of Fredericksburg. Lee had gotten wind of the threat to his left flank, and was moving troops as fast as he could to meet it, leaving but one of his six available divisions to delay the Federals crossing at Fredericksburg itself. John Mangham was among the Georgia infantrymen marching out the Orange Plank Road west of town that night, passing one crossroads marked by little Salem Church, and pulling up short of the intersection with the Orange Turnpike. Here, Semmes's Georgians filed into line on the right of "Fighting Billy" Mahone's brigade, whose left was in turn anchored on the turnpike. Major General Richard H. Anderson was in charge of this sector, and his pickets had been driven in that evening by Federals advancing in great force along the Turnpike and Plank Road, so a general attack was expected in the morning. The 53rd Georgia took position shortly after midnight, so the crackle of rifle fire that greeted the dawn on May 1 interrupted a short night's sleep.[56]

Instead of the anticipated attack, however, the popping muskets of skirmishers soon evidenced a surprising development: the Federals had fallen back to the west! Lee had reinforced Gen. Thomas J. Jackson's 2nd Army Corps with Anderson's and McLaws's divisions of Longstreet's 1st Corps, and Stonewall issued orders to stop digging and start marching west to close with Hooker's army. After some feverish marching and countermarching, Jackson launched some 13,000 men down the turnpike, while another 27,000 marched westward along the plank road. The turnpike was the more northerly of the two routes leading directly towards Hooker's Federals, and John Mangham was among those hiking down it by noon on May 1.[57]

The two leading brigades met resistance near Zoan Church, where the Old Mine Road intersected the turnpike, and Semmes's Brigade double-quicked a mile or more to file into line just south of the turnpike. Deploying under a "scattering fire" from rifles and cannon, the Georgians barely got into line before the fire grew heavier and a "sharp contest" ensued at close range. Most of the fighting was along the road, where the 51st Georgia suffered about one hundred casualties in heavy combat. The firing spread down the line of the 10th Georgia to the 53rd, where John and his comrades fired only one to two rounds apiece toward the nearly invisible foe. The attackers were repulsed handily, and the Georgians eventually pursued them two miles or more through the woods, glorying in the debris of abandoned knapsacks, blankets, and overcoats that marked the trail of the retreating enemy. That evening, the chase ended

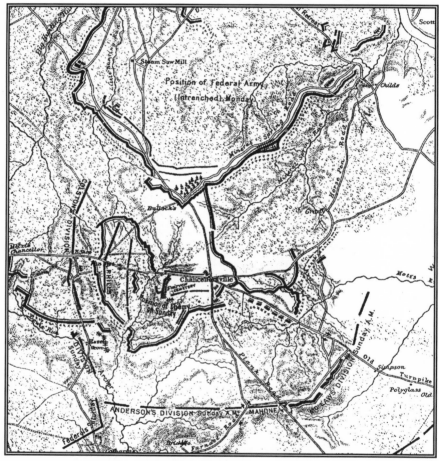

CHANCELLORSVILLE, VIRGINIA, APRIL - MAY, 1863.
PVT. JOHN S. MANGHAM, 53RD GEORGIA, WENT INTO ACTION ALONG THE ORANGE
TURNPIKE EAST OF CHANCELLORSVILLE.
HE SERVED WITH MCLAWS'S DIVISION (LOWER RIGHT).

when the advancing Georgians struck the Federal pickets covering the main line back at Chancellorsville. These bluecoats were not moving anytime soon, so Semmes's men halted in line of battle for the night. Anyone expecting the next days to bring hard

266

fighting would have his expectations met in full, but few could imagine that their army's maneuvers would go down in history as a classic of modern strategy.[58]

The aggressive advance of Jackson's men had caused Hooker to concentrate his force near the Chancellor house, and heavy skirmishing on Saturday, May 2, kept him pinioned there. For John Mangham, this meant a day of marching "backwards and forwards," followed by an advance in line of battle, and then finally stopping to prepare breastworks facing the Federal lines, amidst nearly continuous skirmishing. While these demonstrations kept Hooker's attention oriented east and south of his heavily fortified lines, Jackson swung a heavy column around into the Federal right rear. As skirmishing in Semmes's front waxed during the late afternoon, Jackson landed the blow that has assured Chancellorsville its place in the annals of military history. He smashed and rolled up Hooker's flank in fighting of terrific intensity, which finally sputtered to a close late that night.[59]

Although Stonewall Jackson was mortally wounded that night by North Carolinians who mistook his mounted party for a Union cavalry sortie, Lee continued hammering the Union lines throughout the following day in an attempt to complete his foe's destruction. In heavy skirmishing north and east of Chancellorsville, John Mangham and his regiment approached to within 150 yards of the enemy's breastworks near the Chancellor house itself. There they halted in a low marshy area covered in waist-high alder bushes. Federal pickets firing from covered positions had a field day shooting at the exposed Georgians, and four or five minutes of the unequal contest dropped about twenty-five men in companies B and C, while killing one and wounding four or five more from the Doyal Volunteers. More fortunate than many of his friends, John Wood of Company B was saved by one of the little alders, which deflected a Minie ball bound to hit him at waist level.[60]

The regiment filed by the left flank to escape the hail of bullets, marching at the left oblique until the brigade reformed line of battle and approached the turnpike. The Georgians reveled in the sight that greeted them there. As Wood described in a letter home, the "Vandals had surrendered to the amount of two or three thousand," and the men even got a look at General Lee as he and his staff rode to where Semmes's Brigade lay in line of battle. Captain Peter McGlashan of the 50th Georgia saw Lee talking with Maj. Gen. Lafayette McLaws, the division commander, just a short distance away. As the two commanders concluded their discussion, "Marse Robert" lifted his voice for all to hear, announcing, "Now, General, there is a chance for your young men to distinguish themselves." Semmes's men were called to attention, stood up and filled their cartridge boxes, then filed onto the road where the streams of prisoners cleared hastily out of their way. Wood noted that the "Yanky prisoners, stretched their necks and eyes to get a peep at Gen. Lee" as he passed, and McGlashan was struck by their reaction to the fabled Confederate commander. Noticing an "exciting murmur" passing through the ranks of the Federals, McGlashan heard them calling out: "That's him! that's Lee! Hats off, boys!" The defeated bluecoats pulled off their hats and stared at the man who had engineered their undoing on so many fields, and Lee gravely, even sadly, lifted his hat and bowed in acknowledgement of their salute. The Georgia captain thought Lee "at the zenith of his fame," and Semmes's Brigade cheered the prisoners for their simple and manly recognition of the great chieftain.[61]

Lee, the "gray and bald headed, wise looking old man," was in the process of winning one of the most astounding victories in modern military history, but the ferocious combat just that morning had cost him 8962 dead, wounded and missing. More was yet to come, for couriers informed Lee that additional Federals were coming up the Orange Plank Road from Fredericksburg, bound directly for his army's rear. Although he had intended to commit McLaws's Division to the pursuit of the Federals streaming towards the Rappahannock fords, he now was forced to send the division back towards Fredericksburg to try to prevent a possible disaster.[62]

Brigadier General Cadmus Wilcox's Alabama brigade was the only force between Lee's rear and Maj. Gen. John Sedgwick's approaching host, which had punched a hole through the thinly manned Confederate lines at Fredericksburg before striking out to join Hooker. Wilcox was fighting a skillful delaying action along the Orange Plank Road, and the men of the approaching 53rd Georgia heard heavy skirmish firing before they had proceeded two miles on their eastward march. To Private Wood's ear, the firing sounded as though it was developing into a general engagement before the regiment covered another mile. Continuing on their way towards the roar of battle, they paused for a brief rest about a mile west of Salem Church, the little country church they had passed on their way to Chancellorsville just three days earlier. After their ten-minute rest, the Georgians were called to attention and hustled down the road to Wilcox's aid.[63]

Arriving just as a spattering fire announced a renewed Federal advance, the men saw that the blue tide was about to surge over high ground which would command the Confederate position completely. Veterans that they were, the arriving regiments took in the situation at a glance: unless they moved fast, they were doomed. Regimental commanders led their men forward at the run without awaiting formal orders from the brigade commander, forming "like lightning" by the right into line at a cedar wattle fence on the edge of the field to their front. The 50th Georgia lost fifteen or twenty men to a "terrible fire" at sixty yards' range, before charging forward with a "wild yell" into line with the 53rd Georgia to their left. There, Yankees were only 75 yards away and closing fast as John Mangham and his comrades scrambled into position behind the brush fence, with men dropping right and left "under a storm of bullets." Wilcox's brigade stood astride the road facing east, and Semmes's men fought their way into position on the Alabamians' left flank just in time to prevent them being swamped by the two Federal brigades closing in for the kill. Had the Georgians arrived just moments later, the outnumbered defenders would have faced a hand-to-hand melee that would have negated any advantages of position and cover offered by the defensive line they held.[64]

Lieutenant John Evans of the Jackson Guards, Wiley Mangham's old company, assured his wife later that ". . .you may believe that we gave them buck and ball in a hurry." These compliments were returned with vigor; some fast-firing New Jerseymen desperately tried to reload their badly leaded rifles by inserting the ramrod after the bullet and then jamming it against a tree. Stymied in their frenzied attempts to drive the Minie balls down the barrel, many simply picked up guns from the fallen and resumed their places in the firing line. With both sides pouring it on for all they were worth, the roar mounted to a maddening crescendo of sound. John Wood believed that he had "never heard such a noise in all my life," with the possible exception of

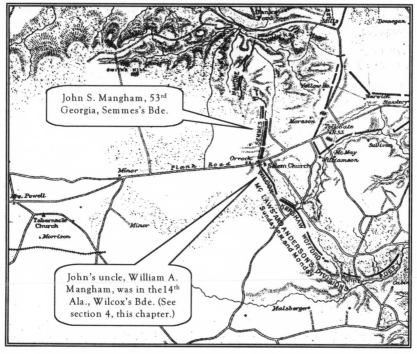

John S. Mangham, 53rd Georgia, Semmes's Bde.

John's uncle, William A. Mangham, was in the 14th Ala., Wilcox's Bde. (See section 4, this chapter.)

SALEM CHURCH, VIRGINIA, MAY 3, 1863.

PVT. JOHN S. MANGHAM, 53RD GEORGIA, SEMMES'S BRIGADE, HELPED HOLD THE LINE JUST ABOVE THE ORANGE PLANK ROAD, SAVING LEE'S ARMY FROM ATTACK IN THE REAR. JOHN WAS MORTALLY WOUNDED SHORTLY THEREAFTER.

Malvern Hill. An awed New Jersey lieutenant to his front noted that the din of musketry and the boom of Federal guns, combined with the crash of shot and shell through the treetops, made it "quite impossible to hear a voice." Several companies of the 53rd Georgia assumed a "beautiful position in a little trench, behind an embankment, formed by the fence," where the men could load and fire without exposing more than their heads and arms to the hurricane of fire. John Mangham's Company A fired only some fifteen rounds per man, since the terrain and vegetation screened their view of the enemy, but their crossfire with Company B and others took a fearful toll of the attackers. Wood noted, "You may well guess, that we made things count when we let loose at them." Companies H, I, and K poured it on, expending 55 to 60 rounds apiece, since "they could see the Vandals" out in the open.[65]

In the ferocious close-range firefight, men dropped like flies, and Lieutenant Colonel Kearse of the 50th Georgia called out to Captain McGlashan in desperation: "I shall have no regiment left if this lasts a half hour longer. Oh, that the sun would set; is there no supports?" At the very peak of the crisis, however, the Alabamians came screaming out of their entrenchments at the stunned Yankees. When the 10th and 51st Georgia joined in the perfectly timed counterattack, retreat turned into rout for the fought-out Federal brigades. Semmes's left flank regiments, the 53rd and 50th Georgia, did not get the word to charge in the smoke-enshrouded forest, but the 53rd captured the national colors of the 2nd Rhode Island Volunteers in the swirling close-range combat. In all probability, the Georgians had shot down the color guard and rendered it impossible for anyone else to approach the fallen colors. Apparently, they dropped the Rhode Islanders' regimental flag at least once as well, but this banner was spared capture. As men of the 50th Georgia made a dash for the colors of a New York regiment, the quick-thinking color bearer tore the flag from its staff and ran for it, leaving the Georgians with nothing but the staff.[66]

After Wilcox's five regiments and Semmes's pair chased their battered quarry almost a mile up the turnpike, the explosion of case shot and shell overhead indicated that they were coming up against a fresh Federal force. When the guns switched to canister, complemented by rifle fire from massed ranks of additional troops, Wilcox halted his charge, surveyed the situation, and ordered his men back into their positions at Salem Church. The two brigades had fought one of the most outstanding small unit actions of the war, deterring any further advance by Sedgwick's corps towards Lee's rear.[67]

John Wood was extremely proud of his regiment's role in the battle, especially its fast and accurate shooting, and informed his aunt, "It is said that our regt. done the best shooting that ever been done since the war commenced." Even so, he admitted that the "dead Yanks" that carpeted the battlefield made it look "more like a slaughter pen, than any thing else." Above all, the "shrieks and groans of the wounded. . .was heart rending, beyond all description. You can't imagine what an awful sight it is to visit a battle field, just after a hard fought battle."[68]

The following day, the men of the 53rd picked up 460 rifles left by their battered opponents, and dug trenches with their bayonets and bare hands in case the conflict resumed. But Sedgwick, like Hooker, had gotten his fill of Rebel soldiers for the time being. Although the Confederates essayed a final effort to cut off their retreating foe near Fredericksburg, the Federals made their way back across the Rappahannock amid torrential rains. The Chancellorsville campaign was over; it had been the costliest battle in the Army of the Potomac's history, with 17,304 Union soldiers killed, wounded, or missing. General Lee's forces likewise had suffered terribly in victory, suffering 1724 dead, 9233 wounded, and 2503 missing. Semmes's Brigade reported 603 casualties, although the casualty lists published in the *Macon Telegraph* listed only 575 of them.[69]

The published list named 15 men of the 53rd Georgia killed in action, as well as another 103 wounded. One of the dead belonged to the Doyal Volunteers, whose casualty list also bore the names of seven men wounded in the fighting. One of those not listed was Pvt. John S. Mangham, who was admitted into the general hospital (as J. T. Mangum) at Camp Winder, near Richmond, on May 12, 1863, suffering from a gunshot wound. It is not known if he was wounded near Chancellorsville or at Salem Church, or perhaps even by accident after the fighting was over. Two days after he arrived at the crowded hospital, however, he died of his wounds in the same hospital where his uncle Wiley Pendleton Mangham died ten months earlier.[70]

John S. Mangham is believed to have been eighteen years old. Although the cause of his injury is uncertain, it is most likely that he was wounded in action. If so, he is the only Mangham Confederate soldier known to have died as a direct result of wounds inflicted by the enemy. In common with the great majority of Confederate soldiers interred in the burial trenches surrounding the army's teeming hospitals, his burial site is known but to God.

Peace to his ashes.

3. MYSTERY LIMPS ON A WOODEN LEG: PVT. JOHN H. MANGHAM, "GEORGE PLAYER CAVALIERS," CO. A, 30TH ALABAMA; ANDERSON'S BATTERY, VIRGINIA ARTILLERY

If John S. Mangham was in fact an orphaned grandson of James M. Mangham of Butts County, he may well have been named after James's son *John Henry Mangham*.

This man is one of the family's great enigmas of the Civil War era, for few pieces of documentary evidence concerning him are fully consistent with each other! Prewar references identify him as Henry Mangham (or Mangum), or as John H. Mangham, whereas wartime and early postwar records consistently use the latter name. From 1881 to 1910, however, veteran's pension documents referring to "W. H. Mangham" clearly are based upon John H. Mangham's service records. Intriguing errors in these files imply that he may have falsified some salient facts about his wartime service record, perhaps in order to qualify for a larger pension. Since seventeen separate pension documents give the applicant's initials as "W. H." (Mangham or Mangum), it may well be that the initial "W." stood for an unknown first or middle name. Many Mangham children of his generation had three given names, including his brother *James M. D. Mangham*, so the possibility is not purely academic.[71]

A less savory alternative that suggests itself is that his brother, *William A. Mangham*, assumed John H. Mangham's identity for pension purposes, and that the misstatements of fact in the pension files arose from his ignorance of certain key events in Henry's wartime service. This seems unlikely, however, since the applicant's wife (and witness) was Eliza A. Mangham, who married Henry Mangham in 1852. Most convincing, perhaps, is the fact that "W. H." Mangham received his disability pension due to the amputation of his left leg, a mishap that befell John H. Mangham during the war. William would have been singularly unfortunate to lose the same limb, especially since he survived the war unmaimed.[72]

Apparently, Henry was born in Butts County, Georgia, on February 2, 1828, although other records indicate he was born as early as 1823 or as late as 1835. The earlier dates seem most consistent with the record of "Henry Mangum," who would have been 21 when he married 15-year-old Eliza T. Devaughn in Coosa County, Alabama, in September 1849. Henry probably was the first of the James M. Mangham family to move westward into Alabama, although he was followed soon by his eldest brother James, who settled in Chambers County. Henry and Eliza lived on a small farm next to the Devaughn family in Coosa's Hatchet Creek district for some time, but she must have died not long after their marriage; in 1852, Henry married one of his other Hatchet Creek neighbors, Eliza Bearden, in neighboring Talladega County. When the census-taker came by their home in Sylacauga in 1860, John was employed as a marble cutter at the rich quarries located nearby, and little Polly (5) and Francis (2) lived at home with 23-year-old Eliza.[73] (See map on page 566.)

There is no way to tell what Henry thought of the outbreak of war in the spring of 1861, or whether he knew that his brother Willis enlisted back in Butts County. In all probability, he was aware that his brother William had signed up that summer in Chambers County, about forty-five miles away. Like his other brothers Wiley and James, Henry decided not to rush things. After the initial victories of 1861, however, bad news from the western battlefronts threatened to drown the glad tidings of the New Year. As historian James McPherson has written, "The urge to defend hearth and home that had impelled so many Southerners to enlist in 1861 took on greater urgency when large-scale invasions became a reality in 1862." Disastrous defeats at Forts Henry and Donelson led to the abandonment of Kentucky and Nashville in February, and President Davis issued a fresh call for volunteers to stem the tide of disaster. At the same time, the Confederate Congress authorized soldiers currently in service to take leave to raise new companies and regiments.[74]

The president gave Alabama a quota of 12,500 men, which equated to twelve new regiments of ten companies each. The state in turn directed Talladega County to raise three of the new companies, and Capt. Charles M. Shelley returned home from the army in Virginia to raise a regiment from eastern Alabama. James Mallory, a southern Talladega County farmer, came into Sylacauga on February 22 for "dinner and speaches" in honor of the company being raised by Dr. William C. Patterson. Mallory noted the "great liberality and effort to provide men for the war," adding, ". . .we lacked them in Tennessee and will now have to put them their at larger expense." Just five days later, Dr. Patterson completed the company's organization, assisted by Mr. Henry P. Oden, owner of one of the local marble works. By the last day of March, the company's rolls had risen to 84 officers and men in anticipation of its acceptance into Confederate service. One of those enrolled in February was Pvt. John H. Mangham, who probably was one of Oden's employees at the marble works. He helped select the company's nickname, the "George Player Cavaliers," in honor of a local citizen who donated money to supply and equip them.[75]

When Henry joined the company, it was encamped at Sylacauga's Camp Curry, a State Camp of Instruction named for local notable J. L. M. Curry. Talladega County had mustered four companies for the new regiment, thus exceeding its quota and ensuring a strong constituency for Captain Shelley, who was duly elected colonel of the newly minted 30th Regiment, Alabama Volunteer Infantry. The raw recruits spent April learning the intricacies of drill, which was relieved a bit by dress parade on Sundays, brief furloughs home, and the April 15 arrival of sixty Union officer prisoners. Henry and his comrades were assigned to guard the prison stockade, where their first military duty gave them a look at real, live Yankees, albeit tame ones. Without a doubt, the Alabamians razzed the "Vandal invaders" about the shoe being on the other foot now, but any thoughtful sentry certainly must have ruminated on the uncertainties he himself faced in the weeks and months to come.[76]

The call to duty came on May 5, 1862. After a day of feverish preparation, the regiment pulled out of Talladega's railroad depot amid a "dense crowd" at 8:00 a.m. on May 7, bound for Chattanooga. The circuitous route followed by the 30th Alabama graphically illustrates the logistical challenges bedeviling Confederate attempts to defend their far-flung borders. In order to reach Chattanooga, which lay about 150 miles north and east of Talladega, the train struck off to the southwest towards Selma! The men were "crowded thick as hops" into eighteen boxcars, but reveled in the spectacle of women throwing flowers while crowds cheered their passing heroes. Lieutenant Kelly of Company E thought it a grand sight, as "All seemed to cheer us on in our cause, the negroes were as intent as their mistresses." When the baggage car came uncoupled from the train, it fell four miles behind before the jam-packed men could pass the word along to the engineer.[77]

Reaching Selma at 4:30 p.m. after a trip of some ninety miles, the regiment filed aboard the *Southern Republic*, "a very large, fine boat," and hove to for Montgomery. As the steamer wended its way up the Alabama River to the capital city, it sounded its whistle at a boat coming in the opposite direction. The blaring noise startled a soldier dozing near the edge, and as he scrambled to his feet he slipped and tumbled overboard to his death. The trip was otherwise uneventful, and the *Southern Republic* docked at Montgomery about 8:30 a.m. on May 8. The next several days were spent aboard trains en route to Atlanta, Big Shanty, and Dalton. Now on the last 25 miles of their roundabout journey, the Alabamians learned first-hand that plans change rapidly in wartime: they passed through Chattanooga and continued on towards Knoxville, 110 miles from Dalton. As they rattled along the rails to their new destination, the men could sense a distinct change in the atmosphere; far from the cheering throngs of Alabama and Georgia, many of the men and women in the mountainous sections of East Tennessee simply "stood and gazed" at the train. Although most folks bade the passing soldiers "God Speed," the Alabama men decided it was easy enough to tell a "Lincolnite" from a secessionist. It was an omen of hard times to come in this desperately poor and largely Unionist section, which would become one of the most bitterly contested areas of the war. With skimpy communications by road and rail, this economic backwater could not support large concentrations of troops on prolonged campaigns, but neither side was willing to forego the effort to secure the region for its cause.[78]

The citizens of Knoxville itself were strongly Southern in sentiment, however, and the ladies welcomed the arriving Alabamians with flowers and buckets of buttermilk on May 11. The regiment drew rifles on May 13 and moved out towards Clinton four days later. The 25-mile route was their first real march, and things went fine for the first eight miles. After eating lunch and moving on again, however, the scorching sun, rough roads, and broken country began to take their toll. An amazed Lt. Sam Kelly thought he "never saw men fail faster"; only about two hundred men arrived at their campsite that evening, while half again that number straggled behind. Sleeping on the ground that night, they awakened to pouring rain and a cold breakfast before hitting the road again. Although in good spirits at the idea of moving on, they were still not conditioned for hard marching. When Lieutenant Kelly arrived at Clinton that evening, he estimated that only about one company's worth of men closed up that night; the other ninety percent were strewn along the roadside back towards Knoxville. (See maps on pp. 125, 519, 566.)[79]

During the next ten days, the 30th Alabama worked its way towards Cumberland Gap, where Tennessee, Kentucky and Virginia intersect at a road that provides the primary north-south communications in the region. There, Lieutenant Kelly took command of a detachment of twenty-seven men from Henry's Company A, supplemented by seven men from Company E. These men stood guard in rifle pits covering the right flank of the Gap, while another eight or ten such detachments outposted the remainder of the strategic passage. The inhospitable mountain terrain offered many unique challenges, even to men from the hills of Talladega. Kelly noted his men had to "sleep steep. . . .We are one part in Virginia and the other in Tennessee." The regiment remained here on guard duty for several weeks, snaring an occasional "Lincolnite" attempting to scout the defenses, and suffering from the camp diseases that began decimating their ranks. Writing on June 3, Lieutenant Kelly mused, "The army is the worst place for measles and mumps. The 30th Ala. regiment would have nine hundred instead of four hundred to-day if it were not for those diseases." Poor rations did not help matters either, and the men ate "bread, meat, and water for breakfast; meat, bread, and water for dinner, and so on day after day." The local inhabitants made a poor impression, too:

> With few exceptions, the corn cribs here are about as large as your ash house. The children are bad looking and the women are pale and nearly all go barefooted. They live on slab floors, and many families do not know a dollar from ten cents. Talking of ignorance and degeneration, East Tennessee is the place.[80]

The middle of June found the regiment "in an uproar" over reports of enemy movements through mountain passes on the flanks of Cumberland Gap. Called into line on the night of June 11, the men formed across the road under the dim light of a lunar eclipse, which eventually passed into complete darkness. Late that night, soaking wet from wading creeks and pouring with sweat from their exertions, they lay down on their arms and slept. It was one of several such confusing nights, as the outnumbered

Confederates were maneuvered out of their positions at Cumberland Gap. For Henry and the 30th Alabama, the retreat began after darkness on June 17, with the men stumbling towards Morristown on what Sam Kelly believed was "the roughest road (I could not see it) that I ever travelled." Wading Powell's River at 10:30 that night, they came to the Clinch River at about three o'clock the next morning. While the men waited to cross on flatboats, pouring rains chilled them to the bone. As the retreat continued, it was impossible to ensure that everyone had a chance to cook rations. Although they worked their few skillets "double quick time all night," the results were uneven: "Some got some, and some got none."[81]

Although the men were disheartened at the retreat, some thought the barrens of East Tennessee were of precious little use to their opponents' cause:

> I see no inducement in this country; there are very few people, the poorest, most ignorant, and worst looking I ever saw,—dirt eaters,—but they have to eat something and there is very little else to eat. The corn is from two blades to knee high except one piece about waist high. The rows run round the hill too steep to walk up.[82]

The regiment remained near Morristown and Clinch Mountain through most of July, but the latter part of that month saw the Confederates resume the offensive. This time, they were part of a larger forward movement which saw General Bragg's army advance from Corinth, Mississippi, to cooperate with Maj. Gen. Edmund Kirby Smith's forces in East Tennessee and Kentucky. Kirby Smith sent Brig. Gen. Carter L. Stevenson's division back north towards Cumberland Gap in early August, and the 30th Alabama marched with it as part of Brig. Gen. Seth M. Barton's brigade.[83]

The men may have seen some action in their retreat from the Gap in mid-June, but they certainly fought a sharp action on August 6, 1862, near Tazewell. There, about twelve miles southeast of the Gap, Stevenson heard reports of a Federal advance in some strength. Barton's Brigade was among those hurled against the force, which apparently comprised an infantry brigade seeking to obtain forage. The Confederates assaulted the enemy line on a crest of hills about a mile from Tazewell, driving them down into and across the valley behind. There the main line halted, skirmishing with the bluecoats until the latter pulled back into the woods and broke contact. The Federals claimed it as a successful foraging expedition, while the 30th Alabama and their comrades viewed it as a victorious repulse of an enemy advance.[84]

The latter part of August saw Stevenson's Division confront the Federal force at Cumberland Gap, while Kirby Smith crossed the remainder of his army into Kentucky via Big Creek Gap. His maneuver made the Cumberland Gap fortifications untenable for Gen. George Morgan's Federals, so they pulled back into Kentucky on September 17-18. But as Barton's Brigade followed them into the Bluegrass State, Pvt. Henry Mangham was no longer marching with the 30th Alabama. On August 31, he had transferred into the brigade's artillery battery, commanded by Capt. Joseph W. Anderson.[85]

Anderson's men hailed from Botetourt County, Virginia, and Henry probably transferred into this outfit to help fill its thinning ranks, as did several other Alabama and Georgia soldiers from the brigade's infantry regiments. At the end of June, only 102 officers and men were present for duty from the battery's normal complement of 165 men, and the hardships of the East Tennessee campaign doubtless disabled many more by August. With active operations resuming at Cumberland Gap, it was critical that the brigade's artillery battery be restored to full capability.[86]

Anderson's Battery moved into Cumberland Gap on September 20 before pushing on through the mountains into Kentucky. After eight days' hard marching through a parched countryside suffering from three months of drought, they arrived at Danville on September 28. Pausing to spruce up for a day, many of the men seized the opportunity to get "very tight" on the plentiful whiskey. Hung-over or not, they passed in review for General Bragg the next day, before moving out of town to camp farther north. On the night of October 1, the artillerymen spent much of the evening serenading the local belles in Lawrenceburg, a town the Rebs dubbed "Little Dixie." While at Rough-and-Ready, they heard reports that the enemy was sallying forth from Louisville. Expecting a fight at last, they ran the wagons to the rear and prepared the guns for action. It turned out to be a false alarm, however, so their preparations were all for naught.[87]

On the evening of October 2, Henry and his Virginia comrades arrived in Frankfort, the capital of Kentucky. Feted by ladies who welcomed them as deliverers from Yankee occupation, one of Anderson's men exulted, "Never was an army in such glorious spirits!" It must have been heady stuff indeed for Henry, who had enlisted that spring when the Confederacy's star seemed in imminent danger of eclipse. Now men wondered what would come next. Was it west to Louisville and the Ohio River, just thirty miles away? Or north to Cincinnati, only eighty miles distant? Or perhaps a showdown with Buell's Federals in Kentucky? Anything seemed possible, as Richard Hawes was inaugurated Confederate governor of Kentucky in ceremonies at Frankfort on a rainy October 4.[88]

On that very day, however, Anderson's Battery was ordered southwards out of Frankfort, and the bridge was set afire behind it. The Confederates were moving to concentrate for battle, and Henry and his comrades marched fourteen miles that night. After resting a couple of days, the battery marched to the vicinity of Harrodsburg, but like many other elements of the army they never were fully concentrated and ordered into the ensuing action. The Battle of Perryville, which occurred on October 8, 1862, was as close as the armies of Bragg and Smith ever got to the climactic battle expected by so many. In a hard-fought struggle that engaged only a portion of Bragg's army, the embattled Federals barely managed to hold the field against less than half of their numbers; the Confederates clearly held both the field and the initiative. Although Barton's Brigade was under fire at Perryville, it was never committed to the fight; instead, it spent the day shuttling back and forth to points of perceived danger. But in one of the strangest and most disastrous decisions of the entire war, Bragg declined to resume the fight the next day, even after combining with Kirby Smith's whole force.

After several days in defensive positions that the Federal forces declined to attack, Bragg decided instead to pull out of Kentucky altogether to avoid being cut off from his base at Chattanooga.[89]

For Henry and the frustrated Virginia artillerymen, the order to turn southward to Tennessee once more was a bitter pill to swallow. Orders being orders, however, they marched back down the road on which they had entered the land of milk and honey. Lieutenant John Johnston wrote home to Botetourt County in utter disgust, declaring that "the demoralization, the disgust, the loss of confidence" had done more damage to morale and efficiency than a pitched battle could have done. The soldiers were astounded that their apparent victory at Perryville, coming on the heels of a victorious campaign throughout Kentucky, resulted in an ignominious retreat. Johnston opined, "I cannot depict to you how great is our mortification at this move. . .Bragg should not only be cashiered, but actually taken out and hanged." Still fuming with impotent rage, the cannoneers eventually marched back through Cumberland Gap on October 20.[90]

Broken down by the hardships of the march, Henry reported sick that same day, but was able to remain with the battery as it moved on to camp on the Holston River three days later. He continued onward with the unit to Knoxville, where they received orders on November 2 to rejoin the brigade southwest of town at Lenoir Station. Apparently, however, Henry's left foot was mangled terribly in an accident during the thirty-mile move. On January 22, 1863, an army surgeon at Knoxville filled out a certificate of disability for discharge:

> I certify, that I have carefully examined the said Priv. J. H. Mangham of Captain Anderson's Battery, and find him incapable of performing the duties of a soldier because of loss of left foot caused by rail-road accident necessitating amputation, above the ankle. I recommend his discharge.

/s/ *James B. Murfree*, Surgeon
Discharged this 22[d] day of January, 1863, at Knoxville, Tenn.
/s/ *J. I. Moseley*, Commanding the Post

With the last flourish of Moseley's pen, the military odyssey of John Henry Mangham was effectively at a close.[91]

Now he faced increasingly hard times back home in Talladega County, where a one-legged stone cutter had little chance to earn a living, and a dwindling chance of receiving assistance from those whose rights he had fought to defend. Planter James Mallory, whose modestly prosperous Selwood Plantation stood some seven miles north of Sylacauga, was appalled at the change of heart apparent among those he believed were "most forward in bringing on the war." By the end of 1863, Mallory was complaining that these erstwhile fire-eaters "close their pockets and hearts against the soldiers and suffering poor." The normally mild-mannered farmer added grimly, "What a poor currency. Thieveing quarter Masters and contracters, misers and poor and weak legislators, with a determined enemy I fear lest God comes to our help we are gone and ruined." By early April of the following year, a Talladega County citizens' council reported their desperate straits to the governor. The second article of their petition read, "At that time, May, 1861, there was a white population in the county of 14,634 persons, and a slave population of about 8,865 persons, and there were only about 30 persons who needed and received aid from the county. Now there are 3,997." The situation would only get worse, however, as powerful columns of Federal cavalrymen passed through Talladega County in July 1864, and again in April 1865. Perhaps the recurring threat convinced Henry Mangham to seek safety elsewhere in the state.[92]

*   *   *   *   *

The name of John H. Mangham next appeared in Hale County, Alabama, where he registered to vote in Greensboro on July 15, 1867. Along with the great majority of his fellow Southerners, he swallowed his pride, signed the Oath of Allegiance to the United States, and "slid back into the Union" after a hiatus of more than six years. Why he had moved west to Hale County is unclear, but he must have struggled to make ends meet. After applying for an artificial leg as John H. Mangham in May 1868, "W. H. Mangum" applied again in 1873. Six years later he applied for relief. In 1881, the Alabama state legislature passed an "Act for the Relief of Maimed Soldiers," and "W. H. Mangum" applied for assistance in Calhoun County, where he then resided. Intriguingly, he stated that his left leg was amputated by Dr. *Murphy* at Knoxville, as a result of wounds received while a member of Company A, 30th Alabama, at the Battle of Perryville, Kentucky, in *September* 1862. In fact, a Dr. *Murfree* recommended his discharge at Knoxville in January 1863, and may well have been the surgeon who removed Henry's lower leg. Henry was a member of Anderson's Battery from August 31, 1862, and that unit and the 30th Alabama were both under fire at Perryville in *October* 1862. Perhaps he stated that he was wounded while serving with his old Alabama unit in order to qualify for a state pension he feared might otherwise be denied him, since his injury occurred while serving in a company from Virginia. His application further stated that he had received an artificial leg, but he "was never able to use the same & it was therefore of no benefit to him whatever."[93]

"W. H. Mangum" regularly applied for pension renewal through the 1880s and 1890s. Although he began signing his name as "Mangham" in 1889, it was 1892 before Calhoun's Probate Judge filled out the form that way! He listed his occupation as farming, and apparently rented properties near Alexandria and Ohatchie in 1896 and 1897, respectively. By 1899, he had moved to Wetumpka in Elmore County, where he worked as a turnkey in the State Penitentiary and joined the local chapter of the United Confederate Veterans (UCV). His detailed pension application that year stated that he was struck in the left leg by a Minie ball at Perryville, resulting in amputation of his left leg. The 1899 application specified that his leg was "off above knee joint," which is significantly worse than was stated on his 1863 discharge form or in his 1868 application for an artificial leg.[94]

By 1900, Henry and Eliza had returned to Alexandria in Calhoun County, where he rented a small farm, assisted by a young farmhand, James Bowden.[95] The following year, Henry served as Doorkeeper of the Gallery for the state constitutional convention in Montgomery; he may have remained in the capital city until October 1906, when he moved into the state Confederate Soldiers' Home at Mountain Creek in Chilton County. He moved out again in May 1907, filing an intriguing pension affidavit in February 1908 with the Chilton County authorities. He testified that he was born in Butts County, Georgia, on February 2, 1828; had enlisted at Sylacauga on February 27, 1862; had served under Colonel Shelley in Company A, 30th Alabama, Barton's Brigade, *Chetom's Division*; and had lost his leg at Perryville on October 8, 1862 (the correct date of the battle). Henry Mangham served under Shelley in Barton's Brigade of Stevenson's Division, not the more famous Cheatham's Division of the late-war Army of Tennessee. Was the old veteran's memory failing? Or was his brother, who had served in the Army of Northern Virginia, giving his *own* birthdate and grasping at straws when asked for the name of his former division commander?[96]

Upon examination of all the evidence, it is possible that the other elements of this man's story were correct (excepting the erroneous reference to Cheatham's Division) and that the error lay in his military records. Was he indeed slightly wounded by a stray bullet at Perryville, losing his leg some weeks later after an infection ensued? Since the discharge papers that referred to his railroad accident were incomplete, it is reasonable to question their accuracy. Likewise, it is plausible that Henry believed he was attached only temporarily to Anderson's Battery, while remaining permanently assigned to the 30th Alabama. Anyone familiar with Civil War medicine and the complexities of military personnel records will recognize that these possibilities are real.

It strains credulity, however, to conclude that John Henry Mangham adopted the name *William* Henry Mangham in honor of his (deceased?) brother, especially when it came time to claim a pension based on the military service records of *John* H. Mangham, 30th Alabama.

*   *   *   *   *

Was this old, disabled pensioner in fact John Henry Mangham, or his brother, William A. Mangham? A mystery to the very end, he took his secret to the grave when he died at the Soldiers' Home on February 28, 1910. He is buried in the Confederate Memorial Park cemetery in Montgomery, Alabama, under a stone marked "W. H. Mangham, Co. A, 30th Ala. Inf., d. Feb. 28, 1910, aged 81 yrs."[97]

4. FIGHTING FOR A SMALL BAY MULE & A COTTON PATCH: PVT. WILLIAM A. MANGHAM, "CUSSETA GREYS," CO. A, 14TH ALABAMA

At least fifty years before "William H. Mangham" was laid to rest in the cemetery at the Soldiers Home, William A. Mangham had moved west from Butts County into Alabama's booming Chambers County. By 1860, he had joined his brother *James M. D. Mangham* and his family on their eighty-acre farm near the village of Oak Bowery, just north of the Russell County line. William owned a small bay mule and a little cotton patch in the hollow just south of his brother's land, and helped James's family and four slaves wrest a living from the land. He also worked on J. M. Moon's little farm near DeSoto, a village that lay just across the county line in Tallapoosa County, earning extra cash by helping cultivate a modest crop of wheat, corn and sweet potatoes, plus a little cotton.[98]

When war broke out a year later, William wasted no time in choosing sides. He was 29 years old but unmarried, so preparing to leave was a simple matter. On May 27, he sold his cotton patch and a "small bay mule supposed to be four years old" to neighbor William Trimble on fire sale terms: one dollar cash as a down payment, with the remainder of the $85 purchase price due by Christmas Day. Like many other Southerners who rallied to the call for armed resistance in 1861, William may have felt impelled by a belief that Lincoln's Republican administration represented an implacable threat to the South's way of life. Perhaps he simply longed above all else to experience adventure of a magnitude normally denied to a poor man plowing a mule, toiling on the lower margins of white society. Although no record exists of his motives for volunteering, the alacrity of his enlistment and the tenacity he displayed over the ensuing four years indicate that he meant the oath he swore in 1861. Undeterred by repeated bouts of illness, wounds, and the horrendous casualties that depleted his regiment's ranks time after time, William A. Mangham stood by the colors to answer the 14th Alabama's final roll call on April 9, 1865, at Appomattox Court House.[99]

His military odyssey began officially on July 26, 1861, when he enlisted in nearby Cusseta, where Captain William D. Harrington was raising a company nicknamed the "Cusseta Greys." The company was one of five from Chambers County that formed the core of Col. Thomas J. Judge's regiment of east Alabamians. Already organized in April, the unit was not recruited and mustered into Confederate service until August 7, probably due to the paucity of arms that hindered rapid mobilization of regiments on both sides of the Mason-Dixon Line. After two months at Camp Johnson, a camp of instruction at nearby Auburn, the regiment moved north to Huntsville in early October. There, as William's comrade Jabez W. Burdett recalled, ". . .we were expecting the Yankees to land troops coming down the river by boats." Although Federals would indeed come swarming up the Tennessee River in the spring of 1862, the threat in October 1861 proved chimerical.[100]

A month later the situation appeared more threatening in Virginia, so the regiment entrained for the "seat of war" in the Old Dominion. Many of the men were recovering from the first onslaught of measles, and the transfer to Richmond on December 7, followed by a move to Evansport just a week later, proved more than they could stand. The December winds blowing in from the Potomac River chilled them to the marrow, and the poorly acclimated Alabamians began dropping by the score. When New Year's Day finally dawned over the bleak shores of the Potomac, fewer than two hundred men were fit for duty. After just five months of service, more than eighty percent were *hors de combat*, and they had never faced a single Yankee gun! The vicious epidemics raging through the camps of the 14th Alabama caused Judah P. Benjamin, Confederate Secretary of War, to consider it "totally disabled by sickness." Its "deplorable condition" resulted in its transfer to Richmond in late December, exchanging the exposure of picket duty for the relative comforts of barracks at Camp Winder. The enfeebled regiment arrived there on January 3, 1862, and one of the men admitted that day to the sprawling Chimborazo Hospital complex was Pvt. William Mangham. Diagnosed with a severe case of rheumatism, he remained confined in the hospital until February 17.[101]

William was hospitalized in March as well, but probably was with the regiment when it was dispatched to the Peninsula on March 27 in response to Federal movements threatening Yorktown. Establishing their camp at Winn's Mill four miles west of town, a week of quiet duty terminated abruptly on April 5, when frantic couriers brought word of an enemy advance against Dam No. 1, just three-quarters of a mile away. For the first time in their service, the regimental drummers beat the long roll in earnest, and the men marched to the threatened point along the banks of the Warwick River and drew up in line of battle. In the face of light skirmishing, the regiment remained at the river for four days, losing as prisoners a four-man outpost "gobbled" by the 6th Maine. Marching back to Winn's Mill on April 9, they commenced improving their works in the face of increasing Federal activity. As the shriek of cannon shells mixed with the zip of sharpshooters' bullets, the 14th Alabama worked night and day in the pouring rain.[102]

This arduous routine characterized the next several weeks of unceasing labor in the muddy trenches near Yorktown, until the regiment received orders to join the general retreat to Williamsburg on May 3. Exhausted from the constant strain and exposure, William and his comrades struggled down the muddy road shedding equipment at every step; as Pvt. Thomas Barron of Company D commented, each soldier had "to toat all he has" or lose it. As they withdrew through Williamsburg itself, the roar of gunfire in the army's rear caused them to face about and retrace their steps, until they finally took position in a redoubt near Fort Magruder. Their position was one of thirteen small redoubts and redans built to cover the earthen fort, which commanded the junction of the Yorktown and Lee's Mill Roads before Williamsburg. These fortifications, strengthened by an abatis of felled trees that impeded any approach to the bristling earthworks, were perfectly positioned to block Federal pursuit of Johnston's retreating army. William and the men of the 14th Alabama probably knew little of the overall plan of battle, but their regiment and the others of Maj. Gen. James Longstreet's division were entrusted with the mission of serving as the army's rear guard as it continued the retreat. The weather conspired to make their task even more difficult, as the rains that began sluicing down that evening turned the already poor roads into bottomless quagmires. Although this slowed the Federal pursuit, it also hindered Johnston's ability to pull back his artillery and wagon trains in sufficient time to escape. After a miserable night sleeping on their arms in the pouring rain, Longstreet's men were about to fight for the salvation of their army.[103]

The ball opened on the morning of May 5. A desultory artillery duel commenced shortly after 8:00 a.m., giving notice that Union forces under Maj. Gen. Joe Hooker were probing for a way to come to grips with the beleaguered grayjackets. After several hours of firing showed that the Federals still hesitated to come forward in a general assault, Longstreet seized the initiative and flung a portion of his line into the attack. Meeting with initial success, he kept feeding more troops into the attack, until more than ten thousand men were in action on each side. Among those ordered to join the assaulting waves of grayclad infantry were the three left flank companies of the 14th Alabama. William's Company A was the regiment's right flank company, and thus stood fast in its redoubt as the combat assumed an intensity that veterans swore exceeded the Battle of Manassas (Bull Run).[104]

Although both sides eventually claimed victory at Williamsburg, 2283 Federal casualties convinced General McClellan that any further pursuit should be decidedly cautious, and Johnston's army was able to pull back to defenses prepared near Richmond itself. The retreat took another two weeks, which the 14th Alabama spent continuously in line of battle or on the march, struggling through quagmires that often held men fast in the viscous muck until comrades pulled them free. Marshall B. Hurst, the regiment's Chief Musician, thought the "whole earth was rotten," and noted dismally that those still able to march faced slim pickings indeed, as the "many thousands of soldiers who were ahead of us, stripped the country of everything eatable." Broken down by the hardships of the march, many of the men were evacuated by ambulance to hospitals at Petersburg, where numbers died from illnesses brought on by exposure, hardship, and exhaustion. Given the sparse food supplies and inadequate nutritional value of army rations, it is little wonder that many succumbed.[105]

If William was one of those who made it to camp at the Fair Field Race Paths east of the capital on May 22, he was probably back in line of battle just nine days later, when the roar of cannon announced that the battle for Richmond itself was joined. Lieutenant Colonel David W. Baine emerged from the hospital when he heard the regiment had orders to move; loading his men with forty rounds of ammunition, he marched them to the battlefield of Seven Pines, just four miles east of the Confederate capital. Here, Gen. Joe Johnston had launched a counterstroke intended to destroy the left wing of McClellan's army before the right wing could cross the Chickahominy River to its support. Baine's 14th Alabama arrived on the field that afternoon, pausing among overrun Federal encampments whose neat rows of tentage and camp kettles filled with beef, peas and coffee bespoke the terrible surprise that befell them that morning. The mangled dead and groaning wounded gave evidence that their resistance had been nonetheless spirited, and Marshall Hurst noted soberly that some of the dead lay covered only by the standing waters of the boggy Chickahominy swamplands. As Baine's troops helped the 6th Alabama's wounded into improvised field hospitals, they encountered places where Union and Confederate dead lay intermingled, with corpses literally impaled on each other's bayonets. Lying on their muskets in the rainy darkness that night, they reflected that the morrow already promised to see them "called upon to perform the severest task for which they volunteered."[106] (See map on page 462.)

They gulped a few mouthfuls of food the next morning, June 1, but a burst of enemy fire sent the Alabamians scrambling into line. General Longstreet had begun an advance intended to develop the Federal positions for a large scale assault by the Confederate army, temporarily commanded by Gen. Gustavus W. Smith due to

Johnston's serious wounds on the previous evening. Smith's movements were tentative, however, and the attack never developed into a general engagement. The fighting on Longstreet's front was vicious in places where the terrain allowed the two opponents to come to grips, but the swamps, woods, and ridges compartmentalized the terrain and made it exceedingly difficult for commanders to control events.[107]

These factors certainly characterized the conditions faced by the men of the 14th Alabama that day. Baine received orders from Brig. Gen. Roger Pryor, his brigade commander, to pull his men out of line on the right of the 8th Alabama, swing behind them into a column covering the left and rear, then march to the sound of the heavy firing in the front. Crossing the Williamsburg Road heading north, the 14th Alabama filed into line of battle when they approached the sound of firing. Flailing their way through a dense swamp, they worked their way across a hill bedecked with small pines and plunged through yet another swamp. There, the 8th Alabama was blasted by heavy fire from Federals posted in a dense thicket, and the terrain frustrated Baine's efforts to maneuver his regiment into a location where his men could fire effectively. Directed to pull back from this profitless position as part of a general withdrawal of Wilcox's and Pryor's brigades, the two Alabama regiments crossed back over the swamp, but became entangled as they clambered up the pine-covered hill. The Federals were pushing forward in their turn, and disaster threatened the Alabamians. After a quick conference with Colonel Winston of the 8th Alabama, Baine pushed his men into position just over the top of the hill while Winston's men hurried to form line on their right. Advancing bluecoats were within thirty yards of Baine's line when the right wing of the 14th Alabama cut loose with a heavy fire that stopped them in their tracks. As Winston's men joined in from the right flank, the Federals reeled back in retreat. With each side having suffered a repulse in its turn, combat ended in this sector when Pryor ordered his brigade to pull back and stand fast.[108]

Although the Confederate counterattacks at the Battle of Seven Pines failed to achieve their immediate goal of crushing one wing of the divided Army of the Potomac, they succeeded in further convincing McClellan that his mighty host was actually outnumbered by a hard-fighting and highly dangerous foe. He could not know that the Confederates lost some 6100 casualties in the two days of fighting, but he considered himself lucky to have lost only 5000-plus instead of his whole left wing. Although neither army had changed its position, the odds against McClellan had in fact grown appreciably longer. Not only did the Southern troops take solace in the fact that they had seized the initiative after weeks of defense and retreat, but their new commander was one whose very name would become synonymous with seizing the initiative in every conceivable circumstance. His name was Gen. Robert Edward Lee.[109]

While Baine's Alabamians returned to rest in their camps in Richmond, Lee quickly began to plot the undoing of McClellan's army. A sharp engagement on June 25 at Oak Grove, just a mile west of the Seven Pines battlefield, signaled the beginning of a week of ferocious combat known as the Seven Days' battles. The next day's fight at Mechanicsville resulted in a repulse for the attacking Confederates, but McClellan shakily concluded that it was high time to "change his base of operations" southward to the James River line, a euphemism for retreating to the cover of Union gunboats operating on that river. It was an incredible blunder, but Lee had taken the measure of his opponent, who proved on this field and many others that the so-called "Young Napoleon" was overwhelmingly a prisoner of his own fears. His engineers rapidly laid out a new defensive line near Gaines's Mill to cover the Chickahominy bridges, critical spans that provided a connection to the army's southern wing as well as an escape route to the James River.[110]

On the other side of the lines, Pryor received orders on the night of June 26 to relieve Colquitt's Brigade on the bloody Mechanicsville battlefield. Pryor's Brigade included regiments from Virginia, Florida, and Louisiana, along with the 14th Alabama, and they filed into line behind Featherston's Brigade expecting that the dawn would bring a renewal of the desperate combat. A Federal thrust against Featherston's men at earliest dawn brought Pryor's troops up in response. William and the other men of the 14th Alabama prepared to charge across Beaver Dam Creek at Ellison's Mill in support of the 14th Louisiana. The leading troops had to throw together a makeshift bridge to bear the weight of supporting artillery batteries, however, so the Alabamians had to wait helplessly in an open field under a "murderous fire." When they finally got the order to cross the river in trace of the advancing Louisianians, they left behind a bloody trail of dead and wounded.[111]

Moving behind Featherston's Brigade down the River Road on the bluffs rising from the northern bank of the Chickahominy, Pryor's men reached the Hogan house by mid-morning. There, Longstreet directed Pryor to assume the advance guard mission and follow up the rapidly retreating Federals. Probing forward to Dr. Gaines's farmstead a mile down the road, skirmishers of the 14th Alabama drove back enemy pickets onto a line of Federals concealed in the woods behind Gaines's property. About 11:00 a.m., Pryor deployed his brigade in the fields approaching the enemy position in an attempt to discover its strength. Crossing a half-mile of open ground under a "galling fire from the enemy's battery over the river," the brigade met a blast of infantry fire that revealed the Yankees posted "in very great force." An incoming artillery shell killed one or two of William's friends in the Cusseta Greys, wounding several others.[112]

Pryor realized he had accomplished his advance guard mission. Having found the enemy posted in sufficient strength to stop his brigade in its tracks, it was time to pull back into cover and report developments. Although William and his Chambers County friends could not have known it, General Lee's plan of battle foresaw a supporting role for Longstreet's Division on his right, while Stonewall Jackson's and D. H. Hill's troops made the main attacks on the left and center. Hill's men began suffering terrific losses, however, as Jackson's troops marched and countermarched through the frustrating tangle of poorly mapped roads and hamlets, unable to strike the Union flank as planned. Lee ordered Longstreet to feint against the Federal left to relieve the pressure against Hill's battered brigades, but a brief effort sufficed to convince "Old Pete" that no feint would make an impression on the strongly posted enemy. He accordingly ordered a general advance, and Pryor and the other brigadiers moved their men out in a direct frontal attack shortly after 2:00 o'clock.[113]

The 14th Alabama moved across a half-mile or more of open ground, paused to adjust its formation, then marched upslope for a hundred yards before emerging into clear view of the defenders. In the words of Musician Marshall Hurst, the enemy then "opened fire on us with terrible effect." Pryor reported that his brigade was "staggered by a terrific volley at the same time that they suffered severely from the battery across

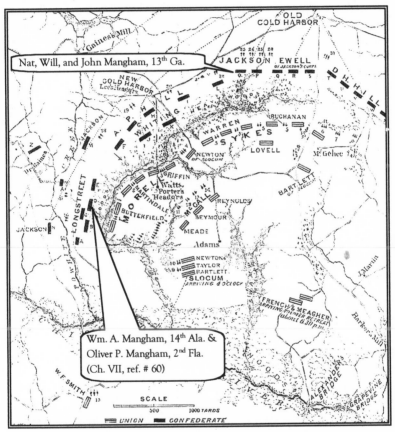

THE BATTLE OF GAINES'S MILL, JUNE 27, 1862.

the Chickahominy." The shock was too much, and although the 14th Alabama advanced to a point only fifty yards from the blazing muzzles, Pryor eventually pulled his men back into the sheltering ravine of Boatswain's Creek. After a brief pause to reorganize, they pushed back uphill once more, where they faced a maelstrom of fire that Pryor described as "impossible to endure." An Alabama corporal in Wilcox's Brigade, adjacent to Pryor's, thought Wilcox's "whole brigade literally *staggered*

285

backward several paces as though pushed by a tornado." Instead of pulling back this time, however, the Alabamians poured return volleys into the blue lines as fast as they could load and fire. Lieutenant Robert Miller of Pryor's 14th Louisiana stood upright in the hailstorm of bullets, tempted momentarily to see "how many I could catch with my open hand stretched out."[114]

The blueclad infantry began drifting rearwards under this unremitting pressure, which came to the boiling point in several other places at the same time. Longstreet's men were screaming "like forty thousand wild cats" as they scrambled up in a furious charge that broke the Federal line "at the point of the bayonet." The foremost defenders began streaming back out of control, and panic ensued as Rebel pursuers loped forward, screaming and firing as they came. They still faced a ferocious fire of grapeshot and canister from the Federal artillery posted in the fields to their front, plus a second line of infantry, and the onrushing attackers fell "at every step." Indeed, the 36,000 Federal troops in the Gaines's Mill position were supported by 96 artillery pieces in commanding positions, and their concentrated fire was murderous. At one point, officers of the 14th Alabama conferred briefly with their Louisiana and Virginia counterparts before deciding to go head-on against a battery that was blasting Pryor's Brigade into bloody ribbons. As they launched another headlong assault, Marshall Hurst noticed with amazement that many of the Louisianians were shedding their empty cartridge boxes and muskets, racing forward with nothing but the naked bayonets in their hands. Faced with this wild onslaught, the blue-coated gunners headed for the rear, and Cpl. James Giles, a color guard member from Company K, planted the 14th Alabama's colors upon the guns of the battery. By this time, Lieutenant Colonel Baine could rally no more than twelve men of the regiment, as the rest were scattered amidst the confusion of the battlefield.[115]

The arrival of two fresh Union brigades in the gloaming facilitated the escape of the battered survivors of Gen. Fitz John Porter's forces that night, although he abandoned twenty-two guns, lost 894 killed and 2829 captured, and suffered 3114 wounded. Overall, McClellan had to count himself lucky that the third of his army north of the Chickahominy had survived the day at all. The price of Lee's victory fell just shy of eight thousand killed, wounded and missing.[116]

The tattered remnants of the 14th Alabama gathered together by 8:00 a.m. on June 28, prepared to pursue the fleeing foe toward the James River, but the Confederates proved unable to bring the enemy to bay. The following day saw Magruder's men fight a sharp engagement at Savage's Station, the baptism of fire for William's brother Wiley and nephew John S. Mangham of the 53rd Georgia, but again McClellan eluded Lee's attempts to bring on a climactic battle.[117]

Lee tried yet again on June 30 at the hamlet of Glendale, where the east-west oriented Long Bridge Road offered him an avenue to cut off McClellan's retreat to the south. Since strong elements of the 2nd and 3rd Corps already were in position covering this key intersection, the Confederate attack actually was an attempt to cut the Army of the Potomac in half and beat it in detail. Once again, however, an array of mistakes and misunderstandings prevented Lee from massing his army at his intended point of attack, but the frustrated commander launched Longstreet's Division into an assault late that afternoon in a desperate attempt to capitalize on his fading opportunity.[118]

Longstreet's first wave of three brigades smashed into McCall's Federal division just west of Glendale itself on the Long Bridge Road, near a piece of land the locals called Frayser's Farm. The assault cracked the Federal line in combat of incredible intensity, overrunning or driving off every one of the twenty-six artillery pieces emplaced on a half-mile front. Confederate Col. E. Porter Alexander, who fought with the Army of Northern Virginia throughout its existence, asserted flatly that the Battle of Frayser's Farm (Glendale) involved "more actual bayonet, & butt of gun, melee fighting than any other occasion I know of in the whole war." Longstreet pushed in three more brigades in an attempt to expand the breach in the enemy lines, and Pryor's Brigade whirled into action just north of the Long Bridge Road against Phil Kearny's Union division.[119]

Kearny was a crusty old soldier, but thought that the Rebel troops swarming to the attack came onward "in such masses as I had never witnessed." Pryor's men were in line with Featherston's Brigade, and Maxcy Gregg's brigade was moving up in support against intense defensive fire. Captain James Thompson's Battery G, 2nd U.S. Artillery massed its fires with a two-gun section from Battery E of the 1st Rhode Island Artillery, and the cannoneers blasted Pryor's right flank mercilessly. Due to the wooded nature of the terrain, Pryor was forced to deploy his brigade in column of regiments, which fed each one into the meatgrinder successively. Thompson's guns riddled Pryor's Brigade with spherical case shot at 400 yards range, with one shot downing six men of the 14th Louisiana and severing a leg from Pryor's horse. It was probably soon after this incident that the desperate brigadier turned to Lieutenant Colonel Baine, asking if the 14th Alabama could take that battery. Baine replied simply, "My boys will take it if I tell them."[120]

Maneuvering his command across a swamp about half a mile in front of the battery, Baine formed his men into line and ordered a charge. Screaming the rebel yell, his Alabamians went howling into a whirlwind of gunfire from front and flank. At 150 yards range Thompson switched to canister, at which the grayclad lines "appeared to falter." They kept coming on, however, until the desperate Thompson switched to double canister, with each discharge spraying the onrushing Rebels with two tin cans full of slugs in the manner of a giant double-barreled shotgun. A Michigan lieutenant thought, "The head of the column seemed to sink into the ground. Beyond a certain point they could not come." Musician Marshall Hurst asserted that the 14th Alabama did not stop until the "battery was but a few yards distant," when the gallant Baine was dropped with a fatal wound. By this point, most of the regiment's officers had been shot down, with only two captains remaining unhurt. Almost leaderless, the gray tide receded some distance until Adjutant Lucius Pinckard and Captains Williamson and McCord rallied the remnants for another try. Although Pryor simply claimed that his men held their ground until the enemy abandoned the field and some of their artillery, Hurst claimed that Captain McCord, Pinckard, and a few other men succeeded in capturing the battery. Federal reports indicate that Thompson's battery and Janstram's section each left one gun on the field that night, admissions that imply that the position was so closely contested that a complete evacuation was impossible. Gunners were trained to get their guns away "at all hazards," just as opposing infantrymen strained every nerve to capture them.[121]

Reinforced during the engagement, Kearny's hard-fighting line was bloodied but unbroken, and a timely combination of reinforcements and darkness saved McCall's shattered line. Their defense of Glendale was a near-run thing, but barely managed to keep open McClellan's line of retreat. Each side suffered about 3700 casualties that day, with Kearny losing more than a thousand from his division alone. Pryor, Featherston, and Gregg lost 882 killed, wounded and missing in their attempt to break his line. Pryor reported an "uncommonly heavy" loss of officers and men, adding the melancholy observation, "The Fourteenth Alabama, bearing the brunt of the struggle, was nearly annihilated." His brigade had crossed the Chickahominy on June 26 with 1400 men; the bitter combats at Gaines's Mill and Frayser's Farm cost him a staggering 849 killed and wounded, plus eleven missing. The 14th Louisiana referred to Frayser's Farm simply as "The Slaughter House," based upon the 122 casualties they suffered there. It is not recorded whether the 14th Alabama ever gave the fight a particular nickname, but their 245 casualties represented a bloodletting of incredible proportions, second in Lee's army only to the 254 men of the Palmetto Sharpshooters who fell that day. On the other side, the 1st New York lost 230 men helping defend Thompson's hard-fighting battery.[122]

As for William Mangham's Cusseta Greys, it was up to Pvt. W. A. Prather to decide what to call the hell they had endured; of the 47 men in ranks on the morning of June 27, he was the only one left to answer roll call on the morning of July 1. Eight sick men had been ordered to the hospital in the interim, and the other 38 had been shot down at Gaines's Mill and Frayser's Farm.[123]

What did people say when the news reached Chambers County?

*   *   *   *   *

The holocaust in the swamps east of Richmond cost the 14th Alabama a total of 71 killed, 253 wounded, and eleven missing. Combined with the losses suffered at Yorktown and Williamsburg, the salvation of the Confederate capital bled the regiment down to a pale shadow of the 700 men who stood in ranks just two months earlier.[124]

The exhausted victors remained on duty east of Richmond until the middle of July, when they were ordered back to their old camp at the fairgrounds to rest and recruit their thinned ranks. Perhaps William was able to visit his brother Wiley of the 53rd Georgia as he lay dying in Richmond's Winder Hospital; was he able to attend to his burial? The sick and wounded Alabamians trickled back to their companies over the next several weeks, until the call came to move north to Gordonsville on August 11. Lee was moving Longstreet's men north to join Stonewall Jackson's wing of the army, since it was now clear that McClellan was evacuating the peninsula altogether and posed no further threat to Richmond. The Confederate commander was striving to mass his forces to "suppress" the depredations of Federal forces ravaging central Virginia at the behest of a man whom an outraged General Lee labeled a "miscreant,"

Maj. Gen. John Pope. In a fashion that became typical of Lee, he sought to achieve his aim by designing the utter destruction of his opponent. Over and above Pope's draconian measures directed against the Southern populace, his army posed a threat to Lee's communications with his army's breadbasket, the Shenandoah Valley.[125]

Within days, the 14th Alabama was marching north from Gordonsville, sloshing across the Rapidan River at Raccoon Ford. Private William Mangham probably was with the regiment as it slogged through the heat and dust of late July. As Lee and Pope commenced a deadly game of maneuvering for positional advantage, it seemed to famished and thirsty grayjackets like Musician Marshall Hurst that the endless "marching and counter-marching on half rations" comprised "hardships and privations unheard of before in the annals of war."[126]

After two weeks of groping for their opponents, the roar of sustained gunfire from Jackson's front on August 29 told the Alabamians that the armies finally had come to grips at Manassas. Pryor's Brigade was in Maj. Gen. Cadmus Wilcox's division, the left flank element of Longstreet's wing of the army. As such, they moved into line just south of Jackson's wing, squarely on the flank of Pope's army. After taking part in a lunge that snared some Federals retreating after a failed attack against Jackson's line, the 14th Alabama fought its way through the Groveton Woods into a position in the woodline just north of the Warrenton Turnpike. Oriented eastward against Union forces now contracted into a solid blocking position buttressed by a dozen or more artillery batteries, Pryor's men remained in place alongside most of Jackson's troops late that afternoon, while the remainder of Longstreet's wing pushed forward to envelop Pope's left.[127]

When William and his mates finally received orders to advance again, the hard-fought battle became a struggle for the very survival of the retreating Federal army. Longstreet's men were held up just long enough in their attacks across Chinn Ridge and onto Henry Hill to allow the left flank of the Union army to maintain its line of retreat eastward along the Warrenton Turnpike, while Pope's center held just north of the Turnpike along Dogan's Ridge. Here the 14th Alabama took part in attacks that steadily pushed back the bluecoats but failed to break their lines. In the course of the afternoon, Corporal Ray and Private Neal were shot down with the regimental colors, which were finally borne safely through the battle by Pvt. J. M. Finley of Company C, the "Tom Watts Greys" of Chambers County. At least five men of the Cusseta Greys were wounded in the fighting, which cost the regiment three killed and 44 wounded. One of those wounded was Third Sgt. Stephen Hodge, acting as company commander after the death, wounding, or transfer of every officer and senior non-commissioned officer since the preceding December.[128]

The Battle of Second Manassas was a resounding victory for the Confederates, who had, in Lee's contemptuous term, "suppressed" Pope so thoroughly that he was relieved of command after his retreat to Centreville. His army limped into Washington's defenses, frustrated and chastened by its latest defeat, but fortunately spared the destruction that Lee had sought, and so nearly achieved. As the Confederate commander pushed his veterans farther north towards Maryland in a bid to take the war into Union territory, however, the large numbers of wounded men who filled Richmond's hospitals were swelled by an ever-growing river of sick men broken down by the hardships of the campaign. One of those admitted to Chimborazo Hospital No. 1 on September 8, 1862, was William Mangham, whose rheumatism had recurred and made him unable to keep up any longer.[129]

He was released from the hospital eight days later, and drew his back pay from an army quartermaster in Richmond the next day. For four months' marching, hardship and exposure, as well as his participation in the battles at Yorktown, Williamsburg, Gaines's Mill, Frayser's Farm, and Second Manassas, he drew the sum of forty-four dollars, along with another twenty-five dollars as commutation for clothing allowance. As meager as it was, he had to count himself one of the fortunate ones, for he was alive and unmaimed. On the same day he received his pay, the 14th Alabama suffered two men killed and another 43 wounded in the Battle of Sharpsburg (Antietam), the bloodiest day in American history.[130]

*   *   *   *   *

William probably rejoined the regiment in Winchester later that month after the army returned from Maryland, and he was present for duty when the 14th Alabama mustered near there for pay at the end of October. In the chill dawn of November 1, they were on the way to Culpeper Courthouse, which they reached that night after wading both branches of the Shenandoah River and both branches of the Rappahannock River as well. With many of the men barefoot, the march certainly must have proved tough for men worn down by the summer campaigns. After sleepless nights spent in the first snows of winter, the regiment was reassigned on November 10 to an all-Alabama brigade under Brig. Gen. Cadmus Wilcox, as part of an initiative to restructure the army's infantry brigades along state lines. Assigned to Anderson's Division of Longstreet's 1st Army Corps, the Cusseta Greys took the road for Fredericksburg on November 19, arriving at camp three miles west of town four days later. They had marched one hundred miles in the previous three weeks. It was just another month in the war for men in the Army of Northern Virginia.[131]

For the Alabamians, the rugged November marching was harder than the battle that thundered along the Rappahannock several weeks later, when the Federals pushed across the river in their latest drive on Richmond. Posted along the heights on the army's extreme left flank, William Mangham and his comrades enjoyed the spectacle of Burnside's crushing defeat without having to lift a finger to help. Battle-hardened veterans they most certainly were, but they were battle-worn as well; Fredericksburg was a welcome respite, as well as a heady tonic. When William mustered for pay with the Cusseta Greys on New Year's Eve, he stood in the ranks of a supremely confident army that considered itself better than anything its opponents could muster. Four months later, General Lee would employ these men in battle with a degree of daring that clearly indicated the feeling was mutual. The stunning victory that resulted at Chancellorsville heightened the mutual confidence between leader and led to a point as lofty as it was unshakeable. At a little brick church west of Fredericksburg along the

Orange Plank Road, Wilcox's hard-marching Alabamians fought a delaying action that proved crucial to the outcome of the entire battle; indeed, it proved to be one of the classic brigade-level operations of the entire war. The name of the church was Salem.[132]

*   *   *   *   *

The winter at Fredericksburg had been a tough one for William. Officially present for duty but sick in his quarters when the regiment mustered for pay at the end of February and again on the last day of April, he also spent the period from March 18 to April 1 in the hospital at Chimborazo No. 4 suffering from scurvy. His malady was a result of the monotonous army diet of meat, flour, and corn meal, which Confederate commissary officers had difficulty supplementing with vegetables and fruit, especially in the winter months. These dietary shortages invited disease, of course; by the spring of 1863, 203 men of the 14th Alabama had succumbed to various non-battle causes, easily exceeding the 139 killed by Federal bullets.[133]

After the long months of picket duty at Banks's Ford on the Rappahannock north of Fredericksburg, the men of Wilcox's Brigade were ordered to prepare for action on April 29, 1863. In a skillfully executed flanking maneuver, Maj. Gen. "Fighting Joe" Hooker had put his Army of the Potomac across the river northwest of Fredericksburg. From this position, his ensuing advance through the desolate Wilderness could place him squarely in Lee's rear if the Confederate commander clung to his prepared defenses. In fact, Hooker was confident that Lee would emerge to fight him, and he hoped to provoke a battle in which his men would fight on the tactical defensive.[134]

He got his defensive battle all right, and much more besides. Although his army bitterly resisted the Rebel assaults, Hooker's line was partially rolled up by Stonewall Jackson's famous flank attack on the evening of May 2. Flying in the face of conventional military theory, Lee had divided his force boldly in the face of the enemy and flung Jackson onto Hooker's flank to achieve a stunning reversal of fortunes. As the bloody hammering continued on May 3, the Federal commander looked back towards Fredericksburg for his salvation. There, Gen. John Sedgwick's VI Corps had crossed the river to threaten the few Confederates remaining in the defenses. Since the latter were badly outnumbered, a successful attack by Sedgwick was highly probable, and it would put him on the Orange Plank Road between Fredericksburg and Lee's rear just eight miles away at Chancellorsville.[135]

By late morning, Sedgwick's corps finally rousted the outnumbered defenders of Marye's Heights from their position, which was the key to the thinly stretched Confederate line. Since the majority of Jubal Early's defenders were forced back south of Fredericksburg, the Orange Plank Road pointed westward like an unsheathed sword aimed at Lee's unprotected back.[136]

Unprotected, that is, but for a lone brigade of Alabama "Yellowhammers," commanded by a man who believed a brigade could make a difference.

Brigadier General Cadmus Wilcox's 8th, 9th, 10th, 11th and 14th Alabama infantry regiments had done little more than march in circles as the Chancellorsville campaign unfolded. After standing ready to move out of their breastworks on April 29, they mustered at Banks's Ford while the cannons roared throughout the next day.[137] On May 1, orders came to move west along the Plank Road, where they approached close enough to Hooker's invasion force to hear stray bullets whistling past. After moving back to the north side of the road and pushing farther westward in a vain search for Yankees in the dense undergrowth south of the Rappahannock, the brigade settled into position in the woods near Duerson's Mills on Mott's Run. From here, they maintained connections with the pickets remaining at Banks's Ford less than two miles away. At 10:00 p.m. that night, however, they were on the march again, this time to a position on the Orange Turnpike in support of the units facing Hooker's men near Chancellorsville. Stumbling into position at 2:30 a.m. the next morning, they stacked arms and lay down to rest, only to receive marching orders once more. This time, they were to return to the very place that they had departed the previous morning: Banks's Ford! After marching a total of some twelve miles that day and night, much of it at the double-quick, the weary Alabamians collapsed asleep at dawn when they got back to their old breastworks.[138]

Private Mangham may have marched the whole way with the Cusseta Greys, if he was not too sick, or perhaps he remained in camp or on picket guard at Banks's Ford when the others marched out (see map on page 266). Unless he was hospitalized or simply collapsed by the roadside, he was probably in ranks at Banks's Ford on May 2, peering across the river as blue-coated infantry and artillerymen moved up to the river on the other side. Some of Wilcox's Alabama veterans were particularly nervous about their position, as they could see blue-coated artillerymen manning "mammoth cannon which were mounted and to all appearances were capable of clearing out the ditch that the Tenth Alabama Regiment occupied at one well directed shot."[139]

Wilcox's orders were to hold the ford "at all hazards" against a possible crossing, but to move west to Chancellorsville if such a crossing appeared unlikely. On May 3, he noticed the enemy's numbers appeared greatly reduced, and saw that their pickets were wearing haversacks. Convinced by these signs that the Yankees were on the move upriver to Hooker's main crossing points, the alert Alabamian determined to leave a token force to watch Banks's Ford and move the rest down the Plank Road to join Lee.[140]

As his brigade formed for the march, one of his pickets came running down from Taylor's Hill to notify Wilcox that Yankees were moving up the River Road out of Fredericksburg! Hurrying to get a look at these troops, Wilcox saw that the leading regiment, one of three visible in the column, was only a thousand yards away. Quickly throwing out his pickets as skirmishers, he then moved his brigade into the old rifle pits on Taylor's Hill, where it had stood during the December battle. The fire of the skirmishers, reinforced by two rifled guns of Huger's Battery, easily checked the initial enemy advance, and Wilcox maneuvered his men southward into the ravine behind Stansbury Hill to await developments.[141]

These movements brought Wilcox into position to spot a group of Confederate officers farther to the south, near Marye's Heights. He rode down to the Marye House and conferred there with Brigadier General Barksdale, whose Mississippi brigade was holding the heights made famous in the December fighting. This reconnaissance made Wilcox aware for the first time that Federals had crossed at and below Fredericksburg in strength. When he learned soon thereafter that Barksdale's men had been pushed off Marye's Heights to the Telegraph Road leading south out of town, he realized that his brigade was the only force now able to protect Lee's rear at Chancellorsville. In clear view of enemy forces that he estimated at treble his own strength, Cadmus Wilcox "felt it a duty to delay the enemy as much as possible," and deployed his troops along the crests of the hills running near the Stansbury House.[142]

Here the Alabamians fought their first delaying action, using skirmishers and two rifled pieces of Lewis's artillery battery to force the Federals to deploy skirmishers, lines of battle, and supporting artillery. The sharp skirmishing cost Wilcox three men killed and about twenty wounded, but convinced him that the slow-moving enemy force was "reluctant to advance." When reports came that blue-coated infantrymen had accompanied a battery along the Plank Road to a position even with his right (southern) flank, Wilcox dispatched forty or fifty attached cavalrymen to a new position astride the road. He ordered the remainder of his brigade to circle back along the River Road, then swung his men at the double-quick southward down a connecting track to the Plank Road. The tentative movements of his enemy had convinced the Alabama brigadier that he need not fear any hard-driving attempts to cut off and destroy his isolated force, so he planned to capitalize on their evident caution. With that intent, he ordered his regiments to march to Salem Church. (See map, p. 269.)[143]

Although the Federals had been cautious so far, they were astride the most direct route to the church. Lieutenant Edmund Patterson of the 9th Alabama put it succinctly: "Although we had been running until our tongues were hanging out still we saw no escape from capture or death unless we could reach that church before the Yankees did." Even worse, "if they arrived there first there would be nothing between them and the main army under Gen'l. Lee, who were fighting at Chancellorsville with their backs to us." With sharpshooters harrying the Alabamians' rear with a brisk fire, Wilcox put the brigade into column of companies to shorten his column's length and allow him to deploy a protective screen of skirmishers to cover his rear.[144]

When his men came puffing into position at the little red brick church, they were relieved to see that they had won the high stakes race. In fact, Wilcox saw that his puny force of cavalrymen had delayed the Yankees long enough to allow him to push his line a half-mile farther east to the old toll gate. Using the same recipe as before, the Alabamians pushed skirmishers into the fields out front and deployed two rifled guns on the road. The Federal response was again cautious, as skirmishers advanced to the front while artillery was called up. While his men traded shots with them, Wilcox received word that Maj. Gen. Lafayette McLaws had dispatched three brigades from the lines near Chancellorsville to his support. Clearly, Lee again felt himself so firmly in possession of the initiative that he believed he could divide his forces before the numerically superior enemy without risking defeat in detail. Despite the fact that he had only some 34,000 men in the lines facing Hooker's 77,000 troops, Lee was right.[145]

Having suffered another three killed and fifteen wounded at the tollgate, Wilcox pulled his men back a half-mile into new positions at Salem Church itself, facing due east. Stationing a company from the 9th Alabama in the brick church and another in the log schoolhouse sixty yards to its right, Wilcox anchored his position on the Plank Road by placing a four-gun battery astride the road. The 14th Alabama filed into position behind a cedar brush fence on the brigade's left flank, with the 11th Alabama on its right, anchored on the guns. The 10th was just to the right of the battery on the south side of the road, and the 8th extended the line farther to the south behind the schoolhouse. The remaining eight companies of the 9th Alabama lay in reserve behind the 10th. With skirmishers in the fields between the tollgate and the brigade's line, the defenders got ready. Towards five o'clock, a twenty-minute artillery duel emptied the caissons of the Confederate gunners, who limbered to the rear as Federal shells began bursting in the woods on either side of the road. The infantrymen would have to go it alone.[146]

As the skirmish fire heated up and two Federal lines of battle advanced to the attack, Semmes's Georgia brigade filed into line on the Alabamians' left, blowing hard from a stiff march at double-quick time. In the ranks of the 53rd Georgia was young *Pvt. John S. Mangham*, separated by three Georgia regiments from his Uncle William in the 14th Alabama. The Georgians were double-quicking into position as the Union line of battle cleared the open fields in front, where they paused at the far edge of a dense growth of scrawny trees just 250 yards from the Confederates.[147]

Giving three cheers, the blue line pushed hard into the woods, causing grayclad skirmishers to hustle back to friendly lines. After the initial burst of "cheering and shouting," the steady "tramp, tramp" of men forcing their way through the woods was all the waiting Alabamians could hear to their front. Skirmishers from the 2nd New Jersey Volunteers led the way, followed by the 1st and 3rd New Jersey regiments in the portion of the line confronting the 11th and 14th Alabama. In some places the line closed to thirty yards range, in other places perhaps eighty, when the Alabama soldiers stood up and "delivered a close and terrible fire" into their faces. Staggered but resolute, the Yankees began "loading and firing as fast as possible." With excited Rebels pouring fire back into them as hard as they could, the battle rose to a white-hot pitch almost immediately. Sergeant English of the 2nd New Jersey saw the clash come "almost to a hand-to-hand contest." Serving in a hard-fighting unit with a good combat record, he observed later that he never had "heard or seen such a fearful fusillade" as he encountered that day.[148]

Determined Federal troops poured up the road, dividing to pass around the brick church and log schoolhouse, while the Rebel riflemen within slashed at the passing columns with deadly flanking fire. Renewed assaults eventually overran these two isolated companies however, and finally began to unhinge the 10th Alabama from its position at the roadside. Shouting "Look at that damned 10th, steady 9th Alabama!", Wilcox turned to his old command to retrieve the desperate situation. Major Jeremiah Williams sang out, "Forward, 9th Alabama!", and the men jumped to their feet. Although they absorbed a staggering close-range volley that cut down men in droves, the survivors went howling into the attack. With the 8th Alabama's leftmost companies volleying directly into the flank of the stunned Federals, the hunter became the hunted. The regiments forming Wilcox's right joined in the furious counterattack, and the fever was spreading fast to the north side of the Plank Road as well. A Chambers County man, Lt. Woody Dozier of the "Yancey Greys," called out "Come on boys, we'll get our blankets back!" and the men of the 14th Alabama clambered over their brush fence and went screaming forward through the woods. Marshall Hurst remembered that the Yankees in their front "retreated slowly and sullenly" at first, but "our boys pressed them closely and they soon struck a trot to keep out of reach of our bayonets."[149]

Two regiments of Semmes's Georgians joined in the counterattack, which swept away a second line of fresh troops as soon as it formed in front of them. Yipping the Rebel yell as they ran after the fleeing Yanks, the seven Alabama and Georgia regiments chased them back all the way to the toll gate. There the counterattack stalled under the fire of three Federal batteries, whose blasts of canister gave notice that the chase was over. As the winded Rebs hove into view of fresh masses of Federal infantry in unbroken lines, they stopped altogether, reformed, and retired to the Salem Church line, posting pickets in the fields near the toll gate on their way back. When the 14th Alabama got back to its brush fence, several men in each company began using bayonets to loosen the earth, while the others used bare hands and tin plates to scoop dirt into crude breastworks should another assault occur the next morning.[150]

But no such assault was even considered, much less undertaken. Salem Church had been a stunning setback for Sedgwick's VI Corps, and its commander spent a sleepless night wondering how to extricate his units from the Rebels swirling about his front and his rear. The VI Corps suffered 1523 casualties at Salem Church, nearly using up Gen. "Bully" Brooks's division. One of his shaken brigades had prided itself in its heretofore perfect record: it had never had a charge repulsed, had never failed to hold a position when ordered, and had never retreated in the face of the enemy. At Salem Church it fought well, but suffered 612 casualties and was lucky to survive intact. The survivors were luckier than they knew, for Mahone's, Kershaw's and Wofford's Confederate brigades were pulling into line on either side of Wilcox and Semmes as the fight began, but none of these brigades was even engaged. The engagement at Salem Church was fought and won by Wilcox and Semmes, whose nine regiments lost 674 men all told. None of Wilcox's five regiments suffered more than the 14th Alabama, which lost eleven killed, 113 wounded, and 36 missing. Thirteen of the wounded and one of the missing were William's friends in the Cusseta Greys. The engagements that day at Salem Church, Chancellorsville, and Fredericksburg resulted in 21,357 casualties in the opposing armies; except for the slaughter at Sharpsburg the previous September, it was the bloodiest day in the Civil War.[151]

Although they worked furiously that night to prepare for a renewed onslaught the next morning, the 14th Alabama's participation in the great Battle of Chancellorsville was effectively at an end. The next day, the men joined the general advance that hurried Sedgwick back across the Rappahannock, then marched west to the lines near

Chancellorsville on May 5 to prepare for the next round with Hooker. But that round remained unfought, for "Fighting Joe" Hooker had had enough. On May 6, the Cusseta Greys and the rest of Wilcox's Brigade marched back into their old camps at Banks's Ford.[152]

After Hooker's army had pulled back across the river, one of his pickets called across the water to one of Barksdale's Mississippians. Writing home afterwards, the Federal soldier recalled, ". . .I asked him what time it was, and he said it was time us Yankees was leaving."[153]

*   *   *   *   *

When the Cusseta Greys next mustered for pay at the end of June, they were stationed at Fayetteville, Pennsylvania. Only 31 men of the company answered roll call that day, and Pvt. William Mangham was one of the many absentees. Hospitalized once more at Richmond, he did not participate in the brutal combat that ensued at Gettysburg during the first days of July.[154]

The 14th Alabama left many dead and wounded behind when it marched back into Virginia as the "high tide" of the Confederacy receded that summer. The Army of Northern Virginia remained a dangerous foe, however, and Maj. Gen. George Meade was satisfied to follow it into its home territory without risking a decisive engagement. Minor skirmishing flared occasionally in the area between the Rappahannock River and the Rapidan to its south, and Lee's army slowly regained strength as the sick and wounded returned from hospitals. William probably returned to the Cusseta Greys in late July or August, so he was most likely present with the army in September 1863 when Longstreet's 1st Corps departed Culpeper Courthouse to reinforce the Army of Tennessee. Anderson's Division had been transferred to Lt. Gen. A. P. Hill's 3rd Corps after Chancellorsville, so William remained in Virginia, where Lee pulled back to the Rapidan to shorten his lines in compensation for Longstreet's absence. Meade tried to capitalize on the chance to strike his depleted opponent, but could find no opportunity to press his advantage.[155]

The shoe was on the other foot several weeks later, when the great Confederate victory at Chickamauga required Meade to send two army corps to reinforce the beaten Federal force besieged at Chattanooga. Lee then flanked Meade out of his positions along the Rapidan, forcing him to pull back to the Rappahannock once more on October 10. Four days later, the 14th Alabama stood in reserve under artillery fire at Bristoe Station, near the old battlegrounds of Manassas, as Hill's Corps struck the retreating Federal columns a glancing blow in a vain attempt to cut them off from Washington. With no further realistic opportunity to wreak havoc on his opponent, Lee pulled back slowly once more to the Rappahannock beginning October 17. Within three days, his forces were arrayed along the river again, but even this minor sideshow in the great war had exacted 1381 Confederate casualties and 2292 on the Union side.[156]

Private Mangham was in ranks when the Cusseta Greys mustered for pay at Brandy Station at the end of October, and he shouldered his musket once more when the opposing armies recommenced jockeying for position on November 7. Meade forced crossings over the Rappahannock at Kelly's Ford and Rappahannock Station despite heavy resistance. Lee, in turn, began withdrawing toward the Rapidan, sparring all the

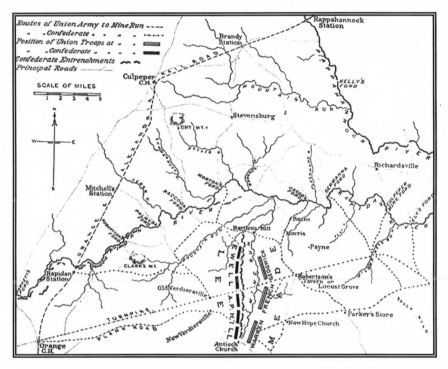

THE MINE RUN CAMPAIGN, NOVEMBER, 1863.

way, but a renewed Federal thrust across that river on November 26 attempted to slice down the small valley of Mine Run between his army and the Confederate capital. There, less than ten miles southwest of the old Chancellorsville battlefields, the 2nd and 3rd Corps of the Army of Northern Virginia dug in to stay. The Cusseta Greys helped repel fierce Federal thrusts over the next five days, until a disappointed Meade pulled his men back across the Rapidan into winter quarters as December began. Lee was likewise disappointed, for he had wanted desperately to smash his foe while he had a chance. A cavalry commander had reported to Lee in the early morning darkness during the Mine Run Campaign, and found the gray-haired warrior aglow with martial ardor: "Captain, if they don't attack us today, we must attack them! We must attack them, sir, and you young men must exert yourselves! You must exert yourselves, sir!" When the Federals managed to retreat intact, the frustrated commander fairly sizzled:

"I am too old to command this army; we should never have permitted these people to get away."[157]

Although the defeat at Gettysburg is often mistaken as the end of the Confederacy's hopes, the autumn campaigning had shown that the Army of Northern Virginia was still capable of hard marching and hard fighting. The 48,500 men who remained in Virginia after Longstreet's Corps departed for Georgia had proved a match for Meade's 85,000 troops in two months of campaigning. It was yet another demonstration of Lee's skill and daring, and his men remained a superb tool for him to wield. The Confederacy's resources were badly overtaxed, however, and Lt. George Clark of the 11th Alabama remembered that winter as a "time of starvation." The normal daily ration was reduced to a mere quarter-pound of bacon and a pint of meal, which was just enough for a single slender repast each day. The gaunt Alabamians ate their daily meal at 11:00 a.m. and tried to make shift as best they could in their bleak hilltop camp a mile or two south of Orange Court House. Other than listening to the banjo music issuing from Jeb Stuart's nearby cavalry encampment, there was precious little to help them while away the long, cold hours. Despite these hardships, many regiments throughout the Confederate armies publicly re-enlisted that winter as their three-year terms were due to expire during the coming campaign season. Not to be outdone was the hard fighting 14th Alabama, which originally had enlisted "for the war" in 1861. In a February 15 letter to Adjutant General Samuel Cooper, General Lee announced that the regiment's soldiers had "reiterated their determination to continue in service."[158]

In mid-February 1864, the drums began beating the long roll throughout the army's camps at about two o'clock one cold morning, as word came that the enemy was on the march. Meade had pushed two army corps across the Rapidan near Madison Court House, some twenty miles away from the point where the 14th Alabama was encamped. Brigadier General Abner Perrin, who assumed command the previous autumn after Wilcox's performance at Salem Church won him a promotion to major general and division command, now led the Alabama brigade. Even so, it often was referred to as "Wilcox's old brigade," and it took position in a line of march that wended its way down dirt roads, now churned into quagmires of icy mud by thousands of men and horses. Thousands straggled along the route of march as the darkness gave way to a weak winter dawn, and some of the Alabamians took note of a small squad of cavalrymen sitting by the side of the road. One trooper was endowed with a "tremendous long nose. . .at least four or five inches long." It was rare that infantry and cavalry encountered each other without trading barbs, and the long-nosed cavalryman was an all-too-obvious target. John Cullen, an Irishman trudging along in the ranks of the 11th Alabama, stepped out of line, bowed politely to the cavalryman, and asked, "My dear sir, won't you please kindly turn your head to one side so the army can pass?" The enraged cavalryman declared his intention to whip Cullen, and the amused onlookers took away their guns and let them go at it. Cullen whipped the unfortunate cavalryman in three rounds. Luckily there was no serious fighting to be done, for near sunset the men were halted and told that Meade had recalled his forces from Madison

Court House. The next day saw Perrin's men slog back to their old camp, where they returned to the drudgery of winter quarters.[159]

Probably William had a chance to visit his elder brother *James M. Mangham*, who arrived in Virginia that February with the 61st Alabama Volunteers, newly assigned to Battle's Brigade in Ewell's 2nd Corps. If so, the brothers must have enjoyed the opportunity to talk about their home in Chambers County, the crops and the weather, the neighbors and the family. Perhaps William took the opportunity to give James some tips about survival in Lee's army as well. Although James was several years older, he certainly was less experienced in the ways of the front-line soldier, since the 61st Alabama had done nothing more strenuous than picket duty since its organization the previous summer. Things would be a whole lot tougher in Virginia.[160]

*   *   *   *   *

Robert E. Lee and his men expected 1864 to be a trying year for the Confederacy, as the Federal armies continued to draw upon seemingly inexhaustible reserves of manpower. After Longstreet's Corps returned from the west on April 20, the Army of Northern Virginia mustered some 65,000 men. When Burnside's troops came from Maryland to join the Army of the Potomac on April 29, the Union forces in Virginia were more than 120,000 strong. Lee also had learned a month earlier that Lincoln had appointed a new commander-in-chief with the rank of lieutenant general: his name was U. S. Grant. He was renowned for victories in the West beginning at Fort Donelson in 1862, where his demand for the garrison's unconditional surrender earned him the nickname "Unconditional Surrender" Grant in contemporary Northern newspapers. Lee's jaunty veterans felt they could teach him lessons that the western armies could not, jibing that his initials stood for "Up the Spout Grant." Longstreet, however, had known Grant since their days at West Point and had stood as best man in his wedding, and "Old Pete" uttered a warning that proved to be prophetic: "That man will fight us every day and every hour till the end of the war." But until Grant launched his army from its winter quarters, Lee felt constrained to rest his hungry men and undernourished horses in their camps south of the Rapidan. He expected Grant would cross the river to interpose his army between Lee and Richmond, then strike the Confederate right flank. When he did so, Lee would attempt to strike first. And if he could get his army out of its covering positions quickly enough, he could hit the Federals where their numbers could not be marshaled to full effect: in the tangled forests of the Wilderness.[161]

*   *   *   *   *

Private Mangham had drawn clothing from Army quartermasters on four different occasions between December and April, so he probably represented a fair specimen of the gray-jacketed, slouch-hatted veterans south of the Rapidan that spring. They began packing up in early May when stirrings across the river showed that the Yankees were on the move again, in this fourth spring of the war. On May 4, word came that the Federals were pouring across the Rapidan downriver of Lee's army, just as the

Confederate commander had expected. He left Anderson's Division, including Perrin's brigade of Alabamians, standing fast along the river line as a rear guard in case more Federals came across in their front. The remainder of Hill's 3rd Corps lit out down the Orange Plank Road towards the Wilderness. Ewell's 2nd Corps fell into line of march just to their north on the Orange Turnpike, also heading east. Encamped farther west was Longstreet's 1st Corps, which had a long way to go to catch up to Hill's hard-marching men.[162]

The huge Federal army committed its full force to the downriver crossings, and the events of May 4 made it clear to Lee that he need not fear any additional crossings in his front or on his left. The advancing blue hordes were streaming through the muggy springtime heat, and they swung west through the Wilderness in an attempt to come up on Lee's right and force a major battle. Many Federals and Confederates shared the expectation that Lee would put his men into their old positions along Mine Run, which ran in a generally north-south direction just west of the dense tangles of the Wilderness. Meade, the titular head of the Army of the Potomac, had cooperated closely with Grant to develop the plan of campaign, and the hawk-nosed commander determined he would not be stymied by the Mine Run defenses in the same manner as the previous November. This time, he would swing a full army corps around the southern end of Lee's line, then lever the Confederates out of their works into the open field, or else roll them up from the south if they were slow to withdraw. Meade stopped his advance on schedule amidst the brambles of the Wilderness on the evening of May 4, confident that he was positioning a steamroller on Lee's flank. The next day would bring it to bear against the outnumbered Confederates.[163]

As historian Gordon Rhea has pointed out in his excellent analysis of Meade's plan, the Federal commander had arrived at a formidable concept of maneuver, although perhaps he should have feinted against Lee's Rapidan defenses to pin the Rebels in position. Certainly, however, he should not have stopped in the Wilderness to allow his supply wagons to catch up to his infantry, because the dense underbrush and second-growth thickets hemmed in his columns and hampered maneuver in both attack and defense. That, of course, is exactly why the heavily outnumbered Lee went hunting for him there. Many Rebel infantrymen had loosened their packstraps as they moved downslope into the valley of Mine Run, expecting the order to halt and occupy their old positions. Surprised when they were ordered across the stream and up the other side, they cheered and laughed at the prospect: "Marse Bob is going for them this time."[164]

On May 5, 1864, Pickett's Division was ensconced in the Richmond defenses, Longstreet's other two were on the road, and Anderson's was moving up from the Rapidan. Nevertheless, Lee hurled his remaining five divisions against a Federal force almost treble their number in the Wilderness. Their mission was to fix Meade's men in place, while Longstreet's two divisions would come up and deliver one of Lee's trademark flank attacks. The fighting centered at the points on the Orange Plank Road and Orange Turnpike where the opposing infantry columns came face to face, and numerous Federal brigades went to pieces under the bone-jarring impact of

Confederate infantry attacks pressed home with the ferocity that was their hallmark. Other Union brigades rushed forward to fill the gaps and pushed hard the other way, displaying a new staying power in the attack that was apparent to their opponents. By late in the day, however, Ewell's three divisions had stopped five Federal divisions dead in their tracks on the Orange Turnpike. Several miles to the south, A. P. Hill's two divisions had fought several times their weight in Yankees, and the seven divisions arrayed against Hill were stopped by the narrowest of margins. Grant planned to send them plowing into Hill's front and northern flank early the next morning. Although Hill had enjoyed perhaps his finest hour on May 5, his exhausted men were scattered crazyquilt fashion throughout the dense thickets, with little semblance of a coherent or defensible line remaining. Directed by Lee to let his men rest until relieved by Longstreet that night, Hill left his units where darkness found them.[165]

If Longstreet's men did not come up on schedule, Hill's Corps faced extinction when the Federals resumed their onslaught. Old Pete's hard-marching veterans had left their positions on the west flank of the Rapidan line about four o'clock on the afternoon of May 4, covering 32 miles in the next twenty-four hours. Unfortunately for Hill, even this forced march left Longstreet's leading units some ten miles from the front, and "Lee's War Horse" recognized that his famished and footsore men required eight hours rest. He knew his orders were to get up "as soon as practicable" the next morning, but did not realize that the fate of the Army of Northern Virginia was entirely in his hands.[166]

Anderson's Division was also en route to the front on the evening of May 5, and William Mangham was in the long column of dusty grayjackets trudging down the Orange Plank Road toward the front. As they pushed through the gathering darkness, they encountered wounded men streaming back to the rear, telling of a hot fight up front. The Alabamians camped that night about a mile behind the front line, then arose before dawn to move into their designated position in Hill's second line. They were held up a short distance behind the battlefront, however, as Longstreet's Corps filed into the Plank Road ahead of them. Since the Federal juggernaut already was grinding into action against Hill's front as dawn broke, these hard-marching Rebs were headed towards one of the closest-run actions in the entire war. They would arrive just in time to stave off disaster.[167]

Hill's subordinate commanders had spent a frantic night awaiting Longstreet's arrival, and their worst nightmares came true on May 6 as Federal divisions rolled into action and began crumbling the Confederate units scattered throughout the forest. One soldier thought the Orange Plank road was a "scene of utter, and apparently, irremediable confusion, such as we had never witnessed before in Lee's army." A desperate Powell Hill even helped man an artillery piece, one of a dozen that sought to stem the waves of blue coats pouring up the road. His troops had borne the brunt of the battle the previous day, and had fought with the desperation of men who knew that they must hold against staggering odds until Longstreet came; their performance was in the finest traditions of the Army of Northern Virginia. This day, however, they had to move to the rear in any way they could, and their predicament was almost as mortifying to the proud veterans as it was dangerous.[168]

As an ever-swelling tide of fugitives sought safety in retreat down the Plank Road, they encountered two separate columns, each four abreast, moving up in the other direction. It was Longstreet at last! From these densely packed ranks came pointed jibes: "Do you belong to General Lee's army? You don't look like the men we left here. You are worse than Bragg's men." Marching his two divisions abreast on the same stretch of road to save time, Old Pete flung brigade after brigade straight from the line of march into a slashing series of counterattacks that staggered the advancing Federals, though at a horrendous cost in casualties. Field's Division smashed the northern half of the Federal pincers, routing Wadsworth's division into panic flight, while Kershaw's Division mauled two divisions of Hancock's corps on the south side of the road.[169]

In slightly more than two hours of furious attacks, Longstreet smashed the Federal spearheads and reestablished a coherent Confederate line across the Orange Plank Road. When Anderson's Division reached the front at about eight o'clock that morning, Lee placed it under Longstreet's command. Old Pete held these fresh troops in reserve for the time being, and William Mangham and the 14th Alabama filed to the left into line of battle with the other men of Perrin's Brigade, whose right flank rested directly upon the Plank Road. There they stood, expecting to go into action at any moment, and Lee himself sat astride Traveler at the right of their line, conferring in undertones with Longstreet. Lieutenant George Clark of the 11th Alabama was standing less than ten feet from the two commanders as two men came from the front, seeking to pass through the line. Looking at one of them sporting a nasty arm wound, Lee asked "My friend, I trust you are not badly hurt." Tipping his hat with his uninjured arm, the soldier responded: "No, General. My right arm is broken, but I hope to be well as soon as possible and take my place in the ranks again." Lee gave the man directions to Dr. Lafayette Guild's tent, adding, "Tell him I sent you there and I want him to dress your arm nicely." The waiting Alabamians then heard Lee order the other man, who was unwounded, to "Go back to the front." When the straggler protested that he was out of ammunition, the general flared "That makes no difference, sir. A true soldier never leaves the field as long as he has his bayonet." Perrin's men began to mutter at the straggler, and one sang out "Old Bob caught you, damn you." Raising his hand for silence, Lee told them, "Stop, boys, maybe we will make a man of him yet." With that final reproof, the chastened straggler turned around and headed back to the front, or perhaps he simply sought a less obtrusive route to the rear![170]

Shortly afterwards, Perrin's men moved into the woods, advancing perhaps four hundred yards before they encountered Yankees in large numbers. Hitting the dirt, the Alabama soldiers loaded and fired as fast as they could for fifteen or twenty minutes, before jumping up and surging forward against a "frightful" volume of fire. They drove these Federals back out of range, but encountered more on front, flanks, and rear in the dense thickets where enemy lines could lie invisible just ten paces away. Lieutenant Clark estimated they pushed forward a mile under these conditions, until they came to a halt and lay down to await orders. There they held their ground until midafternoon, listening to the click of guns as Federals loaded their muskets just 75 yards away. As the Alabamians cautiously watched their front, Longstreet launched a spectacular flanking maneuver that rolled up much of Hancock's corps from south to north. Although Burnside attempted more counterattacks from north of the Plank Road, most of the Federal forces near the road were barely able to hang on against frontal attacks seeking to finish them off.[171]

Accounts of the movements of Perrin's Brigade are conflicting, which is not surprising in a battle that saw Longstreet seriously wounded by a misdirected volley fired by his own men. Likewise, it is not known how many casualties the Confederates suffered in the terrible fighting, although estimates range from 7500 to 11,000 killed, wounded and missing. One of those wounded on May 6 was Pvt. William Mangham, who met a bullet with his name on it during the savage fighting in the tangled thickets. Federal casualties were reported as 17,666 all told, although evidence indicates that some commanders intentionally under-reported their shocking losses. Amidst all the uncertainties, however, Lee's veterans felt sure of one thing: they had licked the Army of the Potomac once more, new commander or not.[172]

*   *   *   *   *

Grant pulled his men out of the Wilderness all right, but they emerged from the forests and turned south towards Spotsylvania Court House, rather than heading back north across the Rapidan to lick their wounds. Union troops, depressed at rumors that they were retreating once more, burst into wild cheering with shouts of "On to Richmond!" They had a general who would spare nothing to get them there, but they would find that the Rebels' saucy ditty of 1863 still held true: Richmond remained a very hard road to travel.[173]

No surviving records provide a clue to the nature or seriousness of William's wound, nor can we determine how long he was absent recovering. Since Lee had directed subordinate commanders to cease reporting minor wounds that left a soldier fit for duty, it is probable that William was unable to serve in the ranks for some time. Perhaps he went home to Chambers County to recover on a 30-, 60-, or 90-day furlough, or perhaps his injuries responded to treatment in a field hospital or a general hospital in Richmond. He certainly was back with the regiment by August 1864, when he again drew replacement items for some of his worn out clothing. In all likelihood, he missed the 14th Alabama's terrible ordeal by fire at Spotsylvania Court House in mid-May, as well as the resulting clashes that brought Grant's forces to the gates of Richmond by early June. Lee was desperate for a chance to smash his opponent's army while it was on the move during its numerous flanking maneuvers, because he feared the final outcome if the Federals reached the James River. "We must destroy this Army of Grant's before he gets to the James River. If he gets there it will become a siege, and then it will be a mere question of time."[174]

William certainly participated in the Petersburg siege that commenced when Grant successfully crossed the James River in mid-June, although a 60-day wounded furlough would have caused him to miss the brilliantly executed counterattack of June 22, led by "Fighting Billy" Mahone, his division commander. In a hard day's fighting, Mahone's men folded up three Union divisions threatening the Weldon Railroad leading south out of Petersburg. As a fellow officer accurately observed, "Whenever Mahone moves out, somebody is apt to be hurt." If William was back in ranks by July 30, then he took part in another Mahone-led riposte that was one of the nastiest battles of the war, and which has become synonymous with the Siege of Petersburg: the Battle of the Crater.[175]

The idea of tunneling under the Confederate entrenchments and blowing them sky-high was the brainchild of Lt. Col. Henry Pleasants of the 48th Pennsylvania Volunteers. A mining and civil engineer before the war, it was natural for Pleasants to view the burgeoning earthworks barring his way into Petersburg as a problem susceptible to his engineering expertise. Obtaining permission to put his Pennsylvanians to work underground, they began burrowing their way towards a portion of the Confederate lines known as Elliott's Salient on June 25, 1864. Many of his men had mined coal for a living before the war, and they improvised the tools necessary to dig a ventilated gallery 510 feet long by July 17, when they reached a point slightly behind the main Rebel trenches. During the ensuing week, the miners constructed 40-foot lateral galleries to left and right, which they began packing with 25-pound kegs of gunpowder on July 27. They completed the job late that night by dragging 320 kegs into position, then laying a fuse and tamping the tunnel to direct the force of the blast upward through the Confederate fortifications.[176]

Major General Ambrose Burnside, commanding the IX Corps facing Elliott's Salient, had the job of planning an infantry assault to exploit the mining operation. Burnside was the same ill-fated commander whose defeat at Fredericksburg in December 1862 resulted in his relief from command of the Army of the Potomac, and the eight thousand pounds of blasting powder under Elliott's Salient promised professional redemption writ large. The salient was just half a mile from Petersburg itself, and a massive rupture of the Confederate lines at such a critical point promised him a sterling opportunity to break the deadlock and precipitate the climactic battle Grant sought. If Grant could shatter Lee's army, he could waltz into Richmond and lay claim to the enemy's capital. With both of these objects achieved, there would be every reason to expect the Confederacy's complete collapse.[177]

Although Burnside initially designated a raw division of black troops to spearhead the infantry assault following the mine explosion, Meade decided such a move was likely to cause terrible recriminations should the attack prove a bloody failure: had they used untried black troops as mere cannon fodder? Although Grant agreed with the rationale for the change, he was unaware that Burnside chose the least rational of solutions: he had his other three division commanders draw lots to see which should be the first into the breach! When Brigadier General Ledlie drew the short straw, it meant that the worst combat outfit of the three assumed the weighty responsibility.[178]

The change was made less than 48 hours before Lieutenant Colonel Pleasants lit the fuse in the predawn darkness of July 30. When the charge failed to detonate, two gutsy Pennsylvanians dug through the tamping to the point where the fuse had sputtered out, lit it anew, and scrambled out of the tunnel as fast as they could go. Minutes later, at 4:44 a.m., ". . .there came a deep shock and tremor of the earth and a jar like an earthquake. . . then a monstrous tongue of flame shot fully two hundred feet into the air, followed by a vast column of white smoke. . .then a great spout or fountain of red earth rose to a very great height. . . ." Amidst the cloud whirled men, guns, and debris of all sorts, which came tumbling to the ground all over the area. Three hundred South Carolina infantrymen and thirty artillerymen manned the trenches and gun positions directly above the mine; of these, 278 were killed or wounded in the explosion. (See map on page 512.)[179]

Immediately following the blast, 110 Federal cannon and 54 mortars cut loose along the two miles of trenchline fronting the crater, which gaped sixty feet wide and thirty feet deep along a front 150-200 feet long. Shortly thereafter, assault troops began pushing through the smoky early morning light, bunching in and around the smoldering hole as stunned Confederates on either flank began firing for all they were worth. Although a few South Carolinians flung themselves at the crater in a desperate counterattack just minutes after the blast, they were shot down in droves as they surged through the open. Ever more blueclad infantrymen scrambled down into the hole as succeeding brigades poured into the breach, but they struggled to clamber up the steep, muddy slope on the opposite side, where the explosion had thrown up a jagged fort-like parapet. Many Federals escorted groups of stunned Rebel survivors to the rear in the chaos, but far too many jammed themselves into the giant pit, where the worsening tangle of men and units quickly reduced the attack into a roiling free-for-all. Although some officers attempted to lead their troops north, south, and west to expand the breach, others had no positive idea what they were to do. Most had never been briefed on the concept of the operation, and simply were flung toward the crater in ever-increasing numbers. Confederate resistance aggravated the confusion, and the Southerners' aggressive response to the penetration brought more and more reinforcements to the battle area, which lay just east of the Jerusalem Plank Road leading southwards out of Petersburg.[180]

Ferrero's black troops comprised the fourth Federal division to cross the seething caldron of cannon and rifle fire and enter the pit, about four hours after the mine had exploded. Their introduction to the bloody fight portended a heightening of Southern desperation, just at the time when an appalled General Grant realized that the grand opportunity to break the Confederate line had gone hopelessly awry. He ordered his troops withdrawn, but General Lee strove to strike fast and hard against the threatened point. He had ordered "Fighting Billy" Mahone to pull two brigades from their positions just west of the Jerusalem Plank Road and repel the assault, but Mahone already knew something was up before he received these orders. As he recalled it, "The first I knew of the crater, beyond the tremendous report of the explosion, came from a soldier who, from thereabouts, hatless and shoeless, passed me, still going, and only time to say, 'Hell has busted!'" Mahone soon got his Virginia and Georgia brigades into position on Cemetery Hill, on rising high ground between Petersburg and the Crater. Seeing the magnitude of the task before him, he sent word to bring up Wilcox's old brigade as quickly as possible. If William Mangham was in ranks that morning, he was one of the 632 Alabamians who pulled out of their trenches and began marching toward the Crater, about a mile away.[181]

Meanwhile, Mahone concluded that the thousands of Yankees milling about the crater were organizing themselves for an attack to seize the high ground, so he decided to strike first. He launched his Virginia and Georgia brigades in a ferocious counterattack just before 9:00 a.m., and they plowed into the jumbled lines of white and black soldiers milling outside the crater. Somehow, word had spread that the black troops were giving no quarter, so the stage truly was set for disaster. Not only were the Confederates well aware that they were facing a desperate tactical and strategic situation, but they were confronting many black troops at the crater.[182]

In Southerners' eyes, armed blacks represented not only an insult to their society and a rejection of their way of life, but also posed an imminent threat to its very survival. In the first place, the image of black soldiers evoked the haunting specter of social equality between white and black. Such seemingly nightmarish visions curdled the blood of white Southerners, whether or not they personally owned slaves; historian James McPherson has shown that such fears were a major factor motivating many Southerners to fight for four long years. One North Carolina dirt farmer's son asserted he would never stop fighting, because the Yankees were "trying to force us to live as the colored race." A Louisiana artilleryman insisted, "I never want to see the day when a negro is put on an equality with a white person. There is too many free niggers. . .now to suit me, let alone having four millions." Asking some Confederate prisoners near Atlanta what they were fighting for, one Wisconsin private was told: "You Yanks want us to marry our daughters to the niggers." With such fears universal throughout the South, many whites viewed the Union army's use of black troops as nothing but an outright Abolitionist bid to incite slave rebellion. Since some Southerners viewed blacks as only one step removed from African savagery, fiery images of slave revolt excited a deep dread of arson, pillage, and rapine. Taking on a sharper edge in the wake of John Brown's abortive slave revolt at Harper's Ferry in 1859, these long-standing fears resonated strongly in 1864. Conscription had pulled almost all able-bodied men into the army, so Confederate soldiers were uncomfortably aware that nothing but young boys and old men stood between a possible slave rampage and their wives and children back home.[183]

Here at the Crater it all came to a boil. Although most soldiers in Lee's army held out hope that the war was not lost, they suspected that the besieged defenders of Atlanta and Petersburg stood almost literally at the proverbial last ditch; their worst fears were nigh upon them. The last straw on July 30, 1864 was to be told that the black troops before them were showing no quarter to Confederates. Their blood boiling over with the full frenzy of battle upon them, Mahone's Virginians and Georgians surged towards either flank of the crater. Mahone's own brigade, commanded by Colonel Weisiger of the 12th Virginia, overran the trenches in front of the crater itself, while Wright's Georgians were shot to pieces by heavy rifle and artillery fire as they came screaming across the open ground towards the southern flank. Those who reached the defensive lines spilled into the trenches and fought hand-to-hand with the defenders; one Reb judged that "Most of the fighting was done with bayonets and butts of muskets." Many Federals, both black and white, lost their nerve and fled for their lives, while enraged Confederates slaughtered many panicked black soldiers as they tried to surrender. Others were murdered in cold blood after they had quit fighting, although blind luck saved some where mercy had failed. One Georgian admitted that four blacks passed safely to the rear, "as we could not kill them as fast as they passed us."[184]

This first counterattack seized the flanks and forward lip of the crater, but thousands of Federals still fired over the parapet of the "horrid pit" itself, either unable to skedaddle or doggedly unwilling to pull back unless ordered. It was 11:00 a.m. when the last available Confederate reinforcements reached the vicinity of the crater. These men were Wilcox's old brigade of Alabamians, now led by Col. John Sanders. The men sheltered in a ravine southwest of the crater, while Capt. John Clark went forward to the lip of the crater to discern the situation from the Virginia and Georgia troops there. While Clark looked over the situation, Mahone briefed Sanders on the plan of attack. If the Alabamians paused in the open to fire and advance, they would never survive the volume of fire that would sweep them from front and flanks. Accordingly, they were to wait for the signal to emerge from cover, oblique to their right to ensure their charge would cover the crater itself as well as the rifle pits to its south, then charge at the double-quick after receiving the first enemy volley. To ensure that nobody would succumb to the overpowering urge to stop and fire in self-defense, muskets were to be carried at a right shoulder shift. Mahone prowled the waiting ranks of Alabama soldiers, spreading the word that black soldiers in the Crater had sworn to give no quarter. He also pointed out the Gee House, where General Lee had located his headquarters, emphasizing that "Marse Robert" himself would be watching them as they attacked. Captain Clark filed down the ranks, ensuring that every single one of the 632 men knew that Lee was prepared to lead the charge personally if necessary. A passing staff officer reinforced this message, calling out to Sanders that Lee would come lead the charge personally if the first attempt were to fail. One Reb spoke for all when he answered, "If the old man comes down here, we will tie him to a sapling while we make the fight."[185]

When the signal guns boomed out early that afternoon, the five Alabama regiments arose and started up the slope of the ravine, crouching low to utilize available cover until the last possible moment. Coming over the crest, they came under fire immediately. Captain Clark noted that "For a moment or two the enemy overshot us and did no damage, but as we reached the works, many were struck down and the gaps became apparent." To a nearby South Carolinian, "The Yankee cannon seemed literally to tear up the ground under the very feet of the brigade." Still the Alabama troops pushed forward, shrilling the Rebel yell as they came. Federals jammed into the human mass at the bottom of the crater could not see them coming, but the dreaded sound made their blood run cold. Some white soldiers turned panic-stricken on their black comrades, shooting them down or bayoneting them for fear that the howling rebels would take no white man prisoner if he were found with the black soldiers. One Federal officer who survived noted that "the men was bound not to be taken prisoner among them niggers."[186]

Some of the first Alabamians to reach the crater flung themselves down in front of its jagged parapet, jumping up to snap off an occasional shot into the blue masses below. Other men flung bayoneted rifles like spears down into the pit, while others hoisted their hats above the rim on their bayonets. When the waiting Yankees blasted a ragged volley at the hats, the Alabamians sprang over the top and down into the crater itself. As one participant recalled it, "This day was the jubilee of fiends in human shape, and without souls." A Massachusetts officer recalled the scene as "one seething cauldron of struggling, dying men," where the dead often remained upright in the writhing mass until they finally were jostled to the ground. Colonel Sanders "had a regular duel" with a big black soldier, but in their excitement neither hit the mark. Two lieutenants of the 11th Alabama flung themselves into the melee with the regimental colors. One of them, Lt. P. M. Vance, was shot through the leg as he leaped into the crater, but managed to come to grips with the black soldier who shot him. As they grappled in the bottom of the pit, the Federal drew a knife to finish off Vance. Fainting from loss of blood and unable to wield his sword, Vance caught his opponent in a desperate bearhug until some of his men came to the rescue, bayoneting and clubbing the black soldier to death.[187]

The slaughter continued for fifteen or twenty agonizing minutes, but an ever-increasing number of Yankees clambered over the rim of the hellhole and ran for their lives. Black soldiers fell victim to savage retaliation at the hands of the attackers. Private W. C. McClellan of the 9th Alabama wrote home that all the black prisoners "would have ben killed had it not been for gen[eral] Mahone who beg our men to Spare them." McClellan saw Mahone confront one enraged Alabama soldier who had killed several blacks, ordering him "For God's sake stop." The man replied grimly, "Well gen[eral] let me kill one more," whereupon he deliberately took out his pocket knife and cut a prisoner's throat. Since both sides assumed the other would grant no quarter, those unable or unwilling to run away remained in the pit fighting for their lives, until Lt. Morgan Cleveland of the 8th Alabama cried out in despair to a nearby Federal colonel, "Why in the hell don't you fellows surrender?" Came the equally despairing answer, "Why in the hell don't you let us?" Lieutenant Kibby of the 4th Rhode Island finally hoisted a white handkerchief affixed to his sword, and the killing subsided around him as Union soldiers dropped their weapons and gave up. A few more black soldiers were shot or bayoneted out of hand as the frenzy subsided, but a Massachusetts soldier saw an Alabama captain finally stop the violence by shouting at his men, "Hold on there; they have surrendered." Although still more men in blue and gray fell victim to incoming Federal artillery fire, the battle was over. As one saddened New Hampshire soldier noted in his diary, "A sad day for our corps. The old story again—a big slaughter, and nothing gained." One lieutenant in the Alabama brigade shared similar feelings: "Troops that our Brigade fought were principally negroe and the slaughter was immense: *heart sickening*."[188]

Private J. J. Autrey of the Cusseta Greys was mortally wounded in the no-holds-barred melee against defenders who outnumbered the attackers by a margin of three to one. If William Mangham was among those who surged into the crater that terrible day, he could count himself a lucky survivor of one of the war's most desperate engagements, as 91 of the 632 attacking Alabamians fell dead or wounded. He and his comrades also could take credit for helping save the Army of Northern Virginia.[189]

As ragged as the army was after three months of intense combat, its troops still inspired a respect bordering on awe among their opponents. Union Lt. Col. Theodore Lyman, a member of General Meade's staff, wrote his wife just eight days after the battle, bemoaning the reticence of Northern volunteers to help carry on the unrelenting fight against these hard cases who simply wouldn't quit:

> By the Lord! I wish these gentlemen who would overwhelm us with Germans, negroes, and the offscourings of great cities, could only see—only *see*—a Rebel regiment, in all their rags and squalor. If they had eyes they would know these men are like wolfhounds, and not to be beaten by turnspits.[190]

*   *   *   *   *

William probably took part in a severe action at Deep Bottom on August 16, where Wilcox's old brigade was almost overrun before it rallied and helped smash a Union penetration north of the James River. Yet another sharp fight occurred near the Weldon Railroad five days later, when Mahone's Division counterattacked a Union encroachment at a critical point. At the Weldon Railroad, however, the hard-fighting Mahone was mistaken in his belief that he had found a vulnerable flank to smash, and his men butted up against a strongly refused Federal flank on the Vaughan Road near Globe Tavern. One Federal remembered that the Rebels came on in four lines of battle, but withered under a concentration of fire in which the "corn stalks were cut off by the bullets as if with a knife." Six times, the starry-crossed battle flag in the first line fell to earth, and six times the color guard took it up again and continued the charge, but all was for naught. Pulling back to seek the flank again, Mahone's men finally gave up the impossible task and withdrew. At Reams Station on August 25, the 14th Alabama took part in another major counterattack, which finally succeeded in administering a severe beating to two of Hancock's divisions along the line of the Weldon Railroad. One North Carolinian wrote that Confederate morale soared after this action: ". . .I never saw men so much elated by any fight. They now think they can storm almost any Yankee's breastworks." At the cost of slightly more than eight hundred casualties, Lee's men had inflicted over 2600 on their besiegers, as well as capturing twelve stands of colors, nine cannon, and 3100 small arms.[191]

William was sick in the division infirmary at the end of October, although he returned to his regiment after muster, so it is uncertain if he participated in the engagement at Hatcher's Run on October 27. Mahone's men were unsuccessful in their attempt to help cut off and destroy Hancock's II Corps after its sortie against the Confederate lines, but the Federals suffered a severe repulse nonetheless. The 14th

Alabama took part in still another counterattack near Hatcher's Run in early February 1865, and this time Mahone's Division helped smash the V Corps near Dabney's Mill. One Alabamian recalled the panic flight of Crawford's and Ayres's Federal divisions with pride, noting: "We drove them back easily and did it handsomely, nothing easier." Despite occasional tactical successes, however, the strategic outlook was growing increasingly grim. According to one discouraged writer back home in Auburn that winter, the Confederacy was "in the category of a schoolboy I once knew, who told the schoolmaster while he was whipping him 'If you'll find hickory, I'll find back.'"[192]

That February, William moved with the remainder of Wilcox's old brigade into the trenches on the extreme left of the Confederate line, anchoring their position on the Howlett Batteries on the James River. Unfortunately, however, the starvation rations of January and February weakened men who already were downhearted at the news that the Army of Tennessee had been practically destroyed at Nashville in December. Other Federal troops had captured Savannah before Christmas, after burning their way across Georgia in a swath of terror and destruction; these same troops had crushed South Carolina under their heels on the way into North Carolina by March 1865. General Lee knew that the end was near. His troops deserted by the thousands as spring approached, their morale destroyed by the steady drumbeat of bad news from their desolated homes throughout the South, and by the army's patent inability to feed or pay them anymore. Although the Federals across the lines had been bled nearly white during the endless campaign of 1864-1865, they were much stronger than the tattered grayclad starvelings who remained defiant in the Petersburg trenches until early April. After a desperate Confederate assault on Fort Stedman left them vulnerable to yet another major Federal thrust, the 35-mile long labyrinth of trenches finally stretched farther than Lee's stalwarts could hold.[193]

The lines at Petersburg collapsed under a series of determined assaults on April 2, 1865, following ten months of nearly continuous combat. Mahone's Division pulled out of the lines north of Petersburg and passed north of town, en route to Goode's Bridge on the Appomattox River. One of the men trudging westward in hopes of uniting with Johnston's army in North Carolina was Pvt. William Mangham. He and the other men of Forney's Brigade struggled vainly on April 7 to hold High Bridge, where his cousin's son, *Pvt. Tom Mangham* of the 10th Alabama, was taken prisoner.[194]

William was still in line of battle a week later at Appomattox Court House when the 14th Alabama met its appointed rendezvous with bitter destiny. Of the 1317 men who had served in the regiment by February 1865, 245 had been killed in action or died of wounds, another 348 died of disease, and 159 had been discharged or transferred. Of the 287 men present for duty at that time, only eleven officers and 180 men remained to stack arms for the last time on April 12, 1865, before a Union contingent headed by Maj. Gen. Joshua Chamberlain. Many years afterwards, the hero of Little Round Top mentally reviewed the columns of Confederates who made their last front before him that April day at Appomattox: "What is this but the remnant of Mahone's Division, last seen by us [Chamberlain's brigade] at the North Anna? its

310

thinned ranks of worn, bright-eyed men recalling scenes of costly valor and ever-remembered history."[195]

William A. Mangham disappeared into the shadows of history on that fateful day when his name was inscribed forever as one of those who fought to the last ditch. Nothing is known of him after April 9, 1865.

5. WHO WILL TAKE CARE OF THE BABIES? PVT. JAMES M. D. MANGHAM, CO. F, 61ST ALABAMA, AND WILEY PAUL MANGHAM, CONFEDERATE SOLDIER

No surviving records indicate whether William came home to Chambers County, where he had lived with his elder brother James M. D. Mangham before the war. Born in January 1824, James was the eldest known son of James M. and Eleanor Mangham of Butts County. As the eldest boy in a large farm family, he must have helped his parents till the land, look out for his younger brothers and sisters, and manage the slaves. He started a family of his own when he married Jane McCoy in Butts County on May 21, 1845, and the couple named their first sons Wiley Paul and Henry J. Mangham after two of James's brothers.[196]

By 1850, James had moved his family to the vicinity of McDonough in neighboring Henry County. The Manghams were only three houses removed from William McWhorter and his wife Francis, who was one of James's elder sisters and the namesake of his seven-month-old daughter. Other close neighbors were the widow Mary Croley and her family, which included 5-year-old *John S. Mangham*, who was probably one of James's nephews. James rented his farm, but owned a horse, milch cow, one sheep and a dozen hogs to provide milk, cheese, and meat for his small family. His small crop comprised a hundred bushels of Indian corn, as well as four 300-pound bales of cotton to provide some ready cash for his little family.[197]

By December of that year, however, he moved west to booming Chambers County, Alabama, moving in temporarily with Green B. Smith. Shortly thereafter, James brought his family from Georgia to join him, and by 1855 he had managed to obtain four slaves to help him work the farm. By 1860, he was working hard on his eighty-acre farmstead near Culebra to feed a large family. This small settlement in the southwestern part of the county was a voting place less than a mile from the Mangham farm, although the nearest post office was in Oak Bowery, about ten miles away. With Wiley in his early teens and Henry now eleven, the boys could help with some of the chores, while Francis was ten and could help with the younger children, Mary (5), James Jr. (4), John C. (2) and an infant son named Jefferson Davis Mangham. James's younger brother *William A. Mangham* lived with the family as well, and farmed a small cotton patch adjoining James's farm. William and Francis Mangham McWhorter lived nearby again, so it was clear that James maintained a close relationship with some of his kin, despite the fact that he had moved away from his early roots in Butts County. In all probability, he also tried to keep track of his brother *Henry* in nearby Sylacauga. The namesake of James's 12-year-old son, Henry had settled briefly in Coosa County about the same time James came to Alabama, before moving across the county line into southern Talladega County about 1852. In all probability the Mangham brothers knew their first cousin *Solomon R. Mangham,* who resided in Chambers County until moving to Dadeville in neighboring Tallapoosa County in the early 1850s; Dadeville was only about fifteen miles away from James's farm. Indeed, since Solomon's father Thomas Mangham had moved his family to Chambers County in the 1830s, it may well be that their experiences there had helped attract his nephews Henry and James Mangham to Alabama a decade later.[198]

THE JAMES M. D. MANGHAM HOME IN CHAMBERS COUNTY, ALABAMA.
(SEE APPENDIX, REF. # 92)

- Courtesy of Jean Ennis

It is unclear what James thought of the national crisis in 1860-1861, but as a small farmer and slaveholder he was probably a typical enough citizen of the Deep South. Regardless of his stance on secession, it is highly likely that he cared little for Yankees and abolitionists. At age 34, with a large family to feed and no sons old enough to take over his farm, however, he clearly was not prepared to drop everything and join William when he sold his cotton patch and mule to enlist in July 1861. Whatever his motives, James remained on his farm until the shifting fortunes of war threatened the Confederacy with disaster in 1863. In May of that year, Col. James H. Clanton received a special commission from the Secretary of War to raise a full brigade of troops from Alabama, for which achievement he expected to receive promotion to brigadier general. As an inducement for men to enlist, he was empowered to promise them duty within the state of Alabama, and he was granted a further special exemption to enlist men who were otherwise liable to conscription.[199]

Since the Confederate Congress had raised the upper limit of the conscription age from 35 to 45 in September 1862, thousands of men like James now were liable for military service, and Clanton's organization seemed attractive in several crucial respects. First of all, service within their home state held out the prospect of frequent visits home, which would enable them to pay some attention to family and business matters. The welfare state was still a hundred years in the future, and the farm family whose husband and father was away in the army had to make shift to get in a crop. With almost all healthy adult male relatives in the service, the only sources of labor were men unfit for military service, slaves, women, and children. Of course, slaves were a mainstay of the Southern economy, but small farmers like James had to work alongside them in the fields and direct their labor throughout the year. Service within Alabama also offered men between 35 and 45 easier physical prospects than did duty with Bragg's Army of Tennessee or Lee's Army of Northern Virginia. Without a doubt, every man of this age group in Chambers County knew robust young men who had marched off to war in 1861 or 1862, only to die within weeks or months from severe exposure or disease, or return home broken down by hard marching on short rations. Robbed of their physical ability to perform hard manual labor, these crippled men faced a questionable future in rural Alabama, condemned to life on the barest margins of subsistence. Many who enlisted under Clanton's plan doubtless did so because it was the most attractive, honorable alternative in a very hard war.[200]

When Alfred F. Zachry of Bluffton (present day Lanett) advertised in Chambers County for a company to serve in one of Clanton's new infantry regiments, one of those who traveled to the county seat of LaFayette to volunteer was James M. D. Mangham. On July 30, 1863, he and 38 other men enrolled for duty in the Confederate Army, signing up "for the war." Over the next month, another eighteen enlisted in the company, allowing Zachry to complete its organization. When the new unit chose officers and non-commissioned officers on August 29, the 44-year-old Zachry was elected captain. Apparently his company was one of the last to complete its organization, for Clanton forwarded twenty-six muster rolls to the War Department at Richmond on July 29; by September 19, he finally could report that his brigade was organized. Along with two cavalry regiments and two artillery batteries, he announced the completion of the 54th and 55th Alabama Volunteer Infantry regiments. The commander of the 55th Alabama was Col. William G. Swanson, whose regiment was redesignated the 59th Alabama in November 1863. After yet another reshuffle, the regiment became known as the 61st Alabama by April 1864. The confusion resulted from the nearly simultaneous reorganization of another all-arms outfit, Hilliard's Alabama Legion, into the 59th and 60th Alabama regiments. Although their regimental designation was fluid for some months, Captain Zachry's Chambers County outfit retained its designation as Company F in Swanson's regiment.[201]

These developments were still in the future when Pvt. James Mangham said his farewells and departed for duty at Camp Pollard, Alabama. In all probability, he boarded the cars of the Montgomery & West Point Railroad in Chambers County, traveled the 80-odd miles to the state capital, and then transferred to the Alabama & Florida Railroad for the 114-mile trip to Pollard. The army camp lay just five miles north of the Florida state line in Conecuh County. The town of Pollard came into being in 1861, when the Alabama & Florida Railroad constructed its southern terminus there, forging a connection with the Florida & Alabama Railroad, which ran north from Pensacola. November 1861 also marked the completion of the Mobile & Great Northern Railroad, which ran 47 miles from Pollard to Tensas Station, on the Tensas River just north of Mobile. Freight and passengers ferried from Mobile to Tensas Station could proceed by rail directly to Pollard, and there turn south to Pensacola or north to Montgomery. To top it all off, the major surface road from Montgomery to Pensacola ran through Pollard as well.[202]

These rail, river, and road communications gave the tiny hamlet a military significance out of all proportion to its size and the uninviting piney woods, swamps, and sandy soil that characterized the area. In 1861, Montgomery was the capital of the young Confederacy, and Mobile and Pensacola were some of the new nation's most important seaports. Since the export of "King Cotton" to northern and European mills was the central pillar of the Deep South's economy, a place like Pollard was an important commercial node. Its significance was magnified by the abandonment of Pensacola in the spring of 1862, when Braxton Bragg's garrison departed for active theaters of war in Tennessee. Thereafter, a garrison held Pollard as insurance against any Federal attempt to stage a sortie from the Florida seaport.[203]

As Clanton's Brigade completed its organization in the late summer of 1863, Pollard offered the perfect rendezvous and duty station. It warranted a substantial garrison of all arms, and Clanton's cavalry provided the capability to screen its approaches against Federal raiders, while his infantry and artillery could hold it against anything less than a sizable invasion force. Since the Federals had shown no sign of mounting a major strike from Pensacola, Pollard also seemed a good place to employ a force comprised of Alabama's young boys and older men, freeing up veteran units for more strenuous duty elsewhere. Had Bragg's army lost the Battle of Chickamauga in September of 1863, Clanton's outfit might have found itself in the Army of Tennessee, but the end of that month saw the defeated Yankees holed up in Chattanooga.

As James got accustomed to military routine at Camp Pollard, he probably encountered some distant cousins in other companies of Swanson's regiment. *Private William T. T. Mangham* was a member of Company E, recruited largely from Butler County, and Francis M. ("Frank") Mangum served as a private in Company H from Macon County. Equipped with Austrian rifles, Zachry's company drilled regularly to learn the intricacies of the manual of arms, as well as the evolutions of company and battalion drill. The men also performed a variety of guard duties in camp, including provost duty at the guardhouse, but their most important duty was detached service protecting the critical lines of communication.[204]

Some troops were posted as far forward as Camp Gonzalez, Florida, also known as Fifteen Mile Station because of its location on the railroad fifteen miles north of Pensacola. The railroad north of that point was denuded of rails, which were removed for use elsewhere after Pensacola's abandonment. Even so, laying new rails would have been a relatively simple task for Federal railroad engineers, so the post at Gonzalez existed to prevent any such unwelcome surprise. Farther north along the old railroad, just a few miles shy of Pollard itself, a guard post at Bluff Springs, Florida, provided additional protection against any Federal movement up the line.[205]

It is uncertain whether Swanson's infantry companies ever pulled tours of duty at these advanced posts, but it is known that soldiers from Zachry's Company F outposted critical railroad bridges in the vicinity of Camp Pollard. The wooden bridges of that era were highly vulnerable to burning or sabotage by Union raiders, disgruntled deserters and draft evaders, runaway slaves, spies, or the pro-Union "Tories" who lurked on the fringes of remote settlements. Sometimes troops from Camp Pollard helped hunt down such men in the surrounding pine forests and swamps, but most of their time was spent guarding the railroad bridges over Burnt Corn Creek, the Escambia River, and the Perdido River. At other times, Company F provided men for the provost guard at Greenville in Butler County; if James was posted there, he may have met Seaborn Moore and his wife Rhoda Callaway Mangham Moore. The stepfather and mother of *William T. T. Mangham*, Seaborn and Rhoda were overwhelmed with ill tidings during November 1863. William was sick in a Greenville hospital, and his brother *Charles A. Mangham*, a corporal in the 18th Alabama, had fallen captive in the disastrous defeat at Missionary Ridge. Rhoda's nephew, *Bush W. Mangham* of Butler County, was hospitalized in Georgia suffering from an extended illness (see Chapter VIII).[206]

The winter of 1863-1864 was a very severe one by the standards of the area, with a great deal of rain, sleet, and ice. The men of Company F benefited from the relaxation of the drill schedule during November, focusing their efforts instead on building small cabins for their winter quarters. As they worked on these homely but important tasks, they looked forward to the packages that came regularly from home via the railroad they protected. Private James Barrow, a six-foot, nine-inch giant from eastern Chambers County, noted that the company had "a general feast" on November 13, when about 25 of Zachry's men received boxes of food just before dinnertime. The fortunate recipients shared the wealth among the whole company, and Barrow modestly understated the case when he observed that the food "seemed to be well enjoyed."[207]

Some of the men received brief furloughs home at some point during the winter, and many busied themselves figuring out ways to get longer ones. Barrow's letters evidence the unhealthy practices arising from the army's desperate manpower needs, as men offered money to potential recruits whose enlistment would entitle the lucky sponsor to a 40-day furlough. Others had their families seek them a "detailed" position, which would allow them to live at home while working in trades deemed essential to the war effort. Although technically still assigned to their company, men performing such long-term detached duties were spared most of the danger, hardships, and crushing boredom of service in the ranks. Many such positions were valid, of course, in an agricultural society where few men were skilled as shoemakers, wheelwrights, apothecaries, or teachers. Women, children, slaves, old men, and the physically disabled could not fill the gaping holes rent in the social and commercial fabric by the wholesale conscription of specialists and tradesmen. Such a system of "details" was vulnerable to abuses, however, as some men bent on a "bomb-proof" position crossed the bounds of propriety. If a few bottles of questionable medicine displayed on a shelf could convince the district enrolling officer that a man was a practicing apothecary, then some were willing to try the dodge.[208]

Others at Camp Pollard were willing to go much further to avoid service in the Confederate Army, since Clanton's recruiting efforts had swept up a number of men interested in peace at any price. Secret organizations known loosely as the "Peace Society" had arisen among the Unionist hill folk of northern Alabama, northern Georgia, east Tennessee, and western North Carolina. Many inhabitants of these areas looked askance at almost any government, but others took their stance primarily against the Confederate authorities. Mountaineers commonly viewed these men as an oligarchy of haughty slaveowners from the lowland plantations of the Black Belt, who shared little in common with the mountain folk. Whether driven by class-consciousness and economic necessity, pacifism, cowardice, or Unionist loyalty, many of these men could be forced into the Confederate Army only by dint of the strictest coercive measures. Accordingly, a great deal of the Southern war effort was absorbed in dealing with this problem in all of its manifestations.[209]

General Clanton and his subordinate commanders began a low-key investigation into the possibility of a "peace conspiracy" within the brigade as early as November, and the Commander of the Department of the Gulf, Maj. Gen. Dabney Maury, reported his own concerns to Secretary of War James Seddon in late December. He was apprehensive that Clanton's men were "much under home influences," which aggravated the fundamental problem that many of the men were unwilling soldiers in the first place. Maury's command comprised four brigades, most of whose regiments were raised in Alabama, and he thought it best to transfer the unreliable ones quietly to active theaters of war. "Intermixed with veteran troops, they would be efficient, and doubtless recover their proper feelings."[210]

While senior commanders and policymakers mulled over their options, the specter of mutiny enveloped Clanton's brigade in the first days of the new year. Some sixty men of the 57th Alabama grounded arms and refused further duty at Camp Gonzalez on January 5, 1864. Captain Bailey Talbot was in command of the 300-man detachment at this forward outpost, and he immediately arrested the mutineers and marched them to Camp Pollard under guard. The fiery Clanton paraded the whole Pollard garrison on January 6 and seized the bull by the horns. Announcing that he had found out the members of the so-called "Peace Society," as well as their secret oaths, passwords, and handshakes, he apparently offered to fight it out with them on the spot. Reporting to General Maury in Mobile the next day, he stated that "They refused a fair fight which I tendered them yesterday with their guns loaded." Afterwards, he invited them to step forward and lay down their arms, and some one hundred men stepped forward and surrendered. Clanton reported scornfully that "They confess everything, and seem badly whipped."[211]

Seven of the conspirators belonged to Swanson's regiment, but a chagrined Private Barrow wrote his wife that none of Zachry's Chambers County men were implicated in the plot: ". . .I fear that the step those reckless and foolish men has taken will cause us to suffer unnecessarily, but I am proud to say that our own company so far as I know is sound even to the core." Asserting that "every true man to his country must feel mortified. . . ," he allowed that "Their object seems to have been to lay down their arms and go home in defiance of any authority whatever." Barrow and some other men of James's company were guarding the Escambia River bridge when the mutiny occurred, while the rest of the unit remained at Pollard. The other companies of Swanson's regiment already were on the way to Montgomery beginning January 5, just before the mutiny erupted. Barrow hit the nail on the head when he suggested, "It is not probable that a brigade so deeply tainted will be trusted with so important a position [as Pollard]."[212]

On January 8, President Jefferson Davis indicated that he assessed the situation the same way: he authorized the exchange of Maury's regiments for veteran regiments on the Confederacy's far-flung battlefronts. In the uproar of mutiny, investigation, and transfer, James Mangham and Company F remained on duty at the Escambia River bridge and Camp Pollard until at least January 22. Three days later, Zachry's company was rattling up the line to Montgomery to rejoin the regiment before it moved. On January 25, Swanson's regiment was ordered to "proceed forthwith to Northern Virginia." The cozy days at Camp Pollard were over.[213]

Zachry's men knew a transfer was afoot, but it was some time before they got wind of their intended destination. In the meantime, Private Barrow noted, "There is great confusion among our men trying to get furloughs to go to see their families as they are much nearer than they have been and the general opinion is that we will not remain here but a short time." At least seven of the Chambers County men got three-day furloughs in the scramble, and these fortunate ones got 72 hours of relief from the cheerless conditions at Camp Mary, where both wood and water were scarce. Barrow and four others were about to depart on a brief leave on February 2 when orders arrived to cancel all furloughs; the gears of military bureaucracy were grinding into action, and it was time to go. Nevertheless, many men in Company F must have enjoyed a momentary reunion with their loved ones at the railroad depot at West Point, Georgia, where the difference in gauges between the Montgomery & West Point Railroad and the Atlanta & West Point Railroad required a change of trains.[214]

For many of these families, it was to be their last glimpse of their soldier husband, father, son, or brother. On February 12, the Adjutant and Inspector General's Office at Richmond published Special Orders No. 36: "Colonel Swanson's regiment of Alabama Volunteers is assigned to duty with and will form a part of Brigadier-General Battle's brigade, to relieve Colonel O'Neal's regiment of the same brigade." Assigned to Rodes's Division of Ewell's 2nd Corps, Army of Northern Virginia, they were about to enter active service in the most unrelenting campaign of the Civil War.[215]

In all likelihood, James enjoyed a reunion with his brother William in camps near Orange Court House, Virginia, and the latter was doubtless glad to renew acquaintances with many old friends and neighbors from back home. Old soldiers like William were a good source of information for the new men, and must have offered them some important insights into the life of a soldier in Lee's army. It would be interesting to know what he and his comrades thought of Swanson's regiment, tainted as it was by the "Peace Society" incidents at Pollard and Gonzalez. If the mutiny incident was common knowledge, then the new regiment surely faced ostracism by Lee's redoubtable veterans.

Besides being much colder than they had been in southern Alabama, Zachry's men doubtless found themselves much hungrier in Virginia, too. The bitter weather and scanty rations were poor preparation for the hardships of the coming campaign, and several of the weakened men fell victim to disease before the shooting started. One of those may have been Private Mangham. On April 28, James was granted a 60-day furlough for disability. In all likelihood, his trip home was rooted in events described by Mrs. Nancy Barrow in a letter to her husband in Company F. Writing on April 8, 1864, she related the health problems besetting some families in the Cusseta area:

> I forgot to mention to you in the proper place that Martha Lee is in very feeble health. . . .She has been lingering for several months and I have been informed that five women around her vicinity has recently died, viz. One of them was Mrs. Vernon. Her husband belongs to Capt Zachry's company I think and I think one of them a Mrs Mangham though I am not certain. The most or all of those ladyes I think had familys of children left behind and their husbands in the service.

With James far away in Virginia, the death of Jane Mangham left their ten children (including two-month-old Eliza) alone in charge of 17-year-old *Wiley Paul Mangham*, the eldest boy, who had just become eligible for conscription in March. If he had already been called up, his duties as head of household devolved upon 16-year-old Henry.[216]

As James left for home on April 28, the men of the 61st Alabama were only seven days away from their baptism of fire at the Wilderness. When Company F mustered on November 17 of that year, James was listed as "Absent—went to his home in Chambers Co. Ala. on furlough of disability for 60 days. Commencing Apr. 28, 1864." Since no other records survive to indicate his status after that point, it is uncertain whether he ever returned to duty with his regiment in Virginia, or if he stayed in Chambers County for the remainder of the war, either with or without leave.[217]

James remarried in Chambers County on August 11, 1864, tying the knot with Matilda A. Love, a young widow who lost her husband earlier in the war. Matilda lived just two houses away from the Manghams, so she was able to move her two daughters Celia Ann and Amanda into her new household with a minimum of difficulty. Just as the circumstances of war had done much to bring James and Matilda together in the first place, it is probable that the South's deteriorating military situation continued to place a huge strain on their family. General Lovell Rousseau's Federal cavalrymen departed their lines at Decatur, Alabama, on July 10, soon thereafter sacking the newspaper offices of James's first cousins (once removed) *Wiley P.* and *Thomas J. Mangham* in Ashville. Later they occupied Sylacauga, where his maimed brother Henry may have stood by helplessly, watching them confiscate rations, horses, and mules. On July 17, Rousseau's troopers fought their way through scratch forces of militiamen near Dadeville, where James's first cousin *Solomon Mangham* and their relative Arthur C.

Mangham may have encountered them. Passing next through DeSoto, where William had helped farm the Moon property before the war, the hard-riding troopers went on to wreck some 26 miles of railroad track along the Atlanta & West Point Railroad, confiscating loads of supplies at Opelika on the way. This town had grown into an important railroad junction in the preceding thirty years, upon land owned originally by James's first cousin (once removed), William Mangham. Just nine days after the raiders left Decatur, they rode through Oak Bowery itself, just a few miles from the Mangham home. Entering the nearby county seat of LaFayette that night, they even dragged some surprised Confederate soldiers out of a congregation celebrating a church service, before paroling them to return home. Rousseau's men eventually entered Sherman's lines near Atlanta on July 22, ending a twelve-day circuit in which they seared the brand of war on the towns and villages that marked the Mangham settlement in eastern Alabama. In a daunting display of their ability to ride literally through the heart of Dixie, Rousseau's men had covered an average of 34 miles daily and destroyed an estimated twenty million dollars worth of property.[218]

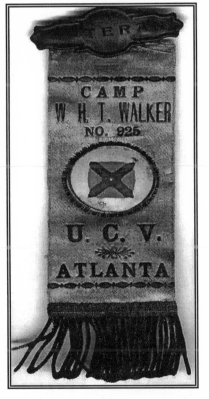

It is not known if James or his sons Wiley and Henry joined the scratch force of Chambers County militia that gathered in Bluffton (modern-day Lanett) as Rousseau passed through, although family lore indicates that both of the Mangham boys served in the Confederate Army in some capacity. Later census records also indicate that Wiley served in the army, but no military records survive to document his service. After the war, he joined the United Confederate Veterans, an organization whose sole requirement for membership was service in the Confederate military; he bequeathed his membership ribbon to posterity, as well as a tale that illustrated the commonplace hardships of military service. It seems that young Wiley was detailed to fetch the water for his mess one night, when close proximity to the enemy forbade the building of conspicuous fires. Creeping down to the nearby branch, the boy dipped out the water needed to cook the hoecakes that comprised that night's supper. The soldiers ate their hoecakes, but the suspicious flavor and texture caused them to

WILEY PAUL MANGHAM'S UNITED CONFEDERATE VETERAN'S MEDAL
(SEE APPENDIX, REF. # 231)
- Courtesy of Steve Mangham

319

take another look at the branch by the light of day. Sure enough, the stagnant water was full of tadpoles![219]

*   *   *   *   *

Although life in Chambers County changed forever with the closing of the war, James Mangham stuck with what he knew: farming. His property was valued at seven hundred dollars in 1870, and his $1370 worth of personal estate made him a relatively wealthy man given the hardships of the time. Wiley had married Mary F. Waldrop in 1869 and moved to Talbot County, Georgia, where they rented a little farm near Talbotton. Henry, now 21 years old, remained at home on his father's farm, helping make ends meet for the other eight children in the household. The family continued to grow, for James and Matilda had eight children born to their union. Fifteen years after the war ended, their home still rang with the sounds of eleven offspring, ranging in age from seven to twenty-five years.[220]

Over the coming years, Wiley and Mary moved back to Alabama, residing near Salem, in Lee County in 1880, and later moving to Tuscaloosa County. Wiley owned a dairy farm there in 1910, when the census-taker recorded that six of Wiley's and Mary's ten children still lived. Although none of the children still lived in his household, his son Robert W. Mangham lived next door with his wife Anna and their two sons. Wiley Mangham was 85 years old when he died of influenza on October 16, 1931, apparently the last Mangham Confederate soldier to pass away. He is buried at McGinty Cemetery in Chambers County.[221]

WILEY PAUL AND MARY F. "FANNIE" MANGHAM
(SEE APPENDIX, REF. # 231)

- Courtesy of Steve Mangham

His brother Henry was 24 years old when he married Mary Ann Thornton in 1872; although Annie was 38 when they married, their marriage was blessed with a son Charlie, born in 1874, and daughter Lella, born two years later. The family lived near Salem in 1880, not far from Wiley and Mary. Henry and Annie lived with Charlie as they got along in years, with both men working as farm laborers near Fredonia in Chambers County in 1900. Ten years later, they lived on Brookwood Road in Tuscaloosa County, again near Wiley and Mary, with Charlie working as a carpenter in a coal mine and Henry helping out by doing odd jobs. Annie apparently had died by this time, so Charlie's wife Ella ran the household. Henry Mangham died sometime after 1920, when he was working as a sweeper in a twine mill in Blue Mountain City, Calhoun County.[222]

James and Matilda Mangham remained at their old home in southwestern Chambers County, and their large family provided them numerous grandchildren. Matilda Love Mangham passed away in 1918, and was buried at Sandy Creek Church. James M. D. Mangham had passed away ten years earlier, on December 18, 1908. He is buried on the grounds of the old homeplace next to his first wife, Jane.[223]

*　　*　　*　　*　　*

Many years earlier, his brother William had gone to war after selling his little bay mule and cotton patch to their neighbor, William Trimble. It seems fitting that the Trimble family lives in the old Mangham homeplace to this day.[224]

---

[1] 1830 and 1860 Censuses, Butts County; Vaughn Ballard, comp., *Solomon Mangham: His Ancestors and Descendants* (Arlington: Family Histories, 1989), pp. 47-49, 54-61; Military Service Record Index, War of 1812, M602, reel 131, NARA; Lois McMichael, comp., *History of Butts County Georgia, 1825-1976* (Atlanta: Cherokee Publishing Co., 1978), pp. 23-24, 34. James Mangham drew land in the 1838 Cherokee Land Lottery based on his war time service (see on-line at http://data.Ancestry.com, Mangham Database Search Results, Georgia Cherokee Land Lottery, 1838).

[2] 1860 Census, Slave Census, and Agricultural Schedule, Butts County; 1860 Censuses, Chambers and Talladega Counties; Ballard, *Solomon Mangham*, pp. 54-57. See the Genealogical Appendix for a fuller discussion of genealogical references; I should emphasize here that the identification of John H. Mangham as James's son is tentative. Evidence indicates that there was another son, as yet unidentified.

[3] 1860 Census, Butts County; Butts County, Marriage Records; McMichael, *Butts County*, pp. 34, 36. The Mangham family lived near the Lindseys and Carmichaels for many years, and James Mangham's daughter Eleanor married John G. Lindsey in 1843. For more on Captain John H. Mangham's branch of the family, see Chapter II.

[4] 1860 Census, Slave Census, and Agricultural Schedule, Butts County; McMichael, *Butts County*, p. 34.

[5] OR IV, pt. 1, pp. 1095, 1098; Carlton McCarthy, *Detailed Minutiae of Soldier Life in the Army of Northern Virginia, 1861-1865* (Richmond: 1862; reprint, Lincoln: Univ. of

Nebraska Press, 1993), p. 37; Bell Irvin Wiley, *The Life of Johnny Reb: The Common Soldier of the Confederacy* (Baton Rouge: LSU Press, 1978), pp. 124-125, 128-129; Emory M. Thomas, *The Confederate Nation: 1861-1863* (New York: Harper & Row, 1979), pp. 152-155.

[6] Quimby Melton, Jr., *The History of Griffin* (Griffin: The Griffin Daily News, n.d.), pp. 88-89, 104; 1860 Census and Slave Census, Spalding County; W. J. Tancig, comp., *Confederate Military Land Units, 1861-1865* (South Brunswick: Thomas Yoseloff, 1967), p. 39.

[7] OR IV, vol. 1, pp. 1098; ORS II, vol. 7, pp. 68-73; CMSR, Wiley P. Mangham, 53rd Georgia. Henderson and Tancig both identify Captain Bond's company as the "Jeff Davis Riflemen," but a letter Bond sent to the *Macon Daily Telegraph* clearly shows that Company I bore the title of "Jackson Guards." See Lillian Henderson, comp., *Roster of the Confederate Soldiers of Georgia 1861-1865* (N.p.: State of Georgia, 1959-64), vol. 5, p. 605; Tancig, *Land Units*, p. 38; MDT, December 13, 1862, p. 2.

[8] CMSR, J. T. Mangham, 53rd Georgia; Tancig, *Land Units*, p. 37; 1860 Census and Census Index, State of Georgia. Although the great majority of the recruits enlisted from the counties discussed above, some enlisted from nearby Pike, Fayette, and Monroe counties. Clearly, Henderson erred in attributing Company A to Spalding County. See Henderson, *Georgia Rosters*, vol. 5, p. 534.

[9] 1850 and 1860 Censuses, Henry County; Henry County, Court of Ordinary, Minutes 1825-1853, p. 249, drawer 8, reel 44, GDAH; Melton, *History of Griffin*, pp. 88-89. One hospital admission record in the service records of J. T. Mangham lists him as J. S. Mangham, duplicating the 1850 Henry County census discussed above. Like many other Manghams, he may have had three given names, a common custom at the time. To date, attempts to trace the Croley family's connections to the Manghams have been fruitless; it is possible that the actual spelling was Crowley or Crawley.

[10] ORS II, vol. 7, pp. 68-73; Stewart Sifakis, *Compendium of the Confederate Armies: South Carolina and Georgia* (New York: Facts on File, 1995), pp. 267-268.

[11] Stephen W. Sears, *To the Gates of Richmond: The Peninsula Campaign* (New York: Ticknor & Fields, 1992), pp. 23-24, 82-84, 138-140, 145-150, 175-176; Philip Katcher, *The Army of Robert E. Lee* (London: Arms and Armour Press, 1994), p. 25.

[12] William R. Stillwell letters, June 26 and July 1, 1862, UDC *Typescripts* vol. 14, pp. 8-10; ORS II, vol. 7, p. 71.

[13] Sears, *Gates of Richmond*, pp. 183, 189, 201-208.

[14] Ibid., pp. 209, 213, 217, 221-223, 241-250; John L. G. Wood letter, June 28, 1862, UDC *Typescripts* vol. 4, p. 115. (The typescript identifies the date of Wood's letter as June 26, but it clearly dates from June 28.)

[15] Sears, *Gates of Richmond*, pp. 255, 260-261, 267-268; William R. Stillwell letter, June 26, 1862, UDC *Typescripts* vol. 14, p. 8; John L. G. Wood letter, June 28, 1862, UDC *Typescripts* vol. 4, p. 115; OR 11, pt. 2, pp. 716-717, 720-721.

[16] OR 11, pt. 2, pp. 720-721.

[17] Ibid., pp. 720-722; John L. G. Wood letter, July 4, 1862, *UDC Typescripts* vol. 4, pp. 117-118. Wood's voluminous correspondence is a valuable resource for anyone researching the 53rd Georgia or associated units. Some of his letters are featured in Bell Irvin Wiley, "North and South: Letters Home Tell Adventures of Two Foes," *Life*, February 3, 1961. Wood lived in Monticello, Georgia, until his death in 1939 (see obituary in *The Monticello News*, September 7, 1939).

[18] John L. G. Wood letter, July 4, 1862, *UDC Typescripts* vol. 4, pp. 117-118; William W. Head letter, July 12, 1862, Civil War Miscellany, Personal Papers, drawer 283, reel 27, GDAH.

[19] Ibid.; OR 11, pt. 2, pp. 717, 720-721. Semmes reported that a "cross-fire from the Fifty-third Georgia and the enemy" struck his aide's horse in three places; perhaps this was the incident Wood mentioned in his letter.

[20] OR 11, pt. 2, pp. 721-722; Sears, *Gates of Richmond*, p. 272; Henderson, *Georgia Rosters*, vol. 5, pp. 605-611.

[21] John L. G. Wood letter, July 4, 1862, *UDC Typescripts* vol. 4, pp. 117-118; Sears, *Gates of Richmond*, pp. 279, 291-293.

[22] John L. G. Wood letter, July 4, 1862, *UDC Typescripts* vol. 4, pp. 117-118; Sears, *Gates of Richmond*, pp. 291-293, 311-315, 332; OR 11, pt. 2, p. 723.

[23] OR 11, pt. 2, pp. 723-724; Henderson, *Georgia Rosters*, vol. 5, pp. 534-543; William W. Head letters, July 3, 1862, July 22, 1862, GDAH.

[24] Sears, *Gates of Richmond*, pp. 337-338.

[25] John L. G. Wood letters, July 4, 1862 and August 25, 1862, *UDC Typescripts* vol. 4, pp. 117-119; William W. Head letter, July 24, 1862, GDAH.

[26] William R. Stillwell letters, July 6 and August 5, 1862, *UDC Typescripts* vol. 14, pp. 14, 37.

[27] Sears, *Gates of Richmond*, pp. 163-165, 347-348; William W. Head letter, July 12, 1862, GDAH.

[28] CMSRs, Wiley P. and J. T. Mangham; Henderson, *Georgia Rosters*, vol. 5, pp. 534-543.

[29] CMSR, Wiley P. Mangham; Sears, *Gates of Richmond*, pp. 163, 344, 355.

[30] CMSR, Wiley P. Mangham; Henderson, *Georgia Rosters*, vol. 5, pp. 605-611. Private Stillwell wrote his wife on the day Wiley died, reporting that nearly one-third of the regiment's men were sick with measles or diarrhea, and that many had died. Less than a week later, he wrote Molly that only one-third of the regiment remained fit for duty. By August 25, Company B had only 37 men fit for duty, while 57 invalids and 5 nurses remained in sick camp. (See William R. Stillwell letters, July 24 and July 30, 1862, *UDC Typescripts* vol. 14, p. 31; John L. G. Wood letter, August 25, 1862, *UDC Typescripts* vol. 4, p. 119.)

[31] Butts County, Superior Court, Deed Book H, p. 269, drawer 6, reel 73, GDAH; Ballard, *Solomon Mangham*, p. 56.

[32] Stephen W. Sears, *Landscape Turned Red: The Battle of Antietam* (New Haven: Ticknor & Fields, 1983), pp. 69-71, 175-76; John Michael Priest, *Antietam: The Soldiers' Battle* (New York: Oxford Univ. Press, 1989), pp. 2, 4-5.

[33] William R. Stillwell letter, undated [from August or early September, 1862], *UDC Typescripts* vol. 14, p. 57; Sears, *Landscape*, p. 69.

[34] Sears, *Landscape*, pp. 144-151, 154-156; OR 19, pt. 1, pp. 860-861, 876-877, 881-882.

[35] Cited in *Antietam, Voices of the Civil War* (Alexandria: Time-Life Books, 1996), p. 49.

[36] Sears, *Landscape*, pp. 112-115, 150-151, 156.

[37] Ibid., pp. 173-176. For the story of the Manghams in the 13th Georgia, see Chapter II.

[38] Sears, *Landscape*, p. 220; OR 19, pt. 1, p. 862; MDT, May 28, 1863.

[39] MDT, May 28, 1863; Sears, *Landscape*, pp. 224-226; Priest, *Antietam*, pp. 118, 125.

[40] MDT, May 28, 1863; OR 19, pt. 1, pp. 874, 877-879; Sears, *Landscape*, p. 226; Priest, *Antietam*, p. 118.

[41] William R. Stillwell letter, September 18, 1862, *UDC Typescripts* vol. 14, p. 59; MDT, May 28, 1863; OR 19, pt. 1, pp. 874-875, 877-880, 883; Sears, *Landscape*, pp. 228-229; Priest, *Antietam*, p. 129.

[42] Sears, *Landscape*, pp. 229-230; Priest, *Antietam*, p. 133.

[43] Sears, *Landscape*, pp. 303-304, 307-308. While the Confederate troops knew they had fought superbly at Sharpsburg, they also knew that they, not the Federals, had retreated afterwards. Opinions doubtless varied, but the legions of Confederate deserters and stragglers provide evidence that many of Lee's troops had enjoyed army life as much as they could stand. Even Lee had to accept that his army was no longer capable of offensive operations until it could rest and recruit.

[44] William R. Stillwell letters, August 5, 1862, and September 18, 1862, *UDC Typescripts* vol. 14, pp. 37, 59; OR 19, pt. 1, p. 875.

[45] William R. Stillwell letter, September 18, 1862; OR 19, pt. 1, pp. 862, 874-875. The 32nd Virginia suffered 45 percent casualties, while the 15th Virginia lost 58 percent of its men. The 10th Georgia took only 147 men into action, suffering 83 killed and wounded for a loss of 57 percent. Every regiment's colors were riddled with bullets, too: the 10th Georgia's flag was hit 46 times, and the flagstaff was twice cut in two. John Mangham's company suffered seven wounded and two captured. See Muster Roll dated December 8, 1862, Company A, 53rd Georgia, NARA. A partial list of the regiment's casualties appeared in the *Macon Daily Telegraph* on October 7, 1862.

[46] Sears, *Landscape*, p. 327; CMSR, J. T. Mangham; ORS II, vol. 7, p. 71; E. B. Long, *The Civil War Day by Day: An Almanac, 1861-1865* (Garden City: Doubleday & Co., 1971), p. 288. Private Mangham was present for duty when Company A mustered at Fredericksburg on December 8, 1862, but only 29 other men were in ranks with him;

55 men were absent, recovering from wounds or illness. See Muster Roll dated December 8, 1862, Company A, 53rd Georgia, NARA.

[47] *MDT*, December 13, 1862. Lieutenant William Willis, secretary of the meeting, was wounded in action on the day this letter was published. Blinded in his right eye, he resigned ten days later. He was nonetheless the *most* fortunate of the four commissioned and non-commissioned officers who managed the meeting: Bond fell at Gettysburg, Gray was killed in action at Cold Harbor, and Pace died in the hospital. See Henderson, *Georgia Rosters*, vol. 5, p. 605.

[48] Theodore P. Savas, "The Battle of Fredericksburg Revisited," *CWR* 4, no. 4 (1995): pp. ii-iv.

[49] John L. G. Wood letter, December 18, 1862, *UDC Typescripts* vol. 4, p. 129; Henderson, *Georgia Rosters*, vol. 5, pp. 537-538; William R. Stillwell letter, December 14, 1862, *UDC Typescripts* vol. 14, p. 115. For an analysis of the fighting within the town itself, see Richard F. Miller and Robert F. Mooney, "The 20th Massachusetts Infantry and the Street Fight for Fredericksburg," *CWR* 4, no. 4 (1995): pp. 101-126.

[50] John L. G. Wood letter, December 18, 1862, *UDC Typescripts* vol. 4, pp. 129-130.

[51] Ibid. The grind of picket duty and fortifying took a toll on the Georgians even though the Yankees remained on their side of the river; Wood got only three nights of good rest between December 11 and December 29.

[52] Savas, "Fredericksburg Revisited," p. iv. For the lyrics, see http://new-www.erols.com/kfraser/ richmond/html. Slightly different lyrics appeared in the *Macon Daily Telegraph* of March 4, 1863.

[53] John L. G. Wood letter, January 5, 1863, *UDC Typescripts* vol. 4, p. 131.

[54] *ORS* II, vol. 7, pp. 65, 73; William R. Stillwell letter, February 22, 1863, *UDC Typescripts* vol. 14, pp. 148-149.

[55] Stephen W. Sears, *Chancellorsville* (Boston: Houghton Mifflin Co., 1996), pp. 153-159; Ernest B. Furgurson, *Chancellorsville 1863: The Souls of the Brave* (New York: Vintage Books, 1993), pp. 97-102; John L. G. Wood letter, May 10, 1863, *UDC Typescripts* vol. 4, p. 134; *OR* 25, pt. 1, p. 833.

[56] Sears, *Chancellorsville*, pp. 197-198; Furgurson, *Chancellorsville 1863*, p. 115; John L. G. Wood letter, May 10, 1863, *UDC Typescripts* vol. 4, p. 134; *OR* 25, pt. 1, p. 833; *MDT*, May 26, 1863.

[57] Sears, *Chancellorsville*, pp. 197-199; Furgurson, *Chancellorsville 1863*, pp. 123-124; John L. G. Wood letter, May 10, 1863, *UDC Typescripts* vol. 4, p. 134; *OR* 25, pt. 1, p. 833; *MDT*, May 26, 1863.

[58] Sears, *Chancellorsville*, p. 206; Furgurson, *Chancellorsville 1863*, pp. 124-127; John L. G. Wood letter, May 10, 1863, *UDC Typescripts* vol. 4, p. 134; *OR* 25, pt. 1, pp. 833-834; *MDT*, May 26, 1863.

[59] Sears, *Chancellorsville*, pp. 219, 364; John L. G. Wood letter, May 10, 1863, *UDC Typescripts* vol. 4, p. 134; *OR* 25, pt. 1, p. 833; *MDT*, May 26, 1863.

[60] Sears, *Chancellorsville*, pp. 293-296, 364-365; Furgurson, *Chancellorsville 1863*, p. 202; John L. G. Wood letter, May 10, 1863, *UDC Typescripts* vol. 4, pp. 134-135; OR 25, pt. 1, pp. 834-835; *MDT*, May 26, 1863.

[61] John L. G. Wood letter, May 10, 1863, *UDC Typescripts* vol. 4, p. 135; OR 25, pt. 1, pp. 834-835; Captain Peter McGlashan, cited in *Chancellorsville*, Voices of the Civil War series, (Alexandria: Time-Life Books, 1996), p. 129.

[62] John L. G. Wood letter, May 10, 1863, *UDC Typescripts* vol. 4, p. 135; Sears, *Chancellorsville*, pp. 365, 372; Furgurson, *Chancellorsville 1863*, pp. 267-268.

[63] Sears, *Chancellorsville*, pp. 374-379; Furgurson, *Chancellorsville 1863*, pp. 273-274; John L. G. Wood letter, May 10, 1863, *UDC Typescripts* vol. 4, pp. 134-135; OR 25, pt. 1, p. 835; *MDT*, May 26, 1863.

[64] Sears, *Chancellorsville*, pp. 379, 382; Furgurson, *Chancellorsville 1863*, pp. 274-278; *MDT*, May 26, 1863.

[65] Ibid.; John L. G. Wood letter, May 10, 1863, *UDC Typescripts* vol. 4, pp. 135-136; OR 25, pt. 1, p. 835; McGlashan, cited in *Chancellorsville*, Voices of the Civil War, pp. 132-133.

[66] Sears, *Chancellorsville*, pp. 383-384; Furgurson, *Chancellorsville 1863*, pp. 278-280; John L. G. Wood letter, May 10, 1863, *UDC Typescripts* vol. 4, pp. 134-135; OR 25, pt. 1, pp. 835-836; *MDT*, May 26, 1863; McGlashan, cited in *Chancellorsville*, Voices of the Civil War, pp. 132-133.

[67] Sears, *Chancellorsville*, p. 384; Furgurson, *Chancellorsville 1863*, p. 279; John L. G. Wood letter, May 10, 1863, *UDC Typescripts* vol. 4, pp. 134-135; OR 25, pt. 1, pp. 835-836; *MDT*, May 26, 1863.

[68] John L. G. Wood letter, May 10, 1863, *UDC Typescripts* vol. 4, p. 135.

[69] Ibid., p. 136; Sears, *Chancellorsville*, pp. 424-430, 440-442; Furgurson, *Chancellorsville 1863*, pp. 311-314; *MDT*, May 26, 1863.

[70] *MDT*, May 11, May 26, 1863; CMSR, J. T. Mangham.

[71] W. H. Mangham and W. H. Mangum Pension Files, ADAH.

[72] Ibid.; Civil War Index, John H. Mangham, ADAH. The latter document is extracted from an Application for Artificial Limb (No. 253) filed by John H. Mangham from Hale County on May 15, 1868. The extract notes that the applicant's left leg had been amputated below the knee, but that the applicant omitted mention of his regiment and the battle in which he was wounded. Although I combed the original State Auditor's files at ADAH, applications numbered from about 200 to 300 were missing, so I was unable to view the original document.

[73] 1850 Census, Coosa County; 1860 Census, Talladega County. Henry Mangum married Elisa T. Devaughn in Coosa County on September 30, 1849 (see Edward F. Hull, comp., *Early Records of Coosa County, 1832-1860* [Birmingham: author, c. 1970], p. 49). Talladega County Marriage Records (typescript), ADAH Reading Room, reflect that Henry Mangum married Eliza Bearden on September 15, 1852. The Mangham family in Butts County had close connections with the Beardens; one of Willis

Mangham's daughters married Fletcher Bearden after the war (see Appendix, ref. # 260).

[74] James M. McPherson, *For Cause and Comrades: Why Men Fought in the Civil War* (New York: Oxford Univ. Press, 1997), pp. 95-96; William Milner Kelly, "A History of the Thirtieth Alabama Volunteers (Infantry), Confederate States Army," *AHQ* 9, no. 1 (Spring 1947): 119.

[75] Kelly, "Thirtieth Alabama," pp. 119-120; *Democratic Watchtower* (Talladega), February 19, 1862; April 2, 1862; Grady McWhiney, Warner O. Moore, Jr., and Robert F. Pace, eds., *"Fear God and Walk Humbly": The Agricultural Journal of James Mallory, 1843-1877* (Tuscaloosa: Univ. of Alabama Press, 1997), p. 301; CMSR, J. H. Mangham, 30th Alabama; Muster Roll, Company A, 30th Alabama Unit Files, ADAH. The original muster roll on file at the state archives reflects J. H. Mangham's enlistment date as March 31, 1862. His CMSR and an original muster-in roll on file at NARA indicate an enlistment date of February 27, as do his pension records. This represents his original enlistment by Captain Patterson in February and muster-in by Colonel Shelley in March. The ADAH roll lists Henry as 38 years old; the one at NARA shows him as 26!

[76] CMSR, J. H. Mangham; Kelly, "Thirtieth Alabama," pp. 120, 123-124; *Democratic Watchtower*, February 19, 1862; Letters, typescript, Samuel C. Kelly, April 9 and April 16, 1862, 30th Alabama Unit Files, ADAH; Capt. George Brewer, "The Thirtieth Alabama Regiment," unpublished manuscript, p. 1, 30th Alabama Unit Files, ADAH; A. B. Self, "Reminiscence," 30th Alabama Unit Files, CRC.

[77] Letter, Samuel Kelly, May 8, 1862, ADAH; Kelly, "Thirtieth Alabama," p. 124. William M. Kelly, author of this unit history, was a descendant of Lt. Sam Kelly of the 30th Alabama.

[78] Letters, Samuel Kelly, May 8, May 11, 1862; Kelly, "Thirtieth Alabama," pp. 124-125; James M. McPherson, *Battle Cry of Freedom: The Civil War Era* (New York: Ballantine Books, 1988), pp. 304-306.

[79] Letters, Samuel Kelly, May 8, May 11, May 14, 1862; Kelly, "Thirtieth Alabama," pp. 125, 127-128.

[80] Letters, Samuel Kelly, May 24, May 27, May 28, May 30, May 31, June 3, 1862; Kelly, "Thirtieth Alabama," p. 128.

[81] Letters, Samuel Kelly, June 12, June 19, June 20, 1862; Kelly, "Thirtieth Alabama," p. 128.

[82] Letter, Samuel Kelly, June 20, 1862; Kelly, "Thirtieth Alabama," p. 128. "Dirt-eating" was caused by severe dietary deficiencies arising from an unvarying diet of "hog and hominy," although this was not understood at the time. Its victims revolted onlookers by eating clay, mud, sand, chalk, or ashes, and were often trussed up with iron gags or wire masks to prevent indulgence in such apparently filthy habits. Southern author W. J. Cash characterized this "addiction" one of the "classical stigmata of true degeneracy" that typified the "backcountry cracker" in his most "abject" form. See W. J. Cash, *The Mind of the South* (Alfred A. Knopf, Inc., 1941;

reprint, New York: Vintage Books, 1991), pp. 23-25; Kenneth M. Stampp, *The Peculiar Institution: Slavery in the Ante-Bellum South* (New York: Vintage Books, 1956), p. 304.

[83] Stanley F. Horn, *The Army of Tennessee* (Bobbs-Merrill, 1941; reprint, Norman: Univ. of Oklahoma Press, 1993), pp. 162-165; Letters, Samuel Kelly, July 1, July 3, 1862; Kelly, "Thirtieth Alabama," p. 128; Brewer, "The Thirtieth Alabama Regiment," p. 2, ADAH; OR 16, pt. 2, p. 719; Stewart Sifakis, *Compendium of the Confederate Armies: Alabama* (New York: Facts on File, 1992), pp. 98-99.

[84] Brewer, "The Thirtieth Alabama Regiment," pp. 2-3, ADAH; Kelly, "Thirtieth Alabama," pp. 128-129; Sifakis, *Confederate Armies: Alabama*, p. 99; Willis Brewer, *Alabama: Her History, Resources, War Record, and Public Men, from 1540 to 1872* (Montgomery: Barrett & Brown, 1872), p. 637; CMH 8, *Alabama (Extended Edition)*, p. 153.

[85] Horn, *Army of Tennessee*, pp. 163-165; Brewer, "The Thirtieth Alabama Regiment," p. 3, ADAH; Kelly, "Thirtieth Alabama," pp. 129-130; OR 16, pt. 2, pp. 719, 984; CMSR, James [sic] H. Mangham, Capt. Douthat's Company (Botetourt Artillery), Virginia Light Artillery; Jerald H. Markham, *The Botetourt Artillery* (Lynchburg: H. E. Howard, 1986), p. 25. During Henry's service with this unit, it was known as Captain Anderson's Battery. Interestingly, his CMSR reflects his first name as James! Since it specifies the date of his transfer from Company A, 30th Alabama, as well as other pertinent enlistment data, there is no doubt that this was actually John H. Mangham.

[86] Markham, *Botetourt Artillery*, p. 13; "Dedication of the Virginia Tablet in the Vicksburg National Military Park, Friday Evening, Nov. 22, 1907, and Exercises in the First Baptist Church, Vicksburg, Mississippi," in Civil War Unit Histories microfiche series, eds. Robert E. Lester, Gary Hoeg, p. 4 (cited hereinafter as "History of Anderson's Battery"). The speeches published in this pamphlet include one by Miss Mary Johnston, the daughter of the battery's second commander. Drawing from the diaries of unit members, she presented a brief narrative history of the unit.

[87] Markham, *Botetourt Artillery*, pp. 16-18; "History of Anderson's Battery," p. 9.

[88] Ibid.; Thomas Lawrence Connelly, *Army of the Heartland: The Army of Tennessee, 1861-1862* (Baton Rouge: LSU Press, 1967), pp. 250-253; Long, *Civil War Day by Day*, p. 275.

[89] "History of Anderson's Battery," p. 10; Markham, *Botetourt Artillery*, pp. 18-19; Horn, *Army of Tennessee*, pp. 179-188; Joseph Bogle, *Some Recollections of the Civil War: By a Private in the 40th Ga. Regiment, C.S.A.* (Dalton: The Daily Argus, 1911), pp. 5-6; Connelly, *Heartland*, pp. 268-270. The 40th Georgia was in Barton's Brigade at Perryville.

[90] Markham, *Botetourt Artillery*, pp. 19-20; "History of Anderson's Battery," p. 10.

[91] Ibid.; "History of Anderson's Battery," pp. 10-11; CMSR, J. H. Mangham.

[92] McWhiney, *Agricultural Journal of James Mallory*, pp. 330, 338, 348; Malcolm C. McMillan, ed., *The Alabama Confederate Reader* (Tuscaloosa: Univ. of Alabama Press, 1963), pp. 377-380.

[93] Civil War Index, W. H. Mangum, ADAH; Alabama, Records of the Secretary of State, Loyalty Oaths, SG 16039, Hale Co., Book 1, p. 463, ADAH; Pension Files, W. H. Mangham and W. H. Mangum, ADAH; CMSR, J. H. Mangham.

[94] Pension Files, W. H. Mangham and Mangum, ADAH; Civil War Index, John H. Mangham, ADAH. His membership in the UCV was based upon service with Co. A, 30th Alabama. Intriguingly, no other member of the Elmore County Camp had served in either the 14th or 30th Alabama regiments (see United Confederate Veterans Association Records, Louisiana and Lower Mississippi Valley Collections, LSU Libraries, Baton Rouge, LA, Box 57, Camp #255).

[95] Perhaps Bowden was actually *Bearden*, a relative of Eliza Bearden Mangham.

[96] Ibid.; 1900 Census, Calhoun County; "Delegates to the Constitutional Convention," on-line at http://www.legislature.state.al.us/misc/...ry/constitutions/1901/1901delegates.html. The 30th Alabama remained in Stevenson's Division for the duration of its service; it never was brigaded under the more famous Cheatham. See Sifakis, *Confederate Armies: Alabama*, p. 99.

[97] Civil War Index, W. H. *Manghum*, ADAH. Note the new variant of his name, as listed here. His wife filed a Widow's Pension application shortly after his death, and her witnesses stated her name as Minnie *Mangram*, widow of W. H. Mangram. Along with records pertaining to his brother James M. Mangham, such references indicate strongly that members of this branch of the family may have pronounced their name with the trill. Minnie Peters Jarrell, already a Confederate widow and resident of Alabama Confederate Soldiers Home, had married W. H. Mangham at the Soldiers Home in 1908 or 1909 (Information courtesy of Bill Rambo of Confederate Memorial Park.). Interestingly, his father James had married Elender (Eleanor?) Jarrell back in Putnam County, Georgia, in 1823.

[98] 1860 Census and Agricultural Schedules, Chambers and Tallapoosa Counties; Chambers County, Chattel Mortgage Records, Book 4, pp. 120-122, ADAH.

[99] 1860 Census, Chambers County; Chambers County, Chattel Mortgage Records, Book 4, pp. 120-122, ADAH; CMSR, William A. Mangham, 14th Alabama; CSA Index, William A. Mangham, ADAH. The 1860 Chambers County census stated William's age as 31, the Tallapoosa census recorded his age as 28, and the CSA Index entry gave William's age as 29 upon enlistment in 1861. The latter was extracted from a muster-in roll dated September 20, 1861.

[100] CMSR, William A. Mangham; M. B. Hurst, *History of the Fourteenth Regiment Alabama Volunteers, with a List of the Names of Every Man that Ever Belonged to the Regiment* (Richmond: 1863; reprint, University: Confederate Publishing Co., 1982), pp. 3, 7-8; Brewer, *Alabama*, pp. 612-613; letter, Green C. Barron to wife, August 31, 1861, in Ray Mathis, *In the Land of the Living: Wartime Letters by Confederates from the Chattahoochee Valley of Alabama and Georgia* (Troy: Troy State Univ. Press, 1981), p. 13; J. W. Burdett, "Some War Experiences," Civil War Miscellany, Personal Papers, drawer 283, reel 19, GDAH.

[101] CMSR, William A. Mangham; Hurst, *Fourteenth Alabama*, p. 8; *The Opelika Post*, December 13, 1901; OR 5, pp. 1020, 1023, 1035.

[102] CMSR, William A. Mangham; Hurst, *Fourteenth Alabama*, p. 9; OR 11, pt. 1, pp. 308-309, 403-404. William's first cousin (once removed), Willoughby Mangham, fought at Dam No. 1 with the 11th Georgia (see Chapter VI).

[103] Hurst, *Fourteenth Alabama*, pp. 9-10; letter, Thomas J. Barron to mother (Spring 1862), in Mathis, *Land of the Living*, p. 45; OR 11, pt. 1, pp. 580-583; Sears, *Gates of Richmond*, p. 70.

[104] Hurst, *Fourteenth Alabama*, pp. 9-10; OR 11, pt. 1, pp. 580-583; Sears, *Gates of Richmond*, pp. 70-84.

[105] Hurst, *Fourteenth Alabama*, pp. 9-10; Sears, *Gates of Richmond*, pp. 70, 82-84.

[106] Hurst, *Fourteenth Alabama*, pp. 10-11; Sears, *Gates of Richmond*, pp. 117-118.

[107] Hurst, *Fourteenth Alabama*, pp. 10-11; Sears, *Gates of Richmond*, pp. 140-145.

[108] OR 11, pt. 1, pp. 986-989; "The 14th Alabama in the Battle of Seven Pines," typescript, 14th Alabama Unit Files, ADAH. This document is a transcribed copy of Lt. Col. D. W. Baine's official after-action report, which was in private hands when the *Official Records* were compiled.

[109] Sears, *Gates of Richmond*, pp. 144-145.

[110] Hurst, *Fourteenth Alabama*, p. 10; Sears, *Gates of Richmond*, pp. 210-217.

[111] OR 11, pt. 2, pp. 779-780; Hurst, *Fourteenth Alabama*, pp. 10-11.

[112] OR 11, pt. 2, pp. 779-780; Hurst, *Fourteenth Alabama*, pp. 11-12; Sears, *Gates of Richmond*, p. 218.

[113] OR 11, pt. 2, pp. 756-757, 779-780; Hurst, *Fourteenth Alabama*, pp. 11-12; Sears, *Gates of Richmond*, pp. 219-226.

[114] OR 11, pt. 2, pp. 779-780; Hurst, *Fourteenth Alabama*, pp. 11-12; Sears, *Gates of Richmond*, p. 240.

[115] OR 11, pt. 2, pp. 779-780; Hurst, *Fourteenth Alabama*, p. 12; Sears, *Gates of Richmond*, pp. 215, 218, 227, 241-246.

[116] Sears, *Gates of Richmond*, pp. 247-250.

[117] Hurst, *Fourteenth Alabama*, p. 12; Sears, *Gates of Richmond*, pp. 255-274.

[118] Sears, *Gates of Richmond*, pp. 277-280, 293.

[119] Ibid., pp. 293-300.

[120] Ibid., p. 302; Hurst, *Fourteenth Alabama*, pp. 12-13.

[121] Hurst, *Fourteenth Alabama*, pp. 12-13; Sears, *Gates of Richmond*, p. 302; OR 11, pt. 2, pp. 780-781; Brewer, *Alabama*, p. 612.

[122] OR 11, pt. 2, p. 781; Hurst, *Fourteenth Alabama*, p. 13; Sears, *Gates of Richmond*, pp. 302-307; William F. Fox, *Regimental Losses in the American Civil War, 1861-1865* (Albany: Brandow Printing, 1898; reprint, Dayton: Morningside, 1985), p. 563.

[123] *The Opelika Post*, December 13, 1901. This article, entitled "Company 'A' Fourteenth Regiment, Alabama Volunteer Infantry, 1861-1865," comprised an annotated unit roster compiled from original records maintained by Captain Hodge,

an original member of the Cusseta Greys and the company commander in the latter part of the war.

[124] OR 11, pt. 2, pp. 503, 980; pt. 3, p. 482.

[125] Hurst, *Fourteenth Alabama*, p. 13; John J. Hennessy, *Return to Bull Run: The Campaign and Battle of Second Manassas* (New York: Simon & Schuster, 1993), pp. 21-22, 25, 30-31.

[126] Hurst, *Fourteenth Alabama*, p. 13.

[127] Ibid.; Hennessy, *Return to Bull Run*, pp. 359, 362-365; OR 12, pt. 2, pp. 597-603.

[128] Hurst, *Fourteenth Alabama*, p. 13; Hennessy, *Return to Bull Run*, pp. 373-375, 407-408; OR 12, pt. 2, pp. 561, 597-603.

[129] Hennessy, *Return to Bull Run*, pp. 451-455; CMSR, William A. Mangham.

[130] CMSR, William A. Mangham; OR 19, pt. 1, p. 812.

[131] CMSR, William A. Mangham; Hurst, *Fourteenth Alabama*, p. 13; ORS II, vol. 1, p. 462; OR 5, pp. 907-908; OR 17, pt. 2, p. 592, OR 19, pt. 2, p. 712; OR 21, pp. 539, 1070; Sifakis, *Confederate Armies: Alabama*, p. 75.

[132] CMSR, William A. Mangham; Hurst, *Fourteenth Alabama*, p. 15; Furgurson, *Chancellorsville 1863*, p. 273.

[133] CMSR, William A. Mangham; Hurst, *Fourteenth Alabama*, p. 34.

[134] OR 25, pt. 1, p. 854; Hurst, *Fourteenth Alabama*, p. 36; Furgurson, *Chancellorsville 1863*, pp. 66-67, 87-88; Sears, *Chancellorsville*, pp. 117-120, 130-132, 171.

[135] Furgurson, *Chancellorsville 1863*, pp. 67, 254-257; Sears, *Chancellorsville*, pp. 181, 308-309.

[136] Furgurson, *Chancellorsville 1863*, pp. 261-267; Sears, *Chancellorsville*, pp. 357, 374-376.

[137] Examination of 14th Alabama CMSRs shows that the regiment mustered for March and April before the battle at Salem Church, no doubt while awaiting orders at Banks's Ford.

[138] OR 25, pt. 1, pp. 854-855; Hurst, *Fourteenth Alabama*, pp. 36-37; Bailey G. McClelen, *I Saw the Elephant: The Civil War Experiences of Bailey George McClelen, Company D, 10th Alabama Infantry Regiment*, ed. Norman E. Rourke (Shippensburg: White Mane Publishing, 1995), p. 35; George Clark, *A Glance Backward, or Some Events in the Past History of My Life* (Houston: Fein & Sons, n.d.), p. 31. Clark served in the 11th Alabama, Wilcox's Brigade, and participated in the Chancellorsville campaign.

[139] CMSR, William A. Mangham; McClelen, *Elephant*, pp. 35-36. When the Cusseta Greys mustered for the period March-April 1863, they were in camp at Banks's Ford near Fredericksburg. William was present in camp, but was excused from the muster formation because he was sick in quarters.

[140] OR 25, pt. 1, p. 855.

[141] Ibid.; Clark, *Glance Backward*, p. 32.

[142] OR 25, pt. 1, pp. 855-857; Clark, *Glance Backward*, pp. 32-33.

[143] Ibid.; McClelen, *Elephant*, p. 36.

[144] Lieutenant Edmund Patterson, cited in *Chancellorsville, Voices of the Civil War*, p. 130.

[145] *OR* 25, pt. 1, p. 857; Sears, *Chancellorsville*, pp. 371-372; Furgurson, *Chancellorsville 1863*, pp. 252-253.

[146] *OR* 25, pt. 1, pp. 857-858; Hurst, *Fourteenth Alabama*, p. 37; Sears, *Chancellorsville*, pp. 379-382; Furgurson, *Chancellorsville 1863*, pp. 274-276.

[147] *OR* 25, pt. 1, p. 858.

[148] Ibid.; Hurst, *Fourteenth Alabama*, p. 37; Clark, *Glance Backward*, pp. 33-34; Sears, *Chancellorsville*, pp. 379-385; Furgurson, *Chancellorsville 1863*, pp. 276-277.

[149] *OR* 25, pt. 1, pp. 858-859; Hurst, *Fourteenth Alabama*, p. 37; Clark, *Glance Backward*, pp. 33-34; Sears, *Chancellorsville*, pp. 382-384; Furgurson, *Chancellorsville 1863*, pp. 277-279.

[150] Ibid.; *ORS* I, vol. 4, pp. 676-678. The unsigned report filed in the *OR Supplement* is clearly an account from the 14th Alabama; much of its text corresponds word for word with Hurst's account.

[151] *OR* 25, pt. 1, pp. 854, 858-859; Hurst, *Fourteenth Alabama*, pp. 37-40; Sears, *Chancellorsville*, pp. 385-388; Furgurson, *Chancellorsville 1863*, pp. 279, 288. Wilcox reported that most of the missing were wounded and captured on the skirmish lines.

[152] *OR* 25, pt. 1, pp. 852, 859-861; Sears, *Chancellorsville*, pp. 417-420, 424-426; Furgurson, *Chancellorsville 1863*, pp. 293-300; McClelen, *Elephant*, p. 36.

[153] Sears, *Chancellorsville*, pp. 425-426.

[154] CMSR, William A. Mangham; John W. Busey and David G. Martin, *Regimental Strengths at Gettysburg* (Baltimore: Gateway Press, 1982), p. 210.

[155] Long, *Civil War Day by Day*, pp. 408-409.

[156] Ibid., pp. 420-424; Clark, *Glance Backward*, p. 43.

[157] CMSR, William A. Mangham; Long, *Civil War Day by Day*, pp. 431-432, 439-441; Clark, *Glance Backward*, pp. 43-44; *The Opelika Post*, December 13, 1901; Gordon C. Rhea, *The Battle of the Wilderness, May 5-6, 1864* (Baton Rouge: LSU Press, 1994), pp. 11-12.

[158] Long, *Civil War Day by Day*, p. 439; Clark, *Glance Backward*, pp. 44-45; *OR* 33, p. 1173.

[159] Clark, *Glance Backward*, pp. 45-46.

[160] CMSR, James M. Mangham, 61st Alabama; *OR* 32, pt. 2, p. 726.

[161] Rhea, *Wilderness*, pp. 18-21, 26-29, 34, 42; Bruce Catton, *Grant Moves South* (Boston: Little, Brown & Co., 1960), pp. 175, 181.

[162] Rhea, *Wilderness*, pp. 26-27, 78-85; Clark, *Glance Backward*, p. 46.

[163] Rhea, *Wilderness*, pp. 52-56, 79, 90.

[164] Ibid., pp. 56, 120-121.

[165] Ibid., pp. 90, 238, 241, 264, 270, 276-277.

[166] Ibid., pp. 273-275.

[167] Clark, *Glance Backward*, pp. 46-47.

[168] Rhea, *Wilderness*, pp. 279-281, 285-289, 293-295.

[169] Rhea, *Wilderness*, pp. 295-300, 308-310.

[170] Ibid., pp. 312-313; Clark, *Glance Backward*, pp. 46-48.

[171] Clark, *Glance Backward*, pp. 48-49; Rhea, *Wilderness*, pp. 304-308, 313, 316, 358-366, 380-394.

[172] *The Opelika Post*, December 13, 1901; Rhea, *Wilderness*, pp. 370, 435-440. It is difficult to reconcile Clark's memoir with Rhea's version of Perrin's activities.

[173] Gordon C. Rhea, *The Battles for Spotsylvania Court House and the Road to Yellow Tavern, May 7-12, 1864* (Baton Rouge: LSU Press, 1997), p. 39.

[174] Lee's General Order no. 63, May 14, 1863, is cited in Fox, *Regimental Losses*, p. 559; CMSR, William A. Mangham; Noah Andre Trudeau, *The Last Citadel: Petersburg, Virginia, June 1864-April 1865* (Baton Rouge: LSU Press, 1991), p. 24.

[175] Trudeau, *Citadel*, pp. 72-80.

[176] Ibid., pp. 100-107.

[177] Ibid., pp. 99-107, 110.

[178] Ibid., pp. 105-108, 126.

[179] Ibid., pp. 108-109.

[180] Ibid., pp. 109-116.

[181] Ibid., pp. 115-118; Richard Wheeler, *On Fields of Fury—From the Wilderness to the Crater: An Eyewitness History* (New York: HarperPerennial, 1991), p. 283; Clark, *Glance Backward*, pp. 57-59.

[182] Trudeau, *Citadel*, pp. 118-121; Clark, *Glance Backward*, p. 60; Wiley, *Johnny Reb*, p. 114.

[183] Ibid.; McPherson, *Cause and Comrades*, pp. 109-110.

[184] Trudeau, *Citadel*, pp. 118-123;

[185] Ibid., pp. 119-123; Clark, *Glance Backward*, p. 59; Michael A. Cavanaugh and William Marvel, *The Battle of the Crater, "The Horrid Pit," June 25 - August 6, 1864* (Lynchburg: H. E. Howard, 1989), pp. 97-98.

[186] Trudeau, *Citadel*, pp. 122-124; Clark, *Glance Backward*, pp. 59-61; Cavanaugh, *Crater*, pp. 97-102.

[187] Ibid.

[188] Ibid.; Wiley, *Johnny Reb*, pp. 314-315; J. Tracy Power, *Lee's Miserables: Life in the Army of Northern Virginia from the Wilderness to Appomattox* (Chapel Hill: UNC Press, 1998), p. 139.

[189] *The Opelika Post*, December 13, 1901. Private J. J. Autrey was one of the original enlistees in the Cusseta Greys. The 14th Alabama lost a total of three killed and seven wounded at the Crater. See George S. Bernard, *War Talks of Confederate Veterans* (Petersburg: Fenn & Owen, 1892), pp. 330-331. Bernard took part in the desperate hand-to-hand fighting in the Crater. For a modern publication that includes his experience, see Rod Gragg, *The Illustrated Confederate Reader* (New York: Harper & Row, 1989), pp. 128-129.

[190] Letter, Theodore Lyman to wife Elizabeth, August 8, 1864.

[191] Trudeau, *Citadel*, pp. 171-172, 181-189; Clark, *Glance Backward*, pp. 62-64; 10th Alabama Unit Files, ADAH.

[192] CMSR, William A. Mangham; Trudeau, *Citadel*, pp. 230-247, 317-321; McMillan, ed., *Alabama Confederate Reader*, p. 391.

[193] Clark, *Glance Backward*, p. 61; Trudeau, *Citadel*, pp. 366-369, 418-421.

[194] Trudeau, *Citadel*, p. 401; Chris M. Calkins, *The Appomattox Campaign, March 29-April 9, 1865* (Conshohocken: Combined Books, 1997), pp. 58, 126-128.

[195] CMSR, William A. Mangham; R. A. Brock, ed., "Paroles of the Army of Northern Virginia," *SHSP* 15 (1887; reprint, New York: Kraus Reprint Co., 1977), pp. 324-326; Joseph H. Crute, *Units of the Confederate States Army* (Midlothian: Derwent Books, 1987), p. 14; Joshua Lawrence Chamberlain, *The Passing of the Armies* (reprint, Dayton: Morningside, 1989), p. 263; "Historical Sketches of Alabama Soldiers," in *Directory of the City of Montgomery, and Sketches of Alabama Soldiers* (N.p.: Perry & Smith, Publishers, 1866), p. 52. The latter source includes tabular data compiled by Alabama regiments serving in the Army of Northern Virginia in February 1865.

[196] Ballard, *Solomon Mangham*, p. 56; letters, Jean Ennis to author, May 1, May 17, 1996, and March 14, 1997; John T. Palmer, *The Mangums of Virginia, North Carolina, South Carolina . . . and Adjoining States* (Santa Rosa: 1992), p. 82; 1900 Census, Chambers County. I am indebted to Miss Ennis for her assistance in learning more about James M. D. Mangham and his family; she descends from his second wife. Note that sources vary on James's age, indicating he was born in 1822, 1824, or 1826. Varying census records compound the confusion, indicating a birthdate as early as 1818 or as late as 1828! I have chosen the date engraved on James's grave marker, which is also consistent with the fact that he wasn't required to join the army until the conscription age was raised from 35 to 45 in late 1862.

[197] 1850 Census and Agricultural Schedule, Henry County.

[198] 1850 Census, Chambers County; 1855 State Census, Chambers County; 1860 Census and Agricultural Schedule, Chambers County; 1860 Census, Tallapoosa County; letter, Jean Ennis to author, March 14, 1997. For more on the Thomas Mangham family group, see Chapter VI.

[199] OR 15, p. 1069; OR 26, pt. 2, pp. 550-552; William H. Davidson, *Word From Camp Pollard, C.S.A.* (West Point: Hester Printing, 1978), pp. 39, 210-211.

[200] OR IV, pt. 2, p. 160.

[201] CMSR, James M. Mangham; Davidson, *Camp Pollard*, pp. 31-34, 38-40, 235, 303-305; OR 26, pt. 2, pp. 239-240; Crute, *Units*, pp. 34-35.

[202] Davidson, *Camp Pollard*, pp. 14-17, 20, 26, 46.

[203] Ibid., pp. 14-21.

[204] Ibid., pp. 51, 121, 123; Muster Roll, October 31, 1863, Company F, 61st Alabama, NARA; CMSRs, William T. T. Mangham and Francis M. Mangum, 61st Alabama. Willie Mangham (Chapter VIII) was a grandson of Josiah Thomas Mangham, and thus

was James's second cousin (once removed). Frank Mangum was born in Edgefield, South Carolina in 1822, and enlisted in Macon County, Alabama. He died there in 1897. See letter, Jean Ennis to author, March 14, 1997, citing records in *Tap Roots*, the journal of the East Alabama Genealogical Society.

[205] Davidson, *Camp Pollard*, pp. v, 26.

[206] Ibid., pp. 21, 25, 115, 117.

[207] Ibid., pp. vi, 33, 47, 51, 65. The 43-year-old Barrow wrote regularly to his wife and family back in Chambers County, where they lived on a large farm in the Providence Church community. His letters form the core of *Word From Camp Pollard*, and provide valuable insights about wartime life in Chambers County and Company F.

[208] Ibid., pp. 45-46, 53-54, 69-70. Draft exemptions, substitutions, and details created many opportunities to avoid military service or mitigate its effects. Many of these positions were perfectly legitimate, but others ranged from questionable to downright dishonest, generating discussion and dissent throughout the South. Perhaps the saving grace was the fact that the Federal draft was even more contentious and less effective system. For discussions of these phenomena, see Gary W. Gallagher, *The Confederate War* (Cambridge: Harvard Univ. Press, 1997), pp. 28-36; Wiley, *Johnny Reb*, p. 114; Bell Irvin Wiley, *The Life of Billy Yank: The Common Soldier of the Union* (reprint, Baton Rouge: LSU Press, 1978), pp. 284-286; Reid Mitchell, *Civil War Soldiers: Their Expectations and Experiences* (New York: Simon & Schuster, 1988), pp. 159-162.

[209] Bessie Martin, *Desertion of Alabama Troops from the Confederate Army: A Study in Sectionalism* (New York: Columbia Univ. Press, 1932), pp. 68, 258; Ella Lonn, *Desertion During the Civil War* (New York: Century, 1928; reprint, Lincoln: Univ. of Nebraska Press, 1998), pp. 62-105; Georgia Lee Tatum, *Disloyalty in the Confederacy* (Chapel Hill: UNC Press, 1934), p. 24.

[210] OR 26, pt. 2, pp. 548-552.

[211] Ibid.

[212] Davidson, *Camp Pollard*, pp. 140, 144-146.

[213] Ibid., pp. 193, 217, 223; OR 26, pt. 2, pp. 549, 629.

[214] Davidson, *Camp Pollard*, pp. 223-225, 229-231, 236, 239. Private Barrow was one of the fortunate ones who saw his wife at the West Point station on February 5, 1864.

[215] OR 26, pt. 2, p. 726.

[216] CMSR, James M. Mangham; Davidson, *Camp Pollard*, p. 238; Palmer, *The Mangums*, pp. 82-84. Eliza was born on February 13, 1864.

[217] CMSR, James M. Mangham; Muster Roll, June 30 to August 31, 1864 (dated November 17, 1864), Company F, 61st Alabama, NARA. This muster roll carried James as one of four men who had overstayed their leaves. It shows that six had been killed in action or died of wounds, while four more had died of disease. Only 23 were present of 56 men on the rolls; a like number were absent, recovering from wounds or illness.

[218] Chambers County marriage records provided by Jean Ennis; letter, Jean Ennis to author, May 1, 1996; David Evans, *Sherman's Horsemen: Union Cavalry Operations in the*

Atlanta Campaign (Bloomington: Indiana Univ. Press, 1996), pp. 106, 127-129, 132-135, 158, 164-169, 172-173; Frank Moore, ed., *The Rebellion Record: A Diary of American Events with Documents, Narratives, Illustrative Incidents, Poetry, etc.* (New York: D. Van Nostrand, 1868), p. 191; *Memorial Record of Alabama: A Concise Account of the State's Political, Military, Professional and Industrial Progress, together with the Personal Memoirs of Many of its People,* vol. 2 (reprint, Spartanburg: The Reprint Company, Publishers, 1976), p. 222; Rev. F. L. Cherry, "The History of Opelika and Her Agricultural Tributary Territory, Embracing More Particularly Lee and Russell Counties, from the Earliest Settlement to the Present Date," in *The Opelika Times,* October 5, 1883-April 17, 1885, reprinted in *AHQ* 15, no. 2 (1953): 201.

[219] 1910 Census, Tuscaloosa County; telephone conversation with Robert Mangham (Wiley's great grandson), April 17, 1999. The 1910 census identified Wiley as a veteran of the Confederate Army. For an informative and tongue-in-cheek account by a boy participant in the Chambers County militia's attempt to confront Rousseau's raiders, see Wilton Burton, "County Militia Called to Stop Raid," in *Lee County and Her Forebears,* ed. Alexander Nunn (Montgomery: Herff Jones, 1983), pp. 247-249. Since the county militia comprised boys aged 16-17 and men between the ages of 50 and 60, it is possible that James Mangham reported for duty with his sons Wiley and Henry.

[220] 1870 and 1880 Censuses, Chambers County; 1870 Census, Talbot County; letter, Jean Ennis to author, May 1, 1996; Claiborne Parish, Louisiana, Deed Index (Direct), Books 1-2, p. 391; and (Indirect), Books 1-2, p. 416. The latter deeds document property bought and sold by Wiley P. Mangham of Tuscaloosa County, Alabama, and his wife Mary F. Mangham, nee Waldrop.

[221] 1880 Census, Lee County; 1910 Census, Tuscaloosa County; Death certificate, District 95013, no. 12, Wiley P. Mangham, Alabama Bureau of Vital Statistics; Margaret P. Milford and Eleanor D. Scott, eds., *A Survey of Cemeteries in Chambers County, Alabama,* Chattahoochee Valley Historical Society Publication no. 14 (Huguley: Genealogical Roving Press, n.d.), p. 26. Mary died in 1918, and Wiley married again, evidently to Annie Scott. Like many of his branch of the family, Wiley may have pronounced his last name with a trill; although his father's name is listed on the death certificate as James M. *Mangham,* Wiley's is misspelled *Wyle Manghrom.*

[222] Letter, Jean Ennis to author, May 1, 1996; 1880 Census, Lee County; 1900 Census, Chambers County; 1910 Census, Tuscaloosa County; 1920 Census, Calhoun County. One wonders if Henry and Wiley knew that Bryant S. Mangham, their second cousin (once removed), was on the crew that surveyed the town of Salem 45 years earlier.

[223] Letter, Jean Ennis to author, May 1, 1996. The kitchen, which originally was set beneath the rest of the house, was repositioned on the same level as the other rooms; additionally, a tin roof replaced the old wooden shingles after a long-ago hailstorm. Otherwise, the home stands as James Mangham built it more than a century ago.

[224] Ibid.

Chapter VI: Farmers, Tradesmen, Cowboys, Professors: The Thomas Mangham & Henry H. Mangham Families

1. Life on the Southern Frontiers: The Thomas Mangham Family

By the time *James M. D. Mangham* moved to Alabama in 1850, most of his uncle Thomas Mangham's family had been there for some fifteen years. One of Solomon Mangham's elder sons, Thomas was born in North Carolina before 1784, and as a young boy accompanied his father to South Carolina and eventually Georgia. By 1805, he was in Hancock County, where he participated in the land lottery with Solomon, Willis Austin, James C., and William Mangham. Although he had attained his majority by this time, he was evidently still a bachelor, receiving only one draw in the lottery; married men were authorized two chances.[1]

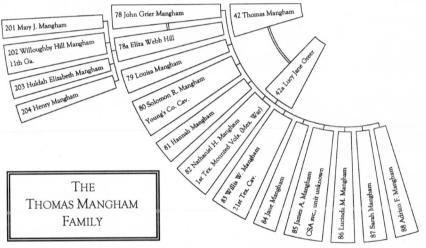

201 Mary J. Mangham

202 Willoughby Hill Mangham
11th Ga.

203 Huldah Elizabeth Mangham

204 Henry Mangham

78 John Grier Mangham

78a Eliza Webb Hill

79 Louisa Mangham

80 Solomon R. Mangham
Young's Co. Cav.

81 Hannah Mangham

82 Nathaniel H. Mangham
1st Tex. Mounted Vols. (Mex. War)

83 Willis W. Mangham
21st Tex. Cav.

84 Jane Mangham

85 James A. Mangham
CSA svc., unit unknown

86 Lucinda M. Mangham

87 Sarah Mangham

88 Adrian F. Mangham

42 Thomas Mangham

42a Lucy Jane Greer

THE
THOMAS MANGHAM
FAMILY

Although unsuccessful in the land lottery, Thomas soon succeeded in establishing a family. He married Lucy Jane Greer about 1805, and their union soon was blessed with a son, John Grier (or Greer) Mangham. Born about 1806, John was the first of Thomas and Jane's eleven known children. Over the coming years, John was joined by Louisa, Hannah, *Solomon R.*, and Nathaniel H. Mangham, as Thomas and Jane moved the family westward from Hancock to Jasper County. It is unclear when they made this move, but post office and land records show that Thomas was established in Jasper County by 1818. Even though he drew land in Irwin County in the 1820 lottery, Thomas seems to have remained in Jasper County, where existing records show that he sold a slave in May 1822. Perhaps he moved to Pike County with his brothers Willis, Wiley, and John for a brief period, because records indicate that Eliza Mangham married Joseph Irwin there in November 1824; this may have been Thomas's daughter Louisa, who is known to have married an Irwin.[2]

In any case, by 1826 Thomas was buying property in newly organized Upson County, which adjoined Pike County near the Mangham settlement in the Springs District. He moved his family there before 1830, when the census taker found Thomas living in Upson with his wife and ten children. The Mangham brood had expanded by this time to include sons *Willis W.* and *James A.*, as well as daughters Lucinda, Jane, and Adrian. Their eldest son John had established his own farm in adjoining Talbot County, where he made his crop with the help of seven slaves.[3]

The opening of eastern Alabama to white settlement over the next several years enticed Thomas into moving across the Chattahoochee River, possibly accompanied by his brother Wiley P. Mangham and his wife Cynthia. Thomas sold his Upson County farm for $1500 to Isaac Collier in December 1835, and probably moved shortly afterwards to Chambers County. The Manghams settled in the town of Wickerville, established where the Creek Indian "Horse Path" crossed the Oseligee River. The following year Thomas staked his daughter Louisa Mangham Irwin (or Irvin) to two hundred dollars when she and her husband moved to Texas, continuing the pattern of westward migration that characterized the times. Not long afterwards, however, Thomas passed away, leaving his widow and a large family. He seems to have died about the same time as his brother and sister-in-law, Wiley and Cynthia Mangham, whose orphans returned to Georgia to live with Mangham and Gray relations in Pike, Crawford, and Talbot counties.[4]

Fortunately for Jane and the younger children, John had moved to Wickerville as well. Thus his mother and younger siblings had an adult male relative to help look after their interests. By 1838, Solomon also attained his majority and established his own household in town, which was one of the many settlements established along the Indian trails that formed the region's road network. Chambers County records nevertheless reflect that the "Widow Mangham" remained the legal guardian of her children and the sole heir to Thomas's estate, so she could afford to keep Willis, James, Jane, and Adrian in school throughout the early 1840s.[5]

2. Six Feet of Dirt on the Texas Frontier: Pvt. Nathaniel H. Mangham, Company F, 1st Texas Mounted Rifles, Mexican War

The allure of Texas and the war with Mexico attracted Thomas and Jane's third son, Nathaniel, to the far southwest by the middle of the decade. He enlisted for a six-month term in Capt. Frank Early's company when it organized in Brenham, Texas, on May 16, 1846. Known as the "Washington Rangers," the company mustered into Federal service at Point Isabel on June 7, before proceeding to Mexico. Many of the men mustered out early, and Nathaniel was among those discharged at Chino, Mexico, on September 11, just twelve days before the unit took part in the Battle of Monterey.[6]

He returned to Washington County after his release from military service and remained there for some time before joining Capt. James Gillet's Company, 1st Texas Mounted Volunteers, in San Antonio on January 18, 1848. Gillet and his men had volunteered the previous summer for a year's service protecting the Texas frontier against hostile Indian raids, and had lost three men in one clash with Indians just a month before 24-year-old Nathaniel enlisted in the company. The outfit was stationed at San Lucas Springs for a time before moving to Arroyo Seco, sixty miles southwest of San Antonio. Although several companies in the regiment organized into a battalion that served in Mexico, Gillet's company continued patrolling the Indian frontier from their post at Camp Arbuckle.[7]

The governor directed Gillet's company to reorganize after it completed a year's service in the summer of 1848, since the Indian threat remained a major factor in frontier life. Accordingly, Nathaniel mustered out of Federal service at Camp Arbuckle on June 15, but he was one of 38 veterans who re-enlisted for another year's service on the following day. Since many of the regiment's men still were soldiering in Mexico under Colonel Hays, the various frontier service companies were augmented and reorganized on July 11 in order to clearly distinguish them from Hays's men. The frontier troopers elected Lieutenant Colonel Bell as their new commanding officer and the regiment accordingly received the title of Bell's Regiment, Texas Mounted Volunteers. Gillet was elected major upon the reorganization, while Lt. Hiram Warfield assumed command of the company and was promoted to captain.[8]

These men continued in service even after the Treaty of Guadalupe Hidalgo terminated the Mexican War on February 2, 1848, since it took some time for regular Federal troops to resume the mission of guarding the frontier. Captain George Blake of the 2nd U. S. Dragoons arrived in Texas that August with orders to muster Bell's Regiment out of service, but not in time to save Pvt. Isaac Heck, who was killed in a skirmish with Indians at Rio Froch on August 29. Colonel George Brooke directed the regiment's discharge in early September, but it was December 16 before the men actually mustered out.[9]

It was too late for Nathaniel, however. About the time Brooke had directed the disbandment of the regiment, men of Warfield's company got into yet another fight with Indians and Nathaniel was severely wounded. He died as a result of these injuries on September 5, 1848, at Camp Leon, Texas. Nathaniel H. Mangham was 24 years old.[10]

3. PASSING THE TORCH IN CHAMBERS COUNTY: JANE, JOHN G., AND SOLOMON R. MANGHAM

The news of Nathaniel's death never reached his mother back in Chambers County. Jane fell gravely ill in 1849, and her last will and testament named Nathaniel as one of the children among whom she divided her estate. Several weeks before preparing her will on July 18, she dictated a letter to her eldest son John, who had returned to Georgia and established himself as a millwright in Cuthbert, Randolph County:[11]

Chambers Cty. Ala[12]
June 23rd 1849

Dear Son   I must now and probberly for the last time. with a dependanc[e] on divine mearcy sit down to dictate a letter to send to you it ___ the balance of the family will through the mearces [mercies] of God I hope it will find you and your family enjoying a peaceable and a tranquil life acompaned with a good health which is the greatest earthly blessing bestowd by providence. I have had a long protracted. spell of sickness in which I have Worn down to be almost helpless in conciquence of which connected with other resons I wish to hear from you if I cannot see you as thair is something hear that Will belong to my children at my death. and I wish to make a will. not to make a differance but to give equality. insomutch as I view that some has had more bestowed on them than the rest will get. which was Louisa when she started to texas. and I wish you to rite amediately. and instruct me how to leve your proportionable part as it is my desire that you get it. plese be in hast to rite Direct to Westpoint Troup.[13] give my pure unalloyd love and respect to Eliza. and the children.[14] tell Eliza that if we mete no more hear that I have confidence to hope We will dwell togeather beyon the skies Collier and family is in tolerable health.[15] the familys Generally sends their respects. I have nothing more only Remane your Affectionate Mother

/s/ Jane Mangham[16]

Although this letter reached John, it is unknown whether he was able to visit his mother during her final illness. Solomon wrote him that fall, informing him that the end had come for their mother on August 17. As the eldest son remaining in close proximity, Solomon assumed the burden of caring for the younger children. Willis, now 21 years old, could assist with legal matters and help make ends meet. Nevertheless, Solomon's letter clearly indicates that Jane's death meant fundamental changes for the family:

Ala. Chambers Cty.   Oct. 4th 1849[17]

Dear Brother

I imbrace this opportunity to inform you that I am well at present hoping this Will find your self and family the same. I have Not as yet recv'd any letter from you. and in conciquence of which I rite you again for fear you did not get my letter whitch would have informed you of the death of our Mother whitch incident occurred on the 17th day of august. She sufferd great affliction during a long protracted illness. She towards the last of her days made a will Leaving each child his and her proportionable part accept Louisa. She left myself and Willis Executors. to the will. I have made Aplication to the Court and gave bond and has had letters testamentary granted and has ordred and Advertised a sale which will be had on the 12th day of November as all the property is to be sold under the will. the family will stay to geather till that time and then brake up then my self or some pearson els will have to make sum provision for Adriann.when the time comes I shal start up the country tomorrow and expect to be gown from two to three weeks. I have nothing more of importance to rite. So I will close my letter by an expresion of friendship and benevolent affection &c.

/s/ Solomon R. Mangham

340

Although it took some time to resolve all the attendant legal matters, Solomon was able to report in April 1852 that everything was satisfactorily settled. As his letter indicates, however, communications between eastern Alabama and southwestern Georgia still posed a challenge for the family:

April, 13th 52[18]

Dear Brother

I take this opportunity to inform you that I have had a settlement of Mothers little Estate and find one shair to be $373.00, and that some time since I lifted your Beard note.[19] And I am ready to settle with you and would like you would rite me how We will arange it as it is out of my power to come at this time to see you and if you cannot come plese rite and give me some directions how to procede. I have had a very savear attact of sickness lately and am very feble yet. I hope this will find your self and family well I have nothing more but remain yours

With Respect   /s/ *Solomon R. Mangham*

Solomon and John stayed in touch with each other, although their correspondence was clearly sporadic at best. Writing from his Chambers County home in 1854, Solomon updated his elder brother on the whereabouts of all of their siblings. Since the death of their mother in 1849, the children had gone in various directions. They clearly maintained close ties with each other, insofar as the constraints of time and distance allowed. Some remained close to home, while those who moved tended to do so in pairs: James and Adrian settled in Mobile, and Willis settled in Washington County, Texas, where Nathaniel had first enlisted in the army in 1846.

Lafayette Ala[20]
August 28th 1854

Dear Brother

I recev'd your letter yestarday which was a source of satisfaction to hear from you and your family being well this leaves us well hope it may find you the same.

for your satisfaction I take my pen to give you a more detaled account of the children. At Mothers death thair was living with her Loucinda Willis James and Adrian. Jane had previously marriad to James Fuller and lives up by Fredonia[.] Loucinda Shortly after her death marrede John Godfry and lives in talapoocy [Tallapoosa].[21] Willis over seed for two or three years.[22] And a year last spring he left my house for Texas whair he lives at this time in Washington Cty. James, after mothers death went to School at westpoint a year.[23] And then went to Mobile whair he now lives he spent the summer with me last summer. Adrian I tuk charge of at mothers death. And put her at Shool a year. Then I married and tuck her home with me and she lived with me two years. Then married a Mr D. Kerby.[24] Of Mobile whair she now lives[.] Brother Nathaniel. I suppose you know was killed in a battle with the indians in the western part of texas. previous to Mothers death.

341

I got a letter from James and Adrian yestarday they air well.[25] I have two children the oldest a girl two years old then a boy three weaks old. I would be very glad to see you and your family. I rote you a second letter in advace of the reseption of yours. But you will plese answer this letter for I would like to keepe a corasponence with you. I would be glad to live near anough for us to see eachother onst amoth [once a month] at least for I all ways enjoyed your company more than any pearson els[e] of my relations. Give my respects to Sister Eliza and the children

I have nothing more of importence to rite so I will Close. Yours &c

/s/ *Solomon R. Mangham*

4. "Ascape the Thieveing Paws of the Yankes": Pvt. Solomon R. Mangham, Young's Company of Cavalry, Alabama State Reserves

Solomon's children, Francis and John W. Mangham, were born in the several years following his marriage on March 6, 1851 to 23-year-old Sarah Shepard. Their second-born child had died young; John arrived about 1855, as the family moved twenty-five miles west to Tallapoosa County. Solomon bought a sizable farm near Dadeville, the county seat, only four miles away from his sister, Lucinda Mangham Godfrey. There he settled down to make a crop with the help of his six slaves. The latter apparently formed one family unit, since the 1860 census indicated that Solomon owned one man aged 31, a woman aged 26, and four children ranging from four to ten years old. Conforming to a typical pattern for his place and time, the $7000 valuation of his slaves was significantly greater than his real estate, which was worth $1500.[26]

As a slave owner, it is likely that Solomon supported the secessionist cause when war came in 1861, but it is unlikely that he intended to enlist at 43 years of age. If he was inclined to shoulder a musket, however, events at home made it impossible to do so. Shortly after Alabama passed its ordinance of secession in January, fate dealt his family a terrible blow. In a letter he wrote to John more than a year later, it is clear that Solomon still anguished over the loss of his wife and infant twins in February 1861. Likewise, the "national troubles" already had exacted a stiff price from him and his relatives, and times threatened to get much worse:

August 2nd 1862[27]

Dear Brother & Sister

I have this morning concluded to preform a duty which I owe to you and you also owe to me and that is to write you a few lines to let you know how my self and children air getting along we air well at this time and I hope this will find yourselves and children well You are awair I suppose that I lost my wife a year agow last February. And left me with 4 children 2 of them was twin Babes that had never sucked the Brest which have Boath since died I have at this time my oldest a daughter 9 years old her name is Francis. And my third. A boy 6 years old his name is John they air boath gowing to school at this time and I live a very lonsome life as well as a distress one in conciquence of national as well as family

342

troubles. Sister Hannahs oldest son was hear to see me the other day her family is well. Though grately distressed in conciquence of the loss of the 2nd son James at the Battle at Richmon from the best information they can get he was killed dead on the battle field Mr. Godfrey is in the searvice and sister Loucinda is hear in 4 miles of me. She has 6 children they air well Brother James was hear in the spring from Mobile he was in the searvice and was trying to get recrutes. I have lost a grate [d]eal already by the war and expect to continue to luse. and ultamaly [ultimately] away gow to the War my self and if I should have to gow I should have to brake up and scatter my children and negrows as it wouldnot dwo [do] to leave them hear alown. and it seems that in that event I should be wors[e] distressed than ever. we have had a long Drought in this country that has ingered [injured] corn very mutch. though we have had some late rains that is helping grately. Brother you must be shure to rite to me as soon as you get this for I wish to hear from you very Bad.

Give my respects to Sister and all the children and tell them to rite to me. as a letter from any of them would be gladly received ___. Your Brother

/s/ Solomon R. Mangham

Direct to Dadeville Tallapoocy

Solomon's next letter to John clearly indicates that he held Yankees in low esteem, to say the least. He was cheered by the good news of Richmond's salvation in the Seven Days' battles of late July and early August, but feared that Federal victories in Louisiana meant trouble for John's business interests there. Obviously it had been a long time since Solomon had heard from Willis, who had moved from Washington County to Bell County before the war. Like many other Southerners, however, the Mangham brothers fretted about Federal incursions that cut off almost all news of their friends and relatives on the Confederate periphery. This was of particular concern since both Louisa and Willis lived in Texas, whose communications with the remainder of the South suffered greatly from the Gulf Coast blockade and the fall of New Orleans in April 1862. One hopes that Solomon was able to follow through on his determination to write John's son Willoughby, a soldier in the 11th Georgia Volunteers, because the young soldier's correspondence was filled with requests for mail!

Sept. 7th 1862[28]

Dear Brother & Sister

your very welcome letter of date August 13th has Just been rec'vd baring the welcom nuse that you was all well. this leaves my self and children Well & hope when it reaches you that under the Cair of providence it will find you the Same We air having some chearing nuse in this country at this time on acount of our late success of the army in virginia. we air tending the office every mail in hope to get the poticulars. you Desired to know whair Brother Willis was befour the war broke out. he lived in washington Cty. Texas though I dwonot [do not] know his address he marriade thair. and settled somewhair in that County. I have not heard from him Since the war began. Sister Louisa lives in Bairstrop Sitty in

343

Bairstrop County Texas I corissponded with her a year or so agow She was thair at that time and I suppose is yet She has her husband by the name of Sheppard.[29] I have just heard from Sister Hannah She has to undergwo Again the loss of a child her oldest daughter Mary dide a few days agow. She had Marriade over a year agow and her husband is in the war. She dide at his Fathers[.] Aunt Sally Greer lives in Randolph Alabama the girls are you ___ ___ ___ ___ about his ___. One of them is a widder and lives with her with one child. John dide in Mobile and Reddick dide some whair in the West. and Gilbert is in the War and is at Richmon I recon if he was not killed Sister Jane lives near Fredonia yet and I suppos is well. I have not had a letter from Brother James since he was hear in the S[p]ring I would like to hear from him very mutch. and I think if my Brothers knew how mutch sattisfaction it was to me in my loansom condition to Read thair letters. and hear from them they would rite often to me for my sattisfaction. I am verry mutch afraid your intrest in Louisana of which you spoke is in dainger though it may ascape the thieveing paws of the yankes and I hope will. State to me in your next letter how I would Back a letter to Willoughby as I want to rite to him. tell Sister Eliza that I have not forgoten her nor her kindness to me. tell Mary and Huldy. that I have the most tender regard for them also. and they must rite to me. my two little Children Francis & John says tell uncle John howdy. and aunt Eliza two. for us I have nothing of importance more to rite. so I will close this letter. by subscribing my self your Brother and friend

/s/ Solomon R. Mangham

Unfortunately, no further correspondence between the Mangham brothers survives to allow us to assess their reactions to subsequent events. As the Confederacy's manpower shortage worsened, however, Solomon's earlier conviction that he would have to enlist in the army probably grew. Indeed, just three weeks after his last letter to John, Congress amended the Conscription Act to include men between the ages of 35 and 45, just missing Solomon.[30]

The next amendment to the law came on February 17, 1864, when Congress expanded conscription to embrace youths of 17 and men aged 45 to 50. The act provided specifically that these new age groups "shall constitute a reserve for State defense and detail duty, and shall not be required to perform service out of the State in which they reside." The law also stipulated that units formed from these sources would undertake guard, labor, or clerical duties in place of soldiers aged 18 to 45 who were fit for field service. Men wishing to volunteer had thirty days to organize their own units and elect officers, but men who awaited the President's summons could do so as well. Anyone failing to enroll his name with the authorities, however, faced immediate conscription and assignment to armies in the field.[31]

Georgia notable Lucius Gartrell identified one of the problems inherent in this system in a letter to Secretary of War James Seddon: "In my efforts to get volunteers I find the young men disposed to come promptly forward, but the men over forty-five, with few exceptions, refuse to volunteer, giving as a reason that it will be time enough to do so when called out by order of the President." Perhaps the same hesitation stayed Solomon's hand, as there is no record of his enlistment during the next six months. In the meantime, he appears to have remarried sometime during the year; his second wife, Emily, could care for the children and calm his fears that military service would force him to break up his family. Since Sherman's advance towards Atlanta in the summer of 1864 made the threat to Tallapoosa's firesides loom ever closer, the likelihood that Solomon would have to take up arms grew accordingly.[32]

Mid-July brought the crisis to a peak, when Federal cavalrymen traversed Tallapoosa County in a daring raid that emphasized the vulnerability of much of the South. The 2700 raiders under General Lovell Rousseau's command rode out of Decatur, Alabama, on the afternoon of July 10, 1864 and maintained a grueling pace during the succeeding week. Passing through Ashville on the fourth day of their march, they ransacked the offices of *Thomas* and *Wiley Mangham's* newspaper, the *Ashville Vidette*, burned some commissary supplies, and then continued on their way. On July 15, Rousseau's column passed through Sylacauga, the home of Solomon's disabled cousin *John Henry Mangham*, and the following day they burned Confederate commissary stores in the town of Youngville.[33]

That night the raiders reached the turbulent Tallapoosa River, where they forced a terrified slave at gunpoint to lead them across a steep-banked ford in pitch darkness. After a rough crossing, some of the men picketed the main road as day was dawning. One picket spotted a Confederate officer prowling nearby and shot him dead, while others captured two of the officer's companions. The dead man was Capt. John W. Browne, a disabled veteran of the 2nd Louisiana Infantry who was stationed at Dadeville as the county enrolling officer. He had mobilized about twenty volunteers in a vain attempt to sink the ferry before the raiders could reach it.[34]

Rousseau urged his exhausted men onward, and they covered the nine miles to Dadeville by eleven o'clock on Sunday morning, July 17. The suspicious troopers feared that the quiet streets portended an ambush by the remnants of Captain Browne's little company of local volunteers, so the whole 8th Indiana Cavalry charged into the courthouse square, shouting wildly as they rode. Snapping off shots at anyone failing to halt promptly, the Federals netted four or five Confederate soldiers as they outposted the town. They faced no resistance from the surprised and terrified citizens, but certainly found themselves unwelcome guests: Rousseau admitted that he found "damned few sympathizers, and they were damned timid." After an hour of swapping their broken-down horses for the citizens' fresh mounts, the dusty blueclads paroled their prisoners and left town, leaving a number of now-horseless buggies and carriages stranded in their wake. Only a few men straggled behind to rob homes of their valuables; most were sufficiently disciplined to remain in column as they marched out, and the specter of Andersonville prison prevented others from lurking about to search for loot. They were hunting for larger game, and would wreck a great deal of important railroad track on their way to an eventual rendezvous with Sherman's forces outside Atlanta on July 22. Although Dadeville's frightened citizens had no conception of the raiders' intentions, they could be certain of one thing: the war had come to their very doorsteps.[35]

Unsurprisingly, the raid provided the impetus to complete the organization of the reserves in Tallapoosa County and summon them to help protect their state. Captain R. G. Young, a 55-year-old citizen of Youngville, already had organized a mounted infantry company for service in Tallapoosa County in January 1864, under the provisions of a law establishing local defense forces. In all likelihood, Young's company provided many of the volunteers who followed Captain Browne in his doomed attempt to stymie Rousseau by burning the Tallapoosa River ferry, which was located just a few miles west of Youngville. This company now served as the nucleus for a new outfit known as Young's Company of State Reserve Cavalry, which mustered into service at Youngville on August 5, 1864. One of the 83 men who enlisted for the war was Pvt. Solomon R. Mangham, whose previous military service was also as a mounted infantryman in the Creek War, almost three decades earlier.[36]

Young's Company was destined for service at the camp for Federal prisoners of war at Cahaba, Alabama, where an influx of captives had threatened to overwhelm both the facility and its tiny guard force. Cahaba Prison, known to its inmates as Castle Morgan in honor of Confederate cavalry raider John Hunt Morgan, was nothing more than a half-built brick warehouse on the Alabama River near its confluence with the Cahaba River. Confederate authorities impressed the warehouse in 1863, along with the one-third acre of land on which it stood, to provide a facility for confining Federal prisoners captured in the Department of Alabama, Mississippi, and East Louisiana. Unfortunately, the directive establishing the prison foresaw accommodations for only five hundred prisoners, so the subsequent breakdown of the prisoner exchange cartel precipitated a crisis at the jam-packed prison.[37]

The cartel system collapsed in early 1864 when Gen. U. S. Grant advised the Lincoln administration to terminate all prisoner exchanges. Since properly exchanged prisoners were eligible to return to the ranks, the system helped to refill Confederate regiments over and over again. Grant had concluded definitely by this time that the war was one of grinding attrition, and thus he assessed the exchange policy as counterproductive. As he put it, "We have got to fight until the military power of the South is exhausted, and if we release or exchange prisoners captured it simply becomes a war of extermination." He was perfectly aware that neither side had a well-developed infrastructure for dealing with massive numbers of prisoners, especially since they had traditionally understood the exchange system as a way of keeping the numbers more manageable. Given the terrible mortality rate that afflicted prisoners of both sides, Grant averred, "It is hard on our men held in Southern prisons not to exchange them, but it is humanity to those left in the ranks to fight our battles."[38]

Already in March 1864, Post Surgeon R. H. Whitfield reported that Cahaba Prison was badly overcrowded, with its rude wooden bunks offering accommodation for only 432 of the 660 men imprisoned there. Sanitary conditions were imperiled even further by the water supply; although nearby artesian wells provided an adequate water source, the life-sustaining liquid flowed into the prison through 200 yards of open street gutter.

As Whitfield bitterly noted, "In its course it has been subjected to the washings of the hands, feet, faces, and heads of soldiers, citizens, and negroes, buckets, tubs, and spittoons of groceries, offices and hospital, hogs, dogs, cows, and horses, and filth of all kinds from the streets and other sources." Whitfield complained repeatedly to the prison commandant, Captain H. A. M. Henderson, who "exerted himself to the extent of his ability to have these defects remedied." Despite their efforts, however, progress was painfully slow.[39]

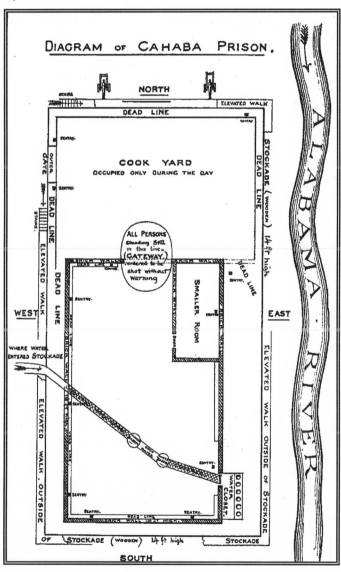

Prison maintenance was very low on the priority list for the resource-strapped Confederacy, and so was the provision of an adequate guard force. Two days before Whitfield composed his report, the Selma *Morning Reporter* published orders that reveal a sense of desperation: all unassigned soldiers in the vicinity were directed to report for duty at Cahaba, where "all the Federal prisoners captured in the Department are confined." Young's Company of State Reserve cavalry was among the units dispatched to help guard the multitudes; they arrived at Cahaba in August 1864 to find the patchwork guard force supervising a prison filled to bursting with Federals netted during the summer campaigns. Records from October 16 of that year show an aggregate of 2151 prisoners incarcerated in Castle Morgan, or more than four times its intended capacity.[40] (See map on page 566.)

Assistant Adjutant and Inspector General D. T. Chandler reported the guard force comprised 55 effective men of the Trans-Mississippi Battalion, 82 in two infantry companies of Alabama reserves, and 24 in one cavalry company [Young's] of Alabama reserves. These 161 men had two small field pieces at their disposal to help guard the teeming masses of prisoners. Chandler held a dim view of the guard force, reporting that "These men are badly armed and their discipline and instruction are very inferior." About fifty of the troops were under orders to return to their various regiments in the Army of Tennessee, but they could not be spared until replacements were scared up from somewhere else. Chandler added that the small numbers of available troops required each man to pull guard shifts every other day, and summarized the situation by asserting that the troops were "totally inadequate for the duties required of them." Lieutenant Colonel Samuel Jones commanded the Post of Cahaba, and his inspection of Young's Company at the end of October generally echoed Chandler's sentiments. Guardedly describing unit discipline as "fair," he rated their instruction, military appearance, and clothing as "not good." Although their arms were "good," Jones rated their accouterments as "insufficient." Only 45 men were present for duty from a total of 89 men on the company rolls, and Pvt. Solomon Mangham was among the twenty-nine privates and four non-commissioned officers absent without leave.[41]

Solomon left ranks on October 15, returning on November 3 along with six other men of the company. Although it is impossible to determine with certainty, Lt. John D. Young and his detail of two sergeants and three privates may have been detailed to bring the laggards back to camp. Young and the others were listed on the rolls as "Absent on detached service since 17th Oct. 1864 by order of Lt. Col. Jones, Commanding Post." Those absent at the end of the month had left ranks before this detail was dispatched, and Solomon was the last of the 33 absentees to leave without authority; most of them had left ranks as early as August or September. Many of these men returned to duty in the course of November and December, but four men deserted outright in November. The only other men who went absent without leave during November and December were Lieutenants Bailey and Young. The latter was declared absent on November 7, just four days after he presumably sent Solomon and six others back to the ranks![42]

Clearly the elderly reservists were torn between their responsibilities to the army and their families, and weak leadership, poor food, sickness, exposure, defeatism, or problems at home may have convinced some to leave camp. Apparently discipline tightened up and perhaps morale improved somewhat as they got accustomed to the army and their duties, for 65 men were present in ranks when Lieutenant Colonel Jones mustered the company for inspection on December 31, while seven more men were absent with proper authority. An additional fourteen remained absent without leave, while two more were under arrest. Jones did not change his opinion of the company's discipline, instruction, and military appearance, although he noted that their clothing was now in good shape and presented a uniform appearance.[43]

Solomon Mangham and the other elderly reservists at Cahaba thus stood guard throughout the fall and winter of 1864, taking their turns at the nine guard posts within the drafty brick warehouse. Several more guards were stationed between the warehouse itself and the twelve-foot tall stockade surrounding the warehouse and prison yard. Still others paced their beats atop a wooden walkway attached to the outside of the stockade, allowing them to observe all activities within the enclosure. Yet another detail stood ready near the two cannon in case of emergency, while a double guard stood outside the front gate near the guard reserve.[44]

One of their prisoners, Pvt. Jesse Hawes of the 9th Illinois Cavalry, arrived at Cahaba on July 26, 1864, about two weeks before Solomon arrived there. As Dawes recollected, "The older men among the guards were perhaps as humane as need be expected, and several certainly were so." It seemed to him that an "atmosphere of sad seriousness enveloped the majority of these more kindly older men, and one could but feel they were depressed by forebodings and homesickness." Most of the incarcerated Federals also respected the commandant, Captain Henderson, for his ongoing efforts to improve conditions at the prison. Henderson was a Methodist minister in civil life, and he worked hard during the course of 1864 to bring to fruition the improvements recommended by Whitfield and Chandler. Workmen routed the water supply through pipes instead of the old open gutters, improved the food rations and cooking facilities, expanded hospital accommodations, and erected and enlarged a prison yard to mitigate overcrowding and provide ventilation for cooking fires. Henderson also met with Union officers at Memphis under a flag of truce, arranging for them to convey clothing, blankets, and cooking utensils to their prisoners at Cahaba in December.[45]

In his mid-October report, however, Chandler expressed his fear that the prisoners could overpower the small guard force and make their escape, especially since the prisoners were organized into squads and companies to ensure efficient ration distribution. This organization provided a ready-made chain of command and potential for unified effort by the prisoners, whose numbers may have exceeded three thousand by the end of the year. Luckily for Solomon and the other guards, no such well-organized effort ever took place. What did take place, however, was a dramatic but ill-prepared attempt to overpower the guards and break out. Captain Hiram Hanchett of the 16th Illinois Cavalry led the attempt, but most of his fellow prisoners did not even recognize him as a soldier, much less respond to his commands in an emergency.

Hanchett had changed into civilian clothes before he was captured, and he maintained a fictitious civilian identity during his internment, in hopes of early release. Of course this meant he was liable to be treated as a spy, so he was desperate to escape before his true identity was revealed. Hanchett proceeded to hatch an elaborate scheme to overpower the guard force, march to Selma and capture the arsenal there, then divide up into groups and walk more than 125 miles to Pensacola.[46]

The plotters went into action before dawn on January 20, 1865, when a corporal marched a nine-man guard detail into the stockade to relieve the posted sentinels. Hanchett's men grappled with the men inside the gate and subdued them, but the wary corporal heard the commotion, slammed the gate shut, and quickly barred it. Two soldiers at the main gate escaped capture as well, and helped sound the alarm. As the reserve guard stood to arms and wheeled a cannon to the gate, a courier got word to Lieutenant Colonel Jones, who promptly ordered out the entire guard force and positioned them to stop the breakout attempt. Meanwhile, Hanchett was shouting for a hundred men to help him rush the gate, but most of the groggy prisoners had no idea who he was or what the ruckus was about. None stepped forward.[47]

Within a few minutes of the first scuffle, the front gate creaked open to reveal a field gun and a solid rank of excited guards brandishing fixed bayonets. Tense moments ensued, as Jones demanded the prisoners release his guards immediately. As Dawes reported it, Jones snarled: "Give up those men in two minutes or I will blow you from hell to breakfast with nine-pound Napoleons." Amidst the threats, shouts, and confusion of three thousand men trying to figure out what was happening in the gloomy stockade, the captured guards finally were hustled to the front of the throng and released.[48]

Although things calmed down until sunrise, Dawes recalled some years later that the aroused Southerners burst into the prison yard at dawn "like a pack of enraged hounds." As he recounted that morning, the guards were shouting "Get up, you G—d d—d Yankee s—n of b—hs, get up or I'll jam a bayonet right through you. You white-livered Blue-Bellies, get out of this." As one guard shouted at a prostrate man to get up, Dawes called to him that the man was too sick to move. The infuriated Confederate responded, "Oh, you d—d nigger-loving abolitionist, I'll see whether you can get up" and thrust his bayonet through the man's thigh. Dawes later learned that the prostrate man had been dead for some hours already, but in the meantime the young Illinoisan hustled to keep out of reach of the riled Alabamians' bayonets. As he put it, the ensuing roll call established that "none of the cursed abolition Yankees had escaped."[49]

Captain Henderson and Lieutenant Colonel Jones investigated the so-called "mutiny" intensely during the succeeding days, cutting off the prisoners' rations for two or three days until their questions were answered satisfactorily. Eventually they determined to try Captain Hanchett by court-martial, although it is unclear if any trial ever took place. The "mutiny" infuriated Brig. Gen. John Imboden, in charge of Confederate States military prisons west of the Savannah River, and he ordered his guards to "instantly fire upon the mutineers" in any future outbreak. He added ominously, "every prisoner found with arms in his hands" during an escape attempt "shall be instantly shot to death," even if he surrendered.[50]

The Federal prisoners at Cahaba survived the January 20 commotion little the worse for wear, but March confronted them with yet another challenge: floodwaters. Cahaba had been the capital of Alabama in 1825 when its citizens first learned, the hard way, that the Alabama River's strong currents acted like a dam at the point of its confluence with the Cahaba River. The phenomenon posed no problem until the Cahaba was swollen by heavy rains, at which point the water had no place to go but up over the riverbanks. After state legislators were forced to enter the statehouse by boat during that first flood, they quickly moved the capital to Tuscaloosa.[51]

Subsequent floods periodically ravaged Cahaba until the once-flourishing town was reduced to a shadow of its former glory by 1860. Five years later, the unfortunate inmates of the prison watched in dread and amazement as the water came seeping through the stockade during the afternoon of March 1. By midnight the water was several feet deep throughout the entire enclosure, and most of the unfortunate denizens had to stand in the water all night long. Lieutenant Colonel Jones refused to allow the prisoners to move to higher ground, although more than sixty of his guards presented him with a petition to allow it. According to one prisoner, Jones told his men: "No! Not if every damned Yankee drowns." After the waterlogged men spent several days in the filthy water, Jones relented enough to allow them to fetch wood and brush to build little islands upon which they could perch. Given that many of the men had become sick with diarrhea (and the disgusting results were floating throughout the prison pen), this measure provided untold relief. Eventually Jones sent about seven hundred prisoners to Selma, and soon thereafter began paroling large groups of the men pending their exchange. General Grant had authorized a resumption of negotiations on the exchange cartel, and an exchange camp was established at Four-Mile Bridge on the Big Black River near Vicksburg. The end was in sight.[52]

Captain Henderson was promoted to lieutenant colonel and assumed duties as a Commissioner of Exchange shortly after Hanchett's January 20 breakout attempt, and he proved instrumental in arranging the release of many of Cahaba's inmates. The Federal commander at Vicksburg reported the receipt of 4700 released prisoners by mid-April, with some 1100 of them noted as sick. Most of the sick had been interned at Andersonville, but the remainder of the released men were "in excellent health, the Cahaba prisoners particularly." Largely due to Captain Henderson's efforts to improve conditions at Cahaba during his tenure as prison commandant, surprisingly few of his hardy captives had succumbed to the stark conditions of the overcrowded prison.[53]

Cahaba's post commander, Lt. Col. Samuel Jones, left an altogether less favorable legacy: he is believed to have ordered the murder of the "spy," Captain Hanchett, on April 3, 1865. Major General James Wilson's army of 13,500 Federal cavalrymen had overrun the thinly-manned Confederate defenses at nearby Selma late on the previous afternoon, so Jones fled across the Alabama River and disappeared into the countryside. The Cahaba town council thereupon met on April 4 and agreed to release the remaining Federal prisoners. Young's Company of State Reserve Cavalry may have been among the militiamen and reservists thrown into the breastworks at Ebenezer Church or Selma to face Wilson, but more likely they remained on the ramparts at Cahaba until the last prisoners departed. In all probability, the company disbanded after Selma fell and the men made their way back to Tallapoosa County as best they could. Wilson's raiders were marching at will towards Columbus, Georgia, and Union forces would finish subduing Mobile's embattled defenders after another week of hard fighting. In the parlance of the times, the Confederacy was going "up the spout."[54]

*   *   *   *   *

Solomon Mangham probably returned home to Emily, Francis (Fanny), and John in April 1865, and their family grew to include four more girls, Cassendra, Susan, Emily, and Mary, by the time the census taker came through Dadeville in 1870. Like most ex-Confederates, Solomon had taken the oath of allegiance in 1867 to allow him to resume the rights of citizenship in the Reconstruction era. With a farm valued at $1200 and personal property worth another seven hundred dollars only five years after the war ended, Solomon was better able than most to care for his family during the aftershocks of war.[55]

The four youngest girls were still at home in 1880, and all were attending school that year. Clearly Solomon strove to secure the benefits of education to his own children, just as he had worked to keep his younger brothers and sisters in school some thirty years before, after the deaths of their parents. One would suppose that Solomon continued to check the mails regularly in hopes of receiving news of his beloved relatives, just as he did before the war. Perhaps he had the opportunity to visit some of them as well, to see for himself how they had withstood the trials and tribulations of four years of war and twelve turbulent years of Reconstruction.[56]

Solomon R. Mangham died at home on July 27, 1881. Emily succumbed to heart disease nine years later.[57]

5. A Mystery Wrapped Within an Enigma: James A. Mangham, Confederate Soldier

Solomon's youngest brother James A. Mangham had moved to the thriving port city of Mobile from Chambers County some thirty years earlier. He was 29 years old when he married 22-year-old Virginia Victoria Spencer on December 6, 1859 at the Government Street Church in Mobile. Virginia was the daughter of Adaline Spencer, a wealthy widow whose Virginia birthplace probably inspired her daughter's name.[58]

James made a modest living as a sawyer, but apparently gave this up to go to war in 1861. The only solid evidence of his military service is provided by Solomon's letter to John G. Mangham on August 2, 1862: "Brother James was hear in the spring from Mobile he was in the searvice and was trying to get recrutes." Regiments organizing in early 1861 typically enlisted for twelve months, but the Conscript Act of April 1862 required them to remain in service and reorganize. Such units generally sent a number of men back home to seek recruits to fill out their ranks, and James almost certainly was engaged in this activity when he visited Solomon in Tallapoosa County.[59]

James may have served in Company A, 1st Alabama Volunteer Infantry, according to one surviving muster roll that lists a "Jas. M. Magnum" as a member of the company. This 35-year-old man enlisted in Mobile on February 20, 1861 for a period of twelve months, so the name, age, and place are approximately correct. This company comprised men from Barbour County's "Eufala Pioneer Guards," however, so this man may have been a more distant Mangum cousin. Annotations on this muster roll report: "Left with Genl. Walker without leave from the Captain, Aug. 2, '61, and has been reported as a deserter." The high-spirited men of the 1st Alabama had enlisted to fight Yankees, and garrison duty in Pensacola left them facing the Federals ensconced on Santa Rosa Island with seemingly little prospect of a fight. When renowned Mexican War veteran William H. T. Walker departed for Virginia just a few days after the great battle at Manassas, many of the Alabamians went with him.[60]

If James A. Mangham served in the 1st Alabama, he may have been captured at Island No. 10 in early 1862, exchanged, and subsequently captured again at Port Hudson in July 1863. The enlisted men were exchanged again that fall, served in Mississippi, then at Camp Pollard and Mobile, and eventually transferred to Johnston's Army of Tennessee in 1864. The regiment was heavily engaged at New Hope Church, Kennesaw Mountain, Peachtree Creek, and Ezra Church during the Atlanta Campaign. The 1st Alabama suffered very heavy losses that winter at Franklin and Nashville, then fought again at Averasboro and Bentonville in 1865. Of the more than 3000 men who served in the regiment during the war, only about one hundred were present at the final surrender at Greensboro in April 1865.[61]

Mobile's 1866 city directory shows that James Mangham survived the war, and lists him as a lumber merchant living on the north side of Government Street, east of Ann Street. For some reason he was not listed with his family in the 1870 census; Virginia and her sons Frank S. (age 3) and James Clarence (age 1) lived in her mother's household, along with several of Virginia's brothers and their families. James again appeared as head of household in 1880, however, with his sons Frank and Clarence now joined by a nine-year-old sister, Virginia Alleen Mangham.[62]

No further records pinpoint the postwar whereabouts of James A. Mangham, who died before 1890. His son Clarence worked for the Southern Pacific Railroad in New Orleans from 1885-1888, before moving to San Antonio and taking a position with the San Antonio & Aransas Pass Railroad. Virginia lived in San Antonio as well, dying there on January 28, 1906, of "asthma of the heart." Her obituary noted that she had "survived her husband by a number of years," and she in turn left behind her children Frank, Clarence, and Alleen Mangham.[63]

Clarence worked for many years as S. A. & A. P. general freight agent in San Antonio and eventually became an executive in the passenger department. When Southern Pacific took over the railroad in 1925, he moved to Houston and served as industrial commissioner for that company. James Clarence Mangham retired due to ill health in May 1933, and returned to San Antonio in October of that year. He died there on November 7, 1933. His brother Frank S. Mangham lived at Cuero, Texas, at that time. Alleen Mangham (Mrs. Watt Hairston) lived in Columbus, Mississippi.[64]

6. "OUR TROOPS WILL FIGHT AS LONG AS THE ENEMY INVADE OUR SOIL": PVT. WILLOUGHBY HILL MANGHAM, "QUITMAN GREYS," CO. I, 11TH GEORGIA[65]

Unlike his Uncle James, whose Civil War experiences remain obscured by the shadows of the intervening decades, much of Willoughby Hill Mangham's personal wartime correspondence survived intact. An only son who bore the name of a maternal uncle, Willoughby wrote these letters to his parents, John Grier and Eliza Hill Mangham, and to his sisters Huldah Elizabeth Mangham and Mary J. Mangham Nichols. John G. Mangham was a prosperous millwright in Cuthbert, owning a mill and farm property valued in 1860 at nearly $30,000, including at least one slave. He also owned land in Louisiana, where Willoughby evidently lived and worked for a time prior to the war. Willoughby's younger sister Huldah remained at home during the war, and their older sister Mary also lived in Cuthbert. Mary's husband, James Nichols, served in the army in Virginia.[66]

Willoughby was a 24-year-old millwright and farmer from Randolph County, Georgia, when he signed up for three years or the war on July 3, 1861. Enlisting as a private in a company that soon organized as part of the 11th Georgia Regiment Volunteer Infantry, he embarked on a military odyssey that took him away from his beloved family in Cuthbert until the guns fell silent almost four years later.[67]

His active field service lasted exactly two years to the day, ending at the Confederacy's high water mark: the Battle of Gettysburg. The end of the young Georgian's active service came on the third day of that bitter contest, as it did for many of his Virginia comrades under General Pickett on a much more famous part of that bloody field. Willoughby was wounded severely in the left hand, probably when the 11th Georgia and other regiments in Brig. Gen. George T. Anderson's brigade engaged a force of Federal cavalry that was threatening the Confederate army's right flank. Evidently unable to move with Lee's retreating army, he was left on the field, taken prisoner, and soon admitted to a Union hospital for treatment. His ensuing sojourn in captivity lasted almost two more years, culminating in his release from Fort Delaware on June 16, 1865. For Willoughby Hill Mangham, the final act of this chapter of his life occurred back in Randolph County on September 27, 1865, when he signed the oath of allegiance to the United States Government.[68]

Only one short note survives from his long period of captivity. He wrote the other eighteen letters from various places in Virginia between July 1861 and June 1863.[69] His thoughts and observations offer numerous interesting insights into the hard realities of life at the "seat of war" in Virginia. Every letter demonstrates his abiding love for his family, his resulting homesickness, and a typical soldier's voracious appetite for mail from loved ones. Likewise, almost every letter evidences the privations exacted by ill health, severe weather, and inadequate diet. Willoughby's obvious preoccupation with his often poor health must be understood in the context of the times; his concerns duly remind the late-20th century reader that the Civil War soldier's most implacable foe was the germ. Indeed, some authorities have suggested that the average Confederate soldier was ill or wounded six times during the war, with cases of sickness outnumbering injuries by a ratio of five to one, while three deaths resulted from sickness for each combat-related fatality.[70]

But Willoughby Mangham's surviving letters offer today's reader much more than a good description of the woes of soldier life. Indeed, his observations offer us clues, I suspect, to the attitudes of the elusive "average" Confederate soldier in many important respects. Above all, he consistently displayed that casual air of confidence and determination that many wartime opponents and postwar chroniclers have identified as a trademark of Southerners in general, but of the Army of Northern Virginia in particular. In his correspondence, however, one sees the immature confidence of the neophyte of 1861 transformed by hard experience into the serious confidence of the veteran soldier of 1863. By this stage, Willoughby was well aware of the dangers of camp and field, as well as the relentless physical hardships of active campaigning. He was nonetheless confident that the Confederate armies would fight as long as the "Yankies" were on Southern soil, and he never betrayed any hint of doubt about the eventual outcome.

As the reader will discern, this confidence underlay Willoughby's bemusement with those who hoped the Mason and Slidell mission to Europe would prove the engine of the Confederacy's salvation. It also colored his amusement at the Federals' military and political discomfiture following the Fredericksburg disaster of December 1862, and his outraged contempt for Confederate soldiers who deserted their cause and countrymen.

His sense of confidence was tempered by realism, however. With minor exceptions during the heady days of 1861, his letters do not have the ring of someone whistling past the graveyard, nor of the self-appointed morale booster for the fainthearted on the home front. In short, his was a simple confidence, not the confidence of the braggart, the fire-eating Southron Yankee-hater, or the self-conscious (or self-styled) hero. On the contrary, Willoughby Mangham's letters provide us a glimpse of a vulnerable, intensely *human* being, who is nonetheless determined to persevere in defense of his home, his family, and his way of life. Through the prism of his letters, the modern-day reader can gain a better understanding of the men who comprised Lee's army, most of them neither urbane literati nor ignorant rustics, neither heroes nor shirkers. Most importantly, these letters allow us to witness, in microcosm, the maturation of the armed enthusiasts of 1861 into the formidable fighting force of 1863, known to history as the Army of Northern Virginia. It is this quality, above all, that imbues Willoughby's letters with significant historical value after an interval of 135 years.

Some modern-day scholars tend to view the error-riddled literary efforts of such men as amusing at best, or mundane and uselessly repetitious at worst. In my opinion, however, yesteryear's Southern yeoman farmer-turned soldier deserves a much kinder fate at modern hands. All overheated "Lost Cause" rhetoric notwithstanding, the very ordinary citizens who filled the ranks of the Army of Northern Virginia accomplished absolutely extraordinary feats of valor and endurance, which earned them the respect of their commander as well as of their foes. Certainly many of their opponents in the Army of the Potomac wondered what made these men tick, and I believe we would be remiss if we denied ourselves the opportunity to examine all obtainable evidence.

In reading Willoughby Mangham's letters home, we are treated to some perhaps unsuspected evidence of a broader awareness than we might have supposed, given his rural background and modest education. His letters stand as he wrote them, a product of Randolph County's private schools of the 1840s and 1850s. They have been edited for neither content nor grammar, and the editorial use of *sic* is avoided altogether. The numerous errors of omission, repetition, capitalization, and misspelling are his, insofar as occasionally erratic penmanship and uneven microfilm quality allowed.[71] These clues help today's reader sense the varying degrees of stress under which he wrote, and thus provide us a deeper understanding of the author and his environment.

*　　*　　*　　*　　*

Ten newly raised companies from across Georgia assembled in the rail center of Atlanta in early July 1861, when they were mustered into service and organized as the 11th Georgia Volunteers on the third day of the month. Willoughby enrolled initially as a private in Company F, but transferred the next day to a company comprised of men from Quitman and Randolph counties. Styling themselves the "Quitman Greys," they became Company I in the newly organized regiment. The eager Georgians, clad in fine gray uniforms, departed immediately for the "seat of war" in Virginia, toting trunks full of spare clothing and old smoothbore muskets. The brand-new soldier dashed off a note to his father straightaway upon arrival in the Old Dominion.[72] His first letter home, written hastily amid a whirlwind of exciting developments, is a good barometer of the young recruit's excitement and his immediate priorities:

July the 6th 1861

My Dear Father

I take my pen this Evening for the purpose of informing you what I am now doing and where I am I am Stationed now in at the citty of Linchburg Va. and do not expect to remain here more than three days and that is dificulty about your geting any thing to me I am first here and there and no teling where we are now eight hundred miles from home we remained atlanta three days went from there on through Tenessee and Va and I hope this will find you well I am well my Self with the exception of a cold we traveled one night in open cars. Father if you wish to Send any thing to me at any time Send it to Lieut Colonel Guary or Capt Dosier[73] one for you Know that a private has not the chance which they have. we are now 120 miles from richmond and they are fighting thereabout Cadwalader came across the Potomac yesterday with 30,000 men we have all arived Safe So far[74]

Your most afectionat Son
W. H. Mangham

*　　*　　*　　*　　*

Writing the very next day to one of his beloved sisters (apparently his younger sister Huldah), a thoroughly homesick young recruit painted a significantly different picture, giving voice to lurking doubts which he probably hesitated to admit to his father. His company commander provided one ray of hope in Willoughby's otherwise gloomy outlook, and later developments would indicate that his initial confidence was well founded:

July the 7th 1861

Dear Sister

I want to See you all now but I do not know when that time will be but I do not think I can Stand a camp life long   I have been Sick ever since yesterday Evening and Sicker than I have been in a long time before   I am now at Lynchburg Va but I can not tel how long I will remain here. I have been in low Spirits ever since I left because I wont see you all before the time will come I know; you must write to as soon as you can and direct your letters in care of Lieut Colonel Guary of the Tenth Regement[75] You must excuse bad writing for I am So nervous that I can not write.

Capt. Dosier and Dr Gilbert are very Good to me. Dosier is a very feeling man I think.

Your only Brother

W. H. Mangham

*   *   *   *   *

By July 10, 1861, the regiment was quartered at Richmond's great Fair Ground, where Col. George T. Anderson commenced the business of drilling his men in earnest. In less than a week, however, Federal movements lent a renewed sense of urgency to events. As the newly raised Federal and Confederate armies groped towards their first major clash in Virginia, the 11th Georgia left camp at Richmond on July 15. They took the Alexandria railroad north, reaching Manassas on the following day. Turning west, they arrived at Strasburg on the following afternoon. Their first foot march took them some twenty miles north to Winchester on July 17, where the footsore Georgians learned that Gen. Joseph E. Johnston's Army of the Shenandoah was evacuating that town in order to reinforce Gen. P. G. T. Beauregard back near Manassas.[76]

Along with their sister regiments of Col. Francis S. Bartow's brigade, the 7th, 8th, and 9th Georgia and the 1st Kentucky, Willoughby and his comrades countermarched some thirty blistering miles in under twelve hours to reach the railway at Piedmont. Lieutenant Bledsoe and four others were the only ones remaining in ranks when they arrived; Willoughby was among the other eighty-two "Grays" who fell behind and straggled into town on blistered and bleeding feet. Bartow and the 7th and 8th Georgia regiments entrained at Piedmont for Manassas, bound for their place in the history books. A railroad mishap blocked the tracks after their departure, however, and stranded the remainder of the brigade at Piedmont. There they fumed in enforced inactivity until July 22, the morning after the battle of Bull Run.[77]

In a letter written a month later, Willoughby fulfilled his father's request to tell him what he knew about the first great battle of the war, and his enthusiasm and state pride clearly colored his second-hand account. From his camp on the northern edge of the deadly ground, his keen sense of disappointment in Bartow's alleged "contrariness" burns brightly through the intervening years, as does his pride in his victorious comrades. Even though he and the soldiers of the Quitman Greys missed this first opportunity to test their mettle as fighting men, however, they too had encountered the specter of death, and it still lurked in their midst:

Manassas Juction Aug 22[d] 1861

Dear Father At Home

I have the Pleasure of informing you that I am well at this time or nearly so and hope this letter will reach you injoying the same pleasure. I have been very Sick with Measles and I tel you I hard time of it Sure we have lost three men out of our Co with them[78] I never was so nervous as I am now before our first Lieut Bledsoe attended on me so well when I was sick I never shall forget him[79] I could not do too much for him he is a Doctor but Recieves nothing that I no of Doctor Gilbert was Paid to go with the Co as does not half the good; I Received your most appreciated letter the other Day which I read with the most gratitude; You told me to tel you all about the Battle of Bullrun I passed Manassas on tuesday and went on to Strawsburg and marched from there to winchester on wednesday and the next day back to Peadmont by Fryday dinner on thursday night about two Oclock we waided Shannandoah river about 15000 of us and it is said there was ten thousand yankies crossed three miles below us the same night; Our Reg did not get here until the Morning after the Battle I went over the field and I never Saw the like of dead men in my life they were lying for miles around they fought Seven miles up and down Bullrun Creek they got our boys awhile in the Morning but did not know it there was two or three of Reg went doubble quick out to field about six miles and they cut them up bad enough Sure Old Bartoes Brigade we belonged to the same Brigade but through his Contrariness we did not get in to the Battle he was Killed he was foolishly Brave any how[80] Thos. Glover was Killed in the Battle.[81] they had Buried all our men when I got out there they just took hoes and Spaids and covered the yankies where they lay Some with their heads out and hands and feet and any way;[82] They Said our boys would Charge Bayonets on them and run and hollow as they would run;[83] I tel you they fought like tigers but they said they Ga boys did not know when they were whiped there were Some Scamps north Say that we had men on the reserve that we run in in fresh but it was not so they had three to our one on the field they fought ten hours;[84] Father I wish you would Send Me one Pair of water Proof boots if you can get them I have run out of Shoes _____ and about two flannel Shirts and one Oil Cloth over coat if you can get it one pair of thick Pants I expect to freeze here this winter any how tel Mother to make the Shirts loose And box them up Send it by express Tel Mother & Sister send me something good to eat we do not get any thing here fit to eat scarcly Just put it in the box and I will Remember them as long as I live I want to see them bad Enough Meat and bread is all we get Old Salt Pork and I can not eat it and I want something I wish you could come Pa if your Business was so as you could but I want you to arrange that Estate affair for the sake of my Sisters and Mother and all becaus they nead it as bad as any I know & you know if you do not attend to it how it will go;[85] Uncle Hayas is our wagoner and O. R. Smith Quarter Master of the Reg;[86] There is no Chance to get a thing here there are so many People there one hundred and ten thousand around this Place;[87] Have those things marked thus

Care of Kent   W. H. Mangham
& Pain & Co   Capt. L.P. Dosier's Co 11th Reg Ga Volunteers
Richmond Va

box them as Compact as posible and they will not cost so much to send them; Tell Sister Mary to write to me; if you Should Ever want to come here when you get to Richmond you would have to tel them you had things for the Soldiers or they would not let you Pass that is So Sure; I have no more to write;

Your most Obedient Son
W. H. Mangham

P. O. I wish you woud Pleas send me some Paper and ink Exvelopes and pen if you Please

W. H. Mangham

*   *   *   *   *

Writing soon afterwards to his mother Eliza Mangham, a desperate Willoughby made a point of asking her assistance with the same sorts of things she doubtless had organized for him while he was home: food and clothing. As his letters amply demonstrate, Confederate soldiers had to scramble to supplement what the new government's freshly minted commissaries and quartermasters could provide, and the unresourceful or unlucky often suffered miserably. The soldiers themselves prepared whatever food they scraped together. In small groups of friends or kinsmen known as a "mess" in Civil War parlance, each group pooled rations and shared cooking duties. As such, the mess comprised a primary social unit and subset of the company.[88]

Willoughby also felt constrained to mention the battlefield at Manassas, although he clearly was not comfortable dwelling upon the gruesome sights he had described to his father. Likewise, he was unable to restrain himself from a brief discussion of the company's rising death toll from disease. As his letter indicates, a raging measles epidemic had rendered the 11th Georgia *hors de combat* before it ever faced an armed Federal, and the stricken regiment was confined to camp for six long, deadly weeks in August and September.[89]

Manassas Juction Aug 28th 1861

Dear Mother At Home

I take my pen to Enroll a lines to inform you that I am about well at this time but I can not tel how long I will remain so I have just come in from drill

359

and I am very much Exausted now and very warm also I wrote to once since I Received your letter I Recd it with much Gratitude; I want all of you to write to me it looks like you do not never write to me I want to hear from you all the time; I Think we will have another Battle before long from the way things are working they are running troops on towards Alexandre & Farefax Court house but I do not know whether our Regiment will be in it or not as it is in such bad order now we have had very bad luck with our Co we have lost four of our men since we have [been] here in three weeks[90] I wrote that I wanted you to send me some thing and for it may be misplaced I write this I wish you would send me one pair of water proof boots No[.] Sevens one Oil Cloth Coat long down to the nees I wish you send them if you Plese & Pair Pants and dawers one Linzy Jacket & two flanel Shirts & Gloves also and Mother send me somthing Good to Eat if you Please I can not eat what we have here the rest gets ____ from home and I wold like be sorter Even with them they think I suppose if I hapen to Pass where they are I want them [to give] me some there are some free hearted I know would give it to me with Pleasure if I were to ask them but I feel a delicacy in doing so though I Do no that I am ____ in the Co the Pittman boys treat me Kind Enough. I am in there mess now and the Davis boys also are frienly as ever you thought were miffed with me for quiting that but you were mistaken they have never mentioned it to me all the boys are friendly with me[91] I went over the Battle field a Day or two after the Battle was fought and it was a sight sure there was dead men lying Every where for seven miles up & down Bull Run Creek they fought ten hours on Sunday we have any amount of rain here and it is very sloppy

Send me writing materials

Mark thus)   W. H. Mangham Capt Dosier Co (I)
In Care of   11th Reg Ga Volunteers Richmond Va
Kent & Paine   Care of Capt Dosier
& Co Richmond Va
Tel Sister Mary & Huldah Howdy my love also

Your only Son   W. H. Mangham

*   *   *   *   *

The 11th Georgia finally left Camp Bartow, named for their fallen brigade commander, on September 11, marching northeastward to the vicinity of Fairfax Court House. After two weeks spent preparing defensive positions to repel an expected Union advance, the regiment moved forward to Falls Church, on the outskirts of present-day Arlington, where the men performed their first picket duty.[92] In a letter composed in early October, Willoughby was proud to tell his sister Huldah of the hardships and dangers he had faced, and one can sense the modest pride of an elder brother as he reassured her on the military situation. He was likewise glad to assure her that spiritual arrangements in camp were satisfactory, as religion was very important to him and his family.[93]

Clearly, however, he was concerned that the diseases ravaging the Quitman Greys and their comrades of the 11th Georgia were exacting an increasingly staggering toll. The proud company had counted 86 officers and men in its ranks as it marched off to war. After only three months of service—and no combat—44 men were already sick, discharged, or dead.[94] Accepted today as a mere childhood inconvenience, the measles were one of the so-called "camp diseases" which Confederate soldiers feared as lethal killers. Typically, Southerners' rural backgrounds precluded the development of immunity to the microbes that thrived among the unprecedented masses of humanity congregated in Civil War encampments.

Compared to these mortal dangers, Willoughby's continuing shortage of writing materials was of secondary importance, but it certainly threatened his ability to remain in contact with his family. Writing materials generally were difficult to obtain in the Confederate Army, which issued such items for official purposes only.[95]

Even worse were the Confederate soldier's financial worries. As Willoughby indicates, the men had a difficult time getting their meager pay, which was disbursed, ideally, at bimonthly musters. Campaigning and other incidents made the schedule much less regular, however, and it was not uncommon for a man's pay to be many months in arrears. Given the inflation that bedeviled the Confederacy's economy, the lag in disbursement often meant that soldiers were paid in devalued currency. For Willoughby, this could (and did) deprive him of the ability to buy needed food and clothing. Fortunately for him, however, his family was not dependent on his military earnings. . .which amounted to the miserable sum of eleven dollars per month.[96]

Camp Near Fairfax Sep 7th 1861[97]

Dear Sister At Home

I Received your letter which I have looked for with wanting Eye I was glad to hear that you were all well; I have wrote severl times since I have received one before and the greatest that I can enjoy is when I am reading a letter from home for you are my greatest Steady indeed I have wrote this nine times to you all at Home & I wrote four of the no[.] to Pa & Received three only. you Said you had Sent my Cloths but I have not Received them yet I fear they have got misplaced and I fear that I will loose those that I have for we had to Send all we had off to the Junction yesterday & I fear they will be robed we are anticipating a great Battle here I. E. About Alexandre or falls Church about fourteen miles above We stood Picket guard up there last week. (Paper Wet) we would stand away off in the Swamp two on a post; and then we were Drawn up in line of Battle Seven Days And I could hear the drums of the Enemy, beating alday long; they Say if they win the next battle or if we win it will be peace I rather think we will win; You wrote somthing about a matrass I can not tel about that yet untill we get to winter quarters we may come back to the Ga[.] coast this winter I hope so at least for then I may get to [see] some of you and get Somthing better to Eat and more of it Somtimes we get Somthing to Eat and then Nothing; Joseph Frith is dead and Capt O. R. Smith also[98] I had handed my Money [to him] and he went to the Hospital and died and I can not tel I will ever get or not I did [not] know when he left; we have lost 7 of our men now and Seven discharged and thirty sick out of the Co. Sister Tel the Girls they must write to me now for it is a bad chance to write here until we get Settled at some place; we have good Preaching every Sabbath and we have all got Bibles; I want you all to write to me now I want to get a letter Every week anyhow from Some one down there Tel Sister Mary to write & Pa & Mother & I will Aswer when I can I have no Paper Ink nor Envelops nor Pen nor Nothing nor a cent of Money we have not drawn any yet;

Your only brother

W. H. Mangham

*   *   *   *   *

Willoughby's next surviving letter is dated almost two months later, and the dark days of epidemic were past. The halving of the meat ration (to six ounces of pork or bacon, or ten ounces of beef daily) was, by contrast, a mere minor inconvenience.[99] In fact, the young Georgian clearly felt that he was in the proverbial "tall cotton," enjoying robust health, new winter clothes from home, fancy stationery printed with a suitably saucy doggerel verse, and solid breastworks to top it all off![100] Although the 11th Georgia still had experienced no combat, its men had stood picket guard within clear view of the U. S. capital and come away unscathed. After five months in Virginia's fields and camps, Willoughby clearly had grown more confident in himself, to complement the pride he already felt in his regiment and his army.

He already had mentioned some of the picket guard dramatics of September 27 in the previous letter to his sister, but he obviously relished the opportunity to recount the story to his parents in detail. Withdrawal in the face of the enemy was indeed a very hazardous business. Performing it at night, from dispersed positions with unseasoned troops, raised the danger level by several orders of magnitude, as one senses in Willoughby's letter. The four-mile nighttime withdrawal from Falls Church to Fairfax was just one of an ongoing series of alarms that kept the Confederates of General Johnston's Department of Northern Virginia on pins and needles throughout much of the winter.[101]

In any event, the men of the 11th Georgia were happy things turned out as they did, and perhaps none were happier on that late September night than Captains E. S. Stokes of Company K and William T. Luffman of Company C, as Willoughby's letter hinted:[102]

Camp Near Centerville Dec 1st 1861

Dear Father & Mother

I take my pen this Evening to write you a few Lines to inform that I am well at this time and hope to Remain so & hope they will reach you enjoing the same Blessing; I am heavier by ten lbs than I ever was before I weigh now 160 lbs[103] We are looking for a fight here now but we do not no whether the Enemy will

Approach or not but the Cavelry Pickets say they are advancing with very heavy forces and they have brought in Severil Prisoners lately and they Say that they will either have to fight or go Some where before long as the Potomack is geting so bogy now that they can not bring there Artilery; I do not think it will be any use of there coming here now to Centerville because we have gotten it so well fortified they work us all the time on breast works and guard duty together[104] We were at one time in five miles of Wasington Citty I could See it very plain but we had to get away from there one night there Came Orders from Gen. Johnson about Seven Oclock that night but we had two Companys Stationed out on Post and they Could not find them until our Reg was behind all the rest Next to the Yankies & we were drawn up in line of battle for three hours and the wind blew very Cold and I came very near frezing Sure and we retreated from there that is from Falls Church back to Balls Cross roads and there we Stand in line of Battle for three days and nights looking them Blue Yankies to come upon us Every minute which maid Seven Days we were in line of Battle at one time and we were expecting about one hundred thousand or more and but three Regiments with ours but they took care not to come I could here there drums when I was on Post away off across a swamp three hundred yds from any other Person I stood there all night and it was so dark I could see nothing at all when a Stick would crack it Appearded like I could hear it a half mile; We have very Cold wether here now and I hear the Virginians say that it is nothing for all the Creeks and rivers to freeze over here & the snow eight or ten inches deep we have had Snow and Sleet already as much as we ever have in Ga I wish they would come on and do somthing now soon and let us go in to winter Quarters The Seccond Ga Brigade are all in front of the [line of] Battle and our Reg. are in front of the whole Brigade but we are just the boys that can face them if they Come[105] I would like very well to hear from you all but I can not here a word about you atall you must all write as soon as you get this letter and give me all the news that you have Tell Sister Mary to write and Give me a full history of Every thing and tell her that I Recieved my Cloths at last I Rec one Coat & Pants two Casmere Shirts two Blue Shirts pair of Shoes & Wescoat some other things too numerous to mention We have Rec for our Services $42 29/100 dollars and we are geting along very well in Money Matters I have got the Money I loaned to O. R. Smith yet & I will try and keep my money in my Pocket now We draw Just half Rassions of meat now. Pleas excuse bad writing; Give my Love to all.

Your Only Son

W. H. Mangham

*   *   *   *   *

Abundant stationery, a kinsman available to carry letters, and the monotonous pace of guard duties combined to allow Willoughby to write his father another brief note just two days later. Also, he had news that he probably felt uncomfortable recounting to the ladies of the family. Writing on December 9 from camp at Centreville, he addressed his "Dear Father At Home":

> I seat myself this Evening to Enroll a few lines to Send to you by Old Uncle Jerry Thompson.[106] I Rec your long looked for letter which I read with the greatest Pleasure indeed I would like to Receive every Day if it was favorable & I have delaid a few days for Mr Thompson to leave; I had just wrote about the time I Rec the Letter from Home; I am guard to day and I have got verry Severe pain in my right Eye I can not tel whether it is caused from cold or what. it feels just like it did when that Steal was in it I hope this will find you all well.[107] There was two of Neworleans Zouaves Shot this morning for taking one of the sentinel's guns away from him They tied them to a Stake and shot them we have some Cold weather now; I have not much time to write now; Tel Sisters & Mother to write soon. No more at this time So goodby; Excuse bad writing & Speling,
>
> Your Most Obedient Son   W. H. Mangham

*   *   *   *   *

The two "Neworleans Zouaves" were Michael O'Brien and Dennis Corcoran of the famous (or infamous) "Tiger Rifles" of Major Roberdeau Wheat's 1st Special Battalion, and the pair were the first soldiers executed in the Confederacy's Virginia army. The "sentinel" they had accosted was their acting commander, Lt. Col. Charles de Choiseul. As villainous in camp as they proved courageous in battle, this company was the source of the nickname "Louisiana Tigers," which Georgians and others eventually applied to all Louisiana infantrymen serving in the Virginia and Tennessee armies. Before they earned a reputation as superb combat troops, however, the appellation was decidedly uncomplimentary, and reflected their reputation as degraded street ruffians from the seedier districts of New Orleans. Indeed, most Southern troops viewed men like O'Brien and Corcoran as dangerous blackguards richly deserving of their fates. Willoughby certainly evinced no sense of horror or injustice at their demise.[108]

Otherwise, camp life in the war's first winter offered little other than constant rumors of enemy advances,[109] discomfort, and poor food, and Willoughby's letter to his mother in February of 1862 reminded her that he was dependent on her help:

> Feb 8th 1862   Fairfax Co. Va
> Camp Centerville
>
> My Dear Mother At Home
> I Received your Letter which I was so glad to hear that you were well and all the rest also it is so much Pleasure to me to hear from home you said that you wished to know how you should mark those Cloths to me; Mark thus: W. H. Mangham, Co (I) 11th Reg Ga Vols. Manassas Junction Va. Major Luffman in Command;[110]
> I expect that Railroad will be to Centerville now in a few days because they goten the road verry near compleet and if I new they would I would let you mark

364

to come to Centerville but I can not tel how that will be; Just mark them in my name to Manassas Va., Our Capt's name is Thacher;[111] I wish you would put in some Sage and Pepper if you have any to Spair I want it to put in beef to make it so as I can eat it, we draw 3/4 lb every ten days of Bacon and then we have to buy all our Shortening for bread We draw nothing but flour and that is not good with out greece & Soda;

John Thomas tels me that Thomas Frith did not take that trunk with him when he left but I did not know it;[112] be Sure and Send a good pair of boots if you can get them No[.] 7; the Mud and Snow is so deep here it goes over my Shoes and wets my feet it is either a Snowing or Sleeting here all the time nearly;

Write Soon all of you

Your Only Son

W. H. Mangham

*　　　*　　　*　　　*　　　*

Less than three weeks after writing home about the incessant sleet and snow, Willoughby Mangham was hospitalized in Richmond, where he remained throughout March. In the meantime, the 11th Georgia broke camp at Centreville and took the field, as General Johnston and Federal commander Gen. George B. McClellan began a deadly ballet of maneuver, later known to history as the Peninsula Campaign. When McClellan began embarking his Army of the Potomac for an eventual landing on the James River below Richmond, Lieutenant Colonel Guerry's 11th Georgia moved by rail down to the Confederate capital.[113]

When the regiment arrived in Richmond on April 11, 1862, it was apparent that they were finally bound for combat, after nine long months in the army. Disregarding his father's admonition to remain in the hospital, Willoughby left his sickbed to rejoin the Quitman Greys at Camp Winder. Soon thereafter, they marched down Main Street to the river, past cheering crowds urging them to victory. Departing on April 13, they disembarked at King's Landing on the next day. Two days later, Lieutenant Colonel Guerry was leading the 11th Georgia at the double-quick under Federal cannon fire, striving to reinforce the center of General Magruder's line at Dam No. 1 as a Union attack developed:[114]

Yorktown Va Apr 26th 1862

My Dear Father at home

I take my pen to inform you that I have received your most appreciated letter which I read with the greatest pleasure imaginable I was glad to hear that you were all well I cannot say that I am exactly well but I have left hospital I have pains about over me You said to stay at the hospital but the Co. came through there and were looking for a fight down here and I wanted to come with them The Soldiers are strung for ten miles here on each side I was glad to here that you had a safe trip out west;[115] we have a greatdeal of rain here now I wish we could all get home and live in peace once again but it appears like the Yankies are so numerous that it will be a long time yet it appears if I was fighting on the same cause that they are I Should dislike verry much indeed; tell Sister Mary that that I saw James day before yesterday and he was well[116] I was with him from dinner til night; I can not tel how long we will stay here at this point but you can direct your letters here and they will be sent to the Reg; Just mail them to Yorktown Va; I want to see little Altha and hear her talk[117] I want to see you all verry bad indeed We have been here two weeks now we had a Skirmish the second day after we arived here we killed some where between three and and four hundred killed and wounded they wounded five men in our Reg there was one of them kid [killed] since where with a Sharp shooter that did it;[118] the other side was not fire on our Reg attall and we got order to fall out of the ditches and we did so but where the orders came from no one knows we ran up the hill about an hundred yards and met Gen. McGruder commanding us to go back and hold our position and we did so and we got back we fired a full volley and that fellow got away from there and did not shoot any more You must write soon; this letter will be mailed in Richmond for I have the chance to send it that far. it is geting dark tell all to write;

Your most obedient Son

W. H. Mangham

*   *   *   *   *

By ignoring his father's advice to remain in the hospital and then justifying it as he did, Willoughby provided his father (and us) an excellent illustration of the comradeship which bound the Quitman Greys into a cohesive fighting force. After all, his friends "came through there and were looking for a fight." Could any Southern man help but respond, especially when the "Yankies" were "so numerous"? And just as the young soldier probably knew his father would approve of such a rationale, it is also clear that both agreed that the Federal cause was an unjust one. Unfortunately, however, we are left wondering exactly *how* the two Georgians defined the enemy's cause. Was it restoration of the Union through coercion? Subjugation of states' rights? Abolition of slavery? Or perhaps all of these?

In any event, the bungled reconnaissance-in-force at Dam No. 1 cost the Federals 165 casualties on April 22, 1862, but the 11th Georgia inflicted few if any of these.[119] The Georgians were several hundred yards from the center of the fray, and their own casualties came from a spattering of cannon fire and long-range rifle fire. Willoughby and his friends then settled down to a routine of trench warfare, with the regiment serving alternate days crouching below ground in the waterlogged forward trenches, as opposing sharpshooters traded shots with deadly effect.[120]

Lieutenant Colonel Luffman led the 11th Georgia, some 573 strong, out of the rifle pits at Dam No. 1 on May 4, as Johnston's army retreated slowly towards Richmond in seemingly ceaseless downpours that transformed the rutted county tracks into muddy sloughs. On May 18, the bone weary Georgians slogged through the city's outskirts and bivouacked three miles west of the city, as the Confederate army prepared to defend its capital.[121]

Shortly after they settled into bivouac, Willoughby sat down to write his mother a brief description of events. As his previous letter had reflected a tone of modest confidence after his first combat at Yorktown, he now remained apparently calm as he and his cause faced potential disaster. Neither desperate firebrand nor woebegone doomsayer, Willoughby Mangham apparently had developed a large measure of the resiliency that marked the veteran soldier. Judging by his letter, he simply was not considering the possibility of defeat:

[About May 18, 1862][122]

My Dear Mother

I am embraced with the opportunity of writing you a few lines to inform you that I am getting well now and hope that these few lines will find you enjoying the Same great Blessing of good heath I have not received any answer for my last letter and I have concluded to write again I hope that I will hear from you Soon for it is the greatest Pleasure that I have is when I am reading a letter from home; we had good Preaching in camps this evening; We have been vacuating untill we have got to Richmond at last and I suppose we will hold this Place if we can We have had a fine time of marching we have been on a march about two weeks now but I guess we will Stop now and fight them awhile I never regreted any thing as much as the giving up Neworleans it I fear will cut off all our western provisions[123] I would like to [see] you all once more if posible I want you all to write me as often as posible I want to hear from you all and tell Sister Mary that I [saw?] Jame the other day and he was well at that time he says he likes it very well but he has the advantage of us for when we are marching with our napsacks he has nothing _____ of _____

All _____ excuse bad [writing?].   *W. H. Mangham*

*   *   *   *   *

The 11th Georgia remained in the immediate vicinity of Richmond until the end of May, when it began to work its way back down the Chickahominy River. It now marched under the overall command of Gen. Robert E. Lee, who replaced General Johnston after the latter fell wounded at Seven Pines on May 31, 1862. Unfortunately none of Willoughby's letters survive from this period, in which the regiment took part in the Seven Days' battles which seared the Chickahominy in late June as Lee delivered a series of stunning counterblows. On the first day of July, the Georgians helped deliver a supporting attack in the most desperate fighting of the war to date, at Malvern Hill. Although their column was in the third line of the assault, they suffered severely from the hurricane of fire that blazed from the strongly entrenched Federal positions, reinforced by massive 9-inch, 11-inch, and 100-pounder shells from the gunboats *Galena*, *Aroostook*, and *Mahaska* on the James River. Their long afternoon and evening of combat roared to a fiery climax from 5:00 to 9:00 p.m. When the shooting sputtered

367

to a halt, the regiment counted its losses: it had suffered six killed in action, fifty wounded and sixteen missing.[124]

A few weeks later, Willoughby scribbled a brief note to his sister Huldah. Although he failed to note his current location, he probably was writing from the 11th Georgia's new picket post: Malvern Hill.[125] As we can tell from the legible portions of the letter, the great battle there had marked the end of the line for Willoughby's old messmate and friend Joe Davis. Writing on July 23, 1862, he addressed his "Dear Sister":

> I take my pen to write you a few lines _____. I am well at this time and hope you are blessed with the same gift I have not heard from you in some time now and I want to hear verry bad we have _____ very ____ time here for _____ a battle to about thirty five miles away the Chickahominy River _____ There was one man killed out of our Co Joe Davis was killed dead;[126] I saw James Nichols in the ___ and he was well ____.
>
> excuse bad writing
>
> W. H. Mangham

*　　*　　*　　*　　*

Another eight-week gap exists in Willoughby's surviving letters. It corresponds to a transition period between the calm following McClellan's evacuation of the Peninsula and a renewed frenzy of activity occasioned by Lee's decision to "suppress" Maj. Gen. John Pope's army in northern Virginia. As Lee moved north to strike Pope, the 11th Georgia engaged in arduous marching and some spirited advanced-guard fighting. At Rappahannock Station on August 23, the opposing artillery engaged in what historian John Hennessy has called "one of the fiercest small artillery duels of the war." When Gen. James Longstreet decided to send in his infantry to resolve the bitterly contested artillery engagement, the 11th Georgia was at the forefront of the assault, along with Holcombe's Legion. "Shouting like demons," they swept upslope and drove off the Union batteries on the near side of the Rappahannock River. As part of George T. "Tige" Anderson's "fine lot of Georgians," they also bore the brunt of seizing Thoroughfare Gap five days later.[127]

Willoughby apparently participated in all of these actions, but they proved merely a prelude to the cauldron of fire into which the Quitman Greys plunged at Manassas on August 30, 1862. On this fateful day, he and slightly fewer than four hundred comrades of the 11th Georgia followed Luffman through heavy artillery fire into their first-ever sustained, close-range, infantry fighting. They doggedly held their place in line and helped drive two Federal brigades from the field, although the brigade's attack eventually stuck fast on the slopes of Henry Hill. The desperate Union stand at this point prevented the destruction of Pope's beaten army, which survived to totter into Washington's defenses. The cost of Lee's resounding but incomplete victory was staggering, as Luffman's men lost twenty killed and 178 wounded in the holocaust; this price in blood ranked second among the Confederate regiments that routed Pope's army that day. The Quitman Greys sadly counted four fallen and 21 wounded, one of whom died soon thereafter from his wounds.[128]

After Manassas, Lee marched his army northward into Maryland in a bold stroke to take the war into the North. The 11th Georgia paused in Leesburg to leave its numerous sick and barefooted men, before passing into Maryland on September 6, 1862.[129] Exhausted and shaking with fever, Willoughby Mangham was one of those left behind. Although his letter's numerous inkblots and erratic penmanship betrayed his continuing weakness, he gamely expressed his hope to catch up to his friends in a letter composed on September 15, 1862:

> My Dear Father
>
> I received yours a few days ago but have not had the chance to answer not until now as I have been on the march ever Since that time and I have been marching four weeks and been Sick but I was able to go again I believe the reg. is gone up to Maryland now and left me at leesburg and we were taken from there to Winchester and I am going to try to get to the Reg[t]. now but they march so hard and fast I do not know whether I can keep up with them or not I have the chills severel days but I have missed the chill two days now I am at a private house now near harpers ferry and better People were ever known than they are the lady is so kind that She reminds me of Mother She does not know when She has done enough for us Soldiers She give us clean cloths to put on while she could wash the ones we had for they were awful black and one Suit is all we have as cant toat any more and keep up I never Shal forget those people; they are so Kind I would like to get home to see you all but there is no chance to get a furlough now at all I hope we Stop marching shortly and then then I can hear you all but I guess you had better direct your letters to Gordenvile and they be sent to the Regt. from there we will be some where in Maryland I reckon I cant tell where we we will be; Tell Sister Mary that I have [not?] heard [from] James since I left Richmond.
>
> Tell Mother & Sisters Huldah & Mary howdy and give them my love and Tell them to write often; And you must write also I shall want Cloths this winter but I can not tell you where to direct them; give my love to all Altha too I wish I could see her.
>
> Excuse bad writing,
> Your Only and most obedient Son
>
> > *W. H. Mangham*

*   *   *   *   *

Since Willoughby had reached Harper's Ferry by September 15, he was actually within some twenty miles of his regiment, and he was almost as close as they were to Sharpsburg. His next letter to his sister, however, seems to indicate that he did not cross into Maryland, where the bloodiest day in American history dawned over Antietam creek on September 17, 1862.

The 11th Georgia had been split into two wings, both serving as wagon train escorts during the advance into Maryland. Only the five companies of the right wing, comprising some 140 men, arrived at Sharpsburg in time to help Brig. Gen. Robert Toombs's small brigade in a counterattack which crumpled the Federal left flank in one of the Civil War's most dramatic small-unit actions. Willoughby's friends in the Quitman Greys played a small role in that action, suffering two of the regiment's ten casualties that day.[130] (See map on page 258.)

After Lee's army pulled back across the Potomac River into Virginia, the Georgians settled into camp near Winchester. By the middle of October, however, smallpox had broken out in parts of the army. Reminiscent of August and September 1861, the regiment once more went into quarantine, this time near Strasburg with the other troops of "Tige" Anderson's and Toombs's brigades.[131]

At some time during the preceding month, Willoughby had rejoined his friends, and he wrote to his sister to catch her up on the news. His reference to the rear guards illustrates the deficiencies of the medical system supporting the invasion of Maryland, as well as the army's stern measures against the rampant straggling that sapped the strength of Lee's northward march. On the positive side, however, it also reflects the strong bond between the officers and men of the Quitman Greys:[132]

Oct 21st 1862

My Dear Sister

I have the opportunity of writing you a few lines this morning to inform you that I am well at this time I have been down with the chills ever since august until about three weeks ago I was left on the road and I got in at a private house and never was treated better in my life I marched severel days when I was hardly able to creep we would march all day and then till midnight and one night I went to Lieut Bledsoe and he being a doctor examaned and gave me a pass and told me to get out in the woods where the rear guards would not find me and then get to a private house and stay untill I got well and as it hapened the gentleman of the house was a Dr and give me medicine ____ long as I staid he give me more ____ than I ever saw before. I wrote a letter while I was there but have not received no answer yet and I getting verry anxtious to hear from you all I have not heard from you since august we are seperated from the army now the troops are resting now Some people think that we will be ordered to the coast shortly and I hope that it may be so and then I could get to see you then we have frost here now every Morning we are now stationed at Strawsburg the place where we first landed at in Va and struck March for Winchester I have not I have not seen James since we left Richmond Some of the [boys?] saw him when I was sick I am sorry that I was not able to go into Maryland with Him. I will want coats shortly I guess for the winter. I reckon I can buy Blankets if we ever get where any are. Tell Pa and all the rest that I am well and would like to see them. Tell them to write soon; I Remain your affectionate Brother

W. H. Mangham

*   *   *   *   *

A week after writing his sister from the quarantined camp at Strasburg, the 11th Georgia hot-footed it south and east out of the Shenandoah Valley, covering nearly one hundred miles in less than five days. Lee was moving his army in response to McClellan's renewed crossing of the Potomac, begun on October 26, 1862. After several weeks of shifting positions in response to the glacial pace of the Federal advance, the Georgians arrived near Fredericksburg on November 22. The Army of Northern Virginia was concentrating there in order to defend the Rappahannock line against crossings threatened by Federal forces, now commanded by Maj. Gen. Ambrose Burnside.[133]

Willoughby and his comrades performed picket guard and built defensive positions in the heights behind the town as they awaited developments. In a letter to his father dated December 14, 1862, he made no mention whatever of the Battle of Fredericksburg, which commenced on December 11 and roared to a fiery climax two days later. It is therefore likely that he wrote the letter about December 10, before Burnside's army began its large-scale river-crossing operations on the following day.[134]

In this brief and conversational letter to his father, Willoughby's heartfelt gratitude for a recently received letter underlines the notorious unreliability of the Confederacy's mails. It was one more major stress factor for soldiers and their families, and the duration, mobility, and intensity of the 1862 campaign further heightened the strain on the creaking postal services. *Every single one* of Willoughby Mangham's surviving wartime letters expressed thanks for a recently received letter, chided his family for not writing often enough, or instructed them on what to send or how to send it. In many letters he addressed several (or all) of these concerns at once. The young soldier viewed himself as the protector of hearth and home, and he clearly found the burden of family separation a very heavy cross to bear.

Willoughby's letter also serves to highlight yet another nagging concern that haunted soldiers of Lee's army, namely their families' struggles to obtain adequate amounts of food staples such as salt. Before the existence of refrigeration technology, large quantities of salt were vitally necessary for food processing and preservation, so any shortage threatened catastrophe. Federal occupation of salt mines in Kentucky and western Virginia had deprived the Confederacy of much of its salt-producing potential, so the danger was very real. Back home in Georgia, which had no saline resources other than its seacoast, Governor Joseph Brown initiated a variety of programs to relieve the shortage. While desperate Southerners dug up smokehouse floors to distill the salt from fat droppings, Brown's administration subsidized issues of the precious substance to soldiers' families to help ward off disaster.[135]

Camp Near Fredricksburg
December the 14th, 1862

My dear Father
 I received yours on the 8 of this month which I was glad enough to receve it Sure for it was the first letter I have got by mail Since July ____ ____ that you

were all well and I hope this will reach you enjoying the Same great Blessing still I do have to hear from if I can not See you but I like to See all of you better _____ _____ _____ __ think there is not hour passes by without my thinking of you all at home I hope that I will see you all before [august?] while Surely I wish I was there now if possible I Saw more pleasure while I was at home than I have ever seen since I was glad to hear of the trade you made with the old building _____ I was afraid that you would be suffering for salt but I am inhops you will have a plenty now and more too Salt Sells here for [3] or 4 Dollars pr [quart Some one][136] offered $5.00 for a Sack the other So I hear them Say, I have known them to give $2.00 pr pint for it; I saw James the other and he was well then John Davis gives you all his love and best respects and tell his folks he is well and one that I think a great deal of Sure[137] I got all the cloths named you must soon Excuse bad writing your most obeient son

W. H. Mangham

*   *   *   *   *

As its contents make clear, Willoughby's next letter certainly postdated the Battle of Fredericksburg, although he mistakenly carried over the previous year's date. His surviving letters indicate a pronounced unwillingness to describe battle scenes in any detail, and this letter confirms the pattern. In any case, he was no longer the rookie soldier of 1861, excitedly recounting his adventures on picket duty. As a veteran of Malvern Hill and Second Manassas, he was not going to get overheated about what "might have been" at Fredericksburg. Quite simply, the Georgians of G. T. Anderson's Brigade were very near the action, but not in the midst of it; their part in the danger was limited to stray bullets and a few casualties. Willoughby apparently figured that a miss was as good as a mile, since none of his friends was wounded. One also notes the utter absence of the bitter disappointment he expressed at missing First Manassas![138]

For Willoughby, Fredericksburg was further proof that he and his friends serving under General Lee enjoyed an advantage in leadership that the Federals could not match, regardless of their numbers. He obviously considered Burnside licked, once and for all. Regarding speculation about a replacement for Burnside, one can almost hear Willoughby chuckling with amusement at a prospect he and his pals obviously considered absurd: President Lincoln himself assuming field command.

Less apparent to him, however, were the implications of the recent Emancipation Proclamation.[139] His enigmatic reference to Lincoln's policy leaves us unable to ascertain precisely his reaction, although his words have the ring of someone whose negative expectations have been fulfilled. After all, Willoughby had grown up in a family that had owned slaves for generations, and John Mangham still owned at least one slave in 1860. Willoughby, in other words, was not just *aware* of the South's "peculiar institution." He and his family were a *part* of it. As a minimum, he and his father understood each other's views on slavery already, and Willoughby therefore felt no need to discuss it in detail in his letter.[140]

Clearly, some of his comrades viewed the Emancipation Proclamation as an act of desperation, but Willoughby was more realistic about the North's ability to continue the war. As a young recruit after First Manassas, he once had allowed himself to speculate about an early peace, but the veteran soldier of 1863 clearly believed any talk of peace was premature; a lot of fighting remained to be done. As far as he was concerned, however, the Army of Northern Virginia clearly would continue to take care of the military side of things handily, as they were healthy, comparatively well-fed and had good tents over their heads. Now all they needed was more mail!

Camp Near Fredricksburg   Jan 9th 1862 [1863]
My Dear Mother
    I Recieved your letter through the Kindness of Mr Davis which I was the gladest to read you ever saw any one in this world I was glad to hear that you were well and all the rest.[141] I am well at this time and hope to remain so   I was vaccinated yesterday all the Co. were vaccinated. I have not Received only two letters by mail Since Aug they are So negligent about the mail we are geting along verry well here now we have good tents now and I hope we will remain in them some time and we are geting more to eat now than we have been hereto fore; I would be So glad to See you all and talk with I think that I could give you a good history of the war but I have no idea how long it will be first there has been some talk of peace here but I think it doutful about it   Linclon Speaks of taking the field in Va in person and I hope he will in prefference to Gen McCleland for he is their best Gen. I think; if he does that we will not have many more fights I do not think Burnsides says he will never attempt to cross the Rapahanock again as long as there is a Rebel gun pointing at him on this anymore I want to Send $50.00 home by Mr Davis;
    To Sister Mary at home
    I want to you and Altha so bad bad I do not know what to do it looks hard to have to stay away so long; I saw James a few days before Mr Davis came up and were speaking of going up to handover Junction about 30 miles from here and Mr Davis Said he understood they were up there I know they are gone from here;[142] And his Cloths are here and do not know what I shall do with them for I can not carry them but I will do the be[st] I know; I want to see Little Altha Bless her little Sweet Self I have not seen no little Children Since I left it is nothing here but big guns and big men and I am geting tired of it and every once and a while march out and face the canon ball. I hope you will write as Soon as you get this letter and let me know how you are geting along; A few lines to Sister Huldah I do not believe she ever writs to me or I would get Some of them I have got a plenty of paper and ink now and I intend to write and Keep writing Every chance I get I got a letter from Father the last letter I got by mail Pa said he was coming to see me and I hope that he will; I Supose Mr Lincoln has passed his Emancipation Bill at last and the Maralanders Say that he has shot his last arrow now but I can tell he has a many a friend yet but they were badly

whiped here the last Battle I think they thew their Bridges a cross one night and began to cross Gen Lee had the news before the first one put his foot on land and he sent word to Gen. Cobb[143] just let them come but in a few minutes the Signal was heard about an hour before day and the drums began beat and the fifes to Play and to the Battle field we marched away and it verry cold the Ground was covered in Snow that morning but our Reg' did not get in to it; and such a roaring of canon you never heard in all your life being so cold maid them roar so loud; You must write as soon as you get this letter; Excuse bad writing and ill composure if you Please

    Your Only Son   W. H. Mangham

    P. O.   Give my love and best respts to all the Girls and tell them I would like to See them too;   To Mrs Eliza W. Mangham

*   *   *   *   *

Several weeks later, we again see the Davis family serving as the conduit for mail between Willoughby and the Mangham family back in Cuthbert. Apparently, Willoughby's good friend, Sgt. John Davis, returned to the company from a home furlough about the time that his father was leaving Virginia to return to Georgia. Mr. Davis probably had come to the army to look after Francis, who had been wounded severely at Sharpsburg in September. Since Joe was killed in action in July at Malvern Hill, it obviously had been a very trying time for the Davis family.

Indeed, Willoughby Mangham's correspondence is filled with references to these networks of friendship and kinship that bound the Quitman Greys to each other and to their home community. Although they were far away from Quitman and Randolph counties, they were well aware that their deeds (or misdeeds) would become a matter of record back home, where individual and family reputations were at stake. As long as civilian morale was intact, these community ties cemented the bonds of individual honor, good leadership, and military discipline into an extremely potent element of individual morale and *esprit de corps*.[144]

Willoughby Mangham's letters provide us glimpses of these bonds in his unit, and other indicators of the Georgians' performance in camp and field confirm their existence. As their original regimental commander Col. "Tige" Anderson proudly reported after commanding the brigade at Second Manassas: "For the desperation of the fight and the fierce tenacity with which my men held their ground let the list of casualties testify." When we apply Anderson's standard of measurement to the Quitman Greys' service from enlistment in July 1861 through the battle of Fredericksburg, we see long-term statistical evidence that supports the proud commander's necessarily subjective assertion. The company had carried a total of 124 men on its rolls, comprising the original 86 upon mustering-in, plus fifteen recruits and twenty-three conscripts. Altogether, 21 had been discharged or resigned for illness; one resigned (reason unknown); nineteen men had been wounded in action, and one of these died of wounds; 23 had died of disease; and five had been killed in action. In short, almost twenty-five percent of the Quitman Greys had died in service, while a further seventeen percent had returned home physically disabled. An additional fifteen percent had been wounded in action.[145] And nothing can quantify the misery of the long marches, the clearly inadequate rations, the exposure to the elements, the mental trauma of combat, inadequate mail, and an unknown (and unknowable) number of family tragedies and complications back home in Georgia.

But not a single man had deserted.

A bemused Willoughby Mangham wrote home in February 1863 from the hills above Fredericksburg, where he had watched Burnside's disastrous "Mud March" result in his replacement by yet another Federal general, this one with a blood'n'thunder nickname. In his homely manner, the young Georgian simply observed: "I guess he will try to do something before long."

The Quitman Greys were playing for keeps, and they were playing to win.

Feb 2ᵈ 1863
Camp Near Fredricksburg Va

My Dear Father at home

I received your letter through the politness of John Davis which I was the gladest to hear that you were all well and doing well I am verry uneasy for fear that you will get the Smalpox in the Family though I hope not I should like to hear from you the oftener on that account I am well and doing well now and hope to remain so I sent by Mr. Davis fifty Dollars which you did not mention whether you had received it or not which I would be glad to know I have not much of interest to write more than we have some verry cold weather here now the Snow was about ten or twelve inches deep here the other day but it has nearly all melted now; And all the Commanding officers have resigned on the yankie's Side Old Burnsides tried to get his army across here the other day and the mud was so deep that he failed and then he desided to come and fight with infantry and have his Artilery on the other side of the river[146] And Old Jo Hooker opposed him and then Said that he would resign as he would not agree and now Old Fighting Jo Hooker as they call has taken command and I guess he will try to do something before long

Please excuse bad writing

Your most obedient Son;   *W. H. Mangham*

A few lines to Sister Mary

I received yours also which I was glad to read and hear that you were well I have nothing to write at present Except that I am well and no peace yet and I can not tell when it will be; You must write soon and tell me all you know

To Sister Huldah

I received one from you which I was gratified verry much to read it I would be so glad to see you all once more and see dear Little Altha and hear her talk I got a letter from James the other day and he was well he was at Ginies Station;[147]

Your Only Brother   *W. H. Mangham*

*   *   *   *   *

When he wrote his father a month later, Willoughby and the remainder of General Longstreet's corps had been encamped on the south side of Richmond for nearly two weeks. A major Federal deployment to Fort Monroe on the coast had posed a threat to the Confederate capital, and General Lee countered it by dispatching Longstreet south from Fredericksburg. As part of Hood's Division, the 11th Georgia force-marched some fifty miles through fierce snowstorms to reach Richmond. The regiment's major, Henry McDaniel of Walton County, described this march in a letter home; he termed it "the severest of the War," and many of the other participants agreed that this was no exaggeration. As they camped in twelve inches of snow during late February, rumors circulated about the regiment's possible transfer to the coastal defenses at Charleston or Savannah.[148] Such possibilities usually made Georgia troops tingle with anticipation of visits home and warmer climes, as a frigid Willoughby clearly implied:

Mar 4th 1863
Camp Near Richmond Va

My Dear Father

I have the opportunity this evening of writing you a few lines to inform you that I am well and hope these few lines will find you enjoying the same Blessing I received a letter from Sister Mary & Huldah through the kindness of Mr Adams which I answered but I do not know whether it it came to hand or not;[149] we have come south of the James now and I hope that we may never go north of it again as long as I live in Service I want to come South every move we have cold weather now; I Sent you $50.00 by Mr Davis and you never Stated whether you had Received it or not I would like to know I fear Mr Davis might have forgotten it as he had money for so Many Give my love to all the ____ and tell them to write to me; I received a letter from Harriet[?] & Lucy & Aunt Sally Graddy the other day;[150] you must excuse this ill writen and crimped letter if you Please as I [am] Seting in Such a critical condition here You must write when you get this; I have nothing more to write; So I will close by Subscribing myself your obedient Son

W. H. Mangham

*   *   *   *   *

A three month hiatus in Willoughby's surviving correspondence obscures our view of the Quitman Greys in the spring of 1863, which saw them participate in Longstreet's month-long siege of Federal forces occupying Suffolk. These operations allowed Longstreet to gather food and forage for Lee's supply-starved army. Describing the food crisis, Virginia Sgt. John Worsham stated simply: "None but the Confederate soldier knows how they lived. For months we had not had a full ration." Maddeningly, the men were losing weight on half-rations and even suffering from scurvy due to the Commissary Department's inability to transport provisions from the bounteous surplus produced in the Deep South. While commissary wagons hauled food north for the main army, Willoughby and other soldiers of Hood's Division shot it out with Yankee gunboats on the Nansemond River, attempting to prevent resupply of the Suffolk garrison.[151]

The period of picket duty, sharpshooting, and occasional shelling ended for the 11th Georgia in early May, however, when the looming clash at Chancellorsville forced Lee to recall Longstreet's Corps to northern Virginia. Although Longstreet's men did not join Lee in time for the battle, the Army of Northern Virginia scored yet another resounding victory. By mid-month, Willoughby and his comrades of Hood's Division finally had resumed their places with the main army, which now was reunited along the Rapidan River west of Fredericksburg. Hooker and his men had pulled back across the Rappahannock to lick their wounds once again, leaving the ever-aggressive Lee to mull over renewed opportunities for taking the war onto Northern soil.[152]

Early June saw Lee's army on the move towards Culpeper Court House, where it staged for its march north into Pennsylvania. When Willoughby sat down to write his sister Huldah on June 14, lead elements of Lt. Gen. Dick Ewell's corps already were engaged at Winchester, fighting to secure the Shenandoah Valley in support of Lee's move north.[153] The young Georgian made no direct mention of these momentous events to his younger sister, simply noting that it would be some time before he expected to come home again.

Perhaps by way of explanation, he made a clearer statement of his convictions than he offered in any other surviving letter. Indeed, he possibly was responding to her repeatedly expressed hopes of an early peace, especially since his previous letters to Huldah and Mary imply that they often asked him about such prospects. He had warned his family previously that "them Blue Yankies" were so numerous that a lot of fighting lay ahead, but in June 1863 he laid all his cards on the table: the war would continue as long as the invader stood on Southern soil. Likewise, Huldah and others should stop looking to English or French intervention for the South's salvation. In his view, all the palaver about the Mason and Slidell missions to Europe only served to obscure the simple reality: the Southern people must rely on their own armies to protect them.[154]

For Willoughby's part, the very idea that these armies might need such pipe dreams for inspiration was insulting. He was painfully aware, however, that some soldiers lacked this spirit of dedication. As he disgustedly pointed out, even the vaunted Army of Northern Virginia had to bribe many such faint-hearts and shirkers with furloughs in order to keep them in ranks.[155]

As homesick as he was, however, he didn't need a furlough as much as he needed cotton socks. He had marching to do!

> June 14th 1863
> Camp Culpepper Va

My Ever Dear Sister
    Yours of the 8th of June came to hand yesterday evening which I read and perused verry carful and was exceeding glad to hear that you were all well with

the exception of Mother and it causes me to be almost misirable to hear that She is Sick for I know it does go so hard with her I would be so [afraid?] ____ ____ her now I think I could ____ a great many things that I think would interest her very much I hope that I will see all of you before long although the prospects do not ___ very fair for at this time yet. Messrs Mason & Slidel keep reporting their prosperity in Europe but I fear it is all a humbug only to encourage the Soldier but then they ought to know that our troops will fight as long as the enemy invade our Soil we are here fighting in Virginia and the Va troops are some of them talking about throughing their arms and stop fighting I met up with one of them yesterday and he was going to take the train to go home on furlough and he was Swearing and grumbling about it he said he had been out here now fifteen months and had never got to go home home before that time but I told him that I had been out here two years with the exceptions of two weeks and had never been home nor did not expect to go until the end of war; They are so mean they have to grant them furlough to keep them from deserting and going to Yankees The night we left _____ there was some of them went over to the Yankees and told them that we were all gone and if they would hurry on in persuit of us they could take a great many that could not keep up with army and they did so immediately and captured a good many And for all that when the fighting is done the Virginians do it if you will just listen to those Richmond papers. Tell Pa & Sister that I wrote to them a few days ago. Tell Pa that he must come to see me as soon as he can for I would like verry well to see you indeed and all the rest I was glad to hear that you had had a plenty of rain because it is better to be too wet than too dry for if it is wet corn will grow. I do not need any Cloths now with the exception of Socks I need Cotton Socks for in marching I wear Socks verry fast yarn hurts my feet [worse?] Cotton; I wrote to you for a tent fly I would like to have that I want it about 4 1/2 ft Sqr to button together at the edge and lap over about 4 or 5 inches and two rows of buttons and direct them to the Georgia Relief and Assosiation Society at Richmond Va[156] I wish I could see little Altha and hear the sweet little thing talk. I got a letter from James a few days ago and he was well at that time. You must write soon for _____ happy ____ any time as when I am reading a letter from home Tell Sister she must write and Pa too I have nothing of interest to write Please excuse this ill written and Composed letter I will close by Subscribing myself your most affectionate Brother

W. H. Mangham

To Miss H. L. G. Mangham

*   *   *   *   *

We don't know if Willoughby ever received his new cotton socks, but he surely needed them over the ensuing weeks. The Quitman Greys hiked northward to a Pennsylvania crossroads town whose name is now borne on courthouse monuments and gravestones throughout the land. At Gettysburg, the Georgians had an opportunity to show "those Richmond papers" the error of their ways, and they stood to the task with the same ferocity and effectiveness they displayed at Second Manassas.

Slightly over three hundred men of Col. Francis H. Little's 11th Georgia went into action on July 2, 1863, as part of "Tige" Anderson's brigade.[157] As the right-center regiment in the brigade's line of battle, they pushed through Rose Woods and across Plum Run to lay claim to a place known ever since simply as "the Wheatfield." There, in a seesaw battle that witnessed the regiment fling itself three times at the enemy lines,

GETTYSBURG, PENNSYLVANIA, JULY 1-3, 1863.
WILLOUGHBY MANGHAM, OF ANDERSON'S DIVISION, FOUGHT IN THE WHEATFIELD
(LOWER LEFT) ON JULY 2, BUT WAS WOUNDED THE NEXT DAY ON THE SOUTHERN FLANK.
HIS SECOND COUSIN, NAT MANGHAM OF THE 13TH GEORGIA, HELPED CAPTURE THE
TOWN ITSELF ON JULY 1 (SEE CH. II AND APPENDIX, REF. # 195).

they finally cleared the field of all Federal resistance by late afternoon. Union forces had held long enough, however, to prevent a breakthrough that would have endangered the integrity of their main defensive line. As night fell, the Georgians pulled back to regroup in the cover of Plum Run. As historian Harry Pfanz has observed, "Longstreet's men could relish the distinct taste of victory in the acrid powder smoke."[158]

For the Quitman Greys, however, it was another victory tempered by its high price. Captain Samuel Thatcher was severely wounded and taken prisoner, dying of his wounds some six weeks later. Frank Bledsoe, the lieutenant who had helped Willoughby on so many occasions, was wounded badly in the arm, which later required amputation. Lieutenant Samuel Belcher died of his wounds, as did Sgt. Daniel McIlvane. Willoughby's friend and messmate, Sgt. Jesse Pittman, was one of the three men killed outright. Of the nine men wounded, five would die of the aftereffects. Clearly, their leaders had led from the front once again, and their men had responded to their example. The same held true for the regiment as a whole. Of an estimated 310 officers and men engaged, it suffered 23 killed in action, 171 wounded, and five missing in action. Only nine regiments in Lee's entire army suffered higher losses at Gettysburg.[159]

The next day saw General Lee choose Pickett's Division to inscribe its name in red in latter-day American history books. As the Virginians' epic drama unfolded at the center of the line, the 11th Georgia was ordered beyond the army's right flank to help other units of the brigade repel a probe by Federal horsemen. Major Henry McDaniel took command, as Colonel Little had been wounded on the previous day and Lieutenant Colonel Luffman fell ill en route to the right flank. McDaniel later reported that the regiment had helped drive the Federals "in confusion" from the field, and the Georgians lashed out again after the cavalrymen returned to harass the pickets. McDaniel, a future Governor of Georgia, added the note: "Our loss was very slight."[160]

By comparison to the previous day's bloodbath in the Wheatfield, McDaniel's report was unquestionably accurate. For John and Eliza Mangham, however, the "slight loss" must have been a fearsome blow. Their son, Pvt. Willoughby Hill Mangham, was wounded badly in the left hand on July 3, 1863. He was left behind when his friends of the Quitman Greys turned southward once more on the following day.[161]

Perhaps the young Georgian pondered the irony of it all. Exactly two years earlier, he had enlisted to defend his homeland against the invader. Now he lay wounded and forlorn, captive in a land where he himself was the invader.

As Lee's army headed back towards refuge in Virginia, the United States celebrated the 87th birthday of a nation born in revolution. For Private Mangham, there was hope of physical recovery and perhaps eventual repatriation, in accordance with the cartel for prisoner exchanges. In the meantime, he could consider only two things certain: pain and imprisonment.

*　　　*　　　*　　　*　　　*

For Willoughby, prison meant Fort Delaware, a damp and gloomy enclosure located on an island in the Delaware River. Along with prison camps such as Johnson's Island

and Rock Island, its name was a bogey around Confederate campfires, just as Libby Prison, Belle Isle, and Andersonville were for their Union counterparts. As daunting as were mortality rates in camp and field, they were positively horrifying in the squalid prison pens of the Civil War. From November 1863 through January 1864, disease killed 311 prisoners at Fort Delaware. According to a Federal medical inspector's calculations, this equated to an annual death rate of nearly 453 per 1000 men, in contrast to a death rate of 52 per 1000 among the Federal garrison. As his report accurately noted, "From previous hard service and short rations [the prisoners'] general condition was considerably below the par of health." Marginal rations and the cold, damp, overcrowded barracks aggravated the problem. Each prisoner possessed only a single blanket to ward off the cold; no other bedding was available, even straw.[162]

Once within the grim prison walls, Willoughby could only await developments and try to avoid incidents with trigger-happy sentries. With reasonable luck, exchange agents eventually would arrange his release, following which he might receive a disability discharge, or perhaps return to duty if his health permitted. Another possible way out was to swear an oath of allegiance to the United States, in which case he might be released on condition he remain north of the Ohio River during the war. Some captured Confederates avoided prolonged captivity by becoming "Galvanized Yankees," enlisting either in the U. S. Navy or in the Army for service on the western frontier.[163]

Given the sentiments he expressed in his earlier letters, it is not surprising that Willoughby found such options unacceptable. Unfortunately for him, however, Federal authorities suspended the exchange cartel at the very time he was captured, amid mutual recriminations over various irregularities, eventually including the treatment of captured black soldiers. There was also a rising consciousness among some in the North that they could afford to lose prisoners for the duration, whereas the South could not. Although exchanges eventually resumed in early 1864, they fell far short of emptying the miserably crowded prisons of both sides.[164]

In his one surviving note from Fort Delaware, Willoughby was still hoping for exchange before the onset of a second winter in captivity. For him, there was simply no other honorable way out:

In Prison at Fort Delaware[165]
Sept. 14, 1864

My dear Father:

I take my pen in hand to inform you that I am well and I hope these few lines may find you the same. You must write as soon as you can. I have written the third time now. Mr. Ham is here and he is well. Tell Mrs. Ham that he has written.[166]

Well I hope that I live to see you all again if it is God's will. I have been here a prisoner over fourteen months now. I hope the authorities will get us away from here before winter. I can't write more than ten lines.

Your only and most obedient son,
W. H. Mangham

* * * * *

As Willoughby composed this note from prison, his old company was in the trenches at Petersburg, Virginia, its ranks thinned by eight major engagements since Gettysburg. Another three were yet to come, flare-ups amidst the steady attrition of trench warfare. Slightly more than six months later, the once-proud Army of Northern Virginia was no more. Only fifteen men stood in the ranks of the Quitman Greys as they stacked arms for the last time at Appomattox Court House, Virginia. Of the 86 men who comprised the original company, a mere nine remained. Three Davis and seven Pittman boys had been Willoughby Mangham's messmates in the long-ago days of 1861, but only Pvt. Francis Marion Davis was there to answer the final roll call.[167]

General Johnston surrendered the Army of Tennessee less than three weeks afterwards at Greensboro, North Carolina. The Confederacy's last major force in the field, the Trans-Mississippi Department, was formally surrendered a month later, on May 26, 1865.[168]

Willoughby Mangham had long since indicated his intention to fight "as long as the enemy invade our soil," and he stuck to his resolution until the Confederacy had breathed its last. Still incarcerated at Fort Delaware, he finally signed the oath of allegiance on June 16, 1865. It was time to go home.

* * * * *

Private Willoughby Hill Mangham occasionally apologized for having "nothing of interest to write," and he commonly asked indulgence for his poorly written letters. As historians Bell I. Wiley and James I. Robertson, Jr., have noted in their landmark studies of Civil War soldiers, these were typical conventions of the Confederate letter-writer.[169] In common with many of his comrades, however, Willoughby decided to soldier through his faulty grammar just as he decided to soldier through good times and bad: "I have got a plenty of paper and ink now and I intend to write and Keep writing Every chance I get."

We are fortunate that he did so, because his letters portray many other typical aspects of life in the Confederate armies, as well. His homesickness and longing for mail, as well as his concerns about scanty rations, inadequate clothing and rampant disease, serve to remind us of the hard realities that characterized service in the Army of Northern Virginia.

He displayed no tendency to minimize these hard realities, although he generally omitted the grimmer details of his experiences. Possibly he sought to spare his family from such things, or perhaps it simply was not his nature to dwell on them. His positive commentaries on people and events shared this rather muted quality in most instances. This quality was certainly not a product of a dull imagination, however, because his sensitivity shows through on every page. He was not above strong feelings of enthusiasm, irritation, or pride; he was neither "marble man" nor callow youth, neither dullard nor polished man of letters. He was confident in victory, but skeptical about rumors of an early peace. He respected his enemy's power, but he was not despondent in retreat. If he ever considered defeat a possibility, it is not apparent in his correspondence.

In a word, he was *steady*. But we see him *become* steady. His lowest moments struck soon after arrival in Virginia, when the sick (and homesick) recruit sought solace by confiding his fears of camp life to his sister. Within weeks, their roles were reversed: he was encouraging her, and even speculating about the possibility of quick victory, as he developed a young soldier's confidence in the victorious army of First Manassas. After a few escapades on picket duty, he developed patience and endurance, along with some self-confidence. This confidence grew noticeably after he first "saw the elephant" at Yorktown, and the summer campaign of 1862 toughened him further, both mentally and physically. Victory at Fredericksburg reinforced these characteristics, and his letters after that period show the morale boost resulting from the mismatch between General Lee and his Federal opponents. His final letter home prior to Gettysburg is perhaps exemplary of the Confederacy at high tide: the reader clearly senses the determination of a no-nonsense campaigner, who has neither time nor patience for shirkers, headline-grabbers, or miracle-seekers.

Were one to judge each of Pvt. Willoughby Mangham's letters after a hasty reading, they might appear to be simply vignettes of soldier life in camp and field, composed in the rather clumsy manner typical of the mid-19th century rural Southerner of moderate education. When studied in context, however, they offer an intriguing perspective on the maturation of the Army of Northern Virginia. Its men were not invincible, nor were they "born soldiers," nor automatons, nor some storybook band of brothers. Many were scoundrels and many were heroes, and the two mixed only reluctantly. But by July 1863, the great majority had developed from good soldier *material* into good *soldiers*.

They were men whom a general could order to take the Wheatfield, and they would take it.

They were men whom a general could order to guide on that clump of trees and break the line *there*, at the angle in the stone wall. And they would break it.

If flesh and blood *could* break it.

*   *   *   *   *

Willoughby Hill Mangham returned home to Cuthbert, Georgia, after almost twenty-four months in captivity. As his letters clearly indicate, it was his first visit to his beloved family since his enlistment in July 1861. The young veteran soon began a family of his own, marrying a young widow, Mrs. Amanda Hillhouse Roper, on September 4, 1866. He settled down to farm and raise nine children of his own, as well as Amanda's two sons. Soon after the war, Willoughby moved back to old-time Mangham country in Hancock County, where he served as postmaster at Minton for many years. In 1877 he moved his family to Worth County, where he organized a Baptist Sunday school that he supervised until 1892. Drawing on his formative experiences in his father's mill, he operated a sawmill and gristmill, and built the first steam gin in Worth County. Willoughby also worked as a contractor, raising the first school building in Sylvester, the county seat of Worth County. He served on the county board of education for several years as well.[170]

Willoughby H. Mangham moved his family to Waresboro, Georgia, in 1892, but soon thereafter passed away. When he died on January 2, 1893, he was only fifty-four years of age. Widowed again after a quarter-century of marriage, Amanda returned to Worth County, where she drew a Confederate widow's pension beginning in 1919. She lived at Sylvester until her death on June 6, 1927.[171]

7. TRAILING A DEAD BROTHER: FIRST SGT. WILLIS W. MANGHAM, CO. D, 21ST TEXAS CAVALRY

Just over three years after Willoughby passed away, his uncle Willis W. Mangham died in faraway Bell County, Texas, where the adventures of his young manhood had fetched him up some fifty years earlier.

Born in Georgia on January 22, 1828, Willis grew up in Chambers County, Alabama, where existing school records document his attendance as late as 1844. As his brother Solomon's correspondence with John G. Mangham shows, Willis worked as an overseer for several years after their mother's death in 1849, but like many others in Alabama, he apparently came down with a case of "Texas fever" in early 1853.[172]

Willis departed in February, traveling down the Alabama River to Mobile on the steamboat *Fashion*, but soon became embroiled in one of the many personal tragedies growing out of the system of chattel slavery. His slave Spencer, doubtless homesick for family or acquaintances left behind in Chambers County, stowed away on the *Fashion* for the trip back upriver. The steamer's crew discovered him some 75 miles upstream, and the captain ordered him confined. Chained to a post on an uncovered deck in the damp chill of late winter, Spencer soon fell gravely ill. Although doctors were summoned to attend him in the Montgomery jail, he died shortly afterwards. Willis later won a thousand-dollar lawsuit against the boat's captain, Jesse J. Cox, who was found negligent in allowing a black person on board without his owner's express permission. (Nine years later, *John Willis Mangham*, a son of Willis's first cousin, James Pendleton Mangham, was soldiering under Cox in his famed Sharpshooter battalion. See Chapter II.)[173]

Willis migrated initially to Washington County, where his brother Nathaniel had lived before enlisting in Captain Early's company during the Mexican War. Although Nathaniel had been killed in a skirmish with Indians several years earlier, it is possible that Willis was the first family member to find out and send word back to Alabama.

He settled down on the central Texas frontier by 1857, raising cattle and horses near Belton, the county seat of Bell County. Wasting no time, he got hitched to 18-year-old Sarah Moore that same year, and their first son Dulane arrived in February 1859. Although he owned no land, the eve of war found him a relatively prosperous stock raiser. That year he raised fifty bushels of wheat and 200 bushels of Indian corn on his rental property, and along with a number of milch cows and draft oxen he owned twenty other cattle and twenty-five horses, with the whole valued at nearly three thousand dollars. Part of Willis's net worth included a 17-year-old slave girl, probably employed as a nurse and house servant, along with her infant daughter. In the following January, the little family was joined by a second son, Clarence W. Mangham.[174]

Like other frontier districts in ante-bellum Texas, Bell County raised small forces, known as ranging companies, which routinely scoured the environs in an attempt to prevent Indian depredations against the isolated white settlements. Surviving rosters of these companies are incomplete, so it is uncertain whether Willis enlisted in one of the several companies securing Bell County in 1859. It is certain, however, that he enrolled in one of the militia companies hurriedly mustered into service when the war emergency arose in 1861. Captain James W. Moore mustered a company of men from Bell County's Beat 4 in June of that year, and Willis was one of 72 privates on the rolls submitted to the state Adjutant General.[175]

As the war entered its second spring in 1862, Willis was among the vast numbers who flocked to the colors in the second great wave of voluntarism. Unlike many other volunteers during this period, however, Willis clearly was not motivated by a fear of conscription, for no such coercive mechanism existed when he signed up for "three years or the war" on March 16, 1862, in a company raised by G. R. Freeman. Although one source refers to this company as "Freeman's Austin Company," 33 of its 63 original members enlisted from Bell County, while another twenty hailed from Milam County. Perhaps the Bell County men hitched up with Freeman since the largely Unionist sentiment prevalent in Belton made it difficult to raise a company in their hometown. Elected captain when the new company completed its organization on March 27, Freeman possessed a commission to recruit men on behalf of George Washington Carter, a charismatic Methodist clergyman and ardent secessionist who resigned the presidency of Soule University to take up arms for the Confederacy.[176]

Commissioned as a colonel and authorized to raise a regiment for three years or the duration of the war, Carter intended to raise a regiment of mounted lancers. He began signing up men in late 1861, but lost both men and companies as fast as he could raise them. Other colonels were enlisting men for twelve months' service, and the temptation to sign up for the shorter term led many of Carter's newly raised companies to renege and offer their services to other regiments. By February 1862, Governor Lubbock was explaining Carter's problems to the War Department, complaining that the colonel had "raised forty companies before he could induce ten to stand to be mustered in as a regiment for the war."[177]

Perhaps due to his recruiting acumen, Carter eventually gained authority to raise thirty companies of Texas cavalry, thus raising his command effectively to brigade strength. After the Conscript Act became law on April 16, recruits flooded into camp to avoid conscription and possible infantry service; most Texans were accustomed to horseflesh and were averse to serving afoot if they could ride instead. As companies rendezvoused in the spring of 1862 at Camp Carter, near Hempstead, Carter drew lots to apportion them across his three regiments, in which the companies likewise ranked by lot, rather than seniority. By this process Freeman's Company, which officially mustered into service on April 24, eventually became Company D in the regiment under Carter's direct command, known grandly as the 1st Texas Lancers. The other two regiments initially were titled the 2nd and 3rd Texas Lancers, but the three units soon thereafter were redesignated as the 21st, 24th, and 25th Texas Cavalry Regiments, respectively.[178]

The three regiments underwent initial cavalry training at Camp Carter, where some men in the 21st received disabling injuries during mock cavalry charges delivered against dismounted comrades. On the whole, however, the troops lived well amid the comforts of plentiful rations, the occasional body servant, and tents sewn by their womenfolk from government-issued fabric. After a brief home furlough for all the men of the regiment, the troops rendezvoused at Crockett, Texas, pending onward movement to Alto, Rusk, and Mount Vernon, in eastern Texas. As they elected field officers to complete their formal regimental organization, many of the Texans were already coming down with the dreaded measles, and numbers died before the regiment marched to Shreveport, Louisiana.[179]

Some of the men were of the sort commonly referred to in those times as ruffians or villains, whereas others were doubtless feeling footloose and fancy free as they entered military service and broke the constraints of civilian society. Numerous complaints attended the march of Carter's brigade through Tyler, Texas, to Shreveport, and their subsequent orders to assist in impressing civilian goods in Louisiana almost brought things to a head. Louisiana's Governor Thomas O. Moore was outraged by the actions of men belonging to Carter's other two regiments, and demanded that Secretary of War George Randolph dismiss the officers in command of the offending units. Moore penned a blunt warning that illustrated the nascent rift between state and Confederate authorities, asserting "You can refuse to dismiss them (the captain and the colonel), but my marksmen may save you the trouble if they come again. There is a point to which patient endurance can extend no further." When men of the 21st Texas were assigned to transport some contraband to Arkansas, they nearly came to blows with Louisiana militiamen and gunboats posted on the Red River at Alexandria and beyond. Fortunately, the officers on the scene kept their heads and clarified the legalities involved before opening fire on each other. In all probability, such incidents inspired Pvt. Willis Mangham and many of his comrades to ruminate on the implications of states' rights within the young Confederacy.[180]

The three regiments eventually arrived in Arkansas, where they came under the command of Gen. Theophilus H. Holmes, commanding the Trans-Mississippi Department. Holmes ordered the regiments to turn in their horses to the government and assume duties as dismounted cavalrymen (i.e. infantrymen), but the 21st Texas kept its horses due to the cleverness of Lieutenant Colonel Giddings, acting commander during Carter's temporary absence. Although Holmes had his order posted on broadsides all over Pine Bluff, Giddings adopted a simple solution: he studiously avoided reading any of the notices! When he received an official copy of the order from a courier, he put it in his pocket unread. In desperate straits, he asked Col. William H. Parsons, 12th Texas Cavalry, to request Holmes to assign the 21st Texas to his command, thus increasing Parsons's outfit to a brigade. And so it was done, with the men of the 21st rejoicing that Giddings had found a way for them to keep their horses. Cavalrymen of any army probably would have felt the same way, but Confederate horse soldiers more than most: their horses were personal property, since army regulations required them to provide their own mounts in return for a small stipend.[181] (See map, p. 558.)

After a couple of months at Pine Bluff and the commencement of an long-lived feud over seniority between Parsons and Carter, the 21st Texas Cavalry received orders to move as part of Parsons's Brigade into the area east of Little Rock. Along with the 12th and 19th Texas cavalry regiments, Carter's men now undertook their first combat duties. Initially encamped several miles east of the bottomlands between the White and Cache Rivers near the town of Cotton Plant, they later moved south to DeVall's Bluff, a village on the White River twelve miles below Des Arc. There the Texans formed part of a screen deployed to shield the Arkansas capital from Federal probes emanating from the line of the Mississippi River. Parsons's 12th Texas had significant combat experience by the fall of 1862, and it had established itself as a capable combat unit. The 19th and 21st Texas were new at the game, however, and it took them some time to become skilled in scouting and patrolling. Lieutenant Buck Walton of Carter's Company B quickly established himself as an expert in leading small groups of picked men on extended forays into contested territory, and after a time his scouting expeditions often grew to include several hundred men from all three regiments.[182]

Possibly Willis took part in these scouting expeditions, because he stated that his time in the army was spent "principally engaged in scout duties."[183] Also, the first surviving muster rolls for Captain Freeman's company show that he had established an outstanding record for reliability. Sometime between August 31, 1862, and February 28, 1863, he achieved the distinction of promotion to first sergeant. Also known as orderly sergeant, a man in this position was the highest-ranking non-commissioned officer in a company's complement of five sergeants and four corporals. As such, he ruled the roost in the company's day-to-day existence. William Watson, an Englishman, served as an orderly sergeant for a time in the 3rd Louisiana Infantry, and his detailed description of the "rather onerous position" provides valuable insight into Willis Mangham's military duties:

> He held the rank of sergeant-major [in British Army parlance], his pay was equal to one-and-a-half that of the first duty-sergeant [i.e., the Second Sgt]. He was the general executive officer of the company. He was secretary of the company, and was allowed a clerk. He went on no special detachments, or guard duty, except in cases of emergency. He kept the roll-book, and all other books, papers or accounts of the company. He was accountable for the men present or absent. He returned every morning to the adjutant a report of the state and effective force of the company.
>
> He made out all requisitions for rations, ammunition, arms, or camp equipage, and all other requirements. He had charge of all the company property, and reported on its condition. He inspected the tents and company

camp ground, and saw that it was properly formed and ditched, and inspected the sanitary arrangements. His signature must be the first, and followed by that of the captain, on all company requisitions and reports, He called the roll at reveille, and noted absentees and delinquents, punished for slight offences, and reported more serious offences. He gave certificates to men who wished to apply for leave of absence. He detailed all men for guard, and detachments for special service, and appointed police guards for the day. He reported the sick to the surgeon, and saw them attended to. He marched up to the colour line, and handed over to the adjutant all details for special service and guard duty. He drilled all squads, and the company in absence of the commissioned officers. He took his place on the right of the company, and acted as guide. He went to the front and centre at parade and heard the orders read. When in front of the enemy, he was generally informed privately of the programme, and of the movements to be made. While the duty sergeants were designated by their respective names as Sergeant T. or Sergeant H., he was designated as *the* Sergeant, and was regarded as the ruling power of the company when on active service.[184]

Whether or not these extensive duties allowed Willis to participate in Lieutenant Walton's undertakings, it is certain that he was heavily involved in the "scouts" that dominated life in the 21st Texas. In the deadly game of tit-for-tat, their scouting patrols strove to outfox, outride, and outshoot the experienced troopers of the 5th Kansas Cavalry under Maj. Samuel Walker. Although Walton's men snared about thirty Kansans in a well-executed raid in September, Walker met the Texan face-to-face under flag of truce and vowed to get even with him; in this small-scale war, things tended to assume a personal nature rarely seen in other theaters. Shortly afterwards, Walker made good on his threat, when he and his men shot up a detachment of Walton's men near Helena. Soon afterwards, men of the 21st Texas overran a careless party of troopers from the 4th Iowa Cavalry at Shell Creek (or Lick Creek). Within minutes, however, a Union relief party cornered Giddings's group and bagged more than twenty of the Texans, including Giddings himself. Afterwards, Walker burned two homes belonging to Southern sympathizers. When Giddings' 17-year-old nephew swore vengeance against Walker, a three-month "war within a war" ensued, only ending when Walker's men cornered young Giddings and shot him down.[185]

Acts of ferocity alternated with acts of magnanimity between some opponents, who grew to respect each other's courage and skill to some extent. Nevertheless, it was a dangerous war of constant scouting and small-scale skirmishing, in which one member of the 21st Texas proudly concluded that his opponents had "a wholesome dread of the Texans—they dont like our mode of fighting. I believe the Texan mode of fighting is to hurt somebody no matter how that is."[186]

Carter's regiment continued to operate from the vicinity of Des Arc Bayou, until an abortive move to save the garrison of Arkansas Post in January brought the men to the Jordan plantation, situated on the banks of the Arkansas River about ten miles north of the captured fort. Each mess chose an abandoned slave cabin for quarters in between their frequent scout and picket duties, as their cavalry brigade and three infantry brigades provided the sole defense of the Arkansas River valley. Since this region was one of the few fertile areas in that portion of the state, General Holmes was desperate to keep it under Confederate control. The 21st Texas remained in this vicinity until April, but no Federal offensive towards Little Rock ensued, as they preferred to concentrate upon tightening the noose on the Rebel garrison at Vicksburg.[187]

The Confederate Trans-Mississippi Department had precious few resources to relieve the growing pressure on Pemberton's army around Vicksburg, but one scheme to rally support in Federal-occupied Missouri offered possible benefit to the bastion on the Mississippi. Major General John S. Marmaduke commanded a Confederate cavalry division in northern Arkansas, and he wanted to repeat an earlier raid into Missouri on a grander scale. It took several months for his idea to gain approval, but early April 1863 saw First Sgt. Willis Mangham and the 21st Texas Cavalry on the march from Jordan's Plantation to Pine Bluff. After a brief halt, the regiment continued on its way to the town of Jackson, along the Eleven Points River near the Missouri state line. Here, where the river rose amid the steep mountain fastnesses, Pvt. William Zuber of Company H was struck by a sight that he and many other Texans had never seen before: "white women working between plow handles."[188] (See map on page 558.)

With Parsons's 12th Texas detached for continued service along the Mississippi River, the 19th and 21st Texas combined with Morgan's Battalion to form Carter's Brigade, and these Texans joined three brigades of Missouri and Arkansas cavalry to comprise Marmaduke's raiding force. Although the force comprised some 5000 men, about 1200 were unarmed, and nine hundred lacked serviceable mounts. Marmaduke divided the force into two columns to facilitate foraging en route, with Colonel Carter commanding the eastern column on its march via Doniphan, Missouri. Both columns aimed to rendezvous at Patterson, Missouri, where they expected to encounter six hundred militiamen before moving on to Bloomfield. If successful, Marmaduke believed they could convincingly demonstrate to the numerous Southern sympathizers in Missouri that the Confederacy had not relegated the state to uncontested Federal domination. Hopefully, their raid would attract numerous recruits, while posing a major threat to traffic on the Mississippi River.[189]

The Texans broke camp on April 18 and marched twenty-five miles to Doniphan, where they were pelted at sundown with the pouring rains that plagued them for much of Marmaduke's Raid. After another twenty-five miles on the following day, they rested for only two hours before climbing into their saddles again towards midnight, bound for Patterson. At daylight they clashed ten or twelve miles outside of town with Federal pickets, who wounded three men of the 21st Texas before they were overwhelmed and captured in an engagement which Marmaduke described as "handsome." Another fight ensued with pickets closer to town, and in the process Lieutenant Colonel Giddings freely used his section of artillery to suppress Federal resistance. Although Lt. John Stranahan of Company A agreed that the well-emplaced pickets were a fairly tough nut to crack, the Texans' deliberate employment of artillery had the disastrous effect of alarming the Federal garrison, while granting it time to set fire to abandoned supplies before fleeing town.[190]

The 21st dismounted before storming the enemy breastworks, but quickly remounted after finding that the defenders had evacuated Patterson. Amid the flames and confusion, Giddings strove to restore order among his command until his horse broke down, whereupon Lieutenant Walton and several company commanders organized their men for the pursuit. Encountering an eighty-man rear guard some three miles outside of town, Walton's company formed for a charge. Most of the Texans carried personally owned double-barreled shotguns and a pistol or two, so there was no thought of a traditional cavalry charge with lance or saber. Once within range, they cut loose with a hail of buckshot from their shotguns, dropping numbers of the enemy and causing a general panic. Walton called upon the disorganized mob to surrender, but when none of the fugitives hoisted a white flag, his Texans rode them down with six-shooters blazing. Although accounts vary as to the numbers killed, wounded, and captured, this rear guard was practically annihilated in bloody fighting that the Federal commander described as "severe in the extreme."[191]

Carter's men reassembled in Patterson under Marmaduke's orders, before departing the next day (April 21) on the march to Bloomfield. Although he intended to attack the Federal garrison stationed there, the muddy roads, flooded rivers, and worn-down horses delayed the column's arrival until April 23, giving the Federal troopers a head start. The 21st Texas rested but two hours in town before moving out again at midnight to rendezvous with Gen. Jo Shelby's column. A detachment of Carter's regiment outflanked and cut to pieces a 57-man Federal picket post on the Cape Girardeau Road, killing, capturing, or wounding forty men of the 1st Wisconsin Cavalry, but the ensuing attempt to cut off the fleeing garrison at Jackson misfired.[192]

The Federals now had consolidated their forces within the defenses at Cape Girardeau, where there was little chance for a cavalry force to storm the works, and they refused Confederate attempts to bluff them into surrender. Under Marmaduke's orders, Shelby's Missourians feigned an assault on the town on April 26, although they feinted so vigorously that the alarmed Marmaduke feared they had launched a headlong assault. The men of the 21st Texas were in close support, but were not directly engaged until it was time for Marmaduke to face the inevitable. With assault out of the question, and scarcity of forage and impending Federal reinforcements rendering a siege equally impractical, Marmaduke turned his raiders southward and employed his Texans as a rear guard to cover his retreat to Arkansas. They camped at Jackson that night, and on the following day the 21st Texas chewed up a Federal company that pressed them too closely at White Water Bridge.[193]

As the retreat continued, the Texans fought delaying actions every day, including especially sharp combats in defense of the crossing at Chalk Bluff on the flooded Saint Francis River. On May 1, Carter's Brigade received a spirited charge by two Federal cavalry regiments, then cut them up badly in a counterattack. As Stranahan proudly noted at the time, the Federals fought bravely and Carter's Brigade "acted as Texicans ought to act and that is as much as I can say for men." Waiting for the Federals' next move that evening, the Texan scribbled grimly in his diary: "I expect we will see sights this evening but we will keep up the reputation of our state." He added, "We are going to put the matter to the test here to see which is the best soldiers though we have no fault to find with the enemy as they have showed today that they are not deficient in courage." Like many other Southerners, Stranahan distinguished between Northern troops from different regions, and he respected Midwesterners as hardy and courageous: "They are the bravest troops that Lincoln has, all Western men. There has been a good many of them killed today."[194]

While Marmaduke's main body crossed the flooded river on a rickety bridge, Carter's Texans stood fast, withheld their fire, and drew their pursuers to within point-blank range of Pratt's section of artillery. When the Texans suddenly pulled aside, the waiting gunners blasted canister into the packed ranks of the astounded Federals. One of Carter's aides estimated that the masked battery's ambush claimed fifty victims. Awestruck, Buck Walton stated: "such a scattering—back going, and confusion, as was produced in the enemy I had never seen." Stranahan agreed, noting "I never saw men get out of the way as fast in my life before." The Texas lieutenant spoke to a captured Union officer a short time afterward, who stated that Pratt's gunners had delivered "the most destructive fire he had ever seen, in such a short time." Despite these tactics, the withdrawal across the Saint Francis remained a close-run thing. The last men of the 21st Texas faced disaster when they found the bridge already cut loose from the far side, but they desperately swam their horses across the swollen river into Arkansas. They arrived on the opposite bank looking "like drowned rats," but glad to be alive. The relieved Federals were content to let them go, but Walton, Zuber, and a number of other men of the 21st Texas crept back into positions to snipe at the Federals across the river. Walton claimed that his group dropped one hundred enemy dead and wounded in a surprise volley, and Lieutenant Stranahan recorded with unfeigned satisfaction: "We killed a good many of them today across the river, with our sharp shooters."[195]

Although several days passed before the Texans determined that the Federals were allowing them to retreat unmolested into Arkansas, the rear guard actions of May 2 on the Saint Francis River effectively marked the end of Marmaduke's Raid. A strategic failure with ill-defined tactical objectives, the operation was a source of discontent for many officers and soldiers mystified by their movements, although others accepted Carter's claim that the raid had stymied Federal intentions to invade Arkansas. Regardless of these strategic ambiguities, the troopers of the 21st Texas Cavalry had acquitted themselves well in their first major campaign, and First Sergeant Mangham and his men could take pride in riding hundreds of miles in just two weeks, while participating in ten fights. As Private Zuber recalled it, the regiment spent thirteen days in Missouri, "and during each twenty four hours of that time we had either a battle with the enemy, an all-night march, or a soaking rain." Of the 161 casualties suffered by Marmaduke's force, the 21st Texas counted one man killed, another missing, and five officers and ten enlisted men wounded in action, out of some 500 men who marched into Missouri. Against these losses, the raiders could count only 150 Missourians who enlisted during the incursion into their bitterly divided border state, even though

Private Zuber and many others encountered many families whose sympathies lay with the South.[196]

The men may have earned a rest, but the closest they got was a steady march in easy stages to Crowley's Ridge, where they outposted the roads from Helena beginning May 9, 1863. Union cavalrymen of the XIII Army Corps were employing scorched earth tactics in the L'Anguille and Saint Francis River valleys, burning crops and killing or confiscating stock, rendering it impossible for the region to offer any support to the Confederate cause. Marmaduke and Carter maneuvered forces into position to destroy a 1200-man force at Taylor's Creek, boxing them in thanks to some sharp fighting by the 21st Texas on May 11. That night, however, a regiment of Arkansas conscripts failed to hold the back door shut and allowed the Federals to escape unmolested down a road the Arkansans were ordered to secure. Although Carter led his men after the escaping force on the following day, a disgusted Lieutenant Stranahan accurately assessed the tardy pursuit to the L'Anguille River as nothing but a "wild goose chase."[197]

Carter admitted to some of his men that he had erred in not pressing the trapped Federals harder, and others like Stranahan criticized the colonel's tactics in conducting mounted charges on May 11 instead of cutting off the enemy with dismounted flanking parties. For his part, Lt. Buck Walton was frustrated that Carter and other leaders were more concerned about casualties than they were about fighting to win. His feelings may have been exacerbated by news of Lee's decisive victory in the bloody Battle of Chancellorsville, which occurred as Marmaduke's raiders were retreating into Arkansas. Things came to a head when recurring complaints indicated that Carter's men were stealing livestock and poultry from the farmers around their Taylor's Creek bivouac; the colonel directed that convicted thieves receive thirty-nine lashes across the bare back. For many of the disgruntled troopers, this edict was the last straw. The spectacle of a free white man being whipped was outrageous in the eyes of Southern volunteers from every state, but perhaps the fiercely independent Texas frontiersmen were still more sensitive to such a display than most. In their world, such brutal discipline was reserved for recalcitrant slaves, if for anyone at all.[198]

The soldiers refused to drill or perform duties of any sort, and Lieutenant Walton feared that the 21st Texas Cavalry might disintegrate as disgusted troopers left for home. Carter reported the magnitude of the crisis in a May 20 missive to General Marmaduke's headquarters, stating: "A good deal of dissatisfaction, verging on mutiny, has manifested itself in the brigade. . .it is avowedly caused by my personal interferences with the men and companies, a written statement to that effect having been handed to Major Hill, inspector general."[199]

The Methodist preacher-turned colonel directed his regiment to assemble one evening to hear him out, and he stepped to the pulpit of an old camp-meeting brush arbor to say his piece. In his charismatic style, Carter tore a strip off the men who "pretended to be soldiers" yet were guilty of such acts, scolding and shaming them thoroughly. He then asked for any man present to step forward and refute him, but none of the malcontents took up the proffered gauntlet. After waiting some minutes in vain, Carter stated bluntly that his "courage had been doubted, his manhood distrusted—and his honor impugned." Accordingly, he announced: "I will waive my rank altogether, and any man, officer or private, may have a fair fight, and we will step out, and settle the matter right now." An impressed Buck Walton stood by as Colonel Carter drew his pistol, stepped down from the pulpit and "took his stand—but no man offered to take up the challenge." After it became clear that nobody planned to step out and face him according to the *code duello*, Carter returned to the pulpit once more. This time he announced that he would withdraw the order, because he saw "how distasteful it was to the men." The resulting roar of approval and general hand-shaking must have threatened to bring down the brush arbor, and Walton believed that Carter was thereafter "more popular than ever." Likewise, all complaints of misconduct ceased as the Texans responded absolutely to a discipline that they understood and respected. As Walton observed many years later, "There were men there who could have shot off any button of his uniform, and who knew not the word fear, but they simply did not wish to have any difficulty with him."[200]

Carter and his men moved down to southeastern Arkansas that summer, since the fall of Vicksburg on July 4 threatened to allow Union forces to push across the river into the Trans-Mississippi. Joining a new division commanded by Maj. Gen. Lucius M. Walker, Carter's Brigade, now comprising the 21st Texas and several independent companies along with Pratt's Battery, was headquartered at the Jordan Plantation again. Shortly afterwards, headquarters displaced to Pine Bluff, but widely dispersed elements fanned out to scout the whole area between the lower White, Saint Francis, and Mississippi Rivers. These lightly-armed units did what they could to harass Union traffic on the Mississippi, but trooper Sam Marr considered that they did little of consequence, writing: "we have bin on the missipie reve picketting & firing into the transports It has not amounted to anything for when we would Shot ontoo them we would have to get out of the way of the gun botes for they would shell the hole contry around thare." Trooper George W. Laurence regretted the widespread sickness that weakened the men, blaming it on the scanty rations of "green corn and peaches."[201]

By early August, however, Walker's cavalrymen were facing a threat much more serious than gunboats. Union Maj. Gen. Frederick Steele was in command of a force with orders to take Little Rock, and his inexorable advance soon pushed the Confederates out of Pine Bluff. After further sharp fighting on Bayou Meto during the last week of the month, Steele eventually flanked his opponents out of Little Rock altogether. The Confederates, under the overall command of Maj. Gen. Sterling Price of Missouri, fell back towards Shreveport, keeping their force interposed between Steele and the critical communications center in northwestern Louisiana.[202]

The 21st Texas was picketing the Arkansas River south of Little Rock before the capital fell, with regimental headquarters located twenty miles south of town. Captain William Rust was acting regimental commander, but he commanded little more than a corporal's guard. Only twenty of his men were fit for duty on the Arkansas River picket posts, and another sixty lay sick in camp. About three hundred more occupied sickbeds at Princeton, so Rust fell back there on his own initiative when no orders came his way after the fall of Little Rock. Obtaining wagons to carry the sickest men, Rust moved the regiment to Arkadelphia. General Price directed him on September 15 to establish a convalescent camp for the 21st Texas Cavalry and some attached units, and the doctor in charge had Rust move first to Cold Springs, then to the town of Washington, about halfway between Arkadelphia and Texarkana.[203]

Arriving there on September 30, Rust found his regiment facing insinuations ranging from plunder to shirking, as some claimed the regiment was trying to get away to Texas. This was the last straw for the frustrated captain, who had struggled to obtain subsistence for his sickly command as he moved from pillar to post, unable to get official assistance for even his most pressing needs. As he pointed out in a letter to General Marmaduke, to whose division the Texans once more belonged, he had only 106 men available for duty when they left Arkadelphia, along with 235 sick cavalrymen and 100 sick infantrymen. Despite these numbers, Generals Price and Holmes had directed him to supply a total of 107 men for various scouting and courier duties; adding insult to injury, Marmaduke directed Rust to concentrate his regiment, while Holmes was ordering its dispersal. With only 33 convalescents remaining in camp to take care of 335 sick men, and Holmes demanding yet another fifteen men to serve as couriers, the irritated captain reached the end of his tether. In his October 4 letter to Marmaduke, Rust asked bluntly, "Now, general, I should like to know who I am to obey." Protesting that his men had been "kept in the swamps until their systems have become poisoned with miasma and malaria," he asserted that they had nevertheless remained ready to perform any duty. Rust flared, "They seem to have an idea at headquarters that we are not as sick as we represent. I know it is difficult to believe that a regiment could get into such a condition, but it is, I am sorry to say, too true."[204]

Apparently Marmaduke took decisive action to clear up the situation for the beleaguered captain, because on October 8 he endorsed a by-name listing of the 21st Texas men to be hospitalized at Washington. One of the names enumerated was Willis W. Mangham.[205]

Willis was back on duty by the end of the month, however, so he probably took part in Marmaduke's attempt to retake Pine Bluff. The town was held by the Texans' long-time foes, the 5th Kansas Cavalry, along with the 1st Indiana Cavalry. Under the command of Colonel Clayton, the two regiments numbered only 550 men, and Marmaduke believed he could gobble them up with his superior force. Unfortunately, however, he allowed Clayton valuable time to prepare his defenses when he sent an emissary to demand the town's surrender. By delaying his reply for an hour, the Federal commander gained time to post sharpshooters and employ several hundred freedmen to erect breastworks from cotton bales. Although Marmaduke's artillerymen shelled the town heavily and dismounted troopers penetrated well into the town itself, he held up his men short of the bastion erected around the courthouse. After five hours of continued sharpshooting and artillery fire, Marmaduke decided to withdraw rather than suffer the consequences of a direct assault. He reported the loss of about forty men, while Clayton counted fifty-six casualties of all ranks, but the town remained in Federal hands. As a disgusted Buck Walton bitterly commented, "The result was that eight hundred men whipped at least 2500 of as good men as we had. . . ."[206]

Although every Confederate commander praised the steadiness of his troops in his after-action reports, the depressing fact remained that Pine Bluff was yet another repulse in a seemingly endless litany of defeat and retreat for the 21st Texas Cavalry. Exaggerated rumors of Indian and Mexican depredations along the Texas frontier added fuel to the fire, and prompted one company to depart in a body for their homes. Resisting attempts to persuade them to return to the army, they proceeded several hundred miles, well into Texas, until they learned to their own satisfaction that the rumors were false. At that point the company returned to the regiment in Arkansas, without a single man deserting.[207]

The disaffection that winter took many other forms, and the other regiments of the brigade approached open mutiny when Brig. Gen. Thomas Churchill was assigned to replace the popular Parsons as commanding officer, sometime after the latter had again assumed brigade command from Carter. The 21st Texas was the only unit to express its support for Churchill, but this was due mostly to the never-ending precedence dispute between their commander and Parsons. Under these conditions, Churchill refrained from pressing the issue, so Parsons's Brigade it remained! Nonetheless, the 21st camped across the Washita River from the rest of the brigade that winter at Camden, Arkansas. It was a visible reminder of the ongoing tension between the two colonels.[208]

That morale was suffering on the home front was readily apparent that winter, too, and Parsons's Brigade was ordered to return to Texas in February 1864 to comb its home counties for deserters and draft evaders. Private Zuber's Company H managed to round up only one man, and Zuber believed this meager haul to be representative of the whole brigade's efforts. By the time the men marched to Texas, spent ten days hunting deserters and another ten days with their families, it was early April before they returned to the army. Following their winter of discontent, Parsons's Texas Brigade would face its sternest test of the war.[209]

As the cavalrymen reassembled at Marshall, Texas, Lt. Gen. Edmund Kirby Smith faced a quandary as to where to dispatch them. The commanding general of the Trans-Mississippi Department knew that Maj. Gen. Frederick Steele and 11,000 Federals were advancing from Little Rock towards Shreveport, while Maj. Gen. Nathaniel Banks was pushing up the Red River towards the city with more than 30,000 soldiers. Admiral David Porter's riverine fleet of some sixty vessels supported Banks's expedition. This Federal land and naval juggernaut was the largest force ever assembled west of the river, and it heralded a massive effort to overrun Shreveport and eastern Texas, thereby crushing the life out of the Trans-Mississippi Confederacy. Operating in tandem, Banks and Porter already were driving back Maj. Gen. Dick Taylor's little Army of Western Louisiana, which struggled to muster even ten thousand troops to defend the embattled region whose name it bore.[210]

Kirby Smith finally made up his mind on April 8, 1864, directing Parsons's Texas Cavalry Brigade to join Taylor's outnumbered band. On this very day, however, Taylor turned on his pursuers and routed them at the Battle of Mansfield, and another savage battle at Pleasant Hill on the next day resulted in a continuation of the Federal retreat. Parsons's men rode hard toward the front, but it was several days after these two decisive battles before they were fully assembled as part of Taylor's effective force. Although the Texas cavalrymen missed out on these pitched battles, there was plenty of work remaining for them over the next six weeks of uninterrupted campaigning. As the David and Goliath drama unfolded on the plains, woodlands, and bayous of Louisiana throughout April and May, the Texans played a conspicuous role, hounding Banks's greatly superior force from the gates of Shreveport all the way back to the Atchafalaya River northwest of Baton Rouge.[211]

Although many men of the 21st Texas Cavalry were still en route to the army on April 12, those who were present took part in the Battle of Blair's Landing on the Red River. Here, some 45 miles north of Grand Ecore, Brig. Gen. Tom Green led some two thousand cavalrymen in a desperate attempt to intercept and destroy seven stranded Federal vessels in a ferocious engagement. The 21st remained mounted and covered the left flank of Green's dismounted force, as the troopers poured volley after volley into the transports and gunboats. Federal gunners returned fire with a vengeance, however, and one canister blast strewed Green's brains along the riverbank. Parsons, already designated by Green as tactical commander of the force, assumed overall command and continued the fight until another half-dozen gunboats arrived to reinforce the desperate bluejackets. The Texas colonel reported with palpable disappointment that his men had forced one gunboat and two transports to hoist the white flag, but the other gunboats' arrival prevented the Texans from taking possession of their captures.[212]

As Parsons's troopers continued to make their way back from Texas, the brigade marched south along the Cane River towards Grand Ecore. Nominally assigned to Wharton's Cavalry Corps and Steele's Division, Parsons's Brigade was effectively Steele's only unit, since the Louisiana cavalry brigade designated for his command never reported for duty under him. Banks soon consolidated his army at Natchitoches, just five miles from Grand Ecore, planning to reunite with Porter's boats before a further retreat to Alexandria, and Parsons's cavalrymen held positions on the picket line outside of town beginning April 12. The ensuing week of light skirmishing was a prelude to sharper engagements on April 19-21, as the Federals drove in the Confederate picket line with heavy forces. On the last day of these attacks, the 21st Texas suffered ten men wounded in the spirited exchange of fire.[213]

These efforts covered Banks's intentions, which were to evacuate Grand Ecore and Natchitoches before commencing a forced march down the island formed by the Cane River on the west and the Red River on the east. Nine companies of Carter's regiment pushed across the Cane River to press the Federal rear at the Prudhomme Plantation on April 22, while Company H remained to secure the ford. In several hours of hard fighting, Carter's Texans and the other men of Parsons's Brigade forced their bluecoated opponents to deploy a line of battle to push them back across the Cane once more. Parsons reported that Carter and his men displayed "conspicuous courage" in the attack, especially praising Major Chenoweth and the two squadrons he led in a flanking attack at the plantation. As Lieutenant Stranahan commented in the diary notes he forwarded to his wife Milda, the river "was not very deep but in crossing over to get to them we was subject to a heavy fire and also while recrossing it to get away, which we done in quick time I assure you."[214]

While the Texas Brigade remained on Banks's rear, pushing hard in repeated attacks to heighten the pressure from that direction, General Taylor dispatched most of

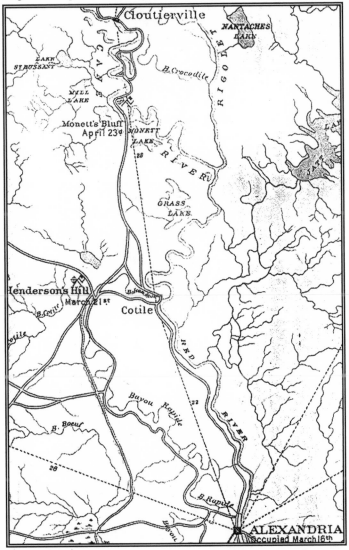

CLOUTIERVILLE TO ALEXANDRIA, LOUISIANA, APRIL 1864.
WILLIS W. MANGHAM HELPED HARASS THE RETREATING FEDERALS, AS DID HIS
RELATIVES HENRY, ARTHUR, JOSIAH THOMAS, & WILLIAM MANGHAM (SEE CH. III,
IX AND APPENDIX, REF. # 83, 140, 141, 157, 180).

Wharton's cavalry corps down to Monett's Ferry, where the Federals had to cross the Cane River to avoid entrapment on the island. He also ordered Polignac's little infantry division, the heroes of Mansfield, to move up to Cloutierville. Willis's second cousins (once removed) *Arthur, Josiah Thomas,* and *William Mangham* served in the diminutive Frenchman's division, and marched with their comrades of the Crescent Louisiana Infantry Regiment and 28th Louisiana to take position in the little hamlet, where they could block Banks's escape to the southwest. Taylor ordered Liddell's cavalry force to Colfax in the east, at the confluence between the Cane and Red Rivers, to hold the line in that direction. These dispositions were skillful, but Banks's most direct route to Alexandria necessarily led southward through Monett's Ferry. There, Brigadier General Bee and 1600 cavalrymen prepared to confront the head of Banks's column. If Bee could hold, Taylor's men would bring to bay a Federal force easily quadruple their strength.[215]

Early on the morning of April 23, the Federal advance guard began to feel out Bee's positions near the ferry. As they did so, Parsons's Texas Brigade spread out a thin line of dismounted cavalrymen to strike at the rear of Banks's column at Lecompte, near Cloutierville, just a few miles distant. Leaving every sixth trooper to hold the horses, the 21st Texas contributed some three hundred men to Parsons's sparse line, and helped drive the Federal skirmishers back onto the rear guard proper. They were tangling with men of Smith's XVI Army Corps, on loan from Sherman's army, and the fight became "very severe" as the Texas cavalrymen traded charge and countercharge with enemy infantry. After the 21st Texas and other elements of Parsons's Brigade pressed the Federals hard on the left, a counterattack pushed them back rapidly until the 12th Texas Cavalry and Barnes's battery provided relief from the right flank.[216]

These engagements on April 22 and 23 convinced Smith that he could not spare a single brigade from his embattled rear guard, although Banks wanted him to send reinforcements to Monett's Ferry in the south. Fighting began there on April 23, and men in the middle of Banks's column began to wonder if disaster was impending. As they listened, they heard firing at the ferry in their front, echoing the heavy firing in their rear, where Parsons's Texans were pushing the Federal rear guard as hard as they could: it sounded like the Rebels had them in the bag. As it turned out, however, historians are left to speculate on the possible outcomes of Bee holding his ground, for the inexperienced commander ordered his outnumbered and outflanked men to pull back that afternoon after inflicting several hundred casualties on their opponents. Taylor was absolutely beside himself with anger, convinced that Bee's flagrant miscues had allowed Banks's trapped army to survive. The Federal advance guard certainly fought skillfully and determinedly to secure their army's egress from the boggy lowlands between the Cane and Red Rivers, so they may have succeeded despite anything Bee did. Regardless, it was an uncomfortably close call for Banks and his men.[217]

Dick Taylor was not about to let this setback keep him from pressing Banks with everything at his disposal, and Willis Mangham and his Texas comrades continued to fling themselves on the Federal rear guard two miles south of Cloutierville. General Wharton was in personal command of the cavalry pursuit, and he sent Parsons forward at 2:00 a.m. on the morning of April 24 to harass the Federals with close range artillery fire, causing havoc in the camps of the sleeping enemy. The 21st Texas was one of two regiments escorting the artillerymen, and their early morning action heralded a full day of heavy combat. After extensive skirmishing, Wharton ordered Parsons to have a regiment charge the enemy ensconced amidst the ruins of a plantation home. Lieutenant Colonel Giddings led the first squadron (companies A and F) of the 21st Texas into the charge, accompanied by one company from Parsons's own regiment. Parsons considered Giddings's assault "one of the most brilliant and daring of the war." Lieutenant John Stranahan of Company A took part in the first squadron's charge, and wrote that it was delivered "in the real Texas style, on horseback and with a yell." The ensuing advance of the rest of Carter's men placed the Federal left under an intolerable strain. As these men fell back, Morgan's Texas Battalion outflanked the enemy right, and the complete unhinging of the rear guard required a full-scale deployment of Federal infantry to salvage the situation. Supported by seven cannon, this line of battle turned the tables, and an awed Stranahan scribbled: "Such a fire I never was under before. It appeared to me if I had held up my hand I could have caught it full of bullets." The 21st Texas fell back hastily with the assistance of a charge by Parsons's 12th Texas, then reformed on the move with the rest of the brigade, "literally bringing order out of chaos," in Private Zuber's opinion. General Taylor, highly pleased with Wharton's offensive spirit and his cavalry's vigorous response, published a general order praising his cavalry commander and his horsemen, singling out Parsons's Brigade for special mention. Himself a veteran of heavy fighting in Virginia in 1861-1862, Taylor declared: "In daring, in vigor, and in soldiership the operations of these three days will compare favorably with any of the war."[218]

Further skirmishing followed on April 25 and 26, as the Texans hounded the Federal retreat towards Alexandria. There, Banks reunited his infantry with Porter's gunboats, but had to mark time as low water levels had stranded the fleet. As his men desperately built wing dams to raise the water sufficiently for Porter's boats to scrape their way over the rapids, the harried Banks strove to fend off the unceasing Confederate probes from all directions. Wharton consolidated his cavalry corps north of town along Bayou Rapides on April 28, and Parsons's Brigade was soon engaged against a large force of Federal infantry and cavalry in support of Major's cavalry division. Carter's regiment formed under heavy fire in an open field, then delivered a dismounted charge to the tune of "a real Texas yell," to succor the embattled 19th Texas Cavalry. Parsons proudly reported "a most gallant fight," in which Carter's attack was "eminently successful in driving the enemy from the timber, then from a ditch, and finally from a breastwork of rails." A pleased Lieutenant Stranahan related, "Our regiment got a great deal of credit for the charge made today."[219]

The 21st Texas stayed busy during the succeeding days as picket duties and incessant skirmishing alternated with movements to various threatened locations. On May 5, a force General Steele described as "immensely superior" drove the thin line of Texans back several miles in steady combat. Lieutenant John Stranahan noted a "full days fighting," adding, "Our loss was heavy today for we fought them close." More of the same followed over the next two days as the Federals fought successfully to obtain elbowroom for their eventual retreat from Alexandria. After Steele repositioned the rest of his cavalry on Bayous Boeuf and Lamourie, he left the 21st Texas alone to "observe and annoy" the enemy along Bayou Rapides. In accordance with Steele's

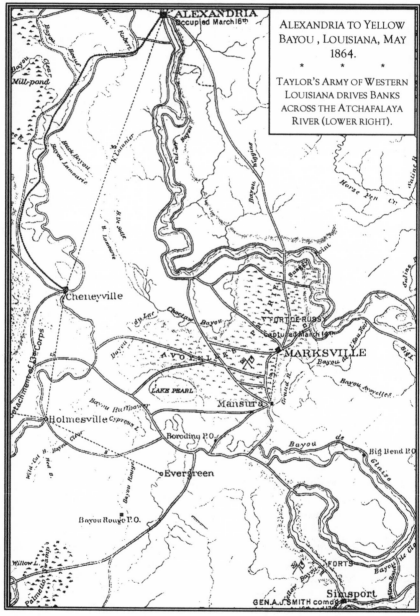

ALEXANDRIA TO YELLOW BAYOU, LOUISIANA, MAY 1864.

* * *

TAYLOR'S ARMY OF WESTERN LOUISIANA DRIVES BANKS ACROSS THE ATCHAFALAYA RIVER (LOWER RIGHT).

orders, the regiment drove in the enemy pickets on May 9, then pulled back in the face of the main body to continue surveillance. Captain Freeman's Company D was on picket that evening, probably along with four other companies of the regiment, when a Federal thrust pushed the Texans' outposts back a mile in the other direction.[220]

In the ongoing tit-for-tat struggle around Alexandria, Carter's companies had to take a turn in the skirmishing every second day, because the 21st Texas was responsible for screening every exit from the north end of the city. Willis and the rest of Freeman's men therefore must have been on duty again on the evening of May 13, when pickets sent back word that the enemy seemed to be retreating out of town. The 21st Texas mounted immediately and started in pursuit, but prudently stopped about two miles short of town after an exchange of shots. That night, they slept holding their horses' bridles before resuming the pursuit the next morning. John Stranahan teased his wife, "We passed through Alexandria and I never saw such a glad looking people in my life. Your antics when I went home was nothing to the shines they kicked up."[221]

Carter's regiment spent the next several days slashing at Banks's flanks and rear, and "had a lively time for about an hour" on May 15 as General Taylor maneuvered forces to hem in the Federals once more. He drew up his little force in battle array at Mansura on May 16, but Parsons's Brigade was overrunning laggards at the rear of the enemy column near Marksville while Taylor's artillery was blasting away at the main body on the Avoyelles Parish prairie. While the Texans were capturing several prisoners in a quick attack, Lieutenant Stranahan noted "the heaviest cannonading. . .I ever heard" from the main battlefield several miles away. Taylor could not risk coming to grips with Banks's superior force in such open country, and when Banks called his bluff with a flanking movement that afternoon, Taylor pulled aside.[222]

Wharton's cavalrymen fell on the Federal rear once more on May 17, as the front of Banks's beleaguered column wended its way towards Simmesport and safety beyond the Atchafalaya River. Carter's regiment was among those striking hard at the Union rear, and only desisted when a heavy force of blueclad artillery and infantry clearly outmatched the thin lines of cavalry. The persistent threat to Banks's rear caused Maj. Gen. A. J. Smith to dispatch General Mower with three infantry brigades back across Yellow Bayou (Bayou de Glaize) the following day, where they encountered Parsons's pickets and began driving them back. Wharton, supported by Polignac's infantry division, counterattacked vigorously, apparently in the belief that other units were in position to help annihilate the Federals. The Confederate cavalry commander launched the 21st and 19th Texas cavalry regiments in a charge against the enemy left in hopes of provoking a real fight, and he certainly got one. The fighting raged for six hours, but soon after their initial charge the 21st Texas was ordered to protect the extreme right flank, where the going was not as rough. As John Stranahan succinctly noted, "Our Regt brought on the fight and then being ordered to the right was what saved us. We were under a heavy fire all the time but did not lose many men." In the center of the fray, by contrast, Polignac's infantrymen stood practically toe-to-toe with four lines of Smith's troops, blasting away at a range of thirty feet while bluecoats shouted, "Surrender you damned Rebels or we'll kill you all."[223]

Although surviving casualty reports are incomplete, partial information indicates that Parsons's Brigade lost about one hundred men of a Confederate casualty toll approximating 608 killed, wounded, and missing in action. Estimates of Federal losses stand at 350 in what turned out to be the last engagement of the Red River Campaign. Many Southerners agreed with sentiments expressed by Sam Marr, a 21st Texas trooper: "it was a foolish fight on our part for the feds were leafing [sic] as fast as they could & we have no men to spare." Writing long after the war, Buck Walton also summed it up pessimistically: "This was one of the bloodiest battles fought West of the Mississippi River—in which we got decently licked." Both sides wound up at or near their original positions after the shooting stopped, however, so many men probably agreed with Stranahan's assessment at the time: "This I call a drawn battle, neither side whipping." Even though he believed the Federals had suffered twice as many casualties as his own side, however, the Texas lieutenant considered the battle "a piece of folly on our part," since ". . .we cannot spare men fighting such unequal fights." Across the lines, many impressed Federals, including General Mower himself, were convinced that the hard-charging rebels had *them* badly outnumbered, even though modern assessments conclude the odds were about even.[224]

Win, lose, or draw, Yellow Bayou turned out to be the last fight of the Red River Campaign. Banks pushed his men to safety across the Atchafalaya River at Simmesport as the cannons boomed at Yellow Bayou, and once across the makeshift bridge they were safely beyond the grasp of Taylor's army and Wharton's hard-riding and hard-fighting cavalrymen. In a general order congratulating his command, Wharton noted with satisfaction: "Your advance guard are now watering their horses in the Mississippi River, whither you will shortly follow."[225]

John Stranahan had served with the 21st Texas Cavalry since its inception, and he observed at the end of the campaign: "We have suffered at times for something to eat, but I have heard less grumbling in the last two months than I ever did before. . . . Nearly every man I saw was willing to suffer any amount of hardship to accomplish the capture of Banks Army." The swath of utter destruction that marked the invaders' trail doubtless helped sharpen the Southerners' commitment to victory, as Stranahan implied to his wife: "Milda, you have no idea what a rich country this was before the Federal army came through it, and if you had you could not form an idea how they have destroyed it. . . .It is now a wilderness."[226]

Even though it proved beyond their means to capture Banks's army, the men of the 21st Texas Cavalry could carry with them the memories of a victorious campaign, which must have been a glorious tonic after their previous experiences in Missouri and Arkansas. First Sergeant Mangham had ridden with the regiment throughout its service, and he probably returned with it to Texas in late summer 1864 to join General Magruder's forces. Shortly after crossing the Sabine River into Texas, however, the regiment countermarched to Arkansas once more, resuming picket duties between Camden and Monticello. On Christmas Eve they got in one more scrape with their old foes, the 5th Kansas Cavalry. The regiment transferred into Lane's Brigade by March

1865 when the War Department finally approved Colonel Carter's assertion of seniority over Parsons, but there was no more fighting to be done.[227]

The 21st Texas Cavalry was eventually ordered back to Texas once again, and made its way to an encampment ten miles east of Bryan on the Little Brazos River. As the Trans-Mississippi Department dissolved in May 1865 after word arrived of the surrenders at Appomattox and Greensboro, the 21st Texas Cavalry went home for good. Private Zuber recollected that about half of the men simply left camp, but the other half hung on grimly, awaiting orders. Major Chenoweth, acting regimental commander in the absence of Carter and Giddings, eventually wearied of the drama and ordered the men to mount up and move out. As they marched slowly towards Bryan, Chenoweth eventually fell back out of sight and disappeared. Others melted away from the column as the regiment disintegrated on its last march, but at least some of the companies returned to their home counties intact. Buck Walton's Company B rendered a further two weeks' service in Austin, helping to maintain order among the chaos of the Confederacy's collapse.[228]

Willis returned home physically unscathed, passing through three years of war without suffering wounds or capture. His wife had died during the war, however, leaving his two little boys without a mother or father until he returned home. There he found his livestock scattered and gone, while law and order had dissolved under the hammer blows of governmental collapse, Indian attack, and the murderous depredations of deserters and draft evaders emboldened by societal turmoil. During the last few months, even the Texas cavalrymen stationed in Bell County had resorted to provisioning themselves by robbing the general stores in Belton and Salado and sacking local farms. Now 37 years of age, Willis was forced to start over amid chaos.[229]

Five years after the end of the war, he traded stock for 193 acres of farmland in the Leon River valley near Belton. That same year he took a second wife, Mrs. L. Bettie Robinson, a widow who had "refugeed" from Georgia to Texas. They soon had two daughters to join sons Dulane and Clarence, but two-year-old Pearlie died in 1874, as did Bettie herself; little Susie survived the dangers of infancy, but died at age 14 in 1885. Willis remarried again in 1877, this time to Mrs. Harriatt Rebecca Scott of Louisiana. Two of their children also died young, but Thomas T. and Eliza Mangham grew to adulthood on their father's 200-acre farm. Willis continued raising livestock, but was also cultivating fifty acres of corn, oats, wheat, and cotton by 1880. Just six years later, however, he was once again a widower: Harriatt died in March 1886, just days after her fiftieth birthday. Willis, a member of the Methodist church, had her gravestone inscribed, "A devoted Christian who's [sic] last prayers were for her children." Just two months after her death, financial disaster struck: a legal judgment arose against his title to the farm he bought in 1871, and the end result was the seizure and auction of 193 acres of his Leon Valley property in late 1887.[230]

His second son Clarence died just a year later at age 27, and apparently the Mangham farmhouse burned with all its contents about the same time. Only Dulane (himself newly widowed, with an infant son), Thomas, and Eliza survived as their father approached old age, with much of his property gone and his home and possessions in ashes. Willis had survived turbulent times and incredible setbacks, to include the Creek Wars in his childhood; three years of military service; the loss of his crops and livestock during the war; the seizure of his land; the destruction of his home; and the death of three wives and five children. Nevertheless, he persevered. Over the next few years he and Dulane built another "good, comfortable residence," and Willis rebuilt his Leon Valley farm to the sum of seventy acres of cultivated property.[231]

When the *Memorial and Biographical History of McLennan, Falls, Bell and Coryell Counties, Texas* was published in 1893, it listed Willis as "one of the representative citizens of Bell County." He and his younger sister Adrian Mangham Kirby, of Fort Smith, Arkansas, were the last survivors of the Thomas and Jane Mangham family. Although the book erroneously listed Willis as the *captain of Company B*, 21st Texas Cavalry, the old veteran had given the definitive data five years previously, when he joined the Bell County Ex-Confederate Veterans' Association as a founding member. Of the numerous brigade, division, and corps assignments of the 21st Texas Cavalry, Willis Mangham chose to list neither their first nor last; stating his rank and unit as first sergeant, Company D, 21st Texas Cavalry, the aging veteran noted his old commanders as "Parsons, Taylor, and E. K. Smith." With these men he had inscribed his name a quarter century earlier in a brilliant chapter of military history. He truly had earned the right to be known as one of the men who had stood "between the enemy and Texas."[232]

*   *   *   *   *

Willis W. Mangham died on July 23, 1896. Sixty-eight years old when he passed away, his tombstone is inscribed: "Blessed art the dead that die in the Lord."[233]

8. FROM ORPHAN BOY TO PLANTATION OWNER: THE HENRY H. MANGHAM FAMILY OF TALBOT AND TAYLOR COUNTIES

Willis's uncle and namesake, Willis Austin Mangham, served as legal guardian for old Solomon Mangham's youngest son, Henry H. Mangham. Born about 1804 in Hancock County, Georgia, Henry was only five or six years old when his father died in 1810. The boy probably remained at home with Sarah and the other young children; his brother Willis lived on a neighboring farm where he could look after his own family as well as his widowed mother's.[234]

The court order that established Willis Mangham's legal responsibilities does not survive, and it is possible that the passage of time required some adjustments to the original arrangements. By October 1823, John Winn (or Wynn) requested that Willis find someone else to serve as security for Willis's guardianship. Two months later, the Putnam County Superior Court duly ordered Winn's release from this financial responsibility, and at the same time discharged Willis as Henry's guardian pending the establishment of some other security. Henry was still a minor at the time, so it is unclear how the courts regulated his situation. In less than two years, however, it became a moot point, as the young man had his eye on a girl named Elizabeth P.

Thweatt. Born in Hancock County on March 3, 1808, Elizabeth was the daughter of John P. Thweatt and his wife Sarah. Henry was 21 and Elizabeth was only a few months past her seventeenth birthday when they married in July 1825.[235]

The next several years brought the young couple a bevy of little girls: Louisa F. and Mary Caroline were born before their mother was twenty years old. Henry moved his family to Meriwether County by 1830, where his household included Elizabeth's parents and ten slaves, some of whom must have belonged to his father-in-law. They did not tarry long in Meriwether before the family was packing up again, moving down the Flint River to neighboring Talbot County by 1832. Talbot was a booming county, headed for real prosperity as hordes of immigrants cleared the lands so recently obtained from the Creek Indians. Henry settled down near his first cousin Josiah Mangum and his sons Arthur, Thomas, Robert, and James Green Mangham, relatively recent immigrants from the "Old North State" (see Chapters VIII and IX). Henry's older brother Thomas lived across the Flint in Upson County with his wife Jane Grier (Greer) Mangham, and their son John Grier Mangham lived in Talbot County itself.[236]

THE
HENRY H. MANGHAM
FAMILY

41 Willis Austin Mangham
42 Thomas Mangham
43 James M. Mangham
44 Unknown Mangham
45 John C. Mangham
46 Wiley P. Mangham
47 Henry H. Mangham
47a Elizabeth P. Thweatt
17 Solomon Mangham
17b Sarah Ann Bennett
112 Louisa F. Mangham
113 Mary Caroline Mangham
114 Martha Winfrey Mangham
115 James O. Mangham
5th Ga. St. Gd.

John's middle name bespoke a probable kinship to many of Henry's neighbors over the following decades; Thomas Greer and Henry Mangham were among the trustees who founded Carsonville's Methodist Episcopal Church in 1842. Henry was only two years older than his nephew, and the two grew up in close proximity to each other. Although John named his first son Willoughby Hill Mangham after the boy's maternal uncle, his second son Henry may well have borne his name in honor of Henry H. Mangham. These dense kinship networks typified community life on the Southern frontier, as each new wave of immigrants commonly comprised groups of close friends and relatives. One of Henry's closest neighbors in the village of Carsonville was Archibald T. Gray, whose sister Cynthia had married Henry's brother Wiley P. Mangham in nearby Pike County in 1821 (see Chapter II).[237]

When Wiley and Cynthia died soon after moving across the Chattahoochee to Chambers County in 1835, Gray assumed the guardianship of one of their orphaned sons, James G. Mangham. By the time the boy was old enough to learn the "three Rs," Henry became his tutor, for which Wiley and Cynthia Mangham's estate paid him the sum of eighteen dollars. These records date from 1842, when Robert Carson formally donated land for the Planters' Academy that had been in operation for seven years. Henry probably served as his younger children's schoolteacher at the same time he was tutoring his orphan nephew; indeed, after Archibald Gray died in 1845, the boy may have lived with his Uncle Henry's family until his untimely death in 1848. By this time, Henry and Elizabeth's little family had undergone a transformation of sorts, as Louisa had married Dr. Benjamin F. Ross in 1847 and Mary Caroline had married John Wynn. The Mangham house still rang with the shouts and laughter of children, however, as Martha Winfrey was born in 1835 and her brother James O. Mangham arrived on the last day of July 1838.[238]

Henry apparently served as the schoolteacher for his own and his neighbors' children at the Planters' Academy throughout the two decades following James's birth, and in 1839 he undertook a term as a county road commissioner. Ten years later he began a three-year stint as Carsonville's postmaster, rounding out a modest but important record of public service. In this respect, as in many others, Henry's life resembled that of many of his brothers, uncles, and cousins. Although he was an active contributor to the development of the prosperous community in which he lived, he made his living primarily as a farmer; the scale of settlement and the nature of rural society in the ante-bellum era inhibited over-specialization. Few men made their living as public servants in this era of limited government intervention in daily life, and the epithet "placeman" still conveyed the sense of distrust towards men who seemed overly attached to their government salary. Like most publicly active men of his milieu, Henry Mangham sought to acquire land and the slaves to work it. By 1850, he had amassed $8000 worth of real estate and 29 slaves to help him farm it. Four years later, tax assessors valued his 3325-acre plantation at $6600, while his slaves added another $14,200 to his net worth of $23,825. Apparently, thirteen of these slaves were actually his mother-in-law's at the time, because John Thweatt had bequeathed them to his wife upon his death in 1849. After her death the slaves "and their increase" were to be apportioned between his daughter Elizabeth Thweatt Mangham and her children, Louisa Ross, Mary Caroline Wynn, Martha, and James.[239]

Martha was only fourteen when her father administered his father-in-law's estate in 1849; four years later she married Patrick H. Mitchell, one of the men who witnessed Thweatt's will. Her brother James was eleven years old when their father had to take on the delicate, time-consuming task of administering Grandpa Thweatt's estate, and ten years later he had barely reached his majority when he had to undertake the same awesome task. His father was only 55 years old in 1859, when an attack of "bilious fever" took hold and would not let go. After nine days of pain and suffering in the oppressive heat of a Georgia August, Henry H. Mangham breathed his last in his Carsonville home.[240]

With all three of his older sisters married and living in the local area, James was able to consult with his extended family about his father's estate, but at 21 he was now the legal head of the household. The estate was certainly sizable, as James had to post $70,000 administrator's bond, with neighbors John T. Gray and W. H. Montfort posting the required security; several months later, his mother Elizabeth and neighbor John Searcy assumed this burden. John Gray had inventoried and appraised Henry's estate in the meantime, assisted by William Mitchell and William Greer. Included among Henry's legal "goods and chattels" were eighteen slaves, ranging in worth from $500 for the "man named Peter Mosely" to $1400 apiece for boys named Ransom and Dave and a man named William. The total value of the eighteen men, women, and children was assessed at $17,850. Some of Henry's other property included several old gins, three buggies, a road wagon, a pair of two-horse wagons, and a Rockaway carriage, along with nine mules, two horses, 52 head of cattle, almost eighty hogs and shoats, 700 bushels of corn, and a like quantity of cotton seed. Clearly a prosperous planter, Henry's parlor carpet, clock, desk, books, plated candlesticks, sideboard, glassware, and glass-overlaid bureau and table bespoke a level of elegance and comfort generally associated with a thriving plantation. Probably one of his hands was a qualified blacksmith, because the estate's blacksmith accounts list almost forty of Henry's relatives and neighbors among those who owed him some $350 for services rendered. Another 48 entries list about $4500 worth of notes and orders payable to his estate, giving a good indication of both his generosity and the relative scarcity of cash in rural Taylor County.[241]

Henry's estate was divided among Elizabeth, James, and his three sisters, with Elizabeth's share assessed in the 1860 census as $18,000 worth of real estate and another $9200 of personal property. James inherited lands valued at another eleven thousand dollars, along with slaves and other property assessed at an equal amount. He was now a family man with responsibilities to a young wife as well as his widowed mother, since he had married 18-year-old Winifred Edwards just three months after his father died. Their marriage further expanded the dense network of kinship that connected neighboring families in the Carsonville area. Winnie was the daughter of William P. Edwards, another well-known local planter who had joined with Henry Mangham and Thomas Greer in 1842 to establish the Methodist Episcopal Church.[242]

9. PLANTER, PRIVATE, PROFESSOR: PVT. JAMES O. MANGHAM, "TAYLOR INFANTRY," RUCKER'S COMPANY, 5TH GEORGIA STATE GUARD

Although his motivations remain cloaked in the shadows of the intervening 140 years, James remained at home when war broke out in 1861. As one 20th century county history recalled, he "entered the teaching profession in the early years of his manhood," and this avocation may have exempted him from military service. He apparently assumed his father's duties at the Planters' Academy when Henry died, and the eventual Conscription Act of 1862 absolved "all presidents and professors of colleges and academies, and all teachers having as many as twenty scholars" from military service. When Congress repealed the original law in favor of a revised conscription system in October 1862, it continued the exemption for academics, as long as they had been "regularly engaged as such for two years previous to the passage of this act." Just as some men had scrabbled together a few bottles of potion and declared themselves apothecaries to avoid the draft, others were desperately organizing a few children into a school class and hurrying to claim exemption as teachers.[243]

JAMES O. MANGHAM

Whereas James may have been exempt as a teacher, his possession of a large number of slaves also qualified him for exemption. The original conscription law made no allowance for white men to remain home to supervise their slaves, and Georgia's contentious Governor Joe Brown was one of those who immediately cried foul. Only a day after the Conscription Act was passed, Brown took pen in hand to warn President Davis of his intention to "respectfully decline all connection with the proposed enrollment" until some questions were clarified. Since he knew of nothing that prevented Confederate enrollment officers from conscripting Georgia's legislators, he even threatened to use "all of the remaining military force of the State" to prevent such an action! The cantankerous governor's other objections embraced a wide variety of demands, including one that helped lay the foundation for exempting some slaveowners:

> I would also respectfully call your attention to the further fact that in portions of our State where the slave population is heavy almost the entire white male population capable of bearing arms (except the overseers on the plantations) are now in the military service of the Confederacy. Most of these overseers are over eighteen and under thirty-five. If they are carried to the field thousands of slaves must be left without overseers, and their labor not only lost at a time when there is great need of it. . .but the peace and safety of helpless women and children must be imperiled for want of protection against bands of idle slaves, who must be left to roam over the country without restraint.[244]

Such language evoked nightmares calculated to raise the blood pressure of any Southerner who recalled John Brown's infamous raid of 1859, and played upon the terror of servile insurrection that lurked just beneath the surface of supposedly placid master-slave relationships. The revised conscription statute of October 1862 accordingly allowed exemptions "to secure the proper police of the country." On "each plantation of twenty negroes, and on which there is no white male adult not liable to military service," one "agent, owner or overseer" was exempted from service. Thus arose the socially divisive "twenty Negro law," that gave rise to the cry "a rich man's war but a poor man's fight." Regardless of its unpopularity in some quarters, the law's provisions clearly exempted James from military service. As the sole adult white male on a plantation embracing 24 slaves in 1860, he could remain at home.[245]

No exemptions barred the way in the summer of 1863, however, when a skillful Federal advance in Tennessee threatened the state of Georgia with direct invasion. President Davis issued a call for local defense corps of draft exempt men to assist the field army there and elsewhere, threatening to conscript the requisite manpower should volunteers hesitate to enroll for six months' service. The War Department established Georgia's quota at 8000 men, and Governor Brown issued a proclamation on June 22calling for their enrollment by the first day of August.[246]

The governor's call summoned Georgians to enlist for six months, during which time recruits would "attend to their ordinary avocations at home, to stand ready at a moment's warning to take up arms and drive back the plundering bands of marauders from their own immediate section of [the] country." Brown chided any potential laggards in advance:

> The man able to bear arms who will wait for a draft before he will join an organization to repel the enemy, whose brutal soldiery comes to his home to destroy his property and insult and cruelly injure his wife and his daughters, is unworthy of the proud name of a Georgian, and should fear lest he be marked as disloyal to the land of his birth and to the government that throws over him the aegis of its protection.

The resulting response indeed bore testimony to Georgians' determination to defend their homes, as well as to Brown's vigorous leadership and effective enforcement by the state's civil and military authorities. Twelve regiments, two legions, and twenty separate battalions organized throughout the state, with muster rolls that bore the names of 18,211 men. Exceeding the state's quota by more than ten thousand men, these units became known as the Georgia State Guard.[247]

One of the companies that organized in response to the looming emergency was the "Taylor Infantry," comprised of men who gathered in the county seat of Butler on August 4, 1863. James signed up as a private soldier when Septimus L. Brewer swore in Captain F. S. Rucker's company for duty in the 2nd, 3rd, and 4th Congressional Districts of the State of Georgia. The Taylor County company became part of the 5th Infantry Regiment, Georgia State Guard, commanded by Col. William L. Salisbury. Having served as a major in *Col. Sam Mangham's* 5th Georgia Volunteers earlier in the war, Salisbury was well qualified to command the regiment in which Sam's first cousin James now found himself (see Chapter IV).[248]

Surviving records indicate that Rucker's Company may have spent time in camp at Cusseta during September, as Rosecrans's invading host began penetrating into the north Georgia hills. Perhaps this was the point in time when Winnie was authorized to purchase salt at discounted rates from the State of Georgia, as James was among those listed as "in service" during the 1863 distribution to soldiers' families in Taylor County. James was at home on September 7, however, when he secured a $10,000 bond for the administrator of James H. Rucker's will; apparently, Captain Rucker had suffered a loss in the family. Later in the month, the looming crisis near the Tennessee state line caused Colonel Salisbury to dispatch his four Muscogee County companies to Atlanta, in response to the governor's call for troops to assist General Bragg in defending the critical rail center. By the time Salisbury's orders went out to his companies, however, they must have had little else to do in Atlanta except escort the prisoners swept up in the great victory at Chickamauga. Although individual soldiers may have volunteered to go north, no evidence exists that the Taylor Infantry headed to Atlanta, possibly due to the provision that allowed each State Guard company to specify its own geographical limits.[249]

The primary mission of Salisbury's regiment was to mobilize against any threat to Columbus, and a mid-December inspection report for General Beauregard's Department of South Carolina, Georgia and Florida listed its four hundred men among the forces available to protect the city and its valuable arsenals. Major General Gilmer's report stated that the regiment was "not as yet called together," however, and its men remained wholly unarmed. The remainder of the available troops comprised Georgia state forces and home defense units too, leaving Gilmer to conclude that the paucity of men and guns made it impossible to defend the earthworks spread across the city's difficult approaches.[250]

Although James's cousin Sam was now lieutenant colonel of a State Guard regiment mobilized from September until February of the following year, it seems unlikely that Salisbury's 5th State Guard spent much time under arms during its brief existence. Along with the other units of Georgia's large-scale home defense force, the Taylor Infantry mustered out of service on February 4, 1864. By this time, however, the disastrous defeat at Missionary Ridge in late November had resulted in the Army of Tennessee's retreat to Dalton, where the troops spent the winter reorganizing under Gen. Joseph E. Johnston. Clearly the next campaign would see a major confrontation in Georgia itself, and the gross disparity in numbers made it clear that Johnston would fight on the defensive. Governor Brown accordingly ordered the complete reorganization of the state militia, in order to transform it from a mere shadow organization to one that had accurate tabs on every man and boy fit to mobilize for the coming crisis.[251]

Taylor County's militia enrollment in early 1864 excluded James, perhaps because of his election as clerk of the county Inferior Court. F. S. Rucker was now first lieutenant of the county's 2nd Militia Company, so membership in the State Guard clearly did not exempt men from enrollment in the militia. Many of the county's militiamen saw sustained action in the operations around Atlanta that summer, the subsequent defense of Macon, and a pitched battle at Griswoldville on November 22. Although James may have participated voluntarily in some of these actions, Governor Brown's mobilization orders of May 18 and 21 specifically authorized exemption for clerks of courts "actually in session." Even his subsequent *levee en masse* order of November 19 acknowledged the exemption of men "engaged in the Legislature or Judicial Departments of the government." These concessions were necessary to salvage any vestiges of local governmental functions, without which all semblance of civil society would have disappeared. Since James was in Taylor County to post bond for the guardianship of Eliza and Angelina Goslin on July 4, just as Sherman's army appeared at Atlanta's very gates, it is likely that he remained at home during most or all of Georgia's protracted agony of 1864. Exempted as a teacher, slave owner, and judicial officer, James was what infantrymen pointedly described as "bomb-proof."[252]

*   *   *   *   *

James and Winnie had two little girls, Annie and Claud, toddling about the Mangham plantation during the long years of bitter war. Their first little brother arrived in the first year after the war ended. Named Henry H. Mangham in remembrance of his grandfather, the little boy was joined by John E. Mangham and little Charlie during the next decade. The early 1880s saw the arrival of a third daughter, Lizzie, probably a namesake of her grandmother, along with little Frank and James O. Mangham, Jr.[253]

The postwar years were indeed eventful ones for the Mangham family. James served as clerk of the Inferior Court until 1866, then continued to teach and operate a successful farm for another ten years, before Taylor County voters elected him County School Commissioner. He held this position for twenty years, also serving as County Surveyor from 1881 to 1883. He had lost his mother in 1871, however, and Winnie died at home on May 27, 1884. Claud was 23 by this time, and she took over the household duties after her mother's untimely death. Claud's loving care for her younger brothers and sisters helped keep the family together without a mother, and James never remarried after Winnie passed away. Annie died in Texas just a year after her mother's death, and Frank died at age 2 only three months afterward. The weight of bereavement grew even heavier the following year, when Henry died at home after suffering a short spell of dysentery.[254]

James had continued to teach throughout his years as School Commissioner, and 1897 saw him move to Worth County with Claud, John, Charlie, and Lizzie. Settling in Sycamore, he rapidly established himself "among the foremost teachers of Southwest Georgia," conducting training institutes that helped provide a steady flow of new teachers for the children of Worth and neighboring counties. His reputation as an educator spread apace over the succeeding years. When Camden County's advertisements for a new school commissioner failed to uncover a qualified applicant in early 1906, the State School Superintendent came looking for James down in Worth County. Mr. W. B. Merritt asked James if he would accept the position, despite the fact that he had never even been in the county! Answering that he would accept the job if

411

the County School Board "should see fit to appoint him," James soon was on his way to St. Mary's on the Georgia coast, along with Claud and Lizzie.[255]

Lizzie, who had received her elementary and high school education in her father's classrooms, soon followed in his professional footsteps. The year they arrived in Camden County, she was elected to teach at St. Mary's High School. Two years later she married one of her father's old Worth County pupils, Elzie Williams, after he took over a school in Camden County. Although James continued his busy schedule of teaching and administrative duties, he served as superintendent of the Methodist Sunday school in town, continuing his lifelong commitment to church activities.[256]

On May 1, 1911, James stopped to visit his youngest son Jim at his home in Jacksonville, Florida, while en route to a convention of Georgia's county school commissioners in Valdosta. He had just arrived and sat down to supper with Jim and his family when "apoplexy. . .seized him in its strong grip." Although he had been active and in good health, his appointed time had come. Back in Taylor County on the following day, a column in the *Butler Herald* bore the heading: "Death Claims Prof. J. O. Mangham." Dr. John E. Mangham, his eldest son, welcomed his four brothers and sisters into his Reynolds home after they conveyed their father's remains to the Butler Methodist Cemetery, where he and his family had attended church for many years before moving away from the county.[257]

Twenty-seven long years after Winnie was laid to rest in the old churchyard, her husband rejoined her there at last.[258]

---

[1] Vaughn Ballard, comp., *Solomon Mangham: His Ancestors and Descendants* (Arlington: Family Histories, 1989), pp. 47-49, 53, 67; 1830 Census, Upson County. Ballard tentatively identifies Thomas Mangham as Solomon's son, but notes that he may have been a brother or nephew. Although I have not found definitive evidence of their relationship, I have found a letter that Willis Austin Mangham's son, John N. Mangham, addressed to "Cous. John G. Mangham" (see Chapter II). If the two Johns were indeed *first* cousins, then Willis and Thomas were brothers. Additionally, the Upson County clerk recorded a Power of Attorney for Thomas in 1830, wherein Philip Graybill appointed him as his attorney for the purpose of settling the Solomon Mangham estate in Hancock County. The reader will recall that Solomon appointed Willis Mangham and Philip Graybill as executors of his estate prior to his death in 1810.

[2] Ballard, *Solomon Mangham*, p. 49; *A Memorial and Biographical History of McLennan, Falls, Bell and Coryell Counties, Texas* (Chicago: The Lewis Publishing Co., 1893), p. 867; Robert Scott Davis, Jr., *Records of Jasper County, Georgia* (Greenville: Southern Historical Press, 1990), pp. 149, 208-209; 1860 Census, Randolph County, Georgia; *Verbatim Copies of Wills, Chambers County, Volumes 1-3, 1818-1861*, p. 200 (Jane Mangham, Will Book 2, p. 193); Fred R. Hartz, *Genealogical Abstracts from the Georgia Journal (Milledgeville) Newspaper, 1809-1840*, vol. 1, excerpt from November 10, 1818; vol. 2, pp.

442, 651; Silas E. Lucas, Jr., *The Third or 1820 Land Lottery of Georgia* (Easley: Southern Historical Press, 1986), p. 209; Pike County Marriages. Jane Mangham's will lists all of her children, to include her daughter Louisa Irwin (Irvin). Jane also allocated a sum of money to "Sarah E. Umphries, the daughter of Sarah Umphries, deceased." In all probability, the deceased Sarah was the daughter (and eleventh child) of Thomas and Jane Mangham. Jane was born in Hancock County on March 13, 1787, and Jasper and Chambers County records indicate that the Thomas Mangham family maintained a close relationship with the Greer (or Grier) family: he and Jane named their first son after John Greer. See the "Greer Family of Julia and Ralph Terry" at http://www. parsonstech.com/ genealogy/trees/rterry1/ d4154.htm#P4154.

³ Upson County, Deed Book B, p. 132; 1830 Censuses, Upson and Talbot Counties.

⁴ Upson County, Deed Book D, p. 57; Bobby L. Lindsey, *"The Reason for the Tears"*: *A History of Chambers County, Alabama 1832-1900* (West Point: Hester Printing Co., 1971), pp. 250-251; *Verbatim Copies of Wills, Chambers County*, p. 200. Isaac Collier was a brother-in-law of Thomas Mangham's daughter, Hannah Mangham Collier, and is another of the present author's great-great-grandparents. His son, Isaac P. "Pete" Collier Jr., was cited for heroism at Kennesaw Mountain in 1864, when he saved a number of his men by throwing a sputtering cannon shell out of a trench just before it exploded. The teenaged sergeant was offered a commission for this action, but he declined promotion in order to stay with his company, the 5th Georgia's Upson Guards (see *MDT*, June 28, 1864; J. H. Harp, "The Bravest Deed I Ever Saw," CV 31 [1923]: 45-46). For more about Wiley P. and Cynthia Mangham, see Chapter II.

⁵ Lindsey, *History of Chambers County*, pp. 209-213, 250-251. Wickerville's population swelled to 2000 people by 1838, benefiting from the continuing influx of settlers from Georgia and the Carolinas.

⁶ CMSR (Mexican War) Nathaniel P. Mangham, Early's Company, 1st Texas Mounted Rifles; Charles D. Spurlin, comp., *Texas Veterans in the Mexican War: Muster Rolls of Texas Military Units* (Victoria: C. D. Spurlin, c. 1984), pp. 25-27; Letter, Washington County Historical Survey Committee, July 7, 1965, TSA.

⁷ CMSR (Mexican War), Nathaniel H. Mangum, Gillet's Company, Bell's Regiment Texas Mounted Volunteers; Spurlin, *Texas Veterans*, pp. 102-104; Henry W. Barton, *Texas Volunteers in the Mexican War* (Wichita Falls: Texian Press, 1970), pp. 101, 104-105. The Washington County tax assessor enumerated "N. H. Mangum" in 1847, assessing his sole taxable property as a horse, valued at one hundred dollars. See Washington County Tax Rolls, reel 1 (1837-1878), reel 637, TSL.

⁸ Spurlin, *Texas Veterans*, pp. 121-122; Barton, *Texas Volunteers*, pp. 105-106.

⁹ Ibid.

¹⁰ Spurlin, *Texas Veterans*, p. 122. See also Solomon R. Mangham letter to John G. Mangham, quoted below.

[11] *Verbatim Copies of Wills, Chambers County*, p. 200; 1850 Census, Randolph County.

[12] Letter, Jane Mangham to John G. Mangham, June 23, 1849, in Family Letters of Willoughby H. Mangham, 1849-1868, drawer 160, reel 72, GDAH.

[13] West Point, Troup County, Georgia. Situated right across the Chattahoochee River from Chambers County on the road to LaGrange, this town was an important railroad terminus.

[14] Jane refers to John's wife Eliza and their children Mary, Huldah, Willoughby and Henry. Born about 1847, Henry apparently died sometime between 1850 and 1860.

[15] Hannah Mangham married Vines H. Collier in Upson County on November 23, 1835. (See Upson County marriage records.)

[16] Jane Mangham's will was signed with a mark, so the signature affixed to this dictated letter is apparently not her own. This is less than definitive proof, however, as I have found documents allegedly signed "by mark" when overwhelming evidence exists to prove the individual's literacy.

[17] Letter, Solomon R. Mangham to John G. Mangham, October 4, 1849, in Family Letters of Willoughby H. Mangham, 1849-1868, GDAH.

[18] Ibid., April 13, 1852.

[19] Since Jane's estate was divided among eight surviving children, the approximate total value equated to $3000. Solomon's reference to the "Beard note" illustrates the customary use of personal notes and loans in the ante-bellum South.

[20] Ibid., August 28, 1854.

[21] James M. Fuller married Jane Mangham in Chambers County on November 16, 1848. County records reflect that John W. Godfrey and Lucinda M. Mangham applied for a marriage license on November 5, 1849. See MFB 18: 12.

[22] Willis worked as an overseer.

[23] The reference is to West Point, Georgia.

[24] Adrian's husband was David R. Kirby.

[25] Solomon generally rendered the word "are" as "air," thus providing modern readers a revealing insight as to his accent and pronunciation.

[26] MFB 18: 12; Chambers County, Superior Court, Deed Book 13 (1857-1860), p. 498, ADAH; 1855 Alabama State Census, Tallapoosa County; 1860 Census and Slave Census, Tallapoosa County. Solomon sold his Chambers County property to Marcus Williams in 1857.

[27] Letter, Solomon R. Mangham to John G. Mangham, August 2, 1862, Willoughby Hill Mangham Letters, GDAH.

[28] Letter, Solomon R. Mangham to John G. Mangham, September 7, 1862, in Family Letters of Willoughby H. Mangham, 1849-1868, GDAH.

[29] Alford Shepherd resided in the town of Bastrop, Texas in 1860 (see 1860 Census, Bastrop County).

[30] OR IV, vol. 2, p. 160.

[31] OR IV, vol. 3, pp. 178-179.

[32] Ibid., p. 196; 1870 Census, Tallapoosa County.

[33] David Evans, *Sherman's Horsemen: Union Cavalry Operations in the Atlanta Campaign* (Bloomington: Indiana Univ. Press, 1996), pp. 98, 106-107, 127-129. For a synopsis of Rousseau's Raid, see Malcolm C. McMillan, ed., *The Alabama Confederate Reader* (Tuscaloosa: Univ. of Alabama Press, 1963), pp. 259-273. For the story of Tom and Wiley Mangham, see Chapter III; for more on John Henry Mangham of Talladega County, see Chapter V.

[34] Evans, *Sherman's Horsemen*, pp. 129-133.

[35] Ibid., pp. 133-135.

[36] Muster rolls, January 22, 1864, Young's Company Mounted Infantry, Alabama Volunteers, and October 31, 1864, Young's Company Cavalry, Alabama State Reserves, in Young's Company Unit Files, ADAH; CMSR, Solomon R. Mangham, Young's Company, Cavalry (State Reserves), Alabama; CMSR Index, Soldiers Serving in the Indian Wars, 1815-1838, M629, reel 23, NARA. Solomon served as a private in House's Company, Webb's Battalion, Alabama Mounted Militia Infantry.

[37] Muster rolls, October 31 and December 31, 1864, Young's Company Cavalry, Alabama State Reserves, Unit Files, ADAH; OR IV, vol. 7, pp. 998-999; William O. Bryant, *Cahaba Prison and the Sultana Disaster* (Tuscaloosa: Univ. of Alabama Press, 1990), pp. 2, 20.

[38] Bryant, *Cahaba Prison*, pp. 9-10; William Marvel, *Andersonville: The Last Depot* (Chapel Hill: UNC Press, 1994), pp. 10, 25-26; OR 2, pt. 7, pp. 606-607. Marvel asserts that the exchange cartel first foundered in 1863 under the influence of U. S. Secretary of War Edwin Stanton, who feared that Federal troops were surrendering for the chance to spend several weeks at home.

[39] OR II, vol. 6, p. 1124.

[40] Bryant, *Cahaba Prison*, p. 21; OR II, vol. 7, pp. 998-1001; Muster roll, December 31, 1864, Young's Company Cavalry, Alabama State Reserves, Unit Files, ADAH. The company muster roll reflects that one soldier enlisted in Young's Company at Cahaba on August 18, indicating that the unit arrived at the prison soon after organization.

[41] OR II, vol. 7, pp. 998-1001; Muster roll, October 31, 1864, Young's Company Cavalry, Alabama State Reserves, Unit Files, ADAH; CMSR, Solomon Mangham.

[42] Muster roll, October 31, 1864, Young's Company Cavalry, Alabama State Reserves, Unit Files, ADAH; CMSR, Solomon Mangham.

[43] Muster roll, December 31, 1864, Young's Company Cavalry, Alabama State Reserves, Unit Files, ADAH.

[44] OR II, vol. 7, pp. 998-1001; Bryant, *Cahaba Prison*, pp. 20-21; Jesse Hawes, *Cahaba: A Story of Captive Boys in Blue* (New York: Burr Printing House, 1888), pp. 19-21.

[45] Hawes, *Captive Boys*, pp. 21, 261; Bryant, *Cahaba Prison*, pp. 2-3, 37.

[46] OR II, vol. 7, pp. 998-1001; Bryant, *Cahaba Prison*, pp. 100-106; Hawes, *Captive Boys*, pp. 403-406.

[47] OR II, vol. 8, p. 117; Bryant, *Cahaba Prison*, pp. 104-105; Hawes, *Captive Boys*, pp. 403-407.

[48] OR II, vol. 8, pp. 117-122; Bryant, *Cahaba Prison*, p. 105; Hawes, *Captive Boys*, pp. 420-423.

[49] Hawes, *Captive Boys*, pp. 423-424. As Bryant explains in his excellent history of Cahaba Prison, Hawes took pains to support his claim that the Alabama prison was fully as terrible as the more notorious Andersonville. Nevertheless, his account is generally accurate. It is certainly believable that the elderly Alabama reservists were fighting mad after the hostage taking and breakout attempt.

[50] OR II, vol. 8, pp. 117-122.

[51] Bryant, *Cahaba Prison*, pp. 108, 128-129.

[52] Ibid., pp. 108-113.

[53] Ibid., pp. 111-112; OR II, vol. 8, pp. 492-493.

[54] OR II, vol. 8, pp. 794-795, 834-835; Noah Andre Trudeau, *Out of the Storm: The End of the Civil War, April-June 1865* (Baton Rouge: LSU Press, 1994), pp. 12-13, 154-167; James Pickett Jones, *Yankee Blitzkrieg: Wilson's Raid Through Alabama and Georgia* (Athens: UGA Press, 1976), pp. 70-73, 82-92.

[55] 1870 Census, Tallapoosa County; 1867 Voter Registration Records, Tallapoosa County, file SG 16054, ADAH.

[56] 1880 Census, Tallapoosa County.

[57] Tallapoosa County, Miscellaneous Probate Records 1835-1947, Record of Deaths, 1881-1888, reel 14, ADAH; Tallapoosa County, Administrator's Records, 1871-1898, p. 84, LGM 87, reel 9, ADAH. Solomon left assets worth some $2500 to his wife Emily and their children.

[58] Mobile County Probate Court, Marriage Records, Book 17, p. 277; 1870 Census, Mobile County.

[59] 1860 Census, Mobile County. Officers and men who reenlisted in the 1st Alabama in April 1862 received furloughs to return home and recruit the regiment. See *Directory of the City of Montgomery, and Historical Sketches of Alabama Soldiers* (Montgomery: Perry & Smith, Publishers, 1866), pp. 53-54.

[60] Muster Roll, Company A, 1st Alabama Unit Files, ADAH; Willis Brewer, *Alabama: Her History, Resources, War Record, and Public Men, from 1540 to 1872* (Montgomery: Barrett & Brown, 1872), pp. 589-590; Edward Y. McMorries, *History of the First Regiment Alabama Volunteer Infantry C.S.A.* (Montgomery: Brown Printing Co., 1904), p. 13.

[61] Brewer, *Alabama*, pp. 589-591; *Directory*, pp. 53-56. For the story of the 1st Alabama's service in Louisiana, see Lawrence Lee Hewitt, *Port Hudson: Confederate Bastion on the Mississippi* (Baton Rouge: LSU Press, 1987).

[62] *Directory*, p. 43; 1870 and 1880 Censuses, Mobile County. James and Virginia had lost their first daughter in August 1864, when little Mary Ida Mangham died at age two

in Mobile. See Lucille Mallon and Rochelle Farris, comp., *Burial Records, Mobile County, Alabama, 1857-1870* (Mobile: Mobile Genealogical Society, 1971), p. 147.

[63] *Houston Morning Post*, May 31, 1933, and additional San Antonio newspaper clippings from November 1933, provided courtesy of Mr. Felix Mangham (Major, USAF, retired) of Denver, Colorado; San Antonio newspaper clippings (1906 and November 8, 1933), provided courtesy of San Antonio Genealogical and Historical Society. An 1890 Mobile directory identifies Virginia Mangham as a widow.

[64] Ibid.

[65] This chapter is republished by permission of the Atlanta Historical Society, which originally published an edited version as "The Civil War Letters of Willoughby Hill Mangham—Private, 'Quitman Greys,' Company I, Eleventh Georgia Volunteer Regiment," Parts 1 and 2, in *Atlanta History: A Journal of Georgia and the South* 46 (Fall 1997, Winter 1998): 40-51, 31-46.

[66] 1860 Census, Randolph County; letter, W. H. Mangham to mother, March 16, 1860, and letter, Solomon R. Mangham to brother John G. Mangham, September 7, 1862, in Family Letters of Willoughby Hill Mangham, 1849-1868, GDAH; Tax in Kind receipt, January 1, 1865, John G. Mangham Papers, Pt. 1, drawer 160, reel 53, GDAH. The author is indebted to John Brannon for providing background information on Eliza Webb Hill Mangham's family.

[67] CMSR, Willoughby H. Mangham, 11th Georgia.

[68] Ibid.; OR 27, pt. 2, pp. 397, 401-403; Private William T. Laseter, cited in Aurelia Austin, *Georgia Boys with "Stonewall" Jackson: James Thomas Thompson and the Walton Infantry* (Athens: UGA Press, 1967), pp. 63-64; Willoughby Hill Mangham Letters, GDAH. Willoughby's CMSR states that he was "wounded at Gettysburg July 3, 1863 and left there." It is not clear why this wound prevented his evacuation, unless severe bleeding and shock made it inadvisable to move him.

[69] With one exception, I have transcribed this correspondence from the Willoughby Hill Mangham Letters, drawer 154, reel 27, GDAH. Since Willoughby's single surviving note from Fort Delaware is almost illegible on microfilm, I have quoted its brief text from a county history that one of his daughters helped prepare in 1934. The book quotes excerpts from four of his other letters, but comparison with the microfilmed originals identifies significant omissions, as well as correction of his (numerous) stylistic errors. See Lillie Martin Grubbs, *History of Worth County Georgia for the First Eighty Years, 1854-1934* (Macon: J. W. Burke Co., 1934; reprint, Sylvester: Barnard Trail Chapter, NSDAR, 1970), pp. 391-393.

[70] Bell Irvin Wiley, *The Life of Johnny Reb: The Common Soldier of the Confederacy* (Baton Rouge: LSU Press, 1978), p. 244.

[71] Grubbs, *Worth County*, p. 390. (I have left an additional space at the end of unpunctuated sentences to enhance clarity without significantly altering the original texts.)

[72] CMSR, Willoughby H. Mangham; Kittrell J. Warren, *Eleventh Georgia Vols., Embracing the Muster Rolls, Together with a Special and Succinct Account of the Marches, Engagements, Casualties, etc.* (Richmond: Smith, Bailey & Co., Printers, 1863), p. 27; J. J. Adams, "History of the Quitman Grays," in Jacquelyn Shepard, *The Quitman Echo: Quitman County, Georgia* (Georgetown: Author, 1991). Mr. Frank Bledsoe, the descendant and namesake of Lieutenant Bledsoe, contributed Adams's memoir to Mrs. Shepard; the current author is indebted to her for providing an electronic copy of it from her book.

[73] The Quitman Greys elected Theodore LeGrand Guerry as their captain upon the company's organization, but regimental elections later that day resulted in his selection as lieutenant colonel. Lewis P. Dozier was elected as the company's first lieutenant and he assumed the captaincy upon Guerry's promotion. See Warren, *Eleventh Georgia*, p. 12; Lillian Henderson, comp., *Roster of the Confederate Soldiers of Georgia 1861-1865* (N.p.: State of Georgia, 1959-64), vol. 2, p. 145.

[74] Perhaps Willoughby is referring to the July 5 skirmish at Newport News. Brigadier General George Cadwalader was the Federal commander of the Department of Annapolis. See E. B. Long, *The Civil War Day by Day: An Almanac, 1861-1865* (Garden City: Doubleday & Co., 1971), pp. 75, 91.

[75] In the initial rush to organize the throngs of volunteers, some confusion ensued in the designation of Georgia's volunteer regiments, which were numbered in order of their acceptance into Confederate service. The distinction was not purely nominal, as it affected precedence of units and often the dates of officers' commissions. It is unclear whether G. T. Anderson's regiment was designated initially as the 10th Regiment, or whether the Quitman Greys were transferred from the 10th to the 11th Georgia. Apparently, the "Walton Infantry" underwent the same process before their designation was established as Co. H, 11th Georgia. See Anita B. Sams, ed., *With Unabated Trust: Major Henry McDaniel's Love Letters From Confederate Battlefields As Treasured in Hester McDaniel's Bonnet Box* (Monroe: The Historical Society of Walton County, 1977), p. 4.

[76] Warren, *Eleventh Georgia*, pp. 28-29; Lieutenant Henry McDaniel, cited in Sams, *Unabated Trust*, pp. 6-8; Captain Matthew T. Nunnally and Pvt. James T. Thompson, cited in Austin, *Georgia Boys*, pp. x, 4-5.

[77] Ibid.; Adams, "History of the Quitman Grays"; Stewart Sifakis, *Compendium of the Confederate Armies: South Carolina and Georgia* (New York: Facts on File, 1995), pp. 196-208. Austin quotes Captain Nunnally of Co. H, who wrote that the march to Piedmont was 34 miles, as well as Private Thompson, who informed his parents that it was 65 miles! Sams cites Lieutenant (later Major) McDaniel, who said it was 27 miles. All sources agree, however, on two salient points: it was a terrible march, and the men were greatly aggrieved at missing the battle. Apparently Thompson's views were representative: "All i want is a crack at a Yankey boy" (Austin, *Georgia Boys*, p. 5).

[78] He is apparently referring to Privates Benjamin W. Apperson, Cicero S. Morgan, and David F. Morris, although Morgan's record indicates he died of pneumonia (Warren, *Eleventh Georgia*, pp. 12-13; Henderson, *Georgia Rosters*, vol. 2, p. 146, 149).

[79] 25-year-old physician Francis M. Bledsoe was elected 2nd Lieutenant upon the company's organization, and he accordingly moved up to the first lieutenancy upon the promotion of Guerry and Dozier (1860 Census, Randolph County; Warren, *Eleventh Georgia*, p. 12; Henderson, *Georgia Rosters*, vol. 2, p. 145).

[80] Lieutenant McDaniel of Co. H, who went on to serve as governor of Georgia in the 1880s, agreed with Willoughby's assessment of Bartow. Although his letter home praised the brigade commander's "manly bearing on the battle-field," he added a bitter postscript: "But it was *his fault* we were left. Had we been with the Georgia boys they might not have been so badly cut up" (emphasis in original). McDaniel, cited in Sams, *Unabated Trust*, pp. 7-8.

[81] Glover belonged to a different regiment.

[82] Federal forces lost some 460 men killed in action, and the Confederates reported 387 deaths (Long, *Civil War Day by Day*, p. 99). Private J. J. Adams of the Quitman Greys recalled that the unburied corpses at Manassas presented "a scene but few had ever seen, the sight of which whipped some of the bravest men we had" (see Adams, "History of the Quitman Grays").

[83] The "hollowing" Willoughby mentions would soon become famous as the "Rebel Yell."

[84] The two armies were more evenly matched than Willoughby asserts, as the Federal force of 37,000 outnumbered Beauregard's force by only some 2000 men (Long, *Civil War Day by Day*, p. 99).

[85] Having just recounted his first impressions of a battlefield, it was perhaps no coincidence that the young soldier now asked his father to arrange his estate.

[86] Private Hayas Graddy, Willoughby's uncle, was wounded at the Wilderness on May 5, 1864, and died of his wounds two months later. Second Lieutenant Osborn R. Smith of the Quitman Greys was appointed regimental quartermaster on July 19, 1861 (letter, Willoughby Mangham to mother, March 16, 1860, Willoughby Hill Mangham Family Letters, 1849-1868, GDAH; Warren, *Eleventh Georgia*, p. 12; Henderson, *Georgia Rosters*, vol. 2, pp. 145, 148). Details to staff and support duties combined with furloughs, desertion, disease and battle injuries to sap the fighting strength of Confederate infantry regiments. From a nominal roll of 800-1000 men, they usually could put only 250-500 in line of battle at any given time.

[87] If he was referring to the strength of Confederate forces there, it represented a considerable overestimate. The earliest returns showing Confederate strength *throughout Virginia* were compiled for October 1861, and these reflected an aggregate strength of approximately 73,000 men (*OR* 5, p. 932).

[88] The Confederacy was notorious for its inability to feed and clothe its troops adequately, and these supply failures had a dramatically adverse impact on the war

effort. For a riveting analysis of these problems from the perspective of the individual soldier, see Wiley, *Johnny Reb*, pp. 90-123.

[89] Warren, *Eleventh Georgia*, p. 29.

[90] Private B. Franklin Pittman died on August 25, 1861 (Warren, *Eleventh Georgia*, p. 12; Henderson, *Georgia Rosters*, vol. 2, p. 150). The other three were Apperson, Morgan, and Morris (see above).

[91] The roster of the Quitman Greys reflects three men named Davis and six named Pittman, all of whom enlisted with Willoughby (Warren, *Eleventh Georgia*, p. 12; Henderson, *Georgia Rosters*, vol. 2, pp. 147, 150).

[92] Warren, *Eleventh Georgia*, pp. 29-30; Lieutenant McDaniel, cited in Sams, *Unabated Trust*, pp. 16-19; Captain Nunnally, cited in Austin, *Georgia Boys*, p. 13.

[93] Ante-bellum Southern society strongly emphasized the importance of religion in daily life. Willoughby's letter illustrates its continuing role in a military environment, as well as indicating the type of camp news he thought would interest his sister. After the war, he was active as a leader in local church affairs. See Gerald F. Linderman, *Embattled Courage: The Experience of Combat in the American Civil War* (New York: The Free Press, 1987), pp. 84-87, 102-110; Grubbs, *Worth County*, p. 389.

[94] Warren, *Eleventh Georgia*, pp. 12-13.

[95] The service records of Confederate commanders typically are cluttered with official forms detailing exact numbers of pens, envelopes, bottles of ink and quires of paper received from unit quartermasters.

[96] General Lee asserted in 1865 that the army's inability to pay and feed its soldiers was the primary cause of desertion (*OR* 46, pt. 2, p. 1143).

[97] Close analysis of the contents of this letter indicates that Willoughby probably composed it on October 7, not September 7, 1861.

[98] Captain (Quartermaster) Smith died at Warrenton on September 14, and Pvt. Thomas D. Frith died there on October 5. The other additional fatality in the company to date was apparently Pvt. David L. Hudspeth, who died on October 6, 1861. Henderson indicates that Pvt. Henry Hudspeth died on the same day; his name does not appear on Warren's roster (Warren, *Eleventh Georgia*, p. 12; Henderson, *Georgia Rosters*, vol. 2, pp. 145, 147).

[99] Wiley, *Johnny Reb*, p. 365.

[100] Willoughby wrote this letter and the succeeding one on stationery printed with a firing cannon and a Confederate flag, encaptioned "God and our rights." This accompanied the rousing (if hastily typeset) verse: "Stand firmly by your cannon, Let ball and grape-shotfly, And trust in Godand Davis, But keep your powder dry."

[101] Warren, *Eleventh Georgia*, p. 30. Writing from headquarters at Centreville on January 14, 1862, General Johnston reported that the danger from enemy movements remained so great that he could not hazard the necessary reorganization of his command (*OR* 5, pp. 1028-1029). Centreville is located six miles west of Fairfax.

[102] Warren, *Eleventh Georgia*, p. 30.

[103] According to Union records, the 23-year-old Georgian carried his 160 lbs. on a 5' 9" frame, with light hair and gray eyes. Regimental records from July 1862 describe him as 5' 8" tall, with blue eyes, light hair and light complexion. See CMSR, Willoughby H. Mangham, and Muster Rolls, 11th Georgia, NARA.

[104] For details of the Confederate position at Centreville, see Lieutenant McDaniel's description in Sams, *Unabated Trust*, pp. 21-24, 32-33.

[105] The 1st Kentucky remained in Brig. Gen. David R. Jones' Brigade through May 1862, so it was not a "Georgia" brigade in the strictest sense. Along with Brig. Gen. Robert Toombs's brigade of four Georgia regiments, they comprised part of G. W. Smith's 2nd Division of General Beauregard's Potomac District in mid-January 1862. Beauregard was in turn subordinate to Johnston's Dept. of Northern Virginia (Lieutenant McDaniel, cited in Sams, *Unabated Trust*, p. 39; OR 5, pp. 1028-1029; OR 11, pt. 3, p. 532).

[106] Three Thompsons appear on the roster of the Quitman Greys. Mr. Thompson's relationship to the Mangham family is not clear.

[107] He is apparently referring to some earlier incident in which a splinter of steel lodged in his eye, perhaps while he was working in his father's mill.

[108] Terry L. Jones, *Lee's Tigers: The Louisiana Infantry in the Army of Northern Virginia* (Baton Rouge: LSU Press, 1987), pp. 39-42, 44; Bromfield L. Ridley, *Battles and Sketches of the Army of Tennessee* (Mexico: Missouri Printing & Publishing Co., 1906; reprint, Dayton: Morningside, 1995), p. 460. Willoughby's brigade-mate Berrien Zettler of the 8th Georgia recounted the execution in some detail in his postwar memoir, so it obviously made the intended impression on the soldiers. See Berrien M. Zettler, *War Stories and School-Day Incidents for the Children* (New York: Neale Publishing, 1912), pp. 78-80. Although few troops had much compassion for executed hooligans, later executions of deserters left them with decidedly mixed feelings. See Wiley, *Johnny Reb*, p. 228; James I. Robertson, Jr., *Soldiers Blue and Gray* (Columbia: USC Press, 1988), pp. 135-136.

[109] Letter, C. C. Farr to brother, December 8, 1861, in *Confederate Reminiscences and Letters*, vol. 2 (Atlanta: Georgia Division, UDC, 1996), p. 246. Farr was stationed near Manassas.

[110] His health failing, Maj. Charles T. Goode resigned from service in January 1862, and Captain Luffman of Co. C was elected his successor. Colonel Anderson had assumed command of the brigade, nominally leaving Lieutenant Colonel Guerry in command. Since Guerry's constitution was failing, too, he was usually unfit for duty and left Major Luffman in command (Warren, *Eleventh Georgia*, p. 32).

[111] Following Capt. Lewis Dozier's resignation on November 23, 1861, Pvt. Samuel Thatcher was elected captain of the Quitman Greys. Born in Ohio, he practiced law in Quitman County before the war (Warren, *Eleventh Georgia*, p. 12; Henderson, *Georgia Rosters*, vol. 2, pp. 145, 151; 1860 Census, Quitman County).

[112] Willoughby is referring to Pvts. Thomas D. Frith and John A. Thomas. Frith was discharged for disability on November 17, 1861 (Warren, *Eleventh Georgia*, pp. 12-13; Henderson, *Georgia Rosters*, vol. 2, pp. 147, 151).

[113] Warren, *Eleventh Georgia*, pp. 32-34; Private Thompson, cited in Austin, *Georgia Boys*, p. 30.

[114] Warren, *Eleventh Georgia*, pp. 32-34; McDaniel, cited in Sams, *Unabated Trust*, p. 63.

[115] John Mangham probably had visited his properties in Concordia Parish, Louisiana, which would have required him to cross the Mississippi River. Federal naval forces began deploying to attack upriver towards New Orleans in mid-March, and the operation was in full swing a month later. See Chester G. Hearn, *The Capture of New Orleans, 1862* (Baton Rouge: LSU Press, 1995), pp. 135, 151.

[116] Willoughby is referring to Sister Mary's husband, James Nichols, who was serving in Virginia.

[117] Altha was Willoughby's niece, and apparently was listed in the 1860 census as one-year-old Eliza A. Nichols (1860 Census, Randolph County).

[118] Those wounded were N. D. Byrun, J. E. Deal, Peter Ran (who died of wounds on May 13), Robert R. Blankenship, and Amos Bishop, none of whom were in the Quitman Greys (Warren, *Eleventh Georgia*, pp. 5-26).

[119] Stephen W. Sears, *To the Gates of Richmond: The Peninsula Campaign* (New York: Ticknor & Fields, 1992), pp. 55-56.

[120] Warren, *Eleventh Georgia*, pp. 34-35; Lieutenant McDaniel, cited in Sams, *Unabated Trust*, pp. 63-65; Captain Nunnally, cited in Austin, *Georgia Boys*, p. 34; OR 11, pt. 1, pp. 1028-1029. A letter signed with Warren's *nom de guerre* "X" appeared in the *Macon Daily Telegraph* of July 22, 1862, giving a spirited account of the 11th Georgia's experiences at Yorktown.

[121] Warren, *Eleventh Georgia*, pp. 35-37. The regiment reported its effective strength on or about April 30, 1862 (OR 11, pt. 3, p. 480).

[122] Although Willoughby normally datelined his letters, he omitted to do so in this instance. A more modern hand had annotated the letter "[About May 1862]". The context indicates he wrote it on May 18 or very shortly thereafter.

[123] The fall of New Orleans on April 29, 1862 did indeed bode ill for the Confederacy's lines of supply to the Trans-Mississippi Department (see Hearn, *Capture of New Orleans*, pp. 258-60). Willoughby's concern about this loss is particularly enlightening, as it indicates the breadth of perspective he possessed. After all, he and his comrades now stood with their backs to the wall at Richmond! One must infer that he believed the Federals would not get any farther in Virginia.

[124] Sears, *Gates of Richmond*, pp. 138, 145, 292; MDT, July 22, 1862. For casualty returns, see OR 11, pt. 2, pp. 707-708, 714-715.

[125] Warren, *Eleventh Georgia*, p. 42. Willoughby certainly was present for duty on July 23, for he signed for $50.00 bounty from the regimental Acting Assistant

Quartermaster, Lieutenant J. M. Jackson, on a roll datelined "Camp near Richmond" (CMSR, Willoughby H. Mangham). The bounty was part of an inducement program to encourage voluntary enlistments; those already serving a three-year term received an equivalent bounty upon completion of their first year of service (OR IV, vol. 1, p. 532).

[126] Private Joe Davis was the first of the Quitman Greys to be killed in battle (Adams, "History of the Quitman Grays").

[127] John J. Hennessy, *Return to Bull Run: The Campaign and Battle of Second Manassas* (New York: Simon & Schuster, 1993), pp. 84-85, 364; OR 12, pt. 2, pp. 593-94.

[128] Warren, *Eleventh Georgia*, pp. 12-13, 45-49; OR 12, pt. 2, pp. 593-595; Hennessy, *Return to Bull Run*, pp. 412-421; William F. Fox, *Regimental Losses in the American Civil War, 1861-1865* (Albany: Brandow Printing, 1898; reprint, Dayton: Morningside, 1985), p. 564. The dead from Co. I were Lt. John B. Guerry, Sgt. William B. Groce, Cpl. D. B. Kirkland, and Pvt. D. L. Chapman. Given the regiment's overall strength, Company I probably carried only 35-40 men into the fight.

[129] Warren, *Eleventh Georgia*, p. 49.

[130] The two wounded men were Willoughby's messmates, Francis Marion Davis and William J. Pittman. Pittman later was killed in action at Funkstown, Maryland, as the 11th Georgia helped secure Lee's withdrawal after Gettysburg. See Ibid., pp. 12-13, 50-55; Henderson, *Georgia Rosters*, vol. 2, pp. 147, 150; OR 19, pt. 1, pp. 885-891, 893, 910-912; John Michael Priest, *Antietam: The Soldiers' Battle* (New York: Oxford Univ. Press, 1989), pp. 251, 271-277, 321.

[131] Warren, *Eleventh Georgia*, p. 56; Captain McDaniel, cited in Sams, *Unabated Trust*, p. 109.

[132] Many of the men who fell out of Lee's columns were truly sick, and the corn and green apples which comprised much of the army's rations in Maryland did precious little to sustain those who made it that far. Others, however, purposefully "lost" their shoes to avoid having to cross into the North, as they objected to waging an "offensive" war. For an excellent discussion of the problem, see Stephen W. Sears, *Landscape Turned Red: The Battle of Antietam* (New Haven: Ticknor & Fields, 1983), pp. 70-71, 175-176.

[133] Warren, *Eleventh Georgia*, pp. 56-57; Long, *Civil War Day by Day*, pp. 281-288. An exasperated President Lincoln finally had relieved McClellan on November 7, 1862.

[134] Warren, *Eleventh Georgia*, p. 57; Long, *Civil War Day by Day*, pp. 294-296. Although filed with the other microfilmed originals, this letter survives only in a typescript labeled "Copy of Dim Letter from W. H. Mangham to Father."

[135] Louise Biles Hill, *Joseph E. Brown and the Confederacy* (Chapel Hill: UNC Press, 1939; reprint, Westport: Greenwood Press, 1972) pp. 112-116; T. Conn Bryan, *Confederate Georgia* (Athens: UGA Press, 1953), pp. 40-41; Clarence L. Mohr, *On the Threshold of Freedom: Masters and Slaves in Civil War Georgia* (Athens: Univ. of Georgia Press, 1986), p. 212; Allen D. Candler, comp., *The Confederate Records of the State of Georgia*, vol. 2 (Atlanta: Charles P. Byrd, State Printer, 1909), pp. 226-231, 728-732;

McMillan, ed., *Alabama Confederate Reader*, p. 371. As Willoughby's letter implies, his family apparently had an adequate salt supply; they are not listed as recipients of salt issued in Randolph County (State of Georgia, Office of the Commissary General, Families Supplied with Salt 1862-1864, pp. 5, 361, 637, 715, 779, drawer 73, reel 4, GDAH).

[136] Words in brackets are cited from a brief excerpt of this letter printed in Grubbs, *Worth County*, p. 393. This excerpt quotes the offering price for a sack of salt as $5.00, whereas the typescript version renders it as $500.00. The former figure was doubtless correct, as confirmed by sack prices quoted in Hill, so I have changed it accordingly. Five dollars was an exorbitant price in its own right, as it represented almost half of a Confederate private's $11.00 monthly wage (CMSR, Willoughby H. Mangham; Hill, *Joseph E. Brown*, p. 113).

[137] Willoughby's friend Private John F. Davis was one of his old messmates, mentioned in the letter of August 28, 1861. John was killed at Gettysburg on July 2, 1863 (Henderson, *Georgia Rosters*, vol. 2, pp. 146).

[138] Warren, *Eleventh Georgia*, pp. 12-13, 57; Major McDaniel, cited in Sams, *Unabated Trust*, p. 109. General G. T. Anderson's Brigade was in Hood's Division of Longstreet's Corps. Its position was well south of the famous stone wall on Marye's Heights and slightly north of A. P. Hill's Division, which helped withstand the assault on Lee's southern flank. See Edward. J. Stackpole, *The Fredericksburg Campaign: Drama on the Rappahannock*, 2nd ed. (Harrisburg: Stackpole Books, 1991), pp. 107, 148, 177.

[139] President Lincoln issued the Proclamation on January 1, 1863 (Long, *Civil War Day by Day*, p. 306).

[140] 1860 Slave Census, Randolph County. In 1830, John Mangham owned seven slaves and his father Thomas owned twelve. When John's grandfather Solomon Mangham died in 1810, his estate inventory reflected ownership of five slaves. See 1830 Censuses, Talbot and Upson Counties; Hancock County, Court of Ordinary, Estate Records, Will Book A, pp. 172-174.

[141] Mr. Davis was clearly a relative of the Davis boys who served in the Quitman Greys. His delivery of mail for the Mangham family is neatly juxtaposed to Willoughby's renewed complaints about the postal system.

[142] He apparently believed that brother-in-law James Nichols's regiment was at Hanover Junction.

[143] Brigadier General Tom Cobb was a popular brigade commander, whose Georgians held the famous stone wall on Marye's Heights. He was mortally wounded there (Stackpole, *Fredericksburg Campaign*, pp. 222-225).

[144] Numerous historians have noted the direct correlation between morale on the home front and morale in the armies. See Wiley, *Johnny Reb*, p. 146; Robertson, *Soldiers Blue and Gray*, p. 136; Linderman, *Embattled Courage*, pp. 83, 86-97.

[145] OR 12, pt. 2, p. 595; Warren, *Eleventh Georgia*, pp. 12-13; Henderson, *Georgia Rosters*, vol. 2, pp. 145-152.

[146] The "Mud March" was the name wags gave to Burnside's attempt on January 21-22, 1863, to outflank Lee's position at Fredericksburg. The ill-fated stratagem floundered in torrential rains and bottomless mud. Lincoln relieved the beleaguered Burnside three days later (Stackpole, *Fredericksburg Campaign*, pp. 244-250, 264).

[147] Guiney's Station, Virginia, some ten miles south of Fredericksburg.

[148] Major McDaniel, cited in Sams, *Unabated Trust*, pp. 133-135; William C. Oates, *The War Between the Union and the Confederacy and its Lost Opportunities* (1905; reprint, Dayton: Morningside, 1985), p. 175; Steven A. Cormier, *The Siege of Suffolk: The Forgotten Campaign, April 11-May 4, 1863*, 2nd ed. (Lynchburg: H. E. Howard, Inc., 1989), pp. 8-9.

[149] Mr. Adams probably was the father of George W. and John J. Adams of the Quitman Greys (Warren, *Eleventh Georgia*, p. 12; Henderson, *Georgia Rosters*, vol. 2, p. 146).

[150] The family of Pvt. Hayas Graddy, Willoughby's uncle.

[151] Cormier, *Siege of Suffolk*, pp. 2-4, 100-104; John H. Worsham, *One of Jackson's Foot Cavalry* (reprint; Wilmington: Broadfoot Publishing Co., 1987), p. 122; Wilbur S. Nye, *Here Come the Rebels!* (Baton Rouge: LSU Press, 1965; reprint, Dayton: Morningside, 1988), pp. 4-6.

[152] Major McDaniel, cited in Sams, *Unabated Trust*, pp. 150-161; Long, *Civil War Day by Day*, pp. 337, 348; Ernest B. Furgurson, *Chancellorsville 1863: The Souls of the Brave* (New York: Vintage Books, 1993), pp. 113-114, 345-346.

[153] Long, *Civil War Day by Day*, pp. 361-367.

[154] James M. Mason and John Slidell were Confederate emissaries to England and France, respectively. They lobbied unsuccessfully for diplomatic recognition and military intervention on the Confederacy's behalf (Sifakis, *Who Was Who in the Civil War*, pp. 436-437, 598).

[155] In some cases, the Confederate armies had to resort to wholesale furloughs in order to lend some semblance of legitimacy to large-scale absenteeism (Wiley, *Johnny Reb*, pp. 142-144).

[156] A tent fly was the forerunner of the modern shelter half; two buttoned together made a small two-man tent. The Confederate soldier who had one was lucky indeed, as most men had nothing more than a blanket and perhaps an oilcloth when on campaign.

[157] Little was elected colonel on November 3, 1862 (Warren, *Eleventh Georgia*, p. 5).

[158] OR 27, pt. 2, pp. 396-403; Harry W. Pfanz, *Gettysburg: The Second Day* (Chapel Hill: UNC Press, 1987), pp. 245-253, 264-66, 294-95, 302.

[159] Henderson, *Georgia Rosters*, vol. 2, pp. 145-152. For calculations estimating the regiment's strength, see John W. Busey and David G. Martin, *Regimental Strengths at Gettysburg* (Baltimore: Gateway Press, 1982), p. 135. William F. Fox calculated that the 11th Georgia's casualties totaled 194 in the three days' fighting, but the regiment reported 199 on July 2 alone. If this official report is correct, then the 11th Georgia

should rank ninth on the regimental casualty lists, rather than tenth. This ignores casualties suffered in the engagement on July 3 (see Fox, *Regimental Losses*, p. 569). John Adams recalled in his memoir that Willoughby was wounded on July 2 at the Wheatfield, where the unit suffered tremendous casualties, but unit muster rolls single him out as the only member of the Quitman Greys injured on July 3.

[160] OR 27, pt. 2, pp. 402-403.

[161] CMSR, Willoughby H. Mangham.

[162] OR II, vol. 6, pp. 1039-1041. Willoughby and his fellow prisoners were crammed into barracks to minimize fuel costs, while several available buildings stood empty. As a result, the prisoners averaged only 176 cubic feet of space apiece, in a building 16 feet tall. Thus, each man's floor space was approximately three feet by four feet. A November 1863 medical inspector described low-lying Fort Delaware as "an utterly unfit location for a prison." A cavalry officer sent to investigate in the following month, however, praised every aspect of the prison operation as perfectly adequate. (See Ibid., pp. 516-518, 651-653.)

[163] Confederate CMSRs typically reflect a number of deserters or prisoners who used these avenues to obtain release from prison. See also D. Alexander Brown, *The Galvanized Yankees* (Urbana: Univ. of Illinois Press, 1963), pp. 1-2, 63-69. For one account of an unprovoked shooting at Fort Delaware, see Rod Gragg, *The Illustrated Confederate Reader* (New York: Harper & Row, 1989), pp. 146-148.

[164] Marvel, *Andersonville*, pp. x-xi, 25-27, 43-44, 233-234.

[165] As this brief letter is almost illegible on microfilm, I have quoted it in full from Grubbs, *Worth County*, pp. 393-394.

[166] The letter was marked "c/o J. W. Hain." Apparently, a relative of one of Willoughby's fellow prisoners was allowed to visit the prison. No family named Ham or Hain appears in the 1860 Randolph County census.

[167] *The Appomattox Roster* (Richmond: The Society, 1887; reprint, New York: Antiquarian Press, 1962), pp. 102-103; Sifakis, *Confederate Armies: Georgia and South Carolina*, pp. 207-208.

[168] Long, *Civil War Day by Day*, pp. 670-671, 682, 690.

[169] Wiley, *Johnny Reb*, p. 202; Robertson, *Soldiers Blue and Gray*, p. 107.

[170] Grubbs, *Worth County*, pp. 389-390.

[171] Ibid.; Confederate Pension Records, Worth County (Mrs. W. H. Mangham), drawer 277, reel 11, GDAH.

[172] Anne Kendrick Walker, *Russell County in Retrospect: An Epic of the Far Southeast* (Richmond: Dietz Press, 1950), pp. 209-213; Letter, Solomon R. Mangham to John G. Mangham, August 28, 1854, in Family Letters of Willoughby H. Mangham, 1849-1868, GDAH; Washington County Tax Rolls, reel 1 (1837-1878), reel 637, TSL. I transcribed Willis Mangham's birthdate from his gravestone in Resthaven Cemetery, Bell County, where it was relocated upon the construction of Belton Lake. For evidence of the "perfect mania on the subject of emmigration to Texas and Louisiana," see Grady

McWhiney, Warner O. Moore, Jr., and Robert F. Pace, eds., *"Fear God and Walk Humbly": The Agricultural Journal of James Mallory, 1843-1877* (Tuscaloosa: Univ. of Alabama Press, 1997), pp. 154, 168.

[173] Case 29 Alabama 81, Mangham v. Cox and Waring, in *Alabama Reports*, June Term, 1856.

[174] *History of McLennan, Falls, Bell and Coryell Counties*, pp. 867-868; 1860 Census, Slave Census, and Agricultural Schedule, Bell County; 1900 Census, Bell County. I have derived his sons' birth months from cemetery inscriptions and the 1900 census. The infant slave girl was a mulatto, which poses the obvious question of paternity. Unfortunately, this will remain an insoluble riddle unless additional source material comes to light. For penetrating discussions on the emotion-laden question of miscegenation in the South, see James C. Cobb, *The Most Southern Place on Earth: The Mississippi Delta and the Roots of Regional Identity* (New York: Oxford Univ. Press, 1992), pp. 26, 156-160; W. J. Cash, *The Mind of the South* (Alfred A. Knopf, Inc., 1941; reprint, New York: Vintage Books, 1991), pp. 84-87; James M. McPherson, *Drawn With the Sword: Reflections on the American Civil War* (New York: Oxford Univ. Press, 1996), pp. 44-47.

[175] Muster Roll of Capt. James W. Morris's Company, Beat No. 4, Bell Co., Texas, 27th Brigade, Texas Militia, June 1861, RG 401, TSA. The author is indebted to the West Bell Genealogical Society, Killeen, Texas, for rosters of Bell County's ranging companies for the year 1859.

[176] CMSR, Willis W. Mangham, 21st Texas Cavalry; Muster Roll of Capt. Freeman's Company, Carter's Regiment, April 2, 1862, RG 401, TSA; B. P. Gallaway, ed., *Texas, The Dark Corner of the Confederacy: Contemporary Accounts of the Lone Star State in the Civil War*, 3rd ed. (Lincoln: Univ. of Nebraska Press, 1994), p. 99.

[177] OR 53, p. 790; Georgianne Bailey, Ph.D. dissertation, *Between the Enemy and Texas: Parsons's Texas Cavalry in the Civil War* (Ann Arbor: UMI, 1987), pp. 41-51; OR IV, vol. 1, pp. 1094-1100; George W. Tyler, *The History of Bell County* (San Antonio: The Naylor Co., 1936), p. 224.

[178] Bailey, *Enemy and Texas*, pp. 48-51, 57; CMSR, Willis W. Mangham; William Physick Zuber, *My Eighty Years in Texas*, ed. Janis Boyle Mayfield (Austin: Univ. of Texas Press, 1971), pp. 134-135.

[179] Zuber, *Eighty Years*, pp. 134-138; Major William Martin "Buck" Walton, *An Epitome of My Life: Civil War Reminiscences* (Austin: The Waterloo Press, 1965), pp. 22-23; Bailey, *Enemy and Texas*, pp. 57-58, 61-62.

[180] Walton, *Epitome*, pp. 23-25; Bailey, *Enemy and Texas*, pp. 63-65.

[181] Bailey, *Enemy and Texas*, pp. 68-69; Zuber, *Eighty Years*, p. 142; OR 13, pp. 883-884. The cavalry regiments-turned-footsloggers fought the rest of the war as "dismounted cavalry," disdaining redesignation as infantry units. See Stephen B. Oates, *Confederate Cavalry West of the River* (Austin: Univ. of Texas Press, 1961), p. 48.

[182] Zuber, *Eighty Years*, pp. 143-146; Walton, *Epitome*, pp. 25-27; Bailey, *Enemy and Texas*, pp. 69-71, 181-187.

[183] *History of McLennan, Falls, Bell and Coryell Counties*, pp. 867-868.

[184] William Watson, *Life in the Confederate Army, Being the Observations and Experiences of an Alien in the South During the American Civil War* (London: Chapman and Hall, 1887; reprint, Baton Rouge: LSU Press, 1995), pp. 140-141.

[185] *History of McLennan, Falls, Bell and Coryell Counties*, pp. 867-868; Zuber, *Eighty Years*, pp. 146-153; Walton, *Epitome*, pp. 26-37; Bailey, *Enemy and Texas*, pp. 187-196.

[186] Bailey, *Enemy and Texas*, p. 197.

[187] Ibid., pp. 199-203; Zuber, *Eighty Years*, pp. 150-157, 160-165.

[188] Bailey, *Enemy and Texas*, pp. 240-243, 247; Zuber, *Eighty Years*, pp. 166-168; letter, John A. Stranahan to wife, May 15, 1863 (typescript), p. 1, in 21st Texas Cavalry Unit Files, CRC. General Holmes was interested in Marmaduke's proposal as early as mid-February (see OR 32, pt. 2, p. 788).

[189] OR 22, pt. 1, pp. 285-286, 300; Bailey, *Enemy and Texas*, pp. 245-251.

[190] OR 22, pt. 1, pp. 286, 300; Bailey, *Enemy and Texas*, pp. 251-253; letter, John A. Stranahan to wife, May 15, 1863, p. 1; Zuber, *Eighty Years*, pp. 167-170. Bailey adopts a position consistent with Carter's critics, who scathingly criticized his lieutenant colonel's slow approach march and use of artillery against enemy videttes; even Marmaduke undertook a brief critique in his after-action report. These criticisms share one fault: they all assume *ex post facto* that the Federal garrison was merely a cipher in the entire equation, and that their hasty evacuation was a foregone conclusion. Available sources fail to prove this assumption, however, and it seems plausible that a more rapid approach march may have resulted in pitting the half-strength 21st Texas against 600 alarmed Federals still ensconced in the town. The outcome of such an engagement was anything but a foregone conclusion.

[191] OR 22, pt. 1, pp. 286, 300; Bailey, *Enemy and Texas*, pp. 251-253; letter, John A. Stranahan to wife, May 15, 1863, p. 1; Zuber, *Eighty Years*, pp. 169-173; Walton, *Epitome*, pp. 46-47. Writing long after the war, Walton declared that he and his men "killed forty two on the ground—wounded thirty seven who died that night—and one man, who was shot through the throat, recovered." Zuber was involved in the pursuit as well, and recalled counting fourteen dead and the same number of wounded. Writing on the day of the fight, Stranahan estimated that the Texans had killed twenty Federals and wounded about the same number, while capturing another thirty. Colonel Carter believed the overall enemy loss was 100 killed, 19 wounded, and 38 captured. Colonel Smart, commanding the 3rd Missouri State Militia Cavalry (U.S.) in the engagement, estimated his losses at fifty, pending an accurate count (OR 22, pt. 1, p. 263.) Initial reports to Brigadier General Davidson, commanding the District of St. Louis, indicated that Smart had suffered 200 casualties. Davidson's report hastened to append copies of orders he had previously issued to Smart, "preparing him for such possible contingency." See OR 22, pt. 1, p. 254.

[192] OR 22, pt. 1, pp. 286-287, 301; Bailey, *Enemy and Texas*, p. 254; letter, John A. Stranahan to wife, May 15, 1863, pp. 1-2; Zuber, *Eighty Years*, pp. 173-175.

[193] OR 22, pt. 1, pp. 287, 301-302; Bailey, *Enemy and Texas*, pp. 254-259; letter, John A. Stranahan to wife, May 15, 1863, pp. 2-3; Zuber, *Eighty Years*, pp. 175-177.

[194] OR 22, pt. 1, pp. 287, 302; Bailey, *Enemy and Texas*, pp. 258-264; letter, John A. Stranahan to wife, May 15, 1863, pp. 2-4; Zuber, *Eighty Years*, pp. 177-184; Walton, *Epitome*, p. 48.

[195] OR 22, pt. 1, pp. 287-288, 302; Bailey, *Enemy and Texas*, pp. 262-266; letter, John A. Stranahan to wife, May 15, 1863, pp. 4-5; Zuber, *Eighty Years*, pp. 184-186; Walton, *Epitome*, pp. 50-53.

[196] OR 22, pt. 1, p. 288, 302; Bailey, *Enemy and Texas*, pp. 266-269; letter, John A. Stranahan to wife, May 15, 1863, pp. 5-8; Zuber, *Eighty Years*, pp. 168, 179, 184; Walton, *Epitome*, p. 45.

[197] OR 22, pt. 1, pp. 323-328; Bailey, *Enemy and Texas*, p. 279; letter, John A. Stranahan to wife, May 15, 1863, pp. 6-7; Zuber, *Eighty Years*, pp. 186-188; Walton, *Epitome*, pp. 53, 55-57.

[198] Letter, John A. Stranahan to wife, May 15, 1863, pp. 6-7; Zuber, *Eighty Years*, p. 187; Walton, *Epitome*, pp. 53-57. For additional perspectives on the Confederate soldier's opinions about army discipline, see Mitchell, *Civil War Soldiers*, pp. 57-59; Wiley, *Johnny Reb*, pp. 217-243. Walton made little secret of his sense of having served in the less-glorious backwaters of the Civil War. This feeling probably was widespread among Trans-Mississippi veterans, given that the postwar South memorialized Lee's Army of Northern Virginia above all others. For a good example of an attempt to combat their relegation to third-class status in the pantheon of Confederate heroism, see ex-Private George H. Hogan, "Parsons's Brigade of Texas Cavalry," CV 33: 17-20. Hogan served in Company E of Parsons's 12th Texas Cavalry.

[199] Walton, *Epitome*, pp. 53-55; OR 22, pt. 2, p. 845.

[200] Walton, *Epitome*, pp. 53-55.

[201] Bailey, *Enemy and Texas*, pp. 277-282, 312-313; Letter, Sam B. Marr to sister, July 16, 1863 (typescript), and Letter, George W. Laurence to Sallie, August 17, 1862, in 21st Texas Cavalry Unit Files, CRC; Zuber, *Eighty Years*, pp. 186-190.

[202] Bailey, *Enemy and Texas*, pp. 312-314; Long, *Civil War Day by Day*, pp. 401-402.

[203] OR 22, pt. 2, pp. 1031-1034.

[204] Ibid.; Bailey, *Enemy and Texas*, pp. 319-321. Sam Marr summarized the epidemic in plain language, writing: "all the regment is sick with the shill nearly them that is not now has bin[.]" See letter, Sam B. Marr to sister, undated (believed to be September or October 1863).

[205] CMSR, Willis W. Mangham.

[206] OR 22, pt. 1, pp. 730-739; Bailey, *Enemy and Texas*, pp. 323-325; Walton, *Epitome*, pp. 74-76.

[207] OR 22, pt. 1, pp. 730-739; Walton, *Epitome*, pp. 77-78; Bailey, *Enemy and Texas*, pp. 325-326.

[208] Bailey, *Enemy and Texas*, pp. 326-331; Zuber, *Eighty Years*, pp. 196-197. The near mutiny at Churchill's appointment to command was a near-replay of events in late 1862, when Brigadier General Hawes was assigned to command the brigade. The resulting uproar convinced Hawes to leave well enough alone, and Parsons remained in charge. See Bailey, *Enemy and Texas*, pp. 201-202.

[209] Zuber, *Eighty Years*, pp. 198-199.

[210] Bailey, *Enemy and Texas*, pp. 342-347; Ludwell H. Johnson, *Red River Campaign: Politics and Cotton in the Civil War* (Johns Hopkins Press, 1958; reprint, Kent: Kent State Univ. Press, 1993), pp. 96-100.

[211] Bailey, *Enemy and Texas*, pp. 348-349; ORS I, vol. 6, p. 378; Letter, John A. Stranahan to wife, May 26, 1864, p. 1; Zuber, *Eighty Years*, p. 202.

[212] Bailey, *Enemy and Texas*, pp. 350-355; ORS I, vol. 6, pp. 378-379; Letter, John A. Stranahan to wife, May 26, 1864, p. 1; Johnson, *Red River*, pp. 211-213.

[213] Bailey, *Enemy and Texas*, pp. 355-356; ORS I, vol. 6, pp. 379-380; Letter, John A. Stranahan to wife, May 26, 1864, pp. 1-2; Zuber, *Eighty Years*, pp. 202-204.

[214] ORS I, vol. 6, p. 380; Letter, John A. Stranahan to wife, May 26, 1864, p. 2; Zuber, *Eighty Years*, pp. 203-204. Also known as Old Cane or Old River, the Cane River previously had been the course of the Red River.

[215] Johnson, *Red River*, pp. 220-226; ORS I, vol. 6, p. 380. For more on Willis Mangham's Louisiana cousins, see Chapter IX. Grandsons of Josiah Mangum (Mangham), these men were his second cousins, once removed.

[216] Johnson, *Red River*, pp. 220-226; ORS I, vol. 6, p. 381; Letter, John A. Stranahan to wife, May 26, 1864, pp. 2-3; Zuber, *Eighty Years*, pp. 206-209.

[217] Johnson, *Red River*, pp. 232-234; ORS I, vol. 6, p. 381; Report of Lt. Gen. Richard Taylor, April 19 to May 21, 1864, dated June 1, 1864, in "Unpublished After-Action Reports From the Red River," *CWR* 4, no. 2, p. 120; Zuber, *Eighty Years*, pp. 206-209; Letter, John A. Stranahan to wife, May 26, 1864, pp. 2-3. Cavalry regiments comprised five squadrons of two companies each, numbered from the right of the line. As the third company in line, Willis Mangham's Company D normally rode as the right-hand company of the 2nd Squadron. See Major William Gilham, *Manual of Instruction for the Volunteers and Militia of the United States* (Philadelphia: Charles Desilver, 1861; reprint, n.d.), pp. 33, 39-42.

[218] OR 34, pt. 1, pp. 596-597; ORS I, vol. 6, pp. 382-383; Zuber, *Eighty Years*, pp. 209-214; Letter, John A. Stranahan to wife, May 26, 1864, pp. 3-4.

[219] Johnson, *Red River*, pp. 248-250; ORS I, vol. 6, p. 384; Letter, John A. Stranahan to wife, May 26, 1864, pp. 4-5.

[220] OR 34, pt. 1, p. 626; ORS I, vol. 6, pp. 384-385; Zuber, *Eighty Years*, pp. 217-218; Letter, John A. Stranahan to wife, May 26, 1864, pp. 6-8.

[221] OR 34, pt. 1, p. 627; *ORS* I, vol. 6, p. 385; Letter, John A. Stranahan to wife, May 26, 1864, pp. 8-9.

[222] OR 34, pt. 1, p. 627; *ORS* I, vol. 6, pp. 385-386; Letter, John A. Stranahan to wife, May 26, 1864, p. 10; Johnson, *Red River*, pp. 273-274.

[223] OR 34, pt. 1, pp. 615-616, 627; *ORS* I, vol. 6, pp. 386-387; Letter, John A. Stranahan to wife, May 26, 1864, pp. 10-11; Johnson, *Red River*, pp. 274-275; Bailey, *Enemy and Texas*, pp. 363-365.

[224] OR 34, pt. 1, pp. 320-321, 615-616; *ORS* I, vol. 6, pp. 386-388; Letter, Sam B. Marr to sister, July 16, 1863; Letter, John A. Stranahan to wife, May 26, 1864, pp. 11-12; Johnson, *Red River*, p. 275; Bailey, *Enemy and Texas*, p. 366; Walton, *Epitome*, p. 83. General Wharton's congratulatory order to his troops asserted that Federal prisoners admitted suffering 800 casualties at Yellow Bayou, and he added that his men had found thirty Federals dead on the field, plus another 65 graves marked "Killed in the action of the 18th May."

[225] OR 34, pt. 1, p. 616.

[226] Letter, John A. Stranahan to wife, May 26, 1864, pp. 12-13.

[227] Bailey, *Enemy and Texas*, pp. 371-372, 383-384; OR 41, pt. 1, pp. 1003, 1458; pt. 3, pp. 915, 950; pt. 4, pp. 1027, 1100, 1131.

[228] Zuber, *Eighty Years*, pp. 225-228; Walton, *Epitome*, pp. 92-93.

[229] *History of McLennan, Falls, Bell and Coryell Counties*, pp. 867-868. For more on the scope of lawlessness in the Bell County area, see David P. Smith's chapter in Daniel E. Sutherland, ed., *Guerrillas, Unionists, and Violence on the Confederate Home Front* (Fayetteville: Univ. of Arkansas Press, 1999).

[230] Ibid.; 1880 Census and Agricultural Schedule, Bell County; Bell County, Deed Book B (1870-1879), p. 344; Deed Book F (1886-1888), p. 343. The 1870 census shows a 25-year-old black woman named Charlotte Mangham living with the Willis Mangham family as a domestic servant, along with her four children. Her oldest child, Jane, was a girl aged 10. Charlotte (unmarried, age 40) and six children still lived next door to Willis in 1880, with her occupation listed as "cook." In all probability, Charlotte was the 17-year-old slave girl and Jane was the infant listed in the 1860 Slave Census.

[231] *History of McLennan, Falls, Bell and Coryell Counties*, pp. 867-868; Bell County Probate Minutes, Book G, p. 29.

[232] *History of McLennan, Falls, Bell and Coryell Counties*, pp. 867-868. The author viewed the original roster of the Bell County Ex-Confederate Veterans Association at the Bell County Museum; it is also available in transcribed format. See Leannell W. Porter, comp., *Roster of Ex-Confederate Veterans, with Remarks and Roster of Camp 122, Texas, Original Members* (N.p.: Bell County Historical Survey Committee, 1966), pp. 39, 77. For a comprehensive listing of the higher headquarters to which the regiment belonged during the war, see Stewart Sifakis, *Compendium of the Confederate Armies: Texas* (New York: Facts on File, 1995), pp. 78-79. Colonel Parsons delivered a written tribute to the survivors of his old brigade in 1878, in which he eloquently eulogized

their contribution to the Confederate war effort. See *A Brief and Condensed History of Parsons' Texas Cavalry Brigade, Composed of Twelfth, Nineteenth, Twenty-First, Morgan's Battalion, and Pratt's Battery of Artillery of the Confederate States* (Waxahatchie: J. M. Flemister, Printer, 1892), pp. 253-266. A fascinating document, it provides subtle postwar evidence of the emotional distance between Carter's Regiment and the brigade's other units. It is no accident that the book's company rosters are either incomplete or non-existent for the 21st Texas. Company D lacks even a list of commissioned officers (see p. 327).

[233] I have transcribed the Mangham gravestones at Resthaven Cemetery. The Bell County Library has an extensive enumeration entitled *Bell County Tombstone Records.*

[234] Putnam County, Court of Ordinary, Minutes 1819-1831, Book AA, pp. 88, 98, drawer 304, reel 58, GDAH; Hancock County, Court of Ordinary, Tax Digest, 1808, drawer 50, reel 78, GDAH. In the 1808 tax rolls prepared for Captain Harper's District of Hancock County, Solomon Mangham's entry was followed immediately by James Mangham, John McArther, and Willis Mangham.

[235] Putnam County, Court of Ordinary, Minutes 1819-1831, Book AA, pp. 88, 98, drawer 304, reel 58, GDAH; Brent H. Holcomb, *Death and Obituary Notices from the Southern Christian Advocate 1867-1878* (Columbia: SCMAR, 1993), issue of May 10, 1871; Talbot County, Court of Ordinary, Estate Records, Wills (1828-1856), pp. 258-262, drawer 123, reel 35, GDAH. Elizabeth's father was a nephew of James Thweatt, who died in Hancock County in 1814. Solomon Mangham's estate records show that he owed money for a judgment Thweatt had obtained against him. See Randy Jones, Thweatt Family homepage, http://www.charweb.org/gen/thweatt/welcome.html; Hancock County, Estate Records, Will Book A, p. 176, drawer 51, reel 60, GDAH.

[236] Silas E. Lucas, *The 1832 Gold Lottery of Georgia: Containing a List of the Fortunate Drawers in Said Lottery* (Easley: Southern Historical Press, 1986), p. 243; 1830 Censuses, Talbot and Upson Counties; 1850 Census, Talbot County. Henry Mangham served with a short-lived Talbot County militia company in May 1836 during the Creek War (see http://www.wso.net/ga/creekwarrecords.htm).

[237] William H. Davidson, *A Rockaway in Talbot: Travels in an Old Georgia County,* 4 vols. (West Point: Hester Printing Co., 1983-1990), vol. 4, p. 189; Frank Lawrence Owsley, *Plain Folk of the Old South* (Baton Rouge: LSU Press, 1949; reprint, 1982), pp. 94-95.

[238] Pike County, Court of Ordinary, Guardians' Bonds, 1829-1955, drawer 168, reel 1, p. 70; reel 2, pp. 137-138, 280-281, 402-403, GDAH; Talbot County Probate Court, Annual Returns vols. A-B, 1828-1848, pp. 289, 373, 474, drawer 123, reel 49, GDAH; Davidson, *Rockaway,* pp. 189-191, 193, 196; Talbot County, Court of Ordinary, Estate Records, Wills (1828-1856), pp. 258-262, drawer 123, reel 35, GDAH; Marriage Records, Talbot County; 1850 Census, Talbot County; Grubbs, *Worth County,* p. 110.

[239] Davidson, *Rockaway,* pp. 188-193; Talbot County, Inferior Court, Minutes for County Purposes (1828-1855), vol. A, January 1839, drawer 124, reel 22, GDAH; 1850

Census, Talbot County; Talbot County, Court of Ordinary, Estate Records, Wills (1828-1856), pp. 258-262, drawer 123, reel 35, GDAH; Owsley, *Plain Folk*, pp. 133-135, 146-149. Owsley notes that the academy system of education was both widespread and successful in the South. The 57 academies operating in Georgia in 1860 charged an average of $15.50 for a year's schooling in elementary subjects, or $26 for high school subjects. Mary Caroline Mangham married John Wynn (or Winn) in Crawford County in 1842; additional research might determine a connection between him and the John Winn (Wynn) who provided security for Willis Mangham's guardianship of Henry Mangham in the mid-1820s. (See Crawford County Marriage Records, 1823-1850.)

[240] Talbot County, Court of Ordinary, Estate Records, Wills (1828-1856), pp. 258-262, drawer 123, reel 35, GDAH; 1860 Mortality Census, Taylor County; Essie Jones Childs, *They Tarried in Taylor (A Georgia County): 1860, 1870, 1880, & 1900 Census Records, Church Records, & Family Records* (Warner Robins: Central Georgia Genealogical Society, 1992), p. 51. Carsonville became part of Taylor County in early 1854, when the legislature gave the young county part of Talbot's eastern districts. See Pat Bryant, comp., *Georgia Counties: Their Changing Boundaries*, 2nd ed. (Atlanta: State Printing Office, 1983), pp. 97-98.

[241] Davidson, *Rockaway*, p. 193; Taylor County, Court of Ordinary, Administrator and Guardians' Bonds (1852-1915), vol. A, p. 88 (see http://www.rootsweb.com/~gataylor/admin.htm); Taylor County, Court of Ordinary, Inventories and Appraisals (1859), pp. 131-140, drawer 169, reel 29, GDAH. John T. Gray was the son of Archibald Gray; Mitchell and Greer were likewise members of the Manghams' extended kinship group. The current author is indebted to Mrs. Virginia Crilley, who maintains the excellent Taylor County homepage, for her assistance in researching the James O. Mangham family.

[242] Davidson, *Rockaway*, pp. 189, 193; 1860 Census, Taylor County; Childs, *Tarried in Taylor*, p. 51; Grubbs, *Worth County*, p. 110; Guelda Hay and Mildred Stewart, *Cemeteries of Taylor County* (Warner Robins: Central Georgia Genealogical Society, 1990), p. 48.

[243] Grubbs, *Worth County*, p. 110; OR IV, vol. 1, p. 1081; vol. 2, pp. 161-162; Albert Burton Moore, *Conscription and Conflict in the Confederacy* (Macmillan, 1924; reprint, Columbia: USC Press, 1996), pp. 54-56. Moore notes that newspaper editors scoffed that a "good soldier was 'frequently spoiled in making up an indifferent pedagogue,'" as well as scorning overnight apothecaries "who could not analyze the simplest compound or put up the plainest prescription in a satisfactory manner if his life depended upon it."

[244] OR IV, vol. 1, pp. 1082-1084.

[245] OR IV, vol. 2, pp. 160-162; Moore, *Conscription and Conflict*, 70-72, 75, 143-145; Oates, *War Between the Union and the Confederacy*, p. 158; 1860 Slave Census, Taylor County.

[246] Candler, comp., *Confederate Records*, vol. 2, pp. 456-462.

[247] Ibid., pp. 456-462; OR IV, vol. 3, pp. 310-311; "Report of the Adjutant and Inspector General of Georgia for the Years 1862-1863," *Atlanta Daily Intelligencer*, November 22, 1863.

[248] ORS II, vol. 6, pp. 215-217; CMSR, James O. Mangham, 5th Georgia State Guard; Record of Events Cards, 5th Georgia State Guard; CMH 6, *Georgia*, p. 28; Sifakis, *Confederate Armies: South Carolina and Georgia*, p. 191; 1860 Census, Taylor County. Militia officers could muster units into the State Guard; Brewer apparently served in this capacity.

[249] Record of Events Cards, 5th Georgia State Guard; Hill, *Joseph E. Brown*, pp. 112-16; Office of the Commissary General, Families Supplied with Salt 1862-1864, drawer 73, reel 4, pp. 46, 318, 577, GDAH; Taylor County, Court of Ordinary, Administrator and Guardians' Bonds (1852-1915), vol. A, p. 127 (see http://www.rootsweb.com/~gataylor/admin.htm); General Order No. 2, Regiment State Troops, September 24, 1863, printed in *Columbus Daily Times*, September 28, 1863, typescript in Civil War Miscellany, Unit Files, 5th Georgia State Guard, drawer 283, reel 58, GDAH.

[250] OR 28, pt. 2, pp. 553-554.

[251] OR IV, vol. 3, pp. 310-311; "An Act to re-organize the Militia of the State of Georgia," December 14, 1863, in *MDT*, December 24, 1863.

[252] State of Georgia, Adjutant General, Military Records, vol. 5 (1861-1866), "Roster of Commissioned Officers in Georgia Militia under the Reorganization Act of 1864," drawer 40, reel 18, GDAH; Childs, *Tarried in Taylor*, p. 11; Candler, comp., *Confederate Records*, vol. 2, pp. 703-704, 800; Taylor County, Court of Ordinary, Administrator and Guardians' Bonds (1852-1915), vol. A, p. 151. Further indications that he may not have served beyond February 1864 are found in Georgia's salt issue records of late 1864, as well as the national Civil War veterans' census of 1910. Neither source reflects that James performed additional military service. See OR IV, vol. 3, pp. 178-180; 1910 Census, Camden County, Georgia.

[253] 1870 and 1880 Censuses, Taylor County; Grubbs, *Worth County*, pp. 110-112.

[254] Childs, *Tarried in Taylor*, pp. 10-11; Grubbs, *Worth County*, pp. 110-112; *Death and Obituary Notices from the Southern Christian Advocate 1867-1878*, issue of May 10, 1871; Marilyn Neisler Windham, *Marriages, Deaths, etc. From The Butler Herald, 1876-1896* (Warner Robins: Central Georgia Genealogical Society, 1995), pp. 50, 59, 72.

[255] Grubbs, *Worth County*, pp. 111-112; *Southeast Georgian*, January 5, 1906. The author is indebted to John H. Christian of the Bryan-Lang Historical Library, Woodbine, Georgia, for his assistance in researching James O. Mangham's career in Camden County.

[256] Ibid.; *Butler Herald*, May 9, 1911.

[257] *Butler Herald*, May 2, May 9, 1911; Grubbs, *Worth County*, p. 111.

[258] *Butler Herald*, May 9, 1911.

Discovering the "Vanished Hand and the Voice That is Stilled" *Basic Research Techniques & Your Civil War Ancestors*

LEVEL ONE research assumes you wish to identify your Civil War ancestor and obtain basic documents such as his service and pension records. Subsequently, you can identify and obtain extant regimental histories and other secondary sources, including battle or campaign histories, to help you understand what he experienced.

Task #1: Identify your ancestor

a. Start with the obvious: family recollections, records, genealogical charts, letters, photos, and copies of county histories that family members may possess. You may identify your ancestor within minutes of starting your research!

b. Go to the websites of major commercial genealogical operations such as Ancestry.com™ and Family Tree Maker™. These have thousands of family trees accessible to you, as well as researchers' forums. Scan the questions, answers, and post your own queries; often you will encounter a researcher who has already studied your family tree in detail. Given the boom in genealogical research and publishing, you may even discover existing books that provide all the answers you're seeking!

c. Enter your family name on an Internet search engine. You will obtain hundreds or even thousands of "hits," which you can scan or refine to determine applicability to your purposes.

d. Census records.

(1) Start on the Internet, which allows you to tap into the GenWeb resources that are growing by leaps and bounds every day. Look up the county names that you suspect are applicable to your search, and you will find their homepages often contain staggering amounts of information. Many sites include transcripts of census records for that county.

(2) In many cases you will need to visit the state archives or a genealogical library to study their microfilmed census records. Call them first to get advice on where to find census records on the region you need. Many repositories maintain regional census rolls, but few have holdings that are national in scope. You may need to visit the National Archives in Washington, the massive holdings of the Church of Latter Day Saints (LDS) in Salt Lake City, or order selected LDS records through a local branch of the LDS. Before undertaking a big trip, however, remember that local and county librarians will often answer your basic census questions for free. Give them a call early in your research. (Find out their locations and contact information from the commercial genealogy sites, or consult a listing from your nearest genealogical library.)

(3) Some census notes:

    - The 1850 census is the first one to name anyone besides the head of household.

    - Bound indexes provide you easy access to the censuses of 1870 and earlier, although they are fraught with transcription and spelling errors. Later censuses use an indexing system called SOUNDEX. This help you avoid errors caused by misspelled names ("Mangham" sounds like "Mangum," and both are coded as M525), but they are bulky and very slow to use. Also, if "Mangham" was transcribed incorrectly as "Maugham," you now have to look at every record filed under M250 as well. Many SOUNDEX rolls indiscriminately combine all cards in a numeric series, so a researcher must comb through every card from M520 to M529, for instance, thus immensely magnifying the required effort.

- The 1890 Census was destroyed by fire. This has had a huge impact on tracing the Civil War generation. (By consolidating state censuses and other records, the commercial genealogical companies are developing many resources that partially offset this shortcoming.)

- Census records in 1850 and 1860 included separate schedules for free population; slave population (by owner's name, number, age, color, and gender, but not by the slave's name); and agricultural production schedules.

- Expect errors in the census records. They are a great starting point to provide you someone's name, gender, age, occupation, nativity, and literacy, but the entries contain enough errors to make experienced users cautious in their application.

Task #2: Identify your ancestor's unit and obtain his pension and service records.

a. The commercial genealogy companies now have databases that may allow you to determine your ancestor's military unit(s) without ever leaving your desk. Try these first! Also check county and regimental websites.

b. Many Southern states have bound indexes of their Civil War soldiers. Look in my bibliography and obtain the appropriate titles from your nearest genealogical library, which may own a copy or can obtain one through Interlibrary Loan (ILL).

c. Contact the appropriate state Department of Archives and History. (See a great list of names and numbers in Segars, *In Search of Confederate Ancestors: The Guide*). Again, you should use the Internet first; many states are creating databases with their soldiers' names and units. In any event, a visit to their website or a call to an archivist will get you on track quickly to obtain what you need.

d. Once you know your Civil War ancestor's name and unit, it is usually easy to order his service and pension records from the state archives. It helps to know his unit first, especially if his name is a common one, but a man with an uncommon name is often found readily. State archives vary significantly in their holdings, so you may need to order your ancestor's Compiled Military Service Records (CMSR or CSR) from the National Archives. Visit their website to learn how to order the appropriate forms.

e. Notes on Compiled Military Service Records

(1) The U.S. War Department, using captured Confederate records, compiled these near the turn of the century. They include unit muster rolls, as well as special

reports, supply transactions, medical logs, court-martial records, and Federal prisoner of war records, among others.

(2) Typically, the CMSR gives basic information on a soldier's name, rank, unit, and status (present, absent, wounded, captured, sick, etc.). In some cases, the CMSR may include personal documentation relative to the soldier or his family. All of these records can be gold mines of information, but they are also subject to errors of spelling and transcription. Many of the original records were lost in battle or in the mails, while others were destroyed intentionally in the final days of the war to delay or prevent possible retribution.

(3) See National Archives Trust Fund Board, *Military Service Records: A Select Catalog of National Archives Microfilm Publications.*

f. Notes on Confederate Pension Records

(1) These are limited to the states of the former Confederacy, and are on file at the respective state archives.

(2) States began to offer veterans' and widows' pensions in the late 1880s, so your ancestors who died before that point will not appear in these files.

(3) Pensions usually were limited to those nearly destitute of other income and resources, such as very elderly men who had already deeded their property to heirs, widows, or the severely disabled. If your ancestor died in good health while still able to work for his living, he will not have received a pension, although you may find that his widow applied for one based on his Confederate service.

(4) These records can provide you some amazing insights into your ancestor's wartime experiences and his character, as exemplified by witness statements about him by former comrades. Sometimes their accuracy suffers from clerical errors, however, as well as from fading memories and survivors' uncertainties about details of the veteran's military service.

Task #3: Identify and obtain any existing regimental history of your ancestor's unit.

a. Regimental histories on Confederate units are surprisingly scarce. Again, the quickest way to find anything about your ancestor's unit is to check with the state archives and search the Internet. Enter the regimental designation on a search engine, and you'll often find that someone maintains a webpage on that unit, or on the brigade in which it served. Also check the United States Civil War Center (USCWC) at Louisiana State University in Baton Rouge, whose website maintains a staggering number of links to Civil War-related sites. One of these is a list of regimental publications, which can give you a quick way to determine which books to seek out.

b. A number of great collections and bibliographies exist that can lead you to fantastic sources about your ancestor's unit. Here are a few of the top ones you may expect to find in a good university or regional library:

(1) Dornbusch, *Military Bibliography of the Civil War. Vol. 2. Regimental Publications and Personal Narratives: Southern, Border, and Western States and Territories;*

Federal Troops. See also Vol. 4, *Regimental Publications and Personal Narratives: Unit and Confederate Biographies.*

(2) Sifakis, *Compendium of the* Confederate *Armies,* is a series of volumes that provides capsule histories of every Confederate unit in service from a given state. The author provides a short bibliography for each unit that can steer the researcher quickly to existing published histories, whether contemporary or modern. Of critical importance is the fact that these volumes provide a quick reference to the brigade(s) in which your ancestor's regiment served. Often you will be unable to find any regimental history on your ancestor's unit, but there may be several that chronicle the exploits of another regiment in the same brigade. In many cases, these may provide welcome details about the specific regiment you are researching. Typically, a brigade's subordinate regiments fought within several hundred yards of each other on Civil War battlefields, so their experiences were very similar.

(3) Lester and Hoeg, eds., *Civil War Unit Histories* microfiche series. This series provides in microfiche format many out-of-print regimental histories written by former members of the units they chronicle. Their works typically include rosters, as well as anecdotes and other information relevant to an understanding of your ancestor's regiment and brigade.

c. In many former Confederate states, veterans and historians of the late nineteenth century compiled resources of inestimable value to the modern-day researcher. Here are some of the most generally useful ones:

(1) *Confederate Military History* (CMH). A multi-volume work compiled by General Clement Evans, each state's volume was written by one of its veterans. Since each author used existing records and his own judgment to prepare his history, *CMH* volumes vary somewhat. Each, however, lists engagements, important officers and commanders, and provides an overview of the war years within the state, as well as its contributions to the Confederacy. Very usefully, the regimental sketches provide an exhaustive cross-reference to the voluminous *Official Records* (OR). Most university libraries in the South will have *CMH* on the shelves, but it is also available for purchase on CD-ROM.

(2) Many states have valuable references compiled by contemporary or modern authors. Consult my bibliography for these, which include Henderson on Georgia's volunteer infantry regiments, Brewer's work on Alabama units, Rietti's on Mississippi, and Booth's and Bergeron's on Louisiana soldiers and units. Each of these can save you a lot of time and provide wonderful insights on their topics.

<u>Task #4: Identify and obtain secondary sources that shed light on the experiences of your ancestor's unit.</u>

a. If you are already involved in Internet research on this project, return to the US Civil War Center to find links that refer you to good books on the appropriate battles and campaigns.

b. Alternatively, consult Sifakis, *Compendium of the Confederate Armies*, to obtain a comprehensive and accurate list of the battles and campaigns in which your ancestor's regiment participated. Since he gives the relevant dates, you can readily compare this listing to the service dates on your ancestor's CSR to narrow down the list to the engagements in which your ancestor may have participated.

c. A less comprehensive, but nevertheless useful source, is Crute, *Units of the Confederate States Army*. Best of all, it includes the nicknames of the various lettered companies, providing you another valuable research tool.

d. Once you have a good reference list of battles and campaigns, consult one of the following bibliographies to determine which books you should seek:

(1) Eicher, *The Civil War in Books: An Analytical Bibliography*.

(2) Nevins, Robertson, and Wiley, eds., *Civil War Books: A Critical Bibliography*. 2 vols.

e. Go to your nearby university library and peruse the shelves for books on the major engagements in which your unit took part, as well as related works on Civil War life and personalities.

LEVEL TWO:

If you want to conduct research at a level similar to Level One, but with the intention of *broadening* your research to allow you to learn about your ancestor's relatives in a similar degree of detail, you will need to repeat (for each relative) the processes described above. The tasks and resources are the same, but you will find the undertaking a lot easier the second time around! After your initial experience, you will have learned where to find the necessary references, made contacts with librarians and archivists, and become familiar with what is (and is not yet) possible on the Internet.

In many cases, your ancestor's relatives served in the same regiment or brigade, so many of the sources are already in your possession. Possibly, however, you will need to revise your work to some degree, since the relatives may have served at different times of the war. For example, Nat, Will, and John Mangham all enlisted in the Confederate Guards (Company A, 13th Georgia Infantry) on the same day in 1861, but Will's wound made him unfit for further service in September 1862. John resigned his commission in early 1864, but Nat remained with the regiment until the surrender at Appomattox in 1865. Had I originally limited my research to Will's time in the regiment, learning about subsequent regimental commanders, brigade reorganizations, battles, and campaigns would have entailed a return to some key sources. You can avoid this problem by copying all relevant material the first time.

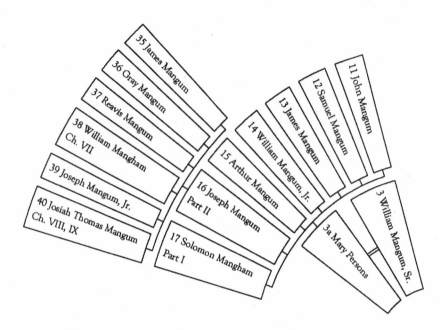

35 James Mangum

36 Gray Mangum

37 Reavis Mangum

38 William Mangham
Ch. VII

39 Joseph Mangum, Jr.

40 Josiah Thomas Mangum
Ch. VIII, IX

15 Arthur Mangum

16 Joseph Mangum
Part II

17 Solomon Mangham
Part I

14 William Mangum, Jr.

13 James Mangum

12 Samuel Mangum

11 John Mangum

3a Mary Persons

3 William Mangum, Sr.

THE JOSEPH MANGUM FAMILY.

AN ELDER BROTHER OF SOLOMON MANGHAM, MANY OF JOSEPH'S
DESCENDANTS RESUMED THE SPELLING MANGHAM BEFORE THE CIVIL WAR,
APPARENTLY INFLUENCED BY THEIR PROXIMITY TO SOLOMON'S DESCENDANTS.
WILLIAM MANGHAM'S (#38) ADULT SONS LATER CHOSE TO RESUME THE MORE
COMMON SPELLING MANGUM, WHILE MOST OF JOSIAH MANGUM'S (#40)
CHILDREN ADOPTED MANGHAM.

PART II

On the Trail of Uncle Solomon: Joseph Mangum's Descendants Move South

Introduction

By the middle of the nineteenth century, most Manghams of the Deep South were descendants of old Solomon Mangham, along with his nephew James C. Mangham. The others who adopted (or re-adopted) the English spelling of their surname were descendants of Joseph Mangum, one of Solomon's brothers. Born about 1747, Joseph arrived shortly after their father, William Mangum, Sr., moved the family from Virginia to North Carolina. Joseph was a few years older than Solomon, and remained in Granville County among numerous Mangum relatives when Solomon struck out for South Carolina and Georgia during the 1780s.[1] Joseph's son William accompanied Solomon to Georgia, where he lived for many years in Hancock and Putnam counties near his uncle. Another of Joseph's sons, Josiah Thomas Mangum, eventually moved his family to Georgia in the 1820s. Many of Josiah's sons, in turn, wound up in Russell County, Alabama, where their Uncle William settled in the mid-1830s. Many of Solomon Mangham's sons and grandsons lived in the Chattahoochee River counties of Georgia and Alabama, too, and thus replicated the dense kinship networks that characterized the earlier Mangham migrations from the Carolinas.

Chapter VII: The William Mangham Family on the Alabama and Texas Frontiers

1. Plantation Life & Public Service: The William Mangham Family of Russell County

William consistently appeared in the early Georgia records in close proximity to both James C. and Solomon Mangham, as well as the latter's sons, Willis and Thomas (Chapters I, II and VI). Born in North Carolina about 1773, he may have been a son of Joseph Mangum, but William moved to Georgia in early manhood and the connection remains speculative. He was established in the Hancock County area by the turn of the century, where his numerous land transactions bespeak a man of prosperity and activity for several decades thereafter.[2]

On a number of occasions, he took part in estate or real estate transactions with James, Solomon, or Willis, but one Putnam County deed implies some intriguing connections to still other Mangham relatives. In November 1820, William purchased a half-acre in the town of Eatonton, the Putnam County seat, from "Solomon Mangham of the State of Louisiana." This was Solomon P. Mangham, a much younger man than his namesake, the patriarch of the Mangham families of Georgia. Born in Orange County, North Carolina in 1786 or early 1787, Solomon P. Mangham was orphaned as a small boy, and was apprenticed at age four to Martin Cooper of Caswell County.

Available evidence indicates that he moved south between 1810 and 1812, and in all likelihood he purchased the little plot in Eatonton while living there among his numerous Mangham relatives. After a short time, however, he pulled up stakes again, moving west to Louisiana. In 1817 he married Zilla Chapman in St. Tammany Parish, where they remained for many years before moving to Mississippi.[3]

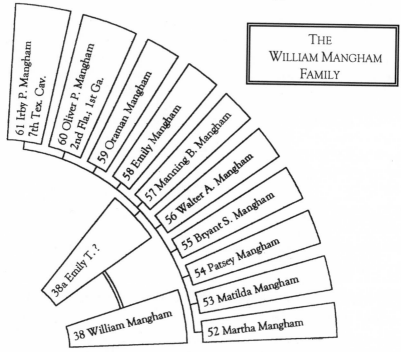

THE
WILLIAM MANGHAM
FAMILY

61 Irby P. Mangham
7th Tex. Cav.

60 Oliver P. Mangham
2nd Fla.; 1st Ga.

59 Oraman Mangham

58 Emily Mangham

57 Manning B. Mangham

56 Walter A. Mangham

55 Bryant S. Mangham

54 Patsey Mangham

53 Matilda Mangham

52 Martha Mangham

38a Emily T.?

38 William Mangham

Within a few years of Solomon P. Mangham's death in Rankin County in 1852, a number of his children moved to Trinity County, Texas, where they lived in the immediate vicinity of William Mangham's sons Bryant and Irby. Interestingly, although Solomon had signed the 1820 deed as *Mangham*, most subsequent documentation referring to him and his family indicates the adoption (or re-adoption) of the spelling *Mangum*. Equally intriguing is the fact that William's sons, all of whom normally used the spelling *Mangham* during their many years in Georgia and Alabama, began signing their names as *Mangum* not long after they removed to Texas in the early 1850s. Interestingly, this change seems to have occurred shortly after William died in Alabama in 1850. Unfortunately, however, the motives for this return to earlier practices remain lost in the shadows, as indeed do the precise relationships between James C., William, and Solomon P. Mangham. Continuous migration, shifting county boundaries, the vagaries of phonetic spelling, and the scarcity of surviving records blur the outlines, but it is likely that they were brothers, half-brothers, or orphaned cousins who grew up with or near each other.[4]

They all appear to have stuck closely to their Uncle Solomon, but his death in 1810 possibly loosened the bonds that had kept his extended family in close contact. As the younger Solomon moved west to Louisiana and James settled on the Georgia coast, William remained in Putnam County, but the names he gave his children break the patterns commonly maintained by old Solomon's direct descendants. William's Putnam County household included daughters Martha, Matilda, Patsey, Oraman, Emily, and sons Bryant S., Manning B., Walter A., Oliver P., and Irby P. Mangham. Martha and Patsey may have been the eldest, because they were both old enough to marry in 1817. Bryant, born about 1804, apparently was William's oldest son, and he certainly became the most prominent. He married Sophronia Varner in 1827, and remained in the Eatonton area for several years after his father moved the family to Henry County about 1825.[5]

In 1830, William was commissioned as a county Justice of the Peace, but he spent most of his time running the family farm with his wife Emily, five children, and eight slaves. The numerous deeds he witnessed or certified accompany the voluminous records of his own land transactions. Bryant certainly proved to be a chip off the old block in this regard. He moved to Houston (later Macon) County about 1829, where the next year saw him operating a plantation with his wife, two children, and 22 slaves. In the early 1830s, however, the promise of new lands convinced him to join the legions of Georgians and Carolinians bound for Alabama. A young boy named F. L. Cherry remembered Bryant coming to the Cherry family's neighboring Macon County plantation to bid them farewell prior to moving across the Chattahoochee to Russell County. Bryant was a land-grant recipient in 1835, and was one of the earliest settlers to clear a plantation on the south side of Chewackla Creek (also known as Uchee Creek). He built a house in a settlement later known as Salem, and opened one of its first boarding houses for wayfarers. He literally helped build the village from the ground up, as he joined Benjamin Baker and Dr. Erastus Jones in surveying the land and laying out the lots. The three men also were leaders in establishing the Salem Male and Female Academy for the education of the community's children. By 1838, Bryant turned his long-standing propensity for land development into a business venture entitled the Salem Town Company, which he established with John T. Riley. Their company traded Russell County properties in great volume, selling acreage to land-hungry settlers arriving in Alabama and buying from those departing for lands farther west. Bryant changed partners by 1841, and his new real estate company bore the title Jones & Mangham.[6]

No record survives of Bryant's activities in the Creek War that flared up in 1836, but some of its most terrifying incidents occurred in his immediate vicinity, including the gory massacre at Nuckoll's Bridge on Big Uchee Creek. Here an Indian war party killed a number of fleeing settlers, scalped the surviving women and children, and then set mules' tails and wagon wheels alight, causing the terrified animals to bolt in blind panic. Maimed women and children were jolted from the careering wagons to die in the roadway in a spectacle of carnage guaranteed to provoke whites to a spirit of bitter revenge. Another event that electrified settlers all along the Chattahoochee River frontier was the ambush, murder, and scalping of Maj. William Flournoy, a Putnam County native whose family was well known to William and his sons. As Indian war parties burned all the bridges on Big and Little Uchee creeks, Russell County settlers evacuated their villages and remote farmsteads in a general flight across the river. Certainly, Bryant must have been one of the hundreds who thus moved his family to safe haven in Georgia. He may well have commanded a militia company before or after the evacuation, for existing records show that he was the captain of Russell County's "Salem Blues" militia company for the community's Fourth of July celebration just two years later, in 1838. Bryant claimed losses totaling $1170 due to Indian depredations during the Creek troubles, so he may have been forced to start from scratch for the second time in just four years. He probably considered himself fortunate to have escaped with his scalp and family intact.[7]

It is highly unlikely that his neighbors would have elected him captain of their company if Bryant had played the role of passive spectator during the Creek War. After all, Southerners of that era placed a high premium on physical courage, and Russell County in 1838 was full of men who had served with distinction in the recent emergency. Likewise, they probably would have been loath to elect him to the State House of Representatives had he absconded during the crisis, but in 1840 they chose him by a 143-vote margin on William Henry Harrison's Whig Party ticket. Bryant was the third man elected to represent booming Russell County in the halls of the state capitol in Montgomery, just as he was the third man appointed postmaster of little Salem, an event that occurred in October of that year. He probably received a lot of family support, because Russell County had attracted Mangham relatives from all branches of the family by that year. His father William had come to Alabama about 1836, settling on land that later became the site of Opelika. Willis A. Mangham's sons Thomas R. and Henry C. Mangham arrived during the next several years. Josiah Mangham's sons Thomas, Arthur, and James lived in Salem itself, with Arthur owning the lot directly across the street from his cousin Bryant.[8] (See map on page 566.)

Within the next couple of years, however, Bryant and his five children were bereaved by Sophronia's death. Young widows and widowers of that era commonly remarried after a decent interval for mourning, because it was next to impossible for a lone adult to run a household, raise children, tend the farm, and conduct business. Bryant was no exception to this pattern, and his second marriage also reflected a common tendency for mature men to marry younger girls. In December 1841, he posted a marriage bond with the county Orphans' Court to marry 20-year-old Angeline Sills. Almost five years later, he again was posting bond with the Orphans' Court, but this time on behalf of his younger brother Oliver. Addressing a note to Judge Thomas H. Burch for Oliver to take to the nearby town of Crawford, Bryant wrote: "My brother O. P. Mangham visits your Town for Marriage License, please attend to it for him, there is no difficulty, all willing, put my name to the Bond, or assign it your Self, or get [Judge] Tate." With all the legalities neatly tied up, Oliver married 20-year-old Mary A. Brannon on March 29, 1846.[9]

By the time Bryant and other community leaders arranged to obtain a formal town charter for Salem in the course of the same year, however, something went terribly wrong with his business dealings. Reverend F. L. Cherry obviously thought highly of him, and his later memoirs circumlocuted Bryant's difficulties in the delicately vague phraseology of the times: "Mr. Mangham being a liberal, generous-hearted man, met with pecuniary reverses, and moved to Texas in 1848." Perhaps some of Bryant's many land transactions foundered on the shoals of unclear titles, or possibly he fell victim to defaulters on money he lent, bonds he secured, or investments he made. Whatever the cause, he looked westward for a new beginning.[10]

Texas was a common destination in those times, as many Alabamians flocked westward with the same enthusiasm that had led them to Russell County a decade earlier. Bryant's brother Walter already had paved the family's way to the new "promised land" in the 1830s, although he died near Mobile in 1839 while returning to visit kinfolks in Russell County. Manning had fallen under the spell of Texas, too, and he had moved to Grimes County by 1846. Irby fought in the Mexican War as a private in Company H, Coffey's 1st Alabama Militia Infantry regiment, and the ensuing victory over Mexico opened up the great southwest to men looking for elbowroom, new lands, or simply a fresh start. They were welcome to take their slaves with them to Texas, and its eastern parts offered a soil receptive to the crops and techniques typical of Southern agriculture.[11]

Bryant got his fresh start by purchasing a 612-acre spread, quaintly titled the "Buck Snort Farm," in Harrison and Panola counties in November 1849, arranging to repay half of the $1225 note in January 1851 and the other half twelve months later. This gave him time to make two crops and sell the proceeds to meet his financial obligations. He and Angeline made a good crop in 1850, helped by his twenty-year-old son William, six younger children ranging from eighteen to four years of age, and ten slaves. They cultivated a total of 130 acres that year, working first and foremost to ensure a good supply of provisions. The harvest yielded five hundred bushels of corn, a like amount of sweet potatoes, another fifty bushels of Irish potatoes, twenty bushels of peas, along with just six bales of cotton as a cash crop.[12]

Oliver, a practicing physician in Russell County, left his father's home and joined Bryant in Harrison County that year with Mary and their children Sarah, Brantly, and Walter. He came back east, however, to attain his formal medical degree by completing the second year of lectures at Georgia Medical College in Augusta in the spring of 1851. Oliver lent his elder brother more than seven thousand dollars in November 1850, and the fact that $3760 was due for repayment by Christmas indicates that Bryant was experiencing what modern-day Americans call a short-term "cash-flow" problem. Apparently, Bryant used some of the money to purchase another 87 ½ acres from Duncan Rodgers in the following year, thus expanding his "Buck Snort Farm" to seven hundred acres. In keeping with the practices of the times, Bryant provided legal security for Oliver's loan by mortgaging the farm itself, as well as his eleven slaves, some horses and mules, wagons, and household furniture. The brothers eventually worked out a joint ownership arrangement of the farm, although surviving records do not document the exact nature of their agreement.[13]

Oliver's medical education must have been a great help to his aging father, and it remains puzzling that he moved to Texas just as William began losing the battle with old age. Old William had lost his wife during the 1840s, and his married daughters Matilda Warlick, Emily Warlick, and Oraman Cates probably helped care for him after Oliver and Mary moved west. Inevitably, however, Father Time exacted the toll owed by mortal man. William was 77 years old in March 1851, when David Lockhart appeared before the county probate judge and asserted that the old man was "insane & not capable of attending to or transacting his own business." Lockhart was Russell County's Overseer of the Poor, and his official responsibilities included intervention in the affairs of the community's disabled citizens. He certainly was well acquainted with William, as both of them are listed among the first five settlers to put down the roots that eventually grew into Opelika. Judge Thomas S. Tate, also an old friend of the Manghams, duly ordered the sheriff to "summon twelve good discreet, & lawful men" from William's neighborhood to visit him at home and make the necessary inquiries. Those deputed for this task included William Sockwell, a near neighbor of William's and the husband of Jemima Mangham Sockwell, a daughter of Josiah Thomas Mangham, William's brother.[14]

Their inquiry resulted in Judge Tate's formal declaration of William Mangham as a "lunatic" on May 1, 1851, and the resulting Writ of Lunacy declared Bryant his guardian in the absence of any other. Before any of William's sons could return from Texas to take charge of affairs, however, the old man passed away. He was buried in the churchyard at Mount Lebanon.[15]

He had made a last will and testament in April 1850, appointing his son Manning as his executor. Manning resided in Harrison County when his father died, and returned to Alabama in July 1851 to settle his father's affairs on behalf of all the children. Things got sticky in November, when his brother-in-law John Warlick, Emily's husband, submitted an affidavit alleging that Manning was about to remove William's property from Alabama. The judge duly ordered Manning to appear before the court, but set aside the ruling when Warlick decided to drop his complaint. The formal legal documentation of this affair merely hints at what must have been an acrimonious dispute between the Manghams and some of their in-laws. The antagonism, if it endured, came to an abrupt end by July 1852, however, when Judge Tate received the news that Manning Mangham had "departed this life." It is not known where he died or whether he left a family of his own.[16]

Earlier that same year, Bryant and Oliver sold the Buck Snort Farm at a handsome profit of $1065, and then prepared to move once again. Bryant's 21-year-old son William had married 14-year-old neighbor Mary Isabella Rutledge in 1851, and two years later he was serving as his mother-in-law's agent in legal affairs involving her 325-acre farm and six slaves. Named after his grandfather, young William also was studying medicine, and in all likelihood his Uncle Oliver served as the preceptor who oversaw his practical training. William may have remained in Harrison County when his father and uncle removed to Tyler County about 1853, but his untimely death that year left his child widow in need of a legal guardian herself. Possibly other tragedies befell Oliver's family in this period as well, for available documentation shows that only Sarah attended school in Tyler County in 1854; the fates of Mary, Brantly, and Walter are uncertain.[17]

Bryant bought a 620-acre farm on the Neches River in Tyler County and began work with his eleven slaves, while Oliver bought a town lot in the county seat of Woodville, whose population could better support his medical practice. In all probability, Oliver's single slave was a house servant who helped him care for little Sarah, his horse, and two cows. Bryant, however, didn't remain long in Tyler before pulling up stakes once again. He established a prosperous 800-acre farm in neighboring Trinity County in 1855 or 1856, and by 1858 he also acquired a town lot in the county seat of Sumpter (now Groveton). Reminiscent of his days as a public official in Alabama, Bryant served as County Clerk beginning in 1858, so he clearly remained a talented man with a flair for leadership. He also retained his accustomed zest for acquiring real estate, which, along with slaves and a large family as a work force, was the basis of prosperity for most Southerners of his time and place. Bryant purchased a 160-acre tract along Piney Creek in 1859, and he obtained a further 160 acres the following year. Even before purchasing the latter properties, the 150 acres he cultivated in 1859-1860 yielded eighteen bales of cotton and five hundred bushels of corn. He may have been limited in his ability to make a larger crop by the fact that his elder children had married or died during the 1850s. When J. A. Murray counted noses at the Mangham residence in August 1860, the only children still living with Bryant and Angeline were Sophronia and her husband, John Gallion, fifteen-year-old Anna, five-year-old Mary, and Bryant S. Mangham, Jr., age three. Mr. Murray failed to note the presence of Bryant's brother Irby in Trinity County, although Irby may have moved into the county sometime after the census count had occurred.[18]

2. With the "Buttermilk Cavalry" in New Mexico: Pvt. & Bugler Irby P. Mangham, "Trinity County Cavalry," Co. E, 7ᵀᴴ Texas Cavalry

As is the case with most other members of the William Mangham family, several factors make it extremely difficult to establish a coherent account of Irby's activities throughout the ante-bellum era. Foremost among these was his astonishing geographic mobility, which was certainly not typical of most branches of the Mangham family. Irby was born in late 1822 or early 1823, doubtless in Putnam County, Georgia. He probably lived with his father or an elder brother until the late 1840s, so census records of the era never accounted for him by name.[19] It was August 12, 1847, before his marriage to Harriet Candle (Chandler?) in Harris County, Georgia, unearths his name from the shadowy obscurity of surviving civil records.[20] Military records evidence his Mexican War service in Company H, Coffey's 1ˢᵗ Alabama Militia Infantry, so apparently he moved from Georgia to Alabama as a youth, served in Texas and Mexico, returned to Georgia to marry, and eventually moved back west about 1850.[21]

Another factor serving to blur his image is the fact that Irby and his brothers began to spell their names as *Mangum* in the decade following their father's death. Perhaps it was due in some way to William's demise, or perhaps it resulted from meeting up with Solomon P. Mangum or other close relatives who revived the old North Carolina spelling after they left Georgia. Regardless of its origin, this shift is observable in documents pertaining to all of William's sons who lived in Texas through the 1850s. The transition is most surprising in Bryant's case, given his twenty years of local prominence in Georgia and Alabama as Bryant S. *Mangham*. Harrison County records of the early 1850s seem to indicate that he and Oliver used both spellings interchangeably, or perhaps county officials simply transcribed their "legal signatures" without even looking at how the brothers actually spelled their own names! Trinity County records from the latter part of the decade remove all lingering uncertainty, however; they were routinely authenticated by the county clerk himself in a bold hand that penned his crystal-clear signature with a flourish: *Bryant S. Mangum.*[22]

*   *   *   *   *

Despite the obscurity of Irby's prewar whereabouts, military records show that he was in Trinity County when war broke out in 1861. As the state of Texas girded itself for conflict that summer, its officers worked hard to revamp a rather sketchy militia organization. Trinity County was in the state's Fifth District, whose militiamen belonged to the 11th Brigade, Texas Militia. Captain William L. Kirksey enlisted volunteers from Beat 1 in an "active militia" company organized at Sumpter on the last day of August, and Irby apparently enlisted that day after the initial muster roll was made out. Far from a conglomeration of old men and young boys cobbled together for local defense, Kirksey's "active militia" of 1861 comprised men enlisting for active service against the Yankees. When Kirksey mustered the company again on September 17, Irby was entered on the rolls as a private; along with the other volunteers since the first muster, Kirksey now had enough men to tender its services for combat duty.[23]

Kirksey's troopers styled themselves the "Trinity County Cavalry," and they brought their horses and double-barreled shotguns with them into cavalry service. These Texans were responding to Brig. Gen. Henry H. Sibley's call for men to march westward into the territories of Arizona and New Mexico, which possessed rich copper and silver resources. One officer asserted in a postwar account that Sibley hoped to claim even greater prizes eventually: California itself, plus territory in northern Mexico. In the heady days of 1861, the fledgling Richmond government hoped Sibley's recent U.S. Army service in New Mexico Territory would enable him to deliver such prizes into their hands. Given the Mexican government's antipathy to the United States, who could rule out spectacular combinations and equally spectacular results?[24]

Confederate Adjutant and Inspector General Samuel Cooper accordingly commissioned Sibley on July 8 to raise two cavalry regiments in Texas, but September 20 found him with only twelve or thirteen companies mustered for service in San Antonio. Since he had arranged with Brig. Gen. Earl Van Dorn to move west with three regiments instead of two, Sibley's brigade lacked seventeen or eighteen companies

448

to complete its organization. Others still hastened to join him, however, and the Trinity County Cavalry was among them. Kirksey had dispatched a hard-riding courier to ride seventy miles to Fifth District headquarters with his September 17 muster roll, asking acceptance into Sibley's Brigade. They were in luck: Joseph Hogg, the district aide-de-camp, directed Kirksey to march from Sumpter on September 30 and report to Sibley in San Antonio as soon as possible.[25]

The men had to cross three hundred miles of south central Texas prairie to reach the brigade rendezvous at San Antonio, where Pvt. Irby P. Mangham and his Trinity County neighbors were mustered-in officially on October 23 for the duration of the war. In all likelihood, this period of service was a terrible hindrance to Sibley's recruitment efforts, just as the three-year hitch hamstrung the organization of Colonel Carter's brigade of Texas Lancers in 1861-1862 (see *Willis W. Mangham*, Chapter VI). Sibley seems to have made no official complaint on this count, however, but emphasized that his initial dependence on the Texas militia system created two major difficulties. The first was a misplaced reliance on inactive units whose sparse rosters failed to meet minimum standards for acceptance. Secondly, many labored under the misapprehension that only companies specified by the governor could serve under Sibley, so many outfits tendered their services to other commanders.[26]

Men willing to overcome all these difficulties and then march 300 miles to rendezvous must have been determined indeed, and their subsequent record bears out this conclusion. Kirksey's outfit eventually became Company E of Col. William Steele's 3rd Regiment, Sibley's Brigade, Texas Mounted Volunteers, although the regiment's tenth company was not mustered in until November 15. In the enumeration of Texas troops, Steele's command comprised the seventh cavalry regiment to achieve formal organization and acceptance; therefore, contemporary reports often refer to it as the 7th Texas Mounted Volunteers, 7th Texas Mounted Militia, 7th Texas Mounted Men, or simply as the 7th Texas Cavalry. They were the last of Sibley's three regiments to organize, and Reily's 4th Cavalry and Green's 5th Cavalry preceded them westward to the vicinity of Fort Bliss, near El Paso.[27]

On November 28, Steele dispatched half of his new command on the trail of their sister regiments, although he personally was required to stay in San Antonio. Apparently he was in charge of the rear detachments of Sibley's grandly styled "Army of New Mexico," whose main body was still at Fort Bliss. The end of 1861 saw Steele still mired in San Antonio; Irby and Company E languished at Fort Clark, where an epidemic of measles had brought their westward progress to a halt. The company was losing men rapidly to various causes: First Lt. S. F. Tullos resigned on December 17, junior Second Lt. John A. Farley died twelve days later, and Second Lt. C. T. Chandler died on January 22, 1862. Of the company's original complement of commissioned officers, therefore, only Captain Kirksey remained as Sibley's Army of New Mexico moved out towards Albuquerque and Santa Fe in early February.[28]

These tribulations eventually kept Company E behind with half of Steele's regiment at Doña Ana, near Las Cruces, New Mexico Territory, where Sibley had established a general hospital. Lieutenant Colonel John S. Sutton took command of the regiment's

1st Battalion and marched with the main body of Sibley's army. Comprised of companies A, B, F, H, and I, the 1st Battalion played a conspicuous part in the victory at Valverde on February 21, when some 1750 Confederates defeated 3800 Federals in

SIBLEY'S NEW MEXICO CAMPAIGN, 1862.

sharp fighting near Fort Craig on the Rio Grande. The colorfully named Capt. Powhatan Jordan took over the 1st Battalion after Sutton was mortally wounded while capturing an artillery battery, and the men moved forward with Sibley's little army through Albuquerque and into Santa Fe. After a small skirmish at Apache Canyon on March 26, another major engagement took place at Glorieta Pass two days later. Here, just twenty-two miles southeast of Santa Fe, several companies of the 7th Texas again played a role in defeating a combination of Colorado volunteers and Federal regular troops.[29]

Unfortunately for Sibley's grand plans, however, a scrappy Unionist detachment had circled into the rear and destroyed the Southerners' vulnerable supply trains. From its inception, the little Texas army had lacked almost every means of formal logistical support, and this blow sounded the death knell of the entire expedition. With a bypassed garrison in his rear at Fort Craig and aroused Federals at Fort Union in his front, Sibley looked gloomily at the barren countryside all about. It was time to retreat.[30]

The withdrawal hazarded the outright annihilation of Sibley's little army, with the exception of the rear detachments at Doña Ana. Other scouting expeditions had probed westward beyond Tucson, Arizona Territory, reaching a point only eighty miles short of the California state line. If these men did not return in a hurry, they would be stranded beyond any hope of salvation. As they hustled back to safety in Texas, the main body of the Army of New Mexico moved southward along the Rio Grande in April 1862. The withdrawal turned into a debacle when approaching Union troops from Fort Craig forced Sibley to seek escape through the trackless San Mateo Mountains, west of the river. Most of their wagons and guns were deserted in the ten-day trek through the forbidding highlands, but the Texans doggedly brought out their two field pieces by dint of sheer grit and determination. Although merely a minor episode in terms of the numbers of men involved, the successful retreat to Doña Ana was an epic saga of desperate perseverance in hopeless circumstances.[31]

Sibley rightly sang the praises of the men in his official report, but his ragamuffin command had lost confidence in his leadership. Many of the men had lost their horses in the retreat, and the government had not yet reimbursed them for their loss. They also lacked almost every other item of military supply. As Sibley noted in his May 4 report from Fort Bliss (El Paso), they had not received a single dollar from Confederate quartermasters for the campaign, and none of the men had been paid since enlistment. As for the New Mexico Territory, they had seen all they wanted to see of its sun-blasted deserts. The defeated commander gloomily opined that the land was "not worth a quarter of the blood and treasure expended in its conquest," and added that his men "manifested a dogged, irreconcilable detestation of the country and the people."[32]

The men who had followed Sibley so confidently into New Mexico now straggled back towards San Antonio in small groups, selling government property and their own guns in order to buy food, clothing, and horses. Colonel Steele remained at Fort Fillmore (near Doña Ana) throughout May and June with a small covering force from his regiment, even though his paltry force was clearly inadequate to repel any significant Federal threat. In all probability, Irby was among the men who maintained this token Confederate presence amidst a hostile Mexican populace, and he and his friends grew increasingly desperate for subsistence. The inhabitants refused to accept Confederate paper money, since its military representatives clearly were on borrowed time. Steele had no specie available, so he had to send out foraging detachments to requisition what they needed. The men acted under proper military orders, but the locals interpreted the resulting seizures as little better than armed robbery, just as Irby's cousins would later view blue-coated foraging parties in the occupied South. Confederate weakness emboldened the residents to armed resistance in many instances, and the ensuing skirmishes cost the 7th Texas Cavalry the lives of Captain Cleaver (Company D) and several enlisted men.[33]

In the early days of July, Steele's men grew increasingly restive. They "were on the point of open mutiny" by this time, and "threatened to take the matter in their own hands unless they were speedily marched back to San Antonio." Federal troops had finally managed to cross the flooded Rio Grande, and men from California and the Colorado Territory were moving into position to attack Fort Fillmore. Steele accepted the inevitable on July 8, and abandoned the Confederacy's "Arizona Territory." Selling the government property he could not transport, he turned over the proceeds to the hospital and pulled back to El Paso. His troopers lacked bread, beef, and transportation to make the trip to San Antonio, and many of them were "almost naked," but remaining in vulnerable El Paso was out of the question. Steele and the remnants of his command struck out for San Antonio shortly after he submitted his official report on July 12. Addressed from "Headquarters, Forces of Arizona," but datelined El Paso, Texas, his report effectively closed the books on Confederate dreams of empire in the great Southwest.[34]

*   *   *   *   *

Irby's horse apparently succumbed to the hardships of this campaign, but he secured a remount on September 3, 1862. The men of the 7th Texas Cavalry and Sibley's Brigade were assembling in Marshall, Texas, preparatory to further service, but Confederate authorities spent the next several months issuing a bewildering series of orders and counterorders. On September 1, the cavalrymen were directed to prepare to join General Taylor's forces in Louisiana. October saw them ordered to Richmond instead, but this order was rescinded in favor of one directing them to Monroe, Louisiana, to join Taylor. In the meantime, they were directed to report to General Hébert in San Antonio, but they proceeded instead to Houston, where Maj. Gen. John B. Magruder had assumed command of the District of Texas, New Mexico, and Arizona. As they were en route to Houston, Lt. Gen. Theophilus Holmes, the Trans-Mississippi Department commander, was promising Sibley's Brigade to Pemberton in Vicksburg. The resulting flurry of telegrams between Pemberton, President Davis, and Adjutant & Inspector General Cooper fairly burned up the wires, resulting in a renewed decision to dispatch the brigade to Taylor in Louisiana![35]

Meanwhile, Magruder was directing the dizzy cavalrymen to Harrisburg, some six miles south of Houston on the road to Galveston. He had warnings of a probable Federal descent on the Texas coast, and was scrambling to gather forces to stem the tide of invasion. Once Magruder got the brigade to Harrisburg, however, he received definitive orders to send the men to Monroe. The destitute state of the brigade quartermaster's fund then stymied this latest plan, but Magruder worked loyally to marshal the funds and supplies needed for their trip.[36]

While the Confederate high command wrangled over the disposition of Sibley's Brigade, the Federal officer commanding the Department of the Gulf, Maj. Gen. Nathaniel P. Banks, landed three infantry companies at Galveston on Christmas Day, 1862. These 280 men of the 42nd Massachusetts Volunteers were intended to serve as the advance party for the remainder of their regiment, which would protect some Unionist refugees bent on returning to Texas. The overall scheme was to establish a foothold on the Texas coast, recruit Texans for the Federal cause, and cripple an important Confederate port in the process. All of this would take place under the protective firepower of the reinforced naval blockading squadron that stood in close ashore. Banks inherited the plan from his predecessor, Maj. Gen. Benjamin "Beast"

452

Butler, and seems to have allowed the ill-conceived operation to unfold of its own momentum.[37]

Banks's opponent, Maj. Gen. "Prince John" Magruder, had a somewhat checkered career in the Confederate Army, but he was renowned for his ability to produce imaginative solutions to seemingly insoluble problems. Given the straitened condition of his department, he cast about for all available organized troops, threw together auxiliary forces of local townsmen, and rapidly developed a plan to drive off the invaders. He directed the armed men of Sibley's Brigade to march to the threatened port, while two steamers, the *Bayou City* and the *Neptune*, were fitted out as cottonclad gunboats. The cavalrymen would provide volunteer crews of "Horse Marines" aboard these boats, using their small arms to supplement the jury-rigged cannon mounts. Colonel Arthur P. Bagby, who had assumed command of the 7th Texas Cavalry upon Steele's promotion, now stepped forward to lead the armed portion of his ill-equipped regiment aboard the *Neptune*. Likewise, Col. Tom Green of the 5th Texas Cavalry took command of his troopers aboard the *Bayou City*. These men carried their accustomed double-barreled shotguns, as well as a number of Enfield rifle muskets Magruder had acquired in Virginia. The remainder of Sibley's Brigade formed part of Magruder's land force under command of Brig. Gen. W. R. Scurry, former commander of the 4th Texas Cavalry. Private Irby Mangham was present for duty and equipped, so he almost certainly numbered among the men who clambered aboard the cottonclad *Neptune* in the darkness of New Year's Eve, 1862.[38]

After detailing his variegated units to mutually supporting tasks on land and sea, Magruder touched off the cannon that opened the fight just three hours into the New Year. The opening volleys soon received a spirited reply from the *Harriet Lane*, the vessel on which Admiral David Porter had received the surrender of Fort Jackson, below New Orleans, in April 1862. The *Harriet Lane* mounted four heavy guns and two 24-pounder howitzers, and she was but one of the five major ships and five lesser men o' war that loosed a "tremendous discharge of shell" from the harbor that night. Most of their attackers were dismounted cavalrymen and local militia manning light field pieces on the beach, and one of the latter deemed it "most trying to the nerves" to have a "green bucket-full of grape thrown at him for a single dose." As the close-range cannonade thundered in full voice, the Massachusetts infantrymen formed line on the wharf and blazed away at Texans wading through the surf with scaling ladders.[39]

Luckily for the heavily outnumbered Bay Staters, the ladders proved too short for the task at hand and that threat receded. The ferocious artillery duel raged unabated for some time, but Magruder's exposed gunners eventually began to flag in the face of the uninterrupted hail of cannon fire from the Federal fleet. Some of the scratch crews of militiamen melted away under the pounding, but General Scurry's dismounted cavalrymen came at a "full run" to get the cannon back in action. In one case they found a lone gunner standing by his piece, loading and firing it by himself. Despite such heroics, Magruder directed his men to begin entrenching, as the clear light of dawn threatened disaster for the exposed gun crews along the beach. At the crucial moment, however, the long-awaited cottonclads hove into view, steaming towards the

453

Harriet Lane. Prince John had realized that the hazards of their 30-mile trip down the Sabine River might foil any attempt to coordinate precisely his land and sea attacks, but he certainly was glad the steamers arrived when they did. Running up the bay towards the *Harriet Lane*, they closed to point-blank range on either side. As cannons roared and rifles and shotguns barked in close combat, the *Neptune* struck the *Lane* a glancing blow forward of the wheel, but she failed to get grappling hooks firmly engaged so that her "Horse Marine" boarding parties could go into action.[40]

If Irby Mangham was indeed on board the *Neptune*, he and his comrades soon had their hands full simply trying to survive. Staggered by the collision and cannon fire, the ship barely reached the edge of the channel before she foundered and began to sink. Nonetheless, she and her crew had fouled the *Lane*'s bowsprit and rigging, and the Federal vessel was unable to steer freely as she turned to tangle with the *Bayou City*. The hard-fighting bluejackets attempted to ram the cottonclad, but missed her and lost their starboard wheelhouse in the process. Close-range rifle- and shotgun-fire continued to rake the *Lane*'s decks, and eventually her gun crews were wiped out or driven from their posts. When the *Bayou City* rammed her full in the wheel, the *Lane* was pinioned and ripe for boarding. Screaming Texans poured onto her decks, and the surviving Federal officers quickly surrendered their swords and their ship. The *Owasco* closed in for one last gun duel with the *Lane*'s Confederate captors and the 7th Texas troopers aboard the foundering *Neptune*, but a storm of musketry convinced her to retreat out of range.[41]

The cavalrymen aboard the *Neptune* were fished safely out of the water, losing only those men who were killed or wounded in the combat preceding their collision with the *Lane*. The Federal flagship *Westfield* ran aground, and Captain Renshaw evidently surrendered his flotilla soon thereafter. Great confusion arose over the ensuing proliferation of flags of truce and surrender flags, however, and Confederate gunners resumed fire at Federal vessels seeking anew to evade capture. When the smoke cleared, the Confederates had captured the *Lane*, two barks, and a schooner, and the *Westfield* was helpless. Captain Renshaw set fire to the grounded vessel, but the men who prepared her for destruction had sloshed turpentine into the forward powder magazine. Just moments after she was set alight the magazine blew up with a roar, killing Renshaw and every man of the small party waiting to row him away from the doomed vessel. The stranded Massachusetts infantrymen had nowhere to go, and wisely surrendered when the debacle in Galveston Bay reduced their chances from slim to none. The surviving vessels of the Union flotilla turned tail for New Orleans, and a volunteer aide aboard the transport *Mary A. Boardman* was stunned to see the navy abandon Galveston Harbor in the general flight to safety.[42]

General Banks truthfully admitted that the Galveston affair was a disaster, allowing ruefully that "It was supposed that the fleet made the occupation of the part of the island adjacent to the gunboats perfectly secure." Magruder, on the other hand, could take great pride in shattering the Federal attempt to establish their "apostate Texans" on the Confederate Gulf Coast. Holding the line at Galveston cost 26 men their lives, and another 117 bore the scars of Federal shot and shell. Combined with a daring victory at Sabine Pass just three weeks later, when raiding parties captured two blockade vessels, the South's victory along the Texas littoral was stunningly complete.[43]

*   *   *   *   *

Irby Mangham was present when the 7th Texas Cavalry mustered for December 31, 1862, so it is all but certain that he took part in the engagement at Galveston. Other than possible skirmishing with recalcitrant New Mexicans the previous summer, however, this would be his only combat experience of the Civil War. He rode through the muddy sloughs that passed as roads when his regiment finally marched to Louisiana in the spring of 1863, but by mid-March he had become seriously ill. Irby languished in the hospital at Opelousas for months; by late summer, the medical authorities diagnosed him with chronic diabetes, contracted while in the service of the Confederate States. Noting that Irby had been completely disabled for the previous five months, Acting Assistant Surgeon J. R. Vaughan provided him a certificate of disability. Brig. Gen. Alfred Mouton approved his discharge from Confederate service on August 28, 1863.[44]

*   *   *   *   *

Irby was forty years old when his two-year military adventure came to a close. As his discharge papers noted, he was 5'2" tall, light complected, with blue eyes and light hair, and he had earned his living as a farmer in more peaceful times. Unfortunately, however, the personal portrait that haltingly emerges from his military record was submerged in the deepening shadows of a Southland fighting for survival. When he was discharged, not even two months had elapsed since the disasters at Gettysburg and Vicksburg, and Federal invasion forces were gaining momentum in Tennessee and rampaging through Louisiana.[45]

Gravely ill, Irby P. Mangham faced a bleak future. Did he ever get home?

3. AN INFANTRYMAN & THE HEALING ARTS: PVT. OLIVER P. MANGHAM, "LEON RIFLES," CO. D, 2ND FLORIDA; AND "COAST RIFLES," CO. F, 1ST GEORGIA (OLMSTEAD'S)

Just as all traces of his brother Irby faded away in the chaos of the wartime Trans-Mississippi Department, all pre-war traces of Oliver P. Mangham vanished from Tyler County, Texas, after 1855. Perhaps he left his home in Woodville and moved elsewhere in Texas, or even returned back east.

The outbreak of war apparently found him in Florida, and his haste to enlist in Confederate service implies that he had strong views on the issues at hand in 1861.[46] Although he may have lost his family before the war, Oliver was nevertheless forty years of age and a practicing physician, hardly the type to enlist for the sheer adventure of war. Just thirty days after the first cannon shots boomed across the waters of Charleston Harbor, he volunteered for twelve months' service as a private in a company organizing in Tallahassee. Oliver was one of many doctors, lawyers, and other professional men throughout the South who rushed to the colors during the spring

455

and summer of 1861, forswearing any chance for a commission in favor of serving in the ranks. Such self-abnegation was quite commonly an individual response to the years of secession rhetoric, in which opinion-makers called for the heights of self-sacrifice on the altar of Southern rights. One also perceives, however, that the rhetoric itself may have been less cause than effect. Was it not the result of a passionate belief structure that enshrined the values of individual freedom and honor? Men who placed service to the cause of Southern rights above their personal well being were making the strongest possible statement of their views.[47]

When D. P. Holland swore Oliver into service at Tallahassee on May 11, 1861, it may well have been in the belief that the new company would assume the defense of the port city of Apalachicola, Florida. Holland had written a letter on March 14 to the Confederacy's new Secretary of the Navy, Floridian Stephen R. Mallory, urging him to provide weapons to the town's four companies so they could contest any Federal attempts to "enforce the revenue" there. Of course, the stakes had risen significantly since the shooting started at Fort Sumter, and thinly populated Florida faced a monumental struggle in preparing to defend her extended coastline. The largest vote ever taken in ante-bellum Florida polled a mere 12,898 men, so each 1000-man regiment made a tremendous dent in the state's adult male population. The first of these units marched to Pensacola in April, and the second began forming that same month in the state's capital city.[48]

As the companies completed their organization and began drilling, they reported to the regimental rendezvous at Jacksonville's "Camp Virginia" in early July. Many of the early militia and volunteer companies underwent reorganization before their services were accepted, and Oliver's apparently was one of these. When formally mustered into Confederate service on July 13 near the "Brick church" outside Jacksonville, Captain Theodore W. Brevard, Jr., was in command of the "Leon Rifles," whose nickname honored their home county. Known throughout 1861 as the 6th Company, Brevard's men eventually were redesignated as Company D, 2nd Florida Infantry Regiment. Their 26-year-old company commander possessed a spectacular resume for a man his age: a commissioned officer in the Third Seminole War, he had served in the state House of Representatives in the late 1850s. The secession crisis of 1860-1861 found him at the pinnacle of Florida's military establishment, serving as the state Adjutant and Inspector General![49]

The new regiment was intended for service in Virginia, and it duly entrained for the "seat of war" on July 15. In common with the experience of many other military organizations crossing the South that year, their passage to the Old Dominion starkly revealed the weakness of the new country's transportation network. No railroad existed to take them northward along the Georgia coast, so they had to board westbound trains whose destination was Lake City. Disembarking there, the rookie soldiers marched some fifty miles northwest to Valdosta, Georgia, where they finally entrained for Richmond. The movement nevertheless was a jubilee celebrating the birth of the infant nation, and bouquets "were showered upon the soldiers by fair hands at many points along the route," while flag-waving crowds vied with local militia escorts in expressing their gratitude to the country's defenders. The Floridians were still relishing memories of their feast at Savannah's Central Depot when they arrived in Richmond on July 21, just in time to hear of the great victory at Manassas Junction.[50]

Although they entertained brief hopes of reaching the battlefield in time to seal the victory, the 2nd Florida's raw levies were ordered into camp near Richmond, where they spent much of the ensuing two months guarding the luckless bluecoats captured at Manassas. They also underwent that inevitable initiation to military service called drill, struggling to master the complex evolutions necessary to move from column of march into fighting line at a moment's notice. Numbingly repetitive, drill was anathema to independent spirits on both sides in 1861, as its undisguised aims of stifling initiative and inculcating instant obedience seemed the very antithesis of individual honor and freedom. As historian Reid Mitchell has reasoned, the juxtaposition of white liberty and black slavery in the South created a context that made drilling the Confederate soldier particularly difficult, as its emphasis on subordination made it clearly comparable to servility. As Mitchell succinctly stated the case: "If regimentation was difficult for most Americans of the 1860s to bear, it was particularly onerous for a Southern white man." Those who lived through the early combats learned that the tedious repetition served a very useful purpose, however, by providing overstimulated nervous systems with mental, emotional, and physical breakwaters against the chaotic riptides of mortal combat.[51]

It would be some time before the 2nd Florida's men finally "saw the elephant," but by September 17 they were en route to garrison duty at Yorktown. Here they occupied a reserve position behind a gristmill owned by Mr. Young, backstopping two brigades under the control of Brig. Gen. Lafayette McLaws. The Young's Mill position was one of several in the vicinity of Yorktown and Williamsburg, where Maj. Gen. John Bankhead Magruder's Army of the Peninsula secured the south bank of the York River approaches to Richmond. When Oliver Mangham took his place in the Yorktown defenses that autumn, he was stationed only some twenty miles from Sgt. Tom Mangham's Georgia outfit down at Sewell's Point (Chapter IV). Although Oliver had moved west while Tom was still a boy, their fathers William and John C. Mangham were first cousins and knew each other well.[52]

Oliver was present for duty in the 2nd Florida's hutments throughout that winter, although the regiment's records seem to have suffered irregularities caused by inexperience with the army's organization and procedures. Surviving muster rolls evidence great delays in conducting the required bimonthly musters: the September-October muster occurred on January 17, while the November-December muster took place on March 6, 1862. The regiment undertook frequent night marches that winter in response to false alarms, and the unavoidable exposure probably combined with monotonous army fare, camp diseases, and endless toil on the fortifications to wear down Oliver's physical resistance. He was admitted to the General Hospital in Petersburg on April 3 with "debilitas" (debility), a common diagnosis that vaguely described the run-down condition of its victims without specifying the root cause of their maladies. Modern research indicates that such men often suffered from scurvy, although the other possibilities are well nigh endless.[53]

Oliver was sufficiently recovered to return to his unit ten days later, but in the meantime he had missed its baptism of fire at Yorktown on April 5, 1862. Their bold sortie against General McClellan's encroaching forces was part of a masterful piece of play-acting by "Prince John" Magruder. He faced some 66,000 Federals with fewer than 14,000 men behind fieldworks along the Warwick River, but he marched and counter-marched these troops in a conspicuous fashion that convinced the notoriously overcautious McClellan that he was badly outnumbered. Rebel columns seemed to be on the move everywhere, and blueclad scouts could not discern that regiments such as the 14th Louisiana had marched from Yorktown to the James River six times, portraying a half-dozen regiments of non-existent reinforcements! Amidst the cacophony of drums, bugles, and shouted commands, McClellan concluded he was facing 100,000 Confederates. This convinced the naturally cautious Federal commander to proceed on tiptoe with his 66,000 troops, for disaster seemed probable if he exposed them to a riposte from the overwhelming Rebel hordes. Of course, these enemy legions existed only in McClellan's mind, but Magruder's masterful performance behind his Warwick River line bought the Confederates precious time and space for counteractions. General Joe Johnston's Army of the Potomac began arriving on April 7, and by April 11 the Confederates could muster almost 35,000 men, with more on the way.[54]

The 2nd Florida was transferred to Maj. Gen. Daniel Harvey Hill's division as Johnston assumed command of the forces on the Peninsula, and Oliver was back in ranks when McClellan directed his units on April 16 to stop the Rebel efforts to improve their positions at Dam No. 1. This position marked the center of the defensive line, and was one of several dams Magruder had constructed in order to turn the approaches into impassable swamps. One Federal brigade directly attacked the redoubt defending the dam, where Oliver's second cousin (once removed) *Willoughby Mangham*, a private in the 11th Georgia, was engaged in the nip-and-tuck defensive action that repelled the attack. The Confederates in the chilly, rain-soaked trenches at Yorktown defiantly faced double their numbers for several more weeks, but it was imperative they evacuate their exposed positions before McClellan turned loose the full weight of his 111 giant siege guns and prepared for an assault.[55]

He planned his grand attack for the morning of May 5, so the time had come for the Floridians to join in a general withdrawal of Johnston's 57,000-man army. Oliver's regiment pulled back as part of Jubal Early's brigade on the night of May 3, while Rebel guns poured out a tremendous volume of fire against the closely opposed Federal siege lines. As the sizzling shells burned their meteoric paths through the darkness, awed Yanks sought safety below ground, while their opponents slipped silently away in a masterful withdrawal. The 2nd Florida passed through Williamsburg the next day and paused that night a mile or two beyond the town, but heavy firing on the morning of May 5 announced that Union forces had come to grips with the army's rear guard. This force was under the command of Maj. Gen. James Longstreet, one of the hardest-hitting commanders in either army, and the Battle of Williamsburg became one of the sharpest actions of the war to date.[56]

Private Oliver Mangham probably was among the 530 men in the regiment's ranks when Longstreet asked Hill for a reserve force that morning, and thus he marched back

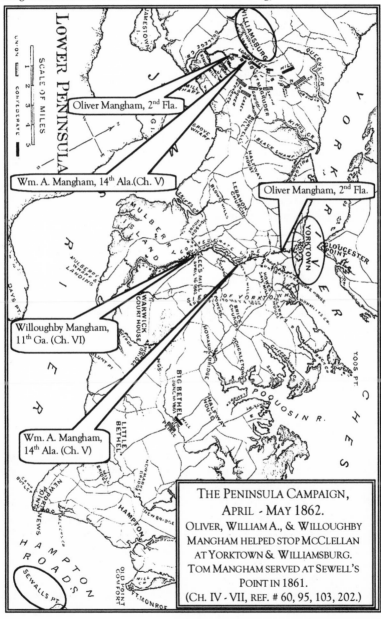

Oliver Mangham, 2nd Fla.

Wm. A. Mangham, 14th Ala.(Ch. V)

Oliver Mangham, 2nd Fla.

Willoughby Mangham, 11th Ga. (Ch. VI)

Wm. A. Mangham, 14th Ala. (Ch. V)

THE PENINSULA CAMPAIGN,
APRIL - MAY 1862.
OLIVER, WILLIAM A., & WILLOUGHBY
MANGHAM HELPED STOP McCLELLAN
AT YORKTOWN & WILLIAMSBURG.
TOM MANGHAM SERVED AT SEWELL'S
POINT IN 1861.
(CH. IV - VII, REF. # 60, 95, 103, 202.)

through the chilly rains to William and Mary College, where Early's Brigade stacked arms and awaited developments. Longstreet, known to his troops as "Old Pete," was loathe to wait within the protection of defensive positions for the coming Yankee assault, and his aggressive counterattacks set the tone for the day's action. His men traded blows with Joe Hooker's Federal division along Lee's Mill Road, southeast of Williamsburg, and were folding them up nicely when Phil Kearny came to Hooker's rescue about 3:00 p.m. The impact of Kearny's division on Longstreet's right flank caused Old Pete to call for two regiments from Early's Brigade, which was en route to reinforce the Confederate left. Early detached Col. George T. Ward's 2nd Florida and the 2nd Mississippi Battalion, and Brig. Gen. Cadmus Wilcox hastened Ward's men forward into the rain-soaked forests in support of the 9th Alabama and 28th Virginia.[57]

These two regiments had been in action since eight o'clock that morning, pushing Hooker's men out of one stretch of forest, through an open field, across a slashing of felled timbers, and finally into the woods beyond. The Alabamians had captured a six-gun battery in the open field, but Wilcox knew that Union infantry in the thick forest some 250 yards beyond the guns could make the position untenable for his men. In their attempt to push into the forest they met with determined resistance, so Wilcox ordered Ward's command in to support their left. The Floridians already had double-quicked two miles through the mud before being ordered to charge, but the excitement kept them going. They moved across the open field and into the slashing, reaching a point within twenty or thirty paces of the woodline, where they came to a halt and poured volley after volley into the nearly invisible enemy line. Colonel Ward was killed in the return fire, and his men must have found it unnerving to duel with shadows. When word spread that Yankees were coming around their flank, they fell back about 300 yards to a ravine before rallying. They soon returned to build up a firing line along a fence about one hundred yards in front of the ravine. From this vantage point they traded shots with the phantoms in the woodline, before changing front to the right to counter a renewed threat to their flank. Apparently Wilcox was satisfied that they had done all the fighting necessary for one day. As the daylong conflict petered out in the rainy twilight, he pulled back his command to prepare for withdrawal.[58]

In fact, Longstreet and Wilcox were highly gratified at the results of the battle, with the former proudly reporting: "This battle was a very handsome affair." Wilcox agreed, adding, "The conduct of both officers and men. . .was in all respects worthy of commendation. . . ." Their fight had gained a day for Johnston's retreating columns, while simultaneously stinging McClellan into following more cautiously. Federal losses totaled almost 2300 men, of whom 1575 were from Hooker's hard-pressed division on the left. The Confederates lost just shy of 1700 men, but had drawn the fangs of their Federal pursuers in the process. The 2nd Florida lost four men killed, 31 wounded, and five missing in the classic delaying action, before pulling back towards Richmond through soupy mud that was often knee-deep. Other creature comforts were imperiled as well. Private D. E. Maxwell of the St. Augustine Rifles bemoaned the fact that the retreating Floridians "lost everything except a change of clothes and a blanket apiece."[59]

The regiment had been planning to reorganize and elect new officers on May 3, in accordance with the provisions of the Conscription Act of April 16. The evacuation of Yorktown and the ensuing fight at Williamsburg had thrown a monkey wrench into this plan, but the elections finally took place soon after the Floridians settled into the defenses outside of Richmond. Clearly, there were internal stresses ravaging the Leon Rifles, almost as thoroughly, if not as fatally, as Yankee bullets. When the company voted on May 11, the general housecleaning offers powerful testimony that all was not well. The men failed to return Brevard as captain, and the same fate befell lieutenants George Cook and Alexander Haywood. Third Lieutenant George Sanders secured election as the new first lieutenant, but "was so disgraced by the character of the other officers elected during the reorganization" that he resigned his office the same day. First Sergeant Baltzell joined corporals Maxwell and Burroughs in transferring to Company H on election day, and Maxwell made it known after the war that he did so because of the inferiority of the officers elected, especially Fourth Sgt. Musgrove, who secured election as captain. The turmoil was general throughout the 2nd Florida, as every company except two elected new captains.[60]

It seems particularly surprising that such strife occurred after the successful engagement at Williamsburg, as one would think experience would make for clear choices. If the company leadership had bungled its duties in combat, one would expect to see evidence that many would simply decline to run for office again; this was a fairly common reaction among early war leaders who found themselves in over their heads. Perhaps Musgrove capitalized on Brevard's honest mistakes, or possibly he appealed to the troops' baser instincts by blaming the discomforts of the retreat on the captain. In any event, the turmoil upon reorganization offers a good example of the weaknesses of the traditional election system, because the election process either caused outright personality conflicts or aggravated those simmering beneath the surface.[61]

*   *   *   *   *

It certainly wasn't a good preparation for the next test these men faced, when Joe Johnston loosed a major assault just three weeks later on McClellan's army outside Richmond. The bloody fight at Seven Pines on May 31 and June 1 was a misfired attempt to destroy two Federal corps posted south of the Chickahominy River, and the result was 6134 Confederate casualties and another 5031 dead, wounded, or missing Federals. For the 2nd Florida Infantry, it was a particularly horrific encounter: they lost 37 killed, 152 wounded, and nine missing in action, from a total of 435 men present for duty. This staggering forty-five percent casualty toll ranked them seventh among all the Confederate regiments engaged in the two-day battle.[62]

Johnston's plan went wrong almost from the beginning, as vaguely articulated orders and skimpy staff work proved glaringly inadequate to the task of moving 22 of his 29 brigades into action against the two exposed Federal corps. Attack preparations floundered on the morning of May 31, as Longstreet's and Huger's divisions jammed

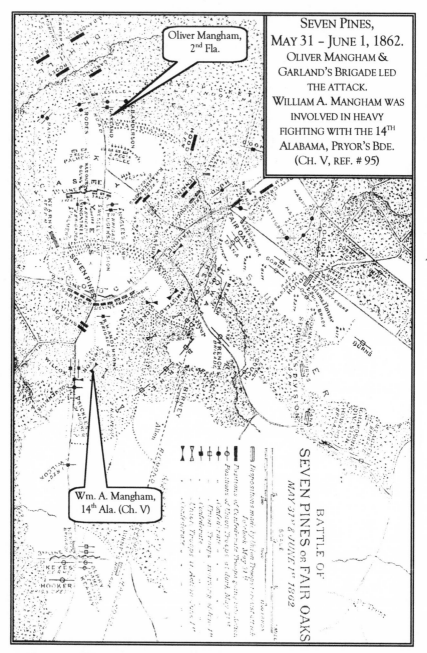

Oliver Mangham, 2nd Fla.

SEVEN PINES,
MAY 31 – JUNE 1, 1862.
OLIVER MANGHAM &
GARLAND'S BRIGADE LED
THE ATTACK.
WILLIAM A. MANGHAM WAS
INVOLVED IN HEAVY
FIGHTING WITH THE 14TH
ALABAMA, PRYOR'S BDE.
(CH. V, REF. # 95)

Wm. A. Mangham,
14th Ala. (Ch. V)

BATTLE OF SEVEN PINES OR FAIR OAKS
MAY 31ST & JUNE 1ST 1862

up a single road. After nail-biting delays of fully five hours, Maj. Gen. Harvey Hill decided to initiate action on his front at 1:00 p.m. His division was supposed to deliver a frontal attack down the Williamsburg Road to fix the Federals near the road intersection known as Seven Pines, while troops under Longstreet delivered the main assault from the northern flank, nearer the Chickahominy River. This maneuver would sweep the two enemy army corps away from the main body of the Army of the Potomac, ensconced in positions north of the river, and allow the destruction of the isolated troops. As it turned out, however, the first Confederate unit to break cover was Jubal Early's old brigade, commanded by Brig. Gen. Samuel Garland since Early was recovering from a serious wound at Williamsburg. If Oliver Mangham was indeed in the ranks that day, he and his butternut- and gray-clad comrades were facing a stern test that dwarfed Williamsburg in its scope.[63]

Garland's advancing battle line included the 2nd Florida, posted on the far left of the brigade. They moved out after signal guns fired three shots, and their unheralded approach caught their opponents off guard. The "sheet of flame" that erupted from the advancing Confederates threw elements of Silas Casey's Federal division into panicked flight, but several Yankee batteries stood their ground along with four infantry regiments. One gunner, a member of Battery A, 1st New York Light Artillery, watched his outfit's deadly spherical case shot cut swathes through the advancing Confederates. Remarking that each shot plowed through the oncoming masses before exploding to scourge them with dozens of lead slugs, he recalled: "Our shot tore their ranks wide open, and shattered them asunder in a manner that was frightening to witness; but they closed up again at once, and came on as steady as English veterans." As Garland's men closed to within four hundred yards, the gunners switched to canister, with still more frightful results. "At each discharge, great gaps were made in their ranks—indeed, whole companies went down before that murderous fire; but they closed up, with an order and discipline that was awe inspiring."[64]

The desperate artillerymen manning the six Napoleon guns poured shot after shot into the Florida, North Carolina, Virginia, and Mississippi troops comprising Garland's Brigade, but the rampaging Southerners came on through the woods, over the fence, and across an open field to the mouths of the guns themselves. Their return fire whizzed around the battery, killing the battery horses and dropping an occasional gunner. One of those killed was Colonel Bailey, commander of the 1st New York Artillery Regiment, who collapsed with a bullet through the head as he ordered his men to spike their cannon. Enough New Yorkers remained at the guns to discharge the last blasts of canister into the faces of the Confederates at fifteen to twenty paces, then some ran while others surrendered.[65]

For the Floridians at the receiving end of the musketry and cannon fire, however, the ordeal had seemed like anything but the relentless advance the New York cannoneer remembered. They had slogged through muddy sloughs in the tangled undergrowth, often wading knee-deep through the muck until they sank in up to their hips. Garland's regiments deployed from column into line of battle as they reached the edge of the woods, where the incoming fire forced them to deploy to return it. At the woodline, the abatis caused further confusion in the advancing ranks, and Garland strove to get his regiments to deploy by the flank to turn the obstacle, rather than plowing straight through it. The regimental columns had overlapped upon forming lines of battle, however, and the bunched up men were falling like flies under the heavy fire. It proved impossible to control them for the relatively complex flanking maneuver, so Garland gave it up as a bad job and ordered them to push straight through the obstacle in a frontal assault.[66]

The 2nd Florida took off in the lead on the left flank, but their formation probably resembled no evolution they had ever practiced on the parade ground. Southerners expected their officers to lead the way in tight spots, and the regiment's officers stood to the task, suffering appalling casualties in the process. Of eleven company commanders in the assault, ten fell wounded or dead, while Major Call was killed and Lieutenant Colonel Pyles critically wounded. As the men clawed through the abatis, their color bearers were shot down wholesale, with a New York gunner claiming that a single blast of canister felled three flags at once. Colonel Smith, commanding the 49th Virginia in Featherston's Brigade, picked up a flag in the abatis and held it until a young man stepped forward asking permission to bear it. The youth belonged to the 2nd Florida, but had lost his regiment and asked to accompany Smith; as for the flag, he was prepared to "plant it in the cannon's mouth" if desired. The Virginian handed over the banner, and was amazed to see that it was actually the standard of the 2nd Florida! As he later reported, ". . .how it reached the spot where I found it is still vailed [sic] in mystery, and probably will ever remain so."[67]

Amidst the fear and confusion of Garland's assault, the 2nd Florida and 38th Virginia reached the fence beyond the abatis, and the firing line they built up was the one that made the position of Battery A untenable. These two regiments "preserved a more distinct organization" in the chaos, and continued the fight as Featherston's Brigade pushed into the field with Garland's men. In a scene that was far from the orderly panorama described by the New York gunner, these men struggled forward and eventually overran the battery. The first man to touch a gun and lay claim to the battery was an officer of the 2nd Florida, believed to be Captain Flagg. He was killed soon afterwards, but Lieutenant Parker of the Leon Rifles survived the melee to bring back the flag of the 8th New York Light Artillery. As the exhausted Floridians herded some fifty prisoners to the rear that afternoon, their part in the battle mercifully drew to a close. Along with D. H. Hill's other brigades, they had smashed Casey's division in the initial onslaught. Although both sides would claim victory in the two-day Battle of Seven Pines, each eventually remained in the positions they held beforehand.[68]

The drama before Richmond continued for several weeks thereafter, but the advent of Robert E. Lee as replacement for the wounded Johnston portended combat of renewed ferocity. The new commander commenced a series of attacks in late June that became known as the Seven Days' battles, and thereby established the reputation for aggressiveness that he sustained throughout the war. After pushing back McClellan at Oak Grove and Mechanicsville, Lee went for the kill once more at Gaines's Mill on June 27. Now in Pryor's Brigade, the 2nd Florida was committed on the Confederate right flank, just north of the Chickahominy. This wing of the army was under Longstreet's command, and Old Pete's half-mile wide tide of butternut and gray went into the assault with screams that reminded one participant of "forty thousand wild cats." At the climax of a fight that sustained a fearsome intensity, Longstreet's men cracked the Federal line wide open. The blue front was dissolving in the center and on the other flank as well, and only the coming of darkness and the arrival of two reinforcing brigades saved the Army of the Potomac that day. If Oliver Mangham was present for duty, he may have helped care for his depleted regiment's eight killed and 52 wounded men. Their unsuccessful attempt to widen the breach in the Federal center at Frayser's Farm three days later was even bloodier, as fourteen died and 62 fell wounded in frontal assaults against Phil Kearny's division. Once again, McClellan's men escaped utter disaster by a very narrow margin, and they eventually managed to retreat to the shelter of their gunboats down on the James River.[69]

Richmond had been saved from the impending doom whose shadow loomed over Confederate hopes throughout the long spring and summer months on the Peninsula, and the spectacular reversal of fortunes heartened the entire South. A grim General Lee, however, knew that the Federals had been allowed to escape and fight another day.

*　　*　　*　　*　　*

Perhaps Oliver encountered his second cousin William Mangham in the ranks of the 14th Alabama during June 1862, as both regiments were in Pryor's Brigade. If so, they must have exchanged pleasantries about their relatives and acquaintances, especially those living in Chambers and Russell counties in eastern Alabama. Any such conversation doubtless would have included a discussion of William's Christian name, and whether it was conferred upon him in honor of Oliver's father.

The two cousins would have had to meet before the Battle of Frayser's Farm, however, for after that conflict William Mangham's Cusseta Grays had only one man standing to answer roll call: Pvt. W. A. Prather.[70]

*　　*　　*　　*　　*

Oliver Mangham apparently went South on furlough in July, and the company he left behind in Virginia was certainly different than the one he had joined in 1861. The survivors were now seasoned veterans, of course, but their painfully thin ranks reflected the hardships of the Peninsula Campaign. The change in leadership among the Leon Rifles may have wrought other changes that weren't immediately visible, however, especially since Captain Musgrove failed to return to duty after being wounded at Seven Pines. It was 1864 before he finally was dropped from the rolls as a deserter, but the troops probably knew much earlier that he had no intention of returning.[71]

Regardless of his reasons for wanting to leave the Leon Rifles, Oliver took decisive action by arranging his discharge from the regiment. He was 41 years old by this time, comfortably over the conscription age, and had declined re-enlistment when the regiment reorganized. By August 11 he had served twelve months plus ninety days, thus fulfilling the conscription clause requiring twelve-months' soldiers under 18 or over 35 to remain for three months in their units, unless sooner replaced by new recruits.

465

Accordingly, Pvt. Oliver P. Mangham accepted his discharge from the 2nd Florida Infantry on August 11, 1862, when his discharge papers described him as 41 years old, 5' 5" tall, with fair complexion, light hair, and blue eyes. Along with $41.03 for back pay since May 1, including commutation for travel, he accepted the "thanks of a grateful nation" and resumed civilian status. . .at least as far as the 2nd Florida was concerned.[72]

In fact, Oliver had made his way to Savannah in July and enlisted in Capt. John S. Turner's "Coast Rifles" on July 17. Turner's outfit was Company F in Col. Charles Olmstead's 1st Volunteer Regiment of Georgia. Accordingly, Oliver was technically a member of two regiments at the same time, just the kind of discrepancy that could drive army bureaucrats to distraction. Perhaps he chose the Coast Rifles due to some family connection, as Miles G. Turner had married Macynthia Ann Mangham in Putnam County on January 31, 1822. Alternatively, Oliver may have selected the Coast Rifles in order to serve in a less strenuous environment than an infantry regiment in Lee's army, where continuous marching and fighting placed a terrific burden on a man his age.[73]

Olmstead's regiment was the first raised in Georgia, and it was comprised of some of Savannah's most prestigious prewar militia companies. Like many other Confederate infantry units, however, they were detailed to serve heavy guns in static positions. The coastal defense batteries that Company F manned at Causton's Bluff through late 1862 offered the opportunity to serve in an important post without exposure to the remorseless physical demands of field service in the infantry. Their prewar roots and static defensive duties at a major port city offered a standard of continuity that lent itself to efficiency in many of the routine details of army life, as comments by their mustering officers attested. After the mud and blood of Virginia's Chickahominy swamps, Oliver must have been glad to pull guard duty in a unit that regularly paid its men, drilled them efficiently, armed them with top-notch Enfield rifles, and clothed them "substantially."[74]

He had suffered from debility in Virginia, and the chill Atlantic winds sent him back to the hospital on December 15, 1862. He was still there at the end of February 1863, and apparently his commanders decided to use his medical talents once he was fit for duty again: before the end of April he was detailed as a hospital nurse, apparently at Guyton in Effingham County. Only 34 men remained on duty with the Coast Rifles at that time, while ten (including Oliver) were detached to perform other duties. A further sixteen were not available due to leave, sickness, or other reasons.[75]

Oliver remained at the hospital at least through the end of 1863, as evidenced by a unit muster roll, clothing records, and a September petition to Secretary of War James Seddon on behalf of John Agee, another nurse at the hospital. Agee had been attached to Guyton Hospital for a year, and requested an official discharge from the 61st Georgia Volunteers when his brother-in-law's death left him as the sole support for fifteen women and children. Given his meager army pay, Agee feared they would starve unless he was discharged to care for them. One of the petition's eighteen signatories was "O. P. Mangum, M.D."[76]

Although Olmstead's regiment was transferred to the Army of Tennessee in May 1864, it is unlikely that Oliver saw action as an infantryman in the bloody Atlanta Campaign of that year. His wife had written the Confederate Adjutant & Inspector General's Office on April 11 to request Oliver's detail to other duties; although her request was disapproved, he again was detached to serve at an army hospital. This time he was posted to Whitesville in Harris County, probably about the time the regiment moved west from Savannah to join Johnston's army in the field. He must have spent an extended period of time there, for he joined the congregation of Bigham Chapel, a Methodist Church in nearby Mulberry Grove. Although it is possible that he went into Tennessee that winter under General Hood, he probably remained busy taking care of wounded and sick soldiers there in the backwater of west Georgia.[77]

* * * * *

"Dr. O. P. *Manghan*" was removed from the probationary list of Bigham Chapel's membership rolls, by letter, on October 1, 1865. As the Confederacy he served for four years slipped into the realm of the history books, Oliver P. Mangham resumed his place among the shadows of the Southland.[78]

* * * * *

Oliver's eldest brother and friend, Bryant S. Mangham, died on March 23, 1867, in Trinity County, Texas. Back east in Salem, Alabama, his old homestead on the banks of Chewackla Creek burned to the ground that same year.[79]

* * * * *

In February 1931, Miss Ruth Horner asked the United States War Department for documents related to Oliver P. Mangum's service in the Civil War, supposing that he had served in a unit from Florida, Georgia, or Louisiana. No record survives of the official reply.[80]

---

[1] *MFB* 25: 7-8. Lynn Parham's invaluable work on the Mangum – Mangham – Mangrum families includes an analysis of the Josiah Thomas Mangum lineage, which is the basis for my assessment here. True to the pattern apparent with Solomon, William, Solomon P. Mangham (later Mangum), and James C. Mangham, the events of the last quarter of the eighteenth century obscure Josiah Mangum's exact antecedents. While frustrating to the researcher, this pattern may indicate that those who reverted to the English spelling were motivated by the curiosity of orphan sons exploring their heritage, or by their Loyalist British (Tory) sentiments during the Revolutionary War. See the Prologue and Chapter I for an examination of the relationship between James C. Mangham, Solomon, and William Mangum "the Loyalist."

[2] 1850 Census, Russell County; Vaughn Ballard, comp., *Solomon Mangham: His Ancestors and Descendants* (Arlington: Family Histories, 1989), pp. 49, 53, 66; Putnam

County, Superior Court, General Index to Deeds and Mortgages, vol. 1 (1806-1832), drawer 1, reel 51, GDAH. The 1808 Hancock County tax rolls reflect that William Mangham owned a quarter section (202 ½ acres) in Wilkinson County, as well as two more in Baldwin County. Nothing is known of Joseph Mangum's son William, but William Mangham's birthdate and later connections to the Josiah Thomas Mangum/Mangham family support the possibility that they were the same person.

[3] Putnam County, Superior Court, Deed and Mortgage Records, Book J (1821-1823), pp. 28-29, drawer 1, reel 55, GDAH; John T. Palmer, *The Mangums of Virginia, North Carolina, South Carolina . . . and Adjoining States* (Santa Rosa: 1992), pp. 85, 191-197; Ballard, *Solomon Mangham*, pp. 49, 53, 185-187; Freda R. Turner, ed., *Henry County, Georgia Land Records*, 3 vols. (McDonough: Henry County Genealogical Society, 1991-1993), vol. 1 (Deed Books A and B), pp. 101, 153.

[4] Palmer, *The Mangums*, pp. 191-197. Many of Solomon P. Mangham's (Mangum's) descendants served in the Confederate Army, and their records typically reflect the spelling *Mangum*. The great majority of Trinity and Rankin County records use this spelling as well.

[5] 1850 Census, Harrison County, Texas; 1860 Census, Trinity County, Texas; Putnam County Marriage Records; Turner, ed., *Henry County, Georgia Land Records*, vol. 1, pp. 67, 110, 153; vol. 2, p. 56. Patsey married William Allen about a month before Martha married Robert Moreland on February 20, 1817, in Putnam County. Later Henry County deeds show that William was a resident of Putnam County in 1823 and 1824 when he bought tracts of land in Henry, but transactions in 1827 no longer identify him as a non-resident of the county. Additionally, Henry County records identify William as a grand juror in March 1825. Bryant was Secretary pro tem of the Masonic Lodge in Eatonton in 1828, but dissolved his business partnership with James A. Meriwether the same year, probably shortly before he moved. See Fred R. Hartz, comp., *Genealogical Abstracts from the Georgia Journal (Milledgeville) Newspaper 1809-1840*, vol. 3, pp. 271, 914, 1016.

[6] Vessie Thrasher Rainer, *Henry County Georgia: The Mother of Counties* (McDonough: N.p., 1971), p. 363; 1830 Censuses, Henry and Houston Counties; Rev. F. L. Cherry, "The History of Opelika and Her Agricultural Tributary Territory, Embracing More Particularly Lee and Russell Counties, from the Earliest Settlement to the Present Date," *AHQ* 15, no. 2 (1953): 201, 264, 268, 386, 428, 465; Russell County Historical Commission, *The History of Russell County, Alabama* (Dallas: National ShareGraphics, 1982), p. C-27; Alexander Nunn, ed., *Lee County and Her Forebears* (Opelika: N.p., 1983), pp. 102-104, 238; Russell County, Superior Court, Deed and Mortgage Records, Book D, pp. 141, 174, 189, 468.

[7] Anne Kendrick Walker, *Russell County in Retrospect: An Epic of the Far Southeast* (Richmond: Dietz Press, 1950), pp. 124-129; Nunn, *Lee County*, pp. 278-279; Robert S. Davis, comp., "Alabama Indian Depredation Claims," *AlaBenton Genealogical Quarterly* 10, no. 1 (1993): 89. The state governor formally commissioned Bryant as a captain in

the state militia just several weeks after the July 4th celebration. According to the Adjutant General's ledger, Bryant S. *Manghum* was appointed captain of the Salem Blues on July 30, 1838. See State of Alabama, Adjutant General's Office, Administrative Files 1820-1865, Register of Officers, vol. 3 (1832-1844), p. 453, ADAH. Extant records show that Josiah Flournoy of Putnam County witnessed at least two land transactions executed by William Mangham (see *Henry County, Georgia Land Records*, vol. 1, p. 110; vol. 2, p. 56).

[8] *The Georgian* (Savannah), August 11, 1840, p. 2; 1840 Census, Russell County; Nunn, *Lee County*, pp. 26, 105, 238; Cherry, "History of Opelika," p. 201; Russell County, Superior Court, Deed and Mortgage Records, Book I, pp. 346-347. Until 1845, Alabama state legislators served for a one-year term (see Cherry, p. 456). See more on Arthur Mangham in Chapters VIII and IX.

[9] Russell County, Miscellaneous Probate Records (Marriages, 1834-1846), LGM 88, reel 16, ADAH.

[10] Nunn, *Lee County*, p. 107; Cherry, "History of Opelika," p. 201. Bryant was a central figure in arranging for the Mobile & Girard Railroad to pass through Salem, thus helping sustain the town he helped survey and incorporate. See Walker, *Russell County in Retrospect*, pp. 171-172.

[11] Buster W. Wright, comp., *Burials and Deaths Recorded in the Columbus (Georgia) Enquirer, 1832-1872* (N.p., 1984), p. 310; 1846 Census, Grimes County; CMSR Index (Mexican War), Irby P. Mangham, Company H, Coffey's 1st Alabama Militia Infantry. The *Columbus Enquirer* of September 25, 1839, announced that Walter A. Mangham, "formerly of Russell Co., Ala.," was on a trip from Texas to visit parents" when he died in Clarke County. In all probability he was taking passage up the Alabama River from Mobile to Montgomery, where further connections to the Tallapoosa River would have brought him within forty miles of his father's home. Walter was at least 28 years old when he died, because he was 21 or older when he drew bounty land in Georgia's Cherokee Land Lottery of 1832. See Silas E. Lucas, Jr., *The 1832 Gold Lottery of Georgia: Containing a List of the Fortunate Drawers in Said Lottery* (Easley: Southern Historical Press, 1986), p. 128.

[12] Harrison County, Deed Book J, pp. 201-202; 1850 Census and Agricultural Schedules, Harrison County; Harrison County, 1850 Tax Rolls, TSL.

[13] 1850 Census, Russell County; *The Medical College of Georgia Alumni Directory 1828-1984* (White Plains: Bernard C. Harris Publishing Co., 1984), pp. v-vi, 123, 238; Harrison County, Deed Book K, pp. 377-380. The November 1850 indenture listed Bryant's slaves as Green, a male age 50, and his wife Mehaly, age 45; Levi, 44, his forty-year-old wife Caroline, and her seven-year-old child Mariah; Dennis, 40; Abraham, 43; Ned, 27; Bob, 21; Adaline, 35; and Jane, 9. This document thus provides clear evidence that Bryant Mangham sanctioned slave marriages in some form, although the reference to Mariah as Caroline's child makes one wonder how Bryant viewed Levi's role as father or guardian. Along with other evidence, this indenture also implies a

surprising geographical mobility for that era, as Oliver apparently moved readily from Alabama to Texas, then back east to Georgia before returning to Texas.

[14] Russell County, Minutes of Probate Court, 1851-1854, pp. 39, 74-75, LGM 89, reel 5, ADAH; Nunn, *Lee County*, p. 26. William Mangham was listed as 75 years old in the 1850 census of Russell County. Josiah Thomas Mangum (Mangham), originally of Granville County, North Carolina, was apparently William's brother. In any case, the interaction of their families implies a close relationship. Probate judges commonly appointed neighbors and relatives to appraise personal estates and participate in like matters; Sockwell's appearance at William's lunacy hearing was doubtless no coincidence.

[15] Russell County, Minutes of Probate Court, 1851-1854, pp. 75, 105, LGM 89, reel 5, ADAH; Cherry, "History of Opelika," p. 201.

[16] Russell County, Minutes of Probate Court, 1851-1854, pp. 105-106, 129-130, 222, LGM 89, reel 5, ADAH. William Mangham's April 1850 will is transcribed from Russell County documents in *MFB* 9: 12-13. One provision gave his daughter Emily Warlick a slave girl named Caroline, aged fifteen.

[17] Harrison County, Deed Book M, pp. 55-56; 1850 Census, Harrison County; Nancy B. Ruff, comp., *Harrison County, Texas, Early Marriage Records 1839-1869* (St. Louis: Ingmire Publications, 1983), p. 20; Harrison County, Probate Court Minutes, vol. MR-C, p. 123; vol. EM-D, p. 81; Harrison County, 1853 Tax Rolls, TSL; Tyler County, 1854 Tax Rolls, TSL; Gifford White, *Texas Scholastics 1854-1855* (Austin: N.p., 1979), p. 345. The 1850 Russell County census listed Sarah Mangham as six years old, although Oliver and Mary were not married until 1846. Although the fates of four-year-old Brantly and one-year-old Walter are not known, the elder boy could be the man who later served in Hilliard's Alabama Legion as "B. W. Mangham" (see Chapter VIII). Little Walter clearly was named for his deceased uncle, Walter A. Mangham.

[18] Tyler County, 1854-1855 Tax Rolls, TSL; Trinity County, 1857-1860 Tax Rolls, TSL; 1860 Census, Slave Census, and Agricultural Schedules, Trinity County. The slave census listed Bryant as owner of nine slaves, which the tax rolls for the previous three years valued at $6000. Tax records for 1860, however, listed only seven slaves valued at $5000. Extant census indexes overlook the "Briant S. Mangum" household on page 340 of the 1860 Trinity County census. The town of Sumpter is now Groveton.

[19] Irby was 38 upon enlistment in 1861, and 40 when discharged in 1863. His discharge papers confirm that he was born in Georgia. See CMSR, Irby P. Mangum, 7th Texas Cavalry.

[20] Transcriptions of Harris County marriage records give Harriet's maiden name as "Candle." Bryant Mangham's overseer in Russell County was named Chandler, however, and several land transactions between the Mangham and Chandler families in Alabama tend to confirm that this was Harriet's actual family name. Lieutenant C. T. Chandler served in Irby's cavalry company during the Civil War, and may have been related to him through marriage. See Cherry, "History of Opelika," p. 268; Russell

County, Superior Court, Deed and Mortgage Records, Book C, p. 217; Book F, p. 795; ORS II, vol. 67, p. 775.

[21] Irby's Mexican War regiment organized in Mobile in June 1846. After serving three months at Brownsville, Texas, the 1st Alabama saw extensive service in Mexico, but no real combat. Of the 900 volunteers in its ranks, one died in a skirmish, 150 succumbed to disease, and about 200 were discharged before the unit mustered out on May 25, 1847. See Willis Brewer, *Alabama: Her History, Resources, War Record, and Public Men, from 1540 to 1872* (Montgomery: Barrett & Brown, 1872), p. 588.

[22] Irby's marriage and Mexican War service records list him as *Mangham*, but Civil War documents uniformly refer to him as *Mangum*. Almost all Alabama records from 1835-1852 indicate that Bryant and Oliver went by *Mangham*, although some transcriptions list Bryant as *Mangum*, *Manghum*, or *Mangrum*, while Oliver graduated Georgia Medical College in 1851 as *Mangum*. Early Texas records use all of these spellings, but surviving documents show that both brothers signed documents as *Mangum* in the Civil War era. Intriguingly, the last known reference to Oliver transcribes his name as *Manghan*.

[23] Muster Roll of Capt. James W. Morris' Company, Beat No. 4, Bell Co., Texas, 27th Brigade, Texas Militia, June 1861, RG 401, TSA; CMSR, Irby P. Mangum.

[24] Ibid.; OR 4, p. 93; Martin Hardwick Hall, *Sibley's New Mexico Campaign* (Austin: Univ. of Texas Press, 1960), pp. 29-32.

[25] OR 4, pp. 93, 107-108; ORS II, vol. 67, pp. 780-781.

[26] CMSR, Irby P. Mangum; ORS II, vol. 67, pp. 780-781; OR 4, pp. 141-143; Hall, *Sibley's New Mexico Campaign*, pp. 33-36. Irby's second cousin, Willis W. Mangham, was a member of Carter's Lancers (see Chapter VI).

[27] ORS II, vol. 67, pp. 777-785; OR 4, pp. 132, 141-143.

[28] ORS II, vol. 67, pp. 775-776, 781; OR 4, p. 164; Hall, *Sibley's New Mexico Campaign*, pp. 51-53. The Company E muster roll for December 31, 1861 shows that it was stationed at Perdro Pinto. Presumably this settlement was near Fort Clark, which stood between Uvalde and today's Del Rio, Texas, where Hall states that the company remained to recuperate. Unfortunately, Hall fails to cite his source for this information, and he omits mention of any dates for the company's stay. In all probability, it remained some weeks at Fort Clark between December 1861 and February 1862, before resuming the march north to join the regiment in New Mexico.

[29] OR 9, pp. 505-509, 513-516, 523, 541-545. Much of *Sibley's New Mexico Campaign* is devoted to analyzing these actions.

[30] Hall points out that Sibley's concept of the campaign was to make his column self-supporting, using captured supplies from the U. S. Army's frontier posts to subsist his column. Unfortunately for Sibley's men, U. S. regular and volunteer troops proved able to hold many of these outposts and prevent their use by the Confederates. Existing documents give us little insight as to how Sibley and Jefferson Davis concluded such a

hazardous logistical arrangement was feasible in the barrens of the far Southwest. See Hall, *Sibley's New Mexico Campaign*, pp. 30-32.

[31] OR 9, pp. 510-511, 707-708; Hall, *Sibley's New Mexico Campaign*, pp. 181-201, 205.

[32] OR 9, pp. 510-512. Federal reports exulted over the destitution of Sibley's force, understanding full well that it meant the complete removal of the threat to the New Mexico Territory. While McClellan demanded ever more reinforcements for his Peninsula Campaign in Virginia, Canby in New Mexico advised the high command to reduce the number of regiments earmarked for duty in New Mexico. See OR 9, pp. 666, 678; Hall, *Sibley's New Mexico Campaign*, pp. 220-222.

[33] OR 9, pp. 719-722; Hall, *Sibley's New Mexico Campaign*, pp. 209-213.

[34] OR 9, pp. 719-722; OR 15, pp. 895-897; Hall, *Sibley's New Mexico Campaign*, pp. 222-224.

[35] CMSR, Irby P. Mangum; OR 13, pp. 888-889; OR 15, pp. 895-897, 902-904, 954, 967-969; OR 17, pt. 2, pp. 767-768. Irby's original horse was appraised at $80 when he mustered in; presumably he eventually received compensation for its loss.

[36] OR 15, pp. 903-904, 968-969.

[37] Ibid., pp. 201-202.

[38] Ibid., pp. 211-213. In his reports of December 6 and December 9, 1862, Magruder described Sibley's Brigade as "not half armed" and "almost without arms." Colonel James Reily, acting commander of the brigade in Sibley's absence, used similar expressions in his reports to Sibley (Ibid., pp. 895-896, 968-969).

[39] Ibid., pp. 212-215; Edward B. Williams, ed., *Rebel Brothers: The Civil War Letters of the Truehearts* (College Station: Texas A&M Press, 1995), pp. 159-160.

[40] OR 15, pp. 209-210, 215; Williams, ed., *Rebel Brothers*, pp. 160-161.

[41] Ibid.

[42] OR 15, pp. 202-204, 209-210, 215-217; Williams, ed., *Rebel Brothers*, p. 161.

[43] OR 15, pp. 201, 216, 219; E. B. Long, *The Civil War Day by Day: An Almanac, 1861-1865* (Garden City: Doubleday & Co., 1971), p. 313.

[44] CMSR, Irby P. Mangum; OR 15, pp. 967-971, 982-983, 999. The 7th Texas Cavalry enhanced its reputation in April 1863 by its performance in action along Bayou Teche, but Irby's illness already had rendered him unfit for duty.

[45] CMSR, Irby P. Mangum.

[46] Page-by-page searches of census records for Leon, Marion, and Hillsborough counties have failed to reveal Oliver's whereabouts in 1860. I have searched tax rolls for Leon, Jefferson, Gadsden, Wakulla, Liberty, and Jackson counties for the period 1859-1862 with equal lack of success. Extant census indexes provide no clue as to his whereabouts in 1860 or after the war.

[47] CMSR, Oliver P. Mangam, 2nd Florida. Note that many of Oliver's Florida service records render his name as *Mangam*. When discharged, however, he signed his pay settlement as *Mangum*.

[48] CMSR, Oliver P. Mangam; OR 1, p. 450; CMH 11, *Florida*, pp. 19-20, 43.

[49] CMH 11, *Florida*, pp. 20, 43; CMSR, Oliver P. Mangam; W. J. Tancig, comp., *Confederate Military Land Units, 1861-1865* (Cranbury: Thomas Yoseloff, 1967), p. 25; David W. Hartman, comp., *Biographical Rosters of Florida's Confederate and Union Soldiers, 1861-1865* (Wilmington: Broadfoot Publishing Co., 1995), p. 169; Fred L. Robertson, comp., *Soldiers of Florida in the Seminole Indian, Civil and Spanish-American Wars* (N.p.: Board of State Institutions, 1903), pp. 84-86. Holland later served as lieutenant colonel of the 4th Florida, as well as of an artillery battalion (see OR 6, pp. 95, 301).

[50] CMH 11, *Florida*, p. 43; Michael W. Evans, "Commands," *America's Civil War* (September 1993): 8; Francis P. Fleming, *Memoir of Capt. C. Seton Fleming, of the Second Florida Infantry, C.S.A.* (Jacksonville: Times-Union Publishing House, 1881; reprint, Alexandria: Stonewall House, 1985), pp. 24, 28-30.

[51] Fleming, *Memoir*, pp. 29-30. For a fine analysis of Civil War soldiers' responses to drill, see Reid Mitchell, *Civil War Soldiers: Their Expectations and Experiences* (New York: Simon & Schuster, 1988), pp. 57-59. Despite the visceral reaction against drill, many soldiers viewed it simply as one more obstacle to overcome. Their letters home nevertheless brim with proud references to their units' achievements on the drill field, even before they learned by experience that well-drilled units were more successful in battle.

[52] Fleming, *Memoir*, p. 30; OR 4, pp. 668-670; ORS II, vol. 5, pp. 211-212. John C. Mangham grew up near William in Putnam County, and his position as an influential businessman and prosperous farmer doubtless facilitated many contacts with William and his family. One documented example is an 1840 indenture between John and Matthew Burnside of Russell County; William's son Bryant Mangham witnessed the transaction. See Russell County, Superior Court, Deed and Mortgage Records, Book D, pp. 61-62. See Chapter IV for more on Sgt. (later Col.) Tom Mangham.

[53] CMSR, Oliver P. Mangam; Fleming, *Memoir*, p. 33. General Magruder ordered his army to construct winter quarters on October 3, 1861. See OR 4, p. 670.

[54] CMSR, Oliver P. Mangam; Fleming, *Memoir*, p. 33; Stephen W. Sears, *To the Gates of Richmond: The Peninsula Campaign* (New York: Ticknor & Fields, 1992), pp. 29-31, 35-37, 43-45.

[55] Stewart Sifakis, *Compendium of the Confederate Armies: Florida and Arkansas* (New York: Facts on File, 1992), pp. 16-17; Sears, *Gates of Richmond*, pp. 48, 55-56. See Willoughby's description of this fight in Chapter VI.

[56] Sears, *Gates of Richmond*, pp. 60-61; Fleming, *Memoir*, p. 34.

[57] Sears, *Gates of Richmond*, pp. 70-78; OR 11, pt. 1, pp. 564-565, 592-593, 602-603, 606-607; Evans, "Commands," *America's Civil War* (September 1993): 8.

[58] OR 11, pt. 1, pp. 592-593; ORS I, vol. 2, pp. 337-338; Fleming, *Memoir*, pp. 34-40, and Letter, Francis P. Fleming, May 10, 1862. (This letter and several others appeared in the Stonewall House reprint as an unpaginated addendum to Fleming's *Memoir*.)

[59] Sears, *Gates of Richmond*, pp. 82-84; OR 11, pt. 1, p. 569; Fleming, *Memoir*, p. 111, and Letter, Francis P. Fleming, May 27, 1862. The casualty listing in Fleming's *Memoir*

names four dead and thirty wounded men. The Leon Rifles lost one killed and two wounded. Maxwell is cited in Evans, "Commands," *America's Civil War* (September 1993): 8.

[60] Fleming, *Memoir*, p. 34; Hartman, comp., *Biographical Rosters*, pp. 169-170; Evans, "Commands," *America's Civil War* (September 1993): 8.

[61] Modern historians, themselves representatives of professionalization in modern Western societies, tend to decry the regimental election system of the Civil War. In so doing, they echo the complaints of some wartime leaders, especially West Pointers, who shared the view that elections undermined discipline and authority. One is entitled to wonder, however, what alternative system could have supplied officers more likely to command the obedience of the volunteers of 1861-1862. Given the social and political realities of that era, it is absurd to think that the volunteers or their state political leaders would have accepted the overthrow of this traditional system until and unless it proved clearly unequal to the emergency. Likewise, in 1861, no pool of reliable senior commanders existed to staff promotion boards that could select officers any more skillfully than the electors themselves could.

[62] Sears, *Gates of Richmond*, pp. 117-118, 146-147; OR 11, pt. 1, pp. 961, 967; William F. Fox, *Regimental Losses in the American Civil War, 1861-1865* (Albany: Brandow Printing, 1898; reprint, Dayton: Morningside, 1985), pp. 561-562.

[63] Sears, *Gates of Richmond*, pp. 118-126.

[64] Ibid., pp. 126-128; Fleming, *Memoir*, pp. 48-50. The 12-pounder case shot carried about ninety shrapnel bullets. See C. S. Ordnance Bureau, *The Field Manual for the Use of the Officers on Ordnance Duty* (Richmond: Ritchie & Dunnavant, 1862; reprint, Gettysburg: Dean S. Thomas, 1984), p. 23.

[65] Fleming, *Memoir*, pp. 48-50; OR 11, pt. 1, pp. 916-922.

[66] OR 11, pt. 1, pp. 961-962, 967.

[67] Ibid., pp. 959, 962-964; Fleming, *Memoir*, pp. 50, 112-114.

[68] OR 11, pt. 1, pp. 962-964, 968; Sears, *Gates of Richmond*, pp. 130-131, 144-145.

[69] Sears, *Gates of Richmond*, pp. 239-250, 293-294, 298-304; Fleming, *Memoir*, pp. 115-117.

[70] See Chapter V for William A. Mangham's experiences in the 14th Alabama. Since his regiment and Oliver's 2nd Florida were in the same brigade at the Seven Days' battles, the two cousins witnessed very similar events.

[71] Hartman, comp., *Biographical Rosters*, p. 170.

[72] CMSR, Oliver P. Mangam; OR IV, pt. 1, p. 1095.

[73] CMSR, Oliver P. Mangum, 1st Volunteer Regiment of Georgia; Marriage Records, Putnam County, Georgia. Further research is necessary to establish the relationships between Miles Turner and Capt. John Turner, as well as Macynthia Mangham and Oliver. Extant records name all of William Mangham's surviving children in 1851, but Macynthia may have predeceased him. On the other hand, she may have been an unidentified daughter of Solomon, who left minor children upon his death in 1810.

When Manning Bowling's will was probated in Putnam County in 1816, Solomon and William Mangham were listed in the document, as was James Turner (see Ballard, *Solomon Mangham*, pp. 186-187). Note also that Oliver's July 17 enlistment in the 1st Georgia is consistent with the law, which had directed that 12-months' men outside conscription age were eligible for discharge on July 16, 1862 (see OR IV, pt. 1, p. 1099).

[74] CMH, vol. 6, *Georgia*, pp. 23-24; Muster Roll, February 28, 1863, 1st Georgia (Olmstead's), NARA.

[75] CMSR, Oliver P. Mangum; Muster Rolls, February 28 and April 30, 1863, 1st Georgia (Olmstead's), NARA. Interestingly, a regimental strength return from December 1862 indicates that Pvt. O. P. *Mangham* was absent, sick. All other regimental records list him as *Mangum*.

[76] CMSR, Oliver P. Mangum; Letter, Isaac S. Toole to James A. Seddon, September 11, 1863, filed in Letters to the Confederate Secretary of War, file no. 289-A-1863, NARA. A receipt roll shows that Oliver signed for clothing at Guyton Hospital on November 9, 1863; interestingly, it claims he signed by mark ("x")! He also received pay for the period July through December 1863 on February 26, 1864, from A. B. Ragan. This officer does not appear on the rolls of Olmstead's 1st Georgia, so Oliver probably remained stationed at Guyton at this time. These two microfilmed records are catalogued with CMSR, Unfiled Slips (Confederate), M347, reel 247, NARA.

[77] Stewart Sifakis, *Compendium of the Confederate Armies: South Carolina and Georgia* (New York: Facts on File, 1995), pp. 173-174; CMSR, Oliver P. Mangum; Records of the Confederate A&IGO, Registers of Letters Received, Chapter I, vol. 64 (July-October 1864), file no. 1120-M-1864, NARA; Records of the Confederate A&IGO, Endorsements, Chapter I, vol. 30 (April-September 1864), p. 214, NARA; Louise Calhoun Barfield, *History of Harris County Georgia: 1827-1961* (Columbus: Columbus Office Supply Co., 1961), pp. 556-557. The A&IGO copyist referred to the writer requesting Oliver's detail as his mother, then wrote "wife" over the word "mother." Since these records refer to "Dr. O. P. Mangum," she probably requested his detail as a medical doctor. Unfortunately, neither her original letter nor the official reply survives, and the endorsement ledgers omit her name and address.

[78] Barfield, *History of Harris County Georgia*, pp. 556-557. The membership list published herein may have copied (or miscopied) a church index, or perhaps the compiler had access to the original letter Oliver submitted to terminate his membership. It would be interesting to know whether he signed it as *Mangum* or *Mangham*, especially since the latter spelling was well known in that part of Georgia.

[79] Patricia B. Hensley and James W. Hensley, *Trinity County Beginnings* (N.p.: Trinity County Book Committee, 1986), pp. 39, 110; Cherry, "History of Opelika," p. 460. Bryant served as County Clerk from 1857 to 1864, and again from 1866 until his death. Bryant left Angeline with their 21-year-old daughter Annie, 10-year-old son Bryant, Jr., and little Jack, age six. Although he had owned almost $8000 worth of property in 1860, this included slaves valued at $5000. His 414 acres of land and

associated livestock depreciated to less than $1500 by 1865, and the following year the same property was worth only $789. Within a year after his death, Angeline had sold 200 acres of their land; the remainder of her property was valued at a mere $180. See 1870 Census, Trinity County; Trinity County, 1860-1868 Tax Rolls, TSL.

[80] CMSR, Oliver P. Mangam, 2nd Florida. Miss Horner's relationship to Oliver is not known.

CHAPTER VIII: THERE'S TALL COTTON IN GEORGIA! THE JOSIAH THOMAS MANGUM FAMILY MOVES TO TALBOT COUNTY

1. "WHAT A TANGLED WEB WE WEAVE!" THE JOSIAH THOMAS MANGUM FAMILY

William Mangham's brother, Josiah Thomas Mangum, was over forty years of age when he moved from Granville County to eastern Talbot County, Georgia, in the late 1820s. Having lost his wife, Susannah Cooper Mangum, sometime in the two decades after their 1807 marriage, Josiah married Louisa Kirkland in 1827 before moving to Georgia. Apparently he left at least one adult son, Josiah Thomas Mangum, Jr., back in Granville County, but another son, Robert, settled nearby in Talbot County in the late 1820s. Yet another son, evidently, was William, commissioned a lieutenant in the militia of adjoining Harris County in 1828.[1] The elder Josiah Mangum's Talbot County household included his sons Arthur, Thomas, James, and daughter Jemima, as the family settled down to the seasonal rhythms of farm life in western Georgia.[2]

Only a few years remained to Josiah, however, before his death in 1836. Arthur served as administrator of his father's estate, and Thomas helped post the necessary security of $2500. In accordance with the laws of that era, Josiah's property was sold at auction on December 25, 1836 and in a second auction on January 27 of the following year. Arthur's report to the county Probate Judge detailed each item sold, its price, and its purchaser, but unfortunately, no records survive to identify each of Josiah's heirs by name. His adult sons Arthur, Robert, and Thomas bought most of the auctioned property, while their widowed stepmother, Louisa, purchased a variety of household items and provisions.[3]

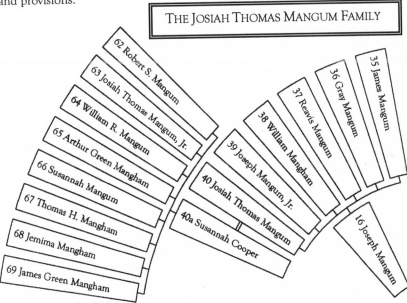

THE JOSIAH THOMAS MANGUM FAMILY

62 Robert S. Mangum
63 Josiah Thomas Mangum, Jr.
64 William R. Mangum
65 Arthur Green Mangham
66 Susannah Mangum
67 Thomas H. Mangham
68 Jemima Mangham
69 James Green Mangham

35 James Mangum
36 Gray Mangum
37 Reavis Mangum
38 William Mangham
39 Joseph Mangum, Jr.
40 Josiah Thomas Mangum
40a Susannah Cooper
16 Joseph Mangum

Arthur and Thomas moved beyond the Chattahoochee River soon after their father died, in the immediate aftermath of the Creek War. In Alabama and (eventually) Louisiana, their renewed ties with Solomon and William Mangham's descendants led them to adopt the earlier English spelling of their surname. This transformation began during their years in Georgia, where records referred to them as Mangum, Mangrum, Mangam, Manghum, or Mangham, but it was under the latter name that their sons marched beneath the Stars and Bars from 1861 to 1865.[4]

*   *   *   *   *

Robert S. Mangum had accepted a commission as first lieutenant in the Talbot County militia the year before his father died, and he remained there another five years before joining the ongoing westward migration in 1841 or 1842.[5] By 1850, he and his family reached Shelby County, Texas, whence they moved to Matagorda County by 1860.[6] Arthur's departure from Talbot County preceded Robert's by four or five years, but he led the younger members of the Josiah Mangum clan only just beyond the Chattahoochee River before settling down at the frontier crossroads of Salem, Alabama. There, in the immediate aftermath of the Creek War, he purchased a lot on the north side of the little town's Main Street, just across from property owned by his first cousin, Bryant S. Mangham.[7]

Bryant and his father William were prominent citizens in Russell County, and Willis Mangham's sons Henry C. and Thomas R. Mangham were likewise well known there (see Chapters II, III, VII). The Thomas and Wiley P. Mangham families had made their mark in neighboring Chambers County as well (see Chapters II and VI), and Josiah's sons Arthur, Thomas, and James began spelling their surname in the English fashion soon after arriving among their numerous cousins in eastern Alabama. They apparently used both spellings for some time, as James's family Bible listed children's names as *Mangum* up to the Civil War. Most surviving records in Alabama, however, indicate that Josiah's sons signed their legal transactions as *Mangham*.

2. "GONE TO ALABAMA": THE THOMAS H. MANGHAM FAMILY

Thomas H. Mangham married Rhoda C. Callaway of Chambers County on November 5, 1840, and they settled down to live in his house on a two-acre lot in Salem. He must have been an important figure in the little town, as he operated a tannery and made shoes to supply the community's needs. Artisans like Thomas were known as mechanics in the terminology of the rural South, and their skills were valued highly. In the era before mass production of such items, shoes were a critical commodity that most farm families could not make for their own use, so a neighborhood shoemaker was a welcome addition to any settlement.[8]

Thomas also owned half of a three-acre lot on which his tan yard was situated, half of a 27-acre lot on which his shoe shop stood, and half of another 20-acre lot in Russell County. He and his young bride were blessed with three children during the six years of their brief marriage: *Charles Arthur*, Martha S., and *William T. T. Mangham*. When

Thomas died sometime in late 1846, two-year-old Charles was the eldest of the three small children.[9]

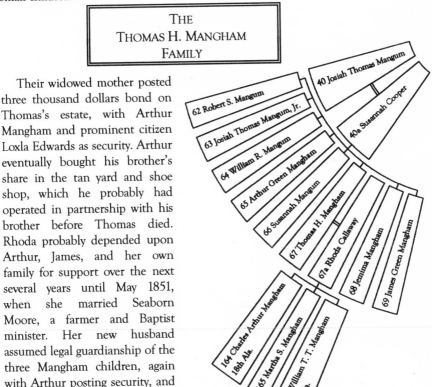

THE
THOMAS H. MANGHAM
FAMILY

40 Josiah Thomas Mangum

40a Susannah Cooper

62 Robert S. Mangum

63 Josiah Thomas Mangum, Jr.

64 William R. Mangum

65 Arthur Green Mangham

66 Susannah Mangum

67 Thomas H. Mangham

67a Rhoda Callaway

68 Jemima Mangham

69 James Green Mangham

164 Charles Arthur Mangham 18th Ala.

165 Martha S. Mangham

166 William T. T. Mangham 61st Ala.

Their widowed mother posted three thousand dollars bond on Thomas's estate, with Arthur Mangham and prominent citizen Loxla Edwards as security. Arthur eventually bought his brother's share in the tan yard and shoe shop, which he probably had operated in partnership with his brother before Thomas died. Rhoda probably depended upon Arthur, James, and her own family for support over the next several years until May 1851, when she married Seaborn Moore, a farmer and Baptist minister. Her new husband assumed legal guardianship of the three Mangham children, again with Arthur posting security, and eventually removed the family to Pine Flat, near Butler Springs in south central Alabama.[10]

3. WITH THE "LITTLE GIANTS" AT CHICKAMAUGA: CPL. CHARLES A. MANGHAM, "TOM WATTS RIFLES," CO. A, 18TH ALABAMA

Thirteen-year-old William ("Willie") T. T. Mangham remained in the elder Moore's prosperous plantation household in 1860, but Charles lived with his sister Martha in the nearby community of Mountain Home. Martha had married her stepbrother, Seaborn Moore, Jr., in December 1857 and the couple established their own household and small farm. There they took care of Charles and their own infant daughter Mary Elna (Madie), and the teenage boy must have been an asset to the younger Moore's farm operations. Born on September 14, 1844, Charles never really knew his own father, and the extended Moore family's prosperous farms and thriving ministry in Alabama's Black Belt comprised the milieu that shaped his outlook on the world. His stepfather, the elder Seaborn Moore, owned eight thousand dollars worth of real estate and eighteen slaves in the South's cotton-growing heartland, and he and his neighbors were utterly appalled at Abraham Lincoln's election in November 1860 on the "Black Republican" ticket. The presidential election triggered the constitutional crisis that had simmered for much of the preceding thirty years. On December 5, the men of Butler County's Beat 4 elected Seaborn J. Moore as one of two voices on a committee empowered to nominate the county's representatives to the state secession convention.[11]

The committee selected Judge S. J. Bolling and John McPherson to speak on the county's behalf, and their pronouncements reflect the fear, loathing, and resentment that Lincoln's election engendered throughout much of the South. Acknowledging this "sense of common danger," Bolling and McPherson opined that Lincoln had "been elected by the Abolitionists of the North to rule over us." They continued, "If we submit the Abolitionists have us in their power, and will, in a few short years, establish

THE SEABORN MOORE HOME IN BUTLER COUNTY, ALABAMA.
CHARLES AND WILLIE MANGHAM LIVED HERE WITH THEIR MOTHER AND STEPFATHER
BEFORE THE WAR. (SEE APPENDIX, REF. # 164, 166.)

- Courtesy of Glenda Owens

the doctrine of Negro equality, and degrade the white men of the South, politically, to the level of the negro." For the Butler County representatives, the choice was clear: secession or submission.[12]

Such fiery rhetoric expressed succinctly the worst fears of a white populace whose social and economic systems were grounded in chattel slavery. Their lingering fears of servile insurrection were stoked by bitter memories of John Brown's sensational Harper's Ferry raid of the previous year, and by his ensuing martyrdom in the Abolitionist press. Generally, white men in Alabama's Black Belt either owned slaves or served as overseers for those who did; even poorer whites who had no direct economic connection to the "peculiar institution" occupied a social status lofty by contrast to the degraded slave. For all of them, the idea of emancipation was anathema. Despite the fact that Lincoln himself, along with most Abolitionists, protested that social equality of whites and blacks was a humbug, white Southerners sensed a clear connection between political and social equality. After all, if freedom were no longer the exclusive province of whites, then on what moral, ethical, or legal basis could one insist upon continued political and social subordination of blacks?[13]

The inexorable logic of the situation led to the ultimate bogey, which Southern newspaper editors and politicians captured for their audiences: any "husky buck Negro" would soon feel free to jostle white women from the sidewalk, and even make lustful advances towards them with impunity. On the one hand, white Southerners found such waking nightmares almost literally unbelievable, for they lived in a world where any such displays of "impudence" met with certain and severe punishment, even death. On the other hand, these visions seemed the likely outcome of a topsy-turvy world in which white-enforced discipline no longer constrained the blacks that surrounded them in such numbers. Such fears were especially dominant in areas where slavery was intensely commercial, such as Alabama's Black Belt, Mississippi's Yazoo Delta, and the rich sugar and cotton lands of Louisiana's Red and Mississippi River valleys. Here, purely exploitative commercial relationships often replaced the familiarity and relative trust that characterized the ties between most small farmers and their slaves. Filled with loathing and fear by such seemingly hellish prospects, men and boys in central Alabama flocked to the colors in 1861. Not for them the hesitation and uncertainty of the mountain districts, where secession met with a decidedly mixed response.[14]

Of course many Southerners enlisted more from a sense of adventure than from any real fear that such worst-case scenarios could actually materialize, and even more volunteered out of a general sense that their homes and firesides were endangered. All of these factors were in the air that summer in Butler County, as Capt. H. Clay Armstrong's company organized on July 16. With their tender of service accepted by Governor A. B. Moore, the "Tom Watts Rifles" went into camp at Butler Springs on July 27. Five days later they were ordered to march to a Camp of Instruction at Auburn, Alabama. As they prepared to depart on August 2, a strapping lad of sixteen, Charles Arthur Mangham, got Captain Armstrong to swear him in as a private, to serve for the duration of the war. The young boy would prove to be a man of his word.[15]

*   *   *   *   *

Armstrong's men were at the regimental rendezvous at Auburn about six weeks before the last companies arrived, so it was September 19 before the 18th Alabama Infantry mustered into Confederate service. Colonel Judge, commanding the 14th Alabama, saw to the completion of the new outfit's organization and served as its interim commander until Col. Edward Bullock arrived to take charge. Private Mangham was one of 86 officers and men in the Tom Watts Rifles, which now became Company F.[16]

The new regiment remained at Auburn until late October, while its officers and men wrestled with the evolutions of company and battalion drill and learned the rudiments of military discipline. Since they were still unarmed, however, the frustrated volunteers could make little progress in the manual of arms. As they awaited developments at Auburn, the camp diseases that ravaged all new Confederate regiments broke out in full fury. Armstrong's Company F had sixteen of its number sick at the unit's first muster, and Company I reported on November 18 that "three-fourths of its members have been sick with measles, besides having suffered much with other diseases." Colonel Bullock himself died within weeks of assuming command, and regimental returns for November show that nineteen men died of disease in that month alone. Most of the sick were able to remain in camp hospitals initially, however, as the same return shows that 868 were present of an aggregate strength of 943 officers and men. One of those on the rolls was Pvt. S. Y. Moore, a son of Seaborn, and Charles Mangham's stepbrother.[17]

The report was compiled at Camp Memminger, at Hall's Mill on the Dog River near Mobile. The regiment had been ordered from Auburn to Huntsville in late October, but barely arrived there before entraining for Corinth, Mississippi, en route to Alabama's premier port city. The epidemic fevers that ravaged Camp Memminger killed men by the hundreds, and some fifteen men succumbed in Company G alone.[18] These tribulations typified the experience of the South's newly recruited legions, just as the regiment's difficulty in obtaining serviceable weapons exemplified the supply crisis that caused the government to suspend the enlistment of new regiments. As their peregrinations evidenced, however, there was a crying need for military presence in the variously threatened portions of the Confederacy at exactly this time. Exacerbating the desperate shortages of arms and men, the badly overtaxed transportation system was inadequate to serve the new country's far-flung frontiers, as the 18th Alabama's circuitous route to Mobile illustrates. Taken as a whole, Charles's experiences in his first months of military service present in microcosm the Confederacy's daunting array of challenges.

Given the 18th Alabama's frequent transfers and rampant sickness, it is no surprise that some of its companies reported themselves "deficient in the various drills" as late as New Year's Eve, 1861. The men of the Tom Watts Rifles remained completely unarmed almost six months after their enlistment. General Braxton Bragg was in command of the Department of Alabama and West Florida at this juncture, and he considered his raw levies "particularly destructive" of the few weapons that were available. Untrained men, under ignorant or inattentive officers and non-commissioned officers, knew little about maintaining weapons in camp and field, and Bragg recognized that it was an uphill struggle to remedy the situation. His efforts paid dividends, however, as the soldiers of his department already had built a reputation for discipline and training that set them above most of the units posted along the Tennessee and Kentucky frontiers; even their enemies had heard of their vaunted superiority. For men like Charles, this had meant clearing acre upon acre of virgin pine forest to provide space for their incessant drill, and one member of the 18th Alabama reckoned that the trees they felled would have provided "millions of feet of lumber."[19]

The Federal threat to Mobile was certainly real, as the blockading squadron anchored outside the harbor reminded its defenders on a daily basis. Nevertheless, Union armies penetrating up the Tennessee and Cumberland Rivers during the disastrous winter of 1862 served notice that the Confederacy faced a life or death situation. Major General U. S. Grant's conquest of Rebel bastions at Forts Henry and Donelson had earned him the sobriquet "Unconditional Surrender Grant," a clever play on his initials and his "hard war" outlook. His successes enabled Union fleets to ferry troops rapidly through the heart of the South's defensive line in Kentucky and Tennessee, and Albert Sidney Johnston began a desperate withdrawal from his unhinged positions. While he struggled to reposition his army, Johnston sent the hero of Fort Sumter, Lt. Gen. Pierre G. T. Beauregard, to organize the defense of the Mississippi River valley and its environs.[20]

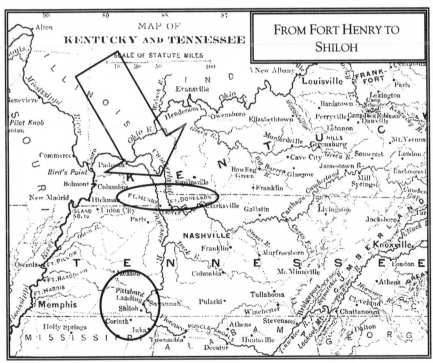

The famous Creole issued calls to the Deep South governors for emergency reinforcements, and their states responded by forwarding troops from various points. In Mobile, Braxton Bragg received word of Beauregard's critical situation from Governor Watts, and he wasted no time in dispatching three regiments from Mobile to rendezvous at Corinth. Here, the Mobile and Ohio Railroad connected with the Memphis and Charleston line, providing the Confederacy with life-sustaining communications between Kentucky and the Gulf of Mexico, and between the Trans-Mississippi states and the Atlantic seaboard. As Bragg explained in a February 27 message to Beauregard, "I am acting on my own responsibility, and doing what it seems to us ought to have been done long ago—concentrating our limited means at some important point to resist a vital blow."[21]

A hurricane blew down many of the 18th Alabama's cabins at Camp Memminger on February 26, and Charles presumably lived through the awe-inspiring storm that his third cousin *Tom Mangham* of the 25th Alabama wrote home about (see Chapter III). If so, the seventeen-year-old soldier had a doubly eventful day, for his regiment was one of the three that Bragg ordered to Corinth that very day, while seven others followed soon thereafter. Unbeknownst to the men clambering into the cars at Mobile for the long ride north, Corinth would mean Shiloh Church, and the little log meeting house in the Tennessee backwoods would mean hell.[22]

*   *   *   *   *

March 1862 witnessed an ongoing buildup of Confederate forces about Corinth, and resulted in the eventual coalescence of the Army of the Mississippi under Johnston's command. Despite these unprecedented comings and goings in the woods of northern Mississippi, however, the army's eventual attack surprised its foes at every level: tactical, operational, and strategic. (See map on page 126.)

Scattered skirmishing between pickets and cavalrymen during the preceding days should have aroused the Union forces at Pittsburg Landing to their imminent peril. Indeed, the unwieldy approach march of the various Confederate commands through the Mississippi and Tennessee backwoods convinced Beauregard to recommend cancellation of the attack. Surely, the Yankees would be ready to smite the awkward columns hip and thigh after all the commotion of their blundering advance! Johnston's emotions had reached fever pitch, however, and he was determined to fight. Maneuvered out of Kentucky and Tennessee, he did not intend to miss an opportunity to strike a blow.[23]

In the early dawn of April 6, his columns came pouring through the woods into a stunning attack against Federal encampments that were scattered unwarily through the fields and woods around Pittsburg Landing. The 413 men of Col. Eli Shorter's 18th Alabama could hear Federal drummers beating the long roll to call their men into line about 4:30, just minutes before popping musketry signaled that bluecoated pickets were firing on the skirmishers who fanned out before the attacking columns.[24]

Shorter's regiment was brigaded with the 17th and 19th Alabama regiments and the 2nd Texas, all commanded by Brig. Gen. John K. Jackson of Georgia. His brigade was in

Maj. Gen. Jones Withers's Division of Bragg's Corps, and occupied a place in the second line behind Gladden's Brigade, with only Chalmers's Mississippi brigade on their right. Jackson's men moved into the front line about 8:30 a.m., advancing with Gladden's and Chalmers's brigades against Union forces posted in Sarah Bell's cotton field. Their opponents were badly weakened by this time, but put on a bold front that convinced the Confederates to probe cautiously rather than attack vigorously. The 18th Alabama was ordered to lie down as enemy cannon fire showered them with fragments, killing two men and wounding three. Skirmishers out front popped away as Jackson brought Girardey's Georgia battery into action, but before the attack developed, Johnston sent orders to move to the right again to counter a Federal division.[25]

This "division" was actually Col. David Stuart's brigade posted in Larkin Bell's fields, overlapping Johnston's extreme right flank. Stuart had no aggressive designs for the moment, but his position posed a terrible threat to which Johnston reacted vigorously. For Charles Mangham and his comrades, this meant a "very fatiguing march" for half a mile or more over hill and dale, until they came to a halt and rested in sight of the enemy's camp. As skirmishers developed the enemy line, Jackson again brought his artillery into play while his infantrymen clambered down into a "swampy bottom." The Alabamians came up into thin air, as the 71st Illinois had given way after a short exchange of fire. The 55th Illinois and 54th Ohio reformed beyond their campgrounds, however, and prepared to hold on until somebody drove them out.[26]

Jackson, determined to accommodate, ordered another charge, but this time the 18th Alabama and 2nd Texas slammed into real resistance. The two regiments formed Jackson's left, and it seemed to them that the Yankees were threatening their left flank and rear. From the Federal perspective, it seemed that Rebs were boiling out of the woods from *their* left, and a desperate combat ensued as both sides fought to save themselves. One soldier in the 17th Alabama's ranks considered this the "most determined and obstinate part of the whole fight," as he and his comrades fired about forty rounds apiece. Forced to ransack the cartridge boxes of the wounded and dead, they had to reduce their volume of fire, but their opponents faltered first and withdrew.[27]

Jackson's men rested a few minutes, looking after the wounded and refilling canteens to quench the thirst caused by exertion, fear, and the acrid taste of cartridges and burnt powder. Then it was off again by the left flank, back down across the creek, and up once more into line of battle east of the Hamburg-Savannah Road, facing north toward the Tennessee River. Here they attacked again, on line between Gladden on their left and Chalmers on the right. The "thundering volley and hail storm of balls" from the fenceline and farm buildings east of the road gave notice that the bluecoats had received reinforcements, but the 17th and 18th Alabama delivered a bayonet charge to clear the fenceline and the Texans and 19th Alabama overran the buildings.[28]

As the Alabamians clambered across the fence and inclined to their left, they were blasted by Federal troops in solid array beyond the next field. Here another ferocious fight ensued, and one awestruck Alabama soldier wrote, "Such a storm of lead whistled around the heads of men as perhaps never was heard upon any battle field." In

Jackson's opinion, this fight at the Cloud Field was the "hottest of the day," and as men fell dead or wounded, others ran low on ammunition. Someone shouted to the 17th Alabama's flag bearer to lower the flag so it wouldn't attract so much fire, but the bearer refused and continued to flaunt it amidst the roar of musketry. More and more men were straggling out of the battle line, seeking ammunition, shelter, orders, or simply a safer place in the rear, and apparently the 19th Alabama wavered and fell back, pleading lack of ammunition. The 18th Alabama on the left and the Texans on the right then wavered as well, and the 17th Alabama followed soon afterwards. As the confused mass tumbled back across the field they had carried with the bayonet, Jackson demanded of Lieutenant Colonel Farris the reason for the retreat. Before he could answer, the men surrounding him were shouting, "Give us ammunition!" and "We are out of cartridges!"[29]

The Georgian sent them all back to the front with orders to hold their positions with the bayonet, but even he must have been relieved when Gladden's Brigade returned to his support. After another resupply of ammunition and some reorganization, Jackson's men attacked across the Hamburg-Savannah Road about five o'clock, in tandem with Chalmers's and Gladden's brigades. Another half-hour of heavy fighting and the Federal position was smashed. Approximately 2200 men under the overall command of General Prentiss grounded their weapons and hoisted the white flag. The Union left was destroyed, but the time and effort it cost the Confederates to reduce this position allowed Grant the opportunity to cobble together a final defensive line along the river.[30]

Men in the 18th Alabama counted twenty of their comrades killed in action, eighty wounded, and another twenty missing and presumed captured; only eight other Southern regiments suffered higher losses. Of these casualties, Butler County's Tom Watts Rifles suffered three killed and ten wounded.[31] The survivors were not alone in their belief that the battle was over and victory complete, and their assignment to escort the prisoners to Corinth took them away from the field before Grant's last line was discovered. As Private Mangham helped herd the defeated Yankees back to Corinth, his nerves must have been tingling with the shocks of the day and the exultation of victory. He and his comrades could bask in the praise of their regimental commander, who reported proudly that his men "conducted themselves throughout the several engagements with much gallantry and spirit." Corporal Edgar Jones, of Company G, recalled that General Prentiss was "a most surly, crusty prisoner, cursing everything in sight, even to the soil of the country; snarling and snapping at everything."[32]

The 18th Alabama Volunteers were not present on the field the next day, when the newly arrived Army of the Cumberland counterattacked to rescue Federal fortunes. It was one of the most stunning reversals of fortune in the entire war, and the Union victory on April 7 sent the disorganized Confederate army reeling back to its lines at Corinth. Most of the men would have agreed with one Irishman, who quipped, "We went to church last Sunday week, didn't we?" Receiving the answer, "Yes, to Shiloh

Church," he responded flatly: "Well, I'm not going anymore, I don't like the sermons they preach there."[33]

*   *   *   *   *

The 18th Alabama helped hold the lines against extremely cautious Federal encroachment over the next two months, standing picket guard in trenches erected to defend the vital railroad junction. In late May, however, they joined the rest of the army in a well-executed withdrawal from the beleaguered town, avoiding its inevitable encirclement by superior Federal forces. On June 3 the regiment was halted and sent back to assume rear guard duties near Blackland, accompanied by the 24th Alabama, a section of Burtwell's Battery, and some 300 cavalrymen. Union cavalry units under the command of Brigadier General Granger tried to rush the rear of Bragg's column by overrunning his rear guard, but on June 4 the Alabamians administered a sharp repulse to Elliott's cavalry brigade. The 18th Alabama suffered five wounded in the exchange, but held the bridge crossing over Twenty Mile Creek for two more days before continuing the retreat to Tupelo. For their efforts, the 18th Alabama was authorized to inscribe the battle honor "Blackland" on colors that already bore the proud name "Shiloh."[34]

The regiment drilled under Jackson's demanding eye at Tupelo and Saltillo that summer, until orders came to return to the Mobile garrison in late July. The existing muster rolls from December 1861 through December 1862 reflect Private Mangham as present, and he probably was glad to trade Mississippi's scarce water and blazing heat for the Gulf breezes of garrison duty in the big city. Harking back to their earlier sojourn in Mobile, the men again cleared away trees and brush to provide open space for a brigade drill ground. This time, however, they were at Camp Forney, about four miles from town, as opposed to their old campsite on Dog River at Hall's Mills. While at Camp Forney, the veteran soldiers were brigaded with untried units, the 36th, 38th, and 40th Alabama Volunteers, and served as the city police force for several months.[35]

Colonel James T. Holtzclaw assumed command of the 18th Alabama that summer, and took it north to Tennessee once more in April 1863 when operational requirements dictated strengthening the Army of Tennessee. This time the clattering railcars led through Chattanooga to Wartrace along the Duck River line, where Bragg's men had wintered after falling back from Murfreesboro in January. The Alabama brigade (minus the 40th Alabama) was assigned to Brig. Gen. Henry D. Clayton, in A. P. Stewart's Division.[36]

Spring turned into summer before Union Maj. Gen. William Rosecrans took the initiative from Bragg, executing a clever series of maneuvers that unhinged the Confederates' ill-posted defensive line. The 18th Alabama was involved in a minor engagement near Wartrace as this operation unfolded, but gradually withdrew all the way to Chattanooga, since the terrain offered the army no place to anchor its flanks for a successful stand.[37] When Rosecrans skillfully crossed the Tennessee River and began making his way past Bragg's army once more, the Confederate commander began casting about desperately for a place to strike back. After the long weeks of

487

maneuvering and positional warfare in Tennessee, he finally got his opportunity in the heavily forested hills of north Georgia. Rosecrans had allowed his army to fragment as it moved through the mountain valleys past Bragg's flank, and the Confederate commander conceived several plans that should have resulted in the utter destruction of large portions of the invading army. Time after time, however, Confederate blunders allowed the widely separated Union army corps to escape seemingly certain destruction, until they finally united once more along Chickamauga Creek.[38]

The 18th Alabama marched hard in the vain attempt to catch two divisions of Maj. Gen. George Thomas's army corps escaping across Stevens's Gap on September 11. The Alabamians had been put in harness, quite literally, as forty-man teams pulled artillery pieces and wagons over the steep mountain roads. As one member of the regiment recalled, "The quartermasters and wagonmasters talked to us as if we were horses sure enough. . .I remember how an old colonel of artillery did curse."[39]

In retrospect, one can only wonder about the ramifications of Bragg's missed opportunities. A one-sided Confederate success against Rosecrans might have altered the outcome of the entire war. Only two months after Lee's defeat at Gettysburg and Pemberton's surrender of Vicksburg, how would North and South have responded to the entrapment and destruction of Rosecrans's army in Georgia?

*   *   *   *   *

Bragg finally landed a glancing blow on his opponent near Gordon's Mills on September 18, and that night his army prepared again to come to grips with the invaders. Lieutenant Bromfield Ridley, an aide on General Stewart's staff, overheard men throughout the division remarking, "Boys, we have retreated far enough; we will whip 'em this time or die." The next two days would prove that they meant what they said.[40]

Charles Mangham's regiment remained in Clayton's Brigade, Stewart's Division, which now comprised part of Breckenridge's Corps of Longstreet's Left Wing. Clayton's men had marched on September 17 from LaFayette, Georgia, rested that night near Rock Spring, and proceeded the following day to Thedford's Ford on Chickamauga Creek. Three cannon shots came sizzling their way, killing a man in the 36th Alabama and breaking the musket of another in the 38th. Stewart's staff worried about the effects on the green regiments, but after the excitement died down, the brigade waded the creek and bivouacked on its banks in the chilly darkness.[41]

Shivering throughout the night without the benefit of campfires, the Alabamians moved forward a mile or two in line of battle the next morning, allowing the remainder of Stewart's Division to cross the creek in their rear. There they waited in Bragg's second line, listening to the growing roar of battle on their right. Several of Charles's second and third cousins, *John W. Mangham* (2nd Georgia Sharpshooters) and *Thomas W.* and *Willis A. Mangham* (30th Georgia), were in the thick of the fighting on that flank. Stewart's men, however, waited vainly for orders until about 1:30 p.m., when they again shifted a mile to the right. As one man reported, "We were 'right-flanked,' and 'left-flanked,' and 'forwarded,' so often and so fast that we were bewildered, somewhat disordered and quite out of breath, before we reached the enemy."[42]

In deference to his background as a mathematics instructor at West Point and Cumberland University, his soldiers knew Maj. Gen. Alexander P. Stewart as "Old Straight." He had been summoned to support Cheatham's hard-pressed division, and that was exactly what he intended to do, despite confusion caused by the fog of war. As "Old Straight" marshaled his division in the dense woods east of the LaFayette Road and south of the Brock Field, he wheeled them left into column of brigades and warned Clayton to use his initiative and be "governed by circumstances" when he contacted the enemy. Clayton's Alabamians formed the blunt end of Stewart's battering ram formation, and they moved behind a screen of skirmishers into the dense woods in search of the enemy. On their way into action, they passed a badly wounded man being carried out by litter-bearers. Although his intestines protruded from his terrible wounds, he excitedly waved his hat at the arriving reinforcements, shouting, "Boys, when I left we were driving 'em!"[43]

Captain Ben Lane led Company K, 38th Alabama through the forest, and his experiences there led him to compose a letter to the Mobile *Register and Advertiser* shortly after the battle. His memorable description of the detritus of combat provides a vivid word-picture in striking contrast to the typical descriptions of serried ranks and parade-ground formations:

> The woods—it was all woods—was full of stragglers, and skulkers, and wounded. Whole companies, regiments and brigades seemed scattered to the winds. Officers, even, with their tinsel on them, seemed to be hunting a safe place in the rear. The fugitives told the wildest tales of flight and massacre, of regiments, and brigades, "cut all to pieces." Of course, they exaggerated the facts, as an excuse for their own flight, but the actual state of the case, was bad enough, without exaggeration. The scene was disgraceful to our army, and at one time, I thought the battle lost, for it seemed that everybody had run, or was running from the enemy.[44]

As the Alabama soldiers forged through the undergrowth and flying fugitives, Col. John Carter of the 38th Tennessee came running up to warn Clayton that he was about to march squarely across the Federal front. Since the brigade was marching by the left flank, the 38th Alabama was in the lead; Clayton hastily ordered it to file double-quick to the left and rear. This timely maneuver sheared his brigade away from its appointment with disaster by allowing its line of battle to confront the enemy when shots rang out just moments later. Even so, the lead files of the 38th Alabama went down in windrows under the close range volley that struck them as they deployed. Corporal Edgar Jones of Company G, 18th Alabama, thought the unseen enemy were within fifty yards when they opened fire unexpectedly, and within "three minutes the engagement was something awful. The slaughter was dreadful."[45]

The men of the 38th Alabama's left flank automatically faced front as the firing began, but were forced to return fire before they could "undouble," or form into the two ranks that constituted a proper line of battle. This meant that the men in the front rank received the enemy's fire in their faces, plus the fire of their own third and fourth ranks from the rear. The problem worsened quickly. Captain Lane observed that "a scramble for the rear rank" ensued, creating a fifth, sixth, and even seventh rank in the confusion. The regiment "kept up a wild fusillade," but the stalwarts in the front rank gradually sidled backwards to escape the fire from both directions. Eventually, the untested regiment recoiled in disorder, with some men claiming they heard orders to retreat, but they rallied and fought on until eventually ordered back by Clayton. Lane saw that the same predicament afflicted the 36th Alabama on his right, which also was undergoing its baptism of fire.[46]

The 18th Alabama was on the right flank, screened from Captain Lane's view, so he was unable to observe how the Shiloh veterans reacted to the close-range encounter. They faced the same murderous, plunging crossfire that riddled their sister regiments, and they, too, returned fire with a will. Their officers soon ordered them to lie down, however, making them cease fire to conserve ammunition. Helplessly exposed to the withering fire for a half-hour, they sprang to their feet to charge when ordered. Whether through a misunderstanding or coincidence, however, they immediately received orders from Clayton to march by the left flank and then fall back. The two leftmost companies fell back in good order, while the rest pulled back with more difficulty, finally reforming several hundred yards to the rear.[47]

Clayton estimated his brigade lost almost 400 officers and men in this hour-long crucible in the claustrophobic Georgia woods. Lieutenant Ridley was appalled at how the Alabamians were "mown down like grain before the reaper" in combat he equated to "the destruction of hail stones to a growing cornfield." Their opponents were eight regiments of Betty's and Dick's brigades, both of which belonged to Brig. Gen. Horatio VanCleve's division. Another five regiments of Grose's brigade had enfiladed their right and rear. Charles Mangham's hard-hit regiment reported a loss of 35 killed and 175 wounded, or some forty percent of its total strength![48]

Despite this bloodletting, they distributed fresh ammunition, regrouped, and returned to the attack at four o'clock that afternoon. Brown's and Bate's brigades of Stewart's Division had continued the seesaw struggle in the thickets, and the sustained combat was wearing down the men in blue. VanCleve received reinforcements too, but his line was shoved backwards across the LaFayette Road to the fields south of the Brotherton House. The desperate Federals were blasting away with muskets and cannon as fast as they could load and fire, but the Confederates were attacking with a force "that seemed irresistible." Stewart's men enjoyed the nickname of the "Little Giant Division," and the hammering they meted out to VanCleve eventually pierced the center of the entire Union line in fighting that Lieutenant Ridley described as "*war to the knife and a fight to the finish.*" Clayton's screaming Alabamians were the ones who pushed through along the road and penetrated a half-mile farther to the Glenn-Kelly Road, reaching the tan yard on the Dyer Farm. From the Glenn House, Rosecrans anxiously watched to see if his center would collapse totally. The 18th Alabama, the brigade's right flank regiment, overran an abandoned howitzer section, with

Lieutenant Holtzclaw's Company G claiming the honor of passing directly over the guns.[49]

The breakthrough petered out for lack of support, however, and Clayton's scattered regiments fell back to consolidate along the LaFayette road, as reports arrived of Yankee divisions arriving to seal off the penetration on the flanks. After tying in their flanks to Bate's and Brown's brigades, the weary Alabama "Yellowhammers" slept on their arms in line of battle, as Yankee axemen felled trees to build breastworks. In a daylong battle of terrible intensity, the Little Giant division had performed magnificently.[50]

The next day General Bragg again launched Stewart's Division at the enemy, after moving them farther to the right, but their resolute assault was unsupported. This was a common predicament for both Rebs and Yanks at Chickamauga, and the result was simply wasted valor. They had suffered under a galling artillery fire before moving into the attack, and guns to their front and both flanks simply slaughtered the attacking waves. Clayton's Brigade was in the supporting line of Stewart's attack, and was called into action near noon. Captain Justice, commanding the 18th Alabama's Company A, cheered his regiment prematurely into a headlong charge, but artillery fire pounded the screaming assault waves into fragments after they pushed through dense woods into an open field. Although their charge compelled the Yankee gunners in their front to abandon their pieces, the exhausted Alabamians' assault stalled at that critical moment, for the field itself became "a sheer slaughter pen." Captain Lane thought, "We were one vast, chaotic, whelming mass of armed men, every man doing as he chose, to stop or go on." They fell back "in some confusion" before a "fire of grape and canister almost too terrible for human nature to endure."[51]

In Lane's assessment, they were now ripe for counterattack, as "great demoralization and panic" threatened to overwhelm the shocked and scattered remnants of the brigade. Instead of facing a counterattack, however, they were given a respite by events elsewhere on the Confederate line. Indeed, their division-sized assault barely anticipated a massive, coordinated attack by the remainder of Longstreet's force to their immediate left. Within the shelter of the dark woods, "Old Pete" massed eight relatively fresh brigades on a two-brigade front, just a half-mile in width. In his nine-brigade assault at Gettysburg just two months earlier, four were badly depleted before they even began their ill-fated attack across the mile of open fields fronting Cemetery Ridge.[52]

This time the result was different, as Longstreet's assault went by chance towards an unintentional gap in the Federal line. A gigantic rupture ensued, and the floodgates of disaster yawned wide for Rosecrans's army over the next several hours. When Clayton's bloodied brigade renewed its attack late that afternoon near Snodgrass Hill, it was an effort to exploit Longstreet's success. Major General Thomas earned his nickname as the "Rock of Chickamauga" by his desperate defense of that hill, and his stand allowed the remainder of Rosecrans's beaten army to flee the field. But even his defense eventually came to an end. When the men of the 18th Alabama surged across the Kelly Field in their final charge of the battle, they helped unhinge the last remnants of the Federal defenses east of the LaFayette Road; the "Yaller Hammers" found themselves marching almost unopposed into deserted breastworks. Clambering across the abandoned entrenchments, they moved out into the open field to fire into the backs of the fleeing enemy and sweep up prisoners.[53]

Corporal Jones of Company G had spent the day lying in the field hospital, listening to savage gunfire that produced "one solid, unbroken wave of awe-inspiring sound." It seemed to him that the "furies of earth and hell had been turned loose in one mighty effort to destroy each other." As evening settled over the woods, however, the "Confederate yell of victory and triumph" signaled that the field was won. The "Southern anthem" that arose that evening on the right wing of Bragg's army soon spread to the left wing and back again. The Rebel yell issued from tens of thousands of throats simultaneously, echoing through the hills and hoarsely heralding total victory. The fighting was over and triumph on the battlefield was complete. Many of Longstreet's veterans well knew the thrill of victory in battle, but Bragg's Army of Tennessee had experienced only the momentary triumphs of Shiloh and Murfreesboro, each of which had turned into galling, dispiriting retreat. Heady though it was that evening, the hecatombs of groaning wounded cast a disquieting pall over the campfires flickering in the Georgia woods. Bragg's men, their blood running hot, reflected with satisfaction that Longstreet's vaunted Virginians had now met "Western Yankees," who "soon taught them as we had learned, that we were of the same blood and meeting foemen worthy of our steel."[54]

*　　*　　*　　*　　*

In another amazing turnabout, the tonic of victory at Chickamauga soon turned once more into the bitter draught of missed opportunity. We will never know how the war's course would have changed had Bragg managed to gobble up Rosecrans's scattered army corps in the maneuvering of mid-September, because the battle that eventually raged in the thickets along Chickamauga Creek resembled nothing more than a lethal brawl of horrific proportions. When Bragg brought Rosecrans to bay on September 18, 1863, the ensuing bloodbath routed the invading force and sent it reeling headlong to safety in Chattanooga. In the process, however, Bragg became convinced that his own terribly bloodied army was unable to pursue and destroy the fleeing enemy. While some subordinate commanders agreed, many others were so enraged by his inactivity that they practically mutinied. Veterans and historians alike have made much of the resulting command shakeups and associated operational blunders, but relatively little has been made of the catastrophic damage that the Army of Tennessee sustained at Chickamauga. How would ensuing events have been different had the holocaust in the north Georgia woods been avoided?

The experience of Charles Mangham and his Alabama regiment was relatively typical of Confederate units in the West's bloodiest battle: it played its part to the hilt, but was practically destroyed in the process. Of the 162 Confederate infantry regiments and separate battalions present at Chickamauga, the 18th Alabama Volunteer Infantry suffered *the highest casualty toll.* Five hundred twenty-seven officers and men had followed its colors into battle on September 19; forty-one were dead and another 256

492

wounded by sundown on the next day. This aggregate casualty rate exceeded 56 percent, coinciding almost exactly with the 54 percent casualty rate suffered by the regiment's 37 officers, of whom four were killed and sixteen wounded. Seventeen of the killed and wounded belonged to the Tom Watts Rifles.[55]

*   *   *   *   *

Charles, who turned nineteen on September 14, was among the men occupying the siege lines that formed around the beleaguered Federals at Chattanooga. Although he was promoted to corporal at some point during 1863, the fearful bickering that beset the Army of Tennessee's high command after Chickamauga gave him and his victorious comrades-in-arms precious little to celebrate. Their generals openly split into pro- and anti-Bragg factions, with many premier commanders importuning President Davis to relieve the man who failed to destroy Rosecrans's routed Army of the Cumberland. Of course, this was merely the latest in the list of Bragg's tactical and strategic failures, which included Perryville, the Kentucky Campaign, Murfreesboro, and the summer campaign in Middle Tennessee.[56]

Even Bragg's dilatory siege tactics at Chattanooga were gravely flawed, as he failed to take positive measures to ensure that his opponent's supply lines were completely interdicted. When Rosecrans was replaced by Ulysses S. Grant in October, active measures to improve the desperate Union supply situation succeeded in reestablishing an adequate flow of logistical support. Their grayclad besiegers not only failed to cut Yankee supply lines, but also suffered a self-inflicted logistical muddle that kept them cold and hungry. The near-starvation of the Army of the Cumberland in October was matched by the hardships besetting the hungry Confederates south of the Tennessee River, with many reduced to scrounging corn meant for army horses, or even scavenging for rats. Still more damaging to Southern prospects, however, was Bragg's next strategic blunder. He seized the chance in early November to dispatch two divisions under his unruly subordinate (and potential rival), James Longstreet, to strike Ambrose Burnside's Union force at Knoxville. On these flimsy strategic grounds, Bragg rid himself of a political enemy at the cost of a huge decrease in his combat power. He aggravated the damage later that month by sending yet another division to East Tennessee. Grant, by contrast, received massive reinforcements in the form of Joe Hooker and two corps from the Army of the Potomac, while William T. Sherman and two divisions were marching in from the west.[57]

Bragg's incredible blunders transformed the tactical situation at Chattanooga in the two months following Chickamauga. He had botched the siege, and now his vendetta against disloyal subordinates apparently blinded him to the tactical implications of ridding himself of Longstreet and his troops. His 37,000 remaining troops now faced some 80,000 bluecoats, and the impregnability of his positions on Lookout Mountain and in front of Missionary Ridge was more apparent than real. In fact, he had never emplaced his troops in anything resembling coherent defensive positions, and the thin skirmish lines on the mountain were highly vulnerable to assault. The bulk of the army was posted on or before Missionary Ridge, but an incredibly flawed defensive scheme

493

split the available forces between rifle pits at its base, a few scattered positions on the slopes, and thinly-manned, poorly sited positions on the topographical crest. Here the fields of fire were limited to a few yards in many sectors, thus ensuring that the thinly spread defenders would have minimal time to react to any attackers popping up in their immediate front. No reserves remained, and artillery pieces were scattered along the crest in positions that made impossible any movement to front or rear. Some of the infantrymen in the rifle pits at the base of the ridge had orders to pull back after firing one volley, while many others never heard anything of such a plan. The men atop the ridge likewise knew nothing of it, so it tragically ensured that some would stand fast while others withdrew, each convinced of his neighbor's failure (or inability) to obey orders. Men retreating uphill were bound to screen their comrades' fields of fire, and were just as certain to arrive on the crest too exhausted to fight, assuming they made it at all. Incredible as it seems, Bragg's army spent two full months at Chattanooga, but these terribly faulty dispositions were not improvised until November 23, 1863. In no major battle of the war would a major army be so poorly prepared to defend itself. But ready or not, the ball was about to open. Grant's forces moved into action against Lookout Mountain on the next day.[58]

*   *   *   *   *

Only six Confederate brigades were strung out for ten miles along the base, mid-slope bench, and upper reaches of Lookout Mountain when the initial attack came, and the ensuing "Battle Above the Clouds" was more accurately a battle *in* the clouds. Joe Hooker's hard-driving troops had a tough time clambering up the slopes against the thinly-spread Rebels they faced, but made so much progress during the day that Bragg decided to abandon the mountain altogether. His primary concern was the northern (right) end of his line, where Sherman's river crossings in his front gave notice of Grant's impending main attack. Lookout Mountain was on the far southern end of the Confederate position, and too few troops were available to defend it. Its utility as an artillery platform had long since proved illusory anyway, since it lay out of effective range of most of Grant's lines. And after the Federals had secured Brown's Ferry in late October, Bragg's forces atop Lookout Mountain were no longer able to interdict the "Cracker Line" supplying Chattanooga via Bridgeport, Alabama. In short, the imposing mountain fastness retained only two significant military advantages: it protected the left flank of the Confederate positions on Missionary Ridge, and the seeming impregnability of its steep slopes offered a distinct morale boost to its possessors.[59]

In order to reposition Lookout's defenders on his threatened right flank before they were cut off by Hooker's advance, Bragg directed them to disengage and abandon the mountain that night. He selected Clayton's Brigade, temporarily commanded by Col. James T. Holtzclaw, to help Maj. Gen. Carter Stevenson secure his troops' passage down the slopes that night. The Alabamians had labored since daybreak to improve their trenches at the Watkins House on the southern flank of the Missionary Ridge position, and the fine, cold rain made for a treacherous approach march across

494

Chattanooga Creek to the mountain. Slipping and sliding on the slick mud, the men double-quicked much of the way, slowed to a quick time, and then double-quicked some more as they made their way to the mountain's base. There they halted to load their muskets and wait for dusk to cover their ascent. Federal batteries dropped a few shells in their assembly area, inflicting several casualties on the waiting men.[60]

As dusk settled down to cloak their movements, Holtzclaw's regiments began the steep climb up the muddy track. They marched by the left flank, with the 38th Alabama in the lead, the 36th following, then the 32nd-58th Alabama (Consolidated), followed by the 18th Alabama, the latter commanded by Lt. Col. Peter F. Hunley. Major General John C. Breckenridge, former Vice President of the United States, was the corps commander responsible for the south and center of the Confederate line, and he directed Holtzclaw to relieve Pettus's and Walthall's brigades and protect the withdrawal of all troops and their supply trains. Holtzclaw filed his column to the right on the Craven House Road, marched to Pettus's position, and filed left into the lines. Conducting a relief in place is tricky business when in direct contact with an enemy force, and the Alabamians were fortunate that most of the Yankees in their front were too busy scratching out breastworks to interrupt the relief.[61]

All went well until Major Thornton accidentally conducted the right wing of the 32nd-58th Alabama and the left wing of the 18th Alabama about fifty yards forward of the original line. This unintentional advance straightened the line from Lookout Point to the Craven House Road, but also pushed the Alabamians into the Federal picket line, triggering a sharp exchange of fire. The foggy mists had dissipated under the impact of a brisk wind, and the wet, chilled soldiers blazed away under a bright "hunter's moon." To observers in the Chattanooga lines, the winking muzzle flashes upon the mountainside presented an awe-inspiring sight, reminding them of thousands of fireflies. On the firing line itself, the Alabamians would shout "Lookout Yanks!" and fire a volley, crowing like roosters to complete the performance. Their antagonists shouted back "Lookout Johnny Reb!" before returning the fire, crowing in their turn.[62]

The extremely rough terrain kept casualties to a minimum, but the engagement was not all sport. Lieutenant Colonel John Inzer's 32nd-58th Alabama lost some three killed and fifteen wounded, while Hunley described the 18th Alabama as facing a "pretty heavy fire," from which it suffered but little. The brisk firing ebbed after Inzer and others forced their men to hold fire until a target presented itself, but the lively exchange impressed Grant and Hooker. Despite the confidence they had felt earlier that afternoon, they each concluded now that Bragg intended to fight for Lookout Mountain after all. Accordingly, Hooker shelved the idea of planning to exploit success, fearing that a counterattack on the western flank of the mountain might undo him. At most, he was content to focus on how to force his way up the mountain the next day. The resulting delay in Hooker's forward movement on November 25 postponed disaster for Bragg's army by a few hours at least, and perhaps prevented complete destruction of the Army of Tennessee.[63]

In Chattanooga Valley, Generals Cheatham, Stevenson, Breckinridge, and John K. Jackson completed plans for the Confederate withdrawal from Lookout Mountain. The men on the heights were to come down first, followed by Holtzclaw's command, with the 18th Alabama in the lead. Cummings's troops, manning the valley perimeter, were to leave next, with Holtzclaw's pickets coming out last. As Corporal Mangham and his fellow Alabamians filed down the mountain at 1:00 a.m. on November 25, three men from each company remained behind for another hour to secure their withdrawal. Perhaps Charles was among these pickets, the last Confederate defenders of Lookout Mountain. A subsequent lunar eclipse effectively cloaked their departure, but caused many to take brutal falls on the treacherous, rocky slopes. Even worse, the freezing men limping and stumbling down the trail knew their situation was desperate. They had been out-generaled and out-maneuvered almost since the siege began, and now the pitch blackness of the eclipse seemed an eerie portent of still worse to come.[64]

Amazingly, the withdrawal was uninterrupted, as the Federals were busily improving their own positions for defense. Every Confederate brigade on the mountain evaded the capture that had threatened them since earlier that day, but November 25 nevertheless would prove their worst day in the war to date. Although the retreating columns set fire to the bridges over swollen Chattanooga Creek as they withdrew, Bragg and Breckenridge were too worried about the right flank to make comprehensive arrangements to defend the left flank of Missionary Ridge. There, the Rossville Gap provided ready ingress for any force wishing to outflank the ridge from the south, and Grant directed Joe Hooker's three divisions to try it. The only Confederates barring the way were the men of Clayton's five understrength Alabama regiments.[65]

Corporal Mangham and his comrades were dispirited, hungry, and worn after their exhausting night on Lookout Mountain. They had pulled into line near Breckenridge's headquarters on Missionary Ridge shortly after daylight, then moved a mile towards the threatened right flank, where Sherman's forces had initiated Grant's main attack. The heavy firing there heralded bitter fighting in which Pat Cleburne's division repulsed Sherman in a brilliant defensive victory. As Sherman's attack bogged down irretrievably and Hooker deliberately forged crossings over Chattanooga Creek to the south, Grant sought to retrieve his fortunes by demonstrating against Bragg's center. Accordingly, he launched George Thomas's Army of the Cumberland against the rifle pits at the base of Missionary Ridge at about 3:30 that afternoon. Holtzclaw was leading his weary Alabamians south towards the Rossville Gap as Thomas's men overran the rifle pits, and the rising thunder of battle gave notice that Federal infantrymen were clawing their way towards the crest itself! The "Yaller Hammers" must have cocked a wary ear to the roar of gunfire in their rear.[66]

Some of the attacking units believed they were supposed to take the rifle pits at the top of the ridge, rather than those at the bottom. Others simply pursued the Rebels apparently fleeing for the crest, little imagining that many of these men had orders to fire one volley and pull back. Still others attacked uphill because they learned the hard way that their original objectives were enfiladed by the positions atop the ridge; they could advance or retreat, but to remain in the first line of rifle pits was to be slaughtered. In an amazing coalescence of miscues, Grant's poorly conceived demonstration against the Confederate center developed into a full-scale attack.[67] The weakly manned, poorly sited, and uncoordinated defensive line repelled some Federal units, but in short order groups of Yankees were clambering onto the crest itself. As they surged into the yawning gaps in Bragg's patchwork line, their unexpected appearance spread panic among defenders who found themselves assailed from front and flanks alike.

Breckenridge himself led Clayton's Brigade down the ridge to the south flank as the emergency unfolded, and Colonel Holtzclaw noticed that his column made its way past two regiments that already had been outflanked. He had been briefed that two other regiments were in front of his column, so he kept his men moving by the left flank with only three companies out front as skirmishers. Since the 18th Alabama was the rightmost regiment, it was marching in the rear behind John Inzer's 32nd-58th Consolidated. These two outfits halted, faced to the right, and moved in line of battle to positions atop Missionary Ridge, facing west. The 36th and 38th Alabama regiments continued along the ridgeline for some four hundred yards, however, before filing left into a line of battle facing southwards. They had little time to prepare for what they were about to face, although extra time probably would have made little difference.[68]

Disaster struck them there, as units from Hooker's advancing corps began to hit them from the front and both flanks. Hooker had ordered one division to sweep northward along the front (west) side of Missionary Ridge, another to move north along the ridgeline itself, and a third to push north along the back side of the ridge. On a grand tactical level, these pincers began rolling up Bragg's southern flank just when Thomas's impromptu assault turned the Confederate center into a sieve. On the minor tactical level, Holtzclaw's men faced Yankees in overwhelming numbers on their front and both flanks. As the shooting began, the skirmishers of the 36th and 38th Alabama came back on the run, causing major confusion among these regiments as they formed a line of battle perpendicular to and across the ridgeline. Commanders struggled to align their men for the fight, as Inzer and Hunley brought up the 32nd-58th and 18th Alabama from positions farther up the ridge.[69]

Holtzclaw filed Inzer's consolidated regiment to the left flank to stem the onrushing tide, but it quickly got into "considerable confusion" as men of the 36th and 38th "came running out over us." Hunley tried to file his regiment to the left flank past Inzer, and Corporal Mangham was among those caught in the melee as Federal bullets whizzed through columns disordered by men fleeing the ranks of the 38th Alabama. Finding it "impossible to get the regiment into line again," Hunley ordered the company commanders to "form their men as best they could and move them forward and form with the Thirty-sixth and Thirty-eighth to the right." Holtzclaw ordered the shattered 38th out of line, telling Hunley to "hold the position at all hazards." The men of the 18th Alabama were in a bad fix, however, and a dismayed Hunley saw that his disordered ranks "were so crowded that some of those in rear killed men in the front line." Nonetheless, Holtzclaw saw that the 18th seemed to be holding the blue tide in check, so he focused his efforts on the terrible threat to his open left flank.[70]

The Federals pressing them in front were from Cruft's division, while C. R. Woods's brigade of Osterhaus's division was sweeping around the Alabamians' left flank. The blueclad flanking column surged around behind Holtzclaw's force, moving up to the top of Missionary Ridge itself. Breckenridge ordered Holtzclaw to withdraw his brigade from the tightening noose, and the desperate Alabama colonel determined to sacrifice his old regiment, the 18th Alabama, to save the rest of the brigade. As he began pulling out his disordered units, a renewed "peremptory order" from Breckenridge directed him to get out immediately and regroup near Chickamauga Creek.[71]

Federals were in both front and rear, and additional columns were closing in from the left and right flanks under covering fire from two artillery batteries. A chastened Holtzclaw thought "discipline and courage alike were gone," and gave his men the order to save themselves as best they could. Scattering weapons, blankets, and anything that hindered their flight, the heroes of Chickamauga ran for their lives. As the despairing colonel rode to the rear, he had eyes only for the confusion that surrounded him, noting that the "greater portion of the command ran out like a mob, each endeavoring to be foremost." Inzer was struggling desperately to restore order in his regiment's dissolving ranks as he moved up to the ridgeline. He had heard no order to retreat, and he stood "begging them to come back and fight the enemy." Pushing through hogweeds that obscured his view, Inzer approached a group of his officers and men to make them cease firing into the retreating fugitives. To his chagrin, he found that they were already prisoners, surrounded by a seemingly endless sea of blue uniforms. Exhausted and hopelessly surrounded, he stuck his sword in the ground and surrendered. As Yankees sealed off every escape route, one thought the Alabamians were reduced to "a whirling, struggling mass of panic-stricken men, signaling frantically to make us understand they surrendered."[72]

As the sun began to set on the debacle, the battle flags of the 36th and 38th Alabama regiments were captured, and Lt. Simeon T. Josselyn of the 13th Illinois Regiment seized the flag of Hunley's doomed 18th Alabama. Brigadier General Carlin was deeply moved by one young Confederate soldier caught up in the rout. As Federal troops were making prisoners of his officers, the young man halted and assumed the position of "order arms." Carlin, riding over to ask if he had surrendered, received the answer, "No, I have not." The Union general told the youth, "Your officers have surrendered, and the best thing you can do is to surrender immediately, for you may be shot down if you don't." After looking around once more at the hopeless scene, the young Rebel lay down his musket and surrendered.[73]

One of the four officers and 153 men declared missing by the 18th Alabama was nineteen-year-old Cpl. Charles Arthur Mangham. He was among the 27 officers and 679 enlisted men reported missing from Clayton's Brigade, of some 1300 carried into action. Butler County's once proud Tom Watts Rifles now counted only seven privates to answer roll call.[74]

*   *   *   *   *

Much of the shattered Army of Tennessee managed to reassemble beyond Chickamauga Creek, and Cleburne's spectacular delaying action at Ringgold ensured the army's survival. Corporal Mangham, however, was heading north. His journey led him through Nashville and Louisville to Rock Island Prison in Illinois, where he arrived on December 9, 1863. He remained in this Mississippi River prison pen through the bone-chilling cold of two winters, surviving the sweltering heat and festering diseases of two torrid summers. He must have rejoiced in the summer of 1864 when fresh well water became available to replace the putrid river water dipped from the Mississippi mud flats, and he may have joined others in gigging rats for food to supplement their starvation rations.[75]

Charles also must have counted himself fortunate to escape the killings that occurred when disgruntled guards fired into the wooden barracks at random, or shot unarmed men on purpose. After a number of such shootings, the desperate prisoners confronted Lieutenant Colonel Carraher, the commanding officer, stating: "Colonel, we have come to the limit of endurance. We are being shot like dogs at all hours of day and night, when we walk on the streets and when we are asleep in our bunks." Voicing a specific complaint against a black soldier who had murdered two prisoners, they added menacingly: "If he ever comes back into this prison, *we'll hang him*, understand that. And you have not got men enough outside to prevent it. If it comes to the point of being murdered like dogs, then you'll have to kill us all." Apparently, the colonel wisely relieved the guard instead of provoking a desperate riot.[76]

Despite this often vicious maltreatment, Charles disdained efforts to recruit prisoners for frontier service in the United States Army, even though 1750 of his fellow Southerners enlisted in two regiments of "U. S. Volunteers" raised at Rock Island in the fall of 1864. Likewise, he spurned offers to earn release from the horrible ennui of captivity by swearing a loyalty oath to the Union, on condition that he remain north of the Ohio River during the war. He stubbornly remained at Rock Island until May 3, 1865, when he was transferred to New Orleans for exchange. Formally exchanged on May 23, he became a free man again on June 2 when he was released at Vicksburg, Mississippi.[77]

A veteran of twenty-eight months' active service in one of the regiments hardest-hit at Shiloh, Chickamauga, and Missionary Ridge, and a survivor of eighteen months at Rock Island, Charles Arthur Mangham was twenty years old.

4. LEE'S LAST GASP—A FORLORN HOPE AT FORT STEDMAN: PRIVATE WILLIAM T. T. MANGHAM, CO. E, 61ST ALABAMA

His nineteen-year-old brother, William T. T. Mangham, was freed from captivity at Point Lookout, Maryland, at the end of the same month, although it is unknown whether the two brothers ever met again after the war.

Willie was born about 1846, shortly before their father's death, and he remained on his stepfather's prosperous plantation when Charles enlisted in 1861. He attended school during the first two years of the war, until deciding to take up arms in the summer of 1863. At age seventeen, he was still too young for conscription, but like many men and boys that summer, he decided to enlist in Col. James H. Clanton's new Alabama brigade. Clanton, a highly reputed cavalry commander, had obtained a special commission to raise a brigade for Confederate service within the state of Alabama. In contravention of the Conscription Act, which funneled all conscription age men into existing units, Clanton was permitted to enlist them in his new regiments. The promise of service within their home state attracted many otherwise reluctant volunteers, who correctly figured that no better offer was forthcoming in the manpower-strapped Confederacy. His recruiting officers also secured a number of boys in their mid- to late teens, eager to enlist with the latest companies forming in their home counties.[78]

One of his aspiring company commanders was Eugenius F. Baber of Butler County, a 21-year-old previously invalided out of the service for wounds. Baber swore in men from ten different counties in central and southern Alabama, which indicates that many of his volunteers had already reported to a camp of instruction for training and assignment to a regiment. Few of them were conscripts in the technical sense, but most were of conscription age and faced mandatory enrollment if they failed to report for service voluntarily. Seventeen-year-old Pvt. Willie Mangham may have reported voluntarily to a camp at Tuskegee, in Macon County, as some surviving records show that he enlisted there on May 29, 1863. Other documents indicate he mustered in at home in Butler County on June 1, while yet another reflects that he volunteered on that date in Montgomery![79]

The documentary confusion of Willie's enlistment mirrors the organizational irregularity of his regiment. Commanded by W. G. Swanson, it was first designated the 55th Alabama, then redesignated in November as the 59th Alabama, and finally became known as the 61st Alabama Volunteer Infantry in April 1864. When the dust finally settled, Captain Baber's outfit became Company E in Swanson's regiment. The newly organized company reported to Camp Pollard in late summer, where Willie may have met his first cousin, *Pvt. Thomas H. Mangham* of the 19th Louisiana. Arthur Green Mangham's eldest son, Thomas was the namesake of Willie's deceased father (see Chapter IX). He was about ten years older than Willie, and doubtless remembered him from their time together in Salem, Alabama, where their fathers had operated the village tannery and shoe shop. Willie also may have made the acquaintance of his second cousin (once removed), *James M. D. Mangham* of Chambers County, whose Company F also served in Swanson's regiment (see Chapter V). James had moved to Chambers County in 1850, and may have known Willie's mother Rhoda Callaway Mangham before she remarried to Seaborn Moore the following year. Yet another distant cousin in the new regiment was Francis M. Mangum, who enlisted at Tuskegee and served in Swanson's Company H.[80]

All of the men serving at Pollard took part in the same camp routines there, as well as performing more important duties guarding the nearby railroad bridges over Burnt Corn Creek, the Escambia River, and the Perdido River. The Alabama & Florida Railroad linked Montgomery to a southern terminus at the town of Pollard, where it met the Florida & Alabama Railroad running north from Pensacola. The Mobile & Great Northern Railroad connected Pollard with Tensas Station, on the river just north of Mobile. Thus, passengers and freight from Alabama's premier port city could proceed by ferry to Tensas Station, thence by rail to Pollard, and thereafter south to Pensacola or north to Montgomery. Since the major surface road from the Alabama capital to the Florida port ran through Pollard as well, the Confederate camp was well posted to guard crucial communications nodes.[81]

Colonel Swanson's regiment built a hutted encampment that winter to help ward off the uncharacteristically cold and wet weather, but nonetheless lost many men to the illnesses that plagued new units. One of those sent to the army hospital at Greenville that fall was Willie Mangham, who was absent sick when the regiment mustered at the end of October. At least he was back home in Butler County, however, so his mother and stepfather must have been able to visit him there. Indeed, he may have been furloughed home from the hospital, as army doctors realized fully that the tender ministrations of loved ones were often the quickest and surest route to recovery. If Willie was still there in late November and early December, he may have shared the shattering news that Charles had been captured in the maelstrom of Missionary Ridge. Likewise, their first cousin, *Pvt. Bush W. Mangham*, was languishing in army hospitals at Ringgold, Georgia, while his unit was cut to pieces in the dark forests along Chickamauga Creek. In all likelihood, it was some time after the September battle before the family learned that he had been spared in the carnage.[82]

Back at Camp Pollard the news was grim, too, although in a fundamentally different way. Willie probably returned to duty there in November or December, and if so he found himself in the middle of an uproar over a mutinous conspiracy that cast a cloud of disgrace over the whole of Clanton's command. Loyal troops arrested some sixty mutineers from the 57th Alabama, and Clanton arrested another hundred who surrendered peaceably after refusing his invitation to a "fair fight." These men belonged to the so-called "Peace Society," whose clandestine members sought to end the war on any terms; seven men who surrendered belonged to Swanson's regiment. Perhaps Willie Mangham was one of the soldiers who helped the angry Clanton face them down.[83]

In any event, he was one of those who went rattling down the rails to Montgomery soon thereafter, as Swanson was ordered to duty in the state capital. Jefferson Davis was personally aware of the Peace Society problem, however, and agreed with other officials that too many of Clanton's men seemed determined to avoid the war by joining a brigade slated for home service. By the time Swanson's regiment arrived at Montgomery in late January 1864, the remedy had been found. The untrustworthy brigade was broken up and its regiments exchanged for reliable units in need of rest and recruitment. The easy garrison duty at Pollard was over. Swanson's 59th Alabama had orders to join the Army of Northern Virginia.[84]

*   *   *   *   *

On February 12, 1864, Special Orders No. 36 from the Adjutant and Inspector General's Office at Richmond assigned Swanson's outfit to Brig. Gen. Cullen Battle's Alabama brigade. Serving in Rodes's Division in Dick Ewell's 2nd Corps, the troops waited for springtime to bring an end to the uneasy peace that reigned in the encampments along the Rapidan River.[85]

Willie doubtless learned a lot that winter about dealing with hardship, for Lee's army was barely able to find enough food to keep body and soul together. They were cut off from much of northern Virginia's prime farmland, and the Orange & Alexandria Railroad was the only lifeline bringing supplies from the Deep South. Most of northern and central Virginia was barren of subsistence after years of marching, countermarching, and heavy fighting had reduced the once-bountiful lands to a shadow of their former splendor. Artillery and cavalry horses had to seek pasturage far away from the Rapidan, and Lee was forced to post General Longstreet's 1st Corps some distance away, where it could eke out a meager existence. Ewell's men joined the veterans of A. P. Hill's 3rd Corps in choking down unappetizing rations of doubtful nutritional value. One Alabama soldier reported that their rations seemed to consist of wheat bran and beef, which reeked like glue when the men tried to cook it. Another recalled, "We had more appetite than anything else, and never got enough to satisfy it— even for a time."[86]

Lee worried about the moral and physical price exacted by the starvation rations, and expressed concerns to President Davis that he might prove unable to keep the army together. His men persevered, however, and tightened their belts in preparation for the coming campaign. Most expected the coming battles to decide the war, and they were amazingly optimistic about the outcome, despite the bare fact that they confronted a numerically superior foe. The Army of Northern Virginia mustered some 65,000 troops at the beginning of May, and the men in its ranks commonly reckoned that Lt. Gen. Ulysses S. Grant's Union forces numbered 150,000 men. The actual count was only slightly less than that as April turned into May: 99,438 were in George Gordon Meade's Army of the Potomac, and another 19,331 filled the ranks of Burnside's attached IX Corps.[87]

Unfortunately, it is not known what the untried Alabamians of Colonel Swanson's contingent thought about the odds they faced. They had welcomed a tenth company into their midst in early April, but the months of delay in completing their regimental organization caused them to lose their claim to precedence as Alabama's 59th Infantry Regiment. This title was transferred to an outfit formed from two battalions of Hilliard's Alabama Legion, whose other two battalions combined to form the 60th Alabama. *Private Bush W. Mangham* served in the newly designated 59th, while his cousin Willie's regiment was renumbered as the 61st Alabama.[88]

In all probability, the regiment bore the unwelcome stigma of political unreliability, although the higher-ranking officers of Lee's army may have been the only ones who knew much about the unsavory story of the Peace Society and Clanton's now-defunct brigade. Lee's Army of Northern Virginia was accustomed to victory and hardship alike, and by May 1864 its soldiers viewed themselves as the Confederacy's sword and shield. These corps, divisions, brigades, and regiments were fiercely proud of their battlefield accomplishments, and intended to uphold their hard-won reputations in the coming campaign. Anyone in this army's ranks had to stand tall or bear the consequences of shame and stigma at the very least, and this atmosphere doubtless proved a shot in the arm to the patriotic men in the 61st Alabama. In the camps along the Rapidan, anyone still sympathizing with the Peace Society's aims had to keep his own counsel.

*   *   *   *   *

Willie's cousin *James M. Mangham* returned to Alabama on sick furlough on April 28, just days before drummers began beating the long roll throughout the camps of Ewell's 2nd Corps. Union forces had commenced crossing the Rapidan to Lee's right on May 4, as part of Grant's plan to synchronize the pressure on the embattled Confederacy. Sherman was about to grapple with Joe Johnston's Army of Tennessee in north Georgia, and Banks and Steele were struggling with Confederate forces in Louisiana and Arkansas. Elsewhere in Virginia itself, Federal armies began movements in the Shenandoah Valley and at Bermuda Hundred, near Petersburg. If Meade could turn Lee's right with the Army of the Potomac, the outnumbered Confederates could be facing utter disaster. He planned to cross the Rapidan, push rapidly westward through the terrible underbrush of the Wilderness, and flush Lee into the open for a decisive battle. When a newspaper correspondent asked General Grant how long it would take him to get to Richmond, the commander responded sensibly: "I will agree to be there in about four days—that is, if General Lee becomes a party to the agreement. But if he objects, the trip will undoubtedly be prolonged."[89]

The Federal plan was indeed bright with possibility, but Meade's decision to slow the advance to protect his ponderous wagon trains was the first of many momentous miscues. Though he outnumbered Lee almost two-to-one, Meade also failed to assign any diversionary force to threaten crossings at other points, so the Confederate commander could concentrate his efforts in one direction. When Jeb Stuart's ubiquitous cavalrymen reported Federal crossings to the east, Lee ordered Ewell and Hill to move their corps towards the Wilderness to strike Meade's columns wherever they found them. If they could hold up the Yankee juggernaut before it rolled into open country, Lee might be able to bring up Longstreet quickly enough to deliver a crushing flank attack in the gloomy forests. Shades of Stonewall Jackson at Chancellorsville![90]

Lieutenant General Dick Ewell, considered by many to be the most eccentric genius in Lee's army, accordingly pushed down the Orange Turnpike with Jubal Early's division in the lead, followed by Edward "Allegheny" Johnson's, with Rodes's men in trail. Powell Hill led his 3rd Corps up the parallel Orange Plank Road, several miles south of Ewell, with two divisions in the van and one remaining in positions overwatching the Rapidan. Lee was pitting only five slim divisions against ten of Meade's larger divisions; when Willie Mangham bedded down on the eve of battle near Locust Grove, the odds were three to one against. The morrow would show whether his 61st Alabama possessed the mettle for the stern tasks that lay ahead.[91]

He was up early the next morning and marching towards the rising sun, with Rodes's Division following Johnson's. Federal pickets of Griffin's division watched in awe as a seemingly endless column of grayclad troops rolled up the turnpike to Saunders's place, where they filed left and right into the forests and began throwing up earthworks about six o'clock that morning. Unbeknownst to any of them, Meade's assumption that Lee would tamely occupy his wintertime defenses along Mine Run, farther west, had led him to carelessly place the Federal corps in positions where Lee could smash his center.[92] (See map on p. 297.)

Ewell placed Johnson's Division on the high ground at the western edge of Saunders's Field, with Jones's Virginia brigade astride the turnpike and the remainder of the division to his left. Rodes's Division formed his second line, several hundred yards to the rear, with Battle's Alabamians backstopping Jones. Several miles to their south, Hill's 3rd Corps was likewise deploying across the Plank Road to block the Federal advance. Until Longstreet could get forward, however, Union forces on high ground at the Chewning place, partway between the two roads, were positioned to cleave Lee's force in twain. If Meade or Grant divined this opportunity, or massed against Hill or Ewell along the main roads, they might destroy the Army of Northern Virginia piecemeal.[93]

As things turned out, however, Warren's V Corps was the only force that came against Ewell's men in the early afternoon of May 5. Harassed by Meade and chafing at the impediments to movement in the Wilderness, Warren finally launched his two divisions up the road some six hours after Meade first ordered an attack. Ayres's Federal brigade slammed into Steuart's Confederates north of the pike, while Bartlett's brigade piled into Jones just south of the road. Both assaults suffered terrible casualties in the first onset, but valor and stubbornness were not qualities monopolized by either side in this engagement. Fortunately for Bartlett, his brigade overlapped Jones's southern (right) flank and managed to push some dismounted cavalrymen aside. The unexpected appearance of heavy Federal assault columns on the Virginians' right flank was too much for them to take, especially since the first incoming volleys had killed Jones and some of his staff officers.[94]

As Bartlett pressed his advantage, Virginians streamed through the ranks of Battle's Brigade in their rear. When a Virginia officer shouted "Fall back to Mine Run!" the 3rd Alabama's commander, Colonel Forsyth, demanded "Is that a general order?" Receiving assurances that it was, the 3rd and 5th Alabama regiments started withdrawing. Bartlett's hard-charging brigade included some of the most famous regiments in the Army of the Potomac, including Joshua Chamberlain's 20th Maine, the 118th Pennsylvania ("Corn Exchange Regiment"), and the 83rd Pennsylvania, along with the 44th New York and 18th Massachusetts. With reinforcements from Sweitzer's brigade, they pushed forward in pursuit of the disordered Confederates, unaware that most of Ayres's men had been stopped cold to their right rear and that nobody was advancing on their left.[95]

General Ewell had instructed Battle and George Doles, commander of a Georgia brigade, "not to allow themselves to become involved, but to fall back slowly if pressed." This was in keeping with Lee's directive to avoid a general engagement until Longstreet arrived, and it largely accounts for the Alabamians' retirement at Bartlett's onslaught. Ewell's brigades began slashing at two isolated regiments of New York Zouaves, resplendent in their French-style uniforms of white leggings, red sashes, and flared pantaloons. These remnants of Ayres's brigade had missed the order to retire as they slanted across the turnpike from the north side of the road. Stranded there amidst ever-increasing opposition, the jauntily attired Zouaves shared the fate of Bartlett's men to their left front: Rebels surrounded them and began cutting them to pieces. Willie Mangham and his comrades of the 61st Alabama played a significant role in the deadly hide-and-seek in the brambles, helping shatter Bartlett's regiments and sending them running to avoid utter destruction.[96]

The mixed up engagement resembled an Indian fight more than the drill field, as opponents appeared on each other's front, flanks, and rear with little warning. The 61st Alabama delivered a "most desperate and successful attack" upon the Zouaves along the turnpike, and probably delivered the volley that felled General Bartlett's horse as he raced back through Rebel lines and vaulted a ditch to safety. The cheers that rang out when the horse went down in mid-jump indicated that the butternut-clad men thought they had killed the general, although some Federal soldiers managed to help the shaken Bartlett to safety. Postwar accounts credited the 61st Alabama with killing "General Jenkins" as they "almost annihilated his New York Zouave brigade." Colonel Jenkins, commander of the 146th New York Zouave Regiment, was indeed killed in action that day, and the Alabamians may have mistaken him for the general they had "killed" in such conspicuous circumstances. They were not far wrong in their claim to have "annihilated" the Zouaves, however, as the 146th New York lost 316 of its 580 officers and men. The 140th New York Zouaves suffered almost as terribly, losing 268 of 529 men engaged.[97]

The 61st Alabama also claimed the honor of capturing two 24-pounder howitzers of Battery D, 1st New York Light Artillery. Commanded by First Lt. William H. Shelton, the pair of guns had taken position in Saunders's Field to blast the Rebel earthworks at close range. During the hour-long melee, however, Confederate bullets had dropped most of Shelton's horses and many of his gunners. When Steuart's Brigade sent forward the 1st and 3rd North Carolina regiments in a ferocious counterattack, the 61st Alabama plunged forward as well. Hand-to-hand combat raged in the field, with clubbed muskets and bayonets freely wielded by both sides until the last of Ayres's Federals surrendered or fled. Shelton's cannoneers got off a few more shots until they were overrun, when an officer of the 61st Alabama jammed a brace of pistols in Shelton's face and demanded his surrender. As the shocked New Yorker was led away, he saw an Alabama regiment "in butternut suits and slouch hats, shooting straggling and wounded Zouaves." These men were doubtless Willie Mangham and his comrades of Swanson's 61st Alabama, engaged in their first combat action.[98]

An officer of Battle's 6th Alabama leapt atop the guns and claimed their capture, at which time Steuart's two North Carolina regiments emerged from nearby ditches and hotly disputed the claim. The argument raged until the three Virginia regiments of Steuart's Brigade emerged to back up their "Tar Heel" brethren, at which time Battle's Alabamians, "persuaded by numbers if not by logic," backed down. Postwar writers continued the argument, leaving it uncertain whether the North Carolina or Alabama regiments had the better claim to capturing the howitzers.[99]

The hot-blooded Southerners' internal dispute soon was overshadowed by another fierce Federal attack into Saunders's Field, which Steuart's and Battle's men combined to repulse decisively. The continuous small arms fire eventually set the underbrush alight, and the woods and overgrown field became a charnel house of smoke and flame. Ammunition in dead men's cartridge boxes cooked off in the heat, and wounded men screamed in terror as the flames swept over them and burned them into gory cinder heaps. In scenes befitting Dante's fictional Inferno, men immobilized by bullet-shattered thighs frantically loaded their muskets one final time to avoid the agonies of slow death amidst the flames.[100]

The bitter fighting in Virginia's Wilderness continued the next day, but Rodes's Division and Battle's Brigade remained in place while desperate engagements were fought elsewhere along the lines. "Old Baldy" Ewell and his subordinate generals had turned in sterling performances on May 5, decisively smashing Meade's attempt to break the Confederate line at the turnpike. The bloody repulse set the stage for Longstreet's attempt to roll up Meade's southern flank and Gordon's envelopment of the northern end of the line, blows which threatened the complete destruction of the Union army. Willie and his Alabama friends watched and waited, but played no part in these actions.[101]

Ewell ordered his divisions to sidle to the right on May 7, extending their line to join with Hill's units to their south. Grant had decided to pull out of the forbidding forests, however, and withdrew his men that night from Lee's front. Many of the blueclad troops concluded gloomily that Bobby Lee had licked them again, but an electric thrill passed down the "retreating" columns when Grant pointed them on the road south, rather than back across the Rapidan. Far from retreating, they were advancing by a different road. It was "On to Richmond" after all![102]

As a popular Southern ditty of 1863 crowed, however, "Richmond was a hard road to travel!" Sung to the tune of "Jordan is a Hard Road to Travel," the song made light of the numerous failed attempts to capture the Confederate capital in the first two years of the war. But Grant had announced his willingness to "fight it out on this line if it takes all summer," and he redoubled his efforts after his defeat in the Wilderness. Although he had lost more than 17,000 men in two days' horrendous fighting, he had come within a whisker of destroying Lee's army on the morning of May 6. Comparable bloody debacles had deterred previous Federal commanders from seeking a rematch with the Army of Northern Virginia, but Grant sought to lunge past Lee's right once more. An examination of his map had revealed a crossroads that would place him between the Confederate commander and the capital he was bound to defend. Grant could not know that his opponent had suffered some 11,000 casualties, but he knew the Confederates were hurt badly. He also knew that he could afford much higher losses than they could. War—hard war—was about to come to sleepy Spotsylvania Court House.[103]

*   *   *   *   *

Robert E. Lee had studied a map of the same ground, and realized that hard marching was required to interpose a force between Grant and Richmond. Lead elements of Longstreet's vaunted 1st Corps, commanded by Maj. Gen. Richard H. Anderson since "Old Pete" was badly wounded in the Wilderness, moved out during the night of May 7. They tramped through smoke-filled forests rent occasionally by the roar of exploding ammunition wagons. After the 1st Corps departed, Rodes's Division led Ewell's 2nd Corps towards Spotsylvania the next morning. "After a very distressing march through intense heat and thick dust and smoke from burning woods," the exhausted men were dropping like flies along the route. Willie and his comrades had barely eaten on May 4, had engaged in heavy combat on May 5 without a bite to eat, then stood to arms throughout the two succeeding days. Worn but intact, the division reached the little crossroads village about five o'clock on the afternoon of May 8.[104]

Their arrival was one of the most dramatic appearances of the entire war. Capitalizing on masterful delaying actions by Jeb Stuart's cavalrymen, two of Anderson's divisions had outmarched the Yankees to Laurel Hill, the high ground just northwest of the courthouse junction. They barred the way to the crucial intersection in heavy fighting against Warren's V Corps throughout the day, but the arrival of "Uncle John" Sedgwick's VI Corps opposite their right flank spelled impending disaster for Anderson's men by late afternoon. In the words of historian Gordon Rhea, Ewell's troops came onto the field in "a breathtaking appearance seemingly orchestrated by fate itself."[105]

Rodes's Division led the way, with Battle's Alabama brigade in the van. Crawford's division of Pennsylvania Reserves was about to sweep past Anderson's right flank when Battle's men struck them head on with a "wild, savage yell." Willie Mangham and the 61st Alabama stood in the center of the brigade's line of battle, with the 6th and 12th Alabama regiments to their left. With fixed bayonets, they went screaming into the assault and shattered the oncoming blue columns with a suddenness that stunned the Federals they overran. One Alabamian recalled that Battle's charge "made the saucy Yankees 'about face' and hunt a more comfortable position a short distance further back." The Pennsylvania troops nonetheless dropped some of Battle's men in their tracks, while others fell victim to errant bullets fired from their own rear ranks.[106]

Ramseur's North Carolina brigade joined the attack, which Battle's men pushed all the way into the Federal entrenchments. Here, some 600 yards from their starting point, Battle's 12th, 6th, and 61st Alabama regiments surged into the enemy works, where the melee continued with musket butts and bayonets. Crowded together and disordered by some of Ramseur's regiments on their right, Battle's exhausted men were unable to hold their lodgment in the Union position, and retreated upon receipt of Rodes's order to fall back. In the fist-and-skull scrap in the Federal trenches, both the 6th and 61st Alabama regiments lost their battle flags and some prisoners. Among these were nine men of Willie's Company E, which also suffered one man wounded. Although the Alabamians continued to engage isolated pockets of Federals stranded between the lines, most of the shooting mercifully died down as night fell. Their slashing counterattack had decisively repulsed Meade's advance, and secured

Confederate control of Spotsylvania Courthouse. Disconsolate, the victor of Gettysburg issued orders for his exhausted army to "remain quiet tomorrow."[107]

Such quietude remained elusive, however, as shooting flared up throughout the night. Eighteen-year-old Willie Mangham must have been as exhausted as the other men in both armies, but he and his comrades worked hard that night and the following day to build earthworks to resist any renewed attack. Battle's Brigade found itself at the western base of the "Mule Shoe," a convex, U-shaped projection on the right of Lee's line that traced the contours of the high ground. The Confederate commander expressed reservations about the awkward salient, but Ewell's confident assurance that his men could hold the line won Lee's approval. After the 3rd Corps arrived to take positions east of the Mule Shoe, the unwieldy salient formed the center of the Confederate line.[108]

Salients tend to attract attention, and Union officers studied the Mule Shoe long and hard. Concluding that its left (west) side offered the best approach routes, a plan developed to storm the Confederate works on the evening of May 10. Twelve of the best regiments in the army were grouped under the command of Col. Emory Upton, an ambitious officer who believed that a massive assault column could penetrate the enemy line if it relied on legwork and the bayonet, rather than halting to exchange fire with entrenched defenders. Upton organized his column into four lines, assigning each a specific mission. Some would turn right and others left, expanding the breach, while others fired to the front and three regiments remained in reserve. Nobody was to cheer or stop to fire until reaching the Confederate works. All officers were enjoined to repeat the command "Forward!" constantly, and nobody was to stop to care for men wounded in the initial rush across the open ground.[109]

Since Federal forces had cleared Rebel pickets out of the woods 200 yards in front of Doles's Georgia brigade, Upton's men assembled there in secrecy during the late afternoon of May 10. After a severe artillery barrage, Meade gave the order for Upton to lead the charge at 6:35 p.m. The massive column rose to charge, as Doles's startled Georgians directed a rapid fire at the apparition looming in their faces. The Federals clawed their way through the abatis below the Georgians and soon flung themselves into the entrenchments, where both sides smashed each other with gun butts and stabbed with bayonets. Spalding County's Thomas Dingler, flag bearer for the 44th Georgia, stood atop the ramparts waving his banner until he was felled with fourteen bayonet wounds. The desperate Georgians were overwhelmed by brute force, and soon poured out of the trenches in surrender. Instead of panicking and withdrawing, however, brigades on the left and right refused their lines and opened fire. Battle's Alabama brigade was just to the left of Daniel's Brigade, which in turn touched Doles's left flank. Daniel's North Carolinians fought it out at point blank range with the attacking Unionists, and Battle's Alabamians flung themselves into yet another furious counterattack against the head of the attacking column. The famed Stonewall Brigade, struggled to hold its position north of the breach, while other brigades piled into the front and flanks of the increasingly confused Federals.[110]

508

Ewell galloped up to Daniel's Brigade shouting, "Don't run, boys, I will have enough men here in five minutes to eat up every damned one of them!" One of Battle's men saw the setting sun, noting that the "immense volumes of smoke" from the intense musketry made it seem like a moonlit night. While Ewell excitedly screamed encouragement and orders to his troops, Lee sat calmly astride Traveller not far away. One shell dug into the ground just five yards from the army commander, while aides noticed at least one Minie ball glance off the horse's saddle. Although Lee seemed of a mind to lead the counterattack himself, the rapidity and ferocity of the Confederate response made it unnecessary. Less than sixty minutes after the attack began, it was finished, with Upton suffering the loss of about one thousand men.[111]

Confederate losses are uncertain since subsequent engagements prevented an accurate accounting, but modern estimates conclude that they exceeded Union casualties by several hundred. Two men in the 61st Alabama's Company E fell wounded during their ferocious counterattack, their third major combat action in six days. One of them was eighteen-year-old Pvt. William T. T. Mangham. Although the entrenchments at Spotsylvania would witness further combat of even greater intensity, the young Alabamian would miss them: he was severely injured and bound for an extended convalescence. The Southerners who remained behind to hold the line against Grant were amazed and dismayed by the Federal commander's persistence during the following days, but many were comforted by the conviction that they were literally destroying his army. One survivor of Doles's Brigade wrote home on May 19, reporting that a Yankee picket had told a captain of the 44th Georgia that "Lee had destroyed half their army." The feisty Georgian added, "Grant is twice as badly whiped [sic] now as was Burnside or Hooker but he is so determined he will not acknowledge it, but I think before he gets through with Lee he will have to own up."[112]

*   *   *   *   *

In all likelihood, Willie required stabilization, surgery, and additional care in army hospitals in Virginia, but he eventually received an extended furlough to recuperate at home. While he slowly mended back in Alabama, Lee's troops continued to stymie Grant's flanking maneuvers all the way to Petersburg, where they eventually were penned up in the static siege lines that Lee feared most of all. The 61st Alabama took part in numerous combats that summer and fall during Jubal Early's Shenandoah Valley campaign and his raid on Washington, but eventually the regiment returned to the main army that winter. It had suffered severely at Winchester and Fisher's Hill, and its numbers were sadly reduced by the time the men settled in at Petersburg. Eight men of Company E had been killed in action or died of wounds that summer. Willie was still home recuperating on November 18, when only ten men of Company E mustered for pay. Another nine were absent without leave, while 22 more were on furlough; most of the latter doubtless were convalescing from wounds or illness. Unit payrolls noted that Willie never had been paid since enlisting in May 1863.[113]

When the company compiled complete historical data in January 1865, its rolls reflected an aggregate strength of eighty men, of whom 72 were volunteers, four conscripts, and four substitutes. By this time, nine men had been killed in action and thirteen more had been wounded. Another nine had died of disease, and two more succumbed to wounds. Six men had retired or been discharged for disabilities, and a like number had deserted. Including transfers and other losses, only 46 men remained on the company rolls. Of these, fourteen were prisoners of war, three were under arrest, five were absent wounded, and ten were detailed to other duties. Only fourteen men were present for duty.[114]

*   *   *   *   *

Perhaps Willie had returned to duty by then, to share the burning hunger and hardship that whittled down the Army of Northern Virginia to skin and bones that winter. Although many discouraged Alabamians deserted during that hard winter, the young veteran returned to his post. New Year's Day of 1865 found his regiment fundamentally changed by its combat experiences, however, for another eight major combat actions had succeeded the concentrated hell of Spotsylvania. A total of 889 men had served in the 61st Alabama, but only 562 remained on its rolls at the end of the year. Seventy men had been killed in action or died of wounds, and a further 148 had been wounded in the regiment's numerous engagements; 98 more had succumbed to the ever-present threat of disease. Fully ten percent of the regiment had deserted; 45 retired, resigned, or received discharges; and another seventeen men transferred to other commands. Many of the 562 names on the regimental rolls appeared there for accountability's sake only, as the enemy had captured 106 and exchanged only one. Of the 26 soldiers absent without leave, it is likely that some returned to duty, and a number of the 73 wounded absentees probably came back, too. Another 51 men were detailed to other duties, so they contributed something to the war effort, if not to their regiment's combat potential. This now rested on the shoulders of exactly 300 officers and men in ranks on December 31, 1864.[115]

Private Mangham was present for duty two months later when General Lee turned to John B. Gordon, now a lieutenant general and corps commander, to ask what should be done in light of the army's desperate situation. Lee summarized reports that lay before him, showing that the army had some 50,000 men remaining, only 35,000 of them effective for combat. Men from A. P. Hill's 3rd Corps were subsisting on one-sixth rations, and others were completely destitute of shoes, coats, and hats in the freezing cold. If Lee could combine his army with Johnston's remnants of the Army of Tennessee, the combined force might muster about 50,000 effective troops. Union armies in the east numbered about 280,000 men, by Lee's reckoning.[116]

Gordon, just thirty-two years old and the only one of Lee's corps commanders who lacked a West Point education, considered three courses of action. First, they should "make terms with the enemy, the best we can get." The next most practical course, he thought, was to break out of Petersburg and unite with Johnston, subsequently striking Sherman with their combined forces. The final option, in the young Georgian's view, was simply to fight without further delay, before starvation and desertion brought the army to its knees. After a lengthy discussion with the revered commanding general,

510

Gordon came away with the impression that Lee agreed with him completely. Given the desires of the government and the practicalities of an attempted retreat to North Carolina, however, only one acceptable option remained: to give battle where they stood. Lee therefore directed Gordon to examine the lines carefully and develop a detailed plan.[117]

The hard-fighting Georgia general devoted himself to intensive reconnaissance throughout the coming week, eventually concluding that the best remaining chance was to mass troops opposite Fort Stedman, on Hare's Hill, and smash the Federal line east of Petersburg. Hopefully, a well-coordinated night attack could capture Stedman and three smaller forts echeloned to its flanks, as well as three additional forts in a second line. This would allow Gordon's attacking column to unhinge Grant's entire left wing south of the Appomattox River. With luck, Lee's army could then deal its opponent a crippling blow, possibly even escaping to North Carolina to join Johnston. The operation faced long odds to say the least, but Gordon nevertheless carefully selected groups of axemen to chop paths through the tangled abatis and sharpened chevaux-de-frise protecting Stedman. Specially briefed 100-man assault units would follow the axemen through the gaps to Stedman and the three flanking forts, which sheltered Battery X, just north of Stedman, Battery XI to its immediate south, and Battery XII a little farther to the south. Their guns commanded the flanks of any Confederates approaching Fort Stedman from its front, which was oriented towards the west.[118]

Officers, identifying themselves in the darkness as Federal commanders assigned to this sector of the lines, would shout that the Rebels had broken through, and imperiously announce that they had orders to immediately occupy and defend the batteries against the penetration. With luck, the uproar, panic, and uncertainty would allow these spearheads to overrun Stedman and its covering bastions, while three additional 100-man assault groups followed specially selected Virginia soldiers, detailed as guides, to take the three second line forts by coup-de-main. If successful, they would open a gap through the entire Federal siege perimeter around Petersburg. Lee assigned almost half of his effective force to Gordon for a full-scale infantry attack meant to cleave the Union line asunder, rolling it back to right and left for a complete breakthrough.[119]

According to one survivor's account, one of the companies Gordon assigned to take Stedman in the initial rush was Company B, 61st Alabama. William H. Philpot commanded this Macon County outfit, and recalled that Gordon told him, "Captain, I want this fort taken with a bayonet. I do not want any noise made because I have other operations that I intend to put into effect immediately after taking this fort." Gordon then told the young commander to have men with "sweethearts and mothers back home" take two steps forward if they wanted to be excused from the hazardous undertaking, for which he promised each participant a gold medal and a thirty-day furlough. The Georgian then pointed out a ditch that Philpot and his men could use to guide their attack in the darkness, as it led directly from the fort. Gordon concluded his instructions by emphasizing that a Federal sentinel stood watch at the point where the ditch entered Fort Stedman: "Do not fire upon him but rush upon him and disarm him and proceed on into the fort."[120]

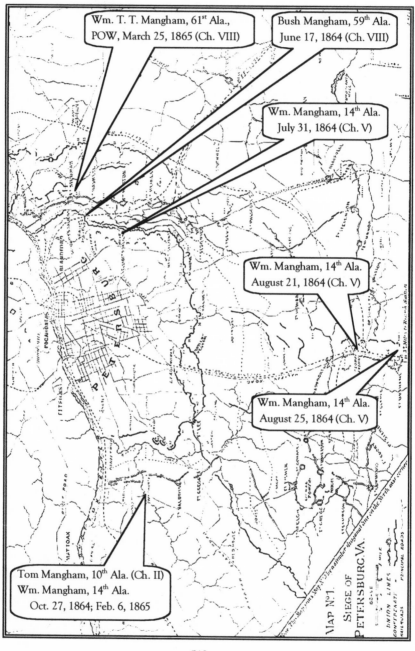

Wm. T. T. Mangham, 61st Ala., POW, March 25, 1865 (Ch. VIII)

Bush Mangham, 59th Ala. June 17, 1864 (Ch. VIII)

Wm. Mangham, 14th Ala. July 31, 1864 (Ch. V)

Wm. Mangham, 14th Ala. August 21, 1864 (Ch. V)

Wm. Mangham, 14th Ala. August 25, 1864 (Ch. V)

Tom Mangham, 10th Ala. (Ch. II)
Wm. Mangham, 14th Ala.
Oct. 27, 1864; Feb. 6, 1865

MAP N°1.
SIEGE OF
PETERSBURG, VA.

Gordon left the Alabamians mulling over his instructions in the darkness, while he went to his chosen spot atop the breastworks in Colquitt's Salient. This sector bore the name of Georgia brigade commander Alfred H. Colquitt, whose lines formed a sally port just 280 yards from Stedman. Gordon stood next to the soldier whose musket shot was to signal the advance, but the muted rustle of men removing obstacles near the Confederate trenches aroused the suspicion of an alert Yankee picket. "What are you doing over there, Johnny? What is that noise? Answer quick or I'll shoot." Gordon stood aghast, fearing that a flurry of picket shots would alert the whole sector and doom his carefully prepared surprise attack.[121]

The quick thinking Rebel private at Gordon's side called out, "Never mind, Yank. Lie down and go to sleep. We are just gathering a little corn. You know rations are mighty short over here." The Georgia general breathed once more when the answer came: "All right, Johnny; go ahead and get your corn. I'll not shoot at you while you are drawing your rations."

Minutes later, when all was ready, General Gordon told the private to fire the signal shot. Raising his musket to fire, the man hesitated until Gordon repeated his command: "Fire your gun, sir." The soldier called out, "Hello, Yank! Wake up; we are going to shell the woods. Look out; we are coming." Then he fired the signal shot and clambered down to charge the enemy lines, satisfied that he had upheld picket line etiquette by returning kindness for kindness.[122]

Captain Philpot quickly made his way through the pre-dawn gloom, coming to the bend in the ditch leading to Fort Stedman. Seeing the Union sentry just beyond, he stopped to wave his men forward. When they saw the sentry, however, Gordon's insistence on a stealthy approach was forgotten in a flash. Yelling "like a bunch of Comanche Indians," they lit out running for the fort, where the surprised guard fired his rifle into the air before disappearing inside. The Alabama soldiers rushed into the emplacement, along with other troops from Georgia and Louisiana. In a trice the fort was theirs, although Federal gunners managed to blast about a dozen rounds of canister blindly into the darkness as Southerners scrambled across the intervening no-man's-land.[123]

If Willie Mangham's Company E did not accompany Philpot's men in the initial race to the fort, he and his mates certainly joined the assault columns that followed fast on the raiders' heels. Troops from all three divisions of Gordon's 2nd Corps swarmed into the trenches around Stedman, also capturing Batteries X and XI on either flank. They overran the camps of two Massachusetts regiments in the supporting line as well, swinging musket butts in a wild fracas that opened a thousand-foot-wide hole in the Federal lines before dawn. Other Union regiments hastily formed a line between Battery XI and Battery XII to its south, even retaking XI for a brief period. These defenders broke under growing pressure from all directions, however, as yelling Rebels flooded around their flanks and streamed past them.[124]

Further exploitation shattered several Federal regiments attempting to block the penetration, but no general panic ensued among the bluecoats. Gordon's attack had driven into the depths of the opposing line, but the assault groups designated to take the second line forts had all lost their Virginia guides in the bedlam. The cork remained firmly in the bottle, which rapidly filled to bursting with Confederate troops. The rising sun gave Federal gunners around the bulging salient the light necessary to aim at masses of men milling in the open. Railroad failures had delayed many of the reinforcing troops intended for Gordon's sector, so his three divisions were stranded and helplessly exposed. Their predicament worsened by the minute as accurate defensive fire turned the Stedman salient into a veritable meatgrinder.[125]

While some officers in the deadly pocket urged their men to renew the assault, Gordon saw that success had become impossible and knew that Lee was right to order a withdrawal. This was easier said than done, however; Federal batteries were raking the entire salient with fire from three directions by 7:00 a.m., when blueclad infantry units sealed off the last gap in the lines. The jubilant Federals were now shooting fish in a barrel, and hundreds of Rebel soldiers huddled in captured bombproof dugouts rather than run through what Gordon viewed as a "literal furnace of fire" back to their own lines. Others decided to risk it, dashing back under fire that mercilessly swept the exposed ground. Some veterans thought that the torrent of lead and iron caused even Malvern Hill and Gettysburg to "pale almost into insignificance," and many Southerners hot-footing it to the rear never made it back. One shaken Northerner recalled, "My mind sickens at the memory of it—a real tragedy in war—for the victims had ceased fighting, and were not struggling between imprisonment and death or home." Miles Huyette of the 208th Pennsylvania was among those who fought his way back into Fort Stedman. Shuddering in horror, he looked down to see men's footprints in "puddles of human blood. Blood was on my boots when the fighting ended. It was hell!"[126]

General Lee was riding back from the debacle when he met his sons Rooney and Robert, Jr. They were riding in advance of Rooney's cavalry division, expecting to receive the commanding general's orders to pass through the breach and cut through the Federal rear. With an air of somber disappointment, their father informed them that the cavalrymen were not needed. The breakthrough attempt had failed.[127]

*　　*　　*　　*　　*

The 61st Alabama was cut to ribbons at Fort Stedman on Hare's Hill, and those who got out counted themselves fortunate indeed. Captain Philpot legged it to the rear after orders came to evacuate the fort, and he was going lickety-split when he overtook his regimental commander near a low rock wall between the original lines. Apparently, this was Lt. Col. Louis Hill of Coosa County, who called out: "Billy, you have stuck with me through all these times; don't desert me now." Without pausing in his flight, Philpot replied, "That is true, but I can't do you a damn bit of good now." Vaulting the rock wall, the young captain "landed upon both hands and both feet, thus ending the taking and losing of Fort Stedman."[128]

Willie Mangham was stranded with much of the remainder of the regiment atop Hare's Hill, perhaps even in Fort Stedman itself. Unable to break contact in time to elude the Federal counterattack, or perhaps unwilling to brave the storms of lead that lashed the withdrawal route from practically all points of the compass, Willie was taken prisoner along with many of his comrades. He was one of about 2700 Southern casualties on this disastrous day, when the Confederacy's last-gasp counterstroke went awry. Aggressive Union counterthrusts seized key portions of the denuded Rebel picket lines later that day, thus establishing the close-quarters toehold that led to the rupture of the Petersburg front just a week later. Most of the 61st Alabama's survivors were killed or captured in the last two weeks of desperate combat that ended at Appomattox. Nineteen-year-old Capt. Augustus B. Fannin of Willie's Company E was serving as regimental commander at the surrender, and he gave the 61st Alabama its final order to stack arms. As Fannin surveyed the ranks for the last time, he may have considered the irony that his first command as a lieutenant was about as numerous as his last: only five officers and forty-two men of the regiment were still with the army.[129]

*   *   *   *   *

Willie's journey into captivity led to Point Lookout, Maryland, where he was imprisoned within days after the catastrophe at Fort Stedman. Established in the backwash of Gettysburg in August 1863, the prison stood upon a low-lying sand spit in Chesapeake Bay. The battles of 1864 had swollen the prison population significantly, as heavy combat in the Wilderness and the Shenandoah Valley harvested a large crop of captives, but the disaster at Fort Stedman nearly doubled the number of Rebs incarcerated in the twenty-acre pen. On the last day of February 1865, the post commander counted 11,332 prisoners under his charge; this figure skyrocketed to 20,110 by the end of March, with a large proportion of the difference credited to Gordon's daring, but ill-fated, breakout attempt at Stedman.[130]

The twelve-foot stockade enclosed a tent city that was a veritable furnace in the summer and icebox in the winter, and the sick list worsened dramatically as more captives poured in. Only 580 Confederate prisoners were on the sick list during March, but the influx of starving, broken-down, and wounded men after the Fort Stedman debacle increased this number to 1731 in April and 1818 in May. The death toll climbed correspondingly, from 175 in March to 203 in April. During the following month a further 324 men died, although Confederate resistance had collapsed. The only Southern army still afield was in the distant Trans-Mississippi Department.[131]

Almost 18,000 prisoners jammed Point Lookout at the end of that month, before the floodgates finally opened in June to send the defeated men back to their homes. Federal authorities had threatened to banish or keep in prison anyone refusing to swear the oath of allegiance to the Union, so the men of Battle's Alabama Brigade "held a meeting and concluded to take the oath." The authorities proceeded to release 18,580 men that month, emptying the prison completely. William T. T. Mangham, lately a private in the 61st Alabama Regiment, signed his parole on June 29, 1865, and thereby gained his release. His captors noted that the light-complexioned young man stood five feet, five inches tall, and had brown hair and gray eyes.[132]

Of the thirty-seven Mangham soldiers who marched beneath the banners of the Confederate States of America, he was the last to start for home at war's end. It is not known if he ever reached Butler County, Alabama, before he faded into the shadows of the defeated Southland.[133]

5. GONE TO TEXAS!

Although Willie Mangham's image receded into the gloom of a South writhing in social, economic, and political turmoil, his older brother Charles left a more visible mark for posterity. In May 1866 he married nineteen-year-old Lucinda E. Williams back home in Butler County and began a family of his own. Eugene was born in November 1869, probably at his parents' rented farmhouse near Brooklyn in Conecuh County. Charles owned personal property worth $150 but no real estate, and worked hard to make ends meet. In the unstable postwar economy, renters and sharecroppers struggled to earn enough to buy the land that gave a man independent status, while subsisting just barely above the level of hired farmhands.[134]

The economic depression of 1873 triggered a renewed flood of emigration from the troubled states of the Deep South to Texas, and many abandoned farmsteads in Dixie bore the initials "GTT" on the front door, indicating that the inhabitants had "Gone to Texas." Charles, Lucinda, and little Eugene joined the hegira, probably due to the desperate economic conditions that beset Alabama's small farmers. Soon after their arrival near Bryan's Mill in Cass County, little Charles, Jr. was born. Charles and Lucinda's second son, he was born in March 1873, and their daughter Ida came along three years later.[135]

By 1880, times had gotten a bit fatter for the Manghams. Charles owned a 100-acre farmstead valued at six hundred dollars, and he cultivated thirty acres of the place with his horse and mule. In the previous year, he and hired hand William Scales wrested six bales of cotton from fourteen acres sown with the crop that characterized the Alabama Black Belt where Charles grew up. He planted another fifteen acres in corn and oats, and grew enough sweet potatoes and sugar cane to round out a diet graced by eighty bushels of apples and peaches, plus beef, pork, milk, and poultry from his beef and dairy cattle, hogs, and poultry. The Mangham family thus served as a fair specimen of the hard-working farm families that populated the area, but Charles's religious zeal also led him into another calling as well. He was a Baptist minister by this time, and organized and became pastor of the Oakridge (later Marietta) Baptist Church, where he also taught school.[136]

By 1900, Charles had moved to the town of San Saba, where he pursued his religious calling full time. Charles Jr. lived nearby, working as a salesman to support his wife Rosa and their two infant sons, while Eugene had moved to Smith County with his own family. Ida was now Mrs. E. J. Lemberg, which left Charles and Lucinda with only a 13-year-old son, C. W. Mangham, still at home.[137]

Charles Mangham moved to Williamson County in 1913, where he continued his ministry in the town of Thrall. Shortly after the end of the World War of 1914-1918, the now aging veteran of an earlier war filed for a Confederate pension from the state of Texas, stating his health as "average good" and owning assessable property worth ninety dollars. His old comrades from Company F, 18th Alabama, K. R. Womack and J.

H. Mullens, filed affidavits on his behalf in Roosevelt, Oklahoma and Goldthwaite, Texas, attesting that Charles had served honorably from 1861-1865. These men, now 75 and 76 years of age respectively, had themselves been but teenaged boys when they enlisted with Charles back in Butler County, Alabama.[138]

Charles Arthur Mangham continued to serve the ministry after he moved with his son Eugene to San Antonio. His membership in the Albert Sidney Johnston Camp, United Confederate Veterans (UCV), showed that he also treasured his memories of faithful service in another, earthly cause of a different era. At age eighty, the old veteran traveled to Dallas to attend the annual UCV convention in 1924, attracting special notice as one of a large group of octogenarians attending from San Antonio. He must have relished the fact that his UCV Camp bore the name of the commander who had led him in his first combat at Shiloh.[139]

In the summer of 1930, the one-time orphan, boy soldier, farmer, and minister commenced his final struggle. This time the foe was hemiplegia, a condition that afflicts one side of the body with paralysis. Supported by his four children, thirteen grandchildren, and eight great-grandchildren, the old fellow resisted stoutly. He knew of no other way. Under the care of his son Eugene, Charles held his position "at all hazards" until the last notes of "Retreat" sounded at 8:45 a.m. on Thursday, July 23, 1931.[140]

Charles Arthur Mangham died at 86 years of age, the last of the Manghams whose service under the Starry Cross is fully documented. He is buried at San Jose Cemetery in San Antonio, Texas.[141]

6. "Corking the Bottle" at Bermuda Hundred: Private Bush W. Mangham, Co. A, 4ᵀᴴ Battalion (Artillery), Hilliard's Alabama Legion, later Co. I, 59ᵀᴴ Alabama

Rhoda Mangham Moore's sons Charles and Willie were not the only Mangham boys who entered Confederate service from Butler County, Alabama. Another seventeen-year-old lad, known in Army records only by his initials B. W. Mangham, enlisted in the county seat of Greenville on March 24, 1862. A company roster compiled many years later by two former members listed the youngster as "Bush Mangham," and thereby provides the only indication of his given name.[142]

It is likely that the young man was one of several orphan sons of Josiah Thomas Mangum, Jr., a brother of Charles and Willie's father, Thomas H. Mangham. Josiah spent most of his life in Granville County, North Carolina, but evidently moved to Dallas County, Alabama, shortly before his death in the 1840s. One of these orphans, Theophilus Fields Mangum (often referred to as Mangham), grew to prominence as a Methodist minister in Alabama, where he served as a chaplain during the Civil War and served his church with distinction into the 20th century. Several other boys, Robert H., *John R., Josiah Thomas,* and *William J. Mangham,* are believed to be his brothers; the latter three served in Confederate units with their Mangham or Mangum cousins, while Robert also became a Methodist minister. Since they grew up in the households of Mangham aunts and uncles scattered from Alabama to Texas, these boys adopted the English spelling of their surname; two subsequently maintained this spelling even after moving in with their Mangum uncles![143]

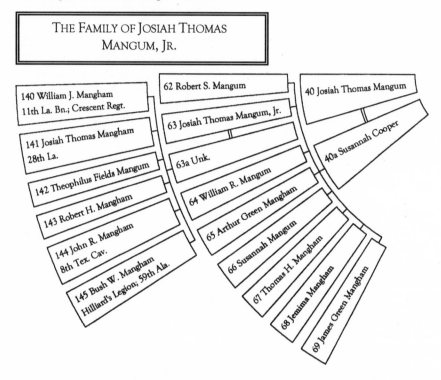

THE FAMILY OF JOSIAH THOMAS MANGUM, JR.

140 William J. Mangham
11th La. Bn.; Crescent Regt.

141 Josiah Thomas Mangham
28th La.

142 Theophilus Fields Mangum

143 Robert H. Mangham

144 John R. Mangham
8th Tex. Cav.

145 Bush W. Mangham
Hilliard's Legion; 59th Ala.

62 Robert S. Mangum

63 Josiah Thomas Mangum, Jr.

63a Unk.

64 William R. Mangum

65 Arthur Green Mangham

66 Susannah Mangum

67 Thomas H. Mangham

68 Jemima Mangham

69 James Green Mangham

40 Josiah Thomas Mangum

40a Susannah Cooper

Bush Mangham probably lived for a time with or near his aunt, Rhoda Mangham Moore, and thus resided in Butler County when he reached enlistment age in 1862. Captain James R. "Bob" Glasgow was seeking recruits to fill out the ranks of his company, which mustered into Confederate service at Greenville on March 13 of that year, and eleven days later Bush Mangham signed up for "three years or the war." Glasgow's volunteers hailed from Butler and Pike counties, and they enlisted at a time when the entire South was swept by a great wave of volunteerism. This patriotic outpouring occurred in response to military disasters on the Cumberland and Tennessee Rivers, threatening the heart of Dixie with invasion just as Northern armies marshaled anew to menace Richmond.[144]

Glasgow recruited his outfit to serve in Col. Henry W. Hilliard's Alabama Legion, a unit comprising troops of all arms of service: infantry, cavalry, and artillery. In the early years of the war, some viewed such all-arms organizations as a handy way to ensure tactical coordination on the battlefield, and several states accordingly commissioned officers to raise legions. Bob Glasgow's men were recruited and organized specifically for artillery service, and thus were authorized an enrollment significantly larger than an infantry company. Soon after mustering in, the company traveled to Montgomery and began drilling at Camp Mary. Other companies assembled there during the succeeding weeks, until Hilliard's Legion of Alabama Volunteers completed its organization on June 25, 1862.[145]

Colonel Hilliard's new command counted some 3000 men, organized into three infantry battalions, one artillery battalion, and a cavalry battalion. Glasgow's troops became Company A in Major Reeves's 4th Battalion (Artillery), evidently ranking as the first of the three artillery companies to complete its organization. The Legion remained in Montgomery fumbling with the intricacies of drill until July 8, when it moved by rail to Atlanta and thence to Chattanooga. Great movements were afoot, as Braxton Bragg was positioning his Army of the Mississippi to move north into Kentucky, where he could cooperate with Edmund Kirby Smith's forces from the Department of East Tennessee.[146]

Glasgow's fledgling artillerists settled in at Chattanooga, progressing markedly in drill during their three-week stay. The Legion received its weapons while in

EAST TENNESSEE AND KENTUCKY
THEATER OF OPERATIONS FOR
HILLIARD'S LEGION, 1862-1864

Chattanooga, but only Kolb's Company drew artillery pieces. Glasgow's would-be cannoneers drew small arms and probably began training as infantrymen, along with the other two unlucky "artillery" companies. These units retained their artillery designation and organization for quite some time, however, so Colonel Hilliard apparently viewed the inconvenience as temporary. Had they only known! If the neophyte redlegs had been able to gaze into a crystal ball, they would have seen visions of themselves slogging up hill and down dale for the remainder of the war, on foot![147]

They postponed the inevitable for one more leg of their journey, though, receiving the coveted transportation warrants that meant they were moving by rail again. This time, Company A was bound for Knoxville in the wilds of northeastern Tennessee. The Legion assembled at this critical communications node, remaining there ten days before taking up the line of march for Tazewell, near Cumberland Gap. On the ensuing 41-mile hike, the Legion's infantry battalions got their first real taste of marching, in the same place where *John Henry Mangham* of the 30th Alabama got his first marching blisters two months earlier (see Chapter V). One of Hilliard's men ruminated on this event shortly after the war, opining: "Every soldier has a *feeling* recollection of his first march—it is invariably associated in his mind with aching limbs and blistered feet." He thought it "probable that no member of the Legion present on that march and still living, has forgotten it." Glasgow's Company A staged into Clinton on the way to Tazewell, and remained there for some days before marching the remainder of the way, thus sparing them some of the agony.[148]

The footsore Alabamians picked a tough spot for this baptism in the rites of the infantryman, as the mountainous terrain, August heat, choking dust, and miserable roads guaranteed the maximum amount of pain. Anyone who has ever marched on blistered feet can sympathize with these "fresh fish" laboring through the inhospitable mountainscape, where each step downslope caused a soldier's foot to slide forward in his shoe, grating mercilessly on the blisters he was gingerly trying to protect. One can imagine the ordeal of marching in leather-soled shoes, in an era when cobblers' patterns did not even distinguish between the left and right shoe!

After resting their sore feet for a few days in Tazewell, most of Hilliard's men joined the Stevenson's Division in besieging Cumberland Gap, although the 4th Battalion remained to garrison Clinton. Federal troops ensconced in the Gap straddled key terrain indeed, where miles of rugged mountains channeled all communications between northeastern Tennessee, southeastern Kentucky, and southwestern Virginia through a single chokepoint. Black Belt Alabamians like Bush Mangham felt uneasy in such a barren moonscape in any case, with its "huge mountain sides, 'rock-ribbed and ancient as the sun,' towering high towards Heaven—bleak, bare, grim, vast and terrible!" The remote mountain fastnesses were worlds apart from their familiar Butler County vistas of bounteous crops, prosperous plantations, and inviting farmsteads. Instead of the hustle and bustle of large farm families and gregarious gangs of field hands, the lonely mountain denizens kept clannishly to themselves, narrowly suspicious of outsiders in general and of flatlanders in particular. One Alabamian viewed the mountain folk contemptuously as "dirt eaters," and his harsh assessment probably reflected an opinion widely held by his comrades. Outsiders to Appalachia, then and since, have commonly shared the uncomfortable feeling that they have blundered somehow into a different world, and Confederate memoirs consistently reflect this combination of fear and loathing.[149]

The stalemate at the Gap ended on September 17, when Union forces withdrew after Kirby Smith's other column passed through Big Creek Gap and turned their position. The bulk of the Legion stood fast, while the 4th Battalion departed Clinton on September 22 and closed into position at Cumberland Gap five days later. Private Mangham and his messmates remained there until October 2, then packed their gear and resumed the march north into Kentucky at the rear of Bragg's column. They pushed forward in nine days of rapid marching to join the remainder of the army as Bragg sought to concentrate it for battle, but his bungling efforts found his forces still scattered a week later at the Battle of Perryville. Badly outnumbered on the field but tactically victorious due to the valor of his troops, Bragg flinched from a rematch with Buell's Federals. After massing his forces briefly in defensive array, he quickly decided to retreat from Kentucky altogether.[150]

On the strategic level, Bragg's ill-conceived actions in the Bluegrass State were disastrous. For Bush and the rest of Glasgow's men, it meant more hard marching. They had marched about 150 miles from Cumberland Gap to reach Camp Dick Robinson, near Bryantsville in eastern Kentucky, in nine days. Arriving there on October 11, they started the return trip just three days later and reached Cumberland Gap again on October 22, 1862. Llewellyn A. Shaver, a member of the Legion, noted that the Alabamians brought up the rear of the army on the way back, as they had in the advance. In so doing, the men "experienced, in all its length and breadth, what it is *to bring up the rear on a retreat.*" Although Shaver left the grim details unspoken, one can imagine the strain involved: broken vehicles and disabled men abandoned to the tender mercies of local Unionist guerrillas, destruction of excess supplies, and disorderly stragglers demoralized by failure and perpetrating outrages on all and sundry. And always the marching! It added up to three hundred miles in twenty days for Bush and the others, including the two days of rest at Camp Dick Robinson. Despite the Legion's subsequent feats of endurance, Shaver considered the retreat from Kentucky to be in a class by itself. In terms of "severity of marching and privation of every description," he thought the campaign was "one of the most trying of the war."[151]

Hilliard's footsore Legion held Cumberland Gap for two weeks before withdrawing further south with the rest of the army on November 4, 1862. In preparation for the movement, Bush was detailed as a teamster on the first of the month; possibly he was broken down by the marching, near-starvation, and general exposure, or perhaps it was simply his turn to tangle with army mules! In any event, five days of marching brought the Alabamians back to Knoxville, where they remained several days before continuing on to Loudon. From there, the Legion took the cars to Bridgeport, Alabama, an important rail junction just southwest of Chattanooga. Arriving there on November 22, they turned around just four days later and returned to Knoxville! Two weeks after arriving in Knoxville, the artillerymen took the road to Clinton again, where they remained until the day after Christmas. Three more days of midwinter marching found Glasgow's men at Big Creek Gap, just a few miles from Cumberland Gap. Hilliard's battalions were now strewn in garrisons at Knoxville, Clinton, Kingston, Big Creek Gap, and even Cumberland Gap. Bush climbed down from his wagon at year's end and resumed his place in ranks.[152]

Since the Department of East Tennessee reverted to its backwater status after the foray into Kentucky, the Alabama Legion remained in its bleak winter garrisons and picket posts while Bragg's Army of Tennessee fought it out with Rosecrans at Murfreesboro over the New Year. Since enlisting in March, Private Mangham had ridden the cars from Alabama to Knoxville, marched from there to within spitting distance of the Ohio River, then legged it back to Cumberland Gap again. Then he drove a wagon back to Alabama, where he promptly turned around and drove it back to the Tennessee-Kentucky line. He may well have participated in a shoot-out or two with the feared and detested East Tennessee bushwhackers, but he and his mates had never been in a proper battle. Nevertheless, they certainly knew something about the hardships of soldiering. And how.[153]

The Alabamians' situation was complicated by the reassignment of the Legion's component battalions to various brigades. The cavalry battalion became the nucleus of the 10th Confederate Cavalry Regiment, thereby losing the last vestiges of its connection to the original Legion. The horsemen had never really operated under Hilliard's control anyway, as the tactical requirements of large-scale maneuver required their attachment to larger cavalry forces able to range far and wide, independent of infantry support. Major Reeves's artillery battalion had never received artillery pieces either, except for Kolb's battery, because experience was proving that brigade-sized infantry units generally could not employ, control, or sustain any artillery organization larger than a battery. Even the companies themselves underwent reorganization, with Bob Glasgow's Company A and Bolling Hall's Company B each dividing into two companies; the new units became Company D and Company E, 4th Battalion.[154]

All in all, the advantages of the Legion's all-arms organization had proved to be more apparent than real, and its battalions were parceled out to various brigades as though they were simply small infantry regiments. Colonel Hilliard eventually resigned his position, leaving his Alabama Legion under the command of Col. Jack Thorington in March 1863. It was about this time that Bush and the rest of the 4th Battalion marched to Williamsburg, Kentucky, probably foraging for beef cattle to augment their rations. Other Legion units conducted similar forays into Kentucky that winter, skirmishing occasionally with bushwhackers who took umbrage at Confederate commissary practices. Glasgow's men covered seventy miles on their expedition in late March, then marched another 48 miles in the first week of April from Big Creek Gap to Lee's Springs, Tennessee. Minor Union troop movements appeared to herald another invasion of East Tennessee, so the Alabamians packed their knapsacks once more in mid-April and hoofed it 74 miles to Cumberland Gap in five days of hard marching. Later that month, they moved another 31 miles to Bean's Station, before shifting over to Morristown.[155]

All of the Legion's units had reassembled at Lee's Springs in April, and there the footloose legionnaires finally received a permanent military "home" in Gracie's Brigade. Brigadier General Archibald Gracie, Jr., was a native New Yorker who had cast his fortunes with the Confederacy, and he provided talented leadership to the Southern troops he commanded. It looked like Gracie might be leading the Alabama Legion into its first taste of real combat in early May, as Union Maj. Gen. Ambrose Burnside continued marshaling forces to strike in East Tennessee. Confederate commanders shuffled their troops once more, so Gracie had to march his brigade on the well-beaten path back to Cumberland Gap. Private Mangham, however, remained in Morristown to guard the commissary stores amassed there, so he missed the long summer of fruitless maneuvering that took his friends of Glasgow's Company A to the Gap, then to Jacksborough, then back to Big Creek Gap by June 21, 1863. The Butler County men had spent the winter here, so they knew the area well as they settled in for another six-week round of boring guard and picket duty. In early August, they pulled up stakes and marched 45 miles to Strawberry Plains, where they remained three weeks before marching another 55 miles to Loudon by month's end.[156]

While his comrades spent a frustrating summer marching in never-ending circles through the wilds of East Tennessee, Bush cooled his heels at Morristown. He apparently drove a wagon again or performed some other special duty during July and August, because he received an additional 25 cents a day in consideration of the duties to which he was detailed. Perhaps he possessed a frail constitution, or his summer of garrison duty may have left him unprepared for hard marching. Regardless of the cause, Bush was ill prepared for the ordeal he faced in early September, when the Alabama Legion began a rapid movement to rendezvous with Bragg's Army of Tennessee. General Simon B. Buckner was moving most of his forces from the Department of East Tennessee to join Bragg near Chattanooga, as Rosecrans's summer campaign had levered Confederate forces out of their lines in Middle Tennessee.[157]

For the Legion, this meant "eighteen days of almost constant marching" during which they covered almost three hundred miles! As Llewellyn Shaver recalled this period, "The heat and dust contributed much to the inconvenience of the troops during the whole march, and the suffering from these and other causes was intense." Bush labored along through the sweltering Tennessee summer heat to the rendezvous with Bragg's Army at Harrison, Tennessee, on September 7. The next two nights he marched southward as part of Bragg's desperate attempt to concentrate forces and bring Rosecrans's onrushing columns to battle. After the last twenty miles of stumbling through the north Georgia darkness, however, the boy reached the end of his tether after hiking 245 miles in thirteen days. He was admitted into the Army hospital at Ringgold, Georgia, on September 13, 1863.[158]

While he lay incapacitated in his hospital bed, the Alabama Legion met the enemy in the forests along Chickamauga Creek on the second day of the great battle. In its baptism of fire, the Legion hurled itself repeatedly at Federal entrenchments atop Snodgrass Hill in some of the most relentless fighting of the war. Bob Glasgow's old company, now commanded by Capt. Robert Fuller Manly, went into action with 48 men, and only nineteen emerged unscathed. Six men were killed outright, and another four died of their wounds over the succeeding two weeks. Their horrendous casualty rate was even worse than the rest of Gracie's Brigade, which lost ninety killed and 615 wounded of the 1870 men in ranks when the battle began. The hardest hit unit was the Legion's 1st Battalion, which lost 169 killed and wounded of the 239 men in ranks. Bolling Hall's 2nd Battalion was in the thick of the fight as well, and the shreds of its battle flag bore the marks of more than eighty bullet holes. The flagstaff had been shot in half three times, and Color Bearer William H. Hiett was hit three times. Major John D. McLennan had succeeded Reeves as commanding officer of the 4th Battalion, and 102 of his 205 men were killed or wounded in the bloodletting.[159]

*   *   *   *   *

Bush Mangham was spared the Calvary atop Snodgrass Hill, but apparently was quite seriously ill in his own right. The young soldier had been present for duty at every one of his company's musters since its inception, excepting cases where he was absent on detached service. In the fall and winter of 1863, however, he remained hospitalized for an extended period. Bush remained absent from his company at the end of February 1864, and his orderly sergeant listed him as absent since entering the hospital at Ringgold. Interestingly, the sergeant also knew that Capt. C. S. Walsh had paid Bush through the last day of December 1863. Apparently the army bureaucracy remained capable of a surprising degree of efficiency in some respects, despite the November catastrophe at Missionary Ridge and the Legion's return to duty in East Tennessee.[160]

When Private Mangham drew two months' pay and clothing from Captain Walsh on January 14, 1864, he stated his unit as Company A, 4th Battalion, Alabama Legion. This is a clear indication that Bush was still convalescing at home or in a hospital well to the rear, because this unit no longer existed. At least, it no longer existed under this name. After spending two months with Bragg's army investing Chattanooga, Gracie's Brigade had departed with Longstreet to besiege Knoxville just before Bragg's debacle at Missionary Ridge. On November 25, 1863, the very day that the great battle at Chattanooga routed Bragg's army, the unwieldy Legion underwent a complete reorganization at distant Charleston, Tennessee. Major McLennan's 4th Battalion (Artillery) combined with Hall's 2nd Battalion into the 59th Alabama Regiment, while the 1st and 3rd Battalions became the 60th Alabama. Kolb's Company, the only outfit in the artillery battalion ever to receive its cannon, was redesignated Kolb's Battery and remained in Gracie's Brigade. Bush Mangham's company swapped its artillery designation for a new title: Company I, 59th Alabama.[161]

The 59th took part in several actions around Knoxville that winter, but Bush was still absent from the ranks. Sometime between March and May he apparently reported back to his company, because he drew clothing from the quartermaster on May 31, 1864. In all likelihood, he rejoined his company in Tennessee or southwestern Virginia during the quiet times of March or early April, when the ill-clad and ill-shod Alabamians eagerly awaited warmer weather. Despite their hardships and setbacks, only two men refused to step forward when the regiment re-enlisted for the war in March.[162]

Events in the latter part of April portended a major change for Gracie's Alabama brigade, however, as General Lee voiced a call for reinforcements in Virginia. A widespread belief existed that the fighting of 1864 would prove decisive, although men on each side confidently believed that victory would be theirs. As Grant mustered his armies for the coming lunge across the Rapidan River, General Buckner dispatched the Department of East Tennessee's largest brigade to Richmond on April 27. Consisting of the 41st, 43rd, 59th, and 60th Alabama regiments and the 23rd Alabama Battalion Sharpshooters, Gracie's Brigade probably counted about 2000 men. The 59th Alabama alone was about six hundred strong, and its men were amused when some of Richmond's knowledgeable citizens mistook them for a brigade, even though the regiment's relatively full ranks dwarfed most others by this point in the war. Other citizens, however, were heard to murmur that the men, fifty of whom were barefooted, clearly "bore marks of service." First Sergeant Preston L. Dodgen of Company F wrote home on April 29 that ". . .we haint had nothing to eat in a day or so. . .but I think we will fare better hear than we did in Tennessee." He added confidently, "I will bee home in 3 months I believe the war will cloes before long."[163]

On the next day, the 59th marched through Richmond en route to camp on the Mechanicsville Road east of town. Captain John Hall, commanding Company B and the brother of regimental commander Col. Bolling Hall, characterized the welcome differences between Virginia ladies and East Tennessee women in a letter to his home folks in Alabama. Approvingly, he noted that ladies in the Old Dominion "share their meals with the soldiers and wear shoes and do not chew tobacco." He added:

> There is such a difference in the Citizens of East Tenn—go to a house and ask for a piece of meat and bread and the answer you would get would be with a long union bushwhacking face, "I haven't got a bite to save my life. I have got three children here and I just know we'll all die this winter. We're bound to starve." Go to a house here and how will you be received? Everything will be given you that can be got—the lady of the house will tell you if she had only two meals—you shall have one.[164]

Gracie's Alabama troops reported for duty with Maj. Gen. Robert Ransom's division. Ransom's Division was assigned to the Richmond and Petersburg defenses, under the overall command of Gen. P. G. T. Beauregard's Department of North Carolina and Southern Virginia. The Creole general's forces comprised a miscellany of infantry brigades, cavalry, artillery, and militia units, with which he had to cover the land and river approaches to the capital and Petersburg, the crucial communications node some 35 miles south of Richmond. Lee's Army of Northern Virginia was entrenched along the Rapidan River far to the north, but only the existence of Beauregard's command gave Lee the freedom to operate this far from Richmond. As early as the spring of 1862 Federal forces had attempted to fight their way up the James River to the capital, and they certainly had the wherewithal to try it again.[165]

Indeed, Grant's campaign plan for summer 1864 dedicated a force under Maj. Gen. Ben Butler to advance up the James River to threaten Richmond and Petersburg while the Army of the Potomac crossed the Rapidan to fight Lee. As the main armies came to grips in the Wilderness and at Spotsylvania, Butler's Army of the James landed on the peninsula of land interposed between the James River on the north and the Appomattox River on the south. Here, the hated occupier of New Orleans established a base at Bermuda Hundred Landing, just ten miles northeast of Petersburg, but then

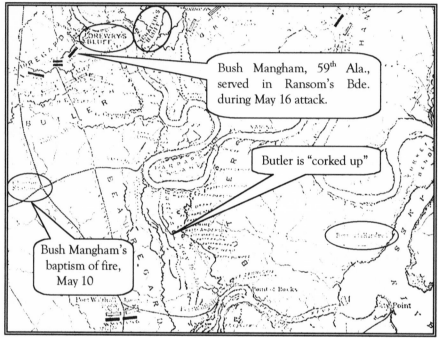

Bush Mangham, 59th Ala., served in Ransom's Bde. during May 16 attack.

Butler is "corked up"

Bush Mangham's baptism of fire, May 10

DREWRY'S BLUFF AND BERMUDA HUNDRED

paused to entrench his lines before advancing further. "Beast" Butler's ensuing advance straddled the Richmond & Petersburg Railroad, threatening the Confederacy's capability to supply its capital. In short, Butler's presence threatened to overthrow the defense of Richmond and force Lee to flee southward to its protection, with Grant and Meade hot on his heels.[166]

As Butler's army threatened Richmond from the south and Petersburg from the north, one of the great dramas of the entire war unfolded. Confederate troop trains poured into Petersburg from the Carolinas, bringing forces to attack the left flank of the powerful invasion force, which numbered more than 30,000 men. Repeatedly, Beauregard juggled his tiny command with admirable panache and a great deal of luck, capitalizing on every Federal mistake. Gracie's Brigade marched to the James River landings on May 6, where it boarded steamers bound for the defenses at Drewry's Bluff, south of the capital. The boat trip was a thrilling experience for the Alabama soldiers after their two-year sojourn in the wilderness of East Tennessee. The novelty wore off quickly enough that night, however, as the brigade bivouacked in line of battle beyond the breastworks, positioned to take the brunt of the enemy's expected attack the next morning. Fatefully, Butler paused to entrench his lines before venturing farther towards Richmond, Petersburg, or the railroad arteries that pumped the South's lifeblood.[167]

The 59th Alabama rested in comfortable quarters within the defensive works during the following two days, before engaging in strenuous maneuvers on May 9. These were barren of results, but resumed on the following day at Chester Station. The regiment played a critical role in this local riposte, trouncing their opponents in a sharp engagement that was probably Bush Mangham's personal baptism of fire. Here, near the Drewry's Bluff defenses, he and his comrades took some sixty Yankee prisoners and killed at least ten more in a brief combat, while suffering no casualties of their own.[168]

Butler tentatively oriented his forces northward in the face of his unexpectedly aroused foe, but his actions lacked the swiftness that would have spelled doom for Beauregard's defensive efforts. As it was, Butler's dilatory movements allowed the Confederate defenders to shuttle forces to and from threatened areas in a dramatic dance with death. When a Federal cavalry raid threatened Richmond on May 11, Beauregard pulled forces from Butler's front to face the new danger. Gracie's Brigade had done some hard work during the two preceding days, but moved out of the line of battle into an assembly area when the call came. While halted on the road, they watched as a dark cloud strategically positioned itself overhead, before proceeding to empty its liquid contents upon their heads. As they settled down afterwards to a damp sleep, the word came: "Get ready to move." In less than ten minutes they were on their way to the capital.[169]

Marching all night, Bush and his comrades reached the town of Manchester at daybreak on May 12. Here, just across the James River from Richmond, barking dogs and crowing cocks announced the passage of the marching men. Shaver noticed that nightcapped heads appeared hastily from windows and retreated just as quickly again, and the laughing Alabamians greeted each "advance and retreat" with a "genuine Confederate cheer." Continuing to march without pausing, they passed through the streets of the capital city towards the sound of cannon booming in the distance. As they did so, the cheers and entreaties of "the beautiful daughters of Richmond" aroused their martial ardor to new heights. It was a "novel experience" for Gracie's men, whose combat experience was limited to the wilds of north Georgia and East Tennessee. Here they were in the capital itself, directly under the eyes of the women and children they had enlisted to protect. As Llewellyn Shaver recalled, "All this was not lost upon the troops. Notwithstanding they had marched during the entire night, their step was brisk and elastic, and the display of a Confederate flag from a window or balcony never failed to elicit a cheer."[170]

Gracie's Alabama soldiers reached the entrenchments on the opposite side of the city, where they formed line of battle and advanced in full view of admiring Richmond militia units. Their steady advance met brisk skirmish fire as they moved across a field and through a half-mile of woods beyond, and elements of the 59th Alabama replaced the 43rd Alabama on the skirmish line. Occasional cannon shots showered tree branches on their heads, but the advance continued until the skirmishers found themselves flanked on the right and accordingly fell back to the brigade line of battle. The main body was too tough for the Federal cavalrymen to crack, and the threat receded. Gracie pulled his brigade back into the works, but repeated alarms kept them marching back and forth to threatened points all day. The Alabamians were soaked from the intermittent rainstorms, but knew they were performing in full view of numerous important officials. Jefferson Davis himself "rode frequently by the troops" before the alarm passed, and they finally encamped after thirty-six straight hours of marching and fighting.[171]

They remained in place for two days until orders came to return to Drewry's Bluff. If their time in East Tennessee prepared them for nothing else, it must have accustomed them to backtracking! At least in Virginia the distances were shorter, the roads better, the terrain flatter, and the women prettier and friendlier. After returning to the entrenchments at Drewry's Bluff on May 14, they made preparations to face Butler's expected attack or to deliver one of their own.[172]

Although Butler had oriented his force northwards towards the Drewry's Bluff defenses, he launched no attack on May 15. Beauregard again capitalized on this opportunity to turn the tide, designing an ambitious plan of attack to destroy his slow-moving opponent. Butler's pause to entrench and ensuing tentative advance had allowed the Louisiana general time to cobble together three small divisions in Butler's front and another in his rear. Ransom's Division, including Gracie's Brigade, occupied the trenches opposite Butler's right wing as it pivoted north. Beauregard planned for Ransom to turn Butler's right flank, thus separating him from naval support on the James River. Hoke's Division would attack Butler's front to prevent reinforcement of his right, while Whiting's Division to the south would march to the sound of the guns. If Whiting pushed hard, he would strike Butler's right rear and precipitate a total collapse. After forcing Butler's surrender, Beauregard hoped to unite with Lee in attacking Grant. Even if these possibilities remained elusive, Beauregard thought it certain that he could shove the Federals back into the Bermuda Hundred peninsula and bottle them up there.[173]

Gracie's Brigade was the left flank unit of Ransom's first line, and his troops moved quietly from their entrenchments before dawn on May 16. Each man in the 59th Alabama carried sixty rounds of .69 caliber ammunition for his musket, and had grounded his knapsack where the quartermaster could keep watch over it. The foggy dampness was "depressing in the extreme," thought one soldier, and the poor visibility hindered the deployment. The line was formed despite harassing fire from suspicious Yankee pickets; the tense Alabamians noticed that the bullets, by some atmospheric quirk, "could be distinctly heard hissing through the dense atmosphere from the time they cleared the muzzles of the guns until they reached their lodgment."[174]

Day was fairly dawning through the "almost perfect obscurity of the densest fog" when Gracie's voice boomed out the command "Forward!" It was 4:45 a.m., and the brigade stepped off into the attack. Within just a few yards, they received a volley from the Federal defenders; instead of sending them reeling in confusion, however, it provoked a Rebel yell and a charge. Heading straight across an open field and past the Willis house, the Alabama brigade fought its way through enemy rifle pits and into the woods beyond, where the main breastworks frowned with muskets and artillery. Dozens were mowed down in the hour of "stubborn fighting" that ensued. Captain John Hall, commanding Company B, 59th Alabama, saw his men "falling right and left" as they overran the enemy defenses. A bullet passed through his coat and settled into his pocket, but left him otherwise untouched; Hall was the only captain in the regiment to survive unhurt. His brother Bolling, commanding the 59th Alabama, was shot three times through the ankle and foot. Their brother Crenshaw, the regimental adjutant, fell gravely wounded by a bullet that struck above his collarbone and ranged downward through his body. The regiment lost twenty men killed and another 142 wounded in their desperate charge, and was left "almost entirely without officers." Companies rated a captain as commander and three lieutenants, but Captain Hall reported that only enough unwounded officers remained to provide each company with a single one.[175]

John Hall rallied the remnants of the regiment and formed them to continue the attack if ordered, but Gracie held them up as Ransom called for fresh troops. Enemy counterattacks drove in some of Hoke's units on Ransom's flank, but Confederate reinforcements pushed them back once more. Whiting, meanwhile, moved hesitantly towards the sound of battle in Butler's rear, failing to strike a powerful blow. Nevertheless, the Union commander's unhinged right flank and battered front suffered 4500 casualties under the relentless hammering; it was punishment enough for Butler, who on May 17 pulled his defeated units back into the snug, defensible confines of the peninsula between the James and Appomattox rivers. Confederate reports accounted for 1388 Federal prisoners taken in the battle at Drewry's Bluff, all but 172 of them taken by the troops attacking from the north. Major General Ransom noted that his two left flank brigades, Gracie's in the first line and Terry's in the second, "deserve special notice" for their gallantry. Total Confederate losses exceeded 2500, but their stunning victory had spectacular results.[176]

Gracie's Brigade remained on the field throughout May 16 and advanced the next day to the vicinity of the Howlet house, where they rapidly erected breastworks to hem in Butler's men. The terrible shells hurled from Union gunboats on the James spurred on the labors of the sweating Alabamians. In John Hall's considered opinion, "These shells weighing 200 lbs. are the worst thing I ever saw." The unremitting rain of metal wore them out and prevented sleep, and Hall personally witnessed the vicious shell fragments cut both legs off of several different men. They held their hard-won positions, however, and made the neck of the Bermuda Hundred peninsula into the graveyard of Federal hopes. A frustrated Beauregard knew he could have destroyed Butler and helped Lee turn on Grant, but mistakes by Ransom and Whiting had prevented complete success. General Grant was frustrated in his own right, observing sourly that Butler's army "was as completely shut off from further operations directly against Richmond as if it had been in a bottle strongly corked." If anybody were going to take the Confederate capital that summer, it would have to be Grant, Meade, and the Army of the Potomac. Richmond was still "a hard road to travel."[177]

*   *   *   *   *

Bush Mangham and the 59th Alabama lay under the fire of the fearsome gunboats until May 21, when they moved back to Chaffin's Farm, leaving others to watch over "Beast" Butler. Captain Hall mused over the fickleness of fate that brought them into comfortable quarters now that the weather was hot, after the regiment had "spent one of the coldest winters ever known without shelter." The rest period gave the quartermaster the opportunity to issue new uniforms at the end of May, and Bush was one of those able to replace some of his tattered clothes. The steady drumbeat of gunfire paused on June 5, causing John Hall to observe gratefully in a letter home, "This morning is the first quiet time we have had in thirty days." Later, however, gunfire swelled again to the north. It marked the ceaseless struggle between Lee and Grant, now approaching Richmond from the north and east.[178]

The 59th Alabama rested at Chaffin's Bluff until Grant's next move created a renewed crisis. Swinging east and then south from Cold Harbor, he crossed his army over the James River in a brilliant maneuver that put him in position to attack Petersburg from the east. While Lee desperately sought to learn where Grant was going and in what strength, Beauregard once more had to play for time with the meager forces at hand. Again, the talented Louisiana general came through in spades, boldly assuming incredible risk in some sectors to mass combat power in areas he judged critical. Time and again, his judgments proved correct, although he benefited greatly from Federal hesitancy, blunders, and the fog of war. The atmosphere of crisis burgeoned on June 15 through June 17, as Lee's army made a desperate bid to get below Richmond in time to save Petersburg. Until it got there in force, Beauregard's magic act would have to suffice.[179]

Beauregard called for the 59th Alabama at 2:00 o'clock in the afternoon on June 17, when the regiment received orders to report to him below town. Rushing to the railcars waiting to speed them through the city, the men were in Petersburg itself within an hour and reported to Beauregard and Maj. Gen. Bushrod Johnson before another hour passed. Ambrose Burnside's IX Corps had seized a portion of the Confederate lines in a predawn assault that morning, but it took him a long time to organize his winded troops for a follow-up attack. One finally got underway just as the 59th Alabama received its orders to leave Chaffin's Farm, and the regiment got mixed up in the resulting action immediately upon its arrival. (See map on page 512.)[180]

As the 59th approached the field, a "most terrible fire of grape and shell" spattered through its ranks, but the fire did not prevent the regiment from occupying its assigned position. Captain Hall was in charge of a detail intended to entrench the line, but after a few minutes work the Yankees came on with a rush against the entire line. As Wise's Brigade collapsed, followed by Elliott's, the 59th Alabama counterattacked headlong into the breach yawning wide on the left. They cleared the enemy from their front and

530

pursued them even beyond the breastworks, but other Federal units already occupied positions beyond their left flank, and were now in rear of it. An intense fight chewed up the regiment's leftmost companies terribly, but the ferocious Confederate counterattacks wore down the attackers and sealed off the dangerous penetration.[181]

Beauregard and his chief engineer had selected a final fallback position earlier that day and marked it clearly with stakes, and had carefully briefed every staff officer in Hoke's and Johnson's divisions. Gracie's men, assigned to Johnson's Division, carefully lit large campfires near the front line and pushed their picket line as close as possible to the Federals. With this bold front well established, the brigades stealthily withdrew at midnight to their assigned positions and began the pick and shovel work necessary to dig them in. As Lee's troops began arriving in force the next morning, renewed Federal attacks were shot to pieces in the open ground between the opposing lines. One Maine regiment began its attack with 900 men in ranks; thirty minutes later it was strangled in its own blood, leaving 632 men dead and wounded on the field. It was the most horrific combat loss suffered by any regiment during the entire Civil War.[182]

The fighting at Petersburg from June 15 to June 18 cost the Union army almost 10,000 casualties, while the Confederates lost perhaps four thousand men. Most of the latter were under Beauregard's skillful command, and again the Creole general had saved the day. Captain John Hall knew his regiment had done well, but the 62 killed and 53 wounded left another terrible rent in its tattered fabric. He put it bluntly: "A few more such fights will wipe us out." In the single month of combat since they arrived in Virginia, the 59th Alabama counted 280 casualties of the 600 who had come to the Old Dominion. Hall's Company B had lost six killed, 24 wounded, and twelve captured, for a total of 42 casualties. The Alabama captain had served in Hilliard's Legion at Chickamauga, where his 2nd Battalion lost 91 men of 230 engaged; nevertheless, he feelingly described the June 17 fracas at Petersburg as "the tightest place I ever got into."[183]

*   *   *   *   *

When a rearrangement of the lines caused Gracie to pull the 59th Alabama out of the front line trenches on June 29, only about 250 effective men remained in ranks. The regiment lost continually during the long siege at Petersburg, and the stream of sick and wounded was swollen by many who deserted the colors in despair after the Battle of the Crater in late July. Bush may have been one of those who tried to go home; surviving records show that Captain Manly wrote the Confederate Adjutant & Inspector General on August 30, requesting commutation of Private Mangham's court-martial sentence. Unfortunately, no documents survive that discuss the nature or disposition of his case, but Manly probably would not have bothered to write such a high official unless Bush faced the ultimate sanction: death by musketry. Many of Lee's men received lighter penalties for desertion or other offenses, but in the life-and-death struggle at Petersburg most of the lesser offenders were sentenced to serve time at hard labor *after* combat operations concluded; few officers troubled themselves to appeal such sentences. Those facing death by firing squad, on the other hand, often benefited

531

from intervention by company- or regimental-level superiors who took into account their knowledge of the soldier's specific background and situation. Bad news from home and a heretofore-solid service record topped the list of extenuating circumstances, but many officers were disturbed by the arbitrariness of military courts that spared some, while exacting the supreme penalty from others.[184]

If Bush was indeed sentenced to die, Manly's plea saved him from an ignominious death at the hands of his own comrades, with a scrap of paper pinned to his jacket as an aiming mark for their muskets. The 59th Alabama lost only one man to this ultimate sanction, and it was Pvt. James Ray of Company C. Just a month after Major Burton had answered Manly's appeal from his desk in Richmond, Ray was blindfolded and tied to a stake while a minister prayed with him. Captain John Hall wrote sadly to his father in Alabama: "His crime was desertion & cowardice. I am sorry for the boy for I do not really think he has any sense. . . .I would give almost any thing to be absent when it is done." Adding a few more lines after General Gracie's final appeals failed and the sentence was carried out, Hall shuddered: "Father I have just witnessed a sight which I pray I may never again be called upon to see. . . .Ray was shot to death by a detail of 15 men made for the purpose." In a grisly postscript, the shaken young captain added, "Several balls took effect but a few moments later after life not being extinct entirely, he was again shot, the last trial finishing life. Twas a sad sight."[185]

Although Bush was spared an end similar to Private Ray's, he was no longer present when his comrades received a badly needed issue of clothing later that fall, nor when the regiment mustered in February 1865. Despite the fact that 438 men still stood by their colors at year's end, few remained after the 59th scraped through a series of tight spots before the end of the war. When Lee launched his last-gasp offensive at Fort Stedman on March 25, the regiment's survivors lashed out at the picket lines of Brig. Gen. Joshua Chamberlain's brigade near the Watkins house. They attacked with the spirit of old; the famous Maine officer was in a position to know, and he described their advance as displaying "great vigor and boldness," although it was "not in heavy force." Counterattacking Federals of the 124th New York shot down the 60th Alabama's regimental commander, cutting off and capturing him and the 164 starving ragamuffins he was leading. The New Yorkers also bagged the colors he was waving. They belonged to the 59th Alabama.[186]

When Company I stacked arms two weeks later at Appomattox, its second lieutenant surrendered with six men. Private Bush Mangham was not among them. In all probability, he stopped a bullet or piece of shell in a lonely stretch of trenchline in September 1864, and lies in an unmarked grave where his comrades buried him.[187]

7. THE WILD WEST COMES TO NASHVILLE: PVT. JOHN R. MANGHAM, CO. C, TERRY'S TEXAS RANGERS

The uncertainty clouding B. W. Mangham's identity and eventual fate also cloaks the origins of John R. Mangham, a young soldier believed to be another orphan son of Josiah Thomas Mangum, Jr. (see diagram on page 518).

Sometime after their father died in the 1840s, John apparently went to live with his aunt, Jemima Mangham Sockwell, in Russell County, Alabama. Jemima was born in 1818 and had moved to Georgia with her father, Josiah Mangum, Sr., in the 1820s. Along with her brothers Thomas, Arthur, and James, she moved to Russell County in the 1830s, when a treaty with the Creek Indians opened the floodgates of white immigration; they settled in the same community as her uncle, old William Mangham, near latter-day Opelika. Their close association with William and his family probably provided the impetus for their adoption, or resumption, of the English spelling of their surname. Jemima married William Sockwell in 1840; ten years later, the census-taker found ten-year-old John Mangham living in the Sockwell home.[188] (See map, p. 566.)

In the early 1850s, William and Jemima Sockwell accompanied her brothers Arthur and James when they moved to Louisiana. A decade earlier, their other brothers, Robert S. and William R. Mangum, had blazed the trail westwards to Texas, where they were the only known sons of Josiah Sr., who maintained, or reverted to, the phonetic *Mangum*. After establishing a prosperous stock farm in Matagorda County with his wife Leacy and their six children, William died in the early 1850s. At about the same time, Robert brought his family from Shelby County to Matagorda.[189]

Leacy moved about 1854 to Gonzales County, where she lived on a prosperous ranch and farm near Rancho. Six years later, her real estate was worth a thousand dollars, and she owned personal property valued at triple that figure. Daughters Susan (23) and Eliza (15) remained at home, as did 25-year-old Caroline, with her husband Hiram and their two small children. William and Leacy's only son, 20-year-old Joseph Marion Mangum, lived with his mother, sisters, brother-in-law, and little cousins, whom he helped support by raising stock. In this last year before the war, two of Joe's other first cousins lived on the ranch as well. The elder was Robert, a 25-year-old North Carolinian who had lived with their uncle, James Green Mangham, back in Russell County in 1850. He had accompanied Green to Louisiana, residing in Claiborne Parish until moving to Gonzales County in late 1859 or early 1860. Joe's other cousin was 20-year old John, who had lived with the Sockwells in 1850; he probably accompanied them from Alabama to Claiborne Parish in the early 1850s, before joining his elder brother for the trip to Texas at the end of the decade. After all, they were entering manhood, and the wide-open western spaces beckoned active young men seeking land, families, and fortunes. Their cousin Joe raised 25 horses and 150 cattle on Leacy's 150-acre ranch in 1860, which was quite an achievement for a young bachelor. Leacy owned another six horses and 200 cattle, so Robert and John certainly were welcome additions to the family work force. The census taker listed their occupations as farmhands, but they doubtless punched cows as part of their daily duties on the prosperous ranch.[190]

When war broke out the next year, Texas cowboys tended to look for cavalry units to join. An English observer, Colonel Fremantle of the Coldstream Guards, made humorous sport of this tendency, which many others acknowledged as well: "At the outbreak of the war it was found very difficult to raise infantry in Texas, as no Texan walks a yard if he can help it." Late summer found Mark L. Evans raising a company in

Gonzales County for service with Col. Benjamin F. Terry, who was commissioned to raise a regiment of Texas Rangers for duty as an independent command in Virginia. Each man was to provide his own six-shooter, a shotgun or rifle, and a bridle, blanket, spurs, lariat, and other equipment necessary for cavalry service. Although most Confederate cavalrymen were required to provide their own mounts, Terry's commission expressed the government's intention to provide his Rangers with horses. Joe and John went with Evans's company to the regimental rendezvous in Houston, where the Rangers were to be mustered into Confederate service by the enrolling officer, Lt. Jesse W. Sparks.[191]

With the various companies formed up on three sides of a hollow square on September 12, 1861, Sparks asked: "Do you men wish to be sworn into service for twelve months or for three years or for during the war?" Private James K. P. Blackburn was among the group, and remembered the answer vividly: "With a unanimity never

JOHN R. MANGHAM AND JOSEPH M. MANGUM?
PERHAPS NOT, BUT THESE UNKNOWN TROOPERS ALSO BELONGED TO
CAPT. MARK EVANS'S CO. C, TERRY'S TEXAS RANGERS.
NOTE THE LONE STAR INSIGNIA ON THEIR HATS.
    - *Courtesy of Texas State Library & Archives Commission*

surpassed, a shout unheard of before, that whole body of men shouted, 'For the war,' 'For the war!'" Sparks obligingly mustered them in for the duration of the war, using company rolls on which Captain Evans recorded Joe's name as J. M. *Mangum*, reflecting the spelling his father had adopted after moving west from Georgia. John, having lived since young boyhood with Mangham aunts and uncles in Alabama and Louisiana, had Captain Evans list his name on the muster roll as J. R. *Mangham*.[192]

Enlisted for the duration, the two young men were now privates in an outfit that became Company C, 1st Texas Rangers, after the captains drew lots for letter assignments within the regimental organization. The regiment was a huge one, as 1170 men had rushed to sign its rolls in less than twenty days after recruiting began. The troopers duly elected their company officers while in Houston, but for some reason the formal election of regimental field officers was delayed. Terry functioned as colonel and regimental commander in the meantime, although he refused to be addressed as "colonel" until his eventual election in October.[193]

They wasted little time in Texas before heading east towards New Orleans, but the disjointed transportation infrastructure of the Deep South prescribed a circuitous route. An 80-mile trip in boxcars brought the men to Beaumont, where they transferred to a steamer to take them down the Neches River, then back up the Sabine River to Niblett's Bluff. Here, on the state line between Texas and Louisiana, they struck out on foot towards New Iberia, facing a 100-mile foot march before they could switch to carts and wagons for another forty miles. Much of the road was covered with watery sloughs between six inches and two feet deep, so most of the Rangers were suffering terribly from blisters before they fairly began the lengthy hike. Private Blackburn was in Strobel's Company, whose men already were suffering badly during the first day's march. Strobel sensibly authorized his troopers to lasso and break the horses they found running free on the west Louisiana prairie, and his south Texas cowboys were all mounted for the second day of the trip! Rangers who wound up riding the carts on the last forty miles to New Iberia found the experience a memorable one, as Creole teamsters drove the springless, seatless oxcarts by wielding a pointed stick instead of a whip. Since New Iberia stood upon the banks of Bayou Teche, the Texans were able to transfer to steamboats for a ride to Brashear City (now Morgan City), then travel by railcar through seemingly endless sugar plantations to the metropolis of New Orleans.[194]

The eye-opening odyssey took upwards of a week, but the regiment almost immediately received orders to proceed north on the Mississippi Central Railroad. The dearth of troops along the Confederacy's northern border necessitated a desperate call for troops, so the Rangers' marching orders were changed from Richmond to Nashville, Tennessee. Some companies learned the news before departing the Crescent City, but others found out only after a prolonged holdover in Mississippi. Likewise, some men were deeply disappointed in their new orders, whereas others rejoiced to find themselves under the command of Albert Sidney Johnston, a general who had made his reputation in Texas. Either way, however, they had to live with the Army's decision. After a long ride in filthy cattle cars to Nashville, they dismounted for the march to encampments at the city's fairgrounds, where they began drilling, guard mount, and camp duties.[195]

In the capital city of Tennessee, the Rangers found themselves holding down center stage in a veritable Wild West show. The Tennesseeans and their ladies had heard tales of the exploits of earlier "Texas Rangers" on the western frontier, and the raw cavalrymen now had to live up to the reputation implied by their famous title. Largely recruited from the stock farms and ranches of south central Texas, many were indeed experienced cowboys, such as Joe Mangum. These men already knew plenty about riding and shooting, even if they were untrained as soldiers. As they received shipments of government horses at the railroad depot, crowds gathered to see the Texans ride, and their performances soon became a regular entertainment at the fairground's racetrack. Spectators would place rows of silver dollars on the ground at twenty-foot intervals, and the Rangers who had drawn horses would run to mount up. At a signal they would gallop toward the line of coins, and Private Blackburn proudly noted that ". . .generally every dollar was picked up the first dash made." Even when the amount was reduced to half- and quarter-dollars, the competition among the riders remained keen, and many performed the trick to pick up bouquets tossed by local belles. Bronco busting was another pastime for all and sundry. Blackburn thought that every "wild, unbroken, vicious horse in that section" was brought in for the Texans to ride, and the troopers rushed to "get first chance at him."[196]

Some of the high-spirited Texans made themselves known by their drunken carousing downtown, too, and Colonel Terry thought it wise to place guards around the camp when orders came to prepare for movement to Kentucky. Some of the undisciplined men viewed this as an unnecessary restriction upon their liberties, and managed to sneak away for a night of amusement despite Terry's efforts. A number had run-ins with the local police, and it came to a head one night at a play about the early Jamestown settlement. When Pocahontas thrust herself between the Indian executioner's bludgeon and the condemned John Smith, a liquored-up trooper whipped out his six-shooter and fired on the "executioner," remarking casually that "his mother had taught him to always protect a lady when in danger." Although the boozy Texan missed his mark, others blazed away more accurately when the police rushed in to collar their comrade. After two policemen died and another lay wounded, the rowdies were given liberty to return unmolested to camp. After the news hummed across the telegraph wires to Governor Isham Harris of Tennessee, he demanded that General Johnston take firm action. Johnston summoned Colonel Terry to report to his headquarters at Bowling Green, Kentucky; the next morning, his unruly Texans were put on trains for the same destination![197] (See map on page 483.)

The green regiment was only one unit in a variety of troops coalescing along the infant Confederacy's north-central frontier. The Rangers belonged to the "Central Geographic Division of Kentucky, Department #2," but that October, they became part of the Reserve, Central Army of Kentucky. As these unwieldy titles indicate, all eyes were on Kentucky, a border state with strong ties to both North and South. President Davis personally chose Sidney Johnston to command the vast region, confident that this noteworthy officer of the old army could handle the complex assignment if anyone could. Johnston inherited a whirlwind, however, because the central frontier was beset with tactical difficulties. On his right was East Tennessee, an undeveloped wilderness populated by clannish mountain folk hostile to the Confederate cause. On the left was the Mississippi River, a veritable highway for the Union Navy unless Johnston could fortify critical points on the river. Some of these points lay in disputed territory, such as Columbus, Kentucky. In his left-center were the Cumberland and Tennessee Rivers, additional invasion routes beckoning the Federals to slice past Johnston's center and outflank his whole line.[198]

Johnston had been putting up a bold front with the unwitting assistance of belligerent newspapermen who trumpeted warnings of his aggressive intentions. The sad truth of the matter, however, was that his "army" was a paper tiger in the autumn of 1861. Numerically, it was sadly inadequate for the task of securing the lengthy frontier, as it consisted of a mere 19,000 men. General Felix Zollicoffer had four thousand of these at Cumberland Gap in the east, while Simon B. Buckner took a like number to Bowling Green in the center. On the western end of the line, Bishop-General Leonidas Polk's 11,000 troops at Columbus accounted for the remainder of Johnston's armed strength. Most of his other troops were raw levies, bellicose to be sure, but unarmed and untrained. The Texas Rangers were one of his most promising outfits, which Johnston pronounced a "capable and well-trained regiment," but they were unable to take the field until every man received his mount. More serious, however, was the health catastrophe that struck the Texans a staggering blow. They barely had brought their Wild West show to town before the measles hit them with a dreadful scourge reminiscent of the Black Death.[199]

Hundreds of young men collapsed under a microbial onslaught of literally epidemic proportions. They overflowed the available hospital space, then flooded the homes of good Samaritans who offered help. Private J. K. P. Blackburn noted that the camp disease that ravaged their encampment in November was a "very violent form" of measles, which was "no respecter of persons." Most men contracted it in one degree or another, regardless of whether they had suffered a case of the disease during childhood. A violent case of measles brought Blackburn to death's door for several weeks, and he credited the tender nursing of local ladies with saving his life. When he crept out of his hospital bed in mid-December, Blackburn was one of only some 150 men fit for duty. Although others would recover eventually, no regimental assembly would ever again muster anything resembling the original strength of 1170 men.[200]

John Mangham was present for duty when the company mustered on October 31, but his cousin Joe was already sick. Joe eventually recovered, but his illness was so debilitating that he was discharged from the army on December 8. Although John managed to withstand the onset of the disease longer than his cousin, he took to his sickbed in November and never arose. Private John R. Mangham died in Nashville on November 25, 1861, one of the hundreds sacrificed to the measles. He had been in the army just 75 days, and was the first Mangham to die in the service of the Confederacy. He would not be the last.[201]

His brother Robert H. Mangham had entered the ministry in 1859, and remained in Texas after the war broke out. He outlived his brother by only two years, dying at Middletown, Texas, in 1863.[202]

*   *   *   *   *

The 1st Texas Rangers were the second cavalry regiment raised in their state, and normally would have received the designation "2nd Texas Cavalry." By waiting to elect field officers until they reached Tennessee, however, their formal date of organization was delayed until late in 1861. Consequently, their official designation became the "8th Texas Cavalry," although John was dead and Joe was discharged by the time this change occurred. Usually, everyone referred to the regiment as Terry's Texas Rangers, and they went down in history as one of the hardest-fighting cavalry outfits in the Confederate service. On December 17, 1861, Colonel Terry led his men in the first-ever charge delivered by the organization that later evolved into the Army of Tennessee. Although he was killed in that successful attack, his men went on to participate in scores of battles, engagements, and skirmishes throughout the war, winning distinction in many. Their final distinction was delivering the last charge of the Army of Tennessee, at Bentonville, North Carolina. It was successful.[203]

---

[1] Josiah Mangham (note spelling) appears in the 1830 Talbot County census, aged between 50 and 59. Robert Mangham, aged 20 to 29, lived nearby. The identification of Robert S. and William R. Mangum (*Mangham*) as Josiah's sons is circumstantial, but Robert's age, proximity, and numerous financial transactions with Arthur make a particularly compelling argument that they were brothers. Likewise, Robert and William lived in very close proximity to each other after moving to Texas. (William's case is discussed in more detail below, under John R. Mangham, 8th Texas Cavalry. Here it is interesting to note, however, that the Georgia Adjutant General's Office issued William *Mangham* a first lieutenant's commission in the 672nd Georgia Militia District [Harris County] on July 28, 1828. See State of Georgia, Military Records, Commissions 1827-1828, drawer 40, reel 7, GDAH.) All references to the Josiah T. Mangum, Sr., family group are complicated by the nearly interchangeable use of *Mangham* and *Mangum* in existing records. Josiah, Sr., probably used *Mangum* until his death, and Robert and William seem to have settled eventually on this spelling. Thomas, Arthur, and James clearly adopted *Mangham* during the quarter century prior to the Civil War, and passed this usage on to the orphaned children of their brother, Josiah, Jr.

[2] I am indebted to Mr. Will Green Mangham for much of the genealogy and history of the Arthur Green and James Green Mangham families. One of James's great-grandsons, Will resides in Baton Rouge, Louisiana, where the present author was born and raised. Again, the paths of the Josiah and Solomon Mangham clans have coincided geographically, leaving future generations to mull over the coincidence!

[3] Talbot County, Court of Ordinary, Sales 1829-1855, pp. 271-274, drawer 124, reel 18, and Index, Case No. 45; Talbot County, Court of Ordinary, Inventories and Appraisals 1831-1855, pp. 219-220, drawer 123, reel 46; Talbot County, Probate Court,

Annual Returns 1828-1848, pp. 353-355, drawer 123, reel 49; Talbot County, Probate Court, Estate Records, p. 26, drawer 124, reel 30, GDAH.

[4] One Talbot County record, showing Arthur as the administrator of Josiah's estate and Thomas as his security, is annotated "Ala." and "gone Ala." underneath their respective names. The further annotation "Cite" implies that a citation was issued for their failure to provide ongoing returns on their father's estate. See Talbot County, Court of Ordinary, Sales 1829-1855, drawer 124, reel 18, Index (Case 45), GDAH. Another source states that Arthur Mangham settled in Salem, Alabama, about 1837. See Alexander Nunn, ed., *Lee County and Her Forebears* (Opelika: N.p., 1983), p. 238.

[5] Robert retained (or reverted to) the surname spelling typical of the North Carolina branch of the family, and his Georgia militia commission reflected this preference (State of Georgia, Military Records, Commissions 1834-1836, drawer 40, reel 9, GDAH). For the approximate date of his departure from Talbot County, see Talbot County, Inferior Court Minutes 1828-1855, entries for court terms dated May 1836, May 1837, January 1838, January 1839, January 1840, March 1841, and March 1842. These records show that Robert received county funds for taking care of Henry Arnold until the final entry, at which point James Boggs assumed Arnold's care.

[6] Robert Mangum's son, Robert S. Mangum, Jr., and nephew, Joseph Marion Mangum, served in the 21st and 8th Texas Cavalry regiments, respectively (see CMSRs; 1850 Census, Shelby County; 1860 Census, Matagorda County; John T. Palmer, *The Mangums of Virginia, North Carolina, South Carolina . . . and Adjoining States* [Santa Rosa: author, 1992], pp. 219-222). Robert moved from Shelby to Matagorda at about the same time as his brother William moved from Matagorda to Gonzales. Additional research might show a specific connection.

[7] Arthur apparently combined resources with Thomas to buy this property, which he eventually sold on October 4, 1852. See Russell County, Superior Court, Deed and Mortgage Records, Book H, pp. 346-347. The record of Thomas's property transactions is discussed below. See more about William Mangham and his family in Chapter VII.

[8] Chambers County, Marriage Licenses and Bonds, LGM 114, reel 25, ADAH; Russell County, Probate Court Minutes 1846-1854, p. 139, LGM 89, reel 5, ADAH.

[9] Russell County, Probate Court Minutes 1846-1850, pp. 139, 160, LGM 89, reel 5, ADAH. These records fortunately identify all of Thomas H. Mangham's heirs by name. Interestingly, little William T. Mangham is listed once as "Thomas W. Mangham," implying that his middle name was in fact Thomas. Later military records give no such hint, but uniformly reflect that he had two middle names, both beginning with the letter "T." For additional information on middle names and nicknames, see *MFB* 21:14, as well as research of Col. William C. Lafield, grandson of Charles A. Mangham (provided courtesy of Mrs. Glenda Owens and Col. William C. Lafield, Jr.).

[10] Russell County, Probate Court Minutes 1851-1854, pp. 87, 122, 128-129, 137, 166, 324; Russell County, Bonds of Administrators and Deceased 1850-1853, p. 106, LGM 89, reel 4, ADAH; Marriage Records, Chambers and Butler Counties.

[11] Death Certificate, Charles A. Mangham, Bexar County, Texas; 1860 Census and Slave Census, Butler County; *Southern Messenger* (Greenville), December 5, 1860; research of Col. William C. Lafield and autobiographical sketch by Madie Elna Moore Owen, (provided courtesy of Mrs. Glenda Owens). The Butler County census-taker rendered William's name as "W. T. Mangum," and Charles' name is rendered incorrectly as "C. Ingragham." Since it is written in a clear hand, one supposes that it was transcribed from illegible notes.

[12] *Southern Messenger* (Greenville), December 12, 1860.

[13] James M. McPherson, *Battle Cry of Freedom: The Civil War Era* (New York: Ballantine Books, 1988), pp. 205-213.

[14] W. J. Cash, *The Mind of the South* (Alfred A. Knopf, Inc., 1941; reprint, New York: Vintage Books, 1991), pp. 82-87, 114-117; James C. Cobb, *The Most Southern Place on Earth: The Mississippi Delta and the Roots of Regional Identity* (New York: Oxford Univ. Press, 1992), pp. 22-26, 156-160.

[15] ORS II, vol. 1, pp. 503-504; CMSR, Charles A. Mangham, 18th Alabama.

[16] Rev. Edgar W. Jones, "History of the 18th Alabama Infantry Regiment," *Jones Valley Times* (reprint, 1994, Zane Geier), p. 1; ORS II, vol. 1, pp. 503-504; Muster-in roll, Company F, in 18th Alabama Unit Files, ADAH.

[17] Jones, "18th Alabama," p. 1; ORS II, vol. 1, pp. 503-507; Company muster-in roll, plus Company F muster roll dated December 31, 1861, and regimental return for November 1861, in 18th Alabama Unit Files, ADAH.

[18] Jones, "18th Alabama," p. 1; ORS II, vol. 1, pp. 498-508.

[19] Jones, "18th Alabama," p. 1; ORS II, vol. 1, pp. 506-507; Muster roll dated December 31, 1861, Company F, 18th Alabama Unit Files, ADAH; Larry J. Daniel, *Shiloh: The Battle That Changed the Civil War* (New York: Simon & Schuster, 1997), p. 63.

[20] Daniel, *Shiloh*, pp. 40-47, 60-63; Wiley Sword, *Shiloh: Bloody April* (New York: William Morrow & Co., 1974), pp. 76-77.

[21] OR 6, p. 836; Daniel, *Shiloh*, pp. 40-47, 60-63; Sword, *Bloody April*, pp. 61-67.

[22] Jones, "18th Alabama," p. 2. See Tom's letter in Chapter III.

[23] Daniel, *Shiloh*, pp. 126-129, 143-144; Sword, *Bloody April*, pp. 104-108, 139-144.

[24] OR 10, pt. 1, p. 557; "Letter From Corinth," typescript, April 11, 1862, copied from *Mobile Advertiser*, in Jackson's Brigade Unit Files, ADAH. The anonymous writer belonged to the 17th Alabama.

[25] OR 10, pt. 1, pp. 532, 554; Daniel, *Shiloh*, pp. 126-127, 196-197; "Letter From Corinth," Jackson's Brigade Unit Files, ADAH.

[26] Daniel, *Shiloh*, pp. 196-199; "Letter From Corinth," Jackson's Brigade Unit Files, ADAH.

[27] Daniel, *Shiloh*, pp. 197-200; "Letter From Corinth," Jackson's Brigade Unit Files, ADAH.

[28] Daniel, *Shiloh*, pp. 223-225; "Letter From Corinth," Jackson's Brigade Unit Files, ADAH. Gladden's Brigade included the 25th Alabama, whose sergeant major was Tom Mangham (See Chapter III).

[29] *OR* 10, pt. 1, pp. 554-555; "Letter From Corinth," Jackson's Brigade Unit Files, ADAH. It was commonly a bone of contention between heavily engaged regiments as to who retreated first, but the identity of the "culprits" in this case is disputed. The anonymous letter-writer from the 17th Alabama identifies the 19th Alabama as the first to waver, but its commander, Colonel (later General) Joe Wheeler, made no mention of the incident in his postwar analysis of the battle (see Joseph Wheeler, "The Battle of Shiloh," *SHSP* 24: 124). Author Larry Daniel states that the 2nd Texas was the first to retreat. Jackson's report mentioned that he rallied one regiment in this incident, but did not name it.

[30] *OR* 10, pt. 1, pp. 554-555; "Letter From Corinth," Jackson's Brigade Unit Files, ADAH; Daniel, *Shiloh*, pp. 236-237.

[31] *OR* 10, pt. 1, p. 557; *ORS* II, vol. 1, p. 504. According to one respected source, the 18th Alabama's casualty toll was exceeded by only eight other Confederate regiments at Shiloh. Wheeler's postwar report, however, claimed 160 casualties for the 19th Alabama in the fight at Cloud Field alone. See William F. Fox, *Regimental Losses in the American Civil War, 1861-1865* (Albany: Brandow Printing, 1898; reprint, Dayton: Morningside, 1985), p. 561; Wheeler, "Battle of Shiloh," *SHSP* 24: 123.

[32] *OR* 10, pt. 1, pp. 533, 555, 557; "Letter From Corinth," Jackson's Brigade Unit Files, ADAH; Daniel, *Shiloh*, pp. 236-237; Jones, "18th Alabama," p. 4.

[33] Cited in William C. Davis, *The Orphan Brigade: The Kentucky Confederates Who Couldn't Go Home* (Baton Rouge: LSU Press, 1980), p. 100.

[34] *ORS* II, vol. 1, pp. 498, 503, 506-507; *OR* 10, pt. 1, pp. 733, 738.

[35] Jones, "18th Alabama," p. 6; *OR* 16, pt. 2, p. 733; *ORS* II, vol. 1, p. 498; *Jacksonville Republican*, July 3, 1862; *History of Company B (Originally Pickens Planters), 40th Alabama Regiment, Confederate States Army, 1862 to 1865* (Anniston: Norwood Printing, 1902), p. 12.

[36] Jones, "18th Alabama," p. 6; *OR* 26, pt. 2, p. 130.

[37] Jones, "18th Alabama," p. 6. The regiment incurred no casualties in the Wartrace affair. A concise summary of Rosecrans's maneuvers and Bragg's inept responses is available in Stanley F. Horn, *The Army of Tennessee* (Bobbs-Merrill, 1941; reprint, Norman: Univ. of Oklahoma Press, 1993), pp. 234-238.

[38] For an assessment of Bragg's ill-fated attempts to destroy the fragments of Rosecrans's army before Chickamauga, see Peter Cozzens, *This Terrible Sound: The Battle of Chickamauga* (Urbana: Univ. of Illinois Press, 1992), pp. 65-85; Glenn Tucker, *Chickamauga: Bloody Battle in the West* (Bobbs-Merrill Co., 1961; reprint, Dayton: Morningside, 1992), pp. 62-71.

[39] Tucker, *Chickamauga*, p. 70.

[40] Bromfield L. Ridley, *Battles and Sketches of the Army of Tennessee* (Mexico: Missouri Printing & Publishing Co., 1906; reprint, Dayton: Morningside, 1995), pp. 208-209.

[41] OR 30, pt. 2, pp. 16, 400-401; Jones, "18th Alabama," p. 7; "Clayton's Brigade at Chickamauga," October 11, 1863, typescript, copied from *Mobile Register and Advertiser*, in Clayton's Brigade Unit Files, ADAH; Ridley, *Battles and Sketches*, p. 209.

[42] Jones, "18th Alabama," p. 7; OR 30, pt. 2, pp. 401, 404, 409; "Clayton's Brigade at Chickamauga," Unit Files, ADAH. See Chapters II and IV for the experiences of Charles's Georgia cousins at Chickamauga. John was his third cousin, while both Tom and Willis were his second cousins (once removed).

[43] OR 30, pt. 2, p. 401; Tucker, *Chickamauga*, pp. 153-154; Ridley, *Battles and Sketches*, p. 219.

[44] "Clayton's Brigade at Chickamauga," Unit Files, ADAH.

[45] Ibid.; OR 30, pt. 2, p. 401; Jones, "18th Alabama," p. 7.

[46] "Clayton's Brigade at Chickamauga," Unit Files, ADAH; OR 30, pt. 2, p. 401, 404-405.

[47] Ibid.

[48] OR 30, pt. 2, pp. 401, 405-406; Ridley, *Battles and Sketches*, pp. 219-220; Cozzens, *Terrible Sound*, pp. 182-183, 231.

[49] OR 30, pt. 2, pp. 402, 404-405; Tucker, *Chickamauga*, pp. 154-161; Cozzens, *Terrible Sound*, pp. 255-256; Ridley, *Battles and Sketches*, p. 220; Jones, "18th Alabama," p. 7. Army regulations positioned Company F second and Company G ninth in the regimental line, numbered from right to left.

[50] OR 30, pt. 2, pp. 402, 405; Tucker, *Chickamauga*, pp. 161-163; Cozzens, *Terrible Sound*, pp. 258-259. All of Bragg's Alabamians were called "Yaller Hammers," after the ubiquitous bird that inhabited their native woods. Charles's Georgia cousins were "Goober Grabblers" (Ridley, *Battles and Sketches*, p. 460).

[51] OR 30, pt. 2, pp. 405-406; Tucker, *Chickamauga*, p. 261; Cozzens, *Terrible Sound*, p. 345; "Clayton's Brigade at Chickamauga," Unit Files, ADAH.

[52] Tucker, *Chickamauga*, pp. 260-264; "Clayton's Brigade at Chickamauga," Unit Files, ADAH.

[53] Tucker, *Chickamauga*, p. 335; Cozzens, *Terrible Sound*, pp. 498-500; OR 30, pt. 2, p. 406.

[54] Jones, "18th Alabama," pp. 7-8; *Atlanta Daily Intelligencer*, Nov. 22, 1863; Cozzens, *Terrible Sound*, p. 501; Sam Watkins, *"Co. Aytch": A Side Show of the Big Show* (reprint, New York: Collier Books, 1962), pp. 109-110; Ridley, *Battles and Sketches*, p. 222.

[55] Fox, *Regimental Losses*, p. 570; OR 30, pt. 2, pp. 404-406; Robert M. Goodgame, Confederate Military Service Memoranda, RG 9, vol. 18, 18th Alabama (Company F), MDAH. Formerly a private in the Tom Watts Rifles, Goodgame composed his memorandum in 1904. It is not known if he stated these figures from memory, or whether he possessed notes, diaries, or reports; therefore, his recollections must be

used with caution. He recalled that Company F suffered 23 casualties at Shiloh, for example, but extant muster roll memoranda indicate a total of 13 casualties.

[56] CMSR, Charles A. Mangham. Records from late 1863 show that Charles was a corporal, but do not identify the date of his promotion. For analyses of the infighting that beset the Army of Tennessee's high command, see Thomas Lawrence Connelly, *Autumn of Glory: The Army of Tennessee, 1862-1865* (Baton Rouge: LSU Press, 1971), pp. 235-251; Cozzens, *Terrible Sound*, pp. 528-536; Peter Cozzens, *The Shipwreck of Their Hopes: The Battles for Chattanooga* (Urbana: Univ. of Illinois Press, 1994), pp. 23-29; Wiley Sword, *Mountains Touched with Fire: Chattanooga Besieged, 1863* (New York: St. Martin's Press, 1995), pp. 29-35, 64-67.

[57] Connelly, *Autumn of Glory*, pp. 262-268; Cozzens, *Shipwreck*, pp. 18, 103-104, 108-109, 125; Sword, *Mountains*, pp. 79-80, 106-111, 164-170.

[58] Cozzens, *Shipwreck*, pp. 250-254; Sword, *Mountains*, pp. 186-188.

[59] Cozzens, *Shipwreck*, pp. 52-100, 187-191; Sword, *Mountains*, pp. 204-208, 212, 222.

[60] Cozzens, *Shipwreck*, pp. 192-193; ORS I, vol. 6, pp. 155, 160, 164; Mattie Lou Teague Crow, ed., *The Diary of a Confederate Soldier, John Washington Inzer, 1834-1928* (Huntsville: The Strode Publishers, Inc., 1977), p. 41.

[61] ORS I, vol. 6, pp. 155-156.

[62] Crow, *Confederate Soldier*, p. 42; ORS I, vol. 6, p. 156; Sword, *Mountains*, pp. 223-224.

[63] Crow, *Confederate Soldier*, p. 42; ORS I, vol. 6, p. 153; Sword, *Mountains*, pp. 223-226.

[64] ORS I, vol. 6, pp. 156, 160, 165; Sword, *Mountains*, pp. 223, 227; Cozzens, *Shipwreck*, p. 197.

[65] ORS I, vol. 6, p. 165; Sword, *Mountains*, pp. 232, 236-237, 262-263; Cozzens, *Shipwreck*, pp. 256, 313-314.

[66] ORS I, vol. 6, pp. 153, 156, 160; Crow, *Confederate Soldier*, p. 43; Sword, *Mountains*, pp. 262-265; Cozzens, *Shipwreck*, pp. 244-247.

[67] Sword, *Mountains*, pp. 279-281; Cozzens, *Shipwreck*, pp. 272-286.

[68] ORS I, vol. 6, pp. 153-154, 156-157, 160; Crow, *Confederate Soldier*, p. 44.

[69] Sword, *Mountains*, pp. 306-307; Cozzens, *Shipwreck*, pp. 314-315; Crow, *Confederate Soldier*, p. 44; ORS I, vol. 6, pp. 154, 157, 160, 163; OR 31, pt. 2, pp. 600-601.

[70] Crow, *Confederate Soldier*, p. 44; ORS I, vol. 6, pp. 154, 157.

[71] Sword, *Mountains*, pp. 307-309; Cozzens, *Shipwreck*, pp. 314-318; Crow, *Confederate Soldier*, pp. 44-46; ORS I, vol. 6, pp. 154, 157-158, 163; OR 31, pt. 2, pp. 601-602.

[72] Crow, *Confederate Soldier*, pp. 44-46; ORS I, vol. 6, pp. 158-159; Cozzens, *Shipwreck*, p. 318.

[73] Cozzens, *Shipwreck*, pp. 318-319; OR 31, pt. 2, p. 606. The state of Illinois returned the 18th Alabama battle flag many years after the war. It is on display at the Alabama Department of Archives and History (see *The Birmingham News*, December 5, 1995, in Unit Flag Files, CRC).

[74] OR 31, pt. 2, p. 745; CMSR, Charles A. Mangham; ORS I, vol. 6, pp. 154-155, 159. Official reports in the OR listed the 18th Alabama's losses as four killed, 48 wounded, and 157 missing. Hunley submitted his report on December 2, 1863, citing losses of five killed, 14 wounded, and 124 missing (supposed captured). Cited in the ORS, the original is on file at the Georgia Historical Society. For the Tom Watts Rifles' losses, see Robert M. Goodgame, Confederate Military Service Memoranda, RG 9, vol. 18, 18th Alabama (Company F), MDAH. Goodgame estimated that the company lost sixty men at Missionary Ridge. His figure seems too high, since Hunley reported a total of 315 officers and men present at the battle, or an average of 31 per company.

[75] CMSR, Charles A. Mangham; J. W. Minnich, *Inside of Rock Island Prison from December, 1863, to June, 1865* (Nashville: Publishing House of the M. E. Church, South, 1908), pp. 6-9.

[76] Minnich, *Rock Island*, pp. 23-30, 34-36.

[77] CMSR, Charles A. Mangham; OR III, vol. 4, pp. 1143, 1203. The Confederacy also attempted to enlist Union soldiers languishing in its prison camps, but with less success.

[78] OR 15, p. 1069; OR 26, pt. 2, pp. 550-552; William H. Davidson, *Word From Camp Pollard, C.S.A.* (West Point: Hester Printing, 1978), pp. 39, 210-211.

[79] Company E, Company Book, 1864, 61st Alabama Unit Files, ADAH; CMSR, William T. T. Mangham, 61st Alabama. In all probability, this contradictory evidence regarding William's enlistment simply recorded different signposts along the company's road to complete organization. He may have traveled to Macon County to enlist, then returned to Butler County for the company's formal mustering-in before the company was accepted into service at Montgomery.

[80] Davidson, *Camp Pollard*, pp. 31-34, 38-40, 235, 303-305; OR 26, pt. 2, pp. 239-240, 549; Joseph H. Crute, *Units of the Confederate States Army* (Midlothian: Derwent Books, 1987), pp. 34-35; CMSR, Francis M. Mangum, 61st Alabama. Francis was born in South Carolina to another branch of the family that had migrated from North Carolina. Although some of his military records reflect the spelling *Mangham*, he clearly used the phonetic spelling generally accepted in the Carolinas. See more on James M. D. Mangham in Chapter V.

[81] Davidson, *Camp Pollard*, pp. 14-17, 20, 26, 46, 51, 121, 123.

[82] Ibid., pp. vi, 33, 47, 51, 65; CMSR, William T. T. Mangham.

[83] OR 26, pt. 2, pp. 548-552.

[84] Davidson, *Camp Pollard*, pp. 140, 144-146, 193, 217, 223; OR 26, pt. 2, pp. 549, 629; OR 32, pt. 2, p. 629; OR 33, p. 1122.

[85] OR 32, pt. 2, p. 726. Swanson's regiment relieved Colonel O'Neal's 26th Alabama. See Willis Brewer, *Alabama: Her History, Resources, War Record, and Public Men, from 1540 to 1872* (Montgomery: Barrett & Brown, 1872), p. 673.

[86] Gordon C. Rhea, *The Battle of the Wilderness, May 5-6, 1864* (Baton Rouge: LSU Press, 1994), pp. 8-10, 19-20.

[87] Ibid., pp. 20-24, 34, 84.

[88] *ORS* II, vol. 1, p. 879.

[89] Rhea, *Wilderness*, pp. 46-55; Richard Wheeler, *On Fields of Fury–From the Wilderness to the Crater: An Eyewitness History* (New York: HarperPerennial, 1991), p. 77.

[90] Rhea, *Wilderness*, pp. 55-58, 82-90.

[91] Ibid., pp. 85, 90.

[92] Ibid., pp. 105, 108-109, 122-123.

[93] Ibid., pp. 124-125, 128-129.

[94] Ibid., pp. 143-145, 152-153.

[95] Ibid., pp. 153-155.

[96] Ibid., pp. 151-152; OR 36, pt. 1, p. 1070.

[97] Ibid., pp. 149-156, 167-168; CMH 7, *Alabama*, p. 229.

[98] Rhea, *Wilderness*, pp. 147-149, 167-168; CMH 7, *Alabama*, p. 229; Brewer, *Alabama*, p. 673.

[99] Rhea, *Wilderness*, pp. 168-169; CMH 7, *Alabama*, p. 229; Brewer, *Alabama*, p. 673; Stephen D. Thruston, "Report of the Conduct of General George H. Steuart's Brigade from the 5th to the 12th of May, 1864, Inclusive," *SHSP* 14: 148-149.

[100] Rhea, *Wilderness*, pp. 170-171.

[101] Ibid., pp. 171-175.

[102] Gordon C. Rhea, *Spotsylvania and the Road to Yellow Tavern, May 7-12, 1864* (Baton Rouge: LSU Press, 1997), p. 39.

[103] Rhea, *Wilderness*, pp. 435-441.

[104] Ibid., p. 123; Rhea, *Spotsylvania*, p. 77; OR 36, pt. 1, p. 1071.

[105] Rhea, *Spotsylvania*, pp. 60, 83.

[106] Ibid., pp. 83-84; William D. Matter, *If It Takes All Summer: The Battle of Spotsylvania* (Chapel Hill: UNC Press, 1988), pp. 91-95; OR 36, pt. 1, p. 1083.

[107] Ibid., pp. 83-86; Matter, *All Summer*, pp. 92-95; OR 36, pt. 1, pp. 1083-1084; Muster Rolls, October 31, 1863, and August 31, 1864 (dated November 18, 1864), 61st Alabama, NARA.

[108] Rhea, *Spotsylvania*, pp. 89-91.

[109] Ibid., pp. 163-165.

[110] Ibid., pp. 164-171; OR 36, pt. 1, p. 1072.

[111] Rhea, *Spotsylvania*, pp. 170-175.

[112] Ibid., pp. 175-177; CMSR, William T. T. Mangham; Letter, Lewis Warlick to wife, May 19, 1864, Southern Historical Collection, McGimsey Papers, http://ils.unc.edu/civilwar/mcgim.html. Lewis Warlick was a member of the 44th Georgia. He probably was related to Hiram Warlick, who married old William Mangham's daughter Emily (see Chapter VII).

[113] Brewer, *Alabama*, p. 673; CMH 7, *Alabama*, p. 229; Muster Roll, August 31, 1864 (dated November 18, 1864), 61st Alabama, NARA.

[114] Unit Historical Roll, Company E, 61st Alabama, ADAH.

[115] Unit Historical Roll, 61st Alabama, ADAH.

[116] General John B. Gordon, *Reminiscences of the Civil War* (Charles Scribner's Sons, 1903; reprint, Baton Rouge: LSU Press, 1993), pp. 385-389.

[117] Ibid., pp. 386-397.

[118] Ibid., pp. 399-405. Chevaux-de-frise comprised barriers made of sharpened logs. When tied together with wire, they constituted a formidable obstacle to the passage of any force.

[119] Ibid., pp. 403-405. Besides Gordon's 11,500 men, another 1700 were nearby under the command of Cadmus Wilcox. George Pickett was to support Gordon with a further 6500 men. See Noah Andre Trudeau, *The Last Citadel: Petersburg, Virginia, June 1864-April 1865* (Baton Rouge: LSU Press, 1991), p. 337.

[120] William Henry Philpot, Jr., "Capture of Fort Steadman," 61st Alabama Unit Files, ADAH. The writer, Captain Philpot's son, prepared this account based on his father's recollections. See also Gordon, *Reminiscences*, pp. 406-407. In his memoirs Gordon recalled that he had offered silver medals to the storming parties, and that veterans occasionally wrote him after the war to request the medals. Laughingly, he noted that these correspondents often told him to forget about the furlough, because they received an even longer one just two weeks later at Appomattox.

[121] Gordon, *Reminiscences*, pp. 407-408; Trudeau, *Citadel*, pp. 335, 338.

[122] Ibid.

[123] Philpot, "Fort Steadman," 61st Alabama Unit Files, ADAH; Trudeau, *Citadel*, pp. 338-340.

[124] Trudeau, *Citadel*, pp. 341-342.

[125] Ibid., pp. 343-346; Gordon, *Reminiscences*, pp. 410-411.

[126] Trudeau, *Citadel*, pp. 346-351; Gordon, *Reminiscences*, pp. 411-412.

[127] Trudeau, *Citadel*, p. 351.

[128] Philpot, "Fort Steadman," 61st Alabama Unit Files, ADAH; Brewer, *Alabama*, p. 673.

[129] CMSR, William T. T. Mangham; Joseph Crute states that the 61st Alabama surrendered five officers and 42 men, which conflicts with Brewer's assertion that only 27 surrendered (see Brewer, *Alabama*, p. 673). Transcribed paroles indicate that Crute's numbers are accurate, but also show that many of the regiment's survivors were detailed to duties outside the regiment. This may be the source of the discrepancy. See "Paroles of the Army of Northern Virginia," *SHSP* 15 (1887): 239, 245-246; Crute, *Units*, pp. 34-35.

[130] CMSR, William T. T. Mangham; OR II, vol. 6, pp. 141-142; and vol. 8, pp. 1000-1003; Eric Mills, *Chesapeake Bay in the Civil War* (Centreville: Tidewater Publishers, 1996), pp. 202-204. The prison's official name was Camp Hoffman, but most knew it by its geographical location: Point Lookout.

[131] OR Series II, vol. 6, pp. 141-142; and vol. 8, pp. 1000-1003; Mills, *Chesapeake Bay*, pp. 202-204. A dismayed Federal sanitation inspector blamed the camp's filthy

conditions on its denizens, asserting that "They live, eat, and sleep in their own filth." Sanitary arrangements were problematical in every Civil War prison camp for a variety of reasons, including prisoner apathy. The large scale imprisonment of otherwise good men was unprecedented in ante-bellum America, and the terrible ennui that developed among bored, hopeless prisoners was an unexpected by-product of nearly four years of war.

[132] Ibid. A surviving company book for Company E, 61st Alabama, reflects that William had blue eyes and dark hair. Otherwise the information agrees with his POW records. See Company E, Company Book, 1864, 61st Alabama Unit Files, ADAH. For an account of life in Point Lookout by a soldier of the 5th Alabama, see Malcolm C. McMillan, ed., *The Alabama Confederate Reader* (Tuscaloosa: Univ. of Alabama Press, 1963), pp. 428-432.

[133] The 1870 Alabama census shows a William T. S. Mangum, a 19-year-old illiterate farmer, living in Autauga County with Isaac C. Morgan. William Mangham would have been 23 or 24 years old, and he certainly could read and write, since enlistment records from 1863 identify him as a student. Given census inaccuracies, however, this Autauga County youth may have been William T. T. Mangham.

[134] 1870 Census, Conecuh County; 1900 Census, San Saba County, Texas; http://data.ancestry.com, Mangham Database Search Results, Alabama Marriages, 1800-1920. Lucinda Williams was the daughter of a plantation owner, G. Barton Williams, and his wife Elizabeth (research of Col. William C. Lafield, provided courtesy of Mrs. Glenda Owens).

[135] 1900 Census, San Saba County; Confederate Pension Records, Williamson County, Texas, C. A. Mangham, file number 36111, TSA. Charles stated in his application that he moved to Texas in 1873.

[136] 1880 Census and Agricultural Schedule, Cass County; research of Col. William C. Lafield, Charles Mangham's grandson, provided by Mrs. Glenda Owens; MariLee Beatty Hageness, *Abstracts of Georgia-Alabama Bible and Family Records*, vol. 2 (Author, 1995), p. 41. Charles performed the marriage services for Stephen C. McMichael and Miss M. A. Frances Coker on July 27, 1879.

[137] 1900 Census, San Saba County; *San Antonio Express*, July 24, 1931.

[138] Confederate Pension Records, Williamson County, C. A. Mangham.

[139] *San Antonio Express*, July 24, 1931; CV 32: 146.

[140] Ibid.; Death certificate #31904, Charles A. Mangham, Texas Dept. of Health, Bureau of Vital Statistics.

[141] Ibid.; Confederate Pension Records, Williamson County, C. A. Mangham. Wiley P. Mangham of Chambers County, Alabama, died in October of 1931. He was a Confederate veteran as well, but I have found no substantial record of his service. See Chapter V for a discussion of the mystery surrounding Wiley Mangham's Civil War experiences.

[142] CMSRs, B. W. Mangham, Hilliard's Legion and 59th Alabama; Unit Roster, Company H, 59th Alabama Unit Files, ADAH. Unit reorganizations in 1862 divided

the original Butler County men into two companies, which became companies H and I, 59th Alabama, in November 1863. When F. M. Cody and Jack Petty listed the members of Company H many years after the war, they included "Bush Mangham," although official records reflect his assignment to Company I. Extensive primary research to date has uncovered only one other contender for the identity of B. W. Mangham. Brantly Mangham, age 4, lived with Oliver P. Mangham in Russell County, Alabama, in 1850 (see Chapter VII). His age corresponds closely, but it seems likely that Cody and Petty would simply have listed Mangham's initials had they not felt sure of his given name. A final twist is the mysterious "B. W. Mangham" who signed a circular petition at Reynolds, in Taylor County, Georgia, on February 15, 1862, requesting that Napoleon Newsom be discharged and commissioned to raise a company. See Letters to the Confederate Secretary of War, file no. 9-N-1862, NARA.

[143] Thomas McAdory Owen, *History of Alabama and Dictionary of Alabama Biography*, 4 vols., (Chicago: S. J. Clarke Publishing Co., 1921), p. 1151. See the Genealogical Appendix for further identification of the Theophilus Fields Mangum family.

[144] CMSR, B. W. Mangham; Unit Roster, Company H, 59th Alabama Unit Files, ADAH.

[145] *Directory of the City of Montgomery, and Historical Sketches of Alabama Soldiers* (Montgomery: Perry & Smith, Publishers, 1866), p. 94; Llewellyn A. Shaver, *Sixtieth Alabama Regiment, Gracie's Alabama Brigade* (N.p., 1867), p. 7; ORS II, vol. 1, pp. 921-922.

[146] *Directory*, p. 94; Shaver, *Sixtieth Alabama*, p. 8; OR 16, pt. 2, pp. 725-726.

[147] *Directory*, p. 94; Shaver, *Sixtieth Alabama*, p. 8; Crute, *Units*, pp. 35, 37.

[148] *Directory*, p. 94; Shaver, *Sixtieth Alabama*, p. 8; ORS II, vol. 1, p. 924. See Chapter V for more about John Henry Mangham and the 30th Alabama.

[149] Letter, typescript, Samuel C. Kelly, June 20, 1862, 30th Alabama Unit Files, ADAH; William Milner Kelly, "A History of the Thirtieth Alabama Volunteers (Infantry), Confederate States Army," AHQ 9, no. 1 (Spring 1947): 128; *Directory*, p. 94; Shaver, *Sixtieth Alabama*, p. 9. Although Lt. Sam Kelly was not in Hilliard's Legion, his 30th Alabama took part in this campaign.

[150] *Directory*, p. 94; Shaver, *Sixtieth Alabama*, pp. 9-10; ORS II, vol. 1, p. 924; Horn, *Army of Tennessee*, pp. 163-165.

[151] Shaver, *Sixtieth Alabama*, pp. 10-11; ORS II, vol. 1, p. 924.

[152] Ibid.; *Directory*, pp. 94-95; CMSR, B. W. Mangham. Presumably, the Legion's peregrinations reflected the high command's original intention to use it in the Murfreesboro campaign, for which the Army of Tennessee marshaled in the Bridgeport-Chattanooga area.

[153] CMSR, B. W. Mangham; ORS II, vol. 1, pp. 924-925. Private Taylor, a soldier in Bush Mangham's company, was killed in action on October 27, 1862 at Richland, Kentucky. Presumably bushwhackers or Union scouts shot him while he stood picket guard or foraged on the Kentucky side of the Gap, where many of the Confederate

forward positions were located. See Company A, 4th Battalion, Hilliard's Legion Unit Files, ADAH.

[154] *ORS* II, vol. 1, pp. 858-860; *CMH* 7, *Alabama*, p. 234; *OR* 20, pt. 2, p. 466; *OR* 23, pt. 2, pp. 644, 711.

[155] *ORS* II, vol. 1, pp. 924-925; *Directory*, p. 95; Charles T. Jones, "Five Confederates: The Sons of Bolling Hall in the Civil War," *AHQ* 24 (1962): 171.

[156] *ORS* II, vol. 1, pp. 924-925; *Directory*, p. 95; Jones, "Five Confederates," p. 171; Shaver, *Sixtieth Alabama*, pp. 11-12.

[157] CMSR, B. W. Mangham; Shaver, *Sixtieth Alabama*, p. 12.

[158] Ibid.; *ORS* II, vol. 1, p. 925; *Directory*, p. 95. If Shaver's estimate of 300 miles total marching distance is correct for the Legion as a whole, then one can calculate how far Bush marched before he was hospitalized. By subtracting the distances from Cumberland Gap to Morristown (45 miles), and from Ringgold to the Chickamauga battlefield (about ten miles), it appears that Bush walked about 245 miles in thirteen days.

[159] *OR* 30, pt. 2, pp. 421-428; *ORS* II, vol. 1, p. 860. General Bragg arranged for Color Bearer Hiett to present the 2nd Battalion's tattered flag to President Jefferson Davis after the battle. See "Letter from Tennessee," October 15, 1863, in Gracie's Brigade Unit Files, ADAH; Jones, "Five Confederates," p. 183, n. 91.

[160] CMSR, B. W. Mangham; see also Unfiled Slips, NARA microform series M347, reel 247. The latter source renders the paymaster's name as Wallach, rather than Walsh.

[161] Ibid.; *Directory*, p. 95; Shaver, *Sixtieth Alabama*, pp. 23-24; *OR* 52, pt. 2, p. 563. Special Orders No. 280 also established the 23rd Alabama Battalion Sharpshooters from three companies of the old 1st Battalion.

[162] *Directory*, pp. 95-96; Jones, "Five Confederates," p. 197; Shaver, *Sixtieth Alabama*, pp. 23-42; CMSR, B. W. Mangham.

[163] *OR* 32, pt. 3, p. 831; Jones, "Five Confederates," pp. 199-200; letter, Preston L. Dodgen to wife Nancy, April 29, 1864, in Ray Mathis, *In the Land of the Living: Wartime Letters by Confederates from the Chattahoochee Valley of Alabama and Georgia* (Troy: Troy State Univ. Press, 1981), pp. 115-117; letter from Crenshaw Hall, April 30, 1864, in Bolling Hall Papers, reel 322, Charles William Ramsdell Collection, University of Texas Center for American History. Gracie's Brigade was the strongest brigade in Buckner's Department of East Tennessee.

[164] Jones, "Five Confederates," p. 201; *ORS* II, vol. 1, p. 857.

[165] *OR* 36, pt. 2, pp. 207-210; G. T. Beauregard, "The Defense of Drewry's Bluff," *B&L* 4, pp. 196-197. General Beauregard arrived in Petersburg on May 10, after it became clear that expected Federal incursions against North Carolina were much less serious than those already underway in Virginia.

[166] Trudeau, *Citadel*, pp. 4-7.

[167] Ibid., pp. 3-7; Beauregard, "Drewry's Bluff," p. 196; Shaver, *Sixtieth Alabama*, pp. 45-46.

168 Shaver, *Sixtieth Alabama*, pp. 45-46.

169 Ibid.; Trudeau, *Citadel*, p. 7.

170 Shaver, *Sixtieth Alabama*, pp. 46-49.

171 Ibid., pp. 49-50; Jones, "Five Confederates," pp. 202-203.

172 Shaver, *Sixtieth Alabama*, pp. 50-51.

173 OR 36, pt. 2, pp. 200-201; Beauregard, "Drewry's Bluff," pp. 198-201.

174 OR 36, pt. 2, pp. 212, 973; Jones, "Five Confederates," pp. 203-204; Shaver, *Sixtieth Alabama*, pp. 51-52.

175 Letter from John E. Hall, May 22, 1864, in Bolling Hall Papers; Jones, "Five Confederates," pp. 203-204; Shaver, *Sixtieth Alabama*, pp. 51-53; OR 36, pt. 2, pp. 212. One of those wounded was Captain Manly of Company I (see Letters Received by the Confederate A&IGO, file no. 1578-M-1864, NARA, granting him a 30-day furlough for wounds received on May 15).

176 OR 36, pt. 2, pp. 205-206, 212-213; Jones, "Five Confederates," p. 204; Shaver, *Sixtieth Alabama*, pp. 53-54; William Farrar Smith, "Butler's Attack on Drewry's Bluff," *B&L* 4, p. 212.

177 Shaver, *Sixtieth Alabama*, p. 54; Jones, "Five Confederates," p. 204; Trudeau, *Citadel*, pp. 7-8; Beauregard, "Drewry's Bluff," p. 204.

178 Jones, "Five Confederates," p. 205; Letter from John E. Hall, June 5, 1864, in Bolling Hall Papers; Shaver, *Sixtieth Alabama*, p. 54.

179 Trudeau, *Citadel*, pp. 33-51.

180 Ibid., pp. 48-50; Jones, "Five Confederates," pp. 206-207.

181 Ibid.

182 Trudeau, *Citadel*, pp. 51-54.

183 Jones, "Five Confederates," p. 207; OR 30, pt. 2, pp. 425-426.

184 OR 40, pt. 2, pp. 703-704; OR 42, pt. 2, pp. 1065; Records of the Confederate A&IGO, Registers of Letters Received, Chapter I, vol. 66 (July-October 1864), file no. 2464-M-1864, NARA; J. Tracy Power, *Lee's Miserables: Life in the Army of Northern Virginia from the Wilderness to Appomattox* (Chapel Hill: UNC Press, 1998), pp. 182-184, 214-215. Manly's letter of August 30 was received on September 5 and Major Burton replied four days later, but no copies of the letter or endorsements survive.

185 *Directory*; Hall cited in Power, *Lee's Miserables*, pp. 214-215.

186 CMSRs, 59th Alabama; *Directory*; OR 46, pt. 1, pp. 233-234, 267-268; pt. 3, pp. 219-220. The *Directory* provides tabulated data for the Alabama regiments in the Army of Northern Virginia, based on Historical Rolls compiled on December 31, 1864. By this point in time, the 59th Alabama had lost 100 men killed in action and 39 more who died of wounds. A further 232 had succumbed to disease. The unfortunate Private Ray was the only man executed.

187 "Paroles of the Army of Northern Virginia," *SHSP* 15 (1887): 413, 417.

188 1850 Census, Russell County; *MFB* 9: 11; *MFB* 10: 16. According to the 1850 Russell County census, 10-year-old John Mangham was born in Alabama. The 1860

census in Gonzales County, Texas, states that 20-year-old John Mangum was born in North Carolina. Nativity annotations were a common source of errors in the census, but the possibility exists that these were different individuals. See the Genealogical Appendix for more context on this identification of J. R. Mangham. William Mangham's family is the subject of Chapter VII.

[189] 1850 Censuses, Matagorda and Shelby Counties; 1860 Census, Gonzales County; Gonzales County Historical Commission, *The History of Gonzales County, Texas* (Dallas: Curtis Media Corp., 1986), p. 402; Palmer, *The Mangums*, pp. 219-222. Robert's son and namesake, Robert S. Mangum, Jr., served in Company C, 21st Texas Cavalry during the Civil War (CMSR, Robert S. Mangum, 21st Texas Cavalry). Willis W. Mangham, a second cousin of Robert, Sr., served in Company D of the same regiment (see Chapter VI).

[190] *History of Gonzales County*, p. 402; 1850 Census, Russell County; 1860 Census, Gonzales County; Gonzales County, 1858-1860 Tax Rolls, TSL. Claiborne Parish records show that R. H. Mangham served on a jury there as late as October 3, 1859. He and his brother may have moved to Texas together, or John may have preceded Robert by several years. See Claiborne Parish District Court Minute Record Book B (1857-1867), pp. 274-276, excerpted in *Claiborne Parish Trails* 6, no. 1 (February 1991): 59.

[191] Lt. Col. Arthur J. L. Fremantle, *Three Months in the Southern States: April-June, 1863* (New York: John Bradburn, 1864; reprint, Lincoln: Univ. of Nebraska Press, 1991), p. 75; L. B. Giles, *Terry's Texas Rangers*, in *Terry Texas Ranger Trilogy*, intro. Thomas W. Cutrer (Austin: State House Press, 1996), p. 11; J. K. P. Blackburn, *Reminiscences of the Terry Rangers*, in *Trilogy*, pp. 95-96.

[192] Blackburn, *Reminiscences*, in *Trilogy*, p. 96; CMSRs, J. R. Mangham and J. M. Mangum, 8th Texas Cavalry. Blackburn ended the war as a captain in the Rangers.

[193] CMSRs, J. R. Mangham and J. M. Mangum; Giles, *Terry's Texas Rangers*, in *Trilogy*, p. 9; Blackburn, *Reminiscences*, in *Trilogy*, pp. 96-97.

[194] Blackburn, *Reminiscences*, in *Trilogy*, pp. 97-100; Giles, *Terry's Texas Rangers*, in *Trilogy*, pp. 11-12.

[195] Ibid.

[196] Blackburn, *Reminiscences*, in *Trilogy*, pp. 100-101; Giles, *Terry's Texas Rangers*, in *Trilogy*, p. 12.

[197] Blackburn, *Reminiscences*, in *Trilogy*, pp. 102-104.

[198] Stewart Sifakis, *Compendium of the Confederate Armies: Texas* (New York: Facts on File, 1995), pp. 58-59; Crute, *Units*, pp. 327-328; Horn, *Army of Tennessee*, pp. 49-51.

[199] Horn, *Army of Tennessee*, pp. 55-59.

[200] Blackburn, *Reminiscences*, in *Trilogy*, p. 102.

[201] CMSRs, J. R. Mangham and J. M. Mangum; *History of Gonzales County*, pp. 402-403. Joe later served with Duff's Regiment until the end of the war. Afterwards he

married and raised seven children, along with champion racehorses such as "Blue Eyes," which broke the Texas state record in 1893 for four and one-half furlongs.

[202] This identification of Robert H. Mangham is necessarily tentative, but it is consistent with available information on the various Mangum/Mangham families in Texas. Robert H. Mangham appeared on a list of deceased Texas Itinerant Ministers published in the *Texas Christian Advocate*, May 17, 1884. (Information courtesy of Linda Emry, Williamson County Genealogical Society, in letter to author dated January 8, 1996.)

[203] *Trilogy*, pp. xiii, xxiv-xxv; Blackburn, *Reminiscences*, in *Trilogy*, p. 104.

Chapter IX: White Gold on the Red River: Arthur G. and James G. Mangham Move West Again

1. From Uchee Creek to the Red River Valley: Arthur and Green Mangham Move West to Louisiana

Although *John R.* and Robert H. Mangham made the fateful decision to join their Uncle William and Aunt Leacy Mangum in Texas during the last months before the Civil War, the kinfolk who cared for them during childhood had put down new roots in Louisiana. Their uncles, Arthur Green and James Green Mangham, departed Alabama about 1853 and settled in thriving Claiborne Parish, accompanied by their sister and brother-in-law, Jemima Mangham Sockwell and William Sockwell.

Arthur had married Sarah Brown in 1833 back in Talbot County, Georgia, and their family grew to include sons *Thomas Hamilton, Arthur Green, Jr.,* Zachary Taylor and Charles John, as well as daughters Francis Ann, Marinda Russell, and Martha Caroline Mangham. Sons Christopher Columbus and Samuel Young Mangham died in childhood, as did little Sarah Lavinia Mangham. When Arthur settled his family on 240 acres of land in Claiborne Parish in early 1854, he probably established a tannery and shoe shop on his farm, just as he had done in Russell County, Alabama.[1]

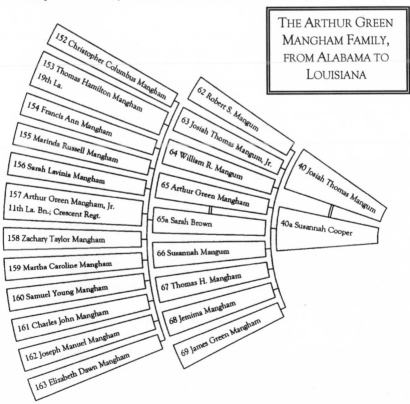

THE ARTHUR GREEN MANGHAM FAMILY, FROM ALABAMA TO LOUISIANA

152 Christopher Columbus Mangham

153 Thomas Hamilton Mangham
19th La.

154 Francis Ann Mangham

155 Marinda Russell Mangham

156 Sarah Lavinia Mangham

157 Arthur Green Mangham, Jr.
11th La. Bn.; Crescent Regt.

158 Zachary Taylor Mangham

159 Martha Caroline Mangham

160 Samuel Young Mangham

161 Charles John Mangham

162 Joseph Manuel Mangham

163 Elizabeth Dawn Mangham

62 Robert S. Mangum

63 Josiah Thomas Mangum, Jr.

64 William R. Mangum

65 Arthur Green Mangham

65a Sarah Brown

66 Susannah Mangum

67 Thomas H. Mangham

68 Jemima Mangham

69 James Green Mangham

40 Josiah Thomas Mangum

40a Susannah Cooper

2. "FIGHTING LIKE HELL A-BEATING TAN BARK": PVT. THOMAS H. MANGHAM, "CLAIBORNE VOLUNTEERS," CO. C, 19TH LOUISIANA

Arthur's eldest son, Thomas Hamilton Mangham, was born in Alabama on August 13, 1836. He had just turned 21 when he married Sarah M. Gray amid the pine-covered hills of Claiborne Parish on September 12, 1857. His uncle, James Green Mangham, had married into the Gray family a decade earlier, and some of their Gray in-laws had joined the Manghams and Sockwells in emigrating from Alabama to north Louisiana in the early 1850s.[2]

Sarah was only seventeen years old in October 1860, when the census taker noted that she and Thomas lived in the house next to his parents in Natchitoches Parish. His father had bought government land near the settlement of Coushatta Chute in 1858, establishing himself in the rich bottomlands near the Red River, south of Claiborne. Two years later the census taker estimated the value of Arthur's real estate holdings at one thousand dollars. He owned double that amount in personal property, including the thirty-year-old slave woman who helped in the Mangham household. Thomas owned no land of his own in Natchitoches Parish, where he made his living as a grinder, probably on his father's farm or at a nearby cotton or sugar plantation.[3]

Just three months earlier, however, Thomas had paid $700 to purchase 320 acres from Josiah Barrow in Claiborne Parish, where his uncle James Green Mangham and cousin *Josiah Thomas Mangham* still lived. Thomas apparently returned to Claiborne to begin working his own farm in late 1860 or early 1861, but the outbreak of war caused a radical change in his little family's plans, as it did for so many others. On June 1, 1861, he sold his land back to Mr. Barrow for the original purchase price, thus clearing his way to go off to war. In all probability, Sarah moved back in with her family or with the Manghams.[4]

Many of the young bloods of Claiborne Parish were joining companies that summer and fall, then making their way to distant Tangipahoa Parish, where regiments were rendezvousing at Camp Moore. One of these companies was Capt. Hyder A. Kennedy's "Claiborne Volunteers," whose ranks included Pvt. Thomas H. Mangham. The men left home in September, reaching Camp Moore later that month. It was October 3, 1861 before Thomas formally enlisted for twelve months' service in Kennedy's company, and it was still later before the Claiborne Volunteers were mustered into Confederate service. Governor Thomas O. Moore, whose name the camp bore, had yielded to the desperate calls from neighboring governors requesting arms in the hectic weeks and months following the outbreak of war at Fort Sumter. Now he could not equip the thousands of his own state's volunteers thronging Camp Moore, and anxious captains schemed to have their companies accepted by regiments that could provide guns for their men.[5]

Although Captain Kennedy's men were designated to join the 19th Louisiana, they and another Claiborne Parish company jumped ship to the 17th Louisiana in early October, since the latter regiment "had the prospect of getting away soon" to active service. The boisterous volunteers also took things into their own hands when corrupt contractors failed to provide meat rations in early October, swarming over several sutler shops and stripping them of everything edible, while company officers wisely stood aside. Things eventually settled down enough in the course of the winter to allow the regiments to complete their organizations, and the Claiborne Volunteers returned to the 19th Louisiana in time to muster into Confederate service as Company C on December 11, 1861. The men generally benefited from Camp Moore's healthy location in the piney woods eighty miles north of New Orleans, where cool spring water and shady groves seemed to promise comfortable accommodations. Lieutenant Silas Grisamore of the 18th Louisiana found that inexperienced officers had botched the job of organizing the camp's sanitary facilities, however, declaring disgustedly: "Two or three days. . .convinced us that the whole camp was one mass of filth and corruption without any system of decency or propriety having been inaugurated. . . ." It was "to the great satisfaction of us all," noted Grisamore, when the regiments of Ruggles's Brigade received orders to move to a new camp just a few days after completing their organization. Their initial destination was Camp Roman, just seven miles upriver of the Crescent City near Carrollton, but the brigade moved to nearby Camp Benjamin in the first days of 1862.[6]

Ruggles tried to whip his unruly troops into shape, confronting the thorny sense of independence that characterized volunteers on both sides at this point in the war. A Bienville Parish company in the 16th Louisiana circulated a petition calling for its commanding officer's resignation, whereupon he threatened to have his lieutenants cashiered for encouraging mutiny. Captain William E. Paxton, quartermaster and commissary officer for the 19th Louisiana, feared the testy captain might "give them trouble," adding, "If he does he had better never come home to Bienville."[7]

Although the Louisiana soldiers had little to fight at Camp Benjamin except rain, mud, and each other, concern mounted about the vulnerability of New Orleans to Federal attack. As state and Confederate authorities struggled to mobilize and equip an army for the state's defense, the fall of Forts Henry and Donelson in February clearly demanded reinforcements in northern Mississippi and western Tennessee. Lead elements of Ruggles's 1st Louisiana Brigade accordingly entrained for Corinth on February 14, but the 19th Louisiana's ammunition was destroyed by fire and required its quartermaster to return to New Orleans to obtain a resupply; nothing whatever was available from Nashville or Memphis. The 16th and 19th Louisiana regiments were preparing to move to Columbus, Kentucky, but the heightening crisis overtook Confederate efforts to marshal reinforcements for the salvation of its north-central frontier. (See maps on pages 125, 126 and 483.)[8]

Corinth became the point of concentration for Confederate forces arriving from across the Deep South, and the 19th Louisiana's baptism of fire would occur at nearby Shiloh rather than on the Kentucky border. By the time the opponents came to grips in the dreary forests of southwest Tennessee, however, the regiment's 873 soldiers were reduced by rampant illness to less than three hundred fit for battle. Shockingly, this seems to have been an *improvement*, as quartermaster William Paxton recorded on March 27, that the "health of our regiment is improving." Thomas was one of the hundreds unable to remain in ranks, stricken with a case of jaundice that hospitalized him at Jackson, Mississippi on March 17. By the time he emerged from his sickbed on April 11, the great Battle of Shiloh had been fought and lost. His regiment had lost twenty percent of its effective strength in pressing home several unsupported attacks against an enemy it could barely see in the dense woods.[9]

Thomas rejoined his company in the trenches at Corinth, and took part in the siege that ensued during April, May, and June. Paxton summed up the prevailing attitude in camp: "Our men are affected by the late disaster—but most of them are possessed of a dogged determination to win the fight or die in the attempt." Private Mangham was among those who accordingly re-enlisted for "three years or the war" on May 8, when the regiment reorganized in accordance with the recent Conscription Act. Perhaps the confusion attending its command reshuffle was the reason the 19th Louisiana remained on duty in the trenches the next day, when other regiments of the brigade took part in the engagement at Farmington. An alternative explanation might be the lingering effects of the "great deal of Sickness in camp," which had left "scarcely a man fit for duty" in late April. As late as May 6, quartermaster Paxton was complaining, "The health of our regiment I believe is improving a little. The water here is very bad. It produces flux and dissentery." The 18th Louisiana's Lieutenant Grisamore added his voice to the chorus of discontent over the unhealthy conditions at Corinth: "The surrounding country was poor and thinly settled, and if there ever was a drink of good water in the place none of us had the good fortune to obtain it." He thought it was "the most abominable stuff that was ever forced down men's throats," adding that the wells his men dug soon filled with "a kind of liquid resembling coal tar, dish water, and soap suds mixed."[10]

The suffering Louisianians remained on duty at Corinth until Beauregard withdrew the entire army to Tupelo in June, where they drilled and reorganized for several weeks. The numerous sick and wounded reduced the Louisiana brigade to a fraction of its nominal strength, and Pvt. Douglas Cater of Company I observed that Colonel Hodge's 19th Louisiana had to combine remnants of three companies to make one full company for drill. Major General William Hardee, commanding Bragg's old 2nd Corps after the latter succeeded to army command, reviewed the troops in mid-July after most had recovered their health. Thomas must have been in the ranks that day, formed up in an open field where the troops could see their own strength. Hodge's men had a clear view of the spectacle, which made a powerful impression. Cater waxed enthusiastic to a cousin about the "long lines of troops with arms bright and bayonets gleaming, the soul stirring strains of martial music from the splendid regimental bands and the proud banners unfurled to the morning breeze"; he thought the effect was "deep and touching."[11]

The retreat to Tupelo had removed the immediate threat of renewed battle, since the Federals remained content with their conquest of Corinth. Braxton Bragg benefited from the opportunity to consider all options, and he mulled over plans to move his troops to Chattanooga and thence into Kentucky. As he positioned his forces for the Kentucky Campaign, however, he had to detach some regiments for garrison duty at Mobile. His headquarters issued Special Orders No. 6 on July 23, assigning the 18th and 19th Louisiana regiments to the job, along with the 17th and 18th Alabama Volunteers. By this coincidence, the same order that sent Thomas's regiment south to Mobile also sent his first cousin, *Charles A. Mangham* of the 18th Alabama, to the same place (see Chapter VIII).[12]

The 19th Louisiana received orders to move on August 3, 1862 and proceeded to Camp Pollard, Alabama. The regiment had to provide soldiers to facilitate the rest of the brigade's movement to Chattanooga, however, and Thomas was among those detailed that day to serve as teamsters in the brigade Quartermaster's Department. As his comrades rode the rails to Mobile, he was learning the finer points of dealing with army mules on the road from Meridian to Columbus, and then to Tuscaloosa, Alabama. Lieutenant Grisamore was in the column, and noticed that the teamsters had become a bit frazzled by the time they reached the hilly country near the Cahaba River on August 13. As they "had to get up and down so often to unlock and lock their wagons, their patience became exhausted, and many of them began to show a disposition to use 'cuss words' for which they became so famous in subsequent times." Their route led onward through Jacksonville to Rome, Georgia, eventually bringing them to Chattanooga on August 26. There they found themselves impressed for the army's northward march into Kentucky, although Grisamore pointed out to General Adams that men from the 18th and 19th Louisiana regiments lacked individual descriptive lists. Without this documentation of their identity, service, and pay status, they could not draw pay and clothing while attached to other units during the coming winter campaign. Unable to impress Adams with their plight, Grisamore and Lieutenant Hodges of the 19th Louisiana took matters into their own hands: they had their men hand over the wagons to anybody willing to take them, then scrambled aboard a southbound train to rejoin their regiments![13]

Thomas rejoined his regiment there on the afternoon of September 1, where its new commander, Col. Wesley P. Winans, devoted a serious effort to training his men. In keeping with the practice of the times, his method was a steady regimen of drills and reviews. Few commanders of that era emphasized live-fire musketry training, probably due to shortage of ammunition for such purposes; there is no evidence that the 19th Louisiana broke the established pattern. Private Mangham apparently mastered the complex drillground evolutions in an exemplary manner, as he earned appointment as the regiment's left general guide on September 23. By regulation, the left and right general guides were to be "selected by the colonel from the sergeants (other than first sergeants) for their accuracy in marching," because many maneuvers were dependent upon the guides who led the deployment. In line of battle, Thomas would be the last man on the regiment's left flank, marching in the rank of the file closers who followed and controlled the movements of the two ranks in the firing line.[14]

Winans may have stuck to traditional training methods, but he did not fail to recognize the value of adding vegetables to the monotonous Army rations of beef, pork, flour, and corn meal. Private Cater marveled at the speed with which the regiment's sweet potato diet at Pollard cured "every man in the regiment" of "that plague, 'camp dysentery' which had so decimated our army at Corinth and Tupelo." Winans planted a vegetable garden in the mild days of February 1863, and the men

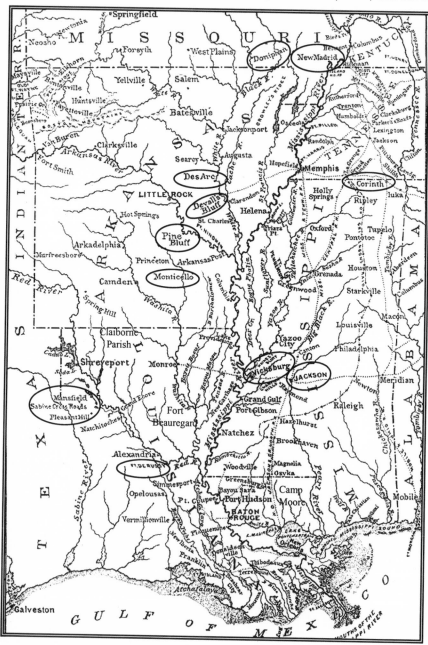

welcomed their non-regulation meals of fresh produce, fried bass, and red perch from the Escambia River. Others amused themselves by dragging gopher turtles from their underground warrens, carrying them about in triumph and crying, "See what Alabama has done!" Their mirthful parody mocked the Mobile newspaper column that daily listed the regiments, battalions, and batteries that Alabama had contributed to the war effort. When they weren't trying their luck with hook and line, gopher turtles, or sweet potatoes, many frolicked in the Escambia's clear running waters, jumping from a diving board they rigged for the purpose.[15]

They were in Pollard to secure its critical railroad connections against Yankee raiders issuing from Pensacola, just fifty miles to the south, but no such threat ever materialized during their tour of duty. Bragg wanted reinforcements for his Army of Tennessee as campaigning season drew nigh in April 1863, so orders duly came for the 19th Louisiana to terminate its idyllic tour in south Alabama and move north. Departing Mobile Camp on April 15, they took a steamboat up the Alabama River to Montgomery, then entrained for Atlanta and eventually Chattanooga. A final journey by train took them through a "wild mountainous region" to Tullahoma, Tennessee, on April 20, where they marched the final mile to their brigade camp (see map on page 483). Their arrival was greeted with shouts of "Hey, you Pollard gardeners, glad to see you!" Plainly, their comrades of Adams's Brigade had read the Mobile newspaper's commentaries about the regiment's solution to the blandness of army rations.[16]

The brigade marched to Wartrace on April 24, wading the knee-deep chill of the Duck River with their socks and shoes held high. They moved to the vicinity of Hoover's Gap in early May, and won a drill competition against the 4th Kentucky on May 21 as Private Cater, the regiment's chief musician, "beat good time on the drum." The following day the 19th Louisiana marched to the Gap itself, where it took a turn on the picket lines in time to witness Federal cavalry engage nearby grayclad troopers; some enemy cannoneers sent a few cannon shots down the road towards the 19th Louisiana. As the Louisiana infantrymen marched to the cavalry's support, they grinned at an old lady who emerged from a roadside house, wringing her hands and declaring, "I didn't mind them little guns, but them cannon, them cannon!"[17]

As Bragg sparred with Rosecrans in Middle Tennessee that month, a developing emergency in Mississippi caused the Confederate government to ask him to reinforce Gen. Joe Johnston's tiny force near Jackson. Johnston was attempting to gather forces to threaten the rear of Grant's force as it approached Vicksburg, but faced serious difficulties in the process. He desperately needed troops, guns, wagons, and cooperation from General Pemberton, whose force stood in the ramparts of the river bastion. Johnston had directed the luckless Pemberton to strike eastward against Grant while Johnston sent his elements against the Federal rear, but two separate attempts to coordinate their movements had failed. The Confederate administration urged Pemberton to defend the city itself, while Johnston's exhortations to save the army and sacrifice the city left Pemberton groping for a suitable compromise.[18]

By the time Maj. Gen. John C. Breckenridge reached Jackson with three of his four brigades in late May, Pemberton's army was cooped up in Vicksburg's defenses.

Brigadier General Daniel Adams's Louisiana brigade had struck its tents at Wartrace on May 23, retraced its steps to Mobile, then entrained for Jackson. Dismounting four miles from town at the point where previous Federal occupiers had destroyed the tracks, the 19th Louisiana marched to a bivouac near the city on the last day of the month. They cooled their heels on picket and camp duties throughout June, as the Vicksburg siege lengthened and Johnston gathered additional forces for a relief effort. (See map on p. 637.)[19]

Having finally gathered adequate guns and wagons to venture from his lines around Jackson, Johnston cautiously probed westward in late June. After mustering for pay on June 30, Private Mangham and the 19th Louisiana took up the line of march the next day, crossing the Big Black River four days later. Probes had convinced Johnston that his small force had no hope of breaking the Union lines north of the railroad, so he determined to strike south of the railroad, create a diversion, and thereby allow Pemberton to cut his way out. Shortly after his courier rode away to carry news of the plan to Pemberton, the dreaded news arrived like a thunderclap: Vicksburg had fallen! Colonel Winans and his men had marched that day in suffocating heat and dust from Bolton to the vicinity of the Baker's Creek battlefield. Bivouacking that night near the site of the recent Confederate defeat, Cater perceived "gloom on every countenance." The enemy had gained almost undisputed possession of the Mississippi River, had captured Pemberton's 31,600 men, and now could turn on Johnston's smaller force.[20]

Private Mangham and his Louisiana comrades marched back to Jackson through the stifling heat and dust, entering the trenches there on July 8, 1863. They spent the night behind the trenches, but the call came at three o'clock the next morning to resume their position: three Union army corps, under the command of William T. Sherman, had appeared in front of Jackson. His was a name the dusty Rebel soldiers would come to know well, but for now he contented himself with besieging his outnumbered opponents. Active skirmishing ensued over the next several days, and increasingly the boom of cannon signaled that Sherman's guns were well emplaced.[21] (See map, p. 211.)

One of his batteries stood in front of the 19th Louisiana's position by July 12, while another was beyond its right flank. These guns opened fire about nine o'clock that morning, searing the regiment's works with a crossfire that kept heads low. Private Cater sat among the men of Slocomb's 5th Company, Washington Artillery, in their emplacements on his regiment's left, serenading them on a piano they had "liberated" from the deserted Cooper residence, which stood forlornly between the opposing lines. Captain Slocomb was enjoying the music amidst the Minie balls and cannon shot swishing overhead, when he heard the distinctive yell of Federal troops, so different from the shrill Rebel yell.[22]

Glancing quickly over the parapet, Slocomb saw several blueclad regiments in line of battle moving from Bailey's Hill up the road to Jackson, straight against the works held by Adams's Brigade. The rush was on, as Slocomb's New Orleans gunners sprang to their pieces and Cater dashed back to his own company. The first gun belched forth the canister kept loaded for just such emergencies, and Slocomb felt relieved that his line was safe when he saw the deadly effect of the first shot; he had feared that the

Yankees had gotten in too close to stop. As the other field guns joined in, so did the muskets of the three leftmost companies of Winans's regiment, which were the only ones able to deliver their fire in the necessary direction. General Adams himself snatched a musket from a man in Cater's company, loosing two shots at the Yankees from an exposed position atop the breastworks. On the other side of the Washington Artillery, the 32nd Alabama cut loose with shattering volleys from its whole line. The only non-Louisiana regiment in Adams's Brigade, its line could rake the entire Federal advance with fire. Although the oncoming blue wave obliqued to the right in an attempt to strike the entrenchments on the brigade's left, the searing fire brought them to a halt about eighty yards from the Confederate line.[23]

Here some of the Federals began to break for the rear "in great confusion and with considerable loss," as it appeared to Adams. Others desperately waved handkerchiefs in token of surrender, realizing that retreat had become almost as hazardous as continuing the attack. The Louisiana brigadier, thinking the enemy's bravery "worthy of a better cause," ordered his men to cease firing. From his left flank, Stovall's Brigade sent out detachments to gather in the prisoners; the catch numbered about 150 all told, about forty of whom came in through Adams's line. In his estimation, which Federal reports subsequently confirmed, another 250 lay killed and wounded. The total loss in Adams's Brigade was one man slightly wounded in Slocomb's Washington Artillery. Two days later the stench of putrefaction grew so strong in the broiling Mississippi heat that an armistice was necessary to bury the dead, 160 of whom found their final resting place in front of the Washington Artillery and the 19th Louisiana.[24]

Local repulses such as this one, along with one delivered by *Col. Thomas Woodward Mangham*'s 30th Georgia on July 16, helped convince Sherman that direct assault was not feasible. Johnston's continued defense of Jackson was likewise impractical, however, as Sherman's forces were numerous enough to outflank the Confederate position. To prevent losing his army entirely, Johnston stealthily pulled back to Brandon on the night of July 16, 1863. Successive rapid marches brought the 19th Louisiana out of harm's way soon thereafter, and Sherman contented himself with burning Jackson to the ground and returning to Vicksburg. Although Thomas Mangham's 19th Louisiana tarried in the stricken state until late August, the only enemies they encountered were the relentless heat and dust of a Mississippi summer.[25]

When the summons came for Breckenridge's Division to return to Bragg's Army of Tennessee, many considered the division "the flower of the Western armies"; Adams's Brigade was widely thought to be the "best-drilled brigade in Bragg's command." The division's services were in demand now because the skillful maneuvers of Union Maj. Gen. William Rosecrans had levered the overmatched Bragg almost completely out of the state of Tennessee. Dan Adams's "splendid brigade" reported back to the main army in Chattanooga, just before Rosecrans's further movements forced Bragg's withdrawal across the Tennessee River into Georgia. Bragg's men were greatly encouraged by the arrival of Lt. Gen. James Longstreet and his famous 1st Corps from Lee's army, but they were deeply offended by the suggestion that they had come to show Bragg's men "how to fight." The 19th Louisiana's Private Cater was not the only man who bridled at the implication, and he and his mates warned the newcomers that they "would find quite a difference in facing these western men from those they had been fighting in Virginia." He allowed smugly, "They acknowledged this before they were sent back to General Lee."[26]

*   *   *   *   *

If Longstreet's men indeed underwent any such conversion, it was due primarily to the events of September 19-20 at Chickamauga. His corps played a major role in smashing the center of Rosecrans's line on the morning of the second day, sending most of the enemy running for Chattanooga, but George Thomas held the Federal left wing together with a tenacity that earned him the sobriquet "Rock of Chickamauga."

One of the Confederate divisions that hammered at Thomas that morning was commanded by 36-year-old Kentuckian John C. Breckenridge, former Vice President of the United States. Posted at the far right end of the Confederate line, his division came close to enjoying a success that would have matched Longstreet's achievement, had it been sustained by reinforcements necessary to make the initial gains stick. Indeed, such sustainment would have reaped the fruits of total victory that eluded the Confederates that day, because Breckenridge had gained a position astride the main Union escape route to Chattanooga. The missed opportunity was one of the many miscues, on both sides, that characterized the savage struggle in the north Georgia forests.

All of this was unknown to Private Mangham as he spent the night of September 19 slogging northward behind the length of Bragg's battlefront, until he and his mates settled wearily into their bivouac behind Cleburne's Division on the extreme right. The rattle of the drummers' long roll called the division into line on Cleburne's right at daybreak the next morning; Breckenridge aligned Helm's Kentucky Brigade as his left flank unit, put Stovall's Brigade in the center, and placed Adams's Brigade on the right. His line was parallel to the LaFayette-Chattanooga Road, and stepped off in the attack at midmorning. Helm's men crashed into the left end of the Federal line, where it bent back to the west to guard against a flanking maneuver. Stovall's men swept up to the LaFayette Road against a regiment in skirmish order, and Adams drove two more regiments of blueclad skirmishers across the road to the edge of the McDonald field. One of the units in the brigade skirmish line was Captain Handley's Company F, 19th Louisiana, which overran two artillery pieces in the fast-moving advance.[27]

Lieutenant Colonel Richard Turner was commanding the 19th Louisiana in this action, and his men occupied the left flank of the brigade line of battle. Amidst the heavy skirmishing, he realized that Stovall's Brigade was nowhere to be seen on his left flank, so he halted the regiment and changed front to protect the brigade's open flank. Now facing due south, the 19th Louisiana was poised to sweep down behind the Federal flank. Adams formed the remainder of the brigade on Turner's right, then had him march by the left flank until he reached the Chattanooga Road. Breckenridge realized that his two brigades were altogether beyond the enemy's flank, and now he arranged them to act in concert. He had Stovall deploy his brigade on Adams's left, then launched the two brigades straight down the road to roll up the Federal line.[28]

562

A series of dreadful miscommunications between Bragg and his subordinate wing and corps commanders had delayed the jump-off of Breckenridge's initial attack from dawn until almost ten o'clock, and now the Louisianians paid for the mistake in blood. The Federal brigade of John Beatty was speeding to the threatened point, and arrived there in time to complicate things considerably. His men were still well behind the Union flank, and the left of Adams's Brigade went ahead unopposed while the right slammed straight into Beatty. A bloody fight developed, with Beatty's right flank units recoiling from the Louisianians streaming past their flank. Lieutenant Colonel Turner had been felled by grapeshot in the initial forward push, so Maj. Loudon Butler had taken command of the 19th Louisiana. He drove forward at the head of his command in a charge that Thomas Mangham's company commander thought was "the most desperate and bloody charge that troops were ever called upon to make." Beatty's right flank regiment, the 42nd Indiana, was rolled up into the 88th Indiana, which managed to change front to the right and continue shooting.[29]

Fortunately for the hard-fighting Beatty, Stanley's Federal brigade was moving into line on his right flank at the critical moment. Stanley's two leading regiments, the 11th Michigan and 19th Illinois, quickly cut down saplings and underbrush to clear fields of fire, then piled up the cuttings and lay down behind them in ambush. The Louisianians were coming forward at the run, chasing skirmishers before them in wild pursuit. When they were barely fifteen yards from the hidden line of battle, regimental flags raised from behind the brush piles, signaling "Fire!" The volley crashed directly into the 13th/20th Louisiana (Consolidated), 16th/20th Louisiana (Consolidated), and 19th Louisiana, dropping men by the score. The attack ground to a bloody halt, as some traded shots with the enemy and others drew away from the unrelenting fire. Major Butler fell dead, leaving Captain Kennedy of the Claiborne Volunteers as the 19th Louisiana's senior surviving officer, and he struggled to bring order from the chaos. Stovall's men were stalled a hundred yards behind his left flank, and the 87th Indiana pushed into the gap, firing into the Louisianians' flank. The two consolidated regiments on his right were falling back under the heavy fire of infantry and artillery. Adams had gone down with a severe arm wound in the melee, and the entire brigade fell back in disorder to the ravine where they had begun their advance.[30]

Many of the men fell back to the point where the brigade originally changed front after crossing the LaFayette-Chattanooga Road, and the regimental commanders eventually managed to halt and reform their shocked units at that point. Colonel Randall Gibson, commander of the 13th/20th Louisiana (Consolidated), assumed command of the brigade and strove valiantly to bring order from the chaos. Another man rallied the troops at this point with the shout, "Rally here, Louisianans, or I'll have to bring up my bobtail cavalry to show you how to fight!" Anyone disposed to argue the point with him was dissuaded by the commanding presence of Gen. Nathan Bedford Forrest, who had ridden in from his post protecting the army's right flank.[31]

Breckenridge's Division shifted around a good deal during the afternoon, eventually settling into reserve positions and stacking arms while the shocked, exhausted men recovered from their ordeal. But in common with much of Bragg's army, the troops were called upon that afternoon to make yet another effort, when their repeated hammer blows finally completed the Federal collapse. General Rosecrans had left the field earlier in the day when his right and center collapsed, but Thomas managed to concentrate the left wing to defend Kelly Field and Snodgrass Hill until dark was approaching. Colonel Gibson led Adams's Brigade in a well-conducted attack, and the 19th Louisiana was in on the kill. The brigade passed through the engaged lines of Wilson's Georgia brigade to help deliver the final blow that sent the remaining Federal units scampering for Chattanooga. The regiment had the satisfaction of overrunning the ground on which they had been repulsed earlier that day, scooping up prisoners and abandoned weapons before receiving orders to halt. It was over.[32]

Captain Kennedy proudly reported that this final assault drove "the enemy in the wildest confusion far beyond his original lines." But the men who gave tongue to the hoarse cheers of victory echoing through the Georgia forests were woefully diminished in number. Lieutenant Colonel Turner had led 349 men into action that morning, but Captain Kennedy was the ranking officer left on his feet when the fighting ended. He reported 28 officers and men killed, with another 106 wounded. Eight more wounded men were missing, as were eleven other unwounded officers and men. The total loss was 153, representing a casualty rate of 44 percent; this toll was the heaviest in Adams's Brigade and the second highest in Breckenridge's Division. Only thirteen regiments in Bragg's army suffered more severely in the bloodiest battle ever fought in the west.[33]

One of the dead men recovered that night was Lt. Rufus Cater of Company I, the elder brother of Douglas. His watch, purse, sword, scabbard, and shoes were all missing, and his pockets were turned inside out. The bullet that felled him had passed through his chest and out his back, and retreating comrades had heard him call weakly "Good-bye boys" as they pulled back from the deadly fire that broke their charge. Douglas was convinced the wound was not a mortal one, however. The fatal wound was from a rifle bullet fired through his forehead at close range. Appalled at what the "devils in human form" had done to his helpless brother, he wrapped his arms around the body and fell asleep amidst the moans and cries of the wounded.[34]

Private Thomas Mangham may have been wounded in the furious engagement of September 20, although available records are not definitive. He received a thirty-day sick furlough on October 1, about the point at which a patient would have stabilized enough to stand the travel. Alternatively, he may have simply broken down from the marching, exposure, and stress of battle. If he attempted to travel home to Claiborne Parish, it doubtless required a great deal of energy and ingenuity to cross the Mississippi River, although some men managed it successfully. Company records list Thomas as absent on October 31, the day his thirty-day furlough should have expired. The next muster, on December 31, 1863, offers the enigmatic annotation: "absent without leave, time unknown." His injury or illness may have required an extension, or perhaps he simply decided to stay away for a while.[35]

*   *   *   *   *

During his extended absence the regiment shared in the catastrophic defeat at Missionary Ridge, although the after action reports of Gibson's Brigade fairly crackle with wounded pride at the circumstances that led to their defeat. In his report on the 19th Louisiana's conduct, Captain Bond offered the following observation: "Never did I witness men who appeared more cool, deliberate, and confident of being able to repel any force that could be brought against them than did our men on this occasion." Private Cater was even more to the point: "We did some good shooting but there were not enough of us." Another soldier, H. A. McFarland of Company D ("Claiborne Greys"), recalled that the enemy "never could have dislodged us had they not flanked us out," even though the regiment's line was so thin that its men were positioned five feet apart. Having handily repulsed two assaults against their position, the troops were amazed that ruptures on the right and left stranded them amidst a flood tide of blue uniforms, from which they had to run for their lives. Only 244 men went into action that November 25, of which the regiment lost seven killed, 23 wounded, and 13 missing, with ten of the casualties coming from the ranks of the Claiborne Volunteers. One of the men killed in action was Colonel Winans, the regiment's beloved commander.[36]

*   *   *   *   *

The grim New Year found the Army of Tennessee licking its wounds at Dalton, Georgia, some thirty miles away from Missionary Ridge. Men were trickling back to their commands throughout the entire army; on December 14, the 19th Louisiana had counted only 270 present for duty, out of 557 men on its rolls. Of those present, only 157 were armed. Even so, it was easily the strongest outfit in the brigade.[37]

One of the returnees was Thomas Mangham, who was back in ranks at Dalton when the Claiborne Volunteers re-enlisted for the war on January 20, 1864. In fact, the whole regiment took the same oath, helping accelerate a spirit of renewed hope and dedication on the heels of the army's disastrous defeat at Missionary Ridge. Less than a week earlier, the 154th Tennessee had been the first regiment in the army to take the plunge of signing on for the duration, and its highly publicized action sent a thrill of excitement and admiration throughout the Army of Tennessee. Entire regiments began to stage mass meetings, passing resolutions to affirm their dedication to Southern liberty and re-enlisting en masse. The soul-stirring ceremonies and patriotic announcements were a shot in the arm to Southern morale, and resulted in part from hope engendered by the reforms, reorganization and discipline instituted by Gen. Joseph E. Johnston, the Army of Tennessee's new commander. Admittedly, whiskey helped fuel some of the re-enlistments, as did promises of new uniforms and Johnston's offer of furloughs to a certain percentage of each re-enlisting unit. The fact remains, however, that a huge proportion of the army declared itself in for the war. This avoided the nightmare of dissolution at the expiration of their enlistments, which roughly coincided with the beginning of the spring campaign. Had the army entered the Atlanta campaign without resolving this issue, certain disaster would have ensued.[38]

Although Johnston got busy reorganizing and re-equipping the army, many of the men rested up and spent the winter in leisurely fashion. Douglas Cater recalled that the 19th Louisiana did very little drilling, but that many attended prayer meetings, organized debating clubs, played cards, chess or checkers, and enjoyed snowball fights whenever opportunity arose. The specter of renewed combat was never too distant, however, and late February saw many units in Hardee's Corps depart their encampment at Dalton for threatened points in Mississippi, although they soon returned when the threats fizzled out. Colonel Richard W. Turner's 19th Louisiana was

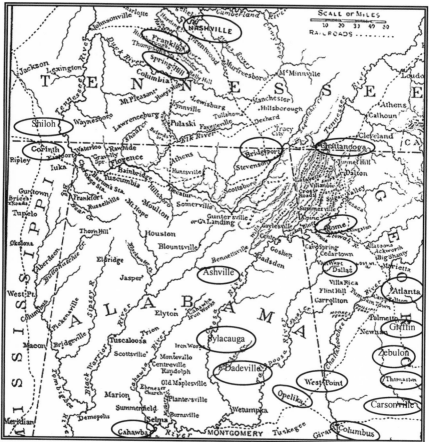

in Gibson's Brigade of Stewart's Division, and hustled out to form a line of battle on Rocky Face Ridge when Federals approached from Ringgold on February 23. The Louisianians remained in line on the northern slopes for three days as skirmishers mixed it up, convincing the Federals that Rocky Face was not to be had without a major engagement. Details of troops had set fire to the regiment's huts on February 24 when it appeared that active operations were underway, so they had to be rebuilt when the threat abated. When a subsequent Federal advance summoned them into line two months later, Turner's men wisely left their huts intact.[39]

Although they were able to reoccupy their cabins when the enemy withdrew that evening, the time for active operations was nigh. Several more false alarms ensued, but the ball finally opened on May 7, when Sherman's drive against Atlanta began in earnest. He sent one part of his army against Rocky Face Ridge once more, seeking to hold Johnston's attention; other units swung well to the west and south to Snake Creek Gap near Resaca, where they could cut the roads to Atlanta. Private Mangham was present at the beginning of the month when his regiment mustered for pay, so he doubtless fell into ranks as the 19th Louisiana moved out of camp for good. The regiment formed line of battle in trenches guarding the left flank of Mill Creek Gap, an avenue of approach from Ringgold that led through the northern end of Rocky Face towards Dalton. The Claiborne Volunteers' old commander, Hyder Kennedy, was now the regiment's lieutenant colonel, and he acted as commander while Turner finished his duties on a corps-level court martial board. Kennedy placed his men on an advanced ridge between the 4th Louisiana Battalion and the 20th Louisiana Regiment, and then settled in to face the music. Each day he dispatched 35 men with two officers to hold the redoubts in front of the main line of works, and at intervals the regiment's line suffered under "tolerably heavy cannonading." The Claiborne Volunteers lost the only man killed and two wounded in these positions, while the nine other companies suffered only two men wounded by enemy fire.[40]

On the evening of May 11, Gibson's Brigade moved across Mill Creek to new positions on Rocky Face itself, but remained there only some twenty-four hours. Although Federal artillery fire and demonstrations against the nearly impregnable defenses kept the Louisiana soldiers fully occupied, Johnston finally awoke to the danger menacing his line of retreat at Resaca. He ordered his forces to fall back toward that town and establish a new defensive front west of the crucial rail junction. Gibson's Brigade belonged to Stewart's Division of Lt. Gen. John Bell Hood's army corps; it was the last division to pull back from Dalton, taking position on the army's right flank at Resaca on the morning of May 14, 1864.[41]

Serious fighting ensued that day at Resaca, but Polk's and Hardee's corps bore the brunt of it. Stewart's men saw little action on the far right, although the 19th Louisiana "suffered considerably from the musketry on the left." Things heated up later in the afternoon, when Hood launched Stewart's Division in a counterattack against the Federal left wing. Although the division's advance attracted a great deal of artillery fire, it suffered few casualties in an effort that petered out in thin air, as the bluecoats in their front pulled back. Stevenson's Division, Stewart's neighbor to the left, tangled with the Yankees in a nasty encounter that folded their left backwards, but Stewart's men apparently went past the Union flank on an angle that led them away from the enemy. About midnight, they received orders to withdraw to their original positions.[42]

The next day, Johnston sent Hood in another attack against the Federal left wing, and this time Stewart's orders had him wheel to the half-left to ensure contact with the enemy. Gibson's Brigade was in the division's second line, supporting Clayton's Alabama brigade, but the dense, prickly chaparral through which they advanced did a great deal to desynchronize the attack. Stewart was pleased that his men advanced "with great spirit and determination," but their inability to see more than a few yards led the Louisianians astray. Pushing too far to the right, they drove forward into a "severe fire" from their direct front. Colonel Turner, who had resumed active command of the 19th Louisiana after its arrival at Resaca, ordered the men to lie down and hold their fire, since he believed that Clayton's Alabama regiments were still fighting in front of him. The incoming fire killed two men and wounded another sixteen in the 19th Louisiana before Turner received orders to pull back to the breastworks from which Clayton had begun his attack. Recognizing that a mix-up had occurred, Gibson was about to order a direct assault when word came to retire.[43]

Stewart recalled his men after suffering about a thousand casualties in an attack that General Johnston had tried to cancel. He had learned that a Federal flanking column had crossed the Oostanaula River to his south, threatening Calhoun and his communications with Atlanta. Unfortunately for Stewart's men, however, the recall order had arrived after their attack was well underway; the division commander decided to withdraw only after Clayton's and Stovall's brigades suffered a repulse, but at least he prevented Gibson's direct assault. That night, Gibson's men again formed part of the army's rear guard, and this time the Yankees pressed him hard as he prepared to cross the Oostanaula at the Resaca bridge. He had control of his own brigade and Stovall's to cover the retreat, and ended up forming a line of battle and sending out a "very heavy line of skirmishers" to cover his line. The 19th Louisiana spent the night in line of battle near the railroad station, where the wounded were being loaded into cars for evacuation as Union shot and shell pounded the town. Gibson proudly reported that the "shelling had no effect" on his men, who showed a "confident tone" and "steadiness" with which he was "especially pleased."[44]

The retreat from Resaca presaged a week of further retreat and jockeying for position near Calhoun, Adairsville, and Cassville, with Turner's Louisiana regiment almost continually on the march or in line of battle. They got a good rest at Allatoona, where the forbidding mountains made the Confederate position obviously impregnable. Here, Johnston's Rebels were astride the Western & Atlantic Railroad leading to Atlanta, so Sherman paused to find a way to maneuver around their flanks once more. He concluded that he could slip his army westward to Dallas, then swing south to Marietta on the railroad and thence move across the Chattahoochee.[45]

The march to Dallas began on May 23, and Sherman expected that his far-flung columns would not encounter significant enemy resistance until they approached Marietta itself. Unbeknownst to Sherman, however, Johnston had sideslipped Hardee's and Polk's corps to block the Atlanta-Marietta road east of Dallas; soon thereafter, he maneuvered Hood's Corps into position on the right of this line, astride roads leading to the little Methodist meeting house named New Hope Church. "Fighting Joe" Hooker was marching the three divisions of his XX Corps towards New Hope on these side roads when he ran into Confederates screening the approaches. The initial skirmishes were but a prelude to Hooker's full-scale assault on the road junction, where the little log church stood as a testament to faith and Christian brotherhood. Before many days had passed, the humble structure would assume a renown reminiscent of other country churches like the Dunker Church at Sharpsburg and Shiloh Meeting House in Tennessee.[46]

The grayclad skirmishers were men of Stewart's Division, primarily Clayton's Alabamians and Gibson's Louisiana troops. Colonel Turner sent forward Company B to reinforce Maj. John Austin's 14th Louisiana Battalion Sharpshooters, and they beat back the Federal skirmishers in repeated clashes. Prisoners indicated that Hooker's entire corps was advancing behind them, and the Louisiana skirmishers drove forward to within two hundred yards of a hastily entrenched line, where Geary's Federal division had gone to ground until its sister divisions could provide support. At one point, Colonel Turner led the entire 19th Louisiana forward to help develop the enemy position, but Stewart soon pulled Gibson's Brigade back into the main defensive line at New Hope Church, where he placed him in support of Stovall's Georgians. Austin's reinforced Sharpshooters followed shortly thereafter, having fought a delaying action that repeatedly wrecked Geary's skirmish line and forced his line of battle to come into action. When the surviving Sharpshooters dashed into the Confederate lines, they had lost 26 killed and wounded of the 85 men engaged.[47]

Geary's Yankees were hot on Gibson's heels, marching in a line of battle that was backed up by two more full divisions bent on brushing aside a force that Sherman presumed was of minimal size. As they reached the northern foot of the slope leading down from the road intersection, however, a veritable hurricane of fire struck them from cannon and small arms. The Battle of New Hope Church was underway, and Hooker's three divisions proceeded to batter themselves to pieces against Stewart's "Little Giants." Gibson's Brigade, having fought the preliminary action, stood in reserve positions at the intersection itself, with Turner's 19th Louisiana "formed along the road just to the right of New Hope Church." Nevertheless, Thomas Mangham and his friends were well within range of Federal musketry, and some of them were hit by Minie balls directed against the brigades of Stovall, Clayton, and Baker, which took the brunt of the assault. Men on both sides fired as fast as they could in an attempt to beat down the enemy's fire, and Stewart accurately characterized the volume of fire as "very heavy." General Johnston sent a message asking Stewart if he needed reinforcements, only to receive the calm reply: "My own troops will hold the position."[48]

Hold it they did, in an engagement that historian Stanley Horn characterized as "one of the most spectacular of the entire war," as a crashing thunderstorm added its lightning bolts and torrents of rain to the roar of gunfire. Major General Alexander P. Stewart, "Old Straight" to his men on account of his background as a university professor, thought "No more persistent attack or determined resistance has anywhere been made," adding that the "calm determination" of his men was "beyond all praise." Hooker's 16,000 men had suffered at least 1665 casualties in a brutal repulse at the hands of four thousand determined defenders, who raised a "prolonged cheer of victory" when the bluecoated attackers pulled back into the rain-drenched forest. One chastened Wisconsin soldier thought, "It was no safer to follow close upon [Johnston's] heels than to fool around the hind feet of an army mule." Stewart's "Little Giants" suffered some three to four hundred casualties of their own in the three hour fight, which ended only with the onset of darkness.[49]

The 19th Louisiana was ordered into the front line when the attacks ceased, and the men spent the night digging breastworks where Stovall's Georgians had fought behind the tombstones in the church cemetery. The ferocity of the initial engagement foreshadowed vicious sharpshooting over the next several days, and Turner's regiment suffered "considerable loss in men and officers" in the stubborn contest. The 19th Louisiana's color bearer, H. A. McFarland, belonged to the Claiborne Greys, and he recalled that the soldiers had to "keep very close during the day" and get water under cover of darkness, as any movement during daylight attracted the deadly attention of Yankee sharpshooters. The Confederates meant to stay, however, and some men from Granbury's Texas brigade made the point plain when they visited the front lines from their reserve positions. They found Georgia troops, probably Stovall's men, in the forward trenches, and Texas Capt. Sam Foster recorded the gist of the conversation: "We find Georgia troops in our front, and our boys tell them that if they run that we will shoot them, and no mistake."[50]

Thomas Mangham's regiment had suffered four killed and forty wounded from Resaca to New Hope Church, so he and his friends probably were grateful that they took part in no more major engagements on the Dallas-New Hope Church line. Their big fight on May 25 was the first time that the citizens of Atlanta, only twenty-five miles away, had heard the rumble of gunfire. The distant muttering became the townspeople's constant companion over the next three months, however, as Johnston fell back to Kennesaw, Smyrna, and eventually crossed the Chattahoochee River. One wonders what Thomas and his comrades thought of the fact that each stand eventually gave way to further repositioning or retreat. Some of Captain Foster's hard-fighting Texans complained that "we are going to Florida and put in a pontoon bridge over to Cuba and go over there." Other men believed implicitly that "Old Joe" Johnston was doing the right thing, conserving their strength for the day when Sherman made a false move and invited a shattering riposte. Historian Richard McMurry makes a convincing case that no real consensus existed in the Army of Tennessee, since opinions depended on a number of factors that varied over time and from one unit to the next.[51]

Beyond all doubt, however, was the wear and tear caused by unrelenting duty in the trenches and on the march. These physical and mental strains were not limited to either side. One Illinois captain grumped, "One should either be wrapped in rubber from head to toe or else go about stark naked, because there is nothing halfway about the rain in Georgia." A New Yorker, jotting down notes in his diary, realized later that daily thunderstorms had drenched the opposing armies for three straight weeks after May 25. For the ragged Rebs, the strain increased exponentially when General Hood replaced Johnston on July 18. Robert Patrick, a quartermaster's clerk in Gibson's Brigade, grumbled in his diary about the "unexpected and startling announcement," which he attributed to the baleful influence of "old Bragg." Like other soldiers throughout the Confederate army, Patrick knew Hood's reputation as a "fighting man," and he had heard about Hood's threat to fight with his corps alone rather than retreat below the Chattahoochee without giving battle. In his view, this was "all very fine talk, but we are not strong enough to go into a pitched battle. If we had been

Johnston would have tried it long before this. From what I can learn the army is dissatisfied with the change."[52]

Hood wasted no time launching major counterattacks. Patrick was in the rear with the quartermaster trains on July 20, when he scribbled down an impression of the sounds reaching him there: "Fighting like 'hell a beating tan b[a]rk.' It appears to be about our centre. They are at it hot and heavy." He was hearing the ferocious gunfire at Peachtree Creek, where a well-conceived but poorly coordinated Confederate assault gave both sides due notice that Hood was living up to his reputation for aggressive tactics. By the next day, Patrick was scribbling the army's unofficial verdict in his notebook: "There seems to be general dissatisfaction among the men on account of the headlong way in which they were put in yesterday, and they think that 'it costs more than it comes to.'" Hood nevertheless struck another hard blow just two days after the first, unleashing a terrific attack that threatened to overwhelm the Union left at a bald hill between Atlanta and Decatur. Despite areas of local success, the ferocious onslaught resulted in yet another costly repulse.[53]

Although the miscues of their acting division commander kept Gibson's troops out of the savage fighting on July 22, further blundering by their new corps commander put them smack in the middle of hard times at Ezra Church on July 28. Mounting casualties among high-level commanders had led to the installation of 30-year-old Stephen Dill Lee as corps commander just days earlier, and he flung his troops impulsively at the Federal right flank in a foredoomed attempt to crush it. Hood had dispatched Lee's Corps to the left to block Sherman's attempt to slip around Atlanta to the west and south, intending to follow up with another corps that would attack the Federals on July 29. Lee thought he had caught the enemy on the move, however, so he launched Brown's Division in a hasty assault upon Maj. Gen. Oliver O. Howard's troops north of the quaintly named Lick Skillet Road.[54]

When Brown's three brigades faltered in their initial assaults, Lee sent a staff officer to order Clayton's Division forward at once. General Henry Clayton had commanded a fine Alabama brigade in Stewart's Division before earning promotion when "Old Straight" took over Polk's Corps. Clayton was forming his men in line of battle on Brown's right, preparing to send them forward with Gibson's Brigade on the left, Holtzclaw on the right, and Baker in support. Gibson had dispatched Austin's Sharpshooters to the front to "develop" the enemy, before riding over to the right to coordinate his attack with Holtzclaw and Clayton. Unfortunately for the Confederates, however, one of Lee's staff officers went straight to Gibson's Brigade while its commander was absent, and apparently issued the attack order to the first colonel he met. This was Leon von Zinken of the 20th Louisiana, whom Gibson had assigned to command the brigade's left. Whatever the staff officer said must have been convincing, because von Zinken obeyed without waiting to consult with Gibson. It was a fateful mistake.[55]

When Gibson rode back to his brigade's position, he encountered a situation that commonly occurs in commanders' nightmares: his brigade had disappeared! As he indignantly reported, ". . .to my astonishment I found it had been moved forward without any order from me or any notice to me. . . ," and one can imagine the fury with which he galloped through the woods to find his errant formation. He was too late, for his troops had advanced briskly to the attack, although they could "smell the biggest kind of rot." Moving out at the quick step, they had driven in the Federal skirmishers and confronted well-built earthworks at the junction between two brigades. Unsupported on either flank, the men lay down in the open and fired at the Federal position in an unequal fight that was a mirror image of New Hope Church. Upholding their reputation as one of the best brigades in the Army of Tennessee, they blazed away with "energy and obstinacy" for an hour. The contest was hopeless from their exposed positions, however, and when Baker's Brigade was unable to force its way through the underbrush in time to join Gibson in a combined assault, the Louisianian pulled his survivors back into a ravine in obedience to Clayton's orders.[56]

Lee continued to fling troops at the well-sited Union position that afternoon, even convincing Stewart to support the uncoordinated assaults as his fresh divisions arrived. These simply added to a horrifically one-sided casualty toll, which apparently reached some three thousand Confederates against only 632 Federals. Fully half the men in Gibson's Brigade were numbered among those killed, wounded, or missing, with two-thirds of the brigade's left wing "completely used up" in the fruitless assaults. The 19th Louisiana was part of the left wing, and Private Cater's memoirs indicate that it lost sixteen killed, 98 wounded, and ten missing in the attack. Gibson sadly reported "the loss of some of my best and bravest officers and men" in the afternoon's fighting, which accomplished precious little for the price paid. Although the attacks stopped Sherman's attempt to cut off Atlanta from the west and south, the Confederates would have achieved the same result simply by placing Lee's Corps in the entrenchments the troops dug that night.[57] Lieutenant General Hardee was dismayed at the headlong assault, commenting acidly: "No action of the campaign probably did so much to demoralize and dishearten the troops engaged in it." Robert Patrick was aghast: "Hood will have our whole army killed off if he doesn't change his policy. . . .He is entirely too reckless." Patrick could only issue all available clothing to his regiment's wounded men and try to help them keep the plague of flies at bay: "The flies are awful. In spite of all that can be done, they will deposit maggots in the wounds of the men, and there is scarcely a wound that is not full of them."[58]

The subsequent skirmishing along the new lines "amounted to almost an engagement" for a week in early August, in Lee's words, but no major assaults disturbed the dangerous and exhausting routine of trench duties throughout the remainder of the month. Apparently Lee took this opportunity to lecture his troops on the offensive-mindedness he sought to re-instill after the "lack of spirit" some brigades had displayed at Ezra Church. Taking his cue from General Hood, the young corps commander believed that his men had lost the spirit necessary to charge the enemy in prepared defenses, although he might have done better to listen to the concerns of men who had seen it and done it throughout the summer. Private Douglas Cater stood near Lee as he addressed the men, and the Louisiana private remembered his scolding: "Soldiers, you can take temporary breastworks, you must and you shall take temporary breastworks." Cater added, "This was what he felt about it, but he was not in the charge on foot with a musket when our men were forced back, and it seemed to me that he might have had better success with his speech if he had used different language." Doubtless many in his regiment and brigade, even the whole army, shared the young private's conclusions: "I was near him when he spoke and it made me feel like he had lost respect for us. He certainly had no more at stake than the rest of us. I was sorry he said it."[59]

The *Official Records* display a number of reports and memoranda on the subject of aggressive action on the picket lines, about which Lee censured his brigade commanders if he found them lacking. But when he next launched his men in a full-scale assault at Jonesboro on August 31, he again found fault with the spirit displayed by many of his units. Hardee's and Lee's corps had marched south of Atlanta to confront Sherman's forces after the Union commander initiated yet another wide sweep to the west and south, but the grayclad infantrymen once more faced overwhelming odds. The bulk of Sherman's army was on the move, and Hood's injunction to Hardee to drive them into the Flint River was unrealistic. About 20,000 Federal troops were on the field at Jonesboro, where they prepared breastworks to receive the assault of an approximately equal number of Confederates. Barring some unexpected failure by the Federals, such an equation was the calculus of disaster.[60]

Private Thomas Mangham was one of Lee's thousands of dog-tired men who marched all night to reach Jonesboro, and most of them had gotten little or no sleep in the last 48 hours. Thousands straggled along the roadside, shoeless, exhausted and "used up." These men had held the trenches on Atlanta's northeastern and northwestern sides during the preceding weeks, and many probably thought the city was lost if the Federals had swung this far south. They nevertheless obeyed orders to charge that afternoon, but many men of Anderson's Division kept their distance from the Yankee earthworks and traded shots at long range. Gibson's men were in the second line of attack with the other brigades of Clayton's Division, and they pressed through the hesitant remnants of the leading waves toward the distant entrenchments. Although .58 caliber slugs dropped man after man as they charged across the open fields east of the Flint River, Gibson reported that "officers and men all behaved with great intrepidity" under the withering fire. Clayton saw Gibson seize a regimental battle flag and lead the charge personally, creating "the greatest enthusiasm throughout his command." Shrieking the Rebel yell, they swept across the enemy's rifle pits and up to the main defensive line. Some of the Louisianians, however, held up at the rifle pits and began firing from the cover of a fenceline. In the face of enemy reinforcements and the hesitation of their own supports, Gibson and his leading troops had to pull back.[61]

In the fifteen-minute charge through the open fields, the Louisiana Brigade lost almost half its numbers in killed and wounded. Nevertheless, the men fell in with a will when Gibson ordered them to prepare for a second effort. The hard-fighting general declared, "I never saw a better spirit manifested than when called upon to reform for the purpose of making a second attack. Every officer and man was in his place and ready to advance."[62] As his report clearly indicates, he was hard pressed to understand what had gone wrong. "I never saw a more gallant charge, or one that so fully promised success." Clayton also was dazzled by the brigade's assault and puzzled by its failure, musing in his report, "Never was a charge begun with such enthusiasm terminated with accomplishing so little." Although 48 of those who fell belonged to the 19th Louisiana, one of the men present when the Claiborne Volunteers mustered after the battle was Private Mangham. Once again, he had survived the long odds faced by the Confederate infantryman.[63]

The desperate charge of Gibson's Brigade on August 31 was clearly an exception, for Confederate and Union observers generally agreed that the assault of Hardee's and Lee's corps was a "feeble effort." General Hardee canceled a renewed attack when staff officers assessed that a Federal counterattack was liable to rout Lee's dispirited troops. Major Taylor of the 47th Ohio commented that the Confederate assault at Jonesboro was the "least determined" he had ever seen Southerners deliver. He was in a good position to recognize the symptoms, because his own regiment suffered from the same malady after four months of relentless pounding. His men had practically mutinied in early August when ordered to retake some rifle pits near Ezra Church, and he had to shove them forward and shame them into advancing at all.[64] In fact, the only reason three Federal army corps were entrenched outside Jonesboro at month's end is because they dug in the moment they glimpsed Confederates entrenched in town in front of them! These grayclad defenders numbered merely four brigades of infantrymen. Acknowledging Howard's report that he had stopped several hundred yards short of the railroad, Sherman had grumbled, "I cannot move the troops 100 yards without their stopping to intrench, though I have not seen an enemy." Men on both sides were tired of charging a foe hidden behind mounds of red Georgia clay, and the results on August 31 simply confirmed the soldiers' conclusions: the entrenched bluecoats reported only 172 casualties in a battle that disorganized Lee's entire corps. Howard's men had shot down their opponents at a rate of thirteen to one, inflicting at least 2200 casualties on the Confederates.[65]

*   *   *   *   *

When Lee's Corps marched back towards Atlanta that night in response to Hood's orders, all hope was gone of hurling the army in a victorious flank attack to destroy Sherman along the Flint River; now its march had the depressing objective of covering the military evacuation of the city. Sherman's forces had a stranglehold on the railroad after surviving Hardee's riposte on August 31, so Atlanta was doomed. So were its defenders unless they withdrew rapidly, and their escape from Atlanta was only due to good fortune and Sherman's negligence. The Federal commander apparently was ready to rest his troops once Atlanta was in his hands, even though Hood's army remained intact. When the opposing armies faced off at Lovejoy's Station for several days after the two-day battle at Jonesboro, Sherman terminated his campaign. He withdrew to Atlanta to rest and refit his troops for their next move. Although it took him six more weeks to get underway, he was bound for the Georgia seacoast.[66]

*   *   *   *   *

574

The Army of Tennessee was down but not out. Men like those in the ranks of the Claiborne Volunteers had marched several hundred miles that summer in the fighting retreat to Atlanta, and General Hood was planning a foray into Tennessee that would call upon every ounce of leg drive they could summon. After regrouping in Palmetto, Georgia, they struck out on September 29, 1864, bound for Sherman's lines of communication to Chattanooga. Snatching up some unlucky garrisons and repelled by others, the army moved rapidly out of Sherman's reach to the west. While he turned back to "make Georgia howl" in his March to the Sea, his antagonists trekked across the mountains into northern Alabama. The 19th Louisiana lost a man in helping Gibson capture crossings over the Tennessee River at Florence, where he routed a 200-man Federal garrison on October 30. The Louisiana soldiers remained there for three weeks to recruit their strength, for the hard marching, mud, rain, cold, and almost non-existent rations were destroying the health of men whose bodies were already worn down by the hardships of the previous months. Official returns dated November 7 indicate that Gibson's Brigade had 1004 men present, but an effective total of only 619. Confederate returns typically excluded officers, the sick, and detailed men such as teamsters and clerks from their "effective totals," which reflected only the number of armed men in ranks. Of 447 men still on the regimental rolls, the 19th Louisiana had only 201 men present, with 140 effectives.[67]

Surviving records imply that Thomas remained in ranks as the tattered legions moved north on November 20, so he probably crossed the Duck River with his regiment on the last day of that month. They could hear the roar of gunfire up ahead at Franklin that evening, and formed line of battle that night upon their arrival. Darkness prevented their employment, however, and the resulting Federal retreat left the Louisianians unmolested to view the field of incredible carnage the next day. Private Douglas Cater's appalled reaction was representative of those who saw the ditch in front of the deserted Federal breastworks: "We found the trenches filled—not half filled—but filled with dead men, both Federals and Confederates." H. A. McFarland of the Claiborne Grays recalled it simply as "a ghastly scene of the dead and dying."[68]

Franklin was the hecatomb of the Army of Tennessee, the army whose commander had reproached its inordinate fear of charging breastworks. Casualty records are spotty at best, due perhaps to Hood's desire to avoid facing the gravity of the disaster, or possibly to the fact that the slaughter annihilated the chain of command that normally prepared such reports. With the loss of 65 regimental, brigade, and division commanders in only five hours' fighting that felled approximately 7000 Confederates (and 2600 Federals), administrative accuracy was a minor concern to many in the aftermath of battle.[69]

Three days later, Gibson's men, in the vanguard of the advancing army with other brigades of Clayton's Division, arrived before Maj. Gen. George Thomas's defenses at Nashville, driving away Union videttes from the hills south of town. Hood promptly went to ground, entrenching his force on ground won by Clayton's Division. Here, where Thomas Mangham's first cousin, *John R. Mangham* (see Chapter VIII), had died during the epidemics that swept Terry's Texas Rangers in the war's early days, the ill-clad Louisianians dug holes to get below the windswept surface as they awaited developments. Hood had little clear idea of doing anything other than provoking an enemy attack, then capitalizing on a defensive victory to follow a defeated enemy into Nashville. As they waited, the chilly weather became deadly cold, plummeting to ten degrees below zero as northwest winds gusted across three inches of ice and snow. Thousands of Confederates in the freezing hills lacked shoes, and few had more than one blanket to compensate for the lack of an overcoat.[70]

Hood certainly provoked the attack he sought, but the only army fleeing its pursuers afterwards was his own, headed back south. The first blow fell on December 15, when Thomas feinted at Hood's right and struck hard at his left. With 70,000

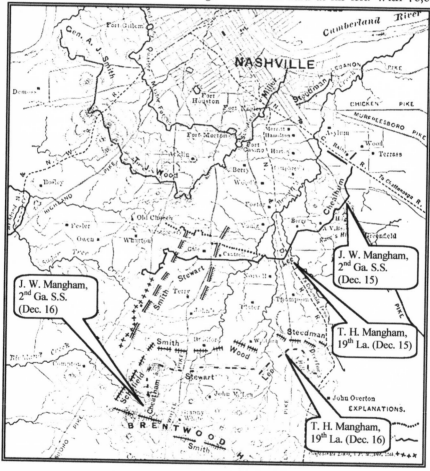

NASHVILLE, DECEMBER 15-16, 1864.
THOMAS MANGHAM WAS IN LEE'S CORPS; JOHN W. MANGHAM (CH. II AND
APPENDIX, REF. #190) WAS IN CHEATHAM'S CORPS.

Federal soldiers opposing 23,000 Confederates, the attackers could reach past the defenders' flanks with relative ease. Gibson's Louisiana troops were the leftmost brigade in Lee's Corps, which was on the center-right of Hood's defensive line. They remained unengaged most of the day, until bad news from the left caused Clayton to order Gibson out of his trenches, which faced north, and form his brigade in line of battle facing due west. Outflanked Confederate units had given way in Stewart's and Cheatham's corps on the left and center, and were fleeing to the rear in a collapse reminiscent of Missionary Ridge. The repositioning of Gibson's Brigade provided Lee's Corps a thin shield between it and the enemy sweeping into its flank and rear.[71]

Although Gibson threw forward a strong skirmish line to engage the approaching enemy in the twilight, the onset of darkness providentially halted the Federal pursuit. Incredibly, however, Hood directed his retreating troops into a new defensive line several miles farther south. Even more incredible, perhaps, is the fact that the routed units obeyed his orders. Stephen Lee marshaled his corps into its new positions, which remained on the army's right. Clayton's Division entrenched Overton Hill with fishhook-shaped works curving around its northern and eastern faces, refusing the line to anchor the extreme right flank. The rightmost brigade, under Stovall, formed the curved portion of the hook, facing east. Holtzclaw's Brigade extended to Stovall's left, aiming its guns down the north face of the hill and stretching across the Franklin Pike. Gibson's Brigade, again the division's left flank unit, formed on Holtzclaw's left, sheltering behind a stone fence on level ground just a stone's throw west of the pike, where they faced due north. As Private Cater recalled, "Our brigade was behind a rock fence, which made us feel pretty safe, but we worked all night to make it stronger."[72]

When Thomas launched a gigantic flanking movement against the Confederate left that morning, he planned for his troops to do little more than occupy the attentions of Hood's right. Thomas, however, gave his two corps commanders in this sector, Wood and Steedman, discretion to push hard against Hood's right if they perceived any attractive opportunities. Wood decided to try to smash the defenses on Overton Hill and cut off any Confederate retreat to the south, and accordingly concentrated six batteries of artillery in a converging fire that devastated the hilltop positions in a two-hour barrage. In the early hours of the afternoon, four Federal brigades surged towards Overton Hill and the stone fence to its west.[73]

Although the attacking brigades fought hard to reach the breastworks, the withering defensive fire cut them down in droves. Gibson could not tell if the men charging his position comprised one large brigade or two small ones, but his Louisiana regiments poured lead into every blue wave that approached their stone fence. Nobody got closer than 75 yards to the rifle muzzles spitting lead over the wall, and Gibson estimated enemy casualties as 200 killed and between seven and nine hundred wounded. Although the assaults nearly reached the breastworks on Overton Hill itself, the slaughter there was just as intense. Clayton supposed that the tenacious attacks had cost the enemy 1500 to 2000 killed and wounded, with one black regiment, the 18th U.S. Colored Troops, losing five color bearers within a few yards of his works. One of Holtzclaw's lieutenants retrieved the trophy after the attackers scattered for safety.[74]

Clayton had received timely succor from two additional brigades in the crisis, affording him much-needed firepower on a front that often had five feet between defenders. They had inflicted a stunningly one-sided defeat on their foes, who suffered more than a thousand casualties in this sector, or about one-third of the entire Federal loss in the two-day battle. Colonel Abel D. Streight commanded a brigade in the second line of attackers, but his men were so roughly handled that he wound up struggling to reform his shattered ranks to resist the counterattack he feared. He labored in vain, however, as nobody from his brigade (or the one in front) would rally short of the protection of friendly breastworks. Clayton's Division "was in the highest state of enthusiasm" over its success when the Alabama general received a puzzling message, which stated that Lee expected him to bring his division off the field "in order." Unbeknownst to the defenders of Overton Hill, Thomas's grand left wheel movement had wrapped around the flank and rear of Cheatham's Corps on the Confederate left, stretching it until it broke. Cheatham's brigades were facing north, west, and south. His men saw Federals in every direction they looked, and when an assaulting column loomed up at point-blank range in front of one poorly sited brigade, the defenders' surprised and inaccurate volley signaled the onset of hand-to-hand combat. As they were swamped, an adjacent brigade took to its heels and the chase began. Unraveling from left to right, the Confederate line completely disintegrated in minutes. With all hope lost, thousands surrendered, while more ran for their lives.[75]

Gibson saw troops fleeing into the Franklin Pike and began changing front to the left as on the previous day, but he had gone to this well one time too many. His report admitted that "at this time confusion prevailed over everything." In other words, some of his brigade melted through his fingers in the race for the rear. The same thing happened to Holtzclaw, leaving Stovall's men as the only fully organized brigade in the army. Clayton was able to form much of his division a mile to the rear, offering enough resistance to keep pursuers at arm's length. That night and throughout the next day, the brigades of Gibson, Holtzclaw, and Stovall played critical roles in desperate rear guard actions; the Confederate division that cleared the way into Nashville two weeks earlier now fought the last actions on the way out. As thousands of bluecoated cavalrymen pushed down every road leading south to Franklin, Gibson's 250 remaining Louisiana troops had to cut their way down to the Harpeth River crossings. A section of artillery provided them some cover in their retreat, and Gibson's men returned the favor by standing in the road and blasting a cavalry charge to pieces. The artillerymen capitalized on the respite to limber to the rear and cross the river, leaving the Louisianians "entirely surrounded" by horsemen. Another desperate action occurred that evening some six miles south of town, where Gibson combined his forces with Stovall's in a 360-degree combat that smashed another cavalry advance, killing many and capturing both enemy colors and prisoners. As the saucy cavalrymen were finding out to their chagrin, the wasp still had a stinger in its tail.[76]

Gibson's exhausted survivors crossed the Duck River on December 19, and Private Mangham and the other men waded the frigid, fast-flowing waters of Shoal Creek on Christmas Day. A day later they crossed the Tennessee River and turned west, heading for Tupelo, which the Claiborne Volunteers reached on the day after New Year's. The scene put Douglas Cater in mind of the hopeful days in the summer of 1862, when he was part of a "fine army" stationed there. Now the decimated, exhausted remnants of the old commands encamped at the same place, but "nearly half of our soldiers were sick." Many had suffered through the butchery at Franklin and the freezing hills outside Nashville in hopes that their sacrifice would redeem long-suffering Tennessee from the invader, but the mid-December disaster proved these hopes to be chimerical.[77]

Thomas moved out once more with the 19th Louisiana as it struck out for West Point on January 25, arriving three days later. The brigade was bound for the defenses of Mobile after another short rest, but many of its men were heading home on furlough instead. Hood had instituted a liberal furlough policy on January 15, granting leave to one out of every seven men in regiments from west of the Mississippi River. Of course, these fortunate ones needed still more luck to cross the enemy-held river, which had barred their way home since the fall of Vicksburg and Port Hudson in July 1863. The men were nonetheless overjoyed at the prospect of seeing loved ones again, and probably viewed the risks as minimal compared to the trials they had undergone.[78]

Hood's furlough scheme merely granted a veneer of official approval to a mass exodus he could no longer control, as many of the shattered survivors were "voting with their feet." One modern estimate concludes that his 38,000-man force had suffered about 23,500 casualties in the Tennessee Campaign, and few survivors had any further doubt about the eventual outcome. One of those who left camp, furlough or no furlough, was Pvt. Thomas Hamilton Mangham, who set course for home on January 29, 1865. The veteran of Jackson, Chickamauga, Rocky Face Ridge, Resaca, New Hope Church, Ezra Church, Jonesboro, and Nashville, as well as many skirmishes in between, joined about half of his fellow survivors in going home. They had given it their best shot, but now concluded that the Confederacy was "gone up the spout" despite their almost superhuman efforts. Union Maj. Gen. John M. Schofield's army had narrowly survived its encounters with them in Tennessee, and he pronounced a fitting epitaph on their dogged endurance: "I doubt if any soldiers in the world ever needed so much cumulative evidence to convince them that they were beaten."[79]

The Claiborne Volunteers, by their count, had marched five hundred miles in the fighting retreat from Dalton to Atlanta, then another *two thousand* miles from Atlanta to Nashville and back to Tupelo. The muster rolls indicate that Private Mangham was present the whole time, although he may have missed some marches or battles due to unrecorded illness or wounds. Last paid by the army at the end of April 1864, he was in no position to pay for transportation home, even if any had been available. When Thomas started out on his final march of the Civil War, he became the only one of thirty-seven Mangham Confederate soldiers officially declared to have deserted his regiment during the four years of bitter warfare.[80]

From West Point, Mississippi to Claiborne Parish, Louisiana, is approximately 350 miles.

* * * * *

Thomas returned home in time to make a small crop that summer. Sketchy parish records from 1866 show that he raised three bales of cotton and two hundred bushels of corn during the preceding year. The parish assessor distinctly inscribed the name "T. H. Mangham" on his tax rolls, but time has meted out rough treatment to these records. The faded rolls provide the last glimpse of Thomas Hamilton Mangham before he faded into the obscurity of his anguished country.[81]

*   *   *   *   *

William C. Oates, the Alabama governor whose empty sleeve bespoke his four years of wartime service as captain and colonel of the 15th Alabama Infantry, mused on the topic of desertion in his postwar memoir. He concluded simply, "I never have had in my heart any ill-feeling nor have I used harsh words toward the poor man who fought faithfully for three years and then, seeing how things were going, deserted to get out of the war."[82]

3. "THE RAVENOUS GARFISH WAX FAT": SGT. ARTHUR G. MANGHAM, JR. AND PVT. WILLIAM J. MANGHAM, "WALMSLEY GUARDS," CO. B, 11TH LOUISIANA BATTALION, LATER CO. K, CRESCENT REGIMENT; AND PVT. JOSIAH T. MANGHAM, "CLAIBORNE INVINCIBLES," CO. D, 28TH LOUISIANA

Three years earlier, Thomas was in the trenches at Corinth when headlines in the *Natchitoches Union* of May 15, 1862 announced the "Occupation of New Orleans by the Federals." Just a few miles down the Red River from the Mangham family's settlement at Coushatta Chute, Natchitoches was a thriving commercial town in the middle of Louisiana's prime cotton producing districts. The port of New Orleans was the destination of Red River cotton, however, and the shocking news of the Crescent City's capture guaranteed economic hardship for the planters of northwestern Louisiana. Thomas's 48-year-old father, Arthur Green Mangham, had listed his occupation as planter when the census taker came around in 1860, but his mechanical skills of tanning and shoemaking soon became priceless in the economic and social upheavals that ravaged wartime Louisiana. With the entire Trans-Mississippi Confederacy absolutely desperate for leather by mid-1862, Arthur probably worked overtime throughout the war to help supply civilians and the army alike.[83]

These hardships resulted in large part from the early capture of New Orleans, but nobody could ascertain the eventual outcome amid the rapid drumfire of military developments. The outcome was a foregone conclusion unless Southerners nerved themselves to renewed exertions, however, and the same mid-May issue of the *Union* announced a resolution by public committees in Bossier and Caddo Parishes to burn their cotton if Federal forces approached. The newspaper also proclaimed the mustering-in of a new military company in Natchitoches: the "Walmsley Guards," commanded by Capt. George W. Holloway. Choosing their nickname in honor of a prominent townsman who probably paid to equip the company, the 110 officers and men mustered into Confederate service for three years or the war on May 6, 1862.[84]

Two of those who raised their right hands that spring day were *Arthur Green Mangham, Jr.*, and his first cousin *William J. Mangham*, both of whom listed themselves as farmers residing in Natchitoches Parish. Young Arthur was born in Russell County, Alabama on February 21, 1844, and his enlistment documents portray a tall youth who stood five feet, eleven and a half inches high, with fair complexion, light hair, and hazel eyes. He apparently had attended little if any school, as he signed the document with the "x" that appears so often in Confederate records. William apparently was a son of Josiah Thomas Mangum, Jr., and like his younger brothers *John*, Robert, *Josiah Thomas*, and *Bush*, he accompanied his aunts and uncles as they migrated westward in the 1850s (see diagram on page 518). Stating his place of birth as Granville County, North Carolina and his age as 34 upon enlistment in May 1862, William was 5' 3 ¼" tall with blue eyes, dark hair, and a fair complexion. Unlike his younger cousin Arthur, he was able to sign "W. J. Mangham" in a crimped hand on his oath of enlistment.[85]

The Walmsley Guards became Company B of Maj. J. D. Shelley's 11th Battalion Louisiana Infantry when they rendezvoused with four other companies from Natchitoches, Sabine, and DeSoto parishes at Mansfield on May 14 and elected field officers. By this time, Holloway had another 32 men on his company rolls, and the battalion was ready to go into camp. The end of June found Arthur and William present for duty at Camp Shelley, near Monroe, where the battalion had grown to a total of six companies and 580 men. In a department starved for military equipment of any description, they probably began learning the rudiments of drill and guard duty with few if any guns. The Conscription Act had become law in April, but the chaos attending the fall of New Orleans had prevented any effective mobilization of the state's remaining military resources. There was not a single Confederate officer in the state west of the Mississippi River to assume the task of training the new volunteer levies, and Governor Moore had no established camps or depots in which to drill the new men. His militia officers were completing the enrollment of men eligible for conscription, but had no place to put the men into camp and no equipment to issue.[86]

Brigadier General Albert G. Blanchard, dispatched by the Confederate government to assist in Louisiana's mobilization, arrived at Monroe on July 12. He established Camp Blanchard near Bawcumville, just outside Monroe, to provide a camp of instruction for the units organizing in the northern part of the state. Shelley's 11th Louisiana Battalion moved there sometime in July or early August, and continued its training while Blanchard desperately sought to organize a force able to prevent Yankee incursions from the Mississippi River. Just sixty miles east of Monroe by rail stood the town of Tallulah, the eastern terminus of the Vicksburg, Shreveport & Texas Railroad; given the growing danger to Vicksburg, just a few miles farther east, it was predictable that Union forces soon would look towards Tallulah and even Monroe. Down at Baton Rouge a Confederate attack in early August convinced the Federals to evacuate the state capital and move downriver, but there was precious little but their own inertia keeping them there. The same applied to the northern approaches to the Vicksburg area, where a Federal flotilla of seven gunboats and five transports provided them the capability of descending without warning on either bank of the river. By the end of

August, the troops in Blanchard's sub-district of the District of Western Louisiana comprised only Shelley's battalion, two green Louisiana infantry regiments, a scattering of Partisan Ranger cavalry companies, and Benton's Battery of light artillery. Confederate inspector Capt. T. J. Mackey reported that these 2500 raw troops had a "heavy sick list" by the end of August, with only about one thousand men fit for duty. They had only 1200 stands of arms all told, mostly shotguns, and the dearth of weapons prevented the enrollment of another 4000 men of military age. This unprepossessing force was supposed to defend all of Louisiana above the Red River.[87]

If Arthur and William had the opportunity to meet Benton's cannoneers, they probably were pleased to meet their third cousin, *Cpl. Henry G. Mangham* (Chapter III). Henry probably remembered Arthur, Sr. and his brothers Thomas H. and James Green Mangham from his days in Russell County, Alabama, where they all lived from the late 1830s through the 1840s. In all likelihood, Henry had seen young Arthur there while the latter was but a babe in arms, and the idea of an all-encompassing civil war was nothing but a will-o'-the-wisp to scare the grown-ups.

*　　*　　*　　*　　*

When the 902 men of Col. Henry Gray's 28th Louisiana Volunteers marched into Camp Blanchard on July 28, another Mangham reunion was imminent. Gray's regiment was a north Louisiana outfit through and through, and Capt. Marcus O. Cheatham's "Claiborne Invincibles" hailed from the parish where William's brother *Josiah Thomas Mangham* lived. Just four days after the regiment's arrival at Blanchard, he mustered into Cheatham's company as a private for three years or the war. Apparently, his regiment was the first to occupy the new camp of instruction, so he probably was there already when Shelley's Battalion arrived. Civil War soldiers always kept an eye out for companies from their home areas, so he probably inquired after relatives with Shelley's two Natchitoches companies. In all probability, it did not take him long to find his brother and cousin in the Walmsley Guards.[88]

Born in North Carolina, he and his brother Robert had moved into the James Green Mangham household in Russell County by 1850, just a short time after his father and namesake died. The census taker that year recorded the 20-year-old youth's name as Thomas, indicating that he went by his middle name, as did his Uncle Green. His ten-year-old brother *John R. Mangham* (see Chapter VIII) lived nearby with their aunt, Jemima Mangham Sockwell, but no records indicate William's whereabouts at that time. When Arthur and Green Mangham moved to Louisiana in the early 1850s, they initially settled in the piney hills of Claiborne Parish, in the far northwestern portion of the state. Arthur moved down to Coushatta Chute near Natchitoches within a few years, but Green remained in Claiborne on a fine 700-acre farm near the hamlet of Gordon. By 1860, he and his wife, Martha Elizabeth Gray Mangham, planted 120 acres of this land in cotton, corn, wheat, and sweet potatoes, harvesting 26 bales of cotton and 500 bushels apiece of corn and sweet potatoes. His real estate alone was valued at four thousand dollars, and the whole concern amounted to a very prosperous farm, if not a small plantation. Although Green and Martha had seven children by this time, the eldest were twins Mary and Sarah, who didn't turn twelve until December of that year. As his nine slaves included only one man and two women of working age, Green obviously did much of his own work, along with hired help.[89]

His 29-year-old nephew Thomas lived in or near the nearby village of Colquit, where he owned real estate worth a thousand dollars and personal property valued at an additional three hundred dollars. The census taker listed him as "J. T. Mangham," which is how most documents of the era record his name. Thomas lived just a few houses away from his aunt and uncle, Jemima Mangham Sockwell and William Sockwell, and gave his occupation as carpenter. Perhaps his 240 acres comprised pinelands yet uncleared for cultivation, because no record exists of his agricultural production in 1860. Since carpentry was a seasonal trade, he may have helped his Uncle Green make his crop in Gordon until he got his own farm underway.[90]

The outbreak of war in 1861 knocked any such plans into a cocked hat, although Thomas waited until conscription was well underway in north Louisiana before volunteering in the summer of 1862. The confusion attending the state's mass mobilization meant that Gray's 28th Louisiana reported at Camp Blanchard on July 28 without so much as a single musket, even though it had been in service since mid-May, drilling at an encampment near Vienna. There was even confusion over the unit's proper designation, as a south Louisiana regiment under the command of Col. Allen Thomas also received the title "28th Louisiana." Months elapsed before the matter of precedence was resolved in favor of Gray's outfit. Major General Richard "Dick" Taylor, newly assigned commander of the District of Western Louisiana, considered Gray's regiment "excellent material"; he noted that autumn, however, that the poorly instructed and ill-equipped men were suffering severely from the camp diseases that typically beset new regiments. They had moved up to a new camp near Bayou Macon, probably near Delhi, where they were performing picket duty near Milliken's Bend on the Mississippi River. Taylor, however, directed Gray to move his men "by easy marches" to the Teche country in the warmer climes of south Louisiana. That November the regiment arrived at Avery Island, and on December 20 it passed through New Iberia en route to garrison Fort Bisland, below Franklin.[91]

Shelley's 11th Louisiana Battalion had transferred from Camp Blanchard back to nearby Camp Shelley that fall, then moved east to Delhi to guard the Vicksburg, Shreveport & Texas Railroad. They got a scare on Christmas morning as Maj. Gen. William T. Sherman landed some 32,000 Federal troops at Milliken's Bend. Although his attention was riveted on the approaches to Vicksburg, Sherman dispatched A. J. Smith's division in the direction of Delhi to block Confederate attempts to supply the riverfront fortress from west of the Mississippi. General Blanchard incurred Taylor's wrath by pulling his puny force back towards Monroe without firing a shot, so it took only forty bluecoated cavalrymen to ransack Delhi and burn the railroad depot. Smith's raiders were only 2000 strong, but Blanchard's timidity prevented a thousand Louisiana troops from striking a single blow in defense of their native soil. When the raiding force pulled back on December 26, it returned unmolested to Sherman's army as it prepared to assault Chickasaw Bluffs. Sherman had no worries about problems in his rear, but the defenders in his front would prove equal to the task of stopping him cold.[92]

Arthur and William Mangham were present in ranks when the Walmsley Guards mustered at Delhi at year's end. Shelley's Battalion soon received orders, however, to march southward to Rosedale, west of Baton Rouge, before moving up to the vicinity of Simmesport. Company B garrisoned Fort DeRussy, a grandly named earthwork on the lower Red River. General Taylor's District of Western Louisiana encompassed a maze of waterways that made a sieve of any possible defensive alignment, and "every little bayou capable of floating a cock-boat called loudly for forts and heavy guns." He could spare only ten 24- and 32-pounder guns salvaged from the waters of Berwick's Bay and Barataria Pass, where they had been dumped after the surrender of New Orleans, so he had to parcel out them out carefully. Even after detailed reconnaissance established the most effective locations, he had to accept significant risk. Eventually he divided the precious ordnance between DeRussy on the Red River, Fort Beauregard on the Ouachita, and Fort Burton at Butte a la Rose on the Atchafalaya. Although he considered these to be "mere water batteries to prevent the passage of gunboats" and did not expect them to repel serious attacks by land, Taylor proudly maintained that they served their intended purpose admirably.[93]

Arthur and William may have been at Fort DeRussy on February 14, 1863, when gunners of the Crescent Battery disabled the Federal steam ram *Queen of the West*. Confederate troops took possession of the vessel and refitted her for operations against her former owners, and General Taylor noted that many Louisiana and Texas troops "smuggled themselves aboard" the *Queen* in anticipation of such exploits. She and the *Webb* rammed and captured the Federal ironclad *Indianola* just two weeks later, but Taylor's memoirs are the only source mentioning Louisianians among her crew of Texas, Tennessee, and even Maryland troops.[94]

Likewise, it is uncertain whether Thomas Mangham was among the men of the 28th Louisiana who helped capture the Federal gunboat *Diana* near Pattersonville on the Atchafalaya River, not far from Fort Bisland. The *Diana* had poked her nose into the network of rivers and bayous above the Union stronghold of Brashear City (now Morgan City), preparatory to a major thrust towards the Red River. Colonel Gray helped set a trap for her on March 28, when two Texas cavalry battalions, the Valverde artillery battery, and 120 of Gray's Louisiana infantrymen triggered a bloody ambush at a range of only fifty yards. The hurricane of fire overwhelmed the Federal gunners, who managed to discharge a few rounds and kill nine cavalry horses before they "were swept away as if they had all been struck by lightening [sic]." The *Diana* drifted downstream for two miles under the relentless gunfire, but eventually ran up the white flag and surrendered to her tormentors. A *Shreveport Weekly News* account asserted that the stricken vessel had 122 men on board, of whom sixty were infantrymen from New York and Connecticut regiments. Ten crewmen were killed in action, another sixteen were wounded, and 95 survivors went unhurt into captivity. Only five escaped by jumping overboard. Once again, Taylor had his men clean up the bloody, bullet-riddled debris and Colonel Gray's Company K filed aboard to provide the vessel its new complement of grayclad infantry.[95]

These newly-minted north Louisiana "marines" did not have long to wait before their role reversal was complete, as barely two weeks elapsed before they manned their battle stations in earnest against Federal infantrymen attacking Fort Bisland.

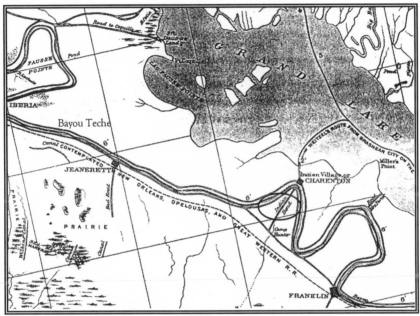

BISLAND AND GRAND LAKE, LOUISIANA, APRIL 12, 1863.
ARTHUR, WILLIAM, AND JOSIAH THOMAS MANGHAM WERE CAPTURED IN FIGHTING
AT INDIAN BEND AND ABOARD *QUEEN OF THE WEST*.

Quartermaster Grisamore had observed in mid-March that life at Bisland was dull, since the "principal occupation of all parties was to get enough to eat." Tongue firmly in cheek, he related the attempts of Gray's regiment to resolve the quandary posed by the unpalatable "blue beef" they received in their rations:

> Gray's 28th La. Regiment was stationed near us, and not having been used to our blue beef, hit upon a very quaint expedient to remedy the defect. The men complained to the officers and the officers to a Board of Inspection. . .which after due and solemn deliberation and consultation condemned the beef, and the result of the board of inspection was forwarded through the regular channels to headquarters.
>
> This settled the matter exactly. The men had no meat that day and were served up with similar rations on the morrow. I believe that was the last board of inspection I ever heard of in our campaigns.[96]

585

Perhaps the men directed their dissatisfaction at the Yankees when General Banks sent his men against Bisland on April 12, as part of a campaign to clean Taylor's rebels out of the Teche country. The Federal commander landed 12,000 men at Berwick City, from which they advanced up Bayou Teche to confront Taylor's four thousand troops in their entrenchments at Fort Bisland, at Bethel Plantation below Franklin. With Confederate attention presumably riveted on the hosts in their front, Banks intended to land Brig. Gen. Cuvier Grover's division of 4000 troops behind Taylor at Indian Bend, above Franklin, and crush the Confederates between two fires. A sound concept of tactical maneuver, it promised to eradicate rebel forces in Acadia once and for all.[97]

Thomas Mangham may have been among the pickets who warned Gray of Federal movements near Berwick as early as April 9, but definitely he was in ranks when the long blue columns arrived before Bisland three days later. The left of Taylor's line comprised two regiments and an infantry battalion oriented to the south, posted between the east bank of the Teche and the swamps fringing Grand Lake farther east. Troops and gangs of impressed slaves dug furiously to prepare entrenchments, as no works had been prepared east of the Teche. The gunboat *Diana* floated on the murky waters of the bayou itself, dividing the Confederate line, and a 24-pounder siege cannon frowned from its emplacement on the western bank. Gray's 28th Louisiana, supported by Semmes's Battery and a section of Cornay's Battery, stretched westward from the bayou to the gun emplacements of the Valverde Battery. These redlegs were stationed on the left flank of Col. Tom Green's reinforced 5th Texas Cavalry, whose dismounted troopers anchored Taylor's right on the salt marshes of Atchafalaya Bay. Two cavalry regiments stood in reserve behind the line.[98]

The defenders filed into their trenches at four o'clock in the morning on April 12, and when the sun burned off a dense fog several hours later they could see Banks's army moving up in their front. Occasional shots marred the profound silence as the blueclad host marshaled less than a mile from the waiting Louisiana and Texas troops. Taylor counted six infantry regiments just in the front line of the enemy force west of Bayou Teche, and a "heavy second line" stood 600 yards farther to the rear. Another "considerable force" took position in front of Taylor's left. At four o'clock that afternoon, Captain Grisamore heard a few shots followed by complete silence. "Suddenly, as if by magic, the artillery on our right and left opened furiously upon the advancing troops." Cornay's "Saint Mary's Cannoneers," posted along the 28th Louisiana's line, fired literally in defense of their own homes. From his vantage point, Captain Cornay could see enemy troops on his own plantation.[99]

The "brisk cannonading" continued until sundown that evening, when Banks retired his line a few hundred yards and encamped, content to wait for Grover's force to prepare its landing in Taylor's rear. The Confederate general had gotten reports of the flotilla moving to his rear on the waters of Grand Lake, and he went to coordinate the actions of his reserve units against a possible landing. He also had sent word for the gunboat *Queen of the West* and her consorts to sortie from the Atchafalaya River into Grand Lake and attack the Federal vessels there. Before leaving Bisland, however, he left orders for General Sibley, commanding the troops west of the Teche, to prepare a spoiling attack for the next morning. If Taylor's ploy worked, he might force Banks to recall Grover's division to his assistance.[100]

Had Sibley obeyed his orders promptly, Thomas Mangham's first major combat action would have been an attack against the greatly superior force to his front. Since Sibley dallied ineffectively, however, Gray's regiment remained in position awaiting the enemy's action. Banks accommodated him with a general advance as the early morning fog lifted, and the sweating Federals sloshed through the knee-high sugar cane and drainage ditches that fronted the Confederate line. Much of the time they remained under cover in the drainage ditches, feasting on the wild blackberries growing there in profusion, while the cannon brayed overhead. As the foot soldiers gradually moved forward and the leading elements opened fire with small arms, Federal batteries blasted away at the whole of the line. The combative Taylor estimated that sixty guns were pounding his lines, and he strolled along the parapets to help steady Gray's raw troops by his example. As he did so, however, Captain Bradford of Company F asked the general for his binoculars and proceeded to climb a tree for a better view of the enemy! Taylor watched admiringly as the "plucky youngster sat in his tree as quietly as in a chimney corner," despite the hail of fire that gradually denuded the tree of its foliage. Emboldened by these examples of bravery, the Louisianians began to expose themselves and suffer some casualties, but their commanding general noticed that they now remained steady, despite these losses.[101]

The oncoming Yankees attempted twice to assault the lines, but west of the Teche the 28th Louisiana and the Texans on their right held firm, repelling the attacks with "considerable loss." Banks met with no more success east of the bayou, but his troops gradually worked their way forward to storming distance along the length of the line. Sundown found men on both sides fixing bayonets in preparation for the grim work to come. The fighting that day had cost the Federals only forty killed and 184 wounded, thanks to the fact that the infantry had played it safe in their drainage ditches. That night, however, Taylor learned that Grover's division had succeeded in landing in his rear near Franklin, threatening the little army's survival. He was furious that the 2nd Louisiana Cavalry's commanding officer had disobeyed his orders and posted a mere picket guard in front of Hudgins's Point, instead of positioning his force to decisively contest a landing operation. Since this negligence allowed the Federal landing force to brush the scattered horsemen easily aside, Taylor had to order an immediate withdrawal from Bisland that night. If the Yankees played for keeps, the men from Louisiana and Texas were doomed.[102]

*　　*　　*　　*　　*

The bluejackets aboard the gunboats *U.S.S. Estrella, Arizona,* and *Calhoun* were definitely on the alert for danger as they stood watch in Grand Lake on the night of April 13. Lookouts had sighted the smoke of Confederate steamers approaching from Lake Chicot earlier that afternoon; by two o'clock the next morning, men on watch were occasionally glimpsing lights approaching from Chicot Pass. The three gunboat captains were not surprised, therefore, when dawn revealed two ships heading their way. The leading vessel, a large black steamer, was the steam ram *Queen of the West*, commanded by Capt. E. W. Fuller. The *Queen*'s engine room sported iron plating, and her gunners manned a 30-pounder Parrott rifle, a 20-pounder of the same make, and three brass 12-pounder field pieces. For sharpshooting and boarding operations, a detachment of riflemen manned battle stations on her upper deck, crouching behind cotton bales for protection against small arms fire and shell splinters. As the *Queen* steamed towards the three Federal gunboats in the gray light of dawn on Grand Lake, the Natchitoches Parish men of Captain Holloway's Walmsley Guards formed the nucleus of the sharpshooting detachment. Among the men peering over the cotton bales were privates Arthur and William Mangham.[103]

Aboard the *Calhoun*, Third Assistant Engineer Baird was now sound asleep after spending an anxious night reporting the lights flickering in the distance. He drowsed in a detached torpor despite the shout "All hands to quarters!" that came at 5:10 a.m., but moments later the grinding of anchor cable and subsequent boom of a cannon brought him awake in a flash. The *Calhoun* was the center of the three Federal vessels, with the *Estrella* on the left and *Arizona* on the right, and all three got underway immediately. The *Calhoun*, however, initially headed in the wrong direction. As her dismayed crew grumbled, "Why, even the *Estrella* is headed toward the enemy," she eventually reversed course. All three vessels opened fire with their 30-pounder Parrott bow guns as soon as they could bear on target.[104]

Captain Fuller steered the *Queen* toward the *Arizona* amid the roar of cannon, apparently intending to close the distance and ram the Federal vessel. The *Queen* was still some three miles distant when the *Calhoun* opened with her bow gun at extreme elevation, and two crewmen standing behind the heavy Parrott saw a shot as it left the muzzle. Tracing its parabola as it arced skyward and back down again in the distance, they saw it thump into the *Queen*'s upper deck. Assistant Engineer Baird heard the distant explosion and the rush of steam that followed. In a miraculous exhibition of gunnery, the crew of the heavy 30-pounder had dropped a percussion shell through the *Queen*'s unarmored roof, where it detonated amidst high-pressure steam machinery. Stricken, she stopped dead in the water, with many of her crew scalded to death. Numerous cotton bales on the upper deck burst into flame, and the fire and scalding steam drove the engineers out before they could start the pumps to fight the conflagration. The hissing inferno killed 26 men, while the remainder of the crew leaped into the water to save their lives. As she burned, her troop-carrying consort turned and pulled for safety.[105]

Lieutenant Commander A. P. Cooke, commanding the *Estrella*, first noticed that the *Queen* had paused in her advance against the storm of rapid and accurate cannon fire, but as the flames spread he realized she was fatally stricken. Bluejackets on all three Union vessels ceased fire and began lowering their boats to rescue the crewmen drifting amid the welter of debris and floating cotton bales. Among the shocked survivors clinging for dear life to the cotton bales were Arthur and William Mangham, grateful to be fished from the waters of Grand Lake with the other ninety who survived the catastrophe. The *Queen* drifted two or three miles down the lake before grounding. There she continued to burn until the fire reached her vitals. At 7:40 a.m. the *Queen of the West* exploded with a "tremendous report" that echoed across the bayou country. Her bid to intervene in the drama unfolding along the Teche had died aborning.[106]

*　　　*　　　*　　　*　　　*

Confederate fortunes that morning stood at their nadir when the *Queen* suffered her death blow, as an overwhelming enemy force snooped around the abandoned earthworks at Bisland and Grover's division was ensconced in Taylor's rear near Franklin. By the time the echoes of the *Queen's* demise stilled over Grand Lake two hours later, however, a reversal of fortunes had occurred that was even more amazing than the chance shot that struck her down.

A fatal combination of extreme hesitancy and poor reconnaissance had characterized Grover's advance into the Teche country on the previous afternoon. Eventually he placed his division near the bayou without ensuring that he blocked all roads leading from Bisland to New Iberia and safety for the retreating Confederates. The miscues continued on April 14 when he marched his men into a bottleneck at Irish Bend, where they had the Teche on their left and one of the ubiquitous swamps on their right. A nasty surprise lurked in their front, where portions of Taylor's army occupied the woods! From ravines hidden by the dense undergrowth, the Southerners launched slashing attacks whose ferocity camouflaged their weakness. At first, Grover's four leading regiments faced a Confederate line comprising only two dismounted cavalry regiments and one infantry battalion. Indeed, the "cavalrymen" that overran one Union battery in the gray light of dawn were actually General Taylor, his staff, and four couriers! The surprised Federals fought back hard, however, and the unequal combat promised only one outcome. It was merely a question of time until they would sweep the field clean of the pesky rebels.[107]

At 7:00 a.m., however, Gray's hard-marching infantrymen reported to Taylor. In the van of the forces falling back from Bisland, the 28th Louisiana's appearance was a godsend for the embattled commander. Ordering the regiment into concealed positions amidst the thickets on his left, Taylor straightaway hurled his entire force into a brazen counterattack, pitting fewer than one thousand men against Grover's five thousand troops. Thomas Mangham and his comrades had been fighting for two solid days and had been on the march since midnight, but they came screaming out of the woods and across the muddy cane fields. Blazing away with "buck and ball" loads whose heavy musket ball and three buckshot made a lethal close range combination, the Louisianians smashed into the flank of the reserve regiments of Grover's leading brigade. The unexpected onslaught caught the 375 men of the 159th New York in a crossfire that exacted 115 casualties before they recoiled in confusion. Grover described the Confederate attack as a "dashing charge" that caused his leading regiments to expend their ammunition and eventually retire, "much overborne by numbers"![108]

The Louisianians' ferocious onset dealt their opponents a nasty reverse, inflicting more than three hundred casualties on the hard-hit 3rd Brigade, but the embattled

Northerners dished out plenty of punishment in return. Grover cautiously stabilized his badly mauled right flank with fresh troops of his 1st Brigade, then arrayed his 2nd Brigade in double line of battle. This accomplished, he risked another push against the thin rebel line. The counterattack drove forward against stubborn resistance, overrunning two caissons and a limber belonging to Cornay's St. Mary's Cannoneers, while capturing the battery's colors and about 120 prisoners. Taken aback by the hornets' nest he had stirred up that morning, however, Grover hunkered down to search the woods on his flanks and front, in case he was facing attack by the whole of Taylor's army. At this point, he got word that the *Diana* was steaming up the Teche on his left flank, so he prepared to parry this latest thrust rather than renew his attack. When his enemy eventually "showed no further disposition to attack," Grover cautiously probed forward into thin air. The only troops in his front were blueclad cavalrymen riding up from Bisland.[109]

As the *Diana* pounded Grover's lines with enfilading fire from her heavy cannon, the bulk of Taylor's army escaped towards New Iberia, marching up the very road that Grover's amphibious flanking operation was supposed to interdict. Gunners aboard the *Diana* blazed away until the Confederate rear guard had withdrawn, then abandoned the ship and set her ablaze. Taylor proudly recounted that "every wagon, pot, or pan was brought off" with the exception of a 24-pounder siege piece and one disabled gun of Cornay's Battery, abandoned at Bisland. The hard-fighting commander singled out the 28th Louisiana for special praise in his after-action report, averring that "Colonel Gray and his regiment, Twenty-eighth Louisiana Volunteers, officers and men, deserve most favorable mention." Contrasting their conduct with some units that lost their cohesion in the retreat from Irish Bend, Taylor added: "Their gallantry in action is enhanced by the excellent discipline which they have preserved, and no veteran soldiers could have excelled them in their conduct during the trying scenes through which they passed."[110]

Although he was the son of former President Zachary Taylor, Maj. Gen. Richard "Dick" Taylor had earned his stars the hard way, by outstanding performance in heavy fighting in Virginia. The fulsome praise that typifies his reports is mixed with stinging censure of those who failed to measure up to his exacting standards. The 28th Louisiana certainly merited approbation as an example of what Civil War soldiers simply called "a fighting regiment," but such distinction came at a high price. Their total casualty figures are lost to history, but extant records make it clear that losses were significant. Colonel Gray and Captain Bradford were both wounded in action at Irish Bend, and Gray fell captive to the advancing Federals. Grover's men buried 21 Confederates on the field and evacuated another 35 who lay wounded on the field; many of these must have been from the 28th Louisiana. All of Company K went into captivity after they abandoned and fired the *Diana*, and many others fell prisoner to the counterattacks that restored the right of Grover's line after their fierce initial onslaught. One of the hard-fighting Louisianians taken prisoner that morning was Pvt. Josiah Thomas Mangham, who joined his brother William and cousin Arthur in captivity.[111]

Captured almost simultaneously in two separate but related actions, the three Manghams probably were transported to Brashear City and eventually on to prison pens in New Orleans. Banks and his army pursued Taylor's remaining force to Opelousas before turning east to invest Port Hudson on the Mississippi River, where they battered themselves almost to pieces in fruitless assaults before settling down to a successful siege. These operations were just getting underway when Banks divested himself of his Confederate captives from the Teche campaign, and the Manghams were released on parole at Prophet's Island, below Port Hudson, on May 11, 1863.[112]

In all probability, the three trekked homeward that summer, awaiting word that Confederate agents had arranged their exchange for Federal prisoners of equal rank.[113] No muster rolls survive from this period for the 11th Louisiana Battalion, but the officer who mustered the 28th Louisiana's Claiborne Invincibles at the end of August marked Thomas "absent, prisoner on parole." If they returned to the army during September, then they must have enjoyed helping thrash an unsuspecting Union force picketing Stirling's Plantation, on Bayou Fordoche near Morganza. The 11th Infantry Battalion, 28th Louisiana Infantry, and 18th Louisiana Infantry now comprised Brig. Gen. Alfred Mouton's brigade, and his was one of four brigades that conducted a successful surprise attack on September 29. The four Confederate brigades crossed the Atchafalaya River during the afternoon and evening, descending next morning upon their startled prey like a bolt from the blue. The unexpected onslaught bagged the 19th Iowa and 26th Indiana regiments en masse, along with a two-gun section of the 1st Missouri Light Artillery. Two cavalry regiments made good their escape with only light losses, but Federal casualties totaled 515, of whom 454 were captured or missing in action. Mouton's Brigade probably secured the approach routes to Bayou Fordoche, because it was not directly involved in the engagement with the unlucky Federals.[114]

The fight at Stirling's Plantation was one of the few substantial engagements that summer and fall for Mouton's Division, which crisscrossed southwestern Louisiana in a fatiguing series of forced marches. Intended to re-establish a Confederate presence after the passage of Banks's force to Port Hudson, their seemingly endless hikes involved little combat. In November the 11th and 12th Battalions merged with the Orleans Parish soldiers of the 24th "Crescent" Regiment, and the Walmsley Guards became Company K in the new Consolidated Crescent Regiment. Although their proud title evoked the original regiment's roots in the "Crescent City" of New Orleans, the fourteen companies of the reorganized outfit would earn their combat reputation in the Red River valley, the haunts of Shelley's old 11th Battalion.[115]

Mouton's Brigade, led by Colonel Gray after Mouton's promotion to division command, moved north to Monroe that December to receive weapon shipments from the cis-Mississippi Confederacy. Foiled by Union interception of these cargoes, Gray received orders to move the brigade north to Bastrop and man remote picket posts along Bayou Bartholomew. January 1864 was a frigid month in north Louisiana, which Grisamore considered "the severest season" his regiment experienced in four years' service. Captain Hyatt, also of the 18th Louisiana, thought it was "Pitiable at night to see [the soldiers] nodding around camp-fires with only one blanket." He concluded grimly, "This is soldiering, this is." Many Confederate reports describe their men as "nearly naked" due to a lack of serviceable clothing, but Mouton's men may have approximated this extreme more literally than most. Known as "the ragged brigade" in an army where good clothing was noticeable by its absence, it is unsurprising that Grisamore saw them leave numerous bloody footprints in the snow and ice on the line of march. Their otherwise frigid and miserable column often resounded with the shouts and cries of families who spied a son or husband in the ranks of the 28th Louisiana. Upon one of these demonstrations, the amused Grisamore heard an envious Irishman exclaim from the ranks of the 18th Louisiana, "Be Jabers, and the 28th must all have three or four wives a pice."[116]

No 28th Louisiana muster rolls survive to document their service after August 1863, but most of the men captured at Irish Bend were exchanged and returned to duty before the spring of 1864; probably Pvt. Josiah Thomas Mangham came back as well. The next surviving Consolidated Crescent muster rolls accounted for the first two months of 1864, and Arthur and William were both present for duty in the regiment's encampment at Pineville. Mouton's Brigade had fetched up there in mid-February after a bitterly cold month on picket duty at Bayou Bartholomew, in the northern part of the state. By the time they returned to the Red River and camped just opposite Alexandria, the Crescent's hard-marching soldiers had covered 225 miles on foot since New Year's. Mouton's men were earning a reputation as "Taylor's foot cavalry."[117]

All signs pointed to a major Federal effort to overrun the Red River heartland of the Confederate Trans-Mississippi that spring. Major General Nathaniel P. Banks, Dick Taylor's longtime foe, marshaled more than 30,000 troops for an advance up the river, in conjunction with 60-odd gunboats and troop transports of Admiral Porter's fleet. Banks intended to conquer Shreveport in far northwestern Louisiana, then continue into east Texas to overrun the budding industrial and commercial centers of Marshall and Tyler. Such a blow would unseat Lt. Gen. Edmund Kirby Smith's command and administrative apparatus at Shreveport, and utterly dislocate his ability to maintain the shaky economic underpinnings of the Trans-Mississippi Department. Often known simply as "Kirby Smithdom," the department had long been dependent largely on its own resources to prosecute the war in Louisiana, Texas, Arkansas, Missouri, and the Indian Territories (modern Oklahoma). The July 1863 capitulation of Vicksburg and Port Hudson had severed all regular communication with the government at Richmond. Kirby Smith was on his own, required to develop political and economic policy in a realm traditionally beyond the pale for American military commanders.[118]

In the spring of 1864, Kirby Smith faced the possibility of renewed Federal descents on the Texas coast, Banks's drive up the Red River, and Maj. Gen. Frederick Steele's advance from Little Rock towards Shreveport. The Federal armies were now under the overall command of Lt. Gen. Ulysses S. Grant, who coordinated the first all-encompassing strategy to overwhelm the Confederacy. He grudgingly authorized two corps stationed in Mississippi to help Banks for thirty days before departing for Sherman's army, but Grant viewed the Red River operation as a sideshow to the main attacks in Virginia and Georgia. Banks accordingly got underway in March, although Sherman and Grant had to wait another month or more for spring grass to grow in quantities adequate to support their armies' draft animals.[119]

Arthur W. Hyatt, a captain in the 18th Louisiana Regiment encamped at Pineville, noted in his journal entry for March 7 that there was "A considerable stir in town about rumors of the enemy." Just one week later, the "stir" had become "Big excitement," as word arrived that Federal forces had captured Fort DeRussy on the river thirty miles below Alexandria. Hampered already by the need to continually move his units just to find forage and rations in the desolated areas of northeast Louisiana and Arkansas, Kirby Smith hardly knew who needed reinforcements more, Taylor in Louisiana or General Price in Arkansas. As he put into motion about seven thousand reinforcements from points in Texas and Arkansas, the six thousand men of Dick Taylor's Army of Western Louisiana fell back before the colossus pushing up the Red River valley.[120]

Mouton's Division, consisting of Polignac's small Texas brigade and Mouton's own Louisiana brigade under Gray's command, had crossed the river and marched 25 miles south to Lecompte as things heated up on March 8. The fall of DeRussy, however, punctured any hope of a forward defense in conjunction with Walker's Division near Simmesport, as the Federal fleet could simply ferry troops up the Red River well into their rear. A bold Yankee thrust upriver towards Alexandria would cut off both divisions, so Taylor ordered them to get out in a hurry. The men of Mouton's Brigade marched for their lives, covering more than fifty miles towards Natchitoches in two days. Major General Andrew J. Smith's Federals, comprising three divisions from the Army of the Tennessee's XVI and XVII Corps, pushed upriver aboard twenty-one transports and occupied Alexandria on March 15. Smith's 11,000 men welcomed the 5000 cavalrymen of Banks's army five days later, and another 15,000 troops of his XIII and XIX Corps arrived on March 25. Banks's infantrymen had departed Franklin on March 15, averaging seventeen miles daily across western Louisiana en route to Alexandria. This force was the largest ever assembled west of the Mississippi, and its ninety field guns complemented the 210 guns mounted aboard 22 gunboats and 40 additional vessels on the Red River.[121]

Although the Red's low water level considerably hindered navigation above Alexandria, the last week of March saw A. J. Smith's men board their transports and steam towards Grand Ecore, the river port that served the nearby town of Natchitoches. Other long columns of cavalry and infantry struck out for these objectives by land, and Federal cavalry entered Natchitoches on March 30. Confederate cavalry detachments evacuated the town with minimal resistance, as Taylor's infantry had set out westward on the road towards Pleasant Hill. Already on March 21, Captain Hyatt of the 18th Louisiana had jotted a brief notation in his diary: "The deuce to play now in Natchitoches, and everything has to be moved. Terrible excitement—everyone on the skeedaddle." For the Walmsley Guards, the evacuation of Natchitoches meant forsaking the town where they had enlisted just under two years earlier, and the abandonment of their nearby families to the tender mercies of the onrushing blue juggernaut. For Arthur and William Mangham, every step towards Pleasant Hill took them farther away from their home in Coushatta Chute, just 20-odd miles upriver from Grand Ecore, on the eastern bank of the river.[122]

Confederate letter-writers, diarists, and newspaper editors often spoke of "striking in defense of their firesides," a turn of phrase that evoked the personal and defensive nature of the war as they generally understood it. For the Manghams of Mouton's

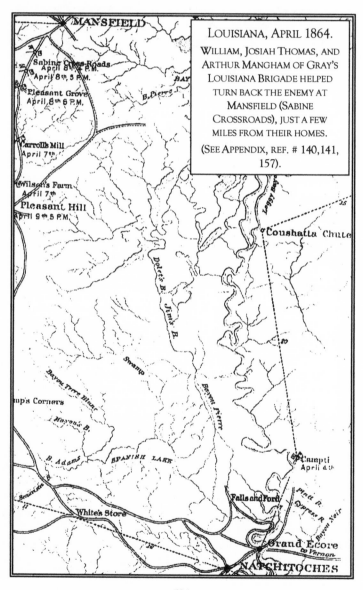

LOUISIANA, APRIL 1864.

WILLIAM, JOSIAH THOMAS, AND ARTHUR MANGHAM OF GRAY'S LOUISIANA BRIGADE HELPED TURN BACK THE ENEMY AT MANSFIELD (SABINE CROSSROADS), JUST A FEW MILES FROM THEIR HOMES.

(SEE APPENDIX, REF. # 140, 141, 157).

Brigade, this metaphor was to apply almost literally just days after they abandoned Natchitoches. The Crescent Regiment's commanding officer, Col. James Beard, was in the same situation, as his family resided in Kingston, just a few miles from Mansfield. While encamped at nearby Pleasant Hill on April 2, Beard wrote his wife confidently about the prospects for striking a blow. "I do not have any fear of our being able to whip the scoundrels here, having the advantage of a good position & the army wants a fight." Despite the long retreat, he believed, "The best of spirits pervades the entire army and no demoralization is produced by our falling back." To ensure that his men were ready when the time came, Beard drilled the Crescent on April 4 at their camp five miles north of Mansfield, having them form line of battle and fire volleys of blank cartridges at an imaginary enemy line.[123]

Although General Taylor had feared he might have to enter Shreveport's defenses before he could offer battle to his vastly superior opponents, reinforcements finally reached him in time to turn his army on his pursuers at Sabine Crossroads, just three miles southeast of Mansfield. Probably Arthur, William, and Thomas Mangham were all in their respective places as General Mouton marched his men back south through Mansfield on the morning of April 8 to form part of Taylor's line astride the Pleasant Hill road. Artillerymen and cavalrymen were trading shots with an advance guard of Federal horsemen, so Gray's arriving Louisianians had to dodge through rearing, terrified mules and cursing teamsters before double-quicking through the trees into line of battle that morning. Taylor eventually posted several dismounted Texas cavalry brigades on his far left beyond Mouton's Division, which in turn stood on the left flank of Randal's Brigade of Walker's Texas Division. The rest of Walker's Division was on the right (south) of the road, forming the right wing of an L-shaped line whose apex straddled the road angling southeastwards through the forests. Taylor had about 8800 men in his two-mile long line of battle, but another four or five thousand were en route. Between Mansfield and Shreveport were two divisions from Maj. Gen. Sterling Price's army in Arkansas, and more Texas cavalry regiments were on the way from winter quarters in their home state.[124]

Mouton arranged his 2200 troops by posting Polignac's Brigade on the right of the division line, with Gray commanding Mouton's old brigade on the left. The 28th Louisiana formed the left of Gray's line of battle, with the 18th Louisiana in the center and the Crescent Regiment on the right flank. From their positions in the woodline north of the Moss Plantation's cleared wheat fields, the three Manghams in Gray's Brigade stood only fifteen miles due west of Arthur and Sarah Mangham's home in Coushatta Chute. In all probability, Arthur, Sarah, and the younger children listened anxiously to the thud of cannon fire that day and prayed for the safe deliverance of their son and nephews. General Taylor paused in front of Gray's Brigade to tell the troops that he wanted them to "draw the first blood" since they were "fighting in defense of their own soil." The distant Mangham family probably could not hear the ripple of musketry that followed almost immediately thereafter, marking the demise of an unwary detachment of Federal cavalrymen. Advancing against scattered cavalry resistance, they had approached the woods as Mouton's Brigade shifted its line to the left. The riderless horses careering across the open field evidenced the deadly effect of the 18th Louisiana's well-timed volley, which emptied saddles at a range of only twenty feet. Mouton cried out joyously, "Louisiana has drawn the first blood to-day, and the victory is ours!", answered immediately by three cheers from his men. Gray directed each regiment to post skirmishers in the open fields facing the Federals taking position atop the opposite slope, but the spiteful crack of their rifles could not have carried very far through the dense pine forests.[125]

By four o'clock that afternoon, however, Taylor decided he had waited long enough for his adversary to attack. Chafing from the seemingly unending weeks of retreat, he had written to Kirby Smith's headquarters on April 4:

> Like the man who has admitted the robber into his bed-chamber instead of resisting him at the door, our defense will be embarrassed by the cries of wives and children. Action, prompt, vigorous action, is required. While we are deliberating the enemy is marching. King James lost three kingdoms for a mass. We may lose three States without a battle.[126]

When Taylor saw continued movement in the Federal lines, he concluded that his enemy's "arrangements were not complete." About 3:30 p.m. he rode to the left flank to speak with Mouton, Gray, and Polignac. Amid the ever-increasing whiz of Minie balls from the skirmishers across the way, Taylor announced to Polignac, "Little Frenchman, I am going to fight Banks here, if he has a million men! Let us charge them right in the face and throw them into the valley!" Taylor had done all the waiting he could stand. It was time for Mouton and his Louisiana and Texas brigades to "draw first blood."[127]

Dick Taylor had learned a lot about combat leadership in three years of warfare in Virginia and Louisiana, and he obviously calculated his words to bring his troops to fever pitch for the stern task ahead. Even so, Taylor was astounded at the response of Mouton's Division, especially the Louisiana troops, "already inflamed by many outrages upon their homes, as well as by camp rumors that it was intended to abandon their State without a fight." Mouton called out, "Throw down that fence, my boys, and charge across that field and drive the enemy away!" The men rose from their position along a little dirt track, moved through a fringe of brush, and then clambered across the fence rails into the open field. With battle flags waving and field officers mounted, the troops surged screaming into the attack at double-quick time. The wrought-up Louisianians faced a half-mile of open field and four Ohio, Illinois, and Kentucky regiments in their direct front, but they did not intend to be denied.[128]

Probably one Federal battery and parts of two others swung their pieces to bear against Mouton's Division, letting fly with solid shot, shell, grape, and canister. The intense fire "beat our soldiers down even as a storm tears down the trees of a forest," shuddered Capt. Felix Poche of the 18th Louisiana. A soldier in the 96th Ohio watched "Shot plow gaps through them, shells burst in their midst and form caverns in the mass of living men." Musketry also exacted a stiff price, and Mouton ordered the survivors to catch their breath in the cover of the creek bed after the 28th Louisiana's skirmishers cleared a small wood in the line of advance. Gray looked at his brigade line of battle and saw that the Crescent Regiment was unable to keep up, as they were advancing into the teeth of an exceptionally heavy fire. He sent his brigade inspector, Lt. Arthur H. Martin, hustling across to bring up the regiment, but the young officer found the men struggling to withstand the horrendous fire.[129]

Although the exact sequence of events remains unclear, it was early in the charge that Colonel Beard seized the Crescent's colors to urge his men forward. Only moments passed before he was shot down and killed, so Maj. Mercer Canfield picked up the banner, only to be shot down in turn. Lieutenant Colonel Franklin Clack dropped, mortally wounded, soon after taking command from Beard, so there were no field officers left standing when Martin arrived with Gray's orders. The lieutenant grabbed the regiment's battle flag and personally ordered the men forward, but immediately suffered the fate of its previous two bearers: he was killed in his tracks. Captain Seth Field of Company A picked up the flag and moved a few steps forward before he, too, dropped fatally wounded. One participant in the charge thought the Confederate line wavered "like a broken reed," but other brave men remained willing to pick up the battle flag and lead the way.[130]

Things got even worse when the Crescent breasted the slope in front of the Federal line. At only fifty yards range, the 130th Illinois delivered a shattering volley into the oncoming men, and the Louisianians fell literally by the score. One shocked observer reported that the deadly close-range fire killed 55 men and wounded another 150 in the Crescent regiment, and he apparently was not far wrong. Unless vagaries of the weather spared the Mangham family in nearby Coushatta Chute, the roar of gunfire must have told them that their relatives were involved in a desperate fight for their lives, their state, and their cause. Little could they have known, however, that Arthur, William, and Thomas stood quite literally in the vortex of the terrible storm.[131]

The 18th Louisiana's colors attracted a hurricane of fire as well, and Colonel Armant took them from the grasp of his dead color bearer only to suffer the same fate. Private Emile Portier picked them up and bore them through the remainder of the battle, earning a promotion to ensign for his valor. On the left flank of Gray's advancing line, the 28th Louisiana's color bearers at first had fared little better than those of the Crescent. When one fell, Sergeant Ganier of the 18th Louisiana picked up the flag and called upon the men to advance. Ganier took a bullet in the knee, so Lt. Wilbur Blackman snatched up the colors and rode towards the fenceline that sheltered the Federal line. Formerly assigned to the 28th Louisiana, Blackman was now serving as Mouton's adjutant, and he halted and turned in full view of the enemy line to urge his old regiment forward. This was truly his lucky day. An awed Federal captive later told the Louisianians that his comrades directed at least two hundred shots at Blackman from the fenceline just fifty yards distant, but none hit its mark.[132]

Apparently Blackman took his stand about the time Gray saw Lieutenant Martin die advancing the Crescent's flag, and the brigade commander sent word for his old regiment to overrun the deadly fenceline position. Most of the 28th Louisiana held their fire until they closed to point-blank range, then poured in a ferocious volley that smashed a gap in the blueclad line. Hurling themselves screaming into the breach, they cracked the line in several minutes of hand-to-hand combat. Gunners began streaming back from their guns and the badly mauled Federal regiments began dissolving, allowing the Crescent and the 18th Louisiana to overrun the fenceline position and destroy all remaining cohesion among the defenders. Shooting down battery horses and snatching frightened prisoners, the furious Louisianians virtually annihilated the 130th Illinois and the 48th Ohio. Polignac's Brigade arrived on their right while Major's cavalry division kept pace on the far left, and Walker's Texas Division now delivered its assault and began to break through as well. The regiments in the outmanned Union center were looking anxiously to the disaster engulfing their right flank, and the onrushing Texans in their front made it clear that resistance was hopeless. Apparently, it was at this point that General Mouton prevented his men from firing by mistake on a group of surrendering Federals, but several of these bluecoats could not resist a last crack at their grayclad nemeses. Picking up the weapons they had dropped, several shot Mouton out of the saddle. His death ensured theirs, however, because the enraged Louisiana soldiers who witnessed the incident slaughtered the whole party.[133]

By five o'clock, the entire Federal battlefront teetered on the edge of catastrophe. Reinforced by Cameron's little division of 1300 men, the embattled defenders falling back from Honeycutt Hill struggled to form a new line in the woods farther to the rear. They held out for almost an hour before Gray's hard-fighting Louisianians flanked them and overran the new position, assisted again by Polignac's Brigade and Randal's Texans. As this second Federal line died aborning, the rout became general. Hundreds of worn out Yankees surrendered, while hundreds more fled for the rear. There they became entangled in a snarl of wagon trains parked close behind their line of battle on the road to Pleasant Hill. Meant to facilitate the rapid advance on Shreveport, the baggage trains now became a deadly ball and chain tethered to divisions that were breaking apart in panic flight. Gray's men had captured several guns atop Honeycutt Hill, but desperate Federal cannoneers now had to abandon another seventeen in the traffic jam on the road. With dense pine forests growing close to both sides of the road, the narrow dirt surface became a fatal bottleneck for the massive trains and for the fighting men trapped in front of them. Taylor had chosen his ground carefully, but the piecemeal manner in which his unwary opponents approached the battlefield was an unexpected bonus. The men in blue were paying a terrible price for their unwary approach march.[134]

Frenzied fugitives rushed rearward in one of the panics that veteran soldiers had long since learned to recognize as one of the most gut-wrenching spectacles of a Civil War battlefield. Some of them had seen it before among friends, foes, or both, and some no doubt had experienced personally the blind, unreasoning terror that reduced brave men and good units to mush. In the throes of panic, organized units dissolved into fleeing mobs, beyond any control, heedless of threats, shame, personal example, or inspiration. Thus the XIII Army Corps, including Landram's and Cameron's divisions, Lee's cavalry division, and every sort and description of teamster, gunner, and camp follower, fled for dear life through the woods and down the road towards Pleasant Hill.

Several miles to the rear, the flood tide of panicked men washed over, around, and through the three brigades of Emory's division of the XIX Corps. Emory had to order his men to fix bayonets and push through the screaming, sweating mass of fugitives, as the latter gasped that his men should run for their lives: certain death awaited anyone who went forward![135]

It was a tribute to the discipline of Emory's 5000 men that they followed orders and deployed into line of battle just south of Chatman's Bayou, at a place known as Pleasant Grove. They enjoyed a brief respite before the demons in gray appeared in their front, and Emory's men proved them only human after all. The winded and thirsty Rebels had double-quicked much of the way from Sabine Crossroads, and were somewhat disorganized from the pounding they had given and received. Nonetheless, they came on hard and fast. They drove in Emory's skirmishers at a run and slammed into his main line, absorbing heavy casualties in the initial onset. Polignac had assumed command of Mouton's Division after Mouton's death, and the enormous casualties of the last few hours limited his two battered brigades to a minor role at Pleasant Grove. Brigadier General Tom Green encountered Gray in advance of the brigade column with the 28th Louisiana, and ordered the arriving regiment into the brush on the right of the road. Under command of Maj. Thomas W. Pool since Lt. Col. William Walker fell at Honeycutt Hill, they thrashed their way through the dense brush without guides or clear orders. After groping blindly through the underbrush, they encountered the enemy along a dry creek bed, hammering them back "with great success" in conjunction with elements of Walker's Division. When the encroaching darkness caused another Confederate regiment to fire a volley into Pool and his men, however, he wisely pulled back from the confused melee. The Crescent and 18th Louisiana had arrived after Green committed the 28th Louisiana to action, and Gray emerged from the woods to find that Polignac had held them back pending clear orders. Colonel Gray praised the good judgment that "wisely kept them from engaging actively in the conflict, to which they could have contributed nothing but additional confusion."[136]

Clearly, the immediate pursuit was at an end, but the hard-fighting Confederates had won the bayou and the precious water it contained. In the humid April heat, this was no minor concern. Banks anxiously held a council of war that night, and one of his generals' main concerns was their inability to get sufficient water to the troops around Pleasant Grove. Thoroughly shaken by the day's events, his subordinates advised him to pull back to Pleasant Hill, where the road network allowed Banks to dispatch his wagon train back towards Grand Ecore. By sending word upriver to Porter's fleet, Banks also could recall T. Kilby Smith's infantrymen aboard ship. The harassed Banks had not yet given up completely on his plan of campaign, but he clearly was setting the conditions for a withdrawal. All these arrangements would take time, of course, and he was not at all sure how much time he had to spare. Just as Dick Taylor considered Banks "easily foiled," Banks must have known a thing or two about his opponent's *modus operandi*. Willing and able to retreat at a killing pace if the odds were insuperable, Taylor would take huge risks and fight desperately if he saw a chance of success. Indeed, he was preparing to do so again the very next day.[137]

First priority for his jubilant Confederates, however, was some rest and reorganization. Of the 8800 men engaged at Mansfield, Taylor's losses approximated one thousand, over three-quarters of whom were infantrymen from Mouton's Division. Although Mouton took only 2200 men into action, 762 were killed, wounded, or missing in the brief but deadly combat on the slopes of Honeycutt Hill and the ensuing fracas at Pleasant Grove. Captain Felix Poche fought with the 18th Louisiana, which lost nineteen killed and 75 wounded, but he noted sadly that Colonel Beard's regiment suffered devastating losses: "The Crescent especially was literally torn to pieces." The regiment's fourteen companies lost 57 killed and 134 wounded, which probably represented almost half of its strength. Seven color bearers had fallen while advancing the Crescent's battle flag across the half mile of open field, and Capt. William Claiborne was the only captain in the regiment to survive unhurt. With Beard, Clack, and Canfield all killed or mortally wounded in the 25-minute charge across the open, the Crescent became the only Louisiana regiment in the war to lose all three field officers killed in a single engagement. Postwar records show that Arthur Mangham came through the whole war untouched, but it is not known if William or his brother Thomas were wounded at Mansfield. The lack of surviving casualty reports leaves it uncertain how many men of the 28th Louisiana suffered death or wounds, but their location and role imply a toll similar to the neighboring 18th Louisiana.[138]

The Calvary atop Honeycutt Hill gutted the leadership of Mouton's old brigade, and cost the command about thirty-five percent of its entire strength. The brigade was barely capable of continuing the fight the next day, but its do-or-die assault, with timely assistance from Polignac's and Randal's brigades, had broken the back of the Federal defense. Their bold attacks inflicted 1888 killed, wounded, and missing upon the seven thousand bluecoats actively engaged at Mansfield, utterly routing the XIII Corps and Lee's cavalry division. Much more important than the casualty ratios, of course, was the fact that the seemingly inexorable advance of Banks's colossus stopped, then spun into reverse after the mauling it absorbed on April 8. By the time Taylor hurled his army at Banks the next day at Pleasant Hill, many Federals were convinced that the north Louisiana woods were some of the least hospitable places on earth.[139]

The initial Confederate attack at Pleasant Hill again routed the lines it struck, and another crack-up seemed imminent. General A. J. Smith's men from the Army of the Tennessee struck back hard from reserve positions, however, folding up much of Taylor's right wing as it unsuspectingly crossed their front. Polignac's battered division was in reserve on the left, and went into action at dusk to support the attack against the badly mauled Federal center. Nearly surrounded by Confederates swirling around it in the gloaming, the beleaguered men in this sector of Banks's line were spared in large part by the poor visibility that caused fratricide among the grayclad brigades. General Major's Texas brigade took fire from Lane's Texans and Polignac's men before their commanders ordered them to cease firing and retire, ending the melee. Taylor expressed his appreciation to several subordinate commanders, among them Polignac and Gray, for heroic efforts that "prevented the confusion on the right from becoming disastrous." Taylor's adversary similarly recognized his own good fortune. Approaching

Smith as the action drew to a close, Banks expressed his heartfelt appreciation, exclaiming, "God bless you, general. . . .You have saved the army." The reported cost was another 1506 Federal casualties of 13,000 engaged, but Taylor's 12,000 men suffered losses that equaled or slightly exceeded this number.[140]

Banks intended to remain in position, just as he had the night before at Mansfield, but the political general from Massachusetts lacked the professional skill to match his pugnacity and personal gallantry. When his shaken subordinates again counseled withdrawal, he changed his mind and acceded in ordering a retreat. Infuriated by this decision, A. J. Smith suggested to Maj. Gen. William B. Franklin, the army's second ranking officer, that he assume command from Banks; Smith rashly promised the support of three army corps for such a coup. Franklin was a bold if unskillful fighter from the old army, more at home leading a charge than maneuvering an army, but he knew trouble when he saw it. Looking at Smith, he retorted: "Smith, don't you know this is mutiny?" This ended the discussion, and the army marched for safety towards Grand Ecore and the retreating gunboats. Since most of the army's wagons were already en route to the Red River, several hundred Federal wounded were abandoned on the field as their comrades departed.[141]

While Banks set his face for the Red River, Taylor initially pulled back most of his force towards Mansfield to get water and reorganize in relative safety. A few artillery shots the next morning drew no return fire from the abandoned Federal positions at Pleasant Hill, however, so Taylor set out to harry his enemy's retreat. He argued vociferously against relinquishing Walker's, Churchill's, and Parsons's infantry divisions for service against Steele in Arkansas, but Kirby Smith was adamant. Polignac's battered division was the only infantry remaining to Taylor, but he soon put it on the road in pursuit of Banks. The main burden of the continuous skirmishing over the following weeks necessarily fell on the cavalry and artillery, who comprised about three-fourths of Taylor's five thousand troops. Detachments of horsemen and cannoneers harried Banks's army along its entire route, delaying the advance guard, hounding the rear guard, and harrying flankers and foragers whenever they ventured into the countryside. Other units ambushed Federal gunboats and transports along the length of the Red River, and their steady stream of successes combined with the treacherously low water level to threaten the entrapment and destruction of Banks's entire invasion force.[142]

Despite plentiful evidence that the diminutive Army of Western Louisiana simply lacked the troops to bring him to bay, Banks never swerved from his conviction that Taylor equaled or outnumbered his forces. The image comes to mind of a man beset by a swarm of angry bees, but one is hard-pressed to apply the metaphor to six weeks of retreat. The assaults of April 8 and 9 bore all too convincing testimony of his opponent's aggressive disposition, so why should Banks expect free rein to retreat from Grand Ecore and Alexandria without facing howling waves of Southerners in another pitched battle? The continuous skirmishing helped mask Taylor's true weakness, of course, but nobody should have mistaken single ranks of dismounted cavalrymen for the smashing power displayed at Mansfield and Pleasant Hill. But outnumbered or not, the very magnitude of Banks's force presented him with an unenviable logistical problem, since the Red River had become completely unreliable as a supply line. The campaigns of 1862 and 1863 had devastated western Louisiana, and A. J. Smith's vengeful Westerners had turned the once lush Red River valley into a "howling wilderness." Banks's only options were to turn on his enemy and destroy him in pitched battle, or continue to retreat. To dispatch forces downriver to secure his supply line would expose them to defeat in detail wherever Taylor marshaled local superiority, and that was a challenge the Confederate leader would have relished. To top it off, Grant was pressing for Smith and his troops to return to Sherman's army in Georgia, although Banks shuddered at the prospect of losing his most reliable troops.[143]

Outside Grand Ecore and later Alexandria, the Mangham infantrymen of Polignac's Division took positions in support of the cavalry outside the enemy's entrenchments. Taylor's tactics throughout the pursuit demonstrated his unwillingness to risk his tiny infantry force against a Federal army still quintuple his strength, since an enemy sally in large force could engage his foot soldiers at a potentially decisive disadvantage. Taylor preferred to leave the close contact to his cavalrymen, who could strike fast, fade back when necessary, and survive to fight another day. At Monett's Ferry on April 23 he brought Polignac's infantry up to throw on Banks's rear in a climactic battle, but Brigadier General Bee's early withdrawal of his cavalry blocking force allowed the Federals to escape across Cane River. By the time the hard marching infantrymen arrived, the bird had flown the coop.[144] (See maps, pp. 397, 400.)

Several weeks later at Mansura, it appeared that Polignac's Division might engage once more in decisive battle, when Taylor drew up his entire force on the open plain before the Federal column as it entered the broad Marksville prairie. Banks cautiously marshaled a force triple the size of Taylor's, however, and both armies engaged in extensive "artillery practice" with little loss in an engagement that lasted throughout the forenoon of May 16. The Federal right wing eventually began a ponderous advance towards Polignac, at which point Taylor gave up the game of bluff and withdrew. Banks resumed his retreat, while grayclad cavalry slashed at his flanks and rear that afternoon and the next day in a highly successful ambush near Moreauville. By now, the harassed Federals were but a day's march from Simmesport on the Atchafalaya River, where they had commenced the campaign on March 12. If Banks could cross his force intact to safe haven on the eastern bank, Federal naval vessels plying the Atchafalaya and the nearby Mississippi River would be able to provide him plentiful supplies, fire support, and reinforcements from New Orleans, Baton Rouge, or Vicksburg. For Dick Taylor, it was now or never.[145]

On May 18, he flung his whole available force at Banks one last time, attacking his rear guard at Norwood's Plantation, near Yellow Bayou and Bayou De Glaize. The Confederates advanced with Major's Texas cavalrymen on the right and Polignac's webfoot infantrymen on the left, against three brigades of infantry and one of cavalry from A. J. Smith's command. Led by Brig. Gen. Joseph Mower, the Federal infantrymen stood fast against Polignac's initial onslaught. They poured a hot fire of musketry and canister into the tangled thicket through which the Louisiana and Texas troops struggled to advance, and followed up the heavy fire with a counterattack at bayonet point. Already discomfited by the natural abatis, the Rebs broke for the rear. In all probability it was at this point that Col. R. D. Stone was killed while leading Polignac's old Texas brigade, because the hard-fighting French general had to personally intervene to "restore order in his left brigade," as Taylor reported. On the other end of the line, Major's cavalrymen had flanked their opponents out of position, but Mower repositioned infantry from the right flank to save his own outmanned horsemen with timely support.[146]

Federal troops began dropping from heatstroke and lack of water in the inhospitable Louisiana steambath, and Mower pulled his men out of the thicket to reorganize. Afterwards, he pushed forward into the underbrush again, only to find that the Confederates were filtering back into the brambles, too. The two lines met in a vicious encounter with musket butt and bayonet, and one Federal praised the Confederates' stubborn impetuosity, which reminded him of Nathan Bedford Forrest's hard-driving assaults. Mower's hard-fighting troops gave a superb account of themselves, too, pushing their adversaries back into the indefensible open field beyond. Posting a heavy force of skirmishers to secure the thicket, Mower again shifted troops to his left to retrieve ground lost by the cavalrymen for a second time. The smoldering thicket soon burst into flame from the sparks generated by thousands of musket discharges, so both sides pulled back from the now-impassable blaze. Taylor's forces broke contact, having suffered losses of five or six hundred men against some 308 Federal casualties reported by Mower. One source indicates that Gray's Louisianians lost forty men killed, 31 wounded and 25 missing at Yellow Bayou; if these figures are accurate, they offer further testimony to the vicious nature of the close-range combat in the thicket. In typical Civil War engagements, the wounded greatly outnumbered those killed in action. Unfortunately, no records indicate regimental losses for the "severely handled" Crescent or the 28th Louisiana, so it is unclear whether William or Thomas Mangham sustained wounds in the final action of the Red River Campaign.[147]

Although Taylor acknowledged that Polignac's Division was "severely repulsed" in the fierce fighting at Yellow Bayou, it seemed to him that its "courage and discipline checked the advancing masses" of "overwhelming numbers." Since Banks's army retreated across the Atchafalaya River the day after the battle, Taylor composed his report in the pleasant afterglow of a victorious campaign. In his judgment, this "little division, decimated at Mansfield and Pleasant Hill by its unflinching bravery and endurance, commands the admiration of the Army." As such, he thought it representative of the entire army, whose men had earned his highest praise: "Officers and men were alike actuated by the earnest resolve to drive the enemy across the Atchafalaya, and no sacrifice, no exertion, no privation could be asked of them to which they did not cheerfully submit."[148]

Indeed, they had not only fought hard and well; they had emerged victorious against unbelievable odds, at a time when the whole Confederacy was staring doom directly in the face. Each day an anxious populace scoured the papers for news of Federal hosts advancing into the very heartland of Dixie, and the armies in Virginia and Georgia were fighting titanic battles ever closer to Richmond and Atlanta. Southerners knew their backs were against the wall; although most still believed they had a significant chance of victory, they also understood that the odds were getting mighty long. These were the only Americans in the age of modern communication ever to face the prospect of real defeat, and the news from Louisiana was indeed a heady tonic. In seventy days of uninterrupted marching and fighting, the tiny Army of Western Louisiana had thoroughly whipped an invader that had seemed irresistible. Could the Army of Northern Virginia and the Army of Tennessee do as well?

*   *   *   *   *

During the long summer of 1864, the news from Georgia and Virginia bore tidings of heretofore unheard of casualties, and Grant and Sherman proved able to sustain colossal losses without loosening their grip. Although Arthur and William Mangham may have taken part in a June 8 engagement against two gunboats and a battery above Simmesport on the Atchafalaya, the Crescent spent most of the summer quietly. It departed for Shreveport on June 20, but received orders to join Taylor in crossing the Mississippi River in August. Kirby Smith noted that it was a large regiment, and felt it would be of more assistance to Taylor than a disorganized brigade comprised of ex-Vicksburg parolees. The entire project was born of desperation, however, and Taylor never had faith in his ability to ferry a large body of troops across the Federal-dominated river. Another major concern was the attitude of his troops, especially Texans, many of whom threatened to go home instead of crossing the Mississippi River. Fortunately, the project faded away amidst a background of benign neglect and bureaucratic inefficiency, so the Crescent Regiment meandered between Alexandria and Shreveport for most of the winter. The 28th Louisiana marched with the remainder of Gray's Brigade to Arkansas, then back via Minden to Alexandria by January. If Thomas remained in the ranks of the Claiborne Invincibles until the end, this march must have been particularly poignant for him, as his regiment passed close by his home in Colquit, Louisiana.[149]

Morale in the Trans-Mississippi was shaky by this point, because the men realized that they were making little contribution to defending a nation in its death throes. Many certainly maintained an almost religious faith in eventual victory, but others were increasingly convinced that the Confederacy was "gone up the spout." The breakdown of law and order in north Louisiana and Arkansas was so complete that many soldiers from these districts had to go home to protect their loved ones from bands of brazen jayhawkers numbering up to five hundred men. Individual morale probably was much higher among units with a successful combat record, such as the Manghams experienced in Gray's Brigade, but surviving correspondence from a Claiborne Parish man of the 31st Louisiana lends substance to Kirby Smith's disparagement of morale in Thomas's Brigade of Vicksburg parolees. Private Henry T. Morgan's letters generally evinced great discouragement and war-weariness, beginning soon after his enlistment in 1862, although in April 1863 he allowed: "Well, i think wee will whip the Yankeys if wee can get plenty to eat. And then we will have as glorious nation. This is all that prompts me to action. I have a litel hope yet."[150]

By early 1865, however, Morgan's letters from camp at Alexandria painted a portrait of almost unrelieved woe. From camps commonly referred to as "Starvation Hollow" by the troops, he wrote his wife on January 14: "Ellen thare is about 19 thousand troops and the worst whipt set i ever saw. The river is very hy but no prospect of a fight yet." Ten days later he confessed, "The Armee hear is very much demoralized. I dont believe that the men will fight much hear." By late February, the spectacle of an official execution moved Morgan to take pen in hand once more: "Ellen thare was six men shot in Alexandria last Friday. It seams that wee have got too many men." On a more prosaic level, he added a comment about the poor rations that dogged his whole service career: "The beef is so poar that wee cant eat it at all and wee dont git meal anuff but after all most of the officers will say that wee git plenty." When the men did get pork, it was occasion for celebration, despite having to pay the transportation costs![151]

By April, Ellen was trying to make arrangements to ship her husband food from their farm in Claiborne, but was repeatedly foiled by uncooperative family and friends: "Henry i wish that all of the men that dont try to git you boys eney thing to eat was thair and had to stay thair till the war ended, that dont care nothing for you all nor your familys." In a telling commentary on the collapse of the Confederacy's transportation and financial systems, she added, "Henry you dont know how bad it hurts me to think you are thar and cant git anuff to eat when you have got plenty at home." In a letter dated April 16, 1865, the young wife summed up her frustrations: "Henry i will bring this to a close fore i have got tothake [toothache] and, i cant send you nothing to eat. I feald mad anuff about not being abel to send you something to eat that i could whip every man in the Confederacy."[152]

Amidst an atmosphere of increasing gloom, the Louisiana troops remained around Alexandria until May 1865, whiling away their time with camp routines and picket duties in a nearly forgotten theater of war. Arthur had earned promotion to fourth sergeant by this time, probably as a reward for outstanding service during the strenuous campaigns of 1864. He was on a well-deserved four-week furlough at the end of February, when the regiment mustered at Fort Randolph. As always, William remained present for duty when the Walmsley Guards fell into line that day, retaining his rank of "high private," and probably a well-deserved reputation for reliability.[153]

While Federal armies ravaged Georgia and the Carolinas and besieged Lee in his entrenchments at Petersburg, those in Louisiana and Arkansas remained quiescent after the thrashings they received in 1864. Few Confederate regimental records survive from the last months of the war in Louisiana, but most soldiers remained at their posts until late April and early May, when ragged men returning home from Virginia brought news of Lee's surrender. Arthur and William remained present or properly accounted for as late as May 15, when the Crescent Regiment's last surviving absentee report showed that twenty of the 84 men assigned to Company K already had slipped away. By this time, returnees from North Carolina were bringing further sad tidings of the Army of Tennessee's surrender; clearly, the jig was up. Except for the pipe dreams of some commanders who considered carrying on resistance in the Trans-Mississippi or fleeing to Mexico, the war had ground inexorably to a halt. After marching from Alexandria to Mansfield in mid-May, Gray's Brigade disbanded on May 19. For the sad Louisianians, the final roll calls amid the lonesome pine woods resounded in a bitter stillness, sanctified by the memories of their greatest victories and haunted forever by the shades of those who made the supreme sacrifice. Thankfully spared the spectacle of a formal surrender on the battlefield, they simply went home; in after years it was known simply as "the breakup." On May 20, the 26th and 28th Louisiana Regiments gathered around the flagpole in Mansfield and lowered the colors. With tears in their eyes, each man tore off a piece as a keepsake before leaving.[154]

4. AFTER "THE BREAKUP": LENGTHENING SHADOWS ALONG THE RED RIVER VALLEY

Although the Trans-Mississippi Department formally surrendered on May 26, 1865, most of its soldiers already had started for home. Arthur and William Mangham remained in ranks until the breakup, and like many others in the Red River valley they came back to Natchitoches on June 20 to accept formal paroles from Federal authorities. With this act, William Mangham disappeared amidst the social, political, and economic maelstrom that engulfed prostrate Louisiana. His brother Josiah Thomas Mangham survived the war, but Claiborne Parish tax records provide the only rays of light in the darkness surrounding his postwar life. The census taker in 1870 made no record of his presence in Louisiana, but tax assessors in 1871 recorded J. T. Mangham as the owner of $250 worth of real estate and fifty dollars worth of other property. Of course, these rock-bottom valuations reflected the scarcity of money in the postwar South. Tax assessments in 1874 and 1875 record that his 240 acres were worth only a dollar per acre. In all probability, he owned this same land in 1860, when it bore a value four times greater than in the hard times after the war. The assessors recorded Thomas as a non-resident in these postwar records, listing his agent as Asberry W. Palmer, a neighbor from Colquit. Asberry probably was a close relative of the Palmers who settled with the Mangham families near Coushatta, and he had served in the 11th Louisiana Battalion with Arthur and William Mangham. The 1879 tax rolls list Thomas as the owner of the same property, but omit any special identification of him as a non-resident.[155]

*   *   *   *   *

Although his cousins William and Thomas left little if any trail in the turbulent postwar South, Arthur Green Mangham, Jr. returned home to Coushatta Chute to marry and settle down. The young veteran was 21 when Parson Clegg officiated at his marriage to 17-year-old Mariah Lewis Murph at her parents' nearby home on October 25, 1865. His mother Sarah died of pneumonia that November, and Arthur Mangham, Sr., married Margaret D. Williams just two months later. Apparently, she passed away soon thereafter, for the elder Mangham married again in November 1867. His third wife was Caroline Amelia Baird, herself a widow with three children.[156]

Arthur and Caroline moved their family to Bell County, Texas in 1869, paying one thousand dollars for half interest in a tannery and lot located in Salado. Located on the banks of Salado Creek, Arthur was a close neighbor of his second cousin *Willis W. Mangham*, who had moved to Bell County in the 1850s (see Chapter VI). Since Willis served with the 21st Texas Cavalry in the Red River Campaign just five years before Arthur moved west, one wonders if they met in Louisiana and established a correspondence that led to Arthur's eventual move to Bell County. Indeed, they may have known each other from earlier days in Alabama, where they lived in neighboring Chambers and Russell counties from the 1830s until Willis left for Texas in 1853.[157]

Maintaining the pattern set in Arthur's earlier moves from North Carolina, Georgia, and Alabama, several relatives joined the migration to Texas. His daughter Frances Mangham Ward moved to neighboring Coryell County, as did his son Arthur, with his little family. The younger Arthur and Mariah settled with their two-year-old son, Charles Warren Mangham, on a farm near Gatesville. Little Charlie was the namesake of Arthur's teenaged brother, Charles John Mangham, who soon moved into their home after his relations soured with his stepmother and her children in Salado. Arthur probably settled along the Leon River, whose bottom lands provided the only arable land in the county. Although the Civil War was over, this part of Texas was still frontier country, and the Indian threat was real. The *Texas Almanac for 1861* had complained: "The Indians have been very troublesome here for the last two or three years; and if something is not soon done for our relief, we will have to give the country up to them, or all turn out in battle, and fight for our lives and property." Three years later, Gatesville was the headquarters for the state's Second Frontier District, and its militia company fought in the disastrous 1864 Indian fight at Dove Creek. If anything, the frontier had rolled back eastward during the war, when most able-bodied white males were fighting Federals, not Indians.[158]

By 1874, the elder Manghams in Salado were unable to keep up the payments on notes they owed, probably because of the massive economic depression that beset the United States in 1873. Through this default, they lost ownership of their tannery and lot in 1876, when Arthur was 65 years old. It is unclear if he managed to recover financially before he passed away on June 7, 1878. Caroline lived for many years afterwards, before she died in 1915. Husband and wife lie buried in Texas.[159]

His son and namesake moved back to Louisiana in 1876, perhaps driven by economic hardship, marauding Indians, or perhaps an inheritance of land at the old home place. His uncle, James Green Mangham, had moved Martha and their family from Claiborne Parish to Coushatta Chute by 1870, possibly renting or buying his elder brother's land when Arthur removed to Texas. Green farmed two hundred acres of land on a spread that included twice that amount of unimproved woodland. The property itself was worth $1500 even in the depressed times shortly after the war, but he apparently rented much of the land he worked, because census records appraised the worth of his personally owned real estate at only $600. In a state so thoroughly ravaged by war, land-rich but livestock-poor, the value of his farm animals was fully one-third higher than the farm itself. By 1874, Green owned 650 acres of land, but the massive economic depression still kept property values low, and it was valued at only $625. Six years later, the long term political, economic, and social upheaval of war and

Reconstruction conspired to keep farm values critically low. Green remained on the same property, but his 590 acres were worth only one thousand dollars.[160]

His nephew, Arthur Mangham, Jr., lived in the second farmhouse down from Green, on 160 acres that he owned. He farmed thirty acres with the help of Mariah, his brother Charles, and John Riley, a middle aged black man who probably had belonged to the nearby Riley family before emancipation. His son Charlie was now eleven and attending school, while daughter Kate was five years old. Typical of the Deep South subsistence farmer of that era, Arthur owned a few cows and hogs, and depended on corn as his main crop. He planted only six acres in cotton, harvesting three bales as a small cash crop to assist in buying goods he could not produce on the farm. Later that year, daughter Winnie was born, and 1884 witnessed the arrival of another daughter, Willie. She was born just months after the death of Arthur's uncle, James Green Mangham, who died on October 10, 1883. Green's wife Martha had died in 1876 after bearing nine children, and his second wife, Julia Murph, had another two before Green passed away. The numerous descendants of Arthur and Green Mangham ensured the clan remained well represented around Coushatta for another century.[161]

Surrounded by members of his extended family, Arthur Green Mangham, Jr. continued to work his little farm well into the 20th century. By 1911, however, he was 67 years old and had suffered from "the gravil" for fifteen years, as well as a condition he described as "nervous prostration." Essentially unable to work due to his ill health, he farmed only three acres. Doubtless, this was a mere vegetable patch, to supplement assistance he received from the children who must have provided for him and Mariah in their advancing age. On May 20 of that year, he appeared before the Red River Parish Clerk of Court to file for a Confederate veteran's pension. Old comrades O. C. Wood and John H. Long attested to his honorable service in Holloway's Company, 11th Louisiana Battalion, and later in Johnston's Company K, Crescent Regiment. Fifty years earlier, as an 18-year-old farm boy whose hands were more accustomed to plow handles than quill pens, he had signed his enlistment papers with a mark. In the twilight years of his life, however, the aging veteran carefully signed his pension application as "A. G. Mangham." That year, Louisiana's state government took a special census of its surviving Confederate veterans, in order to plan for the pension assistance that the old soldiers and their families would require. Along with his third cousin *Thomas Jefferson Mangham* of Lincoln Parish, Arthur Green Mangham Jr. answered this final roll call.[162]

Arthur died at home of Bright's Disease on August 6, 1913, amid the family, woods, and small farms he had fought to defend as a young boy. He lies buried near his uncle, James Green Mangham, in the family "Tan Yard" cemetery that evokes memories of his father's trade. Twenty-five other headstones bearing the family name surround the weathered marker that stands guard over his last resting-place. Although eighty-five years of hot sun and pouring rain have worn the epitaph almost smooth, the proud legacy of a farm boy's youth remains tangible for the visitor whose fingertips carefully trace the inscription. It reads: "A. G. Mangham, Co. K, Crescent La. Inf., C. S."[163]

*   *   *   *   *

Mariah L. Mangham sold their 120 acres to M. C. Spence for $180, then moved in with her son Charlie. She applied for a Confederate widow's pension three months after Arthur died, and received a quarterly stipend of sixty dollars from the state until she passed away on April 30, 1924. When the Pension Board issued a sixty-dollar pensioner's warrant in her name for the quarter ending June 30, her son duly returned it.[164]

[1] Marriage records, Talbot County; Will Green Mangham, "The Arthur Green Mangham Family," in Red River Parish Heritage Society, *Red River Parish–Our Heritage* (N.p.: Everett Publishing Co., 1989), p. 349; Claiborne Parish Conveyance Records, Book 1-2, p. 234. Many of the original Mangham immigrants to Natchitoches (later Red River) Parish lie buried in the family cemetery near Coushatta. The "Tanyard" or "Tan Yard" cemetery's name is a good indication that Arthur pursued his trade in Louisiana. For a list of the 26 Mangham graves, see Gwen Bradford Sealy, *Lest We Forget: A Record of Tombstone Inscriptions, Red River Parish, Louisiana and Vicinity* (Shreveport: author, 1983), pp. 126-127.

[2] Will Mangham, "Arthur Green Mangham Family," *Red River Parish*, p. 349; Claiborne Parish, Louisiana Marriage Records (Hammond: Hunting for Bears, Inc.), p. 51; Russell County Marriage Records. The 1860 census reflects Elbert Gray, William Sockwell, and James Sockwell living in Claiborne Parish.

[3] 1860 Census and Slave Census, Natchitoches Parish.

[4] Claiborne Parish Conveyance Records, Book F, pp. 535, 735. The same records show that Arthur Mangham still owned property in Claiborne Parish.

[5] CMSR, Thomas H. Mangham, 19th Louisiana; John D. Winters, *The Civil War in Louisiana* (Baton Rouge: LSU Press, 1963), pp. 20, 57-58, 71-72; D. W. Harris and B. M. Hulse, comps., *The History of Claiborne Parish, Louisiana, etc.* (New Orleans: W. B. Stansbury & Co., 1886), p. 218. Thomas was mustered into service as *Manghram*, but was carried on subsequent rolls as *Mangham*.

[6] Ken Durham, "'Dear Rebecca': The Civil War Letters of William Edwards Paxton, 1861-1863," *Louisiana History* 20, no. 2 (Spring 1979): 172-173, 175-178; Winters, *Civil War in Louisiana*, pp. 22-25; Arthur W. Bergeron, Jr., ed., *The Civil War Reminiscences of Major Silas T. Grisamore, C. S. A.* (Baton Rouge: LSU Press, 1993), pp. 3, 6, 13.

[7] Durham, "Civil War Letters of William Edwards Paxton," pp. 179-180.

[8] Ibid., p. 181; OR 7, pp. 890-891, 894-895; Bergeron, *Grisamore*, pp. 16-18.

[9] OR 10, pt. 1, pp. 492-494; Durham, "Civil War Letters of William Edwards Paxton," p. 184; CMSR, Thomas H. Mangham. Thomas's brother Arthur and cousin William served in the Consolidated Crescent Regiment when it was stationed in western Louisiana; it suffered 127 casualties at Shiloh ("Memorial to Louisianians at Shiloh," CV 22: 342-343).

[10] CMSR, Thomas H. Mangham; Durham, "Civil War Letters of William Edwards Paxton," pp. 185-186; OR 10, pt. 1, pp. 820-821; Bergeron, *Grisamore*, pp. 18, 51.

[11] Douglas John Cater, *As It Was: Reminiscences of a Soldier of the Third Texas Cavalry and the Nineteenth Louisiana Infantry* (Austin: State House Press, 1990), pp. 137-138. Many years after the war, Cater belonged to San Antonio's Albert Sidney Johnston Camp, UCV. Another member of this camp was Thomas's first cousin Charles A. Mangham, a veteran of the 18th Alabama. *Confederate Veteran* magazine recognized Cater and Mangham as two members of a group of San Antonio octogenarians who attended the 1924 UCV reunion in Dallas, Texas (CV 32: 146).

[12] OR 16, pt. 2, p. 733.

[13] CMSR, Thomas H. Mangham; Record of Events Cards, 19th Louisiana, CMSR; Bergeron, *Grisamore*, pp. 72-78.

[14] Bergeron, *Grisamore*, p. 79; CMSR, Thomas H. Mangham; Cater, *As It Was*, pp. 140-143; Major William Gilham, *Manual of Instruction for the Volunteers and Militia of the United States* (Philadelphia: Charles Desilver, 1861; reprint, n.d.), pp. 33-37. The July-August muster roll for the Claiborne Volunteers noted that Thomas was absent with the Quartermaster's Department, but he probably reported shortly after muster on September 1 with Grisamore and the other 18th and 19th Louisiana teamsters.

[15] Cater, *As It Was*, pp. 140, 145; Bergeron, *Grisamore*, pp. 80-83. Trains coming down from nearby Greenville daily brought farmers selling fresh produce to the soldiers at Pollard, so Thomas may well have had an opportunity to visit his aunt, Rhoda Callaway Mangham Moore, and her son, William T. T. Mangham. Willie enlisted in the 61st Alabama in May 1863 (see Chapter VIII).

[16] Cater, *As It Was*, pp. 145-147.

[17] Ibid., pp. 147-149.

[18] Stanley F. Horn, *The Army of Tennessee* (Bobbs-Merrill, 1941; reprint, Norman: Univ. of Oklahoma Press, 1993), pp. 214-217.

[19] Cater, *As It Was*, pp. 149-150.

[20] Ibid., pp. 152-153; CMSR, Thomas H. Mangham; Record of Events Cards, 19th Louisiana; Horn, *Army of Tennessee*, pp. 218-219.

[21] Cater, *As It Was*, p. 154; Horn, *Army of Tennessee*, pp. 220-221.

[22] Cater, *As It Was*, pp. 153-156. For a soldier's comparison of the "Union hurrah" and the "Rebel yell," see Rod Gragg, *The Illustrated Confederate Reader* (New York: Harper & Row, 1989), pp. 130-131.

[23] Cater, *As It Was*, pp. 153-156; OR 24, pt. 2, pp. 655-657. It is unclear if the Claiborne Grays were in position to fire on the attackers, as Company C was in the right wing of the regiment's line, not the left. Colonel Winans stated in his report, however, that he engaged the enemy with the "three left companies of my right." Perhaps "right" was simply an improper transcription of the word "regiment." If Colonel Winans used the word intentionally, however, it indicates that he had positioned the regiment's right wing companies on the left of his line, and Company C was engaged as the first company on his left. If the regiment filed into the trenches "by

the left flank," however, the normal line of battle was reversed, and Company C was fifth from the left. On such apparently arcane distinctions hung life and death itself.

[24] OR 24, pt. 2, pp. 523-525, 655-657; Cater, *As It Was*, p. 156. The regiment lost one man killed and four wounded in front of Jackson. See OR 24, pt. 2, p. 654.

[25] Cater, *As It Was*, pp. 157-159; Horn, *Army of Tennessee*, p. 220. Chapter IV discusses Colonel Mangham's actions at Jackson in more detail.

[26] Glenn Tucker, *Chickamauga: Bloody Battle in the West* (Bobbs-Merrill Co., 1961; reprint, Dayton: Morningside, 1992), pp. 97, 234; William C. Davis, *The Orphan Brigade: The Kentucky Confederates Who Couldn't Go Home* (Baton Rouge: LSU Press, 1980), p. 170; Cater, *As It Was*, pp. 158-159.

[27] Tucker, *Chickamauga*, pp. 192-193; OR 30, pt. 2, pp. 197-199, 226; Cozzens, *Terrible Sound*, pp. 325-326.

[28] OR 30, pt. 2, p. 199; Tucker, *Chickamauga*, p. 233; Cozzens, *Terrible Sound*, p. 326

[29] OR 30, pt. 2, p. 225; Tucker, *Chickamauga*, pp. 215, 223, 231-236; Cozzens, *Terrible Sound*, pp. 326-329.

[30] Cozzens, *Terrible Sound*, pp. 329-331; OR 30, pt. 2, pp. 221-226; Tucker, *Chickamauga*, pp. 236-237.

[31] Ibid.

[32] OR 30, pt. 2, pp. 221-226; Cozzens, *Terrible Sound*, pp. 500-501. If Thomas Mangham was in this final charge, he passed through the recumbent ranks of Wilson's Georgia Brigade. His second cousins (once removed) Thomas Woodward Mangham and Willis Austin Mangham belonged to the 30th Georgia, although Tom had suffered a severe wound on the previous day (see Chapter IV).

[33] OR 30, pt. 2, pp. 224-226; William F. Fox, *Regimental Losses in the American Civil War, 1861-1865* (Albany: Brandow Printing, 1898; reprint, Dayton: Morningside, 1985), p. 570. The hardest-hit Confederate regiment at Chickamauga was the 18th Alabama, whose ranks included Thomas's first cousin Charles A. Mangham (see Chapter VIII).

[34] Cater, *As It Was*, pp. 162-163.

[35] CMSR, Thomas H. Mangham.

[36] ORS I, vol. 6, pp. 112-130; Cater, *As It Was*, p. 167; Harris and Hulse, *Claiborne Parish*, pp. 200-201; Record of Events Cards, 19th Louisiana.

[37] OR 31, pt. 3, p. 825.

[38] CMSR, Thomas H. Mangham; Record of Events Cards, 19th Louisiana; Larry J. Daniel, *Soldiering in the Army of Tennessee: A Portrait of Life in a Confederate Army* (Chapel Hill: UNC Press, 1991), pp. 139-141.

[39] Cater, *As It Was*, pp. 168-169; Albert Castel, *Decision in the West: The Atlanta Campaign of 1864* (Lawrence: Univ. Press of Kansas, 1992), pp. 49-54. Lieutenant Colonel Turner was promoted after Colonel Winans was killed at Missionary Ridge.

[40] Castel, *Decision*, pp. 128-130, 140, 144; CMSR, Thomas H. Mangham; OR 38, pt. 3, pp. 815, 854, 865; Horn, *Army of Tennessee*, pp. 322-324.

[41] OR 38, pt. 3, pp. 816, 854, 865; Castel, *Decision*, pp. 149-150; Horn, *Army of Tennessee*, pp. 323-325.

[42] Castel, *Decision*, pp. 165-166; OR 38, pt. 3, pp. 817, 854, 866; Horn, *Army of Tennessee*, p. 325.

[43] OR 38, pt. 3, pp. 817, 854, 866; Castel, *Decision*, pp. 175-178; Horn, *Army of Tennessee*, p. 325.

[44] Castel, *Decision*, pp. 180-181; OR 38, pt. 3, pp. 818, 854, 866-867; Horn, *Army of Tennessee*, p. 325.

[45] Castel, *Decision*, pp. 213-217; OR 38, pt. 3, p. 867; Horn, *Army of Tennessee*, p. 329.

[46] Castel, *Decision*, pp. 218-223; Horn, *Army of Tennessee*, p. 329.

[47] OR 38, pt. 3, pp. 855, 862-863, 867. Note: Austin lost fifteen of the 45 men assigned to his battalion. The other losses came from the two companies attached to him for skirmish duty from the 16th and 19th Louisiana regiments.

[48] Castel, *Decision*, pp. 223-226; OR 38, pt. 3, pp. 818, 867; Horn, *Army of Tennessee*, pp. 329-330.

[49] Horn, *Army of Tennessee*, pp. 329-330; OR 38, pt. 2, p. 14; pt. 3, p. 818; Castel, *Decision*, pp. 225-226; Richard A. Baumgartner and Larry M. Strayer, *Kennesaw Mountain, June 1864: Bitter Standoff at the Gibraltar of Georgia* (Huntington: Blue Acorn Press, 1998), p. 13. Horn believed Hooker's casualties were higher than 1665; Stewart estimated his adversary lost 3000-5000 men. Castel's statement that Hooker suffered 665 casualties is apparently a misprint, as Hooker reported 1665 casualties.

[50] OR 38, pt. 3, pp. 818, 855, 867; Harris and Hulse, *Claiborne Parish*, p. 201; Castel, *Decision*, pp. 228-229. Foster is cited in Castel.

[51] OR 38, pt. 3, pp. 855, 867-868; Castel, *Decision*, pp. 226, 230-231, 242-243; Richard M. McMurry, "Confederate Morale in the Atlanta Campaign of 1864," *GHQ* 45, no. 2 (1970): 238-239. McMurry's outstanding article demonstrates convincingly that much of the later anti-Hood feeling was retrospective in nature, although contemporary sources evidence a good deal of such concerns, too. Likewise, many soldiers who supposedly dreaded Hood's accession to command had become increasingly pessimistic that Johnston would ever stand and fight.

[52] Baumgartner, *Kennesaw Mountain*, p. 27; Rice C. Bull, *Soldiering: The Civil War Diary of Rice C. Bull, 123rd New York Volunteer Infantry* (Novato: Presidio Press, 1977), p. 121; F. Jay Taylor, ed., *Reluctant Rebel: The Secret Diary of Robert Patrick, 1861-1865* (Baton Rouge: LSU Press, 1987), p. 197. Patrick's regiment was the 4th Louisiana, which transferred into Gibson's Brigade in July.

[53] Taylor, ed., *Reluctant Rebel*, pp. 199-200.

[54] Castel, *Decision*, pp. 262, 408, 417, 424-428; OR 38, pt. 3, p. 819.

[55] Castel, *Decision*, pp. 429-430; OR 38, pt. 3, pp. 821, 856.

[56] OR 38, pt. 3, pp. 821, 856-857; Castel, *Decision*, pp. 429-430.

[57] Castel, *Decision*, pp. 430-436; Horn, *Army of Tennessee*, pp. 360-361; Cater, *As It Was*, p. 188; OR 38, pt. 3, pp. 856-857. Cater details the numbers of officers and

enlisted men on the regiment's casualty list, but does not specify the date or name of the battle. From context, however, it is clear that he is referring to the Battle of Ezra Church. Many of the regiment's company-level Record of Events Cards named this engagement "Poor House," in reference to the structure that stood near the battlefield.

[58] Colonel T. B. Roy, "General Hardee and the Military Operations Around Atlanta," *SHSP* 8 (1881): 341; Taylor, ed., *Reluctant Rebel*, pp. 202-203. Patrick's 4th Louisiana lost 82 of 240 men engaged.

[59] OR 38, pt. 3, p. 764; Cater, *As It Was*, pp. 186-187. Again, Cater fails to specify the date or place of Lee's speech to the troops, but it clearly came in the aftermath of Ezra Church. For a montage of Atlanta under siege, see A. A. Hoehling, *Last Train from Atlanta* (New York: T. Yoseloff, 1958; reprint, Harrisburg: Stackpole Books, 1992).

[60] OR 38, pt. 3, pp. 762-767; Castel, *Decision*, pp. 495-499.

[61] CMSR, Thomas H. Mangham; Castel, *Decision*, pp. 495-500; OR 38, pt. 3, pp. 857-858.

[62] In direct contrast to Gibson's official report, Castel mentions a color-bearer in Gibson's Brigade, who "could not find a single member of his regiment who was willing to go forward with him in another charge." See Castel, *Decision*, pp. 481, 504.

[63] OR 38, pt. 3, pp. 822, 858; CMSR, Thomas H. Mangham; Cater, *As It Was*, pp. 191-192. It is sometimes difficult to determine the exact date a company mustered, since they mustered *for* a given period but not necessarily on the last day *of* that period, as regulations specified. In this case, however, Company C mustered at Jonesboro. Since August 31 was the only day they spent at this location, they mustered either shortly before or shortly after the battle. The muster roll reflects that Thomas was present. The 4th Louisiana's colonel told Robert Patrick that his regiment went into the fight with 110 men and emerged with only 43. See Taylor, ed., *Reluctant Rebel*, p. 221.

[64] Castel, *Decision*, pp. 481-485, 502. Major Taylor's 47th Ohio practically disintegrated when its enlistments expired in the summer of 1864: only 79 enlisted men remained in the entire regiment.

[65] Ibid., pp. 497-498, 502-504. Castel argues that a "less feeble" attack simply would have resulted in a higher casualty toll, citing the high losses of Gibson's and H. R. Jackson's brigades in their determined assaults. Thomas fought under Gibson's command; his second cousin (once removed) Willis A. Mangham, a sergeant in the 30th Georgia, was critically wounded in Jackson's charge (see Chapter IV).

[66] Ibid., pp. 506-510, 537-541; Horn, *Army of Tennessee*, pp. 365-368.

[67] Record of Events Cards, 19th Louisiana; OR 39, pt. 3, p. 897; Wiley Sword, *The Confederacy's Last Hurrah: Spring Hill, Franklin, and Nashville* (Lawrence: Univ. Press of Kansas, 1992), pp. 66, 80. As Sword illustrates, the delay at Florence was largely a product of Hood's careless logistical planning.

[68] CMSR, Thomas H. Mangham; Cater, *As It Was*, pp. 200-201; Record of Events Cards, 19th Louisiana; Harris and Hulse, *Claiborne Parish*, p. 202.

[69] Sword, *Confederacy's Last Hurrah*, pp. 269-270; OR 45, pt. 1, pp. 255-257, 684-686.

[70] Sword, *Confederacy's Last Hurrah*, pp. 279-282, 303-305; OR 45, pt. 1, p. 697; Horn, *Army of Tennessee*, pp. 405-407.

[71] Sword, *Confederacy's Last Hurrah*, pp. 287, 316; OR 45, pt. 1, pp. 697-698, 702; Horn, *Army of Tennessee*, p. 417. Thomas left about 15,000 men in Nashville itself, employing some 55,000 in his attack. All statistical information regarding Hood's army in the Tennessee Campaign is fraught with uncertainty, as surviving reports are incomplete or even misleading. After the campaign ended, both Hood and his numerous detractors had a distinct interest in making the record support their conflicting claims. Estimates of his strength at Nashville range from 15,000 to about 23,000. See Horn, *Army of Tennessee*, p. 417.

[72] OR 45, pt. 1, pp. 698, 702; Sword, *Confederacy's Last Hurrah*, pp. 358-362; Cater, *As It Was*, p. 202.

[73] Sword, *Confederacy's Last Hurrah*, pp. 354-355, 359-363; OR 45, pt. 1, p. 698.

[74] OR 45, pt. 1, pp. 698, 702; Sword, *Confederacy's Last Hurrah*, pp. 359-363.

[75] Sword, *Confederacy's Last Hurrah*, pp. 359-363, 370-379; OR 45, pt. 1, pp. 294-297, 698, 702; Horn, *Army of Tennessee*, p. 417. General Thomas claimed that his troops captured 4462 Confederate prisoners at Nashville.

[76] OR 45, pt. 1, pp. 698-700, 703; Sword, *Confederacy's Last Hurrah*, pp. 384, 387, 394-399.

[77] CMSR, Thomas H. Mangham; Cater, *As It Was*, pp. 203-205; Record of Events Cards, 19th Louisiana. The muster roll for September 1, 1864 through February 28, 1865 gives no indication that Thomas was absent until late January; apparently he was in ranks during the Tennessee Campaign.

[78] CMSR, Thomas H. Mangham; Record of Events Cards, 19th Louisiana; Richard M. McMurry, *John Bell Hood and the War for Southern Independence* (Lincoln: Univ. of Nebraska Press, 1982), p. 182.

[79] CMSR, Thomas H. Mangham; Sword, *Confederacy's Last Hurrah*, pp. 425-426; Horn, *Army of Tennessee*, p. 417, 422-423. Horn states that 3500 men were furloughed and another 4000 sent to Mobile. Of the remaining 10,000, possibly only 5000 actually went to North Carolina as ordered. Horn also notes, however, that the last figures are given by General Johnston, a bitter enemy of Hood.

[80] Record of Events Cards, 19th Louisiana; CMSR, Thomas H. Mangham.

[81] Claiborne Parish Comptroller's Assessment Rolls, 1866, LSA. A search of personal estate, loyalty oath, and land conveyance records at the Claiborne Parish courthouse turned up no additional information on the fate of Thomas H. Mangham. Further investigation at the Louisiana State Archives included pension records, death certificates, tax assessment rolls for several parishes, an index to State Land Office records, and an index to Confederate proofs and land warrants.

[82] William C. Oates, *The War Between the Union and the Confederacy and its Lost Opportunities* (1905; reprint, Dayton: Morningside, 1985), p. 158. Oates's regiment faced Chamberlain's 20th Maine in the battle for Little Round Top at Gettysburg.

[83] *Natchitoches Union*, May 15, 1862; 1860 Census, Natchitoches Parish; Robert L. Kerby, *Kirby Smith's Confederacy: The Trans-Mississippi South, 1863-1865*, (Tuscaloosa: Univ. of Alabama Press, 1972), pp. 64-68.

[84] *Natchitoches Union*, May 15, 1862.

[85] Ibid.; CMSRs, Arthur G. and William J. Mangham, 11th Louisiana Battalion.

[86] *Natchitoches Union*, May 15, 1862, and May 22, 1862; Arthur W. Bergeron, Jr., *Guide to Louisiana Confederate Military Units, 1861-1865* (Baton Rouge: LSU Press, 1989), p. 164; Winters, *Civil War in Louisiana*, pp. 149-151.

[87] Winters, *Civil War in Louisiana*, pp. 151-155; Record of Events Cards, 11th Louisiana Bn., CMSR; OR 15, p. 805.

[88] Bergeron, *Guide*, p. 138; CMSR, Josiah T. Mangham, 28th Louisiana; OR 15, p. 790. Another member of the Claiborne Invincibles was George Mangum Calhoun Raney, born in Putnam County, Georgia, in 1828. It is likely that his parents, John Raney and Penelope Robinson, were closely related to the Mangum and/or Mangham families prominent in Putnam at that time. See 28th Louisiana Unit Files, CRC.

[89] 1850 Census, Russell County; 1860 Census, Slave Census, and Agricultural Schedule, Claiborne Parish; 1860 Census, Natchitoches Parish; Will Green Mangham, "James Green Mangham," *Red River Parish*, pp. 353-354. Many years after the war, a veteran of the Claiborne Invincibles listed the name "T. J. Mangham" on the unit roster he provided from memory, thus providing another hint that friends and acquaintances called him Thomas. See Harris and Hulse, *Claiborne Parish*, p. 240.

[90] 1860 Census, Claiborne Parish. Josiah T. Mangham purchased 240 acres from the Monroe Land Office on August 20, 1858 (see on-line at http://data.Ancestry.com, Mangham Database Search Results, Louisiana Land Records).

[91] Winters, *Civil War in Louisiana*, p. 154; OR 15, p. 790; Bergeron, *Guide*, p. 139; Terry L. Jones, "The 28th Louisiana Volunteers in the Civil War," *North Louisiana Historical Association Journal* 9 (1978): 85-86; Richard Taylor, *Destruction and Reconstruction: Personal Experiences of the Late War* (reprint, New York: Longmans, Green and Co., 1955), p. 136; Bergeron, *Grisamore*, p. 104; Harris and Hulse, *Claiborne Parish*, p. 238.

[92] Record of Events Cards, 11th Louisiana Bn., CMSR; OR 24, pt. 3, p. 1057; Winters, *Civil War in Louisiana*, pp. 172-173.

[93] CMSRs, Arthur G. and William J. Mangham; Record of Events Cards, 11th Louisiana Bn., CMSR; Taylor, *Destruction and Reconstruction*, pp. 140-141; Bergeron, *Guide*, p. 164.

[94] CMSRs, Arthur G. and William J. Mangham; Bergeron, *Guide*, p. 28; OR 15, p. 348; OR 24, pt. 1, p. 368; Taylor, *Destruction and Reconstruction*, pp. 146-149.

[95] ORS I, vol. 3, pp. 184-187; OR 15, pp. 290-291; Kerby, *Kirby Smith's Confederacy*, p. 98; Bergeron, *Guide*, p. 139. Captain Thomas Abney, commanding officer of Company B, led the 28th Louisiana's detachment in action against the *Diana*.

[96] Bergeron, *Grisamore*, pp. 107-108.

[97] Winters, *Civil War in Louisiana*, pp. 222-223; Jones, "28th Louisiana," p. 87; OR 15, p. 358.

[98] OR 15, pp. 388-389.

[99] Ibid.; Bergeron, *Grisamore*, p. 112; Winters, *Civil War in Louisiana*, p. 223.

[100] OR 15, pp. 359, 389-90; Winters, *Civil War in Louisiana*, pp. 223-225.

[101] Ibid.; Jones, "28th Louisiana," p. 87.

[102] OR 15, p. 391; Winters, *Civil War in Louisiana*, p. 225; Bergeron, *Grisamore*, p. 113.

[103] OR (*Navies*) 20, pp. 134-135, 137 (all references are to Series I); OR 24, pt. 1, pp. 365-366. Sources disagree about the identification of the boat that accompanied the *Queen of the West*. Historian John Winters identifies it as the *Minna Simma*, while General Taylor refers to it as a "tender." Contemporaries also differ, as an official report by Lt. Cdr. A. P. Cooke, commanding *U.S.S. Estrella*, refers to a "white river boat," whereas diarist Baird aboard the *U.S.S. Calhoun* asserts that the *Grand Duke* and the *Mary T.* both accompanied the *Queen* in this action. See Winters, *Civil War in Louisiana*, p. 230; Taylor, *Destruction and Reconstruction*, p. 160; OR *Navies* 20, pp. 134-135, 137.

[104] OR *(Navies)* 20, p. 137.

[105] Ibid., pp. 135, 138.

[106] Ibid.

[107] OR 15, pp. 359-360, 391-392; Jones, "28th Louisiana," p. 88; Bergeron, *Grisamore*, pp. 113-114; Taylor, *Destruction and Reconstruction*, pp. 158-159.

[108] Ibid.

[109] OR 15, pp. 360-362; Taylor, *Destruction and Reconstruction*, p. 159; Winters, *Civil War in Louisiana*, pp. 227-228. Grover's reported loss at Irish Bend totaled 49 killed, 256 wounded, 29 captured, and one missing, of which the 3rd Brigade suffered all but 23. Colonel Birge's official report for the 3rd Brigade, however, admitted these losses for his brigade alone, except that the wounded totaled 259. Probably an error in transcription accounts for the discrepancy of 26 men, since the magnitude of the error is too small to arouse suspicion of under-reporting, and Grover presumably would have squared his story with his subordinate's version.

[110] OR 15, pp. 360-361, 392-395; Taylor, *Destruction and Reconstruction*, p. 159; Winters, *Civil War in Louisiana*, pp. 228-229.

[111] Jones, "28th Louisiana," pp. 88-89; Winters, *Civil War in Louisiana*, p. 229; OR 15, pp. 361, 395; CMSRs, Arthur G., William J., and Josiah T. Mangham.

[112] CMSRs, Arthur G., William J., and Josiah T. Mangham. Although these CMSRs simply annotate the Manghams' release "below Port Hudson," some others specify Prophet's Island. See Jeff McFarland, "History of Colonel Gray's 28th Louisiana Infantry," on Steve Pipes's regimental Internet website at http://members.tripod.com /~pipeslines/mcfarlands28th.html.

[113] The Manghams missed an eventful summer campaign in southern Louisiana due to their imprisonment and parole, including a successful raid against Brashear City itself. For a private's snapshot view of some of these events, see Letter, Jeremiah D. Richardson to J. S. Richardson, July 16, 1863, 28th Louisiana Unit Files, CRC.

[114] OR 15, p. 399; OR 26, pt. 1, pp. 321-325; Kerby, *Kirby Smith's Confederacy*, pp. 242-243; Bergeron, *Grisamore*, pp. 115, 127. Although Mouton was acting as division commander, he was not promoted to the rank of major general. Accordingly, Gray acted as brigade commander while retaining the rank of colonel, and his brigade officially bore Mouton's name until sometime after the Battle of Mansfield.

[115] OR 26, pt. 2, p. 402; Bergeron, *Guide*, pp. 139, 147.

[116] Bergeron, *Guide*, pp. 139, 147; Journal of Arthur W. Hyatt, extracted in Napier Bartlett, "The Trans-Mississippi," in *Military Record of Louisiana, Including Biographical and Historical Papers Relating to the Military Organizations of the State* (reprint; Baton Rouge: LSU Press, 1992), p. 12; Jones, "28th Louisiana," p. 89; Bergeron, *Grisamore*, pp. 133-138.

[117] Record of Events Cards, Consolidated Crescent Regiment, Louisiana Infantry, CMSR; CMSRs, Arthur G. and William J. Mangham, Consolidated Crescent; Kerby, *Kirby Smith's Confederacy*, pp. 250-251.

[118] Kerby, *Kirby Smith's Confederacy*, pp. 136-149, 258-265, 283-292.

[119] Ibid.; Ludwell H. Johnson, *Red River Campaign: Politics and Cotton in the Civil War* (Johns Hopkins Press, 1958; reprint, Kent: Kent State Univ. Press, 1993), pp. 80-83.

[120] Hyatt Journal, in "The Trans-Mississippi," Bartlett, *Military Record*, pp. 12-13; Johnson, *Red River*, pp. 86-89; Kerby, *Kirby Smith's Confederacy*, pp. 286-290; Winters, *Civil War in Louisiana*, p. 324; Arthur W. Bergeron, Jr., "A Colonel Earns His Wreath: Col. Henry Gray's Louisiana Brigade at Mansfield," CWR 4, no. 2 (1994): 1-2.

[121] Bergeron, *Grisamore*, pp. 141-142; Johnson, *Red River*, pp. 89-100; Winters, *Civil War in Louisiana*, pp. 329-331; Jones, "28th Louisiana," pp. 90-91.

[122] Johnson, *Red River*, pp. 110-112; Winters, *Civil War in Louisiana*, pp. 335-337; OR 34, pt. 1, p. 562; Hyatt Journal, in "The Trans-Mississippi," Bartlett, *Military Record*, pp. 12-13.

[123] Theodore P. Savas, "Col. James H. Beard and the Consolidated Crescent Regiment," CWR 4, no. 2 (1994): 86-87.

[124] Ibid., pp. 88-89; Johnson, *Red River*, pp. 119-120; OR 34, pt. 1, pp. 562-564; Taylor, *Destruction and Reconstruction*, pp. 194-195.

[125] Bergeron, "Gray's Louisiana Brigade," pp. 9-11; Savas, "Consolidated Crescent," pp. 90-92; Taylor, *Destruction and Reconstruction*, p. 195; ORS I, vol. 6, p. 375; OR 34, pt. 1, p. 564; Hyatt Journal, in "The Trans-Mississippi," Bartlett, *Military Record*, p. 13; Bartlett, "The Twenty-Eighth Louisiana," *Military Record*, p. 61.

[126] OR 34, pt. 1, p. 522.

[127] Ibid., p. 564; Savas, "Consolidated Crescent," p. 91.

[128] Taylor, *Destruction and Reconstruction*, p. 195; OR 34, pt. 1, p. 564; Bergeron, "Gray's Louisiana Brigade," pp. 12-13; J. E. Sligh, "How General Taylor Fought the Battle of Mansfield, LA.," CV 31: 457. (Sligh's name was originally given as *Sliger*, an error corrected in CV 31: 46.)

[129] Savas, "Consolidated Crescent," pp. 94-96; ORS I, vol. 6, p. 375. Companies A and B served as skirmishers for the 28th Louisiana. See Sligh, "Battle of Mansfield," CV 31: 458.

[130] Bergeron, "Gray's Louisiana Brigade," pp. 13-16; Savas, "Consolidated Crescent," p. 96.

[131] Bergeron, "Gray's Louisiana Brigade," p. 13; Savas, "Consolidated Crescent," pp. 93-94.

[132] Bergeron, *Grisamore*, p. 148; Bergeron, "Gray's Louisiana Brigade," pp. 13-16; Savas, "Consolidated Crescent," p. 96; Bartlett, "The Twenty-Eighth Louisiana," *Military Record*, p. 62.

[133] OR 34, pt. 1, p. 564; ORS I, vol. 6, pp. 375-376; Bergeron, "Gray's Louisiana Brigade," pp. 18-19; Winters, *Civil War in Louisiana*, pp. 342-344; Johnson, *Red River*, pp. 135-136. According to historian Arthur Bergeron, the group of Federals involved in the Mouton incident seems to have numbered between 12 and 35 men. In a postwar account, Lt. J. E. Sligh of Company B asserted that he used a captured Sharps rifle to pick off a mounted Federal officer urging the battery to continue firing, thus precipitating the cannoneers' retreat (Sligh, "Battle of Mansfield," CV 31: 458).

[134] OR 34, pt. 1, pp. 564-565; Bergeron, "Gray's Louisiana Brigade," pp. 17-21; Winters, *Civil War in Louisiana*, pp. 344-346; Johnson, *Red River*, pp. 136-137; OR 34, pt. 1, p. 565.

[135] Johnson, *Red River*, pp. 137-139; Winters, *Civil War in Louisiana*, p. 346.

[136] Johnson, *Red River*, pp. 138-139; Bergeron, "Gray's Louisiana Brigade," p. 21; OR 34, pt. 1, p. 565; ORS I, vol. 6, pp. 376-377.

[137] OR 34, pt. 1, p. 565; Winters, *Civil War in Louisiana*, p. 347; Johnson, *Red River*, pp. 146-147.

[138] Johnson, *Red River*, p. 141; Bartlett, "The Trans-Mississippi," *Military Record*, p. 6; Hyatt Journal, in "The Trans-Mississippi," Bartlett, *Military Record*, p. 13; Savas, "Consolidated Crescent," p. 96; Bergeron, "Gray's Louisiana Brigade," pp. 15, 21-22; Bergeron, *Grisamore*, p. 148; OR 34, pt. 1, p. 564. As Grisamore noted, half of the 18th Louisiana was in reserve, sparing it an even greater casualty toll. It seems probable that the regiment's front line companies suffered losses well above fifty percent; Captain Hyatt's company lost 29 of 42 engaged.

[139] OR 34, pt. 1, pp. 565, 567; Johnson, *Red River*, pp. 140-142; Winters, *Civil War in Louisiana*, pp. 346-348; Bergeron, "Gray's Louisiana Brigade," pp. 21-22. Since Emory's division lost 347 of the 5000 men engaged at Pleasant Grove on the evening of April 8, Federal losses for the day totaled 2235 of 12,000 engaged.

[140] OR 34, pt. 1, pp. 565-568; Johnson, *Red River*, pp. 148-162; Winters, *Civil War in Louisiana*, pp. 348-355.

[141] Johnson, *Red River*, pp. 162-164; Winters, *Civil War in Louisiana*, pp. 356-357.

[142] OR 34, pt. 1, pp. 568-569, 570-572; Winters, *Civil War in Louisiana*, pp. 355, 360-361; Bergeron, "Gray's Louisiana Brigade," p. 24; Report of Lt. Gen. Richard Taylor, in "Unpublished After-Action Reports from the Red River," *CWR* 4, no. 2 (1994): 119-128; Bergeron, *Grisamore*, p. 150.

[143] Johnson, *Red River*, pp. 217-218, 223-225, 244, 268-272; Winters, *Civil War in Louisiana*, pp. 362-366.

[144] OR 34, pt. 1, p. 572; Johnson, *Red River*, pp. 225-234; Taylor's Report, "Unpublished After-Action Reports," pp. 120, 123. While Banks was at Alexandria, Polignac's Division was stationed well to the south at Cheneyville to bar the approach of relief forces. It also was a good position from which to contest Banks's retreat.

[145] Taylor's Report, "Unpublished After-Action Reports," p. 125; Johnson, *Red River*, pp. 273-274.

[146] Winters, *Civil War in Louisiana*, pp. 376-377; Taylor's Report, "Unpublished After-Action Reports," p. 126; Johnson, *Red River*, p. 275.

[147] Winters, *Civil War in Louisiana*, pp. 376-377; Bergeron, "Gray's Louisiana Brigade," pp. 24-25; Johnson, *Red River*, p. 275; Taylor's Report, "Unpublished After-Action Reports," p. 126; Bartlett, "The Trans-Mississippi," *Military Record*, p. 6. Mower's report indicated 38 killed, 226 wounded and three missing. These ratios are more typical, casting further doubt on the figures cited for Gray's Brigade.

[148] Taylor's Report, "Unpublished After-Action Reports," pp. 127-128.

[149] OR 41, pt. 1, pp. 99-100; pt. 3, pp. 950, 953; Bergeron, *Guide*, pp. 139, 147; Jones, "28th Louisiana," pp. 93-94.

[150] John A. Cawthon, ed., "Letters of a North Louisiana Private to His Wife, 1862-1865," *The Mississippi Valley Historical Review* 30 (1944), pp. 541-546; Kerby, *Kirby Smith's Confederacy*, pp. 400-402. See also Donald S. Frazier's chapter in Daniel E. Sutherland, ed., *Guerrillas, Unionists, and Violence on the Confederate Home Front* (Fayetteville: Univ. of Arkansas Press, 1999).

[151] Cawthon, ed., "Letters of a North Louisiana Private," pp. 541-546; Kerby, *Kirby Smith's Confederacy*, p. 382.

[152] Cawthon, ed., "Letters of a North Louisiana Private," pp. 549-550.

[153] Extract, Muster Roll, Company K, Consolidated Crescent Regiment, Mansfield State Park, Mansfield, Louisiana.

[154] Bergeron, *Guide*, pp. 139, 147; Jones, "28th Louisiana," p. 94; OR 41, pt. 1, p. 605; Winters, *Civil War in Louisiana*, pp. 424-425. The author is indebted to Dr. Art Bergeron, Jr., for extracts from the Crescent Regiment's muster roll and from the May 15, 1865 absentee report on file in the Louisiana Adjutant General's Library.

[155] CMSRs, Arthur G. and William J. Mangham; Comptroller Assessment Rolls, Claiborne Parish, 1871, 1873-1881, LSA; 1870 and 1880 Censuses, Claiborne Parish.

For more on taxation and land devaluation in postwar Louisiana, see Roger Wallace Shugg, "Survival of the Plantation System in Louisiana," in Mark T. Carleton, et al., eds., *Readings in Louisiana Politics* (Baton Rouge: Claitor's Publishing Division, 1975), pp. 343-345.

[156] Confederate Pension Applications, Red River Parish, Mrs. M. L. Mangham, LSA; Will Mangham, "Arthur Green Mangham Family," pp. 349-350; *Natchitoches Parish, Louisiana Marriages, 1805-1900* (Hammond: Hunting for Bears, Inc.), p. 160.

[157] Will Mangham, "Arthur Green Mangham Family," pp. 349-350; Bell County, Deed Book M, p. 146. The 1870 Bell County census lists "W. W. Mangham" on page 57 and "A. Mangum" on page 67. All Bell County land transactions refer to "Arthur Mangham," including those he signed. See Willis W. Mangham in Chapter VI.

[158] Will Green Mangham, "Arthur Green Mangham Family," pp. 349-351; 1870 Census, Coryell County, Texas; B. P. Gallaway, ed., *Texas, The Dark Corner of the Confederacy: Contemporary Accounts of the Lone Star State in the Civil War*, 3rd ed. (Lincoln: Univ. of Nebraska Press, 1994), pp. 68-69, 206-207, 220-221.

[159] Bell County, Deed Book T, pp. 381-383, and Deed Book 27, pp. 15-16; Will Green Mangham, "Arthur Green Mangham Family," pp. 349-350.

[160] Confederate Pension Applications, Red River Parish, A. G. Mangham, LSA; 1870 Census and Agricultural Schedule, Natchitoches Parish; 1880 Census and Agricultural Schedule, Red River Parish; Comptroller Assessment Rolls, Red River Parish, 1874-1888, LSA. Although the 1880 agricultural schedule records J. G. Mangham as farming his land on a "fixed rental" basis, this probably was in error. The 1886 tax assessments show his son's 400 acres as comprising part of "the J. G. Mangham place."

[161] 1880 Census and Agricultural Schedule, Red River Parish; Will Green Mangham, "James Green Mangham," pp. 353-356, and "Arthur Green Mangham Family," pp. 349-353.

[162] Confederate Pension Applications, A. G. Mangham, LSA; Index to Census of Confederate Veterans and Widows in Louisiana, 1911, LSA.

[163] Confederate Pension Applications, M. L. Mangham, LSA; Sealy, *Lest We Forget*, pp. 126-127.

[164] Confederate Pension Applications, M. L. Mangham, LSA.

Chapter X: Kissin' Cousins: The John C. Mangham Family of Mississippi

1. In the Shadows of the Southern Frontier: Ante-bellum Years in Georgia, Alabama, and Mississippi

Born in Georgia in 1804, John C. Mangham seems to have grown into adulthood on the Deep South frontiers of Alabama without maintaining the close ties of paternal kinship that characterized most branches of the Mangham family. He may have been the son of Solomon P. Mangham (later Mangum), a North Carolinian known to have lived in Putnam County, Georgia, near old Solomon Mangham and his relatives James C. and William Mangham (see Prologue). The younger Solomon was born about 1786 and orphaned as a young child. Only four years old when he was apprenticed in January 1791 to Martin Cooper in Caswell County, he became a ginwright by trade. Solomon migrated to St. Tammany Parish, Louisiana, in 1817, where he married Zilla Chapman and established a family. In the 1830s he moved once again, this time to east central Mississippi, where he eventually settled in Rankin County with his ever-growing brood. Many of his extended family remained in that part of the state, but others moved to Trinity County, Texas, where they lived in close proximity to several of William Mangham's sons (see Chapter VII).[1]

Although Solomon P. Mangum's life is generally well documented, previously published genealogical information has not accounted for his life in Georgia before moving west to Louisiana. He was about seventeen years old when John was born in Georgia, but it remains unknown whether he was married at that time. If Solomon was indeed John's father, his geographic mobility may have encouraged the younger man to move from Louisiana back to Alabama by 1830. Certainly if John was a child from a first marriage, not to mention if he was born out of wedlock, life with a stepmother and large brood of half-brothers and -sisters also may have encouraged him to move out on his own. Whatever his origins may have been, he was known to his friends as "Jack," and he was about 26 years old when he married Hannah Pharoah in Montgomery County, Alabama, on July 2, 1830.[2]

In later years, Jack earned a living as a skilled carpenter and cabinetmaker, but it is not clear whether he supported his family by working at these trades as a young man or whether he made his living as a farmer. Indeed, the only substantive information about John's marriage to Hannah relates to their two known sons, *Francis Joseph* and *Thomas J. Mangham*. Frank was born in Alabama in 1831 and Thomas was born there on September 6 of the following year. A tradesman like his father and (perhaps) his grandfather before him, Frank became a skilled wheelwright, carpenter, and cabinetmaker, as well as learning how to run a farm.[3]

Eventually, Jack moved his family to Scott County, Mississippi, settling down in an area heavily populated by scions of Jacob Mangum, a North Carolinian who moved to Chesterfield County, South Carolina about 1800. Believed to be the only son of James Mangum, Jacob was a first cousin of Solomon Mangham of Georgia. Jacob put down roots in South Carolina, but his sons Arthur "Asa" and Joseph Edward Mangum moved to the raw frontier of Mississippi. Asa cleared land in Simpson County about 1819, and the settlement of Mangum bore his name for some years before it was renamed Magee. Joseph followed him to Simpson County less than ten years later, but Asa stayed put when his younger brother moved on to Scott County in the course of the 1830s. Eventually putting down roots near Morton, Joseph lived within forty miles of his brother.[4]

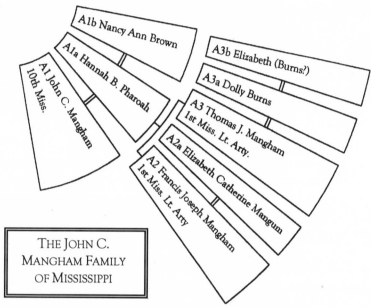

THE JOHN C.
MANGHAM FAMILY
OF MISSISSIPPI

When Jack arrived from Alabama in the early 1850s, he settled very near Joseph Mangum in the Morton area. Both families were ardent Methodists, so they doubtless saw each other extensively at church gatherings. Possibly second cousins (once removed), Jack and Joseph doubtless compared notes closely to identify common relatives and friends. Their antecedents back east are sufficiently vague, however, to make it possible that they were as close as first cousins; Jack Mangham's "coincidental" settlement in Scott County actually may have resulted from much closer communications than one now supposes. The proximity of Solomon P. Mangum at Cato, in adjoining Rankin County just twenty miles from Morton, further expands the network of kinship ties possibly underlying Jack's migration to Mississippi.[5]

Soon after their arrival in Scott County, the existing bonds of kinship between the two families grew even stronger. On February 22, 1855, Frank married Joseph's daughter, Elizabeth Catherine Mangum. Petite, sweet natured, and industrious, Elizabeth was 23 when she married Frank, and they wasted no time in starting a family. The first child was a boy, William Thomas Mangham, born in Scott County on the last day of November that year. Another son, J. R., followed the next year, and little Jane was born in 1859. By this time, however, the family may have moved west to adjoining Rankin County.[6]

Frank was working there as a mechanic and wheelwright in the town of Brandon, just twelve miles east of Jackson on the railroad, as the critical presidential election approached in the fall of 1860. He and his family lived in a modest home in town, on a lot valued at six hundred dollars. Frank's additional three hundred dollars worth of personal property comprised not only the family's household furnishings, but also the tools of his trade. Within weeks of the election, however, the country would sink irretrievably into the secession crisis. Just months later, the utter turmoil of civil war ensued, and the family life of a modest Mississippi tradesman took a fearful turn that few could have imagined at the time.[7]

2. "ALL MISSISSIPPI IS IN A FEVER TO GET TO THE FIELD": PVT. JOHN C. MANGHAM, "RANKIN RIFLES," CO. G, 10TH MISSISSIPPI

Jack Mangham lived in his son's home in Brandon in the last year of peace, and his work as a cabinet carpenter supplemented Frank's income. When the time came for the two men to cast their votes in November, they faced the same choices as every other male citizen in the Deep South. Although we can't know how they cast their ballots, one infers from his later actions that Jack, at least, was a solid Breckenridge man. When Illinois Republican Abe Lincoln secured election with 39 percent of the popular vote, Mississippi was the second state to withdraw from the Union and doubtless did so with Jack's wholehearted support. Governor John J. Pettus worked rapidly to assemble eight regiments for a Mississippi State Army, but on March 1, 1861 he sent out a call for fifteen hundred men to enlist for 12 months' Confederate service at Pensacola. His call was in response to the Confederate government's requisition for five thousand men to reinforce the garrison at the critical port city, where the Mississippians would join new troops from Florida, Georgia, and Louisiana in reinforcing various companies already there.[8]

George N. Miller rapidly went to work organizing a company in Brandon, and within a couple of weeks its ranks were full enough for him to tender its services to the governor. When Captain Yerger came to Brandon on March 27 to muster Miller's "Rankin Rifles" into State service for twelve months, Jack was among the one hundred men who swore the oath. The bombardment at Fort Sumter still lay more than two weeks in the future, obscured by mysteries that none could accurately foretell. In the meantime, the Confederate War Department and Gulf Coast newspapers fairly boiled with speculation that the first armed clash would take place at Pensacola. Private John C. Mangham intended to be there when the shooting started. Although he was old enough to be the grandfather of many of the youths in Miller's company, Jack obviously felt like he had a bone to pick with Abe Lincoln & company. At 56 years of age, he obviously believed fighting was too serious a matter to leave to the young folks![9]

The same day they mustered into Confederate service, the Rankin Rifles joined the stream of Mississippi volunteer companies en route to the threatened Gulf Coast. Traveling by rail to Meridian and thence to Mobile, they camped at the Fair Grounds until shipping out for Hall's Landing on April 8. Two days later they marched fifty miles cross-country to Pensacola, where they took a steamer across the bay to the Warrington Navy Yard on April 12. There they encamped on the bay's northern shore, between Fort Barrancas and the lighthouse to its west. The Mississippi companies organized into two regiments under the guidance of Brig. Gen. Braxton Bragg, Provisional Army of the Confederate States, who accepted them into Confederate service on April 17. Since Mississippi's Adjutant General reserved the first eight regimental numbers for the State Army he was organizing, the two Pensacola outfits became the 9th and 10th Mississippi regiments of infantry. In fact they were the first regiments fully organized by the state and the first Mississippi troops accepted into Confederate service. When the new organization completed these necessary preliminaries, Bragg directed the 10th Mississippi to provide five companies to garrison Fort McRee (see maps on pages 182 and 558).[10]

Miller and his Rankin Rifles became Company G, 10th Mississippi Volunteers, and they remained in camps while companies A, D, E, H, and I garrisoned McRee. Thousands of other Mississippians were yet clamoring for acceptance, arms, and orders in the general pandemonium attendant upon organizing a new country, administration, and army. Governor Pettus wrote to President Jefferson Davis several weeks later about the outlook in the chief executive's home state, and his missive illustrates the rampant excitement: "Suffice it to say, all Mississippi is in a fever to get to the field, and hail an order to march as the greatest favor you can bestow on them, and if you take the field they could not be restrained." His troops in Pensacola felt the same way, as the day they mustered into Confederate service was the same day Virginia seceded from the Union. The secession of the Old Dominion caused some "little excitement" in the Pensacola garrison, where Bragg ordered an eleven-gun salute fired to celebrate the spectacular accession to the infant Confederacy.[11]

Likewise happy to be safely enlisted before the war ended, the men of the 10th Mississippi settled into a busy schedule of camp routine, drilling and performing numerous guard and fatigue duties. As any Civil War soldier could attest, this was a full plate in the early days of the war. Most of the men had to learn their trade beginning with the very basics, although some had militia experience that had instilled the rudiments of company drill. The officers were just as green, and the good ones spent their evenings studying any Army regulations or drill manuals they could obtain. The Confederates assembling at Pensacola had a leavening of "Old Army" officers and non-commissioned officers, of course, and their experience was of inestimable value. On the other hand, their ideas of ironclad discipline were often at variance with the high-spirited volunteers, and it always required some time for the two elements to blend effectively. Braxton Bragg made a reputation at Pensacola for hard-nosed discipline and an unrelenting attention to organization, and it paid big dividends. One Alabama veteran asserted that Bragg's organization of the Army of Pensacola was "the most thorough organization ever made in the Confederate States."[12]

Long after the war, former private Edward McMorries became the 1st Alabama's official historian after obtaining his doctoral degree in history; he and his outfit had served with the Pensacola garrison from its earliest days. The 10th Mississippi's arrival coincided with the Alabamians' displacement from Barrancas Barracks and Fort Barrancas, and McMorries recalled that early April saw his regiment begin the "full routine of soldier duty: company drill in the morning, battalion drill in the afternoon, guard and police duty, and all other duties." He described the process of turning the raw levies into soldiers in terms that doubtless evoked pungent memories for the Gulf Coast troops who had experienced it first-hand at Pensacola:

> Military regulations began to be enforced and penalties to be inflicted for violation. A cordon of guards was kept around the encampment and along the beach; no ingress or egress was permitted without a pass; no intoxicants were allowed within the lines. Whether rising or retiring or whatever else, everything must obey the taps of the drum. Guards were constantly bringing in one or more prisoners and dumping them in the guard house amid frantic execrations of the prisoner that he had come to war to fight for his rights, that he had lost all his rights by the tyranny of his officers, and that he wouldn't stand it. Raw troops and their officers both have a hard time until the former learn that a soldier's first and highest duty is to obey orders, and the latter how to command.[13]

Bragg's exacting discipline made its mark rapidly; by the Battle of Shiloh a year later, his Pensacola troops had established a reputation as the best-trained regiments in the Deep South.[14]

While Jack Mangham and his fellow Mississippians learned the "Army way," they also had to prepare Pensacola for defense. They were stationed, after all, in the very face of the enemy. Forts McRee and Barrancas on the mainland were Confederate controlled, but a Federal garrison remained in Fort Pickens on Santa Rosa Island, just over a mile across the bay. A fresh company reinforced the original company in February, and five more arrived at Pickens on the very day that Bragg received the two new Mississippi regiments into service on April 17, 1861. Fort Pickens originally was intended to be the main fortification for the port's protection, and McRee and Barrancas were merely complementary outworks. Accordingly, Bragg set his neophytes to work in the blazing sands along the beach, constructing a series of thirteen new battery positions despite "clouds of mosquitos, and fleas of prodigious size and bloodthirsty intent." Dubbed "sand batteries" due to their thick, shot-absorbing, parapets of sand, these emplacements already evidenced the hard work of the 1st Alabama, but the Rankin Rifles still had their share of the backbreaking labor. They also performed "coast guard duty," ensuring timely warning if the Yanks across the bay tried a sudden attack.[15]

Jack was in ranks when the Rankin Rifles mustered for their first pay on June 30, and by this time, he may have encountered *Capt. Sam Mangham*, who commanded the "Georgia Battery" of 8-inch Columbiads. Sam's father, also named John C. Mangham (see Chapter IV, and Appendix, ref. #45), was only seven years older than Jack, and in all likelihood the two namesakes had known each other as boys back in Georgia. Now Sam and Jack were working to prepare the defenses of their new country on a beach "astir with busy men." Most of these men had enlisted with the expectation of immediate combat, however, and the exhausting duty schedule and numbing physical labor was anything but inspiring. One minor altercation between the Federal blockade ship *U.S.S. Sabine* and a Confederate supply vessel occurred in early May, and excited gunners went shouting to their battery positions in expectation of a fight. They were disappointed by the *Sabine*'s failure to come into Fort McRee's range, however, and nothing came of the incident. The boom of eleven guns from Fort Pickens a month later appeared to promise action at last, although many Southerners thought the U.S. flag lowered to half-staff signified peaceful intentions. Brigadier General William H. T. Walker, a fiery veteran of the Mexican War, thought the Yankees were up to no good, and scenes of the "wildest excitement prevailed" as his men manned their guns. Once again their adrenaline went for naught, when it turned out that the peaceable garrison at Pickens was simply rendering a salute with blank charges.[16]

When Bragg, now a major general, announced his intention to conduct a formal army review in July, many looked forward excitedly to the colorful panoply of martial display. For weeks the men worked like Trojans, clearing every remnant of underbrush from a half-mile square parade ground amid the pine forests a mile behind the lighthouse. When the appointed time came, they buttoned up their variegated uniforms and filed into ranks some ten thousand strong. Facing into the blazing sun on a windless day when "not a leaf of the forest stirred from its place," the men stood stock-still in the solar furnace while the hot sands slowly broiled their feet inside their shoes. Although every man must have relished the chance to finally exercise cramped muscles, the ensuing pass-in-review entailed another hour of marching in the relentless sun. Legions of dehydrated men fell out before the entire production mercifully came to an end, leaving the disappointed troops convinced that, ". . .as a pleasure affair the whole performance was a stupendous failure."[17]

Many were convinced that such exposure combined with the daily drill, fatigue duties, and hot woolen uniforms to unleash the ravages of disease. Although medical science of their era knew essentially nothing about germ theory, the cumulative stress on their systems doubtless contributed to their susceptibility to disease. The clouds of mosquitoes and fleas helped spread germs from man to man, and the close quarters of camp certainly exposed men to contagions unlike any they had encountered in their largely rural homes. Measles, diarrhea, typhoid fever, jaundice, and malaria scourged the camps and sent thousands to their sickbeds, and hundreds to premature graves. The Marine Hospital stood between Fort Barrancas and the batteries at Warrington, and the spacious three-story brick structure impressed Private McMorries with its "scrupulously clean" walls, furniture, and bedding, as well as an attentive staff of nursing sisters.[18]

Although the general cleanliness was a boon compared to the butcher shop atmosphere of Civil War field hospitals, antiseptics and antibiotics were unknown. Some men feared the hospital itself was an environment guaranteed to cause further problems. Private Langdon Rumph of the 1st Alabama wrote his parents in mid-May complaining of "the Feaver," but concluded: "It would not be prudent for me to go to the hospital as they have the Measles there." A month later he observed that one-half of his company "are down with Diarhea & other diseases & the well ones come on guard 1 day on & 2 off. This with the drilling & other duty is apt to make them sick." By the end of July, the youth observed sadly, "In all my life I never saw such a sickly time. . . .out of 90 men we never get out on parade more than 35 men,—so many sick in Camp & more will not go to the hospital."[19]

Jack Mangham was present at the June 30 and August 31 musters of the Rankin Rifles, but he may have spent a significant amount of time at the Marine Hospital. By early September the cumulative stress had become too much for him, and he had to submit to the reality that ardor alone would not suffice to bring him to grips with the Yankees. Broken down by the rigors of service, he was discharged for disability on September 9, 1861. The second of thirty-seven Manghams to enlist in the Confederate Army, he was the first whose health broke under the strain of soldiering. Had Jack remained in the 10th Mississippi, which later became part of the famed "High Pressure Mississippi Brigade" of the Army of Tennessee, he certainly would have had "a tough row to hoe." Sergeant John Rietti chronicled each day's march in his diary, calculating that the regiment eventually covered 3500 miles on foot and another 5000 miles by boat or train, while participating in eleven major battles and fifteen skirmishes.[20]

When Captain Jones settled the Confederate Army's accounts with Jack on September 30, 1861, his annotation closed out the record of John C. Mangham's military service. It is also the last known record of his life. It is not known if he lived to return to Mississippi.[21]

*   *   *   *   *

Within just a few months of Jack's discharge from the army, desperate commanders and political leaders began wrestling with the best way to keep an army in the field during 1862. Most of the early volunteers had enlisted for only twelve months' service, confident in the belief that a year would suffice to settle the matter. Accordingly, the army faced the dissolution of many existing regiments at the moment of supreme crisis, as military disasters beset the western Confederacy throughout early 1862. With the invading armies and fleets seeking to expand their victories along the Mississippi, Cumberland and Tennessee rivers, the hard-pressed Confederacy would lose the war unless it took heroic measures to retain its veterans and organize additional forces.

The Confederate Congress concluded to pass a Conscription Act that spring, and some of its salient provisions required existing regiments to remain in service. Other clauses declared that every white male between 18 and 35 years of age was subject to enrollment in the service, unless he volunteered prior to being called up. Clearly, the coercive power of America's first-ever military draft encouraged voluntary enlistment to avoid the stigma popularly attached to "conscripts," and Congress authorized these new volunteers to join existing units or organize their own. The Conscription Act became law on April 16, and was published officially twelve days later. Governor Pettus quickly started the wheels turning in President Jefferson Davis's home state, and sent encouraging word to Richmond on the very day the new law was published: "Say to the President that he may rely on Mississippi to the last man."[22]

3. "I Don't Intend To—Eat Rats!" Pvts. Francis J. Mangham, "Jackson Artillery," Co. A, and Thomas J. Mangham, Co. I, 1st Regiment Mississippi Light Artillery

One of those who stepped forward in the looming crisis was Francis Joseph Mangham, Jack's elder son, who traveled to Jackson to enlist in Capt. William T. Withers's "Jackson Light Artillery" on April 28, 1862. The company had mustered into service on March 22, and among its original complement was Pvt. Daniel E. Pharoah, a 27-year-old native Alabamian and close neighbor of Thomas Mangham in Madison County; he probably was the Manghams' first cousin. In all probability, this family connection played a key role in Frank's choice of unit, which continued to receive a stream of recruits while stationed in Jackson: the rolls swelled from 163 men in March to fully 225 by August. Withers was in the process of organizing an entire regiment of light artillery, so he remained in the state capital while coordinating the efforts of the men recruiting companies on his behalf.[23]

Frank was 31 years old when he enlisted, and company records describe him as 5 feet 7 ½ inches tall, with brown hair, light hazel eyes, and a florid complexion. Having worked as wheelwright in Brandon until he joined the army, he may have selected an artillery unit in the hope of using his mechanical abilities. After all, anyone hankering to carry a musket had his choice of the countless infantry companies seeking recruits. Frank mustered into service on the very day that the Conscription Act was published for implementation, even though it became law upon its passage on April 16. The overwhelming tide of enlistments that spring contained thousands of men avoiding conscription, as well as thousands more who had planned to enlist anyway. If Frank was in the former category, he certainly wasted no time in ensuring that he avoided the label of "conscript."[24]

*   *   *   *   *

Just five days after Frank enlisted in Jackson, his brother Thomas mustered into Capt. Robert Bowman's newly organized artillery company at Yazoo City. Born in Montgomery, Alabama, Thomas had turned 29 just a few days before his father's September 9 discharge from the army, but he initially chose to remain at home in Yazoo County. Thomas had resided in neighboring Madison County in 1860, where he worked as an overseer on a large plantation owned by Mary Wells. A widowed South Carolinian, Mrs. Wells owned lands near Canton valued at $44,000 and personal property worth another $35,000. Among the latter were the 53 slaves who worked her plantation under Thomas's supervision.[25]

Although he was far from rich by the standards of that era, Thomas owned five hundred dollars worth of real estate, along with other possessions valued at $550. Apparently he decided it was time to settle down and start a family, because he obtained a license to marry Dolly Burns on Christmas Eve, 1861. An 18-year-old Yazoo

628

City girl, Dolly lived near William H. Mangum, whose ongoing connections with the Mangham family bespeak a close relationship.[26]

Thomas's in-laws probably played an important role in his choice of unit, as Bowman's Company included William and David Burns on its roster. Thomas stated his occupation as "farmer" rather than "overseer" when he enlisted on May 3, 1862, so he apparently had begun working his own place after leaving his overseer's job on Mrs. Wells's Madison County plantation. Standing five feet, eleven inches tall, he was significantly bigger than his brother, and his dark complexion probably resulted from years of toil in the blazing sun of Alabama and Mississippi. Like Frank, however, he had hazel eyes and a predilection for artillery service, for Bowman's men became Company I, 1st Regiment Mississippi Light Artillery on May 15, 1862. The fledgling artillerymen elected Captain Withers as their regimental commander, so the Jackson Light Artillery chose Samuel Ridley to replace him as their captain. Since Ridley's company was the senior one in the regiment, it ranked as Company A.[27]

*   *   *   *   *

Ridley's outfit, certainly the most thoroughly organized and drilled battery under Withers's command, received marching orders just two days after the regiment elected officers. Federal gunboats had appeared below Vicksburg and demanded the surrender of the city, but Brig. Gen. Martin L. Smith duly declined the offer and prepared to defend the city. Ordering the inhabitants to evacuate, Smith alerted his handful of infantry regiments and artillerists, then summoned help from Jackson. Ridley's eight-gun battery left for Vicksburg on May 17, but most of Withers's other batteries followed in the ensuing weeks. Indeed, raw volunteer companies of every arm of service streamed towards the threatened point, with some unarmed men even borrowing guns from other companies in order to make the trip. One of these men was William Pitt Chambers of the "Covington Rebels," who bought a train ticket from DeSoto, Mississippi, in order to catch up with the other armed men of his company. A country boy from southern Mississippi, Chambers confessed himself "somewhat disappointed" by Frank's hometown of Brandon, which seemed to have little of note besides "a good court house (of wood) and several brick buildings near it." When the young soldier first sighted the gunboats riding quietly at anchor in the Mississippi River, he was struck by his reaction to the Stars and Stripes fluttering over each vessel: ". . .once the 'Flag of the Free,' now, to us, the banner of subjugation."[28]

The fleet began firing on the city's defenses on May 26, and Frank and Thomas got their first taste of enemy bombardment less than a month after enlisting. Pitt Chambers's battalion was supporting a detachment of Withers's Artillery at Smede's Point, just four miles below the city, and the bursting shells caused him to record impressions that doubtless represented most of the soldiers' feelings: "I confess I was uneasy and nervous; in fact, was badly demoralized as I beheld the great puffs of smoke from the guns, heard the horrid screaming of the shells, their deafening detonations when they exploded, and beheld the havoc they wrought." Worst of all, in Chambers's opinion, was the sense of helplessness: "One feels utterly defenseless unless there is a

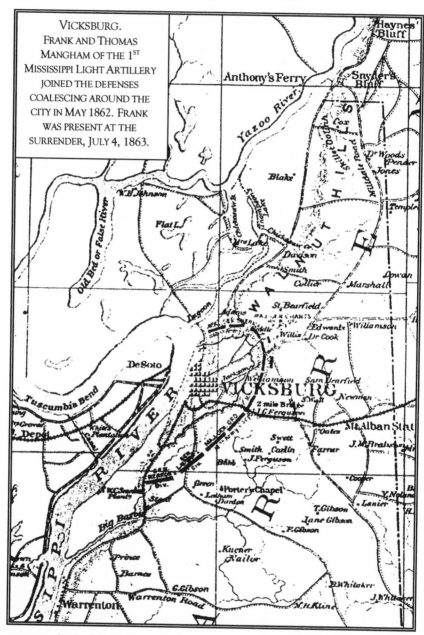

VICKSBURG. FRANK AND THOMAS MANGHAM OF THE 1ST MISSISSIPPI LIGHT ARTILLERY JOINED THE DEFENSES COALESCING AROUND THE CITY IN MAY 1862. FRANK WAS PRESENT AT THE SURRENDER, JULY 4, 1863.

chance to strike back, which in this case is out of the question." The flotilla below Vicksburg belonged to Farragut's fleet, the conquerors of New Orleans during the preceding month. The loss of the commercial capital of the Deep South was a catastrophe of the first magnitude, but it was only one of many that afflicted the Confederacy that spring. Halleck's besieging force succeeded in forcing Beauregard's army to evacuate Corinth just days after the first fleet bombardment of Vicksburg, and McClellan's Army of the Potomac was only a few miles from Richmond, where the Battle of Seven Pines began on May 31. This bloody engagement proved indecisive, and army commander Gen. Joseph E. Johnston received serious wounds during the stubborn fighting that left the enemy within sight of the Confederacy's capital. Only one week afterwards, the port of Memphis fell victim to the Federal power waxing irresistible on the Mississippi River.[29]

In such an atmosphere of sustained crisis, the handful of men at Vicksburg managed to provide enough of a defensive front to prevent a coup-de-main of tremendous magnitude. The outgunned defenders chuckled appreciatively at the spunk displayed by Governor John Pettus, who had hastened to Vicksburg when the first gunboats appeared below town. As the story made the rounds among the Covington Rebels at Smede's Point, Pettus "sent a flag of truce demanding the unconditional surrender of the fleet. It is said that he received a politely worded response of 'If you want them, come and get them.'" At Vicksburg and other places, the embattled Confederacy had little but spunk with which to defend itself. Southern military capability was stretched to the breaking point as commanders sought to marshal forces to defend the important river port, which soon faced fleets operating from both New Orleans and Memphis. By late June, Federal ground forces had appeared on the Louisiana shore opposite Warrenton, just twelve miles below Vicksburg, and Ridley's Jackson Light Artillery again got the first call to respond. Frank and his comrades, accompanied by an infantry regiment, moved out to Warrenton before dawn on June 25. Major General Earl Van Dorn had assumed command of the Vicksburg defenses by this time, and he dispatched infantry and artillery to contest the other landward approaches. Thomas Mangham and the gunners of Bowman's Company I accordingly emplaced their 6-pounder smoothbore guns near Vicksburg, but again the enemy threat failed to materialize into a full-blown offensive. A seven-ship Federal flotilla shot its way past the weak shore batteries at Vicksburg in a "terrific bombardment" on June 27 and 28, but it passed upriver on the second day without landing any infantry force on the east bank of the river.[30]

The Confederate gunners often learned the names of the ships they faced in mortal combat, and the Mangham boys might have been mortified to learn that one of their antagonists was the *U.S.S. George Mangham*, a mortar schooner commissioned into the U.S. Navy in 1861. She had cut her teeth on the fortifications at New Orleans in April 1862, where she received a shot through the hull. She deployed to Pensacola later that month, just missing an opportunity to confront *Col. Sam Mangham* and the 5th Georgia, before returning to duty on the Mississippi River in June.[31]

Her 13-inch mortar and two 32-pounder guns, along with the guns mounted on other craft, gave tongue in thunderous bombardments that rained shells throughout the streets of Vicksburg and environs, but despite their awe-inspiring roar, the incoming shells inflicted few military or civilian casualties. On July 15, the city's denizens experienced another drama on the river, when the Confederate ironclad ram *Arkansas* ran a gauntlet of Federal vessels that a member of Frank's company estimated at thirty men o' war. The *Arkansas* was on her way downriver to Baton Rouge, where she intended to scatter the Federal flotilla while General Breckenridge attacked the garrison. In a hard-fought action there on August 5, Breckenridge's troops were on the verge of decisive victory when word came that the ironclad's engines had broken down. Adrift and in danger of capture, her crew scuttled the vessel, and the stricken gunboat took Breckenridge's hopes to the bottom with her. The hard-pressed Federal line received direct support from the gunboats on the river, and the attackers could not drive home the ground assault merely to face such fire at point-blank range.[32]

Two days after the ill-fated *Arkansas* shot her way through the fleet at Vicksburg, Thomas went home on a week's leave. When he returned on July 23, the Federal fleet still swayed at anchor on the river, but it gave up the naval siege two days later. In six weeks of intermittent bombardment, the fleet had plastered the city with twenty-five to thirty thousand shells, according to one Confederate estimate. As the Union vessels withdrew, the 1ˢᵗ Mississippi Light Artillery used the proffered respite to resume the training interrupted by the fleet's appearance in May. On August 1, Lieutenant Colonel Parker assembled all ten batteries at the Marshall Place outside of the city, and "Camp Parker" quickly became a beehive of activity as "stringent orders" came down to account for absentees. For the next three weeks the encampment resounded to drum and bugle as the regiment conducted training on guard mount, dress parade, and the myriad of camp duties that underlay an efficient combat unit. Withers returned to take charge on August 5, and soon thereafter established a regimental "School of Instruction for Officers" to teach his subordinate leaders their business.[33]

Although Colonel Withers was striving to turn his raw regiment into a well trained, well equipped, and disciplined force, the onset of disease quickly overwhelmed the regimental hospital's ability to care for patients. Bowman's Company I had an initial enrollment of 118 men, but in the course of August the frustrated captain sent Thomas and twenty-five others home "to be taken care of," since he could offer neither surgeons nor medicines. Bowman and the other officers were outraged at the unauthorized absence of Dr. Rice, the regimental surgeon whose negligence eventually resulted in his dismissal from service on August 20. Thomas was desperately ill, apparently remaining on sick furlough from August 24 through November. He seems to have returned to the company once, only to have the surgeon send him to the regimental hospital in Vicksburg. The other raw troops in the area likewise underwent the deadly trial of camp disease. On July 22, Pitt Chambers scrawled a diary entry reflecting the straits to which the Covington Rebels had sunk: "Only three in the company are reported for duty, and they are specially detailed to make beef soup for the rest of us." By early August, he noted that the doctors had little medicine to offer, and the troops had to make shift by skinning the bark from willow and dogwood trees to make tea. This must have been unappetizing to say the least, the more so because the only water available was muddy river water or a milky white liquid drawn from wells sunk into the soapstone soil.[34]

Four days before Thomas left on sick furlough, Frank and the men of Ridley's Company A departed for Snyder's Mills, eleven miles northeast of Vicksburg on the Yazoo River. Several Federal gunboats had debouched from the Mississippi River and probed eastwards up the Yazoo to this point, where they discovered several siege pieces in an incomplete and practically unprotected emplacement on the bluffs. Landing parties quickly spiked the guns and rolled much of the ammunition into the water before departing. General Smith hoped that his Mississippi artillerymen could "get a few shots at the transports," but the hit-and-run raid left him disappointed. By the time Ridley's gunners arrived with companies B and F, the Yankee raiders were long gone.[35]

Stung by the obvious vulnerability of Vicksburg's landward approaches, Smith directed Withers to take charge of fortifying Snyder's Bluff. During much of that fall, several of Withers's companies worked on the fortifications, but fully half the regiment was detached for duties under other commanders in Mississippi and Louisiana. About this time, Captain Ridley detailed Frank as a company teamster, an assignment that lasted until the summer of 1863. His experience as a wheelwright and mechanic probably was the reason for this assignment, because it kept him in a position to work on the entire company's rolling stock. An eight gun battery possessed a wide variety of forage, baggage, and equipment wagons, including the company blacksmith's forge, the caissons and limbers of the firing sections, and of course the guns themselves. Jolting rides down rutted country tracks and cross-country gallops into gun positions were guaranteed to generate a significant repair workload. Private Thomas T. Barnes was the only other wheelwright in the company, so both certainly had plenty of work.[36]

Frank was present at Milldale on November 6, when Colonel Withers reviewed companies A and D at firing practice and judged their firing "excellent." Bowman's Company I was among the three batteries Withers reviewed at the Vicksburg racetrack on the following day, when they experimented by firing at targets across the Mississippi River, but Thomas was still at home on sick furlough. All five companies staged a grand review at the racetrack on November 20 and 21, when Brig. Gen. Martin Smith inspected the troops and Governor Pettus formally presented the regiment its battle flag on behalf of the ladies of Jackson. Although the flag had been in the regiment's possession since its organization, it had never been formally presented with the pomp and ceremony that normally attended such ceremonies, probably due to the Federal fleet's appearance at Vicksburg on May 18.[37]

Barely a week after the festivities, however, Federal gunboats intruded once again. This time they penetrated up the Yazoo to a point level with Blake's plantation, from which they fired a few shots towards the works at Snyder's Bluff. Besides upsetting things generally, the cannon fire sent large numbers of impressed plantation hands scurrying for cover. In conjunction with advice from Colonel Withers, Smith had issued orders earlier in the month impressing fifty percent of the plantation slaves throughout his district, after their owners had proved less forthcoming than the mounting threat required. Although the Confederates could force these unfortunates to work, they didn't intend to face cannonballs for good measure.[38]

Gunboats continued to probe up the Yazoo throughout the month, foretelling a major effort to reach Vicksburg from the north. These efforts came to a head at year's end, when major troop units landed south of Snyder's Bluffs at Chickasaw Bayou. By rapidly shuttling units to the threatened point, however, the Confederates managed to establish a thin line of troops in well-positioned defenses along the bayou. In several days of hard-fought actions, they smashed every attack and sent Sherman and Grant in search of another route to Vicksburg. Lieutenant Frank Johnston's section of the Jackson Light Artillery played a major role in the successful defense, and Bowman's Company I was engaged in a supporting role on the Confederate flank.[39]

Both Frank and Thomas Mangham missed their companies' first major combat actions, however, as Frank was home on leave and his brother was performing detached service in Louisiana. Finally recovered from his extended illness, Thomas had returned to duty in December. As a former overseer, he may well have been sent to Louisiana to help impress additional slaves for work on Vicksburg's fortifications. President Davis had called on November 26 for the several states to pass legislation allowing the impressment of slave labor for military purposes, and both Louisiana and Mississippi responded with alacrity. Louisiana's statute authorized Governor Moore to impress slaves "belonging to any one person or persons, or *under the charge of any person or persons, within the State of Louisiana,*" for work on "fortifications or other works. . .to be erected either *to protect or redeem any portion of the State* (emphasis added). The law further delegated this authority "to the military officer (State or Confederate) commanding the department" where the works were built. Given the act's timing and language, it appears specifically intended to facilitate the defense of Vicksburg, which lay within the Department of Alabama, Mississippi, and East Louisiana. Although the River City lay east of the Mississippi River, its survival was crucial to northeastern Louisiana's defense and economic well being. The Louisiana statute required a joint appraisal of the impressed hands, including one man appointed by the impressing officer, so it seems likely that experienced overseers like Thomas were viewed as indispensable on such forays.[40]

He was back with his company at Camp Lee, near Vicksburg, no later than February 20, 1863, when the men mustered for the months of November and December. By this time, however, he was in the process of arranging his release from service by providing Richard Blanks as a substitute. The 53-year-old Blanks was a native of Granville County, North Carolina, and may have been a longtime acquaintance of the Mangum families of North Carolina, Georgia, and Mississippi. By 1860, he resided in Yazoo County near several members of the Burns family, into which Thomas married during the following year. Any or all of these factors may have helped motivate Blanks to take Thomas's place in ranks, although large cash payments generally comprised the stock-in-trade in the substitute business. Thomas would have been hard pressed to come up with several thousand dollars, which was the going price in the substitute market, although some relative or other benefactor may have done so on his behalf. His army pay certainly would not make even a dent in the going price on the substitute market; even including back pay to June 30, 1862, his mustering out pay totaled only $94.40.[41]

The reaction of Bowman and his men to Thomas's discharge is unrecorded, although soldiers generally felt only contempt and disdain for substitutes and their "principals." Possibly this was ameliorated in Thomas's case by his long-term ill health, although one would suppose his fellow soldiers expected him to serve until and unless he was discharged for disability. In any case, the traffic in substitutes was generating massive abuse and corruption and a corresponding groundswell of public opposition to the practice. In a society that prided itself on manliness, physical courage, and a never-say-die stance against "Yankee subjugation," men who paid for substitutes bore a widespread stigma. Likewise, the implication that the rich could buy their way out of danger gave rise to the complaint that it was "a rich man's war but a poor man's fight."[42]

If Thomas subsequently remained draft exempt by obtaining a surgeon's certificate of disability, he may have kept a relatively low profile back in Yazoo County. If he secured exemption as an overseer, however, then he possibly ran afoul of the widespread irritation associated with another contentious provision of the Conscript Act. Widely reviled as the "twenty nigger law," this provision exempted one white man, either owner or overseer, for each twenty slaves on a farm, plantation, or within the same neighborhood. Clearly, this exemption aimed at keeping white men on hand to exact submission from slaves tempted to "misbehave." A nagging fear among white Southerners was the possibility of servile insurrection, which John Brown's raid on Harper's Ferry in 1859 had done much to aggravate. Many griped, however, that the underlying rationale for the exemption was its all-too-convenient offer of yet another escape route for men of means.[43]

Whites residing in areas where small farmers predominated may have been the most susceptible to this view, but those who lived in the great plantation country may have held a different opinion. Thomas's Yazoo Delta home was perhaps the most plantation-oriented area in the entire country, and slavery there tended to be the roughest sort of economic exploitation. Huge gangs of slaves labored to turn swampy jungles into fertile cotton fields, and the torrid heat, high humidity, and rough frontier conditions exacted a terrible toll. Life on such a slave gang bore little resemblance to the smaller plantations and farms, where personal contact between master and slave had the potential to evoke a much greater degree of humanity in their interpersonal relationships. In the Delta, the impersonal, raw, and exploitative nature of the "peculiar institution" put a premium on ferocious enforcement of black subordination, with less room for the concepts of paternal duty and Christian enlightenment that ameliorated the conditions of bondage in many other environments. Now that Yankee raiders and gunboats were prowling up the Yazoo, whites in the Delta may have been much more concerned than most Southerners about bringing men home from the army to maintain the existing social order.[44]

*   *   *   *   *

The repulse at Chickasaw Bayou had caused General Grant to seek other ways to strike at Vicksburg, such as the giant canal bypass he had his men dig in a vain attempt to re-route the Mississippi River. Numerous other plans also fell victim of the stern climatic and geographical realities of the Delta. By April, however, he had developed the naval and ground strength to prepare a daring plan to destroy Confederate power in the state. If he could march sufficient troops down the river's western bank and run transports past the guns of Vicksburg, he could help General Banks conquer Port Hudson, Louisiana, and then ferry the men across the river for a ground campaign in Mississippi. The catch was logistical support, however, as Confederate batteries at Port Hudson and Vicksburg would not stand idly by while steamers ferried supplies to Grant's army. Sharpshooting gunners at Port Hudson had proved this point emphatically, blasting elements of Farragut's fleet to pieces in a night action on March 13. Grant therefore hatched the daring plan of living off the land in a lightning campaign directed against Jackson itself, then Vicksburg. If he could interpose his army between Johnston's small force and John C. Pemberton's army in Vicksburg, he could beat both in succession. The hard driving Federal commander made his own luck in large measure, aided in due proportion by a befuddled Confederate response. Private Frank Mangham and his comrades would pay the price for such mismanagement.[45]

*   *   *   *   *

For Frank and the rest of Vicksburg's defenders, the early March report that Yankees were massing opposite Warrenton came as an ill omen. When a fleet passed the shore batteries on a successful downriver run on April 22, it became unmistakably clear that a big move was underway. The blow came a week later, when gunboats appeared in front of Ridley's gunners at Snyder's Bluff and shelled the defenders there. This was merely a feint, however, as the real blow landed south of the city, where the Federal fleet ferried the army across the river. Landing near Bayou Pierre, Grant lashed out at Confederate defenders of Grand Gulf and Port Gibson in hard-fought actions. He maintained contact with these defenders as they retreated to the line of the Big Black River, where they joined Pemberton's main army. In less than two weeks of rapid action, Grant started his force northeastwards towards Jackson.[46]

General Joe Johnston, the newly arrived commander of Confederate forces in Mississippi, sent orders from his Jackson headquarters ordering Pemberton to strike Grant's rear while it was exposed. Pemberton, however, ventured with extreme caution across the Big Black towards his adversary and missed the opportunity to smash McClernand's isolated XIII Army Corps. Pemberton hesitated to leave his base too far behind, and refused to obey Johnston's orders to attack. Instead, he seized on the concept of striking southwards to cut off Grant's supply line, little realizing that the Union commander had determined on May 12 to abandon it altogether and live off the land. Even worse, Johnston's small force could not stand alone against Grant's determined advance, which drove the Confederates away from the state capital after a sharp action at Raymond. Appalled, Johnston received notification of Pemberton's disobedience, realizing that his ill-advised move would further divide the Confederates rather than massing them for concerted action. It was too late to remedy the situation, however, as Grant was turning already to confront the blundering Pemberton.[47]

The collision came at Edward's Station on the Southern Railroad, near a meandering watercourse known as Baker's Creek. The overmatched Confederate commander had wanted to remain safely ensconced behind the Big Black River bridges near Bovina, but tardily agreed to leave two divisions on guard between the river and Vicksburg, while advancing eastwards with his remaining three. May 15 found his column bouncing uncertainly along Baker's Creek looking for fording sites, rather than conducting the necessary route reconnaissance with small detachments. The ill-managed army floundered a couple of miles beyond Baker's Creek that day, but was thoroughly tangled up along the roads near Edwards Station as night fell. Stevenson's Division settled down for the night where it stood, not even bothering to post security elements. While Pemberton let the reins go slack with his 22,000-man force, Grant was marshaling 32,000 men in three converging columns.[48]

Amazingly, leading units of the Southern force already had opened fire on Grant's advance guard on the morning of May 16, when Pemberton belatedly decided to obey Johnston's latest order to move north to join forces. Johnston had drafted the order the previous morning in yet another attempt to effect a junction north of the railroad, but certainly without any suspicion that Pemberton would attempt the movement while in direct contact with a superior enemy force! It was up to Maj. Gen. William W. Loring to convince

Mississippi, May – July, 1863

JACKSON (MAY & JULY)
Tom & Willis Mangham,
30th Ga. (See Ch. IV)

BAKER'S CREEK, MAY 16
Frank Mangham,
1st Miss. Lt. Arty.

BIG BLACK, MAY 17
Frank Mangham,
1st Miss. Lt. Arty.

Pemberton that it was necessary to immediately form line of battle, rather than issue orders for the army to reverse its line of march across Baker's Creek. Pemberton fumbled the attempt to arrange both a fight and a withdrawal simultaneously, and setting up an impromptu three-mile battle line while turning his wagon trains westward.[49]

Frank Mangham was still serving as a teamster, so his was among the nearly four hundred wagons churning the dust amidst cracking whips, braying mules, and the muleskinners' fervent oaths. The redirection of the wagon train took place smoothly, thus achieving distinction as one of the few things that went well for Pemberton that day. Had it not gone well, the eventual siege of Vicksburg might never have happened, because Pemberton's army probably would have been destroyed in mid-May. His divisions ended up in a patchwork line whose left was anchored on Champion's Hill, confronting the Federals pouring down the Jackson Road and its northern approaches. A yawning gap separated his left wing from the right wing, which was coalescing into a blocking position along the Raymond Road.[50]

The nucleus of Pemberton's left wing comprised Maj. Gen. Carter Stevenson's division, and Barton's Georgia brigade initially formed his right flank. Captain Ridley supported Barton with Lt. Frank Johnston's and Lt. Allen Sharkey's sections, each with two 12-pounder Napoleons. When Stevenson saw that his left flank was in the air, however, he ordered the 42nd Georgia and Sharkey's section to secure the Jackson Road bridge over Baker's Creek. Situated two miles behind the left of Stevenson's Division on the only available line of retreat, the chokepoint offered any passing Yankee patrol the opportunity to ensure the whole division's entrapment and destruction, simply by burning the bridge. Before long, the enemy's evident intention to outflank Stevenson's left caused him to redeploy the rest of Barton's Brigade to the threatened point. The Georgians double-quicked a mile and a half to the far end of the line, where they immediately attacked to force back the oncoming blueclad skirmishers.[51]

Stevenson's Division had to improvise its position in great haste while in direct contact with the enemy, and the line lacked any natural anchor to prevent the Federals from turning either flank. The rest of Pemberton's haphazard deployment evidenced similar glaring weaknesses, although the Mississippi gunners had no time to see or think about anything but the Yankees closing on their direct front and working around the open flank. Local adjustments by division, brigade, and regimental commanders helped mitigate the vulnerabilities, but competent maneuver by their opponents would find and exploit the fundamental unsoundness of the position. Regardless of the Rebel soldiers' willingness to stand and fight, the entire line of battle was fatally compromised almost from the beginning.[52]

In the give and take developing on the far left, Federal brigades continued sweeping towards and around Champion's Hill, and the threat to Stevenson's left grew exponentially. Upon their arrival on the vulnerable flank, Barton's infantrymen drove the enemy skirmishers back onto their line of battle with a sharp counterattack. The Georgians held firm until 1:30 p.m., but penetrations on their right and the spreading envelopment beyond their left flank threatened their complete destruction. Major

Stephenson, the divisional chief of artillery, ordered Johnston's two-gun section to the embattled Georgians' support. Barton's Brigade was breaking up as the boy lieutenant and his men thundered into position on the army's extreme left, under Captain Ridley's direct command. The two Napoleons went into battery on the northern slope of the hill near the Roberts house, alongside the Cherokee Artillery. Lee's Brigade on their right managed a successful withdrawal to new positions just north of the Jackson Road, but Barton's reserve regiment could not seal off the tidal wave now engulfing the Georgians from two directions.[53]

As their infantry supports melted away, Johnston's Mississippi redlegs and Corput's Georgia Battery poured in canister in a vain attempt to stem the tide. Johnston's Napoleons were doomed, though, as the cauldron of incoming fire steadily swept away men and horses alike. "I had no infantry support," Johnston recalled, "and by the time we could fire four rounds of canister they were right on us." As the blue tide swept in and swirled around the isolated cannoneers, 39 of Johnston's 40 battery horses were shot dead behind the gun positions, and the sole surviving animal was wounded. Captain Ridley refused to leave his pieces even when his cannoneers were killed, wounded, or driven away, despite suffering repeated wounds himself. He continued to serve one piece single-handedly until six Minie balls finally laid him low. One of his Mississippians thought it was "the most deadly fire I ever saw," and counted himself supremely lucky to be among the eight gunners who escaped the maelstrom that engulfed Johnston's section. Less than half of the gunners avoided death or injury in the close range melee.[54]

Stevenson's Division had repelled a number of assaults on its direct front and even delivered several sharp counterblows, but the thin, hastily positioned line lacked the reserves to withstand the hard driving attacks of two enemy divisions. The men of McClernand's XIII and McPherson's XVII Corps smelled victory as Stevenson's brigades sagged and wavered, and Hovey's and Logan's divisions swept up sixteen cannon and hundreds of prisoners in the early afternoon. Pemberton finally made up his mind to assist Stevenson about one o'clock, after the left wing's fate was practically sealed. Bowen's Division held the center of Pemberton's line, and it now received orders to assist Stevenson, even though the flummoxed army commander offered Bowen no advice on how to deal with the masses of Federal troops visible in his direct front. Private William T. Moore, a 17-year-old Mississippian of the Jackson Light Artillery, was stationed near headquarters with a detachment of Ridley's men, and noticed that Pemberton was so overwrought that an aide had to help him into the saddle. Moore's comrades may have included Frank Mangham, as the group apparently comprised support troops rather than a reserve gun section.[55]

In any event, the Mississippians were thrilled to see Bowen's five thousand crack Missouri and Arkansas troops launch a ferocious counterattack at 2:30 p.m. that afternoon, and Lieutenant Sharkey's gun section apparently provided fire support for their charge. Considered by some to be "the best combat troops in either army," Bowen's men swept the Yankees back out of the crossroads where Stevenson's right flank had stood, recapturing four guns of Waddell's Alabama Battery as they advanced.

Learning of their success, Pemberton turned to the nearby detachment of Ridley's artillerymen and directed them to hitch up the recovered guns and pull them back. Private Moore and his buddies accordingly drove down to the crossroads, but a spunky remnant of Waddell's cannoneers had returned to get their own pieces, refusing assistance from the Mississippians. Moore thought Stephen D. Lee's Alabama brigade rallied "as if by magic," inspirited by the successful counterthrust and Lee's appeals.[56]

Bowen's spectacular charge swept Champion's Hill clear of bluecoats, and his leading units spied Yankee ordnance wagons only six hundred yards away. His men smashed Hovey's Federal division in the process, while driving back elements of Crocker's reinforcing division. The Missouri and Arkansas troops had driven deep into the Federal line and almost broken it in twain, but stout resistance on the shoulders of the penetration and reinforcements in front made it clear that a further advance would lead to the division's ultimate destruction. Loring's Division pulled out of contact with the Federals in its front, marching from the far right to Bowen's support, and the hard-bitten Mexican War veteran was building up another full scale counterattack when Pemberton's peremptory retreat order reached him. Loring's attack might only have deepened the Confederate catastrophe by committing the last available division to decisive combat, had McClernand's XIII Corps attacked vigorously into the yawning void on Pemberton's right flank. Fortunately for Pemberton's discombobulated army, the light forces screening Loring's redeployment sufficed to hold his slow-moving opponents at bay.[57]

Nightfall and confusion on both sides allowed Pemberton's trio of battered divisions to pull back from direct contact, and Sharkey's gunners earned Barton's praise for their part in the action at the Baker's Creek bridge, as well as in rear guard actions against enemy cavalry. Loring's Division, however, followed a local guide on a separate route intended to evade his pursuers. Eventually convinced that they could not reach the road to the Big Black River bridges without fighting their way through more Yankees at Edwards Station, the one-armed general and his brigade commanders determined to strike off to the southeast. By May 19, his division had circled around Grant's southern flank and united with General Johnston at Jackson.[58]

The debacle along Baker's Creek might have had a different outcome had Pemberton brought all five divisions of his army east of the Big Black River, rather than pitting only three divisions against three army corps. Of the three divisions engaged, Stevenson's now was essentially demoralized; of its four brigades, only Lee's Alabamians retained real fighting spirit and combat power. Bowen's Division remained a force to be reckoned with, but it had suffered severely during its hell-for-leather counterattack. Loring's was now lost altogether, as far as Pemberton was concerned, since his retreat took him east to Jackson rather than west to Vicksburg. Incomplete casualty returns show that the three battered divisions lost at least 381 killed, 1018 wounded, and 2441 missing at Baker's Creek, along with twenty-seven guns captured or abandoned on the retreat. Two of these pieces were Frank Johnston's Napoleons, but Sharkey brought out his two Napoleons "easily," as Johnston enviously recalled. The teenaged lieutenant certainly was in a good position to judge the matter: he rode out atop one of Sharkey's limbers, since his own horse was killed in the slaughter near Champion's Hill. General Grant, who had left Sherman to confront Joe Johnston's small army at Jackson, reported 410 killed, 1844 wounded and 187 missing in action.[59]

* * * * *

Worse was yet to come, however, as General Pemberton still believed Loring's Division was retreating through the darkness towards the bridge over Big Black River. In a high command already long since riven with dissension over strategy and tactics, this proved to be one more fateful mishap. Pemberton expected his lost division to arrive at the river closely beset by pursuing Federals, in which case the narrow bottleneck at the road and railroad bridges would prove a deadly trap. Accordingly, he placed Vaughn's Brigade of east Tennessee conscripts into the earthworks guarding the bridge approaches on the night of May 16, and reinforced their line with four guns of the Jackson Light Artillery detached from Baldwin's Brigade. Succeeding to company command upon Captain Ridley's death, senior First Lt. Charles E. Hooker turned over his section of 12-pounder Napoleons to 19-year-old Lieutenant Johnston, who had fought so gallantly at Chickasaw Bayou and Baker's Creek. Johnston put his guns into position north of the road, while Lt. Philip Lancaster's section of two 10-pounder Parrott rifles was posted on the south side of the road. Frank Mangham was present for duty at Big Black, but it is unclear if he helped man the guns or whether he drove across the river with the rest of the army's vehicles. Evidently, Pemberton's intent was to clear the withdrawal routes by getting the wagon train safely across the river, but somehow this was translated into orders requiring artillery teams to pull back, too. Intentional or not, this horrific blunder ensured that most of the guns posted east of the river would stay there permanently.[60]

The little force took up its position while Stevenson's battered regiments straggled past, their faces set for the river and safety beyond. Pemberton then directed fiery Brig. Gen. John Bowen, the commander of his hardest-hitting division, to file his troops into the works and assume command of the defense. Bowen obeyed, but placed Cockrell's Missourians south of the road and Green's Arkansas and Missouri brigade on the far north end of the line. Like everyone else in the Confederacy, Bowen was suspicious of the hill folk of East Tennessee, who were noted for their Unionist sympathies. Accordingly, he placed Vaughn's men just north of the Jackson Road, safely ensconced between his own two brigades. Bowen believed that the strong abatis and moat-like bayou in Vaughn's front made that part of the line naturally strong, and thus less likely to be the focus of an attack.[61]

The troops in the defensive works east of the Big Black bridges could not help but look wonderingly over their shoulders at the steep bluffs on the river's western bank. Any private could see that the bluffs themselves offered a formidable defensive position, just as the bridges were a death trap for any closely pursued retreating force. Pitt Chambers of the 46th Mississippi stood in ranks atop the bluffs, and he and his mates dreaded the outcome for the regiments exposed on the low ground across the river: "I do not think a single man. . .believed we could check the enemy's progress."

The open dissatisfaction among subordinate commanders had already sapped the soldiers' confidence in Pemberton, and the catastrophe at Baker's Creek had shaken

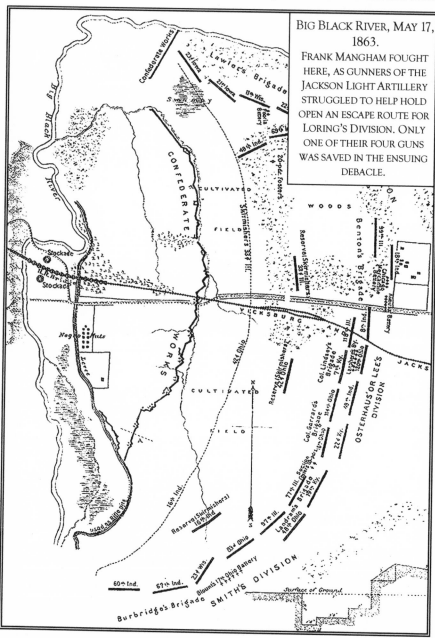

BIG BLACK RIVER, MAY 17, 1863.
FRANK MANGHAM FOUGHT HERE, AS GUNNERS OF THE JACKSON LIGHT ARTILLERY STRUGGLED TO HELP HOLD OPEN AN ESCAPE ROUTE FOR LORING'S DIVISION. ONLY ONE OF THEIR FOUR GUNS WAS SAVED IN THE ENSUING DEBACLE.

them to the core. Now they surveyed their surroundings suspiciously, and many concluded the situation was hopeless. Only five thousand troops were in the bridgehead, and they knew that Grant's whole army was coming down the road from Jackson. What on earth was Pemberton thinking? Probably none of the men in the firing line knew what he intended, for there is no evidence that he rode his lines to inspire his men with the need to stand firm and save Loring's beleaguered heroes.[62]

Faulty as Pemberton's dispositions were, he was motivated purely by his desire to succor Loring's retreating division.[63] Had the army commander simply retreated across the river, leaving Loring's Division to be trapped and shot to pieces at the bridges, he would stand accused of deserting his subordinates. In fact, however, no such result was even remotely possible, since Loring was bound for Jackson; Pemberton was laboring in total ignorance of his subordinate's true situation. Of course Loring should have tried desperately to notify Pemberton of his change of course, and perhaps he did. Nevertheless, one must ask why Pemberton took no positive measures to find Loring. His failure to send out scouts to find Loring or give notice of Grant's arrival was another flagrant violation of security akin to those that brought on the Baker's Creek catastrophe. Additionally, one must wonder how Pemberton supposed that posting a single division in harm's way would save another, in any event. If Loring's men arrived with the Yankees on their heels, then the refugees would block the defenders' field of fire until it was too late to stop the onrushing enemy, and then two divisions would be shot up in the rush for the bridges. The only conceivable positive outcome of Pemberton's dispositions would occur if the Federal pursuit were weak, in which case a solid defensive front might convince the pursuers to go to ground and call for support.

Ensconced in their trenches on low ground, Bowen's men would know the Yankees were there only when the shooting started. Then it would be too late. Only 800 yards deep at its furthest extent, the bridgehead was too shallow for defense against a major force but too large for a single division to man.[64] One must conclude that the army commander could not recognize the difference between terrain suited for warding off hit-and-run attacks by bridge raiders and one suited for sustained defense in broad daylight against a formidable force. Pemberton set up his divisions for the most hazardous operation known to military art: a rearward passage of lines while in contact with the enemy.

Private Marion B. Richmond belonged to one of Johnston's gun crews parked north of the road, and that night he made a point of placing his order for an early breakfast the next day. Captain Ridley, a wealthy planter, had provided a number of servants to cook for his gunners, and Bill had accompanied Richmond's mess into the field. Calling him over, Richmond pointed to woods several hundred yards beyond the lines. "Bill, you see those woods over there? Well, they are full of Yankees, and early to-morrow morning they are going to open fire on us, so you be here with our breakfast by daylight." Bill dutifully appeared with breakfast before full daylight, but soon after the men began eating the whiz of Minies announced that the ball was about to open. When a shell burst about twenty feet away, poor Bill announced, "Good Gaud, Marse Maron! Can't stand dat." The saucy young Rebel gunners hooted at Bill's discomfiture, but Richmond later confessed: "But it was not many minutes before the game took on another aspect, and while we did not exclaim 'Good Gaud, Marse Maron' audibly, things began to get serious, and many of us thought it, no doubt."[65]

Indeed, the shoe was now on the other foot. When the rattle of skirmish fire alerted General Bowen to the Yankees' arrival early on the morning of May 17, it was too late to reconsider his options. The pressure built up rapidly as three Federal divisions deployed across Bowen's front. An artillery duel built up, and some sharpshooting Mississippi or Missouri gun crew hit an ammunition limber serving the 1st Wisconsin Battery's 20-pounder Parrott rifles. The resulting detonation wounded the battery commander, three gunners, and the division commander, Brigadier General Osterhaus. The heavy Parrotts soon began bellowing in response, however, along with two other batteries of light artillery. Before long they managed a direct hit on the axle of Private Richmond's gun, blowing the carriage to bits, dismounting the gun from the trunnion bed, and igniting six boxes of loose ammunition stacked nearby. Richmond watched in horror as the blazing powder set Lieutenant Johnston's clothing aflame, and a bugler standing next to Johnston also struggled to extinguish his own blazing clothing. The flames scorched Johnston's face badly, and severely wounded privates Colquhoun, Smith, and Hooker.[66]

Under cover of the woods just 400 yards in front of Bowen's left wing, an even nastier surprise was brewing. Lawler's Federal brigade had deployed into the cover of the woods and then lunged forward into a swale that offered defilade for the entire brigade. Although Lawler waited for other deployments to secure his left flank, his well-chosen assault position offered him the opportunity to close with the defenders after a short dash across the open. Bowen's concerns about the large force building up in front of his right wing may have kept him from taking proper notice of this threat, although it is difficult to determine what he could have done to stave off the looming threat. It was late morning when Lawler's men poured out of their hidden position in column of battalions, roaring as they came.[67]

Lawler's men bolted across Green's front, absorbing serious casualties from a couple of volleys fired into their exposed flank by the surprised Arkansas and Missouri troops. More than two hundred men fell victim to this fire, but the onrushing brigade wheeled right, fired a volley across the bayou into the defenders' faces, and charged across without flinching. They had struck the line held by the East Tennessee conscripts, many of whom had discovered urgent business in the rear long before this charge came their way. Most of those remaining in line dropped their guns in horror and ran for the bridge when Lawler's men came on the run, and hundreds more milled about looking for a way to surrender. Few showed any fight, and perhaps their obvious irresolution had served as the fatal magnet that attracted the assaulting columns.[68]

The howling charge was one of the shortest and most decisive in the entire war. It took only three minutes from start to finish, but the panicked conscripts' hasty flight opened a yawning hole in the defensive line that was obviously mortal. The 4th Mississippi Battalion, placed next to Vaughn's men as stiffeners, had no choice but to turn tail, and so did the Mississippi gunners of the Jackson Light Artillery. The penetration struck one or two hundred yards to the left of the guns, and the ensuing mass flight of their infantry supports caused at least one gun crew to abandon their piece, still loaded and primed. Private Adkins of the 33rd Illinois jumped atop the captured gun, flapping his arms and crowing like the cock of the roost. In his excitement he reached down and jerked the lanyard, naively supposing that a primed cannon would be unloaded. His was the last shot fired by Company A's four guns at Big Black bridge, and the booming recoil sent Adkins tumbling into the dirt while the shell roared over the regiments coming up in support.[69]

Adkins's bumbling gymnastics were a fitting performance, given the bizarre surroundings. The Tennesseans' collapse convinced Green's Brigade to break and run for the bridges, because any hesitation simply would ensure the Yankees got there first. Since there were no reserves to plug the gap, any major penetration doomed the line irretrievably. Cockrell, south of the road embankment, jumped up on the parapet to look over the embankment toward the heavy firing, little imagining the appalling scene that would greet him. The magnitude of the disaster was apparent at a glance. Turning to his men, he shouted "Retreat, we are flanked!" Some of Cockrell's men fought a minor rear guard action on their way to the bridges, but the real security for the fleeing mobs came from Baldwin's and Lee's brigades, posted atop the hundred-foot high bluffs on the west side. Reinforced by 24-pounder howitzers and a couple of light guns, these infantrymen held the bluffs while the routed refugees raced past. The other saving grace was the requirement for the Federals to disarm and deal with hundreds of prisoners from the nearly instantaneous collapse of the defensive line. Pemberton's chief engineer had prepared the bridges for destruction earlier that morning when he inspected the lines and suspected that the troops' appallingly poor morale promised a nasty setback. Little could he have imagined that the Yankees would bag 1751 demoralized prisoners and eighteen more guns for the price of 279 total casualties. Although Johnston's men miraculously brought out one of their Napoleons, both of Lancaster's Parrott rifles were captured.[70]

The blazing pyres of the bridges marked the end of any thought of defending Vicksburg on the line of the Big Black River. With Loring's Division gone, Stevenson's severely handled at Baker's Creek, and Bowen's needlessly sacrificed, the bumbling of May 16 and 17 had reduced three divisions to the dispirited, disbelieving remnants of only two. Pemberton had only two more fresh divisions remaining to defend the city against Grant's victorious legions. Since he had done very little to prepare Vicksburg's landward approaches for a serious, sustained defense, it remained to be seen if he could make a real fight for the city. And even if he did, few with any knowledge of the situation in Mississippi could imagine any positive outcome to a siege. Johnston, newly placed in command of a skeleton force at Jackson, had his hands more than full facing Sherman's army corps. Any reinforcement large enough to enable him to relieve Vicksburg would have to strip the Army of Tennessee or the Atlantic seacoast defenses. Likewise, few who had witnessed Pemberton's agonizing ineptitude as a field army commander could believe him capable of cutting his way out of Vicksburg in a battle of maneuver. With the Mississippi River bedecked with Yankee gunboats, there was no hope of reinforcement or sustainment from elsewhere in the Confederacy. Barring a miracle, it was only a question of time.[71]

*   *   *   *   *

Frank Mangham was among the downhearted gunners who tramped into Vicksburg under command of Lieutenant Hooker, but many members of the Jackson Light Artillery never made it that far. To Private Richmond, it seemed that the company of nearly 250 men that had sortied beyond the Big Black had melted away to barely more than 150 officers and men. Only three guns were left, since the company had lost two at Baker's Creek and three more at Big Black. Pitt Chambers tramped along with Baldwin's Brigade on rear guard duty, shaken by the impression that his brigade was the only one in the army that retained its organization. His unit served west of the Big Black during the campaign of maneuver, and he was unprepared for the palpable defeatism that marked the regiments returning from across the river: "Instead of the high hopes that animated us last week, a feeling of demoralization seemed to permeate the rank and file, and none of us were hopeful as to the results of the campaign." Others reacted the same way when the despondent columns shuffled into the River City. Newspaperman Augustus S. Abrams, discharged from the Jackson Light Artillery in September for disability, was thunderstruck at the spectacle of the "demoralized mob," devoid of order or discipline, and cursing Pemberton "loud and deep." Lieutenant John L. Power, adjutant of Withers's Light Artillery, summarized the impact on morale: "Confidence appears to be lost in our Department Commander."[72]

Power's confidence lagged even more when he realized on May 20 that the garrison's stock of percussion caps amounted to a mere 250,000, or enough to fill the cartridge boxes of only four thousand men! Likewise, ammunition was short for all light field artillery pieces. The garrison's 40 six-pounder guns had a paltry 3370 rounds available, including spherical case, round shot, and canister; considering that each gun normally carried a basic load of 150 rounds into action, this meant that the gunners had barely over half of their *immediate* needs! Likewise, only two thousand rounds were in stock for the fifteen available 12-pounder howitzers, so each gun crew had slightly more than one basic load. The dozen 12-pounder guns were somewhat better off; sharing 2620 rounds of shot, shell, and canister between them, each piece had approximately two basic loads of ammunition available. With 67 light-caliber guns to serve, the garrison's entire ammunition supply totaled merely 7790 rounds. Further, *nothing at all* was available to feed the army's livestock, so the artillery horses would be too weak to pull their guns after the first few days of starvation. By the time Power recorded these shocking discoveries, the enemy had invested the River City completely. There was no time remaining to remedy such mistakes.[73]

Ulysses S. Grant, quite understandably, sensed total victory within his grasp, and he pushed his army to push into Vicksburg on Pemberton's heels. Delayed by the need to rebuild bridges and marshal forces across a wide front, the pursuers were unable to get there before the Confederates filed into the works, but Grant hoped a quick assault could overwhelm the dispirited troops before they organized an effective defense. The first attempts took place on May 19, but were sharply repulsed amidst heavy firing. This attack went in against the left of Pemberton's semicircular line, which was held by Smith's Division. Lieutenant Philip Lancaster's section of 12-pounder howitzers was positioned with Vaughn's Brigade in this vicinity. In the neighboring sector held by Moore's Brigade of Forney's Division, Sharkey's section of Napoleons dug in at the 2nd Texas Lunette, and Lieutenant Power complimented Sergeant Puttick's Napoleon crew for "some very good firing" in repelling the initial assaults. Farther down Moore's line at the Cox House battery, more redlegs from Company A manned two six-pounder guns. These portions of the line withstood the most determined Federal attacks that day, which cost Sherman's XV Corps 712 men and McPherson's XVII Corps another 129 casualties. Stevenson's Division, holding the southern end of the defensive line, dropped one hundred Federals from McClernand's XIII Corps, which did not press its attacks with the same vigor as Sherman. None of Lieutenant Hooker's guns were stationed in this sector, or with Bowen's Division in reserve.[74]

May 20 saw the besiegers open fire with heavy mortars from positions across the river, and the random devastation of their heavy projectiles soon became a continuous threat. Colonel Lockett, Pemberton's chief engineer, had measured the depth of one mortar crater during the first siege of Vicksburg, and determined that the shell had penetrated seventeen feet into hard packed clay! He blithely concluded, "It was a difficult matter to make bomb-proofs against such destructive engines."[75]

Federal sharpshooters directed a much more precise fire on the Confederates hunched behind their parapets, and it soon became worth a man's life to show his head for a moment. Gunboats, siege guns, and field artillery added their harassing fires to the nerve-wracking concerto of destruction, which swelled ominously throughout that day and the next. Augustus Abrams wondered at the overpowering, inescapable volume of noise:

> The fire was absolutely fearful. Shell after shell came in such rapid succession, that the air seemed alive with them. The noise made by their shrieks, the loud explosion when they bursted, and the silvery sound they made when the fragments were falling, created an uproar almost deafening.

In the face of such a heavy weight of incoming fire, Abrams was appalled that Pemberton ordered his gunners to cease artillery duels to conserve ammunition; nothing discourages friends and encourages the foe half so much as the inability to return fire. Over and above the moral impact of such a lopsided exchange, Abrams noticed that the Yankees used the opportunity to move their guns even closer to their prey.[76]

Lieutenant Power, on Withers's staff, thought the "incessant" firing of May 21 became "perfectly terrific" during the next morning. Grant was trying to force a quick conclusion at Vicksburg, concerned that Johnston might manage to marshal a major relief effort from Jackson. Accordingly, he directed every battery in line to open a furious cannonade at ten o'clock that morning, to be followed by a general assault by all three army corps in his line. Private Richmond of Company A shuddered to recall the mayhem that followed: "Any reader. . .who doesn't think we were in hades during this period, let him imagine the condition of a rat in a hole with a dozen terriers scratching and barking around him." Augustus Abrams was on the receiving end, and pronounced the tornado of fire "the most terrible endured during the siege, and, we believe, the most terrific ever known in civilized warfare." A former member of Ridley's battery, Abrams saw that his old comrades "could scarcely raise from their position to load their pieces."[77]

But load and fire they did, and Lieutenant Sharkey and Cpl. Sylvanus Corson were among the victims of the endless stream of incoming Minie balls, while Lieutenant Hooker was slightly wounded in the arm. Corson died hard, however; he and Sergeant Puttick hit upon the expedient of lighting shell fuses and hurling them over the parapet, where they burst directly among the Yankees crowding below. Their giant hand grenades wiped out one storming party outside their gun embrasure, and point blank volleys of musketry from hard-bitten infantrymen shot down other assaulting columns in windrows. Adjutant Power noted a half-dozen other casualties among the ranks of Withers's Light Artillery, including an artificer and quartermaster sergeant. Even if Frank Mangham was serving primarily as a teamster, the storm of shot, shell, and rifle bullets sweeping the defenses from every angle was utterly undiscriminating in selecting its victims. Grant watched hopefully as elements of all three attacking corps closed with the defenders, and here and there the Stars and Stripes fluttered to the breeze atop the parapets. One Yankee color-bearer leapt over the works next to Pvt. Marion Richmond's gun, but was taken prisoner along with others who miscalculated their chances of success.[78]

Grant reported 147 such men missing or captured, while 2550 fell wounded. Many of these unfortunates lay in no-man's-land between the trenches, where another 502 lay dead. They lay unattended, decomposing rapidly in the sweltering heat, while wounded men expired for lack of help. Since sharpshooters potted away at every Confederate who showed himself, the survivors continued groaning and crying for help. Horrendous spectacles like this became common in the pitiless wars of the 20th century, but such needless suffering was rare in the Civil War, at least before 1864. According to the rules of war then commonly accepted, the commander whose men lay between the lines should have requested a truce to bury his dead and evacuate his wounded. Such a request naturally entailed an acknowledgment that the repulsed attackers were unable to succor their wounded without asking leave from the defenders; perhaps this was an admission that Grant was unwilling to make.[79]

The defenders were appalled at Grant's apparent inhumanity to his own men, and the dreadful stench of decomposition became literally sickening. On the evening of May 25, Pemberton sent out a party with a flag of truce to offer his adversaries permission to bury their dead, and Grant accepted. Both sides mingled freely in no-man's-land, swapping rumors and lies about the likelihood of General Johnston relieving Vicksburg. Lieutenant Power was particularly grateful for the rest it offered the defenders, as well as a chance to improve their works without interruption. Above all, however, it "rid us of an awful stench from decomposing Yankees." The shovels of the burial parties helped put down the noxious odor, and also quieted fears that an epidemic would arise amidst the horrendous corruption of rotting corpses.[80]

According to Lieutenant Power, many of the Federals remarked to their opposite numbers that they "did not intend charging that position again." Their commander came to the same conclusion, deciding to "out-camp the enemy" in a protracted siege. Grant kept the pressure on, to be sure; he knew he had an "inexhaustible supply of ammunition," and he intended to "use it freely." He called upon every West Point graduate in his army to assist in engineering operations, which he pressed vigorously across the entire front. The entire army kept hard at work, building saps and approaches, fieldworks, battery emplacements, and mine tunnels. Since he knew there was no real possibility of a major enemy sortie, Grant withdrew many of his men to covered encampments in the rear, while manning the front lines with continuous reliefs of fresh troops. Their heavy guns blasted away at close range, and solid shot often bored straight through Confederate parapets twelve to sixteen feet thick. Before long, his men had dug approaches within 25 feet of the defenders' lines, and the incessant sharpshooting with rifle and cannon made it extremely hazardous for the Rebs to stray from their ditches. The 2nd Texas lunette was swept with reverse fire from saps to their flank, and already by May 22 the regimental commander reported the middle of his position "was swept within 2 feet of the ground with Minies."[81]

Withers's Mississippi artillerymen struggled continuously to remount and repair guns damaged by enemy fire, as well as clear their embrasures of dirt heaped there by exploding shells. The continual danger reaped a steady harvest of death, and a continuous stream of casualties dots the pages of Lieutenant Power's diary. The young adjutant paused on May 25 to tally the losses of Company A to date. He concluded that he could account for 54 killed, wounded, and missing in the fighting at Baker's Creek, Big Black, and Vicksburg. Nevertheless, Confederate morale had risen significantly after repelling the ferocious assaults of May 19 and May 22. Pemberton's chief engineer, Col. S. H. Lockett, concluded that the troops "were now thoroughly restored to their old-time confidence and aroused to an enthusiastic determination to hold their lines." Confident or not, they were certainly determined to stand and deliver. Due to the close approach of Federal sappers, many regiments kept one-third to one-half of their men under arms at all times; the available reserves were held back for counterattacks, and were not available for routine trench reliefs.[82]

The daily routine of exposure to glaring sunshine, occasional downpours, nighttime chills, mortar shells, and the interminable Minies was a regimen calculated to wear down the men both physically and mentally. Likewise, the inadequate diet undermined a man's constitution just as insidiously as Federal tunnelers undermined the Confederate lines. Men ventured out of the ditches to strip anything green from the landscape, and Vicksburg gradually assumed a nightmarish aspect of shell holes, dirt, and wrecked buildings. Rations dwindled gradually, and by June 8, Lieutenant Power was evincing concern about the probability of mule meat appearing on the ration list. Lieutenant Colonel Smith, commanding the 2nd Texas Infantry, reported that his men grew so emaciated and weak that their ankles began swelling from scurvy.[83]

Federal pickets often chaffed the beleaguered Johnnies about their shortages, and Lieutenant Power and Private Richmond witnessed a spirited exchange one evening. Power had escorted Withers's regimental band out to the lines, where it serenaded the troops with Southern airs like "Dixie" and "The Bonnie Blue Flag." The band also played sentimental favorites of both sides, including "Home, Sweet Home" and "The Girl I Left Behind Me." Doubtless glad to enjoy the pleasant interlude, Yankee sharpshooters allowed the musicians to play unmolested. Captain Sublett of the 46th Mississippi called over to the enemy picket line to ask their opinion of the music, receiving compliments in return, along with a number of requests for "Yankee Doodle." Sublett allowed as how "Yankee Doodle notes" weren't in circulation on his side of the lines, but eventually went outside the lines to continue chatting. Asked whether the Rebs planned to celebrate the 4th of July and what the menu might be, Sublett responded affirmatively. When he held forth on the menu of "hot biscuit, young lamb, butter, coffee, and cake," one Yank yelled back gleefully: *And pea meal!* Everyone within earshot howled with laughter, as the garrison's pea meal bread was utterly notorious on both sides of the line as a "slimy, unpalatable article of food."[84]

Even when it wasn't the topic of across-the-lines repartee, food remained a constant topic of conversation, and three days later Power put down his thoughts on the matter at some length:

> Mule meat is now on sale at the city market; epicures pronounce it very fine. . . Rats command from one to two dollars a piece! There is no reason laid down in the books why rats should not make a good dish. They are as cleanly in their habits as rabbits and squirrels, and infinitely more so than hogs. What more filthy than a hog. People get queer notions in their craniums on the food as well as other questions. I don't consider myself an exception, for I don't intend to— eat rats.[85]

Private Marion Richmond of Company A likewise jested over the matter, although perhaps it was easier in retrospect. Perhaps the wagon driver in his story was Frank Mangham, one of the company teamsters:

> At another time, I was detailed with two other boys to go to the river with a wagon to haul water out to the trenches. The driver drove by a store, loaded on four empty molasses barrels, and drove into the river. In washing out the barrels, I discovered in one barrel quite a bit of sugar sticking to the sides and bottom. I immediately dived into the barrel and was scraping up sugar when the Yanks on the Louisiana side of the river opened fire on us, a shell bursting close by. Mr. Wagon Driver whipped up the mules, they started with a jerk, and head first into the barrel I went, getting covered with sugar and molasses.[86]

Food and even water became truly precious commodities as the siege ground pitilessly on into midsummer, and Col. Ashbel Smith of the 2nd Texas Infantry reported just how bad things really got:

Early during the siege large numbers of animals, chiefly mules and horses, were killed within our lines by the enemy's shot. These were hauled in the night and thrown into the Mississippi River. The water next the bank teemed with maggots, so as to be unfit for any use. The cisterns in the neighborhood being exhausted or forbidden, my men were soon reduced to the sipe [seep] water got from shallow wells dug in the hollows immediately in our rear. This was indifferent in quality and barely sufficient for our scanty cooking and drink. Sentinels were placed over the wells, that none might be wasted for purposes of cleanliness. Our rations were reduced to little more than sufficient to sustain life. Five ounces of musty corn-meal and pea flour were nominally issued daily. In point of fact, this allowance did not exceed three ounces. All the unripe, half-grown peaches, the green berries growing on the briars, all were carefully gathered and simmered in a little sugar and water, and used for food. Every eatable vegetable around the works was hunted up for greens. Some two or three men appeared to succumb and die from inanition [starvation] for want of food, but the health of the men did not seem to suffer immediately from want of rations, but all gradually emaciated and became weak, and toward the close of the siege many were found with swollen ankles and symptoms of incipient scurvy.[87]

The unrelenting hardships deepened throughout June, but Grant's besieging force continued to tighten the vise. By mid-June he had 71,000 troops at his disposal, which easily sufficed to bottle up Pemberton's 30,000 and hold Johnston's 25,000 at bay near Jackson. On some days the firing from his 220 guns was heavier than others, and it seemed to Lieutenant Power that the "terrific cannonade" on June 20 "certainly exceeded anything thus far in the seige [sic]." A major flare-up came five days later, when the Federals detonated a mine under the 3rd Louisiana's redan and followed up with an infantry assault. The Louisianians and the neighboring 6th Missouri drove back their attackers in fighting of furious intensity, and lighted cannon shells again wrought terrible destruction when used as hand grenades. The miners set off another charge in the same place on July 1, but this time positioned a ton of powder underneath their target. The shattering blast gutted the redan, but hundreds of surviving Louisianians steeled themselves for another hand-to-hand fight. No assault followed this time, as Grant admitted that the earlier failure served as a powerful admonition to avoid piecemeal operations of this nature. He continued the mining operations, but planned to detonate a number at one time as the signal for a general assault. Lieutenant John Power visited the wounded men that packed the Vicksburg hospital after the blast and subsequent shelling, and marveled at the fortitude of the patients undergoing amputations there. As one Reb asked the doctor to take his leg off below the knee, he joked that he had flown higher than anyone else, so high in fact that he "could see Joe Johnston in the rear!"[88]

Pemberton, however, felt that further resistance was hopeless, and his generals glumly agreed. Their desperate hope that General Johnston would appear in Grant's rear was doomed to disappointment, as Johnston had only just started cautiously maneuvering toward Vicksburg. His 25,000 troops had streamed by the trainload to Jackson from the Army of Tennessee and various coastal defense units, but they had come without the wagons, horses, and field artillery necessary for maneuver against Sherman's covering force. By the time the little army had the wagons and teams to move itself, it was too late to save Vicksburg. After parleying to obtain more lenient terms of surrender, Pemberton agreed to cease resistance on July 4, 1863. His men marched out of their emplacements at ten o'clock that morning, stacked arms outside their unbroken lines, and marched back inside to await the preparation of formal written paroles. Colonel Withers's artillerymen had drawn rifles on June 23 in case a breakout attempt was ordered, so Pvt. Frank Mangham and his comrades filed out of the works to stack arms, too. The forty-seven days of siege were over.[89]

There were 5496 sick and wounded men hospitalized within the city, so perhaps five times that number underwent the humiliating ceremony. One of those unable to march out was Pvt. Richard Blanks, the 53-year-old substitute for Thomas Mangham. Blanks had been at the company's forge on June 24 when a Minie ball whizzed in and struck him in the leg. Blanks died of his wound in Vicksburg on July 11, 1863.[90]

*   *   *   *   *

Lieutenant Power doubtless voiced the bitter resentment of thousands of soldiers when he heard that General Pemberton refused to furlough his men on his own initiative, confiding to his diary: "Pemberton seems disposed to complete his botch." The young lieutenant knew what General Grant likewise suspected; many of the paroled men would head for home, permission or not. Further, the knowledge that they were disobeying orders by leaving was likely to keep them from ever returning, even after they were duly exchanged. By agreeing to Pemberton's request for immediate parole rather than unconditional surrender, the wily Grant saved his army and navy the transportation required to move 30,000 prisoners up north before paroling them at City Point, Virginia. He also ensured that many never returned to the army at all, as it was easier for them to slip away to their homes from Vicksburg than from Virginia. With the guns silent and the prisoners duly paroled, the defeated army finally marched out of Vicksburg on July 11. Its men began leaving in droves immediately after signing their paroles, as they intended to go home rather than march to a godforsaken parole camp somewhere in eastern Mississippi to await further orders from Pemberton.[91]

Colonel Withers obtained permission for each of his light artillery companies to retain a two-mule wagon for the march to parole camp, so perhaps Frank drove the wagon for the Jackson Light Artillery. Lieutenant William Ratliff was now in command, as Charles Hooker had been hospitalized since May 29. Hooker had been sitting in his tent at company headquarters when a Parrott rifle boomed in the distance; seconds later, a solid shot screamed in and ripped off his arm. The young lieutenant was lucky in comparison to his servant, John, who was struck in the head and killed. As they prepared to march out on the morning of July 11, about 130 men of the 1st Regiment Mississippi Light Artillery had left without permission since signing their paroles four days earlier. Another five refused to sign paroles, thus ensuring that they would go to a northern prison; there they could take the oath, obtain release from prison, and work peacefully until the end of the war. Lieutenant Power added, "No sooner had our Regiment got outside the lines, than the men commenced scattering—but few seeming to place any confidence in Gen. Pemberton's semi-assurance of a furlough, and believing themselves in no way responsible to him until exchanged."[92]

By July 13, "scarcely a Corporal's Guard of the regiment" remained with the disintegrating column. Two days later, only fifteen men still stood by Withers and Power, who themselves obtained leave of absence from Pemberton. The next day, they finally met Johnston's army, the sight that they had longed for since the ill fated attempts to effect a rendezvous back at Baker's Creek two months previously. Unfortunately, it was only his wagon trains. Even worse, they were headed east in full retreat.[93]

Frank Mangham probably stayed with his paroled regiment to drive the company wagon to the bitter end, but now he doubtless walked home to rejoin his family. Rejoicing that he had survived to reach home again, they nonetheless must have been stunned at his physical condition. As for the rest of the Confederacy, well, one must forgive the Manghams if they had concluded sadly that it was "gone up the spout." For the woeful trek of Withers, Power, Mangham, and the dozen other parolees from the once-proud regiment had reached its last stop at Brandon, Mississippi. The dusty columns of Johnston's retreating army were passing through Frank's hometown. The next men marching into town would be under the command of Maj. Gen. William T. Sherman.[94]

*　　*　　*　　*　　*

Frank Mangham and the other parolees of Withers's Artillery subsequently received orders to report to parole camp at Enterprise, Mississippi, by August 23, 1863. An undated record reflects that he was turned over to the enrolling officer at Jackson at one point, possibly indicating that he had overstayed his leave like numerous other Vicksburg parolees. He spent the fall and winter of 1863 detailed to work in government shops at Enterprise as a carpenter and wheelwright, receiving three or four extra dollars daily pay for his skilled labor. His Vicksburg parole declared him ineligible to undertake "duties usually performed by soldiers" until properly exchanged, so assigning him to perform skilled civilian trades was a legal, if artful, dodge by Confederate authorities.[95]

When a Federal advance from central Mississippi smashed up nearby Meridian and appeared to threaten Mobile in early February 1864, Frank's regiment retreated towards Demopolis, Alabama. Apparently Frank soon received orders to report to Selma to work in the Quartermaster's Department there; since his name had appeared on a list of prisoners exchanged the previous December, he should have been cleared to perform duty without any further restrictions. His status obviously was a matter of some dispute, however, because Major Hillger soon sent him packing back to Demopolis.[96]

653

The real problem rested squarely on the shoulders of Lt. Gen. Leonidas Polk, commanding general of the Department of Alabama, Mississippi, and Eastern Louisiana. He was hard at work that spring at his Demopolis headquarters, struggling to rationalize the defense and administration of portions of three different states, each partially occupied by the enemy and beset with threats from land and sea. Among other embarrassments, his department was awash with paroled prisoners from Vicksburg and Port Hudson, and the dreadful state of communications hindered every attempt to sort things out. The only thing not in a state of flux, perhaps, was the constant need for more troops at every point in the Confederacy. On March 5, Polk's assistant adjutant general published General Order No. 41, designed to obtain the maximum production from every available asset:

> Information having reached the lieutenant-general commanding that there is a large class of officers and men in this department who, by wounds received in battle and other causes, are disabled for active field service but capable of other and lighter duty, it is ordered that all such officers and men, whether belonging properly to this department or not, report without delay at the rendezvous to be established at Demopolis, Ala.
>
> Their services should not be lost to the country. They will be encamped at Demopolis and assigned to useful and appropriate duty, as the requirements of the Government may demand.
>
> Commanding officers throughout the department, in the field as well as at posts, will see to the execution of this order, which is not intended, however, to apply to such as may have been heretofore assigned to duty on surgeons' certificates.
>
> By command of Lieutenant-General Polk:
>
> /s/ THOS. M. JACK,
> Assistant Adjutant-General[97]

Major Hillger had anticipated this order by sending Frank to Demopolis already, and Lieutenant Colonel Jack reviewed the road-weary private's situation the same day he published Polk's order. Addressing a note to Hillger, he explained: "I approved the order for F. J. Mangham authorising him to report back to you. As he is <u>unexchanged</u> no formal order for his detail can be made. Let him remain with you for the present." Frank was still working under Hillger in December 1864, listed as a paroled prisoner who was now disabled.[98]

The war ended for Frank when Lt. Gen. Dick Taylor formally surrendered the Department of Alabama, Mississippi, and Eastern Louisiana in May 1865. Frank was among the various detailed personnel working under the supervision of Lt. Col. R. H. Lindsay at Meridian, Mississippi. On July 31, 1865, the erstwhile Rebel appeared before a State Probate Judge and formally swore to "faithfully support, protect and defend the Constitution of the United States, and the union of the States thereunder." He further bound himself to "faithfully support all laws and proclamations which have been made during the existing rebellion with reference to the emancipation of slaves. So help me

God." To use the phrase then current among Southerners adapting to defeat and reunion, Francis Joseph Mangham was "sliding back into the Union." The war was over.[99]

4. "THE MOST SOUTHERN PLACE ON EARTH": POSTWAR YEARS IN THE YAZOO DELTA

At the time of the surrender, Frank's officers listed his residence as Newton County, Mississippi; perhaps he had moved his family there to avoid the devastation attending the constant military movements around Morton, Brandon, and Jackson. He moved the family back to Scott County in February 1866, when he put two hundred dollars into eighty acres of property in time for spring plowing. Cash was tight, however, and he had to mortgage his property for $250 provided by the County Board of Police school fund. Apparently he was able to get his crops in and pay his note the following year, because he remained on this farm for three years. Frank sold out to his brother-in-law John W. Mangum on January 4, 1869, obtaining $300 for his farm. In May he mortgaged his milch cow, two young steers, turning lathe, and his complete outfit of carpentry and cabinetmaking tools for $187 in cash and supplies, apparently to finance his move to Hinds County.[100]

With economic recovery fitfully underway in the Deep South, Frank seems to have decided to leave the farm and return to commercial business as a wheelwright. He listed this as his full time occupation for the 1870 census, which found him living in the town of Edwards. Just a stone's throw from the Baker's Creek battlefield where he experienced his first real combat seven years earlier, Frank lived in a house where he evidently rented or provided rooms to George and Clara Royment, two black laborers.[101]

Five years later he moved his family up to Yazoo City, where he obtained a job as a sawyer and settled into a home at 82 Washington Street. His next door neighbor was William H. Mangum, the 69-year-old city auctioneer with whom Frank and his brother maintained close contacts over the years. Although two younger children apparently had died before reaching maturity, six children still lived at home with Frank and Elizabeth. The eldest was 25-year-old William, a machinist who clearly had his father's talents for the mechanical arts, while his brother J. R. worked as a laborer. Four daughters lived at home, with the three youngest still attending school.[102]

Their father died in Yazoo City on October 21, 1883, only 52 years of age. As a friend eulogized him in a newspaper obituary, Frank had "possessed a loyal Southern heart, full of pure instincts and noble purposes. . . .he became and remained an exemplary citizen, winning the good opinion of all, and especially endearing himself to the many he so often held in kind remembrance." Another writer described him as "an old and respected citizen," as well as an "honest, upright man, energetic and skilled in his trade." He probably never asked for any higher distinction than that.[103]

*   *   *   *   *

For the last eight years of his life, Frank had resided near his brother Thomas, who remained in Yazoo County after his discharge from service in 1863. By 1880, Thomas apparently had remarried to Dolly's older sister Elizabeth. Their house was filled with six children, ranging from fifteen to three years of age. The Yazoo Delta was an overwhelmingly rural area, and the plantation economy of ante-bellum years still formed its socioeconomic backbone. Slavery was gone, of course, but a great proportion of the farmers now worked on a tenant or sharecrop basis of some sort, whether they were black or white. Many others worked as laborers on someone else's farm, an economically marginal role traditionally limited to young men and the desperately poor. In 1880, Thomas toiled as a farm laborer to support his family, assisted by his two teenaged children, Thomas, Jr., and Emily. Apparently none of his four youngest sons attended school, so they must have helped with the numerous chores necessary to wrest a living from the land.[104]

Although Thomas was a big man, he suffered for many years from kidney disease, possibly the same ailment that kept him hospitalized for so much of his brief service in the army. He made a name for himself in the Delta during the 1880s selling horse medicines, but a dangerous bout of fever in the summer of 1888 broke his health. He spent much of May and June 1889 selling his patent medicines in Greenville, but after several weeks in town he fell desperately ill. He sent for Lizzie to join him, but by the time she reached his bedside on June 15 he had lapsed into a coma. Thomas J. Mangham never regained consciousness, dying on the morning of June 16, 1889. He is buried in Greenville.[105]

Thomas was well known in Yazoo City, whose newspaper editor characterized him in a lengthy obituary as a "well known, genial and highly respected gentleman, popular with all his associates and friends." *The Greenville Times* carried a briefer death notice for Thomas, positioned just below a somewhat longer obituary for Gen. William T. Withers. The Mangham brothers' old commander had died at his horse farm in Lexington, Kentucky, of the effects of wounds suffered in the Mexican War. His eulogist concluded, "He served through the war of the rebellion on the Confederate side and was wounded by a shell while in command of the land batteries at Vicksburg."[106]

*   *   *   *   *

Lizzie Mangham eventually moved to Greenville with a number of her children, and was living there with Maggie, Emma, and Robert at the turn of the century. Her son James and his wife Claudia lived nearby, while another son, Francis J. Mangham, lived in neighboring Sunflower County. Twenty-four years old in 1900, his family and friends called him Frank.[107]

*   *   *   *   *

Elizabeth Catherine Mangham died on February 21, 1906, on the anniversary of her marriage. Preceded in death by her husband Frank and six of their eight children, "MyMaw" was beloved by her grandchildren. Her eulogist thought her "happiest when doing for her loved ones." She was 74 years old.[108]

[1] 1860 Census, Rankin County; John T. Palmer, *The Mangums of Virginia, North Carolina, South Carolina . . . and Adjoining States* (Santa Rosa: 1992), pp. 85 (n.154), 191-197; MFB 19: 3. See more on William Mangham's family in Chapter VII.

[2] 1830 Census, Montgomery County; Marriage Records, Montgomery County; Service Memorandum, Sgt. Samuel Rowland Collier, 10th Mississippi Unit Files, RG 9, Confederate Records, container R151, B21 and B22, S2, series 390, vol. 129, MDAH. Tuscaloosa County, Alabama marriage records show that John C. Mangham married Nancy Ann Brown on December 21, 1848. In all probability, this was a second marriage for Jack, but no other evidence survives to dispel the uncertainty (MFB 21: 8).

[3] 1860 Census, Rankin County; CMSR, Francis J. Mangham, 1st Mississippi Light Artillery; undated obituary of F. J. Mangham; Alice Wade and Katherine Branton, eds., *Early Mississippi Records: Washington County 1860-1912*, vol. 4 (Leland: N.p., 1986), pp. 205-206. I am indebted to Frank's great-grandson, William (Bill) Francis Mangham of Banning, California, for a number of newspaper clippings and other genealogical materials related to the Francis J. Mangham family.

[4] Undated obituary of E. C. Mangham; Palmer, *The Mangums*, pp. 98-101, 137-138, 175.

[5] Ibid.; undated obituary of F. J. Mangham. Intriguingly, a younger brother of Asa and Joseph was named John C. Mangum. A well-documented citizen of Chesterfield County, South Carolina, he was born there only a year before John C. Mangham's birth in Georgia, and may have been the latter's namesake. See Palmer, *The Mangums*, pp. 108-110.

[6] Undated obituaries of E. C. and William Thomas Mangham; 1860 Census, Rankin County. Although the evidence establishes the month and day of their marriage with certainty, I have estimated the year based on William's age. Frank and Elizabeth may have married a year or two before 1855.

[7] 1860 Census, Rankin County.

[8] Ibid.; Mark T. Carleton, et al., eds., *Readings in Louisiana Politics* (Baton Rouge: Claitor's Publishing, 1975), pp. 191-192; OR IV, vol. 1, p. 135; "First Regiment Alabama Infantry," in *Directory of the City of Montgomery, and Sketches of Alabama Soldiers* (N.p.: Perry & Smith, Publishers, 1866), p. 53.

[9] John C. Rietti, comp., *Military Annals of Mississippi: Military Organizations Which Entered the Service of the Confederate States of America from the State of Mississippi* (Reprint, Spartanburg: The Reprint Company, Publishers, 1976), p. 13; CMSR, John C. Mangham, 10th Mississippi.

[10] Rietti, *Military Annals*, pp. 85, 97; Dunbar Rowland, "Tenth Regiment—Infantry," in *The Official and Statistical Register of the State of Mississippi* (Nashville: Press of the Brandon Printing Co., 1908), p. 599.

[11] Rietti, *Military Annals*, pp. 13, 84; Rowland, "Tenth Regiment—Infantry," p. 597; OR IV, vol. 1, p. 277; "The Pioneer Banner: A Confederate Camp Newspaper," AHQ 23 (1961): 216. General Bragg directed the regimental headquarters to move to Fort

McRee on July 8, 1861. See 10th Mississippi Regiment, Order Book and Consolidated Morning Reports, RG 9, container R151, B10, S3, series 390, vols. 105, 107, MDAH.

[12] Rietti, *Military Annals*, pp. 84-85; Rowland, "Tenth Regiment—Infantry," p. 599; "First Regiment Alabama Infantry," in *Directory*, p. 53.

[13] Edward Y. McMorries, *History of the First Regiment Alabama Volunteer Infantry C.S.A.* (Montgomery: Brown Printing Co., 1904), pp. 16-17.

[14] Larry J. Daniel, *Shiloh: The Battle That Changed the Civil War* (New York: Simon & Schuster, 1997), p. 63.

[15] J. H. Gilman, "With Slemmer in Pensacola Harbor," *B&L* 1 (Reprint; Edison: Castle, N.d.), p. 32; Henry E. Sterkx and Brooks Thompson, eds., "Letters of A Teenage Confederate," *FHQ* 38: 340; McMorries, *First Alabama*, p. 21; "First Regiment Alabama Infantry," in *Directory*, p. 53; Rietti, *Military Annals*, p. 97.

[16] CMSR, John C. Mangham; Sterkx and Thompson, eds., "Teenage Confederate," pp. 340, 342. Chapter IV focuses on the John C. Mangham of Spalding County, Georgia.

[17] McMorries, *First Alabama*, pp. 23-24.

[18] Ibid., pp. 24-25; Sterkx and Thompson, "Teenage Confederate," pp. 341, 343.

[19] Sterkx and Thompson, "Teenage Confederate," pp. 341, 343-344. Private Rumph died on August 13, 1861.

[20] CMSR, John C. Mangham; Rietti, *Military Annals*, pp. 87, 102-103.

[21] CMSR, John C. Mangham. Disease certainly was no respecter of rank, as Jack outlasted his regimental commander by almost four months. Colonel Phillips died in late May at Pensacola (Rowland, "Tenth Regiment—Infantry," p. 599).

[22] *OR* IV, vol. 1, pp. 1081, 1095-1100; vol. 2, pp. 160-168.

[23] CMSR, Francis J. Mangham; 1860 Census, Madison County; Rowland, "1st Regiment—Light Artillery," pp. 849, 853; Descriptive Roll of Company A, in J. L. Power and Family Papers, 1800-1936, 1958, MDAH. John L Power became adjutant of the 1st Mississippi Light Artillery, and his papers include a diary for 1862-1863, as well as a draft manuscript relative to Yazoo River operations, partial lists of discharges, and descriptive lists of the Jackson Artillery. In 1860, Alabamian Daniel Pharoah was age 25; employed as an overseer by W. J. Dulaney, he lived a few households away from Thomas Mangham.

[24] CMSR, Francis J. Mangham; Historic Roll, Company A, 1st Mississippi Light Artillery, Withers's Artillery Papers, MDAH.

[25] CMSR, Thomas J. Mangham, 1st Mississippi Light Artillery; 1860 Census and Slave Census, Madison County. Bowman's Company organized on May 1, just two days before Thomas enlisted.

[26] 1860 Censuses, Madison and Yazoo Counties; Yazoo County, Office of the Circuit Clerk, Marriage Book D (1858-1870), p. 89, MDAH. Further research on William H. Mangum may hold the key to determining John C. Mangham's correct

place in the family tree. Emsley Burns, Dolly's father, helped Thomas post security for their marriage license.

[27] CMSR, Thomas J. Mangham; J. L. Power Diary, May 15-16, 1862.

[28] J. L. Power Diary, May 17, 1862; A. S. Abrams, *A Full and Detailed History of the Siege of Vicksburg* (Atlanta: Intelligencer Steam Power Presses, 1863), p. 5; William Pitt Chambers, *Blood and Sacrifice: The Civil War Journal of a Confederate Soldier*, ed. Richard A. Baumgartner (Huntington: Blue Acorn Press, 1994), pp. 11-12, 24-26. Pitt Chambers belonged to the 6th Mississippi Battalion, which eventually became the 46th Mississippi Regiment.

[29] Chambers, *Blood and Sacrifice*, pp. 26-27; Abrams, *Siege*, p. 5.

[30] Abrams, *Siege*, pp. 5-6; J. L. Power Diary, June 25, June 27-28, 1862; CMSRs, Francis J. and Thomas J. Mangham; Chambers, *Blood and Sacrifice*, pp. 27, 29-30.

[31] The *George Mangham* was built in 1854 and commissioned into naval service at Philadelphia in 1861. Her namesake was probably one of the few Manghams who lived in the northeast, where immigrating Mangham ancestors apparently arrived later than those who settled in the Southern colonies. See http://www.uss-salem. org/danfs/sail/mangham.txt. See Chapter IV for Sam Mangham's stint at Pensacola.

[32] Abrams, *Siege*, pp. 6-7; Chambers, *Blood and Sacrifice*, pp. 30-35; William A. Spedale, *The Battle of Baton Rouge 1862* (Baton Rouge: Land and Land Publishing Division, 1985), pp. 35-42.

[33] Abrams, *Siege*, pp. 6-7; J. L. Power Diary, July 31, August 4, August 11, 1862.

[34] Regimental Return, August 1862, Company I, 1st Regiment Mississippi Light Artillery, Withers's Artillery Papers, MDAH; CMSR, Thomas J. Mangham; J. L. Power Diary, August 20, 1862; Chambers, *Blood and Sacrifice*, p. 36; William C. Davis, *The Orphan Brigade: The Kentucky Confederates Who Couldn't Go Home* (Baton Rouge: LSU Press, 1980), p. 114. When Company I mustered for July and August on November 11, Thomas remained on sick furlough. The September-October muster roll reflected his admission to hospital in Vicksburg, but it is unclear when this muster took place. A November regimental return reflected him still absent on sick furlough.

[35] J. L. Power Diary, August 20, 1862; Unpublished draft manuscript relative to Yazoo River operations, in J. L. Power and Family Papers.

[36] J. L. Power Papers, unpublished draft manuscript relative to Yazoo River operations (chapters 8, 10); CMSR, Francis J. Mangham. For a glimpse of the disparities between authorized and on-hand equipment in Confederate artillery units, see William Forbes, *Capt. Croft's Flying Artillery Battery, Columbus, Georgia* (Dayton: Morningside, 1993), pp. 75, 79, 83; C. S. Ordnance Bureau, *The Field Manual for the Use of the Officers on Ordnance Duty* (Richmond: Ritchie & Dunnavant, 1862; reprint, Gettysburg: Dean S. Thomas, 1984), pp. 26-33, 89-107. Barnes served as company artificer (see CMSR).

[37] J. L. Power Diary, November 6-7, November 20-21, 1862. General Smith was busy inspecting all of his subordinate units in an effort to improve their combat readiness. See Chambers, *Blood and Sacrifice*, pp. 42-43.

[38] J. L. Power Diary, November 29, 1862. Power's observations typify Confederate views on racial issues, tending to emphasize blacks' apparent unwillingness to face danger. Many soldiers witnessed courageous acts by servants accompanying their masters into battle, but prejudice generally led them to interpret this as evidence of their loyalty and happiness in bondage. Postwar anecdotes abound of personal servants who stood by their masters in battle, even including some who picked up muskets and pitched into the fighting. As Union soldiers, of course, many ex-slaves faced plenty of gunfire, when they had a personal stake in the matter. In desperate assaults at Fort Fisher, Nashville, and elsewhere, they proved to the Confederates' chagrin that they indeed could fight hard and well.

[39] Abrams, *Siege*, pp. 11-13; Edwin C. Bearss, *Vicksburg is the Key*, vol. 1 in *The Campaign for Vicksburg*, 3 vols., (Dayton: Morningside, 1985-86), pp. 163-211.

[40] CMSRs, Francis J. and Thomas J. Mangham; OR IV, vol. 2, pp. 211-212, 249-250; 278-279, 296. Governor Pettus also used slave labor to help mine and import salt from New Iberia, Louisiana, so it is possible that Thomas was involved in these operations.

[41] CMSRs, Francis J. and Thomas J. Mangham, and Richard Blanks, 1st Mississippi Light Artillery; ORS II, vol. 32, p. 558; 1860 Census, Yazoo County; Albert Burton Moore, *Conscription and Conflict in the Confederacy* (Macmillan, 1924; reprint, Columbia: USC Press, 1996), pp. 29-32.

[42] Moore, *Conscription and Conflict*, pp. 27-51.

[43] Ibid., pp. 70-72, 75, 143-145. For the complete text of the Conscription Act of April 1862, see OR IV, vol. 1, pp. 1094-1100.

[44] James C. Cobb, *The Most Southern Place on Earth: The Mississippi Delta and the Roots of Regional Identity* (New York: Oxford Univ. Press, 1992), pp. 21-28, 126-128; Kenneth M. Stampp, *The Peculiar Institution: Slavery in the Ante-Bellum South* (New York: Vintage Books, 1956), pp. 183-185. Cobb's work provides a comprehensive view of the tangled web of racial relations in the Delta, from the earliest settlement through the Civil Rights era. It is an indispensable reference for anyone wishing to understand the environment in which Thomas Mangham lived, worked and eventually died.

[45] Bruce Catton, *Grant Moves South* (Boston: Little, Brown, 1960), pp. 366-387, 407-410, 432-435; Ulysses S. Grant, "The Vicksburg Campaign," *B & L* 3, pp. 493-496; Abrams, *Siege*, pp. 17-18; Lawrence Lee Hewitt, *Port Hudson: Confederate Bastion on the Mississippi* (Baton Rouge: LSU Press, 1987), pp. 72-95.

[46] Abrams, *Siege*, pp. 18, 21; J. L. Power Diary, April 16, 1863; Grant, "The Vicksburg Campaign," *B & L* 3, pp. 496-504; Catton, *Grant Moves South*, pp. 426-430, 436-440.

[47] Bearss, *Vicksburg*, vol. 2, *Grant Strikes a Fatal Blow*, pp. 559-566; Catton, *Grant Moves South*, pp. 440-443; Ulysses S. Grant, "The Vicksburg Campaign," *B & L* 3, pp. 508-510.

[48] Bearss, *Vicksburg*, vol. 2, *Grant Strikes a Fatal Blow*, pp. 571-579.

[49] Ibid., pp. 579-584.

[50] Ibid., pp. 584-587.

[51] OR 24, pt. 2, pp. 99-100; Bearss, *Vicksburg*, vol. 2, *Grant Strikes a Fatal Blow*, pp. 597-599; Rietti, *Military Annals*, pp. 855-856; CMH 9 (*Extended Edition*), Mississippi, p. 146. Charles E. Hooker, the author of the CMH volume for his home state, was a lieutenant in the Jackson Artillery in May 1863.

[52] Rietti, *Military Annals*, p. 856; Bearss, *Vicksburg*, vol. 2, *Grant Strikes a Fatal Blow*, pp. 586-589, 596-598; CMH 9 (*Extended Edition*), Mississippi, p. 146.

[53] OR 24, pt. 2, pp. 99-100; Bearss, *Vicksburg*, vol. 2, *Grant Strikes a Fatal Blow*, p. 604; Letter, Frank Johnston to Capt. William T. Rigby, November 10, 1903, Withers's Artillery Unit Files, VNMP.

[54] Letter, Frank Johnston to Capt. William T. Rigby, November 10, 1903, VNMP; Bearss, *Vicksburg*, vol. 2, *Grant Strikes a Fatal Blow*, p. 604; Abrams, *Siege*, pp. 25-26; CMH 9 (*Extended Edition*), Mississippi, pp. 144, 146; Rietti, *Military Annals*, p. 856.

[55] Bearss, *Vicksburg*, vol. 2, *Grant Strikes a Fatal Blow*, pp. 600-605, 608.

[56] Ibid., pp. 610-613; CMH 9 (*Extended Edition*), Mississippi, p. 146.

[57] Bearss, *Vicksburg*, vol. 2, *Grant Strikes a Fatal Blow*, pp. 611-618, 624-627, 638-640.

[58] Ibid., pp. 632-637; OR 24, pt. 2, pp. 99-100; Rietti, *Military Annals*, p. 856; William L. Calhoun, *History of the 42d Regiment, Georgia Volunteers, Confederate States Army, Infantry* (Atlanta: N.p., 1900), p. 32.

[59] J. L. Power Diary, May 16-17, 1863; Bearss, *Vicksburg*, vol. 2, *Grant Strikes a Fatal Blow*, p. 642; Letter, Frank Johnston to Capt. William T. Rigby, November 30, 1903, VNMP.

[60] Bearss, *Vicksburg*, vol. 2, *Grant Strikes a Fatal Blow*, pp. 657, 667; Rietti, *Military Annals*, p. 856.

[61] Bearss, *Vicksburg*, vol. 2, *Grant Strikes a Fatal Blow*, pp. 653-657.

[62] Ibid., pp. 667-669; Chambers, *Blood and Sacrifice*, p. 71. Fully forty years later, Lieutenant Johnston still had no idea of the true mission of the troops in the bridgehead defenses. He could not conceive of anyone trying to delay the Federal advance on the east side of the river, instead of atop the bluffs on the opposite bank.

[63] Bearss, *Vicksburg*, vol. 2, *Grant Strikes a Fatal Blow*, pp. 654-655, 669-670. Bearss defends Pemberton's decision, but rests his analysis upon the general's intentions alone, as opposed to examining the full tactical implications of such a deployment.

[64] Ibid., p. 655.

[65] Marion B. Richmond, "The Siege of Vicksburg," CV 37 (1929), reprint, Jackson Civil War Round Table, October 1995, p. 4, in 1st Mississippi Light Artillery Unit Files, CRC.

[66] Ibid.; J. L. Power Diary, May 20, 1863; Bearss, *Vicksburg*, vol. 2, *Grant Strikes a Fatal Blow*, pp. 666-667; CMH 9 (*Extended Edition*), *Mississippi*, pp. 148-149; Letter, Frank Johnston to Capt. William T. Rigby, November 14, 1903, VNMP. In his postwar account, Richmond asserted that the explosion wounded the lieutenant, a bugler, and five other men.

[67] Bearss, *Vicksburg*, vol. 2, *Grant Strikes a Fatal Blow*, pp. 672-674.

[68] Ibid.

[69] Ibid., pp. 674-676.

[70] Ibid., pp. 680, 688-689; Rietti, *Military Annals*, p. 856; Letters, Frank Johnston to Capt. William T. Rigby, November 14 and November 30, 1903, VNMP.

[71] In a postwar article, Colonel Lockett, Pemberton's chief engineer, emphasized the great improvements made in Vicksburg's defenses before the siege. Newspaperman Augustus Abrams, a bitter critic of Pemberton's and former member of the Jackson Light Artillery, stressed the paucity of the defenses. The truth lies somewhere in between, but clearly the works were ill-suited for an enemy unafraid to push saps up close to the defenders. See Col. S. H. Lockett, "The Defense of Vicksburg," *B & L* 3, pp. 485-492; Abrams, *Siege*, pp. 43-44, 66.

[72] Richmond, "The Siege of Vicksburg," p. 4; Chambers, *Blood and Sacrifice*, p. 72; Abrams, *Siege*, pp. 3, 29-30.

[73] J. L. Power Diary, May 17, May 18, May 20, 1863; OR 24, pt. 2, p. 376; *Field Manual for the Use of the Officers on Ordnance Duty*, pp. 90-91, 103.

[74] J. L. Power Diary, May 19, 1863; Bearss, *Vicksburg*, vol. 3, *Unvexed to the Sea*, pp. 780-783, 802; OR 24, pt. 2, p. 159. Apparently, Company A drew three new Napoleons and two 12-pounder howitzers to replace the five Napoleons lost at Baker's Creek and Big Black. See Letter, Frank Johnston to Capt. William T. Rigby, November 30, 1903, VNMP, which includes the draft text of one of the plaques destined to adorn the Vicksburg National Military Park.

[75] Lockett, "The Defense of Vicksburg," *B & L* 3, pp. 483-484.

[76] Abrams, *Siege*, pp. 31-32.

[77] Ibid., p. 33; J. L. Power Diary, May 22, 1863; Grant, "The Vicksburg Campaign," *B & L* 3, p. 518; Richmond, "The Siege of Vicksburg," p. 5.

[78] J. L. Power Diary, May 22, 1863; Abrams, *Siege*, pp. 31-32; Grant, "The Vicksburg Campaign," *B & L* 3, p. 518; Richmond, "The Siege of Vicksburg," p. 5.

[79] "The Opposing Forces in the Vicksburg Campaign," *B & L* 3, pp. 549; Grant, "The Vicksburg Campaign," *B & L* 3, pp. 518-519; OR 24, pt. 2, p. 165; Abrams, *Siege*, p. 36.

[80] OR 24, pt. 3, p. 248; J. L. Power Diary, May 25, 1863; Abrams, *Siege*, pp. 36-37.

[81] J. L. Power Diary, May 25, 1863; Grant, "The Vicksburg Campaign," *B & L* 3, pp. 518, 522; OR 24, pt. 2, p. 388; Abrams, *Siege*, p. 41. Grant exempted his 220-pound chief commissary, a West Point graduate who reported that he could make no contribution in engineering "unless he would do for a sap-roller." As mobile parapets,

the cylindrical sap-rollers served to protect men from rifle fire as they dug saps towards enemy fortifications.

[82] J. L. Power Diary, May 25, 1863; Lockett, "The Defense of Vicksburg," *B & L* 3, p. 489; Abrams, *Siege*, p. 41.

[83] OR 24, pt. 2, p. 392; J. L. Power Diary, June 19, 1863.

[84] J. L. Power Diary, June 22, 1863; Richmond, "The Siege of Vicksburg," p. 5.

[85] J. L. Power Diary, June 25, 1863.

[86] Richmond, "The Siege of Vicksburg," p. 5.

[87] OR 24, pt. 2, p. 392.

[88] Grant, "The Vicksburg Campaign," *B & L* 3, pp. 522, 525, 528; J. L. Power Diary, June 20, July 1, 1863.

[89] John C. Pemberton, "The Terms of Surrender," *B & L* 3, pp. 543-546; Grant, "The Vicksburg Campaign," *B & L* 3, pp. 533-537; J. L. Power Diary, June 23, 1863.

[90] OR 24, pt. 2, p. 424; J. L. Power Diary, June 24, 1863; CMSR, Richard Blanks.

[91] J. L. Power Diary, July 6, July 8, July 11, 1863; Grant, "The Vicksburg Campaign," *B & L* 3, p. 536.

[92] J. L. Power Diary, May 29, July 7, July 11, 1863.

[93] Ibid., July 13, July 15-16, 1863.

[94] Ibid., July 16, 1863. Sherman's advance elements fought an action at Brandon on July 19, 1863. See E. B. Long, *The Civil War Day by Day: An Almanac, 1861-1865* (Garden City: Doubleday & Co., 1971), p. 388. Lieutenant Power spent his leave in southern Talladega County, Alabama, at the home of Capt. Tom Patterson of the 30th Alabama, whose brother William had commanded Company A of the same regiment. Perhaps Power encountered John Henry Mangham, an original member of that company, who lost his foot in a train accident near Knoxville in 1862 (see Chapter V).

[95] CMSR and Unfiled Slips, Francis J. Mangham; ORS II, vol. 32, p. 544. A copy of Frank's signed parole is in his service record, and many extracts of records documenting his detached service reside in the alphabetically organized Unfiled Slips.

[96] ORS II, vol. 32, p. 544; CMSR and Unfiled Slips, Francis J. Mangham.

[97] OR 32, pt. 3, p. 589.

[98] CMSR and Unfiled Slips, Francis J. Mangham.

[99] CMSR, Francis J. Mangham; Amnesty Oath, July 31, 1865, Francis J. Mangham, Confederate Records, RG 9, container R151-B11-S1-00344, MDAH.

[100] CMSR, Francis J. Mangham; Scott County Deed Book K, p. 476, Deed Book L, pp. 191-192; Deed Book N, pp. 212-213, 716, reels 15-17, MDAH.

[101] 1870 Census, Hinds County.

[102] Undated obituary of F. J. Mangham; 1880 Census, Yazoo County.

[103] Undated obituary of F. J. Mangham; *Yazoo Sentinel*, October 25, 1883. Three months after Frank's death, his son William married Lucy Davis in Yazoo City. When she died only six months afterwards, the young widower remarried, this time to his first cousin, Frances Catherine ("Kate") Mangum. Kate was a daughter of James Jamison

Mangum and granddaughter of Joseph Edward Mangum. See Yazoo County marriage records; letter, Juanita Strickland to William Francis (Bill) Mangham, January 13, 1992.

[104] 1880 Census, Yazoo County; Cobb, *Most Southern Place*, pp. 54-55, 71-74, 98. Cobb notes that neighboring Washington County reported only 7.5 percent of its farms rented for shares in 1880, but the similar system of "half crop" farming was actually widespread. Under this system, the laborer typically supplied his labor, food, and perhaps half of the stock feed in exchange for housing and half of the crop he raised. In 1860, Elizabeth (18) and Dolly (16) Burns lived in the Emsley Burns household in Yazoo County; presumably this was the Elizabeth whom Thomas later married.

[105] *The Sentinel* (Yazoo City), June 20, 1889; *The Greenville Times*, June 22, 1889.

[106] Ibid.

[107] 1900 Census, Washington and Sunflower Counties, Mississippi.

[108] Undated obituary of E. C. Mangham; letter, Juanita Strickland to William Francis (Bill) Mangham, January 13, 1992.

EPILOGUE: MOONLIGHT, MAGNOLIAS & SHADOWS IN THE GLOAMING

Although even a cursory glance at Civil War sources confronts the reader with voluminous evidence of desertion from both the Federal and Southern armies, only one Mangham soldier in the Confederate Army clearly deserted the colors outright. Private Thomas Hamilton Mangham left the ranks of the 19th Louisiana Volunteers only in late January 1865, after almost four years of war. Probably a veteran of Jackson, Chickamauga, Rocky Face Ridge, Resaca, New Hope Church, Atlanta, Ezra Church, Jonesboro, Nashville, and numberless skirmishes lost to posterity, he went home only when the dreams of Southern secessionists lay in tatters, fully as ragged as the starry crossed flags they had followed so faithfully. The epidemic of desertion among soldiers from states west of the Mississippi was spreading so fast in the Army of Tennessee that their regiments were furloughed *en masse* soon afterward, thus providing a thin veneer of legitimacy to their mass absenteeism.

Lee's Army of Northern Virginia suffered a similar drain from desertions and unauthorized absences towards the end of the war. James M. D. Mangham of the 61st Alabama fell into the latter category after an extended absence due to illness and the death of his wife, although the final disposition of his case is obscured by the chaos of defeat. Bush Mangham of the 59th Alabama was court-martialed under circumstances that imply his desertion at Petersburg in the summer of 1864, but perhaps his commander's appeal for clemency spared the boy for a date with a Yankee bullet.

Although so few deserted, only a handful of Manghams actually remained in service with the Confederate field armies when they stacked arms for the last time in April and May 1865. Frank and Oliver were serving in government factories and hospitals, while Will and Solomon were guarding Federal prisoners at Andersonville and Cahaba. Six others had been discharged for ill health, injuries, or wounds that rendered them unfit for military service—Jack and Irby were so badly debilitated that they might have died before the war ended. Captain John H. Mangham was a different sort of casualty; unable to eat, sleep, or speak during the final weeks of the Confederacy's collapse, he was committed to the Georgia state mental hospital by his heartbroken wife.

Charles and Willoughby languished nearly two years in Federal prison pens, each waiting for the end rather than swearing the oath of allegiance that would have set him free. Tom and Willie were captured during the final agonies at Petersburg and during Lee's retreat to Appomattox Court House, and likewise remained in captivity until war's end. Amazingly, John S. Mangham of the 53rd Georgia was the only one of the thirty-seven Mangham Confederate soldiers known to have died as a direct result of wounds suffered in combat. His relatives John R., William W., Wiley James, and Wiley Pendleton Mangham succumbed to the virulent diseases rife in 19th century army camps; none had been very long in the army, and only the latter ever saw combat.

Many a public man had called loudly for war "to the last ditch" in 1861, but painfully few were left to climb out of that last ditch when the time finally came. Charles A. "Nat" Mangham of the 13th Georgia and William A. Mangham of the 14th Alabama were the only members of the clan left to stack arms when Lee surrendered.

Nat's brother John, a sergeant in the 2nd Georgia Sharpshooters, was the only Mangham remaining with the Army of Tennessee when Johnston surrendered later that month. Those serving in the Trans-Mississippi Department simply went home at "the breakup," like the rest of their dissolving army. The lack of any formal surrender ceremony and associated parole records makes it impossible to determine who remained to the bitter end, although apparently Arthur, William J., Henry, and Willis W. Mangham stood by the colors of their Louisiana and Texas outfits until the last.

*   *   *   *   *

The chaos of Reconstruction followed the collapse in 1865, and the loss, scattering, or destruction of military and civil records that concealed the fates of Bush, Irby, and Jack soon obscured the futures of another half dozen Mangham soldiers known to have survived the war. Such uncertainty was all too common in the defeated South, as one-fourth of its able-bodied male population died or disappeared during the war.[1]

All of the survivors faced greater or lesser challenges in returning to civil life after the war's end. Willis W. Mangham had to start afresh in Bell County, Texas, where long years of war had seen deserters, jayhawkers, and Indians roll back frontier conditions far to the east of the ante-bellum line of settlement. His wife had died during the war and ruffians had stolen or scattered his stock, so he had to remarry and rebuild his life with the help of his two children. Bitter guerrilla warfare had reduced much of Ashville, Alabama to ruins, and their reputation as outspoken secessionists probably made it dangerous for Tom and Wiley Mangham to remain. Both went west to join their brother Henry in Louisiana, wasting little time in finding brides and settling down. Charles, Nat, Will, Willoughby, and Arthur Mangham, plus Col. Tom Mangham of Macon, also found wives "at the double-quick," doubtless eager to begin domestic life after years in the peripatetic, all-male environment of army camps.

Lieutenant Bromfield Ridley, a youthful veteran of Stewart's Division, witnessed this phenomenon in full bloom just weeks after the surrender, when a parlor full of Georgia girls attracted a flock of his comrades on their way home to Tennessee. Forgetting for a moment the anguish of their defeat, the young gallants entered the parlor with gusto, "stepping like peacocks in high grass." Ridley explained this widespread development in his journal entry:

> Whilst the old gentlemen are pondering over the future and grieving over "what I used to was," we young bloods are delving in boyish hope and dwelling in the bright anticipation of meeting a beautiful blonde or brunette, knowing that "all things change as the years pass by, save love, which is the same forever and aye."[2]

Whether single or married, the Manghams had to buckle down to face the multitude of challenges that characterized a world gone topsy-turvy. The first years were very hard indeed, and men like Will and Tom Mangham, probably made fatally vulnerable by serious wounds received at Sharpsburg and Chickamauga, joined the legions of sick, wounded, and exhausted men who died while still young. Nat had to

666

train a horse to support him as he limped on a bad leg, while Henry stumped along on a poorly fitted wooden leg. The shell fragments that wrecked his brother Willis's hearing, eyesight, and back made it impossible for the young farmer to work as he had before the war, but he lived to become one of Butts County's most respected schoolteachers. One of Wiley Person Mangham's lungs was ruined as completely by disease as any Minie ball could have done, but he edited a country newspaper in Louisiana for thirty more years before pneumonia finally stole the last march on him.

For most of the former soldiers, the economic outlook brightened after the South weathered the severe depression of 1873. The following decade brought more hard work, of course, but also a significant degree of economic prosperity, social recovery, and emotional recovery. Many Mangham veterans clearly reveled in the ensuing celebration of the Confederacy that blossomed in the 1880s and continued until the last of the old Confeds died. This era saw the flourishing of the powerful "Lost Cause" mythology, with its mixture of fact, wishful thinking, self-justification, historical revisionism, and simple nostalgia. The wartime and early postwar bitterness between secessionists, "speculators," shirkers, defeatists, and deserters, so pronounced in Tom Mangham's wartime letters to the *Jacksonville Republican*, began to take a backseat to a mellower view of the past. In 1865 it seemed that the war had dragged American society to its nadir; only three decades later, it seemed that every aging Southerner had become a hero of the "Last Stand," just as every Union veteran was a fit champion of the Grand Army of the Republic.

The relative ease with which Northerners could turn to new challenges was largely a function of their victory, of course, and their widespread celebration of wartime heroics seemed to be just one more paving stone in the pathway of America's irresistible national progress. Reminiscent of the way in which Johnny Reb and Billy Yank generally got along while on the picket lines, the burgeoning postwar celebration went a long way towards accommodating the heroic self-image cultivated by each side.[3]

And just as the North's collective memory of the war was shaped by its image as one more victory in an apparently unbroken procession of American victories, the South's was necessarily an adaptation to the realities of defeat. Much of the region's economic and social adaptation to the new order of things, however, was a successful attempt to maintain the essence of the old order *despite* their crushing military defeat. As noted Southern author W. J. Cash mused in his 1941 exposition, *The Mind of the South*, the vanquished never accepted that their defeat on the battlefield necessitated a fundamental change in their world-view:

> And so far from having reconstructed the Southern mind in the large and in its essential character, it was [the] Yankee's fate to have strengthened it almost beyond reckoning, and to have made it one of the most solidly established, one of the least *reconstructible* ever developed.[4]

And although postwar radicals decried the South's dogged refusal to rapidly embrace revolutionary changes in its racial and economic relations, twelve years of resistance during Reconstruction convinced most that the maintenance of some sort of status quo ante-bellum was the only alternative to the worst possible sort of anarchy. Even if the radicals had been willing to enforce a more thoroughgoing outward compliance at the point of the bayonet, most Americans seemed content to let well enough alone. This conclusion was as consistent with Unionist motives and temperament in 1877 as it had been in 1861.

A decade or so after Reconstruction ended, the passage of time was sufficient to allow Southerners to develop a popular historical interpretation of the war, that in some respects practically redefined defeat as victory. This was, of course, but one more facet of their section's successful adaptation to defeat by deflecting its emotional impact. Although many aspects of their "defeated by overwhelming numbers" interpretation were contrived, its underlying theme of indomitability in defeat—so close to *victory* in defeat—was emotionally satisfying. Indeed, it was satisfying enough to help ensure Southern willingness to abide the verdict of the battlefield, just as they would the outcome of an honorable duel, because neither required much adjustment to the "chip on the shoulder individualism" posited by W. J. Cash. Essential to the acceptance of the myth of Southern indomitability, however, was the sizable grain of truth inherent in the concept; veterans of both sides recognized the spectacular stamina displayed by the underfed and outnumbered Rebels of 1861-1865, and both could respect that staying power. Neither Northerners nor Southerners of that era felt any sentiments more noble than pity for helpless (male) victims, and neither was likely to mistake pity for the thing their culture demanded above all else: respect. As a corollary, the blueclad victors derived the respect (and self-respect) due not simply to the winners, but to the men who had *defeated the indomitable.* After all, had the Confederacy been merely a 90-pound weakling doomed to defeat, how could anyone view the badly bloodied victors of four years of warfare as anything but cowardly, incompetent, or both? Despite the contradictions in this mutual accommodation, it enabled each side to glory in their victory, whether real or apparent.

Such views were part of the "Moonlight and Magnolias" view of the war and Southern history, and these rose-tinted interpretations found great favor in North and South alike. One of the greatest advocates of this school of thought was Lt. Gen. John B. Gordon of Georgia, whose early reputation as a brigade commander was secured by men like Will, Nat, and John Mangham of the 13th Georgia Volunteers. Gordon was a successful governor and nationally prominent figure, and his dramatic stage presentations of *American* heroism in the Civil War were fantastically popular throughout the country, because they emphasized the very best qualities inherent in the soldiers of *both* sides. Some of his anecdotes have since been exposed as being more illustrative than factual, but these well-intentioned frauds rang comfortingly true to his audiences of approving veterans, both North and South. Gordon told one story that perfectly illustrates Cash's interpretation of Southern character, as well as the mutually satisfying nature of the myth of Southern indomitability:

> As the Confederates were taking leave of Appomattox. . .many of the Union men bade them cordial farewell.

One of Grant's men said good-naturedly to one of Lee's veterans: "Well, Johnny, I guess you fellows will go home now to stay."

The tired and tried Confederate, who did not clearly understand the spirit in which the playful words were spoken, and who was not at the moment in the best mood for badinage, replied:

"Look here, Yank; you *guess*, do you, that we fellows are going home to stay? Maybe we are. But don't be giving us any of your impudence. If you do, we'll come back and lick you again."[5]

Another tale in this genre was the story of the captured Rebels who appeared before General Ben Butler to take the oath of allegiance to the United States:

One of them, a wag in his way, looked at the General, and with a peculiar Southern drawl, said: "We gave you hell at Chickamauga, General!"

The General was furious at the man's familiar impudence and threatened him with all sorts of punishment, but again came that drawling voice, repeating the first part of the statement, but he was stopped by the General, who ordered him to take the oath of allegiance to the United States at once or he would have him shot. After some hesitation, looking into General Butler's fierce eye, he reluctantly consented to take the oath. After taking the oath, he looked calmly into General Butler's face, and drew himself up as if proud to become a citizen of the United States and a member of the Yankee Army, and said: "General, I suppose I am a good Yankee and citizen of the United States now?"

The General replied in a very fatherly tone, "I hope so."

"Well, General, the rebels did give *us hell* at Chickamauga, didn't they?"[6]

The modern apotheosis of this "Moonlight and Magnolias" history, of course, was Margaret Mitchell's *Gone With the Wind.* Released in 1939, the film became an instant sensation just eight years after Alabama veterans Charles Arthur Mangham and Wiley Paul Mangham passed on to their eternal rewards. Their active membership in the United Confederate Veterans implies that each would have enjoyed the film's depiction of the society he had fought to uphold. The film debuted the same year that ex-Private John Wood died in Monticello, Georgia, where he was lionized as one of the oldest Confederate veterans in Jasper County. Many years earlier, Wood had served with Wiley Pendleton and John S. Mangham in the 53rd Georgia Infantry through the Seven Days' Battles outside Richmond, as well as at Sharpsburg and Chancellorsville. Unlike Wood, both Wiley and John died in Virginia, and probably remain there in the unmarked burial trenches that haunt the grounds of the old hospitals.

With the deaths of Wood and others of his era, including members of the later generations who heard firsthand their tales of America's greatest national drama, our insights into their personalities, hopes, and dreams is limited by our ability to mine nuggets from the written record. Unfortunately, the vicissitudes of war, time, and tide have placed finite limits on what we can learn. For most Confederate soldiers, including the thirty-seven Mangham men and boys who wore the gray, the surviving record is tantalizingly suggestive, but sometimes disappointingly sparse.

For historians and Americans, especially Southerners, the magnetic attraction of the period 1861 to 1865 nonetheless remains powerful indeed, as these events shaped our subsequent cultural and national development in fundamental respects. This attraction is intensified in the modern imagination precisely as it was a century ago, accentuated by the disparity between the publicity attending "Moonlight and Magnolia" deeds of heroism, and the relative obscurity cloaking the ugliest hours in 1865, when the nastiest sorts of violence attended the Confederacy's death agony. Perhaps it was, and remains, a natural defense mechanism for the reunited country to turn its collective back on the excesses of war and Reconstruction, both radical and conservative, consigning them to the back shelf as soon as it seemed safe to do so. It is unfortunate, however, that any attempt to investigate and analyze Southern thoughts and actions, whether objectively or romantically, threatens to awaken the sectional and racial antagonisms imbedded in the war and its aftermath.

We cannot assume that the Manghams, any more than their friends, neighbors, former slaves, or former enemies, made a painless transition to their new world when Reconstruction petered out in 1877, following seventeen years of war and civil emergency. Although the broad outlines of their individual responses to the new order are indeed visible, the impossibility of tracing these in detail ensures that part of the tale, regrettably, must remain forever elusive. For any that seek to discern clearly their faces, lingering in the shadows of a Southland forever gone, the reflections all too often glimmer disappointingly dim in the uncertain moonlight of history.

Nonetheless, it remains in our nature to long for *a touch of the vanished hand and the sound of the voice that is stilled.*

They, too, would understand.

---

[1] Charles P. Roland, *The Confederacy* (Chicago: Univ. of Chicago Press, 1960), p. 154.

[2] Bromfield L. Ridley, *Battles and Sketches of the Army of Tennessee* (Mexico: Missouri Printing & Publishing Co., 1906; reprint, Dayton: Morningside, 1995), pp. 479-481.

[3] For an analysis of the postwar revival and commemoration on both sides of the Mason-Dixon line, see Gerald F. Linderman, *Embattled Courage: The Experience of Combat in the American Civil War* (New York: The Free Press, 1987), pp. 275-297.

[4] W. J. Cash, *The Mind of the South* (Alfred A. Knopf, Inc., 1941; reprint, New York: Vintage Books, 1991), p. 107.

[5] B. A. Botkin, ed., *A Civil War Treasury of Tales, Legends and Folklore* (Reprint; New York: Promontory Press, 1993), pp. 549-550. A nuance of Gordon's tale is the Southerner's emphasis on the Northerner's use of "guess," a colloquialism that highlighted the distinction between its common usage in the North, in contrast to Southerners' use of "reckon."

[6] Ibid., pp. 543-544.

If you are ready to proceed beyond the basic research techniques outlined earlier, you can use the advanced methods and resources of Levels Three and Four. While Level Three techniques allow you to deepen your research by delving into primary resource materials about a specific ancestor, Level Four helps you visualize the approach necessary to broaden such a search across an entire family group.

LEVEL THREE:

If you wish to *deepen* your Level One research on a specific ancestor, you will need to explore a greater variety of primary genealogical and historical sources, rather than limiting yourself to basic data from the census and Compiled Military Service Records. Again, don't overlook the value of published county histories, which can help you find your ancestor and learn a great deal about him. See Filby, A *Bibliography of American County Histories*, and have your local library borrow every relevant history for you through ILL. The Internet allows you to quickly learn the titles of many of these, but leafing through Filby is quicker and more efficient if you can get your hands on a copy.

Indeed, you now have the choice of pursuing much of your research on the Internet, as well as in genealogical libraries and state (or national) archives. The vast majority of the records in the latter repositories are not yet available on the Internet, but the list of available material grows each day. Until and unless images of all archival material are available on the Internet, however, there will always be many good reasons to visit the archives. Only by looking at the original document (or good copies of it), can you avoid the transcription errors arising from the process of entering data into the digital databases. Keep in mind, in any case, that differences between state laws led to the maintenance of different types of records, just as the accidents of fire and war spared some repositories while destroying others. Some counties lost all documents preceding 1865, while others have detailed records dating back into the eighteenth century. Your librarian or archivist can help you clarify these situations as they arise.

Here are some additional avenues you will need to explore as you delve deeper into your Civil War ancestor's past:

a. Genealogical:

(1) Land records. These transactions tell you much about your ancestor's wealth, his associates and family members, as well as his migration pattern. Many were more geographically mobile than you night expect!

(2) Probate records. Wills, estate inventories, and guardianship decrees can identify relationships, key dates, and even the names of the family's slaves. Inventories can identify everything the deceased person owned, giving the modern researcher an amazing glimpse into an ancestor's daily life.

(3) Legal records. Records of lawsuits, paternity suits and the like can tell you a great deal about your ancestor's personality and standing in the community.

(4) Tax records. These rolls often portrayed the populace of a community much more thoroughly than the census, while identifying their financial status in much greater detail. Conducted annually, these records can be of great value in tracking an individual's movements over time.

(5) Registrations. Many states have voluminous records of licenses granted for medical practice, liquor sales, livestock brands and marks, and many other purposes. These help you paint a picture of an individual's whereabouts, lifestyle, and financial status.

(6) Newspapers. If your ancestor lived in a small town or rural community, you can generate a tremendous volume of interesting information on him if the local newspapers from that period still survive today. Call the relevant county library or genealogical society to see whether newspaper collections exist for the time period you need. Another method is to check *Newspapers in Microform*, which lists newspaper holdings across the country. If you dig into these nineteenth century newspapers, plan on spending a long time! The search will be painstaking but captivating.

(7) Every state has unique collections that your archivist or librarian can discuss with you. Land lotteries, letters to the governor or adjutant general, and registries of salt issues can provide you some thrilling discoveries.

(8) Personal papers. If a collection of your ancestor's personal papers survives, you have found the ultimate source to help you understand him as a person. If he had noted relatives or in-laws, you may find detailed discussions of your ancestor and his affairs.

b. Military historical

(1) After consulting CMH and other state-specific sources (discussed above), the *Official Records* (OR) are your point of departure for detailed primary source information about your ancestor's unit and its wartime activities. The OR was compiled near the turn of the century by the War Department, and comprises battle reports and messages, correspondence, casualty and logistics reports, prisoner of war information, and a wealth of other material. Published in 128 volumes, this collection is in many large university libraries, which often hold the important OR Supplement volumes of recent vintage. The OR is now available in an affordable CD-ROM format. See Aimone's reference work for a detailed analysis of the OR's structure, strengths, and weaknesses.

(2) *Southern Historical Society Papers* (SHSP). On the shelves in some libraries, it is more readily available on CD-ROM. Authored by former officers and notable men of the Confederacy, these volumes offer an abundance of material relevant to the career and actions of many Southern units.

(3) *Confederate Veteran*. Published from 1892-1932, this monthly publication was by, for, and about the "Old Confeds." A recently compiled index allows you to comb it quickly for any mention of your ancestor or his old comrades, and is only

limited only by the depth of your own research. Look up company, regimental, and brigade references, as well as battles and engagements about which you want eyewitness information. Some of the material was professionally researched by the veterans who wrote it, while other riveting vignettes were based on memory alone.

(4) Cole, *Civil War Eyewitnesses: An Annotated Bibliography of Books and Articles, 1955-1986*, provides a detailed listing of personal memoirs by former Confederates, indexed by name and unit. This provides you a shortcut to finding memoirs directly relevant to your ancestor, and perhaps even to one that describes him in detail. See also Rowland, Ray, and Dorsey, *Bibliography of the Writings on Georgia History, 1900-1970*, for an example of a state-specific bibliography that can steer you to works relevant to biographical, military, or local history. Also consult U. S. War Department, *Bibliography of State Participation in the Civil War, 1861-1866*, as well as Wright, *Compendium of the Confederacy: An Annotated Bibliography*.

(5) For researchers interested in digging deeper into the available primary materials on the Confederacy, the indispensable bibliography is Beers, *The Confederacy*. This work details holdings across the country's libraries and archives, allowing you to dig out many collections relevant to your unit.

(6) National Archives and Records Administration (NARA). If you can get to Washington, D. C., spend some time in NARA to dig into your unit's history. Consult original muster rolls and surviving unit reports to develop a perspective of a regiment that puts your ancestor's CMSR into context. See my bibliography for a detailed listing of many other types of records that can contribute to your understanding of a Confederate unit.

(7) State archives. Call them or consult their websites. Each has unique collections of official reports, personal memoirs and papers, rosters, and veterans' questionnaires that open up wide vistas for your research.

(8) *National Union Catalog of Manuscript Collections* (NUCMC). Available rarely in bound form, this spectacular resource is increasingly accessible via Internet. Once you learn the names of your ancestor and his officers, you may search NUCMC and find that some small repository has a collection of letters that can shed new light on your subject. By searching NUCMC indexes for the 2nd Georgia Battalion Sharpshooters' officers, I found a collection of letters by Capt. Charlie George, which gave me direct insight into the life and times of my ancestor's unit.

(9) Newspapers. Study local or regional newspapers from 1861-1865 to find reports from the battlefront. Units from rural communities often sent their casualty and battle reports to the larger-circulation newspapers of nearby cities and towns. Once you have learned the enlistment locations of the ten companies in your ancestor's Georgia regiment, for instance, you can easily infer whether you want to concentrate your efforts on the Macon, Atlanta, Columbus, or Augusta newspapers of the period. Letters from local units were likely to appear at any time, but you may wish to focus on a several week period immediately following a unit's

formation, transfer, or participation in a major battle. Since many newspapers were published weekly, your research task can be lightened considerably. Consult your librarian or archivist to help you determine which of these newspapers have name indexes for easy reference.

(10) Library of Congress. Located in Washington, D. C., it offers a spectacular selection of books and newspapers for those who can visit it.

LEVEL FOUR:

Those who wish to conduct in-depth research on their direct ancestor and a number of his family members must combine the approaches described above for Levels Two and Three. Successful research of this scope will require a sustained effort, as well as a thoroughgoing pursuit of bibliographical resources necessary to help you comb the breadth and depth of available genealogical and historical resources.

Early in my research for this book, I compiled a checklist and created a form for each Mangham Confederate's file folder. On this checklist, I kept a ready reference of his unit(s), dates of service, and personal information such as parents' and siblings' names, county history references, and census information (by year and location). Another section was devoted to military source materials, where I kept track of whether I had reviewed Sifakis, Crute, state-specific references such as Brewer and Henderson, *Confederate Veteran*, *CMH*, *Official Records*, and unit histories. Although manual systems remain important, you should obtain one of the several outstanding database programs such as Family Tree Maker™ to help you organize and display the genealogical data you amass, if you plan to do extensive family research.

Modern CD-ROM databases also allow you to cheaply and quickly search for names, addresses, and telephone numbers of everyone listed in current-day telephone books. You may wish to address a direct-mail inquiry to distant relatives in your search for photographs, letters, diaries, and other primary documents. My research for this book benefited significantly from a mass mailing addressed to more than five hundred Manghams throughout the United States.

A Level Four project that encompasses a relatively small portion of an extended family is feasible for the resourceful modern-day researcher to undertake single-handed, but the current project depended heavily upon prior genealogical research by Lynn Parham, John Palmer, and Vaughn Ballard. Without their trailblazing efforts, it would have remained beyond my resources to put the thirty-seven Mangham soldiers of 1861-1865 into a coherent genealogical context. Despite all efforts, however, some of the Mangham genealogy remains speculative, as will be the case in most family research efforts that extend back into the eighteenth century. Extant records make it impossible in many cases to determine exact relationships between individuals, and a boy raised in the household of an elder Mangham could be a son, stepson, nephew, or younger cousin. History demands a tolerance for ambiguity, and so does genealogy!

APPENDIX: MANGHAM FAMILY GENEALOGY

This appendix facilitates ready identification of Mangham Confederate soldiers and their common ancestors, all of whom are listed in bold typeface. Additionally, I have listed the soldiers' wives and children, both to provide insight into their postwar lives and to allow identification by their surviving descendants. For brevity's sake, however, I have had to omit a great deal of additional material relative to succeeding generations. For ease of reference to the text, I have indicated military unit designations and chapter references in parentheses. The numbers assigned to each individual correspond to those used in the genealogical charts displayed throughout this book.

I have used the wealth of genealogical information developed and published by Lynn Parham, Vaughn Ballard, and John Palmer, as well as other genealogical data published in county histories and relevant primary and secondary sources. My own research has provided documentation necessary to correct some previous errors regarding the Solomon and Willis Austin Mangham families, as well as fill in numerous gaps in heretofore published sources on every other Mangham family group explored in this manuscript. My conclusions about these relationships have perforce remained speculative or conjectural in some cases; I have indicated the basis for such conclusions in the text and/or in this appendix.

Descendants of John Mangum of Virginia
GENERATION NO. 1

1. John[1] Mangum was born c. 1670 in England, Ireland, or Virginia? and died c. 1737 in Isle of Wight Co., VA. He married **Frances Bennett** c. 1694.

Children of John Mangum and Frances Bennett are:

2	i.	John[2] Mangum, born c. 1703.
+ 3	ii.	William Mangum, Sr., born c. 1706 in VA.
4	iii.	Frances Mangum, born c. 1708.
5	iv.	Joseph Mangum, born c. 1710.
6	v.	Nicholas Mangum, born c. 1712.
7	vi.	Sarah Mangum, born c. 1714.
8	vii.	James Mangum, born c. 1716.
9	viii.	Mary Mangum, born c. 1718.
10	ix.	Henry Mangum, born c. 1720.

GENERATION NO. 2

3. William[2] Mangum, Sr. (John[1]) was born c. 1706 in VA. He married **Mary Persons** c. 1731 in Isle of Wight Co., VA (not proven).

Children of William Mangum and Mary Persons are:

11	i.	John[3] Mangum, born c. 1732. He married Mary c. 1755 in Isle of Wight Co., VA.
12	ii.	Samuel Mangum, born bef. 1734 in Surry Co., VA; died bef. 1758 in Granville Co., NC.
+ 13	iii.	James Mangum, born June 2, 1734; died Sept. 15, 1757.

+ 14   iv. William Mangum, Jr., born May 16, 1736 in Albemarle Par., Surry Co., VA; died 1818-1819 in Morris Island, Yarmouth Co., Nova Scotia.

+ 15   v. Arthur Mangum, born May 2, 1741; died c. 1793 in Orange Co., NC.

+ 16   vi. **Joseph Mangum, born c. 1750 in Granville Co., NC; died aft. 1809 in Granville Co., NC. (See Part II)**

+ 17   vii. **Solomon Mangham, born c. 1755 in NC; died bef. April 1810 in Putnam/Hancock Co., GA. (See Part I)**

GENERATION No. 3

13. James³ Mangum (William², John¹) was born June 2, 1734, and died Sept. 15, 1757. He married **Unknown**.

Child of James Mangum and Unknown is:

18   i. Jacob⁴ Mangum, born bef. Sept. 15, 1757. (Father of Arthur "Asa" and Joseph Edward Mangum, thus the patriarch of the later Mississippi Mangums.)

14. William³ Mangum, Jr. (William², John¹) was born May 16, 1736 in Albemarle Par., Surry Co., VA, and died 1818-1819 in Morris Island, Yarmouth Co., Nova Scotia. He married **(1) Elizabeth Lithgow**. He married **(2) Unk.** aft. 1786 in Nova Scotia. (Known as *Mangham* in British colony of Nova Scotia, 1786-1819. Used same Christian names for children in both marriages. See Part I and Ch. I for "William the Loyalist.")

Children of William Mangum and Elizabeth Lithgow are:

19   i. Samuel⁴ Mangum, born 1760-1770; died Nov. 12, 1780 near Aug.a, GA.

20   ii. Sarah Mangum, born 1768. She married (1) Juan Jorge Hinsman Nov. 27, 1786. She married (2) Antonio Poncell c. 1798.

21   iii. Mary Mangum, born c. 1769; died 1850 in Glynn Co., GA. She married John Piles, Sr. c. 1783 in Spanish Florida?

+ 22   iv. **James C. Mangham, born c. 1771 in NC; died 1847 in Glynn Co., GA. (See Ch. I)** NOTE: James clearly had a very close relationship to Sarah and Mary Mangum. They featured prominently in his will and correspondence, his son William later lived with the Poncells, and his daughter Sysigambis lived very near the Piles family. Other facets of James's life are fully consistent with identifying him as a son of William "the Loyalist," but the connection remains circumstantial.

Children of William Mangum and Unk. are:

23   i. Sarah⁴ Mangham, born 1792-1794.

24   ii. Jemima Mangham, born 1796-1800.

25   iii. Mary Mangham, born 1797-1800.

26   iv. Solomon Mangham, born c. 1798.

27   v. John Mangham, born aft. 1800.

15. Arthur³ Mangum (William², John¹) was born May 2, 1741, and died c. 1793 in Orange Co., NC. He married **Lucy Person**.

Children of Arthur Mangum and Lucy Person are:

28	i.	William Person⁴ Mangum, born 1762.
29	ii.	Willie Mangum, born c. 1766 in Orange Co., NC.
30	iii.	Sarah Mangum, born 1768 in Orange Co., NC.
31	iv.	Holley Mangum, born c. 1770 in Orange Co., NC.
32	v.	Chaney Mangum, born 1772 in Orange Co., NC.
33	vi.	Arthur Mangum, Jr., born c. 1773 in Orange Co., NC; died 1813 in Orange Co., NC. He married Dicey Carrington.
34	vii.	Clara Mangum, born 1774 in Orange Co., NC.

16. Joseph³ Mangum (William², John¹) was born c. 1750 in Granville Co., NC, and died aft. 1809 in Granville Co., NC. (See Part II)

Children of Joseph Mangum are:

35	i.	James⁴ Mangum.
36	ii.	Gray Mangum, born 1765-1770.
37	iii.	Reavis Mangum, born 1768.
+ 38	iv.	**William Mangham, born c. 1773 in NC; died c. June 1851 in Russell Co., AL. (See Ch. VII)** NOTE: identity as son of Joseph is speculative, although the latter had a son named William. Other details of William Mangham's life, to include age, location, neighbors, and children's names all seem consistent with this identification.
39	v.	Joseph Mangum, Jr., born c. 1778 in Granville Co., NC; died c. 1804.
+ 40	vi.	**Josiah Thomas Mangum, born c. 1782 in NC; died bef. Dec. 1836 in Talbot Co., GA. (See Ch. VIII)**

17. Solomon³ Mangham (William² Mangum, Sr., John¹) was born c. 1755 in NC, and died bef. April 1810 in Putnam/Hancock Co., GA. He married (1) Ann Carrington c. 1780 in NC. He married (2) Sarah Ann Bennett aft. 1780. (See Part I) NOTE: as extant genealogy shows, his identity as son of William, Sr., is fully consistent with the known facts, but nonetheless circumstantial.

Children of Solomon Mangham and Sarah Bennett are:

+ 41	i.	**Willis Austin⁴ Mangham, born 1775-1785 in NC; died c. 1861 in Pike Co., GA. (Ch. II)**
+ 42	ii.	**Thomas Mangham, born bef. 1784 in NC; died bef. 1840 in AL. (Ch. VI)**
+ 43	iii.	**James M. Mangham, born 1786-1790 in NC; died c. 1866 in Butts Co., GA. (Ch. V)**
44	iv.	Unknown Mangham, born bef. 1790. She married Phillip Graybill.
+ 45	v.	**John C. Mangham, born c. 1797 in Hancock Co., GA; died Aug. 14, 1873 in Griffin, Spalding Co., GA. (Ch. IV)**

+ 46   vi.   **Wiley P. Mangham, born bef. 1800; died c. 1835 in Chambers Co., AL. (Ch. II)**

+ 47   vii.   **Henry H. Mangham, born c. 1804 in Hancock Co., GA; died Aug. 1859 in Carsonville, Taylor Co., GA. (Ch. VI)** NOTE: primary evidence of his relationship to Solomon is Willis's guardianship. This is consistent with other existing evidence, but doesn't conclusively prove father-son relationship.

GENERATION NO. 4

22. James C.[4] Mangham (William[3] Mangum, Jr., William[2], John[1]) was born c. 1771 in NC, and died 1847 in Glynn Co., GA. He married (1) Unknown bef. 1807. He married (2) Anne McKenzie bef. 1815. (See Ch. I)

Child of James Mangham and Unknown is:

48   i.   Caroline[5] Mangham, born c. 1807; died Aug. 12, 1824 in Glynn Co., GA.

Children of James Mangham and Anne McKenzie are:

49   i.   **William W.[5] Mangham, born c. 1818 in GA; died March 11, 1862 in Brunswick, GA. (Old Co. L, new Co. K, 13th [later 26th] Ga. Inf., 1861-1862; see Ch. I)**

50   ii.   James Solomon Mangham, born c. 1831 in Glynn Co., GA; died May 1848 in Savannah, GA.

51   iii.   Sysigambis Mangham, born c. 1835 in GA; died July 25, 1852 in Scottsboro, GA.

38. William[4] Mangham (Joseph[3] Mangum, William[2], John[1]) was born c. 1773 in NC, and died c. June 1851 in Russell Co., AL. He married Emily T. (Note: Jan. 10, 1836, Emily T. Mangham witnessed a deed for William Mangham in Henry County, Georgia. Since his daughter Emily appears to have been married prior to this time, this was presumably William's wife. See Ch. VII.)

Children of William Mangham and Emily ? are:

52   i.   Martha[5] Mangham, born c. 1800; died aft. 1851. She married (1) Robert Moreland Feb. 20, 1817 in Putnam Co., GA. She married (2) William Allen bef. 1824 in GA.

53   ii.   Matilda Mangham, born c. 1800. She married Hiram Warlick bef. 1828 in GA.

54   iii.   Patsey Mangham, born c. 1800; died bef. 1824 in GA. She married William Allen Jan. 8, 1817 in Putnam Co., GA.

+ 55   iv.   Bryant S. Mangham, born c. 1804 in Hancock Co., GA; died March 23, 1867 in Sumpter, Trinity Co., TX.

56   v.   Walter A. Mangham, born bef. 1807 in Hancock Co., GA?; died Sept. 1839 in Clarke Co., AL. (Witnessed a deed for William in 1828, so presumably age 21 or older. Walter died while en route from TX to visit parents in Russell Co., AL.)

57	vi.	Manning B. Mangham, born 1810-1815 in Putnam Co., GA; died bef. July 1852 in TX?
58	vii.	Emily Mangham, born bef. 1812. She married John Warlick bef. 1828 in GA.
59	viii.	Oraman Mangham, born bef. 1820. She married P. C. Cates bef. 1834 in GA.
+ 60	ix.	**Oliver P. Mangham, born c. 1821 in Putnam Co., GA; died aft. Sept. 1865. (Co. D, 2nd Fla. Inf., 1861-1862; Co. F, 1st Ga. Inf., 1862-1865; see Ch. VII.)**
61	x.	**Irby P. Mangham, born c. 1823 in Putnam Co., GA?; died aft. Aug. 28, 1863. He married Harriett Chandler Aug. 12, 1847 in Harris Co., GA. (Served in Alabama militia during Mexican War; in Co. E, 7th Tex. Cav., 1861-1863; see Ch. VII.)**

40. Josiah Thomas^4 Mangum (Joseph^3, William^2, John^1) was born c. 1782 in NC, and died bef. Dec. 1836 in Talbot Co., GA. He married (1) Susannah Cooper c. 1799 in Granville Co., NC. He married (2) Louisa Kirkland Jan. 18, 1827 in Granville Co., NC. (See Ch. VIII.)

Children of Josiah Mangum and Susannah Cooper are:

+ 62	i.	Robert S.^{5} Mangum, born c. 1800 in NC; died March 11, 1877 in Matagorda Co., TX.
+ 63	ii.	**Josiah Thomas Mangum, Jr., born 1800-1810 in Granville Co., NC; died c. 1845 (See Ch. VIII.)** Extant genealogy indicates he was a son of Josiah, Sr., but the most important source (Theophilus Fields Mangum's biographical sketch in *Dictionary of Alabama Biographies*) is unfortunately ambiguous.
+ 64	iii.	William R. Mangum, born c. 1810 in NC; died bef. 1853 in Matagorda Co., TX.
+ 65	iv.	**Arthur Green Mangham, born Oct. 6, 1811 in Granville Co. (?), NC; died June 7, 1878 in Salado, Bell Co., TX. (See Ch. IX.)**
66	v.	Susannah Mangham, born bef. 1815.
+ 67	vi.	**Thomas H. Mangham, born 1815-1820 in Granville Co. (?), NC; died bef. Dec. 6, 1847 in Russell Co., AL. (See Ch. VIII.)**
+ 68	vii.	Jemima Mangham, born June 15, 1818 in Granville Co. (?), NC; died 1865 in Coushatta, Red River Parish, LA.
+ 69	viii.	James Green Mangham, born Aug. 29, 1821 in Granville Co. (?), NC; died Oct. 10, 1883 in Coushatta Chute, Red River Parish, LA. (See Ch. IX)

41. Willis Austin^4 Mangham (Solomon^3, William^2 Mangum, Sr., John^1) was born 1775-1785 in NC, and died c. 1861 in Pike Co., GA. He married Temperance Ann Brewer Feb. 26, 1809 in Putnam Co., GA. (See Ch. II)

Children of Willis Mangham and Temperance Brewer are:

70   i.   Henry C.[5] Mangham, born c. 1804 in Hancock Co., GA; died aft. 1860 in GA? He married (1) Elizabeth Barnett Feb. 15, 1831 in Milledgeville, GA. He married (2) Louisa Simpler April 29, 1852 in Muscogee Co., GA. (NOTE: Identity as son of Willis is circumstantial, based on Henry's extremely close relationship with Thomas R. Mangham, and the latter's close relationship to the Pike County Manghams. Either or both could have a different relationship than the one conjectured here.)

+ 71   ii.   Wiley E. Mangham, born Jan. 5, 1805 in Hancock, GA; died June 20, 1891 in Zebulon, Pike Co., GA. (See Ch. II)

+ 72   iii.   **Thomas R. Mangham, born 1806 in Hancock, GA; died Nov. 22, 1861 in Calhoun Co., AL. (See Ch. III)** (See NOTE for Henry C. Mangham above.)

+ 73   iv.   **James Pendleton Mangham, born May 29, 1810 in Hancock or Putnam Co., GA; died April 7, 1874 in Pike Co., GA. (See Ch. II)**

74   v.   Jane Amanda Mangham, born Dec. 14, 1813 in Hancock or Putnam Co., GA; died Oct. 8, 1830 in Pike Co.?, GA.

+ 75   vi.   John N. Mangham, born 1814 in Putnam Co., GA; died bef. July 1866 in Pike Co., GA. (Creek War, Pike County Cav. See Ch. II.)

76   vii.   William D. Mangham, born c. 1816; died March 8, 1838 in Macon, GA.

77   viii.   Frances Anne Mangham, born c. 1823.
(NOTE: extant genealogies incorrectly identified Arthur C. Mangham as a son of Willis, due to his age and Pike Co. connections. 1850 and 1860 census information from Tallapoosa Co., Alabama, however, shows that he was born in NC about 1804-1805, long after Willis moved to Georgia.)

42. Thomas[4] Mangham (Solomon[3], William[2] Mangum, Sr., John[1]) was born bef. 1784 in NC, and died bef. 1840 in AL. He married Lucy Jane Greer c. 1805 in GA. (See Ch. VI)

Children of Thomas Mangham and Lucy Greer are:

+ 78   i.   **John Grier[5] Mangham, born c. 1806 in Hancock Co., GA; died aft. 1865. (See Ch. VI)**

79   ii.   Louisa Mangham, born c. 1807 in Hancock Co., GA. She married (1) Joseph Irwin Nov. 25, 1824 in Pike Co., GA. She married (2) Alford Shepard bef. 1852.

+ 80   iii.   **Solomon R. Mangham, born c. 1818 in GA; died July 27, 1881 in Dadeville, Tallapoosa Co., AL. (Creek War, House's Co., Webb's Bn., Alabama Mounted Militia Inf.; Young's Co. Cav., Alabama State Reserves, 1864-1865; see Ch. VI.)**

81   iv.   Hannah Mangham, born bef. 1820. She married Vines H. Collier Nov. 23, 1835 in Upson Co., GA.

82   v.   Nathaniel H. Mangham, born c. 1824 in GA; died Sept. 5, 1848 in Camp Leon, Texas. (Died of wounds received in skirmish with Indians. Served 1846-1848 with Texas Mounted Vols.; see Ch. VI.)

+ 83   vi.   **Willis W. Mangham, born Jan. 22, 1828 in GA; died July 23, 1896 in Belton, Bell Co., TX. (Co. D, 21ˢᵗ Texas Cavalry, 1862-1865; see Ch. VI.)**

84   vii.   Jane Mangham, born bef. 1830 in GA. She married James M. Fuller Nov. 16, 1848 in Chambers Co., AL.

+ 85   viii. **James A. Mangham, born 1830 in GA; died bef. 1900. (Confederate soldier, 1862-?, unit unknown; see Ch. VI)**

86   ix.   Lucinda M. Mangham, born bef. 1831 in GA. She married John W. Godfrey Nov. 5, 1849 in Chambers Co., AL.

+ 87   x.   Sarah Mangham, born bef. 1831 in GA; died bef. 1849.

88   xi.   Adrian F. Mangham, born c. 1832. She married David R. Kirby.

43. James M.⁴ Mangham (Solomon³, William² Mangum, Sr., John¹) was born 1786-1790 in NC, and died c. 1866 in Butts Co., GA. He married (1) Elender (Eleanor?) Jarrell, Nov. 2, 1823, in Putnam Co., GA; (2) Nancy. (See Ch. V)

Children of James Mangham and Nancy are:

+ 89   i.   Unknown⁵ Mangham, born 1810-1830; died bef. 1860.

+ 90   ii.   Eleanor Mangham, born 1815-1820.

+ 91   iii. Catherine F. Mangham, born c. 1821 in GA.

+ 92   iv.   **James M. D. Mangham, born Jan. 8, 1824 in GA; died Dec. 18, 1908 in Camp Hill, Chambers Co., AL. (Co. F, 61ˢᵗ Ala. Inf., 1863-1865; see Ch. V)**

+ 93   v.   Unk. Mangham, born bef. 1825 in GA; died bef. 1847 in GA. (See Ch. V.)

+ 94   vi.   **John Henry Mangham, born Feb. 2, 1828 in Butts Co., GA; died Feb. 28, 1910 in Montgomery, AL. (Co. A, 30ᵗʰ Ala. Inf., 1862; Anderson's Battery, Va. Artillery, 1862-1863. Later known as William H. Mangham? See Ch. V.)**

95   vii.   William A. Mangham, born 1828-1829 in Butts Co., GA; died aft. April 9, 1865. (Co. A, 14ᵗʰ Ala., 1861-1865; see Ch. V)

+ 96   viii. **Wiley Pendleton Mangham, born c. 1833 in Butts Co., GA; died July 24, 1862 in Richmond, VA. (Co. I, 53ʳᵈ Ga. Inf., 1862; see Ch. V)**

+ 97   ix.   **Willis Austin Mangham, born Feb. 28, 1840 in Butts Co., GA; died Dec. 8, 1907 in Butts Co., GA. (Co. A, 30ᵗʰ Ga. Inf., 1861-1865; see Ch. IV, V)**

45. John C.⁴ Mangham (Solomon³, William² Mangum, Sr., John¹) was born c. 1797 in Hancock Co., GA, and died Aug. 14, 1873 in Griffin, Spalding Co., GA. He married Ann J. Barrett Feb. 26, 1822 in Milledgeville, GA. (See Ch. IV)

Children of John Mangham and Ann Barrett are:

98   i.   John C.⁵ Mangham, Jr., born c. 1824. (Served in Mexican War; died aft. 1850.)

99   ii.   Frances H. Mangham, born c. 1828; died bef. 1857. She married Roswell Ellis Sept. 14, 1848.

+ 100   iii.   **Samuel Watson Mangham, born Sept. 21, 1830 in Zebulon, Pike Co., GA; died Jan. 7, 1888 in Griffin, Spalding Co., GA. (5th Ga. Inf., 1861-1862; 6th Ga. State Guard Inf., 1863-1864; Co. B, 22nd Ga. Bn. Heavy Artillery, 1864-1865; Georgia Militia, 1865; see Ch. IV.)**

101   iv.   Mary E. Mangham, born c. 1833; died Jan. 10, 1884 in Savannah, GA. She married Thomas D. Bertody.

102   v.   James H. Mangham, born 1834 in GA; died Sept. 24, 1858 in Griffin, Spalding Co., GA.

+ 103   vi.   **Thomas Woodward Mangham, born Nov. 1836 in Columbus, GA; died Nov. 1874 in Macon, GA. (Co. D, 2nd Ga. Bn. Inf., 1861; 30th Ga. Inf., 1861-1864; see Ch. IV.)**

+ 104   vii.   **William R. Mangham, born c. April 1847 in GA; died aft. 1900 in Meriwether Co. (?), GA. (Co. A, 22nd Ga. Bn. Heavy Artillery, 1864-1865; see Ch. IV.)**

46. Wiley P.⁴ Mangham (Solomon³, William² Mangum, Sr., John¹) was born bef. 1800, and died c. 1835 in Chambers Co., AL. He married Cynthia Gray March 27, 1821 in Putnam Co., GA. (See Ch. II)

Children of Wiley Mangham and Cynthia Gray are:

+ 105   i.   **John Henry⁵ Mangham, born c. 1827 in Pike Co., GA; died 1867-1898 in GA or AL. (13th Ga. Inf., 1861-1864; see Ch. II.)**

106   ii.   Emily Jane Mangham, born 1828; died May 8, 1850 in Zebulon, Pike Co., GA.

107   iii.   Wiley Adams Mangham, born 1830; died May 9, 1849 in Zebulon, Pike Co., GA.

108   iv.   James G. Mangham, born c. 1831; died 1848 in GA.

+ 109   v.   Cynthia Ann Mangham, born c. 1835.

110   vi.   Elizabeth Mangham, born bef. 1835.

111   vii.   Martha Mangham, born bef. 1835.

47. Henry H.⁴ Mangham (Solomon³, William² Mangum, Sr., John¹) was born c. 1804 in Hancock Co., GA, and died Aug. 1859 in Carsonville, Taylor Co., GA. He married Elizabeth P. Thweatt July 1825 in Putnam or Baldwin Co., GA, daughter of John Thweatt and Sarah. (See Ch. VI)

Children of Henry Mangham and Elizabeth Thweatt are:

112   i.   Louisa F.⁵ Mangham, born c. 1826 in GA. She married Benjamin S. Ross June 10, 1847 in Talbot Co., GA.

113   ii.   Mary Caroline Mangham, born c. 1827 in GA. She married John Wynn.

114   iii. Martha Winfrey Mangham, born 1835 in Carsonville, Talbot Co., GA; died bef. 1886. She married Patrick H. Mitchell Nov. 16, 1853 in Taylor Co., GA.

+ 115   iv. **James O. Mangham, born July 31, 1838 in Carsonville, Talbot Co., GA; died May 1, 1911 in Jacksonville, FL. (Rucker's Co., 5th Ga. State Guard Inf., 1863-1864; see Ch. VI)**

GENERATION NO. 5

55. Bryant S.⁵ Mangham (William⁴, Joseph³ Mangum, William², John¹) was born c. 1804 in Hancock Co., GA, and died March 23, 1867 in Sumpter, Trinity Co., TX. He married **(1) Sophronia Varner** Dec. 23, 1827 in Putnam Co., GA. He married **(2) Angeline Sills** Jan. 5, 1842 in Russell Co., AL. (See Ch. VII)

Children of Bryant Mangham and Sophronia Varner are:

116   i. William⁶ Mangham, born c. 1830 in Houston or Macon Co., GA; died bef. June 18, 1853 in Harrison Co.?, TX. He married Mary Isabella Rutledge June 12, 1851 in Harrison Co., TX.

117   ii. M. Mangham, born c. 1832 in GA.

118   iii. G. Mangham, born c. 1834 in GA.

119   iv. G. Mangham, born c. 1837 in Russell Co., AL.

120   v. Sophronia Mangham, born c. 1838 in Russell Co., AL. She married John W. Gallion bef. 1860.

Children of Bryant Mangham and Angeline Sills are:

121   i. Anna M.⁶ Mangham, born c. 1844 in Russell Co., AL.

122   ii. E. Mangham, born c. 1846 in Russell Co., AL.

123   iii. Mary K. Mangham, born c. 1850 in TX.

+ 124   iv. Bryant S. Mangham, Jr., born May 4, 1857 in Trinity Co., TX; died Sept. 19, 1923 in Trinity Co., TX.

125   v. Jackson Mangham, born c. 1861 in Trinity Co., TX; died aft. 1880.

60. Oliver P.⁵ Mangham (William⁴, Joseph³ Mangum, William², John¹) was born c. 1821 in Putnam Co., GA, and died aft. Sept. 1865. He married **Mary A. Brannon** March 29, 1846 in Russell Co., AL. (Co. D, 2nd Fla. Inf., 1861-1862; Co. F, 1st Ga. Inf., 1862-1865; see Ch. VII)

Children of Oliver Mangham and Mary Brannon are:

126   i. Sarah⁶ Mangham, born c. 1844 in AL. (Age six in 1850 Russell Co. census; possibly a child of an earlier marriage.)

127   ii. Brantly Mangham, born c. 1846 in AL. (Apparently died bef. 1854-55.)

128   iii. Walter Mangham, born c. 1849 in AL. (Apparently died bef. 1854-55.)

62. Robert S.⁵ Mangum (Josiah Thomas⁴, Joseph³, William², John¹) was born c. 1800 in NC, and died March 11, 1877 in Matagorda Co., TX. He married **Ruthie Arnold** Jan. 4, 1819 in Franklin Co. (?), AL.

Children of Robert Mangum and Ruthie Arnold are:

129	i.	James H.⁶ Mangum, born Feb. 28, 1822. He married Mary Lathum.
130	ii.	Thomas P. Mangum, born May 8, 1824; died May 1837.
131	iii.	Josiah (Joseph) Mangum, born April 21, 1827; died Nov. 13, 1882 in Bay City, TX. He married Julia Ellen Wickson Aug. 31, 1869 in Wharton, TX.
132	iv.	Saryan Mangum, born Feb. 1, 1831. She married J. M. Bond Sept. 4, 1848.
133	v.	Ruthie Jane Mangum, born bef. Sept. 1832; died Sept. 24, 1832.
134	vi.	Robert S. Mangum, Jr., born Feb. 2, 1833 in GA; died July 3, 1867 in TX. He married (1) Sarah Chriswell July 13, 1857 in Wharton, TX. He married (2) Jeanie June 19, 1862. (Co. C, 21st Tx. Cav.)
135	vii.	Lucyan Mangum, born Jan. 25, 1834. She married Charles Warren.
+ 136	viii.	Samuel Jackson Mangum, born Jan. 1, 1836 in Talbot Co., GA; died May 11, 1891 in Bay City, Matagorda Co., TX.
137	ix.	George Washington Mangum, born Oct. 8, 1838 in Talbot Co., GA.
138	x.	Dorcus Ann Mangum, born Sept. 7, 1840; died June 6, 1928.
139	xi.	Arthur William Mangum, born March 14, 1846 in AL; died Sept. 15, 1928 in Bay City, Matagorda Co., TX.

63. Josiah Thomas⁵ Mangum, Jr. (Josiah Thomas⁴, Joseph³, William², John¹) was born 1800-1810 in Granville Co., NC, and died c. 1845. He married Unk. bef. 1827. (See Ch. VIII) (NOTE: existing documentation, although frustratingly ambiguous, shows that Theophilus was his son. The identities of the other sons listed here are conjectural, although they are consistent with known birth dates, places, and the relationships apparent in census and military records.)

Children of Josiah Mangum and Unk. are:

140	i.	**William J.⁶ Mangham, born 1827-1828 in Granville Co., NC; died aft. 1865. (Co. B, 11ᵗʰ LA Bn, 1862-1863; Co. K, Consolidated Crescent La. Inf., 1863-1865; see Ch. IX)**
141	ii.	Josiah Thomas Mangham, born c. 1831 in Granville Co. (?), NC; died aft. 1879. (Co. D, 28ᵗʰ La. Inf., 1862-1865? See Ch. IX.)
+ 142	iii.	Theophilus Fields Mangum, born Feb. 11, 1834 in Granville Co., NC; died March 30, 1904 in Eufala, AL.
143	iv.	Robert H. Mangham, born c. 1835 in NC; died 1863 in Middletown, TX(?).(1860-1863, Methodist Minister, TX.)
144	v.	**John R. Mangham, born c. 1840 in NC; died Nov. 25, 1861 in Nashville, TN. (Co. C, Terry's 8ᵗʰ Texas Rangers, 1861; see Ch. VIII.)**

145   vi.   **Bush W. Mangham, born c. 1845; died c. 1864 in near Petersburg, VA?** (Co. A, 4th Bn, Hilliard's Legion, 1862-1863; Co. I, 59th Ala. Inf., 1863-1864; see Ch. VIII)

64. William R.[5] Mangum (Josiah Thomas[4], Joseph[3], William[2], John[1]) was born c. 1810 in NC, and died bef. 1853 in Matagorda Co., TX. He married **Leacy L. Dennis** Jan. 3, 1832 in Harris Co., GA. (See Ch. VIII)

Children of William Mangum and Leacy Dennis are:

146   i.   Francis C.[6] Mangum, born c. 1833 in Harris Co., GA.
+ 147   ii.   Caroline E. Mangum, born c. 1835 in Harris Co., GA.
148   iii.   Leacy Susan Mangum, born 1835-1837 in Harris Co., GA.
+ 149   iv.   Joseph Marion Mangum, born Jan. 31, 1839 in Tallapoosa Co., AL; died in Gonzales Co. TX. (Co. C, Terry's 8th Texas Rangers, 1861; later Co. G, 33rd Tex. Cav. See Ch. VIII.)
150   v.   M. L. Mangum, born c. 1840 in AL.
151   vi.   Eliza Mangum, born c. 1845 in AL.

65. Arthur Green[5] Mangham (Josiah Thomas[4] Mangum, Joseph[3], William[2], John[1]) was born Oct. 6, 1811 in Granville Co. (?), NC, and died June 7, 1878 in Salado, Bell Co., TX. He married (1) Sarah Brown Nov. 17, 1833 in Talbot Co., GA. He married (2) Margaret D. Williams Jan. 1866. He married (3) Caroline Amelia Baird Nov. 1867 in LA. (See Ch. IX) (NOTE: Red River Parish was formed after the Civil War from Natchitoches Parish, including Coushatta Chute.)

Children of Arthur Mangham and Sarah Brown are:

152   i.   Christopher Columbus[6] Mangham, born Aug. 23, 1834 in Talbot Co., GA; died Nov. 5, 1836 in Talbot Co., GA.
153   ii.   **Thomas Hamilton Mangham, born Aug. 13, 1836 in Russell Co., AL; died aft. 1865. He married Sarah Martha Gray Sept. 12, 1857 in Claiborne Parish, LA.** (Co. C, 19th La. Inf., 1861-1865; see Ch. IX.)
+ 154   iii.   Francis Ann Mangham, born May 20, 1838 in Russell Co., AL; died 1871 in Coushatta Chute, Red River Parish, LA.
+ 155   iv.   Marinda Russell Mangham, born Jan. 24, 1840 in Russell Co., AL; died May 18, 1925 in Coryell Co., TX.
156   v.   Sarah Lavinia Mangham, born Aug. 15, 1842 in Russell Co., AL; died March 29, 1843 in Russell Co., AL.
+ 157   vi.   **Arthur Green Mangham, Jr., born Feb. 21, 1844 in Russell Co., AL; died Aug. 16, 1913 in Coushatta Chute, Red River Parish, LA.** (Co. B, 11th LA Bn, 1862-1863; Co. K, Consolidated Crescent La. Inf., 1863-1865; see Ch. IX.)
158   vii.   Zachary Taylor Mangham, born Dec. 21, 1846 in Russell Co., AL; died Aug. 8, 1858 in Russell Co., AL or LA.
+ 159   viii.   Martha Caroline Mangham, born Feb. 24, 1849 in Russell Co., AL; died Oct. 1929 in Bienville Parish, LA.

160   ix.   Samuel Young Mangham, born Feb. 23, 1851 in Russell Co., AL; died Nov. 12, 1851 in Russell Co., AL.

+ 161   x.   Charles John Mangham, born April 14, 1853 in Russell Co., AL; died Feb. 10, 1935 in Coushatta Chute, Red River Parish, LA.

162   xi.   Joseph Manuel Mangham, born Sept. 25, 1855; died bef. 1860.

163   xii. Elizabeth Dawn Mangham, born March 8, 1862 in Natchitoches Parish, LA; died Oct. 8, 1862 in Natchitoches Parish, LA.

67. Thomas H.⁵ Mangham (Josiah Thomas⁴ Mangum, Joseph³, William², John¹) **was born 1815-1820 in Granville Co. (?), NC, and died bef. Dec. 6, 1847 in Russell Co., AL. He married Rhoda Callaway Nov. 5, 1840 in Chambers Co., AL. (See Ch. VIII)**

Children of Thomas Mangham and Rhoda Callaway are:

+ **164**   i.   **Charles Arthur⁶ Mangham, born Sept. 14, 1844 in Russell Co., AL; died July 23, 1931 in San Antonio, TX. (Co. F, 18ᵗʰ Ala. Inf., 1861-1865; see Ch. VIII.)**

165   ii.   Martha S. Mangham, born c. 1845.

166   iii. **William T. T. Mangham, born 1846 in Russell Co., AL; died aft. June 29, 1865. (Co. E, 61ˢᵗ Ala. Inf., 1863-1865; see Ch. VIII.)**

68. Jemima⁵ Mangham (Josiah Thomas⁴ Mangum, Joseph³, William², John¹) was born June 15, 1818 in Granville Co. (?), NC, and died 1865 in Coushatta, Red River Parish, LA. She married **William W. Sockwell** Feb. 6, 1840 in Russell Co., AL.

Child of Jemima Mangham and William Sockwell is:

167   i.   John Dawson⁶ Sockwell, born 1861 in LA; died 1863 in LA.

69. James Green⁵ Mangham (Josiah Thomas⁴ Mangum, Joseph³, William², John¹) was born Aug. 29, 1821 in Granville Co. (?), NC, and died Oct. 10, 1883 in Coushatta Chute, Red River Parish, LA. He married **(1) Martha Elizabeth Gray** Nov. 25, 1846 in Russell Co., AL. He married **(2) Julia Frances Murph** bef. 1880 in Red River Parish, LA. (See Ch. IX)

Children of James Mangham and Martha Gray are:

168   i.   Mary Elizabeth⁶ Mangham, born Dec. 8, 1848 in Russell Co., AL; died June 8, 1876 in LA. She married Unk. Holmes.

169   ii.   Sarah Jemima Mangham, born July 10, 1850 in Russell Co., AL; died Oct. 18, 1904 in Coushatta Chute, Red River Parish, LA. She married Britton C. Lee Dec. 2, 1875.

+ 170   iii. Martha Ann Rebecca Mangham, born Feb. 21, 1852 in Russell Co., AL; died June 30, 1893 in Coushatta Chute, Red River Parish, LA.

+ 171   iv.   James Arthur Mangham, born Dec. 25, 1854 in LA; died March 23, 1929 in Ringgold, Bienville Par., LA.

+ 172   v.   Louisiana Green Mangham, born April 2, 1857 in LA; died Sept. 18, 1882 in Coushatta Chute, Red River Parish, LA.

173 vi. Adolphus Fields Mangham, born Nov. 17, 1858 in LA; died July 1, 1949 in Coushatta Chute, Red River Parish, LA.

174 vii. Susan Harriett Mangham, born April 15, 1860 in LA; died Oct. 1, 1869 in Coushatta Chute, Red River Parish, LA.

+ 175 viii. Green Beauregard Mangham, born Jan. 28, 1862 in LA; died Dec. 16, 1935 in Coushatta Chute, Red River Parish, LA.

176 ix. Thomas John Mangham, born Sept. 8, 1864 in Coushatta Chute, Red River Parish, LA; died Sept. 18, 1864 in Coushatta Chute, Red River Parish, LA.

Children of James Mangham and Julia Murph are:

+ 177 i. Joe[6] Mangham, born Aug. 12, 1880 in Coushatta Chute (?), Red River Parish, LA; died May 4, 1960.

178 ii. Frances Caroline Mangham, born Feb. 26, 1883 in Coushatta Chute, Red River Parish, LA; died July 16, 1884 in Coushatta Chute, Red River Parish, LA.

71. Wiley E.[5] Mangham (Willis Austin[4], Solomon[3], William[2] Mangum, Sr., John[1]) was born Jan. 5, 1805 in Hancock, GA, and died June 20, 1891 in Zebulon, Pike Co., GA. He married **Malinda M. Holmes** Dec. 20, 1827 in Pike Co., GA. (Wiley served in the Pike County Cavalry during the Creek War; see Ch. II.)

Child of Wiley Mangham and Malinda Holmes is:

179 i. Mary Jane[6] Mangham, born Sept. 5, 1831. She married Charles F. Redding 1848 in Pike Co., GA.

72. Thomas R.[5] Mangham (Willis Austin[4], Solomon[3], William[2] Mangum, Sr., John[1]) was born 1806 in Hancock, GA, and died Nov. 22, 1861 in Calhoun Co., AL. He married Matilda Dandridge Grant March 10, 1825 in Pike Co., GA. (See Ch. III)

Children of Thomas Mangham and Matilda Grant are:

+ 180 i. Henry Grant[6] Mangham, born Dec. 9, 1828 in Lee Co., GA; died Dec. 10, 1885 in Alto, Richland Par., LA. (Benton's Battery, a.k.a. Bell Battery, a.k.a. 3rd La. Field Artillery, 1862-1865; see Ch. III.)

181 ii. Ann E. Mangham, born c. 1832 in GA.

182 iii. Matilda C. Mangham, born c. 1834 in GA.

+ 183 iv. Thomas Jefferson Mangham, born Feb. 25, 1835 in Harris Co., GA; died Jan. 12, 1918 in Ruston, Lincoln Par., LA. (Co. D, 1st Ala. Inf. Bn., 1861-1862; Co. D, 25th Ala. Inf., 1862; Co. A, 10th Ala. Inf., 1864-1865; see Ch. III.)

+ 184 v. Wiley Person Mangham, born Jan. 1, 1838 in Russell Co., AL; died Sept. 26, 1896 in Rayville, Richland Par., LA. (Co. D, 1st Ala. Inf. Bn., 1861-1862; Co. D, 25th Ala. Inf., 1862; see Ch. III.)

185 vi. Martha Mangham, born c. 1841 in AL.

186 vii. Sarah Temperance Mangham, born March 26, 1842 in Russell Co., AL; died July 11, 1842 in Russell Co., AL.

187 viii. Amanda H. Mangham, born c. 1845 in AL, died c. Oct. 1875. Married E. S. Landers.

188 ix. Eveline B. Mangham, born c. 1846 in AL.

73. James Pendleton[5] Mangham (Willis Austin[4], Solomon[3], William[2] Mangum, Sr., John[1]) **was born May 29, 1810 in Hancock or Putnam Co., GA, and died April 7, 1874 in Pike Co., GA. He married Winfred Ennis April 16, 1829 in Pike Co., GA.** (See Ch. II.)

Children of James Mangham and Winfred Ennis are:

189 i. Jane Amanda Temperance[6] Mangham, born April 17, 1830. She married (1) Joshah Chapman 1852 in Pike Co., GA. She married (2) Steven W. Elliott, Sr. July 13, 1876 in Pike Co., GA.

+ 190 ii. **John Willis Mangham, born Aug. 3, 1832 in Pike Co., GA; died Nov. 14, 1910 in Hendricks, Upson Co., GA. (Co. L, 5th Ga. Inf., 1862; Co. B, 2nd Ga. Bn. Sharpshooters, 1862-1865; see Ch. II.)**

191 iii. Mary Ann Malinda Harriet Mangham, born Nov. 9, 1833 in Pike Co., GA; died Oct. 17, 1838 in Pike Co., GA.

+ 192 iv. **Wiley James Mangham, born Oct. 16, 1837 in Pike Co., GA; died Feb. 14, 1862 in Manassas, VA. (Co. G, 27th Ga. Inf., 1861-1862; see Ch. II.)**

193 v. Elizabeth Winfred Samithy Mariah Mangham, born April 13, 1838 in Pike Co., GA; died in Pike Co., GA. She married Unk. Thomas.

+ 194 vi. **William Decatur Mangham, born March 2, 1840 in Pike Co., GA; died Nov. 1, 1874 in Pike Co., GA. (Co. A, 13th Ga. Inf., 1861-1864; Co. G, 1st Ga. Reserve Inf., 1864-1865; see Ch. II.)**

+ 195 vii. **Charles Absalem Mangham, born Dec. 30, 1841 in Pike Co., GA; died Nov. 27, 1906 in Kaufman, TX. (Co. A, 13th Ga. Inf., 1861-1865; see Ch. II.)**

196 viii. Rebecca Mangham, born Oct. 12, 1842 in Pike Co., GA; died May 13, 1926 in Barnesville, GA. She married Steven W. Elliott, Jr..

+ 197 ix. **Robert Jackson Mangham, born Sept. 11, 1845 in Pike Co., GA; died July 19, 1929 in Pike Co., GA. (Claimed service in Co. A, 13th Ga. Inf. and Jackson's Ga. Battery, 1862-1864, but unsubstantiated; see Ch. II.)**

75. John N.[5] Mangham (Willis Austin[4], Solomon[3], William[2] Mangum, Sr., John[1]) was born 1814 in Putnam Co., GA, and died bef. July 1866 in Pike Co., GA. He married **Rebecca E. Adams** July 30, 1836. (Served in Pike County Cav. during Creek War; see Ch. II.)

Children of John Mangham and Rebecca Adams are:

198 i. Amanda[6] Mangham, born 1839 in Pike Co., GA; died 1839 in Pike Co., GA.

199 ii. Luella Ann Mangham, born c. 1850 in Pike Co., GA; died aft. 1866.

200   iii.   Rebecca Elizabeth Mangham, born c. 1856 in Pike Co., GA; died bef. Sept. 1880 in Pike Co., GA.

78. John Grier⁵ Mangham (Thomas⁴, Solomon³, William² Mangum, Sr., John¹) was born c. 1806 in Hancock Co., GA, and died aft. 1865. He married Eliza Webb Hill 1836 in GA. (See Ch. VI)

Children of John Mangham and Eliza Hill are:

+   201   i.   Mary J.⁶ Mangham, born c. 1836.

+   202   ii.   **Willoughby Hill Mangham, born April 5, 1838 in Randolph Co., GA; died Jan. 2, 1893 in Ware Co., GA. (Co. I, 11ᵗʰ Ga. Inf., 1861-1865; see Ch. VI.)**

203   iii.   Huldah Elizabeth Mangham, born c. 1845.

204   iv.   Henry Mangham, born c. 1847; died bef. 1860.

80. Solomon R.⁵ Mangham (Thomas⁴, Solomon³, William² Mangum, Sr., John¹) was born c. 1818 in GA, and died July 27, 1881 in Dadeville, Tallapoosa Co., AL. He married (1) Sarah Shepard March 6, 1851 in Chambers Co., AL. He married (2) Emily c. 1864 in Tallapoosa Co., AL. (Creek War, House's Co., Webb's Bn., Alabama Mounted Militia Inf.; Young's Co. Cav., Alabama State Reserves, 1864-1865; see Ch. VI.)

Children of Solomon Mangham and Sarah Shepard are:

205   i.   Francis⁶ Mangham, born aft. Aug. 1852 in Chambers Co., AL; died aft. 1881. She married John E. Duck.

206   ii.   Unknown Mangham, born Aug. 1854; died bef. 1861 in AL.

207   iii.   John W. Mangham, born c. 1856 in Tallapoosa Co., AL; died aft. 1881.

208   iv.   Unknown Mangham, born 1861; died bef. Feb. 1861 in Tallapoosa Co., AL.

209   v.   Unknown Mangham, born 1861; died bef. Feb. 1861.

Children of Solomon Mangham and Emily are:

210   i.   Cassendra E.⁶ Mangham, born c. 1865; died aft. 1881.

211   ii.   Susan E. Mangham, born c. 1866; died aft. 1881.

212   iii.   Emily A. Mangham, born c. 1868; died aft. 1881.

213   iv.   Mary A. Mangham, born c. 1869; died aft. 1881.

83. Willis W.⁵ Mangham (Thomas⁴, Solomon³, William² Mangum, Sr., John¹) was born Jan. 22, 1828 in GA, and died July 23, 1896 in Belton, Bell Co., TX. He married (1) Sarah A. Moore 1857 in Belton, Bell Co., TX. He married (2) L. Bettie Robinson c. 1870. He married (3) Harriatt Rebecca Scott c. 1881 in Bell Co., TX. (Co. D, 21ˢᵗ Tex. Cav., 1862-1865; see Ch. VI.)

Children of Willis Mangham and Sarah Moore are:

+   214   i.   Dulane W.⁶ Mangham, born 1859; died 1954 in Bell Co., TX.

215   ii.   Clarence W. Mangham, born Jan. 31, 1861 in Belton, Bell Co., TX; died Oct. 17, 1888 in Belton, Bell Co., TX.

Children of Willis Mangham and L. Robinson are:

216   i.   Susie Willie[6] Mangham, born Aug. 1870 in Bell Co., TX; died Aug. 1884 in Bell Co., TX.

217   ii.   Pearlie Mangham, born 1872 in Bell Co., TX; died 1874 in Bell Co., TX.

Children of Willis Mangham and Harriatt Scott are:

218   i.   Thomas T.[6] Mangham.

219   ii.   Eliza Mangham.

220   iii.   Unknown Mangham.

221   iv.   Unknown Mangham.

85. James A.[5] Mangham (Thomas[4], Solomon[3], William[2] Mangum, Sr., John[1]) was born 1830 in GA, and died bef. 1900. He married **Virginia Victoria Spencer** Dec. 6, 1859 in Mobile, AL. (**Confederate soldier, 1862-??, unit unknown; see Ch. VI.**)

Children of James Mangham and Virginia Spencer are:

222   i.   Mary Ida[6] Mangham, born 1862; died Aug. 1864 in Mobile, AL.

+ 223   ii.   Frank S. Mangham, born Oct. 1866 in Mobile, AL; died July 14, 1940 in DeWitt Co., TX.

+ 224   iii.   James Clarence Mangham, born March 24, 1868 in Mobile, AL; died Nov. 7, 1933 in San Antonio, TX.

225   iv.   Virginia Alleen Mangham, born Aug. 1871 in Mobile, AL; died aft. 1933 in Columbus, MS? She married Watt Hairston.

87. Sarah[5] Mangham (Thomas[4], Solomon[3], William[2] Mangum, Sr., John[1]) was born bef. 1831 in GA, and died bef. 1849. She married **Unknown Umphries**.

Child of Sarah Mangham and Unknown Umphries is:

226   i.   Sarah E.[6] Umphries, born bef. 1849.

89. Unknown[5] Mangham (James M.[4], Solomon[3], William[2] Mangum, Sr., John[1]) was born 1810-1830, and died bef. 1860. He married **Sarah** bef. 1848.

Child of Unknown Mangham and Sarah is:

227   i.   Charles Thomas[6] Mangham, born 1845-1849 in Butts Co., GA; died aft. 1880.

90. Eleanor[5] Mangham (James M.[4], Solomon[3], William[2] Mangum, Sr., John[1]) was born 1815-1820. She married **John G. Lindsey** Dec. 19, 1843 in Butts Co., GA.

Child of Eleanor Mangham and John Lindsey is:

228   i.   John H[6] Lindsey, born c. 1846.

91. Catherine F.[5] Mangham (James M.[4], Solomon[3], William[2] Mangum, Sr., John[1]) was born c. 1821 in GA. She married **William C. D. McWhorter** Dec. 19, 1843 in Butts Co., GA.

Children of Catherine Mangham and William McWhorter are:

229   i.   R. P.[6] McWhorter, born c. 1845.

230   ii.   W. A. McWhorter, born 1849-1850.

92. James M. D.[5] Mangham (James M.[4], Solomon[3], William[2] Mangum, Sr., John[1]) was born Jan. 8, 1824 in GA, and died Dec. 18, 1908 in Camp Hill, Chambers Co., AL. He married (1) Jane McCoy May 21, 1845 in Butts Co., GA. He married (2) Matilda A. Mitchell Love Aug. 11, 1864 in Camp Hill, Chambers Co., AL. (Co. F, 61st Ala. Inf., 1863-1865; see Ch. V.)

Children of James Mangham and Jane McCoy are:

+ 231   i.   **Wiley Paul[6] Mangham, born March 2, 1846 in Butts or Henry Co., GA; died Oct. 16, 1931 in Riverview, Chambers Co., AL. (Confederate soldier, 1864-1865, unit unknown; see Ch. V.)**

+ 232   ii.   Henry J. Mangham, born Feb. 15, 1848 in GA; died aft. 1920 in AL?

   233   iii.   Eleanor Frances Mangham, born Oct. 9, 1849 in Henry (?) Co., GA; died aft. 1880.

   234   iv.   Mary B. Mangham, born c. 1855 in Camp Hill, Chambers Co., AL. She married Joseph G. Reaves Dec. 24, 1878 in Camp Hill, AL.

+ 235   v.   John C. Mangham, born Aug. 31, 1855 in Camp Hill, Chambers Co., AL; died Dec. 19, 1920.

   236   vi.   James G. Mangham, born Dec. 13, 1856 in Camp Hill, Chambers Co., AL. He married Martha E. Grady.

   237   vii.   Tim Mangham, born c. 1858 in Camp Hill, Chambers Co., AL.

   238   viii.   Adelbert Mangham, born c. 1859 in Camp Hill, Chambers Co., AL.

+ 239   ix.   Jefferson Davis Mangham, born Feb. 15, 1862 in Camp Hill, Chambers Co., AL; died Aug. 27, 1930.

   240   x.   Eliza Mangham, born Feb. 13, 1864 in Camp Hill, Chambers Co., AL. She married William P. Harper Dec. 9, 1886.

Children of James Mangham and Matilda Love are:

   241   i.   William T.[6] Mangham, born June 30, 1866 in Camp Hill, Chambers Co., AL. He married Amanda Waller c. 1890.

   242   ii.   Sarah N. Mangham, born March 27, 1868 in Camp Hill, Chambers Co., AL; died 1901 in Chambers Co., AL. She married Willie Duffy Oct. 26, 1886.

   243   iii.   Callie V. Mangham, born April 5, 1871 in Camp Hill, Chambers Co., AL; died 1901. She married W. R. Reynolds Oct. 21, 1886 in Camp Hill, AL.

   244   iv.   Hassie D. Mangham, born Dec. 18, 1872 in Camp Hill, Chambers Co., AL; died April 13, 1917 in Chambers Co., AL. She married Willie Johnson.

   245   v.   Fulvie Mangham, born 1873 in Camp Hill, Chambers Co., AL. She married Dan Waller.

   246   vi.   Ludie F. Mangham, born March 1, 1874 in Camp Hill, Chambers Co., AL; died Oct. 6, 1955. She married J. D. Waller Aug. 8, 1893 in LaGrange, Troup Co., GA.

247   vii.   Malvie Mangham, born April 27, 1875 in Camp Hill, Chambers Co., AL; died 1900.

248   viii.   James M. Mangham, Jr., born Dec. 17, 1876 in Camp Hill, Chambers Co., AL; died April 24, 1888 in Camp Hill, Chambers Co., AL.

93. Unk.[5] Mangham (James M.[4], Solomon[3], William[2] Mangum, Sr., John[1]) was born bef. 1825 in GA, and died bef. 1847 in GA. He married Unk. (See Ch. V.)

Child of Unk. Mangham and Unk. is:

249   i.   John S.[6] Mangham, born c. 1845. Apprenticed to Mary Croley, McDonough, Henry Co., GA, 1847. (Co. A, 53rd Ga. Inf., 1862-1863; see Ch. V.) (NOTE: possibly another orphaned son of Josiah Thomas Mangum.)

94. John Henry[5] Mangham (James M.[4], Solomon[3], William[2] Mangum, Sr., John[1]) was born Feb. 2, 1828 in Butts Co., GA, and died Feb. 28, 1910 in Montgomery, AL. He married (1) Eliza T. Devaughn Sept. 30, 1849 in Coosa Co., AL. He married (2) Eliza A. Bearden Sept. 16, 1852 in Talladega Co., AL. He married (3) Minnie Peters Jarrell c. 1908 in AL. (Co. A, 30th Ala. Inf., 1862; Anderson's Battery, Virginia Artillery, 1862-1863; see Ch. V.)

Children of John Mangham and Eliza Bearden are:

250   i.   Polly[6] Mangham, born c. 1855 in AL; died aft. 1860.

251   ii.   Francis Mangham, born c. 1858 in AL; died aft. 1860.

96. Wiley Pendleton[5] Mangham (James M.[4], Solomon[3], William[2] Mangum, Sr., John[1]) was born c. 1833 in Butts Co., GA, and died July 24, 1862 in Richmond, VA. He married Mary Ann Heath Oct. 4, 1855 in Butts Co., GA. (Co. I, 53rd Ga. Inf., 1862; see Ch. V.)

Children of Wiley Mangham and Mary Heath are:

252   i.   Eliza R.[6] Mangham, born c. 1857 in Butts Co., GA; died aft. 1870.

253   ii.   John W. Mangham, born c. 1859 in Butts Co., GA; died bef. 1870.

97. Willis Austin[5] Mangham (James M.[4], Solomon[3], William[2] Mangum, Sr., John[1]) was born Feb. 28, 1840 in Butts Co., GA, and died Dec. 8, 1907 in Butts Co., GA. He married Nancy G. Thaxton Feb. 2, 1859 in Butts Co., GA. (Co. A, 30th Ga. Inf., 1861-1865; see Ch. IV.)

Children of Willis Mangham and Nancy Thaxton are:

254   i.   Mary Malissa[6] Mangham, born Sept. 4, 1860 in Butts Co., GA; died aft. 1880 in Butts Co., GA.

255   ii.   Willis Benjamin Franklin Mangham, born Sept. 8, 1862 in Butts Co., GA; died Nov. 22, 1934. He married Molly Ida Benton.

256   iii.   James Wiley Mangham, born March 11, 1866 in Butts Co., GA; died Oct. 19, 1952. He married Eva Grant.

257   iv.   Anna Laura Mangham, born Nov. 21, 1868 in Butts Co., GA; died Jan. 20, 1965. She married Dolfus Cornwell.

258   v.   John Robert Mangham, born Sept. 9, 1870; died c. 1963. He married (1) Anne Barrett. He married (2) Mattie Walker. He married (3) Sallie Mae Williams.

259   vi.   William Henry Mangham, born Sept. 25, 1871 in Butts Co., GA. He married (1) Willie ? He married (2) Maud Bohannon.

260   vii.   Nancy Elizabeth Mangham, born Dec. 19, 1874 in Butts Co., GA. She married Fletcher Bearden.

261   viii.   Minnie Clara Mangham, born Feb. 19, 1879 in Butts Co., GA; died May 13, 1946. She married Henry Jones.

100. Samuel Watson[5] Mangham (John C.[4], Solomon[3], William[2] Mangum, Sr., John[1]) was born Sept. 21, 1830 in Zebulon, Pike Co., GA, and died Jan. 7, 1888 in Griffin, Spalding Co., GA. He married (1) Pope Reeves 1856. He married (2) Harriet L. Reeves Nov. 23, 1859 in Griffin, Spalding Co., GA. (5th Ga. Inf., 1861-1862; 6th Ga. State Guard Inf., 1863-1864; Co. B, 22nd Ga. Bn. Heavy Artillery, 1864-1865; Georgia Militia, 1865; see Ch. IV.)

Child of Samuel Mangham and Pope Reeves is:

262   i.   Pope Reeves[6] Mangham, born April 20, 1857; died May 14, 1877.

Children of Samuel Mangham and Harriet Reeves are:

263   i.   John H.[6] Mangham, born Aug. 28, 1860 in Griffin, Spalding Co., GA; died May 10, 1862 in Griffin, Spalding Co., GA.

264   ii.   Joseph J. Mangham, born March 1867 in Griffin, Spalding Co., GA; died aft. 1910 in Griffin, Spalding Co., GA. He married Ora Boyd.

+ 265   iii.   John Woodward Mangham, born Aug. 1867 in Griffin, Spalding Co., GA; died aft. 1910.

103. Thomas Woodward[5] Mangham (John C.[4], Solomon[3], William[2] Mangum, Sr., John[1]) was born Nov. 1836 in Columbus, GA, and died Nov. 1874 in Macon, GA. He married Ida Louise Winship Sept. 19, 1865 in Macon, GA. (Co. D, 2nd Ga. Inf. Bn., 1861; 30th Ga. Inf., 1861-1864; see Ch. IV.)

Children of Thomas Mangham and Ida Winship are:

266   i.   Fannie Graham[6] Mangham, born c. 1867 in Macon, Bibb Co., GA.

267   ii.   Lizzie Mangham, born c. 1869 in Macon, Bibb Co., GA.

268   iii.   Thomas Woodward Mangham, Jr., born c. 1871 in Macon, Bibb Co., GA.

269   iv.   Ida Louise Mangham, born c. 1872 in Macon, Bibb Co., GA.

104. William R.[5] Mangham (John C.[4], Solomon[3], William[2] Mangum, Sr., John[1]) was born c. April 1847 in GA, and died aft. 1900 in Meriwether Co. (?), GA. He married Fannie Gile (?) in Meriwether County, GA ? (Co. A, 22nd Ga. Bn. Heavy Artillery, 1864-1865; see Ch. IV.)

Child of William Mangham and Fannie (?) is:

270   i.   William Gile[6] Mangham, born 1889 in Woodbury or Griffin; died c. 1974.

105. John Henry⁵ Mangham (Wiley P.⁴, Solomon³, William² Mangum, Sr., John¹) **was born c. 1827 in Pike Co., GA, and died 1867-1898 in GA or AL. He married Rebecca Caldwell. (13ᵗʰ Ga. Inf., 1861-1864; see Ch. II.)**

Children of John Mangham and Rebecca Caldwell are:

271	i.	Willie⁶ Mangham, born Oct. 3, 1851 in Zebulon, GA; died Oct. 31, 1852 in Zebulon, GA.
272	ii.	M. Eliza Mangham, born May 30, 1853 in Zebulon, GA; died June 27, 1854 in Zebulon, GA.
273	iii.	Mary Willie Mangham, born June 16, 1854 in Zebulon, GA; died March 3, 1855 in Zebulon, GA.
274	iv.	Mattie A. Mangham, born c. 1856.
+ 275	v.	Wiley C. Mangham, born Aug. 1858; died aft. 1910 in Oxford, Calhoun Co., AL (?).
276	vi.	Emmie L. Mangham, born c. 1860.
277	vii.	Unknown Mangham, born 1861-1865.

109. Cynthia Ann⁵ Mangham (Wiley P.⁴, Solomon³, William² Mangum, Sr., John¹) was born c. 1835. She married **John C. Redding** Dec. 2, 1853 in Pike Co., GA.

Children of Cynthia Mangham and John Redding are:

278	i.	M. Truman⁶ Redding, born c. 1857.
279	ii.	Willie D. Redding, born c. 1859.

115. James O.⁵ Mangham (Henry H.⁴, Solomon³, William² Mangum, Sr., John¹) **was born July 31, 1838 in Carsonville, Talbot Co., GA, and died May 1, 1911 in Jacksonville, FL. He married Winifred Edwards Nov. 10, 1859 in Taylor Co., GA. (Rucker's Co., 5ᵗʰ Ga. State Guard Inf., 1863-1864; see Ch. VI.)**

Children of James Mangham and Winifred Edwards are:

280	i.	Annie⁶ Mangham, born c. 1861 in Carsonville, Taylor Co., GA; died 1885 in Chatfield, TX. She married Unk. Kenner.
281	ii.	Frances Claud Mangham, born March 31, 1862 in Carsonville, Taylor Co., GA; died Sept. 14, 1942.
282	iii.	Henry H. Mangham, born Oct. 1, 1866 in Carsonville, Taylor Co., GA; died June 6, 1886 in Carsonville, Taylor Co., GA.
283	iv.	John Edward Mangham, born Dec. 1871 in Carsonville, Taylor Co., GA. He married Rachel Respass.
284	v.	Charlie A. Mangham, born c. 1877 in Carsonville, Taylor Co., GA.
+ 285	vi.	Elizabeth Mangham, born May 22, 1880 in Carsonville, Taylor Co., GA; died Dec. 6, 1960 in St. Mary's, Camden Co., GA.
286	vii.	James O. Mangham, Jr., born 1880-1884 in Carsonville, Taylor Co., GA.
287	viii.	Frank Mangham, born 1883 in Carsonville, Taylor Co., GA; died Sept. 26, 1885 in Carsonville, Taylor Co., GA.

GENERATION NO. 6

124. Bryant S.⁶ Mangham, Jr. (Bryant S.⁵, William⁴, Joseph³ Mangum, William², John¹) was born May 4, 1857 in Trinity Co., TX, and died Sept. 19, 1923 in Trinity Co., TX. He married **Nancy** c. 1885 in TX.

Children of Bryant Mangham and Nancy are:

288	i.	Berta⁷ Mangham, born Nov. 1888.
289	ii.	Claud Mangham, born Oct. 1891.
290	iii.	Bulah Mangham, born March 1895.

136. Samuel Jackson⁶ Mangum (Robert S.⁵, Josiah Thomas⁴, Joseph³, William², John¹) was born Jan. 1, 1836 in Talbot Co., GA, and died May 11, 1891 in Bay City, Matagorda Co., TX. He married **(1) Martha Jane White** c. 1857 in TX. He married **(2) Nancy Spaulding** July 22, 1884 in Matagorda Co., TX.

Children of Samuel Mangum and Martha White are:

291	i.	Ruth⁷ Mangum, born c. 1857.
292	ii.	Samuel Jackson Mangum, Jr., born Feb. 23, 1863.
293	iii.	Mary F. Mangum, born 1868.
294	iv.	A. W. Mangum, born 1870.
295	v.	Josiah Mangum, born 1872.
296	vi.	John G. Mangum, born 1874.
297	vii.	Martha Mangum, born 1876.

142. Theophilus Fields⁶ Mangum (Josiah Thomas⁵, Josiah Thomas⁴, Joseph³, William², John¹) was born Feb. 11, 1834 in Granville Co., NC, and died March 30, 1904 in Eufala, AL. He married **Julia Frances Perkins**. (1860-1904, he was a Methodist Minister in Alabama.)

Children of Theophilus Mangum and Julia Perkins are:

298	i.	Daniel Bake⁷ Mangum, born c. 1863 in AL. He married Bessie Lamm.
299	ii.	Theophilus Fields Mangum, Jr., born Oct. 21, 1863 in Dallas Co., AL. He married Alice Fitzhugh Nov. 11, 1891.
300	iii.	William Wightman Mangum, born c. 1868 in AL. He married (1) Mamie McKenzie. He married (2) Nan (Dent) Long.
301	iv.	John Bradfield Mangum, born c. 1873 in AL.
302	v.	Robert Henry Mangum, born April 21, 1875 in Tuskegee, AL. He married Elizabeth Dawson (Hails) McLeod June 15, 1919 in Montgomery, AL.
303	vi.	Josiah Thomas Mangum, born c. 1877 in AL. He married Edith Hooper in Charlotte, NC.
304	vii.	Helen Ira Mangum, born June 1879 in AL. She married G. E. Laughlin.

147. Caroline E.⁶ Mangum (William R.⁵, Josiah Thomas⁴, Joseph³, William², John¹) was born c. 1835 in Harris Co., GA. She married **Hiram**.

Children of Caroline Mangum and Hiram are:

305	i.	Fanny⁷, born c. 1856.
306	ii.	William, born 1859.

149. Joseph Marion⁶ Mangum (William R.⁵, Josiah Thomas⁴, Joseph³, William², John¹) was born Jan. 31, 1839 in Tallapoosa Co., AL, and died in Gonzales Co. TX. He married **Mattie Gillespie** 1876 in Gonzales Co. TX. (Co. C, Terry's 8ᵗʰ Texas Rangers, 1861; later Co. G, 33rd Tex. Cav.; see Ch. VIII.)

Children of Joseph Mangum and Mattie Gillespie are:

307	i.	Edna⁷ Mangum.
308	ii.	Joseph D. Mangum.
309	iii.	Mattie Lee Mangum.
310	iv.	Maude Mangum.
311	v.	Eugene T. Mangum.
312	vi.	Mamie Elizabeth Mangum.
313	vii.	Brown Mangum.

154. Francis Ann⁶ Mangham (Arthur Green⁵, Josiah Thomas⁴ Mangum, Joseph³, William², John¹) was born May 20, 1838 in Russell Co., AL, and died 1871 in Coushatta Chute, Red River Parish, LA. She married **(1) Absolom Cullars** Nov. 24, 1853. She married **(2) Thomas E. Ward** aft. 1854.

Children of Francis Mangham and Thomas Ward are:

314	i.	Susan⁷ Ward, born 1860.
315	ii.	Sarah Ward, born 1861.
316	iii.	Thomas Hamilton Ward, born 1864.
317	iv.	Arthur Green Ward, born 1868.

155. Marinda Russell⁶ Mangham (Arthur Green⁵, Josiah Thomas⁴ Mangum, Joseph³, William², John¹) was born Jan. 24, 1840 in Russell Co., AL, and died May 18, 1925 in Coryell Co., TX. She married **(1) William Peavy** Oct. 15, 1857 in Claiborne Parish, LA. She married **(2) Thomas E. Ward** April 1889 in Coryell Co., TX.

Children of Marinda Mangham and William Peavy are:

318	i.	Fleta⁷ Peavy, born 1858.
319	ii.	Sarah Elizabeth Peavy, born 1860.
320	iii.	Willie Davis Peavy, born 1862.
321	iv.	Eli Green Peavy, born 1866.
322	v.	Unk. Peavy, born 1868.
323	vi.	Martha Peavy, born 1869.
324	vii.	Cora Peavy, born 1872.

157. Arthur Green⁶ Mangham, Jr. (Arthur Green⁵, Josiah Thomas⁴ Mangum, Joseph³, William², John¹) was born Feb. 21, 1844 in Russell Co., AL, and died Aug.

16, 1913 in Coushatta Chute, Red River Parish, LA. He married Mariah Lewis Murph Oct. 25, 1865 in Coushatta Chute, Red River Parish, LA. (Co. B, 11th LA Bn, 1862-1863; Co. K, Consol. Crescent La. Inf., 1863-1865; see Ch. IX.)

Children of Arthur Mangham and Mariah Murph are:

325 i. Charles Warren[7] Mangham, born Oct. 18, 1868 in Coushatta Chute, Red River Parish, LA; died Jan. 29, 1936 in Coushatta Chute, Red River Parish, LA. He married Willie Benbo Broughton 1891 in Coushatta Chute, Red River Parish, LA.

326 ii. Sarah Caroline Mangham, born 1872 in Coushatta Chute, Red River Parish, LA; died 1872 in Coushatta Chute, Red River Parish, LA.

327 iii. Kate Lewis Mangham, born Feb. 1875 in TX; died 1924. She married A. Hawthorn in Red River Parish, LA.

328 iv. Winnie Mangham, born 1880 in Coushatta Chute, Red River Parish, LA.

329 v. Willie Boyleston Mangham, born June 1884 in Coushatta Chute, Red River Parish, LA; died Aug. 5, 1944.

159. Martha Caroline[6] Mangham (Arthur Green[5], Josiah Thomas[4] Mangum, Joseph[3], William[2], John[1]) was born Feb. 24, 1849 in Russell Co., AL, and died Oct. 1929 in Bienville Parish, LA. She married **James Salter** 1870.

Children of Martha Mangham and James Salter are:

330 i. Julius Arthur[7] Salter.
331 ii. Octavia Salter.
332 iii. Fredrick William Salter.
333 iv. Sallie Russell Salter.
334 v. Tuleta Salter.
335 vi. Mary Pauline Salter.
336 vii. Horace Greely Salter.
337 viii. Jamie Caroline Salter.
338 ix. Nellie Minerva Salter.

161. Charles John[6] Mangham (Arthur Green[5], Josiah Thomas[4] Mangum, Joseph[3], William[2], John[1]) was born April 14, 1853 in Russell Co., AL, and died Feb. 10, 1935 in Coushatta Chute, Red River Parish, LA. He married **Caroline Elizabeth Murph** Dec. 10, 1884 in Coushatta Chute, Red River Parish, LA.

Children of Charles Mangham and Caroline Murph are:

339 i. Samuel Brown[7] Mangham, born Feb. 5, 1887 in Coushatta Chute, Red River Parish, LA; died June 12, 1952 in Coushatta Chute, Red River Parish, LA.

340 ii. Sarah Elizabeth Mangham, born 1888.
341 iii. Arthur John Mangham, born 1890.
342 iv. Eugenia Russell Mangham, born 1892.
343 v. Evie Mangham, born 1895.

344   vi. Ruth Mangham, born 1898.

345   vii. Bessie Mangham, born 1900.

346   viii. Unk. Mangham, born July 22, 1894 in Coushatta Chute, Red River Parish, LA; died July 29, 1894 in Coushatta Chute, Red River Parish, LA.

164. Charles Arthur⁶ Mangham (Thomas H.⁵, Josiah Thomas⁴ Mangum, Joseph³, William², John¹) **was born Sept. 14, 1844 in Russell Co., AL, and died July 23, 1931 in San Antonio, TX. He married Lucinda Elizabeth Williams 1866 in AL.** (Co. F, 18ᵗʰ Ala. Inf., 1861-1865; see Ch. VIII.)

Children of Charles Mangham and Lucinda Elizabeth Williams are:

347   i. Eugene⁷ Mangham, born Nov. 1869 in Conecuh Co., AL; died aft. 1931. He married Fannie bef. 1889.

348   ii. Charles A. Mangham, Jr., born March 1873 in TX. He married Rosa 1898 in San Saba (?), TX.

349   iii. Ida Mangham, born c. 1876 in TX; died aft. 1931. She married E. J. Lemberg.

350   iv. C. W. Mangham, born Oct. 1886 in TX.

351   v. Unk. Mangham, born Unknown.

352   vi. Unk. Mangham, born Unknown.

170. Martha Ann Rebecca⁶ Mangham (James Green⁵, Josiah Thomas⁴ Mangum, Joseph³, William², John¹) was born Feb. 21, 1852 in Russell Co., AL, and died June 30, 1893 in Coushatta Chute, Red River Parish, LA. She married **J. R. Palmer** Jan. 28, 1875 in Red River Parish, LA (?).

Children of Martha Mangham and J. Palmer are:

353   i. Paul⁷ Palmer.

354   ii. Fred Palmer.

355   iii. Ethel Palmer.

356   iv. Adolphus Palmer.

357   v. Martha Palmer.

358   vi. Sarah Palmer.

359   vii. Ben Palmer.

171. James Arthur⁶ Mangham (James Green⁵, Josiah Thomas⁴ Mangum, Joseph³, William², John¹) was born Dec. 25, 1854 in LA, and died March 23, 1929 in Ringgold, Bienville Par., LA. He married **Sophia J.**.

Children of James Mangham and Sophia J. are:

360   i. M. Arthur⁷ Mangham, born Oct. 1883.

361   ii. L. Marie Mangham, born April 1885.

362   iii. A. Don Mangham, born June 1886.

363   iv. M. Ruth Mangham, born Oct. 1892.

364   v. Sarah C. Mangham, born May 1900.

172. Louisiana Green[6] Mangham (James Green[5], Josiah Thomas[4] Mangum, Joseph[3], William[2], John[1]) was born April 2, 1857 in LA, and died Sept. 18, 1882 in Coushatta Chute, Red River Parish, LA. She married **W. W. Riley** May 11, 1876.

Children of Louisiana Mangham and W. Riley are:

365   i.   Lovie P.[7] Riley.

366   ii.   Lizzie Riley, born May 1877.

175. Green Beauregard[6] Mangham (James Green[5], Josiah Thomas[4] Mangum, Joseph[3], William[2], John[1]) was born Jan. 28, 1862 in LA, and died Dec. 16, 1935 in Coushatta Chute, Red River Parish, LA. He married **Hallie Anna Lee** Feb. 12, 1889 in Coushatta Chute, Red River Parish, LA.

Children of Green Mangham and Hallie Lee are:

367   i.   Unk.[7] Mangham, born Dec. 2, 1889 in Coushatta Chute, Red River Parish, LA; died Dec. 2, 1889 in Coushatta Chute, Red River Parish, LA.

368   ii.   Walter Lee Mangham, born Dec. 19, 1891 in Coushatta Chute, Red River Parish, LA; died June 2, 1978 in Coushatta, Red River Parish, LA. He married Martha Josephine Wilson April 9, 1915.

369   iii.   James Britton Mangham, born Sept. 28, 1903 in Coushatta Chute, Red River Parish, LA; died Sept. 23, 1904 in Coushatta Chute, Red River Parish, LA.

370   iv.   William Mangham, born Sept. 21, 1905 in Coushatta Chute, Red River Parish, LA; died Sept. 28, 1905 in Coushatta Chute, Red River Parish, LA.

177. Joe[6] Mangham (James Green[5], Josiah Thomas[4] Mangum, Joseph[3], William[2], John[1]) was born Aug. 12, 1880 in Coushatta Chute (?), Red River Parish, LA, and died May 4, 1960. She married **Andrew Lawson Wimberly** Oct. 10, 1905.

Children of Joe Mangham and Andrew Wimberly are:

371   i.   Thomas Lawson[7] Wimberly, born 1907.

372   ii.   James Green Wimberly, born 1909.

373   iii.   Hallie Wimberly, born 1914.

374   iv.   Vashti Wimberly, born 1918.

375   v.   Julia Fannie Wimberly, born 1921.

376   vi.   Frank Wimberly, born Unknown.

377   vii.   Linda Wimberly, born Unknown.

378   viii.   Sarah Wimberly, born Unknown.

180. Henry Grant[6] Mangham (Thomas R.[5], Willis Austin[4], Solomon[3], William[2] Mangum, Sr., John[1]) was born Dec. 9, 1828 in Lee Co., GA, and died Dec. 10, 1885 in Alto, Richland Par., LA. He married Telitha Ann Montgomery April 21, 1859 in Alto, Richland Par., LA. (Benton's Battery, a.k.a. Bell Battery, a.k.a. 3rd La. Field Artillery, 1862-1865; see Ch. III.)

Children of Henry Mangham and Telitha Montgomery are:

379   i.   Harriet[7] Mangham, born c. 1866. She married (1) W. H. Hallack Sept. 25, 1889 in Richland Parish, LA; (2) Robert Louvent.

380   ii.   Caravine ("Carrie") O. Mangham, born c. 1869. She married Robert Lee Binion Jan. 23, 1889, in Alto, LA.

381   iii.   Henry Grant Mangham, born Unknown.

382   iv.   Thomas H. Mangham, born 1860 in Alto, LA; died 1918 in Oklahoma City, OK. He married Maggie H. Smylie March 14, 1880 in Richland Par., LA.

383   v.   Unknown Mangham, born Unknown.

183. Thomas Jefferson[6] Mangham (Thomas R.[5], Willis Austin[4], Solomon[3], William[2] Mangum, Sr., John[1]) was born Feb. 25, 1835 in Harris Co., GA, and died Jan. 12, 1918 in Ruston, Lincoln Par., LA. He married Jennie Yarbrough 1865 in St. Clair County (?), AL. (Co. D, 1st Ala. Inf. Bn., 1861-1862; Co. D, 25th Ala. Inf., 1862; Co. A, 10th Ala. Inf., 1864-1865; see Ch. III.)

Children of Thomas Mangham and Jennie are:

384   i.   Robert[7] Mangham, born c. 1876. (Adopted son, born in Alabama, living with family in 1880.)

385   ii.   John Wiley Mangham, born May 17, 1882; died Sept. 6, 1882.

184. Wiley Person[6] Mangham (Thomas R.[5], Willis Austin[4], Solomon[3], William[2] Mangum, Sr., John[1]) was born Jan. 1, 1838 in Russell Co., AL, and died Sept. 26, 1896 in Rayville, Richland Par., LA. He married Carolyn Frances Emmeline Lynn Oct. 18, 1866 in Girard, LA. (Co. D, 1st Ala. Inf. Bn., 1861-1862; Co. D, 25th Ala. Inf., 1861-1862; see Ch. III.)

Children of Wiley Mangham and Carolyn Lynn are:

386   i.   Jennie L.[7] Mangham, born Oct. 18, 1867 in Rayville, Richland Par., LA; died June 27, 1868 in Rayville, Richland Par., LA.

387   ii.   Mary Alice Mangham, born March 24, 1869 in Rayville, Richland Par., LA; died Sept. 2, 1873 in Rayville, Richland Par., LA.

388   iii.   Wiley Samuel Mangham, born Aug. 11, 1873 in Rayville, Richland Par., LA; died Dec. 4, 1876 in Rayville, Richland Par., LA.

389   iv.   Carolyn Frances Mangham, born Dec. 17, 1875 in Rayville, Richland Par., LA; died Sept. 7, 1876 in Rayville, Richland Par., LA.

390   v.   Jesse Henry Mangham, born bef. 1876; died bef. 1877 in Rayville, Richland Par., LA.

391   vi.   Eunice T. Mangham, born June 15, 1877; died April 13, 1967 in Rayville, Richland Par., LA. She married Unk. Trezevant.

392   vii.   Nettie Irma Mangham, born 1879. She married Duncan Buie.

393   viii.   Horace Albert Mangham, born Aug. 10, 1882; died June 23, 1961.

394   ix.   Hervey Elwyn Mangham, born July 1889. Killed in baseball accident in Baton Rouge, LA, 1908, while playing for LSU.

190. John Willis[6] Mangham (James Pendleton[5], Willis Austin[4], Solomon[3], William[2] Mangum, Sr., John[1]) was born Aug. 3, 1832 in Pike Co., GA, and died Nov. 14, 1910 in Hendricks, Upson Co., GA. He married (1) Amanda G. Barrett Oct. 19, 1852 in Pike Co., GA. He married (2) Amanda Elizabeth Zorn Oct. 7, 1858 in Upson Co., GA. He married (3) Sophronia Victoria Zorn Smith Dec. 3, 1905 in Hillsborough, later Pinellas Co., FL. (Co. L, 5th Ga., 1862; Co. B, 2nd Ga. Bn. Sharpshooters, 1862-1865; see Ch. II.)

Children of John Mangham and Amanda Barrett are:

395	i.	Mary W.[7] Mangham, born Aug. 14, 1853.
396	ii.	Rebecca Mangham, born July 17, 1854. She married Rayford N. "Babe" Hollingsworth Dec. 1, 1874 in GA.

Children of John Mangham and Amanda Zorn are:

397	i.	Charles Banks[7] Mangham, born Dec. 23, 1859 in Hendricks, Upson Co., GA; died Sept. 9, 1930 in Plains, Sumter Co., GA. He married Mariah Emma Hardy Dec. 21, 1880 in Upson Co., GA.
398	ii.	Eliza A. Mangham, born Dec. 1, 1862; died Feb. 27, 1955. She married Thomas A. Hardy Jan. 13, 1884 in Upson Co., GA.
399	iii.	Lella Amee Mangham, born March 15, 1864; died Dec. 20, 1955. She married Will Eason.
400	iv.	Mary Eldora Mangham, born March 21, 1866. She married William B. Collier Oct. 19, 1887 in Upson Co., GA.
401	v.	James Amos Mangham, born Aug. 25, 1868 in Hendricks, Upson Co., GA; died Sept. 9, 1902 in Hendricks, Upson Co., GA. He married Lannie Elizabeth Weathers c. 1888.
402	vi.	Augustus William Mangham, born Oct. 19, 1871 in Hendricks, Upson Co., GA; died Aug. 14, 1886 in Hendricks, Upson Co., GA.
403	vii.	Wiley T. Mangham, born Sept. 17, 1874 in Hendricks, Upson Co., GA; died March 22, 1955. He married Josephine E. Womble Jan. 27, 1895 in Upson Co., GA.
404	viii.	John Jackson Mangham, born July 6, 1877. He married Lizzie Dunn. (He was a Georgia gubernatorial candidate in 1930s.)

192. Wiley James[6] Mangham (James Pendleton[5], Willis Austin[4], Solomon[3], William[2] Mangum, Sr., John[1]) was born Oct. 16, 1837 in Pike Co., GA, and died Feb. 14, 1862 in Manassas, VA. He married Susan Glenn Marshall Oct. 6, 1858 in Pike Co. GA. (Co. G, 27th Ga. Inf., 1861-1862; see Ch. II.)

Children of Wiley Mangham and Susan Marshall are:

405	i.	James Pendleton[7] Mangham II, born Oct. 15, 1859 in Pike Co., GA; died Aug. 18, 1940 in Nacogdoches, TX. He married Mary Eliza Collier.
406	ii.	William Wiley Mangham, born Nov. 3, 1861 in Pike Co., GA; died March 8, 1938 in Nacogdoches, TX. He married Amanda Elizabeth Howard.

NOTE: Susan Marshall Mangham bore two additional children whose father is unknown:

- Robert H. Cager Mangham was born July 8, 1865 in Pike Co., GA, and died 1915 in Spalding Co., GA. He married Mrs. F. E. Reynolds on Nov. 1, 1881.
- John Thomas Mangham was born 1867 in Pike Co., GA, and died in 1942. He married Aug.a Cannon.

194. William Decatur[6] Mangham (James Pendleton[5], Willis Austin[4], Solomon[3], William[2] Mangum, Sr., John[1]) was born March 2, 1840 in Pike Co. GA, and died Nov. 1, 1874 in Pike Co., GA. He married Martha Jane Hagan Feb. 4, 1868 in Pike Co., GA. (Co. A, 13th Ga. Inf., 1861-1864; Co. G, 1st Ga. State Reserve Inf., 1864-1865; see Ch. II.)

Children of William Mangham and Martha Hagan are:

407	i.	Lou Emma[7] Mangham, born c. 1870; died aft. 1880.
408	ii.	Elizabeth Leola Mangham, born c. 1871; died aft. 1880.
409	iii.	Mary Anna Mangham, born June 1873; died aft. 1880. She married Wiley Jimmerson.
410	iv.	James William ("Bud") Mangham, born Dec. 7, 1874 in Lifsey, Pike Co., GA; died Sept. 1912. He married Essie L. Bankston.

195. Charles Absalem[6] Mangham (James Pendleton[5], Willis Austin[4], Solomon[3], William[2] Mangum, Sr., John[1]) was born Dec. 30, 1841 in Pike Co., GA, and died Nov. 27, 1906 in Kaufman, TX. He married (1) Lula Burton Steger Nov. 27, 1866 in Pike Co., GA. He married (2) Lou V. McKnight Aug. 17, 1896 in Nacogdoches, TX. (Co. A, 13th Ga. Inf., 1861-65; see Ch. II.)

Children of Charles Mangham and Lula Steger are:

411	i.	James Newman[7] Mangham, born Aug. 20, 1867. He married Lela Catherine Clayton.
412	ii.	John Charles Mangham, born July 14, 1870. He married (1) Annie McGowan and (2) Mrs. Maude Greenslade.
413	iii.	Mary Winifred Mangham, born Feb. 13, 1872. She married Joseph Lee Akin.
414	iv.	William Burton Mangham, born Feb. 12, 1875; died May 12, 1965. He married Ellie Pearl Lyles.
415	v.	Robert Lee Pearson Mangham, born Sept. 27, 1876; died 1961. He married Emma Trollinger.
416	vi.	Thomas Edward Mangham, born April 9, 1878; died Sept. 25, 1880.
417	vii.	Roy Scott Mangham, born Oct. 2, 1880; died Nov. 15, 1966. He married Naomi Davis.
418	viii.	Arthur Decator Mangham, born March 1, 1882; died Jan. 1940. He married Emma Evelina Flanagan.
419	ix.	Arlin Gordon Mangham, born Dec. 25, 1883; died Nov. 20, 1974. He married Nancy Viola Malone.

420   x. Samuel Lloyd Mangham, born Nov. 1, 1885; died June 5, 1969. He married Vergie Ross.

421   xi. L. D. Mangham, born June 2, 1887; died Oct. 3, 1981. He married Dovie Tuttle.

422   xii. Vera Lucille Mangham, born July 12, 1891; died Nov. 30, 1963. She married (1) John P. Reichert, (2) W. Lowery.

423   xiii. Cleveland Adlai Mangham, born Jan. 30, 1893; died March 7, 1938. He married Margaret Sarah Chamness.

424   xiv. Lula Mangham, born March 10, 1895; died July 28, 1895.

197. Robert Jackson^6 Mangham (James Pendleton^5, Willis Austin^4, Solomon^3, William^2 Mangum, Sr., John^1) was born Sept. 11, 1845 in Pike Co., GA, and died July 19, 1929 in Pike Co., GA. He married (1) Eliza R. Elliott Feb. 24, 1870 in Pike Co., GA. He married (2) Lucy Abby Littlejohn 1891 in Pike Co., GA. (Claimed service with Co. A, 13th Ga. Inf. and Jackson's Ga. Battery, 1862-1864—unsubstantiated; see Ch. II.)

Children of Robert Mangham and Eliza Elliott are:

425   i. Willis Edward^7 Mangham, born Dec. 7, 1870; died March 8, 1875.

426   ii. Carrie Temperance Mangham, born Nov. 4, 1872; died Sept. 28, 1964. She married John Bankston.

427   iii. Lizabeth Uglauno Mangham, born Sept. 9, 1874; died June 8, 1875.

428   iv. Robert Reid Mangham, born Feb. 29, 1876; died March 5, 1955. He married Cora Lee DeMarcus.

429   v. Charles Washington Mangham, born Aug. 28, 1877; died Oct. 30, 1976. He married Eva Jordan Holloway.

430   vi. Ella Mae Mangham, born May 1, 1879. She married James Abner King.

431   vii. Reuben Henry Mangham, born May 15, 1881; died June 28, 1966. He married Lilla Mae Reeves.

432   viii. Luther J. Mangham, born Oct. 18, 1882; died April 12, 1917.

433   ix. Jesse Lee Mangham, born Aug. 29, 1884; died Feb. 10, 1913.

434   x. Trummie Burton Mangham, born March 21, 1886. He married Lizzie Wilson.

435   xi. Claudia Estelle Mangham, born Dec. 20, 1888; died Jan. 8, 1988. She married John Miles Stewart Greene.

436   xii. Lorie James Mangham, born May 11, 1890; died Dec. 25, 1936. He married Rebecca Bush.

Children of Robert Mangham and Lucy Littlejohn are:

437   i. Elmer Floyd^7 Mangham, born April 18, 1893. He married Georgia Adams.

438   ii. Raymond Artis Mangham, born Oct. 30, 1894. He married Lela Buckhanan.

439   iii.   Minnie Ester Mangham, born May 19, 1896; died Aug. 18, 1967. She married Jeff Childree.

440   iv.   Walter Leon Mangham, born Oct. 27, 1897; died July 9, 1898.

441   v.   Mattie Clay Mangham, born Dec. 21, 1898. She married Eddie Lee Duncan.

442   vi.   Edna Mangham, born Dec. 18, 1900. She married Will Henry Waller.

443   vii.   Roy Mangham, born Feb. 26, 1902; died Aug. 3, 1985.

444   viii.   Emma Mangham, born Aug. 6, 1903. She married Douglas Millard Minter.

445   ix.   Harvey Mangham, born April 9, 1906. He married Pearl Fossett.

446   x.   Ruby Grace Mangham, born May 3, 1908. She married Labon Beckham Moore.

447   xi.   Nannie Belle Mangham, born Feb. 28, 1910. She married Roy Lee Moore.

201. Mary J.[6] Mangham (John Grier[5], Thomas[4], Solomon[3], William[2] Mangum, Sr., John[1]) was born c. 1836. She married **James Nichols** bef. 1862.

Child of Mary Mangham and James Nichols is:

448   i.   Altha[7] Nichols, born c. 1861.

202. Willoughby Hill[6] Mangham (John Grier[5], Thomas[4], Solomon[3], William[2] Mangum, Sr., John[1]) was born April 5, 1838 in Randolph Co., GA, and died Jan. 2, 1893 in Ware Co., GA. He married Amanda Hillhouse Roper Sept. 4, 1866 in Randolph Co., GA. (Co. I, 11th Ga. Inf., 1861-1865; see Ch. VI.)

Children of Willoughby Mangham and Amanda Roper are:

449   i.   Ethlyn Virginia[7] Mangham, born June 12, 1867.

450   ii.   Flavius Madison Mangham, born May 1, 1869.

451   iii.   William Thomas Mangham, born Jan. 26, 1872.

452   iv.   Emily Eliza Mangham, born June 28, 1874.

453   v.   Mary Mangham, born Aug. 28, 1876.

454   vi.   Joseph Roper Mangham, born July 10, 1879.

455   vii.   Washington Hill Mangham, born Feb. 21, 1882.

456   viii.   Willoughby Jackson Mangham, born Feb. 21, 1882.

457   ix.   Rosalie Mangham, born aft. 1883. She married J. H. Tipton.

214. Dulane W.[6] Mangham (Willis W.[5], Thomas[4], Solomon[3], William[2] Mangum, Sr., John[1]) was born 1859, and died 1954 in Bell Co., TX. He married (1) **Rebecca Mary** bef. 1885. He married (2) **Mary Ella Estes** aft. July 1886.

Child of Dulane Mangham and Rebecca Mary is:

458   i.   Luther D.[7] Mangham, born June 30, 1886 in Bell Co., TX; died Aug. 5, 1886 in Bell Co., TX.

Children of Dulane Mangham and Mary Estes are:

459   i.   Pearl[7] Mangham, born July 1892.

460   ii.   Clarence Edmond Mangham, born April 1896.

461   iii.   Alice Mangham, born Aug. 1899.
462   iv.   Herbert Mangham, born c. 1902.
463   v.   Dulane Mangham, born c. 1904.
464   vi.   Willis Mangham, born Aug. 1887.

223. Frank S.[6] Mangham (James A.[5], Thomas[4], Solomon[3], William[2] Mangum, Sr., John[1]) was born Oct. 1866 in Mobile, AL, and died July 14, 1940 in DeWitt Co., TX. He married **Minnie** bef. 1898.

Child of Frank Mangham and Minnie is:
465   i.   Frank[7] Mangham, born Jan. 1899.

224. James Clarence[6] Mangham (James A.[5], Thomas[4], Solomon[3], William[2] Mangum, Sr., John[1]) was born March 24, 1868 in Mobile, AL, and died Nov. 7, 1933 in San Antonio, TX. He married **Mary McElroy**.

Children of James Mangham and Mary McElroy are:
466   i.   Clarence Edward[7] Mangham, born Nov. 16, 1896.
467   ii.   Marjorie Mangham.
468   iii.   Renie Mangham. She married Ben W. Freeman ?

231. Wiley Paul[6] Mangham (James M. D.[5], James M.[4], Solomon[3], William[2] Mangum, Sr., John[1]) was born March 2, 1846 in Butts or Henry Co., GA, and died Oct. 16, 1931 in Riverview, Chambers Co., AL. He married Mary F. "Fannie" Waldrop c. 1869. (Confederate soldier, 1864-1865, unit unknown; see Ch. V.)

Children of Wiley Mangham and Mary Waldrop are:
469   i.   James T.[7] Mangham, born Nov. 1869 in AL. He married Ella L.
470   ii.   M. A. Mangham, born c. 1872.
471   iii.   J. L. Mangham, born c. 1874.
472   iv.   Charles E. Mangham, born June 1875. He married Fannie.
473   v.   Annie R. Mangham, born Sept. 1877 in AL.
474   vi.   Robert W. Mangham, born Aug. 1879 in AL.

232. Henry J.[6] Mangham (James M. D.[5], James M.[4], Solomon[3], William[2] Mangum, Sr., John[1]) was born Feb. 15, 1848 in GA, and died aft. 1920 in AL? He married **Mary A. Thornton** Aug. 6, 1872 in AL?

Children of Henry Mangham and Mary Thornton are:
475   i.   Charlie[7] Mangham, born Aug. 1875 in AL. He married Ella E. c. 1898.
476   ii.   Lella Mangham, born 1876.

235. John C.[6] Mangham (James M. D.[5], James M.[4], Solomon[3], William[2] Mangum, Sr., John[1]) was born Aug. 31, 1855 in Camp Hill, Chambers Co., AL, and died Dec. 19, 1920. He married **Celia Ann Mitchell**.

Children of John Mangham and Celia Mitchell are:
477   i.   Amanda J.[7] Mangham, born Nov. 1884.
478   ii.   James M. Mangham, born Aug. 1886.

479   iii.   Wiley P. Mangham, born Dec. 1887.

480   iv.   John L. Mangham, born April 1892.

481   v.   Arthur B. Mangham, born Jan. 1895.

482   vi.   Thomas J. Mangham, born Aug. 1897.

483   vii. Annie W. Mangham, born Dec. 1899.

239. Jefferson Davis⁶ Mangham (James M. D.⁵, James M.⁴, Solomon³, William² Mangum, Sr., John¹) was born Feb. 15, 1862 in Camp Hill, Chambers Co., AL, and died Aug. 27, 1930. He married **Lavinia Lumpkin Harper** Dec. 19, 1888 in Camp Hill, AL.

Children of Jefferson Mangham and Lavinia Harper are:

484   i.   Mattie D.⁷ Mangham, born Jan. 1891.

485   ii.   Francis H. Mangham, born Dec. 1891.

486   iii. Hattie M. Mangham, born June 1893.

487   iv.   Preston Mangham, born Nov. 1894.

488   v.   Wilford O. Mangham, born Aug. 1896.

489   vi.   Unk. dau. Mangham, born Feb. 1898.

265. John Woodward⁶ Mangham (Samuel Watson⁵, John C.⁴, Solomon³, William² Mangum, Sr., John¹) was born Aug. 1867 in Griffin, Spalding Co., GA, and died aft. 1910. He married **Olive Boyd**.

Children of John Mangham and Olive Boyd are:

490   i.   John W.⁷ Mangham, Jr., born Oct. 1895.

491   ii.   Samuel Mangham, born Nov. 1897.

492   iii. David Mangham, born c. 1900 in Spalding Co., GA.

275. Wiley C.⁶ Mangham (John Henry⁵, Wiley P.⁴, Solomon³, William² Mangum, Sr., John¹) was born Aug. 1858, and died aft. 1910 in Oxford, Calhoun Co., AL (?). He married **Delilah** c. 1887.

Child of Wiley Mangham and Delilah is:

493   i.   Daisy⁷ Bolton, born July 1883.

285. Elizabeth⁶ Mangham (James O.⁵, Henry H.⁴, Solomon³, William² Mangum, Sr., John¹) was born May 22, 1880 in Carsonville, Taylor Co., GA, and died Dec. 6, 1960 in St. Mary's, Camden Co., GA. She married **Elzie J. Williams** 1908 in St. Mary's, Camden Co., GA.

Children of Elizabeth Mangham and Elzie Williams are:

494   i.   Mary W.⁷ Williams, born c. 1908.

495   ii.   J. Jack Williams, born c. 1912.

496   iii. Edward J. Williams, born c. 1915.

497   iv.   Mangham Williams, born c. 1917.

Descendants of John C. Mangham of Mississippi

GENERATION NO. 1

A1. John C.[1] Mangham was born 1804-1805 in GA, and died aft. Sept. 1861. He married (1) Hannah B. Pharoah July 2, 1830 in Montgomery, AL. He married (2) Nancy Ann Brown Dec. 21, 1848 in Tuscaloosa Co., AL. (Old Co. G, 10th Miss. Inf., 1861; see Ch. X.)

Children of John Mangham and Hannah Pharoah are:

+ A2   i.   Francis Joseph[2] Mangham, born 1831 in AL; died Oct. 21, 1883 in Yazoo City, Yazoo Co., MS. (Co. A, 1st Miss. Light Artillery, 1862-1865; see Ch. X.)

+ A3   ii.   Thomas J. Mangham, born Sept. 6, 1832 in AL; died June 16, 1889 in Greenville, Washington Co., MS. (Co. I, 1st Miss. Light Artillery, 1862-1863; see Ch. X.)

GENERATION NO. 2

A2. Francis Joseph[2] Mangham (John C.[1]) was born 1831 in AL, and died Oct. 21, 1883 in Yazoo City, Yazoo Co., MS. He married Elizabeth Catherine Mangum Feb. 22, 1855 in Scott Co., MS. (Co. A, 1st Miss. Light Artillery, 1862-1865; see Ch. X.)

Children of Francis Mangham and Elizabeth Mangum are:

+ A4   i.   William Thomas[3] Mangham, born Nov. 30, 1855 in Scott Co., MS; died Jan. 3, 1896 in Yazoo City, Yazoo Co., MS.

A5   ii.   J. R. Mangham, born c. 1857 in MS; died aft. 1884. He married Lucy Burton July 3, 1884 in Yazoo City, Yazoo Co., MS.

A6   iii. Jane Mangham, born c. 1859 in MS.

A7   iv.   A. C. Mangham, born c. 1861 in MS.

+ A8   v.   Callie Mangham, born c. 1865 in MS.

A9   vi.   Zoetta M. Mangham, born c. 1867 in MS. She married Mr. Young.

A10   vii. D. V. M. Mangham, born c. 1870 in MS.

A11   viii. Unknown Mangham, born Unknown.

A3. Thomas J.[2] Mangham (John C.[1]) was born Sept. 6, 1832 in AL, and died June 16, 1889 in Greenville, Washington Co., MS. He married (1) Dolly Burns Dec. 24, 1861 in Yazoo City, Yazoo Co., MS. He married (2) Elizabeth (Burns?) aft. 1862. (Co. I, 1st Miss. Light Artillery, 1862-1863; see Ch. X.)

Children of Thomas Mangham and Elizabeth (Burns?) are:

A12   i.   Margaret[3] Mangham, born Jan. 1863 in MS.

A13   ii.   Thomas J. Mangham, Jr., born c. 1865 in MS; died aft. 1880.

A14   iii. Emily B. Mangham, born c. 1867 in MS.

A15   iv.   Robert Mangham, born July 1870 in MS; died aft. 1900.

A16   v.   James E. Mangham, born Dec. 1873 in MS; died aft. 1900. He married Claudia G.

A17   vi.   Francis J. Mangham, born Nov. 1875 in MS; died aft. 1900.

A18   vii.   George P. Mangham, born c. 1877 in MS; died aft. 1880.

A19   viii.   Emma Mangham, born Jan. 1886 in MS; died aft. 1900.

GENERATION NO. 3

A4. William Thomas[3] Mangham (Francis Joseph[2], John C.[1]) was born Nov. 30, 1855 in Scott Co., MS, and died Jan. 3, 1896 in Yazoo City, Yazoo Co., MS. He married **(1) Lucy Pauline Davis** Jan. 26, 1881 in Yazoo City, Yazoo Co., MS. He married **(2) Frances Catherine Mangum** aft. 1882 in MS.

Child of William Mangham and Frances Mangum is:

A20   i.   William Joseph[4] Mangham, born 1887 in Yazoo City, Yazoo Co., MS; died 1954. He married Edna Belle Walker.

A8. Callie[3] Mangham (Francis Joseph[2], John C.[1]) was born c. 1865 in MS. She married **(1) Mr. Raney**. She married **(2) J. C. Davis** Dec. 22, 1884 in Yazoo City, Yazoo Co., MS.

Child of Callie Mangham and J. Davis is:

A21   i.   Frank[4] Davis.

Glossary

CONTENTS:

1. ARMS OF SERVICE

Artillery—designated as light or heavy artillery depending upon the caliber of their guns. Most light (or field) artillerymen walked, while horses drew the guns, limbers, caissons and assorted support equipment. Batteries typically had four guns, but sometimes six or even eight. Usually, half were field guns and half were howitzers. Nicknamed "redlegs" for the red stripe on their pants.

Cavalry—organized similarly to infantry regiments, Confederate horsemen commonly dismounted once in close contact with the enemy and fought with muskets, carbines or shotguns; most considered sabers and lances superfluous. Scornful infantrymen often referred caustically to the soft life of the "buttermilk cavalry," asking rhetorically: "Who ever saw a dead cavalryman?"

Infantry—the great majority of soldiers served in infantry units, whose foot soldiers bore the brunt of most Civil War actions. Known derisively as "webfeet" by cavalrymen.

2. MILITARY UNIT STRUCTURE

Company—typically raised from men in one or two counties, infantry companies typically comprised about 50 to 125 men. Commissioned "company officers" included a captain and three lieutenants, who were assisted by nine non-commissioned officers: five sergeants and four corporals. Companies bore nicknames, as well as a letter designation (A through K, omitting J.)

Battalion—independent units comprised of two to nine companies, infantry or Sharpshooter battalions were commanded by a major or lieutenant colonel.

Regiment—a formal organization comprising ten companies, whose members elected a colonel, lieutenant colonel, and major as their "field officers." Regimental staffs included several officers and men assigned to commissary, quartermaster, and ordnance duties, as well as a regimental adjutant and sergeant major. Upon completion of their organization, regiments were numbered according to chronological precedence by their home state. Formal designations such as the "5th

Regiment Georgia Volunteer Infantry," were commonly abbreviated as "5th Georgia Volunteers (or Vols.)" or simply "5th Georgia."

Brigade—typically composed of four or five regiments, many included an infantry or Sharpshooter battalion. Confederate brigades bore the names of the brigadier general in command, until and unless he was formally replaced. Thus "Gist's Brigade" bore that name even during the months that Colonel McCullough was in temporary command. (Union brigades were designated by number.)

Division—commanded by a major general whose name it bore, a division commonly comprised four or five brigades. (Union divisions were designated by number.)

Corps (or *Army Corps*)—a grouping of two or more divisions under the command of a lieutenant general, and referred to by his name. (Union corps were designated by Roman numerals.)

Army—a grouping of units, typically two or more corps, into an organization capable of independent action in a theater of operations. Some Confederate field armies originally bore the names of bodies of water, such as the Army of the Potomac and the Army of the Mississippi. During 1862 their names changed to the Army of Northern Virginia and the Army of Tennessee, reflecting the Confederacy's decision to name field armies after geographical regions. (Union armies bore the names of rivers, e.g. "Army of the Potomac.")

Department—a geographic command and control structure. Departmental military forces commonly included a field army and all garrison forces within prescribed geographic limits. Departments were divided into district commands, which in turn were subdivided into subdistricts.

3. CATEGORIES OF MILITARY SERVICE

Conscripts—men drafted for military service. Conscription carried a terrible stigma, and most men liable to conscription volunteered to avoid the shame. Those who waited to be conscripted were therefore doubly suspect; although many conscripts became fine soldiers, most volunteers viewed them with outright contempt.

Militia—each state traditionally organized its available military-age manpower into county militia companies available for local defense service in emergencies. Although most Southern states had allowed their militia organizations to decay in the late antebellum era, they exerted a great deal of energy to reorganize them in 1863-1864.

Regulars—members of the miniscule prewar standing army of the United States. Both sides also established a few regular regiments during the war.

Reserves—in accordance with Congressional mandates passed in 1864, boys aged 16 and men from 45 to 50 had to volunteer for state reserve forces or face conscription. State reserves relieved volunteer units in Confederate service from many local defense duties, to include guarding railroads, depots, and prison camps.

State Guard—special volunteer units recruited for six-months' service by Georgia's Governor Joe Brown in August 1863, in response to the President's requisition for local defense units to augment the field armies. The Georgia State Guard was disbanded in early February 1864.

Volunteers—units recruited from the populace at large by local notables, and officered by men elected to their positions. Later regulations established procedures for examining boards to ensure that volunteer officers were proficient in their duties. Volunteer units bore state designations, e.g. "13th Regiment Georgia Volunteer Infantry," and constituted the great majority of units in the Confederate army.

4. ORDNANCE

A. Weapons and Equipment

Caisson—a two-wheeled carriage mounting two spare ammunition chests and repair parts for field artillery. Attached to a limber for towing, one caisson was assigned to each field piece.

Columbiad—smoothbore artillery pieces of heavy caliber, Columbiads of various calibers were the backbone of Confederate coastal and river defenses against Union vessels.

Limber—a two-wheeled carriage mounting a spare ammunition chest for its assigned field piece, to which it was joined for towing. A second limber was attached to the caisson assigned to each piece.

Musket—a smoothbore percussion or flintlock weapon, whose lack of rifling limited effective ranges to about 100 yards. Rate of fire was about two rounds per minute.

Rifle musket—a percussion weapon whose rifled bore allowed effective shooting out to six or eight hundred yards in expert hands, at a rate of about two rounds per minute. Common patterns in Confederate service were the Enfield (.577 caliber), Springfield (.58), Mississippi (.54), Belgian (.70) and Austrian (.69) rifles.

Field gun—term denoting artillery pieces used in light batteries. Designed to fire at relatively high velocities and flat trajectories, their effective ranges approximated 1000-1500 yards. Common patterns in Confederate service included smoothbores such as the 6-pounder and the 12-pounder Napoleon, plus rifled pieces such as the 10-pounder Parrott. They fired rounds of fixed ammunition, comprising a powder bag strapped to a wooden block, or sabot, with the projectile strapped to the front.

Howitzer—low velocity, high trajectory, light-recoiling weapons that allowed gunners to lob shells over intervening cover. The 12-pounder howitzer was widely used in light field batteries to fire shell and canister. It fired fixed ammunition.

Mortar—heavy, snub-nosed artillery pieces that lobbed giant, low-velocity shells in a great, looping trajectory. Used in siege operations due to their bulk and lack of portability.

B. Ammunition

Musket ball—a lead bullet of the same diameter as the unrifled musket bore from which it was fired, its perfectly round configuration was aerodynamically inefficient. Ranges were short, penetrative power was low, and accuracy was minimal beyond 50-100 yards.

Minie ball—a revolutionary sphero-conical projectile for use in rifle muskets such as the Enfield and Springfield. Known for great penetrating power, long range, and a horrific propensity to shatter bones upon impact. Named for its designer, Captain Minie of the French Army, its soft lead base was smaller than the bore's diameter, but expanded upon firing to engage the rifling. This arrangement equaled the musket in ease and rapidity of loading, while giving the accuracy of a rifle. It eclipsed earlier rifles, whose unwieldy loading mallets, extensive leading problems, and painfully slow rate of fire limited their battlefield use. In short, the Minie ball allowed the widespread use of the rifle musket, thus expanding the battlefield killing zone exponentially. Infantry units, which formerly commanded their fronts out to a range of one or two hundred yards, could now sweep the battlefield at ranges of six to eight hundred yards.

Canister—an antipersonnel projectile of fearsome effect out to 400 yards. The 6-pounder canister shot packed 27 iron balls into a tin cylinder; the 12-pounder howitzer fired 48 balls at a lower velocity.

Grapeshot—a heavy anti-personnel round fired from smoothbore cannon. Its nine iron balls were arranged in three layers of three balls each, held together by two rings and a stand at each end, connected by a rod. The caliber of the individual shot was based upon the caliber of the gun from which it was to be fired.

Shot—solid iron cannon ball able to withstand the stress of firing at high velocities from field guns. Intended for use against fortifications, as well as cutting a swath through troops in massed formation.

Shell—a hollow iron projectile filled with powder. Due to its thin-cased design, it was fired at low velocities by howitzers. When detonated by its fuze, the exploding shell scattered metal fragments at high velocity.

Spherical case shot—also known simply as case shot, this type of artillery projectile comprised a relatively thin iron shell filled with a bursting charge and musket balls, or bullets. It was strong enough to withstand the stress of being fired from high velocity field guns. A 12-pounder case shot contained about 78 bullets, the 6-pounder about 38 bullets. The bullets were often called "schrapnell," after the inventor of the projectile, Colonel Schrapnell of the British Army.

5. TACTICAL TERMINOLOGY

A. Engineering terms

Abatis—an obstacle formed by felling trees in an interlocking pattern facing the enemy's possible approach route. Sharpening the limbs and branches made the abatis even more effective.

Bomb-proof—an earth-covered hole within a system of earthen fortifications, intended to protect its denizens from shells bursting overhead.

Breastworks—typically built by heaping earth, fence rails, or other suitable materials into a chest-high parapet that protected its defenders against enemy musketry.

Enfilade—a position that allows the gunner to fire down the whole length of the
enemy's line.

Lunette—a small fieldwork or fortification for protection of an infantry force and/or
field guns.

Parapet—earth thrown in front of a trench to provide protection from direct fire.

Pontoons—small boats designed to sustain temporary field bridging thrown across
waterways by an army on the march.

Redan—a V-shaped earthwork whose point faced the enemy.

Redoubt—an outlying breastwork, whose parapets were protected by the fire of friendly
artillery.

Trench—commonly referred to as a "ditch," it allowed the troops to fight or move in
close proximity to the enemy. Its front was covered by a parapet.

B. Formations & deployments:

Column—a formation of relatively narrow front and extended length, the column
facilitated movement over extended distances, but prohibited men in the rear
ranks from firing their weapons when in direct contact with the enemy.

Line (or *line of battle*)—a formation that facilitated fighting along a wide front, it allowed
the maximum number of men to fire their muskets at the enemy. Marching over
any extended distance in line of battle (two ranks deep) was impractical, however,
as it was extremely difficult to keep an extended line in proper alignment.

Flank—when a regiment in line faced to the right (or left) and marched in that
direction, it was said to be "moving by the right (or left) flank."

Pickets—dismounted guards posted on the front, flanks and rear of a friendly camp to
give notice of an enemy advance.

Skirmish order—troops scattered in small groups in front of the line of battle. These men
could use cover and concealment to harass the enemy, gather information about
his location and strength, confuse his deployment, and prevent a surprise
onslaught. Their inability to mass fire prevented skirmishers from stopping the
determined advance of an enemy line of battle.

Videttes—mounted picket guards, whose speed of movement allowed their employment
at greater distances from the camps they secured.

C. Marching:

Common time—90 steps per minute.

Quick step—110 steps per minute.

Double-quick step—165 to 180 steps per minute. At 180 steps per minute, a man would
cover 4000 yards in about 25 minutes.

6. OTHER

Census—an enumeration conducted every ten years, the Federal population censuses of
1850 and 1860 listed family members by name, age, color and gender. There were

separate schedules for free and slave populations, as well as agricultural production. The 1890 census was partially destroyed by fire, and the Congress thereafter authorized the complete destruction of the remaining records from that census.

Compiled Military Service Record (CMSR)—prepared around the turn of the century at the National Archives from surviving Civil War records. CMSRs consist of cards abstracted from muster rolls, hospital records, prisoner of war documents, and a variety of unit reports and official correspondence.

Exchange cartel—formal agreement to trade prisoners of war based on a fixed rate of exchange, based on rank. After his exchange, the laws of war allowed a released prisoner to resume hostilities.

Haversack—a linen bag to hold rations, carried slung from the hip.

Muster rolls—the basic document that listed a company's members and their duty status. Mustering officers inspected the men on the last day of even-numbered months, or as soon thereafter as possible. Units and individuals were said to be "mustered in" or "mustered out" upon entry or discharge from military service.

Parole—prisoners were often released on parole, giving their word of honor not to engage in hostilities until properly exchanged. Violation of the parole subjected the soldier to the death penalty.

Bibliography

PRIMARY SOURCES: UNPUBLISHED MANUSCRIPTS
- ALABAMA
Alabama Bureau of Vital Statistics, Tuscaloosa
Death certificate. Wiley P. Mangham.
Alabama Department of Archives and History, Montgomery
  Military Records
Civil War Veterans Service Index File. Microfilm.
Unit Files. 1st Regiment Alabama Volunteer Infantry.
_____. 10th Regiment Alabama Volunteer Infantry.
_____. 14th Regiment Alabama Volunteer Infantry.
_____. 18th Regiment Alabama Volunteer Infantry.
_____. 25th Regiment Alabama Volunteer Infantry.
_____. 30th Regiment Alabama Volunteer Infantry.
_____. 59th Regiment Alabama Volunteer Infantry.
_____. 61st Regiment Alabama Volunteer Infantry.
_____. Hilliard's Alabama Legion.
_____. Young's Company, Alabama State Reserve Cavalry.
_____. Clayton's Brigade.
_____. Gracie's Brigade.
_____. Jackson's Brigade.
_____. Russell County Militia.
  County Records
Chambers County. Direct and Indirect Indexes to Deeds and Mortgages, 1834-1876.
  Microfilm.
_____. Marriage Licenses and Bonds, c. 1840. Microfilm.
_____. Miscellaneous Court Records. Orphans Court Records, 1833-1842.
  Microfilm.
_____. Miscellaneous Probate Records. Inventory Records, 1834-1840. Microfilm.
_____. Orphans Court Records, 1833-1847. Microfilm.
_____. Probate Records. Chattel Mortgages, Book 4, c. 1861. Microfilm.
_____. Superior Court. Deed Book 13, 1857-1860. Microfilm.
Russell County. Bonds of Administrators and Deceased, 1850-1853. Microfilm.
_____. Deed and Mortgage Records Index, 1836-1856. Microfilm.
_____. Inventories, Appraisements and Sales, 1837-1858. Microfilm.
_____. Miscellaneous Probate Records, Marriages, 1834-1855. Microfilm.
_____. Probate Court. Minutes, 1846-1854. Microfilm.
Saint Clair County. Oaths of Allegiance for Officers, 1865. Microfilm.
Talladega County. Marriage Records. Typescript.
Tallapoosa County. Administrator's Records, 1871-1898. Microfilm.
_____. Miscellaneous Probate Records, 1835-1947, Record of Deaths, 1881-1888.
  Microfilm.

State Records

State of Alabama. Adjutant General's Office. Administrative Files, 1820-1865, Register of Officers, vol. 3 1832-1844.

_____. Census of Confederate Soldiers in Alabama, 1907. Microfilm.

_____. Census of Confederate Widows in Alabama, 1927. Microfilm.

_____. 1855 State Census. Microfilm.

_____. 1866 State Census. Microfilm.

_____. Oaths of Allegiance for Officers, 1865. Microfilm.

_____. Pension Files. Microfilm.

_____. Records of the Secretary of State. Loyalty Oath Books.

_____. Voter Registration Records, 1867. Microfilm.

Other

Surname Files. Microfilm.

Verbatim Copies of Wills, Chambers County, Volumes 1-3, 1818-1861. Typescript.

Probate Court of Mobile County, Mobile

Marriage certificate. James A. Mangham.

Auburn University Archives, Opelika

Charles H. George. Confederate Letters, 1859-1866. Typescript.

Russell County Courthouse, Phenix City

Superior Court. Deed and Mortgage Records, c. 1832-1860.

- FLORIDA

Florida State Library, Tallahassee

County Records

Gadsden County. Tax Rolls, 1859-1862. Microfilm.

Hillsborough County. Index to Estate Records. Microfilm.

Jackson County. Tax Rolls, 1859-1862. Microfilm.

Jefferson County. Tax Rolls, 1859-1862. Microfilm.

Leon County. Index to Deeds (Grantees), c. 1830-1869. Microfilm.

_____. Index to Estates, c. 1830-1970. Microfilm.

_____. Tax Rolls, 1859-1862. Microfilm.

Liberty County. Tax Rolls, 1859-1862. Microfilm.

Marion County. Letters Testamentary, c. 1850. Microfilm.

_____. Tax Rolls, 1845-1869. Microfilm.

_____. Wills, c. 1850. Microfilm.

Wakulla County. Tax Rolls, 1859-1862. Microfilm.

State Records

Confederate Pension Records. Pinellas County. Microfilm.

- GEORGIA

Bryan-Lang Historical Library, Woodbine

Camden County School Records.

Georgia Department of Archives and History, Atlanta

Personal Papers

Burwell Atkinson Collection. Microfilm.

Civil War Miscellany. Personal Papers. Microfilm.

Civil War Miscellany. Personal Papers. Unit Files. Microfilm.

John G. Mangham Papers. Microfilm.

Willoughby Hill Mangham Family Letters, 1849-1868. Microfilm.

Willoughby Hill Mangham Letters. Microfilm.

Richard W. Milner Papers. Microfilm.

County Records

Baldwin County. Court of Ordinary. Marriages, c. 1822-1831. Microfilm.

_____. Probate Court. Estate Records. Annual Returns, vols. A-C, 1813-1831. Microfilm.

_____. Probate Court. Estate Records. General Index, Books 1 and 2. Microfilm.

_____. Tax Digest, 1831-1834. Microfilm.

Bibb County. Court of Ordinary. Estate Records. Wills, c. 1873. Microfilm.

Butts County. Superior Court. Deed Book H, c. 1866-1868. Microfilm.

_____. Superior Court. General Index to Deeds and Mortgages, 1825-1895. Microfilm.

Glynn County. Court of Ordinary. Estate Records (Unbound), 1800-1928. Microfilm.

_____. Court of Ordinary. Estate Records. Inventories and Appraisals, 1853-1916. Microfilm.

Hancock County. Court of Ordinary. Estate Records, Will Book A. Microfilm.

_____. Court of Ordinary. Marks and Brands, 1793-1798. Microfilm.

_____. Court of Ordinary. Marriages, 1806-1842. Microfilm.

_____. Court of Ordinary. Will Book F, c. 1810. Microfilm.

_____. Probate Court. Estate Records. Index to Annual Returns, vols. A-D, 1797-1853. Microfilm.

_____. Probate Court. Estate Records. General Index, 1794-1815. Microfilm.

_____. Probate Court. Estate Records. Miscellaneous, 1794-1831. Microfilm.

_____. Superior Court. General Index to Deeds and Mortgages, 1794-1838. Microfilm.

_____. Tax Digests, 1808, 1812. Microfilm.

Harris County. Court of Ordinary. Estate Records. General Index, vols. A-Z, 1828-1940. Microfilm.

_____. Superior Court. General Index to Deeds and Mortgages. Microfilm.

Henry County. Court of Ordinary. Estate Records. Index, 1821-1939. Microfilm.

_____. Court of Ordinary. Minutes, 1825-1853. Microfilm.

_____. Court of Ordinary. Wills and Bonds, Book B, 1822-1834. Microfilm.

_____. General Index of Estate Proceedings, vols. 1-2, 1821-1939. Microfilm.

_____. Inferior Court. Minutes, 1822-1886. Microfilm.

_____. Orphans' Court. Guardianship Letters, 1825-1852. Microfilm.

_____. Probate Court. Guardians' Bonds, 1838-1871. Microfilm.

Jasper County. Court of Ordinary. Index to Probate Records, 1812-1941. Microfilm.

Meriwether County. Court of Ordinary. Estate Records. Inventories and Appraisals, 1858-1863. Microfilm.

_____. Court of Ordinary. Probate Records, Record of Wills, 1859-1903. Microfilm.

_____. Superior Court. Index to Deed and Mortgage Records, 1827-1963. Microfilm.

_____. Tax Digests, 1863. Microfilm.

Monroe County. Superior Court. Reverse Index to Deeds and Mortgages, c. 1820-1830. Microfilm.

Muscogee County. Superior Court. Deed and Mortgage Records, Book C, 1842-1847; Book F, 1851-1854 . Microfilm.

_____. Superior Court. Index to Deed and Mortgage Records, 1838-1887. Microfilm.

Pike County. Court of Ordinary. Confederate Rosters. Microfilm.

_____. Court of Ordinary. Estate Records. Sales, 1861-1868. Microfilm.

_____. Court of Ordinary. Guardians' Bonds, 1829-1955. Microfilm.

_____. Court of Ordinary. Guardians' Bonds, Books A-B, 1829-1898. Microfilm.

_____. Court of Ordinary. Guardians' Letters, Books B-C, 1856-1878. Microfilm.

_____. Court of Ordinary. Letters of Administration (Temporary), 1864-1913. Microfilm.

_____. Court of Ordinary. Minutes, 1819-1831, Book AA. Microfilm.

_____. Court of Ordinary. Probate Records, 1829-1955. Microfilm.

_____. Court of Ordinary. Probate Records. Inventories and Appraisals, 1858-1872. Microfilm.

_____. Court of Ordinary. Probate Records, Record of Wills, 1844-1898. Microfilm.

_____. Superior Court. Deed and Mortgage Records, Book J, 1821-1823. Microfilm.

_____. Superior Court. General Index to Deeds and Mortgages, 1806-1832. Microfilm.

_____. Tax Digests, 1859. Microfilm.

Putnam County. Court of Ordinary. Administrators' Bonds, Books A-E. Microfilm.

_____. Court of Ordinary. Annual Returns (Indexed), c. 1807-1830. Microfilm.

_____. Court of Ordinary. Estate Records. Guardianship (Unbound), 1807-1928. Microfilm.

_____. Court of Ordinary. Estate Records. Minutes, Book AA, 1819-1831. Microfilm.

_____. Court of Ordinary. Estate Records. Miscellaneous, Book Q, 1808-1940. Microfilm.

_____. Court of Ordinary. Index to Estate Records, 1807-1928. Microfilm.

_____. Superior Court. Deeds and Mortgages, Books A-C, 1808-1814; Book J, 1821-1823. Microfilm.

_____. Superior Court. General Index to Deeds and Mortgages, vol. 1, 1806-1832. Microfilm.

Richmond County. Tax Digests, 1850-1852. Microfilm.

Spalding County. Court of Ordinary. Administrators Bonds, Book A, 1852-1878. Microfilm.

_____. Court of Ordinary. Annual Returns and Vouchers, Book C, 1866-1882. Microfilm.

_____. Court of Ordinary. Inventories and Appraisals, Books A-B, 1852-1892. Microfilm.

_____. Court of Ordinary. Letters of Administration (Temporary), Book A, 1859-1881. Microfilm.

_____. Court of Ordinary. Wills, 1881-1929. Microfilm.

_____. Tax Digests, 1866-1871. Microfilm.

Talbot County. Court of Ordinary. Estate Records. Guardians Bonds, 1830-1865. Microfilm.

_____. Court of Ordinary. Estate Records. Inventories and Appraisals, 1831-1855. Microfilm.

_____. Court of Ordinary. Estate Records. Sales, 1829-1855. Microfilm.

_____. Court of Ordinary. Estate Records. Schedule of Administrators, 1829-1853. Microfilm.

_____. Court of Ordinary. Estate Records. Schedule of Guardians, 1829-1853. Microfilm.

_____. Court of Ordinary. Estate Records. Wills, Book A, 1828-1856. Microfilm.

_____. Court of Ordinary. Marriage Records, Book A, 1828-1844. Microfilm.

_____. Inferior Court. Minutes for County Purposes, Vol. A, 1828-1855. Microfilm.

_____. Probate Court. Annual Reports, 1838. Microfilm.

_____. Probate Court. Annual Returns, vols. A-B, 1828-1848. Microfilm.

_____. Superior Court. Deed and Mortgage Records, 1828-1850. Microfilm.

Taylor County. Court of Ordinary. Inventories and Appraisals, 1859. Microfilm.

_____. Index to Estate records. Microfilm.

_____. Superior Court. Index to Deeds and Mortgages (Direct), 1852-1932. Microfilm.

Upson County. Court of Ordinary. Estate Records and Guardians Bonds, 1830-1848. Microfilm.

_____. Superior Court. Deed Books A, B, D, W, c. 1826-1860. Microfilm.

_____. Superior Court. General Index to Deeds and Mortgages, 1825-1879. Microfilm.

State Records

Adjutant General. Incoming Correspondence. 1861-1865.

_____. Letter Book. February 2, 1864-April 4, 1864. Typescript.

_____. Lists of Men Subject to Military Duty, 1862. Microfilm.

_____. Military Records. Commissions, 1824-1866. Microfilm.

_____. Militia Enrollment Lists, 1863-1864. Microfilm.

_____. Commissary General's Department. Families Supplied with Salt, 1862-1864. Microfilm.

Confederate Pension Application Index. Microfilm.

Confederate Pension Records. Microfilm.

Confederate Soldiers' Home of Georgia. Register of Inmates, 1901-1941. 3 vols. Microfilm.

Executive Department. Returns of Qualified Voters under the Reconstruction Act, 1867. Microfilm.

Georgia Military Record Book, 1779-1839. 8 vols. Typescript.

Department of Public Health. Central State Hospital. Medical Case Histories, vol. 3, October 9, 1860-July 31, 1873.

Tallies of Votes Cast in State and Regimental Elections, 1862-1864. Microfilm.

Other

United Daughters of the Confederacy Bound Typescripts. 14 vols.

Garman, James E. "Materials for the Writing of Histories of Georgia Confederate Regiments: A Bibliographical Study." Unpublished M. A. thesis. Emory University, 1961.

Index to Savannah, Georgia, Newspapers, 1811-1888. Microfilm.

Muster Rolls. 53rd Regiment Georgia Volunteer Infantry. Microfilm.

Muster Rolls. 22nd Battalion Georgia Heavy Artillery. Microfilm.

Savannah Newspaper Digest. January 1 to December 31, 1862. Microfilm.

Griffin Historical Society

Griffin Historical Society Papers.

Upson County Historical Society

Jim Smith. Unpublished Reminiscences, 46th Regiment Georgia Volunteer Infantry.

Other

Taylor County. Court of Ordinary. Administrator and Guardians' Bonds, 1852-1915. Online resource.

- LOUISIANA

Claiborne Parish Courthouse, Homer

Claiborne Parish. Conveyance Records.

_____. Deed Indexes, Direct and Indirect, Books 1-2, c. 1850-1880.

Lincoln Parish Courthouse, Ruston

Lincoln Parish. Deed Books J-EE, c. 1890-1918.

_____. Deed Indexes, Direct and Indirect, 1873-1936.

Louisiana State Archives, Baton Rouge

Parish Records

Claiborne Parish. Comptroller's Assessment Rolls, 1866-1881. Microfilm.

Natchitoches Parish. Comptroller's Assessment Rolls, 1871-1880. Microfilm.

Red River Parish. Comptroller's Assessment Rolls, 1874-1888. Microfilm.

State Records
Confederate Pension Records. Microfilm.
Death Certificates, 1912-1944. Microfilm.
Index to Census of Confederate Veterans and Widows in Louisiana, 1911. Microfilm.
State Militia Commissions, 1855-1862. Microfilm.
   Other
Port of New Orleans. Passenger List Index. Microfilm.
Works Progress Administration. Index to State Land Office Records. Microfilm.
   Louisiana State University Archives, Baton Rouge
John Achilles Harris Letters, 1854, 1861-1864.
United Confederate Veterans Association Records, Louisiana and Lower Mississippi
   Valley Collections, 1898-1930.
   Town Clerk's Office, Mangham
Horace B. Chambers. "History of Mangham Louisiana, Richland Parish." Mangham,
   LA: 1951. Unpublished manuscript.

- MISSISSIPPI

   Mississippi Department of Archives and History, Jackson
   County Records
Rankin County. Index of Court Minutes, c. 1850-1880. Microfilm.
_____. Index of Deeds, c. 1850-1880. Microfilm.
_____. Record of Wills, 1858-1905. Microfilm.
_____. Marriage records, 1855-1856. Microfilm.
Scott County. Deed Books K-N, 1860-1871. Microfilm.
_____. Index to Deeds, 1835-1890. Microfilm.
Washington County. Deed Index, vols. 1-4, 1828-1890. Microfilm.
_____. Record of Wills, 1839-1922. Microfilm.
Yazoo County. Administrators' Bonds and Letters, 1872-1917. Microfilm.
_____. Deed Index, 1857-1870. Microfilm.
_____. Deed Index, 1870-1885. Microfilm.
_____. Index to Will Records, 1830-1981. Microfilm.
_____. Office of the Circuit Clerk. Marriage Book D, 1858-1870. Microfilm.
_____. Wills, vols. A-B, 1833-1908. Microfilm.
   Confederate Records
Amnesty Oaths (L-N), 1865.
J. L. Power and Family Papers, 1800-1936, 1958. Microfilm.
Unit Files. 18th Regiment Alabama Volunteer Infantry.
_____. 10th Regiment Mississippi Volunteer Infantry.
10th Regiment Mississippi Volunteer Infantry. Order Book and Consolidated Morning
   Reports, May 28, 1861 – March 6, 1862.
_____. Reports of Guard Mounted at Pensacola, May 28, 1861-March 6, 1862.
Withers' Artillery. Order Book.
_____. Papers.

Vicksburg National Military Park, Vicksburg
Unit Files. Withers's Artillery.

- NORTH CAROLINA

University of North Carolina, Southern Historical Collection, Charlotte
Joseph B. Cumming. War Recollections, 1861-1865. Microfilm.
McGimsey Papers. Online resource.
Jackson-McKinne Papers, 1817-1871. Order Book of Brigadier John K. Jackson's
    Brigade, Withers's Division, March 13, 1862-January 10, 1863. Microfilm.

- TENNESSEE

Tennessee Department of Archives and History, Nashville
Confederate Pension Records.

- TEXAS

Bell County Courthouse, Belton
Bell County. Deed Books A-T, 27, 1850-c. 1900.
_____. General Index to Deeds.
_____. General Index to Probate Minutes, Book 1.
_____. Probate Minutes. Book G.
Bell County Library, Belton
Bell County Tombstone Records. Typescript.
Bell County Museum, Belton
Roster of Original Members, Ex-Confederate Veterans Association, Camp 122, Texas.
    August-September 1888.
Harrison County Courthouse, Marshall
Harrison County. Deed Books J-M, c. 1849-1851.
_____. Direct Deed Index, Book 1, L-R.
_____. Indirect Deed Index, Book 1, L-R.
_____. Probate Court. Index to Probate Record, No. 1, M-Z.
_____. Probate Court. Minutes, vol. MR-C; vol. EM-D.
Texas State Library, Austin
  County Records
Gonzales County. Tax Rolls, 1858-1870. Microfilm.
Harrison County. Tax Rolls, 1840-1876. Microfilm.
Trinity County. Tax Rolls, 1850-1897. Microfilm.
Tyler County. Tax Rolls, 1847-1859. Microfilm.
Washington County. Tax Rolls, 1837-1878. Microfilm.
  Other Records
U. S. City Directories, 1882-1901 (San Antonio). Microfilm.
Texas State Archives, Austin
Adjutant General. Muster Roll of Freeman's Company, Carter's Regiment.
_____. Muster Roll of James W. Moore's Company, Beat 4, Bell County, 27th
    Brigade, Texas Militia.

Bibliography

_____. State Militia Muster Roll Abstracts, 1861-1865. Microfilm.

Confederate Pension Records. Microfilm.

Confederate Records. Indigent Soldiers' Families, 1861-1865. Microfilm.

Texas Department of Health, Bureau of Vital Statistics, Austin

Death certificate. Charles A. Mangham.

University of Texas, Austin
Center for American History

Bolling Hall Papers. Charles William Ramsdell Collection. Microfilm.

Confederate Research Center, Hill College, Hillsboro

Unit Files. 30th Regiment Alabama Volunteer Infantry.

_____. 28th Regiment Louisiana Volunteer Infantry.

_____. 1st Regiment Mississippi Light Artillery.

_____. 21st Regiment Texas Volunteer Cavalry.

Unit Flag Files.

WASHINGTON, D. C.

National Archives and Records Administration

Compiled Records Showing Service of Military Units in Confederate Organizations. Microfilm.

Compiled Service Records of Confederate General and Staff Officers and Non-Regimental Enlisted Men. Microfilm.

Compiled Service Records of Confederate Soldiers Who Served in Organizations from the State of Alabama. Microfilm.

Compiled Service Records of Confederate Soldiers Who Served in Organizations from the State of Florida. Microfilm.

Compiled Service Records of Confederate Soldiers Who Served in Organizations from the State of Georgia. Microfilm.

Compiled Service Records of Confederate Soldiers Who Served in Organizations from the State of Louisiana. Microfilm.

Compiled Service Records of Confederate Soldiers Who Served in Organizations from the State of Mississippi. Microfilm.

Compiled Service Records of Confederate Soldiers Who Served in Organizations from the State of Tennessee. Microfilm.

Compiled Service Records of Confederate Soldiers Who Served in Organizations from the State of Texas. Microfilm.

Compiled Service Records of Confederate Soldiers Who Served in Organizations from the State of Virginia. Microfilm.

Compiled Service Records of Soldiers Who Served in Organizations Raised Directly by the Confederate Government. Microfilm.

Compiled Service Records of Volunteer Soldiers Who Served During the Mexican War in Organizations from the State of Texas. Microfilm.

Confederate States Army Casualties: Lists and Narrative Reports, 1861-1865. Microfilm.

Consolidated Index to Compiled Service Records of Confederate Soldiers. Microfilm.

Index to Compiled Service Records of Volunteer Soldiers Who Served During Indian Wars and Disturbances, 1815-1858. Microfilm.

Index to Compiled Service Records of Volunteer Soldiers Who Served in the War of 1812. Microfilm.

Letters Received by the Confederate Adjutant & Inspector General's Office, 1861-1865. Microfilm.

Letters Received by the Confederate Secretary of War, 1861-1865. Microfilm.

Muster Rolls. 18th Regiment Alabama Volunteer Infantry.

Muster Rolls. 30th Regiment Alabama Volunteer Infantry.

Muster Rolls. 59th Regiment Alabama Volunteer Infantry.

Muster Rolls. 2nd Regiment Florida Volunteer Infantry.

Muster Rolls. 1st Regiment Georgia Volunteer Infantry (Olmstead's).

Muster Rolls. 2nd Battalion Georgia Infantry.

Muster Rolls. 2nd Battalion Georgia Sharpshooters.

Muster Rolls. 6th Regiment Georgia Volunteer Infantry (State Guard).

Muster Rolls. 11th Regiment Georgia Volunteer Infantry.

Muster Rolls. 13th Regiment Georgia Volunteer Infantry.

Muster Rolls. 26th Regiment Georgia Volunteer Infantry.

Muster Rolls. 27th Regiment Georgia Volunteer Infantry.

Muster Rolls. 30th Regiment Georgia Volunteer Infantry.

Muster Rolls. 53rd Regiment Georgia Volunteer Infantry.

Muster Rolls. 22nd Battalion Georgia Heavy Artillery.

Records of the Army and Department of Northern Virginia. Orders and Circulars, 1861-1865. Microfilm.

Records of the Army and Department of Tennessee. General Orders, Army of Tennessee (Bragg-Hardee), November 1862-December 1863.

————. General Orders and Circulars, Army of Tennessee, December 1863-January 1865. Chapter II, vol. 350.

————. Letters Sent and Endorsements, Army of Tennessee, 1863-1864. Chapter II, vol. 158 ½.

————. Special Orders, Army of Tennessee, 1863-1865.

————. Morning Reports of Brigadier General John K. Jackson's Brigade, 1862-1864. Chapter II, vol. 245.

Records of the Army of the Mississippi. Orders and Circulars, 1861-1865, 2nd Army Corps (Bragg).

Records of the Confederate Adjutant & Inspector General. Endorsements, 1864-1865. Chapter I, vols. 29-34.

————. Endorsements on Court-Martial Correspondence, 1864. Chapter I, vol. 201.

————. Inspection Reports and Related Records Received by the Inspection Branch in the Confederate Adjutant and Inspector General's Office. Microfilm.

————. Letters, Telegrams and Endorsements Sent Relating to Courts-Martial, March 1864-March 1865. Chapter I, vol. 42.

————. Registers of Letters Received, March 1861-April 1865. Chapter I, vols. 45-74.

Records of the Department of South Carolina, Georgia & Florida. Orders and Circulars, 1861-1865 (Hardee).

Records of the Department of Mississippi & East Louisiana. Orders and Circulars, 1862-1865.

Records of the Department of North Carolina & Southern Virginia. Orders, Districts of the Department of North Carolina & Southern Virginia, 1864.

Unfiled Papers and Slips Belonging to Confederate Compiled Service Records. Microfilm.

U. S. Bureau of the Census. Fifth Census of the United States, 1830. Microfilm.

————. Sixth Census of the United States, 1840. Microfilm.

————. Seventh Census of the United States, 1850. Free, Slave, Agricultural, and Mortality Schedules. Microfilm.

————. Eighth Census of the United States, 1860. Free, Slave, Agricultural, and Mortality Schedules. Microfilm.

————. Ninth Census of the United States, 1870. Population and Agricultural Schedules. Microfilm.

————. Tenth Census of the United States, 1880. Population and Agricultural Schedules. Microfilm.

————. Twelfth Census of the United States, 1900. Population and Agricultural Schedules. Microfilm.

————. Thirteenth Census of the United States, 1910. Population and Agricultural Schedules. Microfilm.

————. Fourteenth Census of the United States, 1920. Population Schedules. Microfilm.

AUTHOR'S POSSESSION

Jean Ennis. Letters to author, May 1; May 17, 1996, and March 14, 1997.

Mrs. Grady Fowler. Letter to author, August 11, 1996.

Mrs. Gerry Hill. Letters to author, August 8; August 11, 1997.

Craig S. Mangham. Letter to author, December 9, 1995.

Raymond L. Mangham. Letters to author, August 15; September 6; November 12, 1994; November 14, 1995.

Mrs. Roy Mangham. Letter to Ellen Mangham, Beckville, Texas, July 24 (year not stated).

Timothy Mangham. Letters to author, December 2; December 13, 1995.

William Francis Mangham. Letters to author, July 23, 1996; March 25, 1997.

William Lamar Mangham. Letter to author, May 15, 1996.

Mrs. Glenda Owens. Letter to author, November 17, 1999, containing her research and that of Colonel William C. Lafield.

Joseph W. Reichert. Letter to author, July 19, 1996.

Juanita Strickland. Letter to William Francis Mangham, January 13, 1992.

Muster Roll Extract. Company K, Consolidated Crescent Regiment. Prepared by Arthur Bergeron, Jr.

PUBLISHED PRIMARY SOURCE DOCUMENTS:

The Appomattox Roster. Introduction by R. A. Brock. Richmond: The Society, 1887. Reprint. Foreword by Philip Van Doren Stern. New York: Antiquarian Press, 1962.

Booth, A. B., comp. *Records of Louisiana Confederate Soldiers and Louisiana Confederate Commands.* 3 vols. New Orleans: 1920. Reprint. Spartanburg: The Reprint Co., 1984.

Brandenburg, John David and Rita Brinkley Worthy, comps. *Index to Georgia's 1867-1868 Returns of Qualified Voters and Registration Oath Books (White).* Atlanta: N. p., 1995.

Brightwell, Juanita S., comp. *Index to the Roster of the Confederate Soldiers of Georgia 1861-1865.* Spartanburg: The Reprint Co., 1982.

Brock, R. A., ed. "Paroles of the Army of Northern Virginia." *Southern Historical Society Papers* 15 (1887). Reprint. New York: Kraus Reprint Co., 1977.

Candler, Allen D., comp. *The Confederate Records of the State of Georgia.* 3 vols. Atlanta: Charles P. Byrd, State Printer, 1909-1911.

C. S. Ordnance Bureau. *The Field Manual for the Use of the Officers on Ordnance Duty.* Richmond: Ritchie & Dunnavant, 1862. Reprint. Gettysburg, PA: Dean S. Thomas, 1984.

C. S. War Department. *Regulations for the Army of the Confederate States, 1863.* Richmond, VA: J. W. Randolph, 1863. Reprint. Harrisburg: National Historical Society, 1980.

Confederate Veteran. 40 vols. Nashville: 1893-1932. Reprint. 40 vols., plus 3 vols. index. Wilmington: Broadfoot Publishing Co., 1990.

"Delegates to the Constitutional Convention Held at Montgomery, May 21-September 3, 1901." Online resource.

Evans, Clement A. *Confederate Military History.* Extended Edition. Confederate Publishing Co., 1899. 18 vols. Reprint. Wilmington: Broadfoot Publishing Co., 1987.

————. *Confederate Military History.* Extended Edition. Confederate Publishing Co., 1899. 18 vols. CD-ROM. Carmel, IN: Guild Press of Indiana.

Gilham, Major William. *Manual of Instruction for the Volunteers and Militia of the United States.* Philadelphia: Charles Desilver, 1861. Reprint.

Gossett, Joyce Hill. *Abstracts of Pike County Will Books A and B, Part of C.* N.p., n.d.

Henderson, Lillian, comp. *Roster of the Confederate Soldiers of Georgia 1861-1865.* 6 vols. N.p.: State of Georgia, 1959-1964.

Hewett, Janet B. *The Roster of Confederate Soldiers 1861-1865.* 16 vols. Wilmington: Broadfoot Publishing Co., 1996.

Hewett, Janet B., Noah Andre Trudeau, Bryce A. Suderow, eds. *Supplement to the Official Records of the Union and Confederate Armies.* Part 1 (Reports); Part 2 (Records of Events). 92 vols. Wilmington: Broadfoot Publishing, 1994-1999.

Johnson, Robert Underwood and Clarence Clough Buel, eds. *Battles and Leaders of the Civil War.* 4 vols. New York, NY: Century Magazine, 1887-1888. Reprint. Edison, NJ: Castle. N.d.

Mangham, Dana M. "The Civil War Letters of Willoughby Hill Mangham—Private, 'Quitman Greys,' Company I, Eleventh Georgia Volunteer Regiment." Parts 1, 2. *Atlanta History: A Journal of Georgia and the South* 46 (Fall 1997, Winter 1998): 40-51, 31-46.

_____. "Roster of the 2nd Georgia Battalion Sharpshooters, C. S. A." *Georgia Genealogical Magazine* 35, no. 1-2 (Winter/Spring 1995): 65-82.

Natchitoches Parish, Louisiana Marriages, 1805-1900. Hammond, LA: Hunting for Bears, Inc.

Southern Historical Society. *Southern Historical Society Papers.* 52 vols. Richmond: 1876-1959. Reprint. Oakman, AL: H-Bar Enterprises. CD ROM.

Tennesseeans in the Civil War: A Military History of Confederate and Union Units with Available Rosters of Personnel. 2 vols. Nashville: Civil War Centennial Commission, 1965.

U. S. War Department. *The War of the Rebellion: A Compilation of the Official Records of the Union and Confederate Armies.* 128 vols. Washington, D. C., 1890-1901.

_____. *The Civil War CD-ROM: The War of the Rebellion: A Compilation of the Official Records of the Union and Confederate Armies.* 128 vols. Washington, D. C., 1890-1901. Carmel, IN: Guild Press of Indiana.

_____. *Atlas to Accompany the Official Records of the Union and Confederate Armies.* Compiled by Calvin D. Cowles. Washington, D. C., 1891-1895.

U. S. Navy Department. *The War of the Rebellion: A Compilation of the Official Records of the Union and Confederate Navies.* 30 vols. Washington, D. C., 1894-1927.

LETTERS, MEMOIRS, AND CONTEMPORARY UNIT HISTORIES:

"A. J. Harrell." *Confederate Veteran* 19 (1911): 237.

Abell, Richard Bender and Fay Adamson Gecik. *Sojourns of a Patriot: The Field and Prison Papers of An Unreconstructed Confederate.* Journal of Confederate History Series, vol. 19. Murfreesboro: Southern Heritage Press, 1998.

Abrams, A. S. *A Full and Detailed History of the Siege of Vicksburg.* Atlanta: Intelligencer Steam Power Presses, 1863. Microfilm.

Adams, J. J. "History of the Quitman Grays." In Jacquelyn Shepard. *The Quitman Echo: Quitman County, Georgia.* Georgetown, GA: Author, 1991.

Adamson, Augustus Pitt. *Brief History of the Thirtieth Georgia Regiment.* Griffin, GA: Mills Printing Co., 1912.

"Attention, Whitworth Sharpshooters." *Confederate Veteran* 1 (1892): 117.

Austin, Aurelia. *Georgia Boys with "Stonewall" Jackson: James Thomas Thompson and the Walton Infantry.* Athens: Univ. of Georgia Press, 1967.

Bailey, Judith A. and Robert I. Cottom, eds. *After Chancellorsville—Letters from the Heart: The Civil War Letters of Private Walter G. Dunn & Emma Randolph.* Baltimore: Maryland Historical Society, 1998.

Bartlett, Napier. *Military Record of Louisiana, Including Biographical and Historical Papers Relating to the Military Organizations of the State.* Reprint. Baton Rouge: Louisiana State Univ. Press, 1992.

Benson, Susan Williams, ed. *Berry Benson's Civil War Book: Memoirs of a Confederate Scout and Sharpshooter.* Athens: Univ. of Georgia Press, c. 1962.

Bergeron, Arthur W., Jr., ed. *The Civil War Reminiscences of Major Silas T. Grisamore, C. S. A.* Baton Rouge: Louisiana State Univ. Press, 1993.

Bernard, George S. *War Talks of Confederate Veterans.* Petersburg, VA: Fenn & Owen, 1892.

Blackburn, J. K. P. *Reminiscences of the Terry Rangers.* Reprint. *Terry Texas Ranger Trilogy.* Introduction by Thomas W. Cutrer. Austin: State House Press, 1996.

Bogle, Joseph. *Some Recollections of the Civil War, By a Private in the 40th Ga. Regiment, C.S.A.* Dalton, GA: The Daily Argus, 1911. Bethesda: University Publications of America, 1990. Civil War Unit Histories microfiche series. Edited by Robert E. Lester and Gary Hoeg.

Botkin, B. A., ed. *A Civil War Treasury of Tales, Legends and Folklore.* Reprint. New York: Promontory Press, 1993.

Bradwell, I. G. "Second Day's Battle of the Wilderness, May 6, 1864." *Confederate Veteran* 28 (1920): 20-22.

A Brief and Condensed History of Parsons' Texas Cavalry Brigade, Composed of Twelfth, Nineteenth, Twenty-First, Morgan's Battalion, and Pratt's Battery of Artillery of the Confederate States. Waxahatchie, TX: J. M. Flemister, 1892.

Buck, Capt. Irving A. *Cleburne and His Command,* and *Pat Cleburne: Stonewall Jackson of the West.* Edited by Thomas R. Hay. McCowat-Mercer Press, 1957. Reprint. Wilmington: Broadfoot Publishing Co., 1995.

Bull, Rice C. *Soldiering: The Civil War Diary of Rice C. Bull, 123rd New York Volunteer Infantry.* Edited by K. Jack Bauer. Novato, CA: Presidio Press, 1977.

Calhoun, William L. *History of the 42d Regiment, Georgia Volunteers, Confederate States Army, Infantry.* Atlanta: N. p., 1900.

Calvin, Martin V. "The Bloody Angle, Thrilling Events of the Twelfth of May, 1864." *Confederate Veteran* 32 (1924): 460.

"Capt. O. C. Myers." *Confederate Veteran* 33 (1925): 227.

Carnes, W. W. "At Missionary Ridge." *Confederate Veteran* 28 (1920): 185.

Cater, William D. *"As It Was": The Story of Douglas John Cater's Life.* San Antonio: W. Cater, 1981.

Cawthon, John A., ed. "Letters of a North Louisiana Private to His Wife, 1862-1865." *The Mississippi Valley Historical Review* (March 1944): 532-550.

Chamberlain, Joshua Lawrence. *The Passing of the Armies*. Reprint. Dayton: Morningside Press, 1989.

Chambers, C. C. "The Battle of the Wilderness." *Confederate Veteran* 23 (1915): 452-453.

Chambers, William Pitt. *Blood and Sacrifice: The Civil War Journal of a Confederate Soldier*. Edited by Richard A. Baumgartner. Huntington, WV: Blue Acorn Press, 1994.

Cherry, F. L. "The History of Opelika and Her Agricultural Tributary Territory, Embracing More Particularly Lee and Russell Counties, from the Earliest Settlement to the Present Date." *The Alabama Historical Quarterly* 15, no. 2 (1953): 176-537. Reprint. Montgomery: Alabama State Department of Archives and History.

"Civil War Letter." *CHERISH: The Quarterly Journal of the St. Clair Historical Society* 2, no. 2: 50-51.

Clark, George. *A Glance Backward, Or Some Events in the Past History of My Life*. Houston: Pein & Sons, N.d. Bethesda: University Publications of America, 1990. Civil War Unit Histories microfiche series. Edited by Robert E. Lester and Gary Hoeg.

Clark, Walter A. *Under the Stars and Bars or, Memories of Four Years Service with the Oglethorpes, of Augusta, Georgia*. Augusta: Chronicle Printing Co., 1900.

Crow, Mattie Lou Teague, ed. *The Diary of a Confederate Soldier: John Washington Inzer, 1834-1928*. Huntsville, AL: Strode Publishers, 1977.

Cumming, Katharine Hubbell. "Echoes From the Battle of Murfreesboro." *Confederate Veteran* 13 (1905): 410-411.

Davidson, William H. *Word from Camp Pollard, C.S.A.* West Point, GA: Hester Printing, 1978.

"Dedication of the Virginia Tablet in the Vicksburg National Military Park, Friday Evening, Nov. 22, 1907, and Exercises in the First Baptist Church, Vicksburg, Mississippi." Bethesda: University Publications of America, 1990. Civil War Unit Histories microfiche series. Edited by Robert E. Lester and Gary Hoeg.

Dunlop, Major William S. *Lee's Sharpshooters; or, the Forefront of Battle*. Little Rock: Tunnan & Pittard, 1899. Bethesda: University Publications of America, 1990. Civil War Unit Histories microfiche series. Edited by Robert E. Lester and Gary Hoeg.

Durham, Ken. "'Dear Rebecca': The Civil War Letters of William Edwards Paxton, 1861-1863." *Louisiana History* 20, no. 2 (Spring 1979): 169-196.

Fleming, Francis P. *Memoir of Capt. C. Seton Fleming, of the Second Florida Infantry, C.S.A.* Jacksonville: Times-Union Publishing House, 1881. Reprint, Alexandria, VA: Stonewall House, 1985.

Fletcher, William A. *Rebel Private Front and Rear: Memoirs of a Confederate Soldier*. Beaumont: Press of the Greer Print, 1908. Reprint. New York: Meridian, 1995.

Folmar, John Kent, ed. *From That Terrible Field: Civil War Letters of James M. Williams, Twenty-First Alabama Infantry Volunteers*. University: Univ. of Alabama Press, 1981.

Folsom, James M. *Heroes and Martyrs of Georgia: Georgia's Record in the Revolution of 1861*. Macon: Burke, Boykin & Co., 1864. Bethesda: University Publications of America, 1990. Civil War Unit Histories microfiche series. Edited by Robert E. Lester and Gary Hoeg.

"Frank Stovall Roberts." *Confederate Veteran* 32 (1924): 25.

Fremantle, Lt. Col. Arthur J. L. *Three Months in the Southern States: April-June, 1863*. New York: John Bradburn, 1864. Reprint. Lincoln: Univ. of Nebraska Press, 1991.

"Gallantry of a Staff Officer." *Confederate Veteran* 4 (1896): 388.

Giles, L. B. *Terry's Texas Rangers*. Reprint. *Terry Texas Ranger Trilogy*. Introduction by Thomas W. Cutrer. Austin: State House Press, 1996.

Gordon, General John B. *Reminiscences of the Civil War*. Charles Scribner's Sons, 1903. Reprint. Baton Rouge: Louisiana State Univ. Press, 1993.

Harp, J. H. "The Bravest Deed I Ever Saw." *Confederate Veteran* 31 (1923): 45-46.

Hawes, Jesse. *Cahaba: A Story of Captive Boys in Blue*. New York: Burr Printing House, 1888.

Hay, William C. *Reminiscences of the War, In Letters to the Children of Cuthbert, Ga.* N.p.: Confederate Soldiers' Home of Georgia, 1920. Microfilm.

History of Company B (Originally Pickens Planters), 40th Alabama Regiment, Confederate States Army, 1862 to 1865. Anniston, AL: Norwood Printing, 1902. Bethesda: University Publications of America, 1990. Civil War Unit Histories microfiche series. Edited by Robert E. Lester and Gary Hoeg.

Hogan, George H. "Parsons's Brigade of Texas Cavalry." *Confederate Veteran* 33 (1925): 17-20.

Hurst, M. B. *History of the Fourteenth Regiment Alabama Volunteers, with a List of the Names of Every Man that Ever Belonged to the Regiment*. Richmond: 1863. Reprint. Introduction and edited by William Stanley Hoole. Confederate Regimental Series No. 1. University, AL: Confederate Publishing Co., 1982.

Jones, Charles T. "Five Confederates: The Sons of Bolling Hall in the Civil War." *Alabama Historical Quarterly* XXIV (1962): 133-221.

Jones, Edgar W. "History of the 18th Alabama Infantry Regiment," in *Jones Valley Times*. Reprint. N. p.: 1994, Zane Geier.

Lovett, Howard Meriwether. "Notable Georgians." *Confederate Veteran* 28 (1920): 256.

Mathis, Ray. *In the Land of the Living: Wartime Letters by Confederates from the Chattahoochee Valley of Alabama and Georgia*. Troy, AL: Troy State Univ. Press, 1981.

Mathless, Paul, ed. *First Manassas*. Voices of the Civil War Series. Alexandria, VA: Time-Life Books, 1997.

Matthews, J. E. F. *Address Delivered at the Unveiling of Confederate Monument, Thomaston, Georgia, May 1908; Roster of Companies going to the War from Upson County*. Macon: J. W. Burke Co., 1908.

McCarthy, Carlton. *Detailed Minutiae of Soldier Life in the Army of Northern Virginia, 1861-1865*. Richmond, VA: 1862. Reprint. Lincoln: Univ. of Nebraska Press, 1993.

Bibliography

McClelen, Bailey G. *I Saw the Elephant: The Civil War Experiences of Bailey George McClelen, Company D, 10th Alabama Infantry Regiment.* Edited by Norman E. Rourke. Shippensburg, PA: White Mane Publishing, 1995.

McMorries, Edward Young. *History of the First Regiment Alabama Volunteer Infantry, C.S.A.* Montgomery: Brown Printing Co., 1904. Bethesda: University Publications of America, 1990. Civil War Unit Histories microfiche series. Edited by Robert E. Lester and Gary Hoeg.

McMurray, W. J. *History of the Twentieth Tennessee Regiment Volunteer Infantry, C. S. A.* Nashville: The Publication Committee, 1904. Reprint. Nashville: Elder's Bookstore, 1976.

McWhiney, Grady, Warner O. Moore, Jr., and Robert F. Pace, eds. *"Fear God and Walk Humbly": The Agricultural Journal of James Mallory, 1843-1877.* Tuscaloosa: Univ. of Alabama Press, 1997.

"Memorial to Louisianians at Shiloh." *Confederate Veteran* 22 (1914): 342-343.

Minnich, J. W. *Inside of Rock Island Prison from December, 1863, to June, 1865.* Nashville: Publishing House of the M. E. Church, South, 1908.

Morris, Scott, Jr. *John Thomas Pound, Confederate Soldier.* Macon: Southern Press, Inc., Publishers, 1964.

Nelson, H. K. "Tennessee, A Grave or a Free Home." *Confederate Veteran* 15 (1907): 508-509.

Nichols, G. W. *A Soldier's Story of His Regiment (61st Georgia), and Incidentally of the Lawton-Gordon-Evans Brigade, Army Northern Virginia.* Jesup, GA: N.p., [1898].

Nisbet, Colonel James Cooper. *Four Years on the Firing Line.* Chattanooga: Imperial Press, n.d.

Oates, William C. *The War Between the Union and the Confederacy and its Lost Opportunities.* 1905. Reprint. Dayton: Press of Morningside Bookshop, 1985.

Olmstead, Colonel Charles H. *The Memoirs of Charles H. Olmstead.* Edited by Lilla Mills Hawes. Savannah: Georgia Historical Society, 1964.

_____. "Reminiscences of Service with the First Volunteer Regiment of Georgia, Charleston Harbor, in 1863: An address delivered before the Georgia Historical Society, March 3, 1879." Savannah, N. d. Bethesda: University Publications of America, 1990. Civil War Unit Histories microfiche series. Edited by Robert E. Lester and Gary Hoeg.

Peacock, C. L. "Conscription in the Mountains." *Confederate Veteran* 23 (1915): 171.

Peacock, Jane Bonner, ed. "A Georgian's View of War in Virginia." *Atlanta Historical Society Journal* 23 (Summer 1979): 91-136.

"The Pioneer Banner: A Confederate Camp Newspaper." *Alabama Historical Quarterly* 23 (1961): 211-19.

Reid, Whitelaw. *Ohio in the War: Her Statesmen, Generals and Soldiers.* Vol. 2. Cincinnati: The Robert Clarke Co., 1895.

Ridley, Bromfield L. *Battles and Sketches of the Army of Tennessee.* Mexico, MO: Missouri Printing & Publishing Co., 1906. Reprint. Dayton: Morningside, 1995.

Rietti, John C., comp. *Military Annals of Mississippi: Military Organizations Which Entered the Service of the Confederate States of America from the State of Mississippi.* Reprint. Spartanburg: The Reprint Company, Publishers, 1976.

Roberts, Frank S. "C. P. Roberts, Adjutant Second Georgia Battalion." *Confederate Veteran* 22 (1914): 112.

_____. "In Winter Quarters at Dalton, Ga., 1863-64." *Confederate Veteran* 26 (1918): 274-275.

_____. "Old Confeds." *Confederate Veteran* 31 (1923): 45.

_____. "Review of the Army of Tennessee at Dalton, Ga." *Confederate Veteran* 26 (1918): 150.

_____. "Spring Hill-Franklin-Nashville, 1864." *Confederate Veteran* 27 (1919): 58-60.

Roy, Colonel T. B. "General Hardee and the Military Operations around Atlanta." *Southern Historical Society Papers* 8 (1881): 341-386.

Sams, Anita B., ed. *With Unabated Trust: Major Henry McDaniel's Love Letters From Confederate Battlefields As Treasured in Hester McDaniel's Bonnet Box.* Monroe, GA: The Historical Society of Walton County, Inc., 1977.

Sandy, Milton. *Corinth Information Database.* Online resource. 1995.

Shanks, Henry Thomas, ed. *The Papers of Willie Person Mangum.* 2 vols. Raleigh: State Department of Archives and History, 1950.

Shannon, Isaac P. "Sharpshooters in Hood's Army." *Confederate Veteran* 15 (1907): 123-127.

Shaver, Lewellyn A. *A History of the Sixtieth Alabama Regiment, Gracie's Alabama Brigade.* 1867. Bethesda: University Publications of America, 1990. Civil War Unit Histories microfiche series. Edited by Robert E. Lester and Gary Hoeg.

Shellenberger, John K. *The Battle of Franklin, Tennessee, November 30, 1864.* Cleveland: 1916.

Sligh, J. E. "How General Taylor Fought the Battle of Mansfield, LA." *Confederate Veteran* 31 (1923): 456-458.

Smith, Daniel P. *Company K, First Alabama Regiment, or Three Years in the Confederate Service.* Prattville, AL: The Survivors, 1885. Bethesda: University Publications of America, 1990. Civil War Unit Histories microfiche series. Edited by Robert E. Lester and Gary Hoeg.

Sterkx, Henry Eugene and Brooks Thompson, eds. "Letters of a Teenage Confederate." *Florida Historical Quarterly* 38: 339-46.

Taylor, F. Jay, ed. *Reluctant Rebel: The Secret Diary of Robert Patrick, 1861-1865.* Baton Rouge: Louisiana State Univ. Press, 1987.

Taylor, Richard. *Destruction and Reconstruction: Personal Experiences of the Late War.* Edited by Richard B. Harwell. New York: Longmans, Green and Co., 1955.

Thruston, Stephen D. "Report of the Conduct of General George H. Steuart's Brigade from the 5th to the 12th of May, 1864, Inclusive." *Southern Historical Society Papers* 14: 146-154.

Walton, William Martin. *An Epitome of My Life: Civil War Reminiscences*. Austin: Waterloo Press, 1965.

Warren, Kittrell J. *Eleventh Georgia Vols., Embracing the Muster Rolls, Together with a Special and Succinct Account of the Marches, Engagements, Casualties, etc.* Richmond: Smith, Bailey & Co., Printers, 1863. Bethesda: University Publications of America, 1990. Civil War Unit Histories microfiche series. Edited by Robert E. Lester and Gary Hoeg.

Watkins, Sam. *"Co. Aytch": A Side Show of the Big Show*. Reprint. New York: Collier Books, 1962.

Watson, William. *Life in the Confederate Army, Being the Observations and Experiences of an Alien in the South During the American Civil War*. London: Chapman and Hall, 1887. Reprint. Baton Rouge: Louisiana State Univ. Press, 1995.

Wheeler, General Joseph. "The Battle of Shiloh." *Southern Historical Society Papers* 24 (1896): 119-131.

Wiley, Bell Irvin. "The Soldier's Life North and South: Letters Home Tell Adventures of Two Foes." *Life*. February 3, 1961: 64-77.

_____, ed. "The Confederate Letters of John W. Hagan." Parts 1 & 2. *Georgia Historical Quarterly* 38 (1954): 170-200, 268-289.

"William Andrew Griffin." *Confederate Veteran* 25 (1917): 87.

"William H. Hendrix." *Confederate Veteran* 28 (1920): 226.

Williams, Edward B., ed. *Rebel Brothers: The Civil War Letters of the Truehearts*. College Station: Texas A&M Press, 1995.

Woodhead, Henry, ed. *Antietam*. Voices of the Civil War Series. Alexandria, VA: Time-Life Books, 1996.

_____. *Atlanta*. Voices of the Civil War Series. Alexandria, VA: Time-Life Books, 1996.

_____. *Chancellorsville*. Voices of the Civil War Series. Alexandria, VA: Time-Life Books, 1996.

_____. *Gettysburg*. Voices of the Civil War Series. Alexandria, VA: Time-Life Books, 1995.

_____. *Second Manassas*. Voices of the Civil War Series. Alexandria, VA: Time-Life Books, 1995.

Worsham, John H. *One of Jackson's Foot Cavalry*. Edited by James I. Robertson, Jr. Reprint. Wilmington: Broadfoot Publishing Co., 1987.

Young, Y. P. "Hood's Failure at Spring Hill." *Confederate Veteran* 16 (1898): 25-41

Zettler, Berrien M. *War Stories and School-Day Incidents for the Children*. New York: Neale Publishing Co., 1912. Bethesda: University Publications of America, 1990. Civil War Unit Histories microfiche series. Edited by Robert E. Lester and Gary Hoeg.

Zuber, William Physick. *My Eighty Years in Texas*. Edited by Janis Boyle Mayfield. Austin: Univ. of Texas Press, 1971.

NEWSPAPERS

Atlanta Constitution

Atlanta Daily Herald

Atlanta Daily Intelligencer

Atlanta Journal-Constitution

Augusta Constitutionalist

Columbus Enquirer

Daily Columbus Enquirer

Daily Constitutionalist (Atlanta)

The Daily News (Griffin, Ga.)

Democratic Watchtower (Talladega)

Donaldsonville Chief (La.)

Georgia Journal & Messenger (Macon)

The Georgia Messenger (Macon)

The Georgian (Savannah)

The Greenville Times (Miss.)

The Griffin Daily News (Ga.)

Houston Morning Post

Houston Tri-Weekly Telegraph

The Independent South (Griffin, GA)

Jacksonville Republican (Ala.)

LaFayette Sun (Ala.)

Macon Daily Telegraph

Macon Daily Telegraph & Confederate

Macon Weekly Telegraph

The Middle Georgia Times (Thomaston)

Mobile Register and Advertiser

Monroe Morning World (La.)

The Monticello News (Ga.)

Natchitoches Enterprise (La.)

Natchitoches Times (La.)

Natchitoches Union (La.)

The Opelika Post (Ala.)

The Richland Beacon (La.)

Richland Beacon-News (La.)

St. Clair Diamond (Ala.)

The Saint Clair News-Aegis (Ala.)

San Antonio Express

The Savannah Georgian

Southeast Georgian (Woodbine, Ga.)

The Southern Herald (Griffin, Ga.)

Southern Messenger (Greenville, Ala.)

Thomaston Times (Ga.)

Upson Pilot (Ga.)

Yazoo Sentinel (Miss.)

BIBLIOGRAPHIES:

Aimone, Alan C. and Barbara A. Aimone. *A User's Guide to the Official Records of the American Civil War.* Shippensburg, PA: White Mane Publishing Co., 1993.

Beers, Henry Putney, ed. *The Confederacy: A Guide to the Archives of the Government of the Confederate States of America.* Washington, D.C.: U. S. Government Printing Office, 1968. Reprint. 1986.

Cole, Garold L. *Civil War Eyewitnesses: An Annotated Bibliography of Books and Articles, 1955-1986.* Columbia: Univ. of South Carolina Press, 1988.

Dornbusch, Charles E. *Military Bibliography of the Civil War.* Vol. 2. *Regimental Publications and Personal Narratives: Southern, Border, and Western States and Territories; Federal Troops.* New York: The New York Public Library, 1967.

_____. *Military Bibliography of the Civil War.* Vol. 4. *Regimental Publications and Personal Narratives: Unit and Confederate Biographies.* Dayton: Morningside House, 1987.

Eicher, David J. *The Civil War in Books: An Analytical Bibliography.* Urbana: Univ. of Illinois Press, 1997.

Filby, P. William. *A Bibliography of American County Histories.* Baltimore: Genealogical Publishing Co., 1985.

Jones, Charles E. *Georgia in the War, 1861-1865.* Atlanta: Foote & Davies, c. 1909.

National Archives Trust Fund Board. *Military Service Records: A Select Catalog of National Archives Microfilm Publications.* Washington, D.C.: National Archives and Service Administration, 1985.

Nevins, Allan, James I. Robertson, Jr., and Bell I. Wiley, eds. *Civil War Books: A Critical Bibliography.* 2 vols. Baton Rouge: Louisiana State Univ. Press, 1967-1969.

Rowland, Arthur Ray and James E. Dorsey. *Bibliography of the Writings on Georgia History, 1900-1970.* Revised and enlarged edition. Spartanburg: Reprint Co., 1978.

Segars, J. H. *In Search of Confederate Ancestors: The Guide.* Edited by John McGlone. Journal of Confederate History Series, no. IX. Murfreesboro: Southern Heritage Press, 1993.

U. S. War Department. *Bibliography of State Participation in the Civil War, 1861-1866.* 3rd ed. Washington: U. S. Government Printing Office, 1913.

Wright, John H., comp. Compendium of the Confederacy: An Annotated Bibliography. Wilmington: Broadfoot Publishing, 1989.

SECONDARY SOURCES

CITY, COUNTY, AND STATE HISTORIES & SOURCE BOOKS

A History of Pike County, 1822-1989. N.p.: Retired Teachers of Pike County, and "The Pike County Journal & Reporter," 1989.

Allen, Arda Talbot. *Miss Ella of the Deep South of Texas.* San Antonio: The Naylor Co., 1951.

Austin, Jeannette Holland. *30,638 Burials in Georgia.* Baltimore: Genealogical Publishing Co., 1995.

Barfield, Louise Calhoun. *History of Harris County Georgia: 1827-1961.* Columbus: Columbus Office Supply Co., 1961.

Barton, Henry W. *Texas Volunteers in the Mexican War.* Wichita Falls: Texian Press, 1970.

Biographical and Historical Memoirs of Louisiana. 3 vols. Chicago: The Goodspeed Publishing Co., 1892. Reprint. Baton Rouge: Claitor's Publishing, 1975.

Blackford, Randolph F. *Under Seven Flags.* Birmingham: Birmingham Printing Co., 1950.

Bowen, Eliza A. *The Story of Wilkes County, Georgia.* Edited, annotated, and indexed with Introduction by Louise F. Hays. Marietta: Continental Book Co., 1950.

Brewer, Willis. *Alabama: Her History, Resources, War Record, and Public Men, from 1540 to 1872.* Montgomery: Barrett & Brown, 1872.

Brown, Eugene R. *A History of Scott County, Mississippi.* M.A. thesis, Mississippi College, 1967.

Bryant, Pat, comp. *Georgia Counties: Their Changing Boundaries.* 2nd ed. Atlanta: State Printing Office, 1983.

Childs, Essie Jones. *They Tarried in Taylor (A Georgia County): 1860, 1870, 1880, & 1900 Census Records, Church Records, & Family Records.* Warner Robins: Central Georgia Genealogical Society, 1992.

"Claiborne Parish District Court Minute Record Book B (1857-1867)." In *Claiborne Parish Trails* 6, no. 1 (February 1991): 34-59ff.

Collections of Early County Historical Society. 2 vols. Blakely, GA: Early County Historical Society, 1971.

Coffman, Edward. *The Story of Logan County.* Nashville: Parthenon Press, 1962.

Cook, Anna M. G. *History of Baldwin County, Georgia.* Spartanburg: Reprint Co., 1978.

Coy, Howard L., Jr. *Cemetery Records for Alto Baptist Church and Brown Road Cemeteries, Alto, Louisiana.* Author, 1994.

Crow, Mattie Lou Teague. *History of St. Clair County (Alabama).* Huntsville: The Strode Publishers, 1973.

Crump, Ruth R. *Chambers County, Alabama: 19th Century Records.* Huguley, AL: Genealogical Roving Press, 1985.

Davidson, William H. *Brooks of Honey and Butter: Plantations and People of Meriwether County Georgia.* 2 vols. Alexander City, AL: Outlook Publishing Co., 1971.

_____. *Pine Log and Greek Revival: Houses and People of Three Counties in Georgia and Alabama.* Alexander City, AL: Outlook Publishing Co., 1964.

_____. *A Rockaway in Talbot: Travels in an Old Georgia County.* 4 vols. West Point, GA: Hester Printing Co., 1983-1990.

Davis, Robert Scott, Jr. "Alabama Indian Depredation Claims." *AlaBenton Genealogical Quarterly* 10, no. 1 (1993): 60-89ff.

_____. *Records of Jasper County, Georgia.* Greenville: Southern Historical Press, 1990.

Dodd, Donald B. *Historical Atlas of Alabama.* University: Univ. of Alabama Press, 1974.

Flanigan, J. C. *History of Gwinnett County, Georgia: 1818-1943.* Vol. 1. 2nd ed. Reprint. Buford, GA: Moreno Press, 1975.

Fretwell, Mark E. *This So Remote Frontier: The Chattahoochee Country of Alabama and Georgia.* Tallahassee: Historic Chattahoochee Commission, 1980.

Genealogical Committee, Georgia Historical Society, comps. *Register of Deaths in Savannah, Georgia,* vol. 6, *1848-June 1853.* N. p.: Georgia Historical Society, 1989.

Gonzales County Historical Commission. *The History of Gonzales County, Texas.* Dallas: Curtis Media Corp., 1986.

Goolsby, Iva P., comp. *Randolph County, Georgia.* N.p., 1976-77. Published for Randolph County Historical Society.

Grubbs, Mrs. Lillie Martin. *History of Worth County Georgia: For the First Eighty Years 1854-1934.* Macon: J. W. Burke Co., 1934. Reprint. Sylvester, GA: Barnard Trail Chapter, NSDAR, 1970.

Hageness, MariLee Beatty. *Abstracts of Georgia-Alabama Bible and Family Records.* Vol. 2. Published by author, 1995.

Hahn, Marilyn Davis, comp. *Butler County in the Nineteenth Century.* Birmingham: N.p., 1978.

Harris, D. W., and B. M. Hulse, comp. *The History of Claiborne Parish, Louisiana, from Its Incorporation in 1828 to. . .1885. . . .*New Orleans: Stansbury Press, 1886. Reprint. Wadsworth Publishing Co., 1976.

Harris, W. Stuart. *Dead Towns of Alabama.* University: Univ. of Alabama Press, 1977.

Hartz, Fred R. and Emilie K. Hartz, comps. *Genealogical Abstracts from the Georgia Journal (Milledgeville) Newspaper, 1809-1840.* 4 vols. Vidalia, GA: N.p., 1992.

Hay, Guelda and Mildred Stewart. *Cemeteries of Taylor County.* Warner Robins: Central Georgia Genealogical Society, 1990.

Hays, Louise Frederick. *History of Macon County Georgia.* 1933. Reprint. Spartanburg: The Reprint Co., 1979.

Hensley, Patricia B. and James W. Hensley. *Trinity County Beginnings.* N. p.: Trinity County Book Committee, 1986.

Hickson, Bobbe Smith. *A Land So Dedicated: Houston County Georgia.* N. p.: Houston County Library Board, 1976.

Hicky, Louise McHenry. *Rambles Through Morgan County: Her History, Century Old Houses and Churches, and Tales to Remember.* Reprint. N. p.: Morgan County Historical Society, 1971.

History of Calloway County, Kentucky. . . The Ledger & Times, 1931. Reprint. Murray, KY: Kentucky Reprint Co., 1972.

Hodges, Claudie E. and Betty Bishop Hodges, comps. *Ouachita Parish, Louisiana Cemetery Records.* Vol. 2. Shreveport: J&W Enterprises, 1993.

Hull, Edward F., comp. *Early Records of Coosa County, 1832-1860.* Birmingham: author, c. 1970.

Ingram, William Pressley. *A History of Tallapoosa County.* Birmingham: N. p., 1951.

Jemison, E. Grace. *Historic Tales of Talladega.* Montgomery: Paragon Press, 1959.

Jones, Frank S. *History of Decatur County Georgia.* N.p., c. 1971.

Jordan, Judge Robert H. *There Was a Land: A Story of Talbot County, Georgia.* Columbus: Columbus Office Supply Co., 1971.

LaGrone, Leila S. *This Very Unreasonable War: A History of Panola County During the Civil War.* Carthage, TX: N.p., 1972.

Lee County Historical Society. *History of Lee County, Georgia.* Leesburg, AL: The Society, 1983.

Lindsey, Bobby L. *"The Reason for the Tears": A History of Chambers County, Alabama, 1832-1900.* West Point, GA: Hester Printing Co., 1971.

Little, John Buckner. *History of Butler County, Alabama, 1815-1885.* Reprint. N. p., author, 1971.

"Louisiana Masons." *Claiborne Parish Trails* 4, no. 4 (November 1989): 178.

Lucas, Silas E., Jr. *The 1832 Gold Lottery of Georgia: Containing a List of the Fortunate Drawers in Said Lottery.* Easley, SC: Southern Historical Press, 1986.

_____. *The Fourth or 1821 Land Lottery of Georgia.* Easley, SC: Southern Historical Press, 1986.

_____. *Reprint of the Official Register of the Land Lottery of Georgia, 1827*. Easley, SC: Southern Historical Press, 1986.

_____. *The Third or 1820 Land Lottery of Georgia*. Easley, SC: Southern Historical Press, 1986.

Mallon, Lucille and Rochelle Farris, comp. *Burial Records, Mobile County, Alabama, 1857-1870*. Mobile: Mobile Genealogical Society, 1971.

Martin, John H., comp. *Columbus, Geo., From its Selection as a "Trading Town" in 1827, to its Partial Destruction by Wilson's Raid, in 1865*. Columbus: Thos. Gilbert, 1874.

McMichael, Lois, comp. *History of Butts County Georgia, 1825-1976*. Atlanta: Cherokee Publishing Co., 1978.

McSwain, Eleanor D. *The Founding Fathers of the County of Bibb and the Town of Macon, Georgia 1823*. Macon: National Printing Co., 1977.

Melton, Quimby, Jr. *The History of Griffin*. Griffin, GA: The Griffin Daily News, n.d.

Members of the Thronateeska Chapter, D.A.R., comp. *History and Reminiscences of Dougherty County, Georgia*. 1924. Reprint. With new index by Margaret H. Cannon. Spartanburg: The Reprint Co., 1978.

A Memorial and Biographical History of McLennan, Falls, Bell and Coryell Counties, Texas. Chicago: The Lewis Publishing Co., 1893.

Memorial Record of Alabama: A Concise Account of the State's Political, Military, Professional and Industrial Progress, Together with the Personal Memoirs of Many of Its People. Vol. 2. Spartanburg: The Reprint Company, Publishers, 1976.

Milford, Margaret P. and Eleanor D. Scott, eds. *A Survey of Cemeteries in Chambers County, Alabama*. Chattahoochee Valley Historical Society Publication no. 14. Huguley, AL: Genealogical Roving Press, N.d.

Mitchell, Lizzie R. *History of Pike County Georgia, 1822-1932*. With new index by Margaret H. Cannon. Spartanburg: The Reprint Co., 1980.

Moss, Kathleen Borders, and Freda Reid Turner, comps. *Henry County, Georgia Land Records*. 3 vols. McDonough: Henry County, Georgia Genealogical Society, 1993.

Norman, Annie B. and Mr. and Mrs. David N. Brown. *Cemeteries of Marion County, Florida*. Vol. 2. N.p.: Ocala Chapter, NSDAR, 1979.

Nottingham, Carolyn Walker, and Evelyn Hannah. *History of Upson County, Georgia*. 1930. Reprint. Vidalia: Georgia Genealogical Reprints, 1969.

Nunn, Alexander, ed. *Lee County and Her Forebears*. Montgomery: Herff Jones, 1983.

Owen, Thomas McAdory. *History of Alabama and Dictionary of Alabama Biography*. 4 vols. Chicago: S. J. Clarke Publishing Co., 1921.

Pepper, Nina, comp. "Yazoo County, Mississippi, Marriage Book R, 1858-1870." *Mississippi Genealogical Exchange* 32, no. 1 (Spring 1986): 16ff.

Pinkston, Regina P., comp. *Historical Account of Meriwether County, 1827-1974*. Greenville: Gresham Printing Co., 1974.

Portre-Bobinski, Germaine, and Clara Smith. *Natchitoches: The Up-to-Date Oldest Town in Louisiana*. New Orleans: Dameron-Pierson Co., 1936.

Rainer, Vessie Thrasher. *Henry County Georgia: The Mother of Counties*. McDonough, GA: N. p., 1971.

Red River Parish Heritage Society. *Our Heritage*. N.p.: The Society, 1989.

Riley, Benjamin Franklin. *History of Conecuh County, Alabama*. Columbus: Thos. Gilbert, 1881. Reprint. With Introduction and new index by J. Vernon Brantley, 1964.

Rocker, Willard R. *Marriages and Obituaries from the Macon Messenger, 1818-1865*. Easley, SC: Southern Historical Press, 1988.

Rogers, Rev. R. W., comp. *History of Pike County from 1822-1922*. Zebulon: N.p., [1922].

Ruff, Nancy B., comp. *Harrison County, Texas, Early Marriage Records 1839-1869*. St. Louis: Ingmire Publications, 1983.

Russell County Historical Commission. *The History of Russell County, Alabama*. Dallas: National ShareGraphics, 1982.

"St. Clair Diamond, Early Newspaper." *CHERISH: The Quarterly Journal of the St. Clair Historical Society* 2, no. 2: 66-67.

Sams, Anita B. *Wayfarers in Walton: A History of Walton County Georgia, 1818-1967*. Monroe: The General Charitable Foundation of Monroe, Georgia, Inc., 1967.

Sealy, Gwen Bradford. *Lest We Forget: A Record of Tombstone Inscriptions, Red River Parish, Louisiana and Vicinity*. Shreveport: N.p., 1983.

Smith, Clifford L. *History of Troup County*. Atlanta: Foote & Davies, 1933.

Smith, Elizabeth Wiley. *The History of Hancock County, Georgia*. 2 vols. Washington, GA: Wilkes Publishing Co., 1974.

Snead, Rubye S., ed. *Pike County, Georgia, Sesquicentennial, 1822-1972*. Zebulon: Pike County Sesquicentennial Assoc., 1972.

South Central Alabama Development Commission. *Historic Assets: Macon County, Alabama*. Montgomery: N.p., 1975.

Spurlin, Charles D., comp. *Texas Veterans in the Mexican War: Muster Rolls of Texas Military Units*. Victoria, TX: C. D. Spurlin, c. 1984.

Stanley, Lawrence L. *A Little History of Gilmer County*. N.p., 1975.

"State Land Entries." Parts 2 and 3. *Claiborne Parish Trails* 1, no. 4 (November 1986): 148ff.; vol. 2, no. 1 (February 1987): 11ff.

Stewart, Mrs. Frank Ross. *Alabama's Calhoun County*. Vol. 1. Centre, AL: Stewart Univ. Press, 1976.

————. *Cherokee County History: 1836-1956*. 2 vols. Centre, AL: Birmingham Printing Co., 1958.

Terrill, Helen E. and Sara R. Dixon. *History of Stewart County, Georgia*. 2 vols. Columbus: Columbus Office Supply Co., 1958. Reprint. Waycross: Dixon, 1975.

Thaxton, Donna B., ed. *Georgia Indian Depredation Claims*. Americus: The Thaxton Company, N.d.

Turner, Freda R., ed. *Henry County, Georgia Land Records*. 3 vols. McDonough: Henry County Genealogical Society, 1991-1993.

Tyler, George W. *The History of Bell County.* Edited by Charles W. Ramsdell. San Antonio: The Naylor Co., 1936.

Wade, Alice and Katherine Branton, eds. *Early Mississippi Records: Washington County 1860-1912.* Vol. 4. Leland: N. p., 1986.

Walker, Anne Kendrick. *Russell County in Retrospect: An Epic of the Far Southeast.* Richmond: Dietz Press, 1950.

Ward, George Gordon. *The Annals of Upper Georgia, Centered in Gilmer County.* Carrollton: Thomasson Printing & Office Equipment Co., 1965.

White, Gifford. *Texas Scholastics 1854-1855.* Austin: N. p., 1979.

Whitten, Joseph L. *By Murder, Accident, and Natural Causes: Death Notices from St. Clair County, Alabama, Newspapers 1873-1910.*

Williamson, Frederick William, and George T. Goodman, eds. *Eastern Louisiana, A History of the Watershed of the Ouachita River and the Florida Parishes, etc.* 3 vols. Louisville: The Historical Record Association, n. d.

Windham, Marilyn Neisler. *Marriages, Deaths, etc. From The Butler Herald, 1876-1896.* Warner Robins: Central Georgia Genealogical Society, 1995.

Wright, Buster W., comp. *Burials and Deaths Recorded in the Columbus (Georgia) Enquirer, 1832-1872.* N.p., 1984.

Young, Ida, Julius Gholson, and Clara Nell Hargrove. *History of Macon, Georgia.* Macon: Lyon, Marshall & Brooks, 1950.

GENEALOGICAL

Ballard, Vaughn, comp. *Solomon Mangham: His Ancestors and Descendants.* Arlington: Family Histories, 1989.

Palmer, John T. *The Mangums of Virginia, North Carolina, South Carolina, Georgia, Alabama, Mississippi, Tennessee, Arkansas, Texas, Utah and Adjoining States.* Santa Rosa, CA: 1992.

Parham, James Lynn. *Mangum Family Bulletin.* 37 vols. Huntsville: Author, 1969-1991.

_____. *Pleasant Mangum and All His Kin: The Story of the Bennetts, the Mangums and the Parhams.* Baltimore: Gateway Press, 1997.

HISTORICAL

Bailey, Georgianne. *Between the Enemy and Texas: Parsons' Texas Cavalry in the Civil War.* Unpublished dissertation. Ann Arbor: UMI, 1987.

Baumgartner, Richard A. and Larry M. Strayer. *Kennesaw Mountain, June 1864: Bitter Standoff at the Gibraltar of Georgia.* Huntington, WV: Blue Acorn Press, 1998.

Bearss, Edwin C. *The Campaign for Vicksburg.* 3 vols. Dayton: Morningside Press, 1985-86.

_____. *The Siege of Jackson: July 10-17, 1863.* Baltimore: Gateway Press, 1981.

Bergeron, Arthur W., Jr. "A Colonel Earns His Wreath: Col. Henry Gray's Louisiana Brigade at Mansfield," *Civil War Regiments* 4, no. 2 (1994): 1-25.

_____. *Guide to Louisiana Confederate Military Units 1861-1865.* Baton Rouge: Louisiana State Univ. Press, 1989.

Bradley, Mark L. *Last Stand in the Carolinas: The Battle of Bentonville.* Campbell, CA: Savas Woodbury Publishers, 1996.

Bragg, William Harris. *Joe Brown's Army: The Georgia State Line, 1862-1865.* Macon: Mercer Univ. Press, 1987.

Brown, D. Alexander. *The Galvanized Yankees.* Urbana: Univ. of Illinois Press, 1963.

Brown, Russell K. *To the Manner Born: The Life of General William H. T. Walker.* Athens: Univ. of Georgia Press, 1994.

Bryan, T. Conn. *Confederate Georgia.* Athens: Univ. of Georgia Press, 1953.

Bryant, William O. *Cahaba Prison and the Sultana Disaster.* Tuscaloosa: Univ. of Alabama Press, 1990.

Busey, John W. and David G. Martin. *Regimental Strengths at Gettysburg.* Baltimore: Gateway Press, 1982.

Calkins, Chris M. *The Appomattox Campaign, March 29-April 9, 1865.* Great Campaign Series. Conshohocken, PA: Combined Books, 1997.

Cannon, Deveraux Devereaux D. *The Flags of the Confederacy: An Illustrated History.* Memphis: St. Lukes Press. Reprint. Wilmington: Broadfoot Publishing, 1988.

Carleton, Mark T., Perry H. Howard, Joseph B. Parker, eds. *Readings in Louisiana Politics.* Baton Rouge: Claitor's Publishing Division, 1975.

Cash, W. J. *The Mind of the South.* Alfred A. Knopf, Inc., 1941. Reprint. New York: Vintage Books, 1991.

Castel, Albert. *Decision in the West: The Atlanta Campaign of 1864.* Lawrence: Univ. Press of Kansas, 1992.

Catton, Bruce. *Grant Moves South.* Boston: Little, Brown & Co., 1960.

_____. *A Stillness at Appomattox.* New York: Pocket Books, 1953.

Cavanaugh, Michael A. and William Marvel. *The Battle of the Crater, "The Horrid Pit," June 25 - August 6, 1864.* Lynchburg: H. E. Howard, 1989.

Cobb, James C. *The Most Southern Place on Earth: The Mississippi Delta and the Roots of Regional Identity.* New York: Oxford Univ. Press, 1992.

Collier, Kenneth C. *The 13th Georgia Regiment: A Regimental History of the 13th Georgia Infantry Regiment, a Part of the Lawton-Gordon-Evans Brigade.* N. p.: Author, 1997.

Connelly, Thomas Lawrence. *Army of the Heartland: The Army of Tennessee, 1861-1862.* Baton Rouge: Louisiana State Univ. Press, 1967.

_____. *Autumn of Glory: The Army of Tennessee, 1862-1865.* Baton Rouge: Louisiana State Univ. Press, 1971.

Cooling, Benjamin F. *Jubal Early's Raid on Washington, 1864.* Baltimore: Nautical & Aviation Publishing Co. of America, 1989.

Cormier, Steven A. *The Siege of Suffolk: The Forgotten Campaign, April 11-May 4, 1863.* 2nd ed. The Virginia Civil War Battles and Leaders Series. Lynchburg: H. E. Howard, Inc., 1989.

Cozzens, Peter. *No Better Place to Die: The Battle of Stones River.* Urbana: Univ. of Illinois Press, 1990.

_____. *The Shipwreck of Their Hopes: The Battles for Chattanooga.* Urbana: Univ. of Illinois Press, 1994.

_____. *This Terrible Sound: The Battle of Chickamauga.* Urbana: Univ. of Illinois Press, 1992.

Crute, Joseph H. *Confederate Staff Officers, 1861-1865.* Powhatan, VA: Derwent Books, 1982.

_____. *Units of the Confederate States Army.* Midlothian, VA: Derwent Books, 1987.

Cunningham, H. H. *Doctors in Gray: The Confederate Medical Service.* Baton Rouge: Louisiana State Univ. Press, 1958.

Daniel, Larry J. *Cannoneers in Gray: The Field Artillery in the Army of Tennessee, 1861-1865.* Tuscaloosa: Univ. of Alabama Press, 1984.

_____. *Shiloh: The Battle That Changed the Civil War.* New York: Simon & Schuster, 1997.

_____. *Soldiering in the Army of Tennessee: A Portrait of Life in a Confederate Army.* Chapel Hill: Univ. of North Carolina Press, 1991.

Davis, William C. *The Cause Lost: Myths and Realities of the Confederacy.* Modern War Studies. Lawrence: Univ. Press of Kansas, 1996.

_____. *The Orphan Brigade: The Kentucky Confederates Who Couldn't Go Home.* Baton Rouge: Louisiana State Univ. Press, 1980.

Directory of the City of Montgomery and Historical Sketches of Alabama Soldiers. Montgomery: Perry & Smith, 1866. Bethesda: University Publications of America, 1990. Civil War Unit Histories microfiche series. Edited by Robert E. Lester and Gary Hoeg.

Ellingson, Paul, ed. *Confederate Flags in the Georgia State Capitol Collection.* Atlanta: Georgia Office of the Secretary of State, 1994.

Evans, David. *Sherman's Horsemen: Union Cavalry Operations in the Atlanta Campaign.* Bloomington: Indiana Univ. Press, 1996.

Evans, Michael W. "Commands." *America's Civil War* (September 1993).

Forbes, William. *Capt. Croft's Flying Artillery Battery, Columbus, Georgia.* Dayton: Morningside Books, 1993.

Fox, William F. *Regimental Losses in the American Civil War, 1861-1865.* Albany: Brandow Printing, 1898. Reprint. Dayton: Morningside House, 1985.

Furgurson, Ernest B. *Chancellorsville 1863: The Souls of the Brave.* New York: Vintage Books, 1993.

Gallagher, Gary W. *The Confederate War.* Cambridge: Harvard Univ. Press, 1997.

Gallaway, B. P., ed. *Texas, The Dark Corner of the Confederacy: Contemporary Accounts of the Lone Star State in the Civil War.* 3rd ed. Lincoln: Univ. of Nebraska Press, 1994.

Gragg, Rod. *The Illustrated Confederate Reader.* New York: Harper & Row, 1989.

Gunby, Elizabeth W. "Wiley P. Mangham." In *Louisiana Pen Women, Louisiana Leaders.* Baton Rouge: Claitor's Publishing, 1970.

Hall, Martin Hardwick. *Sibley's New Mexico Campaign*. Austin: Univ. of Texas Press, 1960.

Hartman, David W., comp. *Biographical Rosters of Florida's Confederate and Union Soldiers, 1861-1865*. Wilmington: Broadfoot Publishing Co., 1995.

Hearn, Chester G. *The Capture of New Orleans, 1862*. Baton Rouge: Louisiana State Univ. Press, 1995.

Hennessy, John J. *Return to Bull Run: The Campaign and Battle of Second Manassas*. New York: Simon & Schuster, 1993.

Hewitt, Lawrence Lee. *Port Hudson: Confederate Bastion on the Mississippi*. Baton Rouge: Louisiana State Univ. Press, 1987.

Hill, Louise Biles. *Joseph E. Brown and the Confederacy*. Chapel Hill: Univ. of North Carolina Press, 1939. Reprint. Westport, CT: Greenwood Press, 1972.

Hoehling, A. A. *Last Train from Atlanta*. New York: T. Yoseloff, 1958. Reprint. Harrisburg: Stackpole Books, 1992.

_____. *Vicksburg: 47 Days of Siege*. Prentice Hall, 1969. Mechanicsburg, PA: Stackpole Books edition, 1996.

Holcomb, Brent H. *Death and Obituary Notices from the Southern Christian Advocate 1867-1878*. Columbia: SCMAR, 1993.

Horn, Stanley F. *The Army of Tennessee*. Bobbs-Merrill, 1941. Reprint. Norman: Univ. of Oklahoma Press, 1993.

Horwitz, Tony. *Confederates in the Attic: Dispatches from the Unfinished Civil War*. New York: Vintage Books, 1998.

Hughes, Nathaniel Cheairs, Jr. *Bentonville: The Final Battle of Sherman and Johnston*. Chapel Hill: Univ. of North Carolina Press, 1996.

Johnson, Ludwell H. *Red River Campaign: Politics and Cotton in the Civil War*. Johns Hopkins Press, 1958. Reprint. Kent: Kent State Univ. Press, 1993.

Jones, Charles C., Jr. *The Siege of Savannah in December, 1864*. Albany: Joel Munsell, 1874. Reprint. Jonesboro, GA: Freedom Hill Press, 1988.

Jones, Eugene W. *Enlisted for the War: The Struggles of the Gallant 24th Regiment, South Carolina Volunteers, Infantry, 1861-1865*. Hightstown, NJ: Longstreet House, 1997.

Jones, James Pickett. *Yankee Blitzkrieg: Wilson's Raid Through Alabama and Georgia*. Athens: Univ. of Georgia Press, 1976.

Jones, Terry L. *Lee's Tigers: The Louisiana Infantry in the Army of Northern Virginia*. Baton Rouge: Louisiana State Univ. Press, 1987.

_____. "The 28th Louisiana Volunteers in the Civil War." *Journal of the North Louisiana Historical Association* 9 (1973): 85-95.

Katcher, Philip. *The Army of Robert E. Lee*. London: Arms and Armour Press, 1994.

Kelly, William Milner. "A History of the Thirtieth Alabama Volunteers (Infantry), Confederate States Army." *The Alabama Historical Quarterly* 9, no. 1 (Spring 1947): 115-189.

Kennett, Lee. *Marching Through Georgia: The Story of Soldiers and Civilians During Sherman's Campaign*. New York: HarperPerennial, 1995.

Kerby, Robert L. *Kirby Smith's Confederacy: The Trans-Mississippi South, 1863-1865.* Tuscaloosa: Univ. of Alabama Press, 1972.

Krick, Robert K. *Lee's Colonels: A Biographical Register of the Field Officers of the Army of Northern Virginia.* 4th edition, revised. Dayton: Press of Morningside House, 1996.

Leeper, Clare D. "Mangham." In *Louisiana Places: A Collection of the Columns from the Baton Rouge "Sunday Advocate" 1960-1974.* Baton Rouge: Legacy Publishing Co., 1976.

Lewis, Thomas A. *The Guns of Cedar Creek.* New York: Harper & Row, 1988. Reprint. New York: Dell Publishing Co., 1991.

Linderman, Gerald F. *Embattled Courage: The Experience of Combat in the American Civil War.* New York: The Free Press, 1987.

Lockey, Joseph B. "The Florida Banditti, 1783." *FHQ* 24, no. 2 (October 1945): 87ff.

Long, E. B. *The Civil War Day by Day: An Almanac, 1861-1865.* Garden City, NY: Doubleday & Co., 1971.

Lonn, Ella. *Desertion During the Civil War.* New York: Century, 1928. Reprint. Lincoln: Univ. of Nebraska Press, 1998.

————. *Salt as a Factor in the Confederacy.* New York: W. Neale, 1933.

Luvaas, Jay, and Harold W. Nelson, eds. *Guide to the Battles of Chancellorsville & Fredericksburg.* Lawrence: Univ. Press of Kansas, 1994.

————. *The U. S. Army War College Guide to the Battle of Gettysburg.* New York: HarperCollins Publishers, 1987.

Madaus, Howard M. *The Battle Flags of the Confederate Army of Tennessee.* Milwaukee: Milwaukee Public Museum, 1976.

Mangham, Dana M. "Cox's Wild Cats: The 2nd Georgia Battalion Sharpshooters at Chickamauga and Chattanooga." *Civil War Regiments: A Journal of the American Civil War* 7, no. 1 (2000): 91-128.

Markham, Jerald H. *The Botetourt Artillery.* The Virginia Regimental Histories Series. Lynchburg: H. E. Howard, 1986.

Martin, Bessie. *Desertion of Alabama Troops from the Confederate Army: A Study in Sectionalism.* New York: Columbia Univ. Press, 1932.

Martin, David G. *Gettysburg July 1.* Conshohocken, PA: Combined Books, 1995.

Marvel, William. *Andersonville: The Last Depot.* Chapel Hill: Univ. of North Carolina Press, 1994.

Matter, William D. *If It Takes All Summer: The Battle of Spotsylvania.* Chapel Hill: Univ. of North Carolina Press, 1988.

McDonough, James Lee and Thomas L. Connelly. *Five Tragic Hours: The Battle of Franklin.* Knoxville: Univ. of Tennessee Press, 1983.

McDonough, James Lee. *War in Kentucky: From Shiloh to Perryville.* Knoxville: Univ. of Tennessee Press, 1994.

McFarland, Jeff. "History of Colonel Gray's 28th Louisiana Infantry." Steve Pipes's regimental Internet website. Http://members.tripod.com/~pipeslines/mcfarlands28th.html.

McMillan, Malcolm C., ed. *The Alabama Confederate Reader*. Tuscaloosa: Univ. of Alabama Press, 1963.

McMurry, Richard M. "Confederate Morale in the Atlanta Campaign of 1864." *Georgia Historical Quarterly* 45 (1970): 226-243.

_____. *John Bell Hood and the War for Southern Independence*. Lincoln: Univ. of Nebraska Press, 1982.

_____. "Kennesaw Mountain." *Civil War Times Illustrated* 8, no. 9 (1970): 8-9

_____. *Two Great Rebel Armies: An Essay in Confederate Military History*. Chapel Hill: Univ. of North Carolina Press, 1989.

McNeill, William J. "A Survey of Confederate Soldier Morale during Sherman's Campaign through Georgia and South Carolina." *Georgia Historical Quarterly* 54 (1971): 1-25.

McPherson, James M. *Battle Cry of Freedom: The Civil War Era*. New York: Ballantine Books, 1988.

_____. *For Cause and Comrades: Why Men Fought in the Civil War*. New York: Oxford Univ. Press, 1997.

_____. *Drawn With the Sword: Reflections on the American Civil War*. New York: Oxford Univ. Press, 1996.

The Medical College of Georgia Alumni Directory 1828-1984. White Plains, NY: Bernard C. Harris Publishing Co., 1984.

Miles, Jim. *To the Sea: A History and Tour Guide of Sherman's March*. Nashville: Rutledge Hill Press, 1989.

Miller, Richard F. and Robert F. Mooney. "The 20th Massachusetts Infantry and the Street Fight for Fredericksburg." *Civil War Regiments* 4, no. 4 (1995): 101-126.

Mills, Eric. *Chesapeake Bay in the Civil War*. Centreville, MD: Tidewater Publishers, 1996.

Mills, Gary B. *Civil War Claims in the South: An Index of Civil War Damage Claims Filed Before the Southern Claims Commission, 1871-1880*. Laguna Hills, CA: Aegean Park Press, 1980.

Mitchell, Reid. *Civil War Soldiers: Their Expectations and Experiences*. New York: Simon & Schuster, 1988.

Mohr, Clarence L. *On the Threshold of Freedom: Masters and Slaves in Civil War Georgia*. Athens: Univ. of Georgia Press, 1986.

Moore, Albert Burton. *Conscription and Conflict in the Confederacy*. Macmillan, 1924. Reprint. Columbia: Univ. of South Carolina Press, 1996.

Moore, Frank, ed. *The Rebellion Record: A Diary of American Events, with Documents, Narratives, Illustrative Incidents, Poetry, etc.* Vol. 11. New York: D. Van Nostrand, 1868.

Murray, Alton J. *South Georgia Rebels: The True Wartime Experiences of the 26th Regiment Georgia Volunteer Infantry, Lawton-Gordon-Evans Brigade, Confederate States Army, 1861-1865*. St. Marys, GA: Author, 1976.

Newton, Steven H. *Joseph E. Johnston and the Defense of Richmond.* Modern War Studies. Lawrence: Univ. Press of Kansas, 1998.

Nye, Wilbur Sturtevant. *Here Come the Rebels!* Baton Rouge: Louisiana State Univ. Press, 1965. Reprint. Dayton: Press of Morningside Bookshop, 1988.

Oates, Stephen B. *Confederate Cavalry West of the River.* Austin: Univ. of Texas Press, 1961.

Owsley, Frank Lawrence. *Plain Folk of the Old South.* Baton Rouge: Louisiana State Univ. Press, 1949. Reprint. 1982.

Pfanz, Harry W. *Gettysburg: The Second Day.* Chapel Hill: Univ. of North Carolina Press, 1987.

Porter, Leannell W., comp. *Roster of Ex-Confederate Veterans, with Remarks and Roster of Camp 122, Texas, Original Members.* N.p.: Bell County Historical Survey Committee, 1966.

Power, J. Tracy. *Lee's Miserables: Life in the Army of Northern Virginia from the Wilderness to Appomattox.* Chapel Hill: Univ. of North Carolina Press, 1998.

Priest, John Michael. *Antietam: The Soldiers' Battle.* New York: Oxford Univ. Press, 1989.

Rhea, Gordon C. *The Battle of the Wilderness, May 5-6, 1864.* Baton Rouge: Louisiana State Univ. Press, 1994.

_____. *The Battles for Spotsylvania Court House and the Road to Yellow Tavern, May 7-12, 1864.* Baton Rouge: Louisiana State Univ. Press, 1997.

Robertson, Fred L., comp. *Soldiers of Florida in the Seminole Indian, Civil and Spanish-American Wars.* N. p.: Board of State Institutions, 1903.

Robertson, James I., Jr. *Soldiers Blue and Gray.* Columbia: Univ. of South Carolina Press, 1988.

_____. *The Stonewall Brigade.* Baton Rouge: Louisiana State Univ. Press, 1963.

Roland, Charles P. *The Confederacy.* The Chicago History of American Civilization. Chicago: Univ. of Chicago Press, 1960.

Rowland, Dunbar. *The Official and Statistical Register of the State of Mississippi, 1908.* Nashville: Brandon Printing Co., 1908.

Savas, Theodore P. "The Battle of Fredericksburg Revisited." *Civil War Regiments* 4, no. 4 (1995): pp. i-iv.

_____. "Col. James H. Beard and the Consolidated Crescent Regiment." *Civil War Regiments* 4, no. 2 (1994): 68-103.

Sears, Stephen W. *Chancellorsville.* Boston: Houghton Mifflin Co., 1996.

_____. *Landscape Turned Red: The Battle of Antietam.* New Haven: Ticknor & Fields, 1983.

_____. *To the Gates of Richmond: The Peninsula Campaign.* New York: Ticknor & Fields, 1992.

Smedlund, William S. *Camp Fires of Georgia's Troops.* N. p.: Kennesaw Mountain, 1994.

Sifakis, Stewart. *Compendium of the Confederate Armies: Alabama.* New York: Facts on File, 1995.

_____. *Compendium of the Confederate Armies: Florida and Arkansas*. New York: Facts on File, 1992.

_____. *Compendium of the Confederate Armies: Louisiana*. New York: Facts on File, 1995.

_____. *Compendium of the Confederate Armies: Mississippi*. New York: Facts on File, 1995.

_____. *Compendium of the Confederate Armies: South Carolina and Georgia*. New York: Facts on File, 1995.

_____. *Compendium of the Confederate Armies: Texas*. New York: Facts on File, 1995.

_____. *Who Was Who in the Civil War*. New York: Facts on File Publications, 1988.

Sons of Confederate Veterans Ancestor Album. Houston: Heritage Publishers Services, 1986.

Spedale, William A. *The Battle of Baton Rouge 1862*. Baton Rouge: Land and Land Publishing Division, 1985.

Stackpole, Edward J. *The Fredericksburg Campaign: Drama on the Rappahannock*. 2nd ed. Harrisburg: Stackpole Books, 1991.

Stampp, Kenneth M. *The Era of Reconstruction, 1865-1877*. New York: Vintage Books, 1965.

_____. *The Peculiar Institution: Slavery in the Ante-Bellum South*. New York: Vintage Books, 1956.

Summers, Carl, Jr., ed. *Confederate Soldiers from Chambers County, Alabama and Thereabouts*. Chattahoochee Valley Historical Society Publication no. 16. N. p.: Author, 1993.

Sutherland, Daniel E., ed. *Guerrillas, Unionists, and Violence on the Confederate Home Front*. Fayetteville: Univ. of Arkansas Press, 1999.

Sword, Wiley. *The Confederacy's Last Hurrah: Spring Hill, Franklin, and Nashville*. Lawrence: Univ. Press of Kansas, 1992.

_____. *Mountains Touched with Fire: Chattanooga Besieged, 1863*. New York: St. Martin's Press, 1995.

_____. *Shiloh: Bloody April*. New York: William Morrow & Co., 1974.

_____. *Southern Invincibility: A History of the Confederate Heart*. New York: St. Martin's Press, 1999.

Tancig, W. J., comp. *Confederate Military Land Units, 1861-1865*. Cranbury, NJ: Thomas Yoseloff, 1967.

Tatum, Georgia Lee. *Disloyalty in the Confederacy*. Chapel Hill: Univ. of North Carolina Press, 1934.

Thomas, Dean S. *Cannons: An Introduction to Civil War Artillery*. Gettysburg: Thomas Publications, 1985.

Thomas, Emory M. *The Confederate Nation: 1861-1863*. The New American Nation Series. New York: Harper & Row, 1979.

Trefousse, Hans L., ed. *The Causes of the Civil War: Institutional Failure or Human Blunder?* American Problem Studies. New York: Holt, Rinehart and Winston, 1971.

Trelease, Allen W. *White Terror: The Ku Klux Klan Conspiracy and Southern Reconstruction.* Baton Rouge: Louisiana State Univ. Press, 1971.

Troxler, Carole Watterson. "Loyalist Refugees and the British Evacuation of East Florida, 1783-1785." *FHQ* 60, no. 1 (July 1981): 1ff.

Trudeau, Noah Andre. *Bloody Roads South: The Wilderness to Cold Harbor, May-June 1864.* Boston: Little, Brown and Company, 1989.

————. *The Last Citadel: Petersburg, Virginia, June 1864-April 1865.* Baton Rouge: Louisiana State Univ. Press, 1991.

————. *Out of the Storm: The End of the Civil War, April-June 1865.* Baton Rouge: Louisiana State Univ. Press, 1994.

Tucker, Glenn. *Chickamauga: Bloody Battle in the West.* Bobbs-Merrill, 1961. Reprint. Dayton: Morningside, 1992.

United Confederate Veterans. *The Flags of the Confederate States of America.* Baltimore: A. Hoen & Co., 1907.

"Unpublished After-Action Reports from the Red River Campaign." *Civil War Regiments: A Journal of the American Civil War* 4, no. 2 (1994): 118-135.

Wheeler, Richard. *On Fields of Fury—From the Wilderness to the Crater: An Eyewitness History.* New York: HarperPerennial, 1991.

Who Was Who in America: Historical Volume 1607-1896. Chicago: Marquis- Who's Who, 1963.

Wiley, Bell Irvin. *The Life of Billy Yank: The Common Soldier of the Union.* Reprint. Baton Rouge: Louisiana State Univ. Press, 1978.

————. *The Life of Johnny Reb: The Common Soldier of the Confederacy.* Reprint. Baton Rouge: Louisiana State Univ. Press, 1978.

Williams, T. Harry. *Lincoln and His Generals.* New York: Vintage Books, 1952.

Winters, John D. *The Civil War in Louisiana.* Baton Rouge: Louisiana State Univ. Press, 1963.

Index

- Unit references are to chapter/section
- For higher units, see commanders' names.
- Bold face: family group heads & CSA soldiers
- Genealogical ref. # are keyed to Appendix
- Italics denote photos, charts, or maps

392, 420 (n.96), 423 (n.132), 429
(n.198), 464-6, 488, 502-11, 514,
525-32, 561-2, 605
Lee, Gen. Stephen D., 74, 228-9, 571-
4, 577-8, 613 (n.59), 639-40, 645
Lemberg, E. J. #349a: 516, 698
Lifsey, Lt. H. Y., 56, 93 (n.79)
Lifsey Springs (Springs District), GA,
26, 29-30, 45, 50-1, 85, 86 (n.2), 93
(n.79), 338
Lincoln, Pres. Abraham, 11-2, 103,
110, 112, 141, 145, 161 (n.19), 168
(n.60), 181, 202, 253, 262, 280, 299,
346, 372-3, 391, 423 (n.133), 424
(n.139), 425 (n.146), 480-1, 623
Lindsey, John G. #90a: 321 (n.3), 690;
see also 246
Lindsey, John H. #228: 690
Lithgow, Elizabeth #14a: *19*; 676
Little, Col. Francis H. (11ᵗʰ Ga.), 379-
80
Littlejohn, Lucy Abigail #197b: 51,
703
Lofton, Col. William A. (6ᵗʰ Ga. St.
Gd.), 191
Long, Nan (Dent) #300b: 695
Longstreet, Gen. James, 260, 262, 265,
281-90, 296-303, 368, 376-7, 380,
424 (n.138), 458-65, 488, 491-3, 502-
7, 524, 561-2
Lookout Mountain (TN), 66, 493-6
Loring, Gen. William W., 637, 640-1,
643, 645
Lost Mountain (GA), 72
Louvent, Robert #379b: 700
Love, Matilda A. Mitchell #92b: *312*;
318, 320, 321, 691
Lovejoy's Station, GA, 76, 574
Lowery, W. #422b: 703
Luffman, Lt. Col. William T. (11ᵗʰ
Ga.), 362, 364, 366, 368, 380, 421
(n.110)
Lyles, Ellie Pearl #414a: 702

Lynch, Capt. Berry E., 26
Lynn, Carolyn Frances Emmeline
#184a: 155-6, 161, 700
Macon, GA, 29, 42, 45, 181-2, 194-5,
199, 202, 228, 230-1, 411, 666
Macon Co., AL, 314, 500, 511
Macon Co., GA, 192, 443
Macon & Western Railroad, 74-6, 202,
227-8, 574
Madison Co., MS, 628-9
Magruder, Gen. John B., 250-2, 286,
365, 402, 452-4, 457-8, 472 (n.38),
473 (n.53)
Mahaska, 367
Mahone, Gen. William C., 142-5, 171
(n.113), 265, 295, 304-10
Mallory, James, 272, 277
Malone, Nancy Viola #419a: 702
Malvern Hill (VA), 37-8, 46, 88 (n.29),
252-4, 269, 367-8, 372, 374, 514
Manassas, Battle of First, VA, 53, 109,
282, 353, 372-3, 383, 457
Manassas, Battle of Second, VA, 38,
46, 255-6, 289-90, 368-9, 372, 374,
379
Mangham, LA, 159, 161
Mangham & Davis (general store), 156
Mangham & Sons (millinery), 238
(n.72)
Mangham, A. C. #A7: 707
Mangham, A. Don #362: 698
Mangham, Adelbert #238: 691
Mangham, Adolphus Fields #173: 687
Mangham, Adrian F. #88: *337*; 338,
340-2, 404, 414 (n.24), 681
Mangham, Alice #461: 705
Mangham, Amanda #198: 688
Mangham, Amanda H. #187: *102*;
103, 688
Mangham, Amanda J. #477: 705
Mangham, Ann E. #181: *102*; 101,
103, 687
Mangham, Anna (no ref. #): 320